BLACKSTONE'S

LAW OF TORT
INDEX

CASE PRECEDENTS 1900-1997

BLACKSTONE'S

LAW OF TORT
INDEX

CASE PRECEDENTS 1900-1997

Dr Maxwell Barrett

BLACKSTONE
PRESS LIMITED

First published in Great Britain 1998 by Blackstone Press Limited,
Aldine Place, London W12 8AA. Telephone: 0181-740 2277

ISBN: 1 85431 856 X

British Library Cataloguing in Publication Data
A CIP catalogue record for this book is available from the British Library

Typeset by Style Photosetting Limited, Mayfield, East Sussex
Printed by Bell and Bain Limited, Glasgow

CONTENTS

INTRODUCTION

> The decisions . . . of courts are held in the highest regard, and are
> not only preserved as authentic records in the treasuries of the
> several courts, but are handed out to public view in the numerous
> volumes of *reports* which furnish the lawyer's library.[1]

So wrote Blackstone in 1765. Since then those 'numerous volumes of reports' to which he makes reference have multiplied in number to a level that is surely beyond anything he ever imagined. And it is not just that the total number of reports being published has increased in the past two and a half centuries. Mirroring the present tendency among lawyers towards ever greater specialisation into ever more specific fields of legal expertise has been a growing tendency among publishers in recent years to bring out law reports that concentrate on particular subject areas.

All of this has placed lawyers in something of a predicament. Even if it were economically feasible to subscribe to each of the many series of law reports and legal periodicals that have been or become available during this century alone (and even the most generously funded library would surely baulk at such an enormous expense) the amount of overlap in coverage between the different sources could well mean that those cases to which particular lawyers need access are already handsomely covered in the publications to which they or their chambers or firm presently subscribe and that outside reference is so occasional it could be met by a reasonably priced publication which would not only index the reports to which those lawyers or their chambers or firms now subscribe but contain additional comprehensive references to alternative reports and journals that feature relevant case-law and to which occasional recourse might be necessary.

Economic feasibility aside, there is the matter of convenience. However well prepared they are on entering court every barrister and many solicitors have on occasion found themselves on their feet addressing or pressing a perhaps unanticipated argument which they wished they could support by reference to a convincing precedent. That precedent may well exist somewhere among the many sources of case-law now available. Indeed oftentimes a barrister or solicitor may have a very good notion of when a relevant case was decided or with what subject-matter the relevant case was concerned but simply cannot remember its name. Standing before the court, away from law reports and legal periodicals practitioners would at such times undoubtedly find a one-stop, single-volume index relevant to the subject area being litigated, detailing the location and content of many thousands of cases and drawn from a very wide array of sources to be of real usefulness.

Of course such an index would also be of enormous benefit back in the office. It would in a single self-contained book provide lawyers with a cost-effective, hassle-free, easy-to-use means of accessing in their particular subject area many thousands of cases in many thousands of law report and law journal volumes and so open up a whole new world of precedents for them to call in aid when seeking to buttress whatever case they are called upon to make. And with lawyers working ever longer hours, many of them at home, such a reference work that gave immediate access to thousands of cases would be of considerable help there too.

---

[1] Blackstone, *Commentaries on the Laws of England* (Dawsons of Pall Mall, 1966), Volume I, p. 71.

Such a reference work now exists. The publication of the first eight volumes of *Blackstone's Index of Case Precedents*, each volume being an entirely self-contained index to cases in one of eight subject areas means that there is now a reasonably priced, convenient and readily usable one-stop reference source for legal practitioners, academic lawyers and legal students who are seeking to locate a specific twentieth century precedent or trying to discover whether there is a relevant and helpful precedent in a particular area of the law.

Embracing Child Law, Criminal Law, Evidence, Family Law, Marriage Breakdown, Road Traffic Law, Sentencing, and Tort these first eight volumes of *Blackstone's Index* contain over 120,000 references to more than 40,000 cases decided by the English and Welsh courts (and by the Privy Council) throughout the twentieth century. Within the various volumes cases are listed alphabetically as well as by subject. The court which decided each case is also identified. In addition case-entries are followed by brief one or two sentence 'pointers' which seek to indicate in a little greater detail the content of the many decisions that have been indexed. These pointers do not, it should be noted, attempt to summarise the *ratio decidendi* of each case or indeed to encapsulate the entire array of issues that have been considered in a case. They are intended merely to provide a modicum of assistance to the reader in deciding whether it is worth moving on from having unearthed a case in *Blackstone's Index* to actually reading it in its entirety in a case report.

Blackstone's Index is uniquely comprehensive in indexing not only law reports but legal journals and periodicals as well. Cases have been extracted from the *All England Law Reports, Cox's Criminal Cases*, the *Criminal Appeal Reports, Criminal Appeal Reports (Sentencing), Criminal Law Review (Case and Comment), Family Court Reporter, Family Law Reports, Justice of the Peace Reports, Law Journal, Law Journal County Court Reporter, Law Journal Newspaper County Court Appeals, Law Journal Newspaper County Court Reports, Law Journal Reports, Law Reports (Appeal Cases, Chancery Division, Family Division, King's/Queen's Bench Division, Probate, Divorce* and *Admiralty Division), Law Times Reports, New Law Journal, New Law Journal Reports, Road Traffic Reports, Solicitors Journal, Times Law Reports* (old and new series), *Weekly Notes, Weekly Reporter* and *Weekly Law Reports*.

In short *Blackstone's Index of Case Precedents* represents a uniquely powerful low-cost reference tool through which the legal wisdom of the twentieth century is made readily available to lawyers heading into the twenty-first. In addition to publishing each volume of the work as a separate self-contained and easy-to-use book all eight volumes have been published on a single CD-ROM.

HOW TO USE BLACKSTONE'S LAW OF TORT INDEX

This volume contains references to those Law of Tort cases decided by the English and Welsh courts (and the Privy Council) during the twentieth century which have been reported in the wide array of reports and periodicals that form the basis of *Blackstone's Index of Case Precedents*.

Like each other volume of a *Blackstone's Index* this volume is a self-contained reference source. In other words users of the *Law of Tort Index* will not be referred to any other volume in their quest for a particular Law of Tort case.

On the whole the *Law of Tort Index* embraces those areas of law that would feature in a typical Law of Tort syllabus at university. On the whole, Admiralty, trade union and employment law (vicarious liability) cases have been left for later *Index* volumes pertaining to those subject areas.

The *Law of Tort Index* is divided into two Parts. In Part I cases are grouped into subject categories. In Part II cases are listed alphabetically. Readers looking for cases by topic are recommended to consult Part I. Readers with a rough (or indeed exact) idea of a case name and who wish merely to discover where a specific case is located ought to consult Part II.

Each case is succeeded by a brief 'pointer'. The 'pointer' gives a better idea of what exactly each case is concerned with. It cannot be overemphasised that the 'pointer' does not represent an attempt to summarise the entirety of a case nor does it seek to give a one or two line *ratio decidendi* for each case. It is meant merely to provide a flavour of what has been decided in each case and to thereby enable the reader to make a somewhat more informed choice as to whether it is worth consulting a comprehensive account of the case in the relevant source or sources to which the reader is referred.

The Subject Index Cases in the subject index are grouped into generic categories such as NEGLI-GENCE, NUISANCE and TRESPASS. Cases are then listed under a variety of highly specific sub-headings. This has the double advantage that readers can either look up all the cases in a loosely defined area of interest or alternatively can very quickly zone in on the few cases decided in a much more tightly defined area of interest.

Either way the subject index is perfectly easy to use. It is preceded by two Tables of Contents. The first (entitled 'Generic Headings') lists the broad categories into which cases have been divided (NEGLIGENCE, NUISANCE, TRESPASS). The second (entitled 'Generic Headings with Sub-Headings') lists the much more specific headings under which cases are listed within each generic category ('NEGLIGENCE (medical)', 'NUISANCE (smell)', 'TRESPASS (child)'). The reader can turn to the 'Generic Headings' page, see in what generic category the case or type of case being looked for is most likely to be found and turn to the appropriate part of the subject index. Alternatively the reader can move on to (if the reader has not in fact gone straight to) the 'Generic Headings with Sub-Headings' page, find out the sub-headings under which cases are listed, decide which sub-heading most closely matches the reader's subject of inquiry and turn to the page indicated. As with any dictionary or index a degree of creative thinking may very occasionally be required of the reader in judging which category or sub-heading best matches the case or genre of case the reader is seeking to locate.

The Alphabetical Index The alphabetical index follows the traditional format adopted in the contents of case reports. Hence case names are listed both in forward order and in reverse order so that readers can quickly locate the case they are seeking.

Users should note that while every reasonable care has been taken to ensure that the case names and citations in the text of this work are accurate and that the text of the work is correct insofar as it indicates what was decided in each case mentioned the author accepts no responsibility for loss occasioned to any person acting or refraining from acting as a result of material contained in this publication.

ABBREVIATIONS USED

The following abbreviations are used in the text:

AC	*Law Reports (Appeal Cases)*
All ER	*All England Reports*
CA	Court of Appeal
CCA	Court of Criminal Appeal
CCR	Crown Cases Reserved
CC Rep	*Law Journal County Court Reports*
Ch	*Law Reports (Chancery Division)*
Cox CC	*Cox's Criminal Cases*
Cr App R	*Criminal Appeal Reports*
Cr App R (S)	*Criminal Appeal Reports (Sentencing)*
CrCt	Crown Court
Crim LR	*Criminal Law Review*
CyCt	County Court
FamD	*Law Reports (Family Division)*
FCR	*Family Court Reporter*
FLR	*Family Law Reports*
HC ChD	High Court (Chancery Division)
HC FamD	High Court (Family Division)
HC KBD	High Court (King's Bench Division)
HC PDAD	High Court (Probate, Divorce and Admiralty Division)
HC QBD	High Court (Queen's Bench Division)
HL	House of Lords
JP	*Justice of the Peace Reports*
KB	*Law Reports (King's Bench Division)*
LJ	*Law Journal/Law Journal Reports*
LJNCCR	*Law Journal Newspaper County Court Reports*
LJNCCA	*Law Journal Newspaper County Court Appeals*
LTR	*Law Times Reports*
Mag	Magistrates' Court
NLJ	*New Law Journal/New Law Journal Reports*
PC	Privy Council
Police Ct	Police Court
PDAD	*Law Reports (Probate, Divorce and Admiralty Division)*
QB	*Law Reports (Queen's Bench Division)*
RTR	*Road Traffic Reports*
SJ	*Solicitors Journal*
TrTb	Transport Tribunal
TLR	*Times Law Reports*
WN	*Weekly Notes*
WR	*Weekly Reporter*
WLR	*Weekly Law Reports*

ABBREVIATIONS USED

In addition the following letters are sometimes indicated alongside page numbers:

1. dt, g, i, t

These letters when they appear immediately after a page number indicate that the source to which the reader is being referred contains an additional reference to a British newspaper report of the case concerned.

dt	=	*Daily Telegraph*
g	=	*The Guardian*
i	=	*The Independent*
t	=	*The Times*

2. ccr

Not all County Court cases noted by the *Law Journal* were published separately from the main body of the *Journal*. Those notes of County Court reports contained within the *Journal* itself are indicated in the text of this *Index* by prefacing the page number from the relevant volume of the *Law Journal* with the abbreviation 'ccr' to show that the case is contained in the County Court Reporter section of the *Journal*.

3. LB

These letters may appear before the page number in a reference to the *Solicitors Journal* and indicate that the reference is to a page number in the *Lawyer's Brief* section of the relevant *Solicitors Journal*.

4. b, c

These letters when they appear immediately after a page number indicate that the source to which the reader is being referred contains an additional reference to a bar library transcript (b) or Court of Appeal transcript (c) of the case concerned.

5. wr

These letters may appear before the page number in a reference to the *Solicitors Journal* and indicate that the reference is to a page number in the *Weekly Reports* section of the *Solicitors Journal*.

ACKNOWLEDGMENTS

Writing the first eight volumes of *Blackstone's Index of Case Precedents* has been a challenging task rendered all the easier by the consistent kindness of family and friends and the very real generosity of many other people who have freely given their advice and assistance throughout the period in which the volumes were prepared.

My parents, Michael and Della Barrett, yet again provided me with that unqualified encouragement and support which they have afforded me in the past. My two brothers, Conor and Dr Gavin Barrett were similarly helpful.

In addition to my parents and brothers I was privileged throughout the period of writing the various volumes of the *Index* to have a close coterie of generous people around me who were eager to provide me with whatever assistance I needed. My very good friend Jennifer Powell proved herself to be a remarkable bastion of support to whom I owe a particular debt of gratitude. I am also deeply grateful to Sue Bate, the Law Librarian at Manchester University whose unfailing and undeserved kindness towards me has immeasurably facilitated and speeded the completion of this work. Professor Frank B. Wright, my onetime doctoral and later post-doctoral research supervisor at the European Occupational Health and Safety Legal Research Centre willingly provided useful and much-appreciated advice whenever it was solicited. My old friend Dr Jonathan Rush, not only undertook the onerous technical task of formatting *Blackstone's Index* for publication both in book and CD-form but was a constant bedrock of support in many other ways. Bryan and Josie Hallows provided me with a warm and welcome retreat in the Cheshire countryside and so much more besides. So far as places to retreat to with my work were concerned I was in fact rather spoiled for choice with — regrettably as yet unavailed of — offers coming in from Duncan Lennox in San Francisco and from Anna Retoula, Christos Retoulas and Constantina Scholidi in Greece. Others among this 'support team' of friends included Fr Des Doyle, Fr Ian Kelly, Fr John McMahon, Stephano Pistillo and Martin Wai-Chung Leung. I must also acknowledge the very great assistance given to me by the library staff at Cambridge University, Manchester University, Salford University and Trinity College Dublin.

Last but far from least I would like to record my special thanks to Agapi Kapeloni, who when I began this work was my girlfriend, who somewhere along the way found herself changed in status to that of honorary research assistant and whose latest and most agreeable change in status was to become my wife.

Finally, I have taken reasonable care to ensure that the case names and citations in the text of this work are accurate and that the text of the work is correct insofar as it indicates what was decided in each case mentioned. However, I accept no responsibility for loss occasioned to any person acting or refraining from acting as a result of material contained in this publication.

Blackstone's Index of Case Precedents embraces cases from the turn of the twentieth century through to the early Autumn of 1997.

Dr Maxwell Barrett,
Dublin,
Feast of the Immaculate Conception, 1997

GENERIC HEADINGS

ABUSE OF PUBLIC OFFICE
ANIMAL
ASSAULT
BREACH OF CONFIDENCE
CHILD SEX ABUSE
CONFIDENTIAL INFORMATION
CONSPIRACY
CONTRIBUTORY NEGLIGENCE
CONVERSION
COPYRIGHT
CORPORATION
CROWN
DAMAGES
DEFAMATION
DESERTION
DETINUE
DUTY OF CARE
ESTOPPEL
EXPULSION
FALSE IMPRISONMENT
FOREIGN TORT
FRAUD
HARASSMENT
HIGHWAY
HUSBAND AND WIFE
INDUCEMENT
INDUCEMENT TO COMMIT BREACH
  OF CONTRACT
INTERFERENCE

INTIMIDATION
JOINT TORTFEASORS
LIBEL
LIMITATION
LOSS OF CONSORTIUM
MALICIOUS ISSUE OF CIVIL PROCESS
MALICIOUS PROSECUTION
MILITARY
MISFEASANCE IN PUBLIC OFFICE
MISREPRESENTATION
NEGLIGENCE
NERVOUS SHOCK
NUISANCE
OCCUPIER'S LIABILITY
PASSING-OFF
PERSONAL INJURIES
PRIVILEGE
PROCURING ACT DAMAGING THIRD
  PARTY
PUBLIC AUTHORITY PROTECTION
RYLANDS v FLETCHER
SEIZURE
TORT BY PUBLIC OFFICIAL
TRADE UNION
TRESPASS
TROVER
WAIVER OF TORT
WRONGFUL APPROPRIATION

GENERIC HEADINGS WITH SUB-HEADINGS

ABUSE OF PUBLIC OFFICE (general)
ANIMAL (fish)
ANIMAL (general)
ASSAULT (damages)
ASSAULT (general)
ASSAULT (police)
BREACH OF CONFIDENCE (damages)
BREACH OF CONFIDENCE (general)
CHILD SEX ABUSE (damages)
CONFIDENTIAL INFORMATION
  (general)
CONSPIRACY (conspiracy to breach
  contract)
CONSPIRACY (conspiracy to slander)
CONSPIRACY (conspiracy to trespass)
CONSPIRACY (fraudulent conspiracy)
CONSPIRACY (general)
CONSPIRACY (injunction)
CONTRIBUTORY NEGLIGENCE (child)
CONTRIBUTORY NEGLIGENCE
  (damages)
CONTRIBUTORY NEGLIGENCE
  (general)
CONTRIBUTORY NEGLIGENCE (rail)
CONTRIBUTORY NEGLIGENCE (road
  traffic)
CONTRIBUTORY NEGLIGENCE
  (shipping)
CONVERSION (animal)
CONVERSION (bailment)
CONVERSION (bank)
CONVERSION (copyright)
CONVERSION (damages)
CONVERSION (director)
CONVERSION (general)
CONVERSION (road traffic)
COPYRIGHT (general)
CORPORATION (general)
CROWN (general)
CROWN (trespass)
DAMAGES (exemplary)
DAMAGES (foreign tort)
DAMAGES (general)
DAMAGES (innuendo)

DAMAGES (interest)
DAMAGES (mitigation)
DAMAGES (negligence)
DAMAGES (personal injuries)
DAMAGES (remoteness)
DAMAGES (road traffic)
DAMAGES (social security)
DAMAGES (subsidence)
DEFAMATION (bank)
DEFAMATION (class)
DEFAMATION (comment)
DEFAMATION (conspiracy to slander)
DEFAMATION (corporation)
DEFAMATION (damages)
DEFAMATION (diplomatic immunity)
DEFAMATION (fair comment)
DEFAMATION (general)
DEFAMATION (health)
DEFAMATION (husband and wife)
DEFAMATION (innuendo)
DEFAMATION (justification)
DEFAMATION (libel)
DEFAMATION (local authority)
DEFAMATION (malice)
DEFAMATION (malicious falsehood)
DEFAMATION (malicious libel)
DEFAMATION (Parliamentary privilege)
DEFAMATION (payment into court)
DEFAMATION (privilege)
DEFAMATION (slander)
DEFAMATION (slander of goods)
DEFAMATION (slander of office of honour)
DEFAMATION (slander of title)
DEFAMATION (statement in court)
DEFAMATION (trade libel)
DESERTION (general)
DETINUE (animal)
DETINUE (damages)
DETINUE (general)
DETINUE (husband and wife)
DUTY OF CARE (bank)
DUTY OF CARE (coastguard)
DUTY OF CARE (general)
DUTY OF CARE (insurance)

GENERIC HEADINGS WITH SUB-HEADINGS

TRADE UNION (general)
TRESPASS (animal)
TRESPASS (bank)
TRESPASS (building)
TRESPASS (child)
TRESPASS (conspiracy)
TRESPASS (Crown)
TRESPASS (damages)
TRESPASS (estoppel)
TRESPASS (general)
TRESPASS (highway)
TRESPASS (husband and wife)
TRESPASS (landlord and tenant)
TRESPASS (licensee)
TRESPASS (local authority)
TRESPASS (necessity)
TRESPASS (negligence)
TRESPASS (nuisance)
TRESPASS (police)
TRESPASS (rail)
TRESPASS (reasonable force)
TRESPASS (road traffic)
TRESPASS (school)
TRESPASS (trespass to goods)
TRESPASS (trespass to person)
TROVER (general)
WAIVER OF TORT (general)
WRONGFUL APPROPRIATION (general)

SUBJECT INDEX

ABUSE OF PUBLIC OFFICE (general)

Dunlop v Woollahra Municipal Council [1981] 1 All ER 1202; [1982] AC 158; (1981) 125 SJ 199; [1981] 2 WLR 693 PC Can only recover for illegal act not null act; absent malice passing of null act not misfeasance and misfeasance essential to abuse of public office.

ANIMAL (fish)

Stead v Nicholas (1900-1) 45 SJ 467; (1900-01) 49 WR 522 HC KBD Failed appeal against dismissal of information charging person with taking trout from reservoir (reservoirs not covered by Salmon Fishery Act 1865, as amended).

ANIMAL (general)

Paddick v Jones (Morgan) (1931) 72 LJ ccr31 CyCt Person liable in damages for injuries to pigeons occasioned by his cat which he had known to be vicious.

ASSAULT (damages)

Loudon v Ryder [1953] 1 All ER 741; [1953] 2 QB 202; (1953) 97 SJ 170; [1953] 2 WLR 537 CA On exemplary damages for trespass/assault.

ASSAULT (general)

Collins v Wilcock (1984) 79 Cr App R 229; [1984] Crim LR 481; (1984) 148 JP 692; (1984) 128 SJ 660; [1984] TLR 250; [1984] 1 WLR 1172 HC QBD Constable's taking hold of person whom merely wanted to speak to was battery so assault on same not assault on constable in execution of duty.

Gilson v Edwards (1928) 66 LJ ccr25 CyCt Can be sued in tort for assault notwithstanding certificate of conviction (following summary trial) for inflicting grievous bodily harm.

Green v Simmonds (1926) 62 LJ ccr74 CyCt Was assault where person injured self in course of reaction to stated intention of another strike same.

Hughes v Cassares (1967) 111 SJ 637 HC QBD Not assault for police officer to push person aside when in course of moving struggling arrestee to police vehicle.

Hurst v Picture Theatres, Limited (1913-14) XXX TLR 98 HC KBD Recovery for assault/false imprisonment by theatre audience member mistakenly ejected from seat having paid for ticket.

Hurst v Picture Theatres, Limited [1915] 1 KB 1; (1914) 49 LJ 439; [1914] 83 LJKB 1837; (1914-15) 111 LTR 972; (1913-14) XXX TLR 642 CA Recovery for assault/false imprisonment by theatre audience member mistakenly ejected from seat having paid for ticket.

McLeod v McLeod (1963) 113 LJ 420 CyCt Successful action by wife against husband for possession of onetime matrimonial home plus damages for assault (plus injunction restraining acts being done again).

Morriss v Marsden and another [1952] 1 All ER 925; (1952) 102 LJ 219; (1952) 96 SJ 281; [1952] 1 TLR 947; (1952) WN (I) 188 HC QBD Knowledge of nature/quality though not wrongfulness of act opens one to tortious liability.

O'Connor v Hewitson and another [1979] Crim LR 46 CA Valid refusal of aggravated/exemplary damages to prisoner assaulted by police officer given behaviour of prisoner leading up to assault.

Sherbourne v Walker [1955] Crim LR 184 HC QBD Successful action for damages against policeman guilty of assault/wrongful imprisonment/malicious prosecution.

1

Sirros v Moore and another [1974] 3 All ER 776; (1974) 118 SJ 661 CA Judge acting judicially was immune from civil action (as were police acting bona fide under his direction).

Sturley v Commissioner of Police of the Metropolis [1984] TLR 410 HC QBD Successful action for assault against police officers for excessively forceful form of restraint employed on middle-aged female detainee.

Vaughan v McKenzie [1968] 1 All ER 1154; [1968] Crim LR 265; (1968) 118 NLJ 204t; [1969] 1 QB 557; (1968) 112 SJ 212; [1968] 2 WLR 1133 HC QBD Not assault on bailiff in execution of duty where assault occurred when resident sought to impede bailiff's entry (bailiff in so entering was trespassing).

Yardy v Greenwood [1935] LJNCCA 218; (1935) 79 SJ 363 CA Inappropriate staying of action for assault so that prosecution for causing grievous bodily harm with intent/causing grievous bodily harm might be brought.

ASSAULT (police)

White and another v Metropolitan Police Commissioner [1982] TLR 221 HC QBD Exemplary damages from Police Commissioner for false imprisonment/assault/malicious prosecution by police officers.

BREACH OF CONFIDENCE (damages)

National Broach and Machine Co v Churchill Gear Machines Ltd (1965) 109 SJ 511; [1965] 1 WLR 1199 CA General damages could be recovered for breach of duty of confidence where could prove damage; on nature of inquiry as to damages to be undertaken.

BREACH OF CONFIDENCE (general)

Attorney-General v Blake; Jonathan Cape Ltd (third party) [1996] 3 All ER 903; [1997] Ch 84; [1996] 3 WLR 741 HC ChD On nature of duty of confidence owed by onetime Crown servant to Crown: publication of material that was not secret any more was not breach of any such duty.

Dowson and Mason Ltd v Potter and another (1970) 130 SJ 841; [1986] 1 WLR 1419 CA Damages to compensate for loss of manufacturing profits resulting from worker's breach of confidence.

Faccenda Chicken Ltd v Fowler and others; Fowler v Faccenda Chicken Ltd [1986] 3 WLR 288 CA On duty owed by employee towards former employer in respect of confidential information learned during course of employment.

Hellewell v Chief Constable of Derbyshire [1995] TLR 9 HC QBD Was not breach of confidence for police to publicly use photograph of suspect as part of bona fide crime prevention scheme.

Lion Laboratories Ltd v Evans and others [1985] QB 526; (1984) 128 SJ 533; [1984] TLR 185; [1984] 3 WLR 539 CA Court authorised disclosure of documents despite their being published in breach of confidence where public interest in disclosure demanded it.

Maudsley v Palumbo and others [1995] TLR 690 HC ChD On what constitutes breach of confidence in respect of which damages are available.

Re a Company's application [1989] 3 WLR 265 HC ChD Failed action for injunction to restrain employee from disclosing confidential company information to statutory financial regulatory authority.

Schering Chemicals Ltd v Falkman Ltd and others [1982] QB 1; [1981] 2 WLR 848 CA Injunction granted restraining broadcasting of documentary in which chemical company employee spoke about matters in pending litigation: granted because would breach duty of confidence not because would be contempt of court (it would not).

Seager v Copydex Ltd (No 2) [1969] 1 WLR 809 CA On appropriate damages for breach of confidence (disclosure of confidential product information).

Stephens v Avery and others (1988) 132 SJ 822 HC ChD Lesbian did have good basis for breach of confidence action against sometime partner for disclosing details of their relationship to the press.

W v Egdell and others [1990] Ch 359 (also CA); (1989) 133 SJ 570; [1989] 2 WLR 689 HC ChD
On duty of confidentiality owed (and liability for breach of same) by psychiatrist to mental patient
at whose instruction prepare mental health report.

W v Egdell [1990] Ch 359 (also HC ChD); (1990) 134 SJ 286; [1990] 2 WLR 471 CA On duty
of confidentiality owed (and liability for breach of same) by psychiatrist to mental patient at whose
instruction prepare mental health report.

William Summers and Co Limited v Boyce and Kinmond and Co (1907-08) XCVII LTR 505 HC
ChD Injunction granted to restrain disclosure of company secrets by ex-employee to new
employer — damages from ex-employee/new employer for disclosures which had occurred.

Woodward and others v Hutchins and others (1977) 121 SJ 409; [1977] 1 WLR 760 CA Refusal
to grant injunction restraining disclosure of confidential information obtained in course of
employment.

CHILD SEX ABUSE (damages)

Pereira v Keleman [1994] 2 FCR 635; [1995] 1 FLR 428 HC QBD Successful claim by daughters
against father who had physically and sexually assaulted them.

CONFIDENTIAL INFORMATION (general)

Seager v Copydex, Ltd (1967) 111 SJ 335 CA On law as to confidental information: here defendants
liable for improper use of confidential information.

CONSPIRACY (conspiracy to breach contract)

Quinn v Leathem [1900-03] All ER 1; (1901) WN (I) 170 HL Damages available for conspiracy to
induce breaches of contract by employees/customers.

CONSPIRACY (conspiracy to slander)

Ward v Lewis and others [1955] 1 All ER 55; [1955] 1 WLR 9 CA No connection between alleged
slander and special damage meant could be no conspiracy to slander.

CONSPIRACY (conspiracy to trespass)

Byrne and another v Kinematograph Renters Society, Ltd and others [1958] 2 All ER 579 HC ChD
No conspiracy as no trespass when inspectors from trade protection society entered cinema to
monitor operation thereof.

Hesperides Hotels Ltd and another v Muftizade (1978) 142 JP 541; (1978) 122 SJ 507 HL Court
could not hear action regarding conspiracy to trespass on property in foreign country but could
hear action for trespass to chattels in that property.

CONSPIRACY (fraudulent conspiracy)

Price (married woman) and HT Peard v Carter (married woman), WHT Carter and John Carter
(1921) CC Rep X 74 CyCt Successful action for recovery of money mistakenly paid to married
woman and fraudulently transferred by her to husband/father-in-law once learned of mistake.

CONSPIRACY (general)

Allied Arab Bank Ltd v Hajjar and others (No 2) [1988] QB 944; (1988) 132 SJ 1148; [1988]
3 WLR 533 HC QBD Tort of conspiracy only occurs if injury to victim was directly intended by
conspirators — if (as here) was side-effect of alleged conspiracy principally intended to benefit
others (not injure victim) tort of conspiracy does not arise.

Byrne and another v Kinematograph Renters Society, Ltd and others [1958] 2 All ER 579 HC ChD
No conspiracy as no trespass when inspectors from trade protection society entered cinema to
monitor operation thereof.

CONSPIRACY (general)

Corporacion Nacional del Cobre de Chile v Sogemin Metals Ltd and others [1997] 2 All ER 917 HC ChD Contributory negligence not defence to conspiracy claim (arising from alleged bribery).

Crofter Hand Woven Harris Tweed Company, Limited and Others v Veitch and Another [1942] 1 All ER 142; [1942] 111 LJ 17; (1943) 93 LJ 125; (1942) 166 LTR 172 HL On elements of conspiracy to injure.

De Jetley Marks v Greenwood (Lord) and others [1936] 1 All ER 863 HC KBD Must be breach of contract before can sue for conspiracy to cause breach of contract.

Farmer v Wilson (1899-1901) XIX Cox CC 502; (1900) 35 LJ 245; [1900] 69 LJCL 496; (1900) LXXXII LTR 566; (1899-1900) XVI TLR 309 HC QBD Was besetting of persons on board ship (irrespective of whether contract permitting persons to be there was legal or not).

Femis-Bank (Anguilla) Ltd and others v Lazar and another [1991] 2 All ER 865; [1991] Ch 391; [1991] TLR 69; [1991] 3 WLR 80 HC ChD Injunction pending trial which would interfere with freedom of speech only exceptionally available.

Greenhalgh v Mallard [1947] 2 All ER 255 CA Res judicata where having pleaded unlawful purpose or unlawful means later bring action pleading unlawful purpose and unlawful means.

Huntley v Thornton and others [1957] 1 All ER 235; (1957) 107 LJ 73; (1957) 101 SJ 171 HC ChD Trade union liable for conspiracy to prevent party acquiring job.

Lonrho Ltd and others v Shell Petroleum Co Ltd and others [1981] 2 All ER 456; [1982] AC 173; (1981) 125 SJ 429; [1980] 1 WLR 627 HL Breach of sanctions order not breach of statutory duty; conspiracy if do not intend to injure another nor protect oneself.

Lonrho Ltd and another v Shell Petroleum Co Ltd and another (No 2) (1981) 131 NLJ 632; [1981] 3 WLR 33 HL Oil supplies to Zimbabwe-Rhodesia in violation of Southern Rhodesia (Petroleum) Order 1965 did not give rise to tortious liability to injured party.

Lonrho plc and others v Fayed and others (No 5) [1994] 1 All ER 188; (1993) 143 NLJ 1571; [1993] TLR 422; [1993] 1 WLR 1489 CA Tortious conspiracy consists of two or more persons doing acts lawful in themselves with intent to causing injury to another who is thereby injured; damages for injury to reputation/business reputation/feelings available only if defamation.

Marrinan v Vibart and another [1962] 1 All ER 869; [1962] Crim LR 310; (1962) 112 LJ 258; [1963] 1 QB 234; (1962) 106 SJ 511 HC QBD Conspiracy involves agreement plus act/s effecting damage; police evidence to DPP/before Benchers' inquiry immune from civil action.

Metall und Rohstoff AG v Donaldson Lufkin and Jenrette Inc and another [1988] 3 All ER 116; [1990] 1 QB 391 (also CA); (1988) 132 SJ 1149; [1988] 3 WLR 548 HC QBD Conspiracy does not require that sole/principal aim be to injure other party.

Metall und Rohstoff AG v Donaldson Lufkin and Jenrette Inc and another [1990] 1 QB 391 (also HC QBD); (1989) 133 SJ 1200; [1989] 3 WLR 563 CA Conspiracy does not require that sole/principal aim be to injure other party; to commit tort of abuse of legal process sole/principal aim of one's actions must be said abuse.

Midland Bank Trust Co Ltd and another v Green and others (No 3) [1979] 2 All ER 193; (1979) 123 SJ 306; [1979] 2 WLR 594 HC ChD Husband and wife can be liable for tortious conspiracy.

Reynolds v Shipping Federation, Ltd [1923] All ER 383; [1924] 1 Ch 28; (1923-24) 68 SJ 61 HC ChD Trade union/employer agreement that only trade union members be employed deemed not to be conspiracy/unlawful combination.

Scammell (G) and Nephew, Limited v Attlee and others (1928) 66 LJ 406; (1928) WN (I) 296 CA Failed action for alleged conspiracy to discontinue electricity supply which under statutory duty to supply (failed inter alia because out of time under Public Authorities' Protection Act 1893).

Scammell (G) and Nephew, Limited v Hurley and others [1929] 1 KB 419 HC KBD Alleged conspiracy to discontinue electricity supply which under statutory duty to supply.

Singh (Sajan) v Ali (Sandara) [1960] 1 All ER 269 PC Title to property passed in course of conspiracy vests in person to whom passed once conspired act completed and can sue in detinue/trespass.

Sweeney v Coote [1907] AC 221; [1907] 76 LJPC 49; (1907) XCVI LTR 749; (1906-07) 51 SJ 444; (1906-07) XXIII TLR 448; (1907) WN (I) 92 PC Failed claim for injunction to restrain impeding one in carrying on business/job.

CONSPIRACY (injunction)

Midland Bank plc v Laker Airways Ltd (1983) 133 NLJ 537 HC QBD Injunction continued restraining defendant from joining plaintiffs as defendants to conspiracy action before foreign court.

CONTRIBUTORY NEGLIGENCE (child)

Yachuk and Another v Oliver Blais Co, Ld [1949] 2 All ER 150; [1949] AC 386; (1949) LXV TLR 300; (1949) WN (I) 186 PC No contributory negligence by young child purchaser of petrol: seller thereof completely liable for later injuries suffered by child.

CONTRIBUTORY NEGLIGENCE (damages)

Baker v Willoughby [1969] 2 All ER 549; (1969) 113 SJ 37; [1969] 2 WLR 489 CA Equal blameworthiness: appropriate damages.

CONTRIBUTORY NEGLIGENCE (general)

Admiralty Commissioners v North of Scotland and Orkney and Shetland Steam Navigation Co, Ltd [1947] 2 All ER 350 HL Overtaking ships equally negligent in causing collision.

Almeroth v Chivers (WE) and Sons, Ltd [1948] 1 All ER 53 CA Slates left on kerb were nuisance (de minimis non curat lex); not contributorily negligent that did not see.

Brown and another v Thompson [1968] 2 All ER 708; (1968) 112 SJ 464; [1968] 1 WLR 1003 CA Contributory negligence depends on fault; trial judge's finding not interfered with lightly.

Canadian Pacific Railway Company v Frechette [1915] AC 871; [1915] 84 LJPC 161; (1915-16) 113 LTR 1116; (1914-15) XXXI TLR 529 PC Quebecois could not recover damages where real cause of accident was own negligence (despite contributory negligence of party sued).

Capps v Miller [1989] 2 All ER 333; [1989] RTR 312; (1989) 133 SJ 1134; [1989] 1 WLR 839 CA Improperly fastening crash helmet contributory negligence meriting 10% reduction in damages.

Caswell v Powell Duffryn Associated Collieries Limited [1939] 108 LJCL 779; (1939) 161 LTR 374 HL On contributory negligence as defence to action for breach of statutory workplace health and safety duty.

City of Montreal v Watt and Scott, Limited [1922] 2 AC 555; (1923) 128 LTR 147; (1922) WN (I) 271 PC Muncipal authority's liability for overflowing sewer reduced where another was contributorily negligent in causing same.

Cooper v Howatt (1921-22) XXXVIII TLR 721 HC KBD Whether defendant in personal injuries action found to be contributorily negligent (not substantive issue) but not negligent was 'wholly successful defendant'.

Corporacion Nacional del Cobre de Chile v Sogemin Metals Ltd and others [1997] 2 All ER 917 HC ChD Contributory negligence not defence to conspiracy claim (arising from alleged bribery).

Davies v Swan Motor Co (Swansea), Ltd (Swansea Corporation and James, Third Parties) [1949] 1 All ER 620; [1949] 2 KB 291; (1949) LXV TLR 278; (1949) WN (I) 192 CA Lack of proper care (not breach of duty) necessary to show contributory negligence to own death.

Drinkwater and another v Kimber [1951] 2 All ER 713; (1951) 101 LJ 511; (1951) 95 SJ 547; [1951] 2 TLR 630; (1951) WN (I) 496 HC KBD Cannot recover for damage from person contributorily negligent where suffer financial loss but no physical injury.

Drinkwater and another v Kimber [1952] 2 QB 281; [1952] 1 TLR 1486 CA Cannot recover for damage from person contributorily negligent where suffer financial loss but no physical injury.

Fitzgerald v Lane and another (1987) 137 NLJ 316; [1987] QB 781; (1987) 131 SJ 976; [1987] 3 WLR 249 CA Apportionment of liability for personal injuries suffered by pedestrian crossing road (when red light showing for pedestrians) when struck by two cars and rendered tetraplegic (uncertain which collision caused tetraplegia).

5

Fitzgerald v Lane and another [1988] 2 All ER 961; [1989] AC 328; (1988) 138 NLJ 209; [1988] 3 WLR 356 HL Deciding liabilities of co-defendants secondary to deciding liabilities of plaintiff and defendants; plaintiff's conduct to be considered against total conduct of defendants.

Fookes v Slaytor [1979] 1 All ER 137; (1978) 128 NLJ 882t; [1979] RTR 40; (1978) 122 SJ 489; [1978] 1 WLR 1293 CA Judge may only find contributory negligence if was pleaded.

Foskett (an infant) v Mistry [1984] RTR 1 CA Plaintiff infant who ran from hill onto road (75%) contributorily negligent as regarded resulting accident; driver who ought to have seen boy and recognised danger posed (25% negligent).

Franklin v Bristol Tramways and Carriage Co, Ltd [1941] 1 All ER 188; [1941] 1 KB 255; (1942) 92 LJ 59; [1941] 110 LJ 248 CA Contributory negligence where pedestrian (in black-out conditions) did not keep look-out for overtaking traffic.

Gibby v East Grinstead Gas and Water Company (1944) 170 LTR 250 CA Person walking on unfenced gantry at night without light was guilty of contributory negligence.

Glasscock v London, Tilbury, and Southend Railway Company (1901-02) XVIII TLR 295 CA Jury could reasonably arrive at decision that injuries suffered by woman stepping out of train too long for platform were not due to her contributory negligence/were due to negligence of rail company.

Hawkins v Ian Ross (Castings) Ltd [1970] 1 All ER 180 HC QBD No reduction of damages though contributorily negligent.

Hodkinson v Henry Wallwork and Co, Ltd [1955] 3 All ER 236 CA Contributory negligence of ninety per cent despite employer's breach of statutory duty where did something unauthorised.

Jennings v Norman Collison (Contractors) Ltd [1970] 1 All ER 1121 CA Contributory negligence re-appraised where factual error by trial judge.

Jones v Livox Quarries Ld; Same v Same [1952] 2 QB 608 CA Person injured by travelling on towbar of vehicle despite contrary instructions was contributorily negligent towards injuries suffered.

Jones v Staveley Iron and Chemical Co Ld [1955] 1 QB 474 CA Test for negligence versus that for contributory negligence.

Kerry v Carter [1969] 3 All ER 723 CA CA will alter trial judge's apportionment of liability if CA believes mistaken.

Kerry v Keighley Electrical Engineering Co, Ltd [1940] 3 All ER 399; (1940) 90 LJ 28; (1940) 163 LTR 97; (1940) 84 SJ 681 CA Contributory negligence where person stepping through lift door assumed lift was at floor level.

Lasczyk v National Coal Board [1954] 3 All ER 205 Assizes Guilty of contributory negligence where acting under supervisor's instructions but contrary to training officer's ordinance.

Leach v Standard Telephones and Cables, Ltd [1966] 2 All ER 523 HC QBD Employer contributorily negligent towards employee's breach of employee duty under Factory Act 1961.

Machray v Stewarts and Lloyds, Ltd [1964] 3 All ER 716 Assizes No contributory negligence where 'contributory' acts necessitated by other's inaction.

McDonald v British Transport Commission [1955] 3 All ER 789; (1955) 99 SJ 912; [1955] 1 WLR 1323 HC QBD If equipment provided dangerous burden on provider to show took reasonable care of victim's safety.

McLean v Bell [1932] All ER 421; (1932) 73 LJ 411; (1932) 147 LTR 262; (1932) 76 SJ 414; (1931-32) XLVIII TLR 467; (1932) WN (I) 131 HL Contributory negligence by party running another down not complete defence to negligence on part of party run down.

Miller v Evans and another; Pouleuf (Third Party) [1975] RTR 70 CA Driver not contributorily negligent in assuming oncoming traffic travelling at such speed that could stop when lights changed.

Morgan v Aylen [1942] 1 All ER 489; (1943) 93 LJ 115 HC KBD Running in front of motor vehicle to save child not contributory negligence.

Morris v Mayor, Aldermen and Burgesses of the Borough of Luton [1946] 1 All ER 1; (1946) 110 JP 102; [1946] KB 114; [1946] 115 LJ 202; (1946) 174 LTR 26; (1946) 90 SJ 91; (1945-46) LXII TLR 145; (1945) WN (I) 239 CA No rule that party driving in dark must be able to stop within limits of sight or is negligent.

Nance v British Columbia Electric Railway Co, Ltd [1951] 2 All ER 448; [1951] AC 601; (1951) 95 SJ 543; [1951] 2 TLR 137; (1951) WN (I) 373 PC On contributory negligence as defence.

Owens v Brimmell [1976] 3 All ER 765; [1977] QB 859; [1977] RTR 82; (1977) 121 SJ 338; [1977] 2 WLR 943 HC QBD Burden of proving contributory negligence on party alleging; contributory negligence where travel with inebriated driver; join in with party on drinking spree, then travel with party in car.

Pasternack v Poulton [1973] 2 All ER 74; (1973) 123 NLJ 180t; [1973] RTR 334; (1973) 117 SJ 225; [1973] 1 WLR 476 HC QBD Contributory negligence if not wearing seat-belt as chance of car accident foreseeable.

Quintas v National Smelting Co, Ltd [1961] 1 All ER 630 CA Master liable in negligence/plaintiff contributorily so for injury caused in factory by article not machinery under Factories Act 1937, s 14.

Reynolds v Thomas Tilling (Limited) (1902-03) XIX TLR 539 HC KBD Interpretation of findings of jury as to negligence/contributory negligence: non-recovery for personal injuries sustained through injury partly caused by own negligence.

Reynolds v Thomas Tilling (Limited) (1903-04) XX TLR 57 CA Approval of lower court's interpretation of findings of jury as to negligence/contributory negligence: non-recovery for personal injuries sustained through injury partly caused by own negligence.

Sigurdson (Marvin) v British Columbia Electric Railway Co Ld [1953] AC 291; (1952) WN (I) 411 PC On contributory negligence.

Skeen v British Railways Board; Scandle (Third Party); Scandle v Skeen and another [1976] RTR 281 HC QBD British Railways Board fully liable for collision between train and van at very dangerous crossing in respect of which Railways Board took no safeguards despite knowing of danger.

The Towerfield; Owners of the SS Towerfield v Workington Harbour and Dock Board [1948] 2 All ER 736 CA On negligence/contributory negligence under Pilotage Act 1913/Harbours, Docks, and Piers Clauses Act 1847.

Tremayne v Hill [1987] RTR 131 CA Pedestrian not contributorily negligent where did not keep look-out when crossing junction at which vehicle traffic lights red.

William A Jay and Sons v Veevers (JS), Ltd [1946] 1 All ER 646 Assizes Apportionment of liability for contributory negligence on Admiralty Division principles.

Williams v Port of Liverpool Stevedoring Co, Ltd and another [1956] 2 All ER 69; [1956] 1 WLR 551 Assizes Liability of employer for negligence of stevedoring gang and of member of gang for own part in own injury.

Worsfold v Howe [1980] 1 All ER 1028; (1980) 130 NLJ 140; [1980] RTR 131; (1980) 124 SJ 646; [1980] 1 WLR 1175 CA Contributory negligence where collision between motorcyclist on main road and driver edging from lesser road.

CONTRIBUTORY NEGLIGENCE (rail)

Barry Railway Company v White (1900-01) XVII TLR 644 HL On negligence/contributory negligence in action for personal injuries suffered at level crossing.

CONTRIBUTORY NEGLIGENCE (road traffic)

Chapman v Post Office [1982] RTR 165 CA Pedestrian not negligent in standing on kerb (where was hit by side-mirror of van negligently driven too close to kerb).

Chapman v Ward (1974) 124 NLJ 988t; [1975] RTR 7; (1974) 118 SJ 777 HC QBD Front seat passenger without seat belt not guilty of contributory negligence as regards injuries suffered in accident.

Cooper v Swadling [1930] 1 KB 403; (1930) 69 LJ 9; (1930) 99 LJCL 118; (1930) 142 LTR 411; (1929-30) XLVI TLR 73; (1929) WN (I) 273 CA On direction regarding negligence in case where person knocked down in motor collision.

Drage v Smith and another (1974) 124 NLJ 1157t; [1975] RTR 1; (1974) 118 SJ 865 HC QBD Front seat passenger without seat belt guilty of contributory negligence as regards injuries suffered (only 15% as seat belt campaign not at pitch in 1970 — year of accident — as was when case decided).

Freeborn v Thomas [1975] RTR 16 HC QBD Front seat passenger without seat belt not guilty of contributory negligence as regards injuries suffered in accident.

Froom and others v Butcher [1974] 3 All ER 517; (1975) 125 NLJ 843t; [1974] RTR 528; (1974) 118 SJ 758; [1974] 1 WLR 1297 HC QBD No negligence if person acting on reasonably held belief drove without seat belt.

Froom and others v Butcher [1975] 3 All ER 520; [1976] QB 286; [1975] RTR 518; (1975) 119 SJ 613; [1975] 3 WLR 379 CA Is contributory negligence where car passenger does not wear seat belt.

Gregory v Kelly (1978) 128 NLJ 488t; [1978] RTR 426 HC QBD Plaintiff-passenger/defendant-driver 40%/60% liable for injuries/losses arising from collision when travelling in car (plaintiff without seat belt) in car without footbrake: defendant precluded statutorily from pleading volenti non fit injuria.

Hopwood Homes Ltd v Kennerdine [1975] RTR 82 CA Driver not contributorily negligent in assuming oncoming traffic travelling at such speed that could stop when lights changed.

James v Parsons (1974) 124 NLJ 1029t; [1975] RTR 20; (1974) 118 SJ 777 HC QBD Front seat passenger without seat belt not guilty of contributory negligence as regards injuries suffered in accident absent warning from driver of need to wear belt.

Rouse v Squires and others [1973] 2 All ER 903; [1973] QB 889; [1973] RTR 550; (1973) 117 SJ 431; [1973] 2 WLR 925 CA Negligent obstruction of highway contributorily negligent to later negligent collision therewith.

Sparks v Edward Ash, Ltd [1943] 1 All ER 1; (1943) 107 JP 45; (1944) 94 LJ 108; (1942) 86 SJ 322; (1942-43) LIX TLR CA Contributory negligence defence open in breach of statutory duty action.

Swadling v Cooper [1930] All ER 257; [1931] AC 1; (1930) 70 LJ 108; (1931) 100 LJCL 97; (1930) 143 LTR 732; (1930) 74 SJ 536; (1929-30) XLVI TLR 597; (1930) WN (I) 204 HL On direction regarding negligence in case where person knocked down in motor collision.

Tart v Chitty (GW) and Co, Ltd [1931] All ER 826; [1933] 2 KB 453; (1933) 102 LJCL 568; (1933) 149 LTR 261 HC KBD Contributory negligence where driving so fast could not avoid collision or were not keeping proper look-out.

Waller v Levoi (1968) 112 SJ 865 CA Successful plaintiff (who sued person who parked on bend for injuries that arose from collision between them) entitled to appropriate costs though had been contributorily negligent.

Walsh v Redfern and another [1970] RTR 201 HC QBD Person on main road to give way to person on minor road if necessary to avoid accident; lorry driver not contributorily negligent where was driving at reasonable speed on main road and collided with car emerging from minor road without paying heed to warning signs.

CONTRIBUTORY NEGLIGENCE (shipping)

Carsholm (Owners) v Calliope (Owners); The Calliope [1970] 2 WLR 991 HC PDAD Finding of negligence on one hand and intervening negligence on other in shipping collision case.

CONVERSION (animal)

Gelston v King (1918) CC Rep VII 66 CyCt Successful damages for conversion of swarm of bees hived by person who refused to return them to person who formerly hived swarm for one day.

CONVERSION (bailment)

Elvin and Powell, Limited v Plummer Roddis, Limited (1934) 78 SJ 48; (1933-34) L TLR 158 HC KBD Involuntary bailees not liable in conversion for non-negligent act which results in loss of property.

CONVERSION (bank)

Akrokerri (Ashanti) Mines Limited v Economic Bank Limited and Nobbs; Bipposu Mines Limited v Same; Attasi Mines Limited v Same; Ashanti Mines Limited v Same (1904-05) XCI LTR 175 HC KBD Bank's bona fide non-negligent honouring of stolen cheques did not involve conversion.

Australian Bank of Commerce Limited v Perel and others (1926) 135 LTR 586 PC Failed appeal by bank in action brought against bank inter alia for conversion of cheques (failed to establish course of business which had greater effect than written instructions given).

Capital and Counties Bank, Limited v Gordon; London, City and Midland Bank, Limited v Gordon (1903) WN (I) 92 HL On liability of banks for conversion of cheques.

Carpenters' Company of the City of London v British Mutual Banking Company, Limited (1937) 81 SJ 118; (1936-37) LIII TLR 270 HC KBD Bank negligent in accepting cheques fraudulently indorsed and lodging same to fraudster's account.

Carpenters' Company v British Mutual Banking Company, Limited [1938] 1 KB 511; (1937) 81 SJ 701; (1936-37) LIII TLR 1040; (1937) WN (I) 329 CA Bank liable in conversion for accepting cheques fraudulently indorsed and lodging to fraudster's account.

Embiricos v Anglo-Austrian Bank (1904-05) XCI LTR 652; (1903-04) 48 SJ 717; (1904-05) 53 WR 92 HC KBD Bank having obtained good title to originally stolen cheque could pass good title to another whose obtaining payment on foot of same was not therefore conversion.

Embiricos v Anglo-Austrian BAnk (1905) XCII LTR 305 CA Bank having obtained good title to originally stolen cheque could pass good title to another whose obtaining payment on foot of same was not therefore conversion.

Gordon v London, City and Midland Bank, Limited; Gordon v Capital and Counties Bank, Limited [1902] 1 KB 242; (1901-02) 50 WR 276 CA Liability of banks for conversion of cheques.

Lloyds Bank, Ltd v Chartered Bank of India, Australia and China [1928] All ER 285 CA Negligent dealing with cheques resulting in conversion.

Midland Bank, Ltd v Reckitt and others [1932] All ER 90; (1931-32) XLVIII TLR 271 HL Bank liable in negligence/conversion for cashing cheques signed by solicitor whom bank had notice was operating outside authority as agent.

Penmount Estates, Limited v National Provincial Bank, Limited; Stanley Moss and Pilcher (third party) (1945) 173 LTR 344 HC KBD Action for conversion/negligence where bank credited amount of cashed cheque to wrong bank account.

Underwood (AL), Limited v Bank of Liverpool and Martins, Limited (1922-23) XXXIX TLR 606 HC KBD Bank's negligent disposal of cheques was conversion.

Underwood (AL), Ltd v Bank of Liverpool and Martins; Same v Bank (Barclays) [1924] All ER 230; (1924) 131 LTR 271; (1923-24) XL TLR 302 CA Bank's negligent disposal of cheques was conversion.

CONVERSION (copyright)

Ash v Dickie [1936] 105 LJCh 337; (1936) 154 LTR 641; (1936) 80 SJ 364; (1935-36) LII TLR 534; (1936) WN (I) 157 CA Post-copyright infringement: on assessing damage sustained.

Birn Brothers, Lim v Keene and Co, Lim [1919] 88 LJCh 24 HC ChD On rights of action in detinue/conversion open to copyright-owner under Copyright Act 1911, s 7.

Caxton Publishing Co, Ltd v Sutherland Publishing Co, Ltd [1938] 4 All ER 389; [1939] 108 LJCh 5; (1938) 86 LJ 383; (1939) 160 LTR 17; (1938) 82 SJ 1047; (1938-39) LV TLR 123; (1938) WN (I) 367 HL Three-year limitation on post-breach of copyright conversion action; damages available for both infringement and conversion post-breach of copyright.

CBS Songs Ltd and others v Amstrad Consumer Electronics plc and another [1988] Ch 61; [1987] 3 WLR 144 CA Non-enforcement of criminal law (here alleged breach of copyright law) by way of civil action.

CONVERSION (damages)

CBS Songs Ltd and others v Amstrad Consumer Electronics plc and another [1988] AC 1013; (1988) 132 SJ 789; [1988] 2 WLR 1191 HL Manufacturers of stereo hi-fis on which was possible to privately re-record copyright material not liable in tort for incitement to commit breach of copyright legislation.

Graves v Pocket Publications, Limited (1937-38) LIV TLR 952 HC ChD Damages for conversion in context of copyright infringement.

Infabrics Ltd and others v Jaytex Ltd (1980) 124 SJ 309 CA On assessing damages for conversion arising from breach of copyright.

Infabrics Ltd and others v Jaytex Ltd (1981) 125 SJ 257 HL On assessing damages for conversion arising from breach of copyright.

Sutherland Publishing Co, Ltd v Caxton Publishing Co, Ltd (No 2) [1937] 4 All ER; [1938] Ch 174; [1938] 107 LJCh 99; (1936) 154 LTR 367; (1935-36) LII TLR 230; (1937) WN (I) 393 CA On post-breach of copyright damages for conversion.

Tallent v Coldwell [1938] Ch 653; (1937-38) LIV TLR 564 HC ChD Post-copyright infringement damages for conversion.

CONVERSION (damages)

Ash and another v Hutchinson and Company (Publishers), Limited, and others [1936] Ch 489 CA On post-infringement of copyright damages for conversion.

BBMB Finance (Hong Kong) Ltd v Eda Holdings Ltd and others [1991] 2 All ER129; (1990) 134 SJ 425; [1990] TLR 103; [1990] 1 WLR 409 PC General rule is that damages for conversion are gauged by reference to date of conversion.

Building and Civil Engineering Holidays Scheme Management Ltd v Post Office [1964] 2 QB 430; [1964] 2 WLR 967 HC QBD On damages available for conversion of chattel.

Building and Civil Engineering Holidays Scheme Management Ltd v Post Office [1966] 1 QB 247; (1964) 108 SJ 939; [1965] 2 WLR 72 CA Damages for future loss arising from conversion.

Carr v James Broderick and Company, Limited (1941-42) LVIII TLR 373 HC KBD On availability of damages for conversion where owner of hire-purchase property wrongfully retakes possession of same.

Caxton Publishing Co, Ltd v Sutherland Publishing Co, Ltd [1938] 4 All ER 389; [1939] 108 LJCh 5; (1938) 86 LJ 383; (1939) 160 LTR 17; (1938) 82 SJ 1047; (1938-39) LV TLR 123; (1938) WN (I) 367 HL Three-year limitation on post-breach of copyright conversion action; damages available for both infringement and conversion post-breach of copyright.

Chubb Cash Ltd v John Crilley and Son (1983) 127 SJ 153; [1983] 1 WLR 599 CA Damages for conversion were market value of goods (gauged by reference to price raised for goods at wrongful auction of same).

Commonwealth Trust, Limited v Akotey [1925] All ER 270; [1926] AC 72; (1924-25) XLI TLR 641 PC Cocoa-grower precluded by own actions for recovering damages for conversion from ultimate purchaser of cocoa.

IBL Ltd v Coussens [1991] 2 All ER 133; [1990] TLR 538 CA Damages for conversion not gauged by reference to date of judgment or conversion but what is fair compensation to owner for loss.

Montgomery v Hutchins (1906) XCIV LTR 207 HC KBD On appropriate damages for conversion of goods under sale of goods contract.

Solloway and another v McLaughlin [1938] 107 LJPC 1; (1937-38) LIV TLR 69; (1937) WN (I) 358 PC Disposal of client's shares when broker ought not to have been dealing in same was conversion; on appropriate damages therefor.

Wickham Holdings Ltd v Brooke House Motors Ltd [1967] 1 WLR 295 CA Finance company could only recover outstanding amount due under hire-purchase agreement where hirer wrongfully sold goods hired.

CONVERSION (director)

Re Ely, ex parte The Trustee (1899-1900) 44 SJ 483 CA Directors not required to account for their conversion of property on behalf of company where did not personally benefit/appellant had claim against company.

CONVERSION (general)

Ash v Hutchinson and Co (Publishers), Limited [1936] 105 LJCh 303; (1936) 155 LTR 46; (1935-36) LII TLR 429 CA Action for conversion following on infringement of copyright.

Ashley v Tolhurst and others [1937] LJNCCR 78 CyCt Car-park owners liable for breach of contract of bailment for reward and in conversion where handed car to person who did not produce ticket for same and whom it emerged was not the owner.

Baker v Barclays Bank, Ltd [1955] 2 All ER 571; (1955) 105 LJ 376; [1955] 1 WLR 822 Assizes Co-owner of property affecting exclusive possession thereof commits conversion.

Bavins, Junr and Sims v London and South Western Bank, Limited [1900] 69 LJCL 164; (1899-1900) LXXXI LTR 655; [1900] 1 QB 270; (1899-1900) 48 WR 210 CA Party allowed recover money had and received by way of stolen money order.

Beaman v ARTS, Ltd [1949] 1 All ER 465; [1949] 1 KB 550; (1949) 99 LJ 119; (1949) LXV TLR 389 CA Fraud not essential to conversion; fraudulent concealment of action being open held to delay application of limitation.

Belvoir Finance Co Ltd v Harold G Cole and Co Ltd [1969] 1 WLR 1877 HC QBD Successful claim for conversion of hire-purchase goods by hire-purchase finance company against person who bought cars from hirer and then resold them.

Belvoir Finance Co Ltd v Stapleton (1970) 120 NLJ 733t; [1971] 1 QB 210; (1970) 114 SJ 719; [1970] 3 WLR 530 CA Damages awarded for conversion on foot of fully executed illegal hire-purchase contracts.

Bowmakers, Limited v Barnet Instruments, Limited [1945] KB 65; [1945] 114 LJ 41; (1945) 89 SJ 22; (1944-45) LXI TLR 62 CA That have goods as result of illegal agreement not a defence to conversion where plaintiff not raising agreement as issue.

Brightside and Carbrook (Sheffield) Co-operative Society Ltd v Phillips (1964) 108 SJ 53; [1964] 1 WLR 185 CA Can make non-specific claim of conversion.

Bute (Marquess) v Barclays Bank, Ld [1955] 1 QB 202 HC QBD Need not be owner of 'converted' property to claim for conversion; no estoppel by representation where actions had been typical banking practice.

Chabbra Corporation Pte Ltd v Jag Shakti (Owners); The Jag Shakti [1986] AC 337; [1986] 2 WLR 87 PC Appropriate damages to bearers of bills of lading from shipowners for conversion effected by shipowner's wrongful delivery of cargo to buyers.

Clayton v Le Roy and Fils (1910-11) XXVII TLR 206 HC KBD Whether sale of goods in auction room constituted conversion.

Clayton v Le Roy and Fils [1911-13] All ER 284; (1911) 75 JP 521; (1911-12) 105 LTR 430; (1910-11) XXVII TLR 479 CA Whether sale of goods in auction room constituted conversion.

Commercial Banking Company of Sydney, Ltd v Mann [1960] 3 All ER 482; (1960) 104 SJ 846 PC Cannot claim conversion unless own property in issue.

Dobson v North Tyneside Health Authority and Newcastle Health Authority [1997] 2 FCR 651; (1996) 140 SJ LB 165 CA Failed action for conversion of corpse.

Douglas Valley Finance Co, Ltd v S Hughes (Hirers), Ltd [1966] 3 All ER 214; (1965-66) 116 NLJ 1378; [1969] 1 QB 738; (1966) 110 SJ 980; [1967] 2 WLR 503 HC QBD Adverse possession not element of conversion: merely assertion of ownership/control contrary to other's rights of possession/control.

Edwards v Bendall (1953) 103 LJ ccr351 CyCt Liquidator liable in conversion for sale of company property already purchased by another from Official Receiver.

Ellis v John Stenning and Son [1932] All ER 597; [1932] 2 Ch 81; (1932) 76 SJ 232 HC ChD Damages for conversion: action for conversion does not deny owner's title unless/until judgment fully satisfied.

Ellis v Noakes [1930] All ER 382; [1932] 2 Ch 98 CA Liability for conversion of timber which conveyance expressly did not include (even though timber not removed by date specified in conveyance).

Fenton Textile Association, Limited v Thomas [1927] 96 LJCL 1016; (1927) 137 LTR 241; (1928-29) XLV TLR 264 CA Liability of solicitors for conversion of client's funds.

Fenton Textile Association, Limited v Thomas and Clark (1928-29) XLV TLR 113 HC KBD Liability of solicitors for conversion of client's funds.

Finlayson v Taylor (1983) 133 NLJ 720; [1983] TLR 259 HC QBD Landlord liable in detinue/ conversion for seeking to exercise lien over goods bailed with him by tenant where latter owed arrears of rent.

International Factors Ltd v Rodriguez [1979] QB 351; [1978] 3 WLR 877 CA Recovery in conversion by factoring firm of amounts (originally) owed and paid to bank account of company from whom factoring firm had purchased the debts.

Jerome v Bentley and Co [1952] 2 All ER 114; (1952) 102 LJ 343; (1952) 96 SJ 462; [1952] 2 TLR 58 HC QBD Liability for conversion where bought item from person not authorised as/could not be presumed to be agent for sale.

Lancashire and Yorkshire Rail Co and others v MacNicoll [1918-19] All ER 537; [1919] 88 LJCL 601; (1918) 118 LTR 596; (1917-18) 62 SJ 365; (1917-18) XXXIV TLR 280 HC KBD Can commit conversion though do not intend to do wrong; negligence of party did not preclude it recovering for conversion.

Lawrence (Lim) v Lasseter (1924) CC Rep XIII 2 CyCt Successful claim against party guilty of purchase-conversion of furniture which had comprised security for loan to vendor of furniture.

Lewis Trusts v Bambers Stores Ltd [1983] TLR 125 CA Award of damages for conversion under the Copyright Act Act 1956, s 18.

Lowther v Harris (1926-27) XLIII TLR 24 HC KBD Successful action for conversion of tapestries by antique dealer; not estopped from recovering damages for conversion of tapestry which never represented agent had authority to sell.

Mansell v The Valley Printing Company and Rankine (1908) 43 LJ 90; (1908) 77 LJCh 397; (1907-08) XXIV TLR 311 HC ChD Injunction/damages available to author of unpublished matter against anyone who infringes exclusive right to publish/not to publish.

Mansell v The Valley Printing Company (1908) 43 LJ 448; (1908) 77 LJCh 742; (1907-08) XXIV TLR 802 CA Injunction/damages available to author of unpublished matter against anyone who infringes exclusive right to publish/not to publish.

Mills v Brooker [1918-19] All ER 613; [1919] 1 KB 555; [1919] 88 LJCL 950; (1919) 121 LTR 254; (1918-19) 63 SJ 431; (1918-19) XXXV TLR 261 HC KBD Party could abate nuisance of overhanging tree by lopping overhanging branches but was liable in conversion for keeping branches/fruit thereon.

Moorgate Mercantile Co, Ltd v Finch and another [1962] 2 All ER 467; (1962) 112 LJ 402; [1962] 1 QB 701; (1962) 106 SJ 284 CA Not paying instalment breached hire-purchase agreement: owners could bring conversion action; placing uncustomed goods in car then forfeited to customs a conversion as forfeiture natural/probable result of acts.

Munro v Willmott [1948] 2 All ER 983; [1949] 1 KB 295; (1948) 98 LJ 657; [1949] 118 LJR 471; (1948) LXIV TLR 627; (1948) WN (I) 459 HC KBD Appropriate damages for conversion/ detinue.

Nelson, Murdoch and Co v Wood (1921) CC Rep X 76; (1922) 126 LTR 745; (1921-22) XXXVIII TLR 23 HC KBD Improper sale of hire-purchase piano not per se a repudiation of hire-purchase contract and as finance company had not accepted repudiation/terminated contract transfer of piano was not conversion.

North Central Wagon and Finance Co, Ltd v Graham [1950] 1 All ER 780; [1950] 2 KB 7 CA Hirer could sue in conversion for breach of hire-purchase agreement as under particular agreement breach placed property immediately in hirer's possession.

Oakley v Lyster [1930] All ER 234; [1931] 1 KB 148; (1931) 144 LTR 363 CA Cannot convert another's property unless in dealing with same intend to deny owner's rights/assert right inconsistent with that of owner.

Ottoman Bank v Jebara [1928] AC 269 HL Failed action for alleged conversion on foot of sale of goods contract.

Paley (Princess Olga) v Weisz and others (1928-29) XLV TLR 102 HC KBD Failed action in detinue/conversion by Russian exile against defendants who purchased property confiscated by Soviets.

Paley (Princess Olga) v Weisz and others (1928-29) XLV TLR 365 CA Failed action in detinue/conversion by Russian exile against defendants who purchased property confiscated by Soviets.

Payne-Crofts v Aird Bros, Ltd and British Transport Commission (1953) 103 LJ ccr832 CyCt Successful action against warehouse keepers for goods negligently converted/detained/lost.

Re Upton-Cottrell-Dormer (deceased); Upton v Upton and others (1914-15) XXXI TLR 260 HC ChD Personalty (even if converted) had not been devised by testatrix.

RH Willis and Son v British Car Auctions Ltd (1978) 128 NLJ 186t; [1978] RTR 244; [1978] 1 WLR 438 CA Auctioneers liable to car-dealers in conversion for selling hire-purchase car on behalf of hirer who had no title to sell.

Rose v Buckett [1901] 2 KB 449; [1901] 70 LJK/QB 736; (1901) LXXXIV LTR 670; (1900-01) XVII TLR 544; (1901-02) 50 WR 8 CA Right of action for trespass/conversion did not pass to trustee upon plaintiff becoming bankrupt.

Sutherland Publishing Co, Ltd v Caxton Publishing Co, Ltd (No 2) [1937] 1 All ER 338; [1937] Ch 294; [1937] 106 LJCh 104; (1937) 156 LTR 191; (1936-37) LIII TLR 277; (1937) WN (I) 46 HC ChD Appropriate damages for conversion; three-year limitation period for conversion action subsequent to copyright infringement.

The Union Credit Bank and Davies v The Mersey Docks and Harbour Board; Same v Same; Same v The Mersey Docks and Harbour Board and the North and South Wales Bank (1899-1900) LXXXI LTR 44 HC QBD Failed action for damages for conversion of tobacco packages.

Thurston v Charles (1904-05) XXI TLR 659 HC KBD Substantial damages available for wrongful conversion/detention where published another's private correspondence but privilege in communication not destroyed so no libel.

Union Bank of Australia, Limited v McClintock and Others [1922] 1 AC 240; [1922] 91 LJPC 108; (1922) 126 LTR 588 PC Action failed as if ratified act of manager so as to have cause of action would also ratify later conversion.

Union Transport Finance Limited v British Car Auctions Ltd (1977) 127 NLJ 1247b CA Could be conversion of hire purchase item where bailee so acted as to open up right to immediate possession of relevant article by bailor.

United Australia, Ltd v Barclays Bank, Ltd [1939] 1 All ER 676; [1939] 2 KB 53; (1939) 87 LJ 180; [1939] 108 LJCL 477; (1939) 160 LTR 259; (1938-39) LV TLR 457; (1939) WN (I) 81 CA Mere bringing of action in contract waives right to sue in tort.

United Australia, Ltd v Barclays Bank, Ltd [1940] 4 All ER 20; [1941] AC 1; [1940] 109 LJCL 919 HL Earlier contractual action not bar to tortious action as no judgment obtained.

United Fruit Company Limited v Frederick Leyland and Co and Roberts, Brining and Co Limited (1930) 70 LJ 262; (1931) 144 LTR 97; (1930) 74 SJ 735 CA Appropriate interim arrangements regarding stock in action concerning conversion/detinue of bananas.

Van Oppen and Co, Limited v Tredegars, Limited (1920-21) XXXVII TLR 504 HC KBD Was conversion of goods mistakenly delivered by carriers to wrong person for third party in constructive possession of goods to sell them to persons to whom carriers made delivery.

CONVERSION (road traffic)

Whiteley, Limited v Hilt [1918] 2 KB 115; (1918) CC Rep VII 37; (1917-18) XXXIV TLR 402 HC KBD Third party buying hire-purchase item from hirer thereby repudiating hire-purchase of same could be successfully sued in detinue/conversion.

Whiteley, Limited v Hilt [1918] 2 KB 808; (1917-18) XXXIV TLR 592 CA Third party buying hire-purchase item from hirer thereby repudiating hire-purchase of same acquired interest of hirer.

CONVERSION (road traffic)

Bryanston Leasings Ltd v Principality Finance Ltd and another [1977] RTR 45 HC QBD Company/receiver liable in detinue and/conversion where latter refused to assist in obtaining replacement registration books for two lost after leased cars from plaintiffs.

Hillesden Securities Ltd v Ryjack Ltd and another (1983) 133 NLJ 280; [1983] RTR 491; (1983) 127 SJ 521; [1983] 1 WLR 959 HC QBD On damages available to person whose profit earning chattel was subject of conversion.

COPYRIGHT (general)

Carlin Music Corpn, Subiddu Music Ltd and Mechanical-Copyright Protection Society Ltd v Collins (1980) 130 NLJ 218c CA Copyright Protection Society could seek to have unlawful dealings in copyright injuncted as was unlawful interference with its business in that it obtained portion of all licence fees paid.

CORPORATION (general)

Westminster City Council v Haste [1950] 66 (1) TLR 1083 HC ChD Company receiver personally liable in tort for non-payment of rates owed by company.

CROWN (general)

Adams v The War Office [1955] 3 All ER 245; (1955) 105 LJ 666; (1955) 99 SJ 746; [1955] 1 WLR 1116 HC QBD Crown exemption from tortious liability.

Arbon v Anderson and others [1942] 1 All ER 264 CA Secretary of State not liable for torts of officials (unless expressly authorises them).

Arbon v Anderson and others; De Laessoe v Anderson and others (1942-43) LIX TLR 149 HC KBD Non-liability of Secretary of State for actions under wartime detention legislation.

Bell v Secretary of State for Defence (1985) 135 NLJ 847; [1986] QB 322; (1985) 129 SJ 871; [1986] 2 WLR 248 CA Defence Secretary could not plead immunity in respect of tort done to soldier while not on Crown property.

Bell v Secretary of State for Defence [1984] TLR 591 HC QBD Defence Secretary could plead immunity in respect of tort done to off-duty soldier where allegedly negligent acts done on Crown property.

Department of Health and Social Security v Kinnear and others [1984] TLR 433 HC QBD Actions against Government Department for negligent advice regarding giving of whooping cough inoculations allowed to proceed.

Johnstone v Pedlar [1921] 2 AC 262; (1921-25) XXVII Cox CC 68; (1921) 125 LTR 809; (1920-21) XXXVII TLR 870; (1921) WN (I) 229 HL Not good defence to action by friendly alien to recover property wrongfully seized/detained by police that seizure/detention ratified by Crown.

Mackenzie-Kennedy v Air Council [1927] 2 KB 517; (1927) 64 LJ 71; [1927] 96 LJCL 1145; (1928) 138 LTR 8; (1927) 71 SJ 633 (4 July); (1926-27) XLIII TLR 733; (1927) WN (I) 208 CA Cannot sue Air Council in tort.

Pearce v Secretary of State for Defence and another [1988] 2 All ER 348 (also CA); [1988] AC 755 (also HC QBD/CA); (1988) 132 SJ 699; [1988] 2 WLR 1027 HL Secretary of State liable in tort for acts of Atomic Energy Authority.

14

Pearce v Secretary of State for Defence and another [1988] AC 755 (also CA/HL); (1987) 137 NLJ 80; (1987) 131 SJ 362; [1987] 2 WLR 782 HC QBD Secretary of State liable in tort for acts of Atomic Energy Authority.

Pearce v Secretary of State for Defence and another [1988] 2 All ER 348 (also HL); [1988] AC 755 (also HC QBD/HL); (1987) 137 NLJ 922; (1988) 132 SJ 127; [1988] 2 WLR 144 CA Secretary of State liable in tort for acts of Atomic Energy Authority.

Royster v Cavey (1945-46) LXII TLR 709; (1947) WN (I) 8 CA Cannot bring tort action against nominated defendant who owed no duty of care to plaintiff.

Trawnik and another v Ministry of Defence [1984] 2 All ER 791; (1984) 128 SJ 665; [1984] TLR 198/265 HC ChD General claim in tort/seeking declaration of rights may be possible against Crown.

Trawnik and another v Gordon Lennox and another [1985] 2 All ER 368; (1985) 129 SJ 225; [1984] TLR 723; [1985] 1 WLR 532 CA Crown cannot be sued in tort.

CROWN (trespass)

Attorney-General v Nissan [1969] 1 All ER 629; [1970] AC 179; (1969) 119 NLJ 250; (1969) 113 SJ 207; [1969] 2 WLR 926 HL That acts complained of were 'acts of state' not defence in tort action.

Nissan v Attorney-General [1968] 1 QB 286 (also CA); (1967) 111 SJ 195; [1967] 3 WLR 109 HC QBD That acts complained of were 'acts of state' not defence in tort action.

Nissan v Attorney-General [1968] 1 QB 286 (also HC QBD); (1967) 117 NLJ 834t; (1967) 111 SJ 544; [1967] 3 WLR 1044 CA That acts complained of were 'acts of state' not defence in tort action.

DAMAGES (exemplary)

Bishop v Metropolitan Police Commissioner and others (1989) 133 SJ 1626 CA Plaintiff's conduct relevant to setting exemplary damages payable by defendant guilty of malicious prosecution.

McMillan v Singh (1984) 134 NLJ 1087c CA Exemplary damages where defendant seeking to achieve object at expense of of plaintiff.

Warner v Clark, Islip et al (1984) 134 NLJ 763c CA Exemplary damages available where breach of contract proved as liability in tort thereby set up.

DAMAGES (foreign tort)

Boys v Chaplin (1967) 111 SJ 297 HC QBD Damages assessed under English law where was tort effected between British residents if foreign jurisdiction.

Boys v Chaplin [1968] 2 QB 1; (1967) 111 SJ 968 CA Damages assessed under English law where was tort effected between British residents if foreign jurisdiction.

Chaplin v Boys (1969) 113 SJ 608 HL Damages assessed under English law where was tort effected between British residents if foreign jurisdiction.

DAMAGES (general)

Dodd Properties (Kent) Ltd and another v Canterbury City Council and others [1979] 2 All ER 118 HC QBD Generally damages measured by reference to date of damage; entitled to reasonable damages for reasonable repairs.

Dominion Mosaics and Tile Co Ltd and another v Trafalgar Trucking Co Ltd and another [1990] 2 All ER 246; (1989) 139 NLJ 364 CA Restitutio in integrem might mean assessing diminution in value of premises or cost of reinstatement; principle involves 'new for old' restitution in respect of machines.

Doyle v Nicholls (1978) 128 NLJ 711t; (1978) 122 SJ 386 HC QBD Future inflation as a factor when asessing damages in negligence action.

Hall and Co, Ltd v Pearlberg [1956] 1 All ER 297; (1956) 100 SJ 187; [1956] 1 WLR 244 HC QBD On income/profits taxes when gauging damages.

Jones and another v Stroud District Council [1988] 1 All ER 5; (1986) 130 SJ 469; [1986] 1 WLR 1141 CA Cause for negligence action regarding property begins when real/imminent danger to occupiers; that repairs to property paid by another does not disentitle occupier to damages.

Performance Cars Ltd v Abraham [1961] 3 All ER 413; [1955] Crim LR 748; (1961) 111 LJ 644; [1962] 1 QB 33 CA Cannot recover for damage not resulting from tort.

Pigney v Pointers Transport Services, Ltd [1957] 2 All ER 807 Assizes Wife could seek damages for husband's suicide (though felony) arising from negligent injury.

Selvanayagam v University of the West Indies [1983] 1 All ER 824; [1983] TLR 109; (1983) 127 SJ 288; [1983] 1 WLR 585 PC Plaintiff must show refusal of surgery reasonable before damages recoverable; Privy Council can but will not substitute awards for damages.

The Columbus Company, Limited v Clowes [1903] 1 KB 244; [1903] 72 LJKB 330 HC KBD Nominal damages for negligence where suffered no loss.

The Despina R [1978] QB 396 HC QBD Damages for tort awarded in dollars.

The Despina R (1978) 122 SJ 758 HL Damages to be awarded in currency most accurately reflecting loss suffered (unless contract specifically provides otherwise).

The Despina R (1977) 127 NLJ 765t; [1978] QB 396 CA Damages for tort awarded in dollars.

Watt v Watt (1904-05) 49 SJ 400; (1904-05) XXI TLR 386; (1905) WN (I) 60; (1904-05) 53 WR 547 HL Excessive damages in tort action can only be reduced by court where parties agree to same.

DAMAGES (innuendo)

Lewis v Daily Telegraph, Ltd; Rubber Improvement, Ltd v Same; Lewis v Appointed Newspapers, Ltd; Rubber Improvement, Ltd v Same [1962] 2 All ER 698; (1962) 112 LJ 436; [1963] 1 QB 340; (1962) 106 SJ 307 CA Re-trial ordered where was inadequate direction as to innuendo: to wrongly say person subject of Serious Fraud investigation was defamatory but not in same league as saying were guilty of fraud.

DAMAGES (interest)

Blundell v Rimmer (1970) 120 NLJ 1138; (1971) 115 SJ 15 HC QBD On payment of interest on damages payable into court.

Gardner Steel Ltd v Sheffield Brothers (Profiles) Ltd [1978] 3 All ER 399 CA Interest on summary judgment possible.

Saunders and another v Edwards and another [1987] 2 All ER 651 CA In tortious claim arising from fraudulent contract court will look to conduct/culpability of parties in deciding whether to notice illegality; global damages for inconvenience/disappointment should not have interest added.

Wilson v Graham [1990] TLR 485 HC QBD Commercial interest available on damages from when judgment on liability entered.

DAMAGES (mitigation)

Martindale v Duncan (1973) 123 NLJ 129t; [1973] RTR 532; (1973) 117 SJ 168; [1973] 1 WLR 574 CA No violation of onus to mitigate damages where postponed repairs to car until had sorted out insurance claim.

DAMAGES (negligence)

Antcliffe v Gloucester Health Authority [1992] TLR 224 CA On payment of damages in medical negligence cases.

Emeh v Kensington and Chelsea and Westminster Area Health Authority and others (1983) 133 NLJ 352; [1985] QB 1012; (1984) 128 SJ 705; [1984] TLR 484; [1985] 2 WLR 233 CA Damages recovered for birth of child following negligent sterilisation operation.

G v North Tees Health Authority [1989] FCR 53 HC QBD Successful action for damages after hospital negligently mis-diagnosed child's vaginal discharge as having sperm present.

Malyon v Lawrence, Messer and Co (1969) 119 NLJ 38; (1968) 112 SJ 623 HC QBD Recovery of damages from solicitors which would have recovered in action in Germany had not negligence of solicitors led to action being time-barred.

DAMAGES (personal injuries)

Ashley v Vickers (1983) 133 NLJ 642 HC QBD On what living expenses were deductible from road traffic accident damages.

Attree v Baker [1983] TLR 686 HC QBD Personal injuries damages increased in light of tax payable on same.

Baker v Willoughby [1969] 3 All ER 1528; [1970] AC 467; (1968) 118 NLJ 1197t; (1970) 114 SJ 15; [1970] 2 WLR 50 HL Respective duty of motorists/pedestrians to be road wary; personal injury damages are for loss occasioned by injury — here no new loss after second injury so no further damages.

Carroll v Hooper [1964] 1 All ER 845; (1964) 114 LJ 272; (1964) 108 SJ 120; [1964] 1 WLR 345 HC QBD Service disablement pension not relevant when gauging appropriate personal injury damages.

Clarke v Martlew and another (1972) 122 NLJ 586t; [1973] QB 58; (1972) 116 SJ 618; [1972] 3 WLR 653 CA On mutual exchange of results of medical test to which plaintiff acceded at defendant's request.

Cressey v Murray (CP) and Co, Ltd and another (1965) 109 SJ 294 CA Increase in personal injury damages for person who suffered double vision as result of road accident.

Croke and another v Wiseman and another [1981] 3 All ER 852; (1981) 125 SJ 726; [1982] 1 WLR 71 CA Appropriate damages for permanent incapacitation of twenty-one month old infant.

Croke v Brent and Harrow Area Health Authority (1981) 131 NLJ 1237 CA Assessing damages for serious injuries suffered by infant through negligent treatment upon admission to hospital with croup.

Daly v General Steam Navigation Co Ltd [1980] 3 All ER 696; (1981) 125 SJ 100; [1981] 1 WLR 120 CA Can be damages for housekeeping even where housekeeper might not be employed; imagined pre-trial loss irrecoverable.

Dennis v London Passenger Transport Board (1948) LXIV TLR 269 HC KBD Wages paid during absence from work repayable from peronal injury damages awarded.

Donnelly v Joyce [1973] 3 All ER 475; (1973) 123 NLJ 542t; [1974] QB 454; (1973) 117 SJ 488; [1973] 3 WLR 514 CA Damages available for services from third party (whatever basis of services).

Eldridge v Videtta (1964) 108 SJ 137 HC QBD Non-deduction of national assistance payments from personal injury damages.

Elstob v Robinson [1964] 1 All ER 848; (1964) 114 LJ 358; (1964) 108 SJ 543; [1964] 1 WLR 726 HC QBD Personal injury damages not to be reduced in light of service disability pension.

Forrest v Sharp (1963) 107 SJ 536 HC QBD On relevancy of injured person's awareness of affliction to level of damages awarded.

Hall v Avon Area Health Authority (Teaching) (1980) 124 SJ 293; [1980] 1 WLR 481 CA Request that medical examination by doctor nominated by other party to action be conducted in presence of own doctor not reasonable/granted.

Harris (an infant) v Harris (1972) 122 NLJ 1061; (1972) 116 SJ 904 CA On awarding damages for loss of marriage prospects as result of injuries suffered through another's negligence.

Harris v Brights Asphalt Contractors Ld [1953] 1 QB 617; [1953] 1 WLR 341 HC QBD Cannot claim as damages the difference in wages between pre-injury life term and post-injury life term.

Janney v Gentry (1966) 110 SJ 408 HC QBD Allowance made when awarding personal injury damages for civil service pension of which plaintiff in receipt.

Jeffery v Smith (1970) 120 NLJ 272t; [1970] RTR 279; (1970) 114 SJ 268 CA On appropriate damages in negligence for loss to husband of services of wife killed in motor accident.

Jones v Jones [1985] QB 704; (1984) 128 SJ 470; [1984] TLR 415; [1984] 3 WLR 862 CA Person inflicting personal injuries liable for costs incurred by break-up of injured party's marriage (caused directly by injuries inflicted).

Judd v Hammersmith, West London and St Mark's Hospitals Board of Governors and others (1960) 104 SJ 270; [1960] 1 WLR 328 HC QBD Pension awarded on foot of compulsory payments not relevant when assessing level of damages.

Kelly and another v Dawes [1990] TLR 623 HC QBD Personal injury damages payable by way of index-linked annuity earned by investment of total amount of damages.

Lewis v Gardner (1981) 131 NLJ 1134 HC QBD On appropriate damages for motor cycle pillion passenger who suffered brain damage in road traffic accident.

Lian (Lai Wee) v Singapore Bus Service (1978) Ltd [1984] AC 729; (1984) 128 SJ 432; [1984] 3 WLR 63 PC Gauging loss of future earnings by reference to arithmetical table was valid PC could amend damages awarded where was considerable difference between what was and ought to have been awarded.

Littler v GL Moore (Contractors) Ltd (1967) 111 SJ 637; [1967] 1 WLR 1241 Assizes Damages available for possible future loss in quality of vision.

Lolley v Keylock (1984) 128 SJ 471 CA Calculation of deceased person's likely surplus income on percentage of net income basis.

Luker v Chapman (1970) 114 SJ 788 HC QBD Personal injury damages reduced by amount plaintiff would have earned at alternative post-employment he was offered had he not instead elected to become a teacher.

McGinley v Burke (1973) 117 SJ 488; [1973] 1 WLR 990 HC QBD Was not proper for plaintiff in personal injuries action to see medical report prepared for defendant but not vice versa.

McIsaac v Vos (1983) 133 NLJ 185 HC QBD On appropriate damages for previously outgoing girl who was physically and mentally scarred in serious road traffic accident.

McLaren and others v Bradstreet (1969) 119 NLJ 484t CA Compensation unavailable to children for suffering consequent upon accident but prolonged as result of (and avoidable was it not for) actions of neurotic mother of children.

Mitchell v Mulholland and another (1971) 121 NLJ 249; (1971) 115 SJ 227 CA On appropriate means of assessing damages for accident victim.

Naylor v Yorkshire Electricity Board [1966] 3 All ER 327; (1965-66) 116 NLJ 1032t/1432; [1967] 1 QB 244; (1966) 110 SJ 528; [1966] 3 WLR 654 CA Appropriate damages for loss of life of young, engaged man.

Parry v Cleaver [1970] AC 1; (1969) 113 SJ 147; [1969] 2 WLR 821 HL Disability pension to be ignored in assessing personal injury damages.

Paul v Rendell (1981) 131 NLJ 657 PC Only exceptionally will PC interfere with personal injury awards settled on by trial judge/full court and would not do so here.

Rialas v Mitchell (1983) 133 NLJ 378; (1984) 128 SJ 704 HC QBD On appropriate damages for infant child rendered spastic quadraplegic in road traffic accident.

Rialas v Mitchell [1984] TLR 460 CA On appropriate damages for infant child rendered spastic quadraplegic in road traffic accident.

Richards v Highway Ironfounders (West Bromwich), Ltd [1955] 3 All ER 205; [1955] 1 WLR 1049 CA No damages for loss of chance to provide for dependents.

Roberts v J and F Stone Lighting and Radio, Limited and another (1946) 96 LJ 42; (1945) 172 LTR 240; (1944-45) LXI TLR 338 HC KBD On recovery for personal injuries of difference between amount of settlement in first action and total amount claim would have been awarded in personal injuries action had subpoenaed witness (defendant in second action) given evidence in court.

Roberts v Johnstone and another [1989] QB 878; (1988) 132 SJ 1672; [1988] 3 WLR 1247 CA On personal injury damages for nursing care/new accommodation requirements.

Rose v Coventry (1965) 109 SJ 256 CA On appropriate personal injury damages where victim had toes amputated/leg length reduced/was less mobile than previously.

Schneider v Eisovitch; Same v Same [1960] 1 All ER 169; (1960) 110 LJ 137; [1960] 2 QB 430; (1960) 104 SJ 89 HC QBD Damages available for reasonable services arising from tort even if freely given without request; damages available for nervous shock sustained after recover consciousness.

Sparks and another v Pardex Plant Engineers Ltd (1969) 113 SJ 1003 CA On appropriate damages for young girl left with permanent disfiguring scar on leg following negligent collision.

Stanley v Blackstones and Co Ltd (1968) 112 SJ 784 CA On appropriate damages for permanent deforming of middle-aged woman's left hand.

Starr v National Coal Board (1976) 126 NLJ 1120t; (1976) 120 SJ 721; [1977] 1 WLR 63 CA Must submit to medical examination by doctor of defendant's choosing unless have reasonable reason not to do so which reveal to court.

Struthers v British Railways Board (1969) 119 NLJ 249t; (1969) 113 SJ 268 HC QBD British Rail two-thirds liable for injuries suffered by passenger stepping from train that extended beyond the platform.

Thompson v Smiths Shiprepairers (North Shields) Ltd; Gray v Same; Nicholson v Same; Blacklock v Swan Hunter Shipbuilders Ltd; Waggott v Same; Mitchell v Vickers Armstrong Ltd and another [1984] QB 405; (1984) 128 SJ 225; [1984] 2 WLR 522 HC QBD On damages for loss of hearing where loss began before liability of defendant arose.

Waldon v The War Office [1956] 1 All ER 108; (1956) 106 LJ 26; (1956) 100 SJ 33 CA On consideration of relevant awards of damages by judge.

Waller v Lawton (1981) 131 NLJ 1134 HC QBD On appropriate damages for person who suffered inter alia serious brain damage when struck by motor vehicle.

Warwick and another v Jeffery (1983) 133 NLJ 912 HC QBD On awarding of damages following road traffic accident in actions under Fatal Accidents Act 1976/Law Reform (Miscellaneous Provisions) Act 1934 in actions brought by ex-wife (who bore children by deceased) and co-habitee (who bore one child by deceased).

Watson v Powles (1967) 117 NLJ 758t; [1968] 1 QB 596; (1967) 111 SJ 562; [1967] 3 WLR 1364 CA On gauging damages in personal injury actions.

Watson v Smith (1983) 133 NLJ 641 HC QBD On appropriate damages for personal injuries suffered by motor cyclist in road traffic accident with lorry being driven by defendant.

Wright v British Railways Board [1983] 2 AC 773; (1983) 133 NLJ 681; (1983) 127 SJ 478; [1983] TLR 454; [1983] 3 WLR 211 HL On gauging amount of interest due on personal injuries award.

DAMAGES (remoteness)

C Czarnikow Ltd v Koufos [1966] 2 WLR 1397 CA Damages recoverable for reasonably foreseeable damage which occurs.

DAMAGES (road traffic)

Mattocks v Mann [1993] RTR 13; [1992] TLR 303 CA All reasonable car-hire costs available to person whose car was negligently damaged by another and had to be repaired: damages available for period after repairs effected but before received insurance money to pay for same.

Payton v Brooks [1974] RTR 169 CA Valid finding by trial judge that market value of repaired car unaffected by those repairs having been necessitated by damage sustained in car accident: damages for this alleged loss not allowed.

DAMAGES (social security)

Cackett v Earl (1976) 126 NLJ 1090t HC QBD State benefits deductible from expenses being awarded on foot of negligence claim arising from road accident.

Gaskill v Preston [1981] 3 All ER 427; (1981) 131 NLJ 501 HC QBD Family income supplement payments deductible from road traffic accident damages.

DAMAGES (subsidence)

Tunnicliffe and Hampson, Limited v West Leigh Colliery Company, Limited [1905] 2 Ch 390 HC ChD On appropriate damages for damage caused by subsidence.

Tunnicliffe and Hampson, Limited v West Leigh Colliery Company, Limited [1906] 2 Ch 22; (1906) XCIV LTR 715 CA On appropriate damages for damage caused by subsidence.

West Leigh Colliery Company (Limited) v Tunnicliffe and Hampson (Limited) (1907-08) 52 SJ 93; (1907-08) XXIV TLR 146 HL On appropriate damages for damage caused by subsidence.

DEFAMATION (bank)

Frost v London Joint Stock Bank, Limited (1905-06) XXII TLR 760 CA Return of cheque to person seeking payment on same with note attached stating 'Reason assigned: not stated' not per se libellous.

DEFAMATION (class)

Shloimovitz v Clarendon Press (1973) 123 NLJ 679t HC ChD Cannot bring action in respect of defamation of class unless plaintiff can prove that he himself was defamed.

DEFAMATION (comment)

Lloyd (Clive Herbert) v David Syme and Co Ltd [1986] AC 350; (1986) 130 SJ 14; [1986] 2 WLR 69 PC Failure of defence of comment in respect of (defamatory) newspaper article where writer of same did not hold views made therein.

DEFAMATION (conspiracy to slander)

Ward v Lewis and others [1955] 1 All ER 55; [1955] 1 WLR 9 CA No connection between alleged slander and special damage meant could be no conspiracy to slander.

DEFAMATION (corporation)

Citizen's Life Assurance Company, Limited v Brown [1904-07] All ER 925; [1904] AC 423; [1904] 73 LJPC 102; (1904) XC LTR 739; (1903-04) XX TLR 497; (1904-05) 53 WR 176 PC Corporation liable for (unauthorised) malicious libel by its servant acting in course of employment.

D and L Caterers, Ltd and Jackson v D'Ajou [1945] 1 All ER 563; [1945] KB 364; (1946) 96 LJ 199; [1945] 114 LJ 386; (1945) 173 LTR 21; (1944-45) LXI TLR 343; (1945) WN (I) 88 CA Limited company can sue for slander though no proof of actual damage: damage implied to ground action; on cross-examination over credit in defamation suit.

Derbyshire County Council v Times Newspapers Ltd and others [1992] 3 All ER 65; (1992) 142 NLJ 276; [1992] QB 770; [1992] TLR 69; [1992] 3 WLR 28 CA Trading/non-trading corporation with corporate reputation may sue for libel/slander but local authority may not unless actual financial loss.

DEFAMATION (damages)

Anderson v Calvert (1907-08) XXIV TLR 399 CA On considerations for jury when assessing damages for libel.

Associated Newspapers, Ltd v Dingle [1962] 2 All ER 737; [1964] AC 371; (1962) 112 LJ 454; (1962) 106 SJ 488 HL On proper damages for defamation.

Broome v Cassell and Co Ltd and another; Same v Same [1971] 1 All ER 262 HC QBD If claiming exemplary damages must give warning and basis.

Cassell and Co Ltd v Broome and another [1972] 1 All ER 801; [1972] AC 1027; (1972) 122 NLJ 195t; (1972) 116 SJ 199; [1972] 2 WLR 645 HL Rookes v Barnard guidance on exemplary damages applicable to defamation cases; practice when awarding damages.

Damiens v Modern Society (Limited) and another (1910-11) XXVII TLR 164 HC KBD Damages ought not to have been severed in respect of joint defendants.

Davis and another v Rubin and another (1968) 112 SJ 51 CA Re-trial of libel action ordered where damages awarded were excessive.

Dering v Uris and others (1964) 108 SJ 405; [1964] 2 WLR 1298 HC QBD Cannot having accepted money from one defendant seek to extricate damages from another where amount accepted exceeds amount accepted from first defendant; on division of costs where have accepted payment into court (no costs to plaintiff before payment/costs to defendants after payment).

Dingle v Associated Newspapers, Ltd and others [1961] 1 All ER 897; (1961) 111 LJ 237; [1961] 2 QB 162; (1961) 105 SJ 153 CA Can mitigate damages only by showing existing bad reputation; no mitigation on ground that re-publishing another's libel.

English and Scottish Co-operative Property Mortgage and Investment Society, Ltd v Odhams Press, Ltd and Daily Herald (1929), Ltd (1939) 83 SJ 566 HC KBD Newspaper headline libellous by virtue of innuendo to be derived from report that was literally true.

English and Scottish Co-operative Properties Mortgage and Investment Society, Ltd v Odhams Press, Ltd and another [1940] 1 All ER 1; [1940] 1 KB 440; [1940] 109 LJCL 273; (1940) 162 LTR 82; (1940) 84 SJ 112; (1939-40) LVI TLR 195; (1940) WN (I) 9 CA Newspaper headline contained innuendo: one farthing's damages inadequate.

Goody v Odhams Press, Ltd [1966] 3 All ER 369; [1967] 1 QB 333; [1966] 3 WLR 460 CA Evidence of relevant previous convictions admissible to show plaintiff's generally bad reputation; can be partial justification of article if part severable.

Groom v Crocker and others (1937) 84 LJ 158; (1937) 157 LTR 308 HC KBD Failure of solicitor to act equally on behalf of both insurer/insured; damages for breach of duty and for libel.

Hawkins v Express Dairy Co Ltd and Others (1940) 163 LTR 147; (1940) 84 SJ 393 HC KBD Could when assessing damages take into account misbehaviour admitted by person who was victim of libel.

Hobbs v Tinling (CT) and Company, Limited; Hobbs v Nottingham Journal, Limited [1929] 2 KB 1 HC KBD On procedure in libel action; on mitigation of damages where are of bad character.

Hobbs v Tinling (CT) and Co, Ltd; Hobbs v Nottingham Journal, Ltd [1929] All ER 33; (1929) 67 LJ 290; (1929) 98 LJCL 421; (1929) WN (I) 89 CA On libel; on mitigation of damages where are of bad character.

John v MGN Ltd [1996] 2 All ER 35; (1996) 146 NLJ 13; [1997] QB 586; [1995] TLR 675; [1996] 3 WLR 592 CA Judge and counsel may indicate appropriate level of damages to jury; recklessness a ground for exemplary damages.

Kiam v Neill and another (1996) TLR 22/7/96 CA £45,000 damages merited for irresponsible libel.

Lewis and another v Daily Telegraph, Ltd; Same v Associated Newspapers, Ltd [1963] 2 All ER 151; (1963) 113 LJ 317 HL Innuendo not separate cause of action from straightforward defamation by same words; on pleading innuendo; appropriate damages.

Lewis v Daily Telegraph, Ltd; Rubber Improvement, Ltd v Same; Lewis v Associated Newspapers, Ltd; Rubber Improvement, Ltd v Same [1962] 2 Al ER 698; (1962) 112 LJ 436; [1963] 1 QB 340; (1962) 106 SJ 307 CA Re-trial ordered where was inadequate direction as to innuendo: to wrongly say person subject of Serious Fraud investigation was defamatory but not in same league as saying were guilty of fraud.

Ley v Hamilton (1934) 151 LTR 360 CA Re-trial of libel action ordered where damages awarded unreasonable/possible that occasion of publication was privileged contrary to trial judge's ruling.

Ley v Hamilton (1935) 153 LTR 384; (1935) 79 SJ 573 HL Re-trial of libel action unnecessary where damages awarded reasonable/ occasion of publication was not privileged.

Longdon-Griffiths v Smith and others [1950] 2 All ER 662; [1951] 1 KB 295; (1950) 100 LJ 413; (1950) 94 SJ 580; [1950] 66 (2) TLR 627; (1950) WN (I) 448 HC KBD Libel action to be directed at Friendly Society per se not its trustees; special damages available where libel led to losing job; that one of four parties acted maliciously did not affect qualified privilege of others.

Manson v Associated Newspapers, Ltd [1965] 2 All ER 954; (1965) 115 LJ 579; (1965) 109 SJ 457; [1965] 1 WLR 1038 HC QBD Exemplary damages if publish known lies (or are reckless as to truth) knowing will injure other but calculate profits will exceed damages.

McCarey v Associated Newspapers, Ltd and others [Consolidated actions] [1964] 3 All ER 947; (1964) 114 LJ 506; [1965] 2 QB 86; [1965] 2 WLR 45 CA Distinction between compensatory/ punitive damages; when punitive damages appropriate.

McCormick v Bennison and others (1938) 82 SJ 869 CA Onetime boxing champion successfully recovered damages for libellous newspaper article about self.

P v S (1979) 129 (1) NLJ 19c CA Level of damages awarded in personal injury actions not relevant when determining appropriate level of damages for defamation.

Plato Films, Ltd and others v Speidel [1961] 1 All ER 876; (1961) 111 LJ 220; (1961) 105 SJ 230 HL Can mitigate damages by introducing evidence of actual bad reputation (but not that should have bad reputation).

Riches and others v News Group Newspapers Ltd [1985] 2 All ER 845; (1985) 135 NLJ 391; [1986] QB 256; (1985) 129 SJ 401; [1985] 3 WLR 432 CA Exemplary damages to be shared among joint plaintiffs rather than separately awarded to each plaintiff.

Rook v Fairrie [1941] 1 All ER 297; [1941] 1 KB 507; (1942) 92 LJ 61; [1941] 110 LJ 319; (1941) 165 LTR 23; (1941) 85 SJ 297; (1940-41) LVII TLR 297; (1941) WN (I) 37 CA Judge (unlike jury) can condemn otherwise than by heavy damages.

Speidel v Plato Films, Ltd and others; Same v Unity Theatre Society, Ltd [1960] 2 All ER 521 CA In mitigation of damages can prove bad reputation in general/inexorably linked to libel.

Stone v Brewis (1902-03) 47 SJ 70 CA Addressing letter to notorious person care of another's address validly found to be libellous of latter; punitive damages justified.

Weber v Birkett [1925] 1 KB 720; (1925) 60 LJ 294; (1925) WN (I) 77 HC KBD Non-apportionment of damages meant had not been separate verdict on each issue: mistrial; unsatisfactory mode of apology.

Weber v Birkett [1925] All ER 244; (1925) 60 LJ 464; (1925) 133 LTR 598; (1924-25) XLI TLR 451 CA Non-apportionment of damages meant had not been separate verdict on each issue: mistrial.

Wheeler v Somerfield and others [1966] 2 All ER 305; (1965-66) 116 NLJ 837; [1966] 2 QB 94; [1966] 2 WLR 1006 CA Libel damages for injury to health possible (but not here); could be that to include articles of certain section of publication might carry innuendo but not here.

DEFAMATION (diplomatic immunity)

Ghosh v D'Rosario (1962) 106 SJ 352 CA Stay of slander action required where after commencement of action defendant appointed to High Commission staff and thereby acquired diplomatic immunity.

DEFAMATION (fair comment)

Anders v Gas (1960) 110 LJ 350; (1960) 104 SJ 211 HC QBD On defence of fair comment.

Brent Walker Group plc and another v Time Out Ltd and another [1991] 2 All ER 753; [1991] 2 QB 33; [1991] 2 WLR 772 CA Fair comment defence based on prvileged material must give fair/accurate report of occasion of privilege.

Broadway Approvals Ltd and another v Odhams Press Ltd and another (1964) 114 LJ 623; [1964] 2 QB 683; (1964) 108 SJ 564; [1964] 3 WLR 243 HC QBD Cannot be fair comment unless factual basis of comment is basically true.

Burton v Board and another [1928] All ER 659; (1929) 98 LJCL 165; (1929) 140 LTR 289 CA Alleged defamator may give particulars of facts on which made statement (even though does not plead justification).

Burton v Board and another [1929] 1 KB 301 HC KBD Alleged defamator may give particulars of facts on which made statement (even though does not plead justification).

Childs v London Express Newspaper, Ltd and another (1941) 85 SJ 179 HC KBD Plea of innuendo deemed to fail in case where defence of fair comment would in any event have succeeded.

Cohen v Daily Telegraph, Ltd [1968] 2 All ER 407; (1968) 118 NLJ 350t; (1968) 112 SJ 356; [1968] 1 WLR 916 CA Facts when comment made determine if fair comment.

Control Risks Ltd and others v New English Library Ltd and another [1989] 3 All ER 577; (1989) 139 NLJ 1008; [1990] 1 WLR 183 CA On fair comment.

Cunningham-Howe v FW Dimbleby and Sons, Ltd [1950] 2 All ER 882; [1951] 1 KB 360; (1950) 94 SJ 724; [1950] 66 (2) TLR 726; (1950) WN (I) 473 CA If fair comment to be pleaded plaintiff entitled to know factual basis thereof.

Dakhyl v Labouchere [1908] 2 KB 325 [1908] 77 LJCL 728; (1907) XCVI LTR 399; (1906-07) XXIII TLR 364 HL On defence of fair comment.

Digby v The 'Financial News' (Limited) [1907] 76 LJCL 321; (1907) XCVI LTR 172; (1906-07) XXIII TLR 117 CA Further and better particulars of justification unavailable where only pleading fair comment.

Georgius v Oxford University Press (Delegates) and others [1949] 1 All ER 342; [1949] 1 KB 729; [1949] 118 LJR 454; (1949) LXV TLR 101; (1949) WN (I) 47 CA Non-interference with non-allowance of interrogatory seeking source of information in libel.

Grech v Odhams Press Ltd and another; Addis v Same [1957] 3 All ER 556; [1958] 1 QB 310; (1957) 101 SJ 921 HC QBD Reporting of untrue words can be fair comment.

Grech v Odhams Press Ltd and another; Addis v Odhams Press Ltd and another [1958] 2 All ER 462; (1958) 108 LJ 424; [1958] 2 QB 275; (1958) 102 SJ 453 CA Reporting of untrue words can be fair comment.

Hunt v Star Newspaper, Ltd [1908-10] All ER 513; [1908] 2 KB 309; (1908) 43 LJ 193; [1908] 77 LJCL 732; (1908) XCVIII LTR 629; (1907-08) 52 SJ 376; (1907-08) XXIV TLR 452; (1908) WN (I) 80 CA On fair comment.

Jeyaretnam (Joshua Benjamin) v Tong (Goh Chok) (1989) 133 SJ 1032; [1989] 1 WLR 1109 PC Comments of politician at press conference deemed to be fair comments and not defamatory.

Joynt v Cycle Trade Publishing Company [1904] 2 KB 292; (1904) 39 LJ 236; [1904] 73 LJCL 752; (1904-05) XCI LTR 155; (1904) WN (I) 92 CA Could not plead fair comment in respect of baseless criticism of man in piece on matter of public interest.

Kemsley v Foot and others [1951] 1 All ER 331; [1951] 2 KB 34; (1951) 101 LJ 48; (1951) 95 SJ 120; [1951] 1 TLR 197; (1951) WN (I) 88 CA Criticism of newspaper controller for style of newspaper to be treated like criticism of book/play.

Kemsley v Foot and others [1952] 1 All ER 501; [1952] AC 345; (1952) 102 LJ 136; (1952) 96 SJ 165; [1952] 1 TLR 532; (1952) WN (I) 111 HL Fair comment basis open though factual basis thereof not fully stated.

Littler v BBC and another (1966) 110 SJ 585 HC QBD Fair comment plea allowed despite looseness as to factual basis on which grounded.

London Artists, Ltd v Littler [1969] 2 All ER 193; [1969] 2 QB 375; (1969) 113 SJ 37; [1969] 2 WLR 409 CA Untrue claim of plot regarding matter of public interest not fair comment.

London Artists, Ltd v Littler [1968] 1 All ER 1075; (1968) 118 NLJ 1196t; (1968) 112 SJ 194; [1968] 1 WLR 607 HC QBD Where no public interest (or private duty compelling publication) is no qualified privilege.

Lord v Sunday Telegraph Ltd [1970] 3 All ER 504; (1970) 120 NLJ 1066; [1971] 1 QB 235; (1970) 114 SJ 706; [1970] 3 WLR 754 CA Need not separate comments from facts but must explain basic facts if relying on fair comment.

Lyon and Lyon v Daily Telegraph, Ltd [1943] 1 All ER 586; (1943) 168 LTR 251; (1942-43) LIX TLR 193 HC KBD Impossible to determine fair comment where writer of libel unknown; defamation in professional capacity.

Lyon and Lyon v Daily Telegraph, Ltd [1943] 2 All ER 316; [1943] KB 746; (1943) 112 LJ 547; (1944) 94 LJ 108; (1943) 169 LTR 274; (1943) 87 SJ 309; (1942-43) LIX TLR 402; (1943) WN (I) 191 CA Fair comment defence open despite factual error as publication was on matter of public interest and there was no malice involved.

Lyons v Financial News (Lim) and others (1908-09) 53 SJ 671 CA Order as to form of particulars whereby sought to plead truthfulness of some of what stated and that rest was fair comment.

Mangena v Wright [1908-10] All ER 1316; [1909] 2 KB 958; [1909] 78 LJKB 879; (1909) 100 LTR 960; (1908-09) 53 SJ 485; (1908-09) XXV TLR 534 HC KBD Cannot be sued for defamation where publish good faith/non-malicious copy/near-copy of Parliamentary; on mitigation of damages in libel/slander action.

McQuire v Western Morning News Co [1900-03] All ER 673; [1903] 2 KB 100; [1903] 72 LJKB 612; (1903) LXXXVIII LTR 757; (1902-03) XIX TLR 471; (1903) WN (I) 98; (1902-03) 51 WR 689 CA Criticism of play must be reasonably describable as criticism; matter for judge whether something goes beyond fair criticism.

Silkin v Beaverbrook Newspapers, Ltd and another [1958] 2 All ER 516; (1958) 108 LJ 443; (1958) 102 SJ 491 HC QBD Fair comment on matter of public interest if opinion honestly held.

Slim and others v Daily Telegraph, Ltd and another [1968] 1 All ER 497; (1968) 118 NLJ 86t; [1968] 2 QB 157; (1968) 112 SJ 97; [1968] 2 WLR 599 CA Fair comment where words did impugn dishonesty but was public interest/no malice.

South Suburban Co-operative Society, Limited v Orum and others [1937] 2 KB 690; (1937) 83 LJ 410; [1937] 106 LJCL 555; (1937) 157 LTR 93; (1937) 81 SJ 497; (1936-37) LIII TLR 803; (1937) WN (I) 259 CA Writer of allegedly libellous letter to newspaper who pleads fair comment must reveal person/s from whom obtained information.

Stopes v Sutherland and another (1922-23) XXXIX TLR 242 HC KBD Libel action failed where jury found words complained of though unfair were true in substance/fact.

Stopes v Sutherland and another (1923) 58 LJ 366; (1922-23) XXXIX TLR 677 CA Libel action succeeded where jury found words complained of were true in substance/fact but unfair comment.

Sutherland and Others v Stopes et e contra [1924] All ER 19; [1925] AC 47; (1924) 59 LJ 757; [1925] 94 LJCL 166; (1925) 132 LTR 550; (1924-25) 69 SJ 138; (1924-25) XLI TLR 106 HL Plea seeming partly one of justification, partly one of fair comment a plea of fair comment.

Telnikoff v Matusevitch [1990] 3 All ER 865; [1991] 1 QB 102; (1990) 134 SJ 1078; [1990] TLR 423; [1990] 3 WLR 725 CA Court may look to broader context in deciding if material libellous; plea of fair comment raises presumption that comment an honest expression of opinion unless counter-claim of malicious publication.

Telnikoff v Matusevitch [1991] 4 All ER 817; [1992] 2 AC 343; (1991) 141 NLJ 1590; [1991] TLR 513; [1991] 3 WLR 952 HL Letter in reply to article to be looked at in isolation when jury deciding if fair comment/libel; fair comment must be objectively fair.

The Aga Khan v Times Publishing Company [1924] 1 KB 675; (1924) 59 LJ 90; [1924] 93 LJCL 361; (1924) 130 LTR 746; (1923-24) XL TLR 299; (1924) WN (I) 54 CA On 'rolled-up plea' of fair comment.

The Homing Pigeon Publishing Company (Limited) v The Racing Pigeon Publishing Company (Limited) (1912-13) XXIX TLR 389 HC KBD Where fair comment pleaded judge to decide whether statement capable of defamation before leaving matter of whether it was to jury.

Thomas v Bradbury, Agnew, and Company (Limited) and another [1904-07] All ER 220; [1906] 2 KB 627; [1906] 75 LJKB 726; (1906-07) XCV LTR 23; (1905-06) XXII TLR 656; (1905-06) 54 WR 608 CA Proof of malice defeats defence of fair comment on public interest or of privilege.

DEFAMATION (general)

Berkoff v Burchill and another [1996] 4 All ER 1008; (1996) TLR 9/8/96 CA To state of actor that he was 'hideous-looking' could be defamatory.

British Data Management plc v Boxer Commercial Removals plc and another [1996] 3 All ER 707 CA Failed quia timet injunction application: on when such an injunction will be granted.

Broome v Agar (1928) 138 LTR 698 CA Only exceptionally would jury verdict be overturned in defamation action (and was unmerited in instant circumstances).

C v Mirror Group Newspapers and others [1996] 4 All ER 511; [1997] 1 FCR 556; [1996] 2 FLR 532; (1996) 146 NLJ 1093; (1996) TLR 15/7/96; [1997] 1 WLR 131 CA Over five years after newspaper article published woman not allowed/allowed bring defamation/malicious falsehood claim.

Cornwell v Myskow and others (1987) 131 SJ 476; [1987] 1 WLR 630 CA On evidence admissible as to reputation.

E Hulton and Co v Jones [1910] AC 20; (1909) 44 LJ 744; (1910) 79 LJKB 198; (1909-10) 101 LTR 831; (1909-10) 54 SJ 116; (1909-10) XXVI TLR 128; (1909) WN (I) 249 HL That did not intend to defame is not a defence in defamation suit.

Hough v London Express Newspaper, Ltd [1940] 3 All ER 31; [1940] 2 KB 507; (1940) 89 LJ 270; [1940] 109 LJCL 524; (1940) 163 LTR 162; (1940) 84 SJ 573; (1939-40) LVI TLR 758 CA That reasonable people would believe article as referring to plaintiff was defamatory.

Rantzen v Mirror Group Newspapers (1986) Ltd and others [1993] 4 All ER 975; (1993) 143 NLJ 507; [1994] QB 670; [1993] TLR 206; [1993] 3 WLR 953 CA Awards for defamation subject to rigorous scrutiny by Court of Appeal in interests of preserving freedom of publication.

WH Smith and Son v Clinton and another (1908-09) XCIX LTR 840; (1908-09) XXV TLR 34 HC KBD Printer could not recover under libel-indemnity contract with publisher as printer was joint tortfeasor.

DEFAMATION (health)

Janvier v Sweeney and another (1919) 121 LTR 179; (1918-19) XXXV TLR 226 HC KBD Is good cause of action where make statement with intent to injure another who is injured thereby.

Janvier v Sweeney and Barker [1919] 88 LJCL 1231; (1918-19) 63 SJ 430; (1918-19) XXXV TLR 360 CA Is good cause of action where make statement with intent to injure another who is injured thereby.

DEFAMATION (husband and wife)

Barber v Pigden [1937] 1 All ER 115; [1937] 1 KB 664; (1937) 83 LJ 42; [1937] 106 LJCL 858; (1937) 156 LTR 245; (1937) 81 SJ 78; (1936-37) LIII TLR 246; (1937) WN (I) 8 CA Husband not liable for wife's torts unless proceedings begun before Law Reform (Married Women and Tortfeasors) Act 1935; no evidence that wife made slanderous comments as husband's agent.

DEFAMATION (innuendo)

Astaire v Campling and another [1965] 3 All ER 666; (1965) 109 SJ 854; [1966] 1 WLR 34 CA Innuendo cannot make a true and innocent statement libellous.

Childs v London Express Newspaper, Ltd and another (1941) 85 SJ 179 HC KBD Plea of innuendo deemed to fail in case where defence of fair comment would in any event have succeeded.

English and Scottish Co-operative Properties Mortgage and Investment Society, Ltd v Odhams Press, Ltd and another [1940] 1 All ER 1; [1940] 1 KB 440; [1940] 109 LJCL 273; (1940) 162 LTR 82; (1940) 84 SJ 112; (1939-40) LVI TLR 195; (1940) WN (I) 9 CA Newspaper headline contained innuendo: one farthing's damages inadequate.

Fullam v Newcastle Chronicle and Journal Ltd and another [1977] 3 All ER 32; (1977) 127 NLJ 540t; (1977) 121 SJ 376; [1977] 1 WLR 651 CA Where legal innuendo must specify facts raising innuendo/persons understanding it — here latter rare and exceptional so action struck out.

Garbett v Hazell, Watson and Viney, Ltd and others [1943] 2 All ER 359 CA Print and photographs laid out in such a manner that three was a defamatory innuendo.

Grappelli and another v Derek Block (Holdings) Ltd and another [1981] 2 All ER 272; (1981) 125 SJ 169; [1981] 1 WLR 822 CA Material to be libellous must be so upon publication; if plea of innuendo in limited publication must identify those understanding innuendo.

Greenslade and another v Swaffer and others; Same v World's Press News Publishing Co, Ltd and another [1955] 3 All ER 200; (1955) 105 LJ 536; (1955) 99 SJ 725; [1955] 1 WLR 1109 CA On facts to support innuendo (and striking out where not there).

Grubb v Bristol United Press, Ltd [1962] 2 All ER 380; (1962) 112 LJ 369; [1963] 1 QB 309; (1962) 106 SJ 262 CA On innuendo in libel cases.

Lewis and another v Daily Telegraph, Ltd; Same v Associated Newspapers, Ltd [1963] 2 All ER 151; (1963) 113 LJ 317 HL Innuendo not separate cause of action from straightforward defamation by same words; on pleading innuendo; appropriate damages.

Lewis v Daily Telegraph, Ltd; Rubber Improvement, Ltd v Same; Lewis v Associated Newspapers, Ltd; Rubber Improvement, Ltd v Same [1962] 2 All ER 698; (1962) 112 LJ 436; [1963] 1 QB 340; (1962) 106 SJ 307 CA Re-trial ordered where was inadequate direction as to innuendo: to wrongly say person subject of Serious Fraud investiagtion was defamatory but not in same league as saying were guilty of fraud.

Loughans v Odhams Press, Ltd and others [1962] 1 All ER 404; (1962) 112 LJ 137; [1963] 1 QB 299; (1962) 106 SJ 262 CA Can plead innuendo by inference.

Rubber Improvement Ltd and Another v Daily Telegraph Ltd; Same v Associated Newspapers Ltd [1964] AC 234; (1963) 107 SJ 356; [1963] 2 WLR 1063 HL Judge must rule whether words capable of bearing alternative defamatory meanings alleged; on innuendo/justification; damages here too great.

Wheeler v Somerfield and others (1965) 109 SJ 875 HC QBD Failed claim of innuendo in one article based on other articles.

Wheeler v Somerfield and others [1966] 2 All ER 305; [1966] 2 QB 94; [1966] 2 WLR 1006 CA Libel damages for injury to health possible (but not here); could be that to include articles of certain section of publication might carry innuendo but not here.

DEFAMATION (justification)

Arnold and Butler v Bottomley and others [1908] 2 KB 151; [1908] 77 LJCL 584; (1908) XCVIII LTR 777; (1907-08) 52 SJ 300; (1907-08) XXIV TLR 365 CA Must plead specifics of justification.

Aspro Travel Ltd and others v Owners Abroad Group plc and others [1995] 4 All ER 728; (1995) 139 SJ LB 195; [1995] TLR 404; [1996] 1 WLR 132 CA To say of a director that he allowed a company trade while insolvent is defamatory. Sometimes can plead in justification that are merely repeating existing rumours.

Beevis v Dawson and others [1956] 3 All ER 837; [1957] 1 QB 195; (1956) 100 SJ 874; [1956] 3 WLR 1016 CA Various errors justifying re-hearing before judge alone; court may allow plaintiff to delay evidence until defence presents alleged justification.

Bookbinder v Tebbit [1989] 1 All ER 1169; (1989) 139 NLJ 112; [1989] 1 WLR 640 CA Plaintiff withdrawing allegation of general slander meant defendant could not rely on general charge to support justification plea.

Carter v Brand, Montague and Co (1969) 113 SJ 188 HC QBD Justification defence to triumph if alleged libel is substantially true; justified annoyance not malice.

Digby v The 'Financial News' (Limited) [1907] 76 LJCL 321; (1907) XCVI LTR 172; (1906-07) XXIII TLR 117 CA Further and better particulars of justification unavailable where only pleading fair comment.

Godman v Times Publishing Company, Limited [1926] 2 KB 273; (1926) 61 LJ 384; (1926) 135 LTR 291; (1925-26) 70 SJ 606 CA On pleading justification.

Goldschmidt v Constable and Co [1937] 4 All ER 293; (1937) 81 SJ 863 CA Details of justification to accompany delivery of defence.

Goody v Odhams Press, Ltd [1966] 3 All ER 369; [1967] 1 QB 333; (1966) 110 SJ 793; [1966] 3 WLR 460 CA Evidence of relevant previous convictions admissible to show plaintiff's generally bad reputation; can be partial justification of article if part severable.

Howard-Williams v Bearman and Associated Newspapers, Ltd (1962) 106 SJ 1009 CA Party allowed plead partial justification.

Khashoggi v IPC Magazines Ltd and another [1986] 3 All ER 577; (1986) 136 NLJ 1111; (1970) 130 SJ 862; [1986] 1 WLR 1412 CA Interlocutory injunction unavailable regarding unproveable claims if justification to be pleaded regarding connected claims.

Lucas-Box v News Group Newspapers Ltd; Lucas-Box v Associated Newspapers Group plc and others [1986] 1 All ER 177; (1986) 130 SJ 111; [1986] 1 WLR 147 CA Party to specify meaning intends to justify before starting justification.

MacGrath v Black and another (1926) 61 LJ 560; [1926] 95 LJCL 951; (1926) 135 LTR 594 CA Particulars that did not justify specific allegations but supported general tenor of allegedly defamatory piece were admissible in evidence.

Maisel v Financial News, Ltd [1914-15] All ER 671; [1915] 3 KB 336; (1915) 50 LJ 335; [1915] 84 LJKB 2148; (1915-16) 113 LTR 772; (1914-15) 59 SJ 596; (1914-15) XXXI TLR 510; (1915) WN (I) 264 CA Post-libel incidents can be relied on to justify libel.

Maisel v Financial Times (Limited) [1915] 84 LJKB 2145; (1915) 112 LTR 953; (1914-15) 59 SJ 248; (1914-15) XXXI TLR 192 HL Post-libel incidents can be relied on to justify libel.

Marks and another v Wilson-Boyd and others [1939] 2 All ER 605; (1939) 160 LTR 520; (1939) 83 SJ 415; (1938-39) LV TLR 699; (1939) WN (I) 182 CA Need not be order for all particulars of facts sought to be relied on when justification plea raised.

McDonald's Corp and another v Steel and another [1995] 3 All ER 615 CA To plead justification defendant must believe words complained of were true, intend to support plea at trial and have reasonable evidence to buttress allegations.

Moore v News of the World Ltd and another [1972] 1 All ER 915; [1972] 2 WLR 419 CA Must plead justification if going to raise it.

Morrell v Thomson (International) [1989] 3 All ER 733; (1989) 139 NLJ 1007 CA On pleading justification.

R v Studds (Walter John) (1909) 3 Cr App R 207 CCA Must specify elements of (alleged) justification to libel.

Rubber Improvement Ltd and Another v Daily Telegraph Ltd; Same v Associated Newspapers Ltd [1964] AC 234; (1963) 107 SJ 356; [1963] 2 WLR 1063 HL Judge must rule whether words capable of bearing alternative defamatory meanings alleged; on innuendo/justification; damages here too great.

Singh v Gillard (1988) 138 NLJ 144 CA On quality of particulars required when pleading justification.

Stern v Piper and others [1996] 3 All ER 385; [1997] QB 123; (1996) 140 SJ LB 175; (1996) TLR 30/5/96; [1996] 3 WLR 715 CA Failed plea of justification in respect of newspaper publication of claims in affirmation concerning pending court action.

Sutherland and others v Stopes et e contra [1924] All ER 19; [1925] AC 47; (1924) 59 LJ 757; [1925] 94 LJCL 166; (1925) 132 LTR 550; (1924-25) 69 SJ 138; (1924-25) XLI TLR 106 HL Plea seeming partly one of justification, partly one of fair comment, a plea of fair comment.

Wootton v Sievier [1911-13] All ER 1001; [1913] 3 KB 499; (1913) 48 LJ 374; [1913] 82 LJKB 1242; (1913-14) 109 LTR 28; (1912-13) 57 SJ 609; (1912-13) XXIX TLR 596; (1913) WN (I) 187 CA Particulars required when justification pleaded.

DEFAMATION (libel)

Allsop v Church of England Newspaper Ltd and others [1972] 2 All ER 26; (1972) 122 NLJ 129t; [1972] 2 QB 161; (1972) 116 SJ 222; [1972] 2 WLR 600 CA In all cases desirable that plaintiff explain defamatory meaning and in some cases essential.

Anderson v Calvert (1907-08) XXIV TLR 399 CA On considerations for jury when assessing damages for libel.

Associated Leisure Ltd and others v Associated Newspapers Ltd [1970] 2 All ER 754; [1970] 2 QB 450; (1970) 114 SJ 551; [1970] 3 WLR 101 CA Justification not to be pleaded unless solid basis for it; late addition of justification plea possible if done as soon as possible/no irremediable injustice done.

Astaire v Campling and others (1965) 109 SJ 703 HC QBD Suggested innuendoes would not occur to reasonable reader so claims of libel based on same to be struck out.

Atkinson v Fitzwalter and others [1987] 1 All ER 483; [1987] 1 WLR 201 CA Late amendment (even including fraud allegation) allowable if in interests of justice.

Attorney General v News Group Newspapers Ltd [1986] 2 All ER 833; (1986) 136 NLJ 584; [1987] QB 1; (1986) 130 SJ 408; [1986] 3 WLR 365 CA Injunction generally unavailable if justification to be pleaded as defence unless serious risk of prejudice to trial.

Austin (Reginald) v Mirror Newspapers Ltd [1986] AC 299; (1986) 130 SJ 13; [1986] 2 WLR 57 PC Qualified privilege could (under Defamation Act 1974, s 22) attach to newspaper report critical of rugby league team trainer but not here as journalist had not taken reasonable care regarding accuracy of facts.

Australian Consolidated Press, Ltd v Uren [1967] 3 All ER 523; [1969] 1 AC 590; (1967) 117 NLJ 1166; (1967) 111 SJ 741; [1967] 3 WLR 1338 PC Permissible that Rookes v Barnard not be applied to awarding of exemplary libel damages in Australia.

Baird v Wallace-James [1916] 85 LJPC 193 HL Letter from president of parish charity to chair of parish council criticising parish medical officer's under-use of nurse provided by charity was privileged.

Barnes and another v Hill [1967] 1 All ER 347; [1967] 2 WLR 632 CA General verdict terminates case.

Barnet v Crozier and another [1987] 1 All ER 1041; (1987) 131 SJ 298; [1987] 1 WLR 272 CA Statement of court in settlement of one libel claim permissible if no real risk of prejudice to later libel claim.

Bendle and another v United Kingdom Alliance and another (1914-15) XXXI TLR 403 CA Was libel of plaintiffs to print statement to effect that their product did not possess properties claimed.

Bennett and others v Guardian Newspapers Ltd [1995] TLR 719 HC QBD Were not allowed greater leeway in criticisms of public figures before what said could be construed as libellous.

Bennett and others v Guardian Newspapers Ltd [1997] TLR 104 CA On relevant considerations when determining distress occasioned by libel.

Bernstein v The Observer Ltd (1976) 126 NLJ 595t CA Failed appeal against successful libel claim (no misdirection by trial judge/no fair comment).

Beswick v Smith (1907-08) XXIV TLR 169 CA Circular by employers of commercial traveller that he was no longer employed by them and that no orders should be placed/money given to him was not capable of being defamatory.

Beta Construction Ltd and another v Channel Four Television Co Ltd and another [1990] 2 All ER 1012; (1989) 139 NLJ 1561; [1990] 1 WLR 1042 CA Court may order trial by judge of libel cases by two parties where only one plaintiff presents complex evidence if two are sufficiently closely linked.

Boaks v Associated Newspapers Ltd (1967) 111 SJ 703; (1968) 118 NLJ 181t HC QBD Failed appeal against nominal damages awarded for libellous statement of person to effect that was in receipt of national assistance.

Bognor Regis Urban District Council v Campion [1972] 2 All ER 61; (1972) 122 NLJ 377; [1972] 2 QB 169 HC QBD Local government authority can sue in libel to preserve its reputation.

Boston v WS Bagshaw and Sons and others [1966] 2 All ER 906; (1966) 110 SJ 352; [1966] 1 WLR 1126 CA Broadcast seeking criminal enjoyed privilege; leaving general question of malice to jury rather than explaining minutiae thereof valid.

Botham v Khan (1996) TLR 15/7/96 CA On determining whether words capable of bearing defamatory meaning (look to what plaintiff said had been done by defendant).

Bottomley v FW Woolworth and Co, Limited (1931-32) XLVIII TLR 521 CA On liability of distributors (who are not authors) of libellous work.

Bridgmont v Associated Newspapers, Ltd and others [1951] 2 All ER 285; [1951] 2 KB 578; (1951) 95 SJ 529; [1951] 2 TLR 682; (1951) WN (I) 377 CA 'Slanderous' statement that party was person mentioned in libel relevant to question of damages in libel action.

Broome v Cassell and Co Ltd and another [1971] 2 All ER 187; [1971] 2 QB 354; (1971) 115 SJ 289; [1971] 2 WLR 853 CA Rookes v Barnard was per incuriam; exemplary damages available in libel; behaviour fell in second category of Rookes v Barnard; one sum of damages where joint tortfeasors.

Broxton v McClelland (1996) TLR 27/11/96 CA Evidence of ongoing relations between parties properly admitted by judge to enable jury to arrive at balanced conclusion in libel action.

Burns and others v Associated Newspapers, Limited (1925) 89 JP 205; (1925-26) XLII TLR 37 HC ChD Might be libellous to call person a Communist but not statement as to personal character under Municipal Elections (Corrupt and Illegal Practices) Act 1911, s 1(1).

Byrne v Byrne [1937] 2 All ER 204 CA Not defamatory to say person informed police of crime.

Byrne v Deane [1937] 1 KB 818; [1937] 106 LJCL 533; (1937) 157 LTR 10; (1937) 81 SJ 236; (1936-37) LIII TLR 469; (1937) WN (I) 126 CA Allegation that were police informer not defamatory.

Cadam and others v Beaverbrook Newspapers, Ltd [1959] 1 All ER 453; (1959) 109 LJ 184; [1959] 1 QB 413; (1959) 103 SJ 177 CA Just stating that writ issued/particulars of writ might be justifiable; on pleading.

Calvet v Tomkies and others [1963] 3 All ER 610; (1963) 113 LJ 722; (1963) 107 SJ 791; [1963] 1 WLR 1397 CA Evidence of actual loss suffered not admitted as general pecuniary loss claimed.

Carter v Brand, Montague and Co (1969) 113 SJ 188 HC QBD Justification defence to triumph if alleged libel is substantially true; justified annoyance not malice.

Cassidy v Daily Mirror Newspapers, Limited [1929] 2 KB 331 HC KBD Liable for defamatory meaning of one's words though unintended.

Cassidy v Daily Mirror Newspapers, Ltd [1929] All ER 117; (1929) 67 LJ 399; (1929) 98 LJCL 595; (1929) 141 LTR 404; (1929) 73 SJ 348; (1928-29) XLV TLR 485 CA Are liable for defamatory meaning of one's words whether intended defamation or not.

Charleston and another v News Group Newspapers Ltd [1994] TLR 16 CA Photos, headlines and connected articles could not be severed so as to find one element defamatory.

Charleston and another v News Group Newspapers Ltd and another [1995] 2 All ER 313; [1995] 2 AC 65; (1995) 145 NLJ 490; (1995) 139 SJ LB 100; [1995] TLR 171; [1995] 2 WLR 450 HL Photos, headlines and connected articles may not be severed so as to find one element defamatory.

Church of Scientology of California v Johnson-Smith [1972] 1 All ER 378; [1972] 1 QB 522; (1971) 115 SJ 658; [1971] 3 WLR 434 HC QBD Parliamentary proceedings completely and absolutely privileged.

Citizens' Life Assurance Co v Brown [1904-07] All ER 925; [1904] AC 423; [1904] 73 LJPC 102; (1904) XC LTR 739; (1903-04) XX TLR 497; (1904-05) 53 WR 176 PC Corporation liable for (unauthorised) malicious libel by its servant acting in course of employment.

Clerk v Motor-Car Co (1905) Lim and Ford (1904-05) 49 SJ 418 HC ChD Injunction granted where had been unauthorised use of plaintiff's name in connection with defendant's business.

Cohen v Daily Telegraph, Ltd [1968] 2 All ER 407; (1968) 118 NLJ 350t; (1968) 112 SJ 356; [1968] 1 WLR 916 CA Facts when comment made determine if fair comment.

Coke Press Limited v Stevens and Sons, Ltd and Sweet and Maxwell, Ltd (1936) 82 LJ 363 HC KBD Settlement of libel action brought by owners-publishers of 'The Law Journal'/the 'All England Reports' against the owners-publishers of the 'Law Journal Reports' (on foot of certain advertising by latter).

Collins v Jones (1955) 105 LJ 264; [1955] 1 QB 564; (1955) 99 SJ 258; [1955] 2 WLR 813 CA Order for particulars of letter granted to enable plaintiff to make out libel claim with some certainty.

Cookson v Harewood and others [1931] All ER 533; [1932] 2 KB 478; (1932) 101 LJCL 394; (1932) 146 LTR 550 CA Cannot plead innuendo in respect of words properly published under rules of club to which belong.

Corelli v Wall (1905-06) XXII TLR 532 HC ChD Interim injunction on publication of picture postcards refused as alleged libel insufficiently made out.

Crest Homes Ltd v Ascott (1975) 125 NLJ 186t CA No injunction to retrain publication of truth (albeit that publication done in eccentric manner).

Crisp v Daily Herald (1929) and others (1959) 103 SJ 918 CA Impecuniosity no excuse for (twelve year) delay: libel action struck out.

Crowne v Warden and Co Ltd and others (1968) 112 SJ 824 CA Was just possible that newspaper headline and bold introduction could be defamatory though overall article was not.

Daily Mirror Newspapers Ltd v Exclusive News Agency (1937) 81 SJ 924 HC KBD Newspaper had right of indemnity against news agency which supplied it with mistakenly identified photograph that resulted in successful libel action being brought against the newspaper.

Davis and another v Rubin and another (1968) 112 SJ 51 CA Re-trial of libel action ordered where damages awarded were excessive.

Davis v London Express Newspaper, Limited (1939) 83 SJ 96; (1938-39) LV TLR 207 HC KBD Absent malice person to whom letter critical of company written could not sue newspaper which obtained copy of letter and showed it to company officer.

DDSA Pharmaceuticals Ltd v Times Newspapers Ltd and another [1972] 3 All ER 417; (1972) 122 NLJ 609t; [1973] QB 21; (1972) 116 SJ 585; [1972] 3 WLR 582 CA Particulars in pleadings in libel actions.

De L'Isle (Viscount) v Times Newspapers Ltd [1987] 3 All ER 499; (1988) 132 SJ 54; [1988] 1 WLR 49 CA Finding of fact and not a discretion whether trial by judge preferable to trial by jury where many documents/accounts.

De Normanville v Hereford Times Limited (1935) 79 SJ 796 HC KBD Newspaper report deemed a fair and accurate report (slightly inaccurate paraphrasing) of what transpired at public meeting.

De Normanville v Hereford Times Limited (1936) 80 SJ 423 CA Newspaper report deemed a fair and accurate report (slightly inaccurate paraphrasing) of what transpired at public meeting.

Derbyshire County Council v Times Newspapers Ltd and others [1991] 4 All ER 795; [1991] TLR 175 HC QBD Local authority may sue for libel even if no financial loss/property affected.

Derbyshire County Council v Times Newspapers Ltd and others [1992] 3 All ER 65; (1992) 142 NLJ 276; [1992] QB 770; [1992] TLR 69; [1992] 3 WLR 28 CA Trading/non-trading corporation with corporate reputation may sue for libel/slander but local authority may not unless actual financial loss.

Derbyshire County Council v Times Newspapers Ltd and others [1993] 1 All ER 1011; [1993] AC 534; (1993) 143 NLJ 283; (1993) 137 SJ LB 52/81; [1993] TLR 87; [1993] 2 WLR 449 HL Local authority cannot sue for defamation.

Design Yearbook, Ltd v Craig and others (1967) 111 SJ 719 HC QBD Directors who positively authorised secretary to do wrongful act were liable for same.

Dingle v Associated Newspapers, Ltd and others [1961] 1 All ER 897; (1961) 111 LJ 237; [1961] 2 QB 162; (1961) 105 SJ 153 CA Can mitigate damages only by showing existing bad reputation; no mitigation on ground that re-publishing another's libel.

Drummond-Jackson v British Medical Association and others (1970) 114 SJ 152; [1970] 1 WLR 688 CA Statements of claim only struck out where glaringly necessary which was not the case here.

Edmondson v Birch and Co, Ltd [1904-07] All ER 996; [1907] 76 LJCh 347; [1907] 1 KB 371; (1907) XCVI LTR 415; (1906-07) XXIII TLR 234; (1907) WN (I) 18 CA Publication of defamatory material in privileged communication to telegram clerks did not lift privilege.

Electrical, Electronic, Telecommunication and Plumbing Union v Times Newspapers Ltd and others [1980] QB 585; (1980) 124 SJ 31; [1980] 3 WLR 98 HC QBD Trade union could not bring action for libel of itself per se or for libel of all of its members.

Emerson v Grimsby Times and Telegraph Company, Limited (1926) 61 LJ 99; (1925-26) XLII TLR 238 CA Striking out of libel claim on basis that was frivolous/vexatious.

Ex parte Pollard (1900-01) XVII TLR 773 HC KBD Magistrate cannot seek criminal information for libel where has been libelled in capacity as magistrate and has sought apology/threatened action for damages.

Farmer v Morning Post Ltd (1936) 80 SJ 345 CA Possible that words of non-party to action who intervened in court (said intervention being reported) were part of judicial proceedings but converse also possible so ensuing libel action not per se frivolous/vexatious.

Fielding and another v Variety Incorporated [1967] 2 All ER 497; [1967] 2 QB 841; (1967) 111 SJ 257; [1967] 3 WLR 415 CA Absent peculiar damage only damages for financial loss for injurious falsehood; not so with libel.

Fielding v Moiseiwitsch (1946) 174 LTR 265 HC KBD Was breach of contract for pianist not to perform as had contracted; not defamatory for organiser to truthfully state what had occurred — such statement was in any event privileged.

Fielding v Moiseiwitsch (1946) 175 LTR 265 CA Was breach of contract for pianist not to perform as had contracted; not defamatory for organiser to truthfully state what had occurred — such statement was in any event privileged.

Franks v Westminster Press Ltd [1990] TLR 275 HC QBD Absent express waiver complaint to Press Council did not involve waiving right to sue for libel over relevant article.

Fraser v Evans and others (1968) 118 NLJ 956t; (1968) 112 SJ 805 CA Refusal of injunction restraining publication of article which party publishing intended to justify.

Gillick v British Broadcasting Corporation and another [1995] TLR 527 CA Implicit suggestion that person who campaigned for contraceptive information not to be made available to girls was morally responsible for suicides of certain two pregnant girls was libellous.

Goldsmith and another v Bhoyrul and others (1997) 141 SJ LB 151; [1997] TLR 319 HC QBD Political party per se could not bring libel action.

Goldsmith and another v Pressdram Ltd and others [1988] 1 WLR 64 CA Refusal of application for trial of libel action by jury.

Goldsmith v Pressdram Ltd (1976) 126 NLJ 888t; (1976) 120 SJ 606 HC QBD On availability of injunction from stating what was claimed to be a libel.

Goldsmith v Sperrings Ltd [1977] 2 All ER 566; (1977) 121 SJ 304; [1977] 1 WLR 478 CA Abuse of process where action really brought to serve secondary purpose unavailable in law.

Goody v Odhams Press, Ltd [1966] 3 All ER 369; [1967] 1 QB 333; [1966] 3 WLR 460 CA Evidence of relevant previous convictions admissible to show plaintiff's generally bad reputation; can be partial justification of article if part severable.

Greenlands (Limited) v Wilmshurst and others (1912-13) XXIX TLR 64 HC KBD Statements of person acting as confidential agent of member of trade association not privileged.

Greenlands, Limited v Wilmshurst and the London Association for Protection of Trade and another [1913] 3 KB 507; (1913) 48 LJ 471; [1914] 83 LJKB 1; (1913-14) 109 LTR 487; (1912-13) 57 SJ 740; (1912-13) XXIX TLR 685 CA Statements of person acting as confidential agent of member of trade association not privileged.

Griffiths and another v Benn (1910-11) XXVII TLR 346 CA Absent special damage criticism of trader's goods not libel (may be be libel if represents personal attack on trader); criticism of operation of system under patent not per se an attack on operator.

Gros and another v Crook and another (1969) 113 SJ 408 HC QBD Publisher liable for malicious libel published by writer-agent.

Grubb v Bristol United Press, Ltd [1962] 2 All ER 380; (1962) 112 LJ 369; [1963] 1 QB 309; (1962) 106 SJ 262 CA On innuendo in libel cases.

Gulf Oil (GB) Ltd v Page and others [1987] 3 All ER 14; [1987] Ch 327; (1987) 137 NLJ 409; (1987) 131 SJ 695 CA Where conspiracy to injure injunction is available to restrain publication, even one it is later hoped to justify.

Guske v Cooke (1981) 131 NLJ 758 HC QBD Absolute and qualified privilege held to attach to letter from personal doctor to solicitors as to state of client's mental health.

H v H (1899-1900) 44 SJ 706 VacCt Ex parte interim injunction granted to restrain publication of libel.

Harakas and others v Baltic Mercantile and Shipping Exchange Ltd and another [1982] 2 All ER 701; (1982) 126 SJ 414; [1982] TLR 130; [1982] 1 WLR 958 CA If justification/qualified privilege cannot injunct publication unless publisher knows statement untrue.

Hawker v Stourfield Park Hotel Company (1900) WN (I) 51 HC ChD Can restrain making of untrue statement even if not libellous/defamatory if statement operates to injure another.

Haynes v De Beck and others (1914-15) XXXI TLR 115 HC KBD Wholesale newspaper distributors not liable where distributed newspapers which did not know (and were not negligent in not knowing) were defamatory.

Hayward and another v Wegg-Prosser (1978) 122 SJ 792 HC QBD Libel action stayed where plaintiffs sought to rely on documents inadvertently obtained by them after they were disclosed by solicitor to court officer in course of taxation.

Hayward v Thompson and others [1981] 3 All ER 450; (1981) 131 NLJ 926; [1982] QB 47; (1981) 125 SJ 625; [1981] 3 WLR 470 CA Could be one sum of damages for two separate related libels.

Herbage v Pressdram Ltd and others [1984] 2 All ER 769; (1984) 128 SJ 615; [1984] TLR 289; [1984] 1 WLR 1160 CA Damages recoverable for malicious publication of spent convictions.

Hill v Archbold [1967] 2 WLR 1180 HC QBD Master (union) could support servant (officials) in libel action brought against latter arising from their employment.

Hobbs v Tinling (CT) and Company, Limited; Hobbs v Nottingham Journal, Limited [1929] 2 KB 1 HC KBD On procedure in libel action; on mitigation of damages where are of bad character.

Hobbs v Tinling (CT) and Co, Ltd; Hobbs v Nottingham Journal, Ltd [1929] All ER 33; (1929) 67 LJ 290; (1929) 98 LJCL 421; (1929) WN (I) 89 CA On libel; on mitigation of damages where are of bad character.

Holdsworth (TW), Limited v Associated Newspapers, Limited [1938] 107 LJCL 69; (1937) 157 LTR 274; (1937) 81 SJ 685; (1936-37) LIII TLR 1029 CA On whether newspaper comments to effect that employer refusing to implement wages award/pact were libellous.

Horrocks v Lowe [1972] 3 All ER 1098; (1972) 122 NLJ 894t; (1972) 116 SJ 946; [1972] 1 WLR 1625 CA Honest belief in truth of statement rooted in prejudice precludes malice.

Huth v Huth [1914-15] All ER 242; [1915] 3 KB 32; (1915) 50 LJ 195; [1915] 84 LJKB 1307; (1915-16) 113 LTR 145; (1914-15) XXXI TLR 350; (1915) WN (I) 154 CA No libel where unsealed letter sent through post and inadvertently read by addressee's butler.

J Lionel Barber and Co (Limited) v Deutsche Bank (Berlin) London Agency (1916-17) XXXIII TLR 543 CA No damages for libel on privileged occasion as was no express malice proved.

J Trevor and Sons (a firm) v Solomon (1978) 128 NLJ 134t CA Refusal of injunction preventing person from stating what he considered to be the truth.

J v R and another (1984) 128 SJ 333 HC QBD Plaintiff allowed make statement in open court following acceptance of money paid into court by defendants in full satisfaction of plaintiff's libel claim.

Jackson v Mirror Group Newspapers Ltd and another [1994] TLR 174 CA Stay of action merited unless plaintiff to libel action underwent medical test; defendants' medic could seek discovery of medical records from plaintiff's doctor.

Jang Publications Ltd and Rahman v Crescent and Star Publications Ltd and Aziz (1981) 131 NLJ 482c CA £20,000 damages not inappropriate for serious (political) libel.

Jayson v Midland Bank, Ltd (1967) 111 SJ 719 HC QBD Issue whether bank's writing 'refer to drawer' on cheque was libellous left to jury.

Jeyaretnam (Joshua Benjamin) v Tong (Goh Chok) (1989) 133 SJ 1032; [1989] 1 WLR 1109 PC Comments of politician at press conference deemed to be fair comments and not defamatory.

John Leng and Co (Limited) v Langlands (1916) 114 LTR 665; (1915-16) XXXII TLR 255 HL Newspaper criticism of person in public position not unreasonably critical and not libellous.

Jones v E Hulton and Co [1908-10] All ER 29; [1909] 2 KB 444; [1909] 78 LJKB 937; (1909-10) 101 LTR 330; (1908-09) XXV TLR 597; (1909) WN (I) 133 CA No defence to libel that was unintentional.

Jozwiak v Sadek and others [1954] 1 All ER 3; (1954) 104 LJ 10; (1954) 98 SJ 94 HC QBD Later public comments/anonymous telephone calls admissible to prove libel.

Kaye v Robertson and another [1990] TLR 232 CA Is no right to privacy.

Keays v Murdoch Magazines (UK) Ltd and another [1991] 4 All ER 491; (1991) 141 NLJ 893; [1991] 1 WLR 1184 CA Court may order preliminary hearing in libel action to determine if words used can be libellous/import meaning suggested by defendant.

Kemsley v Foot and others [1951] 1 All ER 331; [1951] 2 KB 34; (1951) 101 LJ 48; (1951) 95 SJ 120; [1951] 1 TLR 197; (1951) WN (I) 88 CA Criticism of newspaper controller for style of newspaper to be treated like criticism of book/play.

Kiam v Neill and another (1996) TLR 22/7/96 CA £45,000 damages merited for irresponsible libel.

Knupffer v London Express Newspaper, Limited [1944] 1 All ER 495; [1944] AC 116; (1945) 95 LJ 112; [1944] 113 LJ 251; (1944) 170 LTR 362; (1944) 88 SJ 143; (1943-44) LX TLR 310; (1944) WN (I) 111 HL Cannot claim individually libelled by class/group libel unless can show words refer to one as individual.

Knupffer v The London Express Newspaper, Ltd [1942] 2 All ER 555; [1943] KB 80; (1943) 93 LJ 125; [1943] 112 LJ 176; (1942) 167 LTR 376; (1942) 86 SJ 367; (1942-43) LIX TLR 31; (1942) WN (I) 206 CA Cannot claim individually libelled by class/group libel unless can show words refer to one as individual.

Levene v Roxhan and others [1970] 3 All ER 683; (1970) 120 NLJ 662t; (1970) 114 SJ 721; [1970] 1 WLR 1322 CA Separating of non-/defamatory elements of article possible but inappropriate; striking-out of claim.

Ley v Hamilton (1934) 151 LTR 360 CA Re-trial of libel action ordered where damages awarded unreasonable/possible that occasion of publication was privileged contrary to trial judge's ruling.

Ley v Hamilton (1935) 153 LTR 384; (1935) 79 SJ 573 HL Re-trial of libel action unnecessary where damages awarded reasonable/occasion of publication was not privileged.

Liebrich v Cassell and Co, Ltd [1956] 1 All ER 577 (1956) 100 SJ 188; [1956] 1 WLR 249 HC QBD On statements in open court.

Linklater v Daily Telegraph (1964) 108 SJ 992 HC QBD Left to jury as to whether calling half-Czech/half-Briton a 'Czech' was defamatory (though trial judge personally considered was not).

Linotype Company Limited v British Empire Type-Setting Machine Company Limited (1899-1900) LXXXI LTR 331 HL On libel of tradesman in his conduct of trade.

Lionel Barber and Company, Limited v Deutsche Bank (Berlin) London Agency et e Contra [1918-19] All ER 407; [1919] AC 304; (1918) 53 LJ 436l [1919] 88 LJCL 194; (1919) 120 LTR 288; (1918-19) XXXV TLR 120; (1918) WN (I) 373 HL Libel re-trial order quashed where plaintiffs agreed to reduce damages awarded.

Littler v BBC and another (1966) 110 SJ 585 HC QBD Fair comment plea allowed despite looseness as to factual basis on which grounded.

Lloyd (Clive Herbert) v David Syme and Co Ltd [1986] AC 350; (1986) 130 SJ 14; [1986] 2 WLR 69 PC Failure of defence of comment in respect of (defamatory) newspaper article where writer of same did not hold views made therein.

Lockhart v Harrison [1928] All ER 149; (1928) 139 LTR 521 HL Jury decision that words which need not be defamatory are not defamatory is valid — could be set aside if flew in face of reason.

London Artists, Ltd v Littler [1969] 2 All ER 193; [1969] 2 QB 375; (1969) 113 SJ 37; [1969] 2 WLR 409 CA Untrue claim of plot regarding matter of public interest not fair comment.

London Computer Operators Training Ltd and others v British Broadcasting Corporation and others [1973] 2 All ER 170; (1973) 117 SJ 147; [1973] 1 WLR 424 CA Could amend submission to include evidence of criminal convictions of one claiming libelled by suggestion of dishonesty.

Longdon-Griffiths v Smith and others [1950] 2 All ER 662; [1951] 1 KB 295; (1950) 100 LJ 413; (1950) 94 SJ 580; [1950] 66 (2) TLR 627; (1950) WN (I) 448 HC KBD Libel action to be directed at Friendly Society per se not its trustees; special damages available where libel led to losing job; that one of four parties acted maliciously did not affect qualified privilege of others.

Lord v Sunday Telegraph Ltd [1970] 3 All ER 504; (1970) 120 NLJ 1066; [1971] 1 QB 235; (1970) 114 SJ 706; [1970] 3 WLR 754 CA Need not separate comments from facts but must explain basic facts if relying on fair comment.

Lucas-Box v News Group Newspapers Ltd; Lucas-Box v Associated Newspapers Group plc and others [1986] 1 All ER 177; (1986) 130 SJ 111; [1986] 1 WLR 147 CA Party to specify meaning intends to justify before starting justification.

Lyle-Samuel v Odhams, Ltd [1918-19] All ER 779; [1920] 1 KB 135; (1919) 54 LJ 338; [1919] 88 LJCL 1161; (1920) 122 LTR 57; (1918-19) 63 SJ 748; (1918-19) XXXV TLR 711 CA Absent special circumstances person sued for defamation not obliged to reveal source.

Lyne v Nicholls (1906-07) XXIII TLR 86 HC ChD Absent proof of actual damage disparagement of competitor's goods (rather than advertising puff) was not libel but otherwise would be.

Lyon and Lyon v Daily Telegraph, Ltd [1943] 1 All ER 586; (1943) 168 LTR 251; (1942-43) LIX TLR 193 HC KBD Impossible to determine fair comment where writer of libel unknown; defamation in professional capacity.

Mangena v Wright [1908-10] All ER 1316; [1909] 2 KB 958; [1909] 78 LJKB 879; (1909) 100 LTR 960; (1908-09) 53 SJ 485; (1908-09) XXV TLR 534 HC KBD Cannot be sued for defamation where publish good faith/non-malicious copy/near-copy of Parliamentary; on mitigation of damages in libel/slander action.

Mapp v News Group Newspapers Ltd [1997] 2 Cr App R (S) 562; (1997) 147 NLJ 562; [1997] TLR 124 CA On determining whether words complained of are capable of bearing alleged defamatory meaning.

Martin v Nolan and another [1944] 2 All ER 342; (1943-44) LX TLR 558 HC KBD Conviction and breach of recognisance two offences so Borstal training merited: issue arose in course of successful libel action.

Mason v Brewis Brothers, Ltd [1938] 2 All ER 420; (1938) 82 SJ 523 HC KBD Employers letter to labour exchange not privileged occasion.

Mathew v 'The Times' Publishing Company (Limited) (1912-13) XXIX TLR 471 HC KBD Publication of translated Papal Bull in newspaper was not libellous.

Maulding v Stott and Daily Mirror Newspapers Ltd (1978) 128 NLJ 464t CA Exemplary damages could be sought where newspaper committing libel did so in belief that any damages might have to pay would be less than increased profits made by publishing article.

McCarey v Associated Newspapers Ltd and others (1964) 108 SJ 564; [1964] 1 WLR 855 HC QBD Newspaper account of coroner's court in process clothed by absolute privilege.

McCarey v Associated Newspapers, Ltd and others [Consolidated actions] [1964] 3 All ER 947; (1964) 114 LJ 506; [1965] 2 QB 86; (1964) 108 SJ 916; [1965] 2 WLR 45 CA Distinction between compensatory/punitive damages; when punitive damages appropriate.

McCormick v Bennison and others (1938) 82 SJ 869 CA Onetime boxing champion successfully recovered damages for libellous newspaper article about self.

McManus Associates Ltd v Harms and another (1969) 113 SJ 903 CA Refusal of interlocutory injunction restraining publication of allegedly libellous sign near building estate saying 'Purchasers beware ...'.

Mitchell and another v Hirst, Kidd and Rennie, Ltd, and another [1936] 3 All ER 872; (1936) 82 LJ 425 HC KBD Damages for unfair/inaccurate reporting of court proceedings; judge sitting alone may apportion damages between tortfeasors.

Moore v Lawson and another (1914-15) XXXI TLR 418 CA Court will not strike out claim statement in libel action on basis that words cannot be defamatory — whether are defamatory a matter for trial judge.

Morgan and another v Wallis (1916-17) XXXIII TLR 495 HC KBD Qualified privilege where solicitor in dictating bill of costs included without malice as a point of information a statement that was in fact defamatory.

Morgan v Odhams Press Ltd and another [1970] 2 All ER 544; (1970) 120 NLJ 200t; (1970) 114 SJ 193; [1970] 1 WLR 820 CA Libel action to be grounded in actual words; no libel if no one would have understood referred to plaintiff CA decision that case arguable does not mean libel case must be left to jury.

Morgan v Odhams Press Ltd and another [1971] 2 All ER 1156; (1971) 115 SJ 587; [1971] 1 WLR 1239 HL Article need not clearly point to certain person to be defamatory (though traditional test applies); misdirection on damages where failed to mention low circulation; imprecise, sensationalist article; some persons misled could be told truth by plaintiff; that no apology needed where defendant alleges never impugned plaintiff.

Morris and another v Sandess Universal Products [1954] 1 All ER 47; (1954) 104 LJ 9; (1954) 98 SJ 10 CA Test whether defamatory is would reasonable jury find defamatory.

National Union of General and Municipal Workers v Gillian and others [1945] 2 All ER 593 (also CA); (1945) 89 SJ 543 (also CA); (1945) WN (I) 194 HC KBD Trade union can sue for libel of its name.

National Union of General and Municipal Workers v Gillian and others [1945] 2 All ER 593 (also HC KBD); [1946] KB 81; (1946) 96 LJ 199; [1946] 115 LJ 43; (1945) 89 SJ 543 (also HC KBD); (1945-46) LXII TLR 46; (1945) WN (I) 214 CA Trade union can sue for libel of its name.

Newstead v London Express Newspaper, Limited [1939] 3 All ER 263; [1939] 2 KB 317; [1939] 108 LJCL 618; (1939) 161 LTR 236; (1939) 83 SJ 548; (1938-39) LV TLR 679; (1939) WN (I) 184 HC KBD Words true of one person can be libel of another.

Newstead v London Express Newspaper, Ltd [1939] 4 All ER 319; [1940] 1 KB 377; (1939) 88 LJ 314; [1940] 109 LJCL 166; (1940) 162 LTR 17; (1939) 83 SJ 942; (1939-40) LVI TLR 130; (1939) WN (I) 406 CA Words true of one person can be libel of another.

Pamplin v Express Newspapers Ltd (1985) 129 SJ 190 CA Libel verdict not set aside where plaintiff awarded nominal damages claimed jury not directed to disregard costs issue when reaching their verdict.

Pamplin v Express Newspapers Ltd (No 2) [1988] 1 All ER 282; (1985) 129 SJ 188; [1988] 1 WLR 116 CA Defendant may produce evidence concerning general reputation and previous convictions when arguing for low damages; jury may not take costs into account when reaching verdict.

Perera (MG) v Peiris and Another [1949] AC 1; [1949] 118 LJR 426; (1948) LXIV TLR 590; (1948) WN (I) 388 PC Unsuccessful defamation suit where newspaper published extracts from Government Bribery Commission Report without malice.

Plato Films, Ltd and others v Speidel [1961] 1 All ER 876; (1961) 111 LJ 220; (1961) 105 SJ 230 HL Can mitigate damages by introducing evidence of actual bad reputation (but not that should have bad reputation).

Plunkett and another v Barclay's Bank Limited (1936) 154 LTR 465 HC KBD Marking cheque 'refer to drawer' was not defamatory of plaintiff drawer.

Polly Peck (Holdings) plc and others v Trelford and others [1986] 2 All ER 84; [1986] QB 1000; (1986) 130 SJ 300; [1986] 2 WLR 845 CA Can place words in context of whole work if claimed part of work defamatory; where separate defamatory statements plaintiff can complain of just one; s 5 of Defamation Act inapplicable if not claiming words contain two/more charges.

Ponsford v The 'Financial Times' (Limited) and Hart (1899-1900) XVI TLR 248 HC QBD Newspaper account of shareholders' meeting not a matter of public concern so publishers liable for libel.

Powell v Gelston [1916-17] All ER 953; [1916] 2 KB 615; [1916] 85 LJKB 1783; (1916-17) 115 LTR 379; (1915-16) 60 SJ 696; (1915-16) XXXII TLR 703; (1916) WN (I) 323 HC KBD Opening of confidential letter defamatory of another by third party not libel as writer had been assured of confidentiality.

Prager v Times Newspapers Ltd [1988] 1 All ER 300; (1987) 137 NLJ 810; (1988) 132 SJ 55; [1988] 1 WLR 77 CA Cannot plead wider meaning of words used where if proved would not create less damnable form of statement made; can plead justification of any alternative meaning that might convince jury.

Pryce and Son, Limited v Pioneer Press, Limited (1925-26) XLII TLR 29 HC KBD Printing/publising of another printer's imprint was libellous.

R v Blumenfeld (Ex parte Tupper) (1911-12) XXVIII TLR 308 HC KBD Libel defendant who intends to assert justification will not be committed for contempt unless justification is false/intends to prejudice trial/intends to deter witnesses coming forward.

Ralston v Ralston [1930] All ER 336; [1930] 2 KB 238; (1930) 69 LJ 168; (1930) 99 LJCL 266; (1930) 142 LTR 487 HC KBD Tombstone alleging another woman wife of defendant could be defamatory of actual wife — as did not affect wife in trade/business no action lay under Married Women's Property Act 1882, s 12.

Richards v Naum (1970) 114 SJ 809 CA Libel action struck out for want of prosecution.

Riches and others v News Group Newspapers Ltd [1985] 2 All ER 845; (1985) 135 NLJ 391; [1986] QB 256; (1985) 129 SJ 401; [1985] 3 WLR 432 CA Exemplary damages to be shared among joint plaintiffs rather than separately awarded to each plaintiff.

Rickards v Bartram and others (1908-09) XXV TLR 181 HC KBD Trade union could be sued for alleged libel in its newsletter where was no ongoing/pending trade dispute when published.

Ridge v The 'English Illustrated' Magazine (Limited) (1912-13) XXIX TLR 592 HC KBD Publishers liable (on foot of publishing story falsely ascribed to plaintiff author) in libel if perception of plaintiff would be that of ordinary pen-pusher/in passing off if facts proved and damage inevitable result.

Rost v Edwards and others [1990] 2 All ER 641; [1990] 2 QB 460; [1990] TLR 120; [1990] 2 WLR 1280 HC QBD Reasons for selection/de-selection from Parliamentary committee/member's letter to Speaker privileged; register of Member's Interests not privileged.

Rothermere and others v Times Newspapers Ltd and others [1973] 1 All ER 1013; (1973) 123 NLJ 250t; (1973) 117 SJ 266; [1973] 1 WLR 448 CA Prolonged examination of documents (not complexity/length of trial) can justify no jury but need not.

Rubber Improvement Ltd and Another v Daily Telegraph Ltd; Same v Associated Newspapers Ltd [1964] AC 234; (1963) 107 SJ 356; [1963] 2 WLR 1063 HL Judge must rule whether words capable of bearing alternative defamatory meanings alleged; on innuendo/justification; damages here too great.

S and K Holdings Ltd and others v Throgmorton Publications Ltd and another [1972] 3 All ER 497; (1972) 116 SJ 375; [1972] 1 WLR 1036 CA Plaintiff cannot sever allegedly defamatory parts of article; defendant can plead justification in respect of whole.

Sharp v Skues (1908-09) XXV TLR 336 CA Where sent defamatory letter to plaintiff at business address (only address knew) and was opened by other staff members (which did not envision) were not guilty of libel.

Shaw v London Express Newsaper, Limited (1924-25) XLI TLR 475 HC KBD Newspaper article giving true account of murder in which person coincidentally had name of another who might be mistaken as person in article deemed non-libellous.

Shevill and others v Presse Alliance SA [1992] 1 All ER 409; [1996] AC 959 (also HL); [1991] TLR 132 CA Where conflict of laws in case of tort plaintiff may sue in either jurisdiction.

Shevill and others v Presse Alliance SA [1996] 3 All ER 929; [1996] AC 959 (also CA); (1996) 140 SJ LB 208; (1996) TLR 26/7/96 HL Where conflict of laws in case of tort plaintiff may sue in either jurisdiction.

Shordiche-Churchward v Cordle [1959] 1 All ER 599 CA Action on foot of covenant avoided through libel not a claim in libel: no jury trial.

Sim v Heinz (HJ) Co, Ltd and another [1959] 1 All ER 547; (1959) 109 LJ 200; (1959) 103 SJ 238 CA Interlocutory injunction unavailable for alleged passing off/libel.

Sim v Stretch [1936] 2 All ER 1237; (1936) 80 SJ 703; (1935-36) LII TLR 669 HL Test for defamation is whether would lower opinion of person in eyes of reasonable person/class of persons to whom statement addressed.

Singh and another v Observer Ltd [1989] 2 All ER 751 HC QBD Court may order financial supporter of party's action to pay costs if action fails.

Slazengers (Limited) v C Gibbs and Co (1916-17) XXXIII TLR 35 HC ChD Given that First World War in progress plaintiff firm could sue for libel where was alleged to be German firm.

Slipper v British Broadcasting Corporation [1991] 1 All ER 165; [1991] 1 QB 283; (1990) 134 SJ 1042; [1990] TLR 446; [1990] 3 WLR 967 CA Repetition of libel by third party may expose original publisher to action for damages in respect of repetition.

Smith v Lewis (1916-17) XXXIII TLR 195 HC KBD Need not plead express malice where in defence to claim that publication was malicious privilege is pleaded.

South Suburban Co-operative Society, Limited v Orum and others [1937] 2 KB 690; (1937) 83 LJ 410; [1937] 106 LJCL 555; (1937) 157 LTR 93; (1937) 81 SJ 497; (1936-37) LIII TLR 803; (1937) WN (I) 259 CA Writer of allegedly libellous letter to newspaper who pleads fair comment must reveal person/s from whom obtained information.

Speidel v Plato Films, Ltd and others; Same v Unity Theatre Society, Ltd [1960] 2 All ER 521; (1960) 110 LJ 428; (1960) 104 SJ 602 CA In mitigation of damages can prove bad reputation in general/inexorably linked to libel.

Stone v Brewis (1902-03) 47 SJ 70 CA Addressing letter to notorious person care of another's address validly found to be libellous of latter; punitive damages justified.

Stretch v Sim (1935) 79 SJ 453 CA Was matter for jury whether allegation in telegram that gentleman had been required to borrow money from housemaid was defamatory (certainly was potentially so).

Stubbs, Limited v Russell [1913] AC 386; (1913) 48 LJ 227; (1913) 82 LJPC 98; (1913) 108 LTR 529; (1912-13) XXIX TLR 409; (1913) WN (I) 103 HL Mistaken naming of party in Stubb's Gazette not libellous in light of note at head of list of names.

Stubbs, Ltd v Mazure [1918-19] All ER 1081; [1920] AC 66; (1919) 54 LJ 344; [1919] 88 LJPC 135; (1920) 122 LTR 5; (1918-19) XXXV TLR 697; (1919) WN (I) 234 HL Wrongful publication of name in Stubbs' Gazette deemed defamatory despite qualifier published at head of relevant section.

Sun Life Assurance Co of Canada v WH Smith and Son, Ltd [1933] All ER 432; (1934) 150 LTR 211 CA Vendor liable for libel in negligently not knowing poster contained libel.

Sutcliffe v Pressdram Ltd [1990] 1 All ER 269; (1989) 139 NLJ 1453; [1991] 1 QB 152; [1990] 2 WLR 271 CA Indirect evidence of newspaper payments not adequate to determine if payments made; damages a matter for jury — may be advised of what money is worth but not awards in other cases.

Telnikoff v Matusevitch [1990] 3 All ER 865; [1991] 1 QB 102; (1990) 134 SJ 1078; [1990] TLR 423; [1990] 3 WLR 725 CA Court may look to broader context in deciding if material libellous; plea of fair comment raises presumption that comment an honest expression of opinion unless counter-claim of malicious publication.

Telnikoff v Matusevitch [1991] 4 All ER 817; [1992] 2 AC 343; (1991) 141 NLJ 1590; [1991] TLR 513; [1991] 3 WLR 952 HL Letter in reply to article to be looked at in isolation when jury deciding if fair comment/libel; fair comment must be objectively fair.

Thaarup v Hulton Press, Limited (1943) 169 LTR 309; (1943) WN (I) 184 CA Re-trial ordered where trial judge in libel action found word 'pansy' to be incapable of defamatory meaning.

The London Motor-Cab Proprietors Association and the British Motor-Cab Company (Limited) v The Twentieth Century Press (1912) (Limited) (1917-18) XXXIV TLR 68 HC ChD Injunction on publication pending libel trial refused where would be to no effect (was no intent to publish any more)/action was wrongly framed/publication in issue might not be privileged.

Theaker v Richardson [1962] 1 All ER 229; (1962) 112 LJ 136; (1962) 106 SJ 151 CA Could be anticipated/natural and probable result of writing letter to person that would be opened by spouse.

Thompson v New South Wales Branch of the British Medical Association [1924] AC 764; [1924] 93, 1203; (1924) 131 LTR 162 PC Expulsion rule of Medical Association was to promote trade, not restrain it; Medical Association meeting's resolving to expel member a privileged occasion.

Thomson (DC) and Co v McNulty (1927) 71 SJ 744 HL Failed libel action where was not shown that newspaper article in question referred to respondent to appeal.

Thurston v Charles (1904-05) XXI TLR 659 HC KBD Substantial damages available for wrongful conversion/detention where published another's private correspondence but privilege in communication not destroyed so no libel.

Tolley v Fry (JS) and Sons, Limited [1930] 1 KB 467; (1929) 68 LJ 429; (1930) 99 LJCL 149; (1930) 142 LTR 270; (1929) 73 SJ 818; (1929-30) XLVI TLR 108; (1929) WN (I) 272 CA Something innocently stated could not through circumstance of publication be defamatory.

Tolley v Fry (JS) and Sons, Ltd [1931] All ER 131; [1931] AC 333; (1931) 71 LJ 277; (1931) 100 LJCL 328; (1931) 145 LTR 1; (1931) 75 SJ 220; (1930-31) XLVII TLR 351; (1931) WN (I) 87 HL Something innocently stated may through circumstance of publication be defamatory.

Tudor-Hart v British Union for the Abolition of Vivisection [1937] 4 All ER 475; [1938] 2 KB 329; [1938] 107 LJCL 501; (1938) 158 LTR 162; (1937) 81 SJ 1020; (1937-38) LIV TLR 154 CA Cannot apply for particulars of facts as is application for evidence.

Turner (otherwise Robertson) v Metro-Goldwyn-Mayer Pictures, Ltd [1950] 1 All ER 449; (1950) 94 SJ 145 HL That motivated by financial interest need not mean malicious; opinion need only be genuine not right — here honest views absent malice so qualified privilege remained.

Turner v Metro-Goldwyn-Mayer Pictures Ltd (1947) 97 LJ 389; (1947) 91 SJ 495 HC KBD Was libellous to suggest in writing that critic deliberately sought to damage the industry which provided the matter (film) that critic analysed.

Turner v Metro-Goldwyn-Mayer Pictures, Ltd (1948) 98 LJ 441 CA Potentially libellous to suggest in writing that critic deliberately sought to damage the industry which provided the matter (film) that critic analysed but no malice proved on part of maker of statement.

Turner v Metro-Goldwyn-Mayer Pictures, Limited (1950) 100 LJ 93; [1950] 66 (1) TLR 342; (1950) WN (I) 83 HL On malice; on trial procedure at libel/slander trials.

University of Glasgow v The Economist and another; University of Edinburgh v The Economist and another [1990] TLR 533 HC QBD Defendant had to prove foreign libel laws different where plaintiff raised presumption that were the same.

Vacher and Sons (Limited) v London Society of Compositors and Authors [1912] 81 LJKB 1014; (1911-12) 56 SJ 442; (1911-12) XXVIII TLR 366 CA Libel/conspiracy claim against trade union struck out as Trade Union Disputes Act 1906, s 4 precluded action as libel pertained to trade union per se.

Vacher and Sons (Lim) v London Society of Compositors and others (1912) 47 LJ 706; (1912-13) 57 SJ 75; (1912) WN (I) 268 HL Libel/conspiracy claim against trade union struck out as Trade Union Disputes Act 1906, s 4 precluded action as libel pertained to trade union per se.

Veal and Wife v Heard and another (1929-30) XLVI TLR 448 HC KBD Must be malice for letter to justice's clerk from member of public in course of application for moneylender's licence to be libellous.

Vizetelly v Mudie's Select Library, Limited [1900] 69 LJCL 645; [1900] 2 QB 170; (1899-1900) XVI TLR 352 CA Circulating library who could not show were not negligent liable for publishing libel in book.

Wallersteiner v Moir; Moir v Wallersteiner and others [1974] 3 All ER 217; (1974) 124 NLJ 525t; [1974] 1 WLR 991 CA Libel action used to gag party an abuse of process; consideration of sub judice company affairs at company meeting not contempt.

Ware and De Freville, Ltd v Motor Trade Association and others [1920] All ER 387; [1921] LJCL 949 CA Absent special circumstances statement that intend to do lawful act cannot be defamatory.

Waters v Sunday Pictorial Newspapers [1961] 2 All ER 758; (1961) 111 LJ 518; (1961) 105 SJ 492 CA On pleading in libel action.

Watts v Aldington; Tolstoy v Aldington [1993] TLR 655 CA Settlement agreement between victim and one tortfeasor did not free other tortfeasor from liability.

Watts v Times Newspapers Ltd and others (Schilling and Lom (a firm), third party) [1996] 1 All ER 152; [1995] TLR 488; [1996] 2 WLR 427 CA Respective liability of publisher and client for libel committed in course of apology for earlier libel must be considered separately where qualified privilege may arise in relation to either party.

Weld-Blundell v Stephens [1918] 2 KB 742; [1919] 88 LJCL 689 (also CA); (1917-18) XXXIV TLR 564; (1918) WN (I) 254 HC KBD Non-recovery of damages where ultimate cause of action was one's own.

Weld-Blundell v Stephens [1919] 1 KB 520; [1919] 88 LJCL 689 (also HC KBD); (1919) 120 LTR 494; (1918-19) 63 SJ 301; (1918-19) XXXV TLR 245 CA Nominal damages where ultimate cause of action was one's own behaviour.

Weld-Blundell v Stephens [1920] All ER 32; (1920) 55 LJ 206; [1920] 89 LJCL 705; (1920) 123 LTR 593; (1919-20) 64 SJ 529; (1919-20) XXXVI TLR 640 HL Nominal damages where ultimate cause of action was one's own behaviour/where recovery sought for consequences that were not natural/probable consequences of acts of party against whom claiming.

Weldon v 'The Times' Book Company (Limited) (1911-12) XXVIII TLR 143 CA Book distributors not liable for alleged libel in book distributed where did not know/were not negligent in not knowing of same and need not have been on inquiry as to same.

Wheeler v Somerfield and others [1966] 2 All ER 305; (1965-66) 116 NLJ 837; [1966] 2 QB 94; [1966] 2 WLR 1006 CA Libel damages for injury to health possible (but not here); could be that to include articles of certain section of publication might carry innuendo but not here.

Williams and Hill v London Midland and Scottish Railway Co (1946) 96 LJ 134 HC KBD Intent not necessary to be guilty of libel.

Williams v Associated Newspapers Ltd (1938) 82 SJ 294 CA Newspaper article critical of tennis umpire's actions as umpire deemed not to be defamatory.

Williams v Reason and another; Williams v Reason and others [1988] 1 All ER 262; [1988] 1 WLR 96 CA Fresh evidence inadmissible if no attempt made to obtain before action but admissible in retrial; defendant may introduce evidence of facts to support plea of justification.

Willis and another v Brooks and others [1947] 1 All ER 191; (1947) 91 SJ 55; (1945-46) LXII TLR 745; (1947) WN (I) 3 HC KBD Trade union per se can sue for libel.

Youssoupoff v Metro-Goldwyn-Mayer Pictures, Limited (1934) 78 SJ 617; (1933-34) L TLR 581 CA Defamation via ('talking') cinema film is libel; allegation that woman has been seduced is defamatory of her; on appropriate damages for libel.

DEFAMATION (local authority)

Bognor Regis Urban District Council v Campion [1972] 2 All ER 61; (1972) 122 NLJ 377; [1972] 2 QB 169 HC QBD Local government authority can sue in libel to preserve its reputation.

Derbyshire County Council v Times Newspapers Ltd and others [1992] 3 All ER 65; (1992) 142 NLJ 276; [1992] QB 770; [1992] TLR 69; [1992] 3 WLR 28 CA Trading/non-trading corporation with corporate reputation may sue for libel/slander but local authority may not unless actual financial loss.

Derbyshire County Council v Times Newspapers Ltd and others [1991] 4 All ER 795 HC QBD Local authority may sue for libel even if no financial loss/property affected.

DEFAMATION (malice)

Adam v Ward (1914-15) XXXI TLR 299 CA Letter defaming another but without malice and under moral compulsion was privileged.

Adam v Ward [1916-17] All ER 157; [1917] AC 309; (1917) 52 LJ 126; [1917] 86 LJCL 849; (1917-18) 117 LTR 34; (1916-17) XXXIII TLR 277 HL Letter defaming another but without malice was privileged.

Balden v Shorter and others [1933] All ER 249; [1933] Ch 427; (1933) 102 LJCh 191; (1933) 148 LTR 471; (1933) 77 SJ 138; (1933) WN (I) 37 HC ChD Absent malice no slander.

Broadway Approvals, Ltd and another v Odhams Press, Ltd and another [1965] 2 All ER 523; (1965) 115 LJ 416; (1965) 109 SJ 294; [1965] 1 WLR 805 CA Newspaper article need not be profiting from wrongdoing (so no automatic punitive damages); non-/apology/retraction not per se evidence of malice; knowledge of one area of company need not be imputed to another; editing of article not malice but colouring article could be.

Carter v Brand, Montague and Co (1969) 113 SJ 188 HC QBD Justification defence to triumph if alleged libel is substantially true; justified annoyance not malice.

Davis v London Express Newspaper, Limited (1939) 83 SJ 96; (1938-39) LV TLR 207 HC KBD Absent malice person to whom letter critical of company written could not sue newspaper which obtained copy of letter and showed it to company officer.

Egger v Davies and others (1964) 108 SJ 619 CA Malice of joint defendant in publishing item does not taint others with malice: most be individually motivated by malice to lose qualified privilege.

Groom v Crocker and others [1938] 2 All ER 394; [1939] 1 KB 194; (1938) 85 LJ 308; (1938) 158 LTR 477; (1937-38) LIV TLR 861 CA Failure of solicitor to act equally on behalf of both insurer/insured; malice on ostensibly privileged occasion; nominal damages as action in contract (not tort) and no evidence of actual damage.

Hambrook v The Law Society (1967) 111 SJ 195 HC QBD Non-malicious answers to Ministry of Labour questionnaire enjoyed qualified privilege.

Horrocks v Lowe [1972] 3 All ER 1098; (1972) 122 NLJ 894t; (1972) 116 SJ 946; [1972] 1 WLR 1625 CA Honest belief in truth of statement rooted in prejudice precludes malice.

Horrocks v Lowe [1974] 1 All ER 662; [1975] AC 135; (1974) 118 SJ 149; [1974] 2 WLR 282 HL Privilege/no malice where maker (unreasonably) believes in truth of statement.

Lawrence v Hall and another (1928) 72 SJ 87 HC KBD Letter by club secretary written in context of leasing of premises and in which it was implied (according to the plaintiff-solicitor) that he was incompetent was privileged/not motivated by malice.

Sadgrove v Hole [1901] 2 KB 1; [1901] 70 LJK/QB 455; (1901) LXXXIV LTR 647; (1900-01) 45 SJ 342; (1900-01) XVII TLR 332; (1900-01) 49 WR 473 CA Absent malice communication by way of postcard was privileged.

Smith v Streatfield [1911-13] All ER 362; [1913] 3 KB 764; [1913] 82 LJKB 1237; (1913-14) 109 LTR 173; (1912-13) XXIX TLR 707; (1913) WN (I) 263 HC KBD Author's privilege extended to printers but defeated in respect of both by author's malice.

Thomas v Bradbury, Agnew, and Company (Limited) and another [1904-07] All ER 220; [1906] 2 KB 627; [1906] 75 LJKB 726; (1906-07) XCV LTR 23; (1905-06) XXII TLR 656; (1905-06) 54 WR 608 CA Proof of malice defeats defence of fair comment on public interest or of privilege.

Turner v Metro-Goldwyn-Mayer Pictures, Limited (1950) 100 LJ 93; [1950] 66 (1) TLR 342; (1950) WN (I) 83 HL On malice; on trial procedure at libel/slander trials.

Veal and Wife v Heard and another (1929-30) XLVI TLR 448 HC KBD Must be malice for letter to justice's clerk from member of public in course of application for moneylender's licence to be libellous.

Winstanley v Bampton [1943] 1 All ER 661; [1943] KB 319 HC KBD Privileged letter to plaintiff's commanding officer lost privilege through malice.

DEFAMATION (malicious falsehood)

Allason v Campbell (1996) TLR 8/5/96 HC QBD Cannot succeed in action for malicious falsehood unless can show that have suffered pecuniary loss as result of said falsehood.

Brady v Express Newspapers plc [1994] TLR 690 HC QBD Malicious falsehood prosecution could not be brought by prisoner seeking damages for likely loss of prison privileges on foot of newspaper article.

C v Mirror Group Newspapers and others [1996] 4 All ER 511; [1997] 1 FCR 556; [1996] 2 FLR 532; (1996) 146 NLJ 1093; (1996) TLR 15/7/96; [1997] 1 WLR 131 CA Over five years after newspaper article published woman not allowed/allowed bring defamation/malicious falsehood claim.

Fielding and another v Variety Incorporated [1967] 2 All ER 497; [1967] 2 QB 841; (1967) 111 SJ 257; [1967] 3 WLR 415 CA Absent peculiar damage only damages for financial loss for injurious falsehood; not so with libel.

Joyce v Sengupta and another [1993] 1 All ER 897; (1992) 142 NLJ 1306; (1992) 136 SJ LB 274; [1993] 1 WLR 337 CA Entirely depends on plaintiff whether to bring action for malicious falsehood or libel/slander where defamation.

Leetham v Rank (1912-13) 57 SJ 111 CA Must prove actual loss of customers to succeed in defamation action where allege that have suffered injury as result of malicious falsehoods that are not actionable of themselves.

Shapiro v La Morta (1923-24) 68 SJ 142; (1923-24) XL TLR 39; (1923) WN (I) 290 HC KBD Must prove malice and can only recover damages for actual damage in action for malicious falsehood (failed to do so here).

Shapiro v La Morta [1923] All ER 378; (1923) 58 LJ 513; (1924) 130 LTR 622; (1923-24) 68 SJ 522; (1923-24) XL TLR 201 CA Must prove damage/malice and can only recover damages for actual damage in action for malicious falsehood affecting business/property.

Spring v Guardian Assurance plc and others [1993] 2 All ER 273; [1992] TLR 628 CA Test for malice in malicious falsehood same as that in libel and slander; referee owes no duty of care in negligence to subject of reference when preparing or giving reference.

DEFAMATION (malicious libel)

Watt (Lady Violet) v Watt (Julia) [1905] AC 115; [1904-07] All ER 840 HL Court cannot without defendant's agreement threaten re-trial unless plaintiff agrees to reduced damages where jury award absurd.

DEFAMATION (Parliamentary privilege)

Dingle v Associated Newspapers, Ltd and others [1960] 1 All ER 294 HC QBD On privilege attaching to Parliamentary matters.

Prebble (Richard William) v Television New Zealand Ltd [1995] 1 AC 321; (1994) 144 NLJ 1131; (1994) 138 SJ LB 175; [1994] TLR 393; [1994] 3 WLR 970 PC On praying in aid Parliamentary proceedings to justify alleged defamation.

Re Parliamentary Privilege Act, 1770 (1958) 102 SJ 380 PC Commons would not act contrary to the Parliamentary Privileges Act 1770 if it treated a libel writ against an MP over a speech/ proceeding by him in Parliament as a breach of Parliamentary privilege.

DEFAMATION (payment into court)

Morriss v Baines and Co Limited (1933) 148 LTR 428 HC KBD Plaintiff awarded less than amount paid into court could not be ordered to pay back amount in excess of award where had already withdrawn payment from bank.

DEFAMATION (privilege)

Adam v Ward (1914-15) XXXI TLR 299 CA Letter defaming another but without malice and under moral compulsion was privileged.

Adam v Ward [1916-17] All ER 157; [1917] AC 309; [1917] 86 LJCL 849; (1917) 52 LJ 126; (1917-18) 117 LTR 34; (1916-17) XXXIII TLR 277 HL Letter defaming another but without malice was privileged.

Addis v Crocker and others (1960) 110 LJ 476; [1961] 1 QB 11; (1960) 104 SJ 584 CA Proceedings before solicitors' disciplinary committee similar to judicial trial and therefore absolutely privileged.

Addis v Crocker and others [1959] 2 All ER 773; (1959) 109 LJ 604; [1960] 1 QB 87; (1959) 103 SJ 636 HC QBD Proceedings before solicitors' disciplinary committee are judicial: normal privilege of judicial proceedings applies.

Angel v Bushell (HH) and Co, Ltd and another [1967] 1 All ER 1018; [1968] 1 QB 813; (1967) 111 SJ 116; [1967] 2 WLR 976 HC QBD Business communication with qualified privilege lost it through malice of party.

Attwood v Chapman [1914-15] All ER 1034; (1915) 79 JP 65; [1914] 3 KB 275; (1914) 49 LJ 381; [1914] 83 LJKB 1666; (1914-15) 111 LTR 726; (1913-14) XXX TLR 596; (1914) WN (I) 269 HC KBD Private party's objection to granting of liquor licence not privileged.

Austin (Reginald) v Mirror Newspapers Ltd [1986] AC 299; (1986) 130 SJ 13; [1986] 2 WLR 57 PC Qualified privilege could (under Defamation Act 1974, s 22) attach to newspaper report critical of rugby league team trainer but not here as journalist had not taken reasonable care regarding accuracy of facts.

Baird v Wallace-James [1916] 85 LJPC 193 HL Letter from president of parish charity to chair of parish council criticising parish medical officer's under-use of nurse provided by charity was privileged.

Barratt v Kearns [1905] 1 KB 504; (1905) XCII LTR 255; (1904-05) XXI TLR 212; (1904-05) 53 WR 356 CA Evidence before ecclesiastical commission privileged.

Beach and another v Freeson [1971] 2 All ER 854; [1972] 1 QB 14; (1971) 115 SJ 145; [1971] 2 WLR 805 HC QBD Publication of defamatory letter on foot of one's duties as MP enjoys qualified privilege.

Blackshaw v Lord and another [1983] 2 All ER 311; [1984] QB 1; (1983) 127 SJ 289; [1983] TLR 118; [1983] 3 WLR 283 CA Not everything said by government official in course of employment is privileged under Defamation Act 1952, s 7(1); public to have legitimate interest in report and publisher to have like duty in publishing for qualified privilege to arise; test for varying jury's award of damages stricter than for judge.

Boston v WS Bagshaw and Sons and others [1966] 2 All ER 906; (1966) 110 SJ 352; [1966] 1 WLR 1126 CA Broadcast seeking criminal enjoyed privilege; leaving general question of malice to jury rather than explaining minutiae thereof valid.

Bottomley v Brougham [1908] 1 KB 584; (1908) 43 LJ 59; [1908] 77 LJCL 311; (1908-09) XCIX LTR 111; (1907-08) 52 SJ 225; (1907-08) XXIV TLR 262; (1908) WN (I) 32 HC KBD Court report of official receiver absolutely privileged; on nature of absolute privilege.

Braddock and others v Bevins and others [1948] 1 All ER 450; [1948] 1 KB 580; [1948] 117 LJR 1278; (1948) LXIV TLR 279; (1948) WN (I) 96 CA Candidate's election address clothed with qualified privilege if not malicious/relevant to election.

Brent Walker Group plc and another v Time Out Ltd and another [1991] 2 All ER 753; [1991] 2 QB 33; [1991] 2 WLR 772 CA Fair comment defence based on privileged material must give fair/accurate report of occasion of privilege.

Bryanston Finance Ltd and others v De Vries and another [1975] 2 All ER 609; (1975) 125 NLJ 231; [1975] QB 703; (1975) 119 SJ 287 [1975] 2 WLR 718 CA Qualified privilege between businessman/typist/photocopier if main purpose was usual course of business; not pleading justification does not mean words false; in action against two joint tortfeasors judgment against one bar to action against other.

Burnett and Hallamshire Fuel, Ltd v Sheffield Telegraph and Star, Ltd [1960] 2 All ER 157; (1960) 104 SJ 388 HC QBD Privilege for fair and accurate reporting of judicial proceedings attaches to account of advocate's orations therein.

Burr v Smith [1908-10] All ER 443; [1909] 2 KB 306; [1909] 78 LJKB 889; (1909-10) 101 LTR 194; (1908-09) 53 SJ 502; (1908-09) XXV TLR 542; (1909) WN (I) 115 CA Official receiver's report absolutely privileged.

Cader (Mahomed Abdul) v Kaufman and another (1928) 66 LJ 425; (1928) WN (I) 264 PC Failed petition for special leave to appeal in action concerning the extent of privilege enjoyed when speaking in the Ceylonese Legislative Council.

Chapman v Ellesmere and others [1932] All ER 221; [1932] 2 KB 431; (1932) 73 LJ 274; (1932) 101 LJCL 376; (1932) 146 LTR 538; (1932) 76 SJ 248; (1931-32) XLVIII TLR 309 CA Publication by Jockey Club of decision regarding trainer's licence in Racing Calendar/to news agencies (plus later publication by newspaper) was/was not privileged.

Chenard and Company and others v Arissol (1949) LXV TLR 72 PC Statements made in Colonial Legislature enjoyed absolute privilege.

Church of Scientology of California v Johnson-Smith [1972] 1 All ER 378; [1972] 1 QB 522; (1971) 115 SJ 658; [1971] 3 WLR 434 HC QBD Parliamentary proceedings completely and absolutely privileged.

Co-partnership Farms v Harvey-Smith [1918] 2 KB 405; (1918) 53 LJ 191; [1919] 88 LJCL 472; (1918) 118 LTR 541; (1917-18) XXXIV TLR 414; (1918) WN (I) 175 HC KBD Statements before local military tribunal absolutely privileged.

Collins v Cooper (1902-03) XIX TLR 118 CA Bona fide statements made in course of detecting crime were privileged but re-trial ordered on issue whether statements at issue were bona fide.

Collins v Henry Whiteway and Company, Limited [1927] 2 KB 378; (1927) 63 LJ 537; [1927] 96 LJCL 790; (1927) 137 LTR 297; (1926-27) XLIII TLR 532; (1927) WN (I) 163 HC KBD Communications with Court of Referees not absolutely privileged.

Constable v Jagger (1972) 122 NLJ 268 CA On whether statements in police inquiry privileged.

Cook v Alexander and others [1973] 3 All ER 1037; (1973) 123 NLJ 747t; [1974] QB 279; (1973) 117 SJ 618; [1973] 3 WLR 617 CA Fair representation of Parliamentary proceedings enjoys qualified privilege.

Davidson v Barclay's Bank Limited (1941) 164 LTR 25; (1940) 84 SJ 117; (1939-40) LVI TLR 343 HC KBD Making defamatory of another in genuinely mistaken belief that under duty to make statement not privileged despite mistake.

De Buse and others v McCarthy and Stepney Borough Council [1942] 1 All ER 19; (1942) 106 JP 73; [1942] 1 KB 156; [1942] 111 LJ 170; (1943) 93 LJ 125; (1942) 166 LTR 52; (1941) 85 SJ 468; (1941-42) LVIII TLR 83; (1941) WN (I) 231 CA Council committee report to borough council published to ratepayers not privileged as no common interest/duty.

De Buse and others v McCarthy and others (1941) 105 JP 360; (1941) 165 LTR 255; (1941) 85 SJ 369; (1940-41) LVII TLR 596 HC KBD Publication of elements of allegedly libellous council committee report by distributing notice containing report to council-controlled public libraries was privileged.

Dingle v Associated Newspapers, Ltd and others [1960] 1 All ER 294; [1960] 2 QB 405; (1960) 104 SJ 189 HC QBD On privilege attaching to Parliamentary matters.

Edmondson v Birch and Co, Ltd [1904-07] All ER 996; [1907] 76 LJCh 347; [1907] 1 KB 371; (1907) XCVI LTR 415; (1906-07) XXIII TLR 234; (1907) WN (I) 18 CA Publication of defamatory material in privileged communication to telegram clerks did not lift privilege.

Egger v Chelmsford and others (1964) 108 SJ 218 HC QBD On whether malice by several defendants obviates privilege enjoyed by all defendants.

Egger v Davies and others (1964) 108 SJ 619 CA Malice of joint defendant in publishing item does not taint others with malice: most be individually motivated by malice to lose qualified privilege.

Egger v Viscount Chelmsford and others [1964] 3 All ER 406; (1964) 114 LJ 720; [1965] 1 QB 248; [1964] 3 WLR 714 CA Innocent committee members and (independently) their secretary protected by qualified privilege which other committee members lost through malice.

Elkington v London Association for the Protection of Trade (1911-12) XXVIII TLR 117 HC KBD Insolvency inquiries published in trade society's confidential newsletter not privileged.

Farmer v Hyde [1937] 1 All ER 773; [1937] 1 KB 728; (1937) 83 LJ 167; [1937] 106 LJCL 292; (1937) 156 LTR 403; (1937) 81 SJ 216; (1936-37) LIII TLR 445; (1937) WN (I) 99 CA Fair/accurate publication of interrupter's application was privileged.

Fayed v Al-Tajir [1988] QB 712; (1987) 131 SJ 744; [1987] 3 WLR 102 CA Intra-embassy memorandum was absolutely privileged.

Frank Smythson, Ltd v GA Cramp and Sons, Ltd and The Surrey Manufacturing Co [1943] 1 All ER 322; (1943) 168 LTR 257 CA Copyright owner's letter to persons publishing matter in which copyright infringed was privileged.

Fraser-Armstrong v Hadow and others [1994] TLR 35 CA Not proper to seek to defend self by way of libel action (through reliance upon qualified privilege) from criticisms that were in fact true.

Furniss v The Cambridge Daily News (Limited) (1906-07) XXIII TLR 705 CA Entry in charge sheet not minute/memorandum for purposes of Summary Jurisdiction Act 1848, s 14; on nature of privilege attaching to newspaper reports of court proceedings.

Gerhold v Baker (1918) 53 LJ 417; (1918-19) 63 SJ 135; (1918-19) XXXV TLR 102; (1918) WN (I) 368 CA Third-party letter to Appeal Tribunal over appeal against military service enjoyed qualified privilege (and absent malice could not be libellous).

Glick v Hinchcliffe (1967) 111 SJ 927 CA Judge's words at end of criminal prosecution did enjoy absolute privilege.

Greenlands (Limited) v Wilmshurst and others (1912-13) XXIX TLR 64 HC KBD Statements of person acting as confidential agent of member of trade association not privileged.

Greenlands, Limited v Wilmshurst and the London Association for Protection of Trade and another [1913] 3 KB 507; (1913) 48 LJ 471; [1914] 83 LJKB 1; (1913-14) 109 LTR 487; (1912-13) 57 SJ 740; (1912-13) XXIX TLR 685 CA Statements of person acting as confidential agent of member of trade association not privileged.

Groom v Crocker and others (1937) 84 LJ 158; (1937) 157 LTR 308 HC KBD Failure of solicitor to act equally on behalf of both insurer/insured; damages for breach of duty and for libel.

Groom v Crocker and others [1938] 2 All ER 394; [1939] 1 KB 194; (1938) 85 LJ 308; (1938) 158 LTR 477; (1937-38) LIV TLR 861 CA Failure of solicitor to act equally on behalf of both insurer/insured; malice on ostensibly privileged occasion; nominal damages as action in contract (not tort) and no evidence of actual damage.

Guske v Cooke (1981) 131 NLJ 758 HC QBD Absolute and qualified privilege held to attach to letter from personal doctor to solicitors as to state of client's mental health.

Hambrook v The Law Society (1967) 111 SJ 195 HC QBD Non-malicious answers to Ministry of Labour questionnaire enjoyed qualified privilege.

Hasselblad (GB) Ltd v Orbinson [1985] 1 All ER 173; [1985] QB 475; (1985) 129 SJ 32; [1985] 2 WLR 1 CA On privilege attaching to letter sent voluntarily to European Commission in course of essentially administrative proceedings.

Hayward and another v Wegg-Prosser (1978) 122 SJ 792 HC QBD Libel action stayed where plaintiffs sought to rely on documents inadvertently obtained by them after they were disclosed by solicitor to court officer in course of taxation.

Hope v I'Anson and Weatherby (1901-02) XVIII TLR 201 CA Jockey Club decisions did not enjoy judicial privilege nor did person party to action submit to decision being published as though it were Court decision.

Hope v Sir WC Leng and Co (Sheffield Telegraph) (Limited) (1906-07) XXIII TLR 243 CA On determining whether newspaper report of court proceedings is fair and accurate.

Horrocks v Lowe [1974] 1 All ER 662; [1975] AC 135; (1974) 118 SJ 149; [1974] 2 WLR 282 HL Privilege/no malice where maker (unreasonably) believes in truth of statement.

Horrocks v Lowe [1972] 3 All ER 1098; (1972) 122 NLJ 894t; (1972) 116 SJ 946; [1972] 1 WLR 1625 CA Honest belief in truth of statement rooted in prejudice precludes malice.

Isaacs (M) and Sons, Limited, and others v Cook [1925] 2 KB 391; (1925) 60 LJ 739; [1925] 94 LJCL 886; (1926) 134 LTR 286; (1924-25) 69 SJ 810; (1924-25) XLI TLR 647; (1925) WN (I) 226 HC KBD British High Commissioner to Australia's official communications to Australian Prime Minister (and vice versa) privileged; State document on business concerns could be privileged.

John Jones and Sons (Limited) v The 'Financial Times' (Limited) (1908-09) 53 SJ 614; (1908-09) XXV TLR 677 CA Publication of information in receiverships register entry is privileged.

Khan v Ahmed [1957] 2 All ER 385; (1957) 107 LJ 379; [1957] 2 QB 149; (1957) 101 SJ 447 HC QBD Open meeting a public meeting; letter seeking apology must prescribe formula of apology.

Kingshott and others v Associated Kent Newspapers Ltd and others [1991] 2 All ER 99; [1991] 1 QB 88; [1990] TLR 444; [1990] 3 WLR 675 CA Fairness/accuracy/issues of public benefit and concern are generally matters for jury.

Law v Llewellyn [1904-07] All ER 536; (1906) 70 JP 220; [1906] 1 KB 487; (1906) 41 LJ 137; [1906] 75 LJKB 320; (1906) XCIV LTR 359; (1905-06) 50 SJ 289; (1906) WN (I) 50; (1905-06) 54 WR 368 CA Magistrate absolutely privileged in respect of defamatory statements made in course of acting as magistrate.

Lawrence v Hall and another (1928) 72 SJ 87 HC KBD Letter by club secretary written in context of leasing of premises and in which it was implied (according to the plaintiff-solicitor) that he was incompetent was privileged/not motivated by malice.

Leigh v Gladstone and others (1909-10) XXVI TLR 139 HC KBD Depends on circumstances whether force-feeding of prisoners constituted trespass to the person (here was not); medical officer's reports to prison governor are not privileged.

Ley v Hamilton (1934) 151 LTR 360 CA Re-trial of libel action ordered where damages awarded unreasonable/possible that occasion of publication was privileged contrary to trial judge's ruling.

Ley v Hamilton (1935) 153 LTR 384; (1935) 79 SJ 573 HL Re-trial of libel action unnecessary where damages awarded reasonable/occasion of publication was not privileged.

Lincoln v Daniels [1960] 3 All ER 205; (1960) 104 SJ 625 HC QBD Complaints to Bar Council about barrister have qualified privilege.

Lincoln v Daniels [1961] 3 All ER 740; [1955] Crim LR 647; (1961) 111 LJ 660; [1962] 1 QB 237 CA No absolute privilege letters of complaint to Bar Council where letters did not lead to disciplinary action.

Lincoln v Daniels [1960] 3 All ER 205; (1960) 110 LJ 655 HC QBD Complaints to Bar Council about barrister have qualified privilege.

London Artists, Ltd v Littler [1968] 1 All ER 1075; (1968) 118 NLJ 1196t; (1968) 112 SJ 194; [1968] 1 WLR 607 HC QBD Where no public interest (or private duty compelling publication) is no qualified privilege.

London Association for Protection of Trade and another v Greenlands, Limited [1916-17] All ER 452; [1916] 2 AC 15; (1916) 51 LJ 77; [1916] 85 LJKB 698; (1916) 114 LTR 434; (1915-16) 60 SJ 272; (1915-16) XXXII TLR 281; (1916) WN (I) 45 HL On privilege attaching to communication by trade protection society on foot of bona fide enquiry by trader as to creditworthiness of another trader.

Longdon-Griffiths v Smith and others [1950] 2 All ER 662; [1951] 1 KB 295; (1950) 100 LJ 413; (1950) 94 SJ 580; [1950] 66 (2) TLR 627; (1950) WN (I) 448 HC KBD Libel action to be directed at Friendly Society per se not its trustees; special damages available where libel led to losing job; that one of four parties acted maliciously did not affect qualified privilege of others.

Macintosh and another v Dun and others [1908-10] All ER 664; [1908] AC 390; (1908) 77 LJPC 113; (1908-09) XCIX LTR 64; (1907-08) XXIV TLR 705 PC No qualified privilege in publication out of complete self-interest.

Mangena v Edward Lloyd (Limited) (1908-09) XCIX LTR 824; (1908-09) XXV TLR 26 CA Headline of report based on Parliamentary blue-book fell outside privilege afforded by Parliamentary Papers Act 1840.

Mangena v Edward Lloyd (Limited) (1908) XCVIII LTR 640; (1907-08) XXIV TLR 610 HC KBD Good faith/non-malicious report based on Parliamentary blue-book enjoyed privilege afforded by Parliamentary Papers Act 1840.

Mapey v Baker (1908) 72 JP 511 HC KBD Slanderous words uttered of rate collector at meeting of Board of Guardians were uttered on privileged occasion.

Mapey v Baker (1909) 73 JP 289; (1908-09) 53 SJ 429 CA Slanderous words uttered of rate collector at meeting of Board of Guardians were uttered on privileged occasion.

McCarey v Associated Newspapers Ltd and others (1964) 108 SJ 564; [1964] 1 WLR 855 HC QBD Newspaper account of coroner's court in process clothed by absolute privilege.

Meekins v Henson and others [1962] 1 All ER 899; (1962) 112 LJ 290; [1964] 1 QB 472; (1962) 106 SJ 571 HC QBD Qualified privilege for three partners, one liable in libel action as was motivated by malice.

Minter v Priest [1930] All ER 431; [1930] AC 558; (1930) 69 LJ 250; (1930) 99 LJCL 391; (1930) 143 LTR 57; (1930) 74 SJ 200; (1929-30) XLVI TLR 301; (1930) WN (I) 83 HL Whether occasion privileged a matter for judge; no absolute privilege as solicitor not acting for party and qualified privilege attaching to occasion defeated by solicitor's malice.

Minter v Priest [1929] 1 KB 655; (1929) 67 LJ 378; (1929) 141 LTR 140 HC KBD On professional privilege in defamation actions.

Minter v Priest (1929) 98 LJCL 661; (1929) 73 SJ 529; (1928-29) XLV TLR 393; (1929) WN (I) 94 CA Privilege attaches to communications between solicitor and prospective client regarding possible retainer of former by latter.

Montereale v Longmans Green and Co, Ltd, and another (1965) 109 SJ 215 HC QBD No qualified privilege in relation to commentary on foreign judicial proceedings.

Moore v Canadian Pacific Steamship Co [1945] 1 All ER 128; (1946) 96 LJ 185 Assizes Statutory duty to record entry in ship's log and absence of malice meant qualified privilege.

More v Weaver (1928) 72 SJ 319; (1928) WN (I) 158 HC KBD Absolute privilege attaches to communiciations between solicitor-client in matters pertinent to that relationship.

More v Weaver [1928] All ER 160; [1928] 2 KB 520; (1928) 66 LJ 124; (1928) 97 LJCL 721; (1929) 140 LTR 15; (1928) 72 SJ 556; (1928) WN (I) 207 CA Absolute privilege attaches to communiciations between solicitor-client in matters pertinent to that relationship.

Morgan and another v Wallis (1916-17) XXXIII TLR 495 HC KBD Qualified privilege where solicitor in dictating bill of costs included without malice as a point of information a statement that was in fact defamatory.

O'Connor v Waldron [1934] All ER 281; [1935] AC 76; (1934) 78 LJ 416; (1935) 152 LTR 289; (1934) 78 SJ 859; (1934-35) LI TLR 125; (1934) WN (I) 213 PC Words spoken by commissioner of administrative tribunal in discharge of duties not privileged.

Osborn v Thomas Boulter and Son [1930] All ER 154; [1930] 2 KB 226; (1930) 99 LJCL 556; (1930) 143 LTR 460 CA Privileged communication did not lose privilege through communication to typist.

Phelps v Kemsley (1943) 168 LTR 18 CA On nature of privilege: interested person's communication to another's doctor was privileged.

Plummer v Charman and others [1962] 3 All ER 823; (1962) 112 LJ 800; (1962) 106 SJ 631 CA On amendment of claim to include qualified privilege plea.

Purdew and another v Seress-Smith (1992) 136 SJ LB 244; [1992] TLR 438 HC QBD Letter to social security adjudication officer not absolutely privileged.

R v Rule [1937] 2 All ER 772; (1934-39) XXX Cox CC 599; (1936-38) 26 Cr App R 87; [1937] 2 KB 375; (1937) 83 LJ 362; [1937] 106 LJCL 807; (1937) 157 LTR 48; (1936-37) LIII TLR 720; (1937) WN (I) 215 CCA Constitutent's letter to MP in Parliamentary capacity a privileged occasion.

Richards v Naum [1966] 3 All ER 812; [1967] 1 QB 620; (1966) 110 SJ 794; [1966] 3 WLR 1113 CA Facts to be determined before preliminary point could be decided.

Rivlin v Bilainkin [1953] 1 All ER 534; [1953] 1 QB 485; (1953) 97 SJ 97 HC QBD Publication of document to Member of Parliament not privileged if unconnected with Parliamentary proceedings.

Roff v British and French Chemical Manufacturing Company and Gibson [1918] 2 KB 677; (1918) 53 LJ 272; [1918] 87 LJCL 996; (1918-19) 119 LTR 436; (1917-18) 62 SJ 620; (1917-18) XXXIV TLR 485 CA Privileged communication did not lose privilege through communication to clerks.

Rost v Edwards and others [1990] 2 All ER 641; [1990] 2 QB 460; [1990] TLR 120; [1990] 2 WLR 1280 HC QBD Reasons for selection/de-selection from Parliamentary committee/member's letter to Speaker privileged; register of Member's Interests not privileged.

Russell v Norfolk (Duke) and others [1948] 1 All ER 488; (1948) LXIV TLR 263 HC KBD No implied term in Jockey Club contract to hold inquiry before withdrawing licence; where common interest and agree to publish is qualified privilege unless malice.

Sadgrove v Hole [1901] 2 KB 1; [1901] 70 LJK/QB 455; (1901) LXXXIV LTR 647; (1900-01) 45 SJ 342; (1900-01) XVII TLR 332; (1900-01) 49 WR 473 CA Absent malice communication by way of postcard was privileged.

Sharman v Merritt and Hatcher (Limited) (1915-16) XXXII TLR 360 HC KBD Newspaper report of public meeting of corporation including agenda paper of same was privileged (Law of Libel Amendment Act 1888, s 4).

Smith v Lewis (1916-17) XXXIII TLR 195 HC KBD Need not plead express malice where in defence to claim that publication was malicious privilege is pleaded.

Smith v Streatfield [1911-13] All ER 362; [1913] 3 KB 764; [1913] 82 LJKB 1237; (1913-14) 109 LTR 173; (1912-13) XXIX TLR 707; (1913) WN (I) 263 HC KBD Author's privilege extended to printers but defeated in respect of both by author's malice.

Smith v The National Meter Co, Ltd and another [1945] 2 All ER 35; [1945] KB 543; [1946] 115 LJ 321; (1945) 172 LTR 379; (1945) 89 SJ 306; (1944-45) LXI TLR 366; (1945) WN (I) 103 HC KBD Qualified privilege lapsed because statements motivated by malice; proceedings before medical referee not absolutely privileged as not judicial.

Standen v South Essex Recorders, Limited, and another (1933-34) L TLR 365 HC KBD Newspaper observations on local authority meeting not privileged.

Stone v Association of Official Shorthandwriters, Ltd (1963) 107 SJ 396 HC QBD On privilege attaching to official shorthandwriter's transcripts of summings-up/evidence.

Szalatnay-Stacho v Fink [1946] 1 All ER 303; (1946) 174 LTR 191; (1945-46) LXII TLR 146; (1946) WN (I) 18 HC KBD On absolute privilege of communications of Czech wartime government-in-exile.

Szalatnay-Stacho v Fink [1946] 2 All ER 231; [1947] KB 1; [1946] 115 LJ 455; (1946) 175 LTR 336; (1946) 90 SJ 442; (1945-46) LXII TLR 573; (1946) WN (I) 134 CA On absolute privilege of communications of Czech wartime government-in-exile.

Tadd v Eastwood (1983) 133 NLJ 700; [1983] TLR 392 HC QBD Letter to industrial conciliation committee protected by qualified, not absolute privilege.

Thomas v Bradbury, Agnew, and Company (Limited) and another [1904-07] All ER 220; [1906] 2 KB 627; [1906] 75 LJKB 726; (1906-07) XCV LTR 23; (1905-06) XXII TLR 656; (1905-06) 54 WR 608 CA Proof of malice defeats defence of fair comment on public interest or of privilege.

Thompson v New South Wales Branch of the British Medical Association [1924] AC 764; [1924] 93, 1203; (1924) 131 LTR 162 PC Expulsion rule of Medical Association was to promote trade, not restrain it; Medical Association meeting's resolving to expel member a privileged occasion.

Thorburn v Hermon (Channel 4, third party) [1992] TLR 244 HC QBD On national security as basis for claim of privilege in defamation action.

Thurston v Charles (1904-05) XXI TLR 659 HC KBD Substantial damages available for wrongful conversion/detention where published another's private correspondence but privilege in communication not destroyed so no libel.

Trapp v Mackie (1978) 128 NLJ 1248; (1979) 123 SJ 202; [1979] 1 WLR 377 HL Evidence before commissioner of local inquiry held pursuant to Education (Scotland) Act 1946, s 81(3) was absolutely privileged.

Tsikata v Newspaper Publishing plc [1994] TLR 569 HC QBD Report of government special inquiry was 'public proceeding' so fair and accurate statements concerning the report per se were privileged.

Tsikata v Newspaper Publishing plc [1997] 1 All ER 655 CA Report of government special inquiry was 'public proceeding' so fair and accurate statements concerning the report per se were privileged.

Turner v Metro-Goldwyn-Mayer Pictures Ltd (1947) 97 LJ 389; (1947) 91 SJ 495 HC KBD Was libellous to suggest in writing that critic deliberately sought to damage the industry which provided the matter (film) that critic analysed.

Turner v Metro-Goldwyn-Mayer Pictures, Ltd (1948) 98 LJ 441 CA Potentially libellous to suggest in writing that critic deliberately sought to damage the industry which provided the matter (film) that critic analysed but no malice proved on part of maker of statement.

Turner (otherwise Robertson) v Metro-Goldwyn-Mayer Pictures, Ltd [1950] 1 All ER 449; (1950) 94 SJ 145 HL That motivated by financial interest need not mean malicious; opinion need only be genuine not right — here honest views absent malice so qualified privilege remained.

Waple v Surrey County Council [1997] 2 All ER 836 HC QBD Information passed by solicitor of one party to solicitor of other party upon latter solicitor's request was absolutely privileged.

Watson (Sir Patrick H) v Jones (Mrs JP) or M'Ewan et contra; Watson (Sir Patrick H) v Jones (James) [1905] AC 480; [1905] 74 LJPC 151; (1905-06) XCIII LTR 489; (1905) WN (I) 130 HL Witness privilege in witness box against later slander action extends to communications to solicitor/client in preparing for trial.

Watt v Longsdon (1928-29) XLV TLR 419 HC KBD Absent common interest bona fide voluntary revelation of information believed to be true and pertaining to interest meriting protection on recipient's side is privileged.

Watt v Longsdon [1929] All ER 284; [1930] 1 KB 130; (1929) 68 LJ 76; (1929) 98 LJCL 711; (1930) 142 LTR 4; (1929) 73 SJ 544; (1928-29) XLV TLR 619 CA Absent common interest must be duty on maker's side and interest meriting protection on recipient's side for occasion of statement to be privileged.

Watts v Times Newspapers Ltd and others (Schilling and Lom (a firm), third party) [1996] 1 All ER 152; [1995] TLR 488; [1996] 2 WLR 427 CA Respective liability of publisher and client for libel committed in course of apology for earlier libel must be considered separately where qualified privilege may arise in relation to either party.

Webb v Times Publishing, Ltd [1960] 2 All ER 789; (1960) 110 LJ 590; [1960] 2 QB 535; (1960) 104 SJ 605 HC QBD Qualified privilege attaches to newspaper reports of foreign legal actions if accurate/fair/without malice/of real public interest.

White v J and F Stone Lighting and Radio, Limited [1939] 3 All ER 507; [1939] 2 KB 827; [1939] 108 LJCL 868; (1939) 161 LTR 107; (1939) 83 SJ 603; (1938-39) LV TLR 949; (1939) WN (I) 280 CA On what constitutes a privileged occasion.

Winstanley v Bampton [1943] 1 All ER 661; [1943] KB 319; (1944) 94 LJ 108; [1943] 112 LJ 430; (1943) 168 LTR 206; (1942-43) LIX TLR 183; (1943) WN (I) 55 HC KBD Privileged letter to plaintiff's commanding officer lost privilege through malice.

DEFAMATION (slander)

Aspro Travel Ltd and others v Owners Abroad Group plc and others [1995] 4 All ER 728; (1995) 139 SJ LB 195; [1995] TLR 404; [1996] 1 WLR 132 CA To say of a director that he allowed a company trade while insolvent is defamatory; sometimes can plead in justification that are merely repeating existing rumours.

Balden v Shorter and others [1933] All ER 249; [1933] Ch 427; (1933) 75 LJ 202; [1933] 102 LJCh 191; (1933) 148 LTR 471; (1933) 77 SJ 138; (1933) WN (I) 37 HC ChD Absent malice no slander.

Barber v Pigden [1937] 1 All ER 115; [1937] 1 KB 664; (1937) 83 LJ 42; [1937] 106 LJCL 858; (1937) 156 LTR 245; (1937) 81 SJ 78; (1936-37) LIII TLR 246; (1937) WN (I) 8 CA Husband not liable for wife's torts unless proceedings begun before Law Reform (Married Women and Tortfeasors) Act 1935; no evidence that wife made slanderous comments as husband's agent.

Bookbinder v Tebbit [1989] 1 All ER 1169; (1989) 139 NLJ 112; [1989] 1 WLR 640 CA Plaintiff withdrawing allegation of general slander meant defendant could not rely on general charge to support justification plea.

Bridgman v Stockdale and others (1953) 97 SJ 353; [1953] 1 WLR 704 HC QBD Absent special damage invigilator's statement before examinees that one person had 'cribbed' was not slanderous (was privileged).

Bridgmont v Associated Newspapers, Ltd and others [1951] 2 All ER 285; [1951] 2 KB 578; (1951) 95 SJ 529; [1951] 2 TLR 682; (1951) WN (I) 377 CA 'Slanderous' statement that party was person mentioned in libel relevant to question of damages in libel action.

Bull v Vasquez (1946) 96 LJ 218 HC KBD MP on Parliamentary leave while in Army could sue for slander of self in professional guise of army officer; appropriate damages.

Bull v Vasquez and another [1947] 1 All ER 334; [1947] 116 LJR 551 CA MP on Parliamentary leave while in Army could sue for slander of self in professional guise of army officer; appropriate damages.

Charleston and another v News Group Newspapers Ltd [1994] TLR 16 CA Photos, headlines and connected articles could not be severed so as to find one element defamatory.

Charleston and another v News Group Newspapers Ltd and another [1995] 2 All ER 313; [1995] 2 AC 65; (1995) 145 NLJ 490; (1995) 139 SJ LB 100; [1995] TLR 171; [1995] 2 WLR 450 HL Photos, headlines and connected articles may not be severed so as to find one element defamatory.

Cleghorn v Sadler [1945] 1 All ER 544; [1945] KB 325; (1946) 96 LJ 199; [1945] 114 LJ 508; (1945) 172 LTR 334; (1944-45) LXI TLR 318; (1945) WN (I) 84 HC KBD Firewatching not a profession so 'slanderous' words spoken of firewatcher cannot be spoken of same in professional capacity.

Corporation of Glasgow v Riddell (1911) 104 LTR 354 HL Corporation not liable for slander made by tax collector acting outside scope of his employment.

D and L Caterers, Limited, and another v D'Ajou [1945] 1 KB 210; [1945] 114 LJ 262; (1945) 172 LTR 223; (1945) WN (I) 36 HC KBD Limited company can sue for slander though no proof of actual damage but words an aspersion on its conducting of business.

D and L Caterers, Ltd and Jackson v D'Ajou [1945] 1 All ER 563; [1945] KB 364; (1946) 96 LJ 199; [1945] 114 LJ 386; (1945) 173 LTR 21; (1944-45) LXI TLR 343; (1945) WN (I) 88 CA Limited company can sue for slander though no proof of actual damage: damage implied to ground action; on cross-examination over credit in defamation suit.

Dauncey v Holloway [1901] 2 KB 441; [1901] 70 LJK/QB 695; (1901) LXXXIV LTR 649; (1900-01) 45 SJ 501; (1900-01) XVII TLR 493; (1900-01) 49 WR 546 CA Words spoken of solicitor not actionable absent special damage as did not reflect on same as solicitor.

De Stempel v Dunkels [1937] 2 All ER 215; (1937) 156 LTR 418; (1936-37) LIII TLR 451; (1937) WN (I) 117 HC KBD Statement that person 'a Jew hater' did not refer to person in business conduct — absent special damage could not recover damages.

De Stempel v Dunkels [1938] 1 All ER 238; (1938) 158 LTR 85; (1938) 82 SJ 51; (1937-38) LIV TLR 289 CA Calling person a 'Jew-hater' is defamatory; words said in relation to other's business could be sued on though no proof of special damage.

Derbyshire County Council v Times Newspapers Ltd and others [1992] 3 All ER 65; (1992) 142 NLJ 276; [1992] QB 770; [1992] TLR 69; [1992] 3 WLR 28 CA Trading/non-trading corporation with corporate reputation may sue for libel/slander but local authority may not unless actual financial loss.

Fielding v Moiseiwitsch (1946) 174 LTR 265 HC KBD Was breach of contract for pianist not to perform as had contracted; not defamatory for organiser to truthfully state what had occurred — such statement was in any event privileged.

Fielding v Moiseiwitsch (1946) 175 LTR 265 CA Was breach of contract for pianist not to perform as had contracted; not defamatory for organiser to truthfully state what had occurred — such statement was in any event privileged.

Ghosh v D'Rosario (1962) 106 SJ 352 CA Stay of slander action required where after commencement of action defendant appointed to High Commission staff and thereby acquired diplomatic immunity.

Gray v Jones [1939] 1 All ER 798; (1939) 87 LJ 199; (1939) 160 LTR 361; (1939) 83 SJ 278; (1938-39) LV TLR 437 HC KBD To say that person a convict, if untrue, is defamatory.

Hellwig v Mitchell [1910] 1 KB 609; (1910) 79 LJKB 270; (1910) 102 LTR 110; (1909-10) XXVI TLR 244 HC KBD Must be special damage before statement that person guilty of criminal act for which can be fined/summarily arrested is slanderous.

High Commissioner for India and others v Ghosh (1959) 109 LJ 683; (1959) 103 SJ 939 CA Striking out of counter-claim for slander against High Commissioner/Union of India (sovereign immunity not waived by plaintiffs bringing action for money lent against defendants).

Hopwood v Muirson [1945] 1 All ER 453; [1945] KB 313; (1946) 96 LJ 199; [1945] 114 LJ 267; (1945) 172 LTR 231; (1945) 89 SJ 224; (1944-45) LXI TLR 312; (1945) WN (I) 78 CA Words spoken of solicitor not slander of him in professional rôle as reflected on him personally.

Horrocks v Lowe [1974] 1 All ER 662; [1975] AC 135; (1974) 118 SJ 149; [1974] 2 WLR 282 HL Privilege/no malice where maker (unreasonably) believes in truth of statement.

Jeyaretnam (Joshua Benjamin) v Tong (Goh Chok) (1989) 133 SJ 1032; [1989] 1 WLR 1109 PC Comments of politician at press conference deemed to be fair comments and not defamatory.

Jones v Jones and Wife [1914-17] All ER 560; [1916] 2 AC 481; (1916) 51 LJ 409; [1916] 85 LJKB 1519; (1916-17) 115 LTR 432; (1916-17) 61 SJ 8; (1915-16) XXXII TLR 705; (1916) WN (I) 312 HL Allegation of immorality against schoolteacher not of itself actionable.

Jones v Jones and Wife (1915) 50 LJ 133; [1915] 84 LJKB 1140; (1915-16) 113 LTR 336; (1914-15) XXXI TLR 245; (1915) WN (I) 115 HC KBD Allegation of immorality against schoolteacher actionable without proof of special damage.

Jones v Jones and Wife [1916] 1 KB 351; (1915) 50 LJ 630; [1916] 85 LJKB 388; (1916) 114 LTR 253; (1915-16) 60 SJ 140; (1915-16) XXXII TLR 171; (1915) WN (I) 408 CA Allegation of adultery against schoolmaster not slander unless reflects on same as professional.

Kerr v Kennedy [1942] 1 All ER 412; [1942] 1 KB 409; [1942] 111 LJ 367; (1943) 93 LJ 125; (1942) 166 LTR 238; (1941-42) LVIII TLR 168; (1942) WN (I) 69 HC KBD To state woman is lesbian infers unchastity so (under Slander of Women Act 1891) need not show pecuniary damage to recover damages for slander.

Marks v Samuel [1904] 2 KB 287; (1904) 39 LJ 213; [1904] 73 LJCL 587; (1904) XC LTR 590; (1903-04) 48 SJ 415; (1903-04) XX TLR 430; (1904) WN (I) 86; (1904-05) 53 WR 88 CA Absent special damage can still sue for slander where alleged brought blackmail action.

Michael v Spiers and Pond (Limited) (1909-10) 101 LTR 352; (1908-09) XXV TLR 740 HC KBD Must be special damage for statement that person on licensed premises was drunk to be slander (that might be removed as company director sometime in future too tendentious).

Mycroft v Sleight [1918-23] All ER 509; [1921] LJCL 883; (1921) 125 LTR 622; (1920-21) XXXVII TLR 646; (1921) WN (I) 175 HC KBD Defamatory words not spoken of person in relation to profession inactionable absent special damage.

Oram v Hutt [1913] 1 Ch 259; (1913) 77 JP 110; (1912) 47 LJ 723; (1913) 82 LJCh 152 (1913) 108 LTR 410 HC ChD Trade union acted ultra vires when paid for legal costs of general secretary in slander action.

Oram v Hutt (1914) 78 JP 51; (1913) 48 LJ 659; [1914] 83 LJCh 161; (1914) 110 LTR 187; (1913-14) 58 SJ 80; (1913-14) XXX TLR 55 CA Trade union acted ultra vires when paid for legal costs of general secretary in slander action — money to be repaid with interest.

Ormiston v Great Western Railway Company [1917] 86 LJCL 759; (1917) 116 LTR 479; (1916-17) XXXIII TLR 171 HC KBD Railway company servant cannot arrest passenger for travelling without proper fare unless passenger refuses to show ticket and disclose name and address but what servant says in course of arrest can only be slanderous if is special damage.

Rost v Edwards and others [1990] 2 All ER 641; [1990] 2 QB 460; [1990] TLR 120; [1990] 2 WLR 1280 HC QBD Reasons for selection/de-selection from Parliamentary committee/member's letter to Speaker privileged; register of Member's Interests not privileged.

Russo v Cole [1965] 3 All ER 822; (1965-66) 116 NLJ 245; (1966) 110 SJ 173; [1966] 1 WLR 248 HC QBD Post-slander action can be varied to ensure that do not 'recover more costs than damages'.

Speake v Hughes [1904] 1 KB 138; [1904] 73 LJCL 172; (1903-04) LXXXIX LTR 576 CA Damage allegedly arising from slander (loss of damage) too remote for recovery of damages.

Turner v Metro-Goldwyn-Mayer Pictures, Limited (1950) 100 LJ 93; [1950] 66 (1) TLR 342; (1950) WN (I) 83 HL On malice; on trial procedure at libel/slander trials.

Wakeford v Wright (1922-23) XXXIX TLR 107 CA Absent special damage clergyman could not ring action for words spoken of him in capacity of clergyman unless holding office/in receipt of temporal words spoken when words uttered.

Wernher, Beit, and Co v Markham (1901-02) XVIII TLR 143 CA Particulars that were not pertinent but were embarrassing struck out.

DEFAMATION (slander of goods)

De Beers Abrasive Products Ltd and others v International General Electric Co of New York Ltd and another [1975] 2 All ER 599; (1975) 119 SJ 439; [1975] 1 WLR 972 HC ChD Slander of goods where reasonable person would believe alleged 'puff' was truth.

Interoven Stove Co Ltd v British Broadcasting Corporation (1935) 79 SJ 921 HC KBD Failed action for alleged slander of goods in course of radio broadcast: on elements of 'slander of goods'.

DEFAMATION (slander of office of honour)

Robinson v Ward (1958) 108 LJ 491 HC QBD On elements of slander of office of honour.

DEFAMATION (slander of title)

British Railway Traffic and Electric Company, Limited v The CRC Company Limited and the London County Council [1922] 2 KB 260; [1922] 91 LJCL 824; (1922) 126 LTR 602; (1921-22) XXXVIII TLR 190 HC KBD Failed action for slander of title where was slander but no malice.

Loudon v Ryder (No 2) [1953] Ch 423; (1953) 97 SJ 299; [1953] 2 WLR 863 HC ChD In action for slander of title statements made though false were made absent malice and in belief that were true so no damages/injunction for same.

Mather v Cheetham [1938] LJNCCR 394 CyCt Failed action for slander of title where no actual damage proved to have been occasioned.

Schnitzler v Medley and others (1963) 107 SJ 810 CA On elements/proving of slander of title.

The Dunlop Pneumatic Tyre Company (Limited) v Maison Talbot, the Earl of Shrewsbury and Talbot, and DM Weigel; Clipper Pneumatic Tyre Company v Same (1903-04) 48 SJ 156; (1903-04) XX TLR 88 HC KBD Injunction to restrain slander of title before actual damage transpires is available.

DEFAMATION (statement in court)

Church of Scientology of California v North News Ltd and another (1973) 117 SJ 566 CA On exercise of judicial discretion as regards making of statement in open court.

DEFAMATION (trade libel)

Alcott v Millar's Karri and Jarrah Forests (Limited) and another (1904-05) XCI LTR 722; (1904-05) 49 SJ 32; (1904-05) XXI TLR 30 CA On trade libel.

Concaris v Duncan and Co (1909) WN (I) 51 HC ChD Failed action for damages for alleged trade libel.

Joyce v Motor Surveys Limited [1948] Ch 252; [1948] 117 LJR 935; (1948) WN (I) 84 HC ChD False statements made with intent of ending person's business were malicious.

Lloyds Bank (Limited) v The Royal British Bank (Limited) (1902-03) 47 SJ 603; (1902-03) XIX TLR 548 HC ChD Interlocutory injunction for trade libel only granted in clearest of cases which was not the case here not least because pecuniary loss unproven.

Lloyds Bank (Limited) v The Royal British Bank (Limited) (1902-03) XIX TLR 604 CA Agreement by defendant in interlocutory action not to engage in conduct allegedly giving rise to trade libel pending trial of action.

London and Northern Bank (Limited) v George Newnes (Limited) (1899-1900) XVI TLR 76 HC ChD Injunction granted to restrain publication of unfounded statement that particular bank was in liquidation.

London and Northern Bank (Limited) v George Newnes (Limited) (1899-1900) XVI TLR 433 CA In action for allegedly libellous statement that particular bank was in liquidation court ordered that particulars be given on where was run on bank and for how long.

DESERTION (general)

Guardians of Southwark Union v Guardians of City of London [1906] 2 KB 112 CA Husband ordering drunken (and later adulterous) wife from home was in desertion for purposes of Poor Removal Act, s 3.

DETINUE (animal)

Sorrell v Paget (1949) LXV TLR 595 HC KBD Person impounding straying cattle had lien on same until appropriate amount paid/offered for distress damage feasant.

DETINUE (damages)

Sorrell v Paget [1949] 2 All ER 609; [1950] 1 KB 252 CA Person impounding straying cattle had lien on same until appropriate amount paid/offered for distress damage feasant.

DETINUE (damages)

General and Finance Facilities Ltd v Cooks Cars (Romford) Ltd (1963) 113 LJ 432; [1963] 1 WLR 644 CA Master's decision in detinue action ought to separately itemise value of item in detinue and damages awarded.

Joseph (D), Ltd v Ralph Wood and Co, Ltd (1951) 95 SJ 319; (1951) WN (I) 225 HC KBD On appropriate damages where had been detinue.

Wickham Holdings Ltd v Brooke House Motors Ltd [1967] 1 WLR 295 CA Finance company could only recover outstanding amount due under hire-purchase agreement where hirer wrongfully sold goods hired.

DETINUE (general)

Birn Brothers, Lim v Keene and Co, Lim [1919] 88 LJCh 24 HC ChD On rights of action in detinue/conversion open to copyright-owner under Copyright Act 1911, s 7.

British Economical Lamp Company (Limited) v Empire Mile End (Limited) and another (1912-13) XXIX TLR 386 HC KBD Theatre owners not liable in detinue to owners of lamps rented by former lessees of theatre and remaining in theatre after owners re-entered same.

Bromilow v Howard (1959) 109 LJ ccr268 CyCt Failed claim in detinue by owner of dog who wandered against buyer who purchased dog as stray.

Capital Finance Company Ltd v Bray [1964] 1 All ER 603; [1964] 1 WLR 323 CA No detinue where (absent contractual obligation) do not bring owner's goods to owner.

Curtis v Maloney (1950) 94 SJ 761 CA Application of the Bankruptcy and Deeds of Arrangement Act 1913, s 15.

Curtis v Maloney; R Cheke and Co and another; Third Parties (1950) 94 SJ 437; (1950) WN (I) 307 HC QBD Application of the Bankruptcy and Deeds of Arrangement Act 1913, s 15.

Durrant v Smithfield and Argentine Meat Co Ltd (1956) 106 LJ ccr124 CyCt Was detinue where property in meat had passed to plaintiffs but meat was being retained by defendants.

Eastern Construction Company, Limited v (1) National Trust Company, Limited and Others; (2) Therese Schmidt and Others; Attorney-General for the Province of Ontario (Intervenant) [1914] AC 197; [1914] 83 LJPC 122; (1914) 110 LTR 321 PC Not liable for trespass by person with whom have contract but who is not servant/agent; Crown patentee/licensee a bailee for Crown of trees wrongfully felled so could not sue fellers for trover/detinue.

Finlayson v Taylor (1983) 133 NLJ 720; [1983] TLR 259 HC QBD Landlord liable in detinue/ conversion for seeking to exercise lien over goods bailed with him by tenant where latter owed arrears of rent.

Ghani and others v Jones [1969] 3 All ER 720; [1969] Crim LR 605; (1970) 134 JP 166; (1969) 113 SJ 775 HC QBD Police cannot retain non-evidential items of persons unconnected to crime.

Ghani and others v Jones [1969] 3 All ER 1700; [1970] Crim LR 36t; (1969) 113 SJ 854; [1969] 3 WLR 1158 CA Police cannot retain non-evidential items of persons unconnected to crime.

Glenwood Lumber Co Ltd v Phillips [1904-07] All ER 203; [1904] AC 405; [1904] 73 LJPC 62 PC Damages for trespasser's removal of felled trees from property.

Gollop v Brown (1952) 102 LJ 360 CyCt Failed action in detinue by father against daughter for return of piano originally given to her as birthday present.

Hannah v Peel [1945] 2 All ER 288; [1945] KB 509; (1946) 96 LJ 354; (1945) WN (I) 161 HC KBD Finder entitled to brooch/its worth where owner in whose house find never physically possessed house/never knew of brooch until finder found it/true owner never traced.

Jarvis v Williams [1955] 1 All ER 108; (1955) 105 LJ 40; (1955) 99 SJ 73; [1955] 1 WLR 71 CA Seller seeking to recover property legally passed to buyer's agent could not sue in detinue upon non-return of property.

Kendrick v Sotheby and Co, Elliott (Third Party) (1967) 111 SJ 470 HC QBD Successful action in detinue against innocent defendants who innocently purchased plaintiff's statuette from fraudulent third party.

London Jewellers, Limited v Sutton; Same v Robertsons (London), Limited (1934) 77 LJ 94; (1933-34) L TLR 193; (1934) WN (I) 21 HC KBD Pawnbrokers with whom fraudulently obtained goods were pawned liable to true owners of jewellery in detinue.

Metals and Ropes Co Ltd v Tattersall [1966] 3 All ER 401; (1965-66) 116 NLJ 1460; [1966] 1 WLR 1500 CA Where do not yield up delivery but regard property in items in one's control to rest with other must communicate this to other.

Michael v Michael (1959) 109 LJ ccr464 CyCt Successful action in detinue by one family member against another family member wrongfully retaining family heirloom (authentic balaclava helmet).

Munro v Willmott [1948] 2 All ER 983; [1949] 1 KB 295; (1948) 98 LJ 657; [1949] 118 LJR 471; (1948) LXIV TLR 627; (1948) WN (I) 459 HC KBD Appropriate damages for conversion/detinue.

Paley (Princess Olga) v Weisz and others (1928-29) XLV TLR 102 HC KBD Failed action in detinue/conversion by Russian exile against defendants who purchased property confiscated by Soviets.

Paley (Princess Olga) v Weisz and others (1928-29) XLV TLR 365 CA Failed action in detinue/conversion by Russian exile against defendants who purchased property confiscated by Soviets.

RB Policies at Lloyd's v Butler [1949] 2 All ER 226; [1950] 1 KB 76; (1949) 99 LJ 373; (1949) LXV TLR 436; (1949) WN (I) 299 HC KBD Time for detinue action ran from date of theft though did not then know thief's identity.

Rosenthal v Alderton and Sons, Ltd [1946] 1 All ER 583; [1946] KB 374; [1946] 115 LJ 215; (1946) 174 LTR 214; (1946) 90 SJ 163; (1945-46) LXII TLR 236; (1946) WN (I) 55 CA Value of goods determined at date of decision.

Singh (Sajan) v Ali (Sandara) [1960] 1 All ER 269 PC Title to property passed in course of conspiracy vests in person to whom passed once conspired act completed and can sue in detinue/trespass.

Sir Robert McAlpine and Sons Ltd v Minimax Ltd (1970) 114 SJ 206 HC QBD On remedies for detinue arising from retention of property handed over for scrutiny/preparation of report.

Strand Electric and Engineering Co, Ltd v Brisford Entertainments, Ltd [1952] 1 All ER 796; [1952] 2 QB 246; (1952) 96 SJ 260; [1952] 1 TLR 939; (1952) WN (I) 167 CA Damages for detinue were reasonable cost of hiring goods in relevant period.

Thurston v Charles (1904-05) XXI TLR 659 HC KBD Substantial damages available for wrongful conversion/detention where published another's private correspondence but privilege in communication not destroyed so no libel.

Trucks and Spares, Ltd v Maritime Agencies (Southampton), Ltd [1951] 2 All ER 982 CA Bills of lading proper proof of title justifying interim delivery order.

United Fruit Company Limited v Frederick Leyland and Co and Roberts, Brining and Co Limited (1930) 70 LJ 262; (1931) 144 LTR 97; (1930) 74 SJ 735 CA Appropriate interim arrangements regarding stock in action concerning conversion/detinue of bananas.

Watson v Murray and Co [1955] 1 All ER 350 HC QBD Sheriff committed trespass in taking exclusive possession of party's store/in preparing to hold sale in store; were liable in negligence for goods stolen from store.

Whiteley, Limited v Hilt [1918] 2 KB 115; (1918) CC Rep VII 37; (1917-18) XXXIV TLR 402 HC KBD Third party buying hire-purchase item from hirer thereby repudiating hire-purchase of same could be successfully sued in detinue/conversion.

Whiteley, Limited v Hilt [1918] 2 KB 808; (1917-18) XXXIV TLR 592 CA Third party buying hire-purchase item from hirer thereby repudiating hire-purchase of same acquired interest of hirer.

Willetts v Chaplin and Co (1922-23) XXXIX TLR 222 HC KBD Was reasonable for warehouse-men to sell all furniture deposited with them by plaintiff and not just enough to cover the unpaid costs of storage.

DETINUE (husband and wife)

Healey v Healey [1915] 84 LJKB 1454; (1915) WN (I) 103 HC KBD Married woman could in own name sue husband for detinue of property he assigned under marriage settlement to her trustees.

DUTY OF CARE (bank)

Barclays Bank plc v Khaira and another [1993] 1 FLR 343 (also CA); [1992] 1 WLR 623 HC ChD Bank does not normally owe duty of care to person going guarantor on loan to explain entire transaction/ensure have taken impartial advice on what doing.

Barclays Bank plc v Khaira and another [1993] 1 FLR 343 (also HC ChD) CA Non-party to ChD action not allowed appeal decision that bank does not normally owe duty of care to person going guarantor on loan to explain entire transaction/ensure have taken impartial advice on what doing.

DUTY OF CARE (coastguard)

OLL Ltd v Secretary of State for Transport [1997] 3 All ER 897; [1997] 2 Cr App R (S) 1099; (1997) 147 NLJ 1099; [1997] TLR 407 HC QBD On duty of care owed by coastguard in answering distress call.

DUTY OF CARE (general)

Bell v Arnottt and Harrison, Ltd (1967) 111 SJ 438 CA Employer under duty of care to have ordinary electric drill tested every so often.

Hedley Byrne and Co, Ltd v Heller and Partners, Ltd [1963] 2 All ER 575; [1964] AC 465; (1963) 113 LJ 416; (1963) 107 SJ 454; [1963] 3 WLR 101 HL Duty of care can arise between person seeking advice from other although no contractual/fiduciary relationship exists; disclaimer here excluded liability.

DUTY OF CARE (insurance)

Harvest Trucking Ltd v Davis [1991] TLR 147 HC QBD On duty of care owed by insurance intermediary.

DUTY OF CARE (Law Society)

Wood v Law Society (1993) 143 NLJ 1475 HC QBD Law Society does not owe duty of care to protect client from loss occasioned by solicitor whom are investigating on foot of client's complaint.

DUTY OF CARE (Lloyd's names)

Arbuthnott v Feltrim; Deeny v Gooda Walker; Henderson v Syndicates (Merrett) [1993] TLR 667 CA On extent of duty of care owed by managing/members' agents at Lloyd's towards names.

DUTY OF CARE (police)

Dyer v Bannell [1965] Crim LR 308t; (1965) 109 SJ 216 HC QBD On extent of duty of care owed by police driving police cars.

Swinney and others v Chief Constable of Northumbria Police Force [1996] 3 All ER 449; (1996) 146 NLJ 878; [1997] QB 464; (1996) TLR 28/3/96; [1996] 3 WLR 968 CA Could be that police owe duty of care to informant not to negligently disclose information concerning informant.

W v Commissioner of Police of the Metropolis [1997] TLR 403 CA Failed action in negligence by woman police constable against her superiors for their breach of (non-existent) duty of care towards her.

DUTY OF CARE (reference)

Spring v Guardian Assurance plc and others [1992] TLR 46 HC QBD Employer furnishing reference to prospective employer for employee liable for breach of duty of care to latter.

Spring v Guardian Assurance plc and others [1994] 3 All ER 129; [1995] 2 AC 296; (1994) 144 NLJ 971; (1994) 138 SJ LB 183; [1994] TLR 381; [1994] 3 WLR 354 HL Employer under duty of care not to make negligent mis-statement when giving character reference; reasonable care requirement of employer may be implied term of contract.

DUTY OF CARE (rescuer)

Crossley v Rawlinson [1981] 3 All ER 674; (1981) 131 NLJ 1093; [1982] RTR 442; (1981) 125 SJ 865; [1982] 1 WLR 369 HC QBD Non-liability of driver of burning vehicle for injury suffered by AA man running towards vehicle.

Harrison v British Railways Board and others [1981] 3 All ER 679 HC QBD Rescued person may (as here) owe duty of care towards rescuer who may therefore recover damages for injuries suffered in course of rescue.

DUTY OF CARE (sport)

Smoldon v Whitworth and another (1996) TLR 18/12/96 CA On duty of care owed towards rugby player by rugby referee.

Smoldon v Whitworth and another (1996) TLR 23/4/96 HC QBD Rugby referee owes duty of care in policing scrums to ensure that are conducted safely.

DUTY OF CARE (university)

Thorne v University of London [1966] 2 WLR 1080 CA Degree/examination regulations a matter for Visitor to University not for HC.

ESTOPPEL (general)

In the Estate of Park; Park v Park [1953] 2 All ER 408 HC PDAD No estoppel from re-pleading matters where issue in later case not the same; marriage a readily comprehensible arrangement: capacity necessary to enter marriage set quite low.

EXPULSION (general)

Hunt v Damon (1929-30) XLVI TLR 579 HC KBD Wrongfully expelling child from school is not per se a tort.

FALSE IMPRISONMENT (damages)

Cumber v Chief Constable of Hampshire Constabulary [1995] TLR 32 CA Award of exemplary damages but no compensatory damages for false imprisonment was irrational.

FALSE IMPRISONMENT (general)

Attorney-General of St Christopher Nevis and Anguilla v Reynolds (John Joseph) [1980] AC 637; [1980] 2 WLR 171 PC Exemplary damages for false imprisonment pursuant to emergency legislation was justified.

Boaks v Reece [1956] 2 All ER 750; [1956] Crim LR 563; (1956) 100 SJ 511; [1956] 1 WLR 886 HC QBD Was not wrongful imprisonment for magistrate to remand person in custody pending preparation of medical report prior to sentencing.

Brandeis Goldschmidt and Co Ltd v Western Transport Ltd [1982] 1 All ER 28; [1981] QB 864; [1981] 3 WLR 181 CA Damages for wrongful detention compensatory so need not be gauged by reference to difference in price when detained and when delivered.

Budd v Anderson and others (1941) 91 LJ 294; (1941) 85 SJ 405; (1942-43) LIX TLR 341 HC KBD On procedural irreguularities in detention under wartime detention legislation (Defence (General) Regulations 1939, reg 18B).

Carter v Metropolitan Police Commissioner (1975) 125 NLJ 87t CA Failed action for false imprisonment by woman removed to place of safety by police constable who believed her to be mentally unwell (Mental Health Act 1959, s 136(1)).

Childs v Lewis (1923-24) XL TLR 870 HC KBD Damages allowed for resignation from board of directors following on false imprisonment by police.

Chin (Yap Hon) v GL Jones-Parry and William Cowan (1911-12) XXVIII TLR 89 PC Innocence of any offence not enough under Malaysian Banishment Enactment 1900 to prove imprisonment was false.

Christie and another v Leachinsky [1947] 1 All ER 567; [1947] AC 573; (1947) 111 JP 224; (1947) 97 LJ 165; [1947] 116 LJR 757; (1947) 176 LTR 443; (1947) LXIII TLR 231 HL False imprisonment where arrested without warrant and not told why/not obvious why/inobvious why and do not resist.

Clubb v Wimpey and Co, Ltd [1936] 1 All ER 69 HC KBD Defendant's agent merely signing charge-sheet upon handing into custody was false imprisonment.

Connolly v Smith [1956] Crim LR 834; (1956) 106 LJ 570 Ct of Passage Local health authority officer who acted in good faith not liable in damages for false imprisonment of person whom removed to mental hospital.

Dallison v Caffery [1964] Crim LR 538; (1964) 128 JP 379; [1965] 1 QB 348; (1964) 108 SJ 560; [1964] 3 WLR 385 CA No false imprisonment where policeman held reasonable belief detainee had committed offence and reasonable grounds for delaying release; not malicious prosecution as had been reasonable cause for same.

Davidson v Chief Constable of North Wales and another [1994] 2 All ER 597; [1993] TLR 229 CA Evidence of store detective not directing, procuring, expressly requesting or encouraging arrest by police so not basis for false imprisonment.

Demer v Cook and another (1901-07) XX Cox CC 444; (1903) 67 JP 206; (1903) LXXXVIII LTR 629; (1902-03) 47 SJ 368; (1902-03) XIX TLR 327 HC KBD Action for false imprisonment lay against prison governor not clerk of the peace.

Diamond v Minter and others (1939-40) XXXI Cox CC 468; (1941) 91 LJ 142 HC KBD Unmerited arrest as were not person named in warrant; police officer cannot without warrant arrest person whom reasonably suspects committed criminal act abroad.

Dumbell v Roberts and others [1944] 1 All ER 326; (1944) 108 JP 139; (1945) 95 LJ 112; [1944] 113 LJ 185; (1944) 170 LTR 227; (1943-44) LX TLR 231 CA On special powers of arrest.

Edmondson v Rundle and others (1902-03) XIX TLR 356 HC KBD Failed action for wrongful arrest/imprisonment of soldier by superior officer during wartime: not a matter for civil courts.

Ex parte Docherty [1960] Crim LR 835t HC QBD Habeas corpus order in light of doubts as to identification evidence before magistrates.

Fisher v Oldham Corporation [1930] All ER 96; (1931-34) XXIX Cox CC 154; (1930) 94 JP 132; (1930) 99 LJCL 569; (1930) 143 LTR 281; (1929-30) XLVI TLR 390 HC KBD Police officer acts for Crown in effecting arrest so not liable for false imprisonment.

Green v Garbutt and others (1911-12) XXVIII TLR 575 CA Person bringing false imprisonment action on foot of detention for alleged felony allowed seek details of alleged felony plus basis for suspecting him but not identity of persons who informed on him.

Hague v Deputy Governor of Parkhurst Prison and others; Weldon v Home Office [1991] 3 All ER 733; [1992] 1 AC 58 (also HC QBD/CA); (1991) 141 NLJ 1185; [1991] 3 WLR 340 HL Party cannot launch private law claim for breach of statutory duty unless legislature intended it so; prisoner lawfully imprisoned cannot sue for false imprisonment in respect of residual liberty.

Hanson v Waller [1901] 1 QB 390; [1901] 70 LJK/QB 231; (1900-01) 49 WR 445 HC QBD Master not liable for servant's falsely imprisoning third party.

Harnett v Bond and another (1923-24) XL TLR 414 HC KBD Successful action for false imprisonment of lunatic.

Harnett v Bond and another (1924) 131 LTR 782; (1923-24) XL TLR 653 CA Failed action for false imprisonment of lunatic.

Harnett v Bond and another (1924-25) 69 SJ 445/575; (1924-25) XLI TLR 509 HL Failed action for false imprisonment of lunatic.

Hayward v Commissioner of Police for the Metropolis (1984) 134 NLJ 724; [1984] TLR 175 HC QBD Successful suit for damages for false imprisonment where were arrested and detained by police without reasonable cause.

Herd v Weardale Steel, Coal and Coke Company, Limited and Others [1913] 3 KB 771 HC KBD Action for false imprisonment as defendant not under contractual duty to facilitate exit so that was denied same not imprisonment.

Herd v Weardale Steel, Coal and Coke Company, Limited and Others [1915] AC 67; (1914) 49 LJ 411; (1913) 48 LJ 391; [1915] 84 LJKB 121; (1914-15) 111 LTR 660; (1913-14) XXX TLR 620; (1914) WN (I) 289 HL Party denied relief for false imprisonment on volenti non fit injuria basis.

Herd v Weardale Steel, Coal and Coke Company, Limited and Others [1913] 3 KB 771 (also HC KBD); [1913] 82 LJKB 1354 CA Action for false imprisonment as defendant not under contractual duty to facilitate exit so that was denied same not imprisonment.

Hill (Gary) v Chief Constable of the South Yorkshire Police [1990] 1 All ER 1046 (1990) 134 SJ 197 CA Jury trial necessary if judge satisfied that false imprisonment claim arises; guilty plea/verdict does not preclude claim of false imprisonment.

Hirsch and others v Somervell and others (1946) 90 SJ 369 HC ChD Striking out of false imprisonment/trespass action against successive Home Secretaries.

Hirsch and another v Somervell and others (1946) 90 SJ 394; (1945-46) LXII TLR 592 CA Successful appeal against striking out of false imprisonment/trespass action against successive Home Secretaries.

Holmes and Ward v Hargreaves and Audsley (1923) CC Rep XII 35 CyCt Constables liable to pay damages for false imprisonment for detaining persons merely suspected of committing offence under the Vagrancy Act 1824.

Hook v Cunard Steamship Co (1953) 117 JP 226; (1953) 103 LJ 265; (1953) 97 SJ 334; [1953] 1 WLR 682 HC QBD Master of ship where could reasonably believe is necessary and does believe it to be necessary could detain any person on board ship so as to preserve order/discipline.

Hurst v Picture Theatres, Limited (1913-14) XXX TLR 98 HC KBD Recovery for assault/false imprisonment by theatre audience member mistakenly ejected from seat having paid for ticket.

Hurst v Picture Theatres, Limited [1915] 1 KB 1; (1914) 49 LJ 439; [1914] 83 LJKB 1837; (1914-15) 111 LTR 972; (1913-14) XXX TLR 642 CA Recovery for assault/false imprisonment by theatre audience member mistakenly ejected from seat having paid for ticket.

Hussien (Shaaban Bin) and others v Kam (Chong Fook) and another [1969] 3 All ER 1626; [1970] AC 942; [1970] Crim LR 219; (1970) 114 SJ 55; [1970] 2 WLR 441 PC 'Reasonable suspicion' is not 'prima facie proof'; reasonable suspicion once lies compound circumstantial evidence.

Hyland v Chief Constable of Lancashire Constabulary (1996) TLR 7/2/96 CA Could not bring action for false imprisonment where had been remanded into custody.

Isaacs v Keech (1926-30) XXVIII Cox CC 22; (1925) 89 JP 189; [1925] 2 KB 354; [1925] 94 LJCL 676; (1925) 133 LTR 347; (1924-25) XLI TLR 432; (1925) WN (I) 109 HC KBD Police officer can under Town Police Clauses Act 1847, s 28 arrest anyone whom genuinely believes guilty of inter alia importuning for prostitution.

John Lewis and Co, Ltd v Tims [1952] 1 All ER 1203; [1952] AC 676; (1952) 116 JP 275; (1952) 102 LJ 262; (1952) 96 SJ 342; [1952] 1 TLR 1132; (1952) WN (I) 241 HL Not false imprisonment where store detectives take arrested party before police within reasonable time (not forthwith).

King (J) and King (WH) v Metropolitan District Railway Company (1908) 72 JP 294; (1908-09) XCIX LTR 278 HC KBD On statutory protection afforded special constable (employed by rail company) in effecting arrest.

Lambert v Great Eastern Railway Company (1911-13) XXII Cox CC 165; [1909] 2 KB 776; (1909) 73 JP 445; (1908-09) XXV TLR 734; (1909) WN (I) 186 CA Railway company liable in damages for false imprisonment by their special constables.

Leachinsky v Christie [1945] 2 All ER 395; (1946) 110 JP 23; [1946] KB 124; (1946) 96 LJ 185; [1946] 115 LJ 241; (1946) 174 LTR 13; (1944-45) LXI TLR 584 CA Cannot be arrested for misdemeanour because suspected of felony; on special powers of arrest.

Liversidge v Anderson and Morrisson [1941] 2 All ER 612; (1941) 91 LJ 278; (1942) 92 LJ 51; (1941) 85 SJ 398 CA Home Secretaries not obliged to disclose why person detained under Defence (General) Regulations 1939, reg 18(b).

Liversidge v Anderson and another [1941] 3 All ER 338; [1942] AC 206; (1941) 91 LJ 430; (1941) 85 SJ 439; (1941) WN (I) 223 HL Home Secretaries not obliged to disclose why person detained under Defence (General) Regulations 1939, reg 18(b).

Mee v Cruikshank (1901-07) XX Cox CC 210; (1902) LXXXVI LTR 708; (1901-02) XVIII TLR 271 HC KBD Prison governor liable for illegal detention of acquitted person by prison warders.

Meering v Grahame-White Aviation Company Limited [1918-23] All ER 292; (1920) 122 LTR 44 CA On imprisonment by private prosecutor/police.

Metcalfe v Collett-Ward (1977) 127 NLJ 964b CA On what constitutes false imprisonment: aggravated damages awarded for same.

Middleweek v Chief Constable of the Merseyside Police and another [1990] 3 All ER 662; [1992] 1 AC 179; [1990] 3 WLR 481 CA False imprisonment arises where conditions of detention detrimental to health; police officer acting with good reason to search a detainee does not commit trespass to person.

Millington v Commissioner for the Police (1983) 133 NLJ 806; [1983] TLR 395 HC QBD Damages for false imprisonment where person was detained for longer than necessary by police at police station.

Morriss v Winter and another (1926-30) XXVIII Cox CC 687; [1930] 1 KB 243; (1930) 142 LTR 67; (1928-29) XLV TLR 643 HC KBD No right to early discharge where earn remission marks so no false imprisonment thereafter.

Murray v Ministry of Defence [1988] 2 All ER 521; (1988) 138 NLJ 164; (1988) 132 SJ 852; [1988] 1 WLR 692 HL Arrest can begin before formal words of arrest spoken; formal words usually to be said at moment of arrest.

O'Connor v Isaacs and others [1956] 2 All ER 417; [1956] Crim LR 482; (1956) 106 LJ 392; (1956) 100 SJ 432; [1956] 3 WLR 172 CA Failed action against justices for committal to prison on foot of maintenance order made without jurisdiction; application of public authority limitation.

O'Connor v Isaacs and others [1956] 1 All ER 513; [1956] Crim LR 261; (1956) 120 JP 169; (1956) 100 SJ 171; [1956] 2 WLR 585 HC QBD Absent malice could sue justices for trespass (arising from false imprisonment)/could not sue for money paid on foot of maintenance order made without jurisdiction; application of public authority limitation.

Olotu v Secretary of State for the Home Department and another (1996) TLR 8/5/96 CA Prison governor not liable for false imprisonment of individual kept in remand custody after prescribed time as result of Crown Prosecution Service not applying for extension of time.

Olotu v Home Office and another [1997] 1 All ER 385; (1996) TLR 11/12/96; [1997] 1 WLR 328 CA Person committed to CrCt for trial could not sue Home Secretary/Crown Prosecution Service for false imprisonment/breach of statutory duty where was detained beyond time stipulated.

Peacock and Hoskyn v Musgrave and Porter [1956] Crim LR 414t HC QBD Detention by police of persons whom police reasonably believed to have commiitted offence was not false imprisonment.

Percy (Pauper) v Corporation of City of Glasgow [1922] 2 AC 299; (1922) 86 JP 201; (1922) 127 LTR 501; (1922) WN (I) 181 HL Glasgow City Corporation tramway officials acting in excess of duties might have committed false imprisonment.

Percy and another v Hall and others [1996] 4 All ER 523; (1996) TLR 31/5/96; [1997] 3 WLR 573 CA Bona fide actions under bye-law later deemed invalid did not render persons effecting those actions liable in tort.

Pritchard v Ministry of Defence [1995] TLR 26 HC QBD Failed claim in false imprisonment by individual who claimed was compelled to remain in Army (but such a claim could be successful).

R v Deputy Governor of Parkhurst Prison and others, ex parte Hague [1990] 3 All ER 687; [1992] 1 AC 58 (also HC QBD/HL); (1990) 140 NLJ 1036; [1990] 3 WLR 1210 CA Administrative decisions by prison authorities not subject to private law remedies; intentional unreasonable detention of prisoner beyond term of imprisonment or in conditions detrimental to health is false imprisonment.

R v Linsberg and Leies (1905) 69 JP 107 HC KBD False imprisonment absent assault/battery/belief that had legal authority so to do an indictable crime.

Re Lunacy Act 1890; Re Intended Action by Frost (1936) 80 SJ 464 CA Failed appeal against leave being granted to onetime mental patient (later found not to be unsound) to sue corporation for false imprisonment/wrongful detention.

Reynolds v Commissioner of Police for the Metropolis [1982] Crim LR 600; [1982] TLR 274 CA £12,000 damages merited in serious case of wrongful arrest/false imprisonment.

Robinson (Archibald Nugent) v Balmain New Ferry Company, Limited [1910] AC 295; [1910] 79 LJPC 84 PC No false imprisonment where were merely using reasonable tactic to preempt forcible avoidance of payment for exit from wharf.

Sewell v National Telephone Co, Ltd [1904-07] All ER 457; [1907] 76 LJCL 196; (1907) XCVI LTR 483; (1906-07) 51 SJ 207; (1906-07) XXIII TLR 226 CA False imprisonment not proven through signing of charge-sheet while party in police custody.

Shearer and another v Shields [1914] AC 808; [1914] 83 LJPC 216 HL Malice in fact unnecessary for false imprisonment in pursuance of Glasgow Police Act 1866.

Sherbourne v Walker [1955] Crim LR 184 HC QBD Successful action for damages against policeman guilty of assault/wrongful imprisonment/malicious prosecution.

Sirros v Moore and another [1974] 3 All ER 776; (1974) 118 SJ 661 CA Judge acting judicially was immune from civil action (as were police acting bona fide under his direction).

Stores and Stores v Graham and Bolangaro (1949) 99 LJ 108 CyCt Damages from police for false imprisonment (continued detention in police station after police believed detained suspect to be innocent of alleged offence).

Stuart v Anderson and Morrison [1941] 2 All ER 665; (1941) 91 LJ 286 HC KBD Home Secretary's detention order procedurally correct: court would look no further; detention order under Defence (General) Regulations valid though made against several persons.

Thompson v Commissioner of Police of the Metropolis; Hsu v Same [1997] 2 Cr App R (S) 341; (1997) 147 NLJ 341; [1997] 3 WLR 403 CA On awarding of damages in false imprisonment/ malicious prosecution action.

Tims v John Lewis and Co, Ltd [1951] 1 All ER 814; (1951) 115 JP 265; [1951] 2 KB 459; (1951) 101 LJ 203; (1951) 95 SJ 268; [1951] 1 TLR 719; (1951) WN (I) 188 CA Upon arrest must be taken to police officer/justice of the peace forthwith.

Turner (an infant) v Felton and others [1940] LJNCCR 300 CyCt Absent reasonable basis for questioning person going to police station for questioning in belief that was required to go could claim damages from police for false imprisonment.

Walter v Alltools, Limited (1944) 171 LTR 371; (1944-45) LXI TLR 39; (1944) WN (I) 214 CA On relevant factors when gauging appropriate damages for false imprisonment.

Walters v WH Smith and Son, Ltd [1911-13] All ER 170; (1914) 78 JP 118; [1914] 1 KB 595; [1914] 83 LJKB 335; (1914) 110 LTR 345; (1913-14) 58 SJ 186; (1913-14) XXX TLR 158; (1913) WN (I) 359 HC KBD Private person must to defeat false imprisonment claim show reasonable suspicion that person whom arrested committed an offence that was effected.

Weldon v Home Office [1990] 3 All ER 672; [1992] 1 AC 58 (also HC QBD/HL); [1990] TLR 269; [1990] 3 WLR 465 CA Intentional unreasonable deprivation by prison authorities of residual liberty of prisoner is false imprisonment.

FALSE IMPRISONMENT (police)

Wright v Sharp (1947) 176 LTR 308 HC KBD Failed action for false imprisonment/malicious prosecution following taxi-driver's arrest/failed prosecution after taxi had been hired for robbery.

Yusuf-Ud-Din (Syed Mahamad) v The Secretary of State for India in Council (1902-03) XIX TLR 496 PC Where person released on bail after arrest under warrant which is later set aside the time for bringing false imprisonment action runs from date of release on bail.

FALSE IMPRISONMENT (police)

White and another v Metropolitan Police Commissioner [1982] TLR 221 HC QBD Exemplary damages from Police Commissioner for false imprisonment/assault/malicious prosecution by police officers.

FOREIGN TORT (general)

Kinnear and others v Falconfilms NV and others (hospital Ruber Internacional and another, third parties) [1994] 3 All ER 42 HC QBD Foreign third party to be joined where no alternative or better forum available to those seeking remedy.

Red Sea Insurance Co Ltd v Bouygues SA and others [1994] 3 All ER 749; [1994] TLR 414 PC Rule that tort in other jurisdiction must be actionable there and in England to be actionable not absolute rule — lex loci delicti may take precedence over lex fori.

FRAUD (general)

Kings North Trust Ltd v Bell and others [1985] FLR 948; [1986] 1 WLR 119 CA Non-enforcement on behalf of principals of mortgage deed signed pursuant to fraudulent misrepresentation by their agent.

Shelley v Paddock and another [1978] 3 All ER 129; [1979] QB 120; (1978) 122 SJ 316; [1978] 2 WLR 877 HC QBD Inadvertent unlawful behaviour does not prevent recovery in tort action.

Shelley v Paddock and another [1980] 1 All ER 1009; [1980] QB 348; (1979) 123 SJ 706; [1980] 2 WLR 647 CA Inadvertent illegality in presence of fraud precluded guilty party raising defence of illegality.

HARASSMENT (general)

Devonshire and Smith v Jenkins (1979) 129 (1) NLJ 198c CA Aggravated, not exemplary damages for harassment/nuisance.

HIGHWAY (misfeasance/non-feasance)

Pritchard v Clwyd County Council and another [1992] TLR 353 CA Presence of flood-water on road not per se evidence of non-feasance.

HUSBAND AND WIFE (detinue)

Healey v Healey [1915] 84 LJKB 1454; (1915) WN (I) 103 HC KBD Married woman could in own name sue husband for detinue of property he assigned under marriage settlement to her trustees.

Larner v Larner [1904-07] All ER 1022; [1905] 2 KB 539; (1905) 40 LJ 544; (1905-06) XCIII LTR 537; (1904-05) XXI TLR 637; (1905) WN (I) 116; (1905-06) 54 WR 62 HC KBD Wife can bring detinue action against husband.

HUSBAND AND WIFE (ejectment)

Green v Green (1924) CC Rep XIII 50 CyCt Husband could not bring action of ejectment against wife.

HUSBAND AND WIFE (general)

Beaumont v Kaye and another [1904] 73 LJCL 213; (1904) XC LTR 51; (1903-04) 48 SJ 206; (1903-04) XX TLR 183; (1904) WN (I) 20; (1903-04) 52 WR 241 CA Could sue husband and wife for tort of wife — disparate defences by husband and wife struck out as were sued as unit.

Best v Samuel Fox and Co, Ltd [1951] 2 All ER 116; [1951] 2 KB 639; (1951) 101 LJ 315; (1951) 95 SJ 352; [1951] 1 TLR 1138; (1951) WN (I) 284 CA Wife cannot recover for partial loss of consortium through third party's negligent but not malicious act.

Best v Samuel Fox and Co, Ltd and another [1950] 2 All ER 798; (1950) 100 LJ 511; (1950) 94 SJ 582; (1950) WN (I) 450 HC KBD Wife failed in action for loss of consortium occasioned by tort.

Broom v Morgan (1952) 102 LJ 665; (1952) 96 SJ 803; [1952] 2 TLR 904; (1952) WN (I) 531 HC QBD Wife could sue husband's employers for tort husband did to her in course of his employment.

Broom v Morgan [1953] 1 QB 597; (1953) 97 SJ 247; [1953] 2 WLR 737 CA Wife could sue husband's employers for tort husband did to her in course of his employment.

Burdett v Horne (Elizabeth) and Horne (Frederick Walters) (1910-11) XXVII TLR 402 HC KBD Husband liable for wife's torts.

Burdett v Horne and another (1911-12) XXVIII TLR 83 CA Husband liable for wife's torts.

Cuenod v Leslie [1909] 1 KB 880; (1909) 44 LJ 166; [1909] 78 LJKB 695; (1909) C LTR 675; (1908-09) 53 SJ 340; (1908-09) XXV TLR 374; (1909) WN (I) 65 CA Husband not liable for torts of judicially separated wife committed during coverture.

Earle v Kingscote [1900] 1 Ch 203; [1900] LXIX (1) LJ 202; (1899-1900) LXXXI LTR 775; (1899-1900) XVI TLR 63 HC ChD Husband liable for wife's deceit in respect of contract to purchase shares.

Edwards and Another v Porter and Wife [1923] 1 KB 268; (1923) 58 LJ 34; [1923] 92 LJCL 720 (also CA); (1922-23) XXXIX TLR 124; (1923) WN (I) 9 HC KBD Non-liability of husband for false representation by wife during coverture.

Edwards and Another (Paupers) v Porter [1925] AC 1; (1924) 59 LJ 711; [1925] 94 LJCL 65; (1925) 132 LTR 496; (1924-25) 69 SJ 87; (1924-25) XLI TLR 57; (1924) WN (I) 279 HL Liability of husband for tortious act of wife during coverture.

Edwards and another v Porter and Wife; McNeall v Hawes [1923] 2 KB 538; [1923] 92 LJCL 720; (1923) 129 LTR 170; (1922-23) 67 SJ 482; (1922-23) XXXIX TLR 358/362; (1923) WN (I) 170 CA Non-liability of husband for tortious act of wife during coverture.

Gottliffe v Edelston [1930] 2 KB 378; (1930) 99 LJCL 547; (1930) 143 LTR 595; (1930) 74 SJ 567; (1929-30) XLVI TLR 544; (1930) WN (I) 168 HC KBD Right of action for tort by woman against man ended upon marriage of former to latter.

Lambert and another v Eastern National Omnibus Co, Ltd [1954] 2 All ER 719; (1954) 104 LJ 505; (1954) 98 SJ 493; [1954] 1 WLR 1047 HC QBD Spouse might (but here did not) recover damages for estrangement from other spouse consequent upon negligent act.

Mallett and another v Dunn [1949] 1 All ER 973; [1949] 2 KB 180; [1949] 118 LJR 1650; (1949) LXV TLR 307; (1949) WN (I) 206 HC KBD Husband could sue for medicine/household expenses though wife contributorily negligent.

McNeall v Hawes (1923) 58 LJ 160; [1923] 92 LJCL 729 (also HC KBD); (1922-23) 67 SJ 483; (1922-23) XXXIX TLR 362; (1923) WN (I) 170 CA Non-liability of husband for tortious act of wife during coverture.

McNeall v Hawes [1923] 1 KB 273; [1923] 92 LJCL 729 (also CA); (1922-23) 67 SJ 316; (1922-23) XXXIX TLR 167; (1923) WN (I) 14 HC KBD Liability of husband for tortious act of wife during coverture.

Sarson v Barwell (Sarson Third Party) [1937] LJNCCR 272 CyCt Right of contribution from third party barred by virtue of plaintiff having married third party before judgment signed.

Smith v Moss and another [1940] 1 All ER 469; [1940] 1 KB 424; (1940) 89 LJ 107; [1940] 109 LJCL 271; (1940) 162 LTR 267; (1940) 84 SJ 115; (1939-40) LVI TLR 305; (1940) WN (I) 22 HC KBD Wife could recover for husband's tort against her where he had acted as mother's agent.

William Cuenod and Company v Charles John Leslie and Wife (1908-09) 53 SJ 14; (1908-09) XXV TLR 2 HC KBD Husband liable for torts of judicially separated wife committed during coverture.

HUSBAND AND WIFE (misrepresentation)

Edwards v Taylor (1922-23) 67 SJ 248 HC KBD Husband not liable where wife fraudulently represents that she is authorised to act for him.

INDUCEMENT (general)

Daily Mirror Newspapers, Ltd v Gardner and others [1968] 2 All ER 163; [1968] 2 QB 762; [1968] 2 WLR 1239 CA Interlocutory injunction available; that did not know terms of contract/did not bring about direct pressure no defence; restrictive trade practice prima facie evidence of wrongful interference.

Sefton (Earl) v Tophams, Ltd and Capital and Counties Property Co, Ltd [1965] 3 All ER 1 [1965] Ch 1140 (also HC ChD); [1965] 3 WLR 523 CA Size of money offered evidenced inducement to breach contract.

INDUCEMENT TO COMMIT BREACH OF CONTRACT (general)

Merkur Island Shipping Corp v Laughton and others [1983] 1 All ER 334; (1983) 133 NLJ 186; [1983] 2 WLR 45 CA Elements of 'inducement to commit breach of contract'; immunity from action in tort if purpose of secondary action to frustrate contract between picketed employer and employer facing secondary action.

INTERFERENCE (general)

Boots, Cash Chemists (Lancashire) (Limited), and others v Grundy and another (1900) 35 LJ 413; (1900) LXXXII LTR 769; (1899-1900) XVI TLR 457; (1900) WN (I) 142 HC QBD Cannot bring action against persons combining to induce other persons not to trade with third party.

Brimelow v Casson and others [1923] All ER 40; [1924] 1 Ch 302 HC ChD Justified interference with contractual rights by trade associations.

British Industrial Plastics, Ltd v Ferguson [1938] 4 All ER 504; (1939) 160 LTR 95 CA Not liable for inducing breach of contract where in good faith believed were not so doing.

British Industrial Plastics, Ltd and others v Ferguson and others [1940] 1 All ER 479; (1940) 162 LTR 313 HL That party 'inducing' acted in good faith precluded liability for inducing breach of contract.

British Motor Trade Association v Salvadori and others [1949] 1 All ER 208 HC ChD Trade union could bing action for conspiracy; any person taking active rôle in collective breach of covenant of which are aware guilty of procuring breach of contract.

Carlin Music Corpn, Subiddu Music Ltd and Mechanical-Copyright Protection Society Ltd v Collins (1980) 130 NLJ 218c CA Copyright Protection Society could seek to have unlawful dealings in copyright injuncted as was unlawful interference with its business in that it obtained portion of all licence fees paid.

DC Thompson and Co, Ltd v Deakin and others [1952] 2 All ER 361 CA Cannot procure breach of contract where act procure is not unlawful.

Edwin Hill and Partners (a firm) v First National Finance Corp plc [1988] 3 All ER 801; (1988) 132 SJ 1389; [1989] 1 WLR 225 CA Defendant with equal/superior right interfering with plaintiff's contractual rights via agreement with third party not liable for interference with contractual relations.

Glamorgan Coal Company, Limited and others v South Wales Miners' Federation and others [1903] 1 KB 118 HC KBD Is defence to combination to secure breach of contract that no malice towards other party to contract.

Glamorgan Coal Company, Limited and others v South Wales Miners' Federation and others [1903] 2 KB 545; (1903) 38 LJ 417; (1902-03) XIX TLR 701 CA Liability for procuring breach of contract.

GWK, Limited, and others v Dunlop Rubber Company, Limited (1925-26) XLII TLR 376 HC KBD Substituting own tyres for those on display car (which car company and rival tyre company had come to agreement on regarding display) was interference with contractual rights for which car company/rival tyre company entitled to damages.

GWK, Limited, and others v Dunlop Rubber Company, Limited (1925-26) XLII TLR 593 CA Appeal withdrawn from decision that substituting own tyres for those on display car (which car company and rival tyre company had come to agreement on regarding display) was interference with contractual rights for which car company/rival tyre company entitled to damages.

Hadmor Productions Ltd and others v Hamilton and others (1981) 131 NLJ 445; [1981] 3 WLR 139 CA Trade union liable for unlawful interference with contract between television companies where was not acting in connection with trade dispute.

Hadmor Productions Ltd and others v Hamilton and another (1982) 132 NLJ 348; [1982] 2 WLR 322 HL While trade union might be guilty of unlawful interference (via intimidation) with contract between television companies was immune from liability as acting in connection with trade dispute.

Howard E Perry and Co Ltd v British Railways Board [1980] 2 All ER 579; [1980] 1 WLR 1375 HC ChD Indefinite interference with property rights is wrongful interference; delivery-up order available if damages inappropriate.

Law Debenture Trust Corp plc v Ural Caspian Oil Corp Ltd and others [1995] 1 All ER 157; [1995] Ch 152; [1994] 3 WLR 1221 CA Tort of procuring violation of right extends not only to contractual rights but to right to relief.

Lonrho plc v Fayed and others [1988] 3 All ER 464; (1988) 138 NLJ 225; [1990] 1 QB 490; (1989) 133 SJ 220; [1989] 2 WLR 356 HC QBD Interference with take-over bid not an interference with business interest; if cannot claim for tort cannot claim for conspiracy to commit tort.

Lonrho plc v Fayed and others [1989] 2 All ER 65; (1989) 139 NLJ 539; [1990] 2 QB 479; [1989] 3 WLR 631 CA Interference with trade/business must be intended to hurt plaintiff but not necessarily as principal aim.

Re S (minor) [1993] TLR 185 HC QBD No action for damages lies for interference with parental rights.

Read v The Friendly Society of Operative Stonemasons of England, Ireland and Wales and others [1902] 2 KB 88; [1902] 71 LJCL 634 HC KBD Good faith/absence of malice not enough to justify interfering with contract: only defence is having same/better right than that of person interfered with.

Read v The Friendly Society of Operative Stonemasons of England, Ireland and Wales and others [1902] 2 KB 732; (1902) 37 LJ 543; [1902] 71 LJCL 994; (1902-03) XIX TLR 20 CA Earlier agreement not enough to justify interfering with contract.

Sefton (Earl) v Tophams, Ltd and Capital and Counties Property Co, Ltd [1965] 3 All ER 1; [1965] 3 WLR 523 CA Size of money offered evidenced inducement to breach contract.

South Wales Miners' Federation and others v Glamorgan Coal Company Limited, and others [1905] AC 239; (1904-05) XXI TLR 441 HL Miners federation could be sued for good faith direction to miners not to work on particular days.

INTIMIDATION (general)

Rookes v Barnard and others [1961] 2 All ER 825; [1963] 1 QB 623 (also CA) HC QBD Injury arising through threat to break contract with third person intimidation (if acted alone; otherwise conspiracy) — no protection under Trade Disputes Act 1906, ss 1 and 3.

Rookes v Barnard and others [1962] 2 All ER 579; [1963] 1 QB 623 (also HC QBD) CA Is a tort of intimidation but mere threat to break contract not intimidation: must be fraud/threats/violence.

Rookes v Barnard and others [1964] 1 All ER 367; [1964] AC 1129; [1964] 2 WLR 269 HL Is a tort of intimidation which embraces threatening breach of contract: on exemplary damages for intimidation.

JOINT TORTFEASORS (animal)

Piper v Winnifrith and Leppard (1917) CC Rep VI 93; (1917-18) XXXIV TLR 108; (1917) WN (I) 358 HC KBD Joint savaging of sheep by two dogs owned by two different owners did not mean owners joint tortfeasors.

JOINT TORTFEASORS (damages)

Sims v Foster Wheeler Ltd and another; Plibrico Ltd (Third Party) [1966] 1 WLR 769 CA On liability of joint tortfeasors for damages in presence of warranty contract.

Smith v Bray (Wickham, Third Party) (1940) 84 SJ 170; (1939-40) LVI TLR 200 HC KBD Apportionment of costs/damages in proportion to apportionment of negligence between joint tortfeasors.

JOINT TORTFEASORS (estoppel)

Johnson v Cartledge and Matthews (Matthews, Third Party) [1939] 3 All ER 654 Assizes Damage in two actions was different so no res judicata; cannot be tortfeasor if were not negligent.

JOINT TORTFEASORS (general)

Apley Estates Co and others v De Bernales and others [1946] 2 All ER 338; (1947) 91 SJ 12 HC ChD Agreement with one joint tortfeasor not accord and satisfaction unless so intended.

Apley Estates Co and others v De Bernales and others [1947] 1 All ER 213; [1947] Ch 217; [1947] 116 LJR 705; (1947) 176 LTR 182; (1947) LXIII TLR 71; (1947) WN (I) 13 CA Agreeing not to sue one joint tortfeasor does not release others.

Arneil v Paterson (1931) 71 LJ 425; (1931) 100 LJPC 161; (1931) 145 LTR 393; (1931) 75 SJ 424; (1930-31) XLVII TLR 441; (1931) WN (I) 137 HL Owners jointly liable for entirety of damage where impossible to apportion respective liabilities for damage to cattle by dogs acting in concert.

Bryanston Finance Ltd and others v De Vries and another [1975] 2 All ER 609; (1975) 125 NLJ 231; [1975] QB 703; (1975) 119 SJ 287 [1975] 2 WLR 718 CA Qualified privilege between businessman/typist/photocopier if main purpose was usual course of business; not pleading justification does not mean words false; in action against two joint tortfeasors judgment against one bar to action against other.

Bulmer Rayon Company, Limited v Freshwater and Another [1933] AC 661 HL Non-merger of causes of action.

Burnham v Boyer and Brown [1936] 2 All ER 1165; (1936) 82 LJ 133 HC KBD Under Law Reform (Married Women and Tortfeasors) Act 1965, s 6 contribution available from joint tortfeasor added as third party.

Calvert and another v Pick and another [1954] 1 All ER 566; (1954) 104 LJ 170; (1954) 98 SJ 147 HC QBD Court will not adjudicate on matter that is really settled between various parties.

Cutler and another v McPhail [1962] 2 All ER 474; (1962) 112 LJ 370; [1962] 2 QB 292; (1962) 106 SJ 391 HC QBD Complete release of joint tortfeasors not covenant not to sue so ended all rights of action.

Freshwater and another v Bulmer Rayon Company, Limited [1933] Ch 162 (also CA); (1933) 102 LJCh 102 (also CA) HC ChD Non-merger of causes of action of successive not joint tortfeasors.

Freshwater and another v Bulmer Rayon Company, Limited [1933] Ch 162 (also HC ChD); (1933) 102 LJCh 102 (also HC ChD); (1933) 148 LTR 251; (1932) WN (I) 211 CA Non-merger of causes of action of successive not joint tortfeasors.

Gardiner v Moore and others [1966] 1 All ER 365; [1969] 1 QB 55; [1966] 3 WLR 786 HC QBD No implied term in settlement with two of three joint tortfeasors that would not sue other.

George Wimpey and Co Ld v British Airways Overseas Corporation [1954] 3 All ER 661; [1955] AC 169; (1954) 104 LJ 824; [1954] 3 WLR 932 HL Precluded by public authority special limitation period from recovering contribution from respondent.

Harper v Gray and Walker (a firm) and others [1985] 2 All ER 507; [1985] 1 WLR 1196 HC QBD Contribution notice remained valid after discontinuance of action against joint defendants as liability undetermined.

Hart v Hall and Pickles Ltd; George Reyner and Co Ltd (second defendants and third parties) [1968] 3 All ER 291; (1968) 118 NLJ 980 [1969] 1 QB 405; [1968] 3 WLR 744 CA Dismissal of action against one joint tortfeasor does not mean not liable to other joint tortfeasors.

Harvey v RG O'Dell, Ltd and another (Galway Third Party) [1958] 1 All ER 657; (1958) 108 LJ 266; [1958] 2 QB 78; (1958) 102 SJ 196 HC QBD Negligent master recovering all damages from joint tortfeasor servant.

Howe v Oliver; Haynes Third Party (1907-08) XXIV TLR 781 HC KBD Could not bring action against second partner in respect of same cause of action subject of settlement with one partner.

Ingram v United Automobile Services, Limited, and others [1943] 2 All ER 71; [1943] KB 612; [1943] 112 LJ 447; (1943) 169 LTR 72; (1942-43) LIX TLR 295; (1943) WN (I) 126 CA Trial judge's apportionment of damages between joint tortfeasors will rarely be interfered with by CA if agrees that both parties are tortfeasors.

Lambert and another v Lewis and others [1981] 1 All ER 1185 HL Third party contractor liable to tortfeasor for damages paid by latter if warranted that tortfeasor need no take action which led to tort.

Lampitt and another v Poole Borough Council (Taylor and another, third parties) [1990] 2 All ER 887; [1991] 2 QB 545; [1990] TLR 470; [1990] 3 WLR 179 CA Contribution unavailable under Law Reform (Married Women's and Tortfeasors) Act 1935 but was available under Civil Liability (Contribution) Act 1978.

Lean v Alston [1947] 1 All ER 261 CA Third party recovery from deceased's estate possible though deceased not party to negligence action.

Littlewood v George Wimpey and Co, Ltd; British Overseas Airways Corporation (second defendants and third parties) [1953] 1 All ER 583; (1953) 103 LJ 138; (1953) 97 SJ 152; [1953] 1 WLR 426 HC QBD Corporation a public authority doing public duty so special limitation under Limitation Act 1939, s 2(1) applied and could not be sued: as not sued was not liable for contribution.

Littlewood v George Wimpey and Co, Ltd British Overseas Airways Corporation (second defendants and third parties) [1953] 2 All ER 915; (1953) 117 JP 484; (1953) 103 LJ 589; [1953] 2 QB 501; (1953) 97 SJ 587; [1953] 3 WLR 553 CA Cannot seek contribution from party sued and found not to be liable; time runs for recovery of contribution from date when judgment given against one.

Maxfield v Llewellyn and others [1961] 3 All ER 95; (1961) 105 SJ 550 CA Where assessing contributions of joint tortfeasors court not to look to persons who may be contributorily negligent but not so found/party to action.

Morgan v Ashmore, Benson, Pease and Co, Ltd and another [1953] 1 All ER 328; (1953) 97 SJ 152; [1953] 1 WLR 418 HC QBD Can recover from joint tortfeasor if could have been successfuly sued in past.

Newcombe v Yewen and the Croydon Rural District Council (1912-13) XXIX TLR 299 HC KBD Council could reach indemnity agreement with contractor.

Nolan v Merseyside County Council and Northwest Water Authority (1983) 133 NLJ 616c CA On recovery of contribution from joint tortfeasor.

Nottingham Health Authority v Nottingham City Council (1988) 132 SJ 899; [1988] 1 WLR 903 CA Are only precluded from seeking recovery from joint defendants if they have been sued to judgment and deemed not liable.

Owners of Steamship or Vessel 'British Fame' v Owners of Steamship or Vessel 'MacGregor' [1943] 1 All ER 33 HL Only exceptionally will trial judge's apportionment of liability between tortfeasors be changed on appeal.

Owners of the Steamship Ceramic v Owners of the Steamship Testbank [1942] 1 All ER 281 CA On apportioning liablity and review thereof by CA.

RA Lister and Co Ltd and others v EG Thomson (Shipping) Ltd and others (No 2); The Benarty (No 2) [1987] 3 All ER 1032; [1987] 1 WLR 1614 HC QBD Claim against co-defendant possible even if latter's action stayed and claim not procedurally enforceable.

Rippon v Port of London Authority and J Russell and Co (Port of London Authority, Third Party) [1940] 1 All ER 637 HC KBD Port authority (occupiers) and ship-repairers (notional occupiers) liable for workman's injury.

Romford Ice and Cold Storage Co Ltd v Lister [1955] 3 All ER 460; [1955] 3 WLR 631 CA Damages available to master for servant's failure in duty of care unaffected by being vicariously liable joint tortfeasor.

Ronex Properties Ltd v John Laing Construction Ltd and others (Clarke, Nicholls and Marcel (a firm), third parties) [1982] 3 All ER 961; [1983] QB 398; (1982) 126 SJ 727; [1982] 3 WLR 875 CA Possible limitation defence not good cause for striking out claim; claim against joint tortfeasor for contribution not extinguished in death as not in tort but a right sui generis.

Semtex, Ltd v Gladstone [1954] 2 All ER 206; [1954] 1 WLR 945 Assizes Innocent employer could seek complete indemnity of damages paid from negligent employee.

Sigley v Hale [1938] 3 All ER 87; (1937-38) LIV TLR 967 CA No payment into court possible in case of joint tortfeasors.

Southern Water Authority v Carey and others [1985] 2 All ER 1077 HC QBD Tortious liability excluded by contractual arrangements; breach of duty of care by secondary defendants to primary defendants did not entitle latter to recover damages by indemnity.

Stott v West Yorkshire Road Car Co Ltd and another (Home Bakeries Ltd and another, third parties) [1971] 3 All ER 534; [1971] 2 QB 651; [1971] 3 WLR 282 CA Persons settling action without admitting liability can seek contribution from third parties.

The Koursk [1924] All ER 168 CA To be joint tortfeasor must be some sort of connection/common plan between tortfeasors.

Townsend and another v Stone Toms and Partners and others (1984) 128 SJ 659 CA On apportionment of damages from joint tortfeasors so that plaintiff received only the total amount to which was entitled.

Wah Tat Bank Ltd and another v Kum (Chan Cheng) [1975] 2 All ER 257; [1975] AC 507; (1975) 125 NLJ 133; (1975) 119 SJ 151; [1975] 2 WLR 475 PC Joint tortfeasor not sued to judgment could be sued again.

WH Smith and Son v Clinton and another (1908-09) XCIX LTR 840; (1908-09) XXV TLR 34 HC KBD Printer could not recover under libel-indemnity contract with publisher as printer was joint tortfeasor.

JOINT TORTFEASORS (nuisance)

Hanson v Wearmouth Coal Co, Ltd and Sunderland Gas Co [1939] 3 All ER 47; (1939) 87 LJ 411; (1939) 83 SJ 397; (1938-39) LV TLR 747 CA Gas company negligent in placing mains upon ground being mined underneath; mining company not liable Donoghue v Stevenson-style for loss to other upon ground subsiding.

LIBEL (damages)

Broome v Cassell and Co Ltd and another [1971] 2 All ER 187; [1971] 2 QB 354; (1971) 115 SJ 289; [1971] 2 WLR 853 CA Rookes v Barnard was per incuriam; exemplary damages available in libel; behaviour fell in second category of Rookes v Barnard; one sum of damages where joint tortfeasors.

Kiam v Neil and another [1994] TLR 647 CA Pre-trial settlement offer could not be presented to jury post-trial (by offeror) in effort to mitigate damages to be awarded by jury.

LIBEL (general)

English and Scottish Co-operative Property Mortgage and Investment Society, Ltd v Odhams Press, Ltd and Daily Herald (1929), Ltd (1939) 83 SJ 566 HC KBD Newspaper headline libellous by virtue of innuendo to be derived from report that was literally true.

Morriss v Baines and Co Limited (1933) 148 LTR 428 HC KBD Plaintiff awarded less than amount paid into court could not be ordered to pay back amount in excess of award where had already withdrawn payment from bank.

Wigg v The Spectator, Ltd (1967) 111 SJ 743 CA Leave to administer interrogatories refused where not necessary for fair trial/to save costs.

LIBEL (innuendo)

Pedley v Cambridge Newspapers Ltd (1964) 108 SJ 375; [1964] 1 WLR 988 CA General damages payable for what were technically three actions in respect of three cases of innuendo.

LIBEL (justification)

Godman v Times Publishing Co [1926] 95 LJCL 747 HC KBD On pleading justification.

Stopes v Sutherland and another (1922-23) XXXIX TLR 242 HC KBD Libel action failed where jury found words complained of though unfair were true in substance/fact.

Stopes v Sutherland and another (1923) 58 LJ 366; (1922-23) XXXIX TLR 677 CA Libel action succeeded where jury found words complained of were true in substance/fact but unfair comment.

Sutherland and Others v Stopes et e contra [1924] All ER 19; [1925] AC 47; (1924) 59 LJ 757; [1925] 94 LJCL 166; (1925) 132 LTR 550; (1924-25) 69 SJ 138; (1924-25) XLI TLR 106 HL Plea seeming partly one of justification, partly one of fair comment a plea of fair comment.

LIMITATION (general)

Ackbar v CF Green and Co Ltd [1975] 2 All ER 65; (1975) 125 NLJ 134t; [1975] QB 582; (1975) 119 SJ 219; [1975] 2 WLR 773 HC QBD Action for breach of contract leaving party uninsured against personal injury subject to limitation for contract cases.

Airey v Airey [1958] 2 All ER 59; (1958) 108 LJ 315 HC QBD Action outside negligence limitation but within six months of administering estate allowed.

Airey v Airey [1958] 2 All ER 571; (1958) 108 LJ 457; [1958] 2 QB 300; (1958) 102 SJ 489 CA Negligence action six years after accident but inside six months of estate administration not barred.

Anns and others v Walcroft Property Co Ltd and another [1976] QB 882; (1976) 120 SJ 216; [1976] 2 WLR 512 CA Cause of action from time building defects discovered/ought to have been discovered.

Archer v Catton and Co, Ltd [1954] 1 All ER 896; (1954) 104 LJ 251; (1954) 98 SJ 337; [1954] 1 WLR 775 HC QBD Six-year limitation applied.

Archer v Moss; Applegate v Moss [1971] 1 All ER 747; [1971] 1 QB 406; (1970) 114 SJ 971; [1971] 2 WLR 541 CA Fraud in Limitation Act is equitable fraud; assessment of damages for breach of warranty.

Arnold v Central Electricity Generating Board [1987] 3 All ER 694; [1988] AC 228 (also HC QBD/CA); (1987) 137 NLJ 1014; (1987) 131 SJ 1487; [1987] 3 WLR 1009 HL 1954, 1963 and 1975 Limitation Acts did not/do not obviate existing benefit of time-bar under 1939 Limitation Act.

Arnold v Central Electricity Generating Board [1988] AC 228 (also HC QBD/HL) CA 1954, 1963 and 1975 Limitation Acts did not/do not obviate existing benefit of time-bar under 1939 Limitation Act.

Arnold v Central Electricity Generating Board [1988] AC 228 (also CA/HL); [1986] 3 WLR 171 HC QBD 1954, 1963 and 1975 Limitation Acts obviate existing benefit of time-bar under 1939 Limitation Act.

Baker v Ollard and Bentley and Marsland and Barber (1983) 133 NLJ 422c; (1982) 126 SJ 593 CA Limitation period in negligence action stemming from negligent conveyance ran from date of conveyance.

Balls and another v Lintsbrook Development Ltd (1976) 120 SJ 29 HC ChD Action dismissed for delay (albeit that delay nonetheless meant action being brought inside limitation period).

Bank of America National Trust and Savings Association v Chrismas and others 'The Kyriaki' [1994] 1 All ER 401 HC QBD Court cannot allow new claim after expiry of limitation period.

Barand v British Cellophane plc [1995] TLR 83 CA On deciding whether to allow out-of-limitation action to proceed.

Barnes and another v Pooley (1935) 153 LTR 78; (1934-35) LI TLR 391 HC KBD Action for expenses by parent/person in loco parentis on foot of negligence of defendant's servant an action on the case so six year limitation applicable under Limitation Act 1623, s 3.

Bartlett and others v Barclays Bank Trust Co Ltd [1980] 1 All ER 139 HC ChD Absent fraud can rely on limitation period under Limitation Act 1939, s 26(b).

Battersby and others v Anglo-American Oil Company, Limited, and others (1944-45) LXI TLR 13 CA Court would not exercise discretion to enlarge time for renewing writ where to do so would deprive person of advantage limitation has conferred.

Batting v London Passenger Transport Board [1941] 1 All ER 228 CA No leave to amend outside time under old limitation statute though new limitation statute had come into force since action started.

Beaman v ARTS Ltd [1948] 2 All ER 89; (1948) LXIV TLR 285 HC KBD Limitation as no fraud: bailee acted honestly and in good faith.

Beaman v ARTS, Ltd [1949] 1 All ER 465; [1949] 1 KB 550; (1949) 99 LJ 119; (1949) LXV TLR 389 CA Fraud not essential to conversion; fraudulent concealment of action being open held to delay application of limitation.

Bentley v Bristol and Western Health Authority [1990] TLR 766 HC QBD On when limitation period begins to run in surgical negligence actions.

Biss v Lambeth, Southwark and Lewisham Health Authority [1978] 2 All ER 125; [1978] 1 WLR 382 CA Can be prejudice in conduct of affairs where delayed action; delay before extended limitation can be considered in deciding if prejudice.

Braniff v Holland and Hannen and Cubitts (Southern) Ltd, and another [1969] 3 All ER 959; [1969] 1 WLR 1533 CA Weldon v Neal principles still generally applicable.

British Columbia Electric Railway Company Limited v Pribble (1926) 61 LJ 299; (1926) 95 LJPC 51; (1926) 134 LTR 711; (1925-26) XLII TLR 332 PC Personal injuries action barred by virtue of Consolidated Railway and Light Companies Act 1906, s 60.

Broadley v Guy Clapham and Co [1994] 4 All ER 439; [1993] TLR 375 CA Limitation period in action for negligent surgical operation runs from date when victim broadly knows or could have known with the help of medical advice that injury resulted from surgery.

Brook v Hoar [1967] 3 All ER 395; (1967) 117 NLJ 887t; (1967) 111 SJ 634; [1967] 1 WLR 1336 HC QBD Infant in position of lodger in parent's house not in parent's custody and control.

Brooks v J and P Coates (UK) Ltd [1984] 1 All ER 702 HC QBD Limitation lifted as plaintiff blameless and would suffer greater prejudice if action barred than defendants would in meeting claim after long delay.

Buck v English Electric Co Ltd [1978] 1 All ER 271; [1977] 1 WLR 806 HC QBD Desire not to 'sponge' not good ground for delay; earlier similar cases obviated prejudice to defendants of case with over five year delay: limitation lifted.

Carey v Mayor, etc, of Bermondsey (1903) 67 JP 111 HC KBD Personal injury action not allowed where brought over six months after injury occurred.

Carey v Metropolitan Borough of Bermondsey (1903) 67 JP 447; (1903-04) XX TLR 2 CA Personal injury action not allowed where brought over six months after injury occurred.

Cartledge and others v Jopling (E) and Sons Ltd (1961) 111 LJ 676; [1962] 1 QB 189; (1961) 105 SJ 884 CA Cause of action accrued upon damage/loss even though were unaware of same (workers contracting progressive disease) so action barred.

Cartledge and others v Jopling (E) and Sons Ltd [1963] AC 758; (1963) 113 LJ 120; (1963) 107 SJ 73; [1963] 2 WLR 210 HL Cause of action accrued upon damage/loss even though were unaware of same (workers contracting progressive disease) so action barred.

Central Asbestos Co Ltd v Dodd [1972] 2 All ER 1135; [1973] AC 518; [1972] 3 WLR 333 HL Time from which limitation runs where contracting of disease concerned.

Chappell v Cooper; Player v Bruguiere [1980] 2 All ER 463; (1980) 130 NLJ 317c; (1980) 124 SJ 544; [1980] 1 WLR 958 CA Regardless of reason cannot disapply limitation where second action brought after first action commenced in time but lapsed.

Clark (In re) v Forbes Stuart (Thames Street) Ltd (Intended Action) (1964) 114 LJ 388; (1964) 108 SJ 422; [1964] 1 WLR 836 CA Extension of time limit allowed where identity of occupier became known after limitation period expired.

Clark and another v Woor [1965] 2 All ER 353; (1965) 109 SJ 251; [1965] 1 WLR 650 HC QBD Action not barred where concealment by fraud led to late discovery of damage; damages measured from date of discovery.

Clarkson v Modern Foundries Ltd (1957) 101 SJ 960; [1957] 1 WLR 1210 HC QBD Recovery for entire injury where undistinguishable part of injury occurred outside limitation period.

Clough and others v Clough and others (1968) 118 NLJ 372t; [1968] 1 WLR 525 CA Court exercised discretion to dismiss negligence action for want of prosecution (three years since entry of appearance yet no sign of statement of claim).

Coad v Cornwall and Isles of Scilly Health Authority (1996) 140 SJ LB 168; (1996) TLR 30/7/96; [1997] 1 WLR 189 CA Subjective test required in application of Limitation Act 1980, s 33(3)(a).

Cohen v Snelling; Lubovsky v Snelling [1943] 2 All ER 577 CA No limitation where liability admitted.

Colchester Borough Council v Smith and others [1991] 2 All ER 29 HC ChD Limitation runs from date of trespass with intent to exclude all others; if possession granted by licence are estopped by contract/tradition from claiming title is adversely possessed.

Commissioners of His Majesty's Works and Public Buildings v Pontypridd Masonic Hall Company, Limited [1920] 2 KB 233 HC KBD Corporation were agents of Crown and Crown not affected by Statute of Limitations.

Conry v Simpson and others [1983] 3 All ER 369 CA Court of Appeal will not interfere with judge's disapplying of limitation unless very wrong.

Coote v Eastern Gas Board [1953] 1 All ER 762; (1953) 117 JP 198; [1953] 1 QB 594 HC QBD Limitation period under Gas Act 1948 for tortious liability of gas undertaking absorbed into Gas Board is six years.

Cornish v Kearley and Tonge Ltd (1983) 133 NLJ 870 HC QBD Extension of limitation allowed where had reasonable excuse for delay/had acted with reasonable speed/no undue injustice would result to defendant.

Costa v Georghiou (1984) 134 NLJ 82c HC QBD Failed attempt to have extension limitation disapplied in light of concealed fraud claim.

Cozens v North Devon Hospital Management Committee and another; Hunter v Turners (Soham), Ltd [1966] 2 All ER 276; [1966] 2 QB 318; (1966) 110 SJ 273; [1966] 2 WLR 1134 HC QBD On (extension of) limitation.

Crocker v British Coal Corporation [1995] TLR 389 HC QBD Burden of proof on plaintiff seeking to show personal injuries action not outside relevant limitation period under the Limitation Act 1980, s 11.

Dale v British Coal Corporation (No 1) (1992) 136 SJ LB 197 CA No need for leave to appeal against overriding of limitation period.

Dale v British Coal Corporation (No 2) (1992) 136 SJ LB 199 CA Reversal of disapplication of limitation·period.

Davis v Soltenpur (1983) 133 NLJ 720; [1983] TLR 104 HC QBD Limitation period applied in favour of defendant where plaintiff still had option of bring action against solicitors.

Deeming v British Steel Corporation (1979) 123 SJ 303 CA Delay that did not affect value of evidence to be given in personal injuries action did not justify striking out of personal injuries claim.

Deerness v John R Keeble and Son (Brantham) Ltd and another [1982] TLR 480 CA Could not issue second writ where had already issued writ but allowed limitation period to pass before sought to serve it.

Deerness v John R Keeble and Son (Brantham) Ltd and another (1983) 133 NLJ 641; [1983] TLR 308 HL Correspondence between insurance company and solicitors did not preclude latter from relying on expired limitation period defence.

Dennis and another v Charnwood Borough Council [1982] 3 All ER 486; [1983] QB 409; (1982) 126 SJ 730; [1982] TLR 440; [1982] 3 WLR 1064 CA Local authority owes duty of care in ensuring plans comply with building regulations; time runs from date damage occurs/local authority failure becomes apparent.

Dennis v Charnwood Borough Council (1982) 132 NLJ 349 HC QBD Local authority owes duty of care in ensuring plans comply with building regulations; time ran from date local authority failure became apparent.

Department of Transport v Chris Smaller (Transport) Ltd [1989] AC 1197; (1989) 139 NLJ 363; (1989) 133 SJ 361; [1989] 2 WLR 578 HL Pre-writ delay not punishable where within limitation period; post-writ delay ought not to be punished where does not unduly prejudice other.

Devlin v F (a juvenile) [1982] 2 All ER 450 HC QBD One-judge Divisional Court can deal with time extension application; interests of justice/defendant justify extension.

Dismore v Milton [1938] 3 All ER 762; (1938) 82 SJ 695; (1938-39) LV TLR 20; (1938) WN (I) 305 CA Cause of action remains in personal actions though limitation period has expired.

Dobbie v Medway Health Authority [1994] 4 All ER 450; (1994) 144 NLJ 760t; (1994) 144 NLJ 828; [1994] TLR 278; [1994] 1 WLR 1234 CA Limitation period in personal injury claim runs from date when victim knew injury resulted from action of another even if unaware legal remedy available.

Donovan v Gwentoys Ltd [1990] 1 All ER 1018; (1990) 134 SJ 910; [1990] 1 WLR 472 HL Court has unfettered discretion to allow personal injury action to proceed where limitation period has expired if fair to do so.

Dornan v Ellis (JW) and Co, Ltd [1962] 1 All ER 303; [1962] 1 QB 583; (1961) 105 SJ 1083 CA Leave to amend claim outside limitation period as raised no new ground of recovery.

Dove v Banhams Patent Locks Ltd [1983] 2 All ER 833; (1983) 133 NLJ 538; (1983) 127 SJ 748; [1983] TLR 158; [1983] 1 WLR 1436 HC QBD Time ran from when negligence first apparent not when negligent work completed.

Drinkwater v Joseph Lucas (Electrical) Ltd [1970] 3 All ER 769 CA Where all reasonable steps taken to discover cause of illness failure to discover justified diasapplying limitation.

DW Moore and Co Ltd and others v Ferrier and others [1988] 1 All ER 400; (1987) 137 NLJ 1013; (1988) 132 SJ 227; [1988] 1 WLR 267 CA Client suffers damage from negligently drafted contract when contract executed not when defect discovered.

Eddis and another v Chichester Constable and others [1969] 2 Ch 345; [1969] 3 WLR 48 CA Limitation period in conversion action ran from time fraud discovered.

Eddis v Chichester-Constable and others [1969] 1 All ER 546; (1969) 119 NLJ 224 HC ChD Limitation period did not begin to run where right of action was fraudulently concealed.

Ernst and Young (a firm) v Butte Mining plc (No 2); Butte Mining plc v Ernst and Young (a firm) and others [1997] 2 All ER 471 HC ChD Counterclaim whereby was sought to bring negligence action struck out.

Fettes v Robertson (1920-21) XXXVII TLR 581 CA Statute of Limitations successfully pleaded where written promise to pay had not been unqualified.

Firman v Ellis (1977) 121 SJ 606 HC QBD On extent of discretion of court to disapply limitation period.

Firman v Ellis and other appeals [1978] 2 All ER 851; [1978] QB 886; (1978) 122 SJ 147; [1978] 3 WLR 1 CA Court's discretion to disapply limitation is unfettered.

First National Commercial Bank plc v Humberts [1995] 2 All ER 673; (1995) 145 NLJ 345; [1995] TLR 29 CA Cause of action where loan made following negligent advice runs from date of loss.

Forbes v Wandsworth Health Authority [1996] 4 All ER 881; (1996) 146 NLJ 477; [1997] QB 402; (1996) 140 SJ LB 85; (1996) TLR 21/3/96; [1996] 3 WLR 1108 CA On when possess adequate knowledge for limitation period to commence running.

Forster v Outred and Co (a firm) [1982] 2 All ER 753; [1982] 1 WLR 86 CA Once solicitor's negligent advice acted on to one's detriment time for economic loss action runs.

Forward v Hendricks [1997] 2 All ER 395 CA On whether/when limitation period may be disregarded in personal injury actions (Limitation Act 1980, s 33(1)).

Frisby v Theodore Goddard and Co [1984] TLR 127 CA On concealment of right of action as ground for striking out claim.

Gawthrop v Boulton and others [1978] 3 All ER 615; (1978) 122 SJ 297 HC ChD Limitation period continues to run to defendant's advantage to date added as party.

Goodchild v Greatness Timber Co, Ltd [1968] 2 All ER 25; [1968] 2 QB 372; (1968) 112 SJ 192; [1968] 2 WLR 1283 CA Evidence unnecessary to decide if limitation applied.

Griffiths and another v Smith and others [1941] AC 171; (1941) 105 JP 63; [1941] 110 LJ 156; (1941) 164 LTR 386; (1940-41) LVII TLR 185 HL Public authority limitation period barred action against managers of non-provided elementary school.

Halford v Brookes and another [1991] 3 All ER 559; (1991) 141 NLJ 1367g; [1991] 1 WLR 428 CA Legal advice unnecessary for there to be knowledge of facts causing limitation period to run; ignorance of law relevant when deciding to disapply limitation period.

Hall v Meyrick [1957] 2 All ER 722; (1957) 107 LJ 488; [1957] 2 QB 455; (1957) 101 SJ 574 CA Cannot amend statement of claim to include new statute-barred cause of action.

Hallam-Eames and others v Merrett and others [1995] TLR 20 CA On necessary pre-requisites before may rely on extended limitation period under the Limitation Act 1980, s 14A.

Hamlin and another v Edwin Evans (a firm) (1996) 140 SJ LB 167; (1996) TLR 12/7/96 CA Limitation period ran from time house-buyers knew of valuer's negligence vis-a-vis dry rot.

Harkness v Bell's Asbestos and Engineering Ltd [1967] 2 WLR 29 CA Extension of time on foot of application to registrar who made irregular order.

Harnett v Fisher [1927] 1 KB 402 (also CA); [1927] 96 LJCL 55 (also CA); (1925-26) 70 SJ 737; (1925-26) XLII TLR 486 HC KBD Action by escaped 'lunatic' against doctor for negligent committal to asylum barred by Limitation Act 1623.

Harnett v Fisher [1927] 1 KB 402 (also HC KBD); [1927] 96 LJCL 55 (also HC KBD); (1926) 135 LTR 724; (1925-26) 70 SJ 917; (1925-26) XLII TLR 745 CA Action by escaped 'lunatic' against doctor for negligent committal to asylum barred by Limitation Act 1623.

Harnett v Fisher [1927] AC 573; (1927) 91 JP 175; (1927) 63 LJ 582; [1927] 96 LJCL 856; (1927) 137 LTR 602; (1926-27) XLIII TLR 567 HL Action by escaped 'lunatic' against doctor for negligent committal to asylum barred by Limitation Act 1623.

Harris v Newcastle Health Authority [1989] 2 All ER 273; (1989) 133 SJ 47; [1989] 1 WLR 96 CA Pre-trial disclosure available unless obvious that limitation defence will succeed.

Hartin v London County Council (1926-30) XXVIII Cox CC 618; (1929) 93 JP 160; (1929) 141 LTR 120 HC KBD Special public authority limitation period inapplicable to malicious prosecution action as criminal prosecution not a public duty under Public Authorities Protection Act 1893.

Hartley v Birmingham City District Council [1992] 2 All ER 213; [1992] 1 WLR 968 CA Judge may ignore limitation period if it would be equitable to do so.

Hattam v National Coal Board (1978) 128 NLJ 1149t; (1978) 122 SJ 777 CA Staying of action where all evidence lost/plaintiff had received full industrial benefits since suffered workplace injury.

Hewer v Bryant (1968) 118 NLJ 684t; [1969] 1 QB 415; (1968) 112 SJ 762; [1968] 3 WLR 910 HC QBD 15 year old trainee on farm away from home was in parent's custody: action barred.

Hewer v Bryant [1969] 3 All ER 578; (1969) 119 NLJ 600t; [1970] 1 QB 357; (1969) 113 SJ 525; [1969] 3 WLR 425 CA 15 year old trainee on farm away from home not in parent's custody: action not barred.

Higgins and another v North West Metropolitan Regional Hospital Board and another [1954] 1 All ER 414; (1954) 104 LJ 122; (1954) 98 SJ 147; [1954] 1 WLR 411 HC QBD Hospital specialist acting for local authority enjoys one year limitation under Limitation Act 1939, s 21(1).

Higgins v Arfon Borough Council [1975] 2 All ER 589; [1975] 1 WLR 524 HC QBD Cause of action ran from date of damage not discovery.

Higham v Stena Sealink Ltd [1996] 3 All ER 660; [1996] 1 WLR 1107 CA Cannot disregard two year limitation on personal injury actions by ferry passenger.

Hill v Luton Corporation [1951] 1 All ER 1028; (1951) 115 JP 340; [1951] 2 KB 387; [1951] 1 TLR 853; (1951) WN (I) 269 HC KBD Defective writ served in time and amended out of time allowed to stand.

Hilton v Sutton Steam Laundry [1946] 115 LJ 33; (1946) 174 LTR 31 CA Out of time action disallowed.

Hoare v Tom Pettifer Ltd et al (1984) 134 NLJ 284c CA Extension of time allowed that service of writ might be acknowledged.

Holman v George Elliot and Co, Limited (1943-44) LX TLR 394 HC KBD Validity of fatal accident writ extended in time where had been issued in time but not served in time.

Hopkins v Mackenzie (1994) 138 SJ LB 222; [1994] TLR 546 CA Period of limitation in negligence action against solicitor (whose negligence resulted in loss of right of claim) ran from date of striking out.

Hordern Richmond, Ltd v Duncan [1947] 1 All ER 427; [1947] KB 545; [1947] 116 LJR 1024 HC KBD Third party recovery from person acting in public duty over one year after cause of action.

Howe and others v David Brown Tractors (Retail) Ltd (Rustons Engineering Co Ltd, third party) [1991] 4 All ER 30 CA Amendment of writ where limitation period applies; application to disapply limitation period to be made at same time/beforehand.

Howell v West Midland Passenger Executive (1973) 123 NLJ 13t CA Limitation period disapplied where unaware of rights until shortly before instigated action.

Hyde v Pearce [1982] 1 All ER 1029 CA No adverse possession if uncompleted conveyance would be a defence to charge of possession/if contract terminable upon vendor's demanding return of keys.

Ingall v Moran (1944) 88 SJ 68 CA Administrator could not bring negligence action before letters of administration granted and as that occurred over twelve months after limitation period expired action failed outright.

Iron Trade Mutual Insurance Co Ltd and others v JK Buckenham Ltd [1990] 1 All ER 808 HC QBD Injury caused upon procuring of voidable reinsurance policies; actions in contract/tort to be treated separately under Limitation Act even if same time limits; issue whether latent damage action is time-barred to be decided at trial/as preliminary issue, not in strike-out proceedings.

Islander Trucking Ltd (in liq) v Hogg; Robinson and Gardner Mountain (Marine) Ltd and others [1990] 1 All ER 826 HC QBD Injury caused upon procuring of voidable insurance contract.

Johnson v Chief Constable of Surrey [1992] TLR 551 CA On deciding whether to allow action to be brought after is statute barred.

Jones and another v Stroud District Council [1988] 1 All ER 5; (1986) 130 SJ 469; [1986] 1 WLR 1141 CA Cause for negligence action regarding property begins when real/imminent danger to occupiers; that repairs to property paid by another does not disentitle occupier to damages.

Jones v Bennett (1975) 125 NLJ 870t HC QBD Failed application for extension of limitation where although applicant was illiterate she had been in possession of the relevant facts.

Jones v Trollope Colls Cementation Overseas Ltd and another [1990] TLR 62 CA Foreign Limitation Periods Act 1984 inapplicable where to apply it would be more unfair than fair.

Kaur (Pritam) v S Russell and Sons Ltd [1972] 3 All ER 305; (1972) 122 NLJ 538t; [1972] 3 WLR 663 HC QBD Time runs from day after tort; limitation period includes days on which court office closed.

Kaur (Pritam) (administratrix of Bikar Singh (deceased)) v S Russell and Sons Ltd [1973] 1 All ER 617; (1973) 123 NLJ 16t; [1973] QB 336; [1973] 2 WLR 147 CA Limitation period calculated from day after tort; limitation extended by one day if court office closed for day on last day of limitation period.

Kelly v Bastible and others (1997) 141 SJ LB 5; (1996) TLR 15/11/96 CA On deciding whether limitation period to be disapplied: that solicitor not liable for delay/that defendants insured did not justify disapplication.

72

Kennett v Brown and another [1988] 2 All ER 600; (1988) 132 SJ 752; [1988] 1 WLR 582 CA Claimant need not seek disapplication of limitation period unless and until other party raises it.

Ketteman and others v Hansel Properties Ltd and others [1985] 1 WLR 352; (1984) 128 SJ 800; [1984] 1 WLR 1274 CA Cause of action in relation to defective house arose when physical damage happened; cracks in walls of house meant was imminent danger in respect of which local authority owed duty of care.

Ketteman and others v Hansel Properties Ltd [1988] 1 All ER 38; [1987] AC 189; (1987) 137 NLJ 100; (1987) 131 SJ 134; [1984] TLR 525; [1987] 2 WLR 312 HL Cause of action runs from time latent defect causes damage; party added as defendant when amended writ served unless waive need therefor; party added on date party joined; cannot plead limitation after electing to argue case on merits.

King v Victor Parsons and Co [1972] 2 All ER 625; (1972) 116 SJ 239; [1972] 1 WLR 801 HC QBD Fraudulent failure to warn of risk meant plaintiff not statute-barred from bringing action.

King v Victor Parsons and Co (a firm) [1973] 1 All ER 206; (1972) 122 NLJ 1037t; (1972) 116 SJ 901; [1973] 1 WLR 29 CA Fraudulent non-disclosure of material facts known when making contract meant later action for breach of contract not statute-barred.

Kirby v Leather [1965] 2 All ER 41; [1965] 2 QB 367; (1965) 109 SJ 357; [1965] 2 WLR 1318 CA Incapability of managing own affairs means 'of unsound mind'; adult being looked after by mother is not in her custody.

Kitchen v Royal Air Force Association and others [1958] 2 All ER 241; (1958) 108 LJ 344; (1958) 102 SJ 363 CA Fraud in Limitation Act does not just cover dishonest behaviour; substantial damages where fatal accidents claim barred through negligence.

Knipe v British Railways Board [1972] 1 All ER 673; (1971) 121 NLJ 1025t; [1972] 1 QB 361; [1972] 2 WLR 127 CA If do not know/constructively know that have cause of action cannot waive that cause of action.

Ledingham and others v Bermejo Estancia Co, Ltd; Agar and others v Same [1947] 1 All ER 749 HC KBD Contract valid as legal relationship desired/was consideration; limitation ran once ability to pay under contract ceased.

Letang v Cooper (1964) 114 LJ 622; [1965] 1 QB 232; (1964) 108 SJ 519; [1964] 3 WLR 573 CA Trespass to the person action time-barred under Limitation Act 1939, s 2 (as amended).

Letang v Cooper [1964] 1 All ER 669; (1964) 114 LJ 306; [1964] 2 QB 53; (1964) 108 SJ 180; [1964] 2 WLR 642 HC QBD Trespass to the person action could not be time-barred under Limitation Act 1939, s 2 (as amended).

Liff v Peasley and another [1980] 1 All ER 623; (1980) 124 SJ 360; [1980] 1 WLR 781 CA No extension of limitation period where strong case against defendant/involvement of Motor Insurers' Bureau.

Littlewood v George Wimpey and Co Ltd; British Overseas Airways Corporation (second defendants and third parties) [1953] 2 All ER 915; (1953) 117 JP 484; (1953) 103 LJ 589; [1953] 2 QB 501; (1953) 97 SJ 587; [1953] 3 WLR 553 CA Cannot seek contribution from party sued and found not to be liable; time runs for recovery of contribution from date when judgment given against one.

London Borough Council of Lewisham v Leslie and Co Ltd (1979) 129 (2) NLJ 1179c CA Possible concealed fraud would justify action to determine whether breach of contract action out of time.

London Congregational Union Inc v Harriss and Harriss (a firm) [1985] 1 All ER 335 HC QBD Cause of action ran from time defect caused damage.

London Congregational Union Inc v Harriss and Harriss (a firm) [1988] 1 All ER 15 CA Cause of action runs from time defect causes damage; plaintiff to show cause of action lies in limitation period.

Long v Hepworth [1968] 3 All ER 248; (1968) 118 NLJ 516t; (1968) 112 SJ 485; [1968] 1 WLR 1299 HC QBD Wilful trespass to person is a breach of duty precluding extension of time limit under Limitation Act 1939.

Lovell v Lovell [1970] 3 All ER 721 CA If limitation pleaded interrogatory showing debt due unavailable but interrogatory showing document prceding writ acknowledged debt is available.

Lubovsky v Snelling (1944) 170 LTR 2; (1943-44) LX TLR 52 CA Where party accepts liability and parties agree to go to court on matter of damages only expiry of limitation period cannot be pleaded as defence.

Lucy v WT Henleys Telegraph Works Co Ltd (ICI Ltd, Third Party) [1969] 3 All ER 456 HC QBD If direct action would fail because of Limitation Act cannot be added as defendant to related action.

Lucy v WT Henleys Telegraph Works Co Ltd (ICI Ltd, Third Party); Wild v Siemens Brothers and Co Ltd [1969] 3 All ER 456; [1970] 1 QB 393; (1969) 113 SJ 641; [1969] 3 WLR 588 CA Could not add third party to action where that was precluded by Limitation Act 1963.

Marren v Dawson Bentley and Co, Ltd [1961] 2 All ER 270; (1961) 111 LJ 342; [1961] 2 QB 135; (1961) 105 SJ 383 HC QBD Day of tort not to be included when calculating limitation period.

McCafferty v Metropolitan Police District Receiver [1977] 2 All ER 756; (1977) 121 SJ 678; [1977] 1 WLR 1073 CA Express/non-express reasons for delay in bringing action of relevance in deciding if limitation not to apply.

Melton v Walker and Stanger (1981) 131 NLJ 1238; (1981) 125 SJ 861 HC ChD Date of cause of action ran from date negligently drafted document was signed.

Merlihan v AC Pope, Ltd and JW Hibbert (John Pagnello, Third Party) [1945] 2 All ER 449/354; (1945) 109 JP 231; [1946] KB 166; (1946) 96 LJ 30; [1946] 115 LJ 90; (1945) 173 LTR 257; (1945) 89 SJ 359; (1944-45) LXI TLR 508; (1945) WN (I) 187 HC KBD Cause of action accrues on date of original negligence even in respect of third party later added to claim.

Myers v Bradford Corporation (1914) CC Rep III 102; (1915) 79 JP 130; [1915] 1 KB 417; (1914) 49 LJ 638; [1915] 84 LJKB 306; (1915) 112 LTR 206; (1914-15) 59 SJ 57; (1914-15) XXXI TLR 44; (1914) WN (I) 400 CA Public Authorities Protection Act 1893 limitation period deemed inapplicable to instant action against public authority for negligence.

Myers v Bradford Corporation (1914) 78 JP 177; (1914) 110 LTR 254; (1913-14) XXX TLR 181 HC KBD Equally divided court as to whether Public Authorities Protection Act 1893 limitation period applicable to instant action.

Nash and others v Eli Lilly and Co and others; Berger and others v Eli Lilly and Co and others [1993] 4 All ER 383; [1993] 1 WLR 782 CA Date of action runs from date of knowledge of injury which is when victim did or could reasonably know of injury by himself or with reasonably obtainable medical advice; delay by plaintiff to confirm suspicion delays running of time.

National Westminster Bank plc v Powney and others [1990] 2 All ER 416 CA Application for leave to execute judgment not an action.

Navarro v Larrinaga Steamship Company Ltd; The Niceto de Larrinaga (1965) 109 SJ 633; [1965] 3 WLR 573 HC PDAD Two year limitation on fatal accident claims under Maritime Conventions Act 1911 inapplicable to vessel in which travelling when cause of claim arose.

Newton v Cammell Laird and Co (Shipbuilders and Engineers) Ltd (1969) 119 NLJ 105t; (1969) 113 SJ 89; [1969] 1 WLR 415 CA Decisive material facts outside deceased's knowledge where could not through dying illness meet with lawyer to discuss former employer's liability: limitation therefore ran from date of death.

Newton v Cammell Laird Ltd (1969) 119 NLJ 273t Assizes Decisive material facts outside deceased's knowledge: limitation therefore ran from date of death.

Nitrigin Eireann Teoranta and another v Inco Alloys Ltd and another [1992] 1 All ER 854; (1991) 135 SJ LB 213; [1991] TLR 489; [1992] 1 WLR 498 HC QBD Cause of action arises in negligence not when economic loss occurs but when when physical damage occurs on foot of negligence.

Oyston v Blaker and others [1996] 2 All ER 106; [1995] TLR 590; [1996] 1 WLR 1326 CA Leave to extend limitation period for defamation may not be granted ex parte.

Parker v London County Council (1904) 68 JP 239; [1904] 2 KB 501; [1904] 73 LJCL 561; (1904) XC LTR 415; (1903-04) XX TLR 271; (1903-04) 52 WR 476 HC KBD Special public authority limitation period under Public Authorities Protection Act 1893 applies to county council as tramway owner.

Parsons v FW Woolworth and Co Ltd [1980] 3 All ER 456; (1980) 124 SJ 775 HC QBD Issuing of draft case to parties within 21 days is discretionary and court may hear case where violated.

Peco Arts Inc v Hazlitt Gallery Ltd [1983] 3 All ER 193; (1983) 133 NLJ 682; (1983) 127 SJ 806; [1983] 1 WLR 1315 HC QBD 'Reasonable diligence' depends on facts of case.

Penrose v Mansfield (1970) 120 NLJ 944t HC QBD Failed claim that state of mind following accident caused by another's negligence should have led to limitation period being prolonged.

Penrose v Mansfield (1971) 121 NLJ 249t; (1971) 115 SJ 309 CA Failed claim that state of mind following accident caused by another's negligence should have led to limitation period being prolonged.

Phillips-Higgins v Harper [1954] 2 All ER 51; [1954] 2 WLR 117 CA On when limitation runs where action concerns mistake in contract.

Phillips-Higgins v Harper [1954] 2 WLR 782 CA Affirmation of Phillips-Higgins v Harper (CA).

Phillips-Higgins v Harper [1954] 1 QB 411; (1954) 98 SJ 45 HC QBD On when limitation runs where action concerns mistake in contract.

Pickles v National Coal Board (Intended Action) [1968] 2 All ER 598; [1968] 1 WLR 997 CA Limitation disapplied where all reasonable advice sought.

Pirelli General Cable Works Ltd v Oscar Faber and Partners [1983] 1 All ER 65; [1983] 2 AC 1; (1983) 133 NLJ 63; (1983) 127 SJ 16; [1982] TLR 623; [1983] 2 WLR 6 HL Time runs from date of physical damage in negligent design/workmanship action.

Pirelli General Cable Works Ltd v Oscar Faber and Partners [1982] TLR 54 CA On when limitation period starts to run in negligent design/workmanship action.

Polley v Fordham (1903-04) XX TLR 435 HC KBD Action brought within six months of illegal distress allowed — distress was act complained of not the (quashed) conviction from which distress warrant arose.

Pontin and another v Wood [1961] 3 All ER 992 HC QBD Writ set aside where sought to amend outside limitation period and no special reason justifying disapplication of limitation.

R and H Green and Silley Weir Ltd v British Railways Board [1985] 1 WLR 570 HC ChD Limitation period under indemnity clause ran from when liabilities met not when arose.

R v Bow Street Magistrates' Court, ex parte Paloka [1995] TLR 597 HC QBD Need be no reference to limitation in materials presented as part of extradition request.

R v Bromley Magistrates' Court, ex parte Waitrose Ltd [1980] 3 All ER 464 HC QBD Faulty application within 21 days to state case may be amended within reasonable time.

Ramsden v Lee [1992] 2 All ER 204 CA Court should have regard to all circumstances before disapplying limitation period.

Rath and another v Lawrence (CS) and Partners (a firm) and others (PJ Crook and Co (a firm), third party) [1991] 3 All ER 679 CA Delay in issuing writ not inordinate delay but wilful delay following writ may be.

Razzel v Snowball [1954] 3 All ER 429; (1954) 104 LJ 760; (1954) 98 SJ 787; [1954] 1 WLR 1382 CA Surgeon performing operation did so in execution of National Health Service Act 1946 so covered by Limitation Act 1939, s 2(1).

RB Policies at Lloyd's v Butler [1949] 2 All ER 226; [1950] 1 KB 76; (1949) 99 LJ 373; (1949) LXV TLR 436; (1949) WN (I) 299 HC KBD Time for detinue action ran from date of theft though did not then know thief's identity.

Re an Intended Action Biss v Lewisham Group Hospital Management Committee (1975) 125 NLJ 208t CA Extension of limitation period in negligence action allowed where requirements of Limitation Act 1963, s 7 met.

Re Harper and others v National Coal Board (Intended Action) [1974] 2 All ER 441; [1974] QB 614; (1974) 118 SJ 67; [1974] 2 WLR 775 CA Limitation disapplied where despite all reasonable steps action brought late.

Re S (minors); Dyfed County Council v S [1996] 2 FCR 838; (1995) 139 SJ LB 174; [1995] TLR 390 CA No extension of time to mother of child to appeal against phasing out by local authority of her contact with her children (who were in care).

75

Riches v Director of Public Prosecutions [1973] 2 All ER 935; (1973) 117 SJ 585 CA No presumption that prosecutions initiated by DPP not malicious; court may strike action of defendant who will seek but not succeed in having limitation period disapplied.

Robinson and others v Unicos Property Corporation, Ltd [1962] 2 All ER 24 CA Limitation applied despite amendment to claim as was still same action.

Robinson v Whittle [1980] 3 All ER 459; (1980) 124 SJ 807; [1980] 1 WLR 1476 HC QBD Faulty application within 21 days to state case may be amended anytime before High Court hearing; could not plead defence in respect of killing birds under Protection of Birds Act 1954, s 4(2)(a) where charged with laying poison to kill birds.

Rodriguez v Parker (RJ) (Male) [1966] 3 WLR 546 HC QBD On giving leave for post-limitation period amendment of writs.

Rogers v Exeter and Mid-Devon Hospitals Management Committee (1974) 124 NLJ 1186t; (1975) 119 SJ 86 HC QBD Child taken from mother and placed in cot in another room (where suffered negligently caused injuries) remained in custody of mother.

Ross v English Steel Corporation Limited (1945) 173 LTR 138 HC KBD Preferral of information inside six months of accident was valid.

Ryan v Carr and Marples Ridgeway and Partners Ltd (1971) 115 SJ 206 HC QBD Person who sued another in time, only to discover out of time from particulars that ought to be suing third party had limitation period extended by court.

S v W and another [1995] 3 FCR 649; [1995] 1 FLR 862; [1994] TLR 670 CA Six-year limitation inapplicable to daughter's action in tort against mother for latter's inaction upon discovering father's incest with daughter.

Saxby v Morgan [1997] TLR 242 CA On when limitation period starts to run in personal injury claim.

Seabridge and others v H Cox and Sons (Plant Hire) Ltd and another [1968] 2 WLR 629 CA Extended writ took effect from moment stamped at central office: amendment took place within three years of accident so was valid.

Secretary of State for Foreign and Commonwealth Affairs v Tomlin and others [1990] TLR 758 CA Extended limitation period of thirty years applied to disused embassy building from which Foreign Secretary sought to evict squatters who claimed adverse possession of building.

Secretary of State for the Environment v Essex Goodman and Suggitt (a firm) and others [1986] 2 All ER 69; (1970) 130 SJ 574; [1986] 1 WLR 1432 HC QBD Time runs from date acted on surveyor's report; no action for damage after that date.

Shaw v London County Council; Jacobs v London County Council [1924-35] All ER 696; (1935) 99 JP 10; [1935] 1 KB 67 CA Limitation period does not run for infant until reaches age of twenty-one.

Sheldon and others v RHM Outhwaite (Underwriting Agencies Ltd) and others [1994] 4 All ER 481 (also CA); [1996] 1 AC 102 (also CA/HL); [1993] TLR 632; [1994] 1 WLR 754 HC QBD Limitation period continues to run if concealment of facts post-dates cause of action.

Sheldon and others v RHM Outhwaite (Underwriting Agencies Ltd) and others [1994] 4 All ER 481 (also HC QBD); [1996] 1 AC 102 (also HC QBD/HL); [1994] TLR 359; [1994] 3 WLR 999 CA Limitation period continues to run if concealment of facts post-dates cause of action.

Sheldon and others v RHM Outhwaite (Underwriting Agencies) Ltd and others [1995] 2 All ER 558; [1996] 1 AC 102 (also CA); (1995) 145 NLJ 687; (1995) 139 SJ LB 119; [1995] TLR 258; [1995] 2 WLR 570 HL Concealment of facts postpones time running until concealment was/should have been discovered.

Simpson v Norwest Holst Southern Ltd [1980] 2 All ER 471; (1980) 130 NLJ 391; (1980) 124 SJ 313; [1980] 1 WLR 968 CA Bona fide failure to discover identity of defendant justified disapplying limitation.

Smith v Central Asbestos Co Ltd [Consolidated actions] [1971] 3 All ER 204; (1971) 121 NLJ 500t; [1972] 1 QB 244; [1971] 3 WLR 206 CA Unawareness of extent of injury/right of action could justify disapplying limitation.

Société Commerciale de Réassurance v ERAS (International) Ltd and others; Re ERAS EIL appeals [1992] 2 All ER 82 CA Three year limitation period in latent damage cases applies to purely tortious and not contract-related liability.

Spargo v North Essex District Health Authority (1997) 141 SJ LB 90; [1997] TLR 148 CA Cause of action taken to run from time plaintiff herself believed herself to have been misdiagnosed: action time-barred.

Sparham-Souter and others v Town and Country developments (Essex) Ltd and another [1976] 2 All ER 65; (1976) 126 NLJ 265t; [1976] QB 858; (1976) 120 SJ 216; [1976] 2 WLR 493 CA Cause of action from time building defects discovered/ought to have been discovered.

Sterman v EW and WJ Moore Ltd (a firm) [1970] 1 All ER 581 CA Limit disapplied (where just) to allow amendment of writ.

Stubbings v Webb and another [1991] 3 All ER 949; [1993] 2 FCR 699 (also HL); [1992] 1 FLR 296; [1992] QB 197; [1991] TLR 171; [1991] 3 WLR 383 CA Cause of action for personal injury on foot of sexual abuse ran from date plaintiff realised personal injury attributable to sexual abuse.

Stubbings v Webb and another [1993] 1 All ER 322; [1993] AC 498; [1993] 2 FCR 699 (also CA); [1993] 1 FLR 714; (1993) 143 NLJ 166; (1993) 137 SJ LB 32; [1992] TLR 619; [1993] 2 WLR 120 HL Claim for damages arising from mental ill-health following childhood rape/indecent assault an action for trespass to person and hence subject to six-year limitation period.

Sutherland Publishing Company, Limited v Caxton Publishing Company, Limited [1936] 105 LJCh 150; (1938) 158 LTR 17; (1937-38) LIV TLR 112; (1936) WN (I) 58 CA Six-year limitation on post-breach of copyright conversion action; on gauging damages for such conversion.

Swansea City Council v Glass [1992] 2 All ER 680 CA Cause of action to recover expenses runs from date works completed not date of first demand for payment.

Taylor and others v Taylor [1984] TLR 247 CA On relevant factors when deciding whether or not to disapply time limitation in personal injuries action.

Telfair Shipping Corporation v Insersea Carriers SA [1985] 1 WLR 553 HC QBD Claim under indemnity clause over/under six years after stowage/discharge was statute-barred.

Tew (Yew Bon) alias Tiew (Yong Boon) and another v Mara (Kenderaan Bas) [1983] 1 AC 553; (1982) 126 SJ 729; [1982] TLR 458; [1982] 3 WLR 1026 PC Enactment of special limitation period for public authorities (could but) did not operate retroactively to defeat limitation plea benefitting defendants.

Thomas v Plaistow [1997] TLR 280 CA 'Disability' in the Limitation Act 1980, s 33(3)(d) meant that were minor/mentally imbalanced.

Thompson v Brown and another (1981) 131 NLJ 524; (1981) 125 SJ 377; [1981] 1 WLR 744 HL On allowing extension to claim where if was not allowed plaintff would have guaranteed claim of success against solicitors.

Thompson v Brown Construction (Ebbw Vale) Ltd and others [1981] 2 All ER 296 HL Potential negligence claim against solicitor not ground for refusing to disapply limitation in personal injury/fatal accident action.

Thompson v Edmeads (1978) 128 NLJ 514b CA Valid disregard of three year limitation in personal injuries action where source of delay was negligence on part of plaintiff's solicitors.

Todd (by his next best friend Anne Todd) v Davison [1971] 1 All ER 449; (1971) 115 SJ 144; [1971] 1 WLR 267 Assizes Infant's right of action expires if reasonable parents would have brought action.

Tolley v Morris [1979] 1 All ER 71; (1978) 128 NLJ 712t; (1978) 122 SJ 436; [1979] 1 WLR 205 CA Court would not dismiss for inaction suit of infant plaintiff brought in extended limitation period.

Tolley v Morris (1979) 129 (1) NLJ 518; (1979) 123 SJ 353; [1979] 1 WLR 592 HL Non-dismissal for inaction of suit of infant plaintiff brought in extended limitation period.

Treolar v Nute [1977] 1 All ER 230 CA Time runs from date of possession even if owner not put out by possession.

Turner v Ford Motor Co, Ltd and another [1965] 2 All ER 583; (1965) 115 LJ 448; (1965) 109 SJ 354; [1965] 1 WLR 948 CA Defendant allowed amend claim to allege negligence of plaintiff in not protecting self with equipment given by employers though plaintiff time-barred from claim against employers upon amendment.

UBAF Ltd v European American Banking Corp [1984] 2 All ER 226; [1984] QB 713; (1984) 128 SJ 243; [1984] 2 WLR 508 CA Cause of action following entry into contract on foot of fraudulent misrepresentation might run from later date than that of entry into contract.

Venn v Tedesco (1926) 90 JP 185; [1926] 2 KB 227; [1926] 95 LJCL 866; (1926) 135 LTR 108; (1925-26) 70 SJ 709; (1925-26) XLII TLR 478 HC KBD In action under Lord Campbell's Act 1846 limitation period against public authorities is limitation prescribed in that Act.

Walford and others v Richards (1975) 125 NLJ 1023t CA Limitation period disapplied in light of plaintiff's unawareness of material fact of decisive nature.

Walkin v South Manchester Health Authority [1995] 4 All ER 132; [1995] TLR 380; [1995] 1 WLR 1543 CA Limitation period on claims for physical injury or economic loss arising from unwanted pregnancy after failed sterilisation runs from date of personal injury i.e., date of conception.

Walkley v Precision Forgings Ltd [1979] 2 All ER 548; (1979) 129 (1) NLJ 520; (1979) 123 SJ 354; [1979] 1 WLR 606 HL Courts will rarely disapply limitation to enable second action where earlier action begun in time but allowed lapse.

Walkley v Precision Forgings Ltd [1979] 1 All ER 102; [1978] 1 WLR 1228 CA Plaintiff may ask for disapplication of limitation period in respect of second action even if first dismissed for want of prosecution.

Walter v Yalden [1902] 2 KB 304 HC KBD Lease to expire before limitation ran/lessor could enter property on which trespasser with Statute of Limitations title against lessee.

Weait and another v Jayanbee Joinery, Ltd [1962] 2 All ER 568 CA Can amend defence to show not liable if evidence so showing first emerges after limitation.

Welsh Development Agency v Redpath Dorman Long Ltd [1994] 4 All ER 10; (1994) 138 SJ LB 87; [1994] TLR 190; [1994] 1 WLR 1409 CA Leave to amend unavailable after time limit on claim expires even if application for leave made before expiry; leave to amend by adding new claim not to be given unless defendant has not reasonably arguable case on limitation.

Wilkinson v Ancliff (BLT) Ltd [1986] 3 All ER 427; (1970) 130 SJ 766; [1986] 1 WLR 1352 CA Limitation runs from date victim can with expert advice attribute injury to act/omission.

LIMITATION (statutory authority)

Marriage v East Norfolk Rivers Catchment Board [1949] 2 All ER 50; (1949) 113 JP 362; (1949) LXV TLR 456 HC KBD Action against local authority barred as not brought within one year of cause.

Marriage v East Norfolk Rivers Catchment Board (1950) 114 JP 38 CA Cannot bring action in nuisance for interference with one's rights by statutory authority empowered by statute (which also provides for compensation) to do various works.

LOSS OF CONSORTIUM (general)

Best v Samuel Fox and Co, Ltd [1952] 2 All ER 394; [1952] AC 716; (1952) 102 LJ 415; (1952) 96 SJ 494; [1952] 2 TLR 246; (1952) WN (I) 382 HL Wife cannot seek damages from tortfeasor for loss of husband's consortium.

MALICIOUS ISSUE OF CIVIL PROCESS (general)

Corbett v Burge, Warren and Ridgley, Limited (1931-32) XLVIII TLR 626 HC KBD Failed action in tort for malicious issue of civil process (no malice proven).

MALICIOUS PROSECUTION (damages)

Thompson v Commissioner of Police of the Metropolis; Hsu v Same [1997] 2 Cr App R (S) 341; (1997) 147 NLJ 341; [1997] TLR 84; [1997] 3 WLR 403 CA On awarding of damages in false imprisonment/malicious prosecution action.

MALICIOUS PROSECUTION (general)

Abbott v Refuge Assurance Co, Ltd [1961] 3 All ER 1074; (1961) 111 LJ 836; [1962] 1 QB 432; (1961) 105 SJ 949 CA Desire to recover defrauded money not evidence of malice; prosecuting counsel owe court duty to withdraw baseless cases: that did not showed not malicious; all circumstances including counsel's opinion on taking action showed not malicious prosecution.

Amin (Mohamed) v Bannerjee (Jogendra Kumar) and Others [1947] AC 322; [1947] 116 LJR 963; (1947) 177 LTR 451; (1947) LXIII TLR 433 PC Simply bringing false complaint not malicious prosecution: test whether prosecution malicious is whether action has reached stage that injury done.

Berry v British Transport Commission [1960] 3 All ER 322; (1960) 110 LJ 654; [1961] 1 QB 149; (1960) 104 SJ 826 HC QBD On injury to fair fame as element of malicious prosecution.

Berry v British Transport Commission [1961] 3 All ER 65; [1955] Crim LR 587; (1961) 111 LJ 548; [1962] 1 QB 306 CA Valid malicious prosecution claim where special damages sought are real costs (less costs awarded by quarter sessions).

Bishop v Metropolitan Police Commissioner and others (1989) 133 SJ 1626 CA Plaintiff's conduct relevant to setting exemplary damages payable by defendant guilty of malicious prosecution.

Blaker v Weller [1964] Crim LR 311t HC QBD Successful action against police for false imprisonment/malicious prosecution.

Bostock v Ramsey Urban District Council (1899-1900) XVI TLR 18 HC QBD Not malicious prosecution to bring proceedings for obstruction of highway by employee against employer.

Bradshaw v Waterlow and Sons Limited [1914-17] All ER 36; [1915] 3 KB 527; [1916] 85 LJKB 318; (1915-16) 113 LTR 1101; (1914-15) XXXI TLR 556; (1915) WN (I) 292 CA No want of reasonable and probable cause found.

Corea v Peiris [1909] AC 549; [1910] 79 LJPC 25; (1909) 100 LTR 790; (1908-09) XXV TLR 631 PC Failure of prosecution does not per se mean brought with malice.

Cornford v Carlton Bank, Limited (1899-1900) LXXXI LTR 415; [1900] 1 QB 22; (1899-1900) XVI TLR 12 CA Corporation can be sued for malicious prosecution.

Cox v English, Scottish and Australian Bank [1904-07] All ER 1624; [1905] AC 168; [1905] 74 LJPC 62; (1905) XCII LTR 483 PC Whether reasonable and probable cause a matter for judge.

Dallison v Caffery [1964] Crim LR 538; (1964) 128 JP 379; [1965] 1 QB 348; (1964) 108 SJ 560; [1964] 3 WLR 385 CA No false imprisonment where policeman held reasonable belief detainee had committed offence and reasonable grounds for delaying release; not malicious prosecution as had been reasonable cause for same.

Evans v London Hospital Medical College and others [1981] 1 All ER 715; (1981) 131 NLJ 291 HC QBD Immunity from action for conduct/statement part of (albeit preceding) action.

Everett v Ribbands and another [1951] 2 All ER 818; (1951) 115 JP 582; [1952] 1 KB 113; (1951) 101 LJ 609; (1951) 95 SJ 698; [1951] 2 TLR 829; (1951) WN (I) 554 HC KBD Cannot sue for false imprisonment after binding over order in respect of one.

Everett v Ribbands and another [1952] 1 All ER 823; (1952) 116 JP 221; [1952] 2 QB 198; (1952) 96 SJ 229; [1952] 1 TLR 933; (1952) WN (I) 166 CA Where case could have gone either way is not malicious prosecution.

Ex parte Glick (1967) 111 SJ 982 CA Failed action for malicious prosecution where defendant in action from which malicious prosecution action sprang (plaintiff in instant case) had been unsuccessful.

Glinski v McIver [1959] Crim LR 56t HC QBD Successful action against police officer for malicious prosecution.

Glinski v McIver [1960] Crim LR 428t CA Successful appeal against finding that police officer undertook malicious prosecution: was reasonable and probable cause for prosecution.

Glinski v McIver [1962] 1 All ER 696; [1962] Crim LR 392t; [1962] AC 726; (1962) 112 LJ 220; (1962) 106 SJ 261 HL Whether honest belief in guilt an issue only if doubt; defendant's task in prosecution engendering action was whether reasonable/probable basis for prosecution; if no such basis may be malice but not vice versa.

Green v De Havilland and another (1968) 112 SJ 766 HC QBD On rôle of jury in malicious prosecution action.

Herniman v Smith [1936] 2 All ER 1377 CA On reasonable/probable cause for prosecution.

Herniman v Smith [1938] 1 All ER 1; [1938] AC 305; [1938] 107 LJCL 225; (1938) 82 SJ 192 HL Reasonable and probable cause (a matter for judge) present so no malicious prosecution.

Leibo v D Buckman, Ltd and another [1952] 2 All ER 1057; (1952) 96 SJ 865; [1952] 2 TLR 969; (1952) WN (I) 547 CA Unless reasonable and probable cause is malicious prosecution.

Malz v Rosen [1966] 2 All ER 10; (1965-66) 116 NLJ 753; (1966) 110 SJ 332; [1966] 1 WLR 1008 HC QBD Not malicious prosecution if acting on advice of responsible police officer.

Martin v Watson [1994] 2 All ER 606; (1994) 144 NLJ 463; [1994] QB 425; (1994) 138 SJ LB 55; [1994] TLR 45; [1994] 2 WLR 500 CA That a defendant is not technically the prosecutor precludes finding of malicious prosecution where a prosecution undertaken was a natural and intended consequence of false and malicious actions by defendant.

Martin v Watson [1995] 3 All ER 559; [1996] 1 AC 74; (1995) 145 NLJ 1093; (1995) 139 SJ LB 190; [1995] TLR 408; [1995] 3 WLR 318 HL That a defendant is not technically the prosecutor does not preclude a finding of malicious prosecution where a prosecution undertaken was a natural and intended consequence of false and malicious actions by defendant.

Owen v Lavery (1899-1900) XVI TLR 375 CA Bringing bankruptcy proceedings from ulterior motive different to that envisaged by bankruptcy legislation was malicious prosecution.

Riches v Director of Public Prosecutions [1973] 2 All ER 935; (1973) 117 SJ 585 CA No presumption that prosecutions initiated by DPP not malicious; court may strike action of defendant who will seek but not succeed in having limitation period disapplied.

Sam v Cluney [1956] Crim LR 271t HC QBD Damages for malicious prosecution by police officers whom jury found not to have seen defendant engaged in grossly indecent behaviour in public toilets.

Sherbourne v Walker [1955] Crim LR 184 HC QBD Successful action for damages against policeman guilty of assault/wrongful imprisonment/malicious prosecution.

Stapeley v Annetts and another [1969] 3 All ER 1541; [1970] 1 WLR 20 CA Plaintiff must show malice and no reasonable cause.

Taylor v Anderton (Police Complaints Authority intervening) [1995] 2 All ER 420; (1995) 139 SJ LB 66; [1995] 1 WLR 447 CA Where malicious prosecution allegation met by heavily documented defence trial without jury allowed.

Tempest v Snowden [1952] 1 All ER 1; (1952) 116 JP 28; [1952] 1 KB 130; (1951) 101 LJ 706; (1951) 95 SJ 817; [1951] 2 TLR 1201; (1951) WN (I) 614 CA Whether honest belief in guilt/charge is question to be put to jury.

Tewari (Pandit Gaya Parshad) v Sing (Sardar Bhagat) and another (1907-08) XXIV TLR 884 PC On necessary elements of malicious prosecution.

Thompson v Commissioner of Police of the Metropolis; Hsu v Same [1997] 2 Cr App R (S) 341; (1997) 147 NLJ 341; [1997] TLR 84; [1997] 3 WLR 403 CA On awarding of damages in false imprisonment/malicious prosecution action.

Wiffen v Bailey and others [1914-15] All ER 967; (1915) 79 JP 145; [1915] 1 KB 600; (1914) 49 LJ 674; [1915] 84 LJKB 688; (1914-15) 59 SJ 176; (1914-15) XXXI TLR 64; (1914) WN (I) 434 CA Malicious prosecution action failed where could not show damage to fame; imperiling of life/limb/liberty; financial loss.

Wiffen v Bailey and Romford Urban District Council (1914) 78 JP 187; [1914] 2 KB 5; (1914) 49 LJ 64; [1914] 83 LJKB 791; (1914) 110 LTR 694; (1914) WN (I) 25 HC KBD Can sue for malicious prosecution of action for non-compliance with nuisance abatement notice.

Wright v Sharp (1947) 176 LTR 308 HC KBD Failed action for false imprisonment/malicious prosecution following taxi-driver's arrest/failed prosecution after taxi had been hired for robbery.

MALICIOUS PROSECUTION (police)

White and another v Metropolitan Police Commissioner [1982] TLR 221 HC QBD Exemplary damages from Police Commissioner for false imprisonment/assault/malicious prosecution by police officers.

MILITARY (general)

Heddon v Evans (1918-19) XXXV TLR 642 HC KBD On tortious liability of military officer for his actions.

MISFEASANCE IN PUBLIC OFFICE (general)

Bennett v Commissioner of Police of the Metropolis [1994] TLR 678; [1995] 1 WLR 488 HC ChD Must be actual malice for person to be guilty of tort of misfeasance in public office; Minister does not owe duty of care towards person seeking discovery of documents in respect of which Minister claiming privilege.

Bourgoin SA and others v Ministry of Agriculture, Fisheries and Food [1984] TLR 542 HC QBD On ingredients of tort of misfeasance in public office.

Bourgoin SA and others v Ministry of Agriculture, Fisheries and Food [1986] QB 716; [1985] 3 WLR 1027 CA Was misfeasance in public office/was not innominate tort for Minister to restrict intra-European Community trade on spurious health grounds.

Calveley and others v Chief Constable of the Merseyside Police and other appeals [1989] 1 All ER 1025; [1989] AC 1228; (1989) 139 NLJ 469; (1989) 133 SJ 456; [1989] 2 WLR 624 HL Misfeasance in public office requires that public officer performs act in bad faith/without reasonable cause in respect of which his office shields him.

Calveley and others v Chief Constable of the Merseyside Police; Worrall and others v Same; Park v Chief Constable of the Greater Manchester Police (1988) 138 NLJ 267; [1989] QB 136; (1988) 132 SJ 1244; [1988] 3 WLR 1020 CA No common law duty of care owed by investigating officer (in disciplinary action against police officers) towards officers being investigated.

Elliott v Chief Constable of Wiltshire and others (1996) TLR 5/12/96 HC ChD Could bring action against police officer for misfeance in public office where officer had revealed criminal past of person seeking relief with intent of injuring same.

Jones v Swansea City Council (1989) 139 NLJ 503; (1990) 134 SJ 341; [1990] 1 WLR 54 CA Could be misfeasance in public office for council to refuse change of user of leasehold premises because of ill-will towards lessee's husband, a member of a minority political party on the local authority.

Jones v Swansea City Council (1990) 134 SJ 1437; [1990] 1 WLR 1453 HL Not proven to be misfeasance in public office where council refused change of user of leasehold premises to lessee whose husband was a member of a minority political party on the local authority.

Racz v Home Office [1992] TLR 559 HC QBD Home Office not vicariously liable for misfeasance in public office by prison officers acting outside scope of employment.

Racz v Home Office [1992] TLR 624 CA Home Office not vicariously liable for misfeasance in public office by prison officers acting outside scope of employment.

Racz v Home Office [1994] 1 All ER 97; [1994] 2 AC 45; (1994) 144 NLJ 89; (1994) 138 SJ LB 12; [1993] TLR 660; [1994] 2 WLR 23 HL Home Office vicariously liable for misfeasance in public office by prison officers; that a tort similar to libel, slander, malicious prosecution or false imprisonment irrelevant to determining if presumption against jury trial applies.

Three Rivers District Council and others v Bank of England (No 3) [1996] 3 All ER 558; (1996) TLR 22/4/96 HC QBD On elements of tort of misfeasance in public office (in context of action against Bank of England for alleged misfeasance either in granting/not revoking licence of failed deposit-taking body).

MISREPRESENTATION (general)

Banque Financiére de la Cité SA v Westgate Insurance Co Ltd [1989] 2 All ER 952 CA Failure to fully disclose in contract of utmost good faith not a misrepresentation of full disclosure. Way economic loss suffered by third party need not be foreseeable to be recoverable.

Barclays Bank plc v O'Brien and another [1994] 1 AC 180; [1994] 1 FCR 357; [1994] 1 FLR 1; (1993) 143 NLJ 1511; [1993] TLR 519; [1993] 3 WLR 786 HL Mortgage not enforceable against wife as bank did not take due care to ensure she understood arrangement into which was entering (and here she had been deceived by husband as to effect of arrangement).

Briess and others v Woolley and others [1954] AC 333; [1954] 2 WLR 832 HL Shareholders vicariously liable for fraudulent misrepresentation of agent whom they appointed to sell their shares.

Cremdean Properties Ltd and another v Nash and others (1977) 127 NLJ 940 HC ChD On validity of exclusion clause in light of alleged false representations.

Cremdean Properties Ltd et anor v Nash et al (1978) 128 NLJ 514c CA Failed appeal against finding that exclusion clause in tender that particulars therein might not be (as were not in fact) entirely correct.

Edwards v Taylor (1922-23) 67 SJ 248 HC KBD Husband not liable where wife fraudulently represents that she is authorised to act for him.

Exploring Land and Minerals Company Limited v Kolckmann (1906) XCIV LTR 234 CA On damages available to company from company director for loss suffered by company on foot of its acting on false representation by defendant director.

Gran Gelato Ltd v Richcliff (Group) Ltd and others [1992] 1 All ER 865; [1992] Ch 560; (1992) 142 NLJ 51; [1992] 2 WLR 867 HC ChD Normally conveyancing solicitor for seller does not owe duty to buyer because action already lies against seller; in concurrent claims for negligence/misrepresentation contributory negligence can apply to both claims.

Gross v Lewis Hillman Ltd and another [1969] 3 WLR 787 CA Misrepresentation only fraudulent if intended to be so.

Howard Marine and Dredging Co Ltd v A Ogden and Sons (Excavations) Ltd [1978] 2 All ER 1134; [1978] QB 574; (1978) 122 SJ 48; [1978] 2 WLR 515 CA Misrepresentation acted upon actionable unless misrepresentor has reasonable belief statement true; barge owners/charterers under duty of care when giving advice on specialist matter.

Hussey and another v Eels and another [1990] 1 All ER 449; (1990) 140 NLJ 53 CA Profits made through resale of defective property after negligent misrepresentation not to be set off against damages for latter unless various steps part of a single transaction.

Jewelowski v Propp [1944] 1 All ER 483; (1944) 171 LTR 234; (1943-44) LX TLR 559 HC KBD No duty to mitigate damages in fraudulent misrepresentation action.

Kings North Trust Ltd v Bell and others [1985] FLR 948; [1986] 1 WLR 119 CA Non-enforcement on behalf of principals of mortgage deed signed pursuant to fraudulent misrepresentation by their agent.

Laurence and another v Lexcourt Holdings Ltd [1978] 2 All ER 810; [1978] 1 WLR 1128 HC ChD Common mistake/misrepresentation where incorrectly state premises have unrestricted planning permission for office use; reasonable delay/inaction not acquiesence.

Molloy v The Mutual Reserve Life Insurance Company (1906) XCIV LTR 756; (1905-06) XXII TLR 525 CA Action to recover money paid out on foot of misrepresentation defeated by Statute of Limitations.

Moorgate Mercantile Co Ltd v Twitchings [1976] 2 All ER 641; [1977] AC 890; [1976] QB 225; [1976] RTR 437; (1976) 120 SJ 470; [1976] 3 WLR 66 HL Statement that records indicate certain state not representation that state exists; no duty of care so no estoppel by negligence.

UBAF Ltd v European American Banking Corp [1984] 2 All ER 226; [1984] QB 713; (1984) 128 SJ 243; [1984] 2 WLR 508 CA Cause of action following entry into contract on foot of fraudulent misrepresentation might run from later date than that of entry into contract.

NEGLIGENCE (accountant)

Candler v Crane, Christmas and Co [1951] 1 All ER 426; [1951] 2 KB 164; (1951) 95 SJ 171; [1951] 1 TLR 371; (1951) WN (I) 113 CA Absent contractual/fiduciary relationship accountant did not owe duty of care to third party.

Fox and Son v Morrish, Grant, and Co (1918-19) 63 SJ 193; (1918-19) XXXV TLR 126 HC KBD Accountant owes duty of care to check cash and bank balances where is retained to check account books.

Henry Squire, Cash Chemist, Limited v Ball, Baker and Co; Mead v Ball, Baker, and Co (1912) 106 LTR 197; (1911-12) XXVIII TLR 81 CA Failed action against auditor for negligence: on duty of care owed by auditor.

Mutual Reinsurance Co Ltd v Peat Marwick Mitchell and Co and another (1996) TLR 15/10/96 CA Accountants appointed as company auditors pursuant to Bermudan law/company bylaws could not later be sued for negligence by the company.

NEGLIGENCE (allurement)

Cooke v Midland Great Western Railway of Ireland [1908-10] All ER 16; [1909] AC 229; [1909] 78 LJPC 76; (1909) C LTR 626; (1908-09) 53 SJ 319; (1908-09) XXV TLR 375; (1909) WN (I) 56 HL Liable in negligence for injury to child through allurement.

Culkin v McFie and Sons, Ltd [1939] 3 All ER 613; (1939) 88 LJ 86 HC KBD Lorry carrying leaking sugar bags an allurement to/concealed danger for children.

Cuttress and others v Scaffolding (Great Britain) Ltd and others [1953] 1 All ER 165 Assizes Liable for not taking steps to prevent foreseeable occurrence of children interfering with and being injured by scaffolding.

Cuttress and others v Scaffolding (Great Britain), Ltd and others [1953] 2 All ER 1075; (1953) 97 SJ 741; [1953] 1 WLR 1311 CA Not liable for negligence where children injured by pulling down scaffolding as was safely constructed and events that occurred not reasonably foreseeable.

Donovan v Union Cartage Co, Ltd [1932] All ER 273; [1933] 2 KB 71; (1933) 102 LJCL 270; (1933) 148 LTR 333; (1933) 77 SJ 30; (1932-33) XLIX TLR 125 HC KBD Strict duty of care on owner of unattended vehicle which is allurement to children only if vehicle is dangerous per se.

Dyer v Ilfracombe Urban District Council [1956] 1 All ER 581; (1956) 120 JP 220; (1956) 100 SJ 169; [1956] 1 WLR 218 CA Licensor not liable for allurement not concealing hidden danger.

Glasgow Corporation v Taylor [1921] All ER 1 HL Public authority negligent in allowing children into public playground where knew poisonous berries to be growing.

Gosling v Islington Corporation [1938] LJNCCR 427 CyCt Sand bin by highway was an allurement/trap and defendants were negligent in not making sure that bin was kept locked.

Gough v National Coal Board [1953] 2 All ER 1283; [1954] 1 QB 191; (1953) 97 SJ 811; [1953] 3 WLR 900 CA Child playing on land a licensee under general licence — not trespasser just because did something not supposed to do; slow-moving trucks an allurement; licensor negligently failed to take reasonable care to protect child.

Latham v Richard Johnson and Nephew, Ltd [1911-13] All ER 117; (1913) 77 JP 137; [1913] 1 KB 398; (1912) 47 LJ 748; [1913] 82 LJKB 258; (1913) 108 LTR 4; (1912-13) 57 SJ 127; (1912-13) XXIX TLR 124; (1912) WN (I) 290 CA Occupier of land on which stones owed no special duty of care to children playing thereon — implied term in licence that children to be accompanied by adults.

Morley v Staffordshire County Council [1939] 4 All ER 93; (1939) 83 SJ 848 CA Allurement did not make liable for injury caused by obvious danger.

Shiffman v The Grand Priory in the British Realm of the Venerable Order of the Hospital of St John of Jerusalem [1936] 1 All ER 557; (1936) 80 SJ 346 HC KBD Negligent for non-continuous attention to flagpole (occasioning injury to child allured thereby) erected in public place.

NEGLIGENCE (animal)

Aldham v United Dairies (London), Ltd [1939] 4 All ER 522; [1940] 1 KB 507; (1939) 88 LJ 351; [1940] 109 LJCL 323; (1940) 162 LTR 71; (1940) 84 SJ 43; (1940) WN (I) 14 HC KBD Was negligent to leave milk-cart horse unattended in highway for half-hour.

Aldham v United Dairies (London), Ltd [1939] 3 All ER 478; (1939) 88 LJ 47; (1939) 83 SJ 674; (1939-40) LVI TLR 201 HC KBD Non-recovery for attack by horse negligently left unattended as injury not reasonably to be expected.

Allford v Maton [1936] LJNCCR 167 CyCt Person who had cattle driven down road several times each day liable for damage occasioned by cattle to another's hedge as did not exercise user of highway reasonably.

Andrews v Hendley (1914) CC Rep III 54 CyCt Person harbouring dog which bit another while not being properly kept under restraint was liable for personal injuries sustained by person bitten.

Andrews v Watts and another [1971] RTR 484 HC QBD Cattle owner who did not provide adequate lighting (two-thirds) liable and driver who did not slow down when signalled to do so (one-third) liable for collision with cattle herd on nighttime road.

Bainbridge v Marsay [1937] LJNCCR 218 CyCt Successful action in negligence where cow had been negligently driven onto road into path of oncoming motor cycle.

Barnes v Lucile (Limited) (1906-07) XXIII TLR 389 HC KBD Owner of dog liable for injuries it causes by biting where knows dog to be even occasionally vicious towards humans.

Barton v Ruislip Dog Sanatorium (Limited) (1916-17) XXXIII TLR 458 HC KBD Exception clause meant dogs' home owner not liable in negligence for illness and death of dog lodged there.

Bativala and another v West (1969) 119 NLJ 974t; [1970] 1 QB 716; (1969) 113 SJ 856; [1970] 2 WLR 8 HC QBD Horse-owner liable in negligence for damage caused by straying horse where ought to have known how horse would react to particular situation/sought to prevent it.

Beer v Wheeler (1965) 109 SJ 133 HC QBD Experienced bull-manager ought to have been instructed as to all steps in new bull-keeping procedure but in light of experience was half-liable for accident.

Beer v Wheeler (1965) 109 SJ 457 CA Experienced bull-manager did not have to be instructed in all steps in new bull-keeping procedure.

Behrens and another v Bertram Mills Circus, Ltd [1957] 1 All ER 583; (1957) 107 LJ 250; [1957] 2 QB 1; (1957) 101 SJ 208; [1957] 2 WLR 404 HC QBD Elephants are ferae naturae: absolute duty to keep/control; hiring of booth near circus not volenti non fit injuria; damages for loss of earnings/nervous shock.

Benning v Fox (1925) 60 LJ 1055 CyCt Sane, heroic act to remove danger to public safety caused by another's negligence was not contributory negligence disentitling hero of relief in damages.

Brackenborough v Spalding Urban District Council [1940] 1 All ER 384; (1940) 104 JP 154; [1940] 1 KB 675; (1940) 89 LJ 81; [1940] 109 LJCL 338; (1940) 84 SJ 287 CA Animal never left farmer's control so cattle market pen providers not liable for escape.

Brock v Richards [1951] 1 KB 529; (1951) 95 SJ 75; [1951] 1 TLR 69; (1951) WN (I) 22 CA Not negligent to allow non-vicious horse which had tendency to wander but posed no particular threat to stray onto highway.

Bros (Pinker) v Day (1929) 68 LJ ccr52 CyCt Domestic horse-owner not liable for damage occasioned by horse after strayed (by way of defective fence) onto highway.

Brown-Thomson v Harrods Limited (1924-25) 69 SJ 710 HC KBD Though store-owners may have been prima facie negligent in allowing dogs to be chained at store entrance, person bitten by dog at entrance might nonetheless be contributorily negligent.

Catchpole v Minster (1913) CC Rep II 113; (1913-14) 109 LTR 953; (1913-14) XXX TLR 111 HC KBD Nighttime driving of sheep on highway not per se negligent.

Clinton v J Lyons and Co, Ltd [1911-13] All ER 577; [1912] 3 KB 198; (1912) 81 LJKB 923; (1912) 106 LTR 988; (1911-12) XXVIII TLR 462 HC KBD No liability for injuries caused by cat unnaturally vicious because had kittens.

Cutter v United Dairies (London) Ltd [1933] All ER 594; [1933] 2 KB 297; (1933) 76 LJ 56; (1933) 102 LJCL 663; (1933) 149 LTR 436; (1933) WN (I) 166 CA On liability for acts of (here tame) animal.

De Jong v London and North Western Railway (1914) CC Rep III 13 CyCt Good case for negligence where entrust livestock to rail company and are delivered in damaged condition following delay/where is evidence that inadequate care taken of livestock.

Deen v Davies [1935] All ER 9; [1935] 2 KB 282; [1935] LJNCCA 202; (1935) 153 LTR 90; (1935) 79 SJ 381; (1934-35) LI TLR 398 CA Recovery for natural and probable injuries occasioned upon negliegntly tethered horse escaping.

Draper and another v Hodder [1972] 2 All ER 210; (1972) 122 NLJ 128t; [1972] 2 QB 556; (1972) 116 SJ 178; [1972] 2 WLR 992 CA Can be liable in negligence for reasonably foreseeable injury caused by tame animal.

Ellis v Banyard (1911) 104 LTR 460; (1910-11) 55 SJ 500; (1910-11) XXVII TLR 417 HC KBD
Where field gate open and escaping cattle caused injury to passer-by owner (one judge) was
negligent, victim (other judge) still had to prove negligence of owner.

Ellis v Banyard [1911-13] All ER 303; (1912) 106 LTR 51; (1911-12) 56 SJ 139; (1911-12) XXVIII
TLR 122 CA No duty to fence in cattle (tame animals) — and even if was duty no recovery as
no negligence shown.

Ellis v Johnstone [1963] 1 All ER 286; (1963) 113 LJ 120; [1963] 2 QB 8; (1962) 106 SJ 1030;
[1963] 2 WLR 176 CA No customary/special duty on dog owner to prevent dog straying onto
highway.

Fardon v Harcourt-Rivington (1930-31) XLVII TLR 25 CA Owner not negligent where non-vicious
dog smashed car window from inside injuring pedestrian.

Fardon v Harcourt-Rivington [1932] All ER 81; (1932) 146 LTR 391; (1932) 76 SJ 81; (1931-32)
XLVIII TLR 215 HL Owner not negligent where non-vicious dog smashed car window from
inside injuring pedestrian.

Fitzgerald v Cooke Bourne (ED and AD) (Farms), Ltd and another [1963] 3 All ER 36; (1963)
113 LJ 560; [1964] 1 QB 249; (1963) 107 SJ 459; [1963] 3 WLR 522 CA Animal owner grazing
animals on land across/beside which is public highway not liable for acts done by animals natural
to such animals.

Gayler and Pope, Ltd v B Davies and Son, Ltd [1924] All ER 94; [1924] 2 KB 75; (1924) 59 LJ
282; [1924] 93 LJCL 702; (1924) 131 LTR 507; (1923-24) 68 SJ 685; (1923-24) XL TLR 591;
(1924) WN (I) 158 HC KBD Owner liable for damage by stray horse where was negligent — not
for trespass of horse per se.

Glanville v Sutton and Co [1928] 1 KB 571; (1927) 64 LJ 455; (1928) 97 LJCL 166; (1928) 138
LTR 336; (1927) WN (I) 311 HC KBD That owner knew horse bit horses did not show owner
knew horse would bite humans.

Glazier v Rowlands [1940] LJNCCR 274 CyCt Failed action in negligence against owner of horse
which strayed by way of broken fence onto highway and there occasioned damage by behaving in
uncustomarily wild manner.

Glover v Robertson (1911-13) XXII Cox CC 692; (1912) 76 JP 135 HC KBD Non-liability for
importation of sheep to England from Middle East via Marseilles.

Gomberg v Smith [1962] 1 All ER 725; (1962) 112 LJ 205; [1963] 1 QB 25; (1962) 106 SJ 95 CA
Non-escape but bringing of animal onto highway meant owner liable in negligence for injury
through collision.

Harrison v Jackson [1947] LJNCCR 242 CyCt Person who failed to take reasonable care when
having cattle driven across highway liable in negligence for motor collision which occurred.

Harry and Co v Tuck (1912) CC Rep I 60 CyCt Dog-owner not liable for injury occasioned by dog
absent interference by owner.

Haynes v Harwood [1934] 2 KB 240; (1934) 103 LJCL 410; (1934) 151 LTR 135; (1934) 78 SJ
384; (1933-34) L TLR 371; (1934) WN (I) 106 HC KBD Natural result of one's negligence
cannot be novus actus interveniens; person leaving horses in street owes duty of care to safeguard
persons using highway (including police officer chasing after bolting horse).

Haynes v Harwood (G) and Son [1934] All ER 103; [1935] 1 KB 146; (1934) 77 LJ 340; (1934)
78 LJ 323; (1935) 152 LTR 121; (1934) 78 SJ 801; (1934-35) LI TLR 100; (1934) WN (I) 208
CA Natural result of one's negligence cannot be novus actus interveniens; person leaving horses
in street owes duty of care to safeguard persons using highway (including police officer chasing
after bolting horse): no volenti non fit injuria by highway users.

Heath's Garage (Lim) and another v Hodges (1915) CC Rep IV 67 CyCt Owner of land adjoining
highway liable in negligence for failure to fence in animals.

Heath's Garages, Ltd v Hodges (1916) 80 JP 281; [1916] 1 KB 206; [1916] 85 LJKB 485; (1916)
114 LTR 507; (1915-16) 60 SJ 458; (1915-16) XXXII TLR 134; (1915) WN (I) 390 HC KBD
Non-liability in nuisance/negligence of landowner adjoining highway to fence in tame animals.

Higgins v Searle (1908) 72 JP 449 HC KBD Owner of sow that strayed onto road which frightened horse which in turn caused motor accident could be negligent.

Higgins v Searle (1909) 73 JP 185; (1909) C LTR 280; (1908-09) XXV TLR 301 CA Owner of sow that strayed onto road which frightened horse which in turn caused motor accident found not to be negligent.

Hines (Edith) v Tousley and another (1926) 61 LJ ccr14 CyCt Owner of normally well-behaved dog liable for damage caused by dog.

Hines v Tousley (Newell, third party) (1926) 61 LJ 491 CA Owner of normally well-behaved dog not liable for damage caused by dog.

Jaundrill v Gillett (1996) TLR 30/1/96 CA Horse-owner not liable to driver injured in collision with horses that were on public highway following malicious release by third party onto same.

Jones and another v Lee [1911-13] All ER 313; (1912) 76 JP 137; (1912) 106 LTR 123; (1911-12) 56 SJ 125; (1911-12) XXVIII TLR 92 HC KBD Landowner not liable for damage caused by horse straying — no duty to fence in.

Jones v Hall (1981) 131 NLJ 856 HC QBD Succesful action for damages in negligence for injuries suffered by person kicked by another's horse.

Landau v Railway Executive (1949) 99 LJ 233 CyCt Defendant horse-owners liable in negligence for damage occasioned by runaway horse even though horse had never previously sought to run away.

Lathall v Joyce (A) and Son and others [1939] 3 All ER 854; (1938-39) LV TLR 994 HC KBD Non-recovery for attack by domestic animal not reasonably to be expected.

Lee and Another v Walkers (a firm) and Another (1940) 162 LTR 89; (1939) 83 SJ 925 HC KBD Owner not liable for injury caused by dog whom knew to pose a risk where person injured by dog brought injury upon themself through their own interference.

Ludlam v Peel (WE) and Sons (1939) 83 SJ 832 CA Competent drover who took reasonable care not liable for collision between motor vehicle and cow being driven along road.

Manton v Brocklebank [1923] 1 KB 406; [1923] 92 LJCL 624 (also CA); (1922-23) 67 SJ 213; (1922-23) XXXIX TLR 112; (1922) WN (I) 341 HC KBD Liability of owner of mare (here ferae naturae) in negligence/trespass for injury caused to another's animal by mare.

Manton v Brocklebank [1923] All ER 416; [1923] 2 KB 212; (1923) CC Rep XII 28; [1923] 92 LJCL 624 (also HC KBD); (1923) 129 LTR 135; (1922-23) 67 SJ 455; (1922-23) XXXIX TLR 344; (1923) WN (I) 107 CA Mare not dangerous animal: absent owner negligence not liable for loss occasioned by kicking.

Mashiter v Wilkinson and Sons (Lim) (1923) CC Rep XII 69 CyCt Non-liability of occupation road-owner for injury to cattle straying along (rather than being engaged in ordinary user of) said road.

Mason v Kempson [1939] LJNCCR 203 CyCt Failed action in negligence/nuisance and for breach of statutory duty owed under Dogs Act 1906 for injury suffered in road traffic incident occasioned by dog running across road while being taken for walk by owner.

McQuaker v Goddard [1940] 1 All ER 471; [1940] 1 KB 687; (1940) 89 LJ 119; [1940] 109 LJCL 673; (1940) 162 LTR 232; (1940) 84 SJ 203; (1939-40) LVI TLR 409; (1940) WN (I) 80 CA Camel a domestic animal; camel-owner not negligent in fencing provided.

Nicholls and Son v Devon County Council (1922) CC Rep XI 19 CyCt Licensee not liable in negligence for failure to fence in quarry (where such failure resulted in loss of straying cattle).

North v Wood (1914) CC Rep III 18; [1914] 1 KB 629; [1914] 83 LJKB 587; (1914) 110 LTR 703; (1913-14) XXX TLR 258; (1914) WN (I) 38 HC KBD Father not liable for act of infant daughter's savage dog.

Pacy and another v Field (1937) 81 SJ 160 HC KBD Dog-owner who knew of dog's propensity to bite small boys liable for damages towards plaintiff boy bitten by dog and to father of boy.

Pinn v Rew (1915-16) XXXII TLR 451 HC KBD Drover (whether or not independent contractor) and cattle purchaser liable for damage caused by cow which could reasonably have forseen would be dangerous.

Pirie v Gauler (1930) 70 LJ ccr2 CyCt Dog-owner not liable in damages to owner of another dog where latter dog injured by former.

Pitcher v Martin (1937) 81 SJ 670; (1936-37) LIII TLR 903 HC KBD Dog owner liable in negligence/nuisance for injury caused to person after leashed dog escaped owner's control and ran after cat.

Rands v McNeil (1954) 104 LJ 840; [1955] 1 QB 253; (1954) 98 SJ 851 CA No liability for injury to farm worker entering pen in which dangerous bull kept loose (had not escaped so no strict liability).

Rose v George Hurry Collier, Ltd (1939) WN (I) 19 CA Failed appeal by owners of vicious mare for injuries occasioned by same while left unattended.

Short v British Railways Board (1974) 118 SJ 101; [1974] 1 WLR 781 HC QBD Engine driver not negligent for failing to stop before drove into cattle on track.

Short v Tully [1943] LJNCCR 208 CyCt On liability of cattle-owner for road traffic collision occurring where cattle escape/are driven onto highway.

Smith v Prendergast [1984] TLR 572 CA Owner of yard liable in negligence for injury occasioned to girl walking past open gate of yard by stray dog owner allowed to wander at will in yard.

Stanbury v The Mayor, &c, of Exeter (1906) 70 JP 11; (1905-06) XCIII LTR 795; (1905-06) XXII TLR 3; (1905-06) 54 WR 247 HC KBD Local authority not liable where vet whom they employed carried out duties imposed on him, not them under Diseases of Animals Act 1894.

Sutton v Child (1916) CC Rep V 91 CyCt Absent scienter dog-owner not liable in negligence for to owner of turkey killed by dog.

Sycamore v Ley [1932] All ER 97; (1932) 74 LJ 41; (1932) 147 LTR 342 CA Not negligent to leave non-vicious dog inside car as guard-dog.

Sylvester v GB Chapman Ltd [1935] LJNCCA 261; (1935) 79 SJ 777 CA Circus not liable for injuries to groom who took it upon himself to extinguish cigarette in leopard cage and was mauled in the process.

The Fen Reeves of the Biggleswade Common (by Frederick Gee, Acting Fen Reeve) v MO Seward and Son (1912) CC Rep I 48 CyCt On extent of liability of Fen Reeves — here found not to be liable in negligence.

Toogood v Wright [1940] 2 All ER 306; (1940) 84 SJ 254 CA Absent scienter was no special duty in relation to racing greyhounds.

Turnball v Wieland (1916-17) XXXIII TLR 143 HC KBD Employer liable for unlicensed cattle drover's negligence.

Turner v Coates [1916-17] All ER 264; [1917] 1 KB 670; [1917] 86 LJCL 321; (1916-17) 115 LTR 766; (1916-17) XXXIII TLR 79 HC KBD Owner liable in negligence for injuries arising from putting uncontrolled/unbroken colt on road.

Tutton and others v AD Walter Ltd [1986] QB 61; (1985) 129 SJ 739; [1985] 3 WLR 797 HC QBD Farming company liable for breach of duty of care owed to neighbouring bee-keepers through its spraying of land with insecticide dangerous to bees.

Watts-Russell v Eayrs [1934] LJNCCR 324 CyCt Recovery of damages for loss of sheep through negligence of a shepherd provided by person from whom had acquired grazing rights on certain estate.

Werry v Andrew (1951) 101 LJ 289 CyCt Successful plea by motor cycle rider against cattle-owner whose workers acted negligently when driving cattle from field onto highway so causing accident involving motor cyclist.

White and Wife v Steadman [1913] 3 KB 340; [1913] 82 LJKB 846; (1913-14) 109 LTR 249; (1912-13) XXIX TLR 563; (1913) WN (I) 172 HC KBD Stable keeper liable to wife injured as result of behaviour of horse rented to husband.

Wood v Madders [1935] LJNCCR 253 CyCt Cow-owner liable for injury ocasioned by cow straying from unfenced/poorly fenced field onto adjacent highway.

NEGLIGENCE (architect)

Bagot v Stevens Scanlan and Co [1964] 3 All ER 577; [1966] 1 QB 197; (1964) 108 SJ 604; [1964] 3 WLR 1162 HC QBD Professional's failure to exercise proper care and skill in what contracted to do gives rise to claim in contract: no corollary duty on tort.

BL Holdings Ltd v Robert J Wood and another (1978) 122 SJ 525 HC QBD Architect negligent as regards advice gave to clients concerning planning permission application/process.

BL Holdings Ltd v Robert J Wood and another (1979) 123 SJ 570 CA Architect not negligent as regards advice gave to clients concerning planning permission application/process.

Brickfield Properties Ltd v Newton; Rosebell Holdings Ltd v Newton [1971] 1 WLR 862 CA Claims against architect of negligence as regards erection/design are two different claims.

Chambers v Goldthorpe (1899-1900) 44 SJ 229; (1899-1900) XVI TLR 180 HC QBD Architect acting as arbitrator between builder and builder's client could not be guilty of negligence absent fraud/dishonesty.

Chambers v Goldthorpe (1900-01) 45 SJ 325; (1901) WN (I) 51; (1900-01) 49 WR 401 CA Architect acting as arbitrator between builder and builder's client could not be guilty of negligence.

Clay v Crump (AJ) and Sons Ltd and others (1963) 107 SJ 664; [1964] 1 QB 533; [1963] 3 WLR 866 CA On architect's duty of care to construction worker.

Clayton v Woodman and Son (Builders), Ltd and others [1961] 3 All ER 249; [1962] 2 QB 533 (also CA); (1961) 105 SJ 889 HC QBD Architects owe duty of care to builders to watch out for their safety and are liable for physical (not economic) loss occasioned by breach of duty.

Clayton v Woodman and Son (Builders), Ltd and others [1962] 2 All ER 33; (1962) 112 LJ 288; [1962] 2 QB 533 (also HC QBD); (1962) 106 SJ 242; [1962] 1 WLR 585 CA Architect not liable for manner in which builder performs work.

Cotton v Wallis [1955] 3 All ER 373; (1955) 105 LJ 712; [1955] 1 WLR 1168 CA Low price of building merited architect's certification at lower standard than otherwise.

Kensington and Chelsea Area Health Authority v Wettern (1984) 134 NLJ 887c CA Architects liable in neglience for defective fixing of mullions to building frame.

Lancashire and Cheshire Association of Baptist Churches Inc v Howard and Seddon Partnership (a firm) [1993] 3 All ER 467 HC QBD Tortious duty of care may arise in contractual professional relationship; architect's plans not representation on technical qualities of building; architect not liable for economic loss.

Moresk Cleaners Ltd v Hicks (1965-66) 116 NLJ 1546 Assizes Architect negligent in delegating his design responsibilities to builders.

Restell v Nye (1899-1900) XVI TLR 154 HC QBD House-owner could not recover from architect money paid to builder on foot of architect's negligent certification that builder's work was done.

RL Holdings Ltd v Robert J Wood and Partners (1978) 128 NLJ 978t HC QBD Architect liable in negligence for failing to advise client that planning permission might be legally defective and hence ineffective.

Sutcliffe v Thackrah and others [1973] 2 All ER 1047; (1973) 117 SJ 509; [1973] 1 WLR 888 CA Architect's giving of final certificate an arbitral act clothed with immunity from action for negligence.

Sutcliffe v Thackrah and others [1974] 1 All ER 859; [1974] AC 727; (1974) 124 NLJ 200t; (1974) 118 SJ 148; [1974] 2 WLR 295 HL Architect/valuer acting in arbitral rôle immune from action for negligence in so doing.

The Columbus Company, Limited v Clowes [1903] 1 KB 244; [1903] 72 LJKB 330 HC KBD Nominal damages for negligence where suffered no loss.

Wisbech Rural District Council v Ward (1927) 91 JP 166; (1926-27) XLIII TLR 739; (1927) WN (I) 236 HC KBD Architect in certificating building work was under terms of particular contract not acting in quasi-/arbitral role and so could be (and was) liable in negligence.

Wisbech Rural District Council v Ward (1927) 91 JP 200 CA Architect in certificating building work was not negligent.

Worboys v Acme Investments Ltd (1969) 119 NLJ 322t CA On proving professional negligence on part of architect.

Young v Buckles [1952] 1 KB 220 CA Recoverability of professional charges in excess of that for which building licence allowed (Defence (General) Regulations 1939, r 56(4) applied).

NEGLIGENCE (auctioneer)

Luxmoore-May and another v Messenger May Baverstock (1988) 138 NLJ 341 HC QBD On duty owed to client by provincial auctioneer to establish value of auctioned item before auction.

NEGLIGENCE (auditor)

Al Saudi Banque and others v Clarke Pixley (a firm) [1990] Ch 313; (1989) 139 NLJ 1341; [1990] 2 WLR 344 HC ChD Auditor does not owe duty of care towards potential creditors of company whose accounts auditor audits and certifies.

Anthony and ors v Wright and ors (1994) 144 NLJ 1452i HC ChD Investors who did not act on auditor's work could not sue auditor for non-discovery of misuse of trust money.

Bank of Credit and Commerce International (Overseas) Ltd (in liquidation) and others v Price Waterhouse and others [1997] TLR 60 HC ChD Company accountants who were no auditors of said company held not to owe duty of care to company.

Barings plc and another v Coopers & Lybrand (a firm) and others (1996) TLR 6/12/96 CA On duty of care owed by auditors of subsidiary company towards parent company.

Caparo Industries plc v Dickman and others [1989] 1 All ER 798; (1988) 138 NLJ 289; [1989] QB 653; (1989) 133 SJ 221; [1989] 2 WLR 316 CA Auditor owes duty of care to existing shareholders but not potential shareholders/takeover bidders.

Caparo Industries plc v Dickman and others [1990] 1 All ER 568; [1990] 2 AC 605; (1990) 140 NLJ 248; (1990) 134 SJ 494; [1990] TLR 105; [1990] 2 WLR 358 HL Court will impose duty of care in light of existing case-law; special proximity required before duty of care arises; company auditor owes no duty of care to general public.

Cuff and another v London and County Land and Building Co (1912) 81 LJCh 426 (also CA); (1911-12) 56 SJ 273 HC ChD Injunction refused to require company to give allegedly negligent auditors access to company's books.

Cuff v London and County Land and Building Company Limited (1912) 81 LJCh 426 (also HC ChD); (1912) 106 LTR 285 CA Injunction refused to require company to give allegedly negligent auditors access to company's books.

Deloitte Haskins and Sells v National Mutual Life Nominees Ltd [1993] 2 All ER 1015; [1993] AC 774; (1993) 143 NLJ 883; [1993] 3 WLR 347 PC Auditors owe duty of care in preparing reports but question of insolvency subjective matter for individual auditor.

Galoo Ltd (in liq) and others v Bright Grahame Murray (a firm) and another [1995] 1 All ER 16; [1994] 1 WLR 1360 CA No duty of care on auditor towards potential shareholder or lender who relies on audited accounts.

Henry Squire Cash Chemist (Limited) v Ball, Baker and Co; Mead v Same (1910-11) XXVII TLR 269 HC KBD Failed action against auditor for negligence: on duty of care owed by auditor.

Henry Squire, Cash Chemist, Limited v Ball, Baker and Co; Mead v Ball, Baker, and Co (1912) 106 LTR 197; (1911-12) XXVII TLR 81 CA Failed action against auditor for negligence: on duty of care owed by auditor.

JEB Fasteners Ltd v Marks Bloom and Co [1981] 3 All ER 289; (1981) 131 NLJ 447 HC QBD Auditors owed duty of care to person with whom had no contractual relationship but who relied on audited accounts in deciding whether to purchase company.

JEB Fasteners Ltd v Marks Bloom and Co (a firm) [1983] 1 All ER 583; [1982] TLR 403 CA Auditor not liable to third party for negligent audits unless induce (not encourage) latter to invest in company.

Mutual Reinsurance Co Ltd v Peat Marwick Mitchell and Co and another (1996) TLR 15/10/96 CA Accountants appointed as company auditors pursuant to Bermudan law/company bylaws could not later be sued for negligence by the company.

Re Thomas Gerrard and Son, Ltd [1967] 2 All ER 525; [1968] Ch 455; (1967) 111 SJ 329; [1967] 3 WLR 84 HC ChD Changed invoices put auditors under duty to look further.

West Wiltshire District Council v Garland and others; Cond and others (third parties) [1993] Ch 409; [1993] TLR 112; [1993] 3 WLR 626 HC ChD On duty of care owed by district auditors when auditing local authority accounts.

West Wiltshire District Council v Garland and others; Cond and others (third parties) [1995] Ch 297; (1995) 139 SJ LB 18; [1994] TLR 622; [1995] 2 WLR 439 CA On duty of care owed by district auditors when auditing local authority accounts.

NEGLIGENCE (automatism)

Roberts and others v Ramsbottom [1980] 1 All ER 7; [1980] RTR 261; (1980) 124 SJ 313; [1980] 1 WLR 823 HC QBD Absent automatism are liable for negligent acts.

NEGLIGENCE (aviation)

Blankley v Godley and another [1952] 1 All ER 436 Assizes On negligence in take-off.

Fellowes (or Herd) and another v Clyde Helicopters Ltd [1997] 1 All ER 775; [1997] AC 534; (1997) 141 SJ LB 64 HL Liability of helicopter company towards dependants of police officer killed while being conveyed in helicopter by negligent company pilot was governed by the Warsaw Convention as amended/implemented.

Fosbrooke-Hobbes v Airwork, Limited, and another (1937) 81 SJ 80; (1936-37) LIII TLR 254; (1937) WN (I) 48 HC KBD Carrier but not charterer liable to widow suing for fatal accident damages after pilot husband killed in aeroplane accident; res ipsa loquitur arose where emerged that accident caused by pilot's negligence.

Hesketh v Liverpool Corporation [1940] 4 All ER 429 Assizes Pilot in crash-landing not negligent simply for clipping trees he knew were there.

NEGLIGENCE (bailment)

Aldridge v Franklin (1953) 103 LJ ccr496 CyCt Deemed to be no negligence insofar as loss of coat bailed at cloakroom was concerned.

Andrews v Home Flats, Ltd [1945] 2 All ER 698 CA Landlord liable as bailee for reward for operating negligent system of safeguarding bailed goods.

Ashley v Tolhurst and others [1937] LJNCCR 78 CyCt Car-park owners liable for breach of contract of bailment for reward and in conversion where handed car to person who did not produce ticket for same and whom it emerged was not the owner.

Ballett v Mingay [1943] 1 All ER 143; [1943] KB 281; [1943] 112 LJ 193; (1943) 168 LTR 34 CA Infant could be sued in tort for acts which fell outside bailment contract.

Barlow and others v Heald (1916) CC Rep V 20 CyCt Could bring action for trover/detinue against company seeking to sell discarded bottles subject to deposit arrangement/in respect of which there was an obligation to account.

Becker v Lavender, Limited and another (1946) 90 SJ 502; (1945-46) LXII TLR 504; (1946) WN (I) 135 HC KBD Bailee for reward liable where did not take as much care of bailed property as would of own.

Behrens v Grenville Hotel, (Bude) Limited (1924-25) 69 SJ 346 HC KBD Hoteliers liable for loss of case of jewellery clearly left with them for safe keeping.

Belvoir Finance Co Ltd v Stapleton (1970) 120 NLJ 733t; [1971] 1 QB 210; (1970) 114 SJ 719; [1970] 3 WLR 530 CA Damages awarded for conversion on foot of fully executed illegal hire-purchase contracts.

Blount v War Office (1953) 97 SJ 388; [1953] 1 WLR 736 HC QBD War office liable for theft of goods left (bailed) with War Office's agreement in requisitioned house despite transfer of requisition to Ministry of Agriculture.

British Road Services, Ltd v Arthur Crutchley and Co, Ltd (Factory Guards, Ltd., Third Parties) [1968] 1 All ER 811 CA Bailees liable for negligence of servants/agents; bailees liable in negligence for inadequate security measures.

Bryce v Hornby (1938) 82 SJ 216 HC KBD On duty of care owed by friend-bailee to/with whom property is loaned bailed by friend-bailor.

Bull (AH) and Company v West African Shipping Agency and Lighterage Company [1927] AC 686; (1927) 137 LTR 498 PC Party hiring property liable for negligence of persons under their control responsible for property.

Bullen (AH) v The Swan Electric Engraving Company (1905-06) XXII TLR 275 HC KBD Bailees not liable for loss of goods over which took same degree of care that reasonable person would take of own goods.

Bullen v The Swan Electric Engraving Company (1906-07) XXIII TLR 258 CA Bailees not liable for loss of goods over which took same degree of care that reasonable person would take of own goods.

Chesworth v Farrar and another [1966] 2 All ER 107; (1965-66) 116 NLJ 809; [1967] 1 QB 407; (1966) 110 SJ 307; [1966] 2 WLR 1073 HC QBD Action for failure of bailee to take proper care lies in tort.

Coachcraft, Ltd v Lancegay Safety Glass (1934), Ltd [1938] LJNCCR 380 CyCt Bailees had to prove damage occurring to bailed goods while in their care did not result from their negligence.

Coldman v Hill (1918) CC Rep VII 60; (1917-18) 62 SJ 703; (1917-18) XXXIV TLR 486 HC KBD No finding of negligence on part of deliveree where two cows delivered under contract of agistment were stolen.

Coldman v Hill [1918-19] All ER 434; (1918) CC Rep VII 92; [1919] 1 KB 443; (1918) 53 LJ 428; [1919] 88 LJCL 491; (1919) 120 LTR 412; (1918-19) 63 SJ 166; (1918-19) XXXV TLR 146; (1919) WN (I) 5 CA Finding of negligence on part of deliveree where two cows delivered under contract of agistment were stolen.

Coley v Meteor Garage (Moseley), Ltd [1941] LJNCCR 201 CyCt Garage with whom car bailed during winter not liable in negligence for not having drained radiator/for collapse of garage roof under weight of freak snow onto car.

Cowan v Blackwill Motor Caravan Conversions Ltd (trading as Matador Service Station) [1978] RTR 421 CA Garage owners not liable in negligence for theft of car bailed with them where took all security measures ordinary driver would take on leaving car in street.

Craven v Parkinson (1923) CC Rep XII 26 CyCt On duty of care owed by bailee towards animals left in his keeping.

Cryan v Hotel Rembrandt, Limited (1925) 133 LTR 395; (1924-25) XLI TLR 287 HC KBD Innkeeper liable for loss of coat deposited by dinner-guest and lost through negligence of innkeeper/his servants.

Curtis v Chemical Cleaning and Dyeing Co, Ltd [1951] 1 All ER 631; [1951] 1 KB 805; (1951) 101 LJ 121; (1951) 95 SJ 253; [1951] 1 TLR 452; (1951) WN (I) 148 CA Exception clause inapplicable as misrepresentation as to extent of clause when making bailment.

Eggott (GW) and Son, Ltd v Normanton (CH) and Son, Ltd [1928] All ER 468 HC KBD Permanent employer allowed claim for negligence of servant temporarily in employment of bailee.

Elvin and Powell, Limited v Plummer Roddis, Limited (1934) 78 SJ 48; (1933-34) L TLR 158 HC KBD Involuntary bailees not liable in conversion for non-negligent act which results in loss of property.

Filgate (Macartney) v Bishop and Sons (1964) 108 SJ 897 HC QBD Failed attempt by negligent bailee to rely on liability exemption clause following theft of bailed goods.

Gibaud v Great Eastern Rail Co [1920] 3 KB 689; [1921] LJCL 194; (1919-20) XXXVI TLR 884 HC KBD Exemption clause disclaiming liability for loss effected 'in any way possible' included own negligence.

Gibaud v Great Eastern Rail Co [1921] All ER 35; [1921] 2 KB 426; (1921) CC Rep X 21; (1921) 56 LJ 92; [1921] LJCL 535; (1921) 125 LTR 76; (1920-21) 65 SJ 454; (1920-21) XXXVII TLR 422; (1921) WN (I) 80 CA Exemption clause disclaiming liability for loss effected 'in any way possible' included own negligence.

Giles v Carter (1965) 109 SJ 452 HC QBD Bailee did not fail in duty of care owed to bailor where kept bailed property (fur stole) in unlocked press in locked flat.

Global Dress Co Ltd v WH Boase and Co Ltd (1965-66) 116 NLJ 1544 CA Porters deemed to have been negligent in care they took of dock shed.

Houghland v Low (RR) (Luxury Coaches), Ltd [1962] 2 All ER 159; (1962) 112 LJ 353; [1962] 1 QB 694; (1962) 106 SJ 243; [1962] 2 WLR 1015 CA Non-return of item establishes prima facie case of detinue/negligence which defendant must counter.

Idnani v Elisha (trading as Grafton Service Station) [1979] RTR 488 CA Bailee not negligent where left bailed car in publicly accessible place in such a way that could not be driven away under own power.

J Spurling, Ltd v Bradshaw [1956] 2 All ER 121; (1956) 106 LJ 281; (1956) 100 SJ 317; [1956] 1 WLR 461 CA Exemption clause in bailment contract applied in negligence suit.

Lee Cooper, Ltd v CH Jeakins and Sons, Ltd [1965] 1 All ER 280; (1965) 115 LJ 126; [1967] 2 QB 1; (1965) 109 SJ 794; [1965] 3 WLR 753 HC QBD Bailees owed duty of care to non-bailor owners.

Lockspeiser Aircraft Ltd v Brooklands Aircraft Co Ltd [1990] TLR 183 HC QBD On duty of care owed by bailee.

Martin v London County Council [1947] 1 All ER 783; (1947) 111 JP 310; [1947] KB 628; (1947) 97 LJ 221; [1947] 116 LJR 1231; (1947) 177 LTR 38; (1947) 91 SJ 264; (1947) LXIII TLR 284; (1947) WN (I) 146 HC KBD Local authority running hospital not gratuitous bailee of patient's property/could not assume property bailed of no value; purchase tax relevant in deciding level of damages.

Mitchell v Davis (1920-21) XXXVII TLR 68 HC KBD Bailment relationship continues with tradesman who has been sent goods even after he has completed repairs unless otherwise agree.

O'Sullivan and another v Williams [1992] 3 All ER 385; (1992) 142 NLJ 717; [1992] RTR 402; [1992] TLR 117 CA Bailee ineligible for damages for loss and damage if bailor has already secured damages from third party tortfeasor.

Olley v Marlborough Court, Ltd [1948] 1 All ER 955; (1948) 98 LJ 273; (1948) WN (I) 192 HC KBD Bailee's failure to adequately secure bailed items was negligent.

Olley v Marlborough Court, Ltd [1949] 1 All ER 127; [1949] 1 KB 532; (1948) 98 LJ 699; [1949] 118 LJR 360; (1949) LXV TLR 95; (1949) WN (I) 17 CA Bailee's failure to adequately secure bailed items was negligent; exception clause inapplicable as not clear and not made aware thereof before taken as guest.

Phipps v The New Claridge's Hotel (Limited) (1905-06) XXII TLR 49 HC KBD Person to whom goods entrusted as bailee and who loses them must disprove negligence.

Pye Ltd v BG Transport Service Ltd (1965-66) 116 NLJ 1713 HC QBD Carrier's liable in negligence for loss of goods being carried when they were left unattended.

Rich v Circuits Management Association, Ltd (1957) 107 LJ 556 CyCt Successful reliance on exemption from negligence clause by cloakroom operators with whom lost overcoat bailed.

Rutter v Palmer [1922] All ER 367; [1922] 2 KB 87; (1922) 57 LJ 195; [1922] 91 LJCL 657; (1922) 127 LTR 419; (1921-22) 66 SJ 576; (1921-22) XXXVIII TLR 555 CA Clause exempting bailee from liability for negligence deemed valid.

Saunders (Mayfair) Furs, Ltd v Chas Wm Davies, Ltd (1965-66) 116 NLJ 639; (1965) 109 SJ 922 HC QBD Bailee failed in duty of care by leaving bailed item in shop window where was stolen in smash and grab robbery.

Scriven v Middlesex County Council (1950) 100 LJ 360 CyCt Council did not seem to be under duty to take care of coat left in cloakroom of building by student attending evening classes there but even if it was there was no breach of that duty so council not liable in damages when coat stolen.

Swaffer v Mulcahy; Hooker v Same; Smith v Same (1933-34) L TLR 179 HC KBD Sheep/beasts of plough privileged from seizure if alternative distress possible; wrongful seizure of bailment entitles one to bring action of replevin.

The Winkfield [1900-03] All ER 346; [1902] 71 LJP 21; (1901-02) 46 SJ 162; (1901-02) XVIII TLR 178; (1901-02) 50 WR 246 CA Bailee liable to bailor for damages recovered from third party for negligent loss of goods.

Thorne v Sibley (1913) CC Rep II 11 CyCt Person who had horse on trial not liable for injury horse inflicted on self (no negligence on part of said person), property not having passed to that person.

Warner v Elizabeth Arden, Ltd (1939) 83 SJ 258; (1939) WN (I) 41 HC KBD Beauty salon not liable in negligence or as bailees for necklace removed from handbag left unattended without notice of contents to salon.

Wiehe v Dennis Brothers (1912-13) XXIX TLR 250 HC KBD Person from whom buying horse and with whom left horse for few days during which horse injured liable in negligence as gratuitous bailee who could not show were not negligent.

Woolmer v Delmer Price, Ltd [1955] 1 All ER 377; [1955] 1 QB 291; [1955] 2 WLR 329 HC QBD Could not rely on exception clause where no explanation of disappearance of bailed goods offered: must show either negligence or no negligence.

NEGLIGENCE (bank)

B Liggett (Liverpool), Limited v Barclays Bank, Limited [1928] 1 KB 48; (1927) 137 LTR 443; (1926-27) XLIII TLR 449 HC KBD Action for negligent payment of cheque.

Banbury v Bank of Montreal [1917] 1 KB 409; (1916) 51 LJ 598; [1917] 86 LJCL 380; (1917) 116 LTR 42; (1916-17) 61 SJ 129; (1916-17) XXXIII TLR 104; (1916) WN (I) 412 CA Non-liability of action over letter of introduction; could not bring action on foot of representations/assurances as to credit/ability of company as was not in writing. (Lord Tenterden's Act, s 6).

Banbury v Bank of Montreal [1918] 87 LJCL 1158; (1918-19) 119 LTR 446; (1917-18) 62 SJ 665; (1917-18) XXXIV TLR 518; (1918) WN (I) 231 HL Representation to sustain action for representation as to another's credit need only be in writing where fraudulent misrepresentation claimed. (Lord Tenterden's Act 1828, s 6).

Bank of Montreal v Dominion Gresham Guarantee and Casualty Company, Limited [1930] AC 659; (1931) 144 LTR 6; (1929-30) XLVI TLR 575 PC Banker liable for negligent issuing of drafts — no estoppel precluding action just because had issued in same way several times previously.

Bevan v The National Bank (Limited); Bevan v The Capital and Counties Bank (Limited) (1906-07) XXIII TLR 65 HC KBD Might be negligent for banker to pay crossed cheque into account where suspects is not paying same into payee's account.

Commissioners of Taxation v English, Scottish, and Australian Bank (Limited) (1919-20) XXXVI TLR 305 PC On what constitutes negligence for purposes of (Australian) Bills of Exchange Act 1909, s 88(1)/(Imperial) Bills of Exhange Act 1882, s 82.

Gold Coin Joailliers SA v United Bank of Kuwait plc (1996) TLR 4/11/96 CA Bank not under duty of care when providing reference over telephone regarding financial status of customer to ensure person in respect of whom enquiry was made was actually the person dealing with the enquirer.

Hampstead Guardians v Barclays Bank, Limited (1922-23) XXXIX TLR 229 HC KBD Negligence of bank in receiving payment of cheque meant did not enjoy protection of Bills of Exchange Act 1882, s 82.

Hannan's Lake View Central (Limited) v Armstrong and Co (1899-1900) XVI TLR 236 HC QBD Negligent dealing with cheque by bankers disentitled same to protection of Bills of Exchange Act 1882, s 82.

Hedley Byrne and Co, Ltd v Heller and Partners, Ltd [1961] 3 All ER 891; (1961) 111 LJ 836; [1962] 1 QB 396; (1961) 105 SJ 910 CA Absent special relationship party giving advice does not owe duty to take reasonable care to inquirer.

Hedley Byrne and Co, Ltd v Heller and Partners, Ltd [1963] 2 All ER 575; [1964] AC 465; (1963) 113 LJ 416; (1963) 107 SJ 454; [1963] 3 WLR 101 HL Duty of care can arise between person seeking advice from other although no contractual/fiduciary relationship exists; disclaimer here excluded liability.

Hilton v Westminster Bank, Limited (1925-26) XLII TLR 423 CA Bank were negligent to pay on cheque which customer asked to be stopped quoting wrong number but giving details which enabled bank to know which cheque wanted to be stopped.

Imperial Bank of Canada v Bank of Hamilton (1902-03) LXXXVII LTR 457; (1902-03) 51 WR 289 PC Not negligent for bank to cash certified cheque which did not on face of it seem suspect.

Karak Rubber Co Ltd v Burden and others (No 2) (1971) 115 SJ 888; [1972] 1 WLR 602 HC ChD On duty of care owed by bankers to customers (here not discharged).

Ladbroke and Co v Todd (1914-15) 111 LTR 43 HC KBD Is negligent for banker without making inquiries to open account for person presenting cheque marked 'Account payee only'.

Lipkin Gorman v Karpnale Ltd and another (1986) 136 NLJ 659; [1987] 1 WLR 987 HC QBD On recovery for conversion/negligence where gambling club/bank accepted draft which was not gambler's to present/breached duty to customer to ascertain from where gambler obtaining funds (but where gambler's business partners were contributorily negligent in not inquiring into gambler's affairs once had notice of spending irregularities).

Lipkin Gorman v Karpnale Ltd and another [1989] 1 WLR 1340 CA On liability in conversion/ negligence where gambling club/bank accepted draft which was not gambler's to present/did not ascertain from where gambler obtaining funds.

Lipkin Gorman v Karpnale Ltd and another [1992] 1 All ER 512; [1991] 3 WLR 10 HL On liability in conversion/negligence where gambling club/bank accepted draft which was not gambler's to present/did not ascertain from where gambler obtaining funds.

Lloyds Bank Ltd v Bundy [1975] QB 326; [1974] 3 WLR 501 CA Bank owed fiduciary duty of care to old customer and had breached same by means of undue influence.

Lloyds Bank, Ltd v Chartered Bank of India, Australia and China [1928] All ER 285 CA Negligent dealing with cheques resulting in conversion.

Lloyds Bank, Ltd v Savory (EB) and Co [1932] All ER 106; (1933) 102 LJCL 224; (1933) 148 LTR 291; (1933) WN (I) 6 HL That practice is longstanding and widespread does not mean cannot be negligent.

London Joint Stock Bank, Limited v Macmillan and Arthur [1918] AC 777; (1918) 53 LJ 242; [1919] 88 LJCL 55; (1918-19) 119 LTR 387; (1917-18) XXXIV TLR 509 HL Customer required to bear loss occasioned through own negligent completion of cheque.

Macmillan and another v London Joint Stock Bank (1916-17) XXXIII TLR 140 HC KBD Customer not required to bear loss occasioned through own negligent completion of cheque.

Macmillan and another v London Joint Stock Bank, Limited [1917] 2 KB 439; (1917-18) 117 LTR 202; (1916-17) XXXIII TLR 398; (1917) WN (I) 181 CA Customer not required to bear loss occasioned through own negligent completion of cheque.

Marfani and Co Ltd v Midland Bank Ltd (1968) 112 SJ 396 CA Bank not negligent (though barely so) in allowing person to open new bank account with stolen cheque, then withdraw proceeds.

Midland Bank, Ltd v Reckitt and others [1932] All ER 90; (1931-32) XLVIII TLR 271 HL Bank liable in negligence/conversion for cashing cheques signed by solicitor whom bank had notice was operating outside authority as agent.

Minories Finance Ltd v Arthur Young (a firm) (Bank of England, third party); Johnson Matthey plc v Arthur Young (a firm) (Bank of England, third party) [1989] 2 All ER 105 HC QBD Bank of England not under duty of care to commercial banks/depositors when policing commercial banks.

Morison v London County and Westminster Bank Limited (1914-15) 111 LTR 114 CA On negligence of bank in paying money from account on foot of fraudulently prepared crossed/uncrossed cheques.

National Westminster Bank Ltd v Barclays Bank International Ltd and another [1974] 3 All ER 834; (1974) 124 NLJ 767t; (1974) 118 SJ 627; [1975] 2 WLR 12 HC QBD Bank not negligent in honouring forged cheque; by honouring forged cheque bank did not represent it as genuine so were not estopped by representation (or by negligence) from seeking repayment of cheque.

Ose Gesellschaft, &c v Jewish Colonial Trust (1926-27) XLIII TLR 398 HC KBD Failed action for negligence where cheque was lost and amount was debited from account when cheque later used fraudulently.

Penmount Estates, Limited v National Provincial Bank, Limited; Stanley Moss and Pilcher (third party) (1945) 173 LTR 344 HC KBD Action for covnversion/negligence where bank credited amount of cashed cheque to wrong bank account.

Prefontaine v Grenier [1907] AC 101; [1907] 76 LJPC 4; (1906-07) XCV LTR 623; (1906-07) XXIII TLR 27 PC President of banking company not deemed negligent for having trusted cashier (lead executive officer after directors).

Ross v London County, Westminster and Parr's Bank (Lim) (1918-19) 63 SJ 411; (1919) WN (I) 87 HC KBD Bank negligent in accepting (stolen) cheques and paying them into account.

Savory (EB) and Company v Lloyds Bank, Limited [1932] 2 KB 122; (1932) 101 LJCL 499; (1932) 146 LTR 530; (1931-32) XLVIII TLR 344 CA That practice is longstanding and widespread does not mean cannot be negligent.

Souchette, Limited, v London County Westminster and Parr's Bank, Limited (1919-20) XXXVI TLR 195 HC KBD Negligent cashing by bank of one of five cheques.

Standard Bank London Ltd v Bank of Tokyo Ltd; Girozentrale (Sudwestdeutsche Landesbank) v Bank of Tokyo Ltd and another [1995] TLR 206 HC QBD Person who mistakenly confirmed banking transaction by way of tested telex was guilty of negligent misstatement.

Tai Hing Cotton Mill Ltd v Liu Chong Hing Bank Ltd and others [1986] AC 80; (1985) 135 NLJ 680; [1985] 3 WLR 317 PC On common law duty of care owed by customer to bank: company not estopped from claiming accounts wrongly debited where had not breached its common law (or contractual duty of care).

The Colonial Bank of Australasia (Limited) v Marshall and another [1906] 75 LJPC 76; (1905-06) XXII TLR 746 PC Leaving spaces on cheque that forger might use not negligence on part of customers so were not estopped from denying amended cheques were their cheques.

The Kepitigalla Rubber Estates (Limited) v The National Bank of India (Limited) [1909] 78 LJKB 964; (1909) C LTR 516; (1908-09) 53 SJ 377; (1908-09) XXV TLR 402 HC KBD Company allowed recover from bank amounts bank paid from company account on foot of cheques forged by company secretary.

Walker and another v Manchester and Liverpool District Banking Company Limited (1913) 108 LTR 728; (1912-13) 57 SJ 478 HC KBD Customer could recover amounts bank paid out on foot of forged cheques though customer had not checked pass-book when from time to time was returned to him.

Wealden Woodlands (Kent) Ltd v National Westminster Bank Ltd [1983] TLR 182 CA Company not estopped (by not itself noticing same) from bringing action against bank for clearance of forged cheques drawn on its account.

Welch v Bank of England and another [1955] Ch 508; (1955) 99 SJ 236; [1955] 2 WLR 757 HC ChD On negligence as basis for estoppel in banking stock transfer action.

Westminster Bank, Limited v Hilton (1925-26) 70 SJ 1196; (1926-27) XLIII TLR 124; (1926) WN (I) 332 HL Bank not negligent in not stopping particular cheque where number of cheque were instructed to stop was not number of cheque customer wanted stopped.

Woods v Martins Bank, Ltd and another (1958) 108 LJ 665 HC QBD Bank and manager liable for negligent advice regarding investments given by manager to plaintiff.

NEGLIGENCE (bathing pool)

Simmons v The Mayor, etc, of the Borough of Huntingdon [1936] 1 All ER 596 HC KBD Placing by public authority of diving board at point of public baths where water too shallow for diving was a trap.

NEGLIGENCE (broker)

Ramwade Ltd v WJ Emson and Co Ltd [1987] RTR 72; (1970) 130 SJ 804 CA Brokers who were negligent in not insuring client's lorry liable in damages to latter to amount that insurance company would have paid out for event that transpired.

NEGLIGENCE (building)

Alexander and another v Mercouris and another [1979] 3 All ER 305 CA Defective Premises Act 1972 does not apply to work commenced before Act.

Anns and others v Walcroft Property Co Ltd and another [1976] QB 882; (1976) 120 SJ 216; [1976] 2 WLR 512 CA Cause of action from time building defects discovered/ought to have been discovered.

Birse Construction Ltd v Haiste Ltd; Watson and others (third parties) [1995] TLR 666; [1996] 1 WLR 675 CA Physical faults in reservoir/cost of building new reservoir (losses suffered by two parties respectively) not 'the same damage' so defendant engineers could not recover contribution from third party engineer under Civil Liability (Contribution) Act 1978, s 1(1).

Courage and Co, Ltd v Meakers Garages, Ltd (1948) 98 LJ 163 HC ChD Successful action for damage occasioned by collapse of building maintained in disrepair.

Darngavil Coal Company Limited v McKinlay (1923) 87 JP 66; (1923) 128 LTR 772; (1922-23) 67 SJ 276; (1923) WN (I) 35 HL Action in negligence in respect of injury arising from dangerous gate allowed go to trial.

Department of the Environment v Thomas Bates and Son Ltd (New Towns Commission, third party) [1989] 1 All ER 1075; (1989) 139 NLJ 39 CA No tortious duty on builder to remedy defects in building unless pose threat of imminent physical injury.

Dutton v Bognor Regis United Building Co Ltd and another [1972] 1 All ER 462; (1972) 136 JP 201; (1971) 121 NLJ 617; [1972] 1 QB 373; (1972) 116 SJ 16; [1972] 2 WLR 299 CA Council in exercising building byelaws powers has duty to exercise diligently; can be liable for negligent exercise to purchaser/even if builder not liable (and builder may be liable even if owns premises).

Hicks v Meaker and Brown (1952) 102 LJ 725 CyCt Failed action in negligence in respect of damage arising from allegedly negligent disrepair of houses.

Lovelidge v Anselm Oldling and Sons, Ltd [1967] 1 All ER 459 HC QBD Employers negligent where injury caused to workman not properly dressed (latter contributorily negligent).

McArdle v Andmac Roofing Co and others [1967] 1 All ER 583; (1967) 111 SJ 37; [1967] 1 WLR 356 CA Main contractor liable for (acts of sub-contractors leading to) foreseeable injury of workman.

Murphy v Brentwood District Council [1990] 2 All ER 269; [1991] 1 AC 398 (also HL); (1990) 134 SJ 458; [1990] 2 WLR 944 CA Statutory duty on council to ensure houses properly built meant duty of care on council even though consulting engineers negligent. Damages owed are those necessary to put house in safe condition or enable occupier to move to safe house.

Murphy v Brentwood District Council [1990] 2 All ER 908; [1991] 1 AC 398 (also CA); (1990) 140 NLJ 1111; (1990) 134 SJ 1076; [1990] TLR 558; [1990] 3 WLR 414 HL Local authority does not owe duty of care for pure economic loss to building owner/occupier when discharging statutory functions.

Otto (M) and Otto (E) v Bolton and Norris [1936] 1 All ER 960; [1936] 2 KB 46; [1936] 105 LJCL 602; (1936) 154 LTR 717; (1936) 80 SJ 306; (1935-36) LII TLR 438; (1936) WN (I) 127 HC KBD Builder owes no duty to later residents of property being built to take reasonable care in building same.

Richardson v West Lindsey District Council and others [1990] 1 All ER 296; (1989) 139 NLJ 1263; [1990] 1 WLR 522 CA Local authority does not normally owe duty of care to see that building project complies with building regulations.

Rimmer v Liverpool City Council [1984] 1 All ER 930; [1985] QB 1; (1984) 128 SJ 225; [1983] TLR 762; [1984] 2 WLR 426 CA Landlord who is builder/designer owes duty of care to all affected by build/design of premises.

Sutherland v CR Maton and Sons Ltd (1977) 127 NLJ 291 HC QBD Bungalow-builders liable to first and subsequent owners for defects in construction of house (even though buyers relied on building society inspection and did not employ own surveyor to inspect house).

Walsh v Holst and Co, Ltd, and others [1958] 3 All ER 33 CA Brick falling from construction site and hitting passer-by raised res ipsa loquitur (but was defeated here).

Ward v Cannock Chase District Council [1986] Ch 546; (1986) 130 SJ 316; [1986] 2 WLR 660 HC ChD On damages available upon damage to house resulting from council's disrepair of neighbouring buildings/vandalism consequent upon neglect.

Worlock v SAWS and Rushmoor Borough Council (1981) 131 NLJ 1054 HC QBD Building contractor (breach of contract) and council (breach of building regulations) liable to plaintiff for damages suffered as result of defective building work.

NEGLIGENCE (child)

Bates v Stone Parish Council [1954] 3 All ER 38; (1954) 118 JP 502; (1954) 104 LJ 569; (1954) 98 SJ 698; [1954] 1 WLR 1249 CA By allowing unrestricted playground access to children were liable to child/licensee injured therein.

Bebee v Sales (1915-16) XXXII TLR 413 HC KBD Was negligent to allow son to continue using airgun after had already promised to destroy gun on foot of earlier complaint regarding son's use of same.

Buckland v Guildford Gas Light and Coke Co [1948] 2 All ER 1086; (1949) 113 JP 44; [1949] 1 KB 410; (1948) WN (I) 488 HC KBD Electricity company liable for child's electrocution where allowed tree grow too closely to and obscure electric wires even if child was trespasser.

Carmarthenshire County Council v Lewis [1955] AC 549; (1955) 119 JP 230; (1955) 105 LJ 136; (1955) 99 SJ 167; [1955] 2 WLR 517 HL Is duty to prevent children (unlike animals) from straying onto highway and so imperilling others.

Coates v Rawtenstall Borough Council [1937] 1 All ER 333 Assizes Ordinary duty of care owed to child licensee.

Coates v Rawtenstall Borough Council (1937) 101 JP 483; (1937) 81 SJ 627 CA Local authority liable for injury to child licensee arising from negligent state in which playground maintained.

Cooke v Midland Great Western Railway of Ireland [1908-10] All ER 16; [1909] AC 229; [1909] 78 LJPC 76; (1909) C LTR 626; (1908-09) 53 SJ 319; (1908-09) XXV TLR 375; (1909) WN (I) 56 HL Liable in negligence for injury to child through allurement.

Creed v John McGeogh and Sons, Ltd [1955] 3 All ER 123; (1955) 105 LJ 618; (1955) 99 SJ 563; [1955] 1 WLR 1005 HC QBD Negligence towards child trespasser in builder's trailer; builder's trailer left close to highway not nuisance to highway.

Cuttress and others v Scaffolding (Great Britain) Ltd and others [1953] 1 All ER 165 Assizes Liable for not taking steps to prevent foreseeable occurrence of children interfering with and being injured by scaffolding.

Cuttress and others v Scaffolding (Great Britain), Ltd and others [1953] 2 All ER 1075; (1953) 97 SJ 741; [1953] 1 WLR 1311 CA Not liable for negligence where children injured by pulling down scaffolding as was safely constructed and events that occurred not reasonably foreseeable.

Donovan v Union Cartage Co, Ltd [1932] All ER 273; [1933] 2 KB 71; (1933) 102 LJCL 270; (1933) 148 LTR 333; (1933) 77 SJ 30; (1932-33) XLIX TLR 125 HC KBD Strict duty of care on owner of unattended vehicle which is allurement to children only if vehicle is dangerous per se.

Excelsior Wire Rope Company, Limited v Callan and others [1930] All ER 1; [1930] AC 404; (1930) 94 JP 174; (1930) 69 LJ 218; (1930) 99 LJCL 380; (1930) 142 LTR 531; (1930) WN (I) 55 HL Liable in negligence for injury to child trespasser where knew was probable that children would be near when dangerous machine operated.

French v Sunshine Holiday Camp (Hayling Island), Ltd (1963) 107 SJ 595 HC ChD Holiday camp liable towards child who fell from wall (from which had been ordered down) and through glass: accident reasonably foreseeable/child not contributorily negligent.

Glasgow Corporation v Taylor [1921] All ER 1 HL; (1922) 86 JP 89; (1921) 56 LJ 435; [1922] 91 LJPC 49; (1922) 126 LTR 262; (1921-22) XXXVIII TLR 102; (1921) WN (I) 333 Public authority negligent in allowing children into public playground where knew poisonous berries to be growing.

Gorely and another v Codd and another [1966] 3 All ER 891; (1965-66) 116 NLJ 1658; (1966) 110 SJ 965; [1967] 1 WLR 19 Assizes No offence/negligence if father having taken reasonable care allows child unsupervised use of air gun in non-public place.

Gosling v Islington Corporation [1938] LJNCCR 427 CyCt Sand bin by highway was an allurement/trap and defendants were negligent in not making sure that bin was kept locked.

Gough v Thorne [1966] 3 All ER 398; (1966) 110 SJ 529; [1966] 1 WLR 1387 CA Driver waving child to cross negligent if child struck despite failing to check for overtaking traffic.

Halstead (an Infant, by his next friend) v Bargh (J) and Co (1928) 66 LJ ccr2 CyCt Barn-owner liable in damages for injury to child who enters same without authorisation (and so is trespasser).

Hardy v Central London Rail Co [1920] All ER 205; [1920] 3 KB 459; (1920) 55 LJ 313; [1920] 89 LJCL 1187; (1921) 124 LTR 136; (1919-20) 64 SJ 683; (1919-20) XXXVI TLR 843 CA Absent allurement/malice were not liable to child trespassers.

Harris v Birkenhead Corporation and another (Pascoe and another third party, Alliance Assurance Co Ltd fourth party) [1976] 1 All ER 341; (1976) 120 SJ 200; [1976] 1 WLR 279 CA Legal property occupier liable for reasonably foreseeable injury to child trespasser.

Jackson v London County Council and Chappell (1912) 76 JP 37; (1911-12) XXVIII TLR 66 HC KBD Education authority/building contractor may have been negligent to leave sand mixture in school yard which one child threw at another, causing injury.

Jackson v London County Council and Chappell (1912) 76 JP 217; (1911-12) XXVIII TLR 359 CA Education authority/building contractor may have been negligent to leave sand mixture in school yard which one child threw at another, causing injury.

Jauffur v Akhbar and another [1984] TLR 51 HC QBD On duty of care owed by parent vis-à-vis warning/supervising children regarding/in use of lighted candles.

Latham v Richard Johnson and Nephew, Ltd [1911-13] All ER 117; (1913) 77 JP 137; [1913] 1 KB 398; (1912) 47 LJ 748; [1913] 82 LJKB 258; (1913) 108 LTR 4; (1912-13) 57 SJ 127; (1912-13) XXIX TLR 124; (1912) WN (I) 290 CA Occupier of land on which stones owed no special duty of care to children playing thereon — implied term in licence that children to be accompanied by adults.

Moore (an infant) v Poyner (1974) 124 NLJ 1084t; [1975] RTR 127 CA On duty of care owed by Sunday driver in residential area to children playing in area.

Morley v Staffordshire County Council [1939] 4 All ER 93; (1939) 83 SJ 848 CA Allurement did not make liable for injury caused by obvious danger.

Nesbit and another v Pearson and another (1915) CC Rep IV 69 CyCt Child could recover damages from shopkeeper for injury suffered consequent upon being sold fireworks (parents who ordered child to return fireworks to store — injuries being suffered while child returning — could not).

Newton v Edgerley [1959] 3 All ER 337; (1959) 109 LJ 588; (1959) 103 SJ 919; [1959] 1 WLR 1031 HC QBD Parent negligent in buying gun for child/not giving proper instruction on use before others.

O'Connor v British Transport Commission [1958] 1 All ER 558; (1958) 108 LJ 232; (1958) 102 SJ 214 CA Injury of child on train not negligence of train owner as reasonable care of child responsibility of accompanying adult.

Penny v Northampton Borough Council (1974) 124 NLJ 768t; (1974) 118 SJ 628 CA Failed negligence action for damages on foot of injury suffered by child trespassing on council rubbish tip on which children often trespassed.

Perry v Thomas Wrigley, Ltd and others [1955] 3 All ER 243; (1955) 105 LJ 633; (1955) 99 SJ 781; [1955] 1 WLR 1164 HC QBD On duty of care towards children.

Phipps v Rochester Corporation [1955] 1 All ER 129; (1955) 119 JP 92; (1955) 105 LJ 41; [1955] 1 QB 450; (1955) 99 SJ 45; [1955] 2 WLR 23 HC QBD Occupier not liable in negligence to child as unaccompanied by parent so trespasser/or though child licensee was unreasonable for child to be there unaccompanied.

Prince and another v Gregory and another [1959] 1 All ER 133; (1959) 103 SJ 130 CA Owner/occupier not liable for accident occurring through children playing with lime mortar left outside premises pending repairs.

Proctor v British Northrop Co Ltd (1937) 81 SJ 611 CA Defendants not liable for injury to child trespasser (who knew should not have been where was) where took all reasonable steps/did not lay trap.

Purkis v Walthamstow Borough Council [1934] All ER 64; (1934) 98 JP 244 CA Child using playground swing a licensee.

R Addie and Sons (Collieries), Ltd v Dumbreck [1929] All ER 1; (1929) 67 LJ 254; (1929) 98 LJPC 119; (1929) WN (I) 57 HL Absent malicious intent occupier not liable in negligence to trespasser, even child trespasser.

Ryan v London Borough of Camden [1982] TLR 640 CA Local authority not liable in negligence for injury suffered by child who touched uninsulated heating pipe as could reasonably expect parents to safegard children from doing same.

Schofield v Mayor, &c, of Bolton (1909-10) 54 SJ 213; (1909-10) XXVI TLR 230 CA Persons allowing children to play in field not liable in negligence where left gate to railway line open, child went onto line and was injured.

Tynan v Bailey and others (1972) 116 SJ 922 CA Members of residents' association not liable for injury occasioned to child by barrier association erected at end of private road (accident not reasonably foreseeable).

Videan and another v British Transport Commission [1963] 2 All ER 860; (1963) 113 LJ 529; [1963] 2 QB 650; (1963) 107 SJ 458; [1963] 3 WLR 374 CA Child trespasser could not recover damages for negligence; stationmaster on tracks was reasonably foreseeable so duty of care/damages.

Walder v The Mayor, Aldermen and Burgesses of the Borough of Hammersmith [1944] 1 All ER 490; (1944) 108 JP 224; (1945) 95 LJ 111 HC KBD No duty of care towards (child) trespasser.

Yachuk and Another v Oliver Blais Co, Ld [1949] 2 All ER 150; [1949] AC 386; (1949) LXV TLR 300; (1949) WN (I) 186 PC No contributory negligence by young child purchaser of petrol: seller thereof completely liable for later injuries suffered by child.

NEGLIGENCE (club)

Orchard v Connaught Club, Limited (1930) 74 SJ 169; (1929-30) XLVI TLR 214; (1930) WN (I) 38 HC KBD Club rule precluded liability in negligence for loss of member's goods.

Prole v Allen and others [1950] 1 All ER 476 Assizes Club steward liable to club member for injury caused upon his doing his duties negligently.

Robertson v Ridley and another [1989] 2 All ER 474; (1989) 133 SJ 1170; [1989] 1 WLR 872 CA That certain members responsible for conduct of club does not mean responsible for condition of premises.

NEGLIGENCE (coastguard)

Skinner v Secretary of State for Transport [1995] TLR 2 HC QBD No duty of care owed by coast guard to seafarer.

NEGLIGENCE (company administrator)

Re Charnley Davies Ltd [1990] TLR 481 HC ChD On duty of care owed by company administrator.

NEGLIGENCE (contract)

Vacwell Engineering Co Ltd v BDH Chemicals Ltd (formerly British Drug Houses Ltd) [1969] 3 All ER 1681; [1971] 1 QB 88; [1969] 3 WLR 927 HC QBD Negligent where occurrence — but not scale — of explosion foreseeable; negligent failing to warn of dangers; breach of implied condition that would warn of dangers.

NEGLIGENCE (corporation)

Williams and another v Natural Life Health Foods Ltd and another (1996) 140 SJ LB 43; [1997] TLR 24 HC QBD Company director found liable for tortious acts of company.

NEGLIGENCE (criminal)

Smith v Linskills (a firm) (1996) 146 NLJ 209; (1996) TLR 7/2/96 CA Convict's negligence suit against solicitor who defended him in criminal action a collateral attack on criminal action and so unpermitted.

NEGLIGENCE (Crown Prosecution Service)

Welsh v Chief Constable of the Merseyside Police and another [1993] 1 All ER 692 HC QBD Crown Prosecution Service open to negligence action for failures in administrative but not advocacy duties.

NEGLIGENCE (damages)

Allen v Bloomsbury Health Authority and another [1993] 1 All ER 651 HC QBD Damages available for general discomfort; cost of upkeep until adulthood and, if necessary, additional anxiety caused by unwanted pregnancy following sterilisation.

Allen v Waters and Co [1924-35] All ER 671; [1935] 1 KB 200; [1935] LJNCCA 86; (1935) 152 LTR 179; (1934-35) LI TLR 50; (1934) WN (I) 201 CA Damages untouched though included amount for debt recoverable from but unpaid by person awarded damages.

Ashcroft v Curtin [1971] 3 All ER 1208; (1971) 121 NLJ 665t; [1971] 1 WLR 1731 CA Damages for decrease in profitability of concern too vague to be recovered.

Baker v Willoughby [1969] 2 All ER 549; (1969) 113 SJ 37; [1969] 2 WLR 489 CA Equal blameworthiness: appropriate damages.

Baxter v FW Gapp and Co Ltd and another (1938) 82 SJ 1032 HC KBD On appropriate damages for negligent evaluation of property.

Baxter v Gapp (FW) and Company, Limited, and Gapp [1939] 2 KB 271; [1939] 108 LJCL 522; (1939) 83 SJ 436; (1938-39) LV TLR 739; (1939) WN (I) 201 CA On appropriate damages for negligent evaluation of property.

Benham v Gambling [1941] 1 All ER 7; [1941] AC 157; (1941) 91 LJ 26; (1942) 92 LJ 61; [1941] 110 LJ 49; (1941) 164 LTR 290; (1940) 84 SJ 703; (1940-41) LVII TLR 177 HL On appropriate damages from road death: damages not gauged on actuarial basis.

Bennett v Chemical Construction (GB) Ltd [1971] 3 All ER 822; (1971) 121 NLJ 525t; (1971) 115 SJ 550; [1971] 1 WLR 1571 CA If occurrence which takes place seems impossible otherwise than through defendant's negligence, is for defendants to prove contrary.

Berriello v Felixstowe Dock and Railway Co (1989) 133 SJ 918; [1989] 1 WLR 695 CA Amount paid from seaman's fund not deductible from loss of earning damages.

Billingham v Hughes and another [1949] 1 All ER 684; [1949] 1 KB 643; (1949) LXV TLR 246; (1949) WN (I) 135 CA Damages for loss of future earnings are for gross earnings.

Bishop v Cunard White Star, Ltd; Appleby v Cunard White Star, Ltd; The Queen Mary [1950] 2 All ER 22 HC PDAD On assessment of fatal accident/negligence damages.

Breeze and another v R McKennon and Son Ltd and others (1986) 130 SJ 16 CA On evidence necessary to support request for interim payment of damages.

Cain (Administrator of the estate of Jill M Cain (deceased)) v Wilcock [1968] 3 All ER 817; (1969) 119 NLJ 12; (1968) 112 SJ 844; [1968] 1 WLR 1961 CA On damages for (infant's) loss of expectation of life.

Capps v Miller [1989] 2 All ER 333; [1989] RTR 312; (1989) 133 SJ 1134; [1989] 1 WLR 839 CA Improperly fastening crash helmet contributory negligence meriting 10% reduction in damages.

Chadwick v Parsons (1971) 121 NLJ 177t; (1971) 115 SJ 127 HC QBD On awarding interest on damages.

Cooper v Firth Brown, Ltd [1963] 2 All ER 31; [1963] 1 WLR 418 Assizes Damages for loss of earnings concern net earnings.

Darbishire v Warran [1963] 3 All ER 310; (1963) 107 SJ 631; [1963] 1 WLR 1067 CA Damages greater than cost of replacing damaged chattel irrecoverable.

Davies and another v Powell Duffryn Associated Collieries, Ltd [1942] 1 All ER 657; [1942] AC 601; [1942] 111 LJ 418; (1943) 93 LJ 115; (1942) 167 LTR 74; (1942) 86 SJ 294; (1941-42) LVIII TLR 240; (1942) WN (I) 175 HL Damages obtained under Law Reform (Miscellaneous Provisions) Act 1934 relevant when determining damages under Fatal Accidents Act 1846.

Dodd Properties(Kent) Ltd and another v Canterbury City Council and others [1980] 1 All ER 928 (1980) 130 NLJ 66; (1980) 124 SJ 84; [1980] 1 WLR 433 CA Damages for building repairs are compensatory; cost of repairs that on date of action.

Emeh v Kensington, Chelsea and Fulham Area Health Authority and others [1983] TLR 6 HC QBD No damages for loss associated with birth of child following negligent sterilisation operation (damages for sickness/suffering occasioned by pregnancy and for pain of repeat sterilisation operation).

Gardner (JA) v Fishel (JH) (1977) 127 NLJ 1152 CA On relevancy of law reports to assessment of appropriate damages in negligence action.

Haley v London Electricity Board (1964) 108 SJ 1013 HC QBD On appropriate damages for blind person essentially rendered deaf by negligence of another.

Heatley and another v Steel Co of Wales, Ltd [1953] 1 All ER 489; (1953) 97 SJ 149; [1953] 1 WLR 405 CA Appropriate fatal injury damages.

Jeffery v Smith (1970) 120 NLJ 272t; [1970] RTR 279; (1970) 114 SJ 268 CA On appropriate damages in negligence for loss to husband of services of wife killed in motor accident.

Johnson v Hill [1945] 2 All ER 272; (1945) 173 LTR 38; (1944-45) LXI TLR 398 CA Crown pension relevant when determining fatal accident damages.

Jones v Great Western Railway Company [1924-35] All ER 462; (1931) 144 LTR 194; (1930-31) XLVII TLR 39 HL Fatal accident damages allowed in respect of accident to which no witnesses in action to which defence submitted was no case to answer.

Lory v Great Western Railway Company [1942] 1 All ER 230; (1943) 93 LJ 116; (1942) WN (I) 73 HC KBD Charitable/voluntary pensions deductible from fatal accident damages.

Malcolm and another v Broadhurst [1970] 3 All ER 508 HC QBD Reasonably foreseeable that unstable wife would be affected by negligent injury to husband; no damages for loss of wages by wife.

Malyon v Lawrence, Messer and Co (1969) 119 NLJ 38; (1968) 112 SJ 623 HC QBD Recovery of damages from solicitors which would have recovered in action in Germany had not negligence of solicitors led to action being time-barred.

Meah v McCreamer [1985] 1 All ER 367; (1985) 135 NLJ 80; [1984] TLR 426 HC QBD Damages for imprisonment for offences committed following on personality change occasioned by negligence of defendant.

Meah v McCreamer and others (No 2) [1986] 1 All ER 943; (1986) 136 NLJ 235; (1985) 135 NLJ 80 HC QBD Damages unavailable to meet cost of damages paid to third party for acts arising from earlier negligent action.

Muirhead v Industrial Tank Specialities Ltd and others (1985) 135 NLJ 1106; [1986] QB 507; (1985) 129 SJ 855; [1985] 3 WLR 993 CA On recoverability of damages in negligence for physical loss/pure economic loss.

Oliver and others v Ashman and another [1960] 3 All ER 677; (1960) 110 LJ 830; (1961) 111 LJ 580; [1961] 1 QB 337 HC QBD Shortened lifespan/that most of damages will not be spent on claimant relevant in deciding level of damages.

Parry v Cleaver [1967] 2 All ER 1168; (1967) 117 NLJ 810; [1968] 1 QB 195; (1967) 111 SJ 415; [1967] 3 WLR 739 CA Damages reduced by compulsory pension.

Perry v Sidney Phillips and Son (a firm) [1982] 1 All ER 1005; (1981) 131 NLJ 1135 HC QBD Damages available for cost of repairing defects (not difference between cost/value) where will occupy negligently surveyed house; occupier's delay of repairs undiscovered by negligent surveyor reasonable if no money; damages available for distress/discomfort of repairs/occupying defective house.

Povey v WE and E Jackson (a firm) [1970] 2 All ER 495; (1970) 114 SJ 269; [1970] 1 WLR 969 CA On quantum of damages appeals.

Pryce v Elwood (1964) 108 SJ 583 HC QBD No deduction for income tax for damages payable for loss of trading profits suffered by plaintiff car hirer as reult of collision occasioned by defendant.

Roberts v Naylor Brothers, Ltd [1959] 2 All ER 409; (1959) 103 SJ 491 HC QBD Disablement gratuity deductible from loss of earnings.

Romford Ice and Cold Storage [1955] 3 All ER 460 CA On recovery of damages from joint tortfeasor/from servant.

SCM (United Kingdom) Ltd v WJ Whittall and Son Ltd [1970] 3 All ER 245; (1970) 120 NLJ 684t; [1971] 1 QB 337; (1970) 114 SJ 706; [1970] 3 WLR 694 CA Liable for physical damage and loss of profit where negligently interrupt electricity supply by damaging cable.

Shepherd v Hunter [1938] 2 All ER 587; (1938) 85 LJ 361; (1938) 82 SJ 375 CA Appropriate damages for loss of life expectancy (of infant).

Shiels v Cruikshank (1953) 103 LJ 232; (1953) 97 SJ 208; [1953] 1 WLR 533 HL Widow's own income not relevant when determining damages available after husband's death resulting from another's negligence.

Small v Pilkington Bros Ltd (1971) 121 NLJ 1048t CA On appropriate damages where wrist fractured through negligence of another.

Smith v British European Airways Corporation and another [1951] 2 All ER 737; [1951] 2 KB 893; (1951) 101 LJ 498; [1951] 2 TLR 608 HC KBD Death benefit deductible from fatal accident damages; on infants'/widow's right of recovery despite latter's acceptance of death benefit.

Spartan Steel and Alloys Ltd v Martin and Co (Contractors) Ltd [1972] 3 All ER 557; (1972) 122 NLJ 585t; [1973] QB 27; (1972) 116 SJ 648; [1972] 3 WLR 502 CA Liability for physical damage but not non-consequential economic loss: no doctrine of 'parasitic damages'.

Swingcastle Ltd v Gibson [1990] 3 All ER 463; (1990) 140 NLJ 818; [1990] 1 WLR 1223 CA Negligent surveyor liable to mortgagee for all loss where mortgagee seeks to sell property following mortgagor's default on repayment.

Sykes and others v Midland Bank Executor and Trustee Co Ltd and others [1970] 2 All ER 471; [1971] 1 QB 113; (1970) 114 SJ 225; [1970] 3 WLR 273 CA Solicitor not advising of unusual clause in lease negligent (but nominal damages for breach of contract if client does not prove negligence led to acting as did).

Vernon v Bosley [1997] 1 All ER 577; (1996) 146 NLJ 589; (1997) 141 SJ LB 27; [1997] RTR 1; (1996) TLR 4/4/96 CA Damages available for mental illness (stemming from another's negligence) attributable in part to grief and bereavement.

Warboys (JH) v Sherburn (JA) (1977) 127 NLJ 1151b CA On best means of assessing appropriate damages in negligence actions (by reference to medical reports not law reports).

Ward v Cannock Chase District Council [1986] Ch 546; (1986) 130 SJ 316; [1986] 2 WLR 660 HC ChD On damages available upon damage to house resulting from council's disrepair of neighbouring buildings/vandalism consequent upon neglect.

Warren and another v King and others [1963] 3 All ER 521; (1963) 113 LJ 705; [1964] 1 WLR 1 CA On proper direction on/level of damages (for paralysed infant) and rôle of appellate court regarding jury awards.

Wieland v Cyril Lord Carpets, Ltd [1969] 3 All ER 1006 HC QBD Damages available for second injury on foot of original negligence.

Williamson v John I Thornycroft and Co, Ltd and others; Goulding and another v John I Thornycroft and Co, Ltd and others [1940] 4 All ER 61 CA In assessing damages for negligence which caused death all occurrences before date of trial are relevant.

NEGLIGENCE (dangerous goods)

Andrews v Hopkinson [1956] 3 All ER 422; [1957] 1 QB 229; [1956] 3 WLR 732 Assizes Non-purchaser could rely on warranty that induced hire-purchase arrangement; damages for personal injuries for breach of warranty that was safe car; damages for negligence in delivering unsafe car when defects reasonably discoverable by supplier.

Anglo-Celtic Shipping Company, Limited v Elliott and Jeffery and others (1925-26) XLII TLR 297 HC KBD Manufacturer liable for injuries sustained through use of product dangerous in itself and in respect of using which did not give proper warning.

Barnett v H and J Packer and Co, Ltd [1940] 3 All ER 575 HC KBD Donoghue v Stevenson applicable where injury occurred before examination possible.

Bates and another v Batey and Co, Limited [1913] 3 KB 351; [1913] 82 LJKB 963; (1913) 108 LTR 1036; (1912-13) XXIX TLR 616; (1913) WN (I) 213 HC KBD Manufacturers not liable for injury caused to purchaser via defective bottle even though could have discovered defect had they exercised reasonable care.

Beckett v Newalls Insulation Co, Ltd and another [1953] 1 All ER 250; (1953) 97 SJ 8; [1953] 1 WLR 8 CA Heightened standard of care required where one's task poses heightened risk to others.

Blacker v Lake and Elliot Limited (1912) 106 LTR 533 HC KBD Manufacturer not liable to third-party user of defectively manufactured article that is obviously dangerous/has been revealed by manufacturer to be so.

British Chartered Company of South Africa v Lennon (Limited) [1916] 85 LJPC 111; (1915-16) 113 LTR 935; (1914-15) XXXI TLR 585 PC Recovery of damages for loss suffered through use of cattle dip marketed as particular concentrate but actually stronger.

Castree v ER Squibb and Sons Ltd and another (1980) 124 SJ 743; [1980] 1 WLR 1248 CA Was actionable tort where machine though manufactured abroad was placed on market in England without warning as to special dangers.

Daniels and Wife v R White and Sons Limited and another (1939) 160 LTR 128 HC KBD Failed/successful negligence action against vendor/producer for selling lemonade not fit for human consumption.

Devilez v Boots Pure Drug Co, Ltd and another (1962) 106 SJ 552 HC QBD Manufacturers/ vendors of corn solvent owed special duty of care to purchasers.

Dominion Natural Gas Co v Collins; Same v Perkins and others [1908-10] All ER 61; [1909] AC 640; [1910] 79 LJPC 13; (1909-10) 101 LTR 359; (1908-09) XXV TLR 831 PC Heavy duty of care imposed on supplier of dangerous substance.

Dransfield v British Insulated Cables, Ltd [1937] 4 All ER 382; (1937) 84 LJ 360; (1938) 82 SJ 95; (1937-38) LIV TLR 11 HC KBD Manufacturers escaped liability for death resulting from use of defective product as was chance of intermediate inspection.

Duncan v Cammell Laird and Co, Ltd; Craven v Same; Duncan v Wailes Dove Bitumastic, Ltd; Craven v Same [1943] 2 All ER 621 HC KBD Making an undangerous thing dangerous did not create liability unless reasonable man would have appreciated new danger; contractor liable for danger-causing acts of competent sub-contractor.

Evans v Triplex Safety Glass Co, Ltd [1936] 1 All ER 283 HC KBD Delay between buying car/windscreen smashing; chance to examine windscreen; possible cause other than manufacturer's negligence meant manufacturer not liable in negligence for occurrence.

Farr v Butters Bros and Co [1932] All ER 339; [1932] 2 KB 606; (1932) 74 LJ 144; (1932) 101 LJCL 768; (1932) 147 LTR 427; (1932) WN (I) 171 CA Manufacturer not liable for defect in product that could be and was discovered before use.

Fisher v Harrods, Ltd (1965-66) 116 NLJ 919; (1966) 110 SJ 133 HC QBD Store liable for not exercising adequate care in marketing goods produced by unknown manufacturer.

Haseldine v CA Daw and Son, Ltd and others [1941] 1 All ER 525 HC KBD Flatowner liable for negligence of agent contractors; owner owed duty to warn licensee of dangers of which actually knew (did not know here); defence of having employed competent independent contractor not open as only limited maintenance contract; contractor liable for defective repairs.

Herschthal v Stewart and Arden, Limited [1939] 4 All ER 123; [1940] 1 KB 155; (1939) 88 LJ 299; [1940] 109 LJCL 328; (1939) 161 LTR 331; (1940) 84 SJ 79; (1939-40) LVI TLR 48; (1939) WN (I) 371 HC KBD Interpretation of Donoghue v Stevenson: on intermediate examination of item.

Hill v James Crowe (Cases) Ltd [1978] 1 All ER 812; (1977) 127 NLJ 637 HC QBD Manufacturer vicariously liable for workmen's negligence despite good work system/proper supervision.

Holmes v Ashford and others (1950) 94 SJ 226; (1950) WN (I) 117 HC KBD Manufacturers and commercial buyer of hair-dye, use of which involved certain dangers did not meet duty of care owed to final recipient.

Holmes v Ashford and others [1950] 2 All ER 76; (1950) 94 SJ 337; (1950) WN (I) 269 CA Manufacturers having warned commercial buyer of dangers did not owe duty to final recipient.

Jefferson and others v Derbyshire Farmers, Limited [1921] 2 KB 281; [1921] LJCL 1361; (1921) 124 LTR 775 CA Master liable for negligence of servant in respect of dangerous object regarding which failed to take extra care.

Kubach and another v Hollands and another; Frederick Allen and Sons (Poplar), Limited (Third Party) (1937) 84 LJ 157; (1937) 81 SJ 766; (1936-37) LIII TLR 1024 HC KBD Negligent suppliers of chemicals to school who were successfully sued by student injured through their negligence could not in turn recover against wholesale suppliers.

Larking v Bunnell (1912) CC Rep I 23 CyCt Person bringing article dangerous in itself (here gas) into premises not liable where accident occurs that does not arise from said person not exercising reasonable care.

McAlister (or Donoghue) (Pauper) v Stevenson [1932] All ER 1; [1932] AC 562; (1932) 73 LJ 428; (1932) 101 LJPC 119; (1932) 147 LTR 281; (1932) 76 SJ 396; (1931-32) XLVIII TLR 494; (1932) WN (I) 139 HL Manufacturer owes duty of reasonable care to ultimate consumer to ensure item does not endanger health where intermediate examination not possible.

Miller and others v Ismay Distributors, Ltd [1939] LJNCCR 112 CyCt Mother of child injured by defectively constructed electric washing machine allowed recover damagaes for shock from manufacturer.

Owners of the Steamship Pass of Ballater v Cardiff Channel Dry Docks and Pontoon Co, Ltd [1942] 2 All ER 79 HC PDAD Very strict duty of care on party bringing dangerous substances into place: defence that gave task of policing safety to independent contractor not good.

Paine v Colne Valley Electricity Supply Co, Ltd and British Insulated Cables, Ltd [1938] 4 All ER 803; (1939) 83 SJ 115; (1938-39) LV TLR 181 HC KBD Manufacturer not liable in respect of dangerous article where ample chance of inspection.

Philco Radio and Television Corporation of Great Britain, Ltd v Spurling (J), Ltd and others [1949] 2 All ER 882; (1949) 99 LJ 637; (1949) LXV TLR 757; (1949) WN (I) 271 CA Strict liability where bringing dangerous goods onto premises.

Procter and others v Pauldens, Limited; WT French and Son, Third Party [1934] LJNCCR 263 CyCt Kettle-sellers and manufacturers of kettle liable in negligence for injury occasioned to wife/child of purchaser for injuries suffered short time after purchase as result of defect in kettle.

Ricketts v Erith Borough Council and another [1943] 2 All ER 629; (1944) 108 JP 22; (1944) 94 LJ 108; [1944] 113 LJ 269; (1943) 169 LTR 396 HC KBD Bow and arrow not dangerous thing so no duty on seller; absence of teacher from school playground during breaktime not negligent.

Rock v Smith's, Ltd [1936] LJNCCR 31 CyCt Sellers of piano stool deemed not to be liable for personal injuries suffered as result of latent defect in stool.

Watson v Buckley, Osborne, Garrett and Co, Ltd, and Wyrovoys Products, Ltd [1940] 1 All ER 174; (1940) 89 LJ 45 HC KBD Donoghue v Stevenson applied to goods distributors.

Weaver v Commercial Process Company, Limited, and others (1947) LXIII TLR 466 HC KBD Apportionment of respective negligence of suppliers/receivers of defective jar of nitric acid which resulted in injury to employee of receivers.

Webber v McCausland (1948) 98 LJ 360 CyCt Hairdresser liable in negligence for sale of dangerous hair dye (though plaintiff contributorily negligent in not fully reading warning on bottle).

William Leitch and Co Limited v Leydon; AG Barr and Co Limited v Macgheoghean (1930) 70 LJ 375; (1931) 100 LJPC 10; (1931) 144 LTR 218 HL Water vendor did not owe duty of care to aerated water manufacturer (with whom had no contract) to ensure that bottles supplied for vendor to fill were not those of said manufacturer/put to use of which said manufacturer did not approve.

Wright v Dunlop Rubber Co Ltd and ICI Ltd; Cassidy v Same (1971) 121 NLJ 361 HC QBD Factory owners liable for negligent exposure of workers to carcinogen (liable from moment discovered its effects); manufacturers of chemical liable in negligence for not withdrawing it from sale.

NEGLIGENCE (delay)

Savill v Southend Health Authority [1995] 1 WLR 1254 CA Non-exercise of discretion/dismissal of appeal (against dismissal of claim on want of prosecution basis) where notice of appeal issued five days out of time was valid.

NEGLIGENCE (dentist)

Fish v Kapur and another [1948] 2 All ER 176; (1948) LXIV TLR 328 HC KBD Tooth remaining/fractured jaw not res ipsa loquitur that dentist negligent.

NEGLIGENCE (director)

Al-Nakib Investments (Jersey) Ltd and another v Longcroft and others [1990] 3 All ER 321; (1990) 140 NLJ 741; [1990] 1 WLR 1390 HC ChD Duty of care owed by company directors to persons subscribing for shares in reliance on prospectus does not extend to persons buying shares on stock market in reliance on prospectus.

Dovey and others v Cory (1901-02) LXXXV LTR 257 HL Non-liability of director in negligence for acting in good faith on the false statements of company officers.

Merchants' Fire Office (Lim) v Armstrong and others (1901) 36 LJ 403; (1900-01) 45 SJ 706 CA Negligent company directors liable to repay to company amount paid out negligently.

Morgan Crucible Co plc v Hill Samuel Bank Ltd and others [1991] 1 All ER 148; [1991] Ch 295 (also HC ChD); (1990) 140 NLJ 1605; [1990] TLR 699; [1991] 2 WLR 655 CA Duty of care on directors of/financial advisers to company not to make misleading statements to known bidder.

Morgan Crucible Co plc v Hill Samuel Bank Ltd and others [1990] 3 All ER 330; [1991] Ch 295 (also CA); (1990) 140 NLJ 1271 HC ChD Directors of/financial advisers to company owe no duty of care to known take-over bidder in preparation of documents prepared to contest bid.

Multinational Gas and Petrochemical Co v Multinational Gas and Petrochemical Services Ltd and others [1983] Ch 258 CA Company could not sue directors for negligence where shareholders had ratified actions of directors.

Pavlides v Jensen and others [1956] 3 WLR 224 HC ChD Negligence claim against directors for alleged non-fraudulent sale of company assets at under-value was unmaintainable.

Re Brazilian Rubber Plantations and Estates, Limited [1911] 1 Ch 425; (1911) 80 LJCh 221 HC ChD Director's acceptance of statements in report on which based prospectus not grossly negligent.

Re City of London Insurance Company, Limited (1924-25) XLI TLR 521 HC ChD Company director deemed personally liable where own negligence resulted in loss to company.

Williams and another v Natural Life Health Foods Ltd and another (1996) 140 SJ LB 43 HC QBD Company director found liable for tortious acts of company.

NEGLIGENCE (duty of care)

Adams v Southern Electricity Board [1993] TLR 512 CA On extent of duty of care owed by electricity board towards teenage trespasser — here failed to meet that duty of care.

Bux v Slough Metals [1974] 1 All ER 262 CA Correspondence between common law and statutory duty of care a question of fact in each case.

Hurley v Dyke and others [1979] RTR 265 (also CA/HL) HC QBD Vendors of second-hand car sold via auction at which car stated to be 'As seen and with all its faults' had not discharged their duty of care towards later passenger in car injured as result of its defects.

Hurley v Dyke and others [1979] RTR 265 (also QBD/HL) CA Vendors of second-hand car sold via auction at which car stated to be 'As seen and with all its faults' had discharged their duty of care towards later passenger in car injured as result of its defects.

Nelson Holdings Ltd v British Gas plc and others [1997] TLR 122 HC QBD Generally no duty of care owed by fire authority to owner of burning property.

NEGLIGENCE (ear-piercing)

Phillips v William Whiteley, Limited (1938) 82 SJ 196; (1937-38) LIV TLR 379 HC KBD On duty of care owed by ear-piercer.

NEGLIGENCE (economic loss)

Marc Rich and Co AG and others v Bishop Rock Marine Co Ltd and others 'The Nicholas H' [1994] 3 All ER 686; [1994] TLR 101; [1994] 1 WLR 1071 CA No distinction in law between cases where negligence causes physical damage and where causes economic loss; classification society valuers not under duty of care to shipowners.

Old Gate Estates, Ltd v Toplis and Harding and Russell [1939] 3 All ER 209; (1939) 88 LJ 11; (1939) 161 LTR 227; (1939) 83 SJ 606 HC KBD No recovery for pure economic loss.

NEGLIGENCE (education)

Jones v Lawrence [1969] 3 All ER 267 Assizes Normal carelessness of 7 year old not negligence; damages for loss of grammar school place/concentration.

NEGLIGENCE (electricity)

Lait v AA King (Contractors) Ltd, London Electricity Board and Pitchers (1975) 125 NLJ 432 HC QBD Person who damaged electric cable plates but did not tell Electricity Board was liable along with later worker's employer for injury that followed from damage (Electricity Board not liable).

SCM (United Kingdom) Ltd v WJ Whittall and Son Ltd [1970] 2 All ER 417; (1970) 114 SJ 268; [1970] 1 WLR 1017 HC QBD Damage to electric cable causing electricity loss raised liability in negligence not nuisance.

NEGLIGENCE (escape)

HM Postmaster General v Blackpool and Fleetwood Tramroad Company, Ltd (1918) CC Rep VII 3 CyCt Tram company not liable for damage occasioned to telephone cable by escape of electricity from tram lines absent proof of negligence/non-compliance with relevant regulations.

Irish Linen Manufacturing Co v Lowe (1956) 106 LJ ccr828 CyCt Failed action in negligence where water escaped from one premises into another.

Mason v Levy Auto Parts of England, Ltd [1967] 2 All ER 62; [1967] 2 QB 530; [1967] 2 WLR 1384 Assizes Liable for escape of fire if during non-natural land use keep things likely to ignite and do and fire spreads.

North-Western Utilities, Limited v London Guarantee and Accident Company, Limited, and others [1935] All ER 196; [1936] AC 108; (1935) 80 LJ 378; [1936] 105 LJPC 18; (1936) 154 LTR 89; (1935) 79 SJ 902; (1935-36) LII TLR 93; (1935) WN (1) 176 PC Gas company under duty of care to protect general public from effects of City works close by mains.

Postmaster General v Blackpool and Fleetwood Tramroad Co (1920) CC Rep IX 81; (1920) 55 LJ 387 CA Tram company liable for damage occasioned to telephone cable by escape of electricity from tram lines.

Prosser (A) and Son, Ltd v Levy and others and Barden Morris Incorporated, Ltd (1955) 105 LJ 569 HC QBD On liability for escape of water in office premises.

Prosser (A) and Son, Ltd v Levy and others [1955] 3 All ER 577; (1955) 105 LJ 760; (1955) 99 SJ 815; [1955] 1 WLR 1224 CA Trustees liable in negligence where left pipe in bad condition and water escaped for no apparent reason.

Sturge v Hackett [1962] 3 All ER 166; [1962] 1 WLR 1257 CA Occupier liable for escape of fire and in negligence for starting fire.

NEGLIGENCE (estate agent)

McCullagh v Lane Fox and Ptnrs Ltd (1994) 138 SJ LB 53; [1994] TLR 40 HC QBD Estate agent owed duty of care to client in respect of description of size of property sold (which agent misrepresented).

McCullagh v Lane Fox and Partners Ltd [1995] TLR 700 CA Estate agent did not duty of care to client in respect of description of size of property sold (which agent misrepresented).

NEGLIGENCE (estoppel)

Central Newbury Car Auctions, Ltd v Unity Finance, Ltd and another (Mercury Motors Third Parties) [1956] 3 All ER 905; (1957) 107 LJ 9; [1957] 1 QB 371; [1956] 3 WLR 1068 CA Passing registration book/car itself did not preclude later denial of title of third party as passing did not confer right to sell.

Moorgate Mercantile Co Ltd v Twitchings [1976] 2 All ER 641; [1977] AC 890; [1976] QB 225; [1976] RTR 437; (1976) 120 SJ 470; [1976] 3 WLR 66 HL Statement that records indicate certain state not representation that state exists; no duty of care so no estoppel by negligence.

Nationwide Building Society v Lewis [1997] 3 All ER 498 HC ChD Estopped from denying liability as partner for negligence of other solicitor-partner where relationship really one of master and servant, not partnership but had been held out to plaintiff as partnership.

Orbit Mining and Trading Co, Ltd v Westminster Bank, Ltd (1962) 112 LJ 338; (1962) 106 SJ 373 HC QBD Bank negligent in its collection of cheques; true owner of goods may recover for conversion of same though has assisted in loss suffered through his own negligence.

Orbit Mining and Trading Co, Ltd v Westminster Bank, Ltd (1962) 106 SJ 937 CA Bank not negligent in its collection of cheques.

Talbot v Berkshire County Council [1993] 4 All ER 9; (1993) 143 NLJ 402; [1994] QB 290; [1993] RTR 406; [1993] TLR 168; [1993] 3 WLR 708 CA Rule barring action where one already brought by co-plaintiff for same cause against same defendant applies to personal injuries.

Wilson and Meeson (a Firm) v Pickering [1946] 1 All ER 394; [1946] KB 422; (1945-46) LXII TLR 223; (1946) WN (I) 51 CA Estoppel by negligence could not arise as no duty owed/bias suffered and was fraud not negligence at centre of action; estoppel applying to blank instruments given to agents does not apply to non-negotiable instruments.

NEGLIGENCE (exclusion of liability)

Adler v Dickson and another [1954] 3 All ER 21; (1954) 104 LJ 633; [1955] 1 QB 158; (1954) 98 SJ 592; [1954] 3 WLR 450 HC QBD Company's exemption clauses did not protect servants of company.

Adler v Dickson and another (1954) 104 LJ 761; [1954] 3 WLR 696 CA Company's exemption clauses did not protect servants of company.

Adler v Jackson and another [1954] 3 All ER 397 CA Company's exemption clauses did not protect servants of company.

Arthur White (Contractors) Ltd v Tarmac Civil Engineering Ltd (1967) 111 SJ 831; [1967] 1 WLR 1508 HL Exceptions clause excluding liability for negligence of driver supplied along with hired equipment to hirer valid and enforced.

Ashdown v Samuel Williams and Sons, Ltd and another [1957] 1 All ER 35; (1957) 107 LJ 42; [1957] 1 QB 409; (1956) 100 SJ 945; [1956] 3 WLR 1104 CA Exemption notice applied though plaintiff unaware of specific contents as had been adequately brought to her attention.

Barking and Dagenham London Borough Council v Stamford Asphalt Co Ltd and another [1997] TLR 193 CA Negligent contractor could not avoid liability by way of clause in JCT building contract which required employer to insure self against risk of fire.

Cosgrove v Horsfall (1946) 175 LTR 334; (1945-46) LXII TLR 140 CA Negligent driver of omnibus not protected from liability by exemption clause in free bus pass agreement between London Passenger Transport Board and plaintiff.

Cremdean Properties Ltd et anor v Nash et al (1978) 128 NLJ 514c CA Failed appeal against finding that exclusion clause in tender that particulars therein might not be (as were not in fact) entirely correct.

Forbes, Abbott, and Lennard, Limited v Great Western Railway Company [1927] 96 LJCL 995; (1926-27) XLIII TLR 769 HC KBD Chelsea Dock-owners liable for negligence of their servants notwithstanding attempt to exempt liability by way of exemption clause.

Forbes, Abbott, and Lennard Limited v Great Western Railway Company (1928) 138 LTR 286 CA Chelsea Dock-owners not liable for negligence of their servants by virtue of exemption clause in their by-laws.

Grand Trunk Railway Company of Canada v Robinson (Arthur) [1915] AC 740; [1915] 84 LJPC 194; (1915-16) 113 LTR 350; (1914-15) XXXI TLR 395; (1915) WN (I) 173 PC Valid exemption clause in half-fare travel contract.

James Archdale and Co, Ltd v Comservices, Ltd [1954] 1 All ER 210; (1954) 98 SJ 143; [1954] 1 WLR 459 CA Non-applicability of principle that generally worded exception clause does not apply to own/servant's negligence.

Ludditt and others v Ginger Coote Airways, Limited (1947) LXIII TLR 157 PC Contract exempting liability of carrier of passengers for own negligence was valid.

Penton v Southern Railway [1931] 2 KB 103; (1931) 100 LJCL 228; (1931) 144 LTR 614 HC KBD Exemption clause to be adequately drawn to customer's notice: was done here.

Pyman Steamship Company v Hull and Barnsley Railway Company (1914-15) 111 LTR 41; (1913-14) XXX TLR 430 HC KBD Effective exemption of liability clause.

Pyman Steamship Co, Ltd v Hull and Barnsley Rail Co [1914-15] All ER 292; (1915) 112 LTR 1103; (1914-15) XXXI TLR 243 CA Effective exemption of liability clause.

Re Polemis and Furness, Withy and Co, Ltd [1921] All ER 40; [1921] 3 KB 560; [1921] LJCL 1353; (1922) 126 LTR 154 CA Clause exempting liability for negligence must be clearly worded (insufficiently precise here).

Reynolds v Boston Deep Sea Fishing and Ice Company, Limited (1921-22) XXXVIII TLR 429 CA Exemption clause though did not specifically mention negligence did exclude liability for same.

Sugar v London Midland and Scottish Railway Company (1941) 105 JP 100; (1941) 164 LTR 311; (1941) 85 SJ 32; (1940-41) LVII TLR 197 HC KBD Exemption clause inapplicable where had been blocked out by date stamp.

The Cap Palos (1920-21) XXXVII TLR 921 CA Exception clause did not apply when during relevant period had not been acting under contract.

White v Warwick (John) [1953] 2 All ER 1021; (1953) 97 SJ 740; [1953] 1 WLR 1285 CA Hire contract exception clause found to exclude contractual but not tortious liability.

Wilkie (Arthur Reginald) v London Passenger Transport Board [1946] 1 All ER 650; (1946) 110 JP 215; (1946) 175 LTR 331; (1946) 90 SJ 249; (1945-46) LXII TLR 327; (1946) WN (I) 82 HC KBD Exemption clause on free pass applied to free passholder injured as getting on bus; pass a privilege/licence so Road Traffic Act 1930, s 97 inapplicable as no contract for conveyance.

Woolmer v Delmer Price, Ltd [1955] 1 All ER 377; [1955] 1 QB 291; [1955] 2 WLR 329 HC QBD Could not rely on exception clause where no explanation of disappearance of bailed goods offered: must show either negligence or no negligence.

NEGLIGENCE (explosives)

Miles v Forest Rock Granite Company (Leicestershire) (Limited) (1917-18) 62 SJ 634; (1917-18) XXXIV TLR 500 CA Quarry owner to contain effects of explosions on own land — where fails to do so is liable for acts regardless of negligence.

NEGLIGENCE (financial adviser)

Morgan Crucible Co plc v Hill Samuel Bank Ltd and others [1991] 1 All ER 148; [1991] Ch 295 (also HC ChD); (1990) 140 NLJ 1605; [1990] TLR 699; [1991] 2 WLR 655 CA Duty of care on directors of/financial advisers to company not to make misleading statements to known bidder.

Morgan Crucible Co plc v Hill Samuel Bank Ltd and others [1990] 3 All ER 330; [1991] Ch 295 (also CA); (1990) 140 NLJ 1271 HC ChD Directors of/financial advisers to company owe no duty of care to known take-over bidder in preparation of documents prepared to contest bid.

NEGLIGENCE (fire)

Balfour v Barty-King and another (Hyder and Sons (Builders), Ltd Third Parties) [1957] 1 All ER 156; (1957) 107 LJ 57; [1957] 1 QB 496; (1957) 101 SJ 62; [1957] 2 WLR 84 CA Occupiers liable for damage to neighbour's property by fire negligently started by contractors in occupier's premises as was non-accidental fire/not caused by stranger.

Capital and Counties plc v Hampshire County Council and others; Digital Equipment Co Ltd v Hampshire County Council and others [1996] 4 All ER 336; (1996) TLR 26/4/96; [1996] 1 WLR 1553 HC QBD Fire brigade liable in negligence for turning off fire sprinklers thereby causing fire to spread/worsen (as was reasonably foreseeable).

Capital and Counties plc v Hampshire County Council; Digital Equipment Co Ltd v Same; John Munroe (Acrylics) Ltd v London Fire and Civil Defence Authority and others; Church of Jesus Christ of Latter-Day Saints (Great Britain) v West Yorkshire Fire and Civil Defence Authority [1997] 2 All ER 865; [1997] 2 Cr App R (S) 599; (1997) 147 NLJ 598; (1997) 141 SJ LB 92; [1997] TLR 141; [1997] 3 WLR 331 CA On common law liability of fire brigades as regards attending of fires.

Church of Jesus Christ of Latter-Day Saints (Great Britain) v Yorkshire Fire and Civil Defence Authority (1996) TLR 9/5/96 HC QBD Fire brigade does not owe duty of care to owner of burninig property.

CR Taylor (Wholesale) Ltd and others v Hepworths Ltd [1977] 1 WLR 659 HC QBD On appropriate damages for negligent burning of building where owner never so interested in building per se as development possibilities of land on which stood (and which still remained).

Hartley v Mayoh and Co and another [1953] 2 All ER 525; (1953) 117 JP 369 Assizes Fireman an invitee; presumed fireman has ordinary knowledge of shutting off electricity — here occupier negligent as failed to warn fireman of peculiarity of electrical system (and previously to test system); electricity supply board contributorily negligent for electrocution arising in part from defective installation.

Hartley v Mayoh and Co and another [1954] 1 All ER 375; (1954) 118 JP 178; [1954] 1 QB 383; (1954) 98 SJ 107; [1954] 1 WLR 355 CA Fireman an invitee; presumed fireman has ordinary knowledge of shutting off electricity — here occupier negligent as failed to warn fireman of peculiarity of electrical system (and previously to test system).

John Munroe (Acrylics) Ltd v London Fire and Civil Defence Authority and others [1996] 4 All ER 318; (1996) TLR 22/5/96; [1996] 3 WLR 988 HC QBD On extent of liability in negligence of fire brigade vis-a-vis person whose property goes on fire (no duty of care owed in instant case).

Merrington v Ironbridge Metal Works, Ltd, and others [1952] 2 All ER 1101; (1953) 117 JP 23 Assizes Liability to firemen does not rest on how are there; owner not liable as invitor as fireman would probably have risked danger even if told; owner liable to firemen for keeping building in condition dangerous to them; volenti non fit injuria if fully appreciate risk and freely assume that risk.

Mulholland and Tedd, Ltd v Baker [1939] 3 All ER 253; (1939) 87 LJ 453; (1939) 161 LTR 20 HC KBD Recovery of damages under Rylands and Fletcher for heat, smoke and water arising from occurrence of non-accidental fire.

Musgrove v Pandelis [1918-19] All ER 589; [1919] 1 KB 314; (1919) 54 LJ 106; [1919] 88 LJCL 915 (also CA); (1918-19) 63 SJ 353; (1918-19) XXXV TLR 202; (1919) WN (I) 27 HC KBD Liability for fire negligently started.

Musgrove v Pandelis and others [1919] 88 LJCL 915 (also HC KBD); (1919) 120 LTR 601; (1918-19) XXXV TLR 299; (1919) WN (I) 79 CA Liability for fire negligently started.

Ogwo v Taylor [1987] 1 All ER 668; [1988] AC 431 (also HL); (1987) 137 NLJ 99; (1987) 131 SJ 506; [1987] 2 WLR 988 CA Negligent starter of fire liable to fireman for any foreseeable injuries suffered.

Ogwo v Taylor [1987] 3 All ER 961; [1988] AC 431 (also CA); (1987) 137 NLJ 1110; (1987) 131 SJ 1628; [1987] 3 WLR 1145 HL Negligent starter of fire owes duty of care to firemen for injuries suffered extinguishing fire.

Salmon v Seafarers Restaurants Ltd (British Gas Corp, third party) [1983] 3 All ER 729; (1983) 127 SJ 581; [1983] 1 WLR 1264 HC QBD Fireman owed some duty by occupier as any other save that must exercise skill reasonably expected of fireman.

Tyler Mouldings Ltd v Charles Arckoll Ltd (1982) 132 NLJ 534 HC QBD On damages available to company for losses occasioned through fire started by another company.

Watt v Hertfordshire County Council [1954] 2 All ER 368; (1954) 118 JP 377; (1954) 98 SJ 372; [1954] 1 WLR 835 CA Not liable in negligence to fireman for injury resulting from risk that ought reasonably be assumed by fireman.

NEGLIGENCE (fireman)

Watt v Hertfordshire County Council [1954] 1 All ER 141; (1954) 118 JP 97; (1954) 104 LJ 376; [1954] 1 WLR 208 HC QBD Fireman has heavier burden to discharge in proving what asked to do shows employer not taking reasonable care of him.

NEGLIGENCE (foreseeability)

Bradford v Robinson Rentals, Ltd [1967] 1 All ER 267; (1967) 111 SJ 33; [1967] 1 WLR 337 Assizes Recovery where chance of injury reasonably foreseeable but particular injury not so.

NEGLIGENCE (general)

Admiralty Commissioners v Steamship Amerika (Owners); The Amerika [1916-17] All ER 177 HL Cannot recover damages for voluntary losses sustained on foot of negligence.

Aiken and others v Stewart Wrightson Members' Agency Ltd and others [1995] 3 All ER 449; [1995] TLR 149; [1995] 1 WLR 1281 HC QBD Managing agents of underwriting syndicate owe tortious duty of care to existing syndicate members (and to certain prospective members) for reinsurance against loss.

Allied Maples Group Ltd v Simmons and Simmons (a firm) [1995] 4 All ER 907; (1995) 145 NLJ 1646; [1995] 1 WLR 1602 CA If plaintiff's loss on foot of negligent advice rests on imagined action of another and is a substantial chance that other would have acted to confer benefit on or avoid risk to plaintiff the evaluation of that chance is for judge determining quantum.

Almeroth v Chivers (WE) and Sons, Ltd [1948] 1 All ER 53 CA Slates left on kerb were nuisance (de minimis non curat lex); not contributorily negligent that did not see.

AMF International, Ltd v Magnet Bowling, Ltd and another [1968] 2 All ER 789; (1968) 112 SJ 522; [1968] 1 WLR 1028 HC QBD Application of occupier's liability/negligence principles.

Andrews v Hopkinson [1956] 3 All ER 422; [1957] 1 QB 229; [1956] 3 WLR 732 Assizes Non-purchaser could rely on warranty that induced hire-purchase arrangement; damages for personal injuries for breach of warranty that was safe car; damages for negligence in delivering unsafe car when defects reasonably discoverable by supplier.

Andrews v Schooling and others [1991] 3 All ER 723 CA Interim payment available where court satisfied plaintiff will succeed in action; Defective Premises Act 1972 imposes liability for misfeasance and non-feasance.

Anglo-Algerian Steamship Company, Limited v The Houlder Line, Limited [1908] 1 KB 659; (1908) XCVIII LTR 440; (1907-08) XXIV TLR 235 HC KBD Non-recovery of damages for remoteness.

Anns and others v London Borough of Merton [1977] 2 All ER 492; [1978] AC 728; (1977) 141 JP 526; (1977) 127 NLJ 614t; (1977) 121 SJ 377; [1977] 2 WLR 1024 HL That act done under statute need not mean no breach of common law duty of care; duty of care to supervise builder owed to building owner/occupiers; where breach of duty time runs from date damage caused by negligence.

Anns and others v Walcroft Property Co Ltd and another [1976] QB 882; (1976) 120 SJ 216; [1976] 2 WLR 512 CA Cause of action from time building defects discovered/ought to have been discovered.

Armitage v Nurse [1997] TLR 177 CA Trustee could (as here) validly exclude liability for gross negligence by way of trustee exemption clause.

Aswan Engineering Establishment Co v Lupdine Ltd and another (Thurgar Bolle Ltd, third party) [1987] 1 All ER 135; [1987] 1 WLR 1 CA Manufacturer's duty of care extends to foreseeable occurrences.

Attorney-General and Others v Cory Brothers and Company, Limited, and Others; Kennard and Others v Cory Brothers and Company, Limited [1921] 1 AC 521; (1921) 85 JP 129; [1921] 90 LJCh 221; (1921) 125 LTR 98; (1920-21) XXXVII TLR 343 HL Liability under Rylands v Fletcher and in negligence for landslide occasioned by dumping of colliery waste on mountain-side.

Attorney-General v Cory Brothers and Co (Limited) and others; Kennard and others v Cory Brothers and Co (Limited) (1919) 83 JP 221; [1919] 88 LJCh 410; (1918-19) XXXV TLR 570 CA Non-liability for landslide occasioned by dumping of colliery waste on mountainside.

Attorney-General v Cory Brothers and Co (Limited) and others; Kennard and others v Cory Brothers and Co (Limited) (1917-18) XXXIV TLR 621 HC ChD Liability for landslide occasioned by dumping of colliery waste on mountainside.

Atwill v Plymouth and Stonehouse Gas Light and Coke Co [1934] LJNCCR 361 CyCt Person who lit match following gas leak and so herself caused explosion could not recover damages in nuisance (and was no negligence on part of gas suppliers proved).

Avery v London and North Eastern Ry Co; Harris v London and North Eastern Ry Co; Bonner v London and North Eastern Ry Co; Watson v London and North Eastern Ry Co [1938] 2 All ER 592; (1938) 85 LJ 360 HL Relevant classes of dependents can recover maximum amounts allowed under Employers' Liability Act 1880 and Workmen's Compensation Act 1925 respectively.

Avery v London and North Eastern Ry Co; Harris v London and North Eastern Ry Co; Bonner v London and North Eastern Ry Co; Watson v London and North Eastern Ry Co (1937) 83 LJ 378; [1937] 2 KB 515 CA Relevant classes of dependents can recover maximum amounts allowed under Employers' Liability Act 1880 and Workmen's Compensation Act 1925 respectively.

B v Islington Health Authority [1991] 1 All ER 825; [1991] 1 FLR 483; [1991] 1 QB 638; [1990] TLR 725; [1991] 2 WLR 501 HC QBD Negligence does not require simultaneous duty of care/breach of that duty.

B v Miller and Co [1996] 3 FCR 435; [1996] 2 FLR 23 HC QBD Not collateral attack on order of competent court for plaintiff to bring negligence action against solicitors who advised her in ancillary relief/consent order proceedings.

Baker (Annie Amelia) v Mayor, Aldermen and Burgesses of Bethnal Green [1944] 2 All ER 301; (1945) 95 LJ 111 HC KBD State of staircase made it a concealed danger; stairway not air-raid cause of injury so not a 'war injury'.

Baker v James Brothers and Sons, Limited [1921] 2 KB 674 HC KBD Recovery by servant for injury suffered by means of defective company car (despite awareness of defect).

Balsamo v Medici and another [1984] 2 All ER 304; (1984) 128 SJ 500; [1984] 1 WLR 951 HC ChD Cannot pursue one defendant in contract and other in tort for connected cause; no action against third party whose negligence did not affect cause of contractual action.

Barber and another v Clarke and Co, Ltd and others (1939) 83 SJ 925 HC KBD Failed action by infant against workman on/occupiers of land for injury suffered when dangerously standing gate fell on infant.

Barkway v South Wales Transport Co, Ltd [1950] 1 All ER 392; (1950) 114 JP 172; (1950) 94 SJ 128; [1950] 66 (1) TLR 597; (1950) WN (I) 95 HL On res ipsa loquitur.

Barrett v Ministry of Defence [1995] 3 All ER 87; [1995] TLR 7; [1995] 1 WLR 1217 CA No duty of care on Ministry of Defence to stop navy man becoming very drunk at bar run by Ministry.

Barry v Black-Clawson International, Ltd and others (1967) 111 SJ 135 CA Not per se negligent to use article in manner other than that for which designed.

Batt v Metropolitan Water Board (1911) 75 JP 545; (1911) 80 LJCL 1354; (1910-11) 55 SJ 714; (1910-11) XXVII TLR 579 CA Water Board not liable in negligence for injury occasioned through inadequate maintenance of water stop-cock.

Batt v The Metropolitan Water Board (1911) 80 LJCL 521; (1910-11) XXVII TLR 258 HC KBD Water Board liable in negligence for injury occasioned through its inadequate maintenance of water stop-cock.

Batty and another v Metropolitan Property Realisations Ltd and others [1978] 2 All ER 445; [1978] QB 554; (1978) 122 SJ 63; [1978] 2 WLR 500 CA Relief available in tort and contract for same cause though no common calling/not professional exercising skill.

Baxter v Central Electricity Generating Board and others [1965] 1 WLR 200 Assizes Employer does not owe to person helping employee the same duty of care that owes to employee under common law.

Bennett v Tugwell (an infant) [1971] 2 All ER 248; (1971) 121 NLJ 129t; [1971] 2 QB 267; [1971] RTR 221; (1971) 115 SJ 289; [1971] 2 WLR 847 HC QBD Apparent acceptance of risk raises volenti non fit injuria even if in mind does not really accept.

Berg and Son v Lloyd (Rotterdamsche) (1917-18) XXXIV TLR 272 HC KBD Steamship-owners liable for damage caused to barges which ought to have foreseen would be close by in dock at night.

Billings v Reed [1944] 2 All ER 415; [1945] KB 11; (1945) 95 LJ 111; (1944-45) LXI TLR 27 CA On Personal Injuries (Emergency Provisions) Act 1939 ('war injuries').

Birch v Thomas [1972] 1 All ER 905; (1971) 121 NLJ 1146t; [1972] RTR 130; (1971) 115 SJ 968; [1972] 1 WLR 294 CA Clear waiver of responsibility before reasonably foreseeable event justified volent non fit injuria.

Birchall v J Birby and Sons, Ltd [1953] 1 All ER 163 Assizes Res ipsa loquitur where rope in warehouse snapped and bags fell injuring person; proof that rope maliciously cut discharged res ipsa loquitur.

Bolton v Essex Area Health Authority and Taqui (1977) 127 NLJ 1177 HC QBD On appropriate damages for person left severely paralysed/dumb/nearly blind after negligent hospital operation.

Bottomley and another v Bannister and another (1931-32) XLVIII TLR 39 CA Failed action against landlord for injury to tenant's daughter occasioned by defective gas water heater.

Bowater v Rowley Regis Corporation (1944) 108 JP 163; (1944) WN (I) 105 CA On rarity of application of volenti non fit injuria between master and servant (here not applied).

Bradford Corporation and another v Webster (1920) 84 JP 137; [1920] 2 KB 135; [1920] 89 LJCL 455; (1920) 123 LTR 62; (1919-20) XXXVI TLR 286; (1920) WN (I) 80 HC KBD Corporation could recover wages/special pension from tortfeasor for injury to constable in corporation's service.

Brame v Commercial Gas Co [1915] 84 LJKB 570 HC KBD Local authority resolution did not preclude gas company liability for negligence pursuant to Gasworks Clauses Act 1847.

Brandon and another v Osborne Garrett and Co, Ltd and another [1924] All ER 703; [1924] 1 KB 548; (1924) 59 LJ 76; [1924] 93 LJCL 304; (1924) 130 LTR 670; (1923-24) 68 SJ 460; (1923-24) XL TLR 235; (1924) WN (I) 33 HC KBD Wife could recover for injury suffered in course of non-negligent act to rescue husband from danger.

Brannigen v Harrington (1920-21) XXXVII TLR 349 HC KBD Is implied contract between restauranteur and customer that premises will be kept as safe as reasonably possible but not liable for defects that could not reasonably be discovered.

Branson v Bowes (1922) CC Rep XI 35 CyCt On duty of care owed by agister (and on discharging burden of proving that reasonable care exercised).

Bray v Palmer (1953) 97 SJ 830; [1953] 1 WLR 1455 CA Re-trial merited where trial judge had been unable to fully determine facts of case and apportion blame.

Britannia Hygienic Laundry Company, Limited v John I Thornycroft and Company, Limited [1925] 94 LJCL 858; (1924-25) XLI TLR 667; (1925) WN (I) 227 HC KBD Costs incurred as defendants in earlier action prompted by present defendant's negligence/breach of contract were recoverable by plaintiffs here.

Britannia Hygienic Laundry Company, Limited v John I Thornycroft and Company, Limited [1926] 95 LJCL 237; (1926) 135 LTR 83; (1923-24) 68 SJ 102; (1925-26) XLII TLR 198; (1926) WN (I) 16 CA Costs incurred as defendants in earlier action prompted irrecoverable by plaintiffs as did not prove negligence of instant defendants.

British Columbia Electric Railway Company, Limited v Loach [1916] 1 AC 719; (1915-16) 113 LTR 946 PC Can recover damages where own negligence prior to other's negligence precluded avoidance of effects of other's negligence.

British Road Services, Ltd v Arthur V Crutchley and Co, Ltd (Factory Guards, Ltd., Third Parties) [1967] 2 All ER 785 Assizes Warehouseman vicariously liable for negligence of independent patrol — but no recovery here as negligence did not cause loss.

British Transport Commission v Maxine and Co, Ltd (1963) 107 SJ 1025 CA Employers not vicariously liable for negligence of worker who had not been acting in connection with his work.

Brown and another v Thompson [1968] 2 All ER 708; (1968) 112 SJ 464; [1968] 1 WLR 1003 CA Contributory negligence depends on fault; trial judge's finding not interfered with lightly.

Brown v Rolls Royce, Ltd [1960] 1 All ER 577; (1960) 110 LJ 220 HL Burden of proof on person claiming negligence applies to entirety of evidence, not the various elements thereof.

Brown v T and EC Cotterill (1934-35) LI TLR 21 HC KBD Monumental masons liable for injury suffered by girl when negligently erected tombstone fell on her.

Bruce v Caulfield (1917-18) XXXIV TLR 204 CA Non-liability in negligence for damage caused by piece of tree falling onto and damaging neighbour's stable.

Bryce v Swan Hunter Group plc and others [1988] 1 All ER 659 HC QBD Failure to meet duty to minimise asbestos exposure raised presumption that caused asbestos-related death.

Buckner v Ashby and Horner, Limited (1941) 105 JP 107; [1941] 1 KB 321; [1941] 110 LJ 460; (1941) 85 SJ 106; (1940-41) LVII TLR 238; (1941) WN (I) 11 HC KBD Contractor not liable for post-construction injury following approval by local authority that work had been done to its satisfaction.

Buckner v Ashby and Horner, Limited (1941) 105 JP 220; (1941) 85 SJ 200; (1940-41) LVII TLR 414; (1941) WN (I) 52 CA Contractor not liable for post-construction injury following approval by local authority that work had been done to its satisfaction.

Bull v The Mayor, &c, of Shoreditch (1901-02) XVIII TLR 171 CA Was evidence of misfeasance for jury in respect of personal injuries driver suffered when collided with earth pile (of which authority knew) in course of avoiding part of road made by local authority but unfit for public traffic.

Burnett v British Waterways Board [1973] 2 All ER 631; (1973) 123 NLJ 179t; (1973) 117 SJ 203; [1973] 1 WLR 700 CA Exclusion of liability clause inapplicable if person has no choice in accepting/rejecting it; volenti non fit injuria only if fully and freely consent to risk waiver.

Burnett v British Waterways Board [1972] 2 All ER 1353; (1972) 116 SJ 783; [1972] 1 WLR 1329 HC QBD Employee does not freely do acts required by employer so no defence of volenti non fit injuria as actions not voluntary.

Burnison v Bangor Corporation (1931) 72 LJ 397 CA On liability of waterworks company in negligence for mains escape.

Business Computers International Ltd v Registrar of Companies and others [1987] 3 All ER 465; [1988] Ch 229; (1987) 137 NLJ 758; (1987) 131 SJ 1626; [1987] 3 WLR 1134 HC ChD Litigant does not owe duty of care to other litigant in way in which conducts proceedings.

Butler (or Black) v Fife Coal Company (Limited) (1911-12) XXVIII TLR 150 HL Mineowners liable to widowed miner for negligence as regards appointing competent manager.

C Burley, Limited v Stepney Borough Council (1947) 176 LTR 535 HC KBD No implied warranty that goods to be carried could safely be carried.

C v Hackney London Borough Council [1995] 2 FCR 306; [1996] 1 FLR 427; [1995] TLR 580 CA Res judicata did not apply where child seeking damages for circumstances that led mother to bring earlier successful action at which child not represented.

Callow v Tillstone (1900-01) LXXXIII LTR 411 HC QBD Negligent certification by vet that unsound meat is fit for consumption can ground conviction for aiding and abetting in sale of unsound meat.

Caminer and another v Northern and London Investment Trust, Ltd [1949] 1 All ER 874; [1949] 2 KB 64; (1949) 99 LJ 231; (1949) LXV TLR 302; (1949) WN (I) 212 CA Not liable where non-expert person takes what for it is reasonable care.

Caminer and another v Northern and London Investment Trust, Ltd [1950] 2 All ER 486; [1951] AC 88; (1950) 114 JP 426; (1950) 100 LJ 401; (1950) 94 SJ 518; [1950] 66 (2) TLR 184; (1950) WN (I) 361 HL Occupiers having taken reasonable care were not liable in negligence/nuisance.

Canada Steamship Lines, Ltd v R [1952] 1 All ER 305; [1952] AC 192; [1952] 1 TLR 261 PC Exemption from negligence clause to be clearly worded; if generally worded and covers negligence other basis for action may obviate exemption from negligence suit.

Canadian Pacific Railway Company v Frechette [1915] AC 871; [1915] 84 LJPC 161; (1915-16) 113 LTR 1116; (1914-15) XXXI TLR 529 PC Quebecois could not recover damages where real cause of accident was own negligence (despite contributory negligence of party sued).

Candlewood Navigation Corp Ltd v Mitsui OSK Lines Ltd and another; The Mineral Transportes, The Ibaraki Maru [1985] 2 All ER 935; [1986] AC 1; (1985) 135 NLJ 677; (1985) 129 SJ 507; [1985] 3 WLR 381 PC Non-owner of chattel cannot sue damager of chattel for economic loss.

Canter v Gardner (J) and Co, Ltd and another [1940] 1 All ER 325; (1940) 89 LJ 69; (1940) 84 SJ 289; (1939-40) LVI TLR 305 HC KBD Main contractors were not negligent and did not know of danger; sub-contractors not liable where had left place in safe shape.

Caparo Industries plc v Dickman and others [1990] 1 All ER 568; [1990] 2 AC 605; (1990) 140 NLJ 248; (1990) 134 SJ 494; [1990] TLR 105; [1990] 2 WLR 358 HL Court will impose duty of care in light of existing case-law; special proximity required before duty of care arises; company auditor owes no duty of care to general public.

Carroll v Garford and others (1968) 112 SJ 948 HC QBD Licensees/dog-owner not liable for injury suffered by third party who tripped over generally well-behaved dog that had been brought into pub.

Caudle and others v Sharp; Grove v Sharp [1994] TLR 131 HC QBD That continued not to check risks involved in writing reinsurance contracts a single event from which negligence could be discerned.

Cavanagh v Ulster Weaving Co, Ltd [1959] 2 All ER 745 HL Expert evidence of trade practice not definite as regards negligence: issue properly left to jury.

Chaproniere v Mason (1904-05) XXI TLR 633 CA Presence of stone in bath bun was prima facie evidence of negligent manufacture.

Charlton v Forrest Printing Ink Co Ltd (1978) 122 SJ 730 HC QBD Employer failed to discharge duty of care in respect of employees responsible for collecting wages from bank.

Chesneau v Interhome Ltd (1984) 134 NLJ 341c CA Excess accommodation costs plus damages for distress of holidaymaker who had to find own accommodation abroad when booked accommodation proved to be of lower quality than promised.

Chilvers v London County Council and others (1916) 80 JP 246; (1915-16) XXXII TLR 363 HC KBD No negligence found on part of education authority/school managers where child injured when playing with toy soldiers of another child.

Chipchase v British Titan Products Co, Ltd [1956] 1 All ER 613 CA Negligent management of factory as did not conform with Building (Safety, Health and Welfare) Regulations 1948 though these inapplicable.

Clark and Wife v Brims [1947] 1 All ER 242; [1947] KB 497; (1947) 97 LJ 81; [1947] 116 LJR 853; (1947) 91 SJ 161; (1947) LXIII TLR 148; (1947) WN (I) 65 HC KBD Cannot sue for negligence in performing statutory duty under Road Transport Lighting Act 1927, s 1.

Clark v London General Omnibus Company Limited (1905) XCII LTR 691; (1904-05) XXI TLR 505 HC KBD Father could recover funeral costs from defendants whose negligence had resulted in death of daughter who lived with father.

Clayton v Pontypridd Urban District Council (1918) 82 JP 246; [1918] 87 LJCL 645 HC KBD Negligence action failed where not brought in time against company acting under express and implied statutory duty to supply electricity.

Clifford v Drymond [1976] RTR 134; (1976) 120 SJ 149 CA Pedestrian on zebra crossing contributorily negligent (20%) in failing to keep an eye on oncoming traffic whilst crossing.

Clough and others v Clough and others (1968) 118 NLJ 372t; [1968] 1 WLR 525 CA Court exercised discretion to dismiss negligence action for want of prosecution (three years since entry of appearance yet no sign of statement of claim).

Colvilles, Ltd v Devine [1969] 2 All ER 53; [1969] 1 WLR 475 HL Negligent failure of employers to take adequate safety measures raised res ipsa loquitur.

Coop v Jenkins (1982) 132 NLJ 141 HC QBD Licensee liable in negligence for injuries sustained by bar-manageress who fell through trapdoor left open by barman.

Cooper v Howatt (1921-22) XXXVIII TLR 721 HC KBD Whether defendant in personal injuries action found to be contributorily negligent (not substantive issue) but not negligent was 'wholly successful defendant'.

Cork v Kirby Maclean, Ltd [1952] 2 All ER 402; [1952] 2 TLR 217 CA Half-damages where employers negligent to employee who did not disclose was epileptic.

Corporation of Greenock v Caledonian Railway Company; Corporation of Greenock v Glasgow and South-Western Railway Company [1917] AC 556; (1917) 81 JP 269 HL Liable for flooding resulting from interference with course of stream.

Corstar (Owners) v Eurymedon (Owners), The Eurymedon [1938] 1 All ER 122 CA Negligent act causing negligent mistake by other makes both responsible for result.

Cox v Coulson [1916] 2 KB 177; [1916] 85 LJKB 1081; (1916) 114 LTR 599; (1914-15) XXXI TLR 390 HC KBD Duty owed by theatre owner to member of audience injured during play.

Cox v Coulson (1916) CC Rep V 39; (1916) 51 LJ 205; (1915-16) 60 SJ 402; (1915-16) XXXII TLR 406; (1916) WN (I) 173 CA Duty owed by theatre owner to member of audience injured during play.

Cremdean Properties Ltd et anor v Nash et al (1978) 128 NLJ 514c CA Failed appeal against finding that exclusion clause in tender that particulars therein might not be (as were not in fact) entirely correct.

Cressy v South Metropolitan Gas Co (1906) 70 JP 405 HC KBD Gas company which opened up street not liable for injury caused through local authority servant's negligent repair of street.

Cuckmere Brick Co Ltd and another v Mutual Finance Ltd; Mutual Finance Ltd v Cuckmere Brick Co Ltd and others [1971] 2 All ER 633 CA Mortgagee under duty to mortgagor to obtain real market price of property.

Cummings (or McWilliams) v Sir William Arrol and Co, Ltd and another [1962] 1 All ER 623; (1962) 106 SJ 218 HL Not liable in negligence where injury would have occurred even if breach had not.

Cunard and another v Antifyre, Ltd [1932] All ER 558; [1933] 1 KB 551; (1934) 103 LJCL 321; (1933) 148 LTR 287; (1932-33) XLIX TLR 184 HC KBD Negligence for failure to take steps in relation to overhanging guttering that reasonable man would do in the circumstances.

Curran and another v Northern Ireland Co-ownership Housing Association Ltd and others [1987] AC 718; (1987) 137 NLJ 361; (1987) 131 SJ 506; [1987] 2 WLR 1043 HL No duty of care owed by statutory housing authority to occupiers of houses not to pay money for deficient repairs.

D and F Estates Ltd and others v Church Commissioners for England and others [1988] 2 All ER 992; [1989] AC 177; (1988) 138 NLJ 210; (1988) 132 SJ 1092; [1988] 3 WLR 368 HL Minus contractual obligation pure economic loss irrecoverable; builders not liable for negligence of competent sub-contractor.

D'Urso v Sanson [1939] 4 All ER 26; (1939) 88 LJ 252; (1939) 83 SJ 850 HC KBD Watchman returning inside burning building acted in course of employment: no volenti non fit injuria.

Darling v Attorney-General and another [1950] 2 All ER 793; (1950) 100 LJ 483 Assizes Ministries doing work on private land owe occupier duty not to endanger/cause damage to him (even if entrust work to contractor).

David Taylor and Son Ltd v Bowden Transport Ltd (1965-66) 116 NLJ 726 HC QBD Carriers deemed negligent where their driver left van containing cargo unattended for several minutes in empty street early one morning.

Davie v New Merton Board Mills, Ltd and others [1958] 1 All ER 67; [1958] 1 QB 210 CA Master not liable to servant for defects in manufacture of tools if takes reasonable care to provide safe tools.

Davie v New Merton Board Mills, Ltd [1956] 1 All ER 379; (1956) 100 SJ 170 HC QBD On pleading act of third party as defence to negligence.

Davie v New Merton Board Mills, Ltd and others [1957] 2 All ER 38; [1957] 2 QB 368; (1957) 101 SJ 321 HC QBD Manufacturers and employers liable in negligence for injury to worker by defective tool.

Davie v New Merton Mills Ltd and Another [1959] AC 604; [1959] 2 WLR 331 HL Employers not liable for injury to worker from latent defect in quality tool which could not have discovered.

Davies v Fortior, Ltd [1952] 1 All ER 1359; (1952) 96 SJ 376; (1952) WN (I) 291 HC QBD Comment by dead workman directly after accident admissible as res gestae.

Davies v Swan Motor Co (Swansea), Ltd (Swansea Corporation and James, Third Parties) [1949] 1 All ER 620; [1949] 2 KB 291; (1949) LXV TLR 278; (1949) WN (I) 192 CA Lack of proper care (not breach of duty) necessary to show contributory negligence to own death.

Davies v Tenby Corporation (1974) 124 NLJ 412; (1974) 118 SJ 549 CA Council (75%) liable for paralysis suffered by person who dived from defective diving board put up by corporation.

Davis and another v Radcliffe and others [1990] 2 All ER 536; (1990) 134 SJ 862/1078; [1990] TLR 285; [1990] 1 WLR 821 PC Government bank regulators do not owe duty of care to depositors in failed licensed banks.

De Martell v Merton and Sutton Health Authority [1992] 3 All ER 820; [1992] 2 FCR 832; [1992] 3 WLR 637 (also CA) HC QBD Cause of action for injury to plaintiff at birth runs from date of birth as before that no legal personality.

De Parrell v Walker (1932) 76 SJ 850; (1932-33) XLIX TLR 37 HC KBD Employer of clock-winder who stole property from house to which sent deemed negligent in hiring criminal person as clockwinder.

Dennis v London Co-operative Society, Ltd [1939] LJNCCR 39 CyCt Defendants liable for injury suffered by plaintiff who slipped on piece of fat swepped by defendants into street.

Denton v South West Thames Regional Health Authority (1981) 131 NLJ 240 HC QBD Damages for nurse who suffered injuries as result of collapse of hospital bed.

Department of the Environment v Thomas Bates and Son (New Towns Commission, third party) [1990] 2 All ER 943; [1991] 1 AC 499; (1990) 134 SJ 1077; [1990] TLR 561; [1990] 3 WLR 457 HL Damages unavailable for pure economic loss, for defects that do not damage building/ endanger health.

Deyong v Shenburn [1946] 1 All ER 226; [1946] KB 227 CA No implied term in producer/actor agreement and no common law duty to protect latter's personal property in theatre.

Dollman and another v A and S Hillman, Ltd (1941) 85 SJ 57 HC KBD Fat falling from butcher's shop to pavement causing person to slip was nuisance/negligence.

Dollman and another v A and S Hillman, Ltd [1941] 1 All ER 355; (1942) 92 LJ 91 CA Fat falling from butcher's shop to pavement causing person to slip was nuisance/negligence.

Donaldson v McNiven [1952] 1 All ER 1213 Assizes Parent not liable for negligent firing of air rifle by son.

Donaldson v McNiven [1952] 2 All ER 691; (1952) 102 LJ 594; (1952) 96 SJ 747; (1952) WN (I) 466 CA Parent not liable for negligent firing of air rifle by son.

Doughty v Turner Manufacturing Co Ltd [1964] 1 All ER 98; (1964) 114 LJ 73; (1964) 108 SJ 53; [1964] 2 WLR 240 CA Not liable for unforeseen consequences of unforeseen accident.

Dribbell and another v Robinson (1949) 99 LJ 233 CyCt Landlord liable for injury suffered by child when facia board which landlord knew to be in disrepair but had not repaired collapsed onto highway.

Driver v William Willett Ltd and another [1969] 1 All ER 665; (1969) 119 NLJ 248 Assizes On deciding whether sufficient closeness of relationship to give rise to duty of care.

Duffy v Thanet District Council and another (1984) 134 NLJ 680 HC QBD Employers vicariously liable for act done by worker which was stupid and unauthorised but nonetheless done in course of his employment.

Dumphy v Montreal Light, Heat and Power Company [1907] AC 454; [1907] 76 LJPC 71; (1907-08) XCVII LTR 499; (1906-07) XXIII TLR 770 PC Defendants not liable for deciding to erect overhead (not underground) electric wires in pursuance of statutory duty.

Duncan v Cammell Laird and Co, Ltd; Craven v Cammell Laird and Co, Ltd [1944] 2 All ER 159 CA Resolution of negligence suit.

Earl v Lubbock (1904-05) XCI LTR 73 HC KBD Repairer not liable for injury to driver of van which had recently been in for repair.

Earl v Lubbock [1905] 1 KB 253; (1904-05) XCI LTR 830; (1904-05) 49 SJ 83; (1904-05) XXI TLR 71; (1904-05) 53 WR 145 CA Repairer not liable for injury to driver of van which had recently been in for repair.

Eastern and South African Telegraph Company v Cape Town Tramway Companies [1900-03] All ER 1316; [1902] 71 LJPC 122; (1902) LXXXVI LTR 457; (1901-02) 50 WR 657 PC Non-liability for escape of electricity.

Edinburgh Water Trustees v Sommerville and Son (1906-07) XCV LTR 217 HL Absent negligence water company not liable for accidental pollution of compensation water.

EE Caledonia Ltd v Orbit Valve Co Europe [1993] 4 All ER 165; [1994] 1 WLR 221 HC QBD Unless contrary provision indemnity clause not to be taken as applying to party's own negligence. Concurrent causes of event are each causes unless event would have occurred anyway.

Electrochrome, Ltd v Welsh Plastics, Ltd [1968] 2 All ER 205 Assizes No injury where duty of care owed not to victim but another.

Elliott v CP Roberts and Co (Limited) (1915-16) XXXII TLR 71 HC KBD Contractor liable to other contractor's workers on-site as licensor to licensee.

Elliott v CP Roberts and Co, Limited (1917) 81 JP 20; [1916] 2 KB 518; [1916] 85 LJKB 1689; (1916-17) 115 LTR 255; (1915-16) XXXII TLR 478 CA Contractor liable to other contractor's workers on-site as invitor to invitee.

Esso Petroleum Co Ltd v Mardon [1975] 1 All ER 203; (1974) 124 NLJ 828t; [1975] QB 819; [1975] 2 WLR 147 HC QBD Duty of care if company in pre-contract talks represents certain state of affairs to induce other to sign contract.

Esso Petroleum Co Ltd v Mardon [1976] 2 All ER 5; (1976) 126 NLJ 265t; [1976] QB 801; (1976) 120 SJ 131; [1976] 2 WLR 583 CA Forecast by party of expertise to induce another into contracting is warranty; such party owes duty of care for negligent statements; damages are all losses suffered in light of contract.

Esso Petroleum Co, Ltd and another v Southport Corporation [1955] 3 All ER 864; [1956] AC 218; (1956) 120 JP 54; (1955) 105 LJ 824; (1956) 100 SJ 32; [1956] 2 WLR 81 HL Shipmaster not negligent so owners not vicariously so; on pleadings.

Evans v Edinburgh Corporation and others [1916-17] All ER 1010; [1916] 85 LJPC 200; (1915-16) XXXII TLR 396 HL No duty of care on person owning premises adjoining highway with door opening thereon not to open/have said door.

Everett v Griffiths and another (1919-20) 64 SJ 445 CA Failed action for negligent certification of person as insane.

Everett v Griffiths and another [1920] 3 KB 163; [1921] LJCL 737 HL Failed action for negligent certification of person as insane.

Fagan v Green and Edwards Limited (1926) 134 LTR 191; (1925) WN (I) 266 HC KBD Non-liability of (non-common) carrier-bailees for loss of goods through fire caused by own servant's negligence as had exempted selves from liability in contract.

Fairman (Pauper) v Perpetual Investment Building Society [1923] AC 74; (1923) 87 JP 21; (1922) 57 LJ 392; [1923] 92 LJCL 50; (1923) 128 LTR 386; (1922-23) XXXIX TLR 54; (1922) WN (I) 304 HL Landlord not liable in negligence for injury suffered as consequence of common staircase being in poor repair.

Fellus v National Westminster Bank Ltd [1983] TLR 448 HC QBD Test of what constitutes 'undue negligence' a subjective test.

First Interstate Bank of California v Cohen Arnold and Co [1995] TLR 664 CA Damages recoverable from negligent tortfeasor whose actions resulted in plaintiff losing very real commercial opportunity.

Flower v Prechtel [1934] All ER 810 CA Executors liable in tort personally/as representatives of deceased's estate.

Fookes v Slaytor [1979] 1 All ER 137; (1978) 128 NLJ 882t; [1979] RTR 40; (1978) 122 SJ 489; [1978] 1 WLR 1293 CA Judge may only find contributory negligence if was pleaded.

Foskett (an infant) v Mistry [1984] RTR 1 CA Plaintiff infant who ran from hill onto road (75%) contributorily negligent as regarded resulting accident; driver who ought to have seen boy and recognised danger posed (25% negligent).

Foster v Bush House, Ltd (1952) 96 SJ 763 CA Waitress deemed, in instant circumstances, not to have been negligent in tripping and spilling soup down rear of guest diner's dress.

Foster v Gillingham Corporation [1942] 1 All ER 304; (1942) 106 JP 131; [1942] 111 LJ 364; (1943) 93 LJ 108 CA Failure to light barrier placed across road was negligence.

Fraser-Wallas and another v Elsie and Doris Waters (a firm) [1939] 4 All ER 609; (1939-40) 56 TLR 205; (1940) 89 LJ 8; (1940) 162 LTR 136; (1940) 84 SJ 152 HC KBD Variety programme organisers not liable for dancer's shoe hitting audience member: duty of organisers to audience that of invitee — to take reasonable care.

Frayne v Worsley [1934] LJNCCR 40 CyCt That chattels taken from bailiff when in walking possession of same did not per se mean bailiff had been negligent.

Frensham (George), Ltd v Shorn (M) and Sons, Ltd and another (1950) 94 SJ 553; (1950) WN (I) 406 HC KBD Landlords negligent in leaving central-heating boiler unlit during period of cold weather without even warning tenants.

Frost and others v Chief Constable of the South Yorkshire Police and others; Duncan v British Coal Corp [1997] 1 All ER 540 CA On liability of employer for psychiatric injury suffered by employee in course of rescue operation.

G and K Ladenbau (UK) Ltd v Crawley and de Reya (a firm) [1978] 1 All ER 682; (1977) 127 NLJ 562t; [1978] 1 WLR 266 HC QBD Search of commons register part of duty solicitor owes in certain land sales.

Gibson v C and A Modes (1977) 127 NLJ 416b CA Failed negligence action against store-owners by woman who injured self in not reasonably foreseeable mannner which had not previously occurred (tripped over up-turning tile).

Giles v London County Council (1904) 68 JP 10 HC KBD Council not liable for injury done to man by unconcealed, non-lurking danger present on public cricket ground on which man elects to play.

Glasgow Corporation v Muir and Others [1943] AC 448; (1943) 107 JP 140; [1943] 112 LJ 1; (1943) 169 LTR 53; (1943) 87 SJ182; (1942-43) LIX TLR 266; (1943) WN (I) 113 HL Action failed as cause of accident unproved; duty of care owed by person carrying (or allowing carrying) of tea urn through store is to take care to avoid reasonably foreseeable injury.

Gledhill v Liverpool Abattoir Utility Co, Ltd and another [1957] 3 All ER 117 CA Complete knowledge of unsatisfactory nature of equipment precluded negligence claim.

Goldman v Hargrave and others [1966] 2 All ER 989; [1967] AC 645; (1965-66) 116 NLJ 977; (1966) 110 SJ 527; [1966] 3 WLR 513 PC Failure to obviate/ameliorate danger to neighbour's property gave rise to action in negligence though danger not caused by negligence.

Goodbody v Poplar Borough Council (1915) 79 JP 218; [1915] 84 LJKB 1230 HC KBD Non-liability under Rylands v Fletcher principles for thing (electric/fuse box) made dangerous by presence of another thing (gas) over which had no control.

Goodwill v British Pregnancy Advisory Service [1996] 2 All ER 161; [1996] 2 FCR 680; [1996] 2 FLR 55; (1996) 146 NLJ 173; (1996) 140 SJ LB 37; (1996) TLR 29/1/96; [1996] 1 WLR 1397 CA Must be known/deducible that advice will be acted on by third party before duty of care in respect of same will arise.

Gosse Millard, Limited v Canadian Government Merchant Marine, Limited (1926-27) XLIII TLR 544 HC KBD Recovery of damages for damage to goods where shipowner did not show that neither they nor their servants had been negligent.

Gosse Millard, Limited v Canadian Government Merchant Marine, Limited (1928-29) XLV TLR 63 HL Recovery of damages where negligence of crew resulted in damage to goods.

Gran Gelato Ltd v Richcliff (Group) Ltd and others [1992] 1 All ER 865; [1992] Ch 560; (1992) 142 NLJ 51; [1992] 2 WLR 867 HC ChD Normally conveyancing solicitor for seller does not owe duty to buyer because action already lies against seller; in concurrent claims for negligence/misrepresentation contributory negligence can apply to both claims.

Grand Trunk Railway Company of Canada v Barnett (Walter C) [1911] AC 361; (1911) 80 LJPC 117; (1911) 104 LTR 362; (1910-11) XXVII TLR 359 PC Non-recovery for negligence where no breach of duty/cause of action shown.

Grant v Australian Knitting Mills [1935] All ER 209; (1935) 80 LJ 378; [1936] 105 LJPC 6; (1935) 79 SJ 815; (1935-36) LII TLR 38 PC Where product reached consumer in same state that left manufacturer, latter liable for injury caused by latent defect undiscoverable by reasonable scrutiny.

Great Western Railway Company v Donald Macpherson and Co (Lim) (1918) CC Rep VII 19 CyCt Consignor liable to common carrier for loss occasioned by leakage from consigned goods onto other goods carried even though was no evidence of negligence on part of consignor.

Greater Nottingham Co-operative Society Ltd v Cementation Piling and Foundations Ltd and others [1988] 2 All ER 971; (1988) 138 NLJ 112; [1989] QB 71; (1988) 132 SJ 754; [1988] 3 WLR 396 CA Minus contractual obligation economic loss generally irrecoverable.

Greaves and Co (Contractors) Ltd v Baynham Meikle and Partners [1975] 3 All ER 99 CA Standards expected of professional depend on case — special cases may create special duty.

Green and another v Hills (1969) 113 SJ 385 HC QBD Not negligent for epileptic subject to automatism to go out unaccompanied.

Green and another v The Jockey Club (1975) 119 SJ 258 HC QBD Horse trainer (as possessor of chattel-horse) could sue Jockey Club for negligent injury to horse whilst latter being drug-tested.

Grey v Gee Cars, Ltd (1940) 84 SJ 538 HC KBD Car hire firm not liable in negligence for loss occasioned to client by way of dishonest company chauffeur.

Griffiths v Arch Engineering Co (Newport) Ltd and another [1968] 3 All ER 217; (1968) 118 NLJ 957 Assizes Negligent where foreseeable risk of injury.

Gunter v James (1908) 72 JP 448; (1907-08) XXIV TLR 868 HC KBD Owner of traction-engine (a dangerous spark-emitting machine) liable for damage caused to crops when engine driven along road though no negligent user.

Hales v Kerr [1908] 2 KB 601; [1908] 77 LJCL 870; (1908-09) XCIX LTR 364; (1907-08) XXIV TLR 779 HC KBD Evidence that pointed to continued negligent practice admissible to prove negligence.

Haley v London Electricity Board (1963) 107 SJ 416 HC QBD Corporation doing streetworks owed no special duty of care to the blind.

Haley v London Electricity Board [1963] 3 All ER 1003; (1964) 128 JP 162; (1964) 114 LJ 24; [1964] 2 QB 121; (1963) 107 SJ 1001; [1964] 2 WLR 444 CA Corporation doing streetworks owed no special duty of care to the blind.

Hall and another v Wilson and another [1939] 4 All ER 85; (1939) 88 LJ 276 HC KBD That might have been killed as soldier in Second World War a factor when assessing fatal accident damages.

119

Hall v Kingston and St Andrew Corporation [1941] 2 All ER 1; [1941] AC 284; (1940-41) LVII TLR 397 PC Corporation liable for servant's negligence.

Halliwell v Venables [1930] All ER 284; (1930) 143 LTR 215 CA Re-trial ordered where unusual facts which required defendant to explain them.

Harris v Perry and Co [1903] 2 KB 219; [1903] 72 LJKB 725; (1903-04) LXXXIX LTR 174; (1902-03) XIX TLR 537 CA Contractor liable for servant's failure to take reasonable care of person travelling on engine.

Harris, Newman and Co v Hayles (Cuthbert) (1914) CC Rep III 90 CyCt High Bailiff held to be negligent as regards execution of court judgment.

Harrison v Stepney Borough Council (1942) 86 SJ 234 HC KBD Council which had taken adequate steps to prevent accident arising not liable for injury suffered by person who slipped on soap at public baths.

Hartley v Mayor, &c, of Rochdale [1908] 2 KB 594; (1908-09) XCIX LTR 275; (1907-08) XXIV TLR 625 HC KBD Local authority's failure to remedy subsidence of road caused by water leak did not preclude water company's liability for person injured as result of same.

Hartley v Nayoh and Co and another [1954] 1 All ER 375 CA Electricity board in breach of regulations but company partly negligent to fireman in not familiar with own mains.

Harvey v Road Haulage Executive [1952] 1 KB 120; (1951) 101 LJ 651; (1951) 95 SJ 759; (1951) WN (I) 588 CA Obsolesence of 'last opportunity' doctrine; non-severability of negligent/contributorily negligent acts.

Haseldine v CA Daw and Son, Ltd and others [1941] 1 All ER 525; (1941) 91 LJ 181; (1942) 92 LJ 60; (1941) 85 SJ 265; (1940-41) LVII TLR 431 HC KBD Flatowner liable for negligence of agent contractors; owner owed duty to warn licensee of dangers of which actually knew (did not know here); defence of having employed competent independent contractor not open as only limited maintenance contract; contractor liable for defective repairs.

Haseldine v CA Daw and Son, Ltd, and others [1941] 3 All ER 156; [1941] 2 KB 343; (1941) 91 LJ 359; [1942] 111 LJ 45; (1941) 165 LTR 185; (1941-42) LVIII TLR 1 CA Flatowner's employment of competent contractors relieved liability in negligence; contractors liable to injury occasioned by negligent repairs.

Haynes v Harwood [1934] 2 KB 240; (1934) 103 LJCL 410; (1934) 151 LTR 135; (1934) 78 SJ 384; (1933-34) L TLR 371; (1934) WN (I) 106 HC KBD Natural result of one's negligence cannot be novus actus interveniens; person leaving horses in street owes duty of care to safeguard persons using highway (including police officer chasing after bolting horse).

Haynes v Harwood (G) and Son [1934] All ER 103; [1935] 1 KB 146; (1934) 77 LJ 340; (1934) 78 LJ 323; (1935) 152 LTR 121; (1934) 78 SJ 801; (1934-35) LI TLR 100; (1934) WN (I) 208 CA Natural result of one's negligence cannot be novus actus interveniens; person leaving horses in street owes duty of care to safeguard persons using highway (including police officer chasing after bolting horse): no volenti non fit injuria by highway users.

Henderson and others v Merrett Syndicates Ltd and others; Hallam-Eames and others v Merrett Syndicates Ltd and others; Hughes and others v Merrett Syndicates Ltd and others; Arbuthnott and others v Feltrim Underwriting Agencies Ltd and others; Deeny and others v Gooda Walker Ltd (in liq) and others [1994] 3 All ER 506; [1995] 2 AC 145; [1994] TLR 429; [1994] 3 WLR 761 HL Person undertaking to give quasi-/professional services under duty to exercise reasonable care and skill where reliance by other even if no contract.

Henty v Gregory (1915) CC Rep IV 67 CyCt Damages recoverable from owner of shipwreck for loss suffered through damage to groynes on foreshore by shipwreck.

Hesketh v Birmingham Corporation (1924) 88 JP 77; [1924] 1 KB 260; [1924] 93 LJCL 461; (1924) 130 LTR 476 CA Local authority not liable in nuisance for discharging sewer water into stream/not liable for non-feasance of drainage system.

Hewitson v Steele and Co (1912) CC Rep I 75 CyCt Damages unavailable for skin disease occasioned by negligent cut to neck with scissors by hairdresser's aid (not direct/natural result of injury).

Hewitt v Bonvin and another [1940] 1 KB 189; [1940] 109 LJCL 223; (1939) 161 LTR 360; (1939) 83 SJ 869; (1939-40) LVI TLR 43 CA Father not liable for negligent driving of son who was neither his servant nor agent.

Hicks v Pier House Management Ltd (1984) 134 NLJ 657 HC QBD Employers of flat porter vicariously liable for theft by latter from flat of tenant who entrusted porter with keys while away from flat.

Hinds v London Transport Executive (1978) 128 NLJ 1150t; [1979] RTR 103 CA Expert evidence as to causation unnecessary where could be determined on common sense basis.

HM Postmaster General v Blackpool and Fleetwood Tramroad Company, Ltd (1918) CC Rep VII 3 CyCt Tram company not liable for damage occasioned to telephone cable by escape of electricity from tram lines absent proof of negligence/non-compliance with relevant regulations.

Holliday v National Telephone Company (1899-1900) LXXXI LTR 252 CA Employer of independent contractor liable for injury caused through latter's work.

Honeywill and Stein, Ltd v Larkin Bros (London's Commercial Photographers), Ltd [1933] All ER 77; [1934] 1 KB 191; (1933) 76 LJ 289; (1934) 103 LJCL 74; (1934) 150 LTR 71; (1933-34) L TLR 56; (1933) WN (I) 240 CA Cannot absolve oneself from duty by appointing independent contractor.

Hooper v Furness Railway Company (1906-07) XXIII TLR 451 HC KBD Inadequate notice of exemption clause on ticket meant passenger could recover personal injury damages.

Howard v Furness Houlder Argentine Lines, Ltd and A and R Brown, Ltd [1936] 2 All ER 781; (1936) 80 SJ 554 HC KBD Negligence where supply/fixing of non-dangerous article made it dangerous; Rylands v Fletcher inapplicable as no escape/no unnatural user.

Howard v SW Farmer and Son, Ltd [1938] 2 All ER 296; (1938) 85 LJ 292; (1938) 82 SJ 351 CA Workman unsuccessful in negligence suit as he was careless in uncompleted building.

Hughes v Lord Advocate [1963] 1 All ER 705; [1963] AC 837; (1963) 113 LJ 232; (1963) 107 SJ 232; [1963] 2 WLR 779 HL Act akin to reasonably foreseeable act need not itself be reasonably foreseeable for liability in negligence to arise.

Humphreys v Dreamland (Margate), Ltd [1930] All ER 327; (1931) 100 LJCL 137; (1931) 144 LTR 529; (1930) 74 SJ 862 HL Person having right to possession of land/right to exclude people therefrom liable in negligence for injuries sustained thereon, not landowner.

Hunter and others v Canary Wharf Ltd; Hunter and others v London Docklands Development Corp [1996] 1 All ER 482; (1995) 145 NLJ 1645; (1995) 139 SJ LB 214; [1995] TLR 514; [1996] 2 WLR 348 CA Television interference following erection of tall building not an actionable interference with use and enjoyment of land; excessive dust and physical damage gives rise to action in negligence.

Hunwick v Essex Rivers Catchment Board [1952] 1 All ER 765; (1952) 116 JP 217 Assizes Duty to maintain sea-wall as sea-wall, not walkway.

Hurley v Dyke and others (1979) 129 (1) NLJ 364; [1979] RTR 265 (also HC QBD/CA) HL Vendors of second-hand car sold via auction at which car stated to be 'As seen and with all its faults' had discharged their duty of care towards later passenger in car injured as result of its defects.

Ilford Gas Company v Ilford Urban District Council, Jackson, Third Party (1903) 67 JP 365 CA Contractor not liable to indemnify council for damage to gas pipe which jury found was not effected by manner in which contractor did work.

Imperial Chemical Industries Ltd v Shatwell [1964] 3 WLR 329 HL Volenti non fit injuria held to arise where workman injured after behaving with co-workman in manner contrary to employer's instructions/to law; on causation.

Independent Broadcasting Authority and others v BICC Construction Ltd (1980) 130 NLJ 603 HL Successful action against negligent designers of television mast (sub-contractors) and erectors of mast (main contractors).

Ingall v Moran (1944) 88 SJ 68 CA Administrator could not bring negligence action before letters of administration granted and as that occurred over twelve months after limitation period expired action failed outright.

Inland Revenue Commissioners v Hoogstraten (1984) 128 SJ 484; [1984] TLR 207 CA Three month period given to party within which to sue court officer-sequestrator for alleged negligent management of sequestrated property.

Invercargill City Council v Hamlin [1996] 1 All ER 756; [1996] AC 624; (1996) 146 NLJ 246; (1996) 140 SJ LB 86; (1996) TLR 15/2/96; [1996] 2 WLR 367 PC New Zealand Court of Appeal may take into account local considerations when adjudicating on developing areas of common law; cause of action for latent damage ought generally to run from when economic (and not property) damage occurs.

Jacobs v London County Council and Smith, Gard & Co, Ltd (1949) 99 LJ 52 CyCt Council liable in negligence/nuisance for injury suffered by individual when crossing forecourt in some disrepair.

James McNaughton Paper Group Ltd v Hicks Anderson and Co (a firm) [1991] 1 All ER 134; (1990) 140 NLJ 1311; [1991] 2 QB 113; [1990] TLR 630; [1991] 2 WLR 641 CA Purpose of statement, relationship between maker/giver and other party, knowledge of maker/giver, size of class to which other party belongs are factors when deciding if duty of care on maker/giver of statement to unintended third party recipient.

James v Hepworth and Grandage Ltd [1967] 3 WLR 178 CA Company not negligent where had advertised availability of safety equipment to employees even though injured employee illiterate; non-provision of safety equipment even if negligent was not cause of injury.

Jefferies and A and R Atkey and Co, Limited v Derbyshire Farmers, Limited (1919-20) XXXVI TLR 825 HC KBD Defendant deliverers liable for fire caused as consequence of their servant's acting in breach of their contract with plaintiffs (despite damage being directly caused by servant acting outside his authority).

Jenkins v Great Western Rail Co [1911-13] All ER 216; [1912] 1 KB 525; (1911) 46 LJ 804; (1912) 81 LJKB 378 (1911-12) 105 LTR 882 CA Not liable in respect of injury to child wandering from where had licence to play.

Jennings v British Railways Board (1984) 134 NLJ 584 HC QBD Defendant liable for accident occasioned to plaintiff as result of former's inadequate cleaning system in certain area.

Jeremiah Ambler and Sons, Limited v Bradford Corporation [1902] 2 Ch 585 CA Public Authority Protection Act 1893, s 1(b) — judgment for defendant in action for negligent discharge of statutory function carries costs between solicitor and client — applies to performing duties under provisional electric lights regulation (but does not apply to appeals).

Jerram v Southampton County Council and another (1927) 64 LJ ccr38 CyCt Failed action for negligence/nuisance against local councils for person who injured self in drain-grating.

Johnson v Rea Ltd [1961] 3 All ER 816; [1962] 1 QB 373 CA Persons creating hazard owe duty to take reasonable steps to protect others from hazard.

Johnston v Braham and Campbell, Limited [1917] 1 KB 586 CA Liability of agent for negligent statement to principal.

Jones v Department of Employment [1988] 1 All ER 725; (1987) 137 NLJ 1182; [1989] QB 1; (1988) 132 SJ 128; [1988] 2 WLR 493 CA By statute adjudication officers cannot be sued for negligence; misfeasance, judicial review, statutory appeal only means of challenging decision.

Jones v Staveley Iron and Chemical Co Ld [1955] 1 QB 474 CA Test for negligence versus that for contributory negligence.

Judson v British Transport Commission [1954] 1 All ER 624 CA Wilful violation of company rules meant injury could not be attributed to employer's negligence.

Junior Books Ltd v Veitchi Co Ltd [1982] 3 All ER 201; [1983] 1 AC 520; (1982) 126 SJ 538; [1982] TLR 389; [1982] 3 WLR 477 HL Duty of care if close proximity to prevent harm from work/defects present therein.

K and another v P and others (J, third party) [1993] 1 All ER 521; [1993] Ch 140; [1992] 3 WLR 1015 HC ChD Ex turpi causa not a defence to claim for contribution to damages under Civil Liability (Contribution) Act 1978.

Kealey v Heard [1983] 1 All ER 973; (1983) 127 SJ 288; [1983] 1 WLR 573 HC QBD Cannot plead res ipsa loquitur where injury results from breach of duty of care.

Kelly v London Transport Executive (1981) 131 NLJ 241 HC QBD Failure to discharge burden of proof regarding causation of injuries suffered.

Kerry v Carter [1969] 3 All ER 723 CA CA will alter trial judge's apportionment of liability if CA believes mistaken.

Kimber v Gas Light and Coke Co, Ltd [1918-19] All ER 123; (1918) 82 JP 125; [1918] 1 KB 439; [1918] 87 LJCL 651; (1918) 118 LTR 562; (1917-18) 62 SJ 329; (1917-18) XXXIV TLR 260 CA Person creating danger has duty to warn person unaware of hazard actually/in danger of exposing themselves thereto from doing so.

King v Liverpool City Council [1986] 3 All ER 544; (1986) 136 NLJ 334; (1970) 130 SJ 505; [1986] 1 WLR 890 CA No duty of care to third party injured by trespassing vandals whom unable to stop.

King v Sadler and another (1970) 114 SJ 192 HC QBD Hotel owner and Gas Board equally liable for injury to hotel guest injured by carbon monoxide gas from boiler room below hotel room.

Kinsey v London Borough of St Helens (1977) 127 NLJ 640b CA Failed negligence action by child injured when recently reconstructed school gate pillar collapsed while child swinging on gate.

Kirby v Friend [1945] LJNCCR 90 CyCt Owner of property liable for injury suffered by way of defective coal-plate by person lawfully using highway onto which plate extended.

Knight and another v Demolition and Construction Co, Ltd [1954] 1 All ER 711 CA On negligent acts leading to falling down of wall.

Knightley v Johns and others [1982] 1 All ER 851; [1982] RTR 182; (1982) 126 SJ 101; [1982] 1 WLR 349 CA Novus actus interveniens where ultimate event not natural/probable consequence of original tort.

Konskier v B Goodman, Ltd [1927] All ER 187; [1928] 1 KB 421; (1927) 64 LJ 403; (1928) 97 LJCL 263; (1928) 138 LTR 481 CA Liability in trespass not negligence for leaving waste materials on roof of adjoining property resulting in damage.

Kooragang Investments Pty Ltd v Richardson and Wrench Ltd [1981] 3 All ER 65; (1981) 125 SJ 641; [1981] 3 WLR 493 PC Master not vicariously liable for unauthorised negligent acts of servant.

La Société Anonyme de Remorquage Hélice v Bennetts [1911] 1 KB 243 HC KBD Damages not recoverable despite presence of negligence for results which did not directly flow from same.

Lamb and another v London Borough of Camden and another [1981] 2 All ER 408; (1981) 131 NLJ 474; [1981] QB 625; [1981] 2 WLR 1038 CA Liability of tortfeasor for acts caused by novus actus interveniens.

Lambert and another v Eastern National Omnibus Co, Ltd [1954] 2 All ER 719 HC QBD On action by spouses for injury to one party/consequent loss by estrangement of one party by another.

Lambert and another v Lewis and others; Lexmead (Basingstoke) Ltd (Third Party); B Dixon Bate Ltd (Fourth Party) [1979] RTR 61 HC QBD Owner and manufacturers of defective coupling were liable in negligence for damage caused thereby; retailer of coupling not liable.

Lambert and another v Lewis and others; Lexmead (Basingstoke) Ltd (Third Party); Dixon Bate Ltd (Fourth Party) [1980] RTR 152 CA Owner/retailers of defective coupling were liable in negligence for damage caused thereby; manufacturer of coupling not liable.

Lambert v Corporation of Lowestoft [1901] 1 KB 590; [1901] 70 LJK/QB 333; (1901) LXXXIV LTR 237; (1900-01) 45 SJ 295; (1900-01) XVII TLR 273; (1900-01) 49 WR 316 HC KBD Absent negligence sanitary authority not liable for injury sustained my member of public as result of disrepaired sewer.

Lampert and another v Eastern National Omnibus Co, Ltd [1954] 2 All ER 719; (1954) 104 LJ 505; (1954) 98 SJ 493; [1954] 1 WLR 1047 HC QBD Spouse might (but here did not) recover damages for estrangement from other spouse consequent upon negligent act.

Lancaster v Le Fleming (1920) CC Rep IX 86 CyCt Lord of Manor liable in negligence for failure to fence off quarry (with result that cow was lost).

Langbrook Properties Ltd v Surrey County Council (1969) 113 SJ 983; [1970] 1 WLR 161 HC ChD No nuisance or negligence arose where abstracted water from own land even though affected another's property.

Lasczyk v National Coal Board [1954] 3 All ER 205 Assizes Guilty of contributory negligence where acting under supervisor's instructions but contrary to training officer's ordinance.

Latchford v Beirne (1981) 131 NLJ 856 HC QBD Receiver did not owe duty of care to individual creditors.

Leach v British Oxygen Co, Ltd (1965) 109 SJ 157 CA Employers not liable for injury which occurred to workman directed to do certain task.

Lee Conservancy Board v Leyton Urban District Council (1906-07) XCV LTR 487 HC KBD Single act of negligence in allowing sewage into river did not render council guilty of offence under Lee Conservancy Act 1868.

Lee v Sheard [1955] 3 All ER 777; (1955) 105 LJ 809; [1956] 1 QB 192; (1955) 99 SJ 888; [1955] 3 WLR 951 CA Reduction in share of company profits by third party consequent upon tort recoverable from tortfeasor.

Leigh and Sillavan Ltd v Aliakmon Shipping Co Ltd; The Aliakmon [1985] 2 All ER 44; [1985] QB 350; (1985) 129 SJ 69; [1984] TLR 710; [1985] 2 WLR 289 CA Duty of care but no liability because would create vague liability to vague class; despite forseeability circumstances did not justify recovery for economic loss; negligence that of stevedores not shipowners.

Leigh and Sillivan Ltd v Aliakmon Shipping Co Ltd; The Aliakmon [1986] 2 All ER 145; [1986] AC 785; (1986) 136 NLJ 415; (1986) 130 SJ 357; [1986] 2 WLR 902 HL Buyer of goods cannot claim for loss or damage from negligence unless owns/has title to property.

Lexmead (Basingstoke) Ltd v Lewis and others [1982] AC 225 (also CA); (1981) 131 NLJ 422; [1981] RTR 346; (1981) 125 SJ 310; [1981] 2 WLR 713 HL Warranty expired once person to whom item supplied behaved in negligent manner.

Liebig's Extract of Meat Co (Limited) v Mersey Docks and Harbour Board and others (1916-17) XXXIII TLR 354 HC KBD Damages for goods damaged by reason of negligent failure of Mersey Docks and Harbour Board to maintain quay in manner reasonably fit for receiving goods.

Liebig's Extract of Meat Company (Limited) v The Mersey Docks and Harbour Board and Walter Nelson and Son (Limited) (1917-18) XXXIV TLR 388 CA Damages for goods damaged by reason of negligent failure of Mersey Docks and Harbour Board to maintain quay in manner reasonably fit for receiving goods.

Lister v Romford Ice and Cold Storage Co, Ltd [1957] 1 All ER 125; (1957) 121 JP 98 HL Master could recover damages (including costs of action) paid by them on foot of servant's negligence.

Lloyd v West Midlands Gas Board [1971] 2 All ER 1240; (1971) 115 SJ 227; [1971] 1 WLR 749 CA Retrial where plaintiff succeeded on facts did not plead; res ipsa loquitur inapplicable as defective object in premises of plaintiff.

Lomas v M Jones and Son [1944] KB 4; [1944] 113 LJ 193; (1944) 170 LTR 139; (1943-44) LX TLR 28; (1943) WN (I) 225 CA Farmer voluntarily aiding in delivery of heifer could recover damages for injury sustained through deliverer's negligence.

London General Omnibus Company, Limited v Tilbury Contracting and Dredging Company (1906), Limited (1907) 71 JP 534 HC ChD Successful action for damage to building effected by negligent laying of sewers.

Long v District Messenger and Theatre Ticket Company (Limited) (1915-16) XXXII TLR 596 HC KBD Courier firm's notice of conditions (wherein exempted liability) inapplicable where took delivery of parcel without asking questions as to contents of same.

Longton v Committee of Visitors of Winwick Asylum (1911) 75 JP 348 HC KBD Damages for injury suffered through flooding caused by other's negligence.

Longton v Committee of Visitors of Winwick Asylum (1912) 76 JP 113 CA Out-of-court settlement of appeal from action in which damages awarded for injury suffered through flooding caused by other's negligence.

Lonrho plc v Tebbit and another [1991] 4 All ER 973; (1991) 141 NLJ 1295 HC ChD Striking-out application not appropriate forum for deciding legal points in new field of law; duty of care may arise in respect of discharge of statutory powers implementing, but not deciding policy even where purely economic loss; action against minister rather than judicial review permissible.

Lonrho plc v Tebbit and another [1992] 4 All ER 280 CA Private action for negligence may arise if Secretary of State fails to release firm from undertaking to Secetary regarding purchase of shares.

Lord and another v Pacific Steam Navigation Co, Ltd; The Oropesa [1943] 1 All ER 211; (1944) 94 LJ 108; [1943] 112 LJ 91 CA Capsizing of lifeboat direct result of negligently caused collision between two boats.

Lord Mayor, Aldermen and Citizens of the City of Manchester v Markland [1935] All ER 667; [1936] AC 360; (1935) 99 JP 343; (1935) 153 LTR 302; (1934-35) LI TLR 527 HL Corporation found liable in negligence for failure to attend to water leak which made road dangerous resulting in accident.

Ludgate v Lovett [1969] 2 All ER 1275; (1969) 119 NLJ 414t; (1969) 113 SJ 369; [1969] 1 WLR 1016 CA No evidence capable of rebutting res ipsa loquitur.

MacIntyre v Coles [1966] 1 All ER 723 (1966) 130 JP 189; (1965-66) 116 NLJ 611; (1966) 110 SJ 315; [1966] 1 WLR 831 CA On yielding at junctions (and consequent negligence).

Macrae v HG Swindells (trading as West View Garage Co) (1954) 98 SJ 233; [1954] 1 WLR 597 HC QBD Could recover cost of hiring car where car loaned for period that own car being repaired following garage's negligence was lost through own negligence.

Mallett and another v Dunn [1949] 1 All ER 973; [1949] 2 KB 180; [1949] 118 LJR 1650; (1949) LXV TLR 307; (1949) WN (I) 206 HC KBD Husband could sue for medicine/household expenses though wife contributorily negligent.

Mansfield v Express Dairy Co (London) Ltd, Winter and London and Provincial Poster Group Ltd (1981) 131 NLJ 1112 HC QBD Milkman liable for driving into ladder on which bill-poster standing even though bill-poster had not placed warning sign indicating where was working.

Marc Rich and Co AG and others v Bishop Rock Marine Co Ltd and others 'The Nicholas H' [1995] 3 All ER 307; [1996] 1 AC 211; (1995) 145 NLJ 1033; (1995) 139 SJ LB 165; [1995] TLR 398; [1995] 3 WLR 227 HL Classification society does not owe duty of care to cargo owners who suffer loss.

Marchant Manufacturing Company Limited v Leonard D Ford and Teller Limited (1936) 154 LTR 430 HC KBD Rylands v Fletcher inapplicable to situation where some water in water boiler installed on second floor of commercial premises leaked into ground floor: failed negligence action.

Margarine Union GmbH v Cambay Prince Steamship Co, Ltd [1967] 3 All ER 775; [1969] 1 QB 219; (1967) 111 SJ 943; [1967] 3 WLR 1569 HC QBD Shipowner does not duty of care to party not owning goods when tort committed.

Margereson v JW Roberts Ltd; Hancock v Same (1996) TLR 17/4/96 CA Factory owners liable for deaths occurring to individuals as result of forseeable pulmonary damage arising from dead persons having played as children in asbestos-laden atmosphere adjacent to factory.

Markland v Manchester Corporation (1934) 98 JP 117; [1934] 1 KB 566; (1934) 77 LJ 125; (1934) 103 LJCL 265; (1934) 150 LTR 405; (1934) 78 SJ 103; (1933-34) L TLR 215 CA Corporation found liable in negligence for failure to attend to water leak which made road dangerous resulting in accident.

Marshall v Cellactite and British Uralite Limited and another (1947) LXIII TLR 456 CA Non-liability of factory owner for injury to contractors' employee injured through use of factory owner's defective equipment which contractors had elected to use and chosen themselves.

Marshall v Osmond and another [1982] 2 All ER 610; [1982] Crim LR 441; [1982] QB 857; [1983] RTR 111; (1982) 126 SJ 210; [1982] TLR 38; [1982] 3 WLR 120 HC QBD Police do not owe normal duty of care to person suspected of crime who is unintentionally injured in course of hot pursuit.

Marshall v Osmond and another [1983] 2 All ER 225; [1983] QB 1034; [1983] RTR 475; (1983) 127 SJ 309; [1983] TLR 190; [1983] 3 WLR 13 CA Police owe normal duty of care to person suspected of crime who is unintentionally injured in course of hot pursuit.

Marti v Smith and Home Office (1981) 131 NLJ 1028 HC QBD Failed negligence action against Home Office by person injured by actions of person who escaped from 'open' Borstal.

Mason v Williams and Williams, Ltd and another (1955) 99 SJ 338 HC QBD Manufacturers (not employers) liable for injury occasioned to worker using new work tool for first time.

Maxey Drainage Board v Great Northern Railway Company (1912) 76 JP 236 HC KBD Landowner entitled to do what is necessary and reasonable to protect land from expected flooding.

Maxwell v British Thomson Houston Company (Limited); Blackwell and Co, Third Parties (1901-02) XVIII TLR 278 CA Contractor liable for negligence of sub-contractor.

Mayor, &c, of Shoreditch v Bull (1904) 68 JP 415; (1904) XC LTR 210; (1903-04) XX TLR 254 HL Approval of decision whereby local authority found liable for personal injuries driver suffered when collided with earth pile (of which authority knew) in course of avoiding part of road made by local authority but unfit for public traffic.

McArdle v Andmac Roofing Co and others [1966] 3 All ER 241; (1965-66) 116 NLJ 1404 Assizes Two sub-contractors owed duty of care to worker and were liable in negligence for leaving matter to others.

McArthur v The Dominion Cartridge Company (Limited) [1905] 74 LJPC 30; (1904-05) XXI TLR 47; (1904-05) 53 WR 305 PC Circumstances of injury to workman in ammunition factory could ground successful negligence.

McAuley v Bristol City Council [1992] 1 All ER 749 CA Council right to enter house entailed right to enter garden so duty of care to carry out repairs in garden.

McDowell v FMC (Meat), Ltd, and another (1967) 111 SJ 998 HC QBD Damages for injuries arising from failure to warn participants in agricultural show of presence of high tension electric cable.

McFarlane v Wilkinson and another; Hegarty v EE Caledonia Ltd [1997] TLR 69 CA Failed action for damages by secondary victim of disaster.

McGhee v National Coal Board [1972] 3 All ER 1008 HL If breach of duty causes/contributes to injury are liable in negligence.

McGowan v Stott (1930) 143 LTR 217 CA Re-trial ordered where facts required defendant to explain them.

McLean v Bell [1932] All ER 421; (1932) 73 LJ 411; (1932) 147 LTR 262; (1932) 76 SJ 414; (1931-32) XLVIII TLR 467; (1932) WN (I) 131 HL Contributory negligence by party running another down not complete defence to negligence on part of party run down.

McLean v Redpath Brown and Co Ltd (No 2) (1964) 108 SJ 239 HC QBD On undesirability of lengthy period between date of accident and date of trial.

McLoughlin v O'Brian and another [1982] 2 All ER 298; [1983] 1 AC 410; (1982) 132 NLJ 664; [1982] RTR 209 (also CA); (1982) 126 SJ 347; [1982] TLR 242; [1982] 2 WLR 982 HL Damages for nervous shock if injury foreseeable result of other's negligence; reasonable foreseeability sole criterion in highway negligence cases.

McLoughlin v O'Brian and others [1981] 1 All ER 809; [1981] QB 599; [1982] RTR 209 (also HL); (1981) 125 SJ 169; [1981] 2 WLR 1014 CA Though plaintiff's injury foreseeable no recovery because of lack of proximity.

McMillan v Canadian Northern Railway Company [1923] AC 120; (1923) 128 LTR 293; (1922) WN (I) 312 PC Action brought by Ontario resident in Saskatchewan could not be maintained as cause of action could be 'justified' in Ontario.

Mersey Docks and Harbour Board v Procter [1923] All ER 134; [1923] AC 253; (1923) 58 LJ 14; [1923] 92 LJCL 479; (1923) 129 LTR 34; (1922-23) 67 SJ 400; (1922-23) XXXIX TLR 275; (1923) WN (I) 85 HL Failure of claim against Docks Board as were not negligent/acts were not cause of death.

Metropolitan Police District Receiver v Tatum (1948) 112 JP 209; (1948) WN (I) 152 HC KBD Police receiver allowed recover off-work sums paid for/to officer injured through defendant's negligence.

Midland Silicones Ltd v Scruttons Ltd (1959) 109 LJ 362; [1959] 2 QB 171; (1959) 103 SJ 415 HC QBD Non-party (and non-agent) cannot benefit from terms of contract.

Midland Silicones, Ltd v Scruttons, Ltd [1960] 2 All ER 737; [1961] 1 QB 106 CA Non-party (and non-agent) cannot benefit from terms of contract.

Mills and others v Winchester Diocesan Board of Finance and others [1989] 2 All ER 317; [1989] Ch 428; (1989) 133 SJ 725; [1989] 2 WLR 976 HC ChD Charity Commissioners do not owe duty of care to possible objects of charity.

Ministry of Housing and Local Government v Sharp and another [1970] 1 All ER 1009; (1969) 133 JP 595; [1970] 2 QB 223; [1970] 2 WLR 802 CA Need not be voluntary taking of responsibility to be tortiously liable for misstatement.

Ministry of Housing and Local Government v Sharp and another [1969] 3 WLR 1020 HC QBD Local land charges registrar owed duty of care to ensure search certificate included all entries in local land charges register (and were vicariously liable for negligence of employee).

Mist v Metropolitan Water Board and Creamilk Limited (1915) 79 JP 495; [1915] 84 LJKB 2041; (1915-16) 113 LTR 500 HC KBD Occupier (not Water Board) liable in negligence for injury occasioned by inadequately maintained meter lid.

Moan v Reed Brothers (Engineers), Ltd (1962) 106 SJ 283 CA Judgment set aside where was based on negligence that had not in fact been pleaded.

Monk v Warbey and others (1934) 151 LTR 100; (1933-34) L TLR 263 HC KBD Owner of car liable towards person injured by car when driven by individual accompanying person to whom car loaned.

Monk v Warbey and others (1935) 152 LTR 194; (1934-35) LI TLR 77 CA Owner of car liable towards person injured by car when driven by individual accompanying person to whom car loaned.

Moore v DER Ltd [1971] 3 All ER 517; [1972] RTR 97; (1971) 115 SJ 528; [1971] 1 WLR 1476 CA Purchasing new car, not secondhand car to replace original car damaged through negligence of defendant's driver was reasonable.

Moore v R Fox and Sons [1956] 1 All ER 182; (1956) 106 LJ 57; [1956] 1 QB 596; (1956) 100 SJ 90; [1956] 2 WLR 342 CA Res ipsa loquitir where workman injured in premises controlled by defendants and they cannot show non-negligence/took reasonable care.

Morgan v Incorporated Central Council of the Girls' Friendly Society [1936] 1 All ER 404; (1936) 81 LJ 187; (1936) 80 SJ 323 HC KBD Independent contractors but not landlord liable in negligence to licensee falling down lift shaft when lift gate left open.

Morris v Mayor, Aldermen and Burgesses of the Borough of Luton [1946] 1 All ER 1; (1946) 110 JP 102; [1946] KB 114; [1946] 115 LJ 202; (1946) 174 LTR 26; (1946) 90 SJ 91; (1945-46) LXII TLR 145; (1945) WN (I) 239 CA No rule that party driving in dark must be able to stop within limits of sight or is negligent.

Morris v Murray and another [1990] 3 All ER 801; (1990) 140 NLJ 1459; [1991] 2 QB 6; (1990) 134 SJ 1300; [1990] TLR 610; [1991] 2 WLR 195 CA Person electing to fly with drunken pilot taken to waive rights to damages for negligence by virtue of volenti non vit injuria maxim.

Morris v West Hartlepool Steam Navigation Co, Ltd [1956] 1 All ER 385 HL Non-closure of hatch of hold through which party fell was negligent.

Morrison v Sheffield Corporation (1917) 81 JP 277; [1917] 86 LJCL 1456; (1917-18) 117 LTR 520; (1916-17) 61 SJ 611; (1916-17) XXXIII TLR 492 CA Owners of spiked fence were negligent not to have taken special measures to avoid injury to public during black-out conditions.

Mott and another v The Mayor, Aldermen and Councillors of the Metropolitan Borough of Stepney [1935] LJNCCR 30 CyCt That council lamp bracket fell was of itself evidence of negligence on part of council.

Mulcahy v Ministry of Defence (1996) 146 NLJ 334; [1996] QB 732; [1996] 2 WLR CA Ministry of Defence did not have to provide safe place of work/fellow soldiers do not owe each other duty of care in tort in battlefront conditions.

Mulready v H (J) and W Bell, Ltd and another [1952] 2 All ER 663 Assizes Non-employers not liable in negligence for not safeguarding worker.

Mulready v H (J) and W Bell, Ltd and another [1953] 2 All ER 215; (1953) 103 LJ 381 CA Contractor cannot abdicate safety duties towards workers by employing sub-contractors.

Mulvaine v Joseph and others (1968) 118 NLJ 1078t; (1968) 112 SJ 927 HC QBD Damages from taxi-driver for professional golfer injured in taxi-cab accident caused by negligence of taxi-driver.

Murphy v Bradford Metropolitan Council [1991] TLR 66 CA Local authority liable for breach of duty of care to ensure cleared, salted school path was not slippy.

Murray v Park Bros (Liverpool), Ltd and others (1959) 109 LJ 460 HC QBD Apportionment of liabilites for accident ultimately arising from negligent parking of van.

Mutual Life and Citizens' Assurance Co Ltd and another v Evatt [1971] 1 All ER 150; [1971] AC 793; (1970) 120 NLJ 1090; [1971] 2 WLR 23 PC Absent contract advisor owes duty to be honest in making statements unless fiduciary/styled as expert.

Nabarro v Frederick Cope and Co, Ltd [1938] 4 All ER 565; (1938) 86 LJ 405; (1939) 83 SJ 74 HC KBD Builders not liable for injury suffered by building owner on impromptu visit to site.

Nandreph Ltd v Willmett and Co [1978] 1 All ER 746; (1978) 122 SJ 744 HC ChD Benefit arising from negligence may be deduced from damages if appropriate.

Neushul v Mellish and Harkavy (1967) 111 SJ 399 CA On duty owed by solicitor to client when acting for two parties (here failed to meet duty of care).

Newland v Boardwell; MacDonald v Platt [1983] 3 All ER 179; [1984] RTR 188 CA Admission of liability but denial of liability an abuse of process.

Newman v Bourne and Hollingsworth (1914-15) XXXI TLR 209 HC KBD Shop liable in negligence where through fault of shop employee lost property handed in went missing.

Newman v Francis (1953) 117 JP 214 HC QBD Private individual could not rest cause of action on breach of parks bye-law.

Noel T James, Ltd v Central Electricity Authority (1958) 108 LJ 250 HC QBD Successful claim in negligence against Electricity Board on foot of damage occasioned to plaintiff's property when fire escaped from Board's premises.

Nore v Meyer (1911-12) 56 SJ 109 HC ChD Trustees who advanced money on property without making full inquiry as to property concerned were not (by virtue of the Trustee Act 1893) liable for their actions in negligence.

Northwestern Utilities, Limited v London Guarantee and Accident Company, Limited, and Others [1936] AC 108; (1935) 80 LJ 378; [1936] 105 LJPC 18; (1935) 79 SJ 902; (1935-36) LII TLR 93; (1935) WN (I) 176 PC Gas company under duty of care to protect general public from effects of City works close by mains.

Norwich City Council v Harvey and another (1989) 133 SJ 694; [1989] 1 WLR 828 CA Sub-contractor/sub-contractor's employee deemed not to owe duty of care to building employer for damage occasioned by carelessness of sub-contractor's employee.

O'Connor v Swan and Edgar, Ltd and another (1963) 107 SJ 215 HC QBD Independent contractor (plasterer) liable for latent defect in plastering which five years after completion was responsible for injury.

Oliver v Hinton (1899-1900) LXXXI LTR 212 CA Grossly careless purchaser not allowed deprive prior innocent mortgagee of her priority.

OLL Ltd v Secretary of State for Transport [1997] 3 All ER 897; [1997] 2 Cr App R (S) 1099; (1997) 147 NLJ 1099; [1997] TLR 407 HC QBD On duty of care owed by coastguard in answering distress call.

Osborn v The Metropolitan Water Board (1910) 74 JP 190; (1910) 102 LTR 217; (1909-10) XXVI TLR 283 HC KBD Metropolitan Water Board liable for inadequate maintenance of stop-cock box in pavement and consequent injury to plaintiff.

Osborne v Colenutt (1919) CC Rep VIII 25 CyCt Pedestrian with poor sight who fell through open cellar door that opened onto pavement able to recover damages for injury sustained where normally sighted person would have seen danger and avoided injury.

Overseas Tankship (UK), Ltd v Morts Dock and Engineering Co, Ltd [1961] 1 All ER 404; (1961) 111 LJ 104; (1961) 105 SJ 85 PC Non-foreseeability (by reasonable man) precluded liability in negligence.

Owens v Brimmell [1976] 3 All ER 765; [1977] QB 859; [1977] RTR 82; (1977) 121 SJ 338; [1977] 2 WLR 943 HC QBD Burden of proving contributory negligence on party alleging; contributory negligence where travel with inebriated driver; join in with party on drinking spree, then travel with party in car.

P Perl (Exporters) Ltd v Camden London Borough Council [1983] 3 All ER 161; (1982) 132 NLJ 704; [1984] QB 342; (1983) 127 SJ 581; [1983] 3 WLR 769 CA Generally no duty of care to protect one's own/neighbour's premises from third party access.

Pacific Associates Ltd Inc and another v Baxter and others [1989] 2 All ER 159; (1989) 139 NLJ 41; [1990] 1 QB 993; (1989) 133 SJ 123; [1989] 3 WLR 1150 CA Absent assumption thereof engineer employed to oversee work of contractor does not owe contractor duty of care.

Padbury v Holliday and Greenwood (Limited) and another (1911-12) XXVIII TLR 494 CA Main contractor not liable for injury to third party through negligence of sub-contractor's servant.

Parker v London General Omnibus Company (Limited) (1909) 73 JP 283; (1909) C LTR 409; (1908-09) XXV TLR 429 HC KBD Personal injury victim failed in action against bus company whose driver/placing bus on road was negligent/may or may not have been nuisance.

Parker v London General Omnibus Company (Limited) (1910) 74 JP 20; (1909-10) 101 LTR 623; (1908-09) 53 SJ 867; (1909-10) XXVI TLR 18 CA Personal injury victim failed in action against bus company whose driver/placing bus on road was negligent/may or may not have been nuisance.

Parry v Aluminium Corporation, Ltd (1940) 162 LTR 236 CA Re-trial on question of damages alone where injured employee established machine whereby was injured was dangerous/unfenced.

Paterson v Norris (1913-14) XXX TLR 393 HC KBD Boarding-house keeper owes duty of care to keep door of premises closed.

Pavlides v Jensen and others [1956] 3 WLR 224 HC ChD Negligence claim against directors for alleged non-fraudulent sale of company assets at under-value was unmaintainable.

Payne-Crofts v Aird Bros, Ltd and British Transport Commission (1953) 103 LJ ccr832 CyCt Successful action against warehouse keepers for goods negligently converted/detained/lost.

Pearce v Round Oak Steel Works Ltd [1969] 3 All ER 680; [1969] 1 WLR 595 CA Must show not negligent in acquiring/discovering defect in second hand purchase for res ipsa loquitur not to apply.

Pearson v North Western Gas Board [1968] 2 All ER 699; (1968) 118 NLJ 614 Assizes May be res ipsa loquitur if gas pipe explosion but, if so, negatived here by expert evidence.

Philco Radio and Television Corporation of Great Britain, Ltd v J Spurling, Ltd and others [1949] 2 All ER 129; (1949) 99 LJ 289; (1949) LXV TLR 388 HC KBD Strict liability where bring dangerous material into premises.

Philcox v Civil Aviation Authority (1995) 139 SJ LB 146; [1995] TLR 332 CA Civil Aviation Authority did not owe duty of care to tell person whether maintenance of own aircraft was adequate/deficient.

Pigney v Pointers Transport Services, Ltd [1957] 2 All ER 807 Assizes Wife could seek damages for husband's suicide (though felony) arising from negligent injury.

Pitman v Southern Electricity Board [1978] 3 All ER 901; (1979) 143 JP 156; (1978) 122 SJ 300 CA Metal plate covering new hole a new hazard justifying negligence action.

Pitts v Hunt and another [1990] 1 QB 302; [1989] RTR 365; (1990) 134 SJ 834; [1989] 3 WLR 795 HC QBD Person injured by unlawful acts he encouraged other to undertake barred from recovering damages by virtue of ex turpi causa maxim and absence of duty of care; volenti non fit injuria arose but was defeated by 100% contributory negligence/was here precluded from being relied upon by statute.

Pitts v Hunt and another [1990] 3 All ER 344; [1991] 1 QB 24; [1990] RTR 290; [1990] TLR 312; [1990] 3 WLR 542 CA Person injured by unlawful acts he encouraged other to undertake barred from recovering damages by virtue of ex turpi causa maxim, public policy and absence of duty of care.

Plovidba (Losinjska) v Transco Overseas Ltd and others [1995] TLR 419 HC QBD On duty of care owed by person putting dangerous materials into circulation to neutralise dangers from same.

Porter v Barking and Dagenham London Borough Council and another [1990] TLR 291 HC QBD Not failing to meet duty of care for school caretaker to allow two young teenage boys to practise shot-putting together on school property after school hours.

Possfund Custodian Trustee Ltd and another v Diamond and others (McGrigor Donald (a firm), third party; Parr and others v Diamond and others (McGrigor Donald (a firm), third party) [1996] 2 All ER 774; [1996] 1 WLR 1351 HC ChD Issuers of company share prospectus may owe duty of care to subsequent purchasers of shares.

Post Office v Hampshire County Council [1979] 2 All ER 818 (1979) 129 (1) NLJ 249; [1980] QB 124; (1979) 123 SJ 421; [1979] 2 WLR 907 CA Circuity of action where own negligence led to injury by another.

Postmaster General v Blackpool and Fleetwood Tramroad Co (1920) CC Rep IX 81; (1920) 55 LJ 387 CA Tram company liable for damage occasioned to telephone cable by escape of electricity from tram lines.

Powell v Thorndike and others (1910) 102 LTR 600; (1909-10) XXVI TLR 399 HC KBD Landlords not liable for injury caused by lift which was safe for use if used as intended to be used.

Pratt v Richards and others [1951] 1 All ER 90 HC KBD Fatal accident damages for building site injury occasioned by negligence.

Pritchard v Peto and others [1917] 2 KB 173; [1917] 86 LJCL 1292; (1917-18) 117 LTR 145 HC KBD Houseowner owed duty not to expose calling tradesman to concealed dangers of which owner knew (duty met).

Pritty v Child (1902) 37 LJ 191; [1902] 71 LJCL 512 HC KBD Water-finder liable for reckless statement as to location of water.

Pusey v Peters and another (1974) 124 NLJ 1030t; (1975) 119 SJ 85 HC QBD Gas Board negligent as regards inadequate safeguards regarding ventilation upon change of gas supply to form needing more ventilation.

Pygram v London & Home Counties Electricity Authority [1941] LJNCCR 318 CyCt Absent warning/contributory negligence on part of victim electricity contractors liable in negligence for injury to person whom ought reasonably to have foreseen might be injured by what were doing.

Quainoo v Brent and Harrow Area Health Authority (1982) 132 NLJ 1100 HC QBD On extent of damages recoverable in respect of funeral expenses following fatal accident.

Qualcast (Wolverhampton), Ltd v Haynes [1959] 2 All ER 38 HL In negligence trial by judge only reasoning of judge on what would otherwise be left to jury is not law: no precedent to be cited.

Quebec Railway, Light, Heat and Power Company, Limited v Vandry and others [1920] AC 662; [1920] 89 LJPC 99; (1920) 123 LTR 1; (1919-20) XXXVI TLR 296 PC Party liable in negligence where failed to establish that could not have prevented relevant damage.

Queens of the River Steamship Company v Conservators of the River Thames and Easton Gibb and Son (1905-06) XXII TLR 419 HC KBD Conservators of River Thames not liable in negligence where had taken reasonable care not to expose steamship to navigation danger.

Quintas v National Smelting Co, Ltd [1961] 1 All ER 630 CA Master liable in negligence/plaintiff contributorily so for injury caused in factory by article not machinery under Factories Act 1937, s 14.

Rankine v Garton Sons and Co Ltd [1979] 2 All ER 1185; (1979) 123 SJ 305 CA RSC Judgment available if admission of negligence and liability, not former alone.

Raulin v Fischer (1911) WN (I) 41 HC KBD On enforceability of foreign tribunal's decision as regards negligence of party.

Rawson v Clark (1981) 131 NLJ 1214c CA Non-liability of person for non-negligent behaviour which aggravated and accentuated existing injury that arose from negligence of another.

Re B Johnson and Co (Builders) Ld [1955] Ch 634 CA Companies Act 1948, s 333 did not extend to common law negligence.

Re Linsley; Cattley v West [1904] 2 Ch 785 HC ChD Solicitor trustee liable to indemnify co-trustee for action prompted by solicitor's negligent management of trust (even though was no loss to estate).

Re Raybould; Raybould v Turner [1900] LXIX (1) LJ 249 HC ChD Can recover damages from trust estate for tort committed by trustee in course of trust duties.

Regent Taxi and Transport Company, Limited v Congregation des Petits Fréres de Marie [1932] AC 295; (1932) 146 LTR 399; (1932) WN (I) 25 PC Negligence action barred under Quebec Civil Code, art 2262(2).

Reynolds v Boston Deep Sea Fishing and Ice Company, Limited (1921-22) XXXVIII TLR 22 HC KBD Exemption clause though did not specifically mention negligence did exclude liability for same.

Reynolds v Thomas Tilling (Limited) (1902-03) XIX TLR 539 HC KBD Interpretation of findings of jury as to negligence/contributory negligence: non-recovery for personal injuries sustained through injury partly caused by own negligence.

Reynolds v Thomas Tilling (Limited) (1903-04) XX TLR 57 CA Approval of lower court's interpretation of findings of jury as to negligence/contributory negligence: non-recovery for personal injuries sustained through injury partly caused by own negligence.

RG Stanners Ltd v High Wycombe Borough Council and another (1968) 118 NLJ 614t; (1968) 112 SJ 766 HC QBD Both contractors and local authority for whom working liable for theft from warehouse effected via lean-to which council had been supposed to remove at which time warehouse was to be secured.

Richardson v London County Council (1957) 107 LJ 328 CA Failed appeal against refusal of leave to bring action in which (inter alia) claimed that negligence of public authorities led to purportedly unlawful detention pursuant to the Mental Deficiency Act 1913.

Rickards v Lothian [1911-13] All ER 71; [1913] AC 263; (1913) 82 LJPC 42; (1912-13) XXIX TLR 281; (1913) 108 LTR 225 PC Not liable in negligence/nuisance for damage resulting from third party malicious act in relation to reasonable user.

Riden v Billings (AC) and Sons, Ltd and others [1956] 3 All ER 357; [1957] 1 QB 46; (1956) 100 SJ 748; [1956] 3 WLR 704 CA Damages for negligence as (non-occupying) contractors creating danger owed duty of care to prevent injury.

Rider v Metropolitan Water Board (1949) 113 JP 377 HC KBD Failed action against Water Board for personal injury sustained on foot of alterations it effected.

Rigby and another v Chief Constable of Northamptonshire [1985] 2 All ER 985; (1985) 129 SJ 832; [1985] 1 WLR 1242 HC QBD Bona fide policy decision unimpeachable; necessity a defence to trespass if defendant's negligence did not give rise to necessity; negligent to fire CS canister when no fire equipment.

Riverstone Meat Co Pty Ltd v Lancashire Shipping Co Ltd (1958) 102 SJ 656 HC QBD Non-liability of shipowners for negligence of workman employed by competent repairer obtained by carrier.

Riverstone Meat Co Pty Ltd v Lancashire Shipping Co Ltd [1960] 1 QB 536; (1960) 104 SJ 50 CA Liability of shipowners for negligence of workman employed by competent repairer obtained by carrier.

Riverstone Meat Co Pty, Ltd v Lancashire Shipping Co, Ltd (1961) 105 SJ 148 HL Non-liability of shipowners for negligence of workman employed by competent repairer obtained by carrier.

Roberts v Charing Cross, Euston and Hampstead Rail Co [1900-03] All ER 157 HC ChD Negligence action well-founded despite availability of statutory compensation in respect of cause of action.

Robinson v State of South Australia (1931) 72 LJ 24; (1929) 98 LJPC 136; (1929) 141 LTR 70 PC On liability in negligence of Government of South Australia when performing its duties under the Wheat Harvest Acts 1915-17.

Robinson v The Post Office and another [1974] 2 All ER 737; (1973) 123 NLJ 1017t; [1974] 1 WLR 1176 CA Negligent doctor's act not causing/materially contributing to existing injury not novus actus interveniens.

Robinson v WH Smith and Son (1900-01) XVII TLR 235 HC KBD Dangerous employment (newspaper boys at railway station having to cross lines) put special duty of care on employers which may not have discharged.

Robinson v WH Smith and Son (1900-01) XVII TLR 423 CA Dangerous employment (newspaper boys at railway station having to cross lines) put special duty of care on employers which may not have discharged.

Romford Ice and Cold Storage Co Ld v Lister [1955] 3 WLR 631 CA Damages available to master for servant's failure in duty of care unaffected by being viariously liable joint tortfeasor.

Rosenbaum v The Metropolitan Water Board (1910) 74 JP 378; (1909-10) XXVI TLR 510 HC KBD Water board liable in negligence for injury caused to footpath user by way of inadequately maintained stopcock box.

Rosenbaum v The Metropolitan Water Board (1911) 75 JP 12; (1910-11) XXVII TLR 103 CA Retrial ordered as to whether water board liable in negligence for injury caused to footpath user by way of inadequately maintained stopcock box.

Rowling and another v Takaro Properties Ltd [1988] 1 All ER 163; [1988] AC 473; (1988) 132 SJ 126; [1988] 2 WLR 418 PC Minister exercising statutory duty not liable for negligence despite judicial review finding that he considered irrelevant material as opinion was still reasonable.

Russell v Criterion Film Productions, Ltd and another [1936] 3 All ER 627; (1936) 80 SJ 1036; (1936-37) LIII TLR 117 HC KBD Film production company, not cameraman, liable for injury effected through over-lighting of film scene.

Salsbury v Woodland and others [1969] 3 All ER 863; (1969) 119 NLJ 365t; [1970] 1 QB 324; (1969) 113 SJ 327; [1969] 3 WLR 29 CA No negligence if employ competent person to do work not in itself dangerous.

Saunders v Leeds Western Health Authority and another (1985) 129 SJ 225 HC QBD Successful negligence action (based on res ipsa loquitur) by normal party who went into hospital for routine operation and emerged a partially sighted, mentally retarded spastic quadraplegic.

Schiffahrt und Kohlen GmbH v Chelsea Maritime Ltd; The Irene's Success [1982] 1 All ER 218; [1982] QB 481; (1982) 126 SJ 101; [1982] 2 WLR 422 HC QBD Sea carriers owe duty of care to cif buyers.

Schlarb v London and North Eastern Railway Co [1936] 1 All ER 71; (1936) 80 SJ 168 HC KBD Negligence to wards first-time user of station on foggy night despite white line marking edge of platform off which fell.

SCM (United Kingdom) Ltd v WJ Whittall and Son Ltd [1970] 3 All ER 245; (1970) 120 NLJ 684t; [1971] 1 QB 337; (1970) 114 SJ 706; [1970] 3 WLR 694 CA Liable for physical damage and loss of profit where negligently interrupt electricity supply by damaging cable.

Sellars v Best and another [1954] 2 All ER 389; (1954) 118 JP 326; (1954) 98 SJ 424; [1954] 1 WLR 913 Assizes Electricity supply board not under duty to test electrical equipment to be connected to electricity supply.

Seng (Goh Cheen) v Soo (Lee Kim) [1925] AC 550 PC Master liable for servant's negligence though servant commits unauthorised trespass.

Sharpe v Sweeting (ET) and Son, Ltd [1963] 2 All ER 455; (1963) 113 LJ 399; (1963) 107 SJ 666; [1963] 1 WLR 665 HC QBD Sufficient proximity between builder and later occupier of premises to sustain negligence action.

Shaw v Cates [1909] 1 Ch 389 HC ChD Trustees not liable in negligence for failure to periodically examine state of mortgaged property.

Sheehan v Dreamland, Margate, Limited (1923-24) XL TLR 155 CA Non-liability of freeholder (invitor) to invitee for injury caused in sideshow which was not inherently dangerous and in repect of which neither invitees nor their servants had been negligent.

Sheridan v Boots Co Ltd and Kensington and Chelsea and Westminster Area Health Authority (1981) 131 NLJ 479 HC QBD Failed action for negligence arising from prescription of drug which resulted in plaintiff going blind.

Shiffman v The Grand Priory in the British Realm of the Venerable Order of the Hospital of St John of Jerusalem [1936] 1 All ER 557; (1936) 80 SJ 346 HC KBD Negligent for non-continuous attention to flagpole (occasioning injury to child allured thereby) erected in public place.

Sidwell v British Timken, Ltd (1962) 106 SJ 243 CA Employers not liable for injury occasioned to plaintiff workman as direct result of another workman's prank.

Simaan General Contracting Co v Pilkington Glass [1988] 1 All ER 791; (1988) 138 NLJ 53; [1988] QB 758; (1988) 132 SJ 463; [1988] 2 WLR 761 CA Minus express assumption of resonsibility pure economic loss irrecoverable.

Simmons v Bovis, Ltd and another [1956] 1 All ER 736 Assizes Liable for failure to prevent forseeable occurrences.

Singleton Abbey (Owners) v Paludina (Owners); The Paludina [1926] All ER 220 HL On novus actus interveniens.

Smerkinich v Newport Corporation (1912) 76 JP 454 HC KBD Failed action for negligence by student who lost thumb in saw at technical institute classes: volenti non fit injuria applicable.

Smith and others v Littlewoods Organisation Ltd (Chief Constable, Fife Constabulary, third party) and conjoined appeal [1987] 1 All ER 710; [1987] AC 241; [1987] 2 WLR 480 HL Generally/ exceptionally is/can be duty of care to ensure property not a danger to neighbouring property.

Smith and UMB Chrysler (Scotland) Ltd v South Wales Switchgear Co Ltd (1978) 122 SJ 61 HL Indemnity clause did not indemnify respondents against their own negligence/that of their servants.

Smith v Eric S Bush (a firm); Harris and another v Wyre Forest District Council and another [1989] 2 All ER 514; [1990] 1 AC 831; (1989) 133 SJ 597; [1989] 2 WLR 790 HL Property valuer owes contractual/tortious duty of care to mortgagor/mortgagee; can disclaim duty but disclaimer must be reasonable.

Smith v Leech Brain and Co, Ltd and another [1961] 3 All ER 1159; (1962) 112 LJ 89; [1962] 2 QB 405; (1962) 106 SJ 77 HC QBD Person committing tort must take victim as found — here liable for cancer resulting from burn to malignancy.

Smith v Linskills (a firm) and another [1995] 3 All ER 226 HC QBD Challenge to outcome of criminal trial via negligence action against defence solicitors an abuse of process unless new evidence impugns criminal verdict.

Smith v Littlewoods Organisation Ltd (1987) 137 NLJ 149; (1987) 131 SJ 226 HL Party not liable for damage to neighbour's properties occasioned by trespasser's on party's land unless damage reasonably foreseeable consequence of latter's actions.

Smith v South Eastern Gas Board; Parsons and another v Same; Knopp v Same (1964) 108 SJ 337 HC QBD Damages awarded for negligence of Gas Board workers in failing to pre-empt explosion.

Smith v Southwark Offset (1975) 125 NLJ 42t; (1975) 119 SJ 258 HC QBD Defendants not negligent in loading post office bags contrary to post office guidelines.

Smith v Sudron and Coulson (1982) 132 NLJ 415c CA Successful appeal against finding of negligence where puppy slipped through fence (reasonably designed to keep it in) and caused road accident.

Smith v Taylor (1965-66) 116 NLJ 1518 HC QBD Exclusion clause could not be relied because not adequately brought to plaintiff's notice.

Smith v WH Smith and Sons, Ltd [1952] 1 All ER 528; (1952) 96 SJ 181 CA On damages/costs where both parties equally to blame.

Sole v WJ Hallt Ltd [1973] 1 All ER 1032; [1973] QB 574; (1973) 117 SJ 110; [1973] 2 WLR 171 HC QBD Occupier liable in contract and tort if breach duty of care to party entering property on foot of contract.

Solomons v Stepney Borough Council (1905) 69 JP 360 HC KBD Was evidence of negligence (leakage of electricity in explosive atmosphere) upon which jury could decide.

Spalding v Tarmac Civil Engineering Ltd and another [1966] 1 WLR 156 CA On liability of persons hiring crane to another for negligence of driver supplied with crane (construction of exceptions clause).

St James' and Pall Mall Electric Light Co, Limited v R (1904) 68 JP 288; [1904] 73 LJCL 518 HC ChD Public body to escape liability for compensation had to prove its agents/contractors to be negligent.

Stansbie v Troman [1948] 1 All ER 599; [1948] 2 KB 48; (1948) 98 LJ 175; [1948] 117 LJR 1206; (1948) LXIV TLR 226; (1948) WN (I) 117 CA Decorator owed duty to safeguard premises from thieves when leaving temporarily.

Stansbie v Troman [1947] LJNCCR 134 CyCt Decorator owed duty to safeguard premises from thieves when leaving temporarily.

Stapley v Gypsum Mines, Ltd [1953] 2 All ER 478; [1953] AC 663; [1953] 3 WLR 279 HL Blurring of negligence so that negligence of one tortfeasor inseparable from another.

Stapley v Gypsum Mines, Ltd [1952] 1 All ER 1092; [1952] 2 QB 575 CA Workmen's own negligence resulted in death so no recovery from employer.

Stearn v Gooding and Son (1912) CC Rep I 77 CyCt Painters in meadow who left paints in such a way that animals could (and did) gain access to them and (as happened) get sick were liable in negligence.

Stennett v Hancock and Peters [1939] 2 All ER 578; (1939) 87 LJ 340; (1939) 83 SJ 379 HC KBD Principles in Donoghue v Stevenson applied to repairer.

Stephens v Anglian Water Authority [1987] 1 WLR 1381 CA Landowner abstracting water from under own land owes no duty of care to neighbours in doing so.

Stewart v West African Terminals Ltd, and another (1964) 108 SJ 838 CA On what is meant by foreseeability in context of negligence claim.

Storey v National Coal Board [1983] 1 All ER 375 HC QBD Company officials engaging in dangerous practice of which employees warned not condoning practice: no negligence.

Stovold v Barlows (1995) 145 NLJ 1649; (1995) 139 SJ LB 218; [1995] TLR 550 CA On damages for loss of opportunity through possible third party action had negligent act not occurred.

Stubbs v Anthony (1948) 98 LJ 94 CyCt Defendant liable in negligence for damage occasioned by collapse of his chimney stack onto adjoining property of another.

Swan v Salisbury Construction Co, Ltd [1966] 2 All ER 138; (1965) 109 SJ 195; [1966] 1 WLR 204 PC Res ipsa loquitur arises when crane collapses.

Swingcastle Ltd v Alastair Gibson (a firm) [1991] 2 All ER 353; (1991) 141 NLJ 563; [1991] TLR 197; [1991] 2 WLR 1091 HL Where loan made on foot of negligent valuation only damages available are for loss of use of amount loaned.

Tate and Lyle Food and Distribution Ltd v Greater London Council and another [1981] 3 All ER 716 HC QBD On damages for waste of managerial time in resolving problem created by negligent act; on awarding interest on damages in commercial cases.

Taylor v Rover Co, Ltd and others (Richard W Carr and Co, Ltd, Third Party) [1966] 2 All ER 181; (1965-66) 116 NLJ 809; [1966] 1 WLR 1491 Assizes Manufacturer not liable where employer keeps defective tool (in production of which manufacturer took all reasonable steps) in use when knows it to be dangerous.

Taylor v Sims and Sims [1942] 2 All ER 375; (1943) 93 LJ 108; (1942) 167 LTR 414; (1942) 86 SJ 312; (1941-42) LVIII TLR 339 HC KBD Employers not occupying employee's place of work did not owe duty of care; voluntarily continuing to work in place knowing of danger raised volenti non fit injuria; injury sustained by workman in bomb-blasted house a 'war injury'.

The Ballyalton; Owners of Steamship Ballyalton v Preston Corporation [1961] 1 All ER 459 HC PDAD Harbour authority liable in negligence for failure to adequately supervise berths but were covered by exception clause.

The Guildford; Owners of SS Temple Bar v Owners of MV Guildford [1956] 2 All ER 915; [1956] 3 WLR 474 HC PDAD Refusal of tow/waiting for tug a reasonable act and did not break chain of causation.

The Kite [1933] All ER 234 HC PDAD If can explain act in way that is no less likely than negligence burden reverts to plaintiff to show act was negligent; plaintiffs not allowed recover in tort for negligence for which under their contract with defendants, defendants not liable.

The Stella [1900-03] All ER 184 HC PDAD Fatal accident/negligence action precluded by condition on granting of free travel pass.

The Towerfield; Owners of the SS Towerfield v Workington Harbour and Dock Board [1948] 2 All ER 736 CA On negligence/contributory negligence under Pilotage Act 1913/Harbours, Docks, and Piers Clauses Act 1847.

The Wagon Mound (No 2); Overseas Tankship (UK), Ltd v The Miller Steamship Co Pty Ltd and another [1966] 2 All ER 709; [1967] AC 617; (1966) 110 SJ 447; [1966] 3 WLR 498 PC Negligent where fail to prevent foreseeable injury; foreseeability of injury essential for recovery in nuisance.

Thomas and another v British Railways Board and others [1976] 3 All ER 15; [1976] QB 913; (1976) 120 SJ 334; [1976] 2 WLR 761 CA Juxtaposition of railway/footpath imposed duty of care on Board to provide stile but local authority liable for repair.

Thomas v Gulf Oil Refining Ltd and another (1979) 123 SJ 787 HC QBD Landowner may abstract water from under own land for whatever reason.

Tidy and another v Battman [1933] All ER 259; [1952] Ch 791 (also HC ChD); [1934] 1 KB 319; (1934) 77 LJ 28; (1934) 103 LJCL 158; (1934) 150 LTR 90; (1933) WN (I) 276 CA No rule of law that one must be negligent if one collides with stationary vehicle.

Tilley v Stevenson [1939] 4 All ER 207; (1939) 88 LJ 298; (1939) 83 SJ 943 CA Where burst pipe must show person claimed against knew/ought to have known water being fed to pipe.

Travers v Gloucester Corporation and others [1946] 2 All ER 506; (1946) 110 JP 364; [1947] KB 71; [1946] 115 LJ 517; (1946) 175 LTR 360; (1946) 90 SJ 556; (1945-46) LXII TLR 723 HC KBD Landlord installing defective gas geyser not liable for injuries to tenant's guests/customers: Donoghue v Stevenson inapplicable.

Tremain v Pike and another [1969] 1 WLR 1556 Assizes Non-recovery of damages for disease contracted through contact with rat urine — too remote to be reasonably foreseeable.

Truscott and another v McLaren and another [1982] RTR 34 CA Person on major road was negligent in not taking reasonable steps to avoid collision with car whom saw approaching on minor road.

Turley v Daw (1906) XCIV LTR 216 HC KBD Judgment debtor cannot during duration of committal order bring action aainst County court bailiff for non-service of judgment summons.

Turner v Civil Service Supply Association Limited (1926) 134 LTR 189 HC KBD Non-liability of (non-common) carriers for loss of goods through fire caused by own servant's negligence as had exempted selves from liability in contract.

Turner v Ford Motor Co, Ltd and another [1965] 2 All ER 583; (1965) 115 LJ 448; (1965) 109 SJ 354; [1965] 1 WLR 948 CA Defendant allowed amend claim to allege negligence of plaintiff in not protecting self with equipment given by employers though plaintiff time-barred from claim against employers upon amendment.

Turner v Mansfield Corporation (1975) 125 NLJ 551t; (1975) 119 SJ 629 CA On res ipsa loquitur rule.

Twine v Bean's Express, Ltd [1946] 1 All ER 202; (1946) 174 LTR 239; (1946) 90 SJ 128; (1945-46) LXII TLR 155 HC KBD No duty of care by employers towards trespasser travelling unknown to them in their van.

Vacwell Engineering Co Ltd v BDH Chemicals Ltd (formerly British Drug Houses Ltd) [1970] 3 All ER 553; [1970] 3 WLR 67 CA Settlement of negligence action (involving dangerous chemicals).

Vandyke v Fender and another (1970) 134 JP 487; [1969] 2 QB 581 HC QBD Lender of car liable to injured party for negligence of borrower acting as lender's agent.

Waldock v Winfield [1901] 2 KB 596 CA Master liable for negligence of servant on has hire to another.

Walker v Crabb (1916-17) 61 SJ 219; (1916-17) XXXIII TLR 119 HC KBD Person employing services of auctioneer not liable for negligence of same as auctioneer not person's servant.

Walker v Linom [1907] 2 Ch 104; [1907] 76 LJCh 500; (1907-08) XCVII LTR 92; (1906-07) 51 SJ 483 HC ChD Legal estate of negligent trustees second to equitable interest of purchaser of property who through negligence of trustees bought property without notice of settlement.

Walker v Northumberland County Council [1995] 1 All ER 737; (1994) 144 NLJ 1659; (1995) 139 SJ LB 19 HC QBD Employer owes duty of care not to cause workers psychiatric damage by reason of work burden or character.

Walpole and another v Partridge and Wilson (a firm) [1994] 1 All ER 385; [1994] QB 106; [1993] 3 WLR 1093 CA Collateral attack on final decision in earlier proceedings not necessarily abuse of process.

Walsh v Holst and Co, Ltd, and others [1958] 3 All ER 33; (1958) 108 LJ 537; (1958) 102 SJ 545 CA Brick falling from construction site and hitting passer-by raised res ipsa loquitur (but was defeated here).

Ward v TE Hopkins and Son, Ltd; Baker and another v TE Hopkins and Son, Ltd [1959] 3 All ER 225; [1959] 1 WLR 966 CA Employer liable in negligence to servant also liable to doctor seeking to rescue same: no novus actus interveniens/volenti non fit injuria.

Ward v Tesco Stores Ltd [1976] 1 All ER 219; (1976) 120 SJ 555; [1976] 1 WLR 810 CA Absent explanation of apparent failure of duty of care court could infer breach thereof.

Weeds v Blaney and another (1976) 120 SJ 333 HC ChD Negligence did not preclude rectification of contract.

Weller and Co and another v Foot and Mouth Disease Research Institute [1965] 3 All ER 560; [1966] 1 QB 569; (1965) 109 SJ 702; [1965] 3 WLR 1082 HC QBD Research Institute liable to farmers but not auctioneer at local cattle mart for escape of foot and mouth virus from laboratory.

Wells v Metropolitan Water Board (1938) 102 JP 61; (1937-38) LIV TLR 104 HC KBD Water board liable in negligence for injury caused to child by way of open valve-box lid, it being known to Board that lids were commonly interfered with.

Wheeler and another v New Merton Board Mills, Ltd [1933] All ER 28 CA Cannot be volenti non fit injuria in action for breach of statutory duty.

Wheeler v Copas [1981] 3 All ER 405; (1981) 131 NLJ 367 HC QBD Damages for worker given unsuitable ladder for work by farmer but damages halved given that worker understood danger but used ladder anyway.

Wilkinson v Rea, Ltd [1941] 2 All ER 50 CA Shipowners liable in negligence for workman's fall through hatch.

William A Jay and Sons v Veevers (JS), Ltd [1946] 1 All ER 646 Assizes Apportionment of liability for contributory negligence on Admiralty Division principles.

Williams v Humphrey (1975) 125 NLJ 230/262 HC QBD Person liable for injuries suffered by another whom mischeviously pushed into swimming pool.

Wilson and another v Hodgson's Kingston Brewery Company (Limited) (1916) 80 JP 39; [1916] 85 LJKB 270; (1915-16) 113 LTR 1112; (1915-16) 60 SJ 142; (1915-16) XXXII TLR 60; (1915) WN (I) 352 HC KBD Brewery/tenant of tied pub not liable for injury suffered by independent deliverer who elected to deliver beer by particular route.

Woods v Duncan and others; Duncan and another v Hambrook and others; Duncan and another v Cammell Laird and Co, Ltd [1946] 1 All ER 420; [1946] AC 401; [1947] 116 LJR 120; (1946) 174 LTR 286; (1945-46) LXII TLR 283 HL Resolution of negligence action; on res ipsa loquitur.

Wray v Essex County Council (1936) 82 LJ 296; (1936) 155 LTR 494; (1936) 80 SJ 894 CA Oil can not inherently dangerous: failed negligence action arising from loss of eye occasioned by one pupil running into spout of oil can being carried by another pupil under teacher's instructions to certain part of school.

Wyman or Ferguson (Pauper) v Paterson and others [1900] LXIX (3) LJ 32; (1900) LXXXII LTR 473; (1899-1900) XVI TLR 270 HL Trustees liable for trust funds lost through their gross negligence.

X v Bedfordshire County Council (1995) 145 NLJ 993 HL To ground action for careless performance of duty must prove that common law duty of care arose in circumstances of case.

Yachuk and another v Oliver Blais Co, Ltd [1949] 2 All ER 150; [1949] AC 386; (1949) LXV TLR 300; (1949) WN (I) 186 PC Negligent to sell dangerous substance (petrol) to child; child's later messing with petrol not novus actus interveniens/contributory negligence.

Yeun Kun Yeu and others v Attorney-General of Hong Kong [1988] AC 175; (1987) 137 NLJ 566; (1987) 131 SJ 1185; [1987] 3 WLR 776 PC Hong Kong Commissioner of Deposit-taking Companies did not owe duty of care to individual depositors for losses suffered through misbehaviour of deposit-taking company registered by Commissioner.

NEGLIGENCE (golf)

Langham v Governors of Wellingborough School and Fryer (1932) 96 JP 236; (1932) 73 LJ 361; (1932) 101 LJCL 513; (1932) 147 LTR 91 CA Not negligent/no res ipsa loquitur where school pupil struck by golf ball that other pupil hit from door into schoolground.

NEGLIGENCE (Government department)

Culford Metal Industries Ltd v Export Credit Guarantees Department (1981) 131 NLJ 603 HC QBD Specialist government department liable for negligent advice to first-time exporter.

Gaisford and another v Ministry of Agriculture, Fisheries and Food (1996) TLR 18/7/96 HC QBD Ministry of Agriculture, Fisheries and Food did not owe duty of care towards purchasers of imported animals to discover between importation and expiry of quarantine period whether animals were suffering from disease.

NEGLIGENCE (hairdresser)

Dobbin v Waldorf Toilet Saloons, Ltd [1937] 1 All ER 331 Assizes Negligent permanent waving of bleached/dyed hair by hairdresser.

NEGLIGENCE (highway)

Allison v Corby District Council [1980] RTR 111 HC QBD Local authority not liable in negligence for failure to catch stray dogs (whose presence caused road accident) nor for failure to maintain highway.

Andrews v Merton and Morden Urban District Council (1922) CC Rep XI 3; (1921) 56 LJ 466 HC KBD Non-liability of council for non-feasance of highway.

Andrews v Merton and Morden Urban District Council (1921) CC Rep X 50 CyCt Council/ highway authority liable for injury person suffered by falling into hole in path that occurred when council timber work alongside path fell into disrepair (becoming nuisance).

Attorney-General (on the relation of Thomas Brownlee Paisley) and another v St Ives Rural District Council and another (1959) 123 JP 514 HC QBD Rural district council liable to repair drains did not enjoy similar immunity in respect of non-feasance that highway authority enjoys in respect of roads.

Baker v Longhurst (E) and Sons, Ltd [1932] All ER 102; [1933] 2 KB 461; (1933) 102 LJCL 573; (1933) 149 LTR 264 CA Person driving at night must be able to stop within limits of vision.

Baldwin's, Limited v Halifax Corporation (1916) 80 JP 357; [1916] 85 LJKB 1769 HC KBD Lack of care in technical design of road was misfeasance for which liable in damages to party injured in consequence.

Barnes Urban District Council v London General Omnibus Company (1909) 73 JP 68 HC KBD Bus driver is on face of it negligent where collides in daylight with lamp post (but can prove otherwise to be the case).

Baxter v Stockton-on-Tees Corporation [1958] 2 All ER 675; (1958) 122 JP 443; (1958) 108 LJ 490; [1959] 1 QB 441; (1958) 102 SJ 562 CA Council not liable for non-feasance of highway.

Bird v Pearce and another; Somerset County Council (Third Party) [1978] RTR 290 HC QBD On duty owed towards road users by highway authority re-surfacing road and so obliterating road markings.

Bird v Pearce and another; Somerset County Council (Third Party) (1979) 129 (2) NLJ 681; [1979] RTR 369 CA On duty owed towards road users by highway authority re-surfacing road and so obliterating road markings.

Bradbury v Llandrindod Wells UDC (1921) CC Rep X 3 CyCt Non-liability of highway authority for non-feasance of highway.

Bright v Attorney-General (1971) 121 NLJ 178t; (1971) 115 SJ 226 CA Unusually action in negligence arising from unevenness in road surface caused by council workers was successful.

Bromley v Mercer [1922] 2 KB 126; [1922] 91 LJCL 577; (1922) 127 LTR 282; (1921-22) XXXVIII TLR 496; (1922) WN (I) 112 CA Non-liability to non-user of highway for injury suffered via wall which was public nuisance on highway.

Brown v Harrison (1947) 97 LJ 361; (1947) 177 LTR 281; (1947) LXIII TLR 484; (1947) WN (I) 191 CA Owner of dying tree liable for injury sustained by person on highway on whom fell as ought to have realised and remedied danger tree posed.

Burnside and another v Emerson and another (1969) 133 JP 66; (1968) 112 SJ 565; [1968] 1 WLR 1490 CA Highway authority in part liable for injury arising from inadequate maintenance of highway.

Burton v West Suffolk County Council [1960] 2 All ER 26; (1960) 124 JP 273; [1960] 2 QB 72; (1960) 104 SJ 349 CA Highway authority not negligent where did not warn of ice on road.

Caminer and another v Northern and London Investment Trust, Ltd [1948] 2 All ER 1101; (1948) 98 LJ 685; (1948) LXIV TLR 629; (1948) WN (I) 489 HC KBD Landowners liable in negligence/nuisance for failure to look after tree that falls injuring person on adjoining highway.

Chappell v Mayor, etc of Dagenham (1948) 98 LJ 329; (1948) WN (I) 274 HC KBD Non-liability of local authority for non-feasance of highway.

Crane v South Suburban Gas Co [1914-15] All ER 93; (1916) 80 JP 51; [1916] 1 KB 33; [1916] 85 LJKB 172; (1916) 114 LTR 71; (1915-16) 60 SJ 222; (1915-16) XXXII TLR 74 HC KBD Liability in nuisance and negligence for injury occasioned to person as result of third party intervention on foot of dangerous work by highway.

Cross v Kirklees [1997] TLR 370 CA Presence of snow/ice on highway did not mean (and here was not the case) that highway authority was in breach of its duty of care as regards maintenance of highway.

Daniel v Rickett, Cockerell and Co Limited, and another [1938] 2 All ER 631; [1938] 2 KB 322; (1938) 85 LJ 380; [1938] 107 LJCL 589; (1938) 82 SJ 353; (1937-38) LIV TLR 756; (1938) WN (I) 190 HC KBD Absent adequate warning to passers-by coal deliverer and householder were jointly liable for injury suffered by person falling as result of coal cellar access to pavement being open.

Dawson and Co v Bingley Urban District Council [1911-13] All ER 596 CA Liability for misfeasance.

East Suffolk Rivers Catchment Board v Kent and another [1940] 4 All ER 527; (1941) 165 LTR 65 HL Liability for misfeasance/non-feasance.

Eastbourne County Borough v Fuller and Sons (1929) 93 JP 29 HC KBD Failed action for nuisance/negligence against defendant in respect of its use of agricultural vehicles upon highway.

Evans (Pauper) v Lord Provost, Magistrates, and Council of the City of Edinburgh [1916] 2 AC 45; (1916) 114 LTR 911 HL Door opening outwards onto street not of itself negligence nor was it obstruction of highway.

Farrugia v Great Western Railway Co [1947] 2 All ER 565 CA Person creating risk on highway owes duty of care to others thereon/nearby even if other trespasser or presence otherwise unlawful.

France v Parkinson [1954] 1 All ER 739; (1954) 104 LJ 234; (1954) 98 SJ 214; [1954] 1 WLR 581 CA Absent contrary evidence equal negligence/liability for collision at equal crossroads.

Gould v Birkenhead Corporation (1910) 74 JP 105 HC KBD Nonsuit unjustified where was evidence that malfeasance of defendants' servants resulted in injury to plaintiff.

Griffiths v Liverpool Corporation (1966) 130 JP 376; [1967] 1 QB 374; (1966) 110 SJ 548; [1966] 3 WLR 467 CA Liability of highway authority for non-feasance of highway.

Guilfoyle v Port of London Authority [1931] All ER 365; (1931) 95 JP 217; (1932) 101 LJCL 91; (1931-32) XLVIII TLR 55 HC KBD Port Authority liable for misfeasance/nonfeasance of bridge.

Hale v Hants and Dorset Motor Services, Ltd and another (1948) 112 JP 47 CA On liability of highway authority/omnibus driver for injury to upstairs passenger on omnibus struck by overhanging branches of tree.

Haley v London Electricity Board (1963) 107 SJ 416 HC QBD Corporation doing streetworks owed no special duty of care to the blind.

Haley v London Electricity Board [1964] 3 All ER 185; [1965] AC 778; (1965) 129 JP 14; (1964) 114 LJ 585; (1964) 108 SJ 637; [1964] 3 WLR 479 HL Persons doing street works owed duty of care to blind users of highway.

Hall v Barrow-in-Furness Corporation [1937] LJNCCR 157 CyCt Corporation not liable in negligence for damage to window by stone thrown up by car passing area on road where corporation had recently been doing roadworks.

Hart v St Marylebone Borough Council (1912) 76 JP 257 HC KBD Recovery of cost of repairs necessitated by subsidence in road as result of negligent inattention of council to sewer repair.

Hay (or Bourhill) v Young [1942] 2 All ER 396; [1943] AC 92 HL Tortfeasor in motor vehicle collision not liable to bystander for nervous shock as not reasonably foreseeable.

Hewlett v Great Central Railway Company (1915-16) 60 SJ 428; (1915-16) XXXII TLR 373; (1916) WN (I) 144 CA Railway company deemed in circumstances to be under duty to warn public of presence of post authorised by statute and maintainable by them.

Hill-Venning v Beszant [1950] 2 All ER 1151; (1950) 94 SJ 760; [1950] 66 (2) TLR 921; (1950) WN (I) 538 CA Leaving unlit motorbike on road at night was negligent.

Holloway v Lord Mayor, etc of Birmingham (1905) 69 JP 358 HC KBD Absent evidence of defective construction highway authority could not be found guilty of misfeasance.

Hughes and another v Sheppard and others; Morley and others v Same (1940) 104 JP 357; (1940) 163 LTR 177; (1939-40) LVI TLR 810 HC KBD Not negligent/nuisance for council workers to mark where were painting lines on road with cans and flags — even if was nuisance only negligent driver who failed to see same and collided with another vehicle liable in actions arising from accident.

Irving v Carlisle Rural District Council (1907) 71 JP 212 HC KBD Council found guilty of non-feasance (not misfeasance) of ditch.

Kent and Porter v East Suffolk Rivers Catchment Board [1939] 4 All ER 174; (1940) 104 JP 1; (1939-40) LVI TLR 86 CA Liability/non-liability for misfeasance/non-feasance.

Laurie v Raglan Building Co, Ltd [1941] 3 All ER 332; [1942] 1 KB 152; (1941) 91 LJ 422; (1942) 92 LJ 60; [1942] 111 LJ 292; (1942) 166 LTR 63; (1942) 86 SJ 69 CA Skid requires driver (or here driver's employers) to show were not negligent.

Lavis v Kent County Council [1994] TLR 600 HC QBD County council deemed not to have been negligent in non-erection of road signs in certain place.

Lewys v Burnett and Dunbar and another [1945] 2 All ER 555; (1945) 109 JP 253; (1945) 173 LTR 307; (1945) 89 SJ 415; (1944-45) LXI TLR 527 HC KBD Persons giving free lift negligent for not warning dead passenger of which they knew; highway authority liable in nuisance for negligent raising of road beneath bridge.

Maguire v Corporation of Liverpool (1905) 69 JP 153; [1905] 1 KB 767; (1905) XCII LTR 374; (1904-05) 53 WR 449 CA Liverpool Corporation not liable for non-feasance of roads.

McClelland v Manchester Corporation [1911-13] All ER 562; (1912) 76 JP 21; (1912) 81 LJKB 98; (1911-12) 105 LTR 707; (1911-12) XXVIII TLR 21 HC KBD Liability for misfeasance not nonfeasance.

Miller v Liverpool Co-operative Society, Ltd, and others [1940] 4 All ER 367 Assizes Passenger/licensee recovering against both parties in motor vehicle collision.

Misell v Essex County Council [1994] TLR 648 HC QBD On extent of duty of care owed by highway authority as regards removal of mud from road.

Moul v Croydon Corporation and another [1918-19] All ER 971; (1918) 82 JP 283; (1918) 53 LJ 227; (1918-19) 119 LTR 318; (1917-18) XXXIV TLR 473; (1918) WN (I) 194 HC KBD Highway authority not liable for nonfeasance.

Moul v Thomas Tilling, Lim and another [1919] 88 LJCL 505 HC ChD Non-liability of highway authority for non-feasance.

Nash v Rochford Rural District Council [1916-17] All ER 299; (1917) 81 JP 57; [1917] 86 LJCL 370; (1917) 116 LTR 129 CA Succeeding highway authority not liable for negligence of preceding highway authority.

Newsome v Darton Urban District Council (1938) 102 JP 75; (1938) 158 LTR 149; (1937) 81 SJ 1042; (1937-38) LIV TLR 286 HC KBD Highway authority liable in nuisance/negligence for misfeasance (subsidence in trench had caused to be dug which led to injury to cyclist).

Newsome v Darton Urban District Council (1938) 102 JP 409; (1938) 82 SJ 520; (1937-38) LIV TLR 945 CA Highway and sanitary authority liable as latter in nuisance/negligence for misfeasance (subsidence in trench had caused to be dug which led to injury to cyclist).

Nicholson v Southern Rail Co and Cheam UDC [1935] All ER 168; [1935] 1 KB 558; (1935) 79 LJ 116; (1935) 152 LTR 349 HC KBD Owner of land adjoining highway not under duty to maintain land so as to minimise dangers arising from roadworks: highway authority liable for altering level of highway so as to create danger.

Oakes v Northwich UDC [1943] LJNCCR 203 CyCt On liability of highway authority for misfeasance/non-feasance of highway.

Oldham v Sheffield Corporation (1927) 91 JP 69; (1927) 136 LTR 681; (1926-27) XLIII TLR 222 CA Liable in negligence for placing obstruction on private road and thereby causing invitee injury.

Owens v Thomas Scott and Sons (Bakers), Ltd, and Wastall [1939] 3 All ER 663; (1939) 88 LJ 85 HC KBD Owner of forecourt indistinguishable from and adjoining to highway liable to maintain it so does not endanger passers-by.

Papworth v Battersea Borough Council (1914) 78 JP 172; (1915) 79 JP 309; [1914] 2 KB 89; [1915] 84 LJKB 1881; [1914] 83 LJKB 358; (1914) 110 LTR 385; (1913-14) XXX TLR 240 HC KBD Non-liability/liability as highway/sewer authority.

Papworth v Battersea Borough Council [1914-15] All ER 406; (1916) 80 JP 177; [1916] 1 KB 583; [1916] 85 LJKB 746; (1916) 114 LTR 340; (1915-16) 60 SJ 120 CA Trial ordered as to liability of local authority for negligently constructed road gully.

Parkinson v West Riding of Yorkshire County Council (1921-22) 66 SJ 488 HC KBD Council liable for misfeasance of highway where accident arose as result of state in which workmen left road overnight.

Pether v Kessex Cinemas, Ltd [1937] LJNCCR 314 CyCt Cinema owners liable in negligence for injuries sustained by person falling over sign displayed by another in manner cinema owners ordained.

Quinn v Scott and another [1965] 2 All ER 588; (1965) 109 SJ 498; [1965] 1 WLR 1004 HC QBD Occupier negligent in not felling decaying tree bordering highway whose fall resulted in traffic collision.

Randall v Tarrant [1955] 1 All ER 600; (1955) 105 LJ 168; (1955) 99 SJ 184; [1955] 1 WLR 255 CA Driver of moving vehicle must show not negligent where strikes obvious non-moving vehicle; trespass by driver in field adjoining highway did not mean trespass/nuisance on highway.

Rider v Rider and another [1973] RTR 178 CA On standard of care required of highway authority.

Rouse v Squires and others [1973] 2 All ER 903; [1973] QB 889; [1973] RTR 550; (1973) 117 SJ 431; [1973] 2 WLR 925 CA Negligent obstruction of highway contributorily negligent to later negligent collision therewith.

Rowe v Herman and others [1997] TLR 298 CA Occupier not liable in negligence for hazard created by independent contractor who had been working for occupier and since finished and left.

Ryan v Youngs [1938] 1 All ER 522; (1938) 82 SJ 233 CA Employer not liable in negligence/ nuisance for collision occasioned by act of God (worker in apparent good health dying at wheel).

Scott v Green and Sons (a firm) (1969) 119 NLJ 81t; (1969) 113 SJ 73; [1969] 1 WLR 301 CA Liable (under Highways Act 1959, s 154(5)) for not keeping flagstone in good repair only if negligence/nuisance element present.

Shears v Matthews [1948] 2 All ER 1064; (1949) 113 JP 36; (1949) LXV TLR 194; (1948) WN (I) 472 HC KBD Highway Act 1835, s 78, covers negligence directly connected to driving.

Short and Wife v Hammersmith Corporation (1911) 75 JP 82 HC KBD Highway authority not liable for misfeasance where hole in path occurred after time of last repair to path.

Skilton v Epsom and Ewell Urban District Council (1936) 100 JP 231; [1937] 1 KB 112; [1937] 106 LJCL 41; (1936) 154 LTR 700; (1936) 80 SJ 345; (1935-36) LII TLR 494; (1936) WN (I) 155 CA Local authority's placing of defective stud on highway actionable negligence/nuisance.

Skilton v Urban District Council of Epsom and Ewell [1936] LJNCCR 69 CyCt Local authority's placing of defective stud on highway rendered it liable in negligence.

Stovin v Wise (Norfolk County Council, third party) [1994] 3 All ER 467; [1994] RTR 225; [1994] TLR 134; [1994] 1 WLR 1124 CA Highway authority under common law duty of care to obviate visibility restriction of which it is aware and can eliminate.

Stovin v Wise (Norfolk County Council, third party) [1996] 3 All ER 801; [1996] AC 923; (1996) 146 NLJ 1185; [1996] RTR 354; (1996) 140 SJ LB 201; (1996) TLR 26/7/96; [1996] 3 WLR 388 HL Highway authority not under common law duty of care to obviate visibility restriction of which it is aware and can eliminate.

Tarrant v Rowlands and another [1979] RTR 144 HC QBD Inadequate drainage by highway authority of area where water habitually collected after rain meant authority liable for accident occasioned thereby; person causing collision by driving so fast that fails to observe pool of water and drives into same losing control of car is negligent.

Thompson v Bradford Corporation and another [1914-15] All ER 1176; [1915] 84 LJKB 1440; (1915-16) 113 LTR 506; (1914-15) 59 SJ 495 HC KBD Liability for misfeasance.

Thompson v Bradford Corporation and WS Tinsley (1915) CC Rep IV 27 CyCt Highway authority and telephone company liable in negligence for leaving road in state of disrepair following work on telegraph lines.

Torrance v Ilford Urban District Council (1908) 72 JP 526; (1908-09) XCIX LTR 847 HC KBD Council were perhaps negligent in manner in which left stones on road but damage which occurred not proved to be natural and direct consequence of that action.

Torrance v Ilford Urban District Council (1909) 73 JP 225; (1908-09) XXV TLR 355 CA Council were negligent in manner in which left stones on road but driver could not recover damages as had seen stones, appreciated risk and taken risk anyway.

Watkins v Moffatt and others (1967) 111 SJ 719 CA Person who emerged from side road and drove onto main road at speed was guilty of negligence.

West and another v Buckinghamshire County Council [1985] RTR 306; [1984] TLR 627 HC QBD Highway authority not negligent in not having marked dangerous section of road over twenty feet wide (on which fatal accident occurred) with double white lines.

Wheeler v Morris [1915] 84 LJKB 269; (1915) 112 LTR 412 HC KBD Shopowner could be liable for injury to party caused by two men pulling on external sun-blind in respect of which inadequate precautions taken.

Wheeler v Morris [1914-15] All ER 1196; (1915) CC Rep IV 53; (1915) 50 LJ 335; [1915] 84 LJKB 1435; (1915-16) 113 LTR 644 CA Shopowner not liable for injury to party caused by two men pulling on external sun-blind as was not reasonably foreseeable/had taken all reasonable steps.

Wilson v Kingston-on-Thames Corporation (1948) 112 JP 433; (1948) LXIV TLR 553; (1948) WN (I) 398 HC KBD Highway authorities not liable for injuries resulting from their non-feasance of highway.

Wilson v Kingston-upon-Thames Corporation (1949) 113 JP 184; (1949) 99 LJ 135; (1949) WN (I) 121 CA Highway authorities not liable for injuries resulting from their non-feasance of highway.

NEGLIGENCE (hospital)

Barnett v Chelsea and Kensington Hospital Management Committee [1968] 1 All ER 1068; (1967) 117 NLJ 1218t; [1969] 1 QB 428; (1967) 111 SJ 912; [1968] 2 WLR 422 HC QBD Hospital authority liable for negligence of casualty officer; here link between latter's negligence and victim's death disproved/not proved.

Bolam v Friern Hospital Management Committee [1957] 2 All ER 118; (1957) 107 LJ 315; (1957) 101 SJ 357 HC QBD Doctor not negligent if susbscribes to one of two conflicting views held by responsible bodies of medics; doctor negligent in not giving warning to mentally ill person of what he believes to be minimal dangers of treatment; must show failure to warn not negligent and would not have consented if warned.

Bullard v Croydon Hospital Group Management Committee and another [1953] 1 All ER 596; (1953) 117 JP 182; (1953) 103 LJ 139; [1953] 1 QB 511; (1953) 97 SJ 155 HC QBD Hospital group management committee could be liable in negligence.

Cassidy v Ministry of Health (Fahrni, Third Party) [1951] 1 All ER 574; [1951] 2 KB 343; (1951) 101 LJ 121; (1951) 95 SJ 253; [1951] 1 TLR 539; (1951) WN (I) 147 CA On liability of hospital authorities for negligence of medical staff.

Coles v Reading and District Hospital Management Committee and another (1963) 107 SJ 115 HC QBD Cottage hospital and doctor negligent in not taking adequate care to guard against tetanus infection which led to death of accident victim whose estate brought instant action.

Dryden v Surrey County Council and Stewart [1936] 2 All ER 535; (1936) 82 LJ 9; (1936) 80 SJ 656 HC KBD Nurses' negligence; bases for action against two defendants being different counsel for one could cross-examine witness for other.

Edwards v West Herts Group Hospital Management Committee [1957] 1 All ER 541; (1957) 121 JP 212; (1957) 107 LJ 169 CA Hospital committee not liable as invitor/master or via implied term in employment contract with house physician for personal belongings stolen from staff hostel.

Gold v Essex County Council [1942] 2 KB 293; (1942) WN (I) 161 CA Local authority managing hospital liable for negligent injury of patient by radiographer.

Hillyer v The Governors of St Bartholmew's Hospital (1909) 73 JP 501; [1909] 2 KB 820; (1909) 44 LJ 483; [1909] 78 LJKB 958; (1909-10) 101 LTR 368; (1908-09) 53 SJ 714; (1909) WN (I) 188 CA Hospital governors not liable for injury allegedly sustained by plaintiff at hands of hospital workers.

Knight v Home Office [1990] 3 All ER 237; (1990) 140 NLJ 210 HC QBD On standard of care owed towards mentally unwell prisoner held in prison hospital pending admission to secure hospital.

Roe v Minister of Health and others; Woolley v Same [1954] 2 QB 66; (1954) 98 SJ 30; [1954] 1 WLR 128 HC QBD Hospital not liable for negligence of anesthesist.

Roe v Ministry of Health and others; Woolley v Same [1954] 2 All ER 131; (1954) 104 LJ 313; [1954] 2 QB 66; (1954) 98 SJ 319; [1954] 2 WLR 915 CA Hospital liable for negligence of anesthesist — no negligence here as standard of care was that to be expected of reasonably competent anaesthesist.

Selfe v Ilford and District Hospital Management Committee (1970) 114 SJ 935 HC QBD Hospital negligent in its provision of supervision for suicidal patient (who managed to injure self).

Sherwell v Alton Urban District Council (1908-09) XXV TLR 417 Assizes Diptheria hospital authorities not found liable in negligence for diptheria of child who strayed onto hospital grounds as was not only way in which child could have contracted diptheria.

Strangeways-Lesmere v Clayton and others [1936] 1 All ER 484; [1936] 2 KB 11; [1936] 105 LJCL 385; (1936) 154 LTR 463; (1936) 80 SJ 306; (1935-36) LII TLR 374; (1936) WN (I) 85 HC KBD Hospital not liable/liable for duly qualified nurse acting in professional/administrative capacity.

Thorne v Northern Group Hospital Management Committee (1964) 108 SJ 484 HC QBD Hospital not found to be negligent where suicidal patient managed to slip out, go home and commit suicide.

Vancouver General Hospital v McDaniel and another (1934) 78 LJ 146; (1935) 152 LTR 56; (1934) WN (I) 171 PC Failed negligence action against hospital whose practice accorded with competent general medical practice.

Voller and another v Portsmouth Corporation and others (1947) 97 LJ 233 HC KBD Corporation which maintained hospital liable for negligent injury occasioned to plaintiff when administering spinal injection.

Weigall v Westminster Hospital (Governors) (1935) 79 SJ 560; (1934-35) LI TLR 554 HC KBD Hospital negligent towards mother of patient/invitee slipping on mat on polished floor when entering hospital room for consultation with surgeon.

Weigall v Westminster Hospital [1936] 1 All ER 232; (1936) 80 SJ 146; (1935-36) LII TLR 301 CA Hospital negligent towards mother of patient/invitee slipping on mat on polished floor when entering hospital room for consultation with surgeon.

NEGLIGENCE (husband and wife)

Treharne v Treharne (1967) 111 SJ 34 HC PDAD Wife in maintenance not eligible for maintenance for self where in desertion at date of hearing.

NEGLIGENCE (immunity from suit)

Arenson v Arenson and another [1972] 2 All ER 939 HC ChD Arbitral actions clothed with immunity from negligence suits.

Arenson v Arenson and another [1973] 2 All ER 235; [1973] Ch 346; (1973) 123 NLJ 226t; (1973) 117 SJ 247 CA Arbitration honestly done clothed with immunity from suit for negligence.

Arenson v Casson Beckman Rutley and Co (1972) 122 NLJ 330; (1972) 116 SJ 298 HC ChD Surveyor's valuation of shares immune from suit as discharged in quasi-arbitral manner.

Arenson v Casson Beckman Rutley and Co [1975] 3 All ER 901; [1977] AC 405; (1975) 125 NLJ 1191t; (1975) 119 SJ 810; [1975] 3 WLR 815 HL No immunity for surveyor's negligent valuation of shares unless done judicially.

Boynton v Richardson's (a firm) (1924) WN (I) 262 HC KBD No action in negligence to lie against arbitrator or quasi-arbitrator.

Elguzouli-Daf v Commissioner of Police of the Metropolis and another; McBrearty v Ministry of Defence and others [1995] 1 All ER 833; (1995) 145 NLJ 151; [1995] QB 335; [1994] TLR 598; [1995] 2 WLR 173 CA Crown Prosecution Service immune from actions for negligence.

Home Office v Dorset Yacht Co Ltd [1970] 2 All ER 294 [1970] AC 1004; (1970) 120 NLJ 458t; (1970) 114 SJ 375; [1970] 2 WLR 1140 HL Home Office/its officers do not enjoy immunity from negligence; borstal officers liable for damage to third party vessel caused by persons escaping on foot of their negligence.

Kelley v Corston [1997] 2 Cr App R (S) 1276; (1997) 147 NLJ 1276; [1997] TLR 466 CA On extent of immunity from suit enjoyed by barrister in case concluded by way of settlement of action.

Littrell v United States of America and another (No 2) (1993) 137 SJ LB 278; [1993] TLR 589 CA US government immune from suit in respect of operation of US military hospital in UK.

M and another v London Borough of Newham and others [1993] 2 FLR 575 HC QBD On how far witness immunity from suit extends; parent could not sue local authority for in-/action towards child or local authority psychiatrist/social worker for how performed duties.

Palacath Ltd v Flanagan [1985] 2 All ER 161 HC QBD Surveyor not acting in quasi-/judicial rôle not immune from negligence suit.

Sutcliffe v Thackrah and others [1974] 1 All ER 859; [1974] AC 727; (1974) 124 NLJ 200t; (1974) 118 SJ 148; [1974] 2 WLR 295 HL Architect/valuer acting in arbitral rôle immune from action for negligence in so doing.

Sutcliffe v Thackrah and others [1973] 2 All ER 1047; (1973) 117 SJ 509; [1973] 1 WLR 888 CA Architect's giving of final certificate an arbitral act clothed with immunity from action for negligence.

Wisbech Rural District Council v Ward (1927) 91 JP 166; (1926-27) XLIII TLR 739; (1927) WN (I) 236 HC KBD Architect in certificating building work was under terms of particular contract not acting in quasi-/arbitral role and so could be (and was) liable in negligence.

Wisbech Rural District Council v Ward (1927) 91 JP 200 CA Architect in certificating building work was not negligent.

Zoernsch v Waldock and another (1964) 108 SJ 278 CA Ex-President of European Commission on Human Rights enjoyed privilege in respect of allegedly negligent acts done when acting in official capacity.

NEGLIGENCE (innkeeper)

Bonham-Carter v Hyde Park Hotel, Limited (1948) LXIV TLR 177 HC KBD Innkeeper deemed negligent where security provided ensured privacy but did not afford adequate protection of guests' property.

Brewster v Drennan [1945] 2 All ER 705; (1946) 96 LJ 271; (1946) 174 LTR 62 CA Successful claim against innkeeper for theft of guest's fur cape from unlocked bedroom.

Burke v Purdie [1935] LJNCCR 303 CyCt Innkeeper negligent in leaving guest's car-keys on open access in reception office and so liable for damage occasioned when car taken for 'joy-ride'.

Butler and Co (Limited) v Quilter (1900-01) XVII TLR 159 HC QBD Innkeeper by proving was not negligent does not obviate his liability for loss of goods of guest.

Caldecutt v Piesse (1932) 76 SJ 799; (1932-33) XLIX TLR 26 HC KBD On duty owed in respect of guests' property by (non-innkeeper) person who keeps guest house for reward.

Campbell v Shelbourne Hotel, Ltd [1939] 2 All ER 351; [1939] 2 KB 534; (1939) 87 LJ 303; [1939] 108 LJCL 607; (1939) 160 LTR 436; (1939) 83 SJ 456; (1938-39) LV TLR 938 HC KBD Hotelier negligent in not keeping passageway to communal toilet lit for guest/invitee.

Chamier v De Vere Hotels, Ltd (1928) 72 SJ 155 HC KBD Hotel owner's not liable for theft of guest's jewellery where guest had been negligent in leaving same in unlocked drawer while out.

Clapham v Shearmur [1940] LJNCCR 138 CyCt Failed claim in negligence against innkeeper by patron where loss suffered by patron would not have occurred but for patron's negligence.

Davies v Clarke (1953) 103 LJ ccr141 CyCt Innkeeper liable for loss of bulk of various articles from car parked in inn yard that opened onto road.

Hughes v Bailly (1919-20) XXXVI TLR 398 HC KBD Hotel proprietor not liable for theft by visitor whom boarded out with another where could not reasonably have discovered criminal propensity of visitor.

Maclenan v Segar [1914-17] All ER 409; [1917] 2 KB 325; [1917] 86 LJCL 1113; (1917-18) 117 LTR 376; (1916-17) XXXIII TLR 351 HC KBD Implied warranty in contract with innkeeper that premises as safe as is reasonably possible.

Scarborough and Wife v Cosgrove (1904-05) XXI TLR 570 HC KBD Boarding-house keeper owes no duty to take reasonable care of guest's property in house.

Scarborough and Wife v Cosgrove [1905] 2 KB 805; (1904-05) XXI TLR 754; (1905-06) 54 WR 100 CA Boarding-house keeper owes duty to take reasonable care of guest's property in house.

Seccombe v Clarke, Baker and Co, Ltd (1953) 103 LJ ccr624 CyCt Innkeeper not liable for loss of/damage to goods of guest unless innkeeper has been negligent.

Stewart v Titley [1939] LJNCCR 89 CyCt Innkeeper liable for theft of patron's car from car park left in forecourt though not delivered to innkeeper/her car park attendant.

Watson and others v People's Refreshment House Association Ld [1952] 1 KB 318; (1952) 96 SJ 150; [1952] 1 TLR 361; (1952) WN (I) 74 HC KBD Non-liability of innkeeper for damage to coach parked outside hospitium of inn with his permission but not at his invitation.

Williams v Owen (1955) 105 LJ 794; (1955) 99 SJ 890; [1955] 1 WLR 1293 HC QBD Innkeeper not liable for loss sustained through injury to car; absent negligence Fires Prevention (Metropolis) Act 1774, s 86 affords full defence to injuries resulting from fire.

Winkworth v Raven [1931] All ER 847; (1931) 71 LJ 119; (1931) 100 LJCL 206; (1931) 144 LTR 594; (1931) 75 SJ 120; (1930-31) XLVII TLR 254; (1931) WN (I) 42 HC KBD Responsibilities of innkeeper to guest: no liability as no negligence shown.

Wright and another v Anderton (1909) C LTR 123; (1908-09) 53 SJ 135; (1908-09) XXV TLR 156; (1908) WN (I) 258 HC KBD Relationship of innkeeper and guest (with liability that entails for former) begins where is intent to supply and to take accommodation.

Wright v The Embassy Hotel (1935) 79 SJ 12 HC KBD Innkeeper not liable for theft of property of patron who had been negligent as regards care of same.

NEGLIGENCE (insurance)

Banque Keyser Ullmann SA v Skandia (UK) Insurance Co Ltd and others; Skandia (UK) Insurance Co Ltd v Slavenburg's Banque (Suisse) SA and others; Same v Chemical Bank and another; Banque Keyser Ullmann SA and others v Skandia (UK) Insurance Co Ltd and another [1987] 2 WLR 1300 HC QBD Insurers failed to meet common law duty of care (and so were liable in damages) where failed to reveal to bankers dishonesty of manager of bankers' brokers.

Banque Keyser Ullmann SA v Skandia (UK) Insurance Co Ltd (1988) 138 NLJ 287 CA On extent of duty of care owed by insurer to reveal to bankers the dishonesty of the manager of the bankers' brokers.

Coolee, Limited v Wing, Heath and Co and others (1930-31) XLVII TLR 78 HC KBD Successful action against negligent insurance brokers.

Dickson and Co (Limited) v Devitt (1915-16) XXXII TLR 547 HC KBD Party seeking insurance not under duty to see broker properly carried out insurance sought: could recover for broker's negligence in doing same.

Fraser v BN Furman (Productions) Ltd; Miller Smith and Partners (a firm) Third Party [1967] 1 WLR 898 CA On damages available where insurance broker's negligence meant that were uncovered when event against which 'insured' transpired.

General Accident, Fire and Life Assurance Corporation v Tanter (1984) 134 NLJ 35/82 HC QBD Broker owed duty of care to underwriter to whom gave signing down indication.

McNealy v Pennine Insurance Co Ltd and others [1978] RTR 285 CA Brokers liable where their breach of duty of care owed towards client resulted in latter not being covered by insurance policy.

O'Connor v BDB Kirby and Co (a firm) and another [1972] 1 QB 90; [1971] RTR 440; (1971) 115 SJ 267; [1971] 2 WLR 1233 CA Insurance proposer — not broker — responsible for defective completion of insurance proposal form.

Osman v J Ralph Moss Ltd (1970) 120 NLJ 177t CA Recovery of damages from insurance broker who advised plaintiff to insure car with company that collapsed thereby rendering plaintiff uninsured.

Verderame and others v Commercial Union Assurance Co plc and another [1992] TLR 164 CA Insurance brokers not liable in tort to directors of company for whom were acting.

NEGLIGENCE (invitee)

Bates v Parker [1952] 2 All ER 987 Assizes Occupier not liable to window cleaner for injuries sustained in cleaning but not through defect in property.

Bates v Parker [1953] 2 QB 231; (1953) 97 SJ 226; [1953] 2 WLR 642 CA Invitee (window cleaner) not warned of unusual dangers by invitor who was therefore liable in negligence.

Bell v Travco Hotels, Ltd [1953] 1 All ER 638; [1953] 1 QB 473; [1953] 2 WLR 556 CA That part of drive slippery did not mean hotel had failed in duty to make sure drive as safe as reasonably possible.

Hobson v Bartram and Sons, Ltd [1950] 1 All ER 412 CA That person is under one's control need not mean are one's agents for all purposes.

Johnson v Croggon and Co, Ltd and another [1954] 1 All ER 121 HC QBD Ex turpi causa non oritur actio precluded relief in negligence; could not recover as invitee as had general licence to use equipment but selected defective equipment.

Stein v Gates [1934] LJNCCR 343 CyCt Hotel licensee not liable in negligence towards blind invitee who fell through cellar door on former's premises while door open for goods delivery.

NEGLIGENCE (jeweller)

Philips v William Whiteley, Ltd [1938] 1 All ER 566 HC KBD Surgeon's standard of care not expected of jeweller doing ear-piercing.

NEGLIGENCE (landlord and tenant)

Appah v Parncliffe Investments, Ltd (1964) 114 LJ 288 CA Landlord liable in negligence for not providing licensee for reward with key to mortice lock which resulted in subsequent loss through burglary.

Argy Trading Development Co Ltd v Lapid Developments Ltd [1977] 3 All ER 785; (1976) 126 NLJ 1042t; [1977] 1 WLR 444 HC QBD No duty on landlord to continue insuring property or to notify tenant of insurance stopping.

Ball and another v London County Council [1948] 2 All ER 917 HC KBD Landlord liable to tenant for own negligent installation of boiler.

Ball and another v London County Council [1949] 1 All ER 1056; (1949) 113 JP 315; [1949] 2 KB 159; (1949) WN (I) 223 CA Landlords owe duty of care of ordinary contractor when doing repairs; no duty of care to strangers in installing boiler as not dangerous per se.

Ben Stansfield (Carlisle) v Carlisle City Council (1982) 126 SJ 805 CA Damages for tenants who could not use portion of (and eventually had to quit) leased building in negligent disrepair.

Brooke v Bool [1928] 2 KB 578; (1929) 68 LJ ccr9; (1928) 65 LJ 402; (1928) 97 LJCL 511; (1928) 139 LTR 376; (1928) WN (I) 127 HC KBD Liability for negligent act of one's lodger.

Cameron and others (paupers) v Young and another (1908) 77 LJPC 68 HL On liability of Scots landlord vis-a-vis his tenants in negligence.

Cockburn and another v Smith and others [1924] 93 LJCL 764; (1924) 131 LTR 334 CA On liability of landlord for maintenance of roof of property which has let but in respect of which has not let roof.

Davis v Foots (1939) 83 SJ 780 CA Landlord liable for gassing of honey-mooners following negligent removal of gas fire at behest of same.

Finlay and Co, Ltd v City Business Properties, Ltd [1943] LJNCCR 14 CyCt Landlords liable for damage occurring when water pipe burst during frosty weather (term in lease excluding liability for damage due to weather held not to protect them).

Groves v Western Mansions (Limited) (1917) CC Rep VI 5; (1916-17) XXXIII TLR 76 HC KBD Tenant's wife injuring self on broken stairs failed in negligence action against landlord as could not prove was concealed trap.

Hargroves, Aronson and Co v Hartopp and another [1905] 1 KB 472; (1905) XCII LTR 414; (1904-05) 49 SJ 237; (1905) WN (I) 18 HC KBD Landlord liable in negligence for failure to repair gutter known to them to be defective and which resulted in injury to tenant.

Hart and another v Rogers (1916) 114 LTR 329 HC KBD Landlord of house let in flats owed duty to keep roof in good repair.

Howard v Walker [1947] 116 LJR 1366; (1947) 177 LTR 326; (1947) 91 SJ 494 HC KBD Tenant (but not landlord) liable for injury to tenant's invitee where injured self on negligently maintained forecourt before tenant's shop.

Huggett v Miers [1908-10] All ER 184; [1908] 2 KB 278; (1908) 43 LJ 282; [1908] 77 LJCL 710; (1908-09) XCIX LTR 326; (1908) WN (I) 115 CA Landlord did not owe higher duty of care to invitee of tenant than tenant owed.

Lucy v Bawden [1914] 2 KB 318; [1914] 83 LJKB 523; (1914) 110 LTR 580; (1913-14) XXX TLR 321; (1914) WN (I) 79 HC KBD Owner not to expose tenant's wife to unexpected danger without warning.

Matthews v Smallwood [1910] 1 Ch 777 HC ChD No relief against forfeiture for negligent trustees (Conveyancing and Law of Property Act 1892, s 4).

Targett v Torfaen Borough Council [1992] 3 All ER 27; (1991) 141 NLJ 1698 CA Landlord responsible for design/construction of house under duty of care to ensure house free from injurious defects even where known to victim if victim unable to avoid danger.

NEGLIGENCE (legal adviser)

Acton v Graham Pearce and Co (a firm) [1997] 3 All ER 909 HC ChD Solicitors deemed not to be immune from suit in negligence; award of damages where solicitor's negligence meant had lost chance either not to be prosecuted or (if prosecuted) acquitted.

Al-Kandari v JR Brown and Co (1987) 137 NLJ 36; [1987] QB 514; (1987) 131 SJ 225; [1987] 2 WLR 469 HC QBD Solicitor holding client's passport had been negligent in releasing passport to embassy for amendments thereto but not liable for (not reasonably foreseeable event of) embassy returning passport to client.

Al-Kandari v JR Brown and Co [1988] QB 665; (1988) 138 NLJ 62; (1988) 132 SJ 462; [1988] 2 WLR 671 CA Solcitor liable in damages to party injured through solicitor's negligence regarding client's passport (which had been entrusted to solicitor for safe keeping).

Ali (Saif) v Sydney Mitchell and Co (a firm) and others, P (third party) [1977] 3 All ER 744 (1977) 127 NLJ 638t; [1978] QB 95; (1977) 121 SJ 336; [1977] 3 WLR 421 CA Barrister immune from negligence suits for actions during trial and pre-trial actions connected with trial.

Ali (Saif) v Sydney Mitchell and Co (a firm) and others, P (third party) [1978] 3 All ER 1033 [1980] AC 198; (1978) 128 NLJ 1196t; (1978) 122 SJ 761; [1978] 3 WLR 849 HL Only acts of counsel intrinsically connected with conduct of case in court immune from negligence suit.

Allen v Sir Alfred McAlpine and Sons, Ltd; Bostic v Bermondsey and Southwark Group Hospital Management Committee; Sternberg and another v Hammond and another [1968] 1 All ER 543; [1968] 2 QB 229; (1963) 107 SJ 478; [1968] 2 WLR 366 CA Action can be immediately dismissed for delay leaving only action against solicitor for negligence.

Ashton and others v Wainwright [1936] 1 All ER 805; (1936) 81 LJ 313 HC KBD Solicitor negligent in allowing client open club after clerk's wrongful refusal to register it rather than advise client to seek mandamus order.

Ashton v Philip Conway Thomas and Co (1939) 83 SJ 891 HC KBD Successful claim against firm of solicitors for negligent failure to make workmen's compensation claim in time.

Attard v Samson (Poister, third party) (1965-66) 116 NLJ 640; (1966) 110 SJ 249 HC QBD Failed claim by solicitor for indemnity from one client for solicitor's negligence when dealing with another client.

Bell v Peter Browne and Co (a firm) [1990] 3 All ER 124; (1990) 140 NLJ 701; [1990] 2 QB 495; [1990] 3 WLR 510 CA Solicitor negligently failing to protect client's equitable interest in property being sold is liable in contract for breach of duty and in tort when client parts with legal interest.

Booth and another v Davey (1988) 138 NLJ 104 CA Conveyancing solicitor not liable in negligence where had read out draft contract to clients and given them copy to peruse.

Bristol and West Building Society v Mothew (t/a Stapley and Co) [1996] 4 All ER 698; (1996) TLR 2/8/96; [1997] 2 WLR 436 CA Liability of solicitor towards lender for defective advice given during mortgage deal in which acted for lender and borrower.

British Racing Drivers' Club Ltd and another v Hextall Erskine and Co (a firm) [1996] 3 All ER 667 HC ChD Solicitors liable for negligent advice (failed to advise directors that members required to approve certain transaction which was later rescinded by members thereby occasioning loss).

Bryant v Goodrich (1966) 110 SJ 108 CA Damages for negligent advice of solicitor in divorce case.

Buckland v Mackesy; Buckland v Watts (1968) 112 SJ 841 CA Surveyor but not solicitor deemed to have acted negligently in course of property transaction.

Carr-Glynn v Frearsons (a firm) [1997] 2 All ER 614 HC ChD Negligent solicitor did not owe duty of care to intended beneficiary under will.

Carradine Properties Ltd v DJ Freeman and Co (1982) 132 NLJ 534; [1982] TLR 83 CA Solicitors not negligent where when dealing with client with insurance expertise in insurance case did not ask latter if had particular policy under which was covered for loss at issue.

Clark and another v Kirby-Smith (1964) 114 LJ 604; (1964) 108 SJ 462; [1964] 3 WLR 239; [1964] Ch 506 HC ChD Negligent solicitor liable to client in contract not tort.

Clarke v Bruce Lance and Co (a firm) and others (1987) 137 NLJ 1064; (1987) 131 SJ 1698; [1988] 1 WLR 881 CA Solicitor had not owed duty of care to beneficiary to advise testator when amending will of effect amendment would have on beneficiary.

Computastaff v Ingledew Brown Bennison and Garrett and another (1983) 133 NLJ 598 HC QBD Solicitors liable in negligence for misadvising client as to rateable value of property prior to client's leasing same.

Cook v S [1966] 1 All ER 248; (1966) 110 SJ 964; (1965-66) 116 NLJ 416; [1966] 1 WLR 635 HC QBD Damage flowing from solicitor's negligence not broken by counsel's mistaken advice.

Cook v S [1967] 1 All ER 299 CA Negligent solicitor sued in contract not liable for mental distress occasioned by negligence.

Cook v Swinfen (1965) 109 SJ 972 HC QBD Damages for loss of chances in divorce suit/of receiving maintenance as result of solicitor's negligence.

County Personnel (Employment Agency) Ltd v Alan R Pulver and Co (a firm) [1987] 1 All ER 289; (1986) 136 NLJ 1138; (1987) 131 SJ 474; [1987] 1 WLR 916 CA Strange lease clause to put solicitor on guard/lead him to to draw client's attention to clause; general measure of damages proper if diminution in value principle inappropriate.

Crossan v Bracewell (Ward) (1986) 136 NLJ 849 HC QBD Solicitor liable in negligence to client whom defended on reckless driving charge without first checking if latter's insurers would meet costs.

Davies v Hood and others (1903) LXXXVIII LTR 19; (1902-03) XIX TLR 158 HC KBD Personal representative of dead solicitor liable for negligent acts of latter when alive and on retainer.

Dogma Properties Ltd v Gale (1984) 134 NLJ 453 HC QBD Successful suit against solicitor employed to act for person seeking to purchase property who through solicitor's negligence succeeded only in getting possession, not title to the premises.

Dunn v Fairs, Blissard, Barnes and Stowe (1961) 105 SJ 932 HC QBD Solicitor not negligent in purchasing annuity for old unwell client.

Edward Wong Finance Co Ltd v Johnson Stokes and Master (a firm) [1984] AC 296; (1983) 127 SJ 784; [1984] 2 WLR 1 PC Was negligent (even though conformed with general practice) for solicitor to place mortgagee's money in hands of vendor's solicitor without making provision for relief in case of embezzlement which later occurred.

Edwards v Lee (1991) 141 NLJ 1517 HC QBD Solicitor is liable in negligence if does not reveal that client (for whom is giving business reference) has been charged with a dishonesty offence.

Faithfull v Kesteven [1908-10] All ER 292; (1910-11) 103 LTR 56 CA Must show more than error of judgment on solicitor's part to recover in negligence.

First National Commercial Bank plc v Loxleys (1997) 141 SJ LB 6; (1996) TLR 14/11/96 CA Disclaimer (on standard conveyancing form) had to be proved to be subjectively reasonable in each case.

Fletcher and Son v Jubb, Booth and Helliwell [1920] 1 KB 275; (1919) 54 LJ 411; [1920] 89 LJCL 236; (1920) 122 LTR 258; (1919-20) XXXVI TLR 19; (1919) WN (I) 266 CA Liability of solicitor to client for failure to bring claim before limitation period expires.

Ford and another v White and Co (a firm) (1964) 114 LJ 554; (1964) 108 SJ 542; [1964] 1 WLR 885 HC ChD On quantifying damages available where property purchased on foot of solicitor's negligent advice.

Frank v Seifert, Sedley and Co (1964) 108 SJ 523 HC QBD Failed action for negligence against solicitors in relation to their conduct in failed land deal (mistakenly revealed re-sale price of premises to original vendor in course of dealings).

Goody v Baring [1956] 2 All ER 11; (1956) 106 LJ 266; (1956) 100 SJ 320; [1956] 1 WLR 448 HC ChD Solicitor failed in duty to make proper inquiries on client's behalf.

Gregory v Tarlo (1964) 108 SJ 219 HC QBD Damages awarded against solicitor for failure to prosecute client's claim within statutorily allowed period.

Griffiths v Dawson and Co [1993] 2 FCR 515; [1993] 2 FLR 315; [1993] TLR 201 HC QBD Solicitor negligent as failed to stop divorce decree being made absolute before financial situation resolved so causing wife to lose out financially.

Griffiths v Evans [1953] 2 All ER 1364; (1953) 103 LJ 797; (1953) 97 SJ 812; [1953] 1 WLR 1424 CA Solicitor not negligent in not advising on common law rights when specifically consulted about statutory rights.

Griffiths v Evans [1953] 2 All ER 1364; [1953] 1 WLR 1424 CA Solicitor not negligent in not advising on common law rights when specifically consulted about statutory rights.

Groom v Crocker and others (1937) 84 LJ 158; (1937) 157 LTR 308 HC KBD Failure of solicitor to act equally on behalf of both insurer/insured; damages for breach of duty and for libel.

Groom v Crocker and others [1938] 2 All ER 394; [1939] 1 KB 194; (1938) 85 LJ 308; (1938) 158 LTR 477; (1937-38) LIV TLR 861 CA Failure of solicitor to act equally on behalf of both insurer/insured; malice on ostensibly privileged occasion; nominal damages as action in contract (not tort) and no evidence of actual damage.

Hall v Meyrick [1957] 1 All ER 208; (1957) 107 LJ 74; [1957] 2 QB 455; (1957) 101 SJ 229; [1957] 2 WLR 458 HC QBD Solicitor's negligent failure to advise parties that marriage revoked earlier wills he drafted for them meant liable for damages suffered upon intestacy.

Hemmens v Wilson Browne (a firm) [1995] Ch 223; [1994] 2 FLR 101; [1993] TLR 365; [1994] 2 WLR 323 HC ChD On duty of care owed by solicitor towards envisaged beneficiary of inter vivos arrangement.

Hesketh v Nicholson (1940) 84 SJ 646 HC KBD Solicitor liable for failure to advise client of provisions of Public Authorities Protection Act as regards negligence action against public authority.

Hill v Harris [1965] 2 All ER 359; [1965] 2 QB 601; [1965] 2 WLR 1331 CA Sub-lessee's solicitor negligent if fails to inspect head lease for covenants.

Holmes and another v H Kennard and Son (a firm) (1983) 127 SJ 172 HC ChD Solicitors not negligent in manner in which approached land purchase.

Holmes and another v H Kennard and Son (1984) 128 SJ 854 CA Solictors negligent in manner in which approached land purchase.

Hurlingham Estates Ltd v Wilde and Partners (a firm) [1997] TLR 15 HC ChD Solicitor deemed negligent as regards tax advice that he gave.

Jakeman v Jakeman and Turner [1963] 3 All ER 889; (1964) 114 LJ 10; (1963) 107 SJ 438; [1964] 2 WLR 90 HC PDAD Re-hearing on damages as not originally argued because of solicitor's negligence; solicitor personally liable for costs of first hearing.

Jarvis v T Richards and Co (1980) 124 SJ 793 HC ChD On appropriate damages where negligence of solicitor in property transaction resulted in plaintiff having no place to live.

Jones v Jones and another [1970] 3 All ER 47; [1971] 1 WLR 396 CA Solicitor jeopardising client's claim to interest on damages through late issue of writ open to negligence action.

Kelley v Corston [1997] 2 Cr App R (S) 1276; (1997) 147 NLJ 1276; [1997] TLR 466 CA On extent of immunity from suit enjoyed by barrister in case concluded by way of settlement of action.

Kennedy v Van Emden (KB) and Co (1996) 140 SJ LB 99; (1996) TLR 5/4/96 CA On appropriate damages for loss suffered through negligence of solicitor.

King v Hawkins and Co (1982) 132 NLJ 322 HC QBD On damages available from solicitor-conveyancers to person who received smaller piece of land of different quality to that anticipated through their negligence.

Lake v Bushby and another [1949] 2 All ER 964; (1950) WN (I) 28 HC KBD Solicitor negligent as did not tell client were no approved plans for building of bungalow being bought: damages were difference between building value if were plans and value without plans.

Losner v Michael Cohen and Co (1975) 119 SJ 340 CA Damages against solicitor for failing to ensure proper defendants joined to action under Dogs Act 1871, s 2.

Lynne and another v Gordon Doctors and Walton (a firm) (1991) 135 SJ LB 29 HC QBD Failed action to recoup from allegedly negligent solicitors purported loss personal representatives suffered through solicitors not taking out life assurance for deceased mortgagor.

Mahoney v Purnell and others [1997] 1 FLR 612 HC QBD Agreement between father-in-law and son-in-law set aside as was markedly disadvantageous to former; solicitor liable in negligence for not adequately drawing the father-in-law's attention to disadvantageous nature of transaction.

Mainz v James and Charles Dodd (1978) 128 NLJ 978t HC QBD Damages for negligence of solicitor whose inaction resulted in plaintiff's actions being struck out for want of prosecution.

Malyon v Lawrence, Messer and Co (1969) 119 NLJ 38; (1968) 112 SJ 623 HC QBD Recovery of damages from solictors which would have recovered in action in Germany had not negligence of solicitors led to action being time-barred.

McLeish v Amoo-Gottfried and Co (1993) 137 SJ LB 204 HC QBD Loss of reputation allowed for when assessing mental distress damages where negligence of solicitor had resulted in wrongful conviction.

McLellan v Fletcher (1987) 137 NLJ 593 HC QBD Solicitor negligent as did not make certain that life insurance policy taken out where was part of security on which mortgage advanced.

McNamara v Martin Mears and Co (1983) 127 SJ 69 HC QBD On appropriate damages from negligent solicitor who requested/advised client to accept lower divorce settlement than should have.

Midland Bank Trust Co Ltd and another v Hett, Stubbs and Kemp (a firm) [1978] 3 All ER 571; [1979] Ch 384; (1978) 128 NLJ 33t; (1977) 121 SJ 830; [1978] 3 WLR 167 HC ChD Solicitor always liable in tort for failure to exercise reasonable care and skill.

Montagu v Bird and Bird (a firm) (1973) 117 SJ 448 HC ChD Refusal to strike out professional negligence claim in which plaintiff seeking damages to compensate him for position he would have been in had he not been given allegedly negligent advice.

Morris v Duke-Cohan and Co (1975) 125 NLJ 1222; (1975) 119 SJ 826 HC QBD Successful action in negligence against conveyancing solicitors who advised exchange of contracts without taking usual safeguards.

Mortgage Express Ltd v Bowerman and Partners (a firm) [1994] TLR 285 HC ChD On extent of duty of care owed by solicitor to parties to loan transaction where is acting for both sides.

Mortgage Express Ltd v Bowerman and Partners (a firm) [1995] TLR 450 CA On extent of duty of care owed by solicitor to parties to loan transaction where is acting for both sides.

Murray v Lloyd and others [1990] 2 All ER 92; (1989) 139 NLJ 938; [1989] 1 WLR 1060 HC ChD Damages where solicitor's negligence led to client's failure to become statutory tenant are amount needed for client to become statutory tenant in similar property elsewhere.

National Home Loans Corp plc v Giffen Couch and Archer (a firm) [1997] 3 All ER 808 CA On extent of duty of care owed by solicitor to lender where is acting for borrower and lender in loan transaction.

Neushul v Mellish and Harkavy (1966) 110 SJ 792 HC QBD On duty owed by solicitor to client when acting for two parties (here failed to meet duty of care).

O'Boyle and another v Leiper and others (1990) 134 SJ 316 CA Settlement in full and final settlement of all claims treated as precisely that.

Ochwat and another v Watson Burton (a firm) (1997) 141 SJ LB 163 HC QBD Failed action in negligence against solicitors.

Orchard v South Eastern Electricity Board (1986) 136 NLJ 1112 CA Solicitor (but not barrister) may be liable for opponent's costs.

Otter v Church, Adams, Tatham and Co (a firm) [1953] 1 All ER 168; [1953] Ch 280; (1953) 97 SJ 48; [1953] 1 WLR 156 HC ChD Appropriate damages for solicitor's negligence.

Penn v Bristol and West Building Society and others [1996] 2 FCR 729; [1995] 2 FLR 938; [1995] TLR 348 HC ChD Solicitors liable to wife for selling matrimonial house without realising that wife's signature on documents was forged, and to building society for mortgage loan it gave to purchaser.

Pilkington v Wood [1953] 2 All ER 810; [1953] Ch 770; (1953) 103 LJ 555; (1953) 97 SJ 572; [1953] 3 WLR 522 HC ChD Duty of mitigation does not require bringing complex litigation; unforeseeable damages irrecoverable; no need for resale of land to gauge actual loss caused by solicitor's negligence in purchase.

R v Knutsford Crown Court, ex parte Middleweek [1992] TLR 135 HC QBD On personal liability of negligent solicitor for costs.

R v M; R v W (1968) 118 NLJ 1004t CA On respective liabilities of solicitor/surveyor towards client seeking to buy house.

Raintree Ltd v Holmes and Hills (1984) 134 NLJ 522 HC QBD Solicitor liable in negligence for failing to check expiry date of planning permission on land in respect of purchase of which they were advising client.

Re Foster (a bankrupt); Trustee of Property of Foster and others (bankrupts) v Crusts (a firm) (1985) 129 SJ 333 HC ChD Solicitors owed duty to client company/the personal guarantors of its liabilities to ensure it was aware of (and maybe that it complied with), inter alia, the Companies Act 1948, s 95 (filing particulars of charge).

Re Linsley; Cattley v West [1904] 2 Ch 785 HC ChD Solicitor trustee liable to indemnify co-trustee for action prompted by solicitor's negligent management of trust (even though was no loss to estate).

Re the Coolgardie Goldfields, ex parte Hamilton and Fleming (1899-1900) XVI TLR 161 HC ChD Solicitor personally liable for stamps and penalties payable by client who went insolvent after solicitor put unstamped documents in evidence on client's behalf.

Reggentin v Beecholme Bakeries, Ltd [1968] 1 All ER 566 [1968] 2 QB 276 CA On delay leaving action against solicitor for negligence.

Roberts v JW Ward and Son (1982) 126 SJ 120 CA Solicitors liable for negligent failure not to serve notice to exercise option agreement on company/not stating option purchase price.

Rondel v Worsley [1966] 1 All ER 467; (1965-66) 116 NLJ 501; [1966] 2 WLR 300 HC QBD Counsel not liable in negligence for acts of advocacy.

Rondel v Worsley [1966] 3 All ER 657; [1967] 1 QB 443 (also HC QBD); (1966) 110 SJ 810; [1966] 3 WLR 950 CA Solicitor acting as advocate can be sued for negligence; barrister cannot be sued for acts done pending/in course of litigation.

Rondel v Worsley [1967] 3 All ER 993; [1969] 1 AC 191; (1967) 111 SJ 927; [1967] 3 WLR 1666 HL Counsel immune from negligence action for all work in conduct of/pending litigation; solicitor immune for advocacy work/in settling case.

Ross v Caunters (a firm) [1979] 3 All ER 580; [1980] Ch 297; (1979) 129 (2) NLJ 880; (1979) 123 SJ 605; [1979] 3 WLR 605 HC ChD Solicitor drafting will owes duty of care to beneficiary; beneficiary can recover economic loss.

RP Howard Ltd v Woodman Matthews and Co (1983) 133 NLJ 598 HC QBD Solicitor liable in negligence for failure to seek new tenancy for client under terms of Landlord and Tenant Act 1954, Part II.

Scudder v Prothero and Prothero (1966) 110 SJ 248 HC QBD Small damages for solicitors' technical breach of duty of care regarding calling of witness where had not resulted in damage to case.

Simmons v Pennington and Son (a firm) [1955] 1 All ER 240; (1955) 99 SJ 146; [1955] 1 WLR 183 CA Mistaken answer but which conformed to general conveyancing practice not negligent; damages irrecoverable for fire damage to premises unsold through solicitor's 'negligence'.

Simple Simon Catering Ltd v JE Binstock Miller and Co (1973) 117 SJ 529 CA On appropriate damages for negligence of solicitor in drawing up underlease (as result of which suffered loss).

Simpson v Grove Tompkins and Co (1982) 126 SJ 347; [1982] TLR 265 CA On appropriate damages for person who bought land at inflated price consequent upon negligence of his solicitor.

Smith and another v Haynes (Claremont) [1991] TLR 409 HC QBD Solicitor liable in negligence to intended beneficiaries of will which ought to have prepared swiftly (given perilous health of deceased when orally communicated terms of intended but never-drafted will).

Somasundaram v M Julius Melchior and Co (a firm) [1989] 1 All ER 129; (1988) 138 NLJ 253; (1988) 132 SJ 1732; [1988] 1 WLR 1394 CA Action for negligence against barrister/solicitor struck off if really attack on court of competent jurisdiction.

Stinchcombe and Cooper Ltd v Addison, Cooper, Jesson and Co (1971) 115 SJ 368 HC ChD Solicitor liable in negligence for manner in which conducted land transaction and failure to point to unusual clause in sale contract.

Strefford v Strefford (1966) 110 SJ 568 CA Re-hearing of divorce case ordered in light of negligence of (clerk of) solicitor: costs to be met by solicitor on indemnity basis.

Swindle and others v Harrison [1997] TLR 197 CA On damages recoverable by person who suffered loss as result of negligence of solicitors in context of mortgage-bridging loan-property purchase transaction.

Sykes and others v Midland Bank Executor and Trustee Co, Ltd and others [1969] 2 All ER 1238; (1969) 119 NLJ 297t; [1969] 2 QB 518; (1969) 113 SJ 243; [1969] 2 WLR 1173 HC QBD Solicitor negligent for failing to draw unusual terms in lease to client's attention: cause of action once rent payable; appropriate damages.

Sykes and others v Midland Bank Executor and Trustee Co Ltd and others [1970] 2 All ER 471; [1971] 1 QB 113; (1970) 114 SJ 225; [1970] 3 WLR 273 CA Solicitor not advising of unusual clause in lease negligent (but nominal damages for breach of contract if client does not prove negligence led to acting as did).

Teasdale v Williams and Co (1983) 133 NLJ 105 HC QBD Successful negligence suit against solicitor whose negligent failure to advise client of landlord's application for interim rent meant client failed to apply for new lease.

United Bank of Kuwait v Hammoud and others (1987) 137 NLJ 921 HC QBD On close proximity of relationship between solicitor/client necessary before former liable to latter for loss occasioned through former's inadequate supervision of worker/junior lawyer.

Wardley v Margolis (1981) 131 NLJ 447 HC QBD Damages from solicitor who negligently allowed personal injuries action with every chance of success to lapse.

Webber v Gasquet, Metcalfe and Walton (1982) 132 NLJ 665 HC ChD Recovery of damages for negligence of solicitors vis-à-vis safeguarding plaintiff's property rights during divorce action.

Westway Homes Ltd v Gore Wood and Co [1991] TLR 331 CA How solicitor behaved and not what solicitor thought relevant to determination of whether solicitor behaved negligently.

White and another v Jones and others [1993] 3 All ER 481; [1995] 2 AC 207 (also HL); (1993) 143 NLJ 473; [1993] TLR 124; [1993] 3 WLR 730 CA Non-preparation of will following instruction makes solicitor liable to disappointed beneficiary where instructor dies before will prepared/executed.

White and another v Jones and another [1995] 2 AC 207 (also CA); [1995] 3 FCR 51; (1995) 145 NLJ 251; (1995) 139 SJ LB 83; [1995] TLR 89; [1995] 2 WLR 187 HL Solicitor owed duty of care to intended beneficiary whom it was reasonably foreseeable would suffer loss through solicitor's negligence in relation to preparation of will.

Yager v Fishman and Co and Teff and Teff [1944] 1 All ER 552 CA Solicitor did not owe client duty to state that latest date for option to determine approaching.

Yardley v Coombes (1963) 107 SJ 575 HC QBD On assessing appropriate damages to be awarded against negligent solicitor.

Young v Purdy [1997] 1 FCR 632; [1996] 2 FLR 795 CA Solicitor not liable in damages for negligent actions of client consequent upon solicitor's breach of contract by way of termination of retainer.

NEGLIGENCE (licensee)

Pearson v Lambeth Borough Council [1950] 1 All ER 682; [1950] 2 KB 353 CA Licensor liable only for dangers of which actually knows; meaning of 'actual knowledge'.

Rochman v J and E Hall, Ltd, and another [1947] 1 All ER 895 HC KBD Licensor not responsible for every danger arising from acts of unauthorised persons.

Williams and another v Cardiff Corporation [1950] 1 All ER 250 CA Broken glass on waste ground where children frequently played (so licensees) a concealed danger for which liable.

NEGLIGENCE (lifeguard)

OLL Ltd v Secretary of State for Transport [1997] 3 All ER 897; [1997] 2 Cr App R (S) 1099; (1997) 147 NLJ 1099; [1997] TLR 407 HC QBD On duty of care owed by coastguard in answering distress call.

NEGLIGENCE (liquidator)

Pulsford v Devenish [1903] 2 Ch 625 HC ChD Company liquidator found negligent in performance of his duties.

Re Windsor Steam Coal Company (1901), Limited [1929] 1 Ch 151 CA Liquidator (if acted as agent of company) was liable for misfeasance as a result of his negligence.

NEGLIGENCE (local authority)

Acrecrest Ltd v WS Hattrell and Partners (a firm) and another [1983] 1 All ER 17; (1983) 133 NLJ 64; [1983] QB 260; (1982) 126 SJ 729; [1982] TLR 413; [1982] 3 WLR 1076 CA Local authority owes duty of care to non-negligent owner when checking builder's compliance with building regulations.

Barrett v Enfield London Borough Council [1997] 3 All ER 171; [1997] 2 FLR 167; [1997] TLR 202; [1997] 3 WLR 628 CA Local authority could not be liable in negligence for decisions taken in loco parentis regarding children in care but could be liable for manner in which said decisions effected.

Bint v Lewisham Borough Council (1946) 110 JP 103; (1946) 174 LTR 128; (1946) 90 SJ 80; (1945-46) LXII TLR 238; (1946) WN (I) 12 HC KBD Local authority not negligent in not repairing fence adjacent to railway (adjoining railway fence having being fixed by railway company).

Brown v Lambeth Borough Council (1915) CC Rep IV 86; (1915-16) XXXII TLR 61 HC KBD Council not liable in negligence for collision of taxi with unlit refuge (which was normally lit) as fact that unlit not shown to be due to council's negligence.

Bull v The Mayor, &c, of Shoreditch (1903) 67 JP 37; (1902-03) XIX TLR 64 CA Local authority liable for personal injuries driver suffered when collided with earth pile (of which authority knew) in course of avoiding part of road made by local authority but unfit for public traffic.

Buxton and another v Jayne and others (1960) 104 SJ 602 CA Leave granted to bring action against local authority officer for not exercising reasonable care when deciding to have one plaintiff removed to mental hospital against her will.

Carpenter v Finsbury Borough Council (1920) 84 JP 107; [1920] 2 KB 195; [1920] 89 LJCL 554; (1920) 123 LTR 299; (1919-20) 64 SJ 426; (1920) WN (I) 124 HC KBD Where claim injury due to inadequate street-lighting must examine adequacy of same — cannot accept lighting authority's verdict that was adequate.

Coates v Rawtenstall Borough Council [1937] 1 All ER 333 Assizes Ordinary duty of care owed to child licensee.

Coates v Rawtenstall Borough Council (1937) 101 JP 483; (1937) 81 SJ 627 CA Local authority liable for injury to child licensee arising from negligent state in which playground maintained.

Collins v Hertfordshire County Council and another [1947] 1 All ER 633; (1947) 111 JP 272; [1947] KB 598; [1947] 116 LJR 789; (1947) 176 LTR 456; (1947) LXIII TLR 317; (1947) WN (I) 127 HC KBD County council negligent in operation of county council hospital/not responsible for negligence of part-time surgeon employed; amendment to statement of claim allowed as not new cause of action.

Conelly v West Ham Borough Council (1947) 111 JP 34; (1947) 176 LTR 52; (1946) 90 SJ 614; (1945-46) LXII TLR 739 HC KBD Local authority liable in negligence for injury suffered by pedestrian tripping over paving stone authority caused to be dislocated when acting as civil defence authority.

Corporation of the City of Glasgow v Taylor [1922] 1 AC 44; (1922) 86 JP 89; (1921) 56 LJ 435; [1922] 91 LJPC 49; (1922) 126 LTR 262; (1921-22) XXXVIII TLR 102; (1921) WN (I) 333 HL Corporation possibly negligent for not taking appropriate steps to preempt children eating attractive poisonous berries in public park.

Crump v Torfaen Borough Council (1981) 125 SJ 641 HC QBD Where building would certainly endanger others — though did not have to be about to fall in — a cause of action arose.

Davies v Gellygaer Urban District Council (1954) 104 LJ ccr140 CyCt Council deemed not to have been negligent where child injured self on broken glass bottle in council-maintained pool.

Davy v Spelthorne Borough Council [1984] AC 262; [1983] TLR 604 HL Could bring action against local council for alleged negligent advice from council which led person subject to enforcement notice not to challenge that notice.

Dutton v Bognor Regis Urban District Council [1971] 2 All ER 1003; (1971) 121 NLJ 1146t HC QBD Council owes duty of care through building inspector to later purchaser.

E (a minor) v Dorset County Council and other appeals [1994] 4 All ER 640; [1995] 2 AC 633 (also HL); (1994) 144 NLJ 755; [1994] 3 WLR 853 CA Statutory special education duty of local authority enforceable through judicial review; educational, medical and psychological advisers consulted by local authority on special education of children owe professional duty of care to authority, children and parents.

Ellis v Fulham Borough Council (1937) 101 JP 469; [1938] 1 KB 212; (1937) 84 LJ 47; [1938] 107 LJCL 84; (1937) 157 LTR 380; (1936-37) LIII TLR 884 CA Child using public paddle pool an invitee — glass hidden in sand in pool a concealed danger for which council liable.

Ellis v Sayers Confectioners, Ltd and others (1963) 107 SJ 252 CA Not generally necessary for court to see injured plaintiffs; van driver 80% liable/local authority 20% liable for injuries to deaf and dumb child dismounting from local authority school bus.

Ephraim v London Borough Council (1993) 137 SJ LB 13 CA On extent of duty of care owed by local authority to unintentionally homeless person whom they advise about availability of certain property.

Evans v Mayor, &c, of Liverpool (1905) 69 JP 263; (1904-05) XXI TLR 558 HC KBD Local authority not liable for negligent early discharge of patient by visiting physician whom they employed.

Fellowes v Rother District Council [1983] 1 All ER 513 HC QBD Grounds on which public body liable in negligence for acts ostensibly done pursuant to statutory authority.

Forsyth v Manchester Corporation (1912) 76 JP 246 Assizes Corporation not liable for negligence of gas inspector which resulted in injury to infant.

Forsyth v Manchester Corporation (1912) 76 JP 465; (1912-13) XXIX TLR 15 CA Corporation not liable for negligence of gas inspector which resulted in injury to infant.

Fowles v Bedfordshire County Council [1995] TLR 294 CA Local authority negligent in manner in which allowed gym classes at youth centre to be conducted.

Fox v Newcastle-upon-Tyne Corporation [1941] LJNCCR 165 CyCt Negligent for corporation not to have taken steps to make air-raid shelter more visible.

Fox v Newcastle-upon-Tyne Corporation [1941] 3 All ER 563; (1941) 105 JP 404; [1941] 2 KB 120; (1941) 91 LJ 270; (1942) 92 LJ 59; (1941) 165 LTR 90; (1940-41) LVII TLR 602 CA Local authority not liable in negligence for injury sustained by cyclist through collision with inadequately lit air-raid shelter during black-out conditions.

Franklin v Edmonton Corporation (1965) 109 SJ 876 HC QBD Council one-third liable in negligence for manner in which operated defective vehicle record system.

Gold v Essex County Council [1942] 2 KB 293; (1942) WN (I) 161 CA Local authority managing hospital liable for negligent injury of patient by radiographer.

Governors of the Peabody Donation Fund v Sir Lindsay Parkinson and Co Ltd and others [1983] 3 All ER 417; [1985] AC 210 (also HL); (1983) 127 SJ 749; [1983] 3 WLR 754 CA Local authority not under duty to force compliance with building requirements.

Governors of the Peabody Donation Fund v Sir Lindsay Parkinson and Co Ltd and others [1985] AC 210 (also CA); (1984) 128 SJ 753; [1984] 3 WLR 953 HL Local authority not under duty to force compliance with building requirements.

Greenwood v Central Service Company, Limited and another [1940] 2 KB 447; (1940) 163 LTR 414 CA Non-liability of council for injury sustained in street 'blacked out' pursuant to emergency legislation.

Hanley v Edinburgh Corporation (1913) 77 JP 233 HL Successful claim against corporation for not properly draining burgh.

Harrison v Surrey County Council and others [1994] 2 FCR 1269; [1994] TLR 43 HC QBD Local authority liable for negligent misstatement of employee as to reliability of registered child-minder about whom employee knew there were doubts.

Investors in Industry Commercial Properties Ltd v South Bedfordshire District Council (Ellison and Partners (a firm) and others, third parties) [1986] 1 All ER 787; (1986) 136 NLJ 118; [1986] QB 1034; (1986) 130 SJ 71; [1986] 2 WLR 937 CA Local authority does not owe duty to building owner to ensure building accords with building regulations; professional not responsible for work of specialist consultant unless as professional foresees problem therewith.

Jackson v London County Council and Chappell (1912) 76 JP 37; (1911-12) XXVIII TLR 66 HC KBD Education authority/building contractor may have been negligent to leave sand mixture in school yard which one child threw at another, causing injury.

Jackson v London County Council and Chappell (1912) 76 JP 217; (1911-12) XXVIII TLR 359 CA Education authority/building contractor may have been negligent to leave sand mixture in school yard which one child threw at another, causing injury.

Keating v Elvan Reinforced Concrete Co, Ltd, and another (1967) 111 SJ 743 HC QBD Failed action for breach of statutory duty (Public Utilities Street Works Act 1950, s 8(1)(1)).

Keating v Elvan Reinforced Concrete Co Ltd and another (1968) 118 NLJ 206t; (1968) 112 SJ 193 CA Failed action inter alia in negligence against local authority for street works it had done.

Knight v Sheffield Corporation [1942] 2 All ER 411; (1942) 106 JP 197; (1943) 93 LJ 108; (1942) 167 LTR 203; (1942) 86 SJ 311 HC KBD Local authority had duty to light entrance to shelter where had been in habit of so lighting; was negligent exercise of statutory authority to establish access to air raid shelter by way of unfenced hole in pavement.

Lambert v West Devon Borough Council (1997) 141 SJ LB 66; [1997] TLR 167 HC QBD Defendant council liable for loss to plaintiff on foot of negligent misstatement by council building control officer that he had varied certain planning permission.

Law v Railway Executive and another (1949) LXV TLR 288 HC KBD Railway company/local authority liable in negligence for injury suffered by person colliding with wall and pavement the former had put in place of level crossing gates.

Lyes v Middlesex County Council (1963) 113 LJ 348 HC QBD Education authority liable in negligence for injury to pupil who slipped and put hand through glass in door.

M (a minor) and another v Newham London Borough Council and others; X and others (minors) v Bedfordshire County Council [1994] 4 All ER 602; [1995] 2 AC 633 (also HL); [1994] 2 FCR 1313; [1994] 1 FLR 431 (also HC QBD); (1994) 144 NLJ 357; [1994] TLR 119; [1994] 2 WLR 554 CA Those discharging public law task of child-care owe no private law duty of care for in-/action; psychiatrist/social worker owes duty of care to local authority/health authority, not to mother or child.

M and another v London Borough of Newham and others [1993] 2 FLR 575 HC QBD On how far witness immunity from suit extends; parent could not sue local authority for in-/action towards child or local authority psychiatrist/social worker for how performed duties.

Martin v Middlesbrough Corporation (1965) 109 SJ 576 CA Corporation liable for injury caused to pupil who fell on piece of glass in school playground.

Martine v South East Kent Health Authority [1993] TLR 119 CA No action lay in negligence against health authority in respect of its investigation regarding standards at nursing home.

Mayor, Councillors, and Citizens of Hawthorn v Kannuluik [1904-07] All ER 1422; [1906] AC 105; (1905-06) XCIII LTR 644; (1905-06) 54 WR 285 PC Municipal authority liable in negligence for flooding from drain which when constructed was adequate for purpose for which used.

Morris v Carnarvon County Council (1910) 74 JP 201 (also CA); [1910] 1 KB 159; (1909) 44 LJ 783; (1910) 79 LJKB 169; (1909-10) 101 LTR 914; (1909-10) XXVI TLR 137; (1909) WN (I) 263 HC KBD Local education authority liable for negligent injury suffered by child going through door on teacher's instruction.

Morris v Carnarvon County Council (1910) 74 JP 201 (also HC KBD); [1910] 1 KB 840; (1910) 45 LJ 268; (1910) 79 LJKB 670; (1910) 102 LTR 524; (1909-10) 54 SJ 443; (1909-10) XXVI TLR 391; (1910) WN (I) 94 CA Local education authority liable for negligent injury suffered by child going through door on teacher's instruction.

Murphy v Bradford Metropolitan Council [1991] TLR 66 CA Local authority liable for breach of duty of care to ensure cleared, salted school path was not slippy.

Murphy v Brentwood District Council [1990] 2 All ER 269; [1991] 1 AC 398 (also HL); (1990) 134 SJ 458; [1990] 2 WLR 944 CA Statutory duty on council to ensure houses properly built meant duty of care on council even though consulting engineers negligent; damages owed are those necessary to put house in safe condition or enable occupier to move to safe house.

Murphy v Brentwood District Council [1990] 2 All ER 908; [1991] 1 AC 398 (also CA); (1990) 140 NLJ 1111; (1990) 134 SJ 1076; [1990] TLR 558; [1990] 3 WLR 414 HL Local authority does not owe duty of care for pure economic loss to building owner/occupier when discharging statutory functions.

Newcombe v Yewen and the Croydon Rural District Council (1912-13) XXIX TLR 299 HC KBD Council could reach indemnity agreement with contractor.

Norman v Sheffield Corporation (1917) 52 LJ 298 CA Local authority liable for failure to take reasonable care to avoid injury being occasioned by tree guards during wartime 'black-out' conditions.

P and others v Harrow London Borough Council [1993] 2 FCR 341; [1993] 1 FLR 723; [1992] TLR 215 HC QBD Local authority not guilty of breaching statutory duty where placed children (in care/control of parents) with special educational needs in state-approved boarding school where were sexually abused by headmaster.

Pentecost and another v London District Auditor and others (1951) 115 JP 421; (1951) 95 SJ 432; [1951] 2 TLR 497 HC KBD On what constitutes negligence under Local Government Act 1933, s 228(1)/negligence generally.

Polkinghorn and another v Lambeth Borough Council (1938) 102 JP 131; (1938) 158 LTR 127; (1938) 82 SJ 94 CA Local authority liable in negligence for collision arising from its inadequate lighting of safety island post.

Polkinghorn v Lambeth Borough Council; Leach v Same (1937-38) LIV TLR 345 HC KBD Local authority liable in negligence for collision arising from its inadequate lighting of safety island post.

Provender Millers (Winchester) Limited v Southampton County Council (1939) 161 LTR 162 HC ChD Local authority discharging statutory duty cannot transgress another's rights unless unreasonable to otherwise discharge responsibility.

Ralph v London County Council (1947) 111 JP 246; (1947) 91 SJ 221; (1947) LXIII TLR 239 HC KBD Council liable in negligence for injury suffered by child in course of supervised game in assembly hall (council failed to take steps that reasonably cautious father would have taken).

Ralph v London County Council (1947) 111 JP 548; (1947) LXIII TLR 546 CA Council liable in negligence for injury suffered by child in course of supervised game in assembly hall (council failed to take steps that reasonably cautious father would have taken).

Read and another v Croydon Corporation (1939) 103 JP 25; (1938-39) LV TLR 212 HC KBD Infant who had contracted typhoid could sue local authority for negligence as regards provision of clean water.

Reffell v Surrey County Council (1964) 108 SJ 119; [1964] 1 WLR 358 HC QBD On liability of local education authority in common law/under Education Act 1944, s 10 and Standards for School Premises Regulations 1959, regulation 51 for injury to school pupil.

Richardson v West Lindsey District Council and others (1989) 139 NLJ 1263; [1990] 1 WLR 522; CA Local authority does not normally owe duty of care to see that building project complies with building regulations.

Ryan v London Borough of Camden [1982] TLR 640 CA Local authority not liable in negligence for injury suffered by child who touched uninsulated heating pipe as could reasonably expect parents to safeguard children from doing same.

S and R Steamships Ltd v London County Council (1938) 82 SJ 353 HC KBD Successful action in negligence by shipowner against local authority for loss occasioned on foot of latter's negligent operation of bridge.

S v Walsall Metropolitan Borough Council [1986] 1 FLR 397; (1985) 135 NLJ 986; (1985) 129 SJ 685; [1985] 1 WLR 1150 CA Local authority not vicariously liable for negligence of foster parents.

Sheppard v Mayor, Aldermen and Burgesses of the Borough of Glossop (1921) 85 JP 205; [1921] 3 KB 132 CA Non-liability of local authority for not lighting area around retaining wall which had been source of injury to person.

Shepphard v Devon County Council (1980) 130 NLJ 14 CA Reversal of trial judge's finding that council were liable in negligence where school bus was driven over foot of boy who had jumped off the bus.

Simmons v The Mayor, etc, of the Borough of Huntingdon [1936] 1 All ER 596 HC KBD Placing by public authority of diving board at point of public baths where water too shallow for diving was a trap.

Smith v Martin and the Mayor, &c, of Kingston-upon-Hull (1911) 75 JP 135; (1911-12) 105 LTR 281; (1910-11) XXVII TLR 165 HC KBD Non-liability of local authority for (non-teaching) act of teacher (who was personally liable) resulting in injury to student.

Smith v Martin and the Corporation of Kingston-upon-Hull (1911) 75 JP 433; [1911] 2 KB 775; (1911) 80 LJCL 1256; (1910-11) XXVII TLR 468 CA Local authority liable for (non-teaching) act of teacher (who was also liable) resulting in injury to student.

Surtees v Kingston-upon-Thames Royal Borough Council and Hughes and Hughes [1990] 1 FLR 103 HC QBD Local authority/foster-parents not negligent as regards injuries suffered by plaintiff while in foster-care.

Surtees v Kingston-upon-Thames Borough Council; Surtees v Hughes and another [1991] 2 FLR 559 CA Local authority/foster-parents not negligent as regards injuries suffered by plaintiff while in foster-care.

T (a minor) v Surrey County Council and others [1994] 4 All ER 577; (1994) 144 NLJ 319 HC QBD Local authority failure to de-register child-minder under investigation not statutory breach of duty though to tell parents child-minder posed no significant risk might be negligent misstatement.

Ward v Hertfordshire County Council (1970) 134 JP 261; (1970) 120 NLJ 13t; (1970) 114 SJ 87; [1970] 1 WLR 356 CA Local education authority not liable at common law for injury suffered by child playing in schoolyard before school began — not inherently dangerous area/providing warder would not have prevented accident.

Welton and another v North Cornwall District Council (1996) 140 SJ LB 186; (1996) TLR 19/7/96; [1997] 1 WLR 570 CA Local authority liable for damage occasioned by parties acting on negligent advice of environmental health officer.

Woolfall v Knowlsey Borough Council [1992] TLR 319 CA Local authority liable for injury to child occasioned by explosion of aerosol can which had been part of rubish left uncleared by local authority on foot of industrial dispute.

X and others v Bedfordshire County Council [1994] 1 FLR 431; (1993) 143 NLJ 1783; [1993] TLR 590 HC QBD Failed attempt by children to sue local authority for injuries suffered through authority's alleged negligence/breach of statutory duty as regarded exercise of its care functions.

NEGLIGENCE (lunatic)

De Freville v Dill [1927] 96 LJCL 1056; (1926-27) XLIII TLR 702 HC KBD Successful action for negligent committal of plaintiff to mental hospital.

Everitt (Pauper) v Griffiths and Ankelsaria (1921) 85 JP 149 HL Failed negligence action against chairman of board of guardians/medical doctor for wrongful committal of person to lunatic asylum.

NEGLIGENCE (maternity home)

County Council of the Parts of Lindsey, Lincolnshire v Marshall (Mary), wife of Lewis Alexander Marshall [1936] 2 All ER 1076; [1937] AC 97; (1936) 100 JP 411; [1936] 105 LJCL 614; (1936) 155 LTR 297; (1936) 80 SJ 702; (1935-36) LII TLR 661; (1936) WN (I) 244 HL Negligent admission of/failure to warn nursing home patient in maternity hospital where faced peculiar risk of fever.

Marshall v Lindsey County Council (1935) 99 JP 185; (1935) 152 LTR 421; (1935) 79 SJ 251; (1934-35) LI TLR 279; (1935) WN (I) 32 CA Negligent admission of/failure to warn nursing home patient in maternity hospital where faced peculiar risk of fever.

Marshall v Lindsey County Council [1935] 1 KB 516 HC KBD Admission of/failure to warn nursing home patient in maternity hospital where faced peculiar risk of fever was not negligent.

NEGLIGENCE (medical)

Ashingdon v Tolleth (1951) 101 LJ 235 CyCt Failed action in negligence against osteopath.

Bagley v North Herts Health Authority (1986) 136 NLJ 1014 HC QBD Damages for hospital negligence which resulted in pregnant woman giving birth to still-born child.

Baker v Kaye (1996) TLR 12/12/96 HC QBD In-house company doctor owed duty of care towards prospective employee when carrying out pre-employment medical test and telling company of results of same.

Benarr and anor v Kettering Health Authority (1988) 138 NLJ 179 HC QBD Damages available for future private education of child born of father after negligent vasectomy operation where father's previous children educated privately.

Bolam v Friern Hospital Management Committee [1957] 2 All ER 118 HC QBD Doctor not negligent if susbscribes to one of two conflicting views held by responsible bodies of medics; doctor negligent in not giving warning to mentally ill person of what he believes to be minimal dangers of treatment; must show failure to warn not negligenet and would not have consented if warned.

Burnett, Hood and Hampton v Warden [1935] LJNCCR 245 CyCt That medical treatment given in error did not mean administration of same was perforce negligent.

Burton v Islington Health Authority; De Martell v Merton and Sutton Health Authority [1993] QB 204; [1992] 3 WLR 637 HC QBD Could sue health authorities for negligent treatment in course of pregnancy which resulted baby being born with abnormalities.

Burton v Islington Health Authority; De Martell v Merton and Sutton Health Authority [1992] 2 FCR 845; [1992] 2 FLR 184; (1992) 142 NLJ 565; [1993] QB 204; (1992) 136 SJ LB 104; [1992] TLR 142; [1992] 3 WLR 637 CA Could sue health authorities for negligent treatment in course of pregnancy which resulted baby being born with abnormalities.

Cassidy v Ministry of Health (Fahrni, Third Party) [1951] 1 All ER 574; [1951] 2 KB 343 CA On liability of hospital authorities for negligence of medical staff.

Chapman v Rix (1959) 103 SJ 940 CA Doctor dealing with crisis situation not negligent in not consulting patient's own doctor.

Clark v McLennan and another [1983] 1 All ER 416 HC QBD Burden of proof switches to doctor if pursues unorthodox treatment.

Clarke v Adams (1950) 94 SJ 599 HC KBD Recovery of damages from physiotherapist for inadequate warning to client as to risk posed by certain equipment being used.

Collins v Hertfordshire County Council and another [1947] 1 All ER 633; (1947) 111 JP 272; [1947] KB 598; [1947] 116 LJR 789; (1947) 176 LTR 456; (1947) LXIII TLR 317; (1947) WN (I) 127 HC KBD County council negligent in operation of county council hospital/not responsible for negligence of part-time surgeon employed; amendment to statement of claim allowed as not new cause of action.

Davis v London County Council (1913-14) XXX TLR 275 HC KBD Once competent professionals employed local education authority not liable for negligence of persons whom it agrees to allow conduct medical operations on children.

Defreitas v O'Brien and another [1995] TLR 86 CA On number of medics necessary to constitute 'reasonable body of medical opinion'.

Emeh v Kensington, Chelsea and Fulham Area Health Authority and others [1983] TLR 6 HC QBD No damages for loss associated with birth of child following negligent sterilisation operation (damages for sickness/suffering occasioned by pregnancy and for pain of repeat sterilisation operation).

Gold and others v Essex County Council [1942] 1 All ER 326; (1941-42) LVIII TLR 146 HC KBD County council not liable for county hospital radiographer's negligence.

Gold v Haringey Health Authority [1987] 1 FLR 125 HC QBD Were negligent in not warning patient that sterilisation operation might not succeed.

Gold v Haringey Health Authority [1988] 1 FLR 55; (1987) 137 NLJ 541; [1988] QB 481; (1987) 131 SJ 843; [1987] 3 WLR 649 CA Not negligent in not warning patient that sterilisation operation might not succeed as was substantial body of medical opinion which would not have so warned.

Gray v Mid-Herts Group Hospital Management Committee (1974) 124 NLJ 367t; (1974) 118 SJ 501 HC QBD On appropriate damages for injuries suffered by child as result of negligent hospital operation.

Harrison v Ward [1939] LJNCCR 160 CyCt Doctor liable for increased suffering caused to patient by his negligent treatment of same.

Hills v Potter and others [1983] 3 All ER 716; (1984) 128 SJ 224; [1983] TLR 369; [1984] 1 WLR 641 HC QBD Standard of care expected of doctor is that which one would reasonably expect of doctor.

Hotson v Fitzgerald and others (1985) 129 SJ 558; [1985] 1 WLR 1036 HC QBD On recovery of damages where claiming that but for medical negligence would not have suffered injury to extent which did.

Hucks v Cole and another (1968) 118 NLJ 469t; (1968) 112 SJ 483 CA On heavy burden of proof plaintiff must discharge when alleging negligence against medical practitioner.

Hughes v Waltham Forest Health Authority [1990] TLR 714 CA That surgical decision erroneous or that other surgeons critical of decision did not preclude finding that surgeons being sued not negligent.

Kavanagh v Abrahamson (1964) 108 SJ 320 HC QBD Doctor not negligent in prescribing tablets for longtime patient whom did not see (wife visited and described symptoms).

Keow (Chin) v Government of Malaysia and another (1967) 111 SJ 333 [1967] 1 WLR 813 PC Expert evidence unnecessary for/that doctor followed same practice each day as that challenged in instant case had no bearing on finding of negligent medical practice.

Kralj and another v McGrath and another [1986] 1 All ER 54; (1985) 135 NLJ 913 HC QBD Aggravated damages not appropriate for medical negligence though compensatory damages may be raised; damages for nervous shock, not grief; financial loss in replacing dead child recoverable.

Landau v Werner (1961) 105 SJ 257 HC QBD Psychiatrist who had maintained social relations with patient deemed to have been professionally negligent.

Landau v Werner (1961) 105 SJ 1008 CA Psychiatrist who had maintained social relations with patient deemed to have been professionally negligent.

Langley v Campbell (1975) 125 NLJ 1198t HC QBD Successful action in negligence against doctor for failing to recognise malarial symptoms of person who had just returned from Africa/previously had malaria.

Levenkind v Churchill-Davidson (1983) 133 NLJ 577 HC QBD Failed negligence action following on surgical operation.

Luxmoore-May and another v Messenger May Baverstock (a firm) [1990] 1 All ER 1067; (1990) 140 NLJ 89; [1990] 1 WLR 1009 CA Duty of care expected of provincial auctioneer similar to that of general medical practitioner.

Lybert v Warrington Health Authority [1995] TLR 290 CA On appropriate warning pre-sterilisation operation as to possibility of pregnancy post-sterilisation operation (here warning inadequate).

Mahon v Osborne [1939] 1 All ER 535; [1939] 2 KB 14; [1939] 108 LJCL 567; (1939) 160 LTR 329; (1939) 83 SJ 134 CA Res ipsa loquitur cannot arise in relation to complex surgery; whether leaving swab in patient negligent depends on circumstances.

Maynard v West Midlands Regional Health Authority [1985] 1 All ER 635; (1983) 133 NLJ 641; (1984) 128 SJ 317; [1983] TLR 316; [1984] 1 WLR 634 HL Doctor not proved negligent simply because was reputable body of opinion that disagreed with action he took as well as body of opinion that agreed with action he took.

McKay and another v Essex Area Health Authority and another [1982] 2 All ER 771; (1982) 132 NLJ 466; [1982] QB 1166; [1982] TLR 90; [1982] 2 WLR 890 CA Sole duty to fetus is duty not to injure it.

Morris v Winsbury-White [1937] 4 All ER 494 HC KBD Visiting surgeon not liable for negligence of residence surgeons/nurses (did not act as agents); post-operation finding of tube in patient's body not res ipsa loquitur.

Rance and another v Mid-Downs Health Authority and another [1991] 1 All ER 801; (1990) 140 NLJ 325; [1991] 1 QB 587; [1990] TLR 113; [1991] 2 WLR 159 HC QBD Child 'capable of being born alive' where if born could live and breathe via its own lungs. Failure to advise about abortion of child 'capable of being born alive' not negligent as abortion would be unlawful.

Robinson v The Post Office and another [1974] 2 All ER 737; (1973) 123 NLJ 1017t; [1974] 1 WLR 1176 CA Negligent doctor's act not causing/materially contributing to existing injury not novus actus interveniens.

Roe v Minister of Health and others; Woolley v Same [1954] 2 QB 66; (1954) 98 SJ 30; [1954] 1 WLR 128 HC QBD Hospital not liable for negligence of anaesthesist.

Roe v Ministry of Health and others; Woolley v Same [1954] 2 All ER 131; (1954) 104 LJ 313; [1954] 2 QB 66; (1954) 98 SJ 319; [1954] 2 WLR 915 CA Hospital liable for negligence of anesthesist here — no negligence here as standard of care was that to be expected of reasonably competent anaesthesist.

Salih and another v Enfield Health Authority [1991] 3 All ER 400; (1991) 141 NLJ 460i CA Decision not to have another child and savings made thereby relevant when determining damages for unwanted pregnancy.

Sidaway v Bethlem Royal Hospital Governors and others [1984] 1 All ER 1018; [1984] QB 493; (1984) 128 SJ 301; [1984] TLR 97; [1984] 2 WLR 778 CA Standard expected of surgeon advising on operation is that of experienced, skilled body of medical persons.

Sidaway v Board of Governors of the Bethlem Royal Hospital and the Maudsley Hospital and another (1982) 132 NLJ 814 HC QBD On duty of care owed by surgeon to patient.

Sidaway v Board of Governors of the Bethlem Royal Hospital and the Maudsley Hospital and others [1985] 1 All ER 643; [1985] AC 871; (1985) 135 NLJ 203; (1985) 129 SJ 154; [1985] 2 WLR 480 HL On duty of care owed by surgeon to patient.

Udale v Bloomsbury Area Health Authority [1983] 2 All ER 522; (1983) 127 SJ 510; [1983] TLR 113; [1983] 1 WLR 1098 HC QBD Damages unavailable for birth after sterilisation but can recover for distress, pain, suffering and effect on family finances.

Whichello v Medway and Gravesend Hospital Management Committee and another (1964) 108 SJ 55 HC QBD Decision not to take step which might have proved more fruitful approach to treating patient was not actually negligent.

Wilsher v Essex Area Health Authority [1986] 3 All ER 801; (1986) 136 NLJ 1061; [1987] QB 730; (1970) 130 SJ 749; [1987] 2 WLR 425 CA Health authority can be liable in failing to provide competent medics; 'team negligence' non-existent; standard of care that of ordinary skilled person; burden of proof not transferred by showing step that ought to have been taken not taken; negligence if heightened risk because of action even if other risks present.

Wilsher v Essex Area Health Authority [1988] 1 All ER 871; [1988] AC 1074; (1988) 138 NLJ 78; (1988) 132 SJ 418; [1988] 2 WLR 557 HL Must prove causation between injury and negligent act — not enough that negligent act one of a number of possible causes.

Yeomans v Davies and Camden and Islington Area Health Authority (1981) 131 NLJ 210 HC QBD Damages following negligently performed vasectomy operation.

NEGLIGENCE (misrepresentation)

Anderson (WB) and Sons, Ltd and others v Rhodes (Liverpool), Ltd and others [1967] 2 All ER 850 Assizes Employer owes duty of care to persons acting on business representations of employees.

NEGLIGENCE (mortgagee)

Hudston v Viney [1921] 1 Ch 98 HC ChD Negligence of mortgagees not of such a degree as to relieve them/purchaser from them of the protection of their legal estate.

NEGLIGENCE (nuisance)

Longhurst v Metropolitan Water Board (1947) 111 JP 212; [1947] 116 LJR 612 HC KBD Water board liable for injury suffered through its negligence in repair of leak.

Longhurst v Metropolitan Water Board (1947) 111 JP 477; (1947) 91 SJ 653 CA Water Board owed qualified duty of care to public when effecting repairs under the Waterworks Clauses Act 1847 — here not violated.

Longhurst v Metropolitan Water Board [1948] 2 All ER 834; (1948) 112 JP 470 HL Where act under statutory authority no nuisance absent negligence (and here no negligence).

NEGLIGENCE (nurse)

Hall and Wife v Lees and others (1903-04) 48 SJ 638 CA Nursing association not liable for negligence of trained nurses it supplied as agreement was to provide nurse and it exercised reasonable care in doing so.

NEGLIGENCE (parking)

Stevens v Kelland and others [1970] RTR 445 HC QBD On respective liabilities for collision arising from negligent parking of vehicle.

NEGLIGENCE (planning authority)

Ryeford Homes Ltd v Sevenoaks (1989) 139 NLJ 255 HC QBD Planning authority not liable in negligence for manner in which performs its functions.

NEGLIGENCE (police)

Alexandrou v Oxford [1993] 4 All ER 328; [1990] TLR 127 CA Police not under duty of care to prevent loss to those who inform them of crime being committed or about to be committed.

Ancell and another v McDermott and others [1993] 4 All ER 355; (1993) 143 NLJ 363; [1993] RTR 235; (1993) 137 SJ LB 36; [1993] TLR 42 CA Police not under duty of care to protect road users from road hazards of which police aware.

Ancell v McDermott and others [1992] TLR 62 HC QBD Question as to whether police are under duty of care to protect road users from road hazards of which police aware a subjective question.

Clough v Bussan and another; West Yorkshire Police Authority (Third Party) [1990] RTR 178 HC QBD Police who had been notified of defective traffic lights did not owe duty of care to driver involved in collision thereafter (as result of malfunction).

Great Central Railway Company v Bates [1921] 3 KB 578; (1921) CC Rep X 61; [1921] LJCL 1269; (1920-21) 65 SJ 768; (1920-21) XXXVII TLR 948 HC KBD No duty to policeman entering premises to ascertain whether everything all right.

Hill v Chief Constable of West Yorkshire [1987] 1 All ER 1173; (1987) 137 NLJ 222; [1988] QB 60; (1987) 131 SJ 626; [1987] 2 WLR 1126 CA Police do not owe public duty of care to catch unknown criminal.

Hill v Chief Constable of West Yorkshire (1986) 136 NLJ 238 HC QBD Police do not owe public duty of care to catch unknown criminal (and such a duty of care is anyway too vague and damage occasioned through breach of same too remote to ground suit).

Hill v Chief Constable of West Yorkshire [1988] 2 All ER 238; [1989] AC 53; (1988) 138 NLJ 126; (1988) 132 SJ 700; [1988] 2 WLR 1049 HL Police not liable in damages for failure to catch unknown criminal.

Hughes v National Union of Mineworkers and others [1991] 4 All ER 278; [1991] TLR 301 HC QBD Generally senior police officers not liable to junior police officers for exposure of latter to undue risk.

Kirkham v Chief Constable of the Greater Manchester Police (1990) 140 NLJ 209; [1990] 2 QB 283; (1990) 134 SJ 758; [1990] TLR 21; [1990] 2 WLR 987 CA Police owed (and here had breached) duty of care towards prisoner to inform prison authorities of prisoner's suicidal tendencies.

Kirkham v Chief Constable of the Greater Manchester Police [1989] 3 All ER 882 HC QBD Police owed (and here had breached) duty of care towards prisoner to inform prison authorities of prisoner's suicidal tendencies.

McLeod v Receiver of the Metropolitan Police and another [1971] Crim LR 364 HC QBD Damages for collision arising out of negligent driving by police officer en route to emergency.

Osman and another v Ferguson and another [1993] 4 All ER 344 CA Police not liable for crimes committed by criminal whom they could have but failed to apprehend.

Rivers v Cutting [1982] 3 All ER 69; [1982] Crim LR 525; [1983] RTR 105; (1982) 126 SJ 362; [1982] TLR 213; [1982] 1 WLR 1146 CA Police not vicariously liable for acts of contractor employed to remove broken-down/abandoned vehicle.

NEGLIGENCE (Post Office)

His Majesty's Postmaster-General v Liverpool Corporation (1922) 86 JP 157; (1922) CC Rep XI 51 CA Not liable to pay for repairs caused to telegraph line where damage prompted by original negligence of Postmaster-General or those for whose acts was answerable.

Postmaster-General v Liverpool Corporation (1923) CC Rep XII 53; (1923) 87 JP 157; (1923) 58 LJ 311; (1924) 130 LTR 41; (1922-23) 67 SJ 701; (1922-23) XXXIX TLR 598; (1923) WN (I) 206 HL Not liable to pay for repairs caused to telegraph line where damage prompted by original negligence of Postmaster-General or those for whose acts was answerable.

NEGLIGENCE (principal and agent)

Brown v KMR Services Ltd; Daniels (Sword) v Pitel and others [1994] 4 All ER 385 HC QBD Failure of agent to advise client a breach of contract and a breach of duty of care.

NEGLIGENCE (prison)

D'Arcy v Prison Commissioners [1956] Crim LR 56t HC QBD Successful negligence action against Prison Commissioners for injuries suffered by prisoner during attack by fellow-prisoners.

Dorset Yacht Co Ltd v Home Office [1969] 2 All ER 564; [1969] 2 QB 412; (1969) 113 SJ 227; [1969] 2 WLR 1008 CA Home Office/its officers liable for damage to third party vessel caused by persons escaping on foot of their negligence.

Dorset Yacht Co Ltd v Home Office (1969) 113 SJ 57 HC QBD Home Office/its officers might be liable for damage to third party vessel caused by persons escaping on foot of their negligence.

Egerton v Home Office [1978] Crim LR 494 HC QBD Failed action in negligence against Home Office for injuries suffered by sex offender at hands of fellow prisoners in prison.

Ellis v Home Office [1953] 2 All ER 149; (1953) 103 LJ 380; [1953] 2 QB 135; (1953) 97 SJ 436; [1953] 3 WLR 105 CA No breach of Home Office's duty to take reasonable care of prisoners by giving mental deficient free access to other prisoners.

Greenwell v Prison Commissioners (1951) 101 LJ 486 CyCt Prison Commissioners liable in negligence for damage occasioned by Borstal inmates to third person's property in course of escape.

H v Secretary of State for the Home Department (1992) 136 SJ LB 140; [1992] TLR 226 CA Prisoner could not bring negligence action in respect of actions by prison officials that led to his having to be segregated.

Home Office v Dorset Yacht Co Ltd [1970] 2 All ER 294 [1970] AC 1004; (1970) 120 NLJ 458t; (1970) 114 SJ 375; [1970] 2 WLR 1140 HL Home Office/its officers do not enjoy immunity from negligence; borstal officers liable for damage to third party vessel caused by persons escaping on foot of their negligence.

NEGLIGENCE (professional)

Ashcroft v Mersey Regional Authority [1983] 2 All ER 245 HC QBD Question for professional negligence is whether exercised care to be expected of such a man in such a situation: the more skilled the more care.

Dwyer v Roderick and others [1983] TLR 668 CA On burden of proof as regards proving proving professional persons negligent; on need for greater speed in professional negligence actions.

McCandless (David Noel) v General Medical Council (1996) 140 SJ LB 28; [1995] TLR 668; [1996] 1 WLR 167 PC Gravely negligent treatment of patients could constitute serious professional misconduct.

Re Chien Sing-Shou (1967) 111 SJ 605; [1967] 1 WLR 1155 PC Professional misconduct board could consider negligence which might also be criminal behaviour.

Stafford and another v Conti Commodity Services Ltd [1981] 1 All ER 691 HC QBD Commodities broker's error of judgment may not be negligence and consequent losses not per se evidence of negligence.

Wimpey Construction UK Ltd v Poole [1984] TLR 285 HC QBD On test for determining whether professional man has been negligent.

NEGLIGENCE (property survey/valuation)

Arenson v Arenson and another [1972] 2 All ER 939 HC ChD Arbitral actions clothed with immunity from negligence suits.

Banque Bruxelles Lambert SA v Eagle Star Insurance Co Ltd [1994] TLR 127 HC QBD On liability of valuer for negligent valuation.

Banque Bruxelles Lambert SA v Eagle Star Insurance Co Ltd and others and other appeals [1995] 2 All ER 769 (also HC QBD); (1995) 145 NLJ 343; [1995] QB 375; [1995] TLR 97; [1995] 2 WLR 607 CA Property valuer must exercise reasonable standard of professional care; valuer not guarantor of lender's decision.

Baxter v FW Gapp and Co Ltd and another (1938) 82 SJ 1032 HC KBD On appropriate damages for negligent evaluation of property.

Baxter v Gapp (FW) and Company, Limited, and Gapp [1939] 2 KB 271; [1939] 108 LJCL 522; (1939) 83 SJ 436; (1938-39) LV TLR 739; (1939) WN (I) 201 CA On appropriate damages for negligent evaluation of property.

Beaton and another v Nationwide Anglia Building Society [1990] TLR 645 HC QBD Building society liable for negligence of employee-surveyor despite clause in prescribed form given to every mortgagee stating that the price charged for property did not necessarily indicate its true worth.

Beaumont and another v Humberts (a firm) and others [1990] TLR 543 CA Surveyor held not to have been negligent in his assessment of the reinstatement worth of a three hundred year old house.

Buckland v Mackesy; Buckland v Watts (1968) 112 SJ 841 CA Surveyor but not solicitor deemed to have acted negligently in course of property transaction.

Eagle Star Insurance Co, Ltd v Gale and Power (1955) 105 LJ 458 HC QBD Successful action in negligence against surveyor for making negligent report on basis of which plaintiff had advanced loan.

Eley v King and Chasemore (1989) 139 NLJ 791 CA Surveyor not negligent where did not tell purchaser that underpinning required but did recommend insurance against subsidence.

Fisher v Knowles (1982) 132 NLJ 439 HC QBD Difference in valuation and true value of house awarded to plaintiff who successfully sued surveyor for negligent valuation.

Gardner and another v Marsh and Parsons (a firm) and another [1997] 3 All ER 871; (1996) 140 SJ LB 262; (1996) TLR 2/12/97; [1997] 1 WLR 489 CA Damages available where purchased property in reliance on negligent surveyor's report were difference in cost of property and cost ought to have been were defects known when purchasing.

Humphery v Bowers (1928-29) XLV TLR 297 HC KBD Failed action in negligence against surveyor provided by Lloyd's Register who certified defective yacht as being in good state.

Kenny v Hall (1976) 126 NLJ 1044 HC QBD Bases on which damages awarded for negligent valuation of property by firm of chartered auctioneers/chartered surveyors/estate agents/property experts.

London and South of England Building Society v Stone (1982) 132 NLJ 218 HC QBD Damages awarded in successful negligence action against surveyor was difference between valuation price and true worth at time of survey.

London and South of England Building Society v Stone [1983] 3 All ER 105; (1983) 127 SJ 446; [1983] TLR 407; [1983] 1 WLR 1242 CA Damages for financial burden suffered/not difference between amount lent and amount would have lent on proper valuation; cannot claim for costs arising from unreasonable non-mitigation.

Love v Mack (1905) XCII LTR 345 HC ChD No duty of care found to exist between valuer and person advancing money on basis of valuation where former not agent of latter and had not purported to perform valuation for benfit of latter.

Love v Mack (1905-06) XCIII LTR 352 CA No duty of care found to exist between valuer and person advancing money on basis of valuation where former not agent of latter and had not purported to perform valuation for benfit of latter.

N v C [1997] 2 FCR 600 CA Striking out of negligence action against valuer (regarding valuation of family home as part of divorce proceedings) where issue of valuation had been considered in the ancillary relief proceedings.

Palacath Ltd v Flanagan [1985] 2 All ER 161 HC QBD Surveyor not acting in quasi-/judicial rôle not immune from negligence suit.

Perry v Sidney Phillips and Son (a firm) [1982] 1 All ER 1005; (1981) 131 NLJ 1135 HC QBD Damages available for cost of repairing defects (not difference between cost/value) where will occupy negligently surveyed house; occupier's delay of repairs undiscovered by negligent surveyor reasonable if no money; damages available for distress/discomfort of repairs/occupying defective house.

Philips v Ward [1956] 1 All ER 874; (1956) 106 LJ 281; (1956) 100 SJ 317; [1956] 1 WLR 471 CA Damages for negligent survey/valuation were difference between real value and value in report; damages to be measured at date of report.

R v M; R v W (1968) 118 NLJ 1004t CA On respective liabilities of solicitor/surveyor towards client seeking to buy house.

Roberts and another v J Hampson and Co (a firm) [1989] 2 All ER 504; (1988) 138 NLJ 166; (1989) 133 SJ 1234; [1990] 1 WLR 94 HC QBD Surveyor owes duty of care when carrying out inspection to follow trail of suspicion.

Smith v Bush; Harris v Wyre Forest District Council (1989) 139 NLJ 576 HL On duty of care owed by building society valuer towards mortgagor/mortgagee.

South Australia Asset Management Corporation v York Montague Ltd; United Bank of Kuwait plc v Prudential Property Services Ltd; Nykredit Mortgage Bank plc v Edward Erdman Group Ltd (formerly Edward Erdman) (an unlimited company) [1996] 3 All ER 365; [1997] AC 191; (1996) 146 NLJ 956; (1996) 140 SJ LB 156; (1996) TLR 24/6/96; [1996] 3 WLR 87 HL Damages available where relied on negligent valuation given by surveyor were for losses which mistake in valuation could foreseeably entail.

Stevenson v Nationwide Building Society (1984) 128 SJ 875 HC QBD Building society valuer not liable where despite disclaimer purchaser chose to rely on valuer's report as structural report, not mere valuation.

Strover and another v Harrington and others [1988] 1 All ER 769 HC ChD Absent evidence of general practice surveyor not negligent because relied on vendor's statement.

Sutcliffe v Thackrah and others [1974] 1 All ER 859; [1974] AC 727; (1974) 124 NLJ 200t; (1974) 118 SJ 148; [1974] 2 WLR 295 HL Architect/valuer acting in arbitral rôle immune from action for negligence in so doing.

Sutherland v CR Maton and Sons Ltd (1977) 127 NLJ 291 HC QBD Bungalow-builders liable to first and subsequent owners for defects in construction of house (even though buyers relied on building society inspection and did not employ own surveyor to inspect house).

Swingcastle Ltd v Gibson [1990] 3 All ER 463; (1990) 140 NLJ 818; [1990] 1 WLR 1223 CA Negligent surveyor liable to mortgagee for all loss where mortgagee seeks to sell property following mortgagor's default on repayment.

Yianni v Edwin Evans and Sons [1981] 3 All ER 592; (1981) 131 NLJ 1074; [1982] QB 438; (1981) 125 SJ 694; [1981] 3 WLR 843 HC QBD House purchaser's relying on negligent surveyor's valuation of house (for building society) were owed duty of care by surveyor.

Young v Buckles [1952] 1 KB 220 CA Recoverability of professional charges in excess of that for which building licence allowed (Defence (General) Regulations 1939, r 56(4) applied).

NEGLIGENCE (rail)

Angus v London, Tilbury, and Southend Railway Company (1905-06) XXII TLR 222 CA Where train stopped suddenly causing passenger injury rail company to avoid liability in negligence had to prove stoppage reasonable/that they had not caused need for stoppage through own negligence (which failed to do).

Anthony v Midland Railway Company (1909) C LTR 117; (1908-09) XXV TLR 98 HC KBD Passenger injured by stepping from train which overshot platform before could be warned could not recover damages in negligence.

Atherton v London and North-Western Railway Company (1905-06) XCIII LTR 464; (1904-05) XXI TLR 671 CA Was fair to find rail company negligent for not erecting screen to protect passengers (passing along exit company provided) from sparks from engine.

Barry Railway Company v White (1900-01) XVII TLR 644 HL On negligence/contributory negligence in action for personal injuries suffered at level crossing.

Benson v Furness Railway Company (1903) LXXXVIII LTR 268; (1902-03) 47 SJ 257 HC KBD No negligence where passenger injured by door being slammed shut by railway company employee after train started moving from station.

Booker v Wenborn [1962] 1 All ER 431; (1962) 112 LJ 137; (1961) 105 SJ 1125 CA Person opening moving train door to board owes duty of care not to injure those on platform (including porters).

Brackley v Midland Railway Company [1916] 85 LJKB 1596; (1916) 114 LTR 1150 CA Rail company not liable for inadequate maintenance of railway footbridge/hidden danger it posed where bridge had been dedicated to public.

Braithwaite v South Durham Steel Co, Ltd and another [1958] 3 All ER 161; (1958) 102 SJ 655 HC QBD Master negligent in not providing safe place to work; licensor liable in negligence despite unintended trespass of licencee at moment of accident to escape therefrom.

British Columbia Electric Rail Co, Ltd v Loach [1914-15] All ER 426; [1916] 1 AC 719; [1916] 85 LJPC 23 (1915-16) 113 LTR 946 PC Are liable in negligence despite other's contributory negligence where own negligence precluded avoidance of cause of action.

Brookes v London Passenger Transport Board [1947] 1 All ER 506 HC KBD Board negligent for not closing door before train left station.

Commissioner for Railways v McDermott [1966] 2 All ER 162; [1967] AC 169; (1965-66) 116 NLJ 809; [1966] 3 WLR 267 PC Railway company owed occupier's and more general duty of care to persons using unguarded level crossing.

Conway v British Transport Commission (1962) 106 SJ 78 HC QBD On duty of care owed by driver of train.

Delaney v Metropolitan Railway Company (1919-20) XXXVI TLR 190; (1920) WN (I) 24 HC KBD Once person inside train was no duty on rail company to give warning that train about to move.

Delaney v Metropolitan Railway Company [1920] 89 LJCL 878; (1920) 123 LTR 484; (1919-20) 64 SJ 477; (1919-20) XXXVI TLR 596; (1920) WN (I) 194 CA Though person inside train was duty on rail company to take reasonable care of same when train moved.

Drury v North Eastern Railway Company [1901] 2 KB 322; [1901] 70 LJK/QB 830; (1901) LXXXIV LTR 658 HC KBD Not evidence of negligence that seated passenger's finger crushed when door close by railway employee (who owes no special duty of care to seated passenger).

Dunt v London and North Eastern Railway Co (1942) 86 SJ 203 HC KBD Rail company liable for fire occasioned by sparks flying from engine: on liability of rail companies for flying sparks.

Dyer v The Southern Railway [1948] 1 KB 608; (1948) LXIV TLR 225; (1948) WN (I) 102 HC KBD Railway company liable for negligent look-out system for men working on track.

Dyke v The South-Eastern and Chatham Railways' Managing Committee (1900-01) XVII TLR 651 HC KBD Luggage of passenger carried in same train as passenger came under Carriers Act 1830.

Easson v London and North Eastern Ry Co [1944] 2 All ER 425; [1944] KB 421; (1945) 95 LJ 113; [1944] 113 LJ 449; (1944) 170 LTR 234; (1944) 88 SJ 143; (1943-44) LX TLR 280; (1944) WN (I) 89 CA No res ipsa loquitur that if train door opens in transit railway company negligent.

East Indian Railway Company v Mukerjee (Kalidas) [1901] AC 396; (1901) LXXXIV LTR 210; (1900-01) XVII TLR 284 PC Railway company not liable for injury caused by fireworks brought on board unless parcel carried especial danger.

Edwards v Railway Executive [1952] 2 All ER 430; [1952] AC 737; (1952) 102 LJ 470; (1952) 96 SJ 493; [1952] 2 TLR 237; (1952) WN (I) 383 HL Railway Executive not liable for injuries suffered by boy trespassing on railway line.

Fitton v Lancashire and Yorkshire Railway Co (1914) CC Rep III 68 CyCt Rail company liable for negligent care of luggage entrusted to porter.

French v Hills Plymouth Company and others; Same v Same (1907-08) XXIV TLR 644 HC KBD Rail company's licence to cross line did not include licence to cross when train there.

Geddes v British Railways Board (1968) 112 SJ 194 CA Deceased two-thirds liable for rail accident/engine driver one-third liable for not sounding long whistle in circumstances.

Gilbey v Great Northern Railway Company (1919-20) XXXVI TLR 562 HC KBD Rail company not liable in negligence for stage props carried by passenger as personal luggage though were not personal luggage.

Glasscock v London, Tilbury, and Southend Railway Company (1901-02) XVIII TLR 295 CA Jury could reasonably arrive at decision that injuries suffered by woman stepping out of train too long for platform were not due to her contributory negligence/were due to negligence of rail company.

Grand Trunk Railway Co v Barnett [1911-13] All ER 1624 PC No liability for injury to trespasser occurring through one's negligence.

Great Central Railway Company v Hewlett [1916-17] All ER 1027; [1916] 2 AC 511; (1916) 51 LJ 418; [1916] 85 LJKB 1705; (1916-17) 115 LTR 349; (1915-16) XXXII TLR 707 HL Railway company not under duty to warn public of presence of post authorised by statute and maintainable by them.

Great Northern Railway Company v Woods (1917) CC Rep VI 50 CyCt Rail company liable in negligence for carriage of sheep in overcrowded conditions.

Hallett v London and North Eastern Railway Company (1915) CC Rep IV 4; [1940] LJNCCR 334 CyCt On duty on rail company/passenger regarding ensuring/checking was safe to alight from train which pulled up at station in black-out conditions.

Hare and another v British Transport Commission [1956] 1 All ER 578; (1956) 106 LJ 185; (1956) 100 SJ 189; [1956] 1 WLR 250 HC QBD Guards door need not be closed when train starts but was negligent not to have closed sixty yards after starting.

Hazell v British Transport Commission (1958) 108 LJ 74; (1958) 102 SJ 124 HC QBD Special precautions at rail accommodation crossing to be taken by those seeking to traverse same, not rail authority.

Hearn v Southern Railway Company (1925) 60 LJ 167; (1924-25) XLI TLR 305 CA Exception clause deemed applicable though seemed worded to apply to ordinary and not (as here) special trains.

Henson v London and North Eastern Railway Company (Coote and Warren, Limited, Third Parties) (1945-46) LXII TLR 369 CA Exemption clause ineffective where person purportedly subject thereto had not been given adequate notice of same.

Hicks v British Transport Commission [1958] 1 WLR 493 CA Shunter's/railway company's failure to take reasonable care of self/shunter meant both equally liable in negligence for injury of shunter.

Horton v The Southern Railway Co [1934] LJNCCR 52 CyCt Valid finding of negligence on part of rail company where person injured self in gap between train and inadequately lit platform when alighting from former onto latter.

Hurlstone v London Electric Railway Company and another (1912-13) XXIX TLR 514 HC KBD Railway company liable for negligence of building contractors.

Hurlstone v London Electric Railway Company and another (1913-14) XXX TLR 398 CA Railway company not liable for negligence of building contractors.

Hutchinson v London and North Eastern Railway Company [1942] 1 KB 481 CA Breach of statutory duty in not providing look-out for oncoming train while workmen on line.

Jenner v South-Eastern Railway Company (1911) 75 JP 419; (1911-12) 105 LTR 131; (1910-11) 55 SJ 553; (1910-11) XXVII TLR 445 HC KBD Circumstances justified jury finding that there was inadequate care taken to protect vehicles using level crossing.

Jepps v LMS Railway Co [1944] LJNCCR 129 CyCt Was negligent for train to be pulled up at station in such a way that passenger could not but injure self in alighting from his carriage.

John Lee and Son (Grantham), Limited v Railway Executive (1949) LXV TLR 604 CA Warehouse tenancy agreement with railway company deemed not to preclude recovery in negligence — if there was negligence — for fire in warehouse allegedly started by spark from engine.

Kemshead v British Transport Commission (1956) 106 LJ 601; (1958) 102 SJ 122 CA Foggy conditions put onus on people traversing accommodation crossing, not rail authority, to take special care.

Knight v Great Western Railway [1942] 2 All ER 286; [1943] KB 105; [1943] 112 LJ 321; (1943) 93 LJ 109; (1942) 167 LTR 71; (1942) 86 SJ 331; (1941-42) LVIII TLR 352 HC KBD Is no duty upon train drivers to keep to speed such that can stop within limits of sight.

Law v Railway Executive and another (1949) LXV TLR 288 HC KBD Railway company/local authority liable in negligence for injury suffered by person colliding with wall and pavement the former had put in place of level crossing gates.

Liddiatt v Great Western Railway Co [1946] LJNCCR 22 CyCt Rail company liable for negligent operation of accommodation crossing.

Liddiatt v Great Western Railway Company [1946] KB 545; [1946] LJNCCR 94; (1946) 175 LTR 224; (1946) 90 SJ 369; (1945-46) LXII TLR 345 CA Closeness of accommodation crossing to level crossing traversed by public carriageway did not place special duty of care on railway company.

Lloyds Bank Ltd v Railway Executive (1952) 102 LJ 273; (1952) 96 SJ 313; [1952] 1 TLR 1207 CA Railway Executive liable in negligence for inadequate precautions at level crossing.

London Midland and Scottish Railway Company v The Ribble Hat Works Limited (1936) 80 SJ 1038 HC ChD Was negligent/nuisance for defendants to place red/green neon sign adjacent to rail lights and so render those light signals more difficult to view.

London, Tilbury, and Southend Railway v Paterson (Annie) (1913) CC Rep II 47; (1912-13) XXIX TLR 413 HL Rail company liable in negligence for injury suffered when passenger slipped off platform on foggy evening when other passengers had already slipped off.

Machen v Lancashire and Yorkshire Railway [1919] 88 LJCL 371 CA Rail company not liable for its loading of train: injury over which claim arose not proved directly connected to loading of train in any event.

Manning v London and North-Western Railway Company (1906-07) XXIII TLR 222 CA Evidence of height of train from platform in nearby stations admitted to defeat negligence claim by plaintiff claiming distance between train and platform resulted in her injuring herself.

McDowall v Great Western Rail Co [1900-03] All ER 593; [1903] 2 KB 331; (1903) 38 LJ 316; [1903] 72 LJKB 652; (1903) LXXXVIII LTR 825; (1902-03) 47 SJ 603; (1902-03) XIX TLR 552; (1903) WN (I) 117 CA Railway company not liable for unforeseen acts of trespassers where took all reasonable precautions.

McDowall v Great Western Railway Co [1902] 1 KB 618; [1902] 71 LJCL 330; (1902) LXXXVI LTR 558; (1901-02) XVIII TLR 340 HC KBD Railway company liable for acts of trespassers where did not take all reasonable precautions.

Mercer v South Eastern and Chatham Rail Co's Managing Committee [1922] All ER; [1922] 2 KB 549; [1923] 92 LJCL 25; (1922) 127 LTR 723; (1921-22) XXXVIII TLR 431 HC KBD Gate usually locked when train approaching left open: victim could recover damages in negligence for injuries consequently suffered.

Metropolitan Railway Co v Delaney [1921] All ER 301; (1921) CC Rep X 27; [1921] LJCL 721; (1921) 125 LTR 472; (1920-21) 65 SJ 453; (1920-21) XXXVII TLR 520; (1921) WN (I) 118 HL Injury sustained by passenger upon sharp start of train can justify finding of negligence on part of rail company.

Newbrook v LM and S and GW Joint Railway Companies (1924) CC Rep XIII 10 CyCt On extent of liability of rail company in negligence for damage occasioned by sparks flying from engine.

Norman v Great Western Railway Company [1914-17] All ER 205; (1914) CC Rep III 102; [1915] 1 KB 584; (1914) 49 LJ 638; [1915] 84 LJKB 598; (1914) 110 LTR 306; (1914-15) XXXI TLR 53; (1914) WN (I) 415 CA Duty of railway company to invitees same as that of shopkeeper to invitees.

Norman v Great Western Railway Company [1914] 2 KB 153; [1914] 83 LJKB 669; (1913-14) XXX TLR 241; (1914) WN (I) 15 HC KBD Duty of railway company to invitees.

O'Connor v British Transport Commission [1958] 1 All ER 558; (1958) 108 LJ 232; (1958) 102 SJ 214 CA Injury of child on train not negligence of train owner as reasonable care of child responsibility of accompanying adult.

Page v London, Midland and Scottish Railway Company (1943) 168 LTR 168 HC KBD Construction of rail company's exemption clause in respect of negligence in carriage of luggage: clause ineffective.

Pronek v Winnipeg, Selkirk and Lake Winnipeg Railway Company [1933] AC 61; (1933) 102 LJPC 12; (1933) 148 LTR 193 PC On duty of railway company operating its cars in part on a highway.

R v Broad [1914-17] All ER 90; [1915] AC 1110; (1914-15) XXXI TLR 599 PC Bye-law precluding recovery for negligence was ultra vires.

Sharpe v Southern Rail Co [1925] All ER 372; [1925] 2 KB 311; [1925] 94 LJCL 913; (1925) 133 LTR 693; (1924-25) 69 SJ 775 CA Company though/if negligent not liable to party who was contributorily negligent.

Short v British Railways Board (1974) 118 SJ 101; [1974] 1 WLR 781 HC QBD Engine driver not negligent for failing to stop before drove into cattle on track.

Skeen v British Railways Board; Scandle (Third Party); Scandle v Skeen and another [1976] RTR 281 HC QBD British Railways Board fully liable for collision between train and van at very dangerous crossing in respect of which Railways Board took no safeguards despite knowing of danger.

Slatter v British Railways Board (1966) 110 SJ 688 HC QBD Was foreseeable that rail workman would be startled by unusual shunting activity and hence that injury would occur.

The Canadian Pacific Railway Company v Roy [1902] 71 LJPC 51; (1901-02) XVIII TLR 200; (1901-02) 50 WR 415 PC Statutorily authorised rail company not liable absent negligence for damage caused by locomotive sparks.

The Grand Trunk Railway Company of Canada v McAlpine (since deceased) and others [1914] 83 LJPC 44; (1913-14) 109 LTR 693; (1912-13) XXIX TLR 679 PC Rail company liable for injury at level crossing only if proved that failing to give warning of approach/ring bell led to accident.

Toal (Pauper) v North British Railway Company [1908] AC 352; (1908) 77 LJPC 119; (1908-09) XCIX LTR 173; (1907-08) XXIV TLR 673 HL Leaving railway door open as train pulled from station could be negligent.

Trotman v British Railways Board (1974) 124 NLJ 1030t; (1975) 119 SJ 65 HC QBD Rail board one-third liable for injury to rail workman injured by train whose driver probably did not sound warning.

Trubyfield and another v Great Western Railway Company [1937] 4 All ER 614; (1937) 84 LJ 420; (1938) 158 LTR 135; (1937) 81 SJ 1002; (1937-38) LIV TLR 221; (1938) WN (I) 12 HC KBD On appropriate fatal accident damages to administrator of infant daughter's estate where daughter killed through negligence of rail company's driver.

Trznadel v British Transport Commission [1957] 3 All ER 196 CA On engine-drivers' resposnsibilities to railway employees on track.

Umek v London Transport Executive (1984) 134 NLJ 522 HC QBD Rail Board one-third liable for fatal accident involving member of staff crossing certain point of line (after told not to) as did not advise trains on approaching said point to slow down.

United Machine Tool Company v Great Western Railway Company (1913-14) XXX TLR 312 HC KBD Damages for apparently negligent damage to goods while being consigned by railway.

Vincent v Southern Railway Company (1927) 136 LTR 513; (1927) 71 SJ 34 HL On liability of rail company for non-provision of look-out man where required.

Vosper v Great Western Railway Company (1927) 64 LJ 93; (1928) 97 LJCL 51; (1927) 137 LTR 520; (1927) 71 SJ 605; (1926-27) XLIII TLR 738; (1927) WN (I) 237 HC KBD Recovery of damages for loss of passenger's luggage which rail company failed to prove was through passenger's negligence.

Wilden v London and South Western Railway Co (1919) CC Rep VIII 18 CyCt Rail company not liable where tunnel under rail unlit and person negligently continued to drive under same (albeit that tunnel being unlit was itself negligent).

NEGLIGENCE (rescue)

Baker and another v TE Hopkins and Son, Ltd [1958] 3 All ER 147; (1958) 102 SJ 636 HC QBD Master owed duty of care to doctor seeking to rescue servant; fatal accident damages not to be reduced by portion of estate made up of policy money.

Ward v TE Hopkins and Son, Ltd; Baker and another v TE Hopkins and Son, Ltd [1959] 3 All ER 225; [1959] 1 WLR 966 CA Employer liable in negligence to servant also liable to doctor seeking to rescue same: no novus actus interveniens/volenti non fit injuria.

NEGLIGENCE (revenue)

Attorney-General v Till (1909) 44 LJ 130; [1909] 78 LJKB 708; (1909) C LTR 275 CA Negligence in delivery does not open one to prosecution for refusal/neglect to deliver taxable income statement pursuant to the Income Tax Act 1842, s 55.

NEGLIGENCE (road traffic)

Aitchison v Page Motors, Limited (1936) 154 LTR 128; (1935-36) LII TLR 137 HC KBD Recovery of damages for injury suffered through negligence of bailee for reward's servant (even though latter had been acting outside scope of authority).

Aldham v United Dairies (London), Ltd [1939] 4 All ER 522; [1940] 1 KB 507; (1939) 88 LJ 351; [1940] 109 LJCL 323; (1940) 162 LTR 71; (1940) 84 SJ 43; (1940) WN (I) 14 CA Was negligent to leave milk-cart horse unattended in highway for half-hour.

Amos v Glamorgan County Council (1968) 112 SJ 52 CA Fire service not negligent where collision occurred between stationary fire engine attending daytime fire (no red warning light placed in road) and motorcyclist.

Ancell and another v McDermott and others [1993] 4 All ER 355; (1993) 143 NLJ 363; [1993] RTR 235; (1993) 137 SJ LB 36; [1993] TLR 42 CA Police not under duty of care to protect road users from road hazards of which police aware.

Askew v Bowtell [1947] 1 All ER 883; (1947) 97 LJ 249; (1947) 91 SJ 249; (1947) LXIII TLR 316 HC KBD Tram conductor not negligent in relying on driver to stop at stops/passengers only alighting when tram stopped.

Awad v Pillai and another [1982] RTR 266 CA Motorist owed duty of care to owner of car who bailed same with repairer who in turn loaned it without authority to motorist unaware of true facts.

Bainbridge v Marsay [1937] LJNCCR 218 CyCt Successful action in negligence where cow had been negligently driven onto road into path of oncoming motor cycle.

Baker v Market Harborough Industrial Co-operative Society Ld; Wallace v Richards (Leicester) Ld (1953) 97 SJ 861; [1953] 1 WLR 1472 CA Absent other evidence is presumption of equal blame where two vehicles collide in middle of straight road when dark.

Baldock v Westminster City Council (1919) 83 JP 98 (also CA); (1918-19) 63 SJ 69; (1918-19) XXXV TLR 54; (1918) WN (I) 339 HC KBD Taxi-cab driver successful in negligence suit for inadequate lighting of refuge (even though inadequate lighting a by-result of ongoing war).

Baldock v Westminster City Council (1919) CC Rep VIII 6; (1919) 83 JP 98 (also HC KBD); [1919] 88 LJCL 502; (1918-19) XXXV TLR 188; (1919) WN (I) 22 CA Taxi-cab driver successful in negligence suit for inadequate lighting of refuge (even though inadequate lighting a by-result of ongoing War).

Banfield v Scott and Ranzetta (1984) 134 NLJ 550 HC QBD Death of motor cyclist entirely attributed to negligence of driver pulling out from side-road to main road before was safe to do so.

Barkway v South Wales Transport Co, Ltd [1948] 2 All ER 460; [1949] 1 KB 54 CA Tyre burst causing skid raises presumption of negligence: must show tyre burst not negligent/that took reasonable care.

Barnard v Sully (1931) 72 LJ 122; (1930-31) XLVII TLR 557; (1931) WN (I) 180 HC KBD Where damage proved to have been done by another's motor car is rebuttable presumption that owner of car (or agent/servant) was driving same.

Barry v MacDonald (1966) 110 SJ 56 HC QBD Not negligent to drive within few feet of nearside of road.

Bee-Line Safety Coaches, Ltd v Gosforth, Ltd [1940] LJNCCR 330 CyCt Failed claim against persons who admitted negligence in collision involving lorry already involved in another collision where lorry-owners sought special damages for loss of use of lorry while in for repairs but failed to prove duration of repairs extended by second collision.

Bell v Williamson [1934] LJNCCR 37 CyCt Had good cause for negligence action where could prove roadside fence damaged by defendant's car, no more.

Benham v Gambling [1941] 1 All ER 7; [1941] AC 157; (1941) 91 LJ 26; [1942] 92 LJ 61; [1941] 110 LJ 49; (1941) 164 LTR 290; (1940) 84 SJ 703; (1940-41) LVII TLR 177 HL On appropriate damages for road death: damages not gauged on actuarial basis.

Bowman v Ingram [1938] LJNCCR 425 CyCt Leaving unlit stationary lorry on road was negligent (and violation of Road Transport Lighting Act 1927, s 1) but person who collided with same could not recover damages as was contributorily negligent in driving too fast to pull up in time.

Bramwell v Shaw and others [1971] RTR 167 HC QBD On liabilities of speeding driver, his employer and highway authority for collision occurring on poorly maintained road.

Bright v Ministry of Transport (1970) 120 NLJ 549t; [1970] RTR 401; (1970) 114 SJ 475 HC QBD Ministry of Transport negligent in manner in which had removed white lines from road.

Bright v Ministry of Transport [1971] RTR 253 CA Ministry of Transport vicariously liable for negligent manner in which council workers removed traffic lines from road.

British School of Motoring Ltd v Simms and another (AR Stafford (trading as Mini Countryman School of Motoring) and Cooper, third parties [1971] 1 All ER 317; (1971) 135 JP 103; [1971] RTR 190 Assizes Instructor's mistaken action in emergency was reasonable so not negligent.

Buesnel v Mendelson and another (Eastern Counties Omnibus Co Ltd and another (third parties)) (1959) 109 LJ ccr141 CyCt Person overtaking on inside of bus liable in damages for negligent injury occasioned to passenger on motorcycle waved forward by bus driver at junction.

Burgoyne v Phillips [1983] Crim LR 265; (1983) 147 JP 375; [1983] RTR 49; [1982] TLR 559 HC QBD On what constitutes 'driving' a car.

Burley v Hibell (1916) CC Rep V HC KBD Where car collides into car that has broken down the driver of the latter car (even if was negligent) may recover damages from driver of former if collision could reasonably have been avoided.

Burns v Ellicott (1969) 113 SJ 490 HC QBD On responsibility of driver when overtaking horserider n horse.

Butland v Coxhead and others (1968) 112 SJ 465 HC QBD Not negligent not to place lamp on road indicating presence of broken-down lorry.

Capps v Miller [1989] 2 All ER 333; [1989] RTR 312; (1989) 133 SJ 1134; [1989] 1 WLR 839 CA Improperly fastening crash helmet contributory negligence meriting 10% reduction in damages.

Carberry (formerly an infant but now of full age) v Davies and another [1968] 2 All ER 817; (1968) 118 NLJ 372t; [1968] 1 WLR 1103 CA Owner liable if driver acting on behalf and under authority of owner.

Carryfast Ltd v Hack [1981] RTR 464 HC QBD Van driver negligent in not slowing down/giving wide berth to horse/horse rider (rider not negligent in how behaved).

Carter v Sheath [1990] RTR 12 CA That plaintiff failed to explain how accident occurred meant defendant could not be held to be contributorily negligent.

Chapman v Kirke [1948] 2 All ER 556; (1948) 112 JP 399; [1948] 2 KB 450; [1949] 118 LJR 255; (1948) LXIV TLR 519; (1948) WN (I) 357 HC KBD Negligent injury by tram opens driver to conviction under Stage Carriages Act 1832, s 48.

Chapman v Post Office [1982] RTR 165 CA Pedestrian not negligent in standing on kerb (where was hit by side-mirror of van negligently driven too close to kerb).

Chapman v Ward (1974) 124 NLJ 988t; [1975] RTR 7; (1974) 118 SJ 777 HC QBD Front seat passenger without seat belt not guilty of contributory negligence as regards injuries suffered in accident.

Clarke v Winchurch and others (1968) 112 SJ 909; [1969] 1 WLR 69 CA On duty of care owed by one driver signalling to another.

Clough v Bussan and another; West Yorkshire Police Authority (Third Party) [1990] RTR 178 HC QBD Police who had been notified of defective traffic lights did not owe duty of care to driver involved in collision thereafter (as result of malfunction).

Condon v Condon (1978) 128 NLJ 88t; [1978] RTR 483 HC QBD No reduction in damages where defendant failed to prove that plaintiff's not wearing seat belt contributed to level of injuries suffered.

Connelly v A and W Hemphill Ld (1949) WN (I) 191 HL Failed action in negligence against driver who drove over individual's foot.

Cooper v Swadling [1930] 1 KB 403; (1930) 69 LJ 9; (1930) 99 LJCL 118; (1930) 142 LTR 411; (1929-30) XLVI TLR 73; (1929) WN (I) 273 CA On direction regarding negligence in case where person knocked down in motor collision.

Coote and another v Stone (1970) 120 NLJ 1205; [1971] RTR 66; (1971) 115 SJ 79 CA Order prohibiting waiting on clearways was not intended to create a civil right of remedy.

Cosgrove v Horsfall (1946) 175 LTR 334; (1945-46) LXII TLR 140 CA Negligent driver of omnibus not protected from liability by exemption clause in free bus pass agreement between London Passenger Transport Board and plaintiff.

Cox v Dixon (1984) 134 NLJ 236 HC QBD One-third reduction in damages for driver (injured in collision with speeding police car) who knew the area/should have known that people might speed at night.

Craig v Glasgow Corporation (1918-19) XXXV TLR 214 HL Inferred from circumstances where was no witness that party seeking damages run down as result of tram driver not keeping proper look-out.

Croston v Vaughan [1937] 4 All ER 249; (1938) 102 JP 11; [1938] 1 KB 540; [1938] 107 LJCL 182; (1938) 158 LTR 221; (1937) 81 SJ 882; (1937-38) LIV TLR 54; (1937) WN (I) 361 CA Stop light plus hand-signal needed when stopping; observation of Highway Code not absolute defence to negligence; apportionment of damages best done by trial judge/rarely amended by CA.

Custins v Nottingham Corporation and another [1970] RTR 365 CA Bus-driver not negligent where bus skidded on ice and collided with person after driver had gently pulled to a halt.

Daborn v Bath Tramways Motor Co, Ltd and Trevor Smithey [1946] 2 All ER 333 CA Non-negligence of driver of left-hand drive ambulance to which warning sign affixed/after correct hand-signals given.

Daly v Liverpool Corporation [1939] 2 All ER 142; (1939) 87 LJ 236 HC KBD On dual task of public vehicle driver to keep to schedule and avoid accidents; on driver's duty of care to elderly pedestrians.

Dann v Hamilton [1939] 1 All ER 59; [1939] 1 KB 509; (1939) 87 LJ 46; [1939] 108 LJCL 255; (1939) 160 LTR 433; (1939) 83 SJ 155; (1938-39) LV TLR 297 HC KBD Travelling in car with drunk driver does not raise volenti non fit injuria defence.

Davidson v Leggett (1969) 113 SJ 409 CA Parties to collision between two overtaking vehicles coming from opposite directions were equally responsible for accident.

Davies v Carmarthenshire County Council [1971] RTR 112 CA Council (80%) liable and driver (20%) liable for collision at sunset with lamp left in dangerous position on road after road-widening.

Davies v Journeaux [1976] RTR 111 CA Motorist who hit young girl whom had glimpsed before she ran across road not failing to keep proper look-out as were other legitimate distractions nor was he negligent in not sounding horn.

Davies v Liverpool Corporation [1949] 2 All ER 175; (1949) 113 JP 381; (1949) 99 LJ 301; (1949) WN (I) 268 CA Conductor liable in negligence for not policing dismounting of passengers from tram.

Dawrant v Nutt [1960] 3 All ER 681; (1960) 110 LJ 830; (1961) 105 SJ 129 Assizes Highway user owes duty of care to other highway users to take reasonable care: absence of front lights a breach of duty.

Day v Smith (1983) 133 NLJ 726 HC QBD Person driving several feet over central dividing line liable in negligence for fatal road traffic accident which occurred.

Dickens v Kay-Green (1961) 105 SJ 949 CA Driver who strayed onto wrong side of road during heavy fog deemed to be negligent.

Dixons (Scholar Green) Ltd v JL Cooper Ltd [1970] RTR 222; (1970) 114 SJ 319 CA On assessing appropriate damages for loss of use of vehicle.

Donn v Schacter [1975] RTR 238 HC QBD Driver did not owe duty of care to regular traveller in car to warn and guard same when alighting against risk posed by dangling seat belts.

Drage v Smith and another (1974) 124 NLJ 1157t; [1975] RTR 1; (1974) 118 SJ 865 HC QBD Front seat passenger without seat belt guilty of contributory negligence as regards injuries suffered (only 15% as seat belt campaign not at pitch in 1970 — year of accident — as was when case decided).

Drury v Camden London Brough Council [1972] RTR 391 HC QBD Council (50%) liable in negligence/nuisance for leaving unlit skip projecting into highway; driver equally liable for failing to maintain proper vigilance.

Eastman v South West Thames Health Authority [1990] RTR 315; [1990] TLR 354 HC QBD Ambulance passenger's failure to wear seat-belt not negligent where not informed of need for/availability of same.

Eastman v South West Thames Regional Health Authority [1991] RTR 389; (1991) 135 SJ LB 99; [1991] TLR 352 CA Ambulance authority not negligent in failing to inform passenger of need for/availability of seat-belts.

Elliot v Chiew (1966) 110 SJ 724 CA Owner of-passenger in car could not claim damages where friend-driver involved in non-negligent single car accident which resulted in injury to driver.

Ellor and Wife v Selfridge and Co, Limited (1930) 74 SJ 140; (1929-30) XLVI TLR 236; (1930) WN (I) 45 HC KBD Is prima facie evidence of negligence where motor van by being on pavement causes injury to persons there.

Frank v Cox (1967) 111 SJ 670 CA Pedestrian struck by motorist crossing road when lights for motor traffic were red was not contributorily negligent; on awarding personal injury damages to the elderly.

Franklin v Bristol Tramways and Carriage Co, Ltd [1941] 1 All ER 188; [1941] 1 KB 255; (1942) 92 LJ 59; [1941] 110 LJ 248 CA Contributory negligence where pedestrian (in black-out conditions) did not keep look-out for overtaking traffic.

Freeborn v Thomas [1975] RTR 16 HC QBD Front seat passenger without seat belt not guilty of contributory negligence as regards injuries suffered in accident.

Froom and others v Butcher [1974] 3 All ER 517; (1975) 125 NLJ 843t; [1974] RTR 528; (1974) 118 SJ 758; [1974] 1 WLR 1297 HC QBD No negligence if person acting on reasonably held belief drove without seat belt.

Garston Warehousing Co Ltd v OF Smart (Liverpool) Ltd [1973] RTR 377 CA Van driver driving too fast on wet November morning and ignoring warnings from another driver was two-thirds liable for resultant collision at city crossroads.

Gates v R Bill and Son [1902] 2 KB 38; [1902] 71 LJCL 702; (1902-03) LXXXVII LTR 288; (1901-02) 46 SJ 498; (1901-02) 50 WR 546 CA Unlicensed proprietor of taxi cab could be sued for negligence of driver.

Gaynor v Allen [1959] 2 All ER 644; [1959] Crim LR 786; (1959) 123 JP 413; (1959) 109 LJ 441; [1959] 2 QB 403; (1959) 103 SJ 677 HC QBD Police motorcyclist owes duty of care in negligence though driving at speed in course of duty.

Geeves v London General Omnibus Company (Limited) (1900-01) XVII TLR 249 CA On appropriate direction as regards negligence/contributory negligence where passenger who consented to bus starting was injured when bus started.

Genys v Matthews and another [1965] 3 All ER 24; (1966) 110 SJ 332; [1966] 1 WLR 758 Ct of Passage Free bus pass exception clause did not preclude liability of driver in negligence.

Gillingham v Harris (1949) 99 LJ 416 CyCt Person using major road enjoys no 'right of the road'.

Gleed v Simpkins [1945] LJNCCR 156 CyCt On duty on cattle-owner when driving cattle onto highway after nightfall.

Goke v Willett and another (1973) 123 NLJ 274t; [1973] RTR 422 CA Liability in negligence where failed to give hand-signal when about to undertake dangerous turn.

Gough v Thorne [1966] 3 All ER 398; (1966) 110 SJ 529; [1966] 1 WLR 1387 CA Driver waving child to cross negligent if child struck despite failing to check for overtaking traffic.

Grange Motors (Cwmbrian) Ltd v Spencer and another [1969] 1 All ER 340; (1969) 119 NLJ 154t; (1968) 112 SJ 908; [1969] 1 WLR 53 CA On duty of care owed by one driver signalling to another.

Green v Bunce [1936] LJNCCR 349 CyCt Lorry driver negligent where failed to apply brakes when swerving to avoid pedestrian and so ended up driving onto pavement, there striking the plaintiff.

Gregory v Kelly (1978) 128 NLJ 488t; [1978] RTR 426 HC QBD Plaintiff-passenger/defendant-driver 40%/60% liable for injuries/losses arising from collision when travelling in car (plaintiff without seat belt) in car without footbrake: defendant precluded statutorily from pleading volenti non fit injuria.

Gussman v Grattan-Storey (1968) 112 SJ 884 CA Valid finding that person was better to drive on and possibly kill pheasant than to stop and so (negligently) endanger following traffic.

Haimes v Watson [1981] RTR 90 CA Horse rider not negligent where collision occurred after horse shied.

Hale v Hants and Dorset Motor Services, Ltd and another (1948) 112 JP 47 CA On liability of highway authority/omnibus driver for injury to upstairs passenger on omnibus struck by overhanging branches of tree.

Hannam v Mann [1984] RTR 252 CA Motorcyclist who momentarily took eye off road (75%) contributorily negligent as regards collision with unlit car parked within 15 yards of junction (owner of car 25% liable).

Hardy v Walder [1984] RTR 312 CA Motorcyclist (two-thirds) and driver (one-third) liable for collision where former drove too fast/overtook at blind corner and latter did not stop/look before turning from minor on to main road.

Hargrove v Burn (1929-30) XLVI TLR 59 HC KBD On law of negligence as applied to traffic accident actions.

Harris v Thompson [1938] LJNCCR 69 CyCt Person driving uninsured vehicle could recover damages in negligence against person with whom collided even though should not have been driving uninsured vehicle on road (as was not causative factor).

Harrison v Vincent and others [1982] RTR 8 CA Ordinary standard of care applied where defect in sports motor vehicle was workshop defect; volenti non fit injuria inapplicable where person claimed as being subject to doctrine unaware of facts presenting risk.

Hase v The London General Omnibus Company (Limited) (1906-07) XXIII TLR 616 HC KBD Not negligent of bus driver to turn bus close to kerb and so occasion injury to upstairs passenger struck by small obstruction avoidable by wider turn.

Hay (or Bourhill) v Young [1942] 2 All ER 396; [1942] 111 LJ 97; (1943) 93 LJ 108; (1942) 167 LTR 261; (1942) 86 SJ 349; [1943] AC 92 HL Tortfeasor in motor vehicle collision not liable to bystander for nervous shock as not reasonably foreseeable.

Haydon v Kent County Council (1978) 142 JP 349; [1978] QB 343; (1977) 121 SJ 849; [1978] 2 WLR 485 CA Failed attempt by pedestrian injured by slipping on snowy path to prove highway authority had been negligent in giving priority to salting/sanding/gritting of highway rather than of paths.

Haynes v Harwood [1934] 2 KB 240; (1934) 103 LJCL 410; (1934) 151 LTR 135; (1934) 78 SJ 384; (1933-34) L TLR 371; (1934) WN (I) 106 HC KBD Natural result of one's negligence cannot be novus actus interveniens; person leaving horses in street owes duty of care to safeguard persons using highway (including police officer chasing after bolting horse).

Haynes v Harwood (G) and Son [1934] All ER 103; [1935] 1 KB 146; (1934) 77 LJ 340; (1934) 78 LJ 323; (1935) 152 LTR 121; (1934) 78 SJ 801; (1934-35) LI TLR 100; (1934) WN (I) 208 CA Natural result of one's negligence cannot be novus actus interveniens; person leaving horses in street owes duty of care to safeguard persons using highway (including police officer chasing after bolting horse): no volenti non fit injuria by highway users.

Heng (Chop Seng) v Thevannasan son of Sinnapan and others [1975] 3 All ER 572; [1976] RTR 193 PC Bad parking does not raise presumption of negligence; reasonable foreseeability of collision necessary.

Henley v Cameron (1948) 98 LJ 657; [1949] 118 LJR 989; (1949) LXV TLR 17; (1948) WN (I) 468 CA Apportionment of liability for negligent leaving of unlighted car in highway at night (a nuisance) and negligence of person who collided with same for not seeing it.

Hilder v Associated Portland Cement Manufacturers, Ltd [1961] 3 All ER 709; [1955] Crim LR 725; (1961) 111 LJ 757 HC QBD Not wearing crash helmet not negligent; occupier of green on which children played owed duty to take reasonable steps to prevent injury.

Hill v Phillips and another (1963) 107 SJ 890 CA Driver negligent in that did not anticipate unlit obstruction (broken down trailer) but trailer owner equally negligent in manner in which left trailer on road.

Hill v Stafford (1984) 134 NLJ 264 HC QBD Successful negligence action by person's administratrix against other party to fatal road traffic collision where latter suffered amnesia but balance of probabilities indicated had been to blame.

Hill-Venning v Beszant [1950] 2 All ER 1151; (1950) 94 SJ 760; [1950] 66 (2) TLR 921; (1950) WN (I) 538 CA Leaving unlit motorbike on road at night was negligent.

Hoadley v Dartford District Council and another [1979] RTR 359; (1979) 123 SJ 129 CA No reduction in damages for person not wearing seat belt where no requirement that vehicle have seat belts and it did not in fact have seat belts.

Holdack v Bullock Bros (Electrical), Ltd and another; Martens (third party) (1964) 108 SJ 861 HC QBD Overtaker one-third liable for not sounding horn as overtook; person being overtaken two-thirds liable for not seeing overtaker/for changing course while being overtaken.

Holdack v Bullock Brothers (Electrical), Ltd, and another (Martens Third Party) (1965) 109 SJ 238 CA Was reasonable for trial judge to hold that overtaker ought to have sounded horn though was no general requirement that had to do so.

Homewood and another v Spiller (Hodder, third party) [1963] Crim LR 52; (1962) 106 SJ 900 CA Dotted white lines on approach to junction did not alter duty of care owed by motorists.

Hopwood Homes Ltd v Kennerdine [1975] RTR 82 CA Driver not contributorily negligent in assuming oncoming traffic travelling at such speed that could stop when lights changed.

Howard v Bemrose [1973] RTR 32 CA Parties to accident to which there was no witness properly blamed equally given the circumstances.

Howard v Pickfords, Ltd (1935) 79 SJ 69 HC KBD Driver not negligent where child sitting on running board of van without permission was injured when driver began driving.

Hummingbird Motors Ltd v Hobbs [1986] RTR 276 CA No misrepresentation/breach of warranty where sold second-hand car to another in bona fide but mistaken belief that odometer reading correct.

Humphrey and another v Leigh and another [1971] RTR 363 CA Driver on main road not required to take precaution of taking foot from accelerator and placing above brake as approached/passed side-road.

Hunter v Wright [1938] 2 All ER 621 CA Driver not responsible for consequences of non-negligent skid.

Hurlock v Inglis (1963) 107 SJ 1023 HC QBD Person driving at high speed was negligent in assumption that when overtaking another that other would properly observe rules of the road.

Hurt v Murphy [1971] RTR 186 HC QBD Speeding driver/unvigilant pedestrian 80%/20% liable for collision at pedestrian crossing; husband's damages for loss of wife's services based on costs of keeping a daily help.

Hutchins v Maunder (1920-21) XXXVII TLR 72 HC KBD Placing car on highway in condition where by virtue of defective steering it posed danger to other highway users was negligent even though unaware of defect.

Ironfield v Eastern Gas Board [1964] 1 All ER 544; (1964) 108 SJ 691; [1964] 1 WLR 1125 HC QBD Excess insurance and 'no claims bonus' recoverable as special damages.

Isaac Walton and Co v The Vanguard Motorbus Co (Limited); Gibbons v The Vanguard Motorbus Co (Limited) (1908) 72 JP 505; (1908-09) 53 SJ 82; (1908-09) XXV TLR 13 HC KBD Bus striking permanent structure (in first case) could be due to negligence of driver (and in second case) was negligent use of nuisance placed on highway.

J Sargent (Garages) Ltd v Motor Auctions (West Bromwich) Ltd and another [1977] RTR 121 CA Person giving car/log book to another who wrongfully sold it not estopped — even if negligent — from denying latter's authority to sell; damages set at price plaintiffs had expected to sell (what was a special) car.

James v Audigier (1931-32) XLVIII TLR 600; (1932) WN (I) 181 HC KBD On appropriate questions which may be put to driver in 'running down' case.

James v Audigier (1932) 74 LJ 407; (1932-33) XLIX TLR 36; (1932) WN (I) 250 CA Dismissal of appeal over questions that were asked in running-down case over earlier accident in which defendant involved.

James v Durkin (Civil Engineering Contractors) Ltd [1983] TLR 383 HC QBD Damages in successful negligence claim by estate of deceased driver reduced by 50% in light of contributory negligence of deceased.

James v Parsons (1974) 124 NLJ 1029t; [1975] RTR 20; (1974) 118 SJ 777 HC QBD Front seat passenger without seat belt not guilty of contributory negligence as regards injuries suffered in accident absent warning from driver of need to wear belt.

Jaundrill v Gillett (1996) TLR 30/1/96 CA Horse-owner not liable to driver injured in collision with horses that were on public highway following malicious release by third party onto same.

Jeffery v Smith (1970) 120 NLJ 272t; [1970] RTR 279; (1970) 114 SJ 268 CA On appropriate damages in negligence for loss to husband of services of wife killed in motor accident.

Jeffrey v Fisher (1982) 132 NLJ 490 CA Colleague struck by another who was driving stolen bus found not to have been contributorily negligent.

Jones and another v Dennison [1971] RTR 174 CA Presumption that epileptic involved in collision after blacked out obviated by his proving that did not know/could not reasonably have known was prone to black-outs.

Joseph Eva, Ltd v Reeves [1938] 2 All ER 115; (1938) 102 JP 261; [1938] 2 KB 393; (1938) 85 LJ 242; [1938] 107 LJCL 569; (1938) 82 SJ 255; (1937-38) LIV TLR 608; (1938) WN (I) 140 CA Driver entitled to assume there is no traffic breaking the lights.

Jungnickel v Laing and others (1967) 111 SJ 19 CA To reduce one's driving speed without warning was not negligent.

Karavias v Callinicos (1917) WN (I) 323 CA Successful action for damages for personal injuries suffered as result of negligence of defendant when giving plaintiff a free ride in his car.

Kaye v Alfa Romeo (Great Britain) Ltd and another (1984) 134 NLJ 126 HC QBD Car company deemed two-thirds liable for personal injuries arising at least in part from defective seat belt mechanism.

Kean and another v Boulton (1963) 107 SJ 872 HC QBD Court directions as to agreed damages for infant injured as consequence of negligent driving.

Kemp v Elisha (1918) 82 JP 81; [1918] 1 KB 229; [1918] 87 LJCL 428; (1918) 118 LTR 246; (1917-18) 62 SJ 174; (1917) WN (I) 365 CA Entry as proprietor in Scotland Yard's hackney carriage licence register not uncontrovertible.

Kensington Borough Council v Walters [1960] Crim LR 62; (1959) 103 SJ 921; [1959] 3 WLR 945 HC QBD On expeditious recovery by local authority (pursuant to London Government Act 1939, s 181(3)) of damages for costs incurred by it following road traffic accident.

Kerley and another v Downes [1973] RTR 188 CA Not contributory negligence for pedestrian not to walk on footpath but to walk instead on near side of road.

Klein v Caluori [1971] 2 All ER 701; (1971) 121 NLJ 153; [1971] RTR 354; (1971) 115 SJ 228; [1971] 1 WLR 619 HC QBD Owner not vicariously liable where person who borrowed car without permission returning it under owner's instructions.

Knight v Fellick [1977] RTR 316 CA Motorist found not negligent where (on dark morning as was following other car) struck workman who must have stepped/fallen off pavement leaving no scope for evasive action by motorist.

Knight v Sampson [1938] 3 All ER 309; (1938) 86 LJ 9 HC KBD No negligence/breach of statute if motorist strikes person stepping onto crossing when motor vehicle within very short distance thereof.

Knight v Wiper Supply Services, Ltd and another (1965) 109 SJ 358 HC QBD On appropriate damages for above the knee amputee injured after went through green light by person turning from side-road..

Lancaster v HB and H Transport Ltd and another [1979] RTR 380 CA Articulated lorry driver found completely to blame for collision with car occurring when drove lorry across foggy, wet dual carriageway.

Lang v London Transport Executive and another [1959] 3 All ER 609; (1960) 124 JP 28; (1959) 109 LJ 685; [1959] 1 WLR 1168 HC QBD Driver on major road contributorily negligent for collision with driver emerging from minor road where did not check minor road as passing.

Latchford v Spedeworth International Ltd (1984) 134 NLJ 36; [1983] TLR 587 HC QBD Successful negligence claim by hot-rod racer for injury suffered where tyres on track after another's collision with tyre fence forced him into collision with concrete flower bed.

Launchbury and others v Morgan and others [1971] 1 All ER 642; (1971) 121 NLJ 83t; [1971] 2 QB 245; [1971] RTR 97; (1971) 115 SJ 96; [1971] 2 WLR 602 CA Owner vicariously liable for negligence of third party driving car.

Lawrence v WM Palmer (Excavations), Ltd, and another (1965) 109 SJ 358 HC QBD Two-third/ one-third apportionment of liability between driver/deaf pedestrian for accident at pedestrian crossing.

Leaver v Pontypridd Urban District Council (1911) 75 JP 25 CA Not enough evidence of negligence for matter to go to jury where tram driver did not stop tram when confronted by obstruction.

Leaver v Pontypridd Urban District Council (1910) 74 JP 199 HC KBD Was sufficient evidence of negligence for matter to go to jury where tram driver did not stop tram when confronted by obstruction.

Leaver v Pontypridd Urban District Council (1912) 76 JP 31; (1911-12) 56 SJ 32 HL Was evidence of negligence such that matter should go to jury where tram driver did not stop tram when confronted by obstruction.

Lee v Lever [1974] RTR 35 CA Parties equally liable where negligent driver collided with unlit car left parked at night on well-lit clearway.

Lertora v Finzi [1973] RTR 161 HC QBD Failed attempt to prove injured driver contributorily negligent as regards injuries suffered when not wearing seat belt.

Levine and another v Morris and another [1970] 1 All ER 144; (1970) 134 JP 158; (1969) 119 NLJ 947t; (1969) 113 SJ 798; [1970] RTR 93; [1970] 1 WLR 71 CA In choosing road signs Ministry owes duty not to unduly endanger motorists.

Lewis v Ursell [1983] TLR 282 HC QBD Collision of motor car with gateway an accident that occurred owing to presence of that vehicle on road within meaning of the Road Traffic Act 1972, s 8(2).

Lewys v Burnett and Dunbar and another [1945] 2 All ER 555 HC KBD Persons giving free lift negligent for not warning dead passenger of what they knew; highway authority liable in nuisance for negligent raising of road beneath bridge.

Liffen v Watson (1939) 161 LTR 351; (1939) 83 SJ 871 HC KBD Taxi-driver was negligent where could not explain why had braked and skidded when knew was likely to skid when so braked.

Lloyds Bank Ltd (Administrators of the Estate of Peter Lewis Hughes, deceased) v Budd and others [1982] RTR 80 CA Was negligent to drive defective lorry onto fog-covered motorway but person who occasioned greatest damage in pile-up was most liable as had been driving excessivley fast in fog.

London Electric Supply Corporation, Ltd v Alexander [1942] LJNCCR 49 CyCt Failed action in negligence/trespass against driver who struck lamp post after swerved to avoid dog on road.

Ludlam v Peel (WE) and Sons (1939) 83 SJ 832 CA Competent drover who took reasonable care not liable for collision between motor vehicle and cow being driven along road.

MacIntyre v Coles [1966] 1 All ER 723; (1966) 130 JP 189; (1965-66) 116 NLJ 611; (1966) 110 SJ 315; [1966] 1 WLR 831 CA On yielding at junctions (and consequent negligence).

Madden v Quirk [1989] RTR 304; (1989) 133 SJ 752; [1989] 1 WLR 702 HC QBD Apportionment of liability as regards truck driver whose dangerous driving resulted in injury to person whom had been carrying in open rear.

Maher v Hurst and others (1969) 113 SJ 167 CA Lorry driver/owners, not roadworkers liable for injury which occurred when lorry driver drove through fast through area of roadworks.

Maitland v Raisbeck [1944] 2 All ER 272; [1944] KB 689; (1945) 95 LJ 112; [1944] 113 LJ 549; (1944) 171 LTR 118; (1944) 88 SJ 359; (1943-44) LX TLR 521; (1944) WN (I) 195 CA That rear light of lorry not on did not necessarily make lorry a nuisance.

Malfroot and another v Noxall, Limited (1935) 79 SJ 610; (1934-35) LI TLR 551 HC KBD Fitter of side-car to motor-cycle liable in contract and tort to owner of same and in tort to passenger in same for negligent fitting which resulted in car becoming detached from cycle during use and consequent injury.

Marney v Campbell Symonds and Company, Limited and Others (1946) 175 LTR 283; (1946) 90 SJ 467 HC KBD Company liable for negligence of employee driving requisitioned motor-car.

Martin v Dean and another (1971) 121 NLJ 904; [1971] 3 All ER 279; [1971] 2 QB 208; [1971] RTR 280; (1971) 115 SJ 369; [1971] 2 WLR 1159 HC QBD Judgment debt (arising from negligence action) available against motor bicycle-owner as well as bicycle-driver.

Martin v Stanborough (1923-24) 68 SJ 739; (1923-24) XL TLR 557 HC KBD Was prima facie evidence of negligence to leave parked car with defective brakes on steep hill with only a piece of wood to stop it rolling forwards.

Martin v Stanborough (1924) CC Rep XIII 85; (1924) 59 LJ 680; (1924-25) 69 SJ 104; (1924-25) XLI TLR 1 CA Was negligence to leave parked car with defective brakes on steep hill with only a piece of wood to stop it rolling forwards.

Maynard and another v Rogers [1970] RTR 392 HC QBD Person stepping on to uncontrolled pedestrian crossing without looking in either direction was contributorily negligent but driver also negligent in not yielding to person on uncontrolled pedestrian crossing.

McAll v Brooks [1984] RTR 99; [1983] TLR 115 CA Person unaware of any possible illegaliy in car-replacement agreement with insurance company could recoup reasonable costs of replacement from person responsible for collision which necessitated replacement.

McCready v Miller [1979] RTR 186 CA On duty of care owed by minicab driver towards passengers.

McGee v Francis Shaw and Co Ltd [1973] RTR 409 HC QBD Person choosing not to wear seat belt one-third liable for injuries suffered in accident; no damages for being not being presented because of injury with chance to work abroad.

McKenna v Scottish Omnibuses Ltd and Northumberland County Council (1984) 134 NLJ 681 HC QBD Bus company, not highway authority liable for personal injuries suffered when bus slid on black ice (winter hazard of which driver should have known/which highway authority not here under duty to remove).

McLeod v Receiver of the Metropolitan Police and another [1971] Crim LR 364 HC QBD Damages for collision arising out of negligent driving by police officer en route to emergency.

McNeill and another v Johnstone [1958] 3 All ER 16; (1958) 108 LJ 570; (1958) 102 SJ 602 HC QBD Husband allowed recover portion of expenses incurred through month's leave of absence from work to be near wife.

Miller v Evans and another; Pouleuf (Third Party) [1975] RTR 70 CA Driver not contributorily negligent in assuming oncoming traffic travelling at such speed that could stop when lights changed.

Moore (an infant) v Poyner (1974) 124 NLJ 1084t; [1975] RTR 127 CA On duty of care owed by Sunday driver in residential area to children playing in area.

Moore v Maxwells of Emsworth, Ltd and another [1968] 2 All ER 779; (1968) 118 NLJ 373t; (1968) 112 SJ 424; [1968] 1 WLR 1077 CA Negligence presumption rebutted if show took all reasonable steps to avoid cause of action.

Morales (an infant) v Eccleston [1991] RTR 151 CA Child (75%) negligent and driver (25%) contributorily negligent where child struck when ran onto busy road after football without looking.

Mottram v South Lancashire Transport Co [1942] 2 All ER 452; (1943) 93 LJ 109; (1942) 86 SJ 321 CA Bus conductress not negligent in not policing dismounting of passengers.

Mulligan v Holmes; Yorkshire Bank Ltd v Holmes [1971] RTR 179 CA Driver (80%) liable and pedestrians at studded crossing (20%) liable for collision where former driving too fast/latter not maintaining proper look-out.

Nettleship v Weston [1971] 3 All ER 581; (1971) 121 NLJ 592t; [1971] 2 QB 691; [1971] RTR 425; (1971) 115 SJ 624; [1971] 3 WLR 370 CA Learner-/drivers owe duty to drive with reasonable care/skill; instructor contributorily negligent where learner in accident; volenti non fit injuria only where unqualified express/implied renunciation of any right to claim.

Newberry v Bristol Tramway and Carriage Company (Limited) (1912-13) 107 LTR 801; (1912-13) 57 SJ 172; (1912-13) XXIX TLR 177 CA Tram company not liable for freak injury to passenger where had adopted best practice to avoid injury.

Norwood v Navan [1981] RTR 457 CA Husband-car owner not vicariously liable for wife-provisional licence holder's unsupervised driving as she was not acting as his agent/servant.

O'Connell v Jackson [1971] 3 All ER 129; (1971) 121 NLJ 618t; [1972] 1 QB 270; [1972] RTR 51; (1971) 115 SJ 742; [1971] 3 WLR 463 CA Person contributing to injury but not to accident is contributorily negligent.

Oliver and another v Birmingham and Midland Motor Omnibus Co, Ltd [1932] All ER 820; [1933] 1 KB 35; (1932) 74 LJ 80; (1933) 102 LJCL 65; (1932) 147 LTR 317; (1931-32) XLVIII TLR 540; (1932) WN (I) 156 HC KBD Infant not so identified with grandfather with whom crossing road that grandfather's negligence precluded infant from recovering.

Ormrod and another v Crosville Motor Services, Ltd and another (Murphie, Third Party) [1953] 1 All ER 711; (1953) 97 SJ 154; [1953] 1 WLR 409 HC QBD Car owner vicariously liable for negligence of driver acting at owner's behest.

Ormrod and another v Crosville Motor Services, Ltd and another (Murphie, Third Party) [1953] 2 All ER 753; (1953) 103 LJ 539; (1953) 97 SJ 570; [1953] 1 WLR 1120 CA Car owner vicariously liable for negligence of friend when driving car entirely/partly for owner.

Page v Smith [1995] 2 All ER 736; [1996] 1 AC 155; (1995) 145 NLJ 723; [1995] RTR 210; (1995) 139 SJ LB 173; [1995] TLR 275; [1995] 2 WLR 644 HL Negligent driver liable to primary victim for nervous shock if personal injury reasonably foreseeable as result of accident even if no physical injury.

Page v Smith [1996] 3 All ER 272; (1994) 144 NLJ 756; [1994] TLR 240; [1996] 1 WLR 855 CA Negligent driver not liable to primary victim for nervous shock though personal injury reasonably foreseeable as result of accident.

Parker v Miller (1925-26) XLII TLR 408 CA That car ran down hill when unattended was per se evidence of negligence for which person enjoying right of control over car was liable.

Parkinson and another v Parkinson [1973] RTR 193 CA Not contributory negligence for pedestrians to walk on left hand side of road.

Parkinson v Liverpool Corporation [1950] 1 All ER 367; (1950) 114 JP 146; (1950) 94 SJ 161; [1950] 66 (1) TLR 262; (1950) WN (I) 43 CA Sharp braking to avoid accident resulting in passenger injury not negligent.

Parnell v Metropolitan Police District Receiver [1976] RTR 201 CA No evidence proving that minibus driver had been travelling too close to preceding vehicle/had not seen in time that preceding vehicle stopping.

Parnell v Shields [1973] RTR 414 HC QBD Person deemed one-fifth liability for (fatal) injury through collision where had not been wearing seat belt.

Patel v Edwards [1970] RTR 425 CA On respective liabilities of cyclist pulling to right infront of stationary car and motor-cyclist overtaking car and colliding with cyclist.

Patience v Andrews and another [1983] RTR 447; [1982] TLR 574 HC QBD Damages reduced by 25% where passenger injured in collision not wearing seat-belt.

Phillips v Britannia Hygienic Laundry Company, Limited [1923] 1 KB 539; (1923) CC Rep XII 28; [1923] 92 LJCL 389; (1923) 128 LTR 690; (1922-23) 67 SJ 365; (1922-23) XXXIX TLR 207; (1923) WN (I) 47 HC KBD Apportionment of liability for motor car with hidden defect.

Phillips v Britannia Hygienic Laundry Company, Limited [1924] 93 LJCL 5; (1922-23) XXXIX TLR 530 CA Regulations concerning use and construction of motor cars did not create personal remedy against repairers who returned car with latent defect which meant car did not comply with regulations.

Powell v Moody (1966) 110 SJ 215 CA Party overtaking stationary vehicles on offside was 80% liable for collision which occurred with car emerging from sideroad.

Powell v Phillips [1972] 3 All ER 864; (1973) 137 JP 31; (1972) 122 NLJ 681t; (1972) 116 SJ 713; [1973] RTR 19 CA Highway Code violation does not establish negligence.

Prescott v Lancashire United Transport Co, Ltd [1953] 1 All ER 288; (1953) 117 JP 80; (1953) 97 SJ 64; [1953] 1 WLR 232 CA Conductor on stopped bus liable for not warning passenger not to alight before proper stop reached or preventing passenger alighting/bus re-starting.

Pryce v Elwood (1964) 108 SJ 583 HC QBD No deduction for income tax for damages payable for loss of trading profits suffered by plaintiff car hirer as reult of collision occasioned by defendant.

Pui (Ng Chun) and others v Tat (Lee Chuen) and another [1988] RTR 298; (1988) 132 SJ 1244 PC Plaintiff must still prove negligence though relying on res ipsa loquitur claim; driver not too be judged by too severe a standard when acting in emergency (here driver acted reasonably).

Quinn v Scott and another [1965] 2 All ER 588; (1965) 109 SJ 498; [1965] 1 WLR 1004 HC QBD Occupier negligent in not felling decaying tree bordering highway whose fall resulted in traffic collision.

Radburn v Kemp [1971] 3 All ER 249; (1971) 121 NLJ 618t; [1972] RTR 92; (1971) 115 SJ 711; [1971] 1 WLR 1502 CA No unqualified right to enter junctions upon green light; owe duty of care on entering junction to persons already there.

Radley and another v London Passenger Transport Board [1942] 1 All ER 433; (1942) 106 JP 164; (1943) 93 LJ 109; (1942) 166 LTR 285; (1942) 86 SJ 147; (1941-42) LVIII TLR 364 HC KBD Driver liable in negligence for injury to passenger caused by failure to avoid obstructions (bus clipped trees as drove along).

Rambarran v Gurrucharran [1970] 1 All ER 749; (1970) 120 NLJ 128t; [1970] RTR 195; (1970) 114 SJ 244; [1970] 1 WLR 556 PC Presumption that if using other's motor vehicle are their agent/servant is rebuttable.

Rees v Saville [1983] RTR 332; [1983] TLR 235 CA Seller of second-hand car liable for latent defect in car to buyer who relied on apparent good condition of car and recent MOT test as proof of roadworthiness.

Reichardt v Shard (1913-14) XXX TLR 81 HC KBD Owner of car could be liable for son's negligent driving thereof even though son accompanied by owner's chauffeur.

Reichardt v Shard (1914-15) XXXI TLR 24 CA Owner of car could be liable for son's negligent driving thereof even though son accompanied by owner's chauffeur.

Richley v Faull (Richley, Third Party) [1965] 3 All ER 109; (1965) 129 JP 498; (1965) 115 LJ 609; (1965) 109 SJ 937; [1965] 1 WLR 1454 HC QBD Severe unexcused skid is per se evidence of negligence.

Rivers v Cutting [1982] 3 All ER 69; [1982] Crim LR 525; [1983] RTR 105; (1982) 126 SJ 362; [1982] TLR 213; [1982] 1 WLR 1146 CA Police not vicariously liable for acts of contractor employed to remove broken-down/abandoned vehicle.

Rogers v Night Riders (a firm) and others [1983] RTR 324 CA Mini-cab firm liable for negligent maintenance of car by driver (whether latter an employee/independent contractor).

Rothwell v Davies Brothers (Haulage), Ltd and another [1963] Crim LR 577; (1963) 107 SJ 436 CA Heavy goods vehicle driver 25% liable/car driver 75% liable for collision which occurred where latter distracted former while driving.

Ruoff v Long and Co (1915) CC Rep IV 94; (1916) 80 JP 158; [1916] 1 KB 148; (1915) 50 LJ 546; [1916] 85 LJKB 364; (1916) 114 LTR 186; (1915-16) 60 SJ 323; (1915-16) XXXII TLR 82 HC KBD Non-liability of person leaving lorry on highway for unexpected act of third party.

Samson v Aitchison [1911-13] All ER 1195; [1912] AC 844; (1912-13) 107 LTR 106 PC Owner of vehicle riding in it while driven by another retains control and is liable for driver's negligence.

Saper v Hungate Builders Ltd and others; King v Hungate Builders Ltd and others [1972] RTR 380 HC QBD Presence of poorly lit skip negligent/a nuisance but person who drove into it found contributorily negligent (40%).

Saville v Bache and another (1969) 119 NLJ 226t; (1969) 113 SJ 228; CA Person driving with undipped headlights (and who failed to explain why) held one-third liable for accident which resulted from his lights dazzling another driver.

Scarsbrook and others v Mason [1961] 3 All ER 767; (1961) 111 LJ 726; (1961) 105 SJ 889 HC QBD Passenger sharing costs of trip but not knowing driver liable for driver's negligence as driver acting as agent.

Service v Sundell (1930) 99 LJCL 55; (1928-29) XLV TLR 569; (1929) WN (I) 182 HC KBD No judgment for either side where jury could not decide which party's negligence led to motor collision/personal injuries.

NEGLIGENCE (road traffic)

Service v Sundell (1929) 68 LJ 314; (1929) WN (I) 241 CA No judgment for either side where jury could not decide which party's negligence led to motor collision/personal injuries.

Setchell v Snowdon and another [1974] RTR 389 CA In circumstances car-owner not liable in negligence towards girl injured when learner driver to whom had given car-keys (so that latter and girl could sit in car) drove car despite specifically promising would not.

Shaw v BG Services and Evans [1939] LJNCCR 226 CyCt Failed action in negligence against driver against whom it was alleged that should not have continued to drive van (which was eventually blown over) in windy weather.

Shepherd v West (H) and Son, Ltd, and another (1962) 106 SJ 391 HC QBD Lorry driver liable in negligence where overtook stationary bus at traffic lights changing to green and struck pedestrian.

Shepphard v Devon County Council (1980) 130 NLJ 14 CA Reversal of trial judge's finding that council were liable in negligence where school bus was driven over foot of boy who had jumped off the bus.

Shotter v Gould (1928) 66 LJ ccr8 CyCt Not defence in personal injuries action brought by motor cycle pillion passenger against car driver following accident that motor cycle driver had been contributorily negligent.

Simon v The London General Omnibus Company (Limited) (1906-07) XXIII TLR 463 HC KBD Not negligent where passenger struck by obstruction as bus rounded corner as not proven driver could reasonably have seen obstruction/have foreseen it would injure passenger.

Smith and another v Blackburn (1974) 124 NLJ 524t; [1974] RTR 533 HC QBD Not wearing seat belts not contributory negligence where collided with person driving in wrong direction on one-way road at speed.

Smith v Harris [1939] 3 All ER 960; (1939) 83 SJ 730 CA Equal blame apportioned between motorcyclists involved in collision.

Smith v Samuel Williams and Sons (1972) 122 NLJ 217t HC QBD Failed action for damages on foot of road traffic accident as causation of plaintiff's injuries by defendant's negligence not proved.

Snow v Giddins (1969) 113 SJ 229 CA Pedestrian deemed 25% negligent where in accident occasioned when crossed road at point where was no pedestrian crossing/central refuge.

Southern Railway Company v Gosport Corporation (1926) 135 LTR 630 CA Corporation liable for negligent damage to bridge effected by temporary servant in charge of steam-roller which corporation had hired.

Spenser v H Sinclair and Son [1934] LJNCCR 96 CyCt Was good cause for negligence action by owner of fence damaged by person who repeatedly skidded when out driving.

Stewart v Hancock [1940] 2 All ER 427; (1940) 89 LJ 221; (1940) 84 SJ 440; (1939-40) LVI TLR 572; (1940) WN (I) 141 PC No presumption of negligence where driver collides with unlit obstruction on highway.

Stuart v Rees (1965) 109 SJ 358 HC QBD Immaterial why person driving at night did not see person with whom collided until was too late: was guilty of negligence.

Sudds v Hanscombe [1971] RTR 212 CA Person entering junction after lights red/green was/was not (as had behaved reasonably in circumstances) negligent.

Swadling v Cooper [1930] All ER 257; [1931] AC 1; (1930) 70 LJ 108; (1931) 100 LJCL 97; (1930) 143 LTR 732; (1930) 74 SJ 536; (1929-30) XLVI TLR 597; (1930) WN (I) 204 HL On direction regarding negligence in case where person knocked down in motor collision.

Tan Chye Choo and others v Moi (Chong Kew) [1970] 1 All ER 266; (1969) 113 SJ 1000; [1970] 1 WLR 147 PC No right of action where defect in vehicle not result of negligence.

Tart v Chitty (GW) and Co, Ltd [1931] All ER 826; [1933] 2 KB 453; (1933) 102 LJCL 568; (1933) 149 LTR 261 HC KBD Contributory negligence where driving so fast could not avoid collision or were not keeping proper look-out.

Taylor v Whittle (1931) 72 LJ ccr39 CyCt Other negligent party to road traffic collision could not plead contributory negligence of husband-driver as defence to action brought against him by wife-passenger.

The City of Birmingham Tramways Company Limited v Law (1910) 74 JP 355; [1910] 2 KB 965; (1911) 80 LJCL 80; (1910-11) 103 LTR 44 HC KBD Lessees of tramway could recover compensation paid from party who had contracted with lessor to relay tramway/indemnify lessor for related claims.

Thompson v Spedding [1973] RTR 312 CA On duty/liability of various drivers where 'tailing' each other as drive along road.

Thrower v Thames Valley and Aldershot Bus Co Ltd [1978] RTR 271 CA Precautionary measures plaintiff suggested bus company should have taken were unrealistic: plaintiff failed to establish collision arose from negligence of bus company.

Tingle Jacobs and Co (a firm) v Kennedy [1964] 1 All ER 888; (1964) 108 SJ 196; [1964] 1 WLR 638 CA Traffic lights presumed to be working properly unless contrary evidence.

Tocci v Hankard and another (1966) 110 SJ 835 CA Overtaking when passing side road deemed not to be negligent.

Toperoff v Mor [1973] RTR 419 HC QBD Front-seat passenger not wearing seat belt deemed one-quarter liable for injuries suffered.

Topp v London Country Bus (South West) Ltd [1993] 3 All ER 448 (also CA); [1992] RTR 254; [1991] TLR 552 HC QBD No duty of care by crime victim to victim of accident during criminal act arising from crime victim's negligence.

Topp v London Country Bus (South West) Ltd [1993] 3 All ER 448 (also HC QBD); [1993] RTR 279; (1993) 137 SJ LB 59; [1993] TLR 71; [1993] 1 WLR 976 CA No duty of care by crime victim to victim of accident during criminal act arising from crime victim's negligence.

Toronto Railway Company v King and another [1908-10] All ER 1439; (1908) XCVIII LTR 650 PC That man crossed road at point trams required to run slowly did not establish contributory negligence on man's part when struck by tram.

Tremayne v Hill [1987] RTR 131 CA Pedestrian not contributorily negligent where did not keep look-out when crossing junction at which vehicle traffic lights red.

Trinder v Great Western Railway Company (1918-19) XXXV TLR 291 HC KBD Bus company not liable for injury to passenger on upper level hit by tree which had been cut back by company and where driver not negligent/company unaware was overhanging tree.

Tuey v Clarke [1940] LJNCCR 31 CyCt Driver liable in negligence for colliding with cyclist during black-out even though cyclist did not have required red rear-light as driver not going at such speed that could pull up to avoid collision.

Tysoe v Davies [1983] Crim LR 684; [1984] RTR 88; [1983] TLR 434 HC QBD Were (80%) to blame for accident arising directly from driving with thick clouds of smoke coming from exhaust; person with whom collided (20%) liable for not keeping proper look-out notwithstanding smoke.

Vandyke v Fender and another (Sun Insurance Office Ltd, third party) [1970] 2 All ER 335; (1970) 120 NLJ 250t; [1970] 2 QB 292; [1970] RTR 236; [1970] 2 WLR 929 CA Employers liable for negligence of/not eligible for indemnity from employee acting as agent in using their car to drive fellow employee to work at their request.

Verney v Wilkins [1962] Crim LR 840; (1962) 106 SJ 879 HC QBD That have not complied with driving licence requirements does not of itself mean are guilty of negligence.

Vernon v Bosley [1997] 1 All ER 577; (1996) 146 NLJ 589; (1997) 141 SJ LB 27; [1997] RTR 1; (1996) TLR 4/4/96 CA Damages available for mental illness (stemming from another's negligence) attributable in part to grief and bereavement.

Vincent v Hickman [1936] LJNCCR 320 CyCt Dangerous parking of car in contravention of Road Traffic Act 1930, s 50, meant were guilty of breach of statutory duty for which person injured in consequence could recover damages.

Wagner v West Ham Corporation (1920-21) XXXVII TLR 86 HC KBD Tram owners not liable for tram being started on passenger's prompting (unless conductor's not prompting was negligent).

Waller v Levoi (1968) 118 NLJ 1004t; (1968) 112 SJ 865 CA Driver who parked car on bend in road was 20% liable for injuries suffered by careless motorcyclist who leaped from bike to avoid colliding with car.

Walsh v Redfern and another [1970] RTR 201 HC QBD Person on main road to give way to person on minor road if necessary to avoid accident; lorry driver not contributorily negligent where was driving at reasonable speed on main road and collided with car emerging from minor road without paying heed to warning signs.

Ward v London County Council [1938] 2 All ER 341; (1938) 85 LJ 310; (1938) 82 SJ 274 HC KBD Fire engine driver bound by traffic light regulations.

Ward v Wallach [1937] LJNCCR 86 CyCt Where bolt connecting car and trailer simply fell out there was a presumption of negligence which person owning car/trailer which became detatched was required to rebut.

Wardell-Yerburgh v Surrey County Council [1973] RTR 462 HC QBD Emergency vehicle driver (here one-third liable for collision which occurred) owes that duty of care to public which regular driver owes.

Waring v Kenyon and Co (1927) Limited [1935] LJNCCA 155; (1935) 79 SJ 306 CA Valid finding that person injured in collision between car (in which was passenger) and parked, unlit lorry.

Watkins v Moffatt and others [1970] RTR 205 CA Driver on main road not contributorily negligent where collided with driver suddenly emerging from side road without paying heed to warning signs.

Watson v Heslop [1971] RTR 308; (1971) 115 SJ 308 CA Negligent to park car in narrow, busy road at night; negligent not to have slowed down as soon as dazzled by oncoming lights.

Watson v Thomas S Whitney and Co, Ltd and another [1966] 1 All ER 122; (1966) 130 JP 109; (1966) 110 SJ 73; [1966] 1 WLR 57 CA Person walking near to kerb not contributorily negligent when struck by vehicle.

Werry v Andrew (1951) 101 LJ 289 CyCt Successful plea by motor cycle rider against cattle-owner whose workers acted negligently when driving cattle from field onto highway so causing accident involving motor cyclist.

West v Hughes of Beaconsfield Ltd and another [1971] RTR 298 HC QBD On liabilities of van driver and following car for injuries to cyclist whom former knocked down and latter ran over (latter act not novus actus interveniens).

Western Scottish Motor Traction Company, Limited v Fernie (or Allam) and others [1943] 2 All ER 742; (1944) 94 LJ 109; (1943) 87 SJ 399; (1943-44) LX TLR 34; (1943) WN (I) 223 HL Omnibus operators liable for negligence of driver who rounded corner so quickly that a passenger was thrown from the bus and killed.

Wilkie (Arthur Reginald) v London Passenger Transport Board [1946] 1 All ER 650 HC KBD Exemption clause on free pass applied to free passholder injured as getting on bus; pass a privilege/licence so Road Traffic Act 1930, s 97 inapplicable as no contract for conveyance.

Wilkie v London Passenger Transport Board [1947] 1 All ER 258; (1947) 111 JP 98; [1947] 116 LJR 864; (1947) LXIII TLR 115 CA Free travel pass a licence not contract for conveyance so exception clause applied.

Williams and another v Luff (1978) 122 SJ 164 HC QBD Duty of care owed towards child en ventre sa mére injured in road traffic collision.

Williams v Needham [1972] RTR 387 HC QBD Driver partly liable for collision as did not take precautionary steps when saw pedestrian who had not looked in his direction about to cross road.

Williamson v Tomlinson (1933) 76 LJ ccr6 CyCt Lorry driver negligent as did not drive with additional carefulness expected of driver of large vehicle.

Wills v TF Martin (Roof Contractors) Ltd [1972] RTR 368; (1972) 122 NLJ 81t; (1972) 116 SJ 145 HC QBD Placing skip on highway not proven negligent and though a nuisance person who collided with same, not skip-owner was liable.

Wing v London General Omnibus Company Limited (1909) 73 JP 170; (1909) C LTR 301; (1908-09) 53 SJ 287 HC KBD Recovery of damages for personal injuries sustained by passenger when bus skidded (not proved that passenger knew of/had accepted risk of skidding).

Wing v London General Omnibus Co [1908-10] All ER 496; (1909) 73 JP 429; [1909] 2 KB 652; [1909] 78 LJKB 1063; (1909-10) 101 LTR 411; (1908-09) 53 SJ 713; (1908-09) XXV TLR 729 CA Skidding not per se evidence of negligent driving; on res ipsa loquitur; Rylands v Fletcher applies to unnatural user of highway for traffic.

Winnipeg Electric Company v Geel (Jacob) [1932] AC 690; (1932) 101 LJPC 187; (1933) 148 LTR 24; (1931-32) XLVIII TLR 657 PC Matter for jury whether motor vehicle owner has negatived presumption of negligence under Manitoban law where motor vehicle injures another.

Wintle v Bristol Tramways and Carriage Company Limited (1917) 81 JP 55; [1917] 86 LJCL 240; (1917) 116 LTR 125; (1916-17) 61 SJ 183; (1917) WN (I) 7 HC KBD Though only required to have one lamp by statute driving petrol lorry in instant circumstances with one lamp was negligent.

Wintle v Bristol Tramways and Carriage Company Limited (1917) 52 LJ 188; [1917] 86 LJCL 936; (1917-18) 117 LTR 238; (1917) WN (I) 163 CA Though only required to have one lamp by statute driving petrol lorry in instant circumstances with one lamp could be negligent.

Wood v Clements and Mears (1982) 132 NLJ 141 CA Apportionment of liability for accident arising through interrelated actions involving four vehicles, two stopped on bend in road.

Wooller v London Transport Board and another [1976] RTR 206 CA That single passenger thrown to floor did not mean bus driver negligent in travelling too close to lorry in front and having to brake suddenly when lorry braked so as to avoid collision.

Worsfold v Howe [1980] 1 All ER 1028; (1980) 130 NLJ 140; [1980] RTR 131; (1980) 124 SJ 646; [1980] 1 WLR 1175 CA Contributory negligence where collision between motorcyclist on main road and driver edging from lesser road.

Worsley v Hollins and another (1991) 141 NLJ 425t; [1991] RTR 252; [1991] TLR 153 CA Full service undertaken/MoT certificate issued six weeks/one month before collision negatived presumption of res ipsa loquitur.

Wragg v Grout and London Transport Board (1965-66) 116 NLJ 752t CA Bus driver/company not liable for injuries sustained by passenger on bus where fell because camber of road suddenly changed.

Wright v Hearson (1916) 51 LJ 284; (1916) WN (I) 216 HC KBD Counsel for plaintiff in personal injuries action arising from allegedly negligent driving by defendant ought not to have asked latter if was insured.

Wright v Lodge and another; Kerek v Lodge and others [1993] 4 All ER 299; (1992) 142 NLJ 1269; [1993] RTR 123 CA Negligent driver not liable for acts of reckless driver.

Youde v Chester Corporation [1934] LJNCCR 44 CyCt Matter at issue deemed to be res judicata in second negligence action arising from road traffic incident; could not plead were not at all negligent and that other was contributorily negligent.

Young v Chester [1973] RTR 319 HC QBD Seeking to start car broken down on carriageway with self-starter (which dimmed/extinguished lights) was negligent in that obviated warning to others of presence but so was other's driving too fast with dimmed lights.

Young v Chester [1974] RTR 70 CA Seeking to start car broken down on carriageway with self-starter (which dimmed/extinguished lights) was negligent in that obviated warning to others of presence.

NEGLIGENCE (school)

Abbott v Isham and others (1921) 85 JP 30; [1921] LJCL 309; (1921) 124 LTR 734; (1920-21) XXXVII TLR 7 HC KBD Successful action against school managers for personal injuries suffered by headmaster when defective boiler burst.

Affutu-Nartoy v Clarke and another [1984] TLR 47 HC QBD Was negligent for schoolteacher to participate in rugby football game with students (injuring student through tackle in the process).

Barnes (an infant suing by Leslie Frederick Barnes her next friend) v Hampshire County Council (1969) 133 JP 733; (1969) 119 NLJ 948t; (1969) 113 SJ 834; [1969] 1 WLR 1563 HL School had been negligent in letting children out of school early (by virtue of which act injury to child occurred).

Barnes (an infant) v Hampshire County Council (1968) 112 SJ 599 CA School not negligent in letting children out of school early (by virtue of which act injury to child occurred).

Barnes v London Borough of Bromley (1984) 134 NLJ 312; [1983] TLR 678 HC QBD Teacher one-third negligent for injuries he suffered in use of defective school equipment.

Beaumont v Surrey County Council (1968) 118 NLJ 541t; (1968) 112 SJ 704 HC QBD School were negligent in leaving discarded elastic cord in area so that unsupervised pupils playing with the cord caused injury to the plaintiff.

Black v Kent County Council [1983] TLR 373 CA Failed appeal against successful personal injuries claim by seven year old who stabbed himself in the eye when his chair was moved during art class at Kent County Council-run school.

Camkin v Bishop and another [1941] 2 All ER 713; (1941) 91 LJ 295; (1942) 92 LJ 60; (1941) 165 LTR 246 CA Non-supervision of schoolboys helping farmer not negligence.

Ching v Surrey County Council [1908-10] All ER 305; (1910) 74 JP 187; [1910] 1 KB 737; (1910) 79 LJKB 481; (1910) 102 LTR 414; (1910) WN (I) 74 CA School liable to pupil injuring self on negligently maintained playground.

Ching v Surrey County Council (1909) 73 JP 441; [1909] 2 KB 762; (1909) 100 LTR 940 HC KBD Local education authority could be liable to pupil injuring self on negligently maintained playground.

Clark v Monmouthshire County Council and others (1954) 118 JP 244 CA Schoolmasters not liable for unintended personal injury arising from scuffle between boys, one of whom had knife, as did not involve failure by teachers to maintain reasonable control over boys.

Fryer v Salford Corporation and another (1937) 101 JP 263; (1937) 81 SJ 177 CA Education authority liable for reasonably foreseeable/preventable accident which occurred to girl during school cookery class.

Gibbs v Barking Corporation [1936] 1 All ER 115 CA Education authority liable for injury to boy during PT class whom teacher did not assist.

Jefferey v London County Council (1955) 119 JP 45 HC QBD School not liable for fatal after-hours playground injury to child waiting to be collected.

Langham v Governors of Wellingborough School and Fryer (1932) 96 JP 236; (1932) 73 LJ 361; (1932) 101 LJCL 513; (1932) 147 LTR 91 CA Not negligent/no res ipsa loquitur where school pupil struck by golf ball that other pupil hit from door into schoolground.

Lewis v Carmarthenshire County Council (1953) 117 JP 231 Assizes Teacher owed duty of care to child straying onto highway/person foreseeably injured as result.

Lewis v Carmarthenshire County Council [1953] 2 All ER 1403; (1954) 118 JP 51; (1953) 103 LJ 797; (1953) 97 SJ 831; [1953] 1 WLR 1439 CA Teacher owed duty of care to child straying onto highway/person foreseeably injured as result.

Lyes v Middlesex County Council (1963) 113 LJ 348 HC QBD Education authority liable in negligence for injury to pupil who slipped and put hand through glass in door.

Martin v Middlesbrough Corporation (1965) 109 SJ 576 CA Corporation liable for injury caused to pupil who fell on piece of glass in school playground.

Morris v Carnarvon County Council (1910) 74 JP 201 (also CA); [1910] 1 KB 159; (1909) 44 LJ 783; (1910) 79 LJKB 169; (1909-10) 101 LTR 914; (1909-10) XXVI TLR 137; (1909) WN (I) 263 HC KBD Local education authority liable for negligent injury suffered by child going through door on teacher's instruction.

Morris v Carnarvon County Council (1910) 74 JP 201 (also HC KBD); [1910] 1 KB 840; (1910) 45 LJ 268; (1910) 79 LJKB 670; (1910) 102 LTR 524; (1909-10) 54 SJ 443; (1909-10) XXVI TLR 391; (1910) WN (I) 94 CA Local education authority liable for negligent injury suffered by child going through door on teacher's instruction.

Nwabudike (a minor) v London Borough of Southwark (1996) 140 SJ LB 128 HC QBD Failed claim in negligence against school which took all reasonable steps to ensure child did not run out onto road (as happened).

Ralph v London County Council (1947) 111 JP 246; (1947) 91 SJ 221; (1947) LXIII TLR 239 HC KBD Council liable in negligence for injury suffered by child in course of supervised game in assembly hall (council failed to take steps that reasonably cautious father would have taken).

Ralph v London County Council (1947) 111 JP 548; (1947) LXIII TLR 546 CA Council liable in negligence for injury suffered by child in course of supervised game in assembly hall (council failed to take steps that reasonably cautious father would have taken).

Rich and another v London County Council [1953] 2 All ER 376; (1953) 117 JP 353; (1953) 97 SJ 472; [1953] 1 WLR 895 CA School owes duty of responsible parent towards pupils.

Ricketts v Erith Borough Council and another [1943] 2 All ER 629; (1944) 108 JP 22; (1944) 94 LJ 108; [1944] 113 LJ 269; (1943) 169 LTR 396 HC KBD Bow and arrow not dangerous thing so no duty on seller; absence of teacher from school playground during breaktime not negligent.

Shepherd v Essex County Council and another (1912-13) XXIX TLR 303 HC KBD On duty owed by school teacher to pupils.

Smith v Martin and the Mayor, &c, of Kingston-upon-Hull (1911) 75 JP 135; (1911-12) 105 LTR 281; (1910-11) XXVII TLR 165 HC KBD Non-liability of local authority for (non-teaching) act of teacher (who was personally liable) resulting in injury to student.

Smith v Martin and the Corporation of Kingston-upon-Hull (1911) 75 JP 433; [1911] 2 KB 775; (1911) 80 LJCL 1256; (1910-11) XXVII TLR 468 CA Local authority liable for (non-teaching) act of teacher (who was also liable) resulting in injury to student.

Van Oppen v Clerk to the Bedford Charity Trustees [1989] 1 All ER 273; (1988) 138 NLJ 221 HC QBD No duty of care on schools to insure pupils against sports injuries/advise parents on dangers of particular sports.

Van Oppen v Clerk to the Bedford Charity Trustees (1989) 139 NLJ 900; [1990] 1 WLR 235 CA School not liable in negligence for not insuring school rugby players against accidental injury/for not advising parents on risks rugby posed to players and desirability of insurance against same.

Ward v Hertfordshire County Council (1969) 133 JP 514; (1969) 119 NLJ 272t; (1969) 113 SJ 343; [1969] 1 WLR 790 HC QBD Local education authority liable at common law for failure to adequately protect schoolchildren from reasonably foreseeable risk when playing in schoolyard before school hours.

Woodward and another v Mayor of Hastings and other [1944] 2 All ER 565; (1945) 109 JP 41; [1945] 114 LJ 211 (also HC KBD); (1944-45) LXI TLR 94 CA Grammar school governors not public authority/were liable for caretaker's negligence.

Woodward and another v Mayor of Hastings and others [1944] 2 All ER 119; [1945] KB 174; (1944) 108 JP 247; [1944] KB 671; (1945) 95 LJ 111; [1945] 114 LJ 211 (also CA); (1944) 171 LTR 231; (1943-44) LX TLR 404 HC KBD Suing school governors subject to public authority limitation.

Wray v Essex County Council (1936) 82 LJ 296; (1936) 155 LTR 494; (1936) 80 SJ 894 CA Oil can not inherently dangerous: failed negligence action arising from loss of eye occasioned by one pupil running into spout of oil can being carried by another pupil under teacher's instructions to certain part of school.

Wright v Cheshire County Council [1952] 2 All ER 789; (1952) 116 JP 555; (1952) 102 LJ 581; (1952) 96 SJ 747; [1952] 2 TLR 641; (1952) WN (I) 466 CA Test of reasonable care in sports activities is what is customary practice.

NEGLIGENCE (shipowner)

Arthur Guinness, Son and Co (Dublin) Ltd v SS Freshfield (Owners) and others; The Lady Gwendolen (1964) 108 SJ 524 HC PDAD Shipowner liable for negligence of shipmaster.

Arthur Guinness, Son and Company (Dublin) Ltd v The Freshfield (Owners) and others; The Lady Gwendolen (Limitation) (1965) 109 SJ 336; [1965] 3 WLR 91 CA Duty of person whose secondary business is that of shipowner is same as that of shipowner for whom is principal business.

NEGLIGENCE (shipping)

Admiralty Commissioners v North of Scotland and Orkney and Shetland Steam Navigation Co, Ltd [1947] 2 All ER 350 HL Overtaking ships equally negligent in causing collision.

Admiralty Commissioners v Volute (Owners); The Volute [1921] All ER 193 HL Collision where negligent failure by second ship to avoid consequences of first ship's negligence blamed partly on first ship's negligence.

Anglo-Saxon Petroleum Co, Ltd and others v Damant; Anglo-Saxon Petroleum Co, Ltd and others v Regem [1947] 2 All ER 465; [1947] KB 794; (1947) WN (I) 197 CA Action for negligence of salvor lies in tort; salvor owes duty to take reasonable care to ensure possible plaintiff not injured.

Australian Steam Shipping Co (Limited) v Devitt and others (1916-17) XXXIII TLR 178 HC KBD Failed action by persons who commissioned steamship against management committee of Lloyd's Register for certifying ship as being of certain class when apparently was not.

Carsholm (Owners) v Calliope (Owners); The Calliope [1970] 2 WLR 991 HC PDAD Finding of negligence on one hand and intervening negligence on other in shipping collision case.

Cawood, Wharton and Company, Limited v Samuel Williams and Sons, Limited; The Cawood III [1951] 1 TLR 924 HC PDAD Jetty owners liable for damage to lighter notwithstanding presence of exemption clause.

Compania Mexicana de Petroleo 'El Aguila' v Essex Transport and Trading Company Limited (1929) 141 LTR 106 CA On respective liabilities of shipowners/stevedores in negligence where injury sustained through negligent loading of dangerous substances.

Dee Conservancy Board and others v McConnell and another (1928) 97 LJCL 487; (1928) WN (I) 60 CA Abandonment of wreck sunk through negligence did not preclude liability for expenses of removing same.

Ellerman Lines, Limited v H and G Grayson, Limited [1919] 2 KB 514; [1919] 88 LJCL 904; (1919) 121 LTR 508; (1918-19) XXXV TLR 492 CA Ship-repairers liable for own negligence.

Forbes, Abbott, and Lennard, Limited v Great Western Railway Company [1927] 96 LJCL 995; (1926-27) XLIII TLR 769 HC KBD Chelsea Dock-owners liable for negligence of their servants notwithstanding attempt to exempt liability by way of exemption clause.

Forbes, Abbott, and Lennard Limited v Great Western Railway Company (1928) 138 LTR 286 CA Chelsea Dock-owners not liable for negligence of their servants by virtue of exemption clause in their by-laws.

Fowles v The Eastern and Australian Steamship Company (Limited) (1916-17) 115 LTR 354; (1915-16) XXXII TLR 663 PC Queensland government not liable for negligence of shipping pilots it provided.

Gaselee v Darling; The Millwall [1904-07] All ER 1387 CA Tow owners liable to tug owners.

H and C Grayson, Limited v Ellerman Line, Limited [1920] AC 466; [1920] 89 LJCL 924; (1920) 123 LTR 65; (1919-20) XXXVI TLR 295; (1920) WN (I) 87 HL Shipowners not liable for negligence of ship-repairers.

Hodgson v British Arc Welding Company, Limited and Others (1946) 174 LTR 379 HC KBD Shipwrights not sub-contractors liable for injury to sub-contractor's employee.

Jones v Oceanic Steam Navigation Company, Limited (1924-25) 69 SJ 106; (1923-24) XL TLR 847 HC KBD Construction of contract of passage (failed attempt at precluding liability for injuries to passenger).

Lind v Mitchell (1928-29) XLV TLR 54 CA Recovery of damages where negligence of ship's master resulted in loss of ship.

Mitsui and Co Ltd and another v SA (Flota Mercante Grancolombiana) (1988) 132 SJ 1182; [1988] 1 WLR 1145 CA Shipowner liable in tort in respect of goods damaged on board ship only to owner of goods at time were damaged.

Morris v West Hartlepool Steam Navigation Co, Ltd [1956] 1 All ER 385; (1956) 100 SJ 129 HL Non-closure of hatch of hold through which party fell was negligent.

Norton v Canadian Pacific Steamships, Ltd [1961] 2 All ER 785; (1961) 111 LJ 484; (1961) 105 SJ 442 CA Shipowners not liable for negligence of porter not in any way connected to them other than carrying ship luggage.

Owners of the SS Chittagong v Owners of the SS Kostroma [1901] AC 597 PC Negligent failure to take action when other ship continued in dangerous course.

Page and Co v Darling Brothers and Gaselee and Son; The Millwall [1905] 74 LJP 13 HC PDAD Tow owners liable to tug owners.

Samuel Williams and Sons (Limited) and William Christie and Co (Limited) v Parsons and Parsons (1908-09) XXV TLR 569 HC KBD Wharfingers responsible for canal management liable in negligence for damage caused to barge by sluices being opened and water lowered too far.

Samuel Williams and Sons (Limited) and William Christie and Co (Limited) v Parsons and Parsons (1909-10) 54 SJ 64; (1909-10) XXVI TLR 78 CA Wharfingers responsible for canal management not liable in negligence for damage caused to barge by sluices being opened and water lowered too far.

Smitton v The Orient Steam Navigation Company (Limited) (1906-07) 51 SJ 343; (1906-07) XXIII TLR 359 HC KBD Carrier owed reasonable duty of care towards articles remaining in personal care of passengers (but if not their value was undeclared so Merchant Shipping Act 1894, s 502(ii) applied).

Tarrant v Ramage and others [1997] TLR 434 HC QBD Shipowners must take reasonable care of crew members on ship operating in war zone.

Taylor (J) and Sons, Limited v Union-Castle Mail Steamship Company, Limited (1931-32) XLVIII TLR 249 HC KBD Shipowners not liable for not warning that in course of carriage castor seed had been mixed with maize (thus rendering latter unsuitable for animal feed).

The Ballyalton; Owners of Steamship Ballyalton v Preston Corporation [1961] 1 All ER 459 HC PDAD Harbour authority liable in negligence for failure to adequately supervise berths but were covered by exception clause.

The East London Harbour Board v The Caledonia Landing, Shipping, and Salvage Company (Limited) and The Colonial Fisheries Company (Limited) (1907-08) XXIV TLR 516 PC Harbour board liable for not re-securing tug and coal hulk which had previously moved.

The Snark (1899-1900) XVI TLR 160 CA Owners of sunken barge liable for negligent marking of sunken barge by independent contractor whom they employed.

The Towerfield; Owners of the SS Towerfield v Workington Harbour and Dock Board [1948] 2 All ER 736 CA On negligence/contributory negligence under Pilotage Act 1913/Harbours, Docks, and Piers Clauses Act 1847.

The Vectis (1928-29) XLV TLR 384 HC PDAD Common law principles of negligence applicable in Admiralty action arising from collision.

Wickett v Port of London Authority [1929] 1 KB 216; (1929) 98 LJCL 222; (1928) 138 LTR 668 HC KBD Dock authority exemption clause applicable where injury sustained by person on barge being assisted into London docks by authority servants.

Wilson, Sons and Co, Lim v Barry Railway [1917] 86 LJCL 432 CA Absent concealed danger warehouse-owners not liable to another's employee present as licensee on their premises.

NEGLIGENCE (solicitor)

Aslan v Clintons (a firm) (1984) 134 NLJ 584 HC QBD Solicitor not under duty to warn client who ought to (and did) know that would face successful suit in contract if proved unable to do what contracted self into doing.

Buckland v Farmar and Moody (a firm) (1978) 128 NLJ 365t CA Failed action for alleged negligence on part of firm of solicitors.

NEGLIGENCE (sport)

Bolton and others v Stone [1951] 1 All ER 1078; [1951] AC 850; (1951) 101 LJ 287; (1951) 95 SJ 333; [1951] 1 TLR 977; (1951) WN (I) 280 HL Non-liability where ball from cricket game struck person on highway as foreseeable but negligible risk.

Cleghorn v Oldham (1927) 63 LJ 498; (1926-27) XLIII TLR 465; (1927) WN (I) 147 HC KBD Golfer liable in negligence where struck girl acting as caddie when demonstrating golf stroke to another.

Condon v Basi [1985] 2 All ER 453; (1985) 135 NLJ 485; (1985) 129 SJ 382; [1985] 1 WLR 866 CA Duty of care owed by one sports participant to another.

Conrad v Inner London Education Authority (1965-66) 116 NLJ 1630t; (1967) 111 SJ 684 CA Judo teacher not liable in negligence for injury suffered by first-time judo participant acting on his instructions.

McCord v Swansea City AFC Ltd and another [1997] TLR 64 HC QBD Football player could be liable in negligence for injuries occasioned to another player during football match.

Miller and another v Jackson and another [1977] 3 All ER 338; (1977) 127 NLJ 568t; [1977] QB 966; (1977) 121 SJ 287; [1977] 3 WLR 20 CA Cricket balls emanating from village cricket ground a negligent act.

Morrell v Owen and others [1993] TLR 645 HC QBD On extent of duty of care owed by sports organisers towards persons taking part in disabled persons sports event.

Murray and another v Harringay Arena, Ltd (1951) 95 SJ 123; (1951) WN (I) 38 HC KBD No negligence on part of event-holders where spectator was hit by puck at ice hockey match.

Murray and another v Harringay Arena, Ltd [1951] 2 All ER 320; [1951] 2 KB 529; (1951) 101 LJ 48; (1951) 95 SJ 529; (1951) WN (I) 356 CA No negligence/breach of implied contract/ inadequacy of safety measures/unusual danger in spectator being hit by puck at ice hockey match.

Simms v Leigh Rugby Club, Ltd [1969] 2 All ER 923; (1969) 119 NLJ 649 Assizes Rugby player accepts risks of rugby/pitch conforming to Rugby League specifications; occupier not liable for foreseeable but unlikely events.

Stone v Bolton and others [1949] 1 All ER 237 Assizes Single incident not nuisance; cricket-playing not unnatural land user (Rylands v Fletcher inapplicable); cricket-ball inadvertently striking person on highway not negligent.

Stone v Bolton and others [1949] 2 All ER 851; [1950] 1 KB 201; (1949) 99 LJ 625; (1949) LXV TLR 683; (1949) WN (I) 432 CA Cricket ball flying from ground to highway was negligent/not nuisance.

Tutin v Mary Chipperfield Promotions Ltd (1980) 130 NLJ 807 HC QBD Defendant liable in negligence/under Animals Act 1971 for injury plaintiff suffered when participating in camel race organised by defendants.

Van Oppen v Clerk to the Bedford Charity Trustees [1989] 1 All ER 273; (1988) 138 NLJ 221 HC QBD No duty of care on schools to insure pupils against sports injuries/advise parents on dangers of particular sports.

Van Oppen v Clerk to the Bedford Charity Trustees (1989) 139 NLJ 900; [1990] 1 WLR 235 CA School not liable in negligence for not insuring school rugby players against accidental injury/for not advising parents on risks rugby posed to players and desirability of insurance against same.

White v Blackmore and others [1972] 3 All ER 158; (1972) 122 NLJ 561t; [1972] 2 QB 651; (1972) 116 SJ 547; [1972] 3 WLR 296 CA Volenti non fit injuria inapplicable to motor racecourse visitor injured through race organisers' shortcomings; exclusion clause valid.

Wilks and another v Cheltenham Homeguard Motor Cycle and Light Car Club and another (1971) 115 SJ 127 HC QBD Motor cycle race participant owes duty of care to spectators not to be reckless; race organisers not liable for injuries which could not reasonably have foreseen/ prevented.

Wilks (formerly an infant) and another v The Cheltenham Home Guard Motor Cycle and Light Car Club and another [1971] 2 All ER 369; (1971) 121 NLJ 272t; (1971) 115 SJ 309; [1971] 1 WLR 668 CA Motor cycle race participant owes duty of care to spectators not to be reckless; accident occurring not res ipsa loquitur.

Wooldridge v Sumner and another [1962] 2 All ER 978; (1962) 112 LJ 520; [1963] 2 QB 43; (1962) 106 SJ 489 CA Sports participant not liable in negligence to viewing public injured through non-reckless errors of judgment; volenti non fit injuria not relevant.

NEGLIGENCE (stevedore)

Chapman or Oliver and Another v Saddler and Company and Others [1929] AC 584; (1929) 67 LJ 362; (1929) 98 LJPC 87; (1929) 141 LTR 305; (1928-29) XLV TLR 456; (1929) WN (I) 130 HL Stevedore firm liable to porter injured by defective sling.

Denny v Supplies and Transport Co Ld, and others [1950] 2 KB 374; (1950) 94 SJ 403; [1950] 66 (1) TLR 1168; (1950) WN (I) 294 CA Liability of stevedores for injury sustained by wharfingers' employee in unloading dangerously loaded barge.

Grant v Sun Shipping Co, Ltd and others [1948] 2 All ER 238; [1948] AC 549 HL Stevedore could recover damages from shipowner/repairers where repairers negligently left hatch open.

Karuppan Bhoomidas (Administrator of the Estate of Veeranan S/O Solayappan, dec) v Port of Singapore Authority [1978] 1 WLR 189 PC Port authority liable for injury to stevedore by fellow stevedore.

Treadaway v Dike and Ramsgate Corporation (1967) 117 NLJ 888t HC QBD Crane driver from crane hire company (but not employing stevedores) liable for negligent injury to employee of stevedores.

Williams v Port of Liverpool Stevedoring Co, Ltd and another [1956] 2 All ER 69; [1956] 1 WLR 551 Assizes Liability of employer for negligence of stevedoring gang and of member of gang for own part in own injury.

NEGLIGENCE (stockbroker)

Briggs v Gunner and another (1979) 129 (1) NLJ 116 HC ChD Failed action against stockbroker for allegedly negligent advice rendered.

Merrill Lynch Futures Inc v York House Trading Ltd and another [1984] TLR 340 CA That stockbroker made losses on stock market not per se evidence that stockbroker negligent.

Paul E Schweder and Co v Walton and Hemingway (1910-11) XXVII TLR 89 HC KBD Non-recovery for losses country broker incurred on sale of shares (without consulting clients) following advice from their agent, a London stockbroker firm.

NEGLIGENCE (surgery)

Emeh v Kensington and Chelsea and Westminster Area Health Authority and others (1983) 133 NLJ 352; [1985] QB 1012; (1984) 128 SJ 705; [1984] TLR 484; [1985] 2 WLR 233 CA Damages recovered for birth of child following negligent sterilisation operation.

G v North Tees Health Authority [1989] FCR 53 HC QBD Successful action for damages after hospital negligently mis-diagnosed child's vaginal discharge as having sperm present.

Harrington v Essex Area Health Authority [1984] TLR 632 HC QBD Claim for surgical negligence failed where court could not choose between alternative explanations of situation preferred.

Hendy v Milton Keynes Health Authority [1991] TLR 125 HC QBD On when limitation period began to run in surgical negligence personal injury action.

Hocking v Bell (1948) WN (I) 21 PC Successful action against negligent surgeon.

Moser v Enfield and Haringey Area Health Authority (1983) 133 NLJ 105 HC QBD On appropriate damages for negligently performed minor operation that rendered infant boy brain-damaged quadriplegic.

Thake and another v Maurice [1984] 2 All ER 513; (1985) 129 SJ 86/894; [1984] TLR 225; [1985] 2 WLR 215 HC QBD Absent warning a guarantee of successful vasectomy arose; failure to warn of possible future pregnancies a warranty of completely successful vasectomy; damages for costs of birth and of rearing child ordered.

Thake and another v Maurice [1986] 1 All ER 497; (1986) 136 NLJ 92; [1986] QB 644; [1986] 2 WLR 337 CA Absent express guarantee no guarantee that medical operation will be success; failure to warn of possible future pregnancies a failure of duty of care; damages for distress/pain/ suffering caused by pregnancy/birth available.

Whiteford v Hunter (1950) 94 SJ 758; (1950) WN (I) 553 HL Surgeon found not to be negligent in his mis-diagnosis of patient's ailment.

NEGLIGENCE (taxi)

King v Phillips [1953] 1 All ER 617; (1953) 103 LJ 153; [1953] 1 QB 429 CA No duty of care owed by taxi-driver tipping child with taxi for shock sustained by mother viewing incident from over two hundred deet away.

NEGLIGENCE (tree)

Mackie v Western District Committee of Dumbartonshire County Council (1927) 91 JP 158; (1927) 64 LJ 160; (1927) 71 SJ 710; (1927) WN (I) 247 HL Was actionable issue where alleging that council which had disturbed roots of tree had been negligent in not safeguarding public from danger of tree falling (as eventually occurred).

NEGLIGENCE (trespass)

Excelsior Wire Rope Company, Limited v Callan and others [1930] All ER 1; [1930] AC 404; (1930) 94 JP 174; (1930) 69 LJ 218; (1930) 99 LJCL 380; (1930) 142 LTR 531; (1930) WN (I) 55 HL Liable in negligence for injury to child trespasser where knew was probable that children would be near when dangerous machine operated.

Robert Addie and Sons (Collieries), Limited v Dumbreck [1929] AC 358; (1929) 140 LTR 650; (1928-29) XLV TLR 267 HL Non-liability towards child killed by dangerous machine while trespassing.

NEGLIGENCE (underwriter)

Brown v KMR Services Ltd [1995] 4 All ER 598 CA Underwriting agent owes investor duty to provide proper information on character and risk of business underwritten; loss arising from failure to do so is measured by probable happening if proper advice given; liability is for foreseeable loss irrespective of scale; advice not ongoing: set-off against profits from earlier advice not possible.

NEGLIGENCE (vicarious liability)

Watkins v City of Birmingham (1976) 126 NLJ 442b CA On relationship necessary before milk distributors could be vicariously liable for actions of milk deliverers.

NERVOUS SHOCK (damages)

Alcock and others v Chief Constable of South Yorkshire Police [1992] 1 AC 310 (also CA/HL); [1991] 2 WLR 814 HC QBD Damages available/unavailable for nervous shock caused by injury or risk thereof to another when person shocked watched event on live television/heard of incident on radio and was told of it another but did not see television pictures until some while later.

Alcock and others v Chief Constable of South Yorkshire Police [1992] 1 AC 310 (also HC QBD/HL); [1991] TLR 226 CA Damages unavailable for nervous shock caused by injury/risk thereof to another when person shocked watched event on live television/heard it on radio.

Alcock and others v Chief Constable of the South Yorkshire Police [1991] 4 All ER 908; [1992] 1 AC 310 (also HC QBD/CA); (1992) 136 SJ LB 9; [1991] TLR 547; [1991] 3 WLR 1057 HL Damages unavailable for nervous shock caused by injury/risk thereof to another when person shocked watched event on live television/heard it on radio.

Jones and others v Chief Constable of South Yorkshire (1990) 140 NLJ 1717 HC QBD Damages available to parents/siblings for nervous shock; said damages available when watched live television event in which child/fellow sibling injured.

Jones and others v Wright [1991] 3 All ER 88; (1991) 141 NLJ 635 CA Rebuttable presumption of love between spouse/parent of injured person can arise in relation to other relative/friend if similarly loving relationship with injured at time of injury; proximity requirement for nervous shock cases brought by relations/spouses of victim not satisfied through hearing of event on live television/radio nor visit to morgue if victim killed.

Jones and others v Wright (1991) 141 NLJ 1661 HL Basis on which may recover damages for nervous shock suffered as result of apprehension of physical injury or danger thereof to another.

NERVOUS SHOCK (general)

Alcock and others v Chief Constable of South Yorkshire Police [1992] 1 AC 310 (also CA/HL); [1991] 2 WLR 814 HC QBD Damages available/unavailable for nervous shock caused by injury or risk thereof to another when person shocked watched event on live television/heard of incident on radio and was told of it another but did not see television pictures until some while later.

Alcock and others v Chief Constable of South Yorkshire Police [1992] 1 AC 310 (also HC QBD/HL); [1991] TLR 226 CA Damages unavailable for nervous shock caused by injury/risk thereof to another when person shocked watched event on live television/heard it on radio.

Alcock and others v Chief Constable of the South Yorkshire Police [1991] 4 All ER 908; [1992] 1 AC 310 (also HC QBD/CA); (1992) 136 SJ LB 9; [1991] TLR 547; [1991] 3 WLR 1057 HL Damages unavailable for nervous shock caused by injury/risk thereof to another when person shocked watched event on live television/heard it on radio.

Boardman and another v Sanderson and another (Keel and Block, Third Party) (1961) 105 SJ 152; [1964] 1 WLR 1317 CA Were liable to father who could hear negligent injury to child for shock suffered by father in consequence.

Chadwick v British Railways Board (1967) 111 SJ 562 HC QBD Administratix of rescuer's estate allowed recover damages for shock suffered by rescuer at scene of accident occasioned by defendant's negligence.

Chadwick v British Transport Commission [1967] 2 All ER 945; [1967] 1 WLR 912 HC QBD Damages for nervous shock to rescuer at accident scene.

Dulieu v White and Sons [1900-03] All ER 353; [1901] 2 KB 669; [1901] 70 LJK/QB 837; (1901-02) LXXXV LTR 126; (1900-01) 45 SJ 578; (1900-01) XVII TLR 555; (1901-02) 50 WR 76 HC KBD Damages recoverable where nervous shock followed by physical injury.

Frost and others v Chief Constable of South Yorkshire [1995] TLR 379 HC QBD On recovery of damages for nervous shock by professional rescuers.

Hambrook v Stokes Brothers [1924] All ER 110; [1925] 1 KB 141; (1924) 59 LJ 740; [1925] 94 LJCL 435; (1925) 132 LTR 707; (1924-25) XLI TLR 125; (1924) WN (I) 296 CA Recovery for mental shock where feared for one's children not oneself.

Hevican v Ruane [1991] 3 All ER 65; (1991) 141 NLJ 235 HC QBD Damages for nervous shock after son's injury despite third party relaying of news as each stage in relay foreseeable; damages available for unforeseeably severe nervous shock if nervous shock foreseeable.

Hinz v Berry [1970] 1 All ER 1074; (1970) 120 NLJ 81t; [1970] 2 QB 40; (1970) 114 SJ 111; [1970] 2 WLR 684 CA Appropriate damages for nervous shock.

Jones and others v Chief Constable of South Yorkshire (1990) 140 NLJ 1717 HC QBD Damages available to parents/siblings for nervous shock; said damages available when watched live television event in which child/fellow sibling injured.

Jones and others v Wright [1991] 1 All ER 353 HC QBD Damages for nervous shock on foot of negligent act available to parents and siblings. Proximity in space and time satisified by viewing live television broadcast.

King and another v Phillips [1952] 2 All ER 459 HC QBD Non-liability of taxi-driver tipping child with taxi for shock sustained by mother viewing incident from over two hundred feet away.

King v Phillips [1953] 1 All ER 617; (1953) 103 LJ 153; [1953] 1 QB 429; [1953] 2 WLR 526 CA No duty of care owed by taxi-driver tipping child with taxi for shock sustained by mother viewing incident from over two hundred feet away.

McFarlane v EE Caledonia Ltd [1994] 2 All ER 1; (1993) 143 NLJ 1367; [1993] TLR 476 CA Bystander/witness of awful events ineligible for damages for nervous shock unless proximate to events and victim.

Owens v Liverpool Corporation [1938] 4 All ER 727; [1939] 1 KB 394; (1939) 87 LJ 8; [1939] 108 LJCL 155; (1939) 160 LTR 8; (1938) 82 SJ 1010; (1938-39) LV TLR 246; (1939) WN (I) 6 CA Mental shock damages available even where human injury not envisioned by victim.

Page v Smith [1996] 3 All ER 272; (1994) 144 NLJ 756; [1994] TLR 240; [1996] 1 WLR 855 CA Negligent driver not liable to primary victim for nervous shock though personal injury reasonably foreseeable as result of accident.

Page v Smith [1995] 2 All ER 736; [1996] 1 AC 155; (1995) 145 NLJ 723; [1995] RTR 210; (1995) 139 SJ LB 173; [1995] TLR 275; [1995] 2 WLR 644 HL Negligent driver liable to primary victim for nervous shock if personal injury reasonably foreseeable as result of accident even if no physical injury.

Ravenscroft v Transatlantic (Rederiaktib'laget) [1991] TLR 190 HC QBD Damages for nervous shock of parent over child's death though did not see/hear event or aftermath.

Ravenscroft v Transatlantic (Rederiaktib'laget) [1992] 2 All ER 470; (1991) 141 NLJ 600; [1992] TLR 169 CA Damages for nervous shock of parent over child's death only if saw/heard event or aftermath.

Whitmore and another v Euroways Express Coaches Ltd and others [1984] TLR 290 HC QBD Damages recoverable for shock of being in hospital with/seeing hurt spouse (albeit that were not affected medically/in psychiatric manner by the shock).

NUISANCE (adoption of nuisance)

Page Motors Ltd v Epsom and Ewell Borough Borough Council (1980) 124 SJ 273 HC ChD Adoption of nuisance (posed by gypsies) by landowner.

Page Motors Ltd v Epsom and Ewell Borough Borough Council (1981) 125 SJ 590 CA Adoption of nuisance (posed by gypsies) by landowner.

NUISANCE (animal)

Ex parte Duerdin-Dutton and another [1964] Crim LR 396t HL Refusal of leave to appeal point whether necessary for there to be oral evidence proving facts accepted by defendant's solicitor.

Mason v Kempson [1939] LJNCCR 203 CyCt Failed action in negligence/nuisance and for breach of statutory duty owed under Dogs Act 1906 for injury suffered in road traffic incident occasioned by dog running across road while being taken for walk by owner.

RDC (Berkhamstead) v Duerdin-Dutton and another [1964] Crim LR 307t HC QBD Oral evidence unnecessary to prove facts accepted by defendant's solicitor.

Seligman v Docker [1949] Ch 53; (1948) WN (I) 425 HC ChD Presence of large numbers of wild pheasants on rented land not due to unreasonable act of landlord-defendant who was not under a duty to reduce ther number/rid land of their presence.

The Irish Society and others v Harold and others (1912) 81 LJPC 162; (1911-12) XXVIII TLR 204 PC Drift nets held not to be nuisance.

Tylden-Wright v Watson [1938] LJNCCR 107 CyCt Allowing gypsies to camp on land was not an unnatural user/was transitory so injunctive relief inappropriate/rendered land-owner liable for trespass of gypsies' horses onto land of another.

NUISANCE (bees)

Johnson v Martin (1950) 100 LJ 541 CyCt Failed action in nuisance against bee-keeper by person who had along with her goats been injured by the defendant's bees (one goat dying).

NUISANCE (building)

McGlynn v Marshall: Cotton, Third Party [1944] LJNCCR 96 CyCt Occupier only liable in nuisance for injury occurring on foot of defect in premises if knew of defect and did nothing to fix it/was too slow in fixing it.

Odell v Cleveland House (Limited) (1910) 102 LTR 602; (1909-10) XXVI TLR 410 HC KBD Landlord liable for not taking adequate care not to pull portion of house down in such a way as to create nuisance to tenant.

Sanders-Clark v Grosvenor Mansions Company, Limited and G D'Allessandri [1900] 2 Ch 373; (1900) 35 LJ 363; [1900] LXIX (1) LJ 579; (1900) LXXXII LTR 758; (1899-1900) 44 SJ 502; (1899-1906) XVI TLR 428; (1900) WN (I) 136; (1899-1900) 48 WR 570 HC ChD Reasonable use of property a relevant factor when deciding nuisance cases involving adjoining houseowners.

NUISANCE (damages)

B (A) and others v South West Water Services Ltd [1992] 4 All ER 574; (1992) 142 NLJ 897; [1992] TLR 232 HC QBD Exemplary and aggravated damages available for deliberate public nuisance.

B (A) and others v South West Water Services Ltd [1993] 1 All ER 609; (1993) 143 NLJ 235; [1993] QB 507; [1993] 2 WLR 507 CA Exemplary damages unavailable for public nuisance; water company a commercial operation not exercising executive power so exemplary damages unavailable; aggravated damages unavailable for anger and indignation.

Moss v Christchurch Rural District Council; Rogers v Same [1925] 2 KB 750; [1926] 95 LJCL 81 HC KBD Damages recoverable where house damaged by fire/nuisance were cash difference between value of house pre-/post-fire.

NUISANCE (dangerous goods)

Rainham Chemical Works, Limited (in liquidation), and others v Belvedere Fish Guano Company [1921] All ER 48; [1921] 2 AC 465; (1921) 56 LJ 314; [1921] LJCL 1252; (1922) 126 LTR 70; (1921-22) 66 SJ wr7; (1920-21) XXXVII TLR 973; (1921) WN (I) 281 HL Occupiers and tenants liable under Rylands v Fletcher for explosion occasioned by non-natural user of land.

NUISANCE (easement)

Price v Hilditch [1930] 1 Ch 500; (1930) 99 LJCh 299; (1930) WN (I) 44 HC ChD Failed action for injunction to restrain obstruction of ancient light: right to light not determined by reference to past purpose for which place used.

Sack v Jones [1925] 94 LJCh 229; (1925) 133 LTR 129 HC ChD Failure of one joint owner to give lateral support to party wall not a nuisance.

NUISANCE (electricity)

SCM (United Kingdom) Ltd v WJ Whittall and Son Ltd [1970] 2 All ER 417; (1970) 114 SJ 268; [1970] 1 WLR 1017 HC QBD Damage to electric cable causing electricity loss raised liability in negligence not nuisance.

NUISANCE (escape)

Collingwood v Home and Colonial Stores, Ltd [1936] 1 All ER 74; (1936) 81 LJ 130; (1936) 80 SJ 167 HC KBD Absent negligence in electric fitting/maintenance no Rylands v Fletcher-style liability for escape of water resulting from electrical fault-caused fire; hoarding impeding access a nuisance (despite increase in trade while hoarding present).

NUISANCE (fire)

Job Edwards, Limited v The Company of Proprietors of the Birmingham Navigations [1924] 1 KB 341; [1924] 93 LJCL 261; (1924) 130 LTR 522 CA Non-liability of landowner for failure to abate fire.

NUISANCE (flooding)

Pemberton and another v Bright and others [1960] 1 All ER 792; (1960) 124 JP 265; (1960) 110 LJ 284; (1960) 104 SJ 349 CA Blockable culvert a potential nuisance; blocked culvert a nuisance: council liable for constructing nuisance, occupiers liable for continuing it.

Potter and others v Mole Valley District Council and another [1982] TLR 486 HC QBD Flooding resulting from road works a public/private nuisance for which county council responsible.

NUISANCE (general)

Abbott v Heyman (1925) 60 LJ 1055 CyCt Successful action for damages for nuisances occasioned by removal of door, said removal interfering with exercise of right of way.

Allen v Gulf Oil Refining Ltd [1981] 1 All ER 353; [1981] AC 1001; (1981) 131 NLJ 140; (1981) 125 SJ 101; [1981] 2 WLR 188 HL Statutory immunity for activities at oil refinery of which nuisance inevitable consequence.

Almeroth v Chivers (WE) and Sons, Ltd [1948] 1 All ER 53 CA Slates left on kerb were nuisance (de minimis non curat lex); not contributorily negligent that did not see.

Attorney-General v Barker (1900-01) LXXXIII LTR 245; (1899-1900) XVI TLR 502 HC ChD Newly-constructed level crossings were nuisances which county council did not and could not authorise.

Attorney-General v Cole and Son [1901] 1 Ch 205; (1900) 35 LJ 712; [1901] 70 LJCh 148; (1900-01) LXXXIII LTR 725; (1900) WN (I) 272 HC ChD Own perception as to reasonableness of own behaviour irrelevant in nuisance action; can be guilty of nuisance though carrying out business in ordinary way.

Attorney-General v Hastings Corporation and others; Parsons and others v Same (1950) 94 SJ 225 CA Motor racing in residential area was actionable private, not public nuisance.

Attorney-General v Scott (1903-04) 48 SJ 623; (1903-04) XX TLR 630 HC KBD Perpetual injunction to restrain use of traction engine to carry stone along highway refused (but no use of road for one month until council undertook necessary reconstruction work).

Attorney-General v Scott (1904-05) 49 SJ 221; (1904-05) XXI TLR 211 CA Use of traction engine to carry stone along highway did by level of damage to/obstruction of road constitute nuisance.

Atwill v Plymouth and Stonehouse Gas Light and Coke Co [1934] LJNCCR 361 CyCt Person who lit match following gas leak and so herself caused explosion could not recover damages in nuisance (and was no negligence on part of gas suppliers proved).

Ayers v Hanson, Stanley and Prince (1911-12) 56 SJ 735; (1912) WN (I) 193 HC ChD Use of field for rabbit-coursing matches was a nuisance for which co-tenants (but not landlord) responsible.

Bank View Mill, Ltd and others v Nelson Corpn and Fryer and Co (Nelson), Ltd [1942] 2 All ER 477 Assizes Corporation in occupation and control knowing of obstruction and with chance to remove liable in nuisance; flooding slightly due to weir: nominal damages against weir-owner.

Barber and another v Clarke and Co, Ltd and others (1939) 83 SJ 925 HC KBD Failed action by infant against workman on/occupiers of land for injury suffered when dangerously standing gate fell on infant.

Batcheller v Tunbridge Wells Gas Company (1901) LXXXIV LTR 765; (1900-01) 45 SJ 577; (1900-01) XVII TLR 577 HC ChD Gas company liable in nuisance for leak from gas mains into water pipes which contaminated water.

Bradburn v Lindsay; Bradburn and another v Lindsay [1983] 2 All ER 408 HC ChD Neglected house owner has duty to prevent damage to neighbour's house; right of entry to abate nuisance does not vitiate liability for nuisance.

Brew Brothers Ltd v Snax (Ross) Ltd and another [1970] 1 All ER 587; [1970] 1 QB 612; [1969] 3 WLR 657 CA Repairing covenant from tenants did not preclude them and landlord being liable in nuisance for failed shoring operation.

Bridlington Relay, Ltd v Yorkshire Electricity Board [1965] 1 All ER 264; [1965] Ch 436; (1965) 115 LJ 107; (1965) 109 SJ 12; [1965] 2 WLR 349 HC ChD On interference with television signals as nuisance.

Bullock v Reeve (1901) 84 LTR 55; [1901] 70 LJK/QB 42; (1900-01) 49 WR 93 HC QBD House owner not liable to abate nuisance arising from defective drainage which by virtue of deviation from drainage plan sanctioned by Sewage Commissioners was a sewer, not a drain.

Caminer and another v Northern and London Investment Trust, Ltd [1949] 1 All ER 874; [1949] 2 KB 64; (1949) 99 LJ 231; (1949) LXV TLR 302; (1949) WN (I) 212 CA Not liable where non-expert person takes what for it is reasonable care.

Caminer and another v Northern and London Investment Trust, Ltd [1950] 2 All ER 486; [1951] AC 88; (1950) 114 JP 426; (1950) 100 LJ 401; (1950) 94 SJ 518; [1950] 66 (2) TLR 184; (1950) WN (I) 361 HL Occupiers having taken reasonable care were not liable in negligence/nuisance.

Campbell Davys v Lloyd [1901] 2 Ch 518; (1900-01) 45 SJ 670; (1900-01) XVII TLR 678; (1901) WN (I) 150; (1900-01) 49 WR 710 CA Without special empowerment is no right to repair where is no duty to repair.

Carr v Hackney London Borough Council [1995] TLR 153 HC QBD Could avoid issuance of nuisance order against self by showing that were not responsibility for relevant nuisance.

Charing Cross, West End, and City Electricity Supply Co, Ltd v London Hydraulic Power Co [1914-15] All ER 85; (1914) 78 JP 305; [1914] 3 KB 772; (1914) 49 LJ 244; [1914] 83 LJKB 1352; (1914-15) 111 LTR 198; (1913-14) 58 SJ 577; (1913-14) XXX TLR 441; (1914) WN (I) 170 CA Liability for nuisance (though no negligence) for injury sustained through escape of dangerous thing.

Clayton v Sale Urban District Council [1925] All ER 279; (1926) 90 JP 5; [1926] 1 KB 415; (1925) 60 LJ 962; [1926] 95 LJCL 178; (1926) 134 LTR 147; (1925-26) XLII TLR 72; (1925) WN (I) 278 HC KBD Riparian owner must abate nuisance caused by flooding which has broken flood bank.

Collingwood v Home and Colonial Stores, Ltd [1936] 3 All ER 200; (1936) 155 LTR 550; (1936) 80 SJ 853; (1936-37) LIII TLR 53; (1936) WN (I) 305 CA Rylands v Fletcher inapplicable to domestic use of electricity.

Corporation of Greenock v Caledonian Railway Company; Corporation of Greenock v Glasgow and South-Western Railway Company [1917] AC 556; (1917) 81 JP 269 HL Liable for flooding resulting from interference with course of stream.

Craib v Woolwich Borough Council (1919-20) XXXVI TLR 630 HC KBD Sewer authority not liable for non-feasance that gives rise to nuisance.

Crown River Cruises Ltd v Kimbolton Fireworks Ltd and another (1996) TLR 6/3/96 HC QBD Could claim in nuisance for damage to moored river barge.

Cunliffe v Bankes [1945] 1 All ER 459; (1946) 96 LJ 213 Assizes All reasonable steps taken to gauging safety of tree: no negligence and no nuisance (did not cause defect; did not arise through own act and failed to remedy in reasonable time).

Cushing v Peter Walker and Son (Warrington and Burton), Ltd [1941] 2 All ER 693; (1941) 91 LJ 310; (1942) 92 LJ 61 HC KBD Not liable for continuing undiscoverable nuisance.

Davis v Marrable (1913) 48 LJ 405 HC ChD On extent of right to ancient light.

De Lecavalier v City of Montreal [1930] AC 152; (1930) 99 LJPC 53; (1930) 142 LTR 124 PC Party had no interest on which to ground nuisance action.

Dennis v London Co-operative Society, Ltd [1939] LJNCCR 39 CyCt Defendants liable for injury suffered by plaintiff who slipped on piece of fat swept by defendants into street.

Department of Transport v North West Water Authority [1983] 3 All ER 273; [1984] AC 336 (also HC QBD); (1983) 133 NLJ 1016; [1983] TLR 611; [1983] 3 WLR 707 HL Absent negligence no liability for nuisance caused performing statutory duty.

Devonshire and Smith v Jenkins (1979) 129 (1) NLJ 198c CA Aggravated, not exemplary damages for harassment/nuisance.

Dollman and another v A and S Hillman, Ltd (1941) 85 SJ 57 HC KBD Fat falling from butcher's shop to pavement causing person to slip was nuisance/negligence.

Dollman and another v A and S Hillman, Ltd [1941] 1 All ER 355; (1942) 92 LJ 91 CA Fat falling from butcher's shop to pavement causing person to slip was nuisance/negligence.

Dribbell and another v Robinson (1949) 99 LJ 233 CyCt Landlord liable for injury suffered by child when facia board which landlord knew to be in disrepair but had not repaired collapsed onto highway.

Edwards (Job), Limited v Birmingham Canal Navigations, Limited (1923-24) 68 SJ 501; (1923-24) XL TLR 88 CA Persons not causing/continuing nuisance or negligent in relation thereto not liable to fund protective measures taken by another on foot of nuisance.

Ellwood v Brown [1937] LJNCCR 153 CyCt Recovery of damages for harbouring of bugs but not for invasion of same (where origin of invading bugs unproved).

Gillingham Borough Council v Medway (Chatham) Dock Co Ltd and others [1992] 3 All ER 923; [1993] QB 343; [1991] TLR 440; [1992] 3 WLR 449 HC QBD Nuisance to be decided by reference to neighbourhood despite change of use following planning permission.

Gravesham Borough Council and others v British Railways Board [1978] 3 All ER 853 HC ChD Changing of public ferry service actionable by party suffering direct loss as obstruction/hindrance of ferry public nuisance.

Green v Matthews and Co (1929-30) XLVI TLR 206 HC ChD Cannot claim right to pollute stream/waterway whether by prescription/under lost grant.

Hale v Jennings Brothers [1937] LJNCCR 228 CyCt Fairground operators not liable in negligence/ nuisance for injuries suffered by woman when 'chair-o-plane' (which became detached as result of its occupant's recklessness) struck her, there being no latent defect in the 'chair-o-plane' machine which was not dangerous in itself and where machine not operated negligently.

Hall v Beckenham Corporation [1949] 1 All ER 423; (1949) 113 JP 179; [1949] 1 KB 716; [1949] 118 LJR 965; (1949) LXV TLR 146; (1949) WN (I) 74 HC KBD Local authority not liable for nuisance of persons flying model aeroplanes in public park.

Halsey v Esso Petroleum Co, Ltd [1961] 2 All ER 145; (1961) 111 LJ 290; (1961) 105 SJ 209 HC QBD Oil smuts damaging clothes a private/Rylands v Fletcher-style nuisance; smuts damaging car on highway a public/Rylands v Fletcher-style nuisance; odour from oil depot a nuisance by smell (though no evidence of injury); din from boilers a private nuisance as adversely affected enjoyment of ordinary comforts; din from tankers on highway at night a public nuisance/a private nuisance as connected with use of (though not occurring on) private property.

Hampstead and Suburban Properties, Ltd v Diomedous [1968] 3 All ER 545; [1969] 1 Ch 248; (1969) 119 NLJ 552t; (1968) 112 SJ 656 HC ChD Just because difficult to draw line between acceptable behaviour/nuisance did not justify not granting relief where clearly nuisance; no pre-trial enforcement of obligations after breach of covenant if only balance of convenience demands it.

Harper v Copus [1941] LJNCCR 23 CyCt Owner of wall in negligent disrepair liable in nuisance for damage occasioned by collapse of same (whether or not knew of state in which wall stood).

Hartley v Mayor, &c, of Rochdale [1908] 2 KB 594; (1908-09) XCIX LTR 275; (1907-08) XXIV TLR 625 HC KBD Local authority's failure to remedy subsidence of road caused by water leak did not preclude water company's liability for person injured as result of same.

Harwich Corporation v Brewster (1900-01) XVII TLR 274 HC KBD Local authority allowed bring nuisance action in own name to seek injunction against person discharging noxious matter into storm-water gullies.

Hesketh v Birmingham Corporation (1924) 88 JP 77; [1924] 1 KB 260; [1924] 93 LJCL 461; (1924) 130 LTR 476 CA Local authority not liable in nuisance for discharging sewer water into stream/not liable for non-feasance of drainage system.

Hollywood Silver Fox Farm, Limited v Emmett [1936] 1 All ER 825; [1936] 2 KB 468; (1936) 81 LJ 331; [1936] 105 LJCL 829; (1936) 155 LTR 288; (1936) 80 SJ 488; (1935-36) LII TLR 611 HC KBD Lawful act but extraordinary user of own land rendered liable in nuisance (firing of gun to frighten neighbour's silver foxes).

Home Brewery plc v William Davis and Co (Leicester) Ltd [1987] 1 All ER 637; [1987] QB 339; (1987) 131 SJ 102; [1987] 2 WLR 117 HC QBD Lower land occupier taking steps to prevent water flowing from higher land liable in nuisance to higher land occupier if steps unreasonable and cause damage.

Horridge v Makinson (1915) 79 JP 484; [1915] 84 LJKB 1294; (1915-16) 113 LTR 498; (1914-15) XXXI TLR 389; (1915) WN (I) 180 HC KBD Frontager not liable for nuisance on highway for which highway authority responsible.

Horton v Colwyn Bay Urban District Council (1906-07) 51 SJ 69 HC KBD Failed claim for damages for nuisance (construction of outfall) on another's land where claimant already compensated for laying of sewer through own land.

Hunt v WH Cook, Ltd (1922) 57 LJ 208; (1921-22) 66 SJ 557 HC ChD Noise from poultry farm not a nuisance; plaintiff not estopped from bringing action by fact that predecessor in title had previously brought similar (compromised) action.

Hunter and others v Canary Wharf Ltd; Hunter and others v London Docklands Development Corporation [1997] 2 All ER 426; (1997) 147 NLJ 634; (1997) 141 SJ LB 108; [1997] TLR 219; [1997] 2 WLR 684 HL Television interference following erection of tall building not an actionable interference with use and enjoyment of land; licensee could not sue for nuisance.

Ilford Urban District Council v Beal and Judd [1925] All ER 361; (1925) 89 JP 77; [1925] 1 KB 671; (1924-25) XLI TLR 317 HC KBD Non-liability of landowner in respect of underground sewer of which did not/could not reasonably be expected to know.

Isgoed-Jones v Llanrwst Urban District Council [1911] 1 Ch 393; (1911) 75 JP 68; (1911) 80 LJCh 145; (1910-11) 103 LTR 751; (1910-11) XXVII TLR 133 HC ChD Riparian owner aside natural stream is entitled to have it flow past in its natural state: injunction to prevent council discharging untreated sewage into stream.

J Goldberg and Sons v The Corporation of Liverpool (1900) LXXXII LTR 362; (1899-1900) XVI TLR 320 CA Bona fide placing of pole and fuse-box at entrance to plaintiffs' premises was authorised by statute/was not nuisance.

Jackson v Wimbledon Urban District Council (1904-05) XXI TLR 479 CA Nuisance arising from pipe bringing sewage from house to main sewer was a matter for local authority to remedy.

Jacobs v London County Council and Smith, Gard & Co, Ltd (1949) 99 LJ 52 CyCt Council liable in negligence/nuisance for injury suffered by individual when crossing forecourt in some disrepair.

JH Dewhurst, Ltd v Ratcliffe (1951) 101 LJ 361 CyCt Failed application in nuisance against hedge owner by motorist who on brushing against hedge collided with tree stump hidden by hedge.

Johnstone v Simmons [1937] LJNCCR 289 CyCt Person liable for collapse of wall where if did not know of dangerous condition of wall she ought to have known of it.

Joint Committee of the River Ribble v Halliwell; Same v Shorrock (1899-1900) LXXXI LTR 38 CA Failed action for nuisance arising from alleged placing of putrid solid matter in river.

Jones v Pritchard [1908] 1 Ch 630; (1908) XCVIII LTR 386 HC ChD Person enjoying easements as regards user of common wall not liable for nuisance arising from user so long as is not negligent/careless and uses it for purposes envisioned.

Kennard and others v Cory Brothers and Co, Limited [1922] 1 Ch 265; (1921-22) XXXVIII TLR 213 HC ChD Order given on foot of earlier action to maintain remedial works.

Kennard and others v Cory Brothers and Co, Limited [1922] 2 Ch 1; (1922) 127 LTR 137; (1921-22) XXXVIII TLR 489; (1922) WN (I) 122 CA Order given on foot of earlier action to maintain remedial works approved.

Kennaway v Thompson and another [1980] 3 All ER 329; [1981] QB 88; (1980) 124 SJ 378; [1980] 3 WLR 361 CA Injunction restraining nuisance in use/enjoyment of own land despite public interest in activities constituting nuisance.

Kinney and another v Hove Corporation and others (1950) 94 SJ 551 HC ChD Use of public park by circus deemed not to be a nuisance.

Kirby v Friend [1945] LJNCCR 90 CyCt Owner of property liable for injury suffered by way of defective coal-plate by person lawfully using highway onto which plate extended.

Lagan Navigation Company v Lambeg Bleaching, Dyeing and Finishing Company, Limited [1926] All ER 230; [1927] AC 226; (1927) 91 JP 46; (1927) 96 LJPC 25; (1927) 136 LTR 417 HL No nuisance but had there been court disdained private abatement thereof.

Landeys (Doncaster), Ltd v Fletcher (1959) 109 LJ 204 CyCt Rylands v Fletcher inapplicable to domestic use of electricity/gas/water so not liable under Rylands v Fletcher for escape of water from domestic pipe.

Langbrook Properties Ltd v Surrey County Council (1969) 113 SJ 983; [1970] 1 WLR 161 HC ChD No nuisance or negligence arose where abstracted water from own land even though affected another's property.

Laws and others v Florinplace Ltd and another [1981] 1 All ER 659 HC ChD Injunction possible for nuisance not involving physical emanation.

Lawson v Tuddenham [1945] LJNCCR 141 CyCt Failed claim in nuisance/trespass arising from allegedly excessive user of right of way.

Leakey and others v National Trust for Places of Historic Interest or Natural Beauty [1980] 1 All ER 17; (1979) 129 (2) NLJ 781; [1980] QB 485; (1979) 123 SJ 606; [1980] 2 WLR 65 CA Must take reasonable steps to prevent natural/man-made features on one's land causing damage/becoming danger to another.

Leakey and others v National Trust for Places of Historic Interest or Natural Beauty [1978] 3 All ER 234; (1978) 128 NLJ 242t; [1978] QB 849; (1978) 122 SJ 231; [1978] 2 WLR 774 HC QBD Occupier must take reasonable steps to remove occurrence on land which is hazard for neighbour.

Leyman v The Hessle Urban District Council (1903) 67 JP 56; (1902-03) XIX TLR 73 HC ChD Removal of public urinal from outside plaintiff's house ordered as was nuisance to plaintiff in enjoyment of property.

Lippitt v Jones (1930) 70 LJ ccr30 CyCt Shop-owner liable under principle in Rylands v Fletcher/in nuisance for injury occasioned to person when shop sunblind collapsed on them.

Litchfield-Speer and another v Queen Anne's Gate Syndicate (No 2), Ltd [1918-19] All ER 1075 HC ChD On restraint of anticipated nuisance.

London Borough of Hammersmith v Magnum Automated Forecourts Ltd [1978] 1 All ER 401; (1978) 142 JP 130; (1977) 127 NLJ 691t; (1977) 121 SJ 529; [1978] 1 WLR 50 CA High Court action (for injunction) permissible despite right to bring summary action for nuisance.

Louis v Sadiq (1996) TLR 22/11/96 CA Builder liable in nuisance for damage occasioned to adjoining property by works carried out by him in breach of statutory requirements.

M'Nair v Baker (1903-04) XX TLR 95 HC KBD Club-house not a private house so smoke nuisance a contravention of Public Health (London) Act 1891, s 24.

Maberley (Alan) v Henry W Peabody and Co of London, Ltd, Rowland Smith Motors, Ltd and Rowland Smith [1946] 2 All ER 192 HC KBD Nuisance to wall caused by neighbour piling clay against it and pouring chemicals on clay merited injunction though damage to date of action slight.

Mallock v Mason and Mason [1938] LJNCCR 387 CyCt Barking at night from premises used for breeding of dogs held to be a nuisance.

Masters v London Borough of Brent [1978] 2 All ER 664; (1978) 128 NLJ 34t; [1978] QB 841; (1978) 122 SJ 300; [1978] 2 WLR 768 HC QBD Damages recoverable for nuisance begun before acquired proprietary title.

Matania v National Provincial Bank Limited and Elevenist Syndicate [1937] 106 LJCL 113; (1936) 155 LTR 74 CA Independent contractors found liable for nuisance by noise/dust effected through their work.

Mathias v Davies (1970) 114 SJ 268 CA On appropriate remedy for nuisance.

McCombe v Read and another [1955] 2 All ER 458; (1955) 105 LJ 347; [1955] 2 QB 429; (1955) 99 SJ 370; [1955] 1 WLR 635 HC QBD Roots extending into adjoining land and tapping water were nuisance: post-writ damages available for damage arising from continuation of nuisance.

McKinnon Industries, Ltd v Walker (1951) 95 SJ 559; (1951) WN (I) 401 PC Injunction merited to restrain discharge of noxious vapours/matter from defendant's works onto plaintiff's land.

Metropolitan Properties, Ltd v Jones [1939] 2 All ER 202; (1939) 87 LJ 270; (1939) 83 SJ 399 HC KBD Owner not occupier deemed liable for nuisance.

Midwood and Co Limited v Mayor, Aldermen, and Citizens of Manchester [1904-07] All ER 1364; (1905) 69 JP 348; [1905] 2 KB 597; (1905-06) XCIII LTR 525; (1904-05) XXI TLR 667; (1905-06) 54 WR 37 CA Corporation liable in nuisance for escape of electricity causing explosion.

Mills v Brooker [1918-19] All ER 613; [1919] 1 KB 555; [1919] 88 LJCL 950; (1919) 121 LTR 254; (1918-19) 63 SJ 431; (1918-19) XXXV TLR 261 HC KBD Party could abate nuisance of overhanging tree by lopping overhanging branches but was liable in conversion for keeping branches/fruit thereon.

Mitchell v Fothergill (1917) CC Rep VI 58 CyCt Occupier of house liable for injury sustained by passer-by when coping which occupier knew to be in disrepair fell onto passer-by.

Morris and another v Redland Bricks Ltd [1967] 1 WLR 967 CA On when injunction/damages appropriate remedy for nuisance.

Moul v Shepcott (1924-25) 69 SJ 680 HC ChD Court would not in quia timet action grant interlocutory injunction to restrain apprehended nuisance where subjects of proposed order did not consent to it.

Newman v Real Estate Debenture Corporation, Ltd, and Flower Decorations, Ltd [1940] 1 All ER 131 HC KBD Alteration of premises/business conducted in premises in respect of which covenant that were only for residential purposes was a nuisance.

Nicholls v Ely Beet Sugar Factory, Ltd [1931] All ER 154; [1931] 2 Ch 84; (1931) 100 LJCh 259; (1931) 145 LTR 113 HC ChD Jus tertii defence unavailable because of plaintiff's possessory rights.

Nunn v Parkes and Co (1924) 59 LJ 806 HC KBD Only owner/occupier of property impinged upon by nuisance (here occasioing damage to chattels) could bring action in nuisance.

Osborne v Colenutt (1919) CC Rep VIII 25 CyCt Pedestrian with poor sight who fell through open cellar door that opened onto pavement able to recover damages for injury sustained where normally sighted person would have seen danger and avoided injury.

Parish v The Mayor, &c, of the City of London (1901-02) XVIII TLR 63 HC ChD Order for removal of public urinal which was occasioning nuisance to warehouse owner.

Parker v London General Omnibus Company (Limited) (1909) 73 JP 283; (1909) C LTR 409; (1908-09) XXV TLR 429 HC KBD Personal injury victim failed in action against bus company whose driver/placing bus on road was negligent/may or may not have been nuisance.

Parker v London General Omnibus Company (Limited) (1910) 74 JP 20; (1909-10) 101 LTR 623; (1908-09) 53 SJ 867; (1909-10) XXVI TLR 18 CA Personal injury victim failed in action against bus company whose driver/placing bus on road was negligent/may or may not have been nuisance.

Parker v Williams (1917) CC Rep VI 50 CyCt Landlord liable in nuisance for loss occasioned by collapse into adjoining premises of gutters which previously overhung same.

Paterson and another v Humberside County Council [1995] TLR 224 HC QBD Tree-owner liable in nuisance/negligence for subsidence consequent upon drying out of soil by trees.

Perry v Kendrick's Transport, Ltd [1956] 1 All ER 154; (1956) 106 LJ 40; (1956) 100 SJ 52; [1956] 1 WLR 85 CA Not liable in nuisance as acts in issue were done by starnger over whom had no control.

Phillimore v Watford Rural District Council [1913] 2 Ch 434; (1913) 77 JP 453; (1913-14) 109 LTR 616 HC ChD Injunction to restrain sewage farm discharging effluent into private ditch/ sewer of another; damages also awarded for nuisance by smell/underground passage of sewage.

Price's Patent Candle Company (Limited) v The London County Council (1908) 72 JP 315; (1908) 43 LJ 302; [1909] 78 LJCh 1 (also CA); (1907-08) XXIV TLR 607; (1908) WN (I) 131 HC ChD Council not to create nuisance in course of sewage treatment.

Price's Patent Candle Company (Limited) v The London County Council [1908] 2 Ch 526; (1908) 72 JP 429; (1908) 43 LJ 524; [1909] 78 LJCh 1 (also HC ChD); (1908-09) XCIX LTR 571; (1907-08) XXIV TLR 823; (1908) WN (I) 188 CA Council not to create nuisance in course of sewage treatment.

Pride of Derby and Derbyshire Angling Association, Ltd and another v British Celanese, Ltd and others [1952] 1 All ER 1326; (1952) WN (I) 227 HC ChD Where persons collectively commit nuisance but individually not improper behaviour may be sued collectively for nuisance.

Pride of Derby and Derbyshire Angling Association, Ltd and another v British Celanese, Ltd and others [1953] 1 All ER 179; [1953] Ch 149; (1953) 117 JP 52; (1952) 102 LJ 721; (1953) 97 SJ 28; [1953] 2 WLR 58 CA Local authority liable for nuisance in violating Rivers Pollution Prevention Act 1876; injunction available aginst local authority but suspended where required doing of impossible.

Pwllbach Colliery Co, Ltd v Woodman [1914-15] All ER 124; [1915] AC 634; (1915) 50 LJ 117; [1915] 84 LJKB 874; (1915-16) 113 LTR 10; (1914-15) XXXI TLR 271; (1915) WN (I) 108 HL Authorisation to carry on business not per se authorisation to carry on nuisance (unless cannot otherwise be carried on).

Radstock Co-operative and Industrial Society, Ltd v Norton-Radstock Urban District Council [1968] 2 All ER 59; [1968] Ch 605; (1968) 132 JP 238; (1968) 112 SJ 135; [1968] 2 WLR 1214 CA Something that does not begin as nuisance cannot become so just through passage of time.

Radstock Co-operative and Industrial Society, Ltd v Norton-Radstock Urban District Council [1967] 2 All ER 812; [1967] Ch 1094; (1967) 131 JP 387; [1967] 3 WLR 588 HC ChD Obstruction which does not begin as nuisance cannot become nuisance just by virtue of time.

Reeve v Sadler (1903) 67 JP 63; (1903) LXXXVIII LTR 95; (1902-03) 51 WR 603 HC KBD Subject of sanitary notice cannot recoup part of expenses of work done thereunder from adjoining owner subject to another sanitary notice.

Robinson and another v Urban District Council of Beaconsfield (1911) 75 JP 353 (also CA); (1911) 80 LJCh 647 (also CA); (1910-11) XXVII TLR 319 HC ChD Local authority liable in nuisance for defective manner of sewage disposal by contractor.

Robinson v Beaconsfield Urban District Council [1911-13] All ER 997; [1911] 2 Ch 188; (1911) 75 JP 353 (also HC ChD); (1911) 80 LJCh 647 (also HC ChD); (1911-12) 105 LTR 121; (1910-11) XXVII TLR 478 CA Local authority liable in nuisance for manner of sewage disposal by contractor with whom had not contracted for disposal.

Robinson v London General Omnibus Company (Limited) (1910) 74 JP 161; (1909-10) XXVI TLR 233 HC ChD Over-use of streets for maintenance/repair/turning of buses was nuisance.

Royal Mail Steam Packet Company v George and another [1900-03] All ER 1704; (1900) LXXXII LTR 539 PC On drawing by court of inferences of fact in nuisance action.

Rushmer v Polsue and Alfieri (Limited) [1906] 1 Ch 234; (1905) 40 LJ 867; (1905-06) XCIII LTR 823; (1905-06) 50 SJ 126; (1905-06) XXII TLR 139; (1906) WN (I) 3; (1905-06) 54 WR 161 CA Use of printing machinery by night was nuisance (though in area where much printing took place).

Rushmer v Polsue and Alfieri (Limited) (1904-05) XXI TLR 183 HC ChD Use of printing machinery by night was nuisance (though in area where much printing took place).

Sanders-Clark v Grosvenor Mansions Company, Limited and G D'Allesandri [1900] 2 Ch 373; (1900) 35 LJ 363; [1900] LXIX (1) LJ 579; (1900) LXXXII LTR 758; (1899-1900) 44 SJ 502; (1899-1900) XVI TLR 428; (1900) WN (I) 136; (1899-1900) 48 WR 570 HC ChD Reasonable use of property a relevant factor when deciding nuisance cases involving adjoining houseowners.

Scott and another v Westminster City Council [1995] RTR 327 CA Seizure by highway authority of mobile chestnut braziers placed on path by unlicensed street traders was justified.

Sedleigh-Denfield v St Joseph's Society for Foreign Missions and Hillman [1938] 3 All ER 321; (1938) 86 LJ 26; (1938) 82 SJ 606 HC KBD Occupier only under duty to abate nuisance of which knows, need not go about rooting out nuisances; cannot complain of nuisance brought about purely by freak climactic conditions which could remedy oneself.

Sharpe v Council of the City of Manchester (1978) 128 NLJ 312b CA Successful action in negligence/nuisance where council dealt inadequately with cockroach infestation in council flat.

Smith v Giddy [1904-07] All ER 289; [1904] 2 KB 448; (1904) 39 LJ 346; [1904] 73 LJCL 894; (1904-05) XCI LTR 296; (1903-04) 48 SJ 589; (1903-04) XX TLR 596; (1904) WN (I) 130; (1904-05) 53 WR 207 HC KBD Can lob overhanging branches causing nuisance and claim for damage effected thereby.

Southport Corporation v Esso Petroleum Co, Ltd and another [1953] 2 All ER 1204; (1954) 118 JP 1; (1953) 103 LJ 750; (1953) 97 SJ 764; [1953] 3 WLR 773 HC QBD Private nuisance need not emanate from neighbour's property; public nuisance on public navigable river akin to that on highway; need to prove negligence to establish nuisance.

Southport Corporation v Esso Petroleum Co, Ltd and another [1954] 2 All ER 561; (1954) 118 JP 411; [1954] 2 QB 182; (1954) 98 SJ 472; [1954] 3 WLR 200 CA No trespass/nuisance where act from necessity (unless negligence present); ship-stranding sufficiently abnormal to raise res ipsa loquitur unless show not negligent.

Southport Corporation v Esso Petroleum Co, Ltd and another [1953] 2 All ER 1204; (1954) 118 JPI; (1953) 103 LJ 750; (1953) 97 SJ 764; [1953] 3 WLR 773 HC QBD Private nuisance need not emanate from neighbour's property; public nuisance on public navigable river akin to that on highway; need to prove negligence to establish nuisance.

Southsea Beach Mansions Hotel Ltd v Parkes and Hartry (1918) CC Rep VII 41 CyCt Lessee/occupier liable for nuisance occasioned by way of inadequate drains.

Spicer and another v Smee [1946] 1 All ER 489; (1946) 175 LTR 163 HC KBD Owner liable for nuisance on property though not in occupation; in nuisance can be liable for acts of independent contractor; same liability for private/public nuisance.

St Anne's Well Brewery Co v Roberts [1928] All ER 28; (1928) 92 JP 180; (1929) 140 LTR 1 CA No recovery for nuisance when retaining wall (normal use) collapsed without owner knowing of any defect.

St Anne's Well Brewery Company v Roberts (1928) 92 JP 95 HC KBD Recovery of damages when retaining wall (normal user) collapsed without defective state being known.

Stancomb v Trowbridge Urban District Council [1910] 2 Ch 190; (1910) 102 LTR 647 HC ChD Injunction to restrain council discharging sewage into stream.

Sweetapple v Minett (1976) 126 NLJ 1168b CA Smoke billowing from neighbour's fire into plaintiff's house not an actionable nuisance: people must live and let live.

Tamworth Borough Council v Fazeley Town Council (1978) 122 SJ 699 HC ChD Injunction to prevent operation of new market on same day as franchise market on basis that holding former constituted nuisance.

Tetley and others v Chitty and others [1986] 1 All ER; (1985) 135 NLJ 1009 HC QBD Landlord liable for foreseeable/authorised/impliedly authorised nuisance of tenants; where damages unsuitable injunction given.

The Attorney-General v WH Smith and Son (1910) 74 JP 313; (1910) 45 LJ 390; (1910-11) 103 LTR 96; (1909-10) XXVI TLR 482 HC ChD Whether user of public street in front of business place a nuisance depends on circumstances (here was not).

The Dean and Chapter of Chester and others v The Smelting Corporation (Limited) (1901) 36 LJ 420; (1901-02) LXXXV LTR 67; (1900-01) XVII TLR 743; (1901) WN (I) 179 HC ChD Need not end action for injunction that company which caused nuisance through its operations went into liquidation and ceased operations before trial began.

The Mayor, &c, of Chichester v Foster (1905-06) XCIII LTR 750; (1905-06) XXII TLR 18; (1905-06) 54 WR 199 HC KBD Recovery of damages from driver of traction engine who in driving along road crushed water mains leading to waterworks.

The Wagon Mound (No 2); Overseas Tankship (UK), Ltd v The Miller Steamship Co Pty Ltd and another [1966] 2 All ER 709; [1967] AC 617; (1966) 110 SJ 447; [1966] 3 WLR 498 PC Negligent where fail to prevent foreseeable injury; foreseeability of injury essential for recovery in nuisance.

Thomas and others v National Union of Mineworkers (South Wales Area) and others [1985] 2 All ER 1 HC ChD Peaceful/responsible picketing not watching or besetting/nuisance even if secondary picketing.

Timmis v Pearson [1934] LJNCCR 115 CyCt Overcrowding by tenant need not of itself render tenant guilty of nuisance.

Waterfield v Goodwin (1955) 105 LJ ccr332 CyCt Successful action in nuisance against neighbours (in semi-detached house) whose music lessons/practising of music/fondness for gramophone and radio music created a nuisance by noise.

Wellingborough Council v Gordon (1991) 155 JP 494; [1990] TLR 713 HC QBD Prosecution arising from noise at Friday night birthday party to which all neighbours invited, most attended and none complained, an extreme reaction: nonetheless was no 'reasonable excuse' for noise (Control of Pollution Act 1974, s 58).

Wheeler and another v JJ Saunders Ltd and others [1995] 2 All ER 697; [1996] Ch 19; [1995] TLR 3; [1995] 3 WLR 466 CA Planning consent does not preclude action for nuisance.

Whymark v Abrahams (1922) CC Rep XI 58 CyCt Owner of house not liable for injury occurring to passer-by when brick fell from defective chimney unless proved that owner let house with defect/was under contractual duty to keep chimney in repair.

Wilkins v Leighton [1932] All ER 55; [1932] 2 Ch 106; (1932) 73 LJ 255; (1932) 101 LJCh 385; (1932) 147 LTR 495; (1932) 76 SJ 232; (1932) WN (I) 68 HC ChD Occupier not liable for nuisance unless created it or knowingly allows it to continue when could abate it.

Wood v Conway Corporation [1914-15] All ER 1097; [1914] 2 Ch 47; (1914) 78 JP 249; [1914] 83 LJCh 498; (1914) 110 LTR 917 CA Injunction not damages deemed proper remedy for continuing nuisance.

Woodman v Pwllbach Colliery Company Limited (1914-15) 111 LTR 169 CA No common law right or easement pursuant to lease of colliery to create nuisance..

Wringe v Cohen [1939] 4 All ER 241; [1940] 1 KB 229; (1939) 88 LJ 315; [1940] 109 LJCL 227; (1939) 161 LTR 366; (1939) 83 SJ 923; (1939) WN (I) 386 CA Occupier/owner liable for damage due to want of repair (whether or not aware thereof) but only liable for damage effected by trespasser/hidden act of nature if has actual/constructive knowledge thereof.

NUISANCE (highway)

Attorney-General (at the relation of Knottingley Urban District Council) and Knottingley Urban District Council v Roe (1915) 79 JP 263; (1915) 112 LTR 581 HC ChD Owner of disused quarry ordered to abate nuisance created on adjacent highway through subsidence consequent upon onetime quarrying.

Attorney-General v Brighton and Hove Co-operative Supply Association [1900-03] All ER 216; [1900] 1 Ch 276; (1899-1900) LXXXI LTR 762; (1899-1900) XVI TLR 144; (1899-1900); 48 WR 314 CA On public nuisance/obstruction of highway: was public nuisance to keep up to six vans occupying half of street on regular basis.

Attorney-General v Roe [1914-15] All ER 1190; [1915] 1 Ch 235; [1915] 84 LJCh 322 HC ChD Party liable to fence off from highway adjoining area in which dangerous excavation work being undertaken.

Bromley v Mercer [1922] 2 KB 126; [1922] 91 LJCL 577; (1922) 127 LTR 282; (1921-22) XXXVIII TLR 496; (1922) WN (I) 112 CA Non-liability to non-user of highway for injury suffered via wall which was public nuisance on highway.

Caminer and another v Northern and London Investment Trust, Ltd [1948] 2 All ER 1101; (1948) 98 LJ 685; (1948) LXIV TLR 629; (1948) WN (I) 489 HC KBD Landowners liable in negligence/nuisance for failure to look after tree that falls injuring person on adjoining highway.

Crane v South Suburban Gas Co [1914-15] All ER 93; (1916) 80 JP 51; [1916] 1 KB 33; [1916] 85 LJKB 172; (1916) 114 LTR 71; (1915-16) 60 SJ 222; (1915-16) XXXII TLR 74 HC KBD Liability in nuisance and negligence for injury occasioned to person as result of third party intervention on foot of dangerous work by highway.

Creed v John McGeogh and Sons, Ltd [1955] 3 All ER 123; (1955) 105 LJ 618; (1955) 99 SJ 563; [1955] 1 WLR 1005 HC QBD Negligence towards child trespasser in builder's trailer; builder's trailer left close to highway not nuisance to highway.

Dixon v Chester (1906) 70 JP 380 HC KBD Surveyor empowered under Highway Act 1835, s 73 to seek order requiring that highway be cleared of timber which is nuisance.

Drake v Bedfordshire County Council [1944] 1 All ER 633; (1944) 108 JP 237; [1944] KB 620; (1945) 95 LJ 112; [1944] 113 LJ 328; (1944) 170 LTR 351; (1944) 88 SJ 239; (1943-44) LX TLR 304 HC KBD Gap in railings a continuing nuisance; defence of non-feasance open onty to highway authority and anyway this case involved misfeasance.

Dwyer and another v Mansfield [1946] 2 All ER 247; [1946] KB 437; [1947] 116 LJR 894; (1946) 175 LTR 61; (1946) 90 SJ 443; (1945-46) LXII TLR 401; (1946) WN (I) 93 HC KBD Shopping queue not proved to be nuisance — even if it was had failed to prove defendant caused it/was responsible therefor.

Eastbourne County Borough v Fuller and Sons (1929) 93 JP 29 HC KBD Failed action for nuisance/negligence against defendant in respect of its use of agricultural vehicles upon highway.

Hale v Hants and Dorset Motor Services, Ltd and another (1948) 112 JP 47 CA On liability of highway authority/omnibus driver for injury to upstairs passenger on omnibus struck by overhanging branches of tree.

Harper v Haden (GN) and Sons, Ltd [1932] All ER 59; [1933] Ch 298; (1932) 96 JP 525; (1932) 74 LJ 386; (1933) 102 LJCh 6; (1933) 148 LTR 303; (1932) 76 SJ 849; (1932) WN (I) 267 CA Temporary obstruction of highway/adjoining premises not nuisance where reasonable in scale and duration.

Hughes and another v Sheppard and others; Morley and others v Same (1940) 104 JP 357; (1940) 163 LTR 177; (1939-40) LVI TLR 810 HC KBD Not negligent/nuisance for council workers to mark where were painting lines on road with cans and flags — even if was nuisance only negligent driver who failed to see same and collided with another vehicle liable in actions arising from accident.

Hurst and another v Hampshire County Council [1997] 2 Cr App R (S) 1025; (1997) 147 NLJ 1025; (1997) 141 SJ LB 152; [1997] TLR 339 CA Highway authority liable for damage to house occasioned by roots of tree standing on verge of adjacent highway dedicated to the public.

Jackson v L Obertling, Ltd (1925) 60 LJ 521 CyCt Damages recoverable for nuisance occasioned by broken pavement light (said light not being part of highway repairable by highway authority).

Jones v Rew [1908-10] All ER 955; (1910) 74 JP 321 (also HC KBD); (1910) 79 LJKB 1030; (1910-11) 103 LTR 165 CA Urban sanitary authority liable in nuisance for state of carriage plate (not party who sometimes cleaned it out).

Jones v Rew (1910) 74 JP 321 (also CA) HC KBD Party who sometimes cleaned out carriage plate, not sanitary authority, liable in nuisance for state of same.

Lewys v Burnett and Dunbar and another [1945] 2 All ER 555; (1945) 109 JP 253; (1945) 173 LTR 307; (1945) 89 SJ 415; (1944-45) LXI TLR 527 HC KBD Persons giving free lift negligent for not warning dead passenger of what they knew; highway authority liable in nuisance for negligent raising of road beneath bridge.

Liddle v North Riding of Yorkshire County Council [1934] All ER 222; (1934) 98 JP 319; [1934] 2 KB 101; (1934) 103 LJCL 527; (1934) 151 LTR 202; (1934) 78 SJ 349; (1933-34) L TLR 377; (1934) WN (I) 100 CA Council not liable to child as trespasser as took all reasonable steps, as licensee as danger unconcealed; council not liable in nuisance for piling soil on verge of highway.

Lyons, Son and Co v Gulliver and The Capital Syndicate (Limited) (1912-13) 57 SJ 444; (1912-13) XXIX TLR 428 HC ChD Theatre owners liable in nuisance for obstruction on highway caused by persons queuing outside premises.

Lyons, Sons and Co v Gulliver and The Capital Syndicate (Limited) [1911-13] All ER 537; [1914] 1 Ch 631; (1914) 78 JP 98; [1914] 83 LJCh 281; (1914) 110 LTR 284; (1913-14) 58 SJ 97; (1913-14) XXX TLR 75 CA Theatre owners liable in nuisance for obstruction on highway caused by persons queuing outside premises.

Masters v Hampshire County Council (1915) 79 JP 493; [1915] 84 LJKB 2194 HC KBD Non-liability for non-feasance.

Monmouthshire County Council v Dean (1962) 112 LJ 787 CyCt Failed claim that person whom claimed to have inadequately drained bank was liable in nuisance/for obstruction where bank became waterlogged and slipped onto road.

Newsome v Darton Urban District Council (1938) 102 JP 75; (1938) 158 LTR 149; (1937) 81 SJ 1042; (1937-38) LIV TLR 286 HC KBD Highway authority liable in nuisance/negligence for misfeasance (subsidence in trench had caused to be dug which led to injury to cyclist).

Newsome v Darton Urban District Council (1938) 102 JP 409; (1938) 82 SJ 520; (1937-38) LIV TLR 945 CA Highway and sanitary authority liable as latter in nuisance/negligence for misfeasance (subsidence in trench had caused to be dug which led to injury to cyclist).

Pope v Fraser and Southern Rolling and Wire Mills, Limited (1939) 83 SJ 135; (1938-39) LV TLR 324 HC KBD Employer responsible for servant's non-negligent creation of nuisance on highway which servant did nothing to obviate when informed of same.

Priest v Manchester Corporation [1915] 84 LJKB 1734 HC KBD Sale of land for tipping purposes did not authorise tipping in such a way as to occasion nuisance.

R v Clark [1963] 3 All ER 884; (1964) 48 Cr App R 69; [1964] Crim LR 45; (1964) 114 LJ 8; (1963) 107 SJ 983; [1963] 3 WLR 1067 CCA Obstruction and unreasonable user of street needed in nuisance via obstruction of highway.

Simon v Islington Borough Council and others (1942) 106 JP 212 HC KBD Highway authority not liable for nonfeasance of tramway over which had assumed authority and which had not surfaced.

Simon v Islington Borough Council (1943) 107 JP 59; (1943) 168 LTR 65; (1942-43) LIX TLR 87 CA Council liable for misfeasance of highway by way of obstruction which constituted nuisance.

Skilton v Epsom and Ewell Urban District Council (1936) 100 JP 231; [1937] 1 KB 112; [1937] 106 LJCL 41; (1936) 154 LTR 700; (1936) 80 SJ 345; (1935-36) LII TLR 494; (1936) WN (I) 155 CA Local authority's placing of defective stud on highway actionable negligence/nuisance.

Slater v Worthington's Cash Stores (1930), Limited [1941] 1 All ER 245; (1941) 91 LJ 100; [1942] 111 LJ 91 (also CA); (1941) 165 LTR 293; (1940-41) LVII TLR 294; (1941) WN (I) 26 HC KBD Nuisance/negligence liability where had not removed snow from roof four days after heavy snowstorms ended.

Slater v Worthington's Cash Stores (1930), Ltd [1941] 3 All ER 28; [1941] 1 KB 488; [1942] 111 LJ 91 (also HC KBD); (1940-41) LVII TLR 468 CA Nuisance/negligence liability where had not removed snow from roof four days after heavy snowstorms ended.

The Great House at Sonning Ltd and others v Berkshire County Council [1996] RTR 407; (1996) 140 SJ LB 123 CA Could not claim damages in nuisance against highway authority for obstruction through one-week closure of street for road-works (could seek judicial review of decision).

Turner and another v Deal Corporation (1967) 111 SJ 685 HC QBD Successful action in nuisance for damage to property in course of road-widening.

Tynan v Balmer [1966] Crim LR 223; (1966) 110 SJ 129; [1966] 2 WLR 1181 HC QBD Common law nuisance for picketers to close off public highway.

Vanderpant v Mayfair Hotel Co, Ltd [1929] All ER 296; [1930] 1 Ch 138; (1929) 68 LJ 256; (1930) 99 LJCh 84; (1930) 94 JP 23; (1930) 142 LTR 198; (1929) WN (I) 221 HC ChD Interests of public regarding public highway greater than that of occupier adjoining same but person seeking to restrain latter must show special/direct interest in so doing; on judging when noise a nuisance.

Ware v Garston Haulage Co, Ltd [1943] 2 All ER 558; [1944] KB 30; (1944) 94 LJ 109; [1944] 113 LJ 45; (1944) 170 LTR 155; (1943-44) LX TLR 77 CA Unlit motor vehicle on unlit nighttime road a nuisance.

NUISANCE (hospital)

Frost v The King Edward VII Welsh National Memorial Assocciation for Prevention, Treatment and Abolition of Tuberculosis [1918] 2 Ch 180; (1918) 82 JP 249; (1918) 53 LJ 227; [1918] 87 LJCh 561; (1918-19) 119 LTR 220; (1918) WN (I) 185 HC ChD Operation of tuberculosis hospital deemed not to cause nuisance by virtue of noise/offensiveness/threat of infection.

The Attorney-General v The Mayor, &c, of Nottingham [1904] 1 Ch 673; (1904) 68 JP 125; [1904] 73 LJCh 512; (1904) XC LTR 308; (1903-04) XX TLR 257; (1904) WN (I) 55; (1903-04) 52 WR 281 HC ChD Isolation hospital held not to be nuisance.

NUISANCE (irrigation)

Canadian Pacific Railway Company v Parke and another (1899-1900) LXXXI LTR 127 PC That Crown authorised diversion of water from natural path did not mean could not be liable under common law in performance of same.

NUISANCE (landlord and tenant)

Browne and Wife v Flower, Lightbody, and Kendrick (1910-11) 103 LTR 557 HC ChD Erection of staircase by fellow tenant not a nuisance/breach of covenant.

Cobstone Investments Ltd v Maxim [1985] QB 140 CA On what constitutes an adjoining occupier' (capable of complaining of nuisance of/annoyance by neighbour) for purposes of Rent Act 1977.

Davis v Town Properties Investment Corporation [1903] 72 LJCh 389 CA Assignee of reversion not liable for breach of covenant with lessee (through nuisance).

Elliott and another v London County Freehold and Leasehold Properties, Ltd [1936] LJNCCR 117 CyCt Flat-owners not liable to under-lessees of flat for nuisance (emission into house of smoke/soot) occasioned by under-lessees lighting fire in flat.

Foulger v Arding [1901] 70 LJK/QB 580 HC KBD On covenant in lease necessary to render tenant liable for expense of abating nuisance occasioned by structural defect in leased premises.

Foulger v Arding [1902] 71 LJCL 499 CA On covenant in lease necessary to render tenant liable for expense of abating nuisance occasioned by structural defect in leased premises.

Frederick Platts Company, Limited v Grigor [1950] 66 (1) TLR 859 CA Failed action to recover possession of property on basis of tenant's guilt of nuisance to neighbours in breach of Rent and Mortgage Interest Restrictions (Amendment) Act 1933.

Malzy v Eichholz [1916] 85 LJKB 1132 CA Lessor not liable for nuisance occasioned by one lessee to another towards whom lessor had covenanted quiet enjoyment of property.

Mint and another v Good [1950] 2 All ER 1159; [1951] 1 KB 517; (1950) 100 LJ 691; (1950) 94 SJ 822; [1950] 66 (2) TLR 1110; (1950) WN (I) 555 CA Landlord liable (absent contrary agreement) to maintain premises (here walls adjoining highway) in safe condition.

O'Leary and another v Islington London Borough Council [1983] TLR 307 HC QBD Ought to have brought action in nuisance against neighbours rather than seeking to force landlords to enforce no-nuisance clause in tenancy agreement.

Smith v Scott and others [1972] 3 All ER 645; [1973] Ch 314; (1972) 116 SJ 785; [1972] 3 WLR 783 HC ChD Landlord not liable for tenant's nuisance unless expressly authorises it or it is inevitable from use: neither so here; Rylands v Fletcher inapplicable to landlord with rowdy tenants; landlord's duties well settled law.

Turley v King (1944) 108 JP 73; (1944) 170 LTR 247; (1943-44) LX TLR 197; (1944) WN (I) 51 HC KBD Landlord must comply with order to abate statutory nuisance (war-damaged houses) notwithstanding Landlord and Tenant (War Damage) Act 1939.

Wilchick v Marks and Silverstone (Silverstone, Third Party) (1934) 77 LJ 221; (1934) 151 LTR 60; (1933-34) L TLR 281 HC KBD Tenant liable to passer-by on whom shutter fell and landlord liable to tenant.

Wringe v Cohen [1939] LJNCCR 251 CyCt Landlord of tenanted property liable for damage to another's property occasioned by nuisance upon landlord's premises.

NUISANCE (light)

Ambler v Bishop of Leeds (1904-05) 49 SJ 238; (1904-05) 53 WR 300 HC KBD On, inter alia, extent of user which bestows right not to have light so interfered with as to constitute nuisance.

Anderson v Francis (1906) WN (I) 160 HC ChD Injunction to restrain erection of building in such form as would cause nuisance through interference with ancient windows.

Colls v Home and Colonial Stores, Limited [1904] AC 179 HL Must be considerable interference with light to succeed in action for obstruction of ancient lights.

Cowper and others v Milburn and others (1907-08) 52 SJ 316 HL Interference with ancient lights deemed not, in circumstances, to be a nuisance.

Fishenden v Higgs and Hill Limited (1935) 153 LTR 128 CA Interference with ancient lights sufficiently grave as to constitute nuisance.

Higgins v Betts [1905] 2 Ch 210; (1905) XCII LTR 850; (1904-05) 49 SJ 535; (1904-05) XXI TLR 552; (1904-05) 53 WR 549 HC ChD Considerable deprivation of light rendering occupation of premises difficult is nuisance.

Hortons' Estate, Limited v James Beattie, Limited [1927] 1 Ch 75; (1925-26) XLII TLR 701 HC ChD Particular obstruction of ancient light was actionable nuisance.

Jolly v Kine [1907] AC 1; [1907] 76 LJCh 1; (1906-07) XCV LTR 656; (1906-07) 51 SJ 11; (1906-07) XXIII TLR 1 HL Obstruction of ancient lights a nuisance though room still well-lit.

Kine v Jolly [1905] 1 Ch 480; (1905) XCII LTR 209; (1904-05) 49 SJ 164; (1904-05) XXI TLR 128; (1904-05) 53 WR 462 CA Obstruction of ancient lights a nuisance.

News of the World, Limited v Allen Fairhead and Sons, Limited [1931] 2 Ch 402; (1931) 100 LJCh 394; (1932) 146 LTR 11 HC ChD On gauging degree of nuisance (if nuisance there is) where ancient light reduced by new construction.

Ough v King (1967) 111 SJ 792; [1967] 1 WLR 1547 CA On appropriate test when determining whether reduction of light constituted nuisance.

Paul and another v Robson and others [1914] 83 LJPC 304; (1914-15) 111 LTR 481 PC In action for interference with light and air acts complained of must be nuisance to be successful.

Smith v Evangelization Society (Incorporated) Trust [1933] Ch 515 (also HC ChD); (1933) 102 LJCh 275 (also HC ChD); (1932-33) XLIX TLR 262; (1933) WN (I) 66 CA On nuisance by way of obstruction of ancient light.

Smith v Evangelization Society (Incorporated) Trust [1933] Ch 515 (also CA); (1933) 102 LJCh 275 (also CA); (1932-33) XLIX TLR 32 HC ChD On nuisance by way of obstruction of ancient light.

NUISANCE (mines)

Newcastle-under-Lyme Corporation v Wolstanton, Limited [1947] Ch 92; (1946) 110 JP 376; (1946) 90 SJ 419 HC ChD Damages for nuisance occasioned by mining company to corporation's gas mains/pipes.

Newcastle-under-Lyme Corporation v Wolstanton Ltd (1947) 111 JP 102 CA Damages for nuisance occasioned by mining company to corporation's gas mains/pipes.

NUISANCE (negligence)

Longhurst v Metropolitan Water Board (1947) 111 JP 212; [1947] 116 LJR 612 HC KBD Water board liable for injury suffered through its negligence in repair of leak.

Longhurst v Metropolitan Water Board (1947) 111 JP 477; (1947) 91 SJ 653 CA Water Board owed qualified duty of care to public when effecting repairs under the Waterworks Clauses Act 1847 — here not violated.

Longhurst v Metropolitan Water Board [1948] 2 All ER 834; (1948) 112 JP 470 HL Where act under statutory authority no nuisance absent negligence (and here no negligence).

NUISANCE (noise)

Aitken v South Hams District Council [1994] 3 All ER 400; [1995] 1 AC 262; (1994) 144 NLJ 1096; (1994) 138 SJ LB 167; [1994] TLR 380; [1994] 3 WLR 333 HL Noise abatement order made under repealed legislation is effective.

Andreae v Selfridge and Company, Ltd [1936] 2 All ER 1413; (1936) 82 LJ 174; (1936) 80 SJ 792 HC ChD Noise/dust/grit of construction site was nuisance despite proper use of tools as was done without thought for neighbours.

Andreae v Selfridge and Company, Limited [1938] Ch 1; [1938] 107 LJCh 126; (1937) 157 LTR 317; (1937) 81 SJ 525 CA Limited damages available in nuisance for excesses of noise/dust/grit of construction site.

Becker v Earls' Court (Lim) (1911-12) 56 SJ 73 HC ChD Noise from fairground entertainment/ users of same at Earls' Court exhibition arena was a nuisance.

Bedford v Leeds Corporation (1913) 77 JP 430 HC ChD Action to restrain nuisance occasioned by holding of yearly feast (action successful in part).

Bosworth-Smith v Gwynnes, Limited [1920] 89 LJCh 368; (1920) 122 LTR 15 HC ChD Noise from aeroplane-testing was a nuisance.

Clark v Lloyd's Bank Limited (1910) 74 JP 429; (1910) 45 LJ 537; [1910] 79 LJCh 645; (1910-11) 103 LTR 211; (1909-10) 54 SJ 704 HC ChD Injunction refused to hotel owner seeking to stop builder from carrying on noisy early morning construction work beside hotel.

Colwell v St Pancras Borough Council [1904] 1 Ch 707; (1904) 68 JP 286; (1904) 39 LJ 84; [1904] 73 LJCh 275; (1904) XC LTR 153; (1903-04) XX TLR 236; (1904) WN (I) 40; (1903-04) 52 WR 523 HC ChD Injunction granted to restrain use of engines in power station in manner that their vibration interfered with plaintiffs enjoyment of and depreciated value of his premises.

Compton v Bunting (1939) 83 SJ 398 HC ChD Noise emanating from kindergarten/preparatory school music room deemed not to be such a nuisance as merited injunctive relief.

De Keyser's Royal Hotel (Limited) v Spicer Brothers (Limited) and Minter (1913-14) XXX TLR 257 HC ChD Was nuisance for builders to do pile-driving at night which kept persons in adjoining premises awake.

Delvalle v Thompson and others (1961) 111 LJ 276 CyCt Damages (but no injunction) where noise from parties held by neighbours constituted nuisance.

Dunton v Dover District Council (1977) 127 NLJ 538t HC QBD Injunction restricting opening hours of children's playground noise from hitherto unrestricted use of which had been a nuisance.

Etheridge v Pink (1932) 74 LJ ccr70 CyCt On relief available for nuisance by noise/vibration.

Gilling v Gray (1910-11) XXVII TLR 39 HC ChD Injunction against causing noise by sawing and planing where constituted nuisance plus damages for past nuisance.

Hartland v Mottershead (1956) 106 LJ ccr269 CyCt Damages plus liberty to apply for injunction to elderly plaintiff whose neighbours were guilty of nuisance by noise by way of piano playing/playing the radio.

Heath v The Mayor, &c, of Brighton (1908) 72 JP 225; (1908) XCVIII LTR 718; (1907-08) XXIV TLR 414 HC ChD Noise from electric generator/transformer annoying churchgoers not enough to merit injunction for nuisance.

Knight v The Isle of Wight Electric Light and Power Company (Limited) (1904) 68 JP 266; [1904] 73 LJCh 299; (1904) XC LTR 410; (1903-04) XX TLR 173 HC ChD Injunction to restrain use of engines in such a way as to prevent another's enjoyment of their premises by virtue of the noise, smell and vibrations.

Leeman v Montagu [1936] 2 All ER 1677; (1936) 80 SJ 691 HC KBD Noise from poultry farm a nuisance.

Lipman v George Pulman and Sons Limited (1904) 39 LJ 369; (1904-05) XCI LTR 132; (1904) WN (I) 139 HC ChD On damages recoverable where seeking same in addition to injunction to prevent nuisance by noise/vibration.

Moy v Stoop (1908-09) XXV TLR 262 HC KBD Noise from house used as children's nursery not nuisance.

Polsue and Alfieri, Ltd v Rushmer [1904-07] All ER 586; [1907] AC 121; (1907) 42 LJ 180; [1907] 76 LJCh 365; (1907) XCVI LTR 510; (1906-07) 51 SJ 324; (1906-07) XXIII TLR 362; (1907) WN (I) 67 HL General circumstances of situation relevant when seeking injunction for nuisance by noise.

Prestatyn Urban District Council v Prestatyn Raceway Ltd and another (1969) 113 SJ 899; [1970] 1 WLR 33 HC ChD No relief (absent special injury) for local authority from nuisance which had itself authorised via covenant (plus under Local Government Act 1933, s 276) action ought to have been upon relation of Attorney-General).

R v Clerk to the Birmingham City Justices, ex parte Guppy (1988) 152 JP 159 HC QBD On fomat of noise nuisance abatement notice.

R v Secretary of State for Transport, ex parte Richmond upon Thames London Borough Council and others (No 4) [1996] 4 All ER 93; (1996) 140 SJ LB 98; [1996] 1 WLR 1005 HC QBD On power of Secretary of State for Transport as regards requiring noise reduction at airports.

R v Secretary of State for Transport, ex parte Richmond upon Thames London Borough Council and others (No 4) [1996] 4 All ER 903; [1996] 1 WLR 1460 CA On power of Secretary of State for Transport as regards requiring noise reduction at airports.

Saddleworth Urban District Council v Aggregate and Sand Ltd (1970) 114 SJ 931 HC QBD Unavailability of money/reliance on expert advice not/could be reasonable excuse for non-abatement of nuisance.

Sampson v Hodson-Pressinger and Betts [1981] 3 All ER 710; (1981) 131 NLJ 1212; (1981) 125 SJ 623 CA Damages for nuisance by noise through use of terrazza.

Stretch v Romford Football Club Ltd and others (1971) 115 SJ 741 HC ChD Injunction granted to restrain speedway racing near residential area as was a nuisance.

Tarry v Chandler (1935) 79 SJ 11 HC ChD Noisy manner in which stadium was operated was a nuisance.

White and another v London General Omnibus Co (1914) 49 LJ 114; (1913-14) 58 SJ 339; (1914) WN (I) 78 HC ChD Nuisance by noise/smell from garage not permanent injury to reversion.

NUISANCE (obstruction)

Attorney-General v Wilcox [1938] Ch 934; (1938) 86 LJ 44; [1938] 107 LJCh 425 HC ChD On nuisance through trivial obstruction of public path: injunction on erection of posts on towpath.

NUISANCE (occupier)

Bank View Mill, Ltd and others v Nelson Corpn and Fryer and Co (Nelson), Ltd [1942] 2 All ER 477 Assizes Corporation in occupation and control knowing of obstruction and with chance to remove liable in nuisance; flooding slightly due to weir: nominal damages against weir-owner.

Bank View Mill, Ltd and others v Nelson Corporation and Fryer and Co (Nelson), Ltd [1943] 1 All ER 299; [1943] KB 337; [1943] 112 LJ 306; (1943) 168 LTR 244 CA Corporation not in occupation so not liable for nuisance.

Leanse v Egerton [1943] 1 All ER 489; [1943] KB 323; (1944) 94 LJ 109; [1943] 112 LJ 273; (1943) 168 LTR 218; (1942-43) LIX TLR 191; (1943) WN (I) 56 HC KBD Occupier liable for continuing nuisance occasioned by air raid.

NUISANCE (parking)

Parish v Judd [1960] 3 All ER 33; (1960) 124 JP 444; (1960) 110 LJ 701; (1960) 104 SJ 644 HC QBD Prima facie negligent to leave unlit car in unlit place on road at night (not here as lamp/reasonable care); nuisance if unlit car in unlit place on road at night is dangerous obstruction.

NUISANCE (pollution)

Leake v Wootton and Kelley (trading as the Stoneleigh Quarry Company) (1923) CC Rep XII 68 CyCt Failed action against quarrying company for damages after cattle got sick drinking water polluted (but only inter alia) by local quarry.

Pride of Derby and Derbyshire Angling Association, Ltd and another v British Celanese, Ltd and others [1952] 1 All ER 1326; (1952) WN (I) 227 HC ChD Where persons collectively commit nuisance but individually not improper behaviour may be sued collectively for nuisance.

Pride of Derby and Derbyshire Angling Association, Ltd and another v British Celanese, Ltd and others [1953] 1 All ER 179; [1953] Ch 149; (1953) 117 JP 52; (1952) 102 LJ 721; (1953) 97 SJ 28; [1953] 2 WLR 58 CA Local authority liable for nuisance in violating Rivers Pollution Prevention Act 1876; injunction available against local authority but suspended where required doing of impossible.

NUISANCE (prostitution)

Thompson-Schwab and another v Costaki and another [1956] 1 All ER 652; [1956] Crim LR 274; (1956) 106 LJ 201; (1956) 100 SJ 246; [1956] 1 WLR 335 CA Use of neighbouring premises for prostitution a nuisance.

NUISANCE (public authority)

Dormer and others v Newcastle-upon-Tyne Corporation [1940] 2 All ER 521; (1940) 104 JP 316; [1940] 2 KB 204; (1940) 89 LJ 239; [1940] 109 LJCL 708 (also HC KBD); (1940) 163 LTR 266; (1939-40) LVI TLR 673; (1940) WN (I) 186 CA Safety railings could be erected at side of pavement despite being public/private nuisance.

NUISANCE (quarrying)

Thomas v Lewis [1937] 1 All ER 137; (1937) 81 SJ 98 HC ChD Quarry owner not liable/liable for damage to own land rented to farmer/to farmer's own land adjoining rented land for nuisance arising from quarrying.

NUISANCE (rail)

Ash and another v The Great Northern, Piccadilly, and Brompton Railway Company (1903) 67 JP 417; (1902-03) XIX TLR 639 HC ChD Liability/non-liability of rail company for common law nuisance not clothed/clothed by statutory authority.

Dominion Iron and Steel Company Limited v Burt [1917] 86 LJPC 97; (1917) 116 LTR 261 HL Failed appeal seeking to have rail company found guilty of nuisance in its execution of certain works.

London Midland and Scottish Railway Company v The Ribble Hat Works Limited (1936) 80 SJ 1038 HC ChD Was negligent/nuisance for defendants to place red/green neon sign adjacent to rail lights and so render those light signals more difficult to view.

Smith v Great Western Rail Co and another [1926] All ER 242; (1926) 135 LTR 112; (1925-26) XLII TLR 391 HC KBD Railway company not liable for continuance of nuisance where took all reasonable steps regarding same; party consigning leaking oil tank to rail carriers which resulted in injury to third party liable in nuisance.

NUISANCE (road traffic)

Coote and another v Stone (1970) 120 NLJ 1205; [1971] RTR 66; (1971) 115 SJ 79 CA Parked car on clearway not a common law nuisance.

Demerara Electric Company Limited v White and others [1907] AC 330; (1907) XCVI LTR 752; (1906-07) 51 SJ 497 PC No nuisance condition in lighting order extended to contemporaneous granting of tramways licence.

Drury v Camden London Brough Council [1972] RTR 391 HC QBD Council (50%) liable in negligence/nuisance for leaving unlit skip projecting into highway; driver equally liable for failing to maintain proper vigilance.

Hale v Hants and Dorset Motor Services, Ltd and another (1948) 112 JP 47 CA On liability of highway authority/omnibus driver for injury to upstairs passenger on omnibus struck by overhanging branches of tree.

Isaac Walton and Co v The Vanguard Motorbus Co (Limited); Gibbons v The Vanguard Motorbus Co (Limited) (1908) 72 JP 505; (1908-09) 53 SJ 82; (1908-09) XXV TLR 13 HC KBD Bus striking permanent structure (in first case) could be due to negligence of driver (and in second case) was negligent use of nuisance placed on highway.

Maitland v Raisbeck and RT and J Hewitt, Ltd [1944] LJNCCR 26 CyCt That rear light of lorry not on did not necessarily make lorry a nuisance.

Maitland v Raisbeck [1944] 2 All ER 272; [1944] KB 689; (1945) 95 LJ 112; [1944] 113 LJ 549; (1944) 171 LTR 118; (1944) 88 SJ 359; (1943-44) LX TLR 521; (1944) WN (I) 195 CA That rear light of lorry not on did not necessarily make lorry a nuisance.

R v Wilbraham, ex parte Rowcliffe (1907-09) XXI Cox CC 441; (1907) 71 JP 336; (1907) XCVI LTR 712 HC KBD Non-liability for smoke given out from car as result of carelessness.

T Tilling, Limited v Dick, Kerr and Co Limited (1905) 69 JP 172; (1904-05) 53 WR 380 HC KBD Recovery of damages for injury to omnibuses effected by contractors doing council works.

Ware v Garston Haulage Co, Limited [1943] 2 All ER 558; [1944] KB 30; (1944) 94 LJ 109; [1944] 113 LJ 45; (1944) 170 LTR 155; (1943-44) LX TLR 77 CA Unlit motor vehicle on unlit nighttime road a nuisance.

Wills v TF Martin (Roof Contractors) Ltd [1972] RTR 368; (1972) 122 NLJ 81t; (1972) 116 SJ 145 HC QBD Placing skip on highway not proven negligent and though a nuisance person who collided with same, not skip-owner was liable.

NUISANCE (sewage)

Liverpool Corporation v H Coghill and Son (Limited) [1918] 1 Ch 307; (1918) 82 JP 129; (1918) 118 LTR 336; (1917-18) XXXIV TLR 159 HC ChD Running borax solution into sewer and so causing damage to neighbouring sewage farm was nuisance.

NUISANCE (sheep)

Heath's Garage, Limited v Hodges [1916-17] All ER 358; (1916) 80 JP 321; [1916] 2 KB 370; (1916) 51 LJ 295; [1916] 85 LJKB 1289; (1916-17) 115 LTR 129; (1915-16) 60 SJ 554; (1915-16) XXXII TLR 570; (1916) WN (I) 229 CA Non-liability of sheep-owner for injury caused through sheep straying onto highway.

NUISANCE (smell)

Adams v Ursell [1913] 1 Ch 269; (1913) 48 LJ 42; (1913) 82 LJCh 157; (1913) 108 LTR 292; (1912-13) 57 SJ 227; (1913) WN (I) 18 HC ChD Smell from fried fish shop could ground action for nuisance.

Attorney-General (at the relation of the Chailey Rural District Council) v Keymer Brick and Tile Co, Limited (1903) 67 JP 434 HC ChD Injunction to restrain party bringing house refuse onto land insofar as it constituted a nuisance by smell.

Bainbridge and another v Chertsey Urban District Council (1915) 79 JP 134; [1915] 84 LJCh 626 HC ChD Injunction for nuisance by smell from sewage works: basis on which such injunction to be granted.

Bland v Yates (1913-14) 58 SJ 612 HC ChD Excessive manure (which gave off smell and attracted flies) was nuisance even though area in which located was market gardening area.

Bone and another v Seale [1975] 1 All ER 787; (1975) 119 SJ 137; [1975] 1 WLR 797 CA Appropriate damages for loss of amenity because of smell.

Chesham (Lord) v Chesham Urban District Council (1935) 80 LJ 8 (1935) 79 SJ 453 HC ChD Injunctive relief/damages available against/from party guilty inter alia of nuisance by smell (occasioned by feeding inadequately treated sewage into river).

Dulverton Rural District Council v Tracy (1921) 85 JP 217 HL Damages for nuisance occasioned through killing of fish by piping sewage into river.

Great Central Railway v Doncaster Rural District Council (1918) 82 JP 33; [1918] 87 LJCh 80; (1918) 118 LTR 19; (1917-18) 62 SJ 212 HC ChD Delayed injunction granted to restrain use of tip causing nuisance by smell.

Haigh v Deudraeth Rural District Council [1945] 2 All ER 661; (1946) 110 JP 97; (1946) 96 LJ 213; (1946) 174 LTR 243; (1945) 89 SJ 579 HC ChD Injunction against local authority (having same liability as private individual) to prevent escape of sewage into river.

Knight v The Isle of Wight Electric Light and Power Company (Limited) (1904) 68 JP 266; [1904] 73 LJCh 299; (1904) XC LTR 410; (1903-04) XX TLR 173 HC ChD Injunction to restrain use of engines in such a way as to prevent another's enjoyment of their premises by virtue of the noise, smell and vibrations.

White and another v London General Omnibus Co (1914) 49 LJ 114; (1913-14) 58 SJ 339; (1914) WN (I) 78 HC ChD Nuisance by noise/smell from garage not permanent injury to reversion.

NUISANCE (smoke)

Holling and another v Yorkshire Traction Co, Ltd and others [1948] 2 All ER 662 Assizes Blowing of smoke across road so that view obscured a nuisance.

NUISANCE (sport)

Castle v St Augustine's Links, Limited, and another (1921-22) XXXVIII TLR 615 HC KBD Golf tee and hole found to be public nuisance where were situated.

Miller and another v Jackson and another [1977] 3 All ER 338; (1977) 127 NLJ 568t; [1977] QB 966; (1977) 121 SJ 287; [1977] 3 WLR 20 CA Cricket balls emanating from village cricket ground a negligent act.

Stone v Bolton and others [1949] 1 All ER 237 Assizes Single incident not nuisance; cricket-playing not unnatural land user (Rylands v Fletcher inapplicable); cricket-ball inadvertently striking person on highway not negligent.

Stone v Bolton and others [1949] 2 All ER 851; [1950] 1 KB 201; (1949) 99 LJ 625; (1949) LXV TLR 683; (1949) WN (I) 432 CA Cricket ball flying from ground to highway was negligent/not nuisance.

NUISANCE (statutory authority)

Department of Transport v North West Water Authority [1983] 1 All ER 892; [1984] AC 336 (also HL); [1982] TLR 617; [1983] 3 WLR 105 HC QBD Inapplicability of defence of statutory authority in public nuisance action against water authority.

Tate and Lyle Industries Ltd and another v Greater London Council and another [1983] 1 All ER 1159; [1983] 2 AC 509; (1983) 127 SJ 257 HL Inapplicability of defence of statutory authority in public nuisance action.

NUISANCE (telephone calls)

Khorasandjian v Bush [1993] 3 All ER 669; [1993] QB 727; [1993] 3 WLR 476 CA Court may grant injunction against harrassing telephone calls as private nuisance.

NUISANCE (tree)

British Road Services Ltd v Slater and another [1964] 1 All ER 816; (1964) 114 LJ 290; (1964) 108 SJ 357; [1964] 1 WLR 498 HC QBD Tree branch overhanging road was a nuisance but facts that led to it being nuisance so queer that landowner not liable for same.

Butler v Standard Telephones and Cables, Ltd; McCarthy v Standard Telephones and Cables, Ltd [1940] 1 All ER 121; [1940] 1 KB 399; [1940] 109 LJCL 238; (1940) 163 LTR 145; (1940) 84 SJ 189; (1939-40) LVI TLR 273; (1940) WN (I) 26 HC KBD Tree roots spreading into neighbour's property were deemed nuisance.

Cheater v Cater [1917] 2 KB 516; (1917-18) 117 LTR 335 HC KBD Lessor under Rylands v Fletcher-style liability for death of horse eating yew branches overhanging lessee's property.

Cheater v Cater [1918] 1 KB 247; (1918) 118 LTR 203; (1917) WN (I) 365 CA Lessor not liable for death of horse eating yew branches overhanging lessee's property as lessee took property with yew trees already overhanging.

Davey v Harrow Corporation [1957] 2 All ER 305; (1957) 107 LJ 344; [1958] 1 QB 61; (1957) 101 SJ 405 CA Nuisance to owner of adjoining property if planted/self-sown trees on one's property cause of damage on other's.

Hurst and another v Hampshire County Council [1997] 2 Cr App R (S) 1025; (1997) 147 NLJ 1025; (1997) 141 SJ LB 152; [1997] TLR 339 CA Highway authority liable for damage to house occasioned by roots of tree standing on verge of adjacent highway dedicated to the public.

King and another v Taylor and others (1976) 126 NLJ 916 HC QBD Damages/injunction for nuisance occasioned by encroachment of tree roots onto property.

Morgan (Charles) v Khyatt (Najlo A) (1964) 108 SJ 236; [1964] 1 WLR 475 PC Was nuisance where roots of trees on one person's property ran onto another's and caused structural damage.

Noble v Harrison [1926] All ER 284; (1926) 90 JP 188; [1926] 2 KB 332; [1926] 95 LJCL 813; (1926) 135 LTR 325; (1925-26) 70 SJ 691; (1925-26) XLII TLR 518; (1926) WN (I) 171 HC KBD Overhanging tree not dangerous object/nuisance: no liability if falls and injures person on highway if neither knew/ought to have known might happen.

Russell and another v Barnet London Borough Council [1984] TLR 262 HC QBD Highway authority liable in nuisance for damage occasioned by tree roots to property even though did not actually own the trees.

The PLP Motor Carrying Co, Ltd v Cornwall Legh (1929) 68 LJ 44 CyCt Owner of tree overhanging highway must know of situation before can be liable for damage occasioned by same.

Wallace v Clayton (1962) 112 LJ 208 CyCt Successful action for nuisance occasioned by growing of poplar trees (damages plus suspended injunction).

Walter Scott Motor Co v Horwitt [1937] LJNCCR 30 CyCt Person on whose property tree grew not liable in nuisance when branches overhanging another's property fell and occasioned damage.

NUISANCE (vibration)

Attorney-General (on the relation of Glamorgan County Council and Pontardawe Rural District Council) v PYA Quarries, Ltd [1957] 1 All ER 894; [1957] 2 QB 169; [1957] 2 WLR 770 CA Nuisance a public nuisance if affects class of people in vicinity thereof; on nuisance by vibration.

Colwell v St Pancras Borough Council [1904] 1 Ch 707; (1904) 68 JP 286; (1904) 39 LJ 84; [1904] 73 LJCh 275; (1904) XC LTR 153; (1903-04) XX TLR 236; (1904) WN (I) 40; (1903-04) 52 WR 523 HC ChD Injunction granted to restrain use of engines in power station in manner that their vibration interfered with plaintiffs enjoyment of and depreciated value of his premises.

Etheridge v Pink (1932) 74 LJ ccr70 CyCt On relief available for nuisance by noise/vibration.

Hoare and Co, Ltd v Sir Robert McAlpine, Sons and Co [1922] All ER 759; [1923] 1 Ch 167; [1923] 92 LJCh 81; (1923) 128 LTR 526; (1922-23) 67 SJ 146; (1922-23) XXXIX TLR 97; (1922) WN (I) 329 HC ChD Rylands v Fletcher applied to nuisance by vibration.

Knight v The Isle of Wight Electric Light and Power Company (Limited) (1904) 68 JP 266; [1904] 73 LJCh 299; (1904) XC LTR 410; (1903-04) XX TLR 173 HC ChD Injunction to restrain use of engines in such a way as to prevent another's enjoyment of their premises by virtue of the noise, smell and vibrations.

Lipman v George Pulman and Sons Limited (1904) 39 LJ 369; (1904-05) XCI LTR 132; (1904) WN (I) 139 HC ChD On damages recoverable where seeking same in addition to injunction to prevent nuisance by noise/vibration.

NUISANCE (vicarious liability)

Bird (Vere Cornwall) and others v O'Neal (Joseph Raymond) and another [1960] 3 WLR 584 PC Threats of violence/intimidation at picket sufficient to render individual union members but not trade union liable for nuisance.

NUISANCE (watching and besetting)

Hubbard and others v Pitt and others [1975] 3 All ER 1 CA Watching and besetting with view to securing certain behaviour might be nuisance.

OCCUPIER'S LIABILITY (child)

Pannett v P McGuinness and Co Ltd [1972] 3 All ER 137; [1972] 2 QB 599; (1972) 116 SJ 335; [1972] 3 WLR 386 CA Occupiers owed such duties to trespassing children as common sense/humanity demanded.

OCCUPIER'S LIABILITY (duty of care)

Cotton v Derbyshire Dales District Council [1994] TLR 335 CA Occupier not liable for not posting sign warning of obvious dangers at cliffside.

OCCUPIER'S LIABILITY (fire)

H and N Emanuel Ltd v Greater London Council and another (1970) 120 NLJ 707t; (1970) 114 SJ 653 HC QBD Occupier liable for negligent escape of fire by non-stranger on land.

H and N Emanuel Ltd v Greater London Council and another [1971] 2 All ER 835; (1971) 121 NLJ 226; (1971) 115 SJ 226 CA Occupier liable for negligent escape of fire by anyone on land with consent save strangers (or those with consent who act as strangers).

OCCUPIER'S LIABILITY (general)

AMF International, Ltd v Magnet Bowling, Ltd and another [1968] 2 All ER 789; (1968) 112 SJ 522; [1968] 1 WLR 1028 HC QBD Application of occupier's liability/negligence principles.

Balfour v Barty-King and another (Hyder and Sons (Builders), Ltd Third Parties) [1956] 2 All ER 555; (1956) 106 LJ 379; (1956) 100 SJ 472; [1956] 1 WLR 779 HC QBD Occupiers liable for fire negligently started by others whom could not prove were strangers; Rylands v Fletcher applied as fire started by dangerous/untypical user.

Bermingham v Sher Brothers (1980) 130 NLJ 137; (1980) 124 SJ 117 HL Occupier does not owe duty of care to provide members of fire services with means of escape from place of fire for duration of time they seek to put out fire.

Brand (RA) and Co, Ltd v Samuel Barrow and Co, Ltd (1965) 109 SJ 834 CA Neighbouring occupiers had duty to prevent water seeping into plaintiff occupier's house but plaintiff also had duty to stop same.

Bunker v Charles Brand and Son, Ltd [1969] 2 All ER 59; (1969) 119 NLJ 412; [1969] 2 QB 480; [1969] 2 WLR 1392 HC QBD Tunnel diggers were 'occupiers' of tunnel and digging machine and owed occupier's duty of care (even though victim aware of injury).

Caminer and another v Northern and London Investment Trust, Ltd [1950] 2 All ER 486; [1951] AC 88; (1950) 114 JP 426; (1950) 100 LJ 401; (1950) 94 SJ 518; [1950] 66 (2) TLR 184; (1950) WN (I) 361 HL Occupiers having taken reasonable care were not liable in negligence/nuisance.

Campbell v Thompson and another (1953) 97 SJ 229 HC QBD Representation order naming two unincorporated club members as representative of unincorporated club which plaintiff sought to sue.

Collier v Anglian Water Authority [1983] TLR 223 CA Water authority liable as occupiers of promenade for injury suffered by member of public when tripped on irregular paving.

Cunningham and others v Reading Football Club Ltd (1991) 141 NLJ 425i; [1991] TLR 153 HC QBD Football club liable as occupiers for not so maintaining concrete that it could not be torn up and hurled at police (as occurred).

Davies v British Railways Board (1984) 134 NLJ 888 HC QBD On duty of occupier towards (child) trespasser.

Dobson v Horsley and another (1913-14) XXX TLR 148 HC KBD Landlord not liable for injury suffered by child falling through defective railing.

Dobson and another v Horsley and another [1915] 1 KB 634; [1915] 84 LJKB 399; (1915) 112 LTR 101 CA Landlord not liable for injury suffered by child falling through defective railing (not trap/concealed danger).

Ferguson v Welsh and others [1987] 3 All ER 777; (1987) 137 NLJ 1037; (1987) 131 SJ 1552; [1987] 1 WLR 1553 HL Usually occupier not liable to contractor's employees but exceptionally may be.

Fisher v CHT, Ltd and others [1966] 1 All ER 88; [1966] 2 QB 475; (1965-66) 116 NLJ 334; (1965) 109 SJ 933; [1966] 2 WLR 391 CA Licensor and licensee were occupiers under Occupiers' Liability Act 1957 but licensee was occupier for purposes of Electricity (Factories Act) Special Regulations 1908 and 1944.

Green v Fibreglass, Ltd [1958] 2 All ER 521; (1958) 108 LJ 473; [1958] 2 QB 245; (1958) 102 SJ 472 HC QBD Occupier not liable for negligence of competent contractor employed to do work requiring expert knowledge.

Greenhalgh v British Railways Board [1969] 2 QB 286; (1969) 113 SJ 108; [1969] 2 WLR 892 CA Non-liability under Railways Clauses Consolidation Act 1845/Occupiers' Liability Act 1957 for injury sustained by person using disrepaired public right of way.

Hartley v British Railways Board (1981) 125 SJ 169 CA Occupier liable for injury to fireman when undertook hazardous task of searching burning building for person whom reasonably believed to be inside.

Hilder v Associated Portland Cement Manufacturers, Ltd [1961] 3 All ER 709; [1955] Crim LR 725; (1961) 111 LJ 757 HC QBD Not wearing crash helmet not negligent; occupier of green on which children played owed duty to take reasonable steps to prevent injury.

Holden v White [1982] 2 All ER 328; (1981) 131 NLJ 476; [1982] QB 679; (1982) 126 SJ 230; [1982] TLR 165; [1982] 2 WLR 1030 CA Not visitor if using public/private right of way.

Irving v London County Council (1965) 109 SJ 157 HC QBD Occupiers not required to light common staircase at all times without special cause.

Kearney v Waller (Eric) Ltd and another [1965] 3 All ER 352; [1966] 2 WLR 208 HC QBD Contractors did not owe occupiers' liability to non-employee injured in area under occupation/control of sub-contractors.

Knight v Whitbread (Wales) Ltd (1980) 130 NLJ 116c CA Defendant pub-owners liable as occupiers to barmaid for failing to provide safe means of access to garage in which pub watchdog kept.

Mack v Somertons of Harrow, Ltd (1965) 109 SJ 53 HC QBD Shop-owner liable in common law/for breach of statutory duty for injury to customer who slipped on inadequately secured metal strip around store doormat.

McGeown v Northern Ireland Housing Executive [1994] 3 All ER 53; [1995] 1 AC 233; (1994) 144 NLJ 901; (1994) 138 SJ LB 156; [1994] TLR 343; [1994] 3 WLR 187 HL Owner of land over which public right of way not liable for negligent nonfeasance; person exercising public right of way not licensee or invitee.

McGinlay (or Titchener) v British Railways Board [1983] 3 All ER 770; (1984) 134 NLJ 36; (1983) 127 SJ 825; [1983] 1 WLR 1427 HL Occupier owes reasonable care to person on premises; reasonableness depends on case.

Moloney v Lambeth Borough Council (1966) 110 SJ 406 HC QBD Occupier liable where staircase railing had gaps so wide that child whom could expect to use staircase fell through gaps and injured self.

Munro v Porthkerry Park Holiday Estates Ltd [1984] TLR 138 HC QBD On duty of care owed by licensee towards customer who has consumed large quantity of alcohol.

Murphy v William Henderson Sons, Ltd; McBride v Same (1963) 107 SJ 534 CA Occupiers liable in negligence for having fire doors open or for not closing them as soon as possible after became aware of fire.

Rochman v J and E Hall, Ltd, and another [1947] 1 All ER 895 HC KBD Licensor not responsible for every danger arising from acts of unauthorised persons.

Roles v Nathan and others; Roles v Corney and others [1963] 2 All ER 908; (1963) 113 LJ 496; (1963) 107 SJ 680; [1963] 1 WLR 1117 CA Occupier not liable for death of chimney sweeps whom had warned of special risks.

Salmon v Seafarer Restaurants Ltd (British Gas Corp, third party) [1983] 3 All ER 729; (1982) 132 NLJ 882; (1983) 127 SJ 581; [1983] 1 WLR 1264 HC QBD Fireman owed same duty by occupier as any other save that must exercise skill reasonably expected of fireman.

Savory v Holland, Hannen and Cubitts (Southern), Ltd [1964] 3 All ER 18; [1964] 1 WLR 1158 CA Occupier owed duty of reasonable care to servant but not breached here.

Sims v L Goodall and Sons, Ltd and Another (1965-66) 116 NLJ 472t HC QBD Contractors who left gas cylinder on site not liable in negligence for subsequent injury to member of public who sought to put out fire caused when cylinder exploded.

Staples v West Dorset District Council (1995) 139 SJ LB 117; [1995] TLR 246 CA Occupiers did not owe duty of care plaintiff who knew all the relevant facts necessary to avoid injuring self.

Stone v Taffe [1974] 3 All ER 1016; (1974) 118 SJ 863 CA Occupier liable for injury to licensee who fell down unlit staircase when leaving public house premises after-hours.

Turner v Waterman (1961) 105 SJ 1011 HC QBD Landlord failed in duty of care owed to all visitors as did not take adequate safeguards with regard to floorboards exposed to dry rot.

Wheat v E Lacon and Co, Ltd [1966] 1 All ER 582; [1966] AC 552; (1965-66) 116 NLJ 611; (1966) 110 SJ 149; [1966] 2 WLR 581 HL Husband and wife running split premises occupied whole; no occupiers' liability where accident reasonably avoidable.

Wheat v E Lacon and Co, Ltd and others [1965] 2 All ER 700; (1965) 115 LJ 464; [1966] 1 QB 335; (1965) 109 SJ 334; [1965] 3 WLR 142 CA Brewer not in control of part of inn run as private boarding-house so not occupier.

White v St Albans City and District Council [1990] TLR 196 CA On extent of liability of occupier towards trespasser.

Whiting v Hillingdon London Borough Council (1970) 114 SJ 247 HC QBD Highway authority not occupier of footpath/not liable in negligence for person who injured self on concealed tree stump.

Wood v Morland and Co Ltd (1971) 115 SJ 569 HC QBD Occupiers not liable for not sweeping away snow on which persons exiting premises slipped as could have done nothing to render situation less dangerous.

Wright v Lefever (1902-03) 47 SJ 109; (1902-03) 51 WR 149 CA House-owner liable to person-invitee injured at house when (after getting key from house-agent) went to look over same with view to renting it.

OCCUPIER'S LIABILITY (invitee)

Bates v Parker [1952] 2 All ER 987 Assizes Occupier not liable to window cleaner for injuries sustained in cleaning but not through defect in property.

Bates v Parker [1953] 2 QB 231; (1953) 97 SJ 226; [1953] 2 WLR 642 CA Invitee (window cleaner) not warned of unusual dangers by invitor who was therefore liable in negligence.

Blackman v Railway Executive [1953] 1 All ER 4; (1953) 97 SJ 10 HC QBD No failure to keep station safe for passengers/licensees so no liability.

Blackman v Railway Executive [1953] 2 All ER 323; (1954) 98 SJ 61; [1954] 1 WLR 220 CA On responsibility towards invitees.

Bloomstein v Railway Executive [1952] 2 All ER 418; (1952) 102 LJ 455; (1952) 96 SJ 496; (1952) WN (I) 378 HC QBD British Transport Commission invitor even on properties run by Railway Executive and London Transport Executive; duty of care not obviated where maintenance of machine causing accident has been entrusted to manufacturers thereof.

Bywater v Bennett and Pye [1934] LJNCCR 117 CyCt House-owner (but not estate agent) liable in negligence towards person injured whilst being shown around unoccupied house by estate agent.

Carroll v Garford and others (1968) 112 SJ 948 HC QBD Licensees/dog-owner not liable for injury suffered by third party who tripped over generally well-behaved dog that had been brought into pub.

Christmas v General Cleaning Contractors, Ltd (1951) 95 SJ 452; (1951) WN (I) 294 HC KBD Occupier and employer of invitee (window-cleaner) liable in negligence for injury to latter while at work..

Christmas v General Cleaning Contractors, Ltd and others [1952] 1 All ER 39; [1952] 1 KB 141; (1951) 101 LJ 706; (1951) 95 SJ 802; [1951] 2 TLR 1218 CA Occupier need not warn invitee of something that is ordinarily safe though could be dangerous to invitee.

Corporation of Glasgow v Muir and others [1943] 2 All ER 44; (1944) 94 LJ 108 HL Occupier not liable to invitee for unforeseeable danger.

Dalby v West Ham Borough Council (1945) 109 JP 180; (1945) 173 LTR 191; (1945) 89 SJ 270; (1944-45) LXI TLR 467 HC KBD Invitors liable for scalding of invitee using shower-bath (even though he had not tested water temperature) as he had not been told how to use same properly/not been warned about dangers of same/had through usage come to expect water of certain temperature.

Doherty v London Co-operative Society, Ltd (1965-66) 116 NLJ 388; (1966) 110 SJ 74 HC QBD Shop-owner not liable for injury suffered by customer who tripped over obstruction between three to four feet high.

Elliott v CP Roberts and Co, Limited (1917) 81 JP 20; [1916] 2 KB 518; [1916] 85 LJKB 1689; (1916-17) 115 LTR 255; (1915-16) XXXII TLR 478 CA Contractor liable to other contractor's workers on-site as invitor to invitee.

Ellis v Fulham Borough Council [1937] 1 All ER 698; (1937) 101 JP 198; (1937) 83 LJ 150; (1937) 156 LTR 220; (1937) 81 SJ 140; (1936-37) LIII TLR 387 HC KBD Child using public paddle pool an invitee — glass hidden in sand in pool a concealed danger for which council liable.

Goldstone v Cheshire Lines Committee [1938] LJNCCR 130 CyCt Rail company liable for injury suffered by person alighting from unlit carriage onto insufficiently lit platform.

Green v Fibreglass, Ltd [1958] 2 All ER 521; (1958) 108 LJ 473; [1958] 2 QB 245; (1958) 102 SJ 472 HC QBD Occupier not liable for negligence of competent contractor employed to do work requiring expert knowledge.

Hart v Liverpool Corporation (1949) 99 LJ 594; (1949) LXV TLR 677 CA Tenant coming back to flat by different approach to normal was nonetheless invitee and hole into which fell was unusual danger so landlord liable.

Hartley v Mayoh and Co and another [1953] 2 All ER 525; (1953) 117 JP 369 Assizes Fireman an invitee; presumed fireman has ordinary knowledge of shutting off electricity — here occupier negligent as failed to warn fireman of peculiarity of electrical system (and previously to test system); electricity supply board contributorily negligent for electrocution arising in part from defective installation.

Hartley v Mayoh and Co and another (1954) 118 JP 178; [1954] 1 QB 383; (1954) 98 SJ 107; [1954] 1 WLR 355 CA Fireman an invitee; presumed fireman has ordinary knowledge of shutting off electricity — here occupier negligent as failed to warn fireman of peculiarity of electrical system (and previously to test system).

Hayward v Drury Lane Theatre, Ltd and another [1916-17] All ER 405; [1918] 87 LJCL 18; (1917-18) 117 LTR 523; (1916-17) 61 SJ 665 CA Person voluntarily under another's control allowed recover as invitee for negligent acts of that other's servant.

Henaghan v Forangirene (Rederiet) [1936] 2 All ER 1426 Assizes Stevedore an invitee.

Hillen and another v ICI (Alkali), Limited [1934] 1 KB 455; (1934) 150 LTR 147; (1933-34) L TLR 93; (1933) WN (I) 266 CA No liability to party to illegal act other than not to injure same.

Hillen and Pettigrew v ICI (Alkali), Limited [1935] All ER 555; [1936] AC 65; (1935) 153 LTR 403; (1934-35) LI TLR 532 HL No liability to trespasser (if trespasser was invitee was contributorily negligent).

Hobson v Bartram and Sons, Ltd [1950] 1 All ER 412 CA That person is under one's control need not mean are one's agents for all purposes.

Hornsey v John Gardner (London), Limited [1934] LJNCCR 293 CyCt Liable towards customer-invitee in restaurant who fell through open trap-door having being given inadequate warning about its being opened.

Hornsey v John Gardner (London), Limited [1935] LJNCCA 97 CA Liable towards customer-invitee in restaurant who fell through open trap-door having being given inadequate warning about its being opened.

Horton v London Graving Dock Co, Ltd [1949] 2 All ER 169; [1949] 2 KB 584; (1949) 99 LJ 356; [1949] 118 LJR 1639; (1949) LXV TLR 386; (1949) WN (I) 281 HC KBD Invitor's duty to warn of unusual dangers means dangers unusual to invitee.

Horton v London Graving Dock Company, Ltd [1950] 1 All ER 180; [1950] 1 KB 421; (1950) 100 LJ 20; (1950) 94 SJ 14; [1950] 66 (1) TLR 246; (1950) WN (I) 33 CA An 'unusual danger' is an abnormal danger (albeit one of which victim knew).

Howard and Wife v Walker and Lake (Trustees) and Crisp [1947] KB 860; [1947] 116 LJR 1366; (1947) 177 LTR 326; (1947) 91 SJ 494; (1947) LXIII TLR 518; (1947) WN (I) 216 HC KBD Landlord not liable to invitee of tenant injured while on tenanted property.

Hyett v Great Western Railway Company [1947] 2 All ER 264; [1948] 1 KB 345; [1947] 116 LJR 1243; (1947) 177 LTR 178; (1947) 91 SJ 434; (1947) LXIII TLR 411; (1947) WN (I) 220 CA Invitors owed duty of reasonable care to protect invitee; invitee injured while seeking to extinguish fire on invitor's premises could recover damages.

Jennings v Cole [1949] 2 All ER 191 HC KBD Neighbour doing agreed task in neighbour's house which materially benefitted latter an invitee.

Jerred and others v T Roddam Dent and Son, Ltd (Glen Line, Ltd Third Party) [1948] 2 All ER 104 Assizes Duty of invitor to invitee did not extend to third party.

Johnson v Croggon and Co, Ltd and another [1954] 1 All ER 121 HC QBD Ex turpi causa non oritur actio precluded relief in negligence; could not recover as invitee as had general licence to use equipment but selected defective equipment.

Lee v Luper [1936] 3 All ER 817; (1937) 81 SJ 15 HC KBD Publican not liable to invitee sustaining injury in private area of pub.

Leonard v London Corporation [1940] LJNCCR 267 CyCt Non-liability on basis of principle of volenti non fit injuria in respect of injury suffered by invitee.

Letang v Ottawa Electric Railway Company [1926] All ER 546; [1926] AC 725; (1926) 95 LJPC 153; (1926) 135 LTR 421; (1925-26) XLII TLR 596 PC Invitee must freely/voluntarily accept risk inherent in visiting dangerous premises for volenti non fit injuria to apply.

London Graving Dock Co, Ltd v Horton [1951] 2 All ER 1; [1951] AC 737; (1951) 101 LJ 301; (1951) 95 SJ 465; [1951] 1 TLR 949; (1951) WN (I) 278 HL Contractor had to show safe system of work/defendant accepted risk — this a question of fact.

Mendelovitch v Eastern Cinemas (GCF) Ltd [1940] LJNCCR 158 CyCt Cinema-owners not liable in negligence for injury suffered by patron-invitee who slipped on floor despite all reasonable efforts being taken by cinema to prevent any such occurrence.

Norman v Great Western Railway Company [1914-17] All ER 205; (1914) CC Rep III 102; [1915] 1 KB 584; (1914) 49 LJ 638; [1915] 84 LJKB 598; (1914) 110 LTR 306; (1914-15) XXXI TLR 53; (1914) WN (I) 415 CA Duty of railway company to invitees same as that of shopkeeper to invitees.

Norman v Great Western Railway Company [1914] 2 KB 153; [1914] 83 LJKB 669; (1913-14) XXX TLR 241; (1914) WN (I) 15 HC KBD Duty of railway company to invitees.

Pearson v Coleman Brothers [1948] 2 All ER 274; [1948] 2 KB 359; (1948) 98 LJ 371; [1948] 117 LJR 1781; (1948) WN (I) 270 CA Liability to child invitee disobeying danger sign.

Perkowski v City of Wellington Corporation [1958] 3 All ER 368; (1958) 108 LJ 712; (1958) 102 SJ 794 PC No breach of duty between licensor/licensee where no concealed danger; whether relationship that of licensor/licensee or invitor/invitee.

Pope v St Helen's Theatre Ltd [1946] 2 All ER 440; [1947] KB 30; (1946) 90 SJ 644; (1945-46) LXII TLR 588; (1946) WN (I) 192 HC KBD Injury to theatre caused by bomb blast but injury arose from defendant's negligence in not doing anything to remedy damage: negligent injury not 'war injury'.

Raum v British Holiday Estates, Ltd (1952) 102 LJ 416 CyCt Hotel-owners liable for personal injuries sustained by patron upon collapse of garden chair on which victim seated.

Silverman v Imperial London Hotels, Ltd [1927] All ER 712; (1927) 137 LTR 57; (1926-27) XLIII TLR 260 HC KBD Breach of implied term of contract (and negligent) allowing invitee into premises knowing of a danger (and failing to address danger).

Simons v Winslade [1938] 3 All ER 774; (1938) 86 LJ 142; (1938) 82 SJ 711 CA Person quitting pub for outside toilet to rear of pub is still invitee.

Slade v Battersea and Putney Group Hospital Management Committee [1955] 1 All ER 429; (1955) 119 JP 212; (1955) 105 LJ 138; (1955) 99 SJ 169; [1955] 1 WLR 207 HC QBD Hospital liable to visitor slipping on newly polished floor as invitee/as licensee (concealed danger) where no warning given.

Slater v Clay Cross Co, Ltd [1956] 2 All ER 625; (1956) 106 LJ 442; [1956] 2 QB 264; (1956) 100 SJ 450; [1956] 3 WLR 232 CA Volenti non fit injuria inapplicable as did not accept negligence of other; invitor/licensor owes duty to take reasonable care to prevent injury to person lawfully present on property.

Smith v Austin Lifts, Ltd and others [1959] 1 All ER 81 HL Occupiers liable to invitee for failure to take reasonable care to maintain safe premises; employers also liable in negligence.

Stein v Gates [1935] LJNCCA 171; (1935) 79 SJ 252 CA Re-trial ordered as to whether had been negligent not to take special precautions for protection of frequent (unsighted) customer from peril of falling through open trap-door which had been adequately signposted for sighted persons.

Stowell v Railway Executive [1949] 2 All ER 193; [1949] 2 KB 519; (1949) 99 LJ 356; [1949] 118 LJR 1482; (1949) LXV TLR 387; (1949) WN (I) 288 HC KBD Person meeting train passenger an invitee at railway station: oil on platform an unusual danger.

Thomson v Cremin and others [1953] 2 All ER 1185; (1956) 100 SJ 73; [1956] 1 WLR 103 HL Invitor's duty to invitee vests in invitor personally and cannot be arrogated to a third party; stevedores unloading ship not under duty to inspect it for safety purposes.

Turner v Arding and Hobbs, Ltd [1949] 2 All ER 911 HC KBD Vegetable matter on shop floor an unusual danger in consequence of which were found liable to invitee.

Weigall v Westminster Hospital [1936] 1 All ER 232; (1936) 80 SJ 146; (1935-36) LII TLR 301 CA Hospital negligent towards mother of patient/invitee slipping on mat on polished floor when entering hospital room for consultation with surgeon.

Weigall v Westminster Hospital (Governors) (1935) 79 SJ 560; (1934-35) LI TLR 554 HC KBD Hospital negligent towards mother of patient/invitee slipping on mat on polished floor when entering hospital room for consultation with surgeon.

Wells v Cooper [1958] 2 All ER 527; (1958) 108 LJ 377; [1958] 2 QB 265; (1958) 102 SJ 508 CA Occupier not liable for injury sustained through own failure at everyday repair if exercised skill of competent carpenter.

Woodman v Richardson (1937) 84 LJ 144; (1937) 81 SJ 70 CA Non-liability of invitor towards invitee for not reasonably foreseeable course of events (not instigated by invitor's employees) that resulted in injury to invitee.

Yardley v Yardley and Robinson (1956) 106 LJ ccr412 CyCt Where tenant did not know/could not reasonably have known of personal danger to plaintiff neither he nor landlord were liable in personal injuries action brought by plaintiff.

OCCUPIER'S LIABILITY (licensee)

Anderson v The Guinness Trust [1949] 1 All ER 530; (1949) LXV TLR 679; (1949) WN (I) 127 HC KBD Wife keeping house for tenant a licensee (not invitee) of landlords.

Ashdown v Samuel Williams and Sons, Ltd and another [1956] 2 All ER 384; (1956) 106 LJ 378; [1956] 2 QB 580; (1956) 100 SJ 420 [1956] 3 WLR 128 HC QBD Licensor not liable to licensee where latter aware sign excluding liability exists and of its nature but not its contents; employer liable to worker for not warning her of known dangers on short cut they allow her to use.

Attorney-General v Corke (on relation of Bromley Rural District Council) [1932] All ER 711; [1933] Ch 89; (1933) 102 LJCh 30; (1933) 148 LTR 95; (1932) 76 SJ 593; (1931-32) XLVIII TLR 650; (1932) WN (I) 217 HC ChD Injunction can issue to stop person allowing licensee on property where licensee causing nuisance on neighbouring property.

Bates v Stone Parish Council [1954] 3 All ER 38; (1954) 118 JP 502; (1954) 104 LJ 569; (1954) 98 SJ 698; [1954] 1 WLR 1249 CA By allowing unrestricted playground access to children were liable to child/licensee injured therein.

Billings (AC) and Sons, Ltd v Riden [1957] 3 All ER 1; [1958] AC 240; (1957) 107 LJ 521; (1957) 101 SJ 645 HL Contractors could not rely on occupier's liability (as occupier) to licensee to preclude their own liability.

Braithwaite v South Durham Steel Co, Ltd and another [1958] 3 All ER 161; (1958) 102 SJ 655 HC QBD Master negligent in not providing safe place to work; licensor liable in negligence despite unintended trespass of licencee at moment of accident to escape therefrom.

Burley (C), Limited v Edward Lloyd, Limited (1928-29) XLV TLR 626 HC KBD Milton Creek Conservancy Act 1899, s 78 did not empower licensee to erect obstruction in creek.

Caseley v Bristol Corporation [1944] 1 All ER 14; (1945) 95 LJ 112 CA On extent of duty owed to licensee.

Coates v Rawtenstall Borough Council [1937] 1 All ER 333 Assizes Ordinary duty of care owed to child licensee.

Coates v Rawtenstall Borough Council (1937) 101 JP 483; (1937) 81 SJ 627 CA Local authority liable for injury to child licensee arising from negligent state in which playground maintained.

Coleshill v Lord Mayor, Aldermen and Citizens of the City of Manchester [1928] 1 KB 776; (1928) 65 LJ 95; (1928) 97 LJCL 229; (1928) 138 LTR 537 CA Non-liability towards licensee falling into trench which was not hidden danger/trap.

Cullen (suing by her mother) and Cullen v Manchester Corporation [1940] LJNCCR 255 CyCt Defendants not liable to plaintiff licensees for injury occurring from danger of which defendants had hitherto been unaware.

Dickson v JA Scott (Limited) (1914) 49 LJ 112; (1913-14) XXX TLR 256 CA Occupier owes duty to man whom allows onto land in darkness to alert/save same as to/from danger posed by hatchway.

Dunster v Abbott [1953] 2 All ER 1572; (1953) 103 LJ 828; (1954) 98 SJ 8 CA Person canvassing for business a licensee: here duty of care to licensee not breached as bridge over ditch not concealed danger/no negligence as regards nighttime lighting.

Dyer v Ilfracombe Urban District Council [1956] 1 All ER 581; (1956) 120 JP 220; (1956) 100 SJ 169; [1956] 1 WLR 218 CA Licensor not liable for allurement not concealing hidden danger.

Edwards v Railway Executive [1952] 2 All ER 430; [1952] AC 737; (1952) 102 LJ 470; (1952) 96 SJ 493; [1952] 2 TLR 237; (1952) WN (1) 383 HL Executive not liable for injuries suffered by boy trespassing on railway line.

Elliott v CP Roberts and Co (Limited) (1915-16) XXXII TLR 71 HC KBD Contractor liable to other contractor's workers on-site as licensor to licensee.

Fern v London County Council [1938] LJNCCR 76 CyCt Owners of public recreation ground liable in negligence for injury suffered by person onto whom previously broken branch fell on them while they were sitting on a bench.

Gilmour v Belfast Harbour Commissioners (1934) 150 LTR 63 HL Workman held to have taken risk of injury upon self where elected to walk along unlit route (instead of lit route) containing potential hazards of which knew.

Gough v National Coal Board [1953] 2 All ER 1283; [1954] 1 QB 191; (1953) 97 SJ 811; [1953] 3 WLR 900 CA Child playing on land a licensee under general licence — not trespasser just because did something not supposed to do; slow-moving trucks an allurement; licensor negligently failed to take reasonable care to protect child.

Greene v Chelsea Borough Council [1954] 2 All ER 318; (1954) 118 JP 346; [1954] 2 QB 127; (1954) 98 SJ 389; [1954] 3 WLR 12 CA Requisitioning authority owed duty to residents as licensees; negligent for failing to remedy foreseeable danger.

Haseldine v CA Daw and Son, Ltd and others [1941] 1 All ER 525; (1941) 91 LJ 181; (1942) 92 LJ 60; (1941) 85 SJ 265; (1940-41) LVII TLR 431 HC KBD Flatowner liable for negligence of agent contractors; owner owed duty to warn licensee of dangers of which actually knew (did not know here); defence of having employed competent independent contractor not open as only limited maintenance contract; contractor liable for defective repairs.

Hawkins v Coulsdon and Purley Urban District Council [1953] 2 All ER 364; (1953) 117 JP 360; (1953) 103 LJ 414; [1954] 1 QB 319; (1953) 97 SJ 473; [1953] 1 WLR 882 HC QBD Licensee did not accept at night risks which were obvious by day; occupier owed duty to remedy risks which reasonable man would have recognised.

Hawkins v Coulsdon and Purley Urban District Council [1954] 1 All ER 97; (1954) 118 JP 101; (1954) 104 LJ 25; (1954) 98 SJ 44; [1954] 2 WLR 122 CA Licensors liable in negligence where knew of physical circumstances constituting trap.

Jacobs and another v London County Council [1949] 1 All ER 790; [1949] 1 KB 685; (1949) 99 LJ 219; (1949) WN (I) 179 CA Person on forecourt not open to public a licensee; no nuisance adjoining highway proved as was not using highway when encountered 'nuisance'.

Jacobs v London County Council [1950] 1 All ER 737; [1950] AC 361; (1950) 114 JP 204; (1950) 100 LJ 175; (1950) 94 SJ 318; [1950] 66 (1) TLR 659; (1950) WN (I) 170 HL Person on forecourt not open to public a licensee; no nuisance adjoining highway proved as was not using highway when encountered 'nuisance'.

Malone v Laskey and another [1904-07] All ER 304; [1907] 2 KB 141; (1907-08) XCVII LTR 324; (1906-07) 51 SJ 356; (1906-07) XXIII TLR 399 CA Licensee not allowed recover for private nuisance (vibration).

Mumford v Naylor (1951) 95 SJ 383; [1951] 1 TLR 1068; (1951) WN (I) 241 HC KBD Person injured crossing private forecourt to front of shop could recover damages as licensee from shop-owner where injured self in hole/concealed trap of which shopowner knew.

Mumford v Naylor (1951) 95 SJ 742; (1951) WN (I) 579 CA On what constitutes a concealed trap — such a trap found not to exist here.

Nicholls and Son v Devon County Council (1922) CC Rep XI 19 CyCt Licensee not liable in negligence for failure to fence in quarry (where such failure resulted in loss of straying cattle).

Norris (an infant) and Norris v Tomlinson [1941] LJNCCR 211 CyCt Butcher liable for injury occasioned to child-licensee who placed hand in sausage machine (an allurement/trap) while was running.

Pearson v Lambeth Borough Council [1950] 1 All ER 682; (1950) 114 JP 214; [1950] 2 KB 353; (1950) 100 LJ 133; (1950) 94 SJ 269; [1950] 66 (1) TLR 561; (1950) WN (I) 148 CA Licensor liable only for dangers of which actually knows; meaning of 'actual knowledge'.

Pearson v Lambeth Borough Council (1950) 100 LJ 51 CyCt Council not liable for injury occasioned by danger of which council did not actually know to person using public toilets (a licensee).

Perkowski v City of Wellington Corporation [1958] 3 All ER 368; (1958) 108 LJ 712; (1958) 102 SJ 794 PC No breach of duty between licensor/licensee where no concealed danger; whether relationship that of licensor/licensee or invitor/invitee.

Phipps v Rochester Corporation [1955] 1 All ER 129; (1955) 119 JP 92; (1955) 105 LJ 41; [1955] 1 QB 450; (1955) 99 SJ 45; [1955] 2 WLR 23 HC QBD Occupier not liable in negligence to child as unaccompanied by parent so trespasser/or though child licensee was unreasonable for child to be there unaccompanied.

Pitt v Jackson [1939] 1 All ER 129; (1939) 87 LJ 64; (1939) 83 SJ 216 HC KBD Polished linoleum not a trap for which liable to licensee slipping thereon.

Purkis v Walthamstow Borough Council [1934] All ER 64; (1934) 98 JP 244 CA Child using playground swing a licensee.

Slade v Battersea and Putney Group Hospital Management Committee [1955] 1 All ER 429; (1955) 119 JP 212; (1955) 105 LJ 138; (1955) 99 SJ 169; [1955] 1 WLR 207 HC QBD Hospital liable to visitor slipping on newly polished floor as invitee/as licensee (concealed danger) where no warning given.

Slater v Clay Cross Co, Ltd [1956] 2 All ER 625; (1956) 106 LJ 442; [1956] 2 QB 264; (1956) 100 SJ 450; [1956] 3 WLR 232 CA Volenti non fit injuria inapplicable as did not accept negligence of other; invitor/licensor owes duty to take reasonable care to prevent injury to person lawfully present on property.

Sutton v Bootle Corporation [1947] 1 All ER 92; (1947) 111 JP 81; [1947] KB 359; (1947) 97 LJ 23; (1947) 177 LTR 168 CA Licensor only obliged to warn licensee of dangers actually known.

Turner v Haslam [1939] LJNCCR 267 CyCt Visitor to hotel (licensee) could recover damages from occupier where injured self on (what constituted trap) an unlit accessible flight of stairs which knew to be customarily either lit/inaccessible.

Williams v Cardiff Corporation [1950] 1 All ER 250; (1950) 114 JP 126; [1950] 1 KB 514; (1950) 94 SJ 161; [1950] 66 (1) TLR 243; (1950) WN (I) 44 CA Broken glass/tins on property where child playing a trap rendering occupier liable for injuries child sustained.

OCCUPIER'S LIABILITY (negligence)

Clelland v Edward Lloyd, Ltd [1937] 2 All ER 605; (1936-37) LIII TLR 644 HC KBD Occupier not liable for negligence of independent contractor over whom has no control.

Lewis v Ronald [1908-10] All ER 782; (1909-10) 101 LTR 534; (1909-10) XXVI TLR 30 HC KBD Landlord not liable for injuries suffered by person visiting premises in area which landlord had contracted to light for tenants but had not done so.

OCCUPIER'S LIABILITY (trespass)

Barker v Herbert [1911-13] All ER 509; (1911) 75 JP 481; [1911] 2 KB 633; (1911) 80 LJCL 1329; (1911-12) 105 LTR 349; (1910-11) XXVII TLR 488 CA Owner of premises adjoining highway not liable for nuisance caused by trespasser unless permitted its continuance.

Barker v Herbert (1911) 75 JP 355; (1910-11) XXVII TLR 252 HC KBD Owner of premises adjoining highway not liable for injury not directly stemming from nuisance caused by trespasser.

British Railways Board v Herrington [1972] 1 All ER 749; [1972] AC 877; (1972) 116 SJ 178; [1972] 2 WLR 537 HL Occupier owes duty of care to trespasser to take reasonable acts to prevent injury.

Buckland v Guildford Gas Light and Coke Co [1948] 2 All ER 1086; (1949) 113 JP 44; [1949] 1 KB 410; (1948) WN (I) 488 HC KBD Electricity company liable for child's electrocution where allowed tree grow too closely to and obscure electric wires even if child was trespasser.

Caminer and another v Northern and London Investment Trust, Ltd [1948] 2 All ER 1101; (1948) 98 LJ 685; (1948) LXIV TLR 629; (1948) WN (I) 489 HC KBD Landowners liable in negligence/nuisance for failure to look after tree that falls injuring person on adjoining highway.

Commissioner for Railways v Quinlan (Francis John) [1964] 1 All ER 897; [1964] AC 1054; (1964) 114 LJ 304; (1964) 108 SJ 296; [1964] 2 WLR 817 PC On occupier's duty of care towards trespasser (not to do reckless act endangering same).

Creed v John McGeogh and Sons, Ltd [1955] 3 All ER 123; (1955) 105 LJ 618; (1955) 99 SJ 563; [1955] 1 WLR 1005 HC QBD Negligence towards child trespasser in builder's trailer; builder's trailer left close to highway not nuisance to highway.

Edwards v Railway Executive [1952] 2 All ER 430; [1952] AC 737; (1952) 102 LJ 470; (1952) 96 SJ 493; [1952] 2 TLR 237; (1952) WN (1) 383 HL Executive not liable for injuries suffered by boy trespassing on railway line.

Gough v National Coal Board [1953] 2 All ER 1283; [1954] 1 QB 191; [1953] 3 WLR 900 CA Child playing on land a licensee under general licence — not trespasser just because did something not supposed to do; slow-moving trucks an allurement; licensor negligently failed to take reasonable care to protect child.

Grand Trunk Railway Co v Barnett [1911-13] All ER 1624 PC No liability for injury to trespasser occurring through one's negligence.

Halstead (an Infant, by his next friend) v Bargh (J) and Co (1928) 66 LJ ccr2 CyCt Barn-owner liable in damages for injury to child who enters same without authorisation (and so is trespasser).

Hardy v Central London Rail Co [1920] All ER 205; [1920] 3 KB 459; (1920) 55 LJ 313; [1920] 89 LJCL 1187; (1921) 124 LTR 136; (1919-20) 64 SJ 683; (1919-20) XXXVI TLR 843 CA Absent allurement/malice were not liable to child trespassers.

Harris v Birkenhead Corporation and another (Pascoe and another third party, Alliance Assurance Co Ltd fourth party) [1976] 1 All ER 341; (1976) 120 SJ 200; [1976] 1 WLR 279 CA Legal property occupier liable for reasonably foreseeable injury to child trespasser.

Harris v Birkenhead Corporation and another (Pascoe and another third party, Alliance Assurance Co Ltd, fourth party) [1975] 1 All ER 1001; (1975) 119 SJ 186; [1975] 1 WLR 379 HC QBD Legal occupiers liable to child trespasser sustaining injury in unmaintained vacant property.

Herrington v British Railways Board [1971] 1 All ER 897; (1970) 120 NLJ 1136t; [1971] 2 QB 107; (1970) 114 SJ 954; [1971] 2 WLR 477 CA No duty of care to trespasser save where acts done aimed at/or reckless as to whether would injure trespasser.

Hillen and another v ICI (Alkali), Limited [1934] 1 KB 455; (1934) 150 LTR 147; (1933-34) L TLR 93; (1933) WN (I) 266 CA No liability to party to illegal act other than not to injure same.

Hillen and Pettigrew v ICI (Alkali), Limited [1935] All ER 555; [1936] AC 65; (1935) 153 LTR 403; (1934-35) LI TLR 532 HL No liability to trespasser (if trespasser was invitee was contributorily negligent).

Kingzett v British Railways Board (1968) 112 SJ 625 CA Rail board not liable for injury to child by way of detonator he acquired from boys who stole same while trespassing on rail property.

Moulton v Poulter [1930] All ER 6; (1930) 94 JP 190; [1930] 2 KB 183; (1930) 69 LJ 187; (1930) 99 LJCL 289; (1930) 143 LTR 20; (1930) 74 SJ 170; (1929-30) XLVI TLR 257; (1930) WN (I) 63 HC KBD Feller owed duty of care to warn person on land of danger even though person trespassing.

Pannett v P McGuinness and Co Ltd [1972] 3 All ER 137; [1972] 2 QB 599; (1972) 116 SJ 335; [1972] 3 WLR 386 CA Occupiers owed such duties to trespassing children as common sense/humanity demanded.

Penny v Northampton Borough Council (1974) 124 NLJ 768t; (1974) 118 SJ 628 CA Failed negligence action for damages on foot of injury suffered by child trespassing on council rubbish tip on which children often trespassed.

Periscinotti v Brighton West Pier, Ltd (1961) 105 SJ 526 CA Pier managers not liable to trespasser injured in diving from pier diving board.

Phipps v Rochester Corporation [1955] 1 All ER 129; (1955) 119 JP 92; (1955) 105 LJ 41; [1955] 1 QB 450; (1955) 99 SJ 45; [1955] 2 WLR 23 HC QBD Occupier not liable in negligence to child as unaccompanied by parent so trespasser/or though child licensee was unreasonable for child to be there unaccompanied.

Proctor v British Northrop Co Ltd (1937) 81 SJ 611 CA Defendants not liable for injury to child trespasser (who knew should not have been where was) where took all reasonable steps/did not lay trap.

R Addie and Sons (Collieries), Ltd v Dumbreck [1929] All ER 1; (1929) 67 LJ 254; (1929) 98 LJPC 119; (1929) WN (I) 57 HL Absent malicious intent occupier not liable in negligence to trespasser, even child trespasser.

Revill v Newberry [1996] 1 All ER 291; (1996) 146 NLJ 50; [1996] QB 567; (1995) 139 SJ LB 244; [1995] TLR 563; [1996] 2 WLR 239 CA Duty of care to trespassers extends to trespassers engaged in criminal enterprise.

Sedleigh-Denfield v O'Callaghan and Others [1940] AC 880; [1940] 3 All ER 349; (1940) 90 LJ 27; [1940] 109 LJCL 893; (1941) 164 LTR 72; (1940) 84 SJ 657; (1939-40) LVI TLR 887; (1940) WN (I) 260 HL On 'continuing'/'adopting' nuisance; party presumed to have known of act of trespasser and so were liable for nuisance resulting therefrom where to took no action in relation thereto.

Sedleigh-Denfield v St Joseph's Society for Foreign Missions [1939] 1 All ER 725; (1939) 83 SJ 236 CA Occupier had no duty to abate nuisance of which did not know and which was caused by trespasser.

Southern Portland Cement Ltd v Cooper [1974] 1 All ER 87; [1974] AC 623; (1974) 118 SJ 99; [1974] 2 WLR 152 PC Duty of occupier towards trespassers gauged by reference to humaneness.

Videan and another v British Transport Commission [1963] 2 All ER 860; (1963) 113 LJ 529; [1963] 2 QB 650; (1963) 107 SJ 458; [1963] 3 WLR 374 CA Child trespasser could not recover damages for negligence; stationmaster on tracks was reasonably foreseeable so duty of care/damages.

Walder v The Mayor, Aldermen and Burgesses of the Borough of Hammersmith [1944] 1 All ER 490; (1944) 108 JP 224; (1945) 95 LJ 111 HC KBD No duty of care towards (child) trespasser.

Westwood v Post Office (1972) 122 NLJ 1086t; [1973] QB 591 CA Non-liability of occupier towards trespassing worker.

Wringe v Cohen [1939] 4 All ER 241; [1940] 1 KB 229; (1939) 88 LJ 315; [1940] 109 LJCL 227; (1939) 161 LTR 366; (1939) 83 SJ 923; (1939) WN (I) 386 CA Occupier/owner liable for damage due to want of repair (whether or not aware thereof) but only liable for damage effected by trespasser/hidden act of nature if has actual/constructive knowledge thereof.

PASSING-OFF (general)

Ad-Lib Club Ltd v Granville [1971] 2 All ER 300; (1971) 121 NLJ 13t; (1971) 115 SJ 74 HC ChD Passing-off action grounded in goodwill which can attach to defunct business.

Aerators, Ltd v Tollitt [1900-03] All ER 564 HC ChD Action dismissed as name complained of was commonplace words/unconfusing.

Anheuser-Busch Inc v Budejovicky Budvar Narodni Podnik and others (1984) 128 SJ 398 CA 'Budweiser' beer found to have dual reputation in United Kingdom; sales of US 'Budweiser' on US military bases in UK did not create necessary goodwill in market at large to support passing off action.

Associated Newspapers Group plc v Insert Media Ltd and others [1988] 1 WLR 509 HC ChD On bases on which passing off injunction will be granted.

Associated Newspapers plc v Insert Media Ltd and others [1990] 2 All ER 803; (1990) 134 SJ 636; [1990] TLR 1; [1990] 1 WLR 900 HC ChD Third party inserts in newspapers do involve misrepresentation as somehow connected with paper even where insert states contrary.

Associated Newspapers plc v Insert Media Ltd and others [1991] 3 All ER 535; [1991] TLR 127; [1991] 1 WLR 571 CA If substantial body of public believes unauthorised newspaper inserts authorised/made by newspaper owners there is misrepresentation.

Bach and Johnson, Ltd v Cowan and another (1969) 113 SJ 38 HC ChD Passing off injunction granted to owners of name 'Pembridge Gardens Hotel' against owners of name 'Pembridge Hotel'.

Bass, Ratcliff and Gretton v Wright (1924-25) 69 SJ 695 HC KBD Settlement of claim in which was accepted that was 'passing off' to provide some other ale to person who requested Bass ale.

Baume and Co, Ltd v AH Moore, Ltd [1958] 2 All ER 113; [1958] Ch 907; (1958) 102 SJ 329 CA Passing off even though using own name.

Baume and Co, Ltd v Moore (AH), Ltd [1957] 3 All ER 416; [1958] Ch 137 HC ChD Use of own name could not be passing off.

Biba Group v Gill (1981) 131 NLJ 262 HC ChD Injunction against person from using nickname which was also the business name of a competitor.

Bollinger (J) and others v Costa Brava Wine Company, Ltd [1959] 3 All ER 800; (1959) 109 LJ 735; (1961) 105 SJ 180; [1959] 3 WLR 966 HC ChD Goodwill attaching to geographical name could be protected by class of people producing goods in that area.

Bollinger (J) and others v Costa Brava Wine Co, Ltd (No 2) [1961] 1 All ER 561; [1960] Ch 262; (1961) 111 LJ 155; (1959) 103 SJ 1028 HC ChD Goodwill could vest in geographical name and be protected from passing off.

Boord and Son v Huddart (1903-04) LXXXIX LTR 718; (1903-04) 48 SJ 143 HC ChD Injunction granted to restrain passing off sloe gin as established brand of sloe gin.

Bostik Ltd v Sellotape GB Ltd [1994] TLR 14 HC ChD Failed passing off action by makers of 'Blu-Tack' against makers of 'SelloTak' — get-up at point of sale central to action.

Bourne v Swan and Edgar (1902-03) 47 SJ 92 HC ChD On type of evidence admissible in support of passing off action.

Box Television Ltd v Haymarket Magazines Ltd (1997) 141 SJ LB 47; [1997] TLR 111 HC ChD Failed passing off action by owners of 'The Box' cable channel to restrain publication of unrelated magazine entitled 'The Box'.

British Broadcasting Corporation v Talbot Motor Co Ltd (1981) 131 NLJ 237 HC ChD Successful passing off action restraining defendants from using same name in respect of same product which plaintiffs had tested some years previously.

British Diabetic Association v Diabetic Society Ltd and others [1995] 4 All ER 812 HC ChD Passing-off includes (unintentional) deception by one fund-raising charity that enables it to appropriate goodwill of and donations to another.

British Vacuum Cleaner Company (Limited) v New Vacuum Cleaner Company (Limited) [1907] 2 Ch 312; (1907-08) XCVII LTR 201; (1906-07) XXIII TLR 587 HC ChD 'Vacuum cleaner' was descriptive term not fancy term: same principles applicable to use of similar company names as apply to passing off.

Bulmer (HP) Ltd and another v J Bollinger SA and others [1974] Ch 401; (1977) 127 NLJ 914t; [1974] 3 WLR 202 CA Article 177 reference to European Court of Justice in course of passing off action (on EEC wine/champagne legislation).

Burberrys v JC Cording and Co (Limited) (1909) 100 LTR 985; (1908-09) XXV TLR 576 HC ChD Failed injunction to prevent firm using name that was at once descriptive and distinctive.

C and T Harris (Calne), Limited v Harris (1933-34) L TLR 338 CA Failed action to prevent person using own name where was no real risk of confusion/passing off.

C and T Harris (Calne), Limited v Harris (1934) 78 SJ 13; (1933-34) L TLR 123 HC ChD Failed action to prevent person using own name where was no real risk of confusion/passing off.

Cadbury Schweppes Pty Ltd and others v Pub Squash Co Pty Ltd [1981] 1 All ER 213; (1980) 130 NLJ 1095; (1981) 125 SJ 96; [1981] 1 WLR 193 PC Passing off extends to distinctive ads. to which goodwill attached.

Champagne Heidsieck et Cie Monopole Societe Anonyme v Buxton [1930] 1 Ch 330; (1930) 69 LJ 43; (1930) 99 LJCh 149; (1930) 142 LTR 324 HC ChD Failed action for passing off where defendant sold plaintiff's French wine under plaintiff's label in England.

Chancellor, Masters and Scholars of the University of Oxford v Pergamon Press Ltd (1977) 127 NLJ 1103t; (1977) 121 SJ 758 CA Successful application by Oxford University for interlocutory injunction restraining pergamon Press from publishing the 'Pergamon Oxford Dictionary of Perfect Spelling'.

Chanel Ltd v Three Pears Wholesale Cash and Carry Ltd (1981) 131 NLJ 145 HC ChD Consent order (agreeing not to deal in certain goods) not set aside where later case meant that Chanel Ltd would probably not succeed in trade mark infringement/passing off action against Three Pears Ltd.

Choo (Lee Kar) (trading as Yeen Thye Co) v Choon (Lee Lian) (trading as Chuan Lee Co) [1966] 3 All ER 1000; [1967] AC 602; [1966] 3 WLR 1175 PC That no trade mark violations does not mean no passing-off; injunction/ancillary relief available where contrive to implement passing off.

Ciba Geigy plc v Parke Davis and Co Ltd [1993] TLR 202 HC ChD No interlocutory injunction merited preventing advertisement by alleged tortfeasor in pending passing off action that alleged tortfeasor's drug was as effective as but less expensive than competitor (bringing passing off action).

Claudius Ash, Son and Co (Lim) v Invicta Manufacturing Co (Lim) (1910-11) 55 SJ 348 HC ChD Injunction will be granted to restrain manufacturer from marketing goods under name that is not own/is that of rival manufacturer.

Coleman and Co (Limited) v Stephen Smith and Co (Limited) (1910-11) XXVII TLR 533 HC ChD Failure of action brought by makers of 'Wincarnis' meat wine on trade mark, get up and passing off grounds against makers of 'Carvino' meat wine.

Coleman and Co (Limited) v Stephen Smith and Co (Limited) [1911] 2 Ch 572; (1911-12) XXVIII TLR 65 CA Failure of action brought by makers of 'Wincarnis' meat wine on trade mark, get up and passing off grounds against makers of 'Carvino' meat wine.

Dalgety Spillers Foods Ltd v Food Brokers Ltd and others [1993] TLR 618 HC ChD On conduct of parties as relevant factor in passing off action.

Dental Manufacturing Company, Limited v C De Trey and Co [1912] 3 KB 76; (1912) 81 LJKB 1162; (1912-13) 107 LTR 111; (1911-12) XXVIII TLR 498; (1912) WN (I) 190 CA Sole agent could not maintain passing off action for loss of profits where had not sold item under own get-up.

Draper v Trist and others [1939] 3 All ER 513 CA On damages for passing-off.

Edge (W) and Sons (Limited) v Niccolls (W) and Sons (Limited) (1909-10) XXVI TLR 588 HC ChD Injunction granted restraining use of particular get-up which had come to be identified with plaintiff's product.

Edge (W) and Sons (Limited) v Niccolls (W) and Sons (Limited) [1911] 1 Ch 5; (1910) 45 LJ 805; (1911) 80 LJCh 154; (1910-11) 103 LTR 579; (1910-11) XXVII TLR 101; (1910) WN (I) 250 CA Injunction restraining use of particular get-up which had come to be identified with plaintiff's product refused as general confusion unlikely.

Electromobile Company (Limited) v British Electromobile Company (Limited) and others (1907-08) XCVII LTR 196; (1906-07) XXIII TLR 61 HC ChD Injunction refused to prevent company using word 'electromobile' in its name as was generic descriptive word.

Electromobile Company (Limited) v British Electromobile Company (Limited) and others (1907-08) XXIV TLR 192 CA Injunction refused to prevent company using word 'electromobile' in its name as was generic descriptive descriptive word.

Erven Warnink BV and others v J Townend and Sons (Hull) Ltd and others [1979] 2 All ER 927; [1979] AC 731; (1979) 129 (1) NLJ 631; (1979) 123 SJ 472; [1979] 3 WLR 68 HL Passing-off relief if goodwill in descriptive name of product (whether because of ingredients/place of origin).

Ewing (trading as the Buttercup Dairy Co) v Buttercup Margarine Co (Lim) (1916-17) 61 SJ 369; (1917) WN (I) 89 HC ChD Injunction granted to restrain use of trade name in circumstances where use in said way would give rise to confusion.

Ewing v Buttercup Margarine Company, Limited [1917] 2 Ch 1; (1917) 52 LJ 172; (1917-18) 117 LTR 67; (1916-17) 61 SJ 443; (1917) WN (I) 153 CA Injunction granted to restrain use of trade name in circumstances where use in said way would give rise to confusion.

F Reddaway and Co, Limited v Hartley (1931) 71 LJ — see special supplement to issue of February 7, 1931; (1930-31) XLVII TLR 226; (1928) WN (I) 189 CA Injunction granted to restrain sale of products in such a way as was insufficient to distinguish them from plaintiff's goods.

Fels v Thomas Hedley and Co (Limited) (1902-03) XIX TLR 340 HC ChD Use of word 'naphta' in description of soap not so closely identified with plaintiff's products as to merit passing off injunction.

Fels v Thomas Hedley and Co (Limited) (1903-04) XX TLR 69 CA Use of word 'naphta' in description of soap not so closely identified with plaintiff's products as to merit passing off injunction.

Forbes v Kemsley Newspapers, Limited [1951] 2 TLR 656 HC ChD On propietorial rights of journalist in pseudonym under which writes.

Francis Day and Hunter, Limited v Twentieth Century Fox Corporation, Limited, and others (1939) 83 SJ 796; (1939-40) LVI TLR 9 PC For there to be passing off the work passed off must be similar to that which it is passing off.

General Council and Register of Osteopaths Ltd and another v Register of Osteotherapists and Naturopaths Ltd and another (1968) 112 SJ 443 HC ChD Successful passing off action for poprietors of name 'MRO' for osteopaths against persons using name 'MRO' followed by 'registered osteotherapist'.

George Outram and Co (Limited) v The London Evening Newspapers Company (Limited) (1910-11) 55 SJ 255; (1910-11) XXVII TLR 231 HC ChD Injunction to use same newspaper name refused where use of name would not result in any confusion/injury.

Gillette Safety Razor Company and Gillette Safety Razor, Limited v Franks (1923-24) XL TLR 606 HC ChD Injunction granted to restrain sale of second-hand Gillette razor blades as new blades.

Gillette UK Ltd and another v Edenwest Ltd [1994] TLR 135 HC ChD Defendant who did not behave dishonestly could nonetheless be liable in damages in passing off action.

Habib Bank Ltd v Habib Bank AG Zurich [1981] 2 All ER 650; (1981) 131 NLJ 470; (1981) 125 SJ 512; [1981] 1 WLR 1265 CA International business itself retains goodwill/reputation despite establishing branch in England.

Harris v Warren and Phillips (1918) 53 LJ 213; [1918] 87 LJCh 491; (1918-19) 119 LTR 217; (1917-18) 62 SJ 568; (1917-18) XXXIV TLR 440; (1918) WN (I) 173 HC ChD Failed passing off action against persons who had acquired copyright over old song newly publishing same.

Harrods Ltd v Harrodian School (1996) TLR 3/4/96 CA Failed passing off action by Harrods' department store against private preparatory school called 'The Harrodian School'.

Havana Cigar and Tobacco Factories, Limited v Oddenino [1923] 2 Ch 243; (1923) 58 LJ 238; [1924] 93 81 (also CA); (1922-23) 67 SJ 640; (1923) WN (I) 171 HC ChD Corona cigar manufacturers could bring passing off action where person sold cigar not of their make (but of Corona size and shape) as a Corona cigar: on elements of said passing off.

Havana Cigar and Tobacco Factories, Limited v Oddenino [1924] 1 Ch 179; [1924] 93 81 (also HC ChD); (1923) 58 LJ 568; (1924) 130 LTR 428; (1923-24) XL TLR 102 CA Corona cigar manufacturers could bring passing off action where person sold cigar not of their make (but of Corona size and shape) as a Corona cigar: on elements of said passing off.

Henry Faulder and Co (Limited) v O and G Rushton (Limited) (1902-03) XIX TLR 452 CA Injunction granted to restrain sale of jams as 'Silverpan' jams when were not made by plaintiffs.

Henry Thorne and Co Limited v Sandow Limited (1912) 106 LTR 926 HC ChD Failed action for passing off in respect of use of term 'Health' in relation to cocoa.

Hines v Winnick [1947] 2 All ER 517; [1947] Ch 708; [1948] 117 LJR 187; (1947) 91 SJ 560; (1947) LXIII TLR 520; (1947) WN (I) 244 HC ChD Stage name of musician protected in passing off action.

Hodgkinson and Corby Ltd and another v Wards Mobility Services Ltd [1994] TLR 446; [1994] 1 WLR 1564 HC ChD Must be deception for there to be passing off (no deception here so no passing off).

Horlick's Malted Milk Company v Summerskill (W) (1915-16) XXXII TLR 63 HC ChD Term 'malted milk' a descriptive term use of which by rival sellers of malted milk was not passing off.

Horlick's Malted Milk Company v Summerskill [1916] 85 LJP 338; (1916) 114 LTR 484; (1915-16) 60 SJ 320; (1915-16) XXXII TLR 311 CA Term 'malted milk' a descriptive term use of which by rival sellers of malted milk was not passing off.

Horlick's Malted Milk Company v Summerskill (1916) 51 LJ 129; [1917] 86 LJCh 175; (1916-17) 61 SJ 114; (1916-17) XXXIII TLR 83 HL Term 'malted milk' a descriptive term use of which by rival sellers of malted milk was not passing off.

Howard Cundey (trading as Henry Poole and Co) v Lerwill and Pike (1908-09) XCIX LTR 273; (1907-08) XXIV TLR 584 HC ChD No injunction to restrain longtime employee who left to run own business from using connection with earlier firm to advertise own worth.

Hunt, Roope, Teage and Co v Ehrmann Brothers [1910] 2 Ch 198; [1910] 79 LJCh 533; (1910-11) 103 LTR 91 HC ChD Failed action for passing off: on what constitutes passing off.

Illustrated Newspapers, Limited v Publicity Services (London), Limited [1938] Ch 414; [1938] 107 LJCh 154; (1938) 158 LTR 195; (1938) 82 SJ 76; (1937-38) LIV TLR 364; (1938) WN (I) 59 HC ChD Injunction to restrain placing of unauthorised supplement in certain publication of plaintiff as were passing off former as being part of latter.

Imperial Tobacco Company of Great Britain and Ireland v Pasquali; Re Imperial Tobacco Company's Trade Marks [1918] 2 Ch 207 CA Using word 'Regiment' in respect of one's products where rival company's trade mark is 'Regimental' is not breach unless inter alia is real risk of passing off.

Imperial Tobacco Company of India v Albert Bonnan and Bonnan and Co (1924) 131 LTR 642 PC Not passing off to sell manufacturer's cigarettes as such even though had previously sold same cigarettes under particular trade mark.

J and J Cash, Ltd v Cash (1901) 36 LJ 122; (1901) LXXXIV LTR 349; (1901) WN (I) 46 HC ChD Restraint ordered on trading in own name.

J and J Cash, Ltd v Cash [1900-03] All ER 562; (1901-02) XVIII TLR 299 CA No restraint on trading in own name but must be careful to avoid confusion.

Jaeger (Professor Dr G) v The Jaeger Company, Limited (1926-27) XLIII TLR 220 HC ChD Injunction to prevent use of trade name where was danger of confusion resulting.

Jay's, Ltd v Jacobi and another [1933] All ER 690; [1933] Ch 411; (1933) 102 LJCh 130; (1933) 149 LTR 90; (1933) 77 SJ 176; (1933) WN (I) 54 HC ChD No passing off where traded under own name (even if caused some confusion) absent intent to confuse consumers that were another.

JH Coles Proprietary Limited (in liquidation) v Need (John Francis) (1934) 150 LTR 166 PC Injunction granted to restrain use of another's trade names after that other's licence to do so had been revoked.

John Bright and Brothers, Limited v John Bright (Outfitters) Limited (1922-23) 67 SJ 112 CA Refusal of 'passing off' injunction where was good faith use of same name/no competition between the two firms/defendants prepared to make it clear their business was not that of plaintiffs.

John Brinsmead and Sons (Limited) v EG Stanley Brinsmead and Waddington and Sons (Limited) (1912-13) 57 SJ 322; (1912-13) XXIX TLR 237 HC ChD Court would not injunct person from using own name on pianos he made even though might be connected with other well-known piano firm.

John Brinsmead and Sons (Limited) v EG Stanley Brinsmead and Waddington and Sons (Limited) (1912-13) 57 SJ 716; (1912-13) XXIX TLR 706 CA Court would not injunct person from using own name on pianos he made even though might be connected with other well-known piano firm.

John H Andrew and Co (Limited) v Kuehnrich (1912-13) XXIX TLR 771 CA Person using un/registered trade mark can oppose registration of similar mark likely to cause confusion.

John Jacques and Son, Ltd v Chess (a firm) [1939] 3 All ER 227; (1939) 83 SJ 585; (1939-40) LVI TLR 543 HC ChD Though brand name not firmly established as unique to party's goods use of word 'genuine' by another party before that brand name was passing off.

John Jacques and Son, Ltd v 'Chess' (1940) 89 LJ 195; (1940) 84 SJ 302 CA Where brand name not firmly established as unique to party's goods use of word 'genuine' by another party before that brand name was not passing off.

John Walker and Sons Ltd and others v Henry Ost and Co Ltd and another [1970] 2 All ER 106; (1970) 114 SJ 417; [1970] 1 WLR 917 HC ChD Whisky blenders are whisky producers; tort to enable person abroad to manufacture goods under false trade description.

Keith Garner and Associates Ltd v Ingham White Ltd (1980) 130 NLJ 1208c CA Though 'Business' a regular word in publishing titles, target market of publications meant passing off injunction justified.

King and Co (Lim) v Gillard and Co (Lim) (1904-05) 49 SJ 401 CA Failed action for passing off by one dried soup manufacturer against another (no fraudulent intent/risk of confusion).

Kingston, Miller, and Co (Limited) v Thomas Kingston and Co (Limited) (1912) 47 LJ 143; (1912) 81 LJCh 417; (1911-12) XXVIII TLR 246 HC ChD Injunction against firm from using personal name of prorpietor where public likely as result to mistake it for existing firm in same trade.

La Radiotechnique v Weinbaum (1927) 64 LJ 121; (1928) 97 LJCh 17; (1927) 71 SJ 824; (1927) WN (I) 211 HC ChD On when HC will order particulars of defence.

Lecouturier and others v Rey and another; Lecouturier and others v Rey and others [1910] AC 262; (1910) 45 LJ 205; (1909-10) 54 SJ 375; (1909-10) XXVI TLR 368; (1910) WN (I) 79 HL Foreign manufacturer could succeed in passing off action where locus of passing off was England as had acquired reputation there.

Lee Kar Choo (trading as Yeen Thye Co) v Lee Lian Choon (trading as Chuan Lee Co) [1966] 3 All ER 1000; [1967] AC 602; (1966) 110 SJ 946; [1966] 3 WLR 1175 PC That no trade mark violations does not mean no passing-off; injunction/ancillary relief available where contrive to implement passing off.

Legal and General Assurance Society Ltd v Daniel and Others (1967) 117 NLJ 113t CA Successful passing off action by Legal and General Assurance Society against the 'Legal and General Enquiry Bureau'.

Lever Brothers Limited v Masbro' Equitable Pioneer Society Limited (1911-12) 105 LTR 948; (1911-12) 56 SJ 161 HC ChD Injunction for passing off properly refused: on passing off/'trap' orders.

Lever Brothers Limited v Masbro' Equitable Pioneer Society Limited (1912) 106 LTR 472 CA Injunction for passing off properly refused: on passing off/'trap' orders.

Lloyd's and Dawson Brothers v Lloyds Southampton (Limited) (1911-12) XXVIII TLR 338 CA Injunction granted prohibiting Lloyds Southampton, Ltd carrying on business under that or any name which would induce belief that were the Lloyd's.

Lloyds Bank Limited v The Lloyds Investment Trust Company (Limited) and others (1911-12) XXVIII TLR 379 HC ChD Injunction granted upon application of Lloyds Bank prohibiting use of name Lloyds in connection with banking-finance or together with word 'Trust'.

Löwenbräu Mnchen and another v Grnhalle Lager International and another (1974) 118 SJ 50 HC ChD Interlocutory injunction to Löwenbräu Mnchen beer to restrain sales of Grnhalle Löwen-bräu pending full passing off action.

Marengo v Daily Sketch and Sunday Graphic, Limited (1946) 96 LJ 317 CA Failed passing off action by cartoonist with name highly similar to that being used by another cartoonist.

Marengo v Daily Sketch and Sunday Graphic, Limited [1948] 117 LJR 787; (1948) LXIV TLR 160; (1948) WN (I) 92 HL On form of passing-off injunction.

Maxim's Ltd and another v Dye [1978] 2 All ER 55; (1977) 127 NLJ 715t; (1977) 121 SJ 727; [1977] 1 WLR 1155 HC ChD Passing-off relief available to business in other jurisdiction but goodwill in England.

McCulloch v Lewis A May (Produce Distributors), Ltd [1947] 2 All ER 845; (1947) 97 LJ 691; (1947) WN (I) 318 HC ChD Use of stage name in area of manufacture where artiste had no proprietary interest not passing off.

Morecambe and Heysham Corporation v Mecca, Ltd (1966) 110 SJ 70 HC ChD Failed passsing off action brought by organisers of 'Miss Great Britain' contest against organisers of 'Miss Britain' contest.

Morning Star Newspaper Co-operative Society Ltd v Express Newspapers Ltd (1978) 128 NLJ 1100t HC ChD Failed action by The Morning Star newspaper for interim injunction to restrain launch of The Daily Star newspaper as was slim chance of confusion between the two.

Morris Motors Ltd v Lilley [1959] 1 WLR 1184 HC ChD Injunction available to stop person selling manufacturer's cars as new where were not (interfered with goodwill of manufacturer).

Morris Motors Ltd v Phelan [1960] 1 WLR 352 HC ChD On appropriate form of injunction for passing off.

Mothercare Ltd v Robson Books Ltd (1979) 129 (1) NLJ 317 HC ChD Injunction granted to Mothercare Ltd to restrain Robson Books from publishing book entitled 'Mother Care' (or other similarly deceptive name).

Motor Manufacturers' and Trading Society, Ltd v Motor Manufacturers' and Traders' Mutual Insurance Co, Ltd [1925] All ER 616; [1925] Ch 675 (also HC ChD); (1925) 133 LTR 330 CA On granting injunctions to stop passing off (here injunction refused).

New Zealand Netherlands Society 'Oranje' Incorporated v Kuys (Laurentius Cornelius) and another (1973) 117 SJ 565; [1973] 1 WLR 1126 PC Person in fiduciary position in a society held to owe no fiduciary duty to society as regards newspaper person published himself: granted injunction against society publishing newspaper under same name.

Newsweek Inc v The British Broadcasting Corporation (1979) 129 (2) NLJ 952 CA Failed application by proprietors of 'Newsweek' magazine to restrain the BBC from screening a weekly news programme entitled 'Newsweek'.

Norman Kark Publications, Ltd v Odhams Press, Ltd [1962] 1 All ER 636; (1962) 112 LJ 239; (1962) 106 SJ 195 HC ChD Must show proprietary right in goodwill of name and likely confusion to succeed.

Office Cleaning Services, Limited v Westminster Window and General Cleaners, Limited (1946) 174 LTR 229; (1946) WN (I) 24 HL No passing off where names were 'Office Cleaning Sevices' and 'Office Cleaning Association'.

Office Cleaning Services, Ltd v Westminster Office Cleaning Association [1944] 2 All ER 269 CA No passing off where names were 'Office Cleaning Sevices' and 'Office Cleaning Association'.

Park Court Hotel Ltd v Trans-World Hotels Ltd (1970) 120 NLJ 202t; (1970) 114 SJ 166 HC ChD Failed action by owners of 'Hotel International' (a hotel in London) to restrain party from using name 'London International Hotel' in respect of latter's hotel.

Parker and Smith v Satchwell and Co (Lim) (1900-01) 45 SJ 502 HC ChD On form of injunction in passing off/patent action.

Payton and Co (Limited) v Snelling, Lampard, and Co (Limited) (1899-1900) XVI TLR 56 CA Failed action for passing off based on get-up of goods.

Payton and Co, Limited v Snelling, Lampard and Co, Limited [1901] AC 308; [1901] 70 LJCh 644; (1901-02) LXXXV LTR 287 HL Role of judge/witnesses in passing off trial.

Pearks, Gunston and Tee (Limited) v Thompson, Talmey, and Co (1900-01) XVII TLR 250 HC ChD Injunction granted to prominent company trading as 'Talmey and Co' precluding new rival company from trading as 'Thompson, Talmey and Co'.

Pearks, Gunston and Tee (Limited) v Thompson, Talmey, and Co (1900-01) XVII TLR 354 CA Settlement pending appeal against injunction granted to prominent company trading as 'Talmey and Co' precluding new rival company from trading as 'Thompson, Talmey and Co'.

Perry and Co (Lim) v T Hessin and Co (1912) 47 LJ 180; (1911-12) 56 SJ 176 HC ChD Failed action to restrain selling of pens of similar shape/in similar get-up to those of plaintiffs: pen-shape common to trade/get-up unlikely to result in confusion.

Perry and Co v T Hessin and Co (1911-12) 56 SJ 572 CA Failed action to restrain selling of pens of similar shape/in similar get-up to those of plaintiffs: plaintiffs failed to prove intent to deceive on part of defendants.

Pink v Sharwood (JA) and Co Limited (No 2); Re Sidney Ord and Co's Trade Mark (1913-14) 109 LTR 594 HC ChD Failed action for passing off where plaintiff's business had ceased to trade.

Preston v Raphael Tuck and Sons, Limited (1925-26) XLII TLR 440 HC ChD Failed action for passing off of drawings as those of plaintiff.

Re Davis' Trade Marks; Davis v Sussex Rubber Company, Limited [1927] 2 Ch 345 (also CA) HC ChD Injunction granted to restrain passing off through use of name very similar to plaintiff's registered trade name.

Re Davis' Trade Marks; Davis v Sussex Rubber Company, Limited [1927] 2 Ch 345 (also HC ChD); (1928) 97 LJCh 8 CA Injunction granted to restrain passing off through use of name very similar to plaintiff's registered trade name.

Reckitt and Colman Products Ltd v Borden Inc and others [1990] 1 All ER 873; (1990) 134 SJ 784; [1990] TLR 101; [1990] 1 WLR 491 HL Can be misrepresentation as to whole or part of product get-up; get-up may have secondary significance of indicating not only class of product but particular brand.

Repford, Ltd v Mather and Crowther, Ltd, and another (1939) 83 SJ 691 HC KBD Was no cause of action where sued individual as 'passing off' self as author of another's book.

Revlon Inc and others v Cripps and Lee Ltd and others (1980) 130 NLJ 418c CA Failed action in which company sought injunction to restrain sale in the United Kingdom of products it marketed in the United States.

Rey v Lecouturier [1908] 2 Ch 715; [1909] 78 LJCh 181; (1908) XCVIII LTR 197 CA Foreign manufacturer could succeed in passing off action where locus of passing off was England as had acquired reputation there.

Ridge v The 'English Illustrated' Magazine (Limited) (1912-13) XXIX TLR 592 HC KBD Publishers liable (on foot of publishing story falsely ascribed to plaintiff author) in libel if perception of plaintiff would be that of ordinary pen-pusher/in passing off if facts proved and damage inevitable result.

Ridgway v Hutchinson (1923) 58 LJ 296 HC ChD Failed passing-off action by proprietors of 'Adventure' magazine against the proprietors of 'Hutchinson's Adventure-Story Magazine'.

Ripley v Arthur and Co (1902) LXXXVI LTR 495; (1900-01) 45 SJ 165 HC ChD Where as result of judgment by default defendants were estopped from denying alleged passing off attachment would not issue.

Ripley v Arthur and Co (1902) LXXXVI LTR 735 CA Where as result of judgment by default defendants were estopped from denying alleged passing off attachment would not issue.

Sales Affiliates, Limited v Le Jean, Limited [1947] Ch 295; (1947) 97 LJ 106; [1947] 116 LJR 729; (1947) 176 LTR 251; (1947) 91 SJ 100 HC ChD Injunction to prevent giving 'Jamal' hair-wave without using 'Jamal' products: absent actual sale of goods passing-off can be proved by evidence from trade witness.

Samuelson v Producers' Distributing Company, Limited [1932] 1 Ch 201 (also CA); (1932) 101 LJCh 168 (also CA) HC ChD Passing off of film as cinema version of written work.

Samuelson v Producers' Distributing Co, Ltd [1931] All ER 74; [1932] 1 Ch 201 (also HC ChD); (1932) 101 LJCh 168 (also HC ChD); (1932) 146 LTR 37 CA Passing off of film as cinema version of written work.

Serville v Constance and another [1954] 1 All ER 662; (1954) 104 LJ 186; (1954) 98 SJ 179; [1954] 1 WLR 487 HC ChD No chance of confusion meant no recovery for passing-off.

Sim v Heinz (HJ) Co, Ltd and another [1959] 1 All ER 547; (1959) 109 LJ 200; (1959) 103 SJ 238 CA Interlocutory injunction unavailable for alleged passing off/libel.

Societe Anonyme des Anciens Etablissements Panhard et Levassor v Panhard Levassor Motor Co Ltd and others [1900-03] All ER 477; (1901) 36 LJ 393; [1901] 70 LJCh 738; (1901-02) LXXXV LTR 20; (1900-01) XVII TLR 680 HC ChD Foreign company can recover directly in passing off though sells through intermediary into England.

Society of Accountants and Auditors v Goodway and London Association of Accountants, Limited [1907] 1 Ch 489; (1907) XCVI LTR 326; (1907) WN (I) 45 HC ChD Injunction to prevent improper use of term 'incorporated acountant' and to stop defendant society advertising its members as being able to use such a title.

Spalding (AG) and Brothers v Gamage (AW) (Limited) and Benetfink and Co (Limited) (1912-13) XXIX TLR 541 HC ChD Passing off where sold goods of inferior quality made by particular trader as goods of higher quality made by same.

Spalding and Brothers v AW Gamage Limited and Benetfink and Co Limited (1914) 49 LJ 142; (1914) 110 LTR 530 CA Failed action for passing off where by mistake (for which apologised and which sought to remedy upon discovery) sold goods of inferior quality made by particular trader as goods of higher quality made by same.

Spalding (AG) Brothers v Gamage (AW), Ltd [1914-15] All ER 147; [1915] 84 LJCh 449; (1915-16) 113 LTR 198; (1914-15) XXXI TLR 328; (1915) WN (I) 151 HL Passing off where sold goods of inferior quality made by particular trader as goods of higher quality made by same.

Stringfellow and another v McCain Foods (GB) Ltd and another (1984) 128 SJ 701; [1984] TLR 423 CA Failed passing off action by a Mr. Stringfellow (owner of prestigious dining/disco club) against manufacturers of 'Stringfellows' chips, television advertisement for which included disco dancing scene.

Taittinger v Allbev (1993) 143 NLJ 332; [1993] TLR 62 HC ChD 'Elderflower Champagne', a non-alcoholic, carbonated drink produced and marketed in England unlikely to adversely impinge on goodwill in name 'champagne' of real champagne producers.

Taittinger and others v Allbev Ltd and others [1994] 4 All ER 75; [1993] TLR 358 CA 'Elderflower Champagne', a non-alcoholic, carbonated drink produced and marketed in England could adversely impinge on goodwill in name 'champagne' of real champagne producers.

Tallerman v The Dowsing Radiant Heat Company (Limited) (1899-1900) 48 WR 146 HC ChD No injunction to stop inventor circulating publication which quoted from another's article on similar process of treating disease without mentioning other's name as was no passing off.

Tallerman v Dowsing Radiant Heat Company [1900] 1 Ch 1; [1900] LXIX (1) LJ 46 CA No injunction to stop inventor circulating publication which quoted from another's article on similar process of treating disease without mentioning other's name as was no passing off.

Tavener Rutledge Ltd v Trexapalm (1975) 125 NLJ 869t; (1975) 119 SJ 792 HC ChD Suspended interlocutory judgment granted in favour of 'Kojapop' manufacturers against 'Kojak' lollipop manufacturers.

Teofani and Co, Limited v Teofani (A); Re Teofani and Co's Trade Mark [1913] 2 Ch 545 CA Injunction granted to producer of 'A Teofani's cigarettes' to restrain rival producing cigarettes marked in any way with name 'Teofani'.

The Apollinaris Company (Limited) and another v Duckworth and Co (1905-06) XXII TLR 638 HC ChD Failed action for passing off where merely sold product as having properties akin to that of another and did not enable purchasers to do something they ought not to do.

The Apollinaris Company (Limited) and another v Duckworth and Co (1905-06) XXII TLR 744 CA Failed action for passing off where merely sold product as having properties akin to that of another and did not enable purchasers to do something they ought not to do.

The Dental Manufacturing Company (Limited) v C De Trey and Co (Limited) (1911-12) XXVIII TLR 272 HC KBD Sole agent could not maintain passing off action for loss of profits through sale of profits under similar get-up of product for which is sole agent.

The Dunlop Pneumatic Tyre Company, Limited v The Dunlop Motor Company [1907] AC 430; (1907-08) XCVII LTR 259; (1906-07) 51 SJ 715; (1906-07) XXIII TLR 717; (1907) WN (I) 187 HL No passing off by latter party to case; nobody enjoys right to sole use of name 'Dunlop'.

The Fine Cotton Spinners' and Doublers' Association (Limited) and John Cash and Sons (Limited) v Harwood Cash and Co (Limited) [1907] 2 Ch 184; (1907-08) XCVII LTR 45; (1906-07) XXIII TLR 537; (1907) WN (I) 127 HC ChD Injunction granted to prevent new company using name of existing company.

The Ridgway Company v The Amalgamated Press (Limited) (1911-12) XXVIII TLR 149 HC ChD Failed action by proprietors of 'Everybody's Magazine' to restrain publication of competing periodical under title 'Everybody's Weekly'.

The Scotch Whisky Association and others v Glen Kella Distillers Ltd (1997) 141 SJ LB 91; [1997] TLR 186 HC ChD Inunction granted to restrain marketing as Scotch whisky of redistilled Scotch whisky (or 'white whiskey').

The Society of Motor Manufacturers and Traders, Limited v Motor Manufacturers' and Traders' Mutual Insurance Company, Limited [1925] Ch 675 (also CA); (1924-25) 69 SJ 428 HC ChD On granting injunctions to stop passing off (here injunction refused).

The Standard Bank of South Africa (Limited) v The Standard Bank (Limited) (1908-09) XXV TLR 420 HC ChD Defendant injuncted from using its name or any other name that would cause confusion between it and plaintiff bank.

The Valentine Meat Juice Company v The Valentine Extract Company (1899-1900) XVI TLR 33; (1899-1900) 48 WR 127 HC ChD Failed action to injunct opponent from using own name as part of product name where claimant contended confusion would arise as to identity of manufacturer.

The Valentine Meat Juice Company v The Valentine Extract Company (1900-01) LXXXIII LTR 259; (1899-1900) XVI TLR 522 CA Successful action to injunct opponent from using own name as part of product name where claimant contended confusion would arise as to identity of manufacturer.

W and G Du Cros v Gold (1912-13) XXIX TLR 163 HC ChD Restraint by injunction on using particular get-up to pass one taxi-firm off as another.

W Truman (Limited) v Attenborough (Robert) (1910-11) 103 LTR 218; (1909-10) 54 SJ 682; (1909-10) XXVI TLR 601 HC KBD On passing of property under approbation contract — on whether estopped from denying title.

W Woodward (Limited) v Boulton Macro (Limited); Re W Woodward (Limited) (1915) 50 LJ 147; [1916] 85 LJCh 27; (1914-15) XXXI TLR 269; (1915) WN (I) 124 HC ChD Passing off action failed where not proved that 'gripe water' had come to identify plaintiffs' product alone.

Walter v Ashton [1902] 2 Ch 282; [1902] 71 LJCh 839; (1902-03) LXXXVII LTR 196; (1902) WN (I) 66 HC ChD On granting injunctions for unauthorised use of name: injunction to restrain sale of cycles in such a way that they appeared to be connected with 'The Times' newspaper.

Warwick Tyre Company, Limited v New Motor and General Rubber Company, Limited [1910] 1 Ch 248; (1910) 45 LJ 36; [1910] 79 LJCh 177; (1909-10) 101 LTR 889; (1910) WN (I) 8 HC ChD Injunction to stop use of name 'Warwick' in respect of motor tyres as calculated to deceive consumers that defendant's tyres produced by plaintiffs.

Weiner v Harvey and Co, Ltd [1936] LJNCCR 94 CyCt Injunction refused where further incident of passing off (of tobacco blend) not likely; on entrapment of person guilty of passing off.

Weingarten Brothers v Bayer and Co [1904-07] All ER 877; (1905) XCII LTR 511; (1904-05) XXI TLR 418 HL Passing-off found where used another's distinctive logo on own products.

Weingarten Brothers v Charles Bayer and Co (1903) LXXXVIII LTR 168; (1902-03) XIX TLR 239 HC ChD Injunction granted prohibiting sale of goods not made by plaintiff under plaintiff's distinctive trade-name where was possibility of confusion among buyers.

Weingarten Brothers v Charles Bayer and Company (1903-04) LXXXIX LTR 56; (1902-03) XIX TLR 604 CA Reversal of injunction granted by HC KBD prohibiting sale of goods not made by plaintiff under plaintiff's distinctive trade-name where was possibility of confusion among buyers.

WH Dorman and Company, Limited v Henry Meadows, Limited [1922] 2 Ch 332; [1922] 91 LJCh 728; (1922) 127 LTR 655; (1922) WN (I) 164 HC ChD Injunction restraining use of surname as part of product-name insofar as would cause confusion.

White Hudson and Co, Ltd v Asian Organisation, Ltd [1965] 1 All ER 1040; (1964) 108 SJ 937; [1964] 1 WLR 1466 PC Can be passing-off by get-up even though writing on items distinguishes them.

William Edge and Sons, Limited v William Nicholls and Sons, Limited [1911] AC 693; (1910-11) 55 SJ 737; (1911) WN (I) 176 HL Injunction granted to restrain passing off by get-up.

WN Sharpe, Lim v Solomon Bros, Lim; Re WN Sharpe, Lim's Trade Mark [1915] 84 LJCh 290 CA Failed action for passing-off in get-up of Christmas card boxes.

Worsley (E) and Co, Ltd v Cooper [1939] 1 All ER 290; (1939) 87 LJ 103 HC ChD Misrepresenting that another business (of same kind as one's own) had ceased was (absent malice/special damage) passing off.

Yeatman and others v Homberger and Co (1912-13) 107 LTR 742; (1912-13) XXIX TLR 26 CA Not to repeat action not satisfactory response to passing off complaint: must seek to redress damage done.

Yeatman v L Homberger and Co (1912-13) 107 LTR 43; (1911-12) 56 SJ 614 HC ChD Injunction granted to restrain passing off in price circular of one wine as another.

Zimmer Orthopaedic Ltd v Zimmer Manufacturing Co Ltd (1968) 118 NLJ 1053t; [1968] 1 WLR 1349 CA Claim and counterclaim dismissed for want of prosecution in action involving inter alia passing off.

PERSONAL INJURIES (animal)

Marlor v Ball (1899-1900) XVI TLR 239 CA Person who meddled with wild animals (zebras) could not recover damages where suffered consequent personal injuries.

PERSONAL INJURIES (child)

Shrimpton v Hertfordshire County Council (1910) 74 JP 305 CA Education authority not liable for personal injury suffered by child on school transportation (where child not supposed to be using same).

Shrimpton (Florence M) (an infant by her father and next friend), Pauper, v Hertfordshire County Council (1911) 75 JP 201; (1911) 104 LTR 145; (1910-11) 55 SJ 270; (1910-11) XXVII TLR 251 HL Education authority liable for personal injury suffered by child on school transportation (though child not supposed to be using same).

PERSONAL INJURIES (damages)

Abbott v Isham and others (1921) 85 JP 30; [1921] LJCL 309; (1921) 124 LTR 734; (1920-21) XXXVII TLR 7 HC KBD Successful action against school managers for personal injuries suffered by headmaster when defective boiler burst.

Adair v General Motors Ltd [1968] 1 All ER 481 (1968) 118 NLJ 182t HC QBD On damages for personal injuries (severe asthma).

Adams and another v Railway Executive (1952) 96 SJ 361 HC QBD Loss of consortium must be entire before can recover for same.

Agar v Elliott and another (1970) 114 SJ 887 CA On farm labour rendered quadraplegic in car collision.

Andrews v Freeborough [1966] 2 All ER 721; (1965-66) 116 NLJ 1032; [1967] 1 QB 1; (1966) 110 SJ 407; [1966] 3 WLR 342 CA Damages for loss of expectation of life (despite victim's coma)/injuries suffered available to administrator of deceased victim's estate.

Andrews v Hopkinson [1956] 3 All ER 422; [1957] 1 QB 229; [1956] 3 WLR 732 Assizes Non-purchaser could rely on warranty that induced hire-purchase arrangement; damages for personal injuries for breach of warranty that was safe car; damages for negligence in delivering unsafe car when defects reasonably discoverable by supplier.

Attia v British Gas plc [1987] 3 All ER 455; (1987) 137 NLJ 661; [1988] QB 304; (1987) 131 SJ 1248; [1987] 3 WLR 1101 CA Damages for nervous shock/psychiatric damage where personal injury/view destruction of property.

Auty and others v National Coal Board [1985] 1 All ER 930; (1985) 129 SJ 249; [1984] TLR 205; [1985] 1 WLR 784 CA Future inflation not relevant to personal injury damages; non-payment of fatal accident compensation to dead man's wife inelgible for after-retirement widow's pension.

Auty, Mills, Rogers and Popow v National Coal Board (1981) 131 NLJ 927 HC QBD Future inflation not relevant to personal injury damages; on recoverability of damages for reduced widow's pension available where husband died in retirement/course of employment.

Bailey v Howard [1938] 4 All ER 827; [1939] 1 KB 453; (1939) 87 LJ 9; [1939] 108 LJCL 182; (1939) 160 LTR 87; (1938) 82 SJ 1030; (1938-39) LV TLR 249; (1939) WN (I) 17 CA On appropriate damages for loss of life expectancy (of child).

Baillie v Birmingham and Midland Motor Omnibus Co, Ltd (1964) 108 SJ 258 HC QBD On appropriate damages for music teacher who suffered negligent injury to her arm.

Baker v Willoughby [1968] 2 All ER 236; (1968) 118 NLJ 277t; [1969] 1 QB 38; (1968) 112 SJ 234; [1968] 2 WLR 1138 HC QBD Post-personal injury wounding with which original injury merged did not disentitle one to damages for original injury.

Bass v Hendon Urban District Council (1912) 76 JP 13 HC KBD Damages for personal injuries sustained by fire brigade volunteer through negligence of council employee.

Bastow v Bagley and Co Ltd (1961) 111 LJ 820; (1961) 105 SJ 885; [1961] 1 WLR 1494 CA On appropriate damages for personal injuries (here loss of eye).

Bellingham v Dhillon and another [1973] 1 All ER 20; [1973] QB 304; (1972) 116 SJ 566; [1972] 3 WLR 730 HC QBD Projected profits less actual profits yields amount of damages in contract/tort for loss of profits.

Bird v Cocking and Sons, Ltd [1951] 2 TLR 1260 CA On gauging personal injury damages: relevancy of awards in similar cases/relevancy of age.

Birkett v Hayes and another [1982] 2 All ER 710; (1982) 126 SJ 399; [1982] TLR 157; [1982] 1 WLR 816 CA Interest usual when awarding general damages for pain/suffering/loss of amenities.

Booth and another v Chrystal Springs Ltd (1968) 112 SJ 51 CA On appropriate personal injuries damages for young woman and her husband (for loss of consortium) where former's leg injured/permanently affected in negligent accident.

Bowker v Rose (1977) 121 SJ 274 HC QBD State mobility/attendance allowances not deductible from personal injury damages.

Bowker v Rose (1978) 122 SJ 147 CA State mobility/attendance allowances not deductible from personal injury damages.

Brice and others v Brown and others [1984] 1 All ER 997; (1984) 134 NLJ 204 HC QBD Tortfeasor liable for nervous shock and its consequences even where not those normal person would suffer.

British Transport Commission v Gourley [1955] 3 All ER 796; [1956] AC 185; (1955) 105 LJ 808; [1956] 2 WLR 41 HL Income tax and surtax factors to be considered when awarding damages.

Brown v New Empress Saloons Limited (1937) 156 LTR 427; (1937) WN (I) 156 CA On practice as regards awarding costs as element of damages in personal injuries action.

Browning v The War Office (1962) 106 SJ 452 HC QBD Veterans benefits payable to injured US military employee disregarded when assessing personal injuries damages payable to same.

Browning v The War Office and another (1962) 112 LJ 849; [1963] 1 QB 750; (1962) 106 SJ 957; [1963] 2 WLR 52 CA Disability pension deductible from personal injury damages; damages for negligence are intended to compensate victim not punish tortfeasor.

Choo (Lim Poh) v Camden and Islington Area Health Authority [1979] 1 All ER 332; (1978) 128 NLJ 63t; [1979] QB 196; [1978] 3 WLR 895 HC QBD Damages to include lost earnings; not to be adjusted for inflation.

Choo (Lim Poh) v Camden and Islington Area Health Authority [1979] 1 All ER 332; (1978) 128 NLJ 933; (1978) 122 SJ 509; [1979] QB 196; [1978] 3 WLR 895 CA Damages to include lost earnings; not to be adjusted for inflation.

Choo (Lim Poh) v Camden and Islington Area Health Authority [1979] 2 All ER 910; [1980] AC 174; (1979) 129 (2) NLJ 656; (1979) 123 SJ 457; [1979] 3 WLR 44 HL Damages for loss of earnings available but to be reduced by damages for cost of future care.

Clark v The London General Omnibus Company (Limited) (1906) 41 LJ 492; [1906] 75 LJKB 907; (1906-07) XCV LTR 435; (1905-06) 50 SJ 631; (1905-06) XXII TLR 691 CA Funeral expenses of unmarried daughter living with father irrecoverable as fatal accident damages by father.

Clarke v Rotax Aircraft Equipment Ltd [1975] 3 All ER 794; [1975] 1 WLR 1570 CA No interest on damages for loss of earning capacity.

Cluer v Chiltern Works (Engineering) Ltd (1975) 119 SJ 85 HC QBD On whether plaintiff entitled to require disclosure of medical report as pre-requisite to submitting to joint medical examination.

Colledge v Bass Mitchells and Butlers Ltd [1988] 1 All ER 536 CA Redundancy payment stemming from personal injury can be deducted from damages.

Connolly v Camden and Islington Area Health Authority [1981] 3 All ER 250; (1981) 131 NLJ 802 HC QBD Young child can claim damages for loss of earnings in lost years.

Cook v JL Kier and Co Ltd [1970] 2 All ER 513; (1970) 120 NLJ 248t; (1970) 114 SJ 207; [1970] 1 WLR 774 CA Appropriate damages for severe brain injury.

Cozens v North Devon Hospital Management Committee and another [1966] 2 All ER 799; (1965-66) 116 NLJ 1061; [1966] 2 QB 330; (1966) 110 SJ 428; [1966] 3 WLR 279 CA Cannot apply for ex parte order disapplying limitation to be discharged before trial.

Crossgrove and another v Barkers Traffic Services Ltd and others (1966) 110 SJ 892 HC QBD On appropriate damages for head injuries where was uncertain whether would worsen over time.

Cunningham v Harrison and another [1973] 3 All ER 463; (1973) 123 NLJ 542t; [1973] QB 942; (1973) 117 SJ 547; [1973] 3 WLR 97 CA Damages not reduced by ex-gratia payments from employer; damages for nursing/attendants/accommodation to be reasonable.

Cutler v Vauxhall Motors Ltd [1970] 2 All ER 56; (1970) 120 NLJ 249t; [1971] 1 QB 418; (1970) 114 SJ 247; [1970] 2 WLR 961 CA No damages where would have had to undergo operation necessitated by personal injury anyway.

Cutts and another v Chumley and another (1967) 111 SJ 458; [1967] 1 WLR 742 HC QBD On appropriate damages for personal injuries leaving wife permanently incapacitated; on damages for husband for adverse impact of injuries on consortium.

Daish (an infant by his next friend Albert Edward Daish) v Walton [1972] 1 All ER 25; (1971) 121 NLJ 928t; [1972] 2 QB 262; (1971) 115 SJ 891; [1972] 2 WLR 29 CA Damages not to be reduced by National Health Service benefits.

Davids v Turner (1946) 96 LJ 56 HC KBD Failed person injuries action brought by licensee (who fell down stairs) where was no trap/hidden danger — plaintiff in fact knew of danger and failed to take reasonable precautions.

Denman v Essex Area Health Authority [1984] 2 All ER 621; (1984) 134 NLJ 264; [1984] QB 735; (1984) 128 SJ 318; [1984] TLR 1 HC QBD When benefits to be deducted from damages fully defined in Law Reform (Personal Injuries) Act 1948.

Dews v National Coal Board [1986] 2 All ER 769; [1987] QB 81; [1986] 3 WLR 227 CA Missed compulsory pension contributions not to be included in damages.

Dews v National Coal Board [1988] AC 1; (1987) 137 NLJ 545; [1987] 3 WLR 38 HL Missed compulsory pension contributions not to be included in damages.

Dexter v Courtaulds Ltd [1984] 1 All ER 70; (1984) 128 SJ 81; [1983] TLR 688; [1984] 1 WLR 372 CA Half-rate interest on special damages in ordinary personal injuries case is proper.

Dodds and another v Dodds (1977) 121 SJ 619 HC QBD One dependant could claim fatal accident injuries from another dependant whose negligence led to fatal accident; multiplier to be fixed at date of trial.

Dowman v Wolverhampton Die Casting Co Ltd [1968] 3 All ER 692 Assizes On personal injury damages (for dermatitis).

Dowman v Wolverhampton Die Casting Co Ltd [1968] 3 All ER 692 CA On personal injury damages (for dermatitis).

Eagus v Leonard (1962) 106 SJ 918 CA On rôle of agreed medical reports in assessment of personal injuries damages.

Edmeades v Thames Board Mills Ltd (1969) 119 NLJ 105t; [1969] 2 QB 67; [1969] 2 WLR 668 CA Proceedings stayed to allow for new medical evidence required by new claims.

Eley v Bedford [1971] 3 All ER 285; (1971) 115 SJ 369; [1971] 3 WLR 563 HC QBD Damages not to be reduced by time-barred injury benefits of which were unaware.

Ellis and another v Raine [1939] 108 LJCL 292; (1939) 161 LTR 234; (1939) 83 SJ 152; (1938-39) LV TLR 344 CA Re-trial ordered where despite direction from judge jury in action brought by parents of child killed through negligence awarded damages under Fatal Accidents Act 1846 but not under Law Reform (Miscellaneous Provisions) Act 1934.

Feay v Barnwell [1938] 1 All ER 31 HC KBD Appropriate damages where overlapping of damages under Fatal Accidents Acts and Law Reform (Miscellaneous Provisions) Act 1934.

Fitzgerald v Lane and another [1988] 2 All ER 961; [1989] AC 328; (1988) 138 NLJ 209; [1990] RTR 133; (1988) 132 SJ 1064; 3 WLR 356 HL Deciding liabilities of co-defendants secondary to deciding liabilities of plaintiff and defendants; plaintiff's conduct to be considered against total conduct of defendants.

Fletcher v Autocar Transporters, Ltd [1968] 1 All ER 726; (1968) 118 NLJ 84t; [1968] 2 QB 322; (1968) 112 SJ 96; [1968] 2 WLR 743 CA Fair not perfect compensation sought; damages a single sum: heads of compensation merely an aid.

Fletcher v Sanderson (1976) 126 NLJ 1068t CA £6,500 damages for three year old who had to spend three weeks in hospital and suffered serious pelvic injuries after being knocked down.

Flint v Lovell [1934] All ER 200; [1935] 1 KB 354; (1934) 78 LJ 381; (1935) 152 LTR 231; (1934) 78 SJ 860; (1934-35) LI TLR 127; (1934) WN (I) 223 CA Shorter life expectancy a separate head of damage.

Flowers v George Wimpey and Co, Ltd [1955] 3 All ER 165; (1955) 105 LJ 602; [1956] 1 QB 73; (1955) 99 SJ 564; [1955] 3 WLR 426 HC QBD No special damages for loss of earnings where benefits exceeded loss.

Foster v Tyne and Wear County Council [1986] 1 All ER 567 CA Half the value of social security benefits paid for five years after cause of action deductible from award for loss of earning capacity.

Fowler and another v Grace (1970) 120 NLJ 200t; (1970) 114 SJ 193 CA On appropriate damages for person paralysed in all her limbs as a result of a motor accident.

Fowler v AW Hawksley, Ltd (1951) 95 SJ 788 CA On appropriate damages for personal injuries to already disabled man.

Foxley and another v Olton [1964] 3 All ER 248; [1965] 2 QB 306; (1964) 108 SJ 522; [1964] 3 WLR 1155 HC QBD On deduction/non-deduction of unemployment benefit/national assistance grants.

Gage and another v King [1960] 3 All ER 62; (1960) 110 LJ 541; [1961] 1 QB 188; (1960) 104 SJ 644 HC QBD Party legally liable for expenses entitled to recover.

Gambling v Benham [1940] 1 All ER 275; (1940) 84 SJ 132 CA On appropriate damages for loss of life expectancy (of infant).

Gammell v Wilson and another [1980] 2 All ER 557; [1982] AC 27 (also HL); (1980) 130 NLJ 510; (1980) 124 SJ 329; [1980] 3 WLR 591 CA Estate can sue for lost earnings in lost years; gravestone is funeral expense; sum for loss of life expectation changeable/not constantly reviewable.

Gammell v Wilson and others; Furness and another v B and S Massey Ltd [1981] 1 All ER 578; [1982] AC 27 (also CA); (1981) 131 NLJ 197; (1981) 125 SJ 116; [1981] 2 WLR 248 HL Estate of deceased can recover damages for deceased's loss of earnings in lost years.

Gardner v Dyson [1967] 3 All ER 762; (1967) 117 NLJ 1087t; (1967) 111 SJ 793; [1967] 1 WLR 1497 CA Appropriate damages upon loss of eye.

George and another v Pinnock and another [1973] 1 All ER 926; (1973) 117 SJ 73; [1973] 1 WLR 118 CA Appropriate damages for total incapacity.

Haggar v De Placido [1972] 2 All ER 1029; (1972) 116 SJ 396; [1972] 1 WLR 716 CrCt Victim may recover costs/losses of third parties to whom has legal liability for reasonable costs/losses they suffered (even if family members).

Haley v London Electricity Board (1965) 109 SJ 295 CA On appropriate damages for blind person rendered deaf through negligence of another.

Hall v Wilson and another [1939] 4 All ER 85; (1939) 88 LJ 276; (1939) 83 SJ 961; (1939-40) LVI TLR 15 HC KBD Allowance for risk of death in war made when gauging fatal personal injury damages.

Hambridge v Harrison (1973) 117 SJ 343 CA On appropriate personal injury damages for person who endured personality change/unhappiness with way of life; agreed medical reports must be 'agreed' — court must not have to choose between them.

Harper v John Harper and Co Ltd (1979) 129 (1) NLJ 198c CA £700 damages for sixty year old who through negligence of another suffered an inguinal hernia.

Harris v Brights Asphalt Contractors Ld [1953] 1 QB 617; [1953] 1 WLR 341 HC QBD Cannot claim as damages the difference in wages between pre-injury life term and post-injury life term.

Hartley v Sandholme Iron Co Ltd [1974] 3 All ER 475; (1974) 118 SJ 702; [1974] 3 WLR 445 HC QBD Personal injury damages can be reduced by income tax savings resulting from injury.

Harun (Jamil Bin) v Rasdi (Yang Kamsiah Bte Meor) and another [1984] AC 529; (1984) 128 SJ 281; [1984] 2 WLR 668 PC Malaysian Federal Court could itemise rather than award general damages for child's permanent incapacitation on foot of accident.

Haste v Sandell Perkins Ltd [1984] 2 All ER 615; (1984) 134 NLJ 681; [1984] QB 735; (1984) 128 SJ 334; [1984] 3 WLR 73 HC QBD When benefits to be deducted from damages fully defined in Law Reform (Personal Injuries) Act 1948.

Hawkins v New Mendip Engineering, Ltd [1966] 3 All ER 228; (1965-66) 116 NLJ 1377; [1966] 1 WLR 1341 CA Possibility of serious supervening illness a legitimate factor when assessing damages.

Hayes v Bowman [1989] 1 WLR 456 CA Court could (but did not here) strike out personal injuries action where want of prosecution led to increase in (loss of earnings) damages available.

Heaps v Perrite, Ltd [1937] 2 All ER 60; (1937) 83 LJ 186 CA Appropriate damages for personal injuries (loss of hands).

Hewson v Downes and another [1970] 1 QB 73; (1969) 119 NLJ 274t; (1969) 113 SJ 309; [1969] 2 WLR 1169 HC QBD State pension relevant to level of damages awarded to person who suffered injuries in motor car accident.

Hicks and another v Chief Constable of the South Yorkshire Police; Wafer v Chief Constable of the South Yorkshire Police [1992] 1 All ER 690 CA Horror and fear not heads of damages unless result in real psychiatric damage; no damages for pain and suffering if part of death.

Hindmarsh v Henry and Leigh Slater, Ltd (1965-66) 116 NLJ 868t; (1966) 110 SJ 429 CA On appropriate personal injury damages for person left with physical deformity/personality change but who could not understand consequences of his injuries.

Hodgson v Trapp and another [1988] 3 All ER 870; [1989] AC 807; [1988] 1 FLR 69; (1988) 138 NLJ 327; (1988) 132 SJ 1672; [1988] 3 WLR 1281 HL Attendance/mobility allowances deductible from personal injuries awards; damages multiplier not to be increased to allow for tax.

Hole and Son (Sayers Common) Ltd and another v Harrisons of Thurnscoe Ltd and others (1972) 116 SJ 922 HC QBD On appropriate damages following accident which demolished cottage.

Hotson v East Berkshire Area Health Authority [1987] AC 750 (also CA); (1987) 137 NLJ 638; [1987] 3 WLR 232 HL Tortious damages available for lost chance of recovery if can prove causation (which here failed to do).

Housecroft v Burnett [1986] 1 All ER 332; (1985) 135 NLJ 728 HC QBD £75,000 appropriate for pain/suffering/loss of tetraplegic; no damages in respect of national health care nursing; sham contract for services will not yield extra damages; awards for non-economic loss altered only if clearly too high/low.

Hughes v McKeown (1985) 129 SJ 543; [1985] 1 WLR 963 HC QBD On determining personal injury damages for young woman who because of injury has limited future earning ability and no chance of marriage.

Hultquist v Universal Pattern and Precision Engineering Co, Ltd [1960] 2 All ER 266; [1960] 2 QB 467; (1960) 104 SJ 427 CA Appropriate personal injury damages.

Hurditch v Sheffield Health Authority [1989] 2 All ER 869; [1989] QB 562; (1989) 133 SJ 630; [1989] 2 WLR 827 CA Parties agreeing on need for provisional damages but disagreeing on some evidence enough basis for taxing master to make order.

Hussain v New Taplow Paper Mills Ltd [1987] 1 All ER 417; [1987] 1 WLR 336 CA Long-term sickness benefit an earning which if not paid for are deductible from damages.

Hussain v New Taplow Paper Mills Ltd [1988] 1 All ER 541; [1988] AC 514; (1988) 138 NLJ 45; [1988] 2 WLR 266 HL Long-term sickness benefit deductible from personal injury damages.

Ichard and another v Frangoulis [1977] 2 All ER 461; (1977) 121 SJ 287; [1977] 1 WLR 556 HC QBD Loss of enjoyment of holiday recoverable as general damages in personal injuries action, not as specific head.

Jackman v Corbett [1988] QB 154; (1987) 131 SJ 808; [1987] 3 WLR 586 CA Half of invalidity benefit in five-year period from date when cause of action arose was deductible from personal injury damages.

James v Woodall Duckham Construction Co Ltd [1969] 2 All ER 794; (1969) 113 SJ 225; [1969] 1 WLR 903 CA Damages for loss of earnings reduced where delay deferred return to work.

Jefford and another v McGee [1970] 1 All ER 1202; (1970) 114 SJ 206 CA On interest on fatal accident damages.

Jobling v Associated Dairies Ltd [1980] 3 All ER 769; [1981] QB 389; (1980) 124 SJ 631; [1980] 3 WLR 704 CA Tortious liability falls if tortious injury overtaken by supervening illness.

Jobling v Associated Dairies Ltd [1981] 2 All ER 752; [1982] AC 794; (1981) 125 SJ 481; [1981] 3 WLR 155 HL Supervening illness to be taken into account when assessing liability of tortfeasor for injury.

Johnston v Great Western Railway Company (1904) 39 LJ 224; [1904] 73 LJCL 568; (1904-05) XCI LTR 157; (1903-04) 48 SJ 435 CA On appropriate damages for personal injuries resulting in loss of earning capacity.

Jones v Griffith [1969] 2 All ER 1015; (1969) 113 SJ 309; [1969] 1 WLR 795 CA Appropriate damages where epilepsy induced by accident.

Jordan v Limmer and Trinidad Lake Asphalt Co, Ltd and another [1946] 1 All ER 527; [1946] KB 356; (1946) 175 LTR 89; (1945-46) LXII TLR 302; (1946) WN (I) 76 HC KBD Income tax not to be deduced from future earnings when assessing personal injury damages.

Kaiser (an infant) v Carlswood Glassworks, Ltd, and another (1965) 109 SJ 537 CA On need for recent medical report when deciding on damages for personal injuries.

Kansara v Osram [1967] 3 All ER 230 CA Appropriate damages in cases meriting small awards.

Kirby v Vauxhall Motors Ltd (1969) 113 SJ 736 CA On appropriate damages for disablement of young man's leg; itemisation of heads of damages appropriate though ultimately regard must be had to overall damages.

Kitcat v Murphy (1969) 113 SJ 385 HC QBD On appropriate damages for personal injuries that resulted in quadraplegia.

Kralj and another v McGrath and another [1986] 1 All ER 54; (1985) 135 NLJ 913 HC QBD Aggravated damages not appropriate for medical negligence though compensatory damages may be raised; damages for nervous shock, not grief; financial loss in replacing dead child recoverable.

Lane v Willis; Same v Beach (1972) 116 SJ 102; [1972] 1 WLR 326 CA Case properly stayed where plaintiff refused to undergo medical examination.

Liffen v Watson [1940] 2 All ER 213; [1940] 1 KB 556; (1940) 89 LJ 183; [1940] 109 LJCL 367; (1940) 84 SJ 368; (1939-40) LVI TLR 442; (1940) WN (I) 100 CA Damages for traumatic neurosis and for loss of board and lodging at place of employment.

Lim v Camden and Islington Area Health Authority (1978) 122 SJ 82 HC QBD On making allowances for inflation when awarding personal injury damages.

Lincoln v Hayman and another [1982] 2 All ER 819; [1982] RTR 336; (1982) 126 SJ 174; [1982] 1 WLR 488 CA Supplementary benefits to be deducted from special damages.

Martin v Stirk (1969) 113 SJ 527 HC QBD On personal injuries damages for person rendered quadraplegic by another's negligence and who had awareness of her injuries.

McCamley v Cammell Laird Shipbuilders Ltd [1990] 1 All ER 854; [1990] 1 WLR 963 CA Payment of pre-set sum from benevolent insurance policy not to be deducted from personal injury damages.

McKew v Holland and Hannen and Cubitts (Scotland) Ltd [1969] 3 All ER 1621 HL Careless act broke causation between first injury and later injury.

Millikin v Smith (1951) 95 SJ 560 CA On procedure as regards assessment of damages in personal injury actions.

Mills v Stanway Coaches, Ltd and another [1940] 2 All ER 586; [1940] 2 KB 334; (1940) 89 LJ 250; [1940] 109 LJCL 648; (1940) 163 LTR 68; (1940) 84 SJ 595; (1939-40) LVI TLR 790; (1940) WN (I) 199 CA Appropriate damages for reduction of life expectancy/pain and suffering.

Mitchell (by his next friend Hazel Doreen Mitchell) v Mulholland and another (No 2) [1971] 2 All ER 1205; [1972] 1 QB 65; [1971] 2 WLR 1271 CA Multiplier method better than actuarial method of assessing damages; effect of post-trial inflation inadmissible; evidence of 'productivity' inflation admissible.

Moeliker v A Reyrolle and Co Ltd [1977] 1 All ER 9; [1977] 1 WLR 132 CA Damages for loss of earning capacity to employed only if real prospect of job loss; how to measure loss of earning capacity.

Morey v Woodfield [1963] 3 All ER 533; (1963) 107 SJ 651; [1964] 1 WLR 16 CA On appeals concerning personal injury damages.

Moriarty v McCarthy [1978] 2 All ER 213; (1977) 127 NLJ 1049t; (1977) 121 SJ 745; [1978] 1 WLR 155 HC QBD Marriage/children consideration in deciding young woman's loss of future earnings; if no marriage prospects loss of husband's financial support heading for damages.

Morris v Johnson Matthey and Co Ltd (1968) 112 SJ 32 CA On appropriate damages for fifty-two year old craftsman who suffered permanent injury to his hand.

Murphy v Stone Wallwork (Charlton) Ltd [1969] 2 All ER 949; (1969) 119 NLJ 600t HL Lords may allow fresh evidence pointing to mistaken assessment of damages.

Nabi v British Leyland [1980] 1 All ER 667; (1980) 124 SJ 83; [1980] 1 WLR 529 CA Special damages to be reduced by unemployment benefit.

Neal v Bingle [1997] TLR 409 CA Could claim in damages social security payments that would have received but for personal injury in respect of which bringing claim.

Newall v Tunstall [1970] 3 All ER 465; (1971) 115 SJ 14 Assizes No interest where order made not order against defendant.

Nicholls v Rushton [1992] TLR 303 CA Damages irrecoverable for nervous injury incapable of psychological definition from which suffered after road accident.

O'Brien v Meadows (1965) 109 SJ 316 CA On appropriate personal injury damages for person who suffered venous thrombosis after accident arising from another's negligent driving.

Oakley v Walker and another (1977) 121 SJ 619 HC QBD Personal injury damages avaialble for collapse of marriage consequent upon negligent road traffic accident.

Oliver and others v Ashman and another [1960] 3 All ER 677; (1960) 110 LJ 830; (1961) 111 LJ 580; (1960) 104 SJ 1036 HC QBD Shortened lifespan/that most of damages will not be spent on claimant relevant in deciding level of damages.

Oliver and others v Ashman and another [1961] 3 All ER 323; [1955] Crim LR 608; [1962] 2 QB 210 CA Loss of life expectation to include loss of earnings estimate.

Owen v Sykes [1935] All ER 90; [1936] 1 KB 193; (1935) 80 LJ 418; [1936] 105 LJCL 32; (1936) 80 SJ 15 CA Awards of damages amended on appeal only where grossly wrong.

Page v Smith [1995] 2 All ER 736; [1996] 1 AC 155; (1995) 145 NLJ 723; [1995] RTR 210; (1995) 139 SJ LB 173; [1995] TLR 275; [1995] 2 WLR 644 HL Negligent driver liable to primary victim for nervous shock if personal injury reasonably foreseeable as result of accident even if no physical injury.

Parry v English Electric Co Ltd [1971] 2 All ER 1094; [1971] 1 WLR 664 CA Appopriate personal injury damages to be assessed in each case.

Payne v Railway Executive [1952] 1 KB 26; (1951) 95 SJ 710; [1951] 2 TLR 929; (1951) WN (I) 547 CA Service pension not to be taken into account when assessing personal injury damages.

Payne v Railway Executive (1951) 95 SJ 268; [1951] 1 TLR 921; (1951) WN (I) 240 HC KBD Service pension not to be taken into account when assessing personal injury damages.

Perez v CAV, Ltd [1959] 2 All ER 414; (1959) 103 SJ 492 HC QBD Proportion of disablement gratuity deductible from loss of earnings.

Pickett v British Rail Engineering Ltd (1977) 121 SJ 814 CA Loss of earnings in lost years unavailable to plaintiff suffering work related injury/disease whose action came to court during his lifetime.

Pickett v British Rail Engineering Ltd; British Rail Engineering Ltd v Pickett [1979] 1 All ER 774; [1980] AC 136; (1978) 128 NLJ 1198t; (1978) 122 SJ 778; [1978] 3 WLR 955 HL Loss of earnings damages where life expectancy diminished are for whole of pre-injury life expectancy; interest available on inflation-adjusted damages.

Plummer v PW Wilkins and Son Ltd [1981] 1 All ER 91; (1980) 130 NLJ 1043; (1981) 125 SJ 399; [1981] 1 WLR 831 HC QBD Special damages to be reduced by amount of supplementary benefits.

Pope and others v D Murphy and Son, Ltd [1960] 2 All ER 873; (1960) 110 LJ 542; [1961] 1 QB 222; (1960) 104 SJ 427 HC QBD Loss of earning capacity to be gauged by pre-injury life expectancy.

Povey v Governors of Rydal School [1970] 1 All ER 841 Assizes Appropriate damages for tetraplegia.

Pritchard v JH Cobden Ltd and another [1987] 1 All ER 300; [1988] Fam 22; [1987] 2 FLR 30; (1970) 130 SJ 715; [1987] 2 WLR 627 CA Date of trial date on which to assess actual/future loss of earnings; divorce costs cannot be included in damages as not a loss.

Rees (D) v West Glamorgan County Council (1993) 143 NLJ 814 CA Status of payment to Compensation Recovery Unit controverted.

Richards v Highway Ironfounders (West Bromwich), Ltd [1955] 3 All ER 205; [1955] 1 WLR 1049 CA No damages for loss of chance to provide for dependants.

Robertson v Turnbull (1981) 131 NLJ 1211 HL Refusal of damages (expenses/solatium) to husband whose wife suffered non-fatal injury in road accident.

Robinson v Post Office and another (1973) 117 SJ 915 CA On appropriate personal injuries damages from employer (doctor not negligent) to worker who contracted encephalitis on foot of anti-tetanus injection.

Rodriguez v Rodriguez (1989) 133 SJ 1134 CA Work incapacity benefits not deductible from benefits.

Rose v Ford [1936] 1 KB 90; (1935) 80 LJ 273; [1936] 105 LJCL 21; (1936) 154 LTR 77; (1935) 79 SJ 816; (1935-36) LII TLR 7; (1935) WN (I) 168 CA On availability of personal injury damages to deceased victim's personal representative (claiming on behalf of deceased's estate).

Rose v Ford [1937] AC 826; (1937) 84 LJ 29; [1937] 106 LJCL 576; (1937) 157 LTR 174; (1936-37) LIII TLR 873; (1937) WN (I) 275 HL Deceased's personal representative could claim damages for loss of life expectancy.

Rourke v Barton and others [1982] TLR 330 HC QBD Amount included in personal injury damages for fact that injured party was unable to aid terminally ill husband.

Rowden v Clarke Chapman and Co, Ltd [1967] 3 All ER 608 HC QBD On personal injury damages (loss of fingers/earnings).

Rushton v National Coal Board [1953] 1 All ER 314; [1953] 1 QB 495; (1953) 97 SJ 94; [1953] 1 WLR 292 CA Appropriate damages in personal injury cases.

S and another v Distillers Co (Biochemicals) Ltd; J and others v Distillers Co (Biochemicals) Ltd and others [1969] 3 All ER 1412; (1969) 113 SJ 672; [1970] 1 WLR 114 HC QBD Appropriate personal injury damages to thalidomide children.

Samways v Westgate Engineers, Ltd (1962) 106 SJ 937 CA Refuse collector/disposers equally negligent in not wearing gloves when collecting/not warning of particular hazard attaching to certain rubbish.

Scott v Musial [1959] 3 All ER 193; [1959] 2 QB 429; [1959] 3 WLR 437 CA Only interfere with jury awards where out of all proportion to injuries.

Seecharran v Streets of London Ltd [1983] TLR 239 CA No entitlement to increased damages simply because duration of case extended by way of appeal.

Senior v Barker and Allen, Ltd [1965] 1 All ER 818; (1965) 109 SJ 178; [1965] 1 WLR 429 CA On personal injury damages (loss of use of hand).

Sharp v Avery and Kerwood [1938] 4 All ER 85; (1938) 86 LJ 309; (1938) 82 SJ 908 CA Lead motorcyclist responsible to second motorcyclist and pillion passenger for whom he has expressly/impliedly agreed to act as navigator.

Shearman v Folland [1950] 1 All ER 976; [1950] 2 KB 43; (1950) 100 LJ 245; (1950) 94 SJ 336; [1950] 66 (1) TLR 853; (1950) WN (I) 206 CA Bed and board but not cost of hotels in which plaintiff would have stayed deducted from personal injury damages.

Shephard v H West and Son, Ltd, and another (1962) 106 SJ 817 CA On appropriate injuries for brain damaged accident victim who was possibly aware of her condition.

Shutt and another v Extract Wool and Merino Co Ltd (1969) 113 SJ 672 HC QBD On damages available for temporary loss of sexual intercourse with wife as result of personal injury.

Singh (an infant) v Toong Fong Omnibus Co, Ltd [1964] 3 All ER 925; (1965) 115 LJ 24; (1964) 108 SJ 818; [1964] 1 WLR 1382 PC On uniformity of awards/interference by appellate court in level of damages.

Slater v Hughes and another (Jones, third party); Hughes v Slater and another; Slater v Hughes and another (Slater and another, third parties) [1971] 3 All ER 1287; [1971] RTR 491; (1971) 115 SJ 428; [1971] 1 WLR 1438 CA Date from which interest payable.

Smith v Manchester City Council (1974) 118 SJ 597 CA Real prospects of getting new job to be considered when determining personal injury damages.

Smoker v London Fire and Civil Defence Authority [1991] 2 WLR 422 HC QBD Damages for loss of earnings not to be reduced by amount of disablement pension.

Smoker v London Fire and Civil Defence Authority; Wood v British Coal Corp [1991] 2 All ER 449; [1991] 2 WLR 1052 HL Damages for loss of earnings not to be reduced by amount of disablement pension.

Stevens v William Nash Ltd [1966] 3 All ER 156; (1965-66) 116 NLJ 1203; (1966) 110 SJ 710; [1966] 1 WLR 1550 CA Generally CA will not seek to examine personal injuries.

Stott v Sir William Arrol and Co, Ltd [1953] 2 All ER 416; [1953] 2 QB 92; [1953] 3 WLR 166 HC QBD One half of all injury benefits accruing to party during and post-incapacity to be considered when awarding damages.

Swift v Prout (1964) 108 SJ 317 CA On appropriate personal injury damages for person whose injuries had shortened his lifespan to three years from date of accident.

Taylor v Bristol Omnibus Co Ltd and another [1975] 2 All ER 1107; (1975) 125 NLJ 574t; (1975) 119 SJ 476; [1975] 1 WLR 1054 CA Damages for future loss of earnings available to child though speculative; reasonableness of entire damages considered after damages under various heads awarded.

Taylor v RV Chuck (Transport) Ltd, and another (1963) 107 SJ 910 HC QBD On appropriate damages for disfiguring of face.

Thomas v Brighton Health Authority [1995] TLR 579 HC QBD On gauging quantum of damages in personal injuries action.

Thomas v Bunn; Wilson v Graham; Lea v British Aerospace plc [1991] 1 AC 362; (1990) 140 NLJ 1789; [1990] TLR 783; [1991] 2 WLR 27 HL Interest on personal injury damages rightly ran from date of judgment in which damages payable gauged.

Thomas v Wignall and others [1987] 1 All ER 1185; [1987] QB 1098; (1987) 131 SJ 362; [1987] 2 WLR 930 CA Court may take into account effect of tax on award when deciding multiplier.

Thompson (Christopher Bernard) v Faraonio (Karan) (1979) 123 SJ 301; [1979] 1 WLR 1157 PC On awarding of interest on personal injuries damages (none on portion of damages concerning post-judgment losses).

Tong (Chan Wai) and another v Sum (Li Ping) [1985] AC 446; (1985) 129 SJ 153; [1985] 2 WLR 396 PC On appropriate damages for personal injuries; on damages for loss of future earnings.

Waite v Redpath Dorman Long Ltd [1971] 1 All ER 513 HC QBD No interest on order made under RSC Ord 22, r 5.

Wales v Wales and another (1967) 111 SJ 946 HC QBD On appropriate personal injury damages (following negligent road traffic collision) follwing great delay in litigation.

Walker v John McLean and Sons Ltd [1979] 2 All ER 965; (1979) 129 (1) NLJ 294; (1979) 123 SJ 354/374; [1979] 1 WLR 760 CA Damages to reflect value of money; need not be reduced to counter inflation.

Walton v Jacob (1938) 82 SJ 586 HC KBD On assessing apppropriate damages for loss of expectation of life for healthy twenty-one year old man killed in negligent road traffic collision.

Ward v James [1965] 1 All ER 563; (1965) 115 LJ 228; (1965) 109 SJ 111; [1965] 2 WLR 455 CA On damages/when jury trial appropriate in personal cases.

Watson v Fowles [1967] 3 All ER 721 CA Damages awarded as one sum: need not be divided under headings; actuarial approach undesirable.

Wells v Wells; Thomas v Brighton Health Authority; Page v Sheerness Steel Co plc [1997] 1 All ER 673; (1996) 140 SJ LB 239; (1996) TLR 24/10/96; [1997] 1 WLR 652 CA On gauging damages for future expenses and losses in personal injury cases.

West (H) and Son, Ltd and another v Shephard [1963] 2 All ER 625; [1964] AC 326; (1963) 113 LJ 432; (1963) 107 SJ 454; [1963] 2 WLR 1359 HL Purpose/measurement of personal injury damages.

Wharton v Sweeney (1961) 105 SJ 887 CA On appropriate damages for loss of eye.

White v London Transport Executive (1982) 126 SJ 277 HC QBD Assessment of fatal accident damages.

Willson v Ministry of Defence [1991] 1 All ER 638 HC QBD 'Chance of serious deterioration': 'chance' means something more than fanciful/'serious deterioration' more than ongoing detrioration and greater than ordinary deterioration.

Wilson v Pilley [1957] 3 All ER 525; (1957) 107 LJ 744; (1957) 101 SJ 868 CA CA varied damages awarded though generally reluctant to do so.

Wilson v Stag (1986) 136 NLJ 47 CA Extravagant expenditure on girlfriend by deceased when alive not relevant when calculating 'living expenses'.

Wise v Kaye and another [1962] 1 All ER 257; (1962) 112 LJ 104; [1962] 1 QB 638; (1962) 106 SJ 14 CA Assessment of personal injury damages.

PERSONAL INJURIES (delay)

Browes v Jones and Middleton (a firm) and another (1979) 123 SJ 489 CA On deciding whether to allow extension of limitation period in personal injuries action.

Fitzpatrick v Batger and Co, Ltd [1967] 2 All ER 657 CA Five year delay caused by plaintiff's solicitor inordinate delay justifying dismissal of action.

Marlton (an infant) and another v Lee-Leviten and another [1968] 2 All ER 874 CA Inexcusable delay excused as no prejudice, action certain of success, plaintiff's infancy, payment into court.

Paxon v Allsopp (1971) 115 SJ 446 CA Stay of action in light of ten year delay since settlement offer made.

Roebuck v Mungovin [1994] 2 AC 224; (1994) 138 SJ LB 59; [1994] 2 WLR 290 HL Appropriate that personal injuries claim be struck out where plaintiff guilty of great delay even though defendant's behaviour not entirely blameless.

PERSONAL INJURIES (fire)

Solomons v R Gertzenstein Ld and others (1954) 104 LJ 266; [1954] 1 QB 565; (1954) 98 SJ 270; [1954] 2 WLR 823 HC QBD Liability of rackrent receiver for personal injuries suffered by tenants of building that went on fire.

Solomons v R Gertzenstein Ld and others (1954) 104 LJ 442; [1954] 2 QB 243 CA Liability of rackrent receiver for personal injuries suffered by tenants of building that went on fire.

PERSONAL INJURIES (general)

Allen and others v Jambo Holdings Ltd and others [1980] 2 All ER 502; (1980) 124 SJ 742 CA Mareva injunction available in personal injuries action.

Baker (Annie Amelia) v Mayor, Aldermen and Burgesses of Bethnal Green [1944] 2 All ER 301 HC KBD State of staircase made it a concealed danger; stairway not air-raid cause of injury so not a 'war injury'.

Baker (Annie Amelia) v Mayor, Aldermen and Burgesses of Bethnal Green [1945] 1 All ER 135; (1945) 109 JP 72 CA Injury in air-raid shelter due to poorly maintained staircase was negligent personal injury, not 'war injury'.

Berryman v Hounslow London Borough Council (1996) TLR 18/12/96 CA Failed action against landlord for personal injuries for spinal injuries suffered through having to use stairs where lift was not functioning.

Carter v Tesco Stores Ltd (1980) 130 NLJ 604 HC QBD Damages for personal injury suffered when negligently stacked meat fell on plaintiff but not for collapse of foot attributable to pre-existing illness.

Castanho v Brown and Root (UK) Ltd and another [1980] 1 All ER 689 HC QBD Court would strike out discontinuance as abuse of process where was done in hope of getting higher damages abroad.

Castanho v Brown and Root (UK) Ltd and another (1980) 124 SJ 375 CA Successful appeal against striking out of discontinuance as abuse of process (where was done in hope of getting higher damages abroad).

Castanho v Brown and Root (UK) Ltd and another [1981] 1 All ER 143; (1980) 124 SJ 884 HL No discontinuance if is abuse of process; injunction restraining foreign action available unless foreign court better forum for action.

Coddington v International Harvester Co Ltd of GB (1969) 119 NLJ 249t HC QBD Employers not vicariously liable for act of worker which resulted in train if events causing injury to another worker/the plaintiff.

Davies (Joseph Owen) v Eli Lilly and Co and others (1987) 131 SJ 807 HC QBD On division of costs in multiple pesonal injuries action.

Davies (Joseph Owen) v Eli Lilly and Co and others [1987] 3 All ER 94; (1987) 131 SJ 842 CA Court may impose costs on persons not party to case at (or sometimes before) end of trial.

Davies v Rustproof Metal Window Co, Ltd [1943] 1 All ER 248; (1942-43) LIX TLR 151 CA Cannot pay money into court denying liability, then admit liability in defence.

Dawson v Spaul (1934-35) LI TLR 247 HC KBD Adjudication in personal injuries action ordered in interest of defendant despite death of plaintiff.

Eggington v Reader [1936] 1 All ER 7 HC KBD Driver an independent contractor (despite company's contribution to petrol costs) so company not liable for driver's negligence.

Ellen v The Great Northern Railway (1900-01) XVII TLR 338; (1900-01) 49 WR 395 HC KBD Question for jury whether person who took money in full settlement of claims arising from injuries could bring action when new injuries occurred consequent upon same accident.

Ellen v The Great Northern Railway (1900-01) XVII TLR 453 CA Question for jury whether person who took money in full settlement of claims arising from injuries could bring action when new injuries occurred consequent upon same accident.

Gahan v Szerelmey (UK) Ltd and another [1996] 1 WLR 439 CA Non-dismissal of personal injuries action for want of prosecution where defendant's having money during period of delay which would otherwise have paid as compensation meant could not plead undue prejudice arising from delay.

Gibson v C and A Modes (1977) 127 NLJ 416b CA Failed negligence action against store-owners by woman who injured self in not reasonably foreseeable mannner which had not previously occurred (tripped over up-turning tile).

Glasgow Corporation v Sutherland (1951) 95 SJ 204; (1951) WN (I) 111 HL Tram driver who braked suddenly to avoid injury to animal and so occasioned injury to passenger who fell held not to be negligent.

Guinnear v LPT Board (1948) 98 LJ 217 HC KBD Fifty percent of damages otherwise available to plaintiff who was negligent in boarding a moving bus whose driver in turn was negligent for moving on without proper regard for plaintiff's safety.

H v Ministry of Defence [1991] 2 All ER 834; (1991) 141 NLJ 420; (1991) 141 NLJ 425i; [1991] 2 QB 103; [1991] 2 WLR 1192 CA Trial by jury generally inappropriate in personal injuries action.

Haines v Minister of Pensions (1944-45) LXI TLR 181 HC KBD On recovery for nervous debility arising from civil defence duties.

Hassall v Secretary of State for Social Security; Pether v Secretary of State for Social Security [1995] 3 All ER 909; [1995] RTR 316; [1994] TLR 667 CA Secretary of State can deduct full amount of post-accident benefits from sums awarded as personal injuries damages.

Hawley and another v Alexander and Wife (1930) 74 SJ 247 HC KBD Parents of young teenage son liable in negligence for personal injuries occasioned consequent upon their allowing son to use airgun without adequate supervision.

Hennell v Ranaboldo [1963] 3 All ER 684 CA Judge only trials desirable in personal injury cases.

Hodges v Harland and Wolff, Ltd [1965] 1 All ER 1086 CA Exceptional action in which trial by jury justified.

Hoffman v Sofaer (1982) 126 SJ 611; [1982] 1 WLR 1350 HC QBD Appropriate that United States resident suffering personal injury while in Britain be awarded damages in dollars.

Howgate v Bagnall and another [1951] 1 KB 265; (1950) 94 SJ 725; [1950] 66 (2) TLR 997 HC KBD Injuries sustained through crash landing of aircraft not war injuries: damages available.

Ilkiw v Samuels and others (1963) 107 SJ 680; [1963] 1 WLR 991 CA Employers liable for negligence of employee who acting within scope of responsibility behaved in unauthorised way; appropriate damages for personal injuries.

Jones and another v London County Council (1931-32) XLVIII TLR 368 HC KBD Failed action against council where its servant had ordered boy on instruction course to take part in rough game whereby boy suffered injury.

Jones and another v London County Council (1932) 96 JP 371; (1931-32) XLVIII TLR 577 CA Failed action against council where its servant had ordered boy on instruction course to take part in rough game whereby boy suffered injury.

Jones v Watney, Combe, Reid, and Co (Limited) (1911-12) XXVIII TLR 399 HC KBD Can/cannot recover for aggravation of personal injury in respect of which claiming where aggravation due to own carelessness/natural causes.

Kennedy v Bowater Containers Ltd [1990] 1 All ER 669; (1989) 133 SJ 1606 HC QBD High Court cannot transfer personal injuries action to county court.

Lane v Willis; Same v Beach (1972) 116 SJ 102; [1972] 1 WLR 326 CA Case properly stayed where plaintiff refused to undergo medical examination.

Larby v Thurgood (1992) 136 SJ LB 275; [1992] TLR 493 HC QBD Refusal to order interview between plaintiff and employment consultant in order that plaintiff's real employment prospects might be gauged.

Leather v Kirby [1965] 3 All ER 927; (1965-66) 116 NLJ 275; [1965] 1 WLR 1489 HL On claim compromises by persons under disability.

Lofthouse v Leicester Corporation (1948) LXIV TLR 604 CA On reversal of decisions of trial judge in Fatal Accident/running down actions (here unreversed).

McFarlane v EE Caledonia Ltd [1994] 2 All ER 1; (1993) 143 NLJ 1367; [1993] TLR 476 CA Bystander/witness of awful events ineligible for damages for nervous shock unless proximate to events and victim.

McLoughlin v Warrington Corporation (1911) 75 JP 57 CA Town corporation could be found negligent where through defective repair of fountain person was injured when another climbing on fountain dislodged stone therefrom.

Minister of Pensions v Ffrench (1945-46) LXII TLR 227 HC KBD On meaning of 'injurious act' under Personal Injuries (Emergency Provisions) Act 1939, s 8(1).

Morgan v Scoulding [1938] 1 All ER 28; [1938] 1 KB 786; [1938] 107 LJCL 299; (1938) 158 LTR 230; (1937) 81 SJ 1041; (1937-38) LIV TLR 253; (1938) WN (I) 13 HC KBD Cause of action in motor collision is collision so that die instantly does not mean no cause of action.

Olsen v Magnesium Castings and Products, Ltd [1947] 1 All ER 333 CA Employer must show (if so claiming) that workman accepted workmen's compensation in lieu of common law entitlements.

Parker v London General Omnibus Company (Limited) (1909) 73 JP 283; (1909) C LTR 409; (1908-09) XXV TLR 429 HC KBD Personal injury victim failed in action against bus company whose driver/placing bus on road was negligent/may or may not have been nuisance.

Parker v London General Omnibus Company (Limited) (1910) 74 JP 20; (1909-10) 101 LTR 623; (1908-09) 53 SJ 867; (1909-10) XXVI TLR 18 CA Personal injury victim failed in action against bus company whose driver/placing bus on road was negligent/may or may not have been nuisance.

Pattenden v Beney (1933) 77 SJ 732; (1933-34) L TLR 10 HC KBD Failed claim by widow of dustman against doctor for fatal injuries suffered by dustman after collected gas containers from doctor's house.

Pattenden v Beney (1934) 78 SJ 121 CA Failed claim by widow of dustman against doctor for fatal injuries suffered by dustman after collected gas containers from doctor's house.

Pritchard v Post Office (1950) 114 JP 370; (1950) 94 SJ 404; (1950) WN (I) 310 CA Failed action against Post Office by non-sighted woman who suffered personal injuries after falling into open manhole adequately signposted to sighted people.

Re Kemp [1945] 1 All ER 571 HC KBD Personal Injuries (Emergency Provisions) Act 1939 to be interpreted narrowly as so greatly qualifies common law rights.

Reynolds v British Leyland Ltd [1991] 1 WLR 675 CA Appeal dismissed for want of prosecution (and defendants had not behaved in such a way as to warrant continuance of action).

Reynolds v Murphy (1965) 109 SJ 255 HC QBD On need for swift conclusion to personal injuries actions.

Reynolds v Thomas Tilling (Limited) (1902-03) XIX TLR 539 HC KBD Interpretation of findings of jury as to negligence/contributory negligence: non-recovery for personal injuries sustained through injury partly caused by own negligence.

Reynolds v Thomas Tilling (Limited) (1903-04) XX TLR 57 CA Approval of lower court's interpretation of findings of jury as to negligence/contributory negligence: non-recovery for personal injuries sustained through injury partly caused by own negligence.

Roach v Yates [1938] 1 KB 256; [1938] 107 LJCL 170; (1937) 81 SJ 610 CA On assessment of personal injury damages for person rendered unable to look after self.

Sayers v Harlow Urban District Council [1958] 2 All ER 342; (1958) 122 JP 351; (1958) 108 LJ 392; (1958) 102 SJ 419 CA Damages recoverable for injuries sustained in attempted escape from locked toilet cubicle.

Stott v Sir William Arrol and Co, Ltd [1953] 2 All ER 416; [1953] 2 QB 92; (1953) 97 SJ 439; [1953] 3 WLR 166 HC QBD One half of all injury benefits accruing to party during and post-incapacity to be considered when awarding damages.

Suchcicka v Grabowski (1973) 117 SJ 58 CA On personal injuries damages (and interest awardable thereon) for foreigner injured in collision (exchange rate being particularly difficult to calculate).

PERSONAL INJURIES (invitee)

Warren v Railway Executive (1950) 100 LJ 344; (1950) 94 SJ 457 HC KBD Rail company liable where invitee-passenger got into unlighted train waiting on platform and injured self while looking for seat.

PERSONAL INJURIES (landlord and tenant)

Heap v Ind Coope and Allsopp, Limited (1940) 84 SJ 536; (1939-40) LVI TLR 948 CA
Appropriate that personal injuries action be brought against landlord as despite lease requiring
tenant to do internal repairs landlord did all repairs (claimant's action arose through injury
suffered by way of defective outside repairs).

PERSONAL INJURIES (local authority)

Clarke and another v Bethnal Green Borough Council (1939) 103 JP 160; (1939) 83 SJ 218;
(1938-39) LV TLR 519 HC KBD Local authority found not liable for personal injuries suffered
by individual in public swimming pool.

PERSONAL INJURIES (Post Office)

Bainbridge v Postmaster-General and another [1904-07] All ER 1326; (1905) 40 LJ 805; [1906] 75
LJKB 366; (1906) XCIV LTR 120; (1905-06) 54 WR 221 CA Cannot bring personal injury
action against Postmaster-General under Telegraph Act 1868.

PERSONAL INJURIES (rail)

Re Saunderton Glebe Lands, ex parte The Rector of Saunderton [1903] 1 Ch 480 HC ChD Portion
of money railway company used to buy land set aside for limited owner as compensation inter
alia for personal injury.

PERSONAL INJURIES (repetitive strain injury)

Mughal v Reuters Ltd (1993) 137 SJ LB 275 HC QBD Non-recognition of repetitive strain injury
as medical condition.

PERSONAL INJURIES (road traffic)

Bridgeford v Weston [1975] RTR 189 HC QBD Person travelling to work in another's car (not
public service vehicle) could agree to be carried at own risk.

Dublin United Tramways v Fitzgerald (1902-03) XIX TLR 78 HL Tramway company liable for
injury sustained as result of their failure to keep portion of road for which were responsible in safe
condition (Tramways Act 1870, s 28).

Liffen v Watson (1939) 161 LTR 351; (1939) 83 SJ 871 HC KBD Taxi-driver was negligent where
could not explain why had braked and skidded when knew was likely to skid when so braked.

Smith v Harris [1939] 3 All ER 960; (1939) 83 SJ 730 CA Equal blame apportioned between
motorcyclists involved in collision.

Whittaker v London County Council (1915) 79 JP 437; [1915] 2 KB 676; (1915-16) 113 LTR 544;
(1915) WN (I) 212 HC KBD Recovery of damages for injuries sustained when wrongfully ejected
physically from tramway.

PRIVILEGE (Parliamentary privilege)

Allason v Haines (1995) 145 NLJ 1576; [1995] TLR 438 HC QBD Member of Parliament's libel action
to be stayed if Member's privilege precludes defendants from putting forward their preferred defence.

PROCURING ACT DAMAGING THIRD PARTY (general)

Davies v Thomas and others [1920] All ER 438; [1920] 2 Ch 189; (1919-20) XXXVI TLR 571
CA No injunction restraining implementation of legally void rule as persons concerned not acting
in unlawful conspiracy.

PUBLIC AUTHORITY PROTECTION (estoppel)

Hewlett v London County Council (1908) 72 JP 136; (1907-08) XXIV TLR 331 HC KBD
Defendants could plead public authority limitation despite plaintiff's claim that action brought
out of time because defendants indicated wanted out of court settlement.

PUBLIC AUTHORITY PROTECTION (general)

Attorney-General v Company of Proprietors of Margate Pier and Harbour [1900] 1 Ch 749 HC ChD Profit-making public utility incorporated by Parliament does not enjoy benefits of Public Authorities Protection Act 1893.

Barnett v Woolwich Borough Council (1910) 74 JP 441 HC ChD Failed action for injunction to restrain nuisance as was brought out of time allowed under Public Authorities Protection Act 1893.

Bradford Corporation v Myers [1916] 1 AC 242; (1916) CC Rep V 4; (1916) 80 JP 121; (1915) 50 LJ 555; [1916] 85 LJKB 146; (1916) 114 LTR 83; (1915-16) 60 SJ 74; (1915-16) XXXII TLR 113; (1915) WN (I) 367 HL Public Authorities Protection Act 1893 limitation period deemed inapplicable to instant action against public authority for negligence.

Broadbent v Mayor, Aldermen and Burgesses of the Borough of Burlington [1935] LJNCCR 258 CyCt Local authority not liable in negligence for injuries occasioned through sewer explosion from cause not previously known of.

Clarke v Mayor, Aldermen, and Burgesses of the Borough of St Helens (1915) 79 JP 529; [1916] 85 LJKB 17; (1915-16) 113 LTR 681; (1914-15) 59 SJ 509 CA Public authority limitation deemed inapplicable to action where public authority whose employee had been driving car which caused injury had not been acting in course of duty.

Copper Export Association, Inc v Mersey Docks and Harbour Board (1932) 147 LTR 320; (1931-32) XLVIII TLR 542 HC KBD Action in negligence against docks and harbour authority precluded by six-month public authority limitation.

Dickens v London Passenger Transport Board [1935] LJNCCR 171 CyCt London Passenger Transport Board enjoyed the protection afforded public authorities by the Public Authorities Protection Act 1893.

Duncan v Lambeth London Borough Council [1968] 1 All ER 84; [1968] 1 QB 747; (1967) 111 SJ 909; [1968] 2 WLR 88 HC QBD Limitation period had not expired where had been infant when cause of action accrued and not properly in custody of a parent who could have bought action.

Edwards v Metropolitan Water Board (1922) 86 JP 33 (also HC KBD); [1922] 1 KB 291 (also HC KBD); (1921) 56 LJ 472; [1922] 91 LJCL 210 (also HC KBD); (1921-22) 66 SJ 195; (1921-22) XXXVIII TLR 153; (1921) WN (I) 354 CA Journey out and back was on behalf of public authority so public authority limitation applied.

Edwards v Metropolitan Water Board (1922) 86 JP 33 (also CA); [1922] 1 KB 291 (also CA); [1922] 91 LJCL 210 (also CA) HC KBD Journey out and back was on behalf of public authority so public authority limitation applied.

Firestone Tire and Rubber Company (SS) Ltd v Singapore Harbour Board (1952) 96 SJ 448; [1952] 1 TLR 1625 PC Failure of action against harbour board where not brought within six-month limitation prescribed by public authority protection ordinance.

Freeborn v Leeming (1926) 90 JP 179; [1926] 1 KB 160 (also CA); (1925) 60 LJ 637/823; [1926] 95 LJCL 114 (also CA); (1924-25) 69 SJ 663/692; (1928-29) XLV TLR 567 HC KBD Six month limitation against public authority ran from moment patient stopped being in doctor's care.

Freeborn v Leeming (1926) 90 JP 53; [1926] 1 KB 160 (also HC KBD); (1925) 60 LJ 1007; [1926] 95 LJCL 114 (also HC KBD); (1926) 134 LTR 117; (1925-26) 70 SJ 264; (1925-26) XLII TLR 119; (1925) WN (I) 273 CA Six month limitation against public authority ran from moment patient stopped being in doctor's care.

Gerrard v Birkenhead Corporation [1937] LJNCCR 325 CyCt Day of accident not included when calculating limitation period for purpose of the Public Authorities Protection Act 1893.

Government of Malaysia v Ning (Lee Hock) [1974] AC 76; (1973) 117 SJ 617; [1973] 3 WLR 334 PC Special public authority limitation period did not apply in respect of action based on private contract.

Greenwood v Atherton (1939) 103 JP 41; [1939] 1 KB 388; [1939] 108 LJCL 165; (1939) 160 LTR 37; (1938-39) LV TLR 222; (1938) WN (I) 410 CA Public authority limitation applied to managers of non-provided public elementary school (and here barred out-of-time action for negligence).

Greenwood v Atherton (1938) 85 LJ 328 HC KBD Public authority limitation applied to managers of non-provided public elementary school (and here barred out-of-time action for negligence).

Griffiths and another v Smith and others [1941] AC 171; (1941) 105 JP 63; [1941] 110 LJ 156; (1941) 164 LTR 386; (1940-41) LVII TLR 185 HL Public authority limitation period barred action against managers of non-provided elementary school.

Griffiths and another v Smith and others (1939) 103 JP 163; (1938-39) LV TLR 630 CA Six-month public authority limitation applied in favour of school sued by invitee attending school exhibition.

Hague v Doncaster Rural District Council (1909) 73 JP 69; (1909) C LTR 121; (1908-09) 53 SJ 135; (1908-09) XXV TLR 130 HC KBD Public authority limitation applicable but as action concerned ongoing damage (pollution of stream) was of no effect.

Hawkes v Torquay Corporation (1938) 86 LJ 294 HC KBD Public Authorities Protection Act povisions did not apply to pavilion built and operated by local authority.

Huyton and Roby Gas Company v Liverpool Corporation [1925] All ER 153; (1926) 90 JP 45; [1926] 1 KB 146; (1926) 61 LJ 9; [1926] 95 LJCL 269; (1925-26) 70 SJ 226; (1925) WN (I) 273 CA Public authority limitation did not begin to run until continuing duty had been discharged.

Jacoby v Prison Commissioners [1940] 2 All ER 499 HC KBD Special public authority time limitation applicable in suit against prison commissioners.

Jacoby v Prison Commissioners [1940] 3 All ER 506 CA Special public authority time limitation applicable in suit against prison commissioners.

Jeremiah Ambler and Sons, Limited v Bradford Corporation [1902] 2 Ch 585 CA Public Authority Protection Act 1893, s 1(b) — judgment for defendant in action for negligent discharge of statutory function carries costs between solicitor and client — applies to performing duties under provisional electric lights regulation (but does not apply to appeals).

Kaufmann Brothers v Liverpool Corporation (1916) 80 JP 223; [1916] 85 LJKB 1127; (1916) 114 LTR 699; (1915-16) 60 SJ 446; (1915-16) XXXII TLR 402; (1916) WN (I) 155 HC KBD Public authority limitation did not apply in respect of action against same for compensation for riot damage.

Lyles v Southend-on-Sea Corporation (1905) 69 JP 193; [1905] 2 KB 1; (1905) 40 LJ 282; (1905) XCII LTR 586; (1904-05) XXI TLR 389; (1905) WN (I) 63 CA Six-month public authority limitation applied in negligence action against municipal corporation acting as tramway operator.

Markey and another v The Tolworth Joint Isolation Hospital District Board [1900] 69 LJCL 738; (1900-01) LXXXIII LTR 28; [1900] 2 QB 454; (1899-1900) XVI TLR 411 HC QBD Hospital Board enjoyed special six-month limitation period under Public Authorities Protection Act 1893.

Marshall v London Passenger Transport Board [1936] 3 All ER 83; (1936) 82 LJ 296; (1936) 80 SJ 893 CA Amendment of pleadings introducing new cause of action precluded by Public Authorities Protection Act 1893, s 1.

Mountain v Bermondsey Borough Council [1942] 1 KB 204; [1942] 111 LJ 534 HC KBD Action for recovery of debt from council defeated as brought out of time (outside one year period).

Nelson v Cookson and another [1939] 4 All ER 30; (1939) 103 JP 363; [1940] 1 KB 100; (1939) 88 LJ 241; [1940] 109 LJCL 154; (1939) 161 LTR 346; (1939) 83 SJ 871; (1939-40) LVI TLR 2; (1939) WN (I) 350 HC KBD Public authority limitation period applied in respect of county hospital assistant medical officers.

Newell v Starkie (1919) 83 JP 113; [1920] 89 LJPC 1 HL Absent proof of malice (of which was none) action against Education Commissioner out of time under Public Authorities Protection Act 1893.

O'Connor v Isaacs and others [1956] 1 All ER 513; [1956] Crim LR 261; (1956) 120 JP 169; (1956) 100 SJ 171; [1956] 2 WLR 585 HC QBD Absent malice could sue justices for trespass (arising from false imprisonment)/could not sue for money paid on foot of maintenance order made without jurisdiction; application of public authority limitation.

O'Connor v Isaacs and others [1956] 2 All ER 417; [1956] Crim LR 482; (1956) 106 LJ 392; (1956) 100 SJ 432; [1956] 3 WLR 172 CA Failed action against justices for committal to prison on foot of maintenance order made without jurisdiction; application of public authority limitation.

Parker v London County Council (1904) 68 JP 239; [1904] 2 KB 501; [1904] 73 LJCL 561; (1904) XC LTR 415; (1903-04) XX TLR 271; (1903-04) 52 WR 476 HC KBD Special public authority limitation period under Public Authorities Protection Act 1893 applies to county council as tramway owner.

Rawlins v Gillingham Corporation (1932) 96 JP 153; (1932) 146 LTR 486 HC KBD Negligence action failed where brought out of time under Public Authorities Protection Act 1893.

Reeves v Deane-Freeman (1952) 102 LJ 457; (1952) 96 SJ 531; [1952] 2 TLR 361; (1952) WN (I) 415 HC QBD One-year public authority limitation on tort actions applies to soldier driving military truck in course of duty.

Reeves v Deane-Freeman (1953) 103 LJ 121; [1953] 1 QB 459; (1953) 97 SJ 132 CA One-year public authority limitation on tort actions applies to soldier driving military truck in course of duty.

Riley v Mayor, Aldermen, and Burgesses of Halifax (1907) 71 JP 428; (1907-08) XCVII LTR 278; (1906-07) XXIII TLR 613 HC ChD Damages for trespass rather than injunction to stop same merited in the circumstances.

Scammell (G) and Nephew, Limited v Hurley and others [1929] 1 KB 419 HC KBD Alleged conspiracy to discontinue electricity supply which under statutory duty to supply.

Shaw and others v London County Council and another (1934) 98 JP 398; (1934) 78 LJ 44; (1933-34) L TLR 489 HC KBD Six month limitation on action against public authority applicable to claims of infants.

Scammell (G) and Nephew, Limited v Attlee and others (1928) 66 LJ 406; (1928) WN (I) 296 CA Failed action for alleged conspiracy to discontinue electricity supply which under statutory duty to supply (failed inter alia because out of time under Public Authorities' Protection Act 1893).

Shaw and others v London County Council and another (1935) 99 JP 10; [1935] 1 KB 67; (1934) 78 LJ 286; [1935] 104 LJCL 84; (1934) 78 SJ 734; (1934-35) LI TLR 16; (1934) WN (I) 183 CA Six month limitation on action against public authority applicable to claims of infants.

Swain v Southern Railway Co [1938] 3 All ER 705; [1939] 1 KB 77; (1937-38) LIV TLR 1119 HC KBD Railway company not a public authority enjoying benefit of Public Authorities Protection Act 1893, s 1.

Swain v Southern Railway Company (1939) 160 LTR 606; (1939) 83 SJ 476; (1938-39) LV TLR 805 CA Railway company not a public authority enjoying benefit of Public Authorities Protection Act 1893, s 1.

The Burns (1906-07) XXIII TLR 258 HC PDAD Action in rem does not come under Public Authorities Protection Act 1893, s 1.

The Burns (1906-07) XXIII TLR 323 CA Action in rem does not come under Public Authorities Protection Act 1893, s 1.

The Danube II (1919-20) XXXVI TLR 321 HC PDAD Public Authorities Protection Act 1893 applicable to Crown servants.

The Danube II (1921) 125 LTR 156; (1920-21) XXXVII TLR 421 CA Public Authorities Protection Act 1893 applicable to Crown servants.

The Earl of Harrington v The Mayor, &c, of Derby [1905] 1 Ch 205; (1905) 69 JP 62; (1904) 39 LJ 686; (1904-05) XXI TLR 98; (1904) WN (I) 210 HC ChD Consideration of Public Authorities Protection Act 1893, s 1, in context of nuisance action.

Western India Match Company, Limited v Lock and others [1946] KB 601; [1946] 115 LJ 497; (1945-46) LXII TLR 419; (1946) WN (I) 125 HC KBD Public authority limitation applied to War Transport Ministry officials unloading ship under direction of Minsitry representative.

Williams v Mersey Docks and Harbour Board (1905) 69 JP 196; [1905] 1 KB 804; (1905) 40 LJ 301; (1905) XCII LTR 444; (1904-05) 49 SJ 417; (1904-05) XXI TLR 397; (1904-05) 53 WR 488 CA Action could not be continued by deceased's representative where deceased could not have continued action.

Woodward and another v Mayor of Hastings and others [1944] 2 All ER 565; (1945) 109 JP 41; [1945] KB 174; [1945] 114 LJ 211 (also HC KBD); (1945) 172 LTR 16; (1944-45) LXI TLR 94; (1944) WN (1) 239 CA Grammar school governors not public authority/were liable for caretaker's negligence.

Woodward and another v Mayor of Hastings and others [1944] 2 All ER 119; (1944) 108 JP 247; [1944] KB 671; (1945) 95 LJ 111; [1945] 114 LJ 211 (also CA); (1944) 171 LTR 231; (1943-44) LX TLR 404 HC KBD Suing school governors subject to public authority limitation.

Woodward v Mayor of Hastings and Others; Same v Same (1945) 172 LTR 16; (1944) WN (I) 239 CA School governors not entitled to protection of public authority limitation period in negligence action.

Yorkshire Electricity Board v British Telecommunications plc (1970) 130 SJ 613; [1986] 1 WLR 1029 HL Cause of action where owning undertakers' appartus damaged by operating undertakers did not run from date of damage but date owning undertakers suffered expense of repair.

PUBLIC AUTHORITY PROTECTION (joint tortfeasors)

George Wimpey and Co Ld v British Airways Overseas Corporation [1954] 3 All ER 661; [1955] AC 169; (1954) 104 LJ 824; [1954] 3 WLR 932 HL Precluded by public authority special limitation period from recovering contribution from respondent.

PUBLIC AUTHORITY PROTECTION (libel)

Reid v Blisland School Board (1900-01) XVII TLR 626 Assizes Libel action against School Board by ex-schoolmaster claiming Board resolution outlining why was dismissed was libellous ought to have been brought inside six months.

PUBLIC AUTHORITY PROTECTION (police)

Betts v Receiver for the Metropolitan Police District and Carter Paterson and Company, Limited (1932) 96 JP 327; [1932] 2 KB 595; (1932) 74 LJ 60; (1932) 101 LJCL 588; (1932) 147 LTR 336; (1932) 76 SJ 474; (1931-32) XLVIII TLR 517; (1932) WN (I) 15i HC KBD Public authority limitation precluded police authority liability for conversion/detinue of seized goods.

RYLANDS V FLETCHER (general)

Attorney-General v Cory Brothers and Co (Limited) and others; Kennard and others v Cory Brothers and Co (Limited) (1917-18) XXXIV TLR 621 HC ChD Liability for landslide occasioned by dumping of colliery waste on mountainside.

Attorney-General v Cory Brothers and Co (Limited) and others; Kennard and others v Cory Brothers and Co (Limited) (1919) 83 JP 221; [1919] 88 LJCh 410; (1918-19) XXXV TLR 570 CA Non-liability for landslide occasioned by dumping of colliery waste on mountainside.

Attorney-General and Others v Cory Brothers and Company, Limited, and others; Kennard and others v Cory Brothers and Company, Limited [1921] 1 AC 521; (1921) 85 JP 129; [1921] 90 LJCh 221; (1921) 125 LTR 98; (1920-21) XXXVII TLR 343 HL Liability under Rylands v Fletcher and in negligence for landslide occasioned by dumping of colliery waste on mountainside.

Balfour v Barty-King and another (Hyder and Sons (Builders), Ltd Third Parties) [1956] 2 All ER 555; (1956) 106 LJ 379; (1956) 100 SJ 472; [1956] 1 WLR 779 HC QBD Occupiers liable for fire negligently started by others whom could not prove were strangers; Rylands v Fletcher applied as fire started by dangerous/untypical user.

Belvedere Fish Guano Company, Limited v Rainham Chemical Works, Limited, Feldman and Partridge; Ind Coope and Company, Limited v Same (1920) 84 JP 185; [1920] 2 KB 487; (1920) 55 LJ 108; [1920] 89 LJCL 631; (1920) 123 LTR 211; (1919-20) XXXVI TLR 362; (1920) WN (I) 111 CA Manufacturers and directors of company personally liable for nuisance under Rylands v Fletcher rules.

British Celanese, Ltd v AH Hunt (Capacitors) Ltd [1969] 2 All ER 1252; (1969) 119 NLJ 364t; (1969) 113 SJ 368; [1969] 1 WLR 959 HC QBD Rylands v Fletcher inapplicable as no special use of land.

Cambridge Water Co Ltd v Eastern Counties Leather plc [1994] 1 All ER 53; [1994] 2 AC 264; [1994] 2 WLR 53 CA Foreseeability of relevant damage necessary before strict liability for escape likely to do mischief.

Cambridge Water Co Ltd v Eastern Counties Leather plc [1994] 1 All ER 53; [1994] 2 AC 264; (1994) 144 NLJ 15; (1994) 138 SJ LB 24; [1993] TLR 641; [1994] 2 WLR 53 HL Foreseeability of relevant damage necessary before strict liability for escape likely to do mischief.

Charing Cross, West End, and City Electricity Supply Co, Ltd v London Hydraulic Power Co (1913) 77 JP 378; [1913] 3 KB 442; [1914] 83 LJKB 116; (1913-14) 109 LTR 635; (1912-13) XXIX TLR 649 HC KBD Liability for nuisance (though no negligence) for injury sustained through escape of dangerous thing from property over which enjoyed licence.

Collingwood v Home and Colonial Stores, Ltd [1936] 3 All ER 200; (1936) 155 LTR 550; (1936) 80 SJ 853; (1936-37) LIII TLR 53; (1936) WN (I) 305 CA Rylands v Fletcher inapplicable to domestic use of electricity.

Dunne and others v North Western Gas Board and another [1963] 3 All ER 916; (1964) 114 LJ 56; [1964] 2 QB 806; (1963) 107 SJ 890; [1964] 2 WLR 164 CA Not liable under Rylands v Fletcher if do what statute requires non-negligently.

Gilson v Kerrier District Council (1976) 120 SJ 572; [1976] 1 WLR 904 CA Council not liable inter alia in nuisance/under Rylands v Fletcher for escape of water from watercourse on land to which owner when watercourse being built consented to building of same.

Goodbody v Poplar Borough Council (1915) 79 JP 218; [1915] 84 LJKB 1230 HC KBD Non-liability under Rylands v Fletcher principles for thing (electric/fuse box) made dangerous by presence of another thing (gas) over which had no control.

Hale v Jennings Brothers [1938] 1 All ER 579; (1938) 85 LJ 157; (1938) 82 SJ 193 CA Rylands v Fletcher applied in case of defective chair-o-plane.

Halsey v Esso Petroleum Co, Ltd [1961] 2 All ER 145; (1961) 111 LJ 290; (1961) 105 SJ 209 HC QBD Oil smuts damaging clothes a private/Rylands v Fletcher-style nuisance; smuts damaging car on highway a public/Rylands v Fletcher-style nuisance; odour from oil depot a nuisance by smell (though no evidence of injury); din from boilers a private nuisance as adversely affected enjoyment of ordinary comforts; din from tankers on highway at night a public nuisance/a private nuisance as connected with use of (though not occurring on) private property.

Hoare and Co, Ltd v Sir Robert McAlpine, Sons and Co [1922] All ER 759; [1923] 1 Ch 167; [1923] 92 LJCh 81; (1923) 128 LTR 526; (1922-23) 67 SJ 146; (1922-23) XXXIX TLR 97; (1922) WN (I) 329 HC ChD Rylands v Fletcher applied to nuisance by vibration.

Howard v Furness Houlder Argentine Lines, Ltd and A and R Brown, Ltd [1936] 2 All ER 781; (1936) 80 SJ 554 HC KBD Negligence where supply/fixing of non-dangerous article made it dangerous; Rylands v Fletcher inapplicable as no escape/no unnatural user.

Kiddle v City Business Premises, Ltd [1942] 2 All ER 216; [1942] 1 KB 269; [1942] 111 LJ 196; (1942) 166 LTR 302 HC KBD No nuisance by landlords as no negligence: taker of part of premises must take part as finds it.

Lippitt v Jones (1930) 70 LJ ccr30 CyCt Shop-owner liable under principle in Rylands v Fletcher/in nuisance for injury occasioned to person when shop sunblind collapsed on them.

Mansel v Webb [1918-19] All ER 794; [1919] 88 LJCL 323 CA Rylands v Fletcher-style liability for emission of sparks from locomotive engine travelling along highway.

Marchant Manufacturing Company Limited v Leonard D Ford and Teller Limited (1936) 154 LTR 430 HC KBD Rylands v Fletcher inapplicable to situation where some water in water boiler installed on second floor of commercial premises leaked into ground floor: failed negligence action.

Mulholland and Tedd, Ltd v Baker [1939] 3 All ER 253; (1939) 87 LJ 453; (1939) 161 LTR 20 HC KBD Recovery of damages under Rylands and Fletcher for heat, smoke and water arising from occurrence of non-accidental fire.

Peters v Prince of Wales Theatre (Birmingham), Limited [1942] 2 All ER 553; (1943) 93 LJ 117; (1943) 168 LTR 241; (1943) 87 SJ 83 CA Rylands v Fletcher inapplicable where implied consent to hazard.

Rainham Chemical Works, Limited (in liquidation), and others v Belvedere Fish Guano Company [1921] All ER 48; [1921] 2 AC 465; (1921) 56 LJ 314; [1921] LJCL 1252; (1922) 126 LTR 70; (1921-22) 66 SJ wr7; (1920-21) XXXVII TLR 973; (1921) WN (I) 281 HL Occupiers and tenants liable under Rylands v Fletcher for explosion occasioned by non-natural user of land.

Read (Norah) v J Lyons and Co, Ltd [1944] 2 All ER 98; [1945] KB 216; (1944) 170 LTR 418; (1944) 88 SJ 298; (1943-44) LX TLR 363 HC KBD High explosives manufacturer subject to strict liability (Rylands v Fletcher applies — non-natural user); no volenti non fit injuria as victim was employed against her will.

Read (Norah) v J Lyons and Co, Ltd [1945] 1 All ER 106; (1946) 96 LJ 213; (1947) 91 SJ 54; (1944-45) LXI TLR 148 CA Rylands v Fletcher inapplicable to explosion in high explosives manufacturers and no volenti non fit injuria.

Read v J Lyons and Co, Ltd [1946] 2 All ER 471; [1947] AC 156; [1947] 116 LJR 39; (1946) 175 LTR 413; (1945-46) LXII TLR 646 HL Manufacturer of explosive shells not absolutely liable for personal injuries caused; unwilling worker an invitee to whom strict but not absolute liability; notion of 'escape' in Rylands v Fletcher.

Rogers (Mollie) v Kaus (Otto) (1976) 126 NLJ 544t CA Escape of grime/oil from cars not covered by Rylands v Fletcher but was negligent to allow escaped material to heap up.

Smeaton v Ilford Corporation [1954] 1 All ER 923; [1954] Ch 450; (1954) 118 JP 290; (1954) 104 LJ 264; (1954) 98 SJ 251; [1954] 2 WLR 668 HC ChD Escape of sewage not result of negligent act by corporation so not guilty of nuisance; Rylands v Fletcher applicable but statutory requirement to allow public use of sewers (which resulted in problem) a defence (Public Health Act 1936, s 34(1)).

Smith v Scott and others [1972] 3 All ER 645; [1973] Ch 314; (1972) 116 SJ 785; [1972] 3 WLR 783 HC ChD Landlord not liable for tenant's nuisance unless expressly authorises it or it is inevitable from use: neither so here; Rylands v Fletcher inapplicable to landlord with rowdy tenants; landlord's duties well settled law.

Sterling Wharfage Co, Ltd v Peek Brothers and Winch, Ltd [1935] LJNCCA 235 CA Persons from whose property water leaked into another's premises held to be under duty to show escape of water did not result from their negligence (failed to discharge this duty).

The Sterling Wharfage Co, Ltd v Peek Brothers and Winch, Ltd [1935] LJNCCR 134 CyCt Persons from whose property water leaked into another's premises held to be under duty to show escape of water did not result from their negligence (failed to discharge this duty).

Thomas and Evans, Limited v Mid-Rhondda Co-operative Society, Limited [1941] 1 KB 381; [1941] 110 LJ 699; (1940) 84 SJ 682; (1940-41) LVII TLR 228 CA Non-liability of riparian owner in negligence/nuisance or under Rylands v Fletcher for flooding consequent upon pulling down of flood wall which had itself erected.

Weller and Co and another v Foot and Mouth Disease Research Institute [1965] 3 All ER 560; [1966] 1 QB 569; (1965) 109 SJ 702; [1965] 3 WLR 1082 HC QBD Research Institute liable to farmers but not auctioneer at local cattle mart for escape of foot and mouth virus from laboratory.

West v Bristol Tramways Company (Limited) (1908) 72 JP 145; (1907-08) 52 SJ 264; (1907-08) XXIV TLR 299 HC KBD Rylands v Fletcher applied to creosoting as non-natural user of land.

West v Bristol Tramways Co [1908-10] All ER 215; (1908) 72 JP 243; [1908] 2 KB 14; [1908] 77 LJCL 684; (1908-09) XCIX LTR 264; (1907-08) 52 SJ 393; (1907-08) XXIV TLR 478; (1908) WN (I) 95 CA Rylands v Fletcher applied to creosoting as non-natural user of land.

Western Engraving Co v Film Laboratories, Ltd [1936] 1 All ER 106; (1936) 80 SJ 165 CA Bringing large quantities of water into factory premises a non-natural user upon escape of which Rylands v Fletcher-style liability arose.

Whitmores (Edenbridge), Limited v Stanford [1909] 1 Ch 427 HC ChD Rylands v Fletcher inapplicable to owner of land on which another keeps/impounds water (or other dangerous element) for that other's purposes; injunction to restrain interference (inter alia by trespass) with full use and enjoyment of stream.

RYLANDS V FLETCHER (road traffic)

Wing v London General Omnibus Company Limited (1909) 73 JP 170; (1909) C LTR 301; (1908-09) 53 SJ 287 HC KBD Recovery of damages for personal injuries sustained by passenger when bus skidded (not proved that passenger knew of/had accepted risk of skidding).

Wing v London General Omnibus Co [1908-10] All ER 496; (1909) 73 JP 429; [1909] 2 KB 652; [1909] 78 LJKB 1063; (1909-10) 101 LTR 411; (1908-09) 53 SJ 713; (1908-09) XXV TLR 729 CA Skidding not per se evidence of negligent driving; on res ipsa loquitur; Rylands v Fletcher applies to unnatural user of highway for traffic.

RYLANDS V FLETCHER (sport)

Stone v Bolton and others [1949] 1 All ER 237 Assizes Single incident not nuisance; cricket-playing not unnatural land user (Rylands v Fletcher inapplicable); cricket-ball inadvertently striking person on highway not negligent.

SEIZURE (damages)

Moore v Lambeth County Court Registrar and others [1970] 2 WLR 87 CA Excessive seizure was tort even though malice unproved.

TORT BY PUBLIC OFFICIAL (general)

Marshal Shipping Company v Board of Trade [1923] 2 KB 343; (1923) WN (I) 115 CA Liability of Board of Trade for acts of Shipping Controller.

TRADE UNION (general)

Boulting and another v Association of Cinematograph, Television and Allied Technicians [1963] 2 WLR 529 CA Court can grant injunction to prevent apprehended tort by trade union.

TRESPASS (animal)

Buckle v Holmes [1925] All ER 676; (1926) 90 JP 47; (1925) 60 LJ 1029; [1926] 95 LJCL 158 (also CA); (1926) 134 LTR 284; (1925-26) 70 SJ 284; (1925-26) XLII TLR 147 HC KBD Cat-owner not liable for damage caused by trespassing cat unless aware of peculiar tendency of cat to cause damage.

Buckle v Holmes [1926] All ER 90; (1926) 90 JP 109; [1926] 2 KB 125; (1926) 61 LJ 324; [1926] 95 LJCL 547; (1926) 134 LTR 743; (1925-26) 70 SJ 464; (1925-26) XLII TLR 369; (1925) WN (I) 295 CA Cat-owner not liable for cat trespass unless aware of peculiar tendency of cat to cause damage; cats and dogs treated the same in law of trespass.

Cooke v Skinner; Cooke v Wilson; Cooke v Ellarby (1948) 98 LJ 38 CyCt On liability for trespass by sheep coming onto another's property by way of highway from common where pasturing.

Creasy v Bell [1945] LJNCCR 148 CyCt Cattle-owner liable absent proof of negligence for trespass of straying cattle onto another's property.

Cresswell v Sirl (1947) WN (I) 310 HC KBD On criminal liability for shooting of trespassing dog.

Cresswell v Sirl (1948) 112 JP 69; [1948] 1 KB 241; (1947) 97 LJ 648; [1948] 117 LJR 654; (1947) 91 SJ 653; (1947) LXIII TLR 620 CA On test of criminal liability for shooting of trespassing dog.

Crow v Wood [1970] 3 All ER 425; [1971] 1 QB 77; (1970) 114 SJ 474; [1970] 3 WLR 516 CA Party failing in duty to maintain walls cannot complain of cattle trespass by neighbour's sheep.

Cummings v Grainger (1975) 125 NLJ 256t; (1975) 119 SJ 425; [1975] 1 WLR 1330 HC QBD Successful action for damages under Animals Act 1975 from owner-keeper of particularly fierce Alsatian dog.

Cunningham v Cripwell (1914) CC Rep III 85 CA May be custom requiring owner of adjoining fields to maintain fence so as to prevent damage by animals.

Egerton v Harding and another [1974] 3 All ER 689; [1975] QB 62; (1974) 118 SJ 565; [1974] 3 WLR 437 CA Duty to fence against common arose from immemorial custom.

Eustace v Ayre [1947] LJNCCR 106 CyCt Could recover damages for having to destroy bull after bull broke its leg chasing cow that strayed/trespassed onto/on field where bull kept.

Gayler and Pope, Ltd v B Davies and Son, Ltd [1924] All ER 94; [1924] 2 KB 75; (1924) 59 LJ 282; [1924] 93 LJCL 702; (1924) 131 LTR 507; (1923-24) 68 SJ 685; (1923-24) XL TLR 591; (1924) WN (I) 158 HC KBD Owner liable for damage by stray horse where was negligent — not for trespass of horse per se.

Goldston v Bradshaw [1934] LJNCCR 355 CyCt Absent negligence/intent on part of pig drover/his employer could not recover damages from same for damage occasioned by straying pig.

Gould v McAuliffe [1941] 1 All ER 515; (1941) 91 LJ 191; (1942) 92 LJ 60; (1941) 85 SJ 215; (1940-41) LVII TLR 369 HC KBD Customer looking for outside pub lavatory could recover for animal injury though trespasser.

Hadwell v Righton (1907) 71 JP 499; [1907] 2 KB 345; [1907] 76 LJKB 891; (1906-07) XXIII TLR 548 HC KBD Owner of fowl not liable for injury caused by same while trespassing on highway footpath as was too remote.

Hammond v Mallinson and Bowie [1939] LJNCCR 357 CyCt Agister (not owner) liable for trespass by agisted sheep.

Hamps v Darby (1948) 98 LJ 303 CyCt On liability of farmer for shooting and killing pigeons without first trying to scare them off.

Hamps v Darby [1948] 2 KB 311; (1948) 98 LJ 427; [1949] 118 LJR 487; (1948) LXIV TLR 440; (1948) WN (I) 313 CA Liability of farmer for shooting and killing pigeons without first trying to scare them off.

Holgate v Bleazard [1916-17] All ER 817; (1917) CC Rep VI 13; [1917] 1 KB 443; [1917] 86 LJCL 270; (1916-17) 115 LTR 788; (1916-17) XXXIII TLR 116; (1916) WN (I) 432 HC KBD Animal-owner liable for damage caused by esacaping animal (horses).

Hopkins v R and S Jenkins (1919) CC Rep VIII 74 CyCt On liability of owners of cattle with right of common in two areas for damage occasioned when strayed from public highway between two areas into another's land.

Jones v Price (1965) 115 LJ 512; [1965] 2 QB 618; [1965] 3 WLR 296 CA Absent agreement to do so was no obligation on landowner to fence property so as to stop neighbour's cattle straying.

Lowery v Walker [1909] 2 KB 433; (1909) 44 LJ 356; [1909] 78 LJKB 874; (1909-10) 101 LTR 78; (1908-09) 53 SJ 544; (1908-09) XXV TLR 608; (1909) WN (I) 130 HC KBD Owner not liable for injuries to trespassers by vicious animal.

Lowery v Walker [1910] 1 KB 173; (1909) 44 LJ 745; (1910) 79 LJKB 297; (1909-10) 101 LTR 873; (1909-10) 54 SJ 99; (1909-10) XXVI TLR 108; (1909) WN (I) 249 CA Owner not liable for injuries to trespassers by vicious animal.

Lowery v Walker [1911] AC 10; (1910) 45 LJ 738; (1911) 80 LJCL 138; (1910-11) 103 LTR 675; (1910-11) 55 SJ 62; (1910-11) XXVII TLR 83; (1910) WN (I) 241 HL Owner who had erected warning notice liable for injuries to trespassers by vicious animal.

Matthews v Cowan (1915) CC Rep IV 84 CyCt Non-recovery of damages in trespass for liability suffered by straying cattle where person owning land onto which cattle strayed had not discharged duty of fencing out said cattle.

Morris v Curtis [1947] LJNCCR 284 CyCt Absent proof that third party had left field gate open cattle owner was liable for damage occasioned to vegetable plot onto which cattle strayed/trespassed by way of open gate.

Park v J Jobson and Son [1944] LJNCCR 153 CyCt Person who was author of own troubles in that created situation whereby cattle could trespass on own property could not recover damages from cattle owner when cattle so trespassed.

Park v J Jobson and Son [1945] 1 All ER 222; (1946) 96 LJ 213 CA No duty on allotment holder to keep allotment fenced; no liability on one allotment holder with defective fence to others as no evidence of animal trespass through particular part of fence.

Poupart v Brazil [1941] LJNCCR 223 CyCt Pony-owner liable in trespass where ponies strayed through fence in disrepair onto highway and onto another's property.

Pratt v Martin (1911-13) XXII Cox CC 442; (1911) 75 JP 328; [1911] 2 KB 90; (1911) 80 LJCL 711; (1911-12) 105 LTR 49; (1910-11) XXVII TLR 377; (1911) WN (I) 102 HC KBD Not trespass to send one's dog across another's land to search for game.

Searle v Wallbank [1947] 1 All ER 12; [1947] AC 341; (1947) 97 LJ 9; [1947] LJNCCR 34; [1947] 116 LJR 258; (1947) 176 LTR 104; (1947) 91 SJ 83; (1947) LXIII TLR 24; (1947) WN (I) 60 HL No duty to highway users to maintain fence to prevent animals straying onto highway; no duty to prevent undangerous animals straying onto highway.

Sharp v Harvey [1935] LJNCCR 261 CyCt Sheep-owner not liable for damage occasioned by trespassing sheep where trespass occurred through fault of third party.

Sloan v Windle (1921) CC Rep X 60 CyCt Gamekeeper could shoot trespassing dog chasing hare over master's property where chase presented real chance of hare being killed.

Smith v Richardson and others (1923) CC Rep XII 2 CyCt Agisters not liable for trespass of horses onto allotments where responsibility of maintaining fence at allotments fell on certain rail company.

Stearn v Prentice Bros, Ltd [1918-19] All ER 495; (1919) CC Rep VIII 13; [1919] 1 KB 394; [1919] 88 LJCL 422; (1919) 120 LTR 445; (1918-19) 63 SJ 229; (1918-19) XXXV TLR 207 HC KBD Bone merchant not liable for trespass of rats running to and from premises.

Sutcliffe v Holmes and another [1946] 2 All ER 599; [1947] KB 147; [1947] 116 LJR 415; (1946) 175 LTR 487; (1945-46) LXII TLR 733; (1947) WN (I) 7 CA Sheep trespass: could not claim other party liable to fence as no evidence of same; could not claim due to third party's non-fencing as had known of third party's failure and should have guarded against it.

Theyer v Purnell [1918] 2 KB 333; [1919] 88 LJCL 263; (1918-19) 119 LTR 285; (1918) WN (I) 174 HC KBD Recovery of damages consequent upon trespass of sheep: doctrine of scienter inapplicable.

Timothy Whites Ltd v Byng [1934] LJNCCR 47 CyCt Animal owners under positive duty to restrain their animals trespassing on another's property.

Wormald v Cole [1954] 1 All ER; (1954) 104 LJ 201; [1954] 1 QB 614; (1954) 98 SJ 232; [1954] 2 WLR 613 CA Cattle owner liable for personal injury caused to neighbour upon trespass of quiet cattle.

TRESPASS (bank)

Henniker v Howard (1904) XC LTR 157 HC KBD Maintenance of bank, fence and ditch for almost fifty years held not rebut presumption of ownership in respect of another.

TRESPASS (building)

Truckell v Stock [1957] 1 WLR 161 CA That footings extended beyond boundary of wall (wall rested on footings) was trespass.

TRESPASS (child)

Davis v St Mary's Demolition and Excavation Co, Ltd [1954] 1 All ER 578; (1954) 98 SJ 217; [1954] 1 WLR 592 HC QBD Liability to child trespasser as neighbour where child trespass frequent.

Liddle v North Riding of Yorkshire County Council [1934] All ER 222; (1934) 98 JP 319; [1934] 2 KB 101; (1934) 103 LJCL 527; (1934) 151 LTR 202; (1934) 78 SJ 349; (1933-34) L TLR 377; (1934) WN (I) 100 CA Council not liable to child as trespasser as took all reasonable steps, as licensee as danger unconcealed; council not liable in nuisance for piling soil on verge of highway.

Robert Addie and Sons (Collieries), Limited v Dumbreck [1929] AC 358; (1929) 140 LTR 650; (1928-29) XLV TLR 267 HL Non-liability towards child killed by dangerous machine while trespassing.

TRESPASS (conspiracy)

Byrne and another v Kinematograph Renters Society, Ltd and others [1958] 2 All ER 579 HC ChD No conspiracy as no trespass when inspectors from trade protection society entered cinema to monitor operation thereof.

Hesperides Hotels Ltd and another v Muftizade (1978) 142 JP 541; (1978) 122 SJ 507 HL Court could not hear action regarding conspiracy to trespass on property in foreign country but could hear action for trespass to chattels in that property.

TRESPASS (Crown)

Attorney-General v Nissan [1969] 1 All ER 629; [1970] AC 179; (1969) 119 NLJ 250; (1969) 113 SJ 207; [1969] 2 WLR 926 HL That acts complained of were 'acts of state' not defence in tort action.

Nissan v Attorney-General [1968] 1 QB 286 (also CA); (1967) 111 SJ 195; [1967] 3 WLR 109 HC QBD That acts complained of were 'acts of state' not defence in tort action.

Nissan v Attorney-General [1968] 1 QB 286 (also HC QBD); (1967) 117 NLJ 834t; (1967) 111 SJ 544; [1967] 3 WLR 1044 CA That acts complained of were 'acts of state' not defence in tort action.

TRESPASS (damages)

Ashover Fluor Spar Mines, Limited v Jackson (1911) WN (I) 163 HC ChD On assessment of damages for trespass on mine.

Drane v Evangelou and others [1978] 2 All ER 437; [1978] 1 WLR 455 CA Judge can raise issue of trespass though not pleaded; exemplary damages need not be pleaded.

Jaggard v Sawyer and another [1995] 2 All ER 189 CA Court may award 'once and for all' damages insead of injunction to restrain trespass or breach of covenant; oppression to be judged as facts stand on date injunction sought.

Loudon v Ryder [1953] 1 All ER 741; [1953] 2 QB 202; (1953) 97 SJ 170; [1953] 2 WLR 537 CA On exemplary damages for trespass/assault.

Swordheath Properties Ltd v Tabet and others [1979] 1 All ER 240; (1979) 129 (1) NLJ 40; [1979] 1 WLR 285 CA Damages for continuing trespass whether or not land would have been let; measure of damages.

TRESPASS (estoppel)

Kelsen v Imperial Tobacco Co (of Great Britain and Ireland), Ltd [1957] 2 All ER 343; (1957) 107 LJ 377; [1957] 2 QB 334; (1957) 101 SJ 446 HC QBD Incursion by advertisements into air space above shop a trespass against which injunction granted; three year non-objection to sign did not raise estoppel as other party had not acted to detriment on representation of intention not to object (which in itself could not create estoppel).

TRESPASS (general)

Adams v Naylor [1944] 2 All ER 21 Assizes No duty of care to trespassers.

Adams v Naylor [1944] 2 All ER 21; (1945) 95 LJ 111; [1944] 113 LJ 499; (1944) 171 LTR 105; (1944) 88 SJ 325 CA No duty of care to trespassers.

Alliance Building Society v Varma [1949] Ch 724; (1949) LXV TLR 576 CA Court could (under RSC Or 55, r 5A) order delivery up of mortgaged premises to mortgagee though person in occupation a trespasser.

Armstrong v Sheppard and Short, Ltd [1959] 2 All ER 651; (1959) 123 JP 401; (1959) 109 LJ 477; [1959] 2 QB 384 CA Oral consent to acts done defeats trespass action even though not fully aware of proprietary rights when consented.

Balls and another v Lintsbrook Development Ltd (1976) 120 SJ 29 HC ChD Action dismissed for delay (albeit that delay nonetheless meant action being brought inside limitation period).

Bannister v Bracewell (1960) 110 LJ 208 CyCt Damages plus leave to apply for injunction for trespass by sheep.

Barbara v Home Office (1984) 134 NLJ 888 HC QBD Trespass by Government (prison) officials punished by way of damages/aggravated damages but not exemplary damages.

Barclays Bank, Ltd v Roberts (1954) 104 LJ 617 CA Failed action in trespass following on improper execution of writ of possession.

Bartley v Capel (1932) 74 LJ ccr78 CyCt Erection of fence was a trespass; unlawful exercise of right of way a trespass.

Behrens v Richards [1905] 2 Ch 614; (1905) 69 JP 381; (1905-06) XCIII LTR 623; (1904-05) 49 SJ 685; (1905-06) 54 WR 141 HC ChD Nominal damages but no injunction in respect of trespass whereby owner not injured.

Berkeley Estates Co, Ltd and Phillips v Smith [1946] LJNCCR 105 CyCt Injunction granted to owners of profit a prendre to restrain past trespasser who declared intent to trespass in future.

Betts Limited v Pickfords Limited (1906) XCIV LTR 363 HC ChD Injunction to restrain trespass occasioned by unconsented to building of party wall.

Burton v Winters and another [1993] 3 All ER 847; [1993] 1 WLR 1077 CA Common law right to self-redress for trespass by encroachment if urgency requires it/legal action unmerited.

Byrne and another v Kinematograph Renters Society, Ltd and others [1958] 2 All ER 579 HC ChD No conspiracy as no trespass when inspectors from trade protection society entered cinema to monitor operation thereof.

Campbell-Davys v Lloyd [1901] 2 Ch 518; (1901-02) LXXXV LTR 59; (1900-01) 45 SJ 670; (1900-01) XVII TLR 678; (1901) WN (I) 150; (1900-01) 49 WR 710 CA Entry onto land to abate nuisance was trespass.

Canadian Pacific Rail Co v R [1931] All ER 113; (1931) 100 LJPC 129 PC No trespass where was evidence of longtime occupation of land.

Canadian Pacific Wine Co v Tuley and others [1921] LJPC 233 PC Police not rendered trespassers by seizing goods absent search warrant in course of lawful search/seizure.

Canvey Island Commissioners v Preedy [1922] 1 Ch 179; (1922) 86 JP 21; [1922] 91 LJCh 203; (1922) 126 LTR 445; (1921) WN (I) 363 HC ChD Damages for trespass upon foreshore.

Carver v Jones [1944] LJNCCR 31 CyCt Refusal of injunction preventing trespass into house of person to whom person seeking injunction had placed self in loco parentis by marrying mother of person against whom injunction sought.

Cave v Capel [1953] 1 WLR 1185 HC QBD Trespass to person and goods were one where trespass occurred while bailiff (mistakenly) seizing caravan in which person residing.

Chatterton v Gerson and another [1981] 1 All ER 257; (1981) 131 NLJ 238; [1981] QB 432; (1980) 124 SJ 885; [1980] 3 WLR 1003 HC QBD Trespass to person requires lack of real consent; no such lack where general explanation of operation/risks by doctor (which obliged to give).

Christie and another v Leachinsky [1947] 1 All ER 567; [1947] AC 573; (1947) 111 JP 224; (1947) 97 LJ 165; [1947] 116 LJR 757; (1947) 176 LTR 443; (1947) LXIII TLR 231 HL False imprisonment where arrested without warrant and not told why/not obvious why/inobvious why and do not resist.

Christie v Corporation of Trinity House (1918-19) XXXV TLR 480 HC KBD Owner of wrecked ship entitled to damages from Trinity House Corporation which had blown up ship without jurisdiction for doing so.

Clarke (Loftus Otway) v Chowdhry (Brojendra Kissore Roy); The Same v Chowdhurani (Srimati Biseswari Debi) (1911-12) XXVIII TLR 486 PC Forced search of cutcherry where was no one to admit searchers was justified under Code of Civil Procedure.

Clissold v Cratchley and another (1909-10) 101 LTR 911 HC KBD Absent malice solicitor/client not liable in action for trespass on foot of fi fa writ sued out/executed after debt paid.

Clissold v Cratchley [1910] 2 KB 244; (1910) 45 LJ 306; (1910) 102 LTR 520 CA Absent malice solicitor/client not liable in action for trespass on foot of fi fa writ sued out/executed after debt paid.

Conway v George Wimpey and Co, Ltd [1951] 1 All ER 363; [1951] 1 TLR 587 CA No duty of care to trespasser.

Cope v Sharpe [1910] 1 KB 168; (1910) 45 LJ 8; (1910) 79 LJKB 281; (1910) 102 LTR 102; (1909-10) XXVI TLR 172; (1910-11) XXVII TLR 396; (1910) WN (I) 10 HC KBD Trespass through necessity not trespass.

Cope v Sharpe [1911-13] All ER 1212; [1912] 1 KB 496; (1912) 47 LJ 8; (1912) 81 LJKB 346; (1912) 106 LTR 56; (1911-12) 56 SJ 187; (1911-12) XXVIII TLR 157; (1912) WN (I) 17 CA Trespass through necessity not trespass.

Cope v Sharpe (No 2) [1911] 2 KB 837; (1911) 80 LJCL1008; (1911) 104 LTR 718 HC KBD Trespass through genuine necessity justified.

Cross v Rix (1912) CC Rep I 97 HC KBD New trial necessary where person non-suited (in light of provisions of Public Authorities Protection Act) without person consenting to same/having evidence heard.

Cubitt v Gamble (1918-19) 63 SJ 287; (1918-19) XXXV TLR 223 HC KBD Person seeking debt execution after tender of amount of debt is guilty of trespass.

Cummings v Grainger (1977) 141 JP 95; (1976) 126 NLJ 665t; [1977] QB 397; (1976) 120 SJ 453; [1976] 3 WLR 842 CA Person with untrained guard dog not liable for injuries suffered by trespasser (who in any event entered guarded place knowing of dog and so assumed risk of injury).

Cunningham v Cripwell (1914) CC Rep III 85 CA May be custom requiring owner of adjoining fields to maintain fence so as to prevent damage by animals.

Davies v British Railways Board (1984) 134 NLJ 888 HC QBD On duty of occupier towards (child) trespasser.

Davis v Bromley Urban District Council (1903) 67 JP 275 CA Punitive damages appropriate for trespass by local authority.

Day v Tidball (1929) 68 LJ ccr24 CyCt Damages available from CyCt in action for trespass following order by court of summary jurisdiction pursuant to the Small Tenements Recovery Act 1838.

De Coppett v Barnett and others (1900-01) XVII TLR 273 CA Sheriff not protected from action for trespass where substantial grievance had resulted to plaintiff as result of sheriff's actions.

Delaney v TP Smith, Limited [1946] 2 All ER 23; [1946] KB 393; [1946] 115 LJ 406; [1946] LJNCCR 141; (1946) 175 LTR 187; (1946) 90 SJ 296; (1945-46) LXII TLR 398; (1946) WN (I) 79 CA No tenancy as no note or memorandum thereof: party continuing occupancy without permission of landlord in trespass.

Department of the Environment v James and others (1972) 116 SJ 712 HC ChD Court would not delay recovery of possession of property occupied by trespassers.

Dibben v Holloway (1929) 68 LJ ccr8 CyCt Building-owner not in possession of same could recover damages in trespass for loss sustained through person without authority affixing radio wires to building.

Dickinson v Ead and others (1914-15) XXIV Cox CC 308; (1914) 78 JP 326; (1914-15) 111 LTR 378; (1913-14) XXX TLR 496 HC KBD Genuine (and reasonable) belief that were allowed onto land meant was no trespass.

Director of Public Prosecutions v Jones and another [1997] 2 All ER 119; [1997] 2 Cr App R (S) 162 HC QBD On elements of offence of trespassory assembly.

Drane v Evangelou and others [1978] 2 All ER 437; [1978] 1 WLR 455 CA Judge can raise issue of trespass though not pleaded; exemplary damages need not be pleaded.

EE Bevan, Ltd v Harfoot [1945] LJNCCR 136 CyCt On liability for wilful trespass.

Ellwood v West Cumberland Relay Service, Ltd (1948) 98 LJ 660 CyCt On extent of liability for trespass occasioned when installing wireless rediffusion service.

Erith Corporation v Holder [1949] 2 KB 46 CA House-owner rendered trespasser in own home by virtue of emergency (requisitioning) legislation.

Farrugia v Great Western Railway Co [1947] 2 All ER 565 CA Person creating risk on highway owes duty of care to others thereon/nearby even if other trespasser or presence otherwise unlawful.

Fitzhardinge (Lord) v Purcell (1908-09) XCIX LTR 154 HC ChD Injunction granted to restrain trespass by wildfowler going from river to foreshore in exercise of purported right.

Ford v Scarth (1951) 101 LJ 289 CyCt Failed action in trespass by aged aunt who took in niece and her family as tenants/occupiers and then sought to evict them when she decided to sell the house.

Fowley Marine (Emsworth) Ltd v Gafford [1967] 2 All ER 472; [1967] 2 QB 808 HC QBD Quality claims to ownership plus paper title could not sustain trespass action; failure to prove sixty years' adverse possession meant did not displace Crown title to tidal creek.

Fowley Marine (Emsworth), Ltd v Gafford [1968] 1 All ER 979; (1968) 118 NLJ 110t; [1968] 2 QB 618; [1968] 2 WLR 842 CA Quality of claims to ownership plus paper title could sustain trespass action.

Freeman v Home Office [1984] 1 All ER 1036; (1984) 128 SJ 298; [1984] TLR 132; [1984] 2 WLR 802 CA Doctrine of informed consent not part of English law.

Fuller v Chippenham Rural District Council (1915) 79 JP 4 HC ChD One of three paths in trespass action found to be public footway.

Gale and another v Rhymney and Aber Valleys Gas and Water Company (1903) 67 JP 430 CA Water company guilty of trespass where unlawfully cut houseowners connection with water mains.

George v Commissioner of Police of the Metropolis [1984] TLR 199 HC QBD Successful action against Police Commissioner for trespass/assault by the police.

Glenwood Lumber Company, Limited v Phillips [1904-07] All ER 203; [1904] AC 405; [1904] 73 LJPC 62 PC Damages for trespasser's removal of felled trees from property.

Greenwell and another v Howell and another [1900] 69 LJCL 461; (1899-1900) XVI TLR 235 CA County surveyor/deputy clerk committing trespass for purpose of bringing test action protected by provisions of Public Authorities Protection Act 1893.

Greenwell v Welch (1904-05) 49 SJ 538 HC KBD Not allowed to treat as distress what have dealt with as trespass.

Greyvensteyn (Samuel Jacobus) v Daniel Wilhelmus Hattingh and Others [1911] AC 355; (1911) 80 LJPC 158; (1910-11) XXVII TLR 358 PC Not liable for results of driving locusts from one's property in act of self-protection.

Grove v Eastern Gas Board [1951] 2 KB 586; (1951) WN (I) 312 HC KBD Forcible entry by Gas Board officials to inspect supply pipes/gas meter and empty coins from meter not trespass.

Grove v Eastern Gas Board [1952] 1 KB 77; (1951) 101 LJ 331; (1951) 95 SJ 789; (1951) WN (I) 615 CA Forcible entry by Gas Board officials to inspect supply pipes/gas meter and empty coins from meter not trespass.

Haringey London Borough Council v Wright and another (1969) 113 SJ 900 VacCt Interim injunction restraining two onetime students of college of art from returning to same.

Heath v Keys (1984) 134 NLJ 888; [1984] TLR 349 HC QBD Recovery of damages in trespass for dumping of spoil on land.

Helm v Facey (1981) 131 NLJ 291 HC ChD Refusal of injunction against trespasser whose continued occupation of premises raised the sale price of those premises.

Hemmings and Wife v Stoke Poges Golf Club, Ltd, and another [1918-19] All ER 798; [1920] 1 KB 720; [1920] 89 LJCL 744; (1920) 122 LTR 479; (1919-20) XXXVI TLR 77 CA Landlord may enter premises and use reasonable force to remove trespasser/trespasser's property.

Henniker v Howard (1904) XC LTR 157 HC KBD Maintenance of bank, fence and ditch for almost fifty years held not rebut presumption of ownership in respect of another.

Hicks, Arnold and Co and another v Bloch (1964) 108 SJ 336 HC QBD Damages for trespass on firm/assault on solicitor and injunction restraining future trespass.

Hindley v Pemberton (1957) 107 LJ ccr620 CyCt On trespass by person acting under licence.

Hirsch and others v Somervell and others (1946) 90 SJ 369 HC ChD Striking out of false imprisonment/trespass action against successive Home Secretaries.

Hirsch and another v Somervell and others (1946) 90 SJ 394; (1945-46) LXII TLR 592 CA Successful appeal against striking out of false imprisonment/trespass action against successive Home Secretaries.

Hope v Osborne [1913] 2 Ch 349; (1913) 77 JP 317; (1913) 48 LJ 393; (1913) 82 LJCh 457; (1913-14) 109 LTR 41; (1912-13) XXIX TLR 606; (1913) WN (I) 201 HC ChD Liable in damages for excessive trespass in entering onto another's land to remove nuisance.

Hornby v Gillam (1912) CC Rep I 23 CyCt Seller of property who entered onto same after conveyance/sale complete was trespasser.

Inverugie Investments Ltd v Hackett [1995] 3 All ER 841; [1995] 1 WLR 713 PC Hirer of goods or letter of property may recover damages for wrongful use arising from trespass regardless of actual loss suffered.

Jarvis v Smith (1957) 107 LJ ccr476 CyCt RSPCA inspector did not trepass on land when entered on same when investigating allegations but did commit trespass when removed carcase from land.

Jenkins v Great Western Rail Co [1911-13] All ER 216; [1912] 1 KB 525; (1911) 46 LJ 804; (1912) 81 LJKB 378 (1911-12) 105 LTR 882 CA Not liable in respect of injury to child wandering from where had licence to play.

John Trenberth Ltd v National Westminster Bank Ltd (1979) 129 (1) NLJ 566; (1979) 123 SJ 388 HC ChD Injunction granted to restrain trespass (even though the damage caused by the trespass was not great).

Jolliffe v Willmett and Co and another [1971] 1 All ER 478; (1970) 120 NLJ 707t; (1970) 114 SJ 619 HC QBD Person entering home of separated spouse (not family home) with permission of other spouse is trespasser; employer not responsible for torts of independent contractor unless commssioned tort/negligence in choosing same led to tort.

King v Brown, Durant, and Co [1913] 2 Ch 416; (1913) 48 LJ 471; (1913) 82 LJCh 548 HC ChD Commoner cannot sue other commoner/stranger for simple trespass (but can sue for interference with his rights).

Kinsey v London Borough of St Helens (1977) 127 NLJ 640b CA Failed negligence action by child injured when recently reconstructed school gate pillar collapsed while child swinging on gate.

Kirby v Chessum (1913-14) XXX TLR 15 HC KBD Commissioners of Works not liable to indemnify contractor who committed trespass unauthorised by former in course of its work.

Kirby v Chessum (1915) 79 JP 81; (1913-14) XXX TLR 660 CA Commissioners of Works liable to indemnify contractor who in course of work committed trespass authorised by former's architect.

Konskier v B Goodman, Ltd [1927] All ER 187; [1928] 1 KB 421; (1927) 64 LJ 403; (1928) 97 LJCL 263; (1928) 138 LTR 481 CA Liability in trespass not negligence for leaving waste materials on roof of adjoining property resulting in damage.

Kynoch, Limited v Rowlands [1912] 1 Ch 527 (also CA); [1912] 81 LJCh 340 (also CA); (1910-11) 55 SJ 617 HC ChD Trespass found where was inadequate evidence of discontinuance of possession.

Kynoch Limited v Rowlands [1911-13] All ER 1258; [1912] 1 Ch 527 (also HC ChD); (1912) 81 LJCh 340 (also HC ChD); (1912) 106 LTR 316 CA Trespass found where was inadequate evidence of discontinuance of possession.

Lawson v Tuddenham [1945] LJNCCR 141 CyCt Failed claim in nuisance/trespass arising from allegedly excessive user of right of way.

Leachinsky v Christie [1945] 2 All ER 395; (1946) 110 JP 23; [1946] KB 124; (1946) 96 LJ 185; [1946] 115 LJ 241; (1946) 174 LTR 13; (1944-45) LXI TLR 584 CA Cannot be arrested for misdemeanour because suspected of felony; on special powers of arrest.

League Against Cruel Sports Ltd v Scott and others [1985] 2 All ER 489; [1986] QB 240; (1985) 129 SJ 543 HC QBD Master of hounds liable for hounds' trespass where knew real risk of entry/negligently failed to prevent trespass; master liable for persons over whom has control; intent/negligence judged by conduct.

Letang v Cooper (1964) 114 LJ 622; [1965] 1 QB 232; (1964) 108 SJ 519; [1964] 3 WLR 573 CA Trespass to the person action time-barred under Limitation Act 1939, s 2 (as amended).

Letang v Cooper [1964] 1 All ER 669; (1964) 114 LJ 306; [1964] 2 QB 53; (1964) 108 SJ 180; [1964] 2 WLR 642 HC QBD Trespass to the person action could not be time-barred under Limitation Act 1939, s 2 (as amended).

Lewis v Gunter-Jones (1949) LXV TLR 181 CA Failed action for trespass under Small Tenements Recovery Act 1838, s 3.

London and North-Western Railway v Westminster Corporation [1904] 73 LJCh 386; (1903-04) 48 SJ 330; (1903-04) 52 WR 596 CA Injunction to restrain trespass by local authority in erection of public toilets.

London Borough of Southwark v Williams and another; London Borough of Southwark v Anderson and another [1971] 2 All ER 175; [1971] Ch 734; [1971] 2 WLR 467 CA Trespass on foot of homelessness not justifiable as necessity.

Lord Bernstein of Leigh v Skyviews and General Ltd [1977] 2 All ER 902; (1977) 127 NLJ 242t; [1978] QB 479; (1977) 121 SJ 157; [1977] 3 WLR 136 HC QBD Rights of owner in land extend to airspace over it necessary for reasonable use/enjoyment; aerial trespass action against aerial photographer barred by Civil Aviation Act 1949, s 40(1).

Manchester Corporation v Connolly and others (1970) 114 SJ 108 CA Vice Chancellor ought not to have granted order for possession at interlocutory hearing.

Mann v Nurse (1900-01) XVII TLR 569 HC KBD Justices' jurisdiction ousted where person charged with trespass in pursuit of game had reasonably held belief was allowed to shoot on land in issue.

Marriott v East Grinstead Gas and Water Company [1909] 1 Ch 70 HC ChD Owner of soil under which water board laying unauthorised pipes can sue for trespass/seek injunction (without joining Attorney-General).

Mason and others v Clarke (1955) 105 LJ 232 HL Successful action inter alia for trespass arising from breach of covenant regarding hunting/shooting.

McLeod v McLeod (1963) 113 LJ 420 CyCt Successful action by wife against husband for possession of onetime matrimonial home plus damages for assault (plus injunction restraining acts being done again).

McPhail v Unknown (Persons); Bristol Corporation v Ross and another (1973) 117 SJ 448 CA On non-availability of suspension of possession order where latter made against squatter-trespassers.

Mills and another v Silver and others [1991] 1 All ER 449; [1990] TLR 535 CA Use with landowner's acquiescence/tolerance does not preclude use as of right. Improvement of easement well beyond repair is trespass.

Mills v Brooker and Son (1918) CC Rep VII 90 CyCt Picking and selling on of fruit from branches of neighbour's trees that overhung defendant's property involved amounted to trespass and conversion.

Minister of Health v Bellotti (1943-44) LX TLR 228; (1944) WN (I) 45 CA Compulsory evacuees not given enough notice to quit premises but period between commencement of action and hearing of appeal had been adequate time to arrange new accomodation.

National Coal Board v JE Evans and Co (Cardiff), Ltd and another [1951] 2 All ER 310; [1951] 2 KB 861; (1951) 101 LJ 345; (1951) 95 SJ 399; [1951] 2 TLR 415; (1951) WN (I) 354 CA No trespass in action where plaintiffs partly to blame for occurrence and defendants blameless.

Newman v Bennett [1981] QB 726 HC QBD Right of common pur vicinage gives right to graze on adjoining land and is not therefore a mere defence to trespass.

Ocean Estates Ltd v Pinder (Norman) [1969] 2 AC 19; (1969) 113 SJ 71; [1969] 2 WLR 1359 PC Enough possession of land (use/architect's surveys) found to sustain action for trespass.

Osborne v Mead and others (1928) 66 LJ ccr18 CyCt Where unlawfully place chattels on another's land that other is allowed to remove same.

Palmer v Conservators of the River Thames (1901-02) LXXXV LTR 537; (1901-02) 46 SJ 84 HC ChD Unauthorised dredging under River Thames Conservancy Act 1894 constituted trespass.

Parry and others v Bulmer and Allington (1913) CC Rep II 108 CyCt No damages for non-repair of fences voluntarily erected and maintained by owner of land adjoining common.

Patel and others v WH Smith (Eziot) Ltd and another [1987] 1 WLR 853 CA On granting of injunction to landowner to halt trespass onto land to which holds unchallenged title.

Percy v Director of Public Prosecutions [1995] 3 All ER 124; [1995] Crim LR 714; (1995) 159 JP 337; (1995) 139 SJ LB 34; [1994] TLR 644; [1995] 1 WLR 1382 HC QBD Civil trespass not a breach of peace unless violence a natural consequence of trespass; criminal standard of proof necessary to establish breach of peace.

Peters v Shaw [1965] Crim LR 429t HC QBD Nominal damages awarded against police officer who entered on to property absent permission/without warrant/when not in hot pursuit.

Plascott v Southampton Bill-Posting Co (1921) CC Rep X 75 CyCt Is trespass for person posting bills to vandalise bills of other person authorised by occupier to post bills on same premises.

Porter v Tottenham Urban District Council (1913-14) XXX TLR 251 HC KBD Building owner not liable under building contract for delay in obtaining of possession by virtue of trespasser's actions.

Porter v Tottenham Urban District Council (1914-15) XXXI TLR 97 CA Building owner not liable under building contract for delay in obtaining of possession by virtue of trespasser's actions.

Portland Managements Ltd v Harte and others [1976] 1 All ER 225 CA Trespasser in possession to confess/avoid trespass if absolute owner proves title/intent to regain possession; Court of Appeal can order new trial even if defendant had adduced no evidence at original hearing.

Price v Shean [1939] LJNCCR 395 CyCt Declaration of title granted plus damages for cost of removing construction works improperly extending onto plaintiff's land.

Pridgeon v Mellor and others (1911-12) XXVIII TLR 261 HC KBD Treasury solicitor and aides not liable in trespass for seizure on foot of writ issued as result of judicial proceedings.

R v Ayres [1956] Crim LR 129t/210t CCA Civil trespass not sufficient to support conviction for shopbreaking.

R v Collins [1972] 2 All ER 1105; (1972) 56 Cr App R 554; [1972] Crim LR 498; (1972) 136 JP 605; [1973] QB 100; (1972) 116 SJ 432; [1972] 3 WLR 243 CA Only enter premises as trespasser if know/reckless as to whether entering without permission.

R v Laing [1995] Crim LR 395 CA Could not be guilty of burglary where were not trespasser when entered building.

R v Thornley (William James) (1981) 72 Cr App R 302; [1981] Crim LR 637 CA Police not trespassing where spend reasonable time on premises after being invited in by one co-occupier though are ordered out by another.

Re Wykeham Terrace, Brighton, ex parte Territorial Auxiliary and Volunteer Reserve Association for the South East Territorial Association v Hales (1969) 113 SJ 921 HC ChD Refusal to restrain trespass by way of ex parte application.

Riddiford v R [1905] AC 147 PC Lands surrendered to Crown subject to existing contracts did not include conveyance to appellant who was consequently trespasser.

Riley v Mayor, Aldermen, and Burgesses of Halifax (1907) 71 JP 428; (1907-08) XCVII LTR 278; (1906-07) XXIII TLR 613 HC ChD Damages for trespass rather than injunction to stop same merited in the circumstances.

Robson and another v Hallett [1967] 2 All ER 407; (1967) 51 Cr App R 307; (1967) 131 JP 333; [1967] 2 QB 939; (1967) 111 SJ 254; [1967] 3 WLR 28 HC QBD Police have implied licence to enter garden in course of duty; once licence revoked by owner have reasonable time to go before become trespasser; if breach of peace in garden police can enter to stop it.

Rogers v Tarratt (1931) 72 LJ ccr43 CyCt Person failing to establish title to near-abandoned property that adjoined own held to have trespassed on near-abandoned property.

Rose v Buckett [1901] 2 KB 449; [1901] 70 LJK/QB 736; (1901) LXXXIV LTR 670; (1900-01) XVII TLR 544; (1901-02) 50 WR 8 CA Right of action for trespass/conversion did not pass to trustee upon plaintiff becoming bankrupt.

Rouse v Gravelworks, Ltd [1940] 109 LJCL 408; (1940) 84 SJ 112; (1940) WN (I) 12 CA Failed trespass action trespass where water blown from pond formed after natural user (quarrying) caused erosion to neighbour's land.

Salisbury and Fordingbridge District Drainage Board v Southern Tanning Company (1920), Limited (1927) 137 LTR 754; (1926-27) XLIII TLR 824 HC KBD Successful counter-claim for trespass by mill-owners whose alleged enhancement of weir was torn down by drainage commissioners.

Sampson v Duke; Same v Huxtable (1913) CC Rep II 74 CyCt Persons who illegally seized goods of wife of debtor against whom had obtained judgment were liable in trespass.

Saunby v Water Commissioners of the City of London and the Corporation of the City of London (Ontario) [1906] AC 110; [1906] 75 LJPC 25 PC Allowed seek injunction for trespass (arbitration requirements in Ontario Act inapplicable).

Schweder v Worthing Gas Light and Coke Company [1912] 1 Ch 83 HC ChD Injunction to prevent trespass by laying pipes through/against plaintiff's premises.

Seng (Goh Cheen) v Soo (Lee Kim) [1925] AC 550 PC Master liable for servant's negligence though servant commits unauthorised trespass.

Sheffield Conservative and Unionist Club (Limited) v Brighton [1916] 85 LJKB 1669; (1915-16) XXXII TLR 598 HC KBD Action for trespass unsustainable against military authority comandeering premises under emergency legislation for clerical rather than 'military' staff (Defence of the Realm (Consolidation) Regulations 1914, regulation 2).

Simpson v Weber (1925) 133 LTR 46; (1924-25) XLI TLR 302 HC KBD Growing of creeper in such a way as blocked another's gutter was trespass for which damages available.

Singh (Sajan) v Ali (Sandara) [1960] 1 All ER 269 PC Title to property passed in course of conspiracy vests in person to whom passed once conspired act completed and can sue in detinue/trespass.

Smith v Littlewoods Organisation Ltd (1987) 137 NLJ 149; (1987) 131 SJ 226 HL Party not liable for damage to neighbour's properties occasioned by trespasser's on party's land unless damage reasonably foreseeable consequence of latter's actions.

Southam v Smout [1963] Crim LR 637; [1964] 1 QB 308; (1963) 107 SJ 513; [1963] 3 WLR 606 CA Bailiff's entry by closed/unlocked door rendered lawful as person whom wanted was found in house entered: in consequence houseowner could not order bailiffs out.

Southern Portland Cement Ltd v Cooper [1974] 1 All ER 87; [1974] AC 623; (1974) 118 SJ 99; [1974] 2 WLR 152 PC Duty of occupier towards trespassers gauged by reference to humaneness.

Southport Corporation v Esso Petroleum Co, Ltd and another [1954] 2 All ER 561; (1954) 118 JP 411; [1954] 2 QB 182; (1954) 98 SJ 472; [1954] 3 WLR 200 CA No trespass/nuisance where act from necessity (unless negligence present); ship-stranding sufficiently abnormal to raise res ipsa loquitur unless show not negligent.

Spry v Mortimore [1946] LJNCCR 83 CyCt Owner of ponies pasturing on common not liable for trespass by ponies (by way of public highway) onto private property adjoining common.

Staffordshire and Worcestershire Canal Navigation v Bradley [1912] 1 Ch 91 HC ChD Injunction to restrain trespass by way of unauthorised fishing in canal from towing paths.

Stevens v Stevens (1906-07) 51 SJ 825 HC KBD Injunction granted to restrain forty-nine year old son from imposing self on mother and insisting on living with her.

Stiff v Billington (1901) LXXXIV LTR 467; (1900-01) 45 SJ 448; (1900-01) XVII TLR 430 HC KBD 'Search and pursuit' of game under Game Act 1831, s 30 includes search and pursuit without intent to kill.

Swift v Ellis [1939] LJNCCR 384 CyCt Failed action for trespass by sheep from common onto land adjoining common which plaintiff-owner was under duty to fence off.

Syed Hussain Bin Abdul Rahman Bin Shaikh Alkaff and others [1985] 1 WLR 1392 PC Stayed possession order valid where trespassers had conceded were such (and so not protected under Control of Rent Act) in consenting to stayed possession order.

The Denaby and Cadeby Main Collieries (Limited) v Anson (1909-10) XXVI TLR 310 HC KBD Was trespass for coal hulk to be permanently moored in harbour without permission.

The Earl of Craven v Pridmore and others (1900-01) XVII TLR 399 HC KBD Neighbour's longtime repairing of fence/cutting of trees in ditch bounding rented land (actions known to tenant but not to landlord of rented land) held to rebut presumption that fence was on landlord's land.

The Earl of Craven v Pridmore and others (1901-02) XVIII TLR 282 CA Neighbour's longtime repairing of fence/cutting of trees in ditch bounding rented land (actions known to tenant but not to landlord of rented land) did not rebut presumption that fence was on landlord's land.

The Ocean Accident and Guarantee Corporation, Limited, and others v The Ilford Gas Company [1905] 2 KB 493; (1905-06) XCIII LTR 381; (1904-05) XXI TLR 610 CA Post-entry right of mortgagee to bring action against pre-entry trespasser.

Thompson v Earthy [1951] 2 All ER 235; (1951) 115 JP 407; [1951] 2 KB 596; (1951) 101 LJ 358 HC KBD Deserted wife in family home a trespasser/had no equitable rights to house.

Thompson v Park [1944] 2 All ER 477; [1944] KB 408; (1945) 95 LJ 112; [1944] 113 LJ 561; (1944) 170 LTR 207 CA Injunction available to stop licensee whose licence is revoked committing trespass.

Thornhill v Weeks (1914) 78 JP 154 HC ChD Injunction to restrain trespass where trespassers failed to establish public right of way.

Tideway Investment and Property Holdings Ld v Wellwood; Same v Orton; Same v Jones; Same v Friedentag; Same v Thornley [1952] Ch 791 (also CA); (1952) 96 SJ 579; [1952] 1 TLR 1177 HC ChD Erection of flue pipes on undemised portion of premises was trespass (albeit minor).

Tideway Investment and Property Holdings Ld v Wellwood; Same v Orton; Same v Jones; Same v Friedentag; Same v Thornley [1952] 2 TLR 365 CA Erection of flue pipes on undemised portion of premises was trespass (albeit minor).

Titchmarsh v Royston Water Company Limited (1899-1900) LXXXI LTR 673 HC ChD Injunction granted to halt trespass on private road.

Towcester Gas Co v Beck and Pollitzer (1917) CC Rep VI 42 CyCt Wighbridge-owners had no basis of recovery against driver of heavy vehicle who damaged same when drove over it whilst driving driving on wrong side of the road.

Townend v Askern Coal and Iron Company [1934] Ch 463; (1934) 151 LTR 197; (1933-34) L TLR 200 HC ChD Landowner only allowed ordinary (not punitive) damages for inadvertent trespass committed by mining company which had applied to Railway and Canal Commission for permission to commit.

Truro Corporation v Rowe [1902] 71 LJCL 974 CA Successful claim by corporation against oyster fisherman who trespassed upon foreshore in course of trade.

University of Essex v Ratcliffe (1969) 119 NLJ 1118t CA University graduate who entered university premises could be dealt with as trespasser.

Upjohn v Seymour Estates, Limited (1937-38) LIV TLR 465 HC KBD Damage to party wall in course of demolition of neighbour's buildings did not involve trespass.

Van Diemen's Land Company v Marine Board of Table Cape [1904-07] All ER 1427; [1906] AC 92; [1906] 75 LJPC 28; (1905-06) XCIII LTR 709; (1905-06) XXII TLR 114; (1905-06) 54 WR 498 PC Pre-Crown grant occupation/user of land granted admissible to show land included in grant.

Vaughan v McKenzie [1968] 1 All ER 1154; [1968] Crim LR 265; (1968) 118 NLJ 204t; [1969] 1 QB 557; (1968) 112 SJ 212; [1968] 2 WLR 1133 HC QBD Not assault on bailiff in execution of duty where assault occurred when resident sought to impede bailiff's entry (bailiff in so entering was trespassing).

Videan and another v British Transport Commission [1963] 2 All ER 860; (1963) 113 LJ 529; [1963] 2 QB 650; (1963) 107 SJ 458; [1963] 3 WLR 374 CA Child trespasser could not recover damages for negligence; stationmaster on tracks was reasonably foreseeable so duty of care/damages.

Walkley v Fox (1914) CC Rep III 66 CyCt Prescription Act 1832 deemed inapplicable insofar as Dean Forest Re-afforestation Act 1668 applied so person acquired no right of user after forty years.

Walter v Yalden [1902] 2 KB 304 HC KBD Lease to expire before limitation ran/lessor could enter property on which trespasser with Statute of Limitations title against lessee.

Wandsworth, Wimbledon and Epsom District Gas Company v Grant (1926) 62 LJ ccr70 CyCt Failed action in trespass against gas company which laid gas mains along road without agreement of soil-owner.

Waterhouse v Waterhouse (1906) XCIV LTR 133; (1905-06) 50 SJ 169 HC ChD On father's obtaining injunction against trespass in father's house by his son.

Watson v Murray and Co [1955] 1 All ER 350 HC QBD Sheriff comitted trespass in taking exclusive possession of party's store/in preparing to hold sale in store; were liable in negligence for goods stolen from store.

Webb and another v Sandown Urban District Council (1925) 60 LJ 606 CyCt Person did not by virtue of occasional trespass of cattle upon another's land for under twelve years acquire title to same to exclusion of owner.

Webb v Knight; Hedley v Webb [1901] 70 LJCh 663 HC ChD Action for trespass effected in course of constructing sewage system.

Webster v Bakewell Rural District Council (1916) 80 JP 437 HC ChD Trespass action (for minor trespass) an abuse of process: dismissed with costs.

Wellaway v Courtier [1916-17] All ER 340; (1917) CC Rep VI 94; [1918] 1 KB 200; (1917) 52 LJ 451; [1918] 87 LJCL 299; (1918) 118 LTR 256; (1917-18) 62 SJ 161; (1917-18) XXXIV TLR 115; (1917) WN (I) 368 HC KBD Crop-purchaser can maintain action in trespass.

White v St Albans City and District Council [1990] TLR 196 CA On extent of liability of occupier towards trespasser.

Whittaker v Bailey (1925) 60 LJ 521 CyCt Where house sold and conveyance did not mention existing right of way use of the way held to pass to buyer of house.

Willcox v Kettell [1937] 1 All ER 222; (1937) 83 LJ 58 HC ChD Leave to underpin wall did not prevent extension of foundations thereof onto other's property being trespass.

Williams v Williams and others (1937) 81 SJ 435 CA Failed action for trespass which allegedly arose in course of execution by sherrif's officer of court order for possession after action for possession brought by landlord.

Williams-Ellis v Cobb and others (1935) 152 LTR 133 CA On providing adequate of evidence of public user so as to prove that certain land was public highway and so no trespass had been committed.

Wiltshire County Council and others v Frazer and others (1985) 129 SJ 871 HC QBD On granting writ of restitution in respect of persons trespassing once more following possession order having been made.

Woollerton and Wilson Ltd v Richard Costain Ltd [1970] 1 All ER 483; (1969) 119 NLJ 1093t; (1970) 114 SJ 170; [1970] 1 WLR 411 HC ChD Postponed injunction granted against party guilty of trespass when swang crane to and fro.

Wuta-Ofei v Danquah [1961] 3 All ER 596; [1955] Crim LR 806 PC Little evidence needed for person to establish possession against other who never enjoyed title to land.

TRESPASS (highway)

Fielden v Cox (1905-06) XXII TLR 411 HC ChD Trespass injunction against insect-catchers refused given trivial nature of trespasses.

Hanscombe v Bedfordshire County Council [1938] Ch 944; [1938] 107 LJCh 433 HC ChD Highway authority not authorised under Highway Acts 1864/1835 to trespass by laying pipes in ditch without permission from adjacent landowners.

Hue v Whiteley (1928) 66 LJ 304; (1929) 98 LJCh 227; (1929) 140 LTR 531; (1928) WN (I) 257 HC ChD On inferring right of way from traditional user of pathway/roadway (in action for injunction to restrain alleged trespass).

Randall v Tarrant [1955] 1 All ER 600; (1955) 105 LJ 168; (1955) 99 SJ 184; [1955] 1 WLR 255 CA Driver of moving vehicle must show not negligent where strikes obvious non-moving vehicle; trespass by driver in field adjoining highway did not mean trespass/nuisance on highway.

Rochford v Essex County Council [1916] 85 LJP 281 HC PDAD Raising of footpath so that covered part of previously existing fence was trespass.

Webb v Baldwin (1911) 75 JP 564 HC ChD On proving dedication of highway to public (and so no trespass).

TRESPASS (husband and wife)

Shipman v Shipman (1923-24) XL TLR 348 HC ChD Injunction granted excluding husband from wife's property where effect of husband's being there was to reduce value of property.

TRESPASS (landlord and tenant)

Burrows v Brent London Borough Council (1996) TLR 4/11/96 HL Agreement whereby landlord would not seek posession order if 'tenant' complied with certain conditions meant tenant was a tolerated trespasser.

Cruise v Terrell [1922] 91 LJCL 499; (1922) 126 LTR 750 CA Actual damages may be claimed in trespass action by statutory tenant against landlord who re-takes possession of premises.

Daphne v Bailey (1919) CC Rep VIII 66 CyCt Landlord who after giving tenant notice to quit forcibly entered premises and threw tenant's furniture into street held to be liable in damages for trespass.

Delaney v TP Smith, Ltd [1946] LJNCCR 16 CyCt Tenant enjoying tenancy under parol agreement can bring trespass action if improperly evicted.

Frederick Betts (Limited) v Pickford (Limited) [1906] 2 Ch 87; (1905-06) XXII TLR 315 HC ChD Use of non-party walls as party walls could be trespass.

Grunnell v Welch [1905] 2 KB 650; (1905-06) 54 WR 216 HC KBD Trespass ab initio in proceeding under first trespass warrant.

Grunnell v Welch (1905-06) 54 WR 581 CA Trespass ab initio in proceeding under first trespass warrant.

Gunter v Davis (1924) WN (I) 288 HC KBD Order for ejectment of trespasser (costs to landlord).

Hope Brothers, Limited v Cowan [1913] 2 Ch 312 HC ChD Was not trespass for lessee to put flower boxes on outside of outer wall of leased office.

Jeeves v Sutton [1934] LJNCCR 288 CyCt Was trespass for owner of premises not to allow statutory tenant return to premises.

Jeffrey v Sherry [1947] LJNCCR 29 CyCt Rooms held to have been lawfully sub-let by tenant so was no trespass.

Northumberland Hotels, Ltd v Turnbull [1943] LJNCCR 50 CyCt Tenant not liable for trespass where remains in property after date specified in invalid notice to quit.

Perera v Vandiyar (1953) 97 SJ 332; [1953] 1 WLR 672 CA Landlord's cutting off gas and electricity not tortious (not trespass).

Phelps v Mayor, Commonalty, and Citizens of the City of London [1916] 2 Ch 255; (1916) 114 LTR 1200 HC ChD On construction of lease defendants found not to have committed trespass in their actions.

Smith v Abraham, Hague and Mew, Langton and Co, Ltd [1937] LJNCCR 205 CyCt Failed action for trespass by licensee entitled to supply refreshments at dance hall against owners/tenants of same who notwithstanding licence arrangement with plaintiff obtained occasional excise licences and sold alcohol to patrons of dance hall.

Thompson v Ward (1953) 97 SJ 352; [1953] 2 WLR 1042 CA Tenant who had abandoned premises and lost entitlement to possession could not sustain trespass action against occupier.

Walker v Trustees of Upwell Branch of Independent Order of Oddfellows and Overland [1934] LJNCCR 426 CyCt Failed action for trespass against landlord entering onto property following non-payment of rent (not estopped by letter had sent from entering onto said property).

White and another v Eastaugh (1921) CC Rep X 11 CyCt Order for possession available against tenant who through refusal to quit property upon cessation of tenancy renderes self a trespasser.

TRESPASS (licensee)

Coates v Wembley Stadium, Ltd and another (1940) 84 SJ 370 HC KBD Damages for excessive use of force in eviction from premises licensee who through his conduct converted himself into a trespasser.

Young v Edward Box and Co, Limited [1951] 1 TLR 789 CA Person allowed by foreman to be carried in defendant's lorry by their employee was licensee not trespasser.

TRESPASS (local authority)

Andrews v Abertillery Urban District Council (1911) 75 JP 449; (1911) 104 LTR 335 HC ChD Not trespass for council to place electricity standard on land owned by plaintiff but dedicated to public.

Andrews v Abertillery Urban District Council (1911) WN (I) 133 CA Was trespass for council to place electricity standard on land owned by plaintiff but dedicated to public.

Consett Urban District Council v Crawford (1903) 67 JP 309; (1902-03) 47 SJ 549; (1902-03) XIX TLR 508; (1902-03) 51 WR 669 HC KBD Urban council members had no right to enter premises to check whether nuisance abated unless owner permitted same or magistrate ordered it (Public Health Act 1875, s 102).

Escott v The Mayor, &c, of Newport [1904] 2 KB 369; [1904] 73 LJCL 693; (1904) XC LTR 348; (1903-04) XX TLR 158 HC KBD Failed action for trespass against local corporation for erecting tramway pole in plaintiff's soil.

Grant v Derwent (1929) 93 JP 113; (1929) 67 LJ 12; (1929) 98 LJCh 70; (1929) 140 LTR 330 CA Council's trespass in laying sewage pipe did not render person who requested council to connect house to sewer liable for trespass.

Grant v Derwent (1929) 93 JP 1; (1928) 97 LJCh 434 HC ChD Council not liable for trespass in laying sewage pipe as plaintiff's rights over soil subject to those of council in respect of sewer.

Isgoed-Jones v Llanrwst Urban District Council [1911] 1 Ch 393; (1911) 75 JP 68; (1911) 80 LJCh 145; (1910-11) 103 LTR 751; (1910-11) XXVII TLR 133 HC ChD Riparian owner aside natural stream is entitled to have it flow past in its natural state: injunction to prevent council discharging untreated sewage into stream.

London and North-Western Railway v Westminster Corporation [1902] 71 LJCh 34; (1901-02) 50 WR 268 HC ChD Injunction to restrain trespass by local authority in erection of public toilets.

Mayor, &c, of Westminster v London and North-Western Railway Co (1905-06) 54 WR 129 HL Injunction to restrain trespass by local authority in erection of public toilets.

Sheringham Urban District Council v Holsey (1903-04) XX TLR 402 HC ChD District council could sue for damages where post was removed and public path used as carriageway.

TRESPASS (necessity)

Rigby and another v Chief Constable of Northamptonshire [1985] 2 All ER 985; (1985) 129 SJ 832; [1985] 1 WLR 1242 HC QBD Bona fide policy decision unimpeachable; necessity a defence to trespass if defendant's negligence did not give rise to necessity; negligent to fire CS canister when no fire equipment.

TRESPASS (negligence)

Periscinotti v Brighton West Pier, Ltd (1961) 105 SJ 526 CA Pier managers not liable to trespasser injured in diving from pier diving board.

TRESPASS (nuisance)

Barker v Herbert [1911-13] All ER 509; (1911) 75 JP 481; [1911] 2 KB 633; (1911) 80 LJCL 1329; (1911-12) 105 LTR 349; (1910-11) XXVII TLR 488 CA Owner of premises adjoining highway not liable for nuisance caused by trespasser unless permitted its continuance.

Barker v Herbert (1911) 75 JP 355; (1910-11) XXVII TLR 252 HC KBD Owner of premises adjoining highway not liable for injury not directly stemming from nuisance caused by trespasser.

Sedleigh-Denfield v O'Callaghan and Others [1940] AC 880; [1940] 3 All ER 349; (1940) 90 LJ 27; [1940] 109 LJCL 893; (1941) 164 LTR 72; (1940) 84 SJ 657; (1939-40) LVI TLR 887; (1940) WN (I) 260 HL On 'continuing'/'adopting' nuisance; party presumed to have known of act of trespasser and so were liable for nuisance resulting therefrom where to took no action in relation thereto.

TRESPASS (police)

Lamb v Director of Public Prosecutions (1990) 154 JP 381 HC QBD Trespassing police officer was nonetheless acting in course of duty when stayed in place to prevent expected breach of the peace.

McVittie v Turner [1916] 85 LJKB 23; (1915-16) 113 LTR 982; (1915-16) 60 SJ 238 CA Secondary motives of police officer entering theatre pursuant to Cinematograph Act 1909 for valid purpose did no render entry a trespass.

Valentine v Jackson [1972] 1 WLR 528 HC QBD Police officer to have suspicion that crime committed/about to be committed before may insist on entering licensed premises under Licensing Act 1964, s 186(1).

TRESPASS (rail)

Arnold v Morgan [1908-10] All ER 392 HC KBD magistrates' jurisdiction to hear trespass action ended upon public right of way being established.

TRESPASS (reasonable force)

Farrell v Secretary of State for Defence [1980] 1 All ER 166; (1980) 70 Cr App R 224; (1980) 124 SJ 133; [1980] 1 WLR 172 HL Defence of reasonable force under Criminal Law Act (NI) 1967, s 3, open to those in immediate situation requiring force.

TRESPASS (road traffic)

London Electric Supply Corporation, Ltd v Alexander [1942] LJNCCR 49 CyCt Failed action in negligence/trespass against driver who struck lamp post after swerved to avoid dog on road.

Morris v Beardmore (1980) 71 Cr App R 256 (also HL); [1979] RTR 393; (1979) 123 SJ 300; [1979] 3 WLR 93 HC QBD Request to take breath test valid though police officer trespassing on property of person requested at time of request.

Morris v Beardmore [1980] 2 All ER 753; [1981] AC 446; (1980) 71 Cr App R 256 (also HC QBD); [1979] Crim LR 394; (1980) 144 JP 331; (1980) 130 NLJ 707; [1980] RTR 321; (1980) 124 SJ 512; [1980] 3 WLR 283 HL Request to take breath test invalid where police officer trespassing on property of person requested at time of request.

TRESPASS (school)

Blencowe v Northamptonshire County Council [1907] 76 LJCh 276 HC ChD Non-provided school managers appointed under Education Act 1902 unable to bring action for trespass on school.

TRESPASS (trespass to goods)

Elliott v Yates and another (1899-1900) 44 SJ 591 CA Was lawful to levy distress after financial year ended for taxes that became owing during the last financial year.

Horner v Dents (Lim) (1917) CC Rep VI 2 CyCt Nominal damages for unauthorised removal of company name from watch by company whose name had featured on watch/to whom watch entrusted for repair.

Owen and Smith (trading as Nuagin Car Sevice) v Reo Motors (Britain), Ltd [1934] All ER 734; (1934) 151 LTR 274 CA Considerable (but not exemplary) damages awarded for trespass to goods (bailor entry and seizure absent notice).

Wilson v Lombank Ltd [1963] 1 All ER 740; (1963) 113 LJ 249; [1963] 1 WLR 1294 HC QBD Person taking property thought to be own and which later surrendered to true owner liable to person from whom took property who honestly thought had good title to property.

TRESPASS (trespass to person)

Farrell v Secretary of State for Defence [1980] 1 All ER 166; (1980) 70 Cr App R 224; (1980) 124 SJ 133; [1980] 1 WLR 172 HL Defence of reasonable force under Criminal Law Act (NI) 1967, s 3, open to those in immediate situation requiring force.

Fowler v Lanning [1959] 1 All ER 290; (1959) 109 LJ 201; [1959] 1 QB 426; (1959) 103 SJ 157 HC QBD No trespass to person if injury was not negligent and was unintended (though foreseeable): here not proved.

Freeman v The Home Office [1983] 3 All ER 589; (1983) 133 NLJ 726; [1984] QB 525; (1983) 127 SJ 825; [1983] TLR 360; [1984] 2 WLR 130 HC QBD Where drugs given for medical reason prison doctor acts as doctor not disciplinarian; informed consent irrelevant to battery.

Lane v Holloway [1967] 3 All ER 129; (1967) 117 NLJ 731t; [1968] 1 QB 379; (1967) 111 SJ 655; [1967] 3 WLR 1003 CA Disproportionate reaction to provocative conduct precludes ex turpi causa non oritur actio; provocation not ground for reducing damages.

Re F (1989) 133 SJ 265 CA Order that sterilisation operation on mentally retarded individual who had formed sexual liaison with another mental patient would not be unlawful.

Re F (1989) 133 SJ 785 HL Approval of order that sterilisation operation on mentally retarded individual who had formed sexual liaison with another mental patient would not be unlawful; on whether/when such orders necessary.

Robertson v The Balmain New Ferry Company (Limited) (1909-10) XXVI TLR 143 PC Use of reasonable force to impede person trying to leave wharf without making required payment was not assault.

T v T and another [1988] Fam 53; [1988] 1 FLR 400; [1988] 2 WLR 189 HC FamD Abortion/sterilisation operation on mentally handicapped adult allowed despite absence of consent.

W v Meah; D v Meah and another [1986] 1 All ER 935; (1986) 136 NLJ 165 HC QBD Damages for trespass primarily compensatory.

Wilson v Pringle [1986] 2 All ER 440; (1986) 136 NLJ 416; [1987] QB 237; (1986) 130 SJ 468; [1986] 3 WLR 1 CA Intended hostile act not intent to injure necessary for trespass to person to occur.

TROVER (general)

Eastern Construction Company, Limited v (1) National Trust Company, Limited and Others; (2) Therese Schmidt and Others; Attorney-General for the Province of Ontario (Intervenant) [1914] AC 197; [1914] 83 LJPC 122; (1914) 110 LTR 321 PC Not liable for trespass by person with whom have contract but who is not servant/agent; Crown patentee/licensee a bailee for Crown of trees wrongfully felled so could not sue fellers for trover/detinue.

Rice v Reed [1900] 69 LJCL 33; (1899-1900) LXXXI LTR 410; [1900] 1 QB 54 CA Did not waive right to bring action against second tortfeasor by settling action with first tortfeasor.

WAIVER OF TORT (general)

Verschures Creameries, Limited v Hull and Netherlands Steamship Company, Limited [1921] 2 KB 608; [1922] 91 LJCL 39; (1921) 125 LTR 165 CA Owner having sought and received judgment against customer could not later seek damages from negligent forwarding agent.

WRONGFUL APPROPRIATION (general)

Bank of England v Gibson and others [1994] TLR 253 HC QBD Standard of proof in action for wrongful appropriation of money is the civil standard.

ALPHABETICAL INDEX

AA King (Contractors) Ltd, London Electricity Board and Pitchers, Lait v (1975) 125 NLJ 432 HC QBD Person who damaged electric cable plates but did not tell Electricity Board was liable along with later worker's employer for injury that followed from damage (Electricity Board not liable).

A and S Hillman, Ltd, Dollman and another v [1941] 1 All ER 355; (1942) 92 LJ 91 CA Fat falling from butcher's shop to pavement causing person to slip was nuisance/negligence.

A and S Hillman, Ltd, Dollman and another v (1941) 85 SJ 57 HC KBD Fat falling from butcher's shop to pavement causing person to slip was nuisance/negligence.

A and W Hemphill Ld, Connelly v (1949) WN (I) 191 HL Failed action in negligence against driver who drove over individual's foot.

A Ogden and Sons (Excavations) Ltd, Howard Marine and Dredging Co Ltd v [1978] 2 All ER 1134; [1978] QB 574; (1978) 122 SJ 48; [1978] 2 WLR 515 CA Misrepresentation acted upon actionable unless misrepresentor has reasonable belief statement true; barge owners/charterers under duty of care when giving advice on specialist matter.

A Reyrolle and Co Ltd, Moeliker v [1977] 1 All ER 9; [1977] 1 WLR 132 CA Damages for loss of earning capacity to employed only if real prospect of job loss; how to measure loss of earning capacity.

Abbott v Heyman (1925) 60 LJ 1055 CyCt Successful action for damages for nuisances occasioned by removal of door, said removal interfering with exercise of right of way.

Abbott v Isham and others (1921) 85 JP 30; [1921] LJCL 309; (1921) 124 LTR 734; (1920-21) XXXVII TLR 7 HC KBD Successful action against school managers for personal injuries suffered by headmaster when defective boiler burst.

Abbott v Refuge Assurance Co, Ltd [1961] 3 All ER 1074; (1961) 111 LJ 836; [1962] 1 QB 432; (1961) 105 SJ 949 CA Desire to recover defrauded money not evidence of malice; prosecuting counsel owe court duty to withdraw baseless cases: that did not showed not malicious; all circumstances including counsel's opinion on taking action showed not malicious prosecution.

Abbott, Dunster v [1953] 2 All ER 1572; (1953) 103 LJ 828; (1954) 98 SJ 8 CA Person canvassing for business a licensee: here duty of care to licensee not breached as bridge over ditch not concealed danger/no negligence as regards nighttime lighting.

Abertillery Urban District Council, Andrews v (1911) 75 JP 449; (1911) 104 LTR 335 HC ChD Not trespass for council to place electricity standard on land owned by plaintiff but dedicated to public.

Abertillery Urban District Council, Andrews v (1911) WN (I) 133 CA Was trespass for council to place electricity standard on land owned by plaintiff but dedicated to public.

Abraham, Hague and Mew, Langton and Co, Ltd, Smith v [1937] LJNCCR 205 CyCt Failed action for trespass by licensee entitled to supply refreshments at dance hall against owners/tenants of same who notwithstanding licence arrangement with plaintiff obtained occasional excise licences and sold alcohol to patrons of dance hall.

Abraham, Performance Cars Ltd v [1961] 3 All ER 413; [1955] Crim LR 748; (1961) 111 LJ 644; [1962] 1 QB 33 CA Cannot recover for damage not resulting from tort.

Abrahams, Whymark v (1922) CC Rep XI 58 CyCt Owner of house not liable for injury occurring to passer-by when brick fell from defective chimney unless proved that owner let house with defect/was under contractual duty to keep chimney in repair.

Abrahamson, Kavanagh v (1964) 108 SJ 320 HC QBD Doctor not negligent in prescribing tablets for longtime patient whom did not see (wife visited and described symptoms).

Allbev, Taittinger v (1993) 143 NLJ 332; [1993] TLR 62 HC ChD 'Elderflower Champagne', a non-alcoholic, carbonated drink produced and marketed in England unlikely to adversely impinge on goodwill in name 'champagne' of real champagne producers.

Allbev Ltd and others, Taittinger and others v [1994] 4 All ER 75; [1993] TLR 358 CA 'Elderflower Champagne', a non-alcoholic, carbonated drink produced and marketed in England could adversely impinge on goodwill in name 'champagne' of real champagne producers.

Allen and others v Jambo Holdings Ltd and others [1980] 2 All ER 502; (1980) 124 SJ 742 CA Mareva injunction available in personal injuries action.

Allen and others, Prole v [1950] 1 All ER 476 Assizes Club steward liable to club member for injury caused upon his doing his duties negligently.

Allen Fairhead and Sons, Limited, News of the World, Limited v [1931] 2 Ch 402; (1931) 100 LJCh 394; (1932) 146 LTR 11 HC ChD On gauging degree of nuisance (if nuisance there is) where ancient light reduced by new construction.

Allen v Bloomsbury Health Authority and another [1993] 1 All ER 651 HC QBD Damages available for general discomfort; cost of upkeep until adulthood and, if necessary, additional anxiety caused by unwanted pregnancy following sterilisation.

Allen v Gulf Oil Refining Ltd [1981] 1 All ER 353; [1981] AC 1001; (1981) 131 NLJ 140; (1981) 125 SJ 101; [1981] 2 WLR 188 HL Statutory immunity for activities at oil refinery of which nuisance inevitable consequence.

Allen v Sir Alfred McAlpine and Sons, Ltd; Bostic v Bermondsey and Southwark Group Hospital Management Committee; Sternberg and another v Hammond and another [1968] 1 All ER 543; [1968] 2 QB 229; (1963) 107 SJ 478; [1968] 2 WLR 366 CA Action can be immediately dismissed for delay leaving only action against solicitor for negligence.

Allen v Waters and Co [1924-35] All ER 671; [1935] 1 KB 200; [1935] LJNCCA 86; (1935) 152 LTR 179; (1934-35) LI TLR 50; (1934) WN (I) 201 CA Damages untouched though included amount for debt recoverable from but unpaid by person awarded damages.

Allen, Gaynor v [1959] 2 All ER 644; [1959] Crim LR 786; (1959) 123 JP 413; (1959) 109 LJ 441; [1959] 2 QB 403; (1959) 103 SJ 677 HC QBD Police motorcyclist owes duty of care in negligence though driving at speed in course of duty.

Allford v Maton [1936] LJNCCR 167 CyCt Person who had cattle driven down road several times each day liable for damage occasioned by cattle to another's hedge as did not exercise user of highway reasonably.

Alliance Building Society v Varma [1949] Ch 724; (1949) LXV TLR 576 CA Court could (under RSC Or 55, r 5A) order delivery up of mortgaged premises to mortgagee though person in occupation a trespasser.

Allied Arab Bank Ltd v Hajjar and others (No 2) [1988] QB 944; (1988) 132 SJ 1148; [1988] 3 WLR 533 HC QBD Tort of conspiracy only occurs if injury to victim was directly intended by conspirators — if (as here) was side-effect of alleged conspiracy principally intended to benefit others (not injure victim) tort of conspiracy does not arise.

Allied Maples Group Ltd v Simmons and Simmons (a firm) [1995] 4 All ER 907; (1995) 145 NLJ 1646; [1995] 1 WLR 1602 CA If plaintiff's loss on foot of negligent advice rests on imagined action of another and is a substantial chance that other would have acted to confer benefit on or avoid risk to plaintiff the evaluation of that chance is for judge determining quantum.

Allison v Corby District Council [1980] RTR 111 HC QBD Local authority not liable in negligence for failure to catch stray dogs (whose presence caused road accident) nor for failure to maintain highway.

Allsop v Church of England Newspaper Ltd and others [1972] 2 All ER 26; (1972) 122 NLJ 129t; [1972] 2 QB 161; (1972) 116 SJ 222; [1972] 2 WLR 600 CA In all cases desirable that plaintiff explain defamatory meaning and in some cases essential.

Allsopp, Paxon v (1971) 115 SJ 446 CA Stay of action in light of ten year delay since settlement offer made.

Anderson and others, Arbon v; De Laessoe v Anderson and others (1942-43) LIX TLR 149 HC KBD Non-liability of Secretary of State for actions under wartime detention legislation.

Anderson and others, Arbon v [1942] 1 All ER 264 CA Secretary of State not liable for torts of officials (unless expressly authorises them).

Anderson and others, Budd v (1941) 91 LJ 294; (1941) 85 SJ 405; (1942-43) LIX TLR 341 HC KBD On procedural irregularities in detention under wartime detention legislation (Defence (General) Regulations 1939, reg 18B).

Anderson v Calvert (1907-08) XXIV TLR 399 CA On considerations for jury when assessing damages for libel.

Anderson v Francis (1906) WN (I) 160 HC ChD Injunction to restrain erection of building in such form as would cause nuisance through interference with ancient windows.

Anderson v The Guinness Trust [1949] 1 All ER 530; (1949) LXV TLR 679; (1949) WN (I) 127 HC KBD Wife keeping house for tenant a licensee (not invitee) of landlords.

Anderton (Police Complaints Authority intervening), Taylor v [1995] 2 All ER 420; (1995) 139 SJ LB 66; [1995] 1 WLR 447 CA Where malicious prosecution allegation met by heavily documented defence trial without jury allowed.

Anderton, Wright and another v (1909) C LTR 123; (1908-09) 53 SJ 135; (1908-09) XXV TLR 156; (1908) WN (I) 258 HC KBD Relationship of innkeeper and guest (with liability that entails for former) begins where is intent to supply and to take accommodation.

Andmac Roofing Co and others, McArdle v [1966] 3 All ER 241; (1965-66) 116 NLJ 1404 Assizes Two sub-contractors owed duty of care to worker and were liable in negligence for leaving matter to others.

Andmac Roofing Co and others, McArdle v [1967] 1 All ER 583; (1967) 111 SJ 37; [1967] 1 WLR 356 CA Main contractor liable for (acts of sub-contractors leading to) foreseeable injury of workman.

Andreae v Selfridge and Company, Ltd [1936] 2 All ER 1413; (1936) 82 LJ 174; (1936) 80 SJ 792 HC ChD Noise/dust/grit of construction site was nuisance despite proper use of tools as was done without thought for neighbours.

Andreae v Selfridge and Company, Limited [1938] Ch 1; [1938] 107 LJCh 126; (1937) 157 LTR 317; (1937) 81 SJ 525 CA Limited damages available in nuisance for excesses of noise/dust/grit of construction site.

Andrew, Werry v (1951) 101 LJ 289 CyCt Successful plea by motor cycle rider against cattle-owner whose workers acted negligently when driving cattle from field onto highway so causing accident involving motor cyclist.

Andrews and another, Patience v [1983] RTR 447; [1982] TLR 574 HC QBD Damages reduced by 25% where passenger injured in collision not wearing seat-belt.

Andrews v Abertillery Urban District Council (1911) 75 JP 449; (1911) 104 LTR 335 HC ChD Not trespass for council to place electricity standard on land owned by plaintiff but dedicated to public.

Andrews v Abertillery Urban District Council (1911) WN (I) 133 CA Was trespass for council to place electricity standard on land owned by plaintiff but dedicated to public.

Andrews v Freeborough [1966] 2 All ER 721; (1965-66) 116 NLJ 1032; [1967] 1 QB 1; (1966) 110 SJ 407; [1966] 3 WLR 342 CA Damages for loss of expectation of life (despite victim's coma)/injuries suffered available to administrator of deceased victim's estate.

Andrews v Hendley (1914) CC Rep III 54 CyCt Person harbouring dog which bit another while not being properly kept under restraint was liable for personal injuries sustained by person bitten.

Andrews v Home Flats, Ltd [1945] 2 All ER 698 CA Landlord liable as bailee for reward for operating negligent system of safeguarding bailed goods.

Andrews v Hopkinson [1956] 3 All ER 422; [1957] 1 QB 229; [1956] 3 WLR 732 Assizes Non-purchaser could rely on warranty that induced hire-purchase arrangement; damages for personal injuries for breach of warranty that was safe car; damages for negligence in delivering unsafe car when defects reasonably discoverable by supplier.

Anns and others v Walcroft Property Co Ltd and another [1976] QB 882; (1976) 120 SJ 216; [1976] 2 WLR 512 CA Cause of action from time building defects discovered/ought to have been discovered.

Ansell v McDermott and another (1993) 143 NLJ 363 CA Police not under duty of care to warn motorists of dangers discovered but not caused by or within realms of responsibility of police.

Anselm Oldling and Sons, Ltd, Lovelidge v [1967] 1 All ER 459 HC QBD Employers negligent where injury caused to workman not properly dressed (latter contributorily negligent).

Anson, The Denaby and Cadeby Main Collieries (Limited) v (1909-10) XXVI TLR 310 HC KBD Was trespass for coal hulk to be permanently moored in harbour without permission.

Antcliffe v Gloucester Health Authority [1992] TLR 224 CA On payment of damages in medical negligence cases.

Anthony and ors v Wright and ors (1994) 144 NLJ 1452i HC ChD Investors who did not act on auditor's work could not sue auditor for non-discovery of misuse of trust money.

Anthony v Midland Railway Company (1909) C LTR 117; (1908-09) XXV TLR 98 HC KBD Passenger injured by stepping from train which overshot platform before could be warned could not recover damages in negligence.

Anthony, Stubbs v (1948) 98 LJ 94 CyCt Defendant liable in negligence for damage occasioned by collapse of his chimney stack onto adjoining property of another.

Antifyre, Ltd, Cunard and another v [1932] All ER 558; [1933] 1 KB 551; (1934) 103 LJCL 321; (1933) 148 LTR 287; (1932-33) XLIX TLR 184 HC KBD Negligence for failure to take steps in relation to overhanging guttering that reasonable man would do in the circumstances.

Apley Estates Co and others v De Bernales and others [1946] 2 All ER 338; (1947) 91 SJ 12 HC ChD Agreement with one joint tortfeasor not accord and satisfaction unless so intended.

Apley Estates Co and others v De Bernales and others [1947] 1 All ER 213; [1947] Ch 217; [1947] 116 LJR 705; (1947) 176 LTR 182; (1947) LXIII TLR 71; (1947) WN (I) 13 CA Agreeing not to sue one joint tortfeasor does not release others.

Appah v Parncliffe Investments, Ltd (1964) 114 LJ 288 CA Landlord liable in negligence for not providing licensee for reward with key to mortice lock which resulted in subsequent loss through burglary.

Arbon v Anderson and others; De Laessoe v Anderson and others (1942-43) LIX TLR 149 HC KBD Non-liability of Secretary of State for actions under wartime detention legislation.

Arbon v Anderson and others [1942] 1 All ER 264 CA Secretary of State not liable for torts of officials (unless expressly authorises them).

Arbuthnott v Feltrim; Deeny v Gooda Walker; Henderson v Syndicates (Merrett) [1993] TLR 667 CA On extent of duty of care owed by managing/members' agents at Lloyd's towards names.

Arch Engineering Co (Newport) Ltd and another, Griffiths v [1968] 3 All ER 217; (1968) 118 NLJ 957 Assizes Negligent where foreseeable risk of injury.

Archbold, Hill v [1967] 2 WLR 1180 HC QBD Master (union) could support servant (officials) in libel action brought against latter arising from their employment.

Archer v Catton and Co, Ltd [1954] 1 All ER 896; (1954) 104 LJ 251; (1954) 98 SJ 337; [1954] 1 WLR 775 HC QBD Six-year limitation applied.

Archer v Moss; Applegate v Moss [1971] 1 All ER 747; [1971] 1 QB 406; (1970) 114 SJ 971; [1971] 2 WLR 541 CA Fraud in Limitation Act is equitable fraud; assessment of damages for breach of warranty.

Arding and Hobbs, Ltd, Turner v [1949] 2 All ER 911 HC KBD Vegetable matter on shop floor an unusual danger in consequence of which were found liable to invitee.

Arding, Foulger v [1901] 70 LJK/QB 580 HC KBD On covenant in lease necessary to render tenant liable for expense of abating nuisance occasioned by structural defect in leased premises.

Arding, Foulger v [1902] 71 LJCL 499 CA On covenant in lease necessary to render tenant liable for expense of abating nuisance occasioned by structural defect in leased premises.

Attorney-General v Nissan [1969] 1 All ER 629; [1970] AC 179; (1969) 119 NLJ 250; (1969) 113 SJ 207; [1969] 2 WLR 926 HL That acts complained of were 'acts of state' not defence in tort action.

Attorney-General v Roe [1914-15] All ER 1190; [1915] 1 Ch 235; [1915] 84 LJCh 322 HC ChD Party liable to fence off from highway adjoining area in which dangerous excavation work being undertaken.

Attorney-General v Scott (1903-04) 48 SJ 623; (1903-04) XX TLR 630 HC KBD Perpetual injunction to restrain use of traction engine to carry stone along highway refused (but no use of road for one month until council undertook necessary reconstruction work).

Attorney-General v Scott (1904-05) 49 SJ 221; (1904-05) XXI TLR 211 CA Use of traction engine to carry stone along highway did by level of damage to/obstruction of road constitute nuisance.

Attorney-General v Till (1909) 44 LJ 130; [1909] 78 LJKB 708; (1909) C LTR 275 CA Negligence in delivery does not open one to prosecution for refusal/neglect to deliver taxable income statement pursuant to the Income Tax Act 1842, s 55.

Attorney-General v Wilcox [1938] Ch 934; (1938) 86 LJ 44; [1938] 107 LJCh 425 HC ChD On nuisance through trivial obstruction of public path: injunction on erection of posts on towpath.

Attorney-General, Bright v (1971) 121 NLJ 178t; (1971) 115 SJ 226 CA Unusually action in negligence arising from unevenness in road surface caused by council workers was successful.

Attorney-General, Nissan v [1968] 1 QB 286 (also CA); (1967) 111 SJ 195; [1967] 3 WLR 109 HC QBD That acts complained of were 'acts of state' not defence in tort action.

Attorney-General, Nissan v [1968] 1 QB 286 (also HC QBD); (1967) 117 NLJ 834t; (1967) 111 SJ 544; [1967] 3 WLR 1044 CA That acts complained of were 'acts of state' not defence in tort action.

Attree v Baker [1983] TLR 686 HC QBD Personal injuries damages increased in light of tax payable on same.

Attwood v Chapman [1914-15] All ER 1034; (1915) 79 JP 65; [1914] 3 KB 275; (1914) 49 LJ 381; [1914] 83 LJKB 1666; (1914-15) 111 LTR 726; (1913-14) XXX TLR 596; (1914) WN (I) 269 HC KBD Private party's objection to granting of liquor licence not privileged.

Atwill v Plymouth and Stonehouse Gas Light and Coke Co [1934] LJNCCR 361 CyCt Person who lit match following gas leak and so herself caused explosion could not recover damages in nuisance (and was no negligence on part of gas suppliers proved).

Audigier, James v (1932) 74 LJ 407; (1932-33) XLIX TLR 36; (1932) WN (I) 250 CA Dismissal of appeal over questions that were asked in running-down case over earlier accident in which defendant involved.

Audigier, James v (1931-32) XLVIII TLR 600; (1932) WN (I) 181 HC KBD On appropriate questions which may be put to driver in 'running down' case.

Austin (Reginald) v Mirror Newspapers Ltd [1986] AC 299; (1986) 130 SJ 13; [1986] 2 WLR 57 PC Qualified privilege could (under Defamation Act 1974, s 22) attach to newspaper report critical of rugby league team trainer but not here as journalist had not taken reasonable care regarding accuracy of facts.

Austin Lifts, Ltd and others, Smith v [1959] 1 All ER 81 HL Occupiers liable to invitee for failure to take reasonable care to maintain safe premises; employers also liable in negligence.

Australian Bank of Commerce Limited v Perel and others (1926) 135 LTR 586 PC Failed appeal by bank in action brought against bank inter alia for conversion of cheques (failed to establish course of business which had greater effect than written instructions given).

Australian Consolidated Press, Ltd v Uren [1967] 3 All ER 523; [1969] 1 AC 590; (1967) 117 NLJ 1166; (1967) 111 SJ 741; [1967] 3 WLR 1338 PC Permissible that Rookes v Barnard not be applied to awarding of exemplary libel damages in Australia.

Australian Knitting Mills, Grant v [1935] All ER 209; (1935) 80 LJ 378; [1936] 105 LJPC 6; (1935) 79 SJ 815; (1935-36) LII TLR 38 PC Where product reached consumer in same state that left manufacturer, latter liable for injury caused by latent defect undiscoverable by reasonable scrutiny.

B Davies and Son, Ltd, Gayler and Pope, Ltd v [1924] All ER 94; [1924] 2 KB 75; (1924) 59 LJ 282; [1924] 93 LJCL 702; (1924) 131 LTR 507; (1923-24) 68 SJ 685; (1923-24) XL TLR 591; (1924) WN (I) 158 HC KBD Owner liable for damage by stray horse where was negligent — not for trespass of horse per se.

B Goodman, Ltd, Konskier v [1927] All ER 187; [1928] 1 KB 421; (1927) 64 LJ 403; (1928) 97 LJCL 263; (1928) 138 LTR 481 CA Liability in trespass not negligence for leaving waste materials on roof of adjoining property resulting in damage.

B Liggett (Liverpool), Limited v Barclays Bank, Limited [1928] 1 KB 48; (1927) 137 LTR 443; (1926-27) XLIII TLR 449 HC KBD Action for negligent payment of cheque.

B v Islington Health Authority [1991] 1 All ER 825; [1991] 1 FLR 483; [1991] 1 QB 638; [1990] TLR 725; [1991] 2 WLR 501 HC QBD Negligence does not require simultaneous duty of care/breach of that duty.

B v Miller and Co [1996] 3 FCR 435; [1996] 2 FLR 23 HC QBD Not collateral attack on order of competent court for plaintiff to bring negligence action against solicitors who advised her in ancillary relief/consent order proceedings.

Bach and Johnson, Ltd v Cowan and another (1969) 113 SJ 38 HC ChD Passing off injunction granted to owners of name 'Pembridge Gardens Hotel' against owners of name 'Pembridge Hotel'.

Bache and another, Saville v (1969) 119 NLJ 226t; (1969) 113 SJ 228 CA Person driving with undipped headlights (and who failed to explain why) held one-third liable for accident which resulted from his lights dazzling another driver.

Bagley and Co Ltd, Bastow v (1961) 111 LJ 820; (1961) 105 SJ 885; [1961] 1 WLR 1494 CA On appropriate damages for personal injuries (here loss of eye).

Bagley v North Herts Health Authority (1986) 136 NLJ 1014 HC QBD Damages for hospital negligence which resulted in pregnant woman giving birth to still-born child.

Bagnall and another, Howgate v [1951] 1 KB 265; (1950) 94 SJ 725; [1950] 66 (2) TLR 997 HC KBD Injuries sustained through crash landing of aircraft not war injuries : damages available.

Bagot v Stevens Scanlan and Co [1964] 3 All ER 577; [1966] 1 QB 197; (1964) 108 SJ 604; [1964] 3 WLR 1162 HC QBD Professional's failure to exercise proper care and skill in what contracted to do gives rise to claim in contract: no corollary duty on tort.

Bailey and others, Tynan v (1972) 116 SJ 922 CA Members of residents' association not liable for injury occasioned to child by barrier association erected at end of private road (accident not reasonably foreseeable).

Bailey and others, Wiffen v [1914-15] All ER 967; (1915) 79 JP 145; [1915] 1 KB 600; (1914) 49 LJ 674; [1915] 84 LJKB 688; (1914-15) 59 SJ 176; (1914-15) XXXI TLR 64; (1914) WN (I) 434 CA Malicious prosecution action failed where could not show damage to fame; imperiling of life/limb/liberty; financial loss.

Bailey and Romford Urban District Council, Wiffen v (1914) 78 JP 187; [1914] 2 KB 5; (1914) 49 LJ 64; [1914] 83 LJKB 791; (1914) 110 LTR 694; (1914) WN (I) 25 HC KBD Can sue for malicious prosecution of action for non-compliance with nuisance abatement notice.

Bailey v Howard [1938] 4 All ER 827; [1939] 1 KB 453; (1939) 87 LJ 9; [1939] 108 LJCL 182; (1939) 160 LTR 87; (1938) 82 SJ 1030; (1938-39) LV TLR 249; (1939) WN (I) 17 CA On appropriate damages for loss of life expectancy (of child).

Bailey, Daphne v (1919) CC Rep VIII 66 CyCt Landlord who after giving tenant notice to quit forcibly entered premises and threw tenant's furniture into street held to be liable in damages for trespass.

Bailey, Whittaker v (1925) 60 LJ 521 CyCt Where house sold and conveyance did not mention existing right of way use of the way held to pass to buyer of house.

Baillie v Birmingham and Midland Motor Omnibus Co, Ltd (1964) 108 SJ 258 HC QBD On appropriate damages for music teacher who suffered negligent injury to her arm.

Bailly, Hughes v (1919-20) XXXVI TLR 398 HC KBD Hotel proprietor not liable for theft by visitor whom boarded out with another where could not reasonably have discovered criminal propensity of visitor.

Baker, M'Nair v (1903-04) XX TLR 95 HC KBD Club-house not a private house so smoke nuisance a contravention of Public Health (London) Act 1891, s 24.

Baker, Mapey v (1908) 72 JP 511 HC KBD Slanderous words uttered of rate collector at meeting of Board of Guardians were uttered on privileged occasion.

Baker, Mapey v (1909) 73 JP 289; (1908-09) 53 SJ 429 CA Slanderous words uttered of rate collector at meeting of Board of Guardians were uttered on privileged occasion.

Baker, Mulholland and Tedd, Ltd v [1939] 3 All ER 253; (1939) 87 LJ 453; (1939) 161 LTR 20 HC KBD Recovery of damages under Rylands and Fletcher for heat, smoke and water arising from occurrence of non-accidental fire.

Bakewell Rural District Council, Webster v (1916) 80 JP 437 HC ChD Trespass action (for minor trespass) an abuse of process: dismissed with costs.

Balden v Shorter and others [1933] All ER 249; [1933] Ch 427; (1933) 75 LJ 202; [1933] 102 LJCh 191; (1933) 148 LTR 471; (1933) 77 SJ 138; (1933) WN (I) 37 HC ChD Absent malice no slander.

Baldock v Westminster City Council (1919) 83 JP 98 (also CA); (1918-19) 63 SJ 69; (1918-19) XXXV TLR 54; (1918) WN (I) 339 HC KBD Taxi-cab driver successful in negligence suit for inadequate lighting of refuge (even though inadequate lighting a by-result of ongoing war).

Baldock v Westminster City Council (1919) CC Rep VIII 6; (1919) 83 JP 98 (also HC KBD); [1919] 88 LJCL 502; (1918-19) XXXV TLR 188; (1919) WN (I) 22 CA Taxi-cab driver successful in negligence suit for inadequate lighting of refuge (even though inadequate lighting a by-result of ongoing war).

Baldwin's, Limited v Halifax Corporation (1916) 80 JP 357; [1916] 85 LJKB 1769 HC KBD Lack of care in technical design of road was misfeasance for which liable in damages to party injured in consequence.

Baldwin, Webb v (1911) 75 JP 564 HC ChD On proving dedication of highway to public (and so no trespass).

Balfour v Barty-King and another (Hyder and Sons (Builders), Ltd Third Parties) [1956] 2 All ER 555; (1956) 106 LJ 379; (1956) 100 SJ 472; [1956] 1 WLR 779 HC QBD Occupiers liable for fire negligently started by others whom could not prove were strangers; Rylands v Fletcher applied as fire started by dangerous/untypical user.

Balfour v Barty-King and another (Hyder and Sons (Builders), Ltd Third Parties) [1957] 1 All ER 156; (1957) 107 LJ 57; [1957] 1 QB 496; (1957) 101 SJ 62; [1957] 2 WLR 84 CA Occupiers liable for damage to neighbour's property by fire negligently started by contractors in occupier's premises as was non-accidental fire/not caused by stranger.

Ball and another v London County Council [1948] 2 All ER 917 HC KBD Landlord liable to tenant for own negligent installation of boiler.

Ball and another v London County Council [1949] 1 All ER 1056; (1949) 113 JP 315; [1949] 2 KB 159; (1949) WN (I) 223 CA Landlords owe duty of care of ordinary contractor when doing repairs; no duty of care to strangers in installing boiler as not dangerous per se.

Ball, Baker and Co, Henry Squire Cash Chemist (Limited) v; Mead v Same (1910-11) XXVII TLR 269 HC KBD Failed action against auditor for negligence: on duty of care owed by auditor.

Ball, Baker and Co, Henry Squire, Cash Chemist, Limited v; Mead v Ball, Baker, and Co (1912) 106 LTR 197; (1911-12) XXVIII TLR 81 CA Failed action against auditor for negligence: on duty of care owed by auditor.

Ball, Marlor v (1899-1900) XVI TLR 239 CA Person who meddled with wild animals (zebras) could not recover damages where suffered consequent personal injuries.

Ballett v Mingay [1943] 1 All ER 143; [1943] KB 281; (1943) 112 LJ 193; (1943) 168 LTR 34 CA Infant could be sued in tort for acts which fell outside bailment contract.

Balls and another v Lintsbrook Development Ltd (1976) 120 SJ 29 HC ChD Action dismissed for delay (albeit that delay nonetheless meant action being brought inside limitation period).

Balmain New Ferry Company, Limited, Robinson (Archibald Nugent) v [1910] AC 295; [1910] 79 LJPC 84 PC No false imprisonment where were merely using reasonable tactic to preempt forcible avoidance of payment for exit from wharf.

Balmer, Tynan v [1966] Crim LR 223; (1966) 110 SJ 129; [1966] 2 WLR 1181 HC QBD Common law nuisance for picketers to close off public highway.

Balsamo v Medici and another [1984] 2 All ER 304; (1984) 128 SJ 500; [1984] 1 WLR 951 HC ChD Cannot pursue one defendant in contract and other in tort for connected cause; no action against third party whose negligence did not affect cause of contractual action.

Baltic Mercantile and Shipping Exchange Ltd and another, Harakas and others v [1982] 2 All ER 701; (1982) 126 SJ 414; [1982] TLR 130; [1982] 1 WLR 958 CA If justification/qualified privilege cannot injunct publication unless publisher knows statement untrue.

Bambers Stores Ltd, Lewis Trusts v [1983] TLR 125 CA Award of damages for conversion under the Copyright Act 1956, s 18.

Bampton, Winstanley v [1943] 1 All ER 661; [1943] KB 319; (1944) 94 LJ 108; [1943] 112 LJ 430; (1943) 168 LTR 206; (1942-43) LIX TLR 183; (1943) WN (I) 55 HC KBD Privileged letter to plaintiff's commanding officer lost privilege through malice.

Banbury v Bank of Montreal [1918] 87 LJCL 1158; (1918-19) 119 LTR 446; (1917-18) 62 SJ 665; (1917-18) XXXIV TLR 518; (1918) WN (I) 231 HL Representation to sustain action for representation as to another's credit need only be in writing where fraudulent misrepresentation claimed (Lord Tenterden's Act 1828, s 6).

Banbury v Bank of Montreal [1917] 1 KB 409; (1916) 51 LJ 598; [1917] 86 LJCL 380; (1917) 116 LTR 42; (1916-17) 61 SJ 129; (1916-17) XXXIII TLR 104; (1916) WN (I) 412 CA Non-liability of action over letter of introduction; could not bring action on foot of representations/assurances as to credit/ability of company as was not in writing (Lord Tenterden's Act, s 6).

Banfield v Scott and Ranzetta (1984) 134 NLJ 550 HC QBD Death of motor cyclist entirely attributed to negligence of driver pulling out from side-road to main road before was safe to do so.

Bangor Corporation, Burnison v (1931) 72 LJ 397 CA On liability of waterworks company in negligence for mains escape.

Banhams Patent Locks Ltd, Dove v [1983] 2 All ER 833; (1983) 133 NLJ 538; (1983) 127 SJ 748; [1983] TLR 158; [1983] 1 WLR 1436 HC QBD Time ran from when negligence first apparent not when negligent work completed.

Bank of America National Trust and Savings Association v Chrismas and others 'The Kyriaki' [1994] 1 All ER 401 HC QBD Court cannot allow new claim after expiry of limitation period.

Bank of Credit and Commerce International (Overseas) Ltd (in liquidation) and others v Price Waterhouse and others [1997] TLR 60 HC ChD Company accountants who were no auditors of said company held not to owe duty of care to company.

Bank of England (No 3), Three Rivers District Council and others v [1996] 3 All ER 558; (1996) TLR 22/4/96 HC QBD On elements of tort of misfeasance in public office (in context of action against Bank of England for alleged misfeasance either in granting/not revoking licence of failed deposit-taking body).

Bank of England and another, Welch v [1955] Ch 508; (1955) 99 SJ 236; [1955] 2 WLR 757 HC ChD On negligence as basis for estoppel in banking stock transfer action.

Bank of England v Gibson and others [1994] TLR 253 HC QBD Standard of proof in action for wrongful appropriation of money is the civil standard.

Bank of Hamilton, Imperial Bank of Canada v (1902-03) LXXXVII LTR 457; (1902-03) 51 WR 289 PC Not negligent for bank to cash certified cheque which did not on face of it seem suspect.

Bank of Liverpool and Martins, Limited, Underwood (AL), Limited v (1922-23) XXXIX TLR 606 HC KBD Bank's negligent disposal of cheques was conversion.

Bank of Liverpool and Martins, Underwood (AL), Ltd v; Same v Bank (Barclays) [1924] All ER 230; (1924) 131 LTR 271; (1923-24) XL TLR 302 CA Bank's negligent disposal of cheques was conversion.

Bank of Montreal v Dominion Gresham Guarantee and Casualty Company, Limited [1930] AC 659; (1931) 144 LTR 6; (1929-30) XLVI TLR 575 PC Banker liable for negligent issuing of drafts — no estoppel precluding action just because had issued in same way several times previously.

Bank of Montreal, Banbury v [1917] 1 KB 409; (1916) 51 LJ 598; [1917] 86 LJCL 380; (1917) 116 LTR 42; (1916-17) 61 SJ 129; (1916-17) XXXIII TLR 104; (1916) WN (I) 412 CA Non-liability of action over letter of introduction; could not bring action on foot of representations/assurances as to credit/ability of company as was not in writing (Lord Tenterden's Act, s 6).

Bank of Montreal, Banbury v [1918] 87 LJCL 1158; (1918-19) 119 LTR 446; (1917-18) 62 SJ 665; (1917-18) XXXIV TLR 518; (1918) WN (I) 231 HL Representation to sustain action for representation as to another's credit need only be in writing where fraudulent misrepresentation claimed (Lord Tenterden's Act 1828, s 6).

Bank of Tokyo Ltd, Standard Bank London Ltd v; Girozentrale (Sudwestdeutsche Landesbank) v Bank of Tokyo Ltd and another [1995] TLR 206 HC QBD Person who mistakenly confirmed banking transaction by way of tested telex was guilty of negligent misstatement.

Bank View Mill, Ltd and others v Nelson Corpn and Fryer and Co (Nelson), Ltd [1942] 2 All ER 477 Assizes Corporation in occupation and control knowing of obstruction and with chance to remove liable in nuisance; flooding slightly due to weir: nominal damages against weir-owner.

Bank View Mill, Ltd and others v Nelson Corporation and Fryer and Co (Nelson), Ltd [1943] 1 All ER 299; [1943] KB 337; [1943] 112 LJ 306; (1943) 168 LTR 244 CA Corporation not in occupation so not liable for nuisance.

Bankes, Cunliffe v [1945] 1 All ER 459; (1946) 96 LJ 213 Assizes All reasonable steps taken to gauging safety of tree: no negligence and no nuisance (did not cause defect; did not arise through own act and failed to remedy in reasonable time).

Bannell, Dyer v [1965] Crim LR 308t; (1965) 109 SJ 216 HC QBD On extent of duty of care owed by police driving police cars.

Bannerjee (Jogendra Kumar) and Others, Amin (Mohamed) v [1947] AC 322; [1947] 116 LJR 963; (1947) 177 LTR 451; (1947) LXIII TLR 433 PC Simply bringing false complaint not malicious prosecution: test whether prosecution malicious is whether action has reached stage that injury done.

Bannister and another, Bottomley and another v (1931-32) XLVIII TLR 39 CA Failed action against landlord for injury to tenant's daughter occasioned by defective gas water heater.

Bannister v Bracewell (1960) 110 LJ 208 CyCt Damages plus leave to apply for injunction for trespass by sheep.

Banque Bruxelles Lambert SA v Eagle Star Insurance Co Ltd [1994] TLR 127 HC QBD On liability of valuer for negligent valuation.

Banque Bruxelles Lambert SA v Eagle Star Insurance Co Ltd and others and other appeals [1995] 2 All ER 769 (also HC QBD); (1995) 145 NLJ 343; [1995] QB 375; [1995] TLR 97; [1995] 2 WLR 607 CA Property valuer must exercise reasonable standard of professional care; valuer not guarantor of lender's decision.

Banque Financiére de la Cité SA v Westgate Insurance Co Ltd [1989] 2 All ER 952 CA Failure to fully disclose in contract of utmost good faith not a misrepresentation of full disclosure. Way economic loss suffered by third party need not be foreseeable to be recoverable.

Banque Keyser Ullmann SA v Skandia (UK) Insurance Co Ltd and others; Skandia (UK) Insurance Co Ltd v Slavenburg's Banque (Suisse) SA and others; Same v Chemical Bank and another; Banque Keyser Ullmann SA and others v Skandia (UK) Insurance Co Ltd and another [1987] 2 WLR 1300 HC QBD Insurers failed to meet common law duty of care (and so were liable in damages) where failed to reveal to bankers dishonesty of manager of bankers' brokers.

Banque Keyser Ullmann SA v Skandia (UK) Insurance Co Ltd (1988) 138 NLJ 287 CA On extent of duty of care owed by insurer to reveal to bankers the dishonesty of the manager of the bankers' brokers.

Banyard, Ellis v (1911) 104 LTR 460; (1910-11) 55 SJ 500; (1910-11) XXVII TLR 417 HC KBD Where field gate open and escaping cattle caused injury to passer-by owner (one judge) was negligent, victim (other judge) still had to prove negligence of owner.

Banyard, Ellis v [1911-13] All ER 303; (1912) 106 LTR 51; (1911-12) 56 SJ 139; (1911-12) XXVIII TLR 122 CA No duty to fence in cattle (tame animals) — and even if was duty no recovery as no negligence shown.

Baring, Goody v [1956] 2 All ER 11; (1956) 106 LJ 266; (1956) 100 SJ 320; [1956] 1 WLR 448 HC ChD Solicitor failed in duty to make proper inquiries on client's behalf.

Barings plc and another v Coopers & Lybrand (a firm) and others (1996) TLR 6/12/96 CA On duty of care owed by auditors of subsidiary company towards parent company.

Barker and Allen, Ltd, Senior v [1965] 1 All ER 818; (1965) 109 SJ 178; [1965] 1 WLR 429 CA On personal injury damages (loss of use of hand).

Barker v Herbert (1911) 75 JP 355; (1910-11) XXVII TLR 252 HC KBD Owner of premises adjoining highway not liable for injury not directly stemming from nuisance caused by trespasser.

Barker v Herbert [1911-13] All ER 509; (1911) 75 JP 481; [1911] 2 KB 633; (1911) 80 LJCL 1329; (1911-12) 105 LTR 349; (1910-11) XXVII TLR 488 CA Owner of premises adjoining highway not liable for nuisance caused by trespasser unless permitted its continuance.

Barker, Attorney-General v (1900-01) LXXXIII LTR 245; (1899-1900) XVI TLR 502 HC ChD Newly-constructed level crossings were nuisances which county council did not and could not authorise.

Barkers Traffic Services Ltd and others, Crossgrove and another v (1966) 110 SJ 892 HC QBD On appropriate damages for head injuries where was uncertain whether would worsen over time.

Barking and Dagenham London Borough Council and another, Porter v [1990] TLR 291 HC QBD Not failing to meet duty of care for school caretaker to allow two young teenage boys to practise shot-putting together on school property after school hours.

Barking and Dagenham London Borough Council v Stamford Asphalt Co Ltd and another [1997] TLR 193 CA Negligent contractor could not avoid liability by way of clause in JCT building contract which required employer to insure self against risk of fire.

Barking Corporation, Gibbs v [1936] 1 All ER 115 CA Education authority liable for injury to boy during PT class whom teacher did not assist.

Barkway v South Wales Transport Co, Ltd [1948] 2 All ER 460; [1949] 1 KB 54 CA Tyre burst causing skid raises presumption of negligence: must show tyre burst not negligent/that took reasonable care.

Barkway v South Wales Transport Co, Ltd [1950] 1 All ER 392; (1950) 114 JP 172; (1950) 94 SJ 128; [1950] 66 (1) TLR 597; (1950) WN (I) 95 HL On res ipsa loquitur.

Barlow and others v Heald (1916) CC Rep V 20 CyCt Could bring action for trover/detinue against company seeking to sell discarded bottles subject to deposit arrangement/in respect of which there was an obligation to account.

Barlows, Stovold v (1995) 145 NLJ 1649; (1995) 139 SJ LB 218; [1995] TLR 550 CA On damages for loss of opportunity through possible third party action had negligent act not occurred.

Barnard and others, Rookes v [1961] 2 All ER 825; [1963] 1 QB 623 (also CA) HC QBD Injury arising through threat to break contract with third person intimidation (if acted alone; otherwise conspiracy) — no protection under Trade Disputes Act 1906, ss 1 and 3.

Barnard and others, Rookes v [1962] 2 All ER 579; [1963] 1 QB 623 (also HC QBD) CA Is a tort of intimidation but mere threat to break contract not intimidation: must be fraud/threats/violence.

Barnard and others, Rookes v [1964] 1 All ER 367; [1964] AC 1129; [1964] 2 WLR 269 HL Is a tort of intimidation which embraces threatening breach of contract: on exemplary damages for intimidation.

Barnard v Sully (1931) 72 LJ 122; (1930-31) XLVII TLR 557; (1931) WN (I) 180 HC KBD Where damage proved to have been done by another's motor car is rebuttable presumption that owner of car (or agent/servant) was driving same.

Barnes (an infant) v Hampshire County Council (1968) 112 SJ 599 CA School not negligent in letting children out of school early (by virtue of which act injury to child occurred).

Barnes (an infant suing by Leslie Frederick Barnes her next friend) v Hampshire County Council (1969) 133 JP 733; (1969) 119 NLJ 948t; (1969) 113 SJ 834; [1969] 1 WLR 1563 HL School had been negligent in letting children out of school early (by virtue of which act injury to child occurred).

Barnes and another v Hill [1967] 1 All ER 347; [1967] 2 WLR 632 CA General verdict terminates case.

Barnes and another v Pooley (1935) 153 LTR 78; (1934-35) LI TLR 391 HC KBD Action for expenses by parent/person in loco parentis on foot of negligence of defendant's servant an action on the case so six year limitation applicable under Limitation Act 1623, s 3.

Barnes Urban District Council v London General Omnibus Company (1909) 73 JP 68 HC KBD Bus driver is on face of it negligent where collides in daylight with lamp post (but can prove otherwise to be the case).

Barnes v London Borough of Bromley (1984) 134 NLJ 312; [1983] TLR 678 HC QBD Teacher one-third negligent for injuries he suffered in use of defective school equipment.

Barnes v Lucile (Limited) (1906-07) XXIII TLR 389 HC KBD Owner of dog liable for injuries it causes by biting where knows dog to be even occasionally vicious towards humans.

Barnet Instruments, Limited, Bowmakers, Limited v [1945] KB 65; [1945] 114 LJ 41; (1945) 89 SJ 22; (1944-45) LXI TLR 62 CA That have goods as result of illegal agreement not a defence to conversion where plaintiff not raising agreement as issue.

Barnet London Borough Council, Russell and another v [1984] TLR 262 HC QBD Highway authority liable in nuisance for damage occasioned by tree roots to property even though did not actually own the trees.

Barnet v Crozier and another [1987] 1 All ER 1041; (1987) 131 SJ 298; [1987] 1 WLR 272 CA Statement of court in settlement of one libel claim permissible if no real risk of prejudice to later libel claim.

Barnett (Walter C), Grand Trunk Railway Company of Canada v [1911] AC 361; (1911) 80 LJPC 117; (1911) 104 LTR 362; (1910-11) XXVII TLR 359 PC Non-recovery for negligence where no breach of duty/cause of action shown.

Barnett and others, De Coppett v (1900-01) XVII TLR 273 CA Sheriff not protected from action for trespass where substantial grievance had resulted to plaintiff as result of sheriff's actions.

Barnett v Chelsea and Kensington Hospital Management Committee [1968] 1 All ER 1068; (1967) 117 NLJ 1218t; [1969] 1 QB 428; (1967) 111 SJ 912; [1968] 2 WLR 422 HC QBD Hospital authority liable for negligence of casualty officer; here link between latter's negligence and victim's death disproved/not proved.

Barnett v H and J Packer and Co, Ltd [1940] 3 All ER 575 HC KBD Donoghue v Stevenson applicable where injury occurred before examination possible.

Barnett v Woolwich Borough Council (1910) 74 JP 441 HC ChD Failed action for injunction to restrain nuisance as was brought out of time allowed under Public Authorities Protection Act 1893.

Barnett, Grand Trunk Railway Co v [1911-13] All ER 1624 PC No liability for injury to trespasser occurring through one's negligence.

Barnwell, Feay v [1938] 1 All ER 31 HC KBD Appropriate damages where overlapping of damages under Fatal Accidents Acts and Law Reform (Miscellaneous Provisions) Act 1934.

Barratt v Kearns [1905] 1 KB 504; (1905) XCII LTR 255; (1904-05) XXI TLR 212; (1904-05) 53 WR 356 CA Evidence before ecclesiastical commission privileged.

Barrett v Enfield London Borough Council [1997] 3 All ER 171; [1997] 2 FLR 167; [1997] TLR 202; [1997] 3 WLR 628 CA Local authority could not be liable in negligence for decisions taken in loco parentis regarding children in care but could be liable for manner in which said decisions effected.

Barrett v Ministry of Defence [1995] 3 All ER 87; [1995] TLR 7; [1995] 1 WLR 1217 CA No duty of care on Ministry of Defence to stop navy man becoming very drunk at bar run by Ministry.

Barrow-in-Furness Corporation, Hall v [1937] LJNCCR 157 CyCt Corporation not liable in negligence for damage to window by stone thrown up by car passing area on road where corporation had recently been doing roadworks.

Barry Railway Company v White (1900-01) XVII TLR 644 HL On negligence/contributory negligence in action for personal injuries suffered at level crossing.

Bates v Stone Parish Council [1954] 3 All ER 38; (1954) 118 JP 502; (1954) 104 LJ 569; (1954) 98 SJ 698; [1954] 1 WLR 1249 CA By allowing unrestricted playground access to children were liable to child/licensee injured therein.

Bates, Great Central Railway Company v [1921] 3 KB 578; (1921) CC Rep X 61; [1921] LJCL 1269; (1920-21) 65 SJ 768; (1920-21) XXXVII TLR 948 HC KBD No duty to policeman entering premises to ascertain whether everything all right.

Batey and Co, Limited, Bates and another v [1913] 3 KB 351; [1913] 82 LJKB 963; (1913) 108 LTR 1036; (1912-13) XXIX TLR 616; (1913) WN (I) 213 HC KBD Manufacturers not liable for injury caused to purchaser via defective bottle even though could have discovered defect had they exercised reasonable care.

Batger and Co, Ltd, Fitzpatrick v [1967] 2 All ER 657 CA Five year delay caused by plaintiff's solicitor inordinate delay justifying dismissal of action.

Bath Tramways Motor Co, Ltd and Trevor Smithey, Daborn v [1946] 2 All ER 333 CA Non-negligence of driver of left-hand drive ambulance to which warning sign affixed/after correct hand-signals given.

Bativala and another v West (1969) 119 NLJ 974t; [1970] 1 QB 716; (1969) 113 SJ 856; [1970] 2 WLR 8 HC QBD Horse-owner liable in negligence for damage caused by straying horse where ought to have known how horse would react to particular situation/sought to prevent it.

Batt v Metropolitan Water Board (1911) 75 JP 545; (1911) 80 LJCL 1354; (1910-11) 55 SJ 714; (1910-11) XXVII TLR 579 CA Water Board not liable in negligence for injury occasioned through inadequate maintenance of water stop-cock.

Batt v The Metropolitan Water Board (1911) 80 LJCL 521; (1910-11) XXVII TLR 258 HC KBD Water Board liable in negligence for injury occasioned through its inadequate maintenance of water stop-cock.

Battersby and others v Anglo-American Oil Company, Limited, and others (1944-45) LXI TLR 13 CA Court would not exercise discretion to enlarge time for renewing writ where to do so would deprive person of advantage limitation has conferred.

Battersea and Putney Group Hospital Management Committee, Slade v [1955] 1 All ER 429; (1955) 119 JP 212; (1955) 105 LJ 138; (1955) 99 SJ 169; [1955] 1 WLR 207 HC QBD Hospital liable to visitor slipping on newly polished floor as invitee/as licensee (concealed danger) where no warning given.

Battersea Borough Council, Papworth v [1914-15] All ER 406; (1916) 80 JP 177; [1916] 1 KB 583; [1916] 85 LJKB 746; (1916) 114 LTR 340; (1915-16) 60 SJ 120 CA Trial ordered as to liability of local authority for negligently constructed road gully.

Battersea Borough Council, Papworth v (1914) 78 JP 172; (1915) 79 JP 309; [1914] 2 KB 89; [1915] 84 LJKB 1881; [1914] 83 LJKB 358; (1914) 110 LTR 385; (1913-14) XXX TLR 240 HC KBD Non-liability/liability as highway/sewer authority.

Batting v London Passenger Transport Board [1941] 1 All ER 228 CA No leave to amend outside time under old limitation statute though new limitation statute had come into force since action started.

Battman, Tidy and another v [1933] All ER 259; [1952] Ch 791 (also HC ChD); [1934] 1 KB 319; (1934) 77 LJ 28; (1934) 103 LJCL 158; (1934) 150 LTR 90; (1933) WN (I) 276 CA No rule of law that one must be negligent if one collides with stationary vehicle.

Batty and another v Metropolitan Property Realisations Ltd and others [1978] 2 All ER 445; [1978] QB 554; (1978) 122 SJ 63; [1978] 2 WLR 500 CA Relief available in tort and contract for same cause though no common calling/not professional exercising skill.

Baume and Co, Ltd v AH Moore, Ltd [1958] 2 All ER 113; [1958] Ch 907; (1958) 102 SJ 329 CA Passing off even though using own name.

Baume and Co, Ltd v Moore (AH), Ltd [1957] 3 All ER 416; [1958] Ch 137 HC ChD Use of own name could not be passing off.

Bavins, Junr and Sims v London and South Western Bank, Limited [1900] 69 LJCL 164; (1899-1900) LXXXI LTR 655; [1900] 1 QB 270; (1899-1900) 48 WR 210 CA Party allowed recover money had and received by way of stolen money order.

Beardmore, Morris v [1980] 2 All ER 753; [1981] AC 446; (1980) 71 Cr App R 256 (also HC QBD); [1979] Crim LR 394; (1980) 144 JP 331; (1980) 130 NLJ 707; [1980] RTR 321; (1980) 124 SJ 512; [1980] 3 WLR 283 HL Request to take breath test invalid where police officer trespassing on property of person requested at time of request.

Beardmore, Morris v (1980) 71 Cr App R 256 (also HL); [1979] RTR 393; (1979) 123 SJ 300; [1979] 3 WLR 93 HC QBD Request to take breath test valid though police officer trespassing on property of person requested at time of request.

Bearman and Associated Newspapers, Ltd, Howard-Williams v (1962) 106 SJ 1009 CA Party allowed plead partial justification.

Beaton and another v Nationwide Anglia Building Society [1990] TLR 645 HC QBD Building society liable for negligence of employee-surveyor despite clause in prescribed form given to every mortgagee stating that the price charged for property did not necessarily indicate its true worth.

Beaumont and another v Humberts (a firm) and others [1990] TLR 543 CA Surveyor held not to have been negligent in his assessment of the reinstatement worth of a three hundred year old house.

Beaumont v Kaye and another [1904] 73 LJCL 213; (1904) XC LTR 51; (1903-04) 48 SJ 206; (1903-04) XX TLR 183; (1904) WN (I) 20; (1903-04) 52 WR 241 CA Could sue husband and wife for tort of wife — disparate defences by husband and wife struck out as were sued as unit.

Beaumont v Surrey County Council (1968) 118 NLJ 541t; (1968) 112 SJ 704 HC QBD School were negligent in leaving discarded elastic cord in area so that unsupervised pupils playing with the cord caused injury to the plaintiff.

Beaverbrook Newspapers, Ltd and another, Silkin v [1958] 2 All ER 516; (1958) 108 LJ 443; (1958) 102 SJ 491 HC QBD Fair comment on matter of public interest if opinion honestly held.

Beaverbrook Newspapers, Ltd, Cadam and others v [1959] 1 All ER 453; (1959) 109 LJ 184; [1959] 1 QB 413; (1959) 103 SJ 177 CA Just stating that writ issued/particulars of writ might be justifiable; on pleading.

Bebee v Sales (1915-16) XXXII TLR 413 HC KBD Was negligent to allow son to continue using airgun after had already promised to destroy gun on foot of earlier complaint regarding son's use of same.

Beck and Pollitzer, Towcester Gas Co v (1917) CC Rep VI 42 CyCt Weighbridge-owners had no basis of recovery against driver of heavy vehicle who damaged same when drove over it whilst driving driving on wrong side of the road.

Beckenham Corporation, Hall v [1949] 1 All ER 423; (1949) 113 JP 179; [1949] 1 KB 716; [1949] 118 LJR 965; (1949) LXV TLR 146; (1949) WN (I) 74 HC KBD Local authority not liable for nuisance of persons flying model aeroplanes in public park.

Becker v Earls' Court (Lim) (1911-12) 56 SJ 73 HC ChD Noise from fairground entertainment/ users of same at Earls' Court exhibition arena was a nuisance.

Becker v Lavender, Limited and another (1946) 90 SJ 502; (1945-46) LXII TLR 504; (1946) WN (I) 135 HC KBD Bailee for reward liable where did not take as much care of bailed property as would of own.

Beckett v Newalls Insulation Co, Ltd and another [1953] 1 All ER 250; (1953) 97 SJ 8; [1953] 1 WLR 8 CA Heightened standard of care required where one's task poses heightened risk to others.

Bedford v Leeds Corporation (1913) 77 JP 430 HC ChD Action to restrain nuisance occasioned by holding of yearly feast (action successful in part).

Bedford, Eley v [1971] 3 All ER 285; (1971) 115 SJ 369; [1971] 3 WLR 563 HC QBD Damages not to be reduced by time-barred injury benefits of which were unaware.

Bedfordshire County Council, Drake v [1944] 1 All ER 633; (1944) 108 JP 237; [1944] KB 620; (1945) 95 LJ 112; [1944] 113 LJ 328; (1944) 170 LTR 351; (1944) 88 SJ 239; (1943-44) LX TLR 304 HC KBD Gap in railings a continuing nuisance; defence of non-feasance open only to highway authority and anyway this case involved misfeasance.

Benham, Gambling v [1940] 1 All ER 275; (1940) 84 SJ 132 CA On appropriate damages for loss of life expectancy (of infant).

Benn, Griffiths and another v (1910-11) XXVII TLR 346 CA Absent special damage criticism of trader's goods not libel (may be be libel if represents personal attack on trader); criticism of operation of system under patent not per se an attack on operator.

Bennett and others v Guardian Newspapers Ltd [1995] TLR 719 HC QBD Were not allowed greater leeway in criticisms of public figures before what said could be construed as libellous.

Bennett and others v Guardian Newspapers Ltd [1997] TLR 104 CA On relevant considerations when determining distress occasioned by libel.

Bennett and Pye, Bywater v [1934] LJNCCR 117 CyCt House-owner (but not estate agent) liable in negligence towards person injured whilst being shown around unoccupied house by estate agent.

Bennett v Chemical Construction (GB) Ltd [1971] 3 All ER 822; (1971) 121 NLJ 525t; (1971) 115 SJ 550; [1971] 1 WLR 1571 CA If occurrence which takes place seems impossible otherwise than through defendant's negligence, is for defendants to prove contrary.

Bennett v Commissioner of Police of the Metropolis [1994] TLR 678; [1995] 1 WLR 488 HC ChD Must be actual malice for person to be guilty of tort of misfeasance in public office; Minister does not owe duty of care towards person seeking discovery of documents in respect of which Minister claiming privilege.

Bennett v Tugwell (an infant) [1971] 2 All ER 248; (1971) 121 NLJ 129t; [1971] 2 QB 267; [1971] RTR 221; (1971) 115 SJ 289; [1971] 2 WLR 847 HC QBD Apparent acceptance of risk raises volenti non fit injuria even if in mind does not really accept.

Bennett, Jones v (1975) 125 NLJ 870t HC QBD Failed application for extension of limitation where although applicant was illiterate she had been in possesssion of the relevant facts.

Bennett, Newman v [1981] QB 726 HC QBD Right of common pur vicinage gives right to graze on adjoining land and is not therefore a mere defence to trespass.

Bennetts, La Société Anonyme de Remorquage Hélice v [1911] 1 KB 243 HC KBD Damages not recoverable despite presence of negligence for results which did not directly flow from same.

Benning v Fox (1925) 60 LJ 1055 CyCt Sane, heroic act to remove danger to public safety caused by another's negligence was not contributory negligence disentitling hero of relief in damages.

Bennison and others, McCormick v (1938) 82 SJ 869 CA Onetime boxing champion successfully recovered damages for libellous newspaper article about self.

Benson v Furness Railway Company (1903) LXXXVIII LTR 268; (1902-03) 47 SJ 257 HC KBD No negligence where passenger injured by door being slammed shut by railway company employee after train started moving from station.

Bentley and Co, Jerome v [1952] 2 All ER 114; (1952) 102 LJ 343; (1952) 96 SJ 462; [1952] 2 TLR 58 HC QBD Liability for conversion where bought item from person not authorised as/could not be presumed to be agent for sale.

Bentley v Bristol and Western Health Authority [1990] TLR 766 HC QBD On when limitation period begins to run in surgical negligence actions.

Berg and Son v Lloyd (Rotterdamsche) (1917-18) XXXIV TLR 272 HC KBD Steamship-owners liable for damage caused to barges which ought to have foreseen would be close by in dock at night.

Berkeley Estates Co, Ltd and Phillips v Smith [1946] LJNCCR 105 CyCt Injunction granted to owners of profit a prendre to restrain past trespasser who declared intent to trespass in future.

Berkoff v Burchill and another [1996] 4 All ER 1008; (1996) TLR 9/8/96 CA To state of actor that he was 'hideous-looking' could be defamatory.

Berkshire County Council, Talbot v [1993] 4 All ER 9; (1993) 143 NLJ 402; [1994] QB 290; [1993] RTR 406; [1993] TLR 168; [1993] 3 WLR 708 CA Rule barring action where one already brought by co-plaintiff for same cause against same defendant applies to personal injuries.

Berkshire County Council, The Great House at Sonning Ltd and others v [1996] RTR 407; (1996) 140 SJ LB 123 CA Could not claim damages in nuisance against highway authority for obstruction through one-week closure of street for road-works (could seek judicial review of decision).

Birmingham Corporation, Hesketh v (1924) 88 JP 77; [1924] 1 KB 260; [1924] 93 LJCL 461; (1924) 130 LTR 476 CA Local authority not liable in nuisance for discharging sewer water into stream/not liable for non-feasance of drainage system.

Birn Brothers, Lim v Keene and Co, Lim [1919] 88 LJCh 24 HC ChD On rights of action in detinue/conversion open to copyright-owner under Copyright Act 1911, s 7.

Birse Construction Ltd v Haiste Ltd; Watson and others (third parties) [1995] TLR 666; [1996] 1 WLR 675 CA Physical faults in reservoir/cost of building new reservoir (losses suffered by two parties respectively) not 'the same damage' so defendant engineers could not recover contribution from third party engineer under Civil Liability (Contribution) Act 1978, s 1(1).

Bishop and another, Camkin v [1941] 2 All ER 713; (1941) 91 LJ 295; (1942) 92 LJ 60; (1941) 165 LTR 246 CA Non-supervision of schoolboys helping farmer not negligence.

Bishop and Sons, Filgate (Macartney) v (1964) 108 SJ 897 HC QBD Failed attempt by negligent bailee to rely on liability exemption clause following theft of bailed goods.

Bishop of Leeds, Ambler v (1904-05) 49 SJ 238; (1904-05) 53 WR 300 HC KBD On, inter alia, extent of user which bestows right not to have light so interfered with as to constitute nuisance.

Bishop Rock Marine Co Ltd and others 'The Nicholas H', Marc Rich and Co AG and others v [1994] 3 All ER 686; [1994] TLR 101; [1994] 1 WLR 1071 CA No distinction in law between cases where negligence causes physical damage and where causes economic loss; classification society valuers not under duty of care to shipowners.

Bishop Rock Marine Co Ltd and others 'The Nicholas H', Marc Rich and Co AG and others v [1995] 3 All ER 307; [1996] 1 AC 211; (1995) 145 NLJ 1033; (1995) 139 SJ LB 165; [1995] TLR 398; [1995] 3 WLR 227 HL Classification society does not owe duty of care to cargo owners who suffer loss.

Bishop v Cunard White Star, Ltd; Appleby v Cunard White Star, Ltd; The Queen Mary [1950] 2 All ER 22 HC PDAD On assessment of fatal accident/negligence damages.

Bishop v Metropolitan Police Commissioner and others (1989) 133 SJ 1626 CA Plaintiff's conduct relevant to setting exemplary damages payable by defendant guilty of malicious prosecution.

Biss v Lambeth, Southwark and Lewisham Health Authority [1978] 2 All ER 125; [1978] 1 WLR 382 CA Can be prejudice in conduct of affairs where delayed action; delay before extended limitation can be considered in deciding if prejudice.

BL Holdings Ltd v Robert J Wood and another (1978) 122 SJ 525 HC QBD Architect negligent as regards advice gave to clients concerning planning permission application/process.

BL Holdings Ltd v Robert J Wood and another (1979) 123 SJ 570 CA Architect not negligent as regards advice gave to clients concerning planning permission application/process.

Black and another, MacGrath v (1926) 61 LJ 560; [1926] 95 LJCL 951; (1926) 135 LTR 594 CA Particulars that did not justify specific allegations but supported general tenor of allegedly defamatory piece were admissible in evidence.

Black v Kent County Council [1983] TLR 373 CA Failed appeal against successful personal injuries claim by seven year old who stabbed himself in the eye when his chair was moved during art class at Kent County Council-run school.

Black-Clawson International, Ltd and others, Barry v (1967) 111 SJ 135 CA Not per se negligent to use article in manner other than that for which designed.

Blackburn, Smith and another v (1974) 124 NLJ 524t; [1974] RTR 533 HC QBD Not wearing seat belts not contributory negligence where collided with person driving in wrong direction on one-way road at speed.

Blacker v Lake and Elliot Limited (1912) 106 LTR 533 HC KBD Manufacturer not liable to third-party user of defectively manufactured article that is obviously dangerous/has been revealed by manufacturer to be so.

Blackman v Railway Executive [1953] 1 All ER 4; (1953) 97 SJ 10 HC QBD No failure to keep station safe for passengers/licensees so no liability.

Blackman v Railway Executive [1953] 2 All ER 323; (1954) 98 SJ 61; [1954] 1 WLR 220 CA On responsibility towards invitees.

Blount v War Office (1953) 97 SJ 388; [1953] 1 WLR 736 HC QBD War office liable for theft of goods left (bailed) with War Office's agreement in requisitioned house despite transfer of requisition to Ministry of Agriculture.

Blumenfeld (Ex parte Tupper), R v (1911-12) XXVIII TLR 308 HC KBD Libel defendant who intends to assert justification will not be committed for contempt unless justification is false/intends to prejudice trial/intends to deter witnesses coming forward.

Blundell v Rimmer (1970) 120 NLJ 1138; (1971) 115 SJ 15 HC QBD On payment of interest on damages payable into court.

BN Furman (Productions) Ltd; Miller Smith and Partners (a firm) Third Party, Fraser v [1967] 1 WLR 898 CA On damages available where insurance broker's negligence meant that were uncovered when event against which 'insured' transpired.

Boaks v Associated Newspapers Ltd (1967) 111 SJ 703; (1968) 118 NLJ 181t HC QBD Failed appeal against nominal damages awarded for libellous statement of person to effect that was in receipt of national assistance.

Boaks v Reece [1956] 2 All ER 750; [1956] Crim LR 563; (1956) 100 SJ 511; [1956] 1 WLR 886 HC QBD Was not wrongful imprisonment for magistrate to remand person in custody pending preparation of medical report prior to sentencing.

Board and another, Burton v [1929] 1 KB 301 HC KBD Alleged defamator may give particulars of facts on which made statement (even though does not plead justification).

Board and another, Burton v [1928] All ER 659; (1929) 98 LJCL 165; (1929) 140 LTR 289 CA Alleged defamator may give particulars of facts on which made statement (even though does not plead justification).

Board of Governors of the Bethlem Royal Hospital and the Maudsley Hospital and another, Sidaway v (1982) 132 NLJ 814 HC QBD On duty of care owed by surgeon to patient.

Board of Governors of the Bethlem Royal Hospital and the Maudsley Hospital and others, Sidaway v [1985] 1 All ER 643; [1985] AC 871; (1985) 135 NLJ 203; (1985) 129 SJ 154; [1985] 2 WLR 480 HL On duty of care owed by surgeon to patient.

Board of Trade, Marshal Shipping Company v [1923] 2 KB 343; (1923) WN (I) 115 CA Liability of Board of Trade for acts of Shipping Controller.

Boardman and another v Sanderson and another (Keel and Block, Third Party) (1961) 105 SJ 152; [1964] 1 WLR 1317 CA Were liable to father who could hear negligent injury to child for shock suffered by father in consequence.

Boardwell, Newland v; MacDonald v Platt [1983] 3 All ER 179; [1984] RTR 188 CA Admission of liability but denial of liability an abuse of process.

Bognor Regis United Building Co Ltd and another, Dutton v [1972] 1 All ER 462; (1972) 136 JP 201; (1971) 121 NLJ 617; [1972] 1 QB 373; (1972) 116 SJ 16; [1972] 2 WLR 299 CA Council in exercising building byelaws powers has duty to exercise diligently; can be liable for negligent exercise to purchaser/even if builder not liable (and builder may be liable even if owns premises).

Bognor Regis Urban District Council v Campion [1972] 2 All ER 61; (1972) 122 NLJ 377; [1972] 2 QB 169 HC QBD Local government authority can sue in libel to preserve its reputation.

Bognor Regis Urban District Council, Dutton v [1971] 2 All ER 1003; (1971) 121 NLJ 1146t HC QBD Council owes duty of care through building inspector to later purchaser.

Bolam v Friern Hospital Management Committee [1957] 2 All ER 118; (1957) 107 LJ 315; (1957) 101 SJ 357 HC QBD Doctor not negligent if susbscribes to one of two conflicting views held by responsible bodies of medics; doctor negligent in not giving warning to mentally ill person of what he believes to be minimal dangers of treatment; must show failure to warn not negligent and would not have consented if warned.

Bollinger (J) and others v Costa Brava Wine Company, Ltd [1959] 3 All ER 800; (1959) 109 LJ 735; (1961) 105 SJ 180; [1959] 3 WLR 966 HC ChD Goodwill attaching to geographical name could be protected by class of people producing goods in that area.

Bollinger (J) and others v Costa Brava Wine Co, Ltd (No 2) [1961] 1 All ER 561; [1960] Ch 262; (1961) 111 LJ 155; (1959) 103 SJ 1028 HC ChD Goodwill could vest in geographical name and be protected from passing off.

Bolton and Norris, Otto (M) and Otto (E) v [1936] 1 All ER 960; [1936] 2 KB 46; [1936] 105 LJCL 602; (1936) 154 LTR 717; (1936) 80 SJ 306; (1935-36) LII TLR 438; (1936) WN (I) 127 HC KBD Builder owes no duty to later residents of property being built to take reasonable care in building same.

Bolton and others, Stone v [1949] 1 All ER 237 Assizes Single incident not nuisance; cricket-playing not unnatural land user (Rylands v Fletcher inapplicable); cricket-ball inadvertently striking person on highway not negligent.

Bolton and others, Stone v [1949] 2 All ER 851; [1950] 1 KB 201; (1949) 99 LJ 625; (1949) LXV TLR 683; (1949) WN (I) 432 CA Cricket ball flying from ground to highway was negligent/not nuisance.

Bolton and others v Stone [1951] 1 All ER 1078; [1951] AC 850; (1951) 101 LJ 287; (1951) 95 SJ 333; [1951] 1 TLR 977; (1951) WN (I) 280 HL Non-liability where ball from cricket game struck person on highway as foreseable but negligible risk.

Bolton v Essex Area Health Authority and Taqui (1977) 127 NLJ 1177 HC QBD On appropriate damages for person left severely paralysed/dumb/nearly blind after negligent hospital operation.

Bond and another, Harnett v (1923-24) XL TLR 414 HC KBD Successful action for false imprisonment of lunatic.

Bond and another, Harnett v (1924-25) 69 SJ 445/575; (1924-25) XLI TLR 509 HL Failed action for false imprisonment of lunatic.

Bond and another, Harnett v (1924) 131 LTR 782; (1923-24) XL TLR 653 CA Failed action for false imprisonment of lunatic.

Bone and another v Seale [1975] 1 All ER 787; (1975) 119 SJ 137; [1975] 1 WLR 797 CA Appropriate damages for loss of amenity because of smell.

Bonham-Carter v Hyde Park Hotel, Limited (1948) LXIV TLR 177 HC KBD Innkeeper deemed negligent where security provided ensured privacy but did not afford adequate protection of guests' property.

Bonvin and another, Hewitt v [1940] 1 KB 189; [1940] 109 LJCL 223; (1939) 161 LTR 360; (1939) 83 SJ 869; (1939-40) LVI TLR 43 CA Father not liable for negligent driving of son who was neither his servant nor agent.

Bookbinder v Tebbit [1989] 1 All ER 1169; (1989) 139 NLJ 112; [1989] 1 WLR 640 CA Plaintiff withdrawing allegation of general slander meant defendant could not rely on general charge to support justification plea.

Booker v Wenborn [1962] 1 All ER 431; (1962) 112 LJ 137; (1961) 105 SJ 1125 CA Person opening moving train door to board owes duty of care not to injure those on platform (including porters).

Bool, Brooke v [1928] 2 KB 578; (1929) 68 LJ ccr9; (1928) 65 LJ 402; (1928) 97 LJCL 511; (1928) 139 LTR 376; (1928) WN (I) 127 HC KBD Liability for negligent act of one's lodger.

Boord and Son v Huddart (1903-04) LXXXIX LTR 718; (1903-04) 48 SJ 143 HC ChD Injunction granted to restrain passing off sloe gin as established brand of sloe gin.

Booth and another v Chrystal Springs Ltd (1968) 112 SJ 51 CA On appropriate personal injuries damages for young woman and her husband (for loss of consortium) where former's leg injured/permanently affected in negligent accident.

Booth and another v Davey (1988) 138 NLJ 104 CA Conveyancing solicitor not liable in negligence where had read out draft contract to clients and given them copy to peruse.

Bootle Corporation, Sutton v [1947] 1 All ER 92; (1947) 111 JP 81; [1947] KB 359; (1947) 97 LJ 23; (1947) 177 LTR 168 CA Licensor only obliged to warn licensee of dangers actually known.

Boots Co Ltd and Kensington and Chelsea and Westminster Area Health Authority, Sheridan v (1981) 131 NLJ 479 HC QBD Failed action for negligence arising from prescription of drug which resulted in plaintiff going blind.

Boots Pure Drug Co, Ltd and another, Devilez v (1962) 106 SJ 552 HC QBD Manufacturers/ vendors of corn solvent owed special duty of care to purchasers.

Boots, Cash Chemists (Lancashire) (Limited), and others v Grundy and another (1900) 35 LJ 413; (1900) LXXXII LTR 769; (1899-1900) XVI TLR 457; (1900) WN (I) 142 HC QBD Cannot bring action against persons combining to induce other persons not to trade with third party.

Borden Inc and others, Reckitt and Colman Products Ltd v [1990] 1 All ER 873; (1990) 134 SJ 784; [1990] TLR 101; [1990] 1 WLR 491 HL Can be misrepresentation as to whole or part of product get-up; get-up may have secondary significance of indicating not only class of product but particular brand.

Bosley, Vernon v [1997] 1 All ER 577; (1996) 146 NLJ 589; (1997) 141 SJ LB 27; [1997] RTR 1; (1996) TLR 4/4/96 CA Damages available for mental illness (stemming from another's negligence) attributable in part to grief and bereavement.

Bostik Ltd v Sellotape GB Ltd [1994] TLR 14 HC ChD Failed passing off action by makers of 'Blu-Tack' against makers of 'SelloTak' — get-up at point of sale central to action.

Bostock v Ramsey Urban District Council (1899-1900) XVI TLR 18 HC QBD Not malicious prosecution to bring proceedings for obstruction of highway by employee against employer.

Boston Deep Sea Fishing and Ice Company, Limited, Reynolds v (1921-22) XXXVIII TLR 22 HC KBD Exemption clause though did not specifically mention negligence did exclude liability for same.

Boston Deep Sea Fishing and Ice Company, Limited, Reynolds v (1921-22) XXXVIII TLR 429 CA Exemption clause though did not specifically mention negligence did exclude liability for same.

Boston v WS Bagshaw and Sons and others [1966] 2 All ER 906; (1966) 110 SJ 352; [1966] 1 WLR 1126 CA Broadcast seeking criminal enjoyed privilege; leaving general question of malice to jury rather than explaining minutiae thereof valid.

Bosworth-Smith v Gwynnes, Limited [1920] 89 LJCh 368; (1920) 122 LTR 15 HC ChD Noise from aeroplane-testing was a nuisance.

Botham v Khan (1996) TLR 15/7/96 CA On determining whether words capable of bearing defamatory meaning (look to what plaintiff said had been done by defendant).

Bottomley and another v Bannister and another (1931-32) XLVIII TLR 39 CA Failed action against landlord for injury to tenant's daughter occasioned by defective gas water heater.

Bottomley and others, Arnold and Butler v [1908] 2 KB 151; [1908] 77 LJCL 584; (1908) XCVIII LTR 777; (1907-08) 52 SJ 300; (1907-08) XXIV TLR 365 CA Must plead specifics of justification.

Bottomley v Brougham [1908] 1 KB 584; (1908) 43 LJ 59; [1908] 77 LJCL 311; (1908-09) XCIX LTR 111; (1907-08) 52 SJ 225; (1907-08) XXIV TLR 262; (1908) WN (I) 32 HC KBD Court report of official receiver absolutely privileged; on nature of absolute privilege.

Bottomley v FW Woolworth and Co, Limited (1931-32) XLVIII TLR 521 CA On liability of distributors (who are not authors) of libellous work.

Boulting and another v Association of Cinematograph, Television and Allied Technicians [1963] 2 WLR 529 CA Court can grant injunction to prevent apprehended tort by trade union.

Boulton and others, Gawthrop v [1978] 3 All ER 615; (1978) 122 SJ 297 HC ChD Limitation period continues to run to defendant's advantage to date added as party.

Boulton Macro (Limited), W Woodward (Limited) v; Re W Woodward (Limited) (1915) 50 LJ 147; [1916] 85 LJCh 27; (1914-15) XXXI TLR 269; (1915) WN (I) 124 HC ChD Passing off action failed where not proved that 'gripe water' had come to identify plaintiffs' product alone.

Boulton, Kean and another v (1963) 107 SJ 872 HC QBD Court directions as to agreed damages for infant injured as consequence of negligent driving.

Bourgoin SA and others v Ministry of Agriculture, Fisheries and Food [1984] TLR 542 HC QBD On ingredients of tort of misfeasance in public office.

Bourgoin SA and others v Ministry of Agriculture, Fisheries and Food [1986] QB 716; [1985] 3 WLR 1027 CA Was misfeasance in public office/was not innominate tort for Minister to restrict intra-European Community trade on spurious health grounds.

Bradford Metropolitan Council, Murphy v [1991] TLR 66 CA Local authority liable for breach of duty of care to ensure cleared, salted school path was not slippy.

Bradford v Robinson Rentals, Ltd [1967] 1 All ER 267; (1967) 111 SJ 33; [1967] 1 WLR 337 Assizes Recovery where chance of injury reasonably foreseeable but particular injury not so.

Bradley, Staffordshire and Worcestershire Canal Navigation v [1912] 1 Ch 91 HC ChD Injunction to restrain trespass by way of unauthorised fishing in canal from towing paths.

Bradshaw v Waterlow and Sons Limited [1914-17] All ER 36; [1915] 3 KB 527; [1916] 85 LJKB 318; (1915-16) 113 LTR 1101; (1914-15) XXXI TLR 556; (1915) WN (I) 292 CA No want of reasonable and probable cause found.

Bradshaw, Goldston v [1934] LJNCCR 355 CyCt Absent negligence/intent on part of pig drover/his employer could not recover damages from same for damage occasioned by straying pig.

Bradshaw, J Spurling, Ltd v [1956] 2 All ER 121; (1956) 106 LJ 281; (1956) 100 SJ 317; [1956] 1 WLR 461 CA Exemption clause in bailment contract applied in negligence suit.

Bradstreet, McLaren and others v (1969) 119 NLJ 484t CA Compensation unavailable to children for suffering consequent upon accident but prolonged as result of (and avoidable was it not for) actions of neurotic mother of children.

Brady v Express Newspapers plc [1994] TLR 690 HC QBD Malicious falsehood prosecution could not be brought by prisoner seeking damages for likely loss of prison privileges on foot of newspaper article.

Braham and Campbell, Limited, Johnston v [1917] 1 KB 586 CA Liability of agent for negligent statement to principal.

Braithwaite v South Durham Steel Co, Ltd and another [1958] 3 All ER 161; (1958) 102 SJ 655 HC QBD Master negligent in not providing safe place to work; licensor liable in negligence despite unintended trespass of licencee at moment of accident to escape therefrom.

Brame v Commercial Gas Co [1915] 84 LJKB 570 HC KBD Local authority resolution did not preclude gas company liability for negligence pursuant to Gasworks Clauses Act 1847.

Bramwell v Shaw and others [1971] RTR 167 HC QBD On liabilities of speeding driver, his employer and highway authority for collision occurring on poorly maintained road.

Brand (RA) and Co, Ltd v Samuel Barrow and Co, Ltd (1965) 109 SJ 834 CA Neighbouring occupiers had duty to prevent water seeping into plaintiff occupier's house but plaintiff also had duty to stop same.

Brand, Montague and Co, Carter v (1969) 113 SJ 188 HC QBD Justification defence to triumph if alleged libel is substantially true; justified annoyance not malice.

Brandeis Goldschmidt and Co Ltd v Western Transport Ltd [1982] 1 All ER 28; [1981] QB 864; [1981] 3 WLR 181 CA Damages for wrongful detention compensatory so need not be gauged by reference to difference in price when detained and when delivered.

Brandon and another v Osborne Garrett and Co, Ltd and another [1924] All ER 703; [1924] 1 KB 548; (1924) 59 LJ 76; [1924] 93 LJCL 304; (1924) 130 LTR 670; (1923-24) 68 SJ 460; (1923-24) XL TLR 235; (1924) WN (I) 33 HC KBD Wife could recover for injury suffered in course of non-negligent act to rescue husband from danger.

Braniff v Holland and Hannen and Cubitts (Southern) Ltd, and another [1969] 3 All ER 959; [1969] 1 WLR 1533 CA Weldon v Neal principles still generally applicable.

Brannigen v Harrington (1920-21) XXXVII TLR 349 HC KBD Is implied contract between restauranteur and customer that premises will be kept as safe as reasonably possible but not liable for defects that could not reasonably be discovered.

Branson v Bowes (1922) CC Rep XI 35 CyCt On duty of care owed by agister (and on discharging burden of proving that reasonable care exercised).

Bray (Wickham, Third Party), Smith v (1940) 84 SJ 170; (1939-40) LVI TLR 200 HC KBD Apportionment of costs/damages in proportion to apportionment of negligence between joint tortfeasors.

Bray v Palmer (1953) 97 SJ 830; [1953] 1 WLR 1455 CA Re-trial merited where trial judge had been unable to fully determine facts of case and apportion blame.

Bristol and Western Health Authority, Bentley v [1990] TLR 766 HC QBD On when limitation period begins to run in surgical negligence actions.

Bristol City Council, McAuley v [1992] 1 All ER 749 CA Council right to enter house entailed right to enter garden so duty of care to carry out repairs in garden.

Bristol Corporation, Caseley v [1944] 1 All ER 14; (1945) 95 LJ 112 CA On extent of duty owed to licensee.

Bristol Omnibus Co Ltd and another, Taylor v [1975] 2 All ER 1107; (1975) 125 NLJ 574t; (1975) 119 SJ 476; [1975] 1 WLR 1054 CA Damages for future loss of earnings available to child though speculative; reasonableness of entire damages considered after damages under various heads awarded.

Bristol Tramway and Carriage Company (Limited), Newberry v (1912-13) 107 LTR 801; (1912-13) 57 SJ 172; (1912-13) XXIX TLR 177 CA Tram company not liable for freak injury to passenger where had adopted best practice to avoid injury.

Bristol Tramways and Carriage Co, Ltd, Franklin v [1941] 1 All ER 188; [1941] 1 KB 255; (1942) 92 LJ 59; [1941] 110 LJ 248 CA Contributory negligence where pedestrian (in black-out conditions) did not keep look-out for overtaking traffic.

Bristol Tramways and Carriage Company Limited, Wintle v (1917) 81 JP 55; [1917] 86 LJCL 240; (1917) 116 LTR 125; (1916-17) 61 SJ 183; (1917) WN (I) 7 HC KBD Though only required to have one lamp by statute driving petrol lorry in instant circumstances with one lamp was negligent.

Bristol Tramways and Carriage Company Limited, Wintle v (1917) 52 LJ 188; [1917] 86 LJCL 936; (1917-18) 117 LTR 238; (1917) WN (I) 163 CA Though only required to have one lamp by statute driving petrol lorry in instant circumstances with one lamp could be negligent.

Bristol Tramways Company (Limited), West v (1908) 72 JP 145; (1907-08) 52 SJ 264; (1907-08) XXIV TLR 299 HC KBD Rylands v Fletcher applied to creosoting as non-natural user of land.

Bristol Tramways Co, West v [1908-10] All ER 215; (1908) 72 JP 243; [1908] 2 KB 14; [1908] 77 LJCL 684; (1908-09) XCIX LTR 264; (1907-08) 52 SJ 393; (1907-08) XXIV TLR 478; (1908) WN (I) 95 CA Rylands v Fletcher applied to creosoting as non-natural user of land.

Bristol United Press, Ltd, Grubb v [1962] 2 All ER 380; (1962) 112 LJ 369; [1963] 1 QB 309; (1962) 106 SJ 262 CA On innuendo in libel cases.

Britannia Hygienic Laundry Company, Limited v John I Thornycroft and Company, Limited [1925] 94 LJCL 858; (1924-25) XLI TLR 667; (1925) WN (I) 227 HC KBD Costs incurred as defendants in earlier action prompted by present defendant's negligence/breach of contract were recoverable by plaintiffs here.

Britannia Hygienic Laundry Company, Limited v John I Thornycroft and Company, Limited [1926] 95 LJCL 237; (1926) 135 LTR 83; (1923-24) 68 SJ 102; (1925-26) XLII TLR 198; (1926) WN (I) 16 CA Costs incurred as defendants in earlier action prompted irrecoverable by plaintiffs as did not prove negligence of instant defendants.

Britannia Hygienic Laundry Company, Limited, Phillips v [1923] 1 KB 539; (1923) CC Rep XII 28; [1923] 92 LJCL 389; (1923) 128 LTR 690; (1922-23) 67 SJ 365; (1922-23) XXXIX TLR 207; (1923) WN (I) 47 HC KBD Apportionment of liability for motor car with hidden defect.

Britannia Hygienic Laundry Company, Limited, Phillips v [1924] 93 LJCL 5; (1922-23) XXXIX TLR 530 CA Regulations concerning use and construction of motor cars did not create personal remedy against repairers who returned car with latent defect which meant car did not comply with regulations.

British Airways Overseas Corporation, George Wimpey and Co Ld v [1954] 3 All ER 661; [1955] AC 169; (1954) 104 LJ 824; [1954] 3 WLR 932 HL Precluded by public authority special limitation period from recovering contribution from respondent.

British and French Chemical Manufacturing Company and Gibson, Roff v [1918] 2 KB 677; (1918) 53 LJ 272; [1918] 87 LJCL 996; (1918-19) 119 LTR 436; (1917-18) 62 SJ 620; (1917-18) XXXIV TLR 485 CA Privileged communication did not lose privilege through communication to clerks.

British Arc Welding Company, Limited and Others, Hodgson v (1946) 174 LTR 379 HC KBD Shipwrights not sub-contractors liable for injury to sub-contractor's employee.

British Broadcasting Corporation and another, Gillick v [1995] TLR 527 CA Implicit suggestion that person who campaigned for contraceptive information not to be made available to girls was morally responsible for suicides of certain two pregnant girls was libellous.

British Broadcasting Corporation and others, London Computer Operators Training Ltd and others v [1973] 2 All ER 170; (1973) 117 SJ 147; [1973] 1 WLR 424 CA Could amend submission to include evidence of criminal convictions of one claiming libelled by suggestion of dishonesty.

British Broadcasting Corporation v Talbot Motor Co Ltd (1981) 131 NLJ 237 HC ChD Successful passing off action restraining defendants from using same name in respect of same product which plaintiffs had tested some years previously.

British Broadcasting Corporation, Interoven Stove Co Ltd v (1935) 79 SJ 921 HC KBD Failed action for alleged slander of goods in course of radio broadcast: on elements of 'slander of goods'.

British Broadcasting Corporation, Slipper v [1991] 1 All ER 165; [1991] 1 QB 283; (1990) 134 SJ 1042; [1990] TLR 446; [1990] 3 WLR 967 CA Repetition of libel by third party may expose original publisher to action for damages in respect of repetition.

British Car Auctions Ltd, RH Willis and Son v (1978) 128 NLJ 186t; [1978] RTR 244; [1978] 1 WLR 438 CA Auctioneers liable to car-dealers in conversion for selling hire-purchase car on behalf of hirer who had no title to sell.

British Car Auctions Ltd, Union Transport Finance Limited v (1977) 127 NLJ 1247b CA Could be conversion of hire purchase item where bailee so acted as to open up right to immediate possession of relevant article by bailor.

British Celanese, Ltd and others, Pride of Derby and Derbyshire Angling Association, Ltd and another v [1953] 1 All ER 179; [1953] Ch 149; (1953) 117 JP 52; (1952) 102 LJ 721; (1953) 97 SJ 28; [1953] 2 WLR 58 CA Local authority liable for nuisance in violating Rivers Pollution Prevention Act 1876; injunction available against local authority but suspended where required doing of impossible.

British Celanese, Ltd and others, Pride of Derby and Derbyshire Angling Association, Ltd and another v [1952] 1 All ER 1326; (1952) WN (I) 227 HC ChD Where persons collectively commit nuisance but individually not improper behaviour may be sued collectively for nuisance.

British Celanese, Ltd v AH Hunt (Capacitors) Ltd [1969] 2 All ER 1252; (1969) 119 NLJ 364t; (1969) 113 SJ 368; [1969] 1 WLR 959 HC QBD Rylands v Fletcher inapplicable as no special use of land.

British Cellophane plc, Barand v [1995] TLR 83 CA On deciding whether to allow out-of-limitation action to proceed.

British Chartered Company of South Africa v Lennon (Limited) [1916] 85 LJPC 111; (1915-16) 113 LTR 935; (1914-15) XXXI TLR 585 PC Recovery of damages for loss suffered through use of cattle dip marketed as particular concentrate but actually stronger.

British Coal Corporation (No 1), Dale v (1992) 136 SJ LB 197 CA No need for leave to appeal against overriding of limitation period.

British Coal Corporation (No 2), Dale v (1992) 136 SJ LB 199 CA Reversal of disapplication of limitation period.

British Coal Corporation, Crocker v [1995] TLR 389 HC QBD Burden of proof on plaintiff seeking to show personal injuries action not outside relevant limitation period under the Limitation Act 1980, s 11.

British Columbia Electric Rail Co, Ltd v Loach [1914-15] All ER 426; [1916] 85 LJPC 23 PC Are liable in negligence despite other's contributory negligence where own negligence precluded avoidance of cause of action.

British Columbia Electric Railway Co Ld, Sigurdson (Marvin) v [1953] AC 291; (1952) WN (I) 411 PC On contributory negligence.

British Columbia Electric Railway Co, Ltd, Nance v [1951] 2 All ER 448; [1951] AC 601; (1951) 95 SJ 543; [1951] 2 TLR 137; (1951) WN (I) 373 PC On contributory negligence as defence.

British Mutual Banking Company, Limited, Carpenters' Company of the City of London v (1937) 81 SJ 118; (1936-37) LIII TLR 270 HC KBD Bank negligent in accepting cheques fraudulently indorsed and lodging same to fraudster's account.

British Mutual Banking Company, Limited, Carpenters' Company v [1938] 1 KB 511; (1937) 81 SJ 701; (1936-37) LIII TLR 1040; (1937) WN (I) 329 CA Bank liable in conversion for accepting cheques fraudulently indorsed and lodging to fraudster's account.

British Northrop Co Ltd, Proctor v (1937) 81 SJ 611 CA Defendants not liable for injury to child trespasser (who knew should not have been where was) where took all reasonable steps/did not lay trap.

British Oxygen Co, Ltd, Leach v (1965) 109 SJ 157 CA Employers not liable for injury which occurred to workman directed to do certain task.

British Pregnancy Advisory Service, Goodwill v [1996] 2 All ER 161; [1996] 2 FCR 680; [1996] 2 FLR 55; (1996) 146 NLJ 173; (1996) 140 SJ LB 37; (1996) TLR 29/1/96; [1996] 1 WLR 1397 CA Must be known/deducible that advice will be acted on by third party before duty of care in respect of same will arise.

British Racing Drivers' Club Ltd and another v Hextall Erskine and Co (a firm) [1996] 3 All ER 667 HC ChD Solicitors liable for negligent advice (failed to advise directors that members required to approve certain transaction which was later rescinded by members thereby occasioning loss).

British Rail Engineering Ltd, Pickett v (1977) 121 SJ 814 CA Loss of earnings in lost years unavailable to plaintiff suffering work related injury/disease whose action came to court during his lifetime.

British Rail Engineering Ltd, Pickett v; British Rail Engineering Ltd v Pickett [1979] 1 All ER 774; [1980] AC 136; (1978) 128 NLJ 1198t; (1978) 122 SJ 778; [1978] 3 WLR 955 HL Loss of earnings damages where life expectancy diminished are for whole of pre-injury life expectancy; interest available on inflation-adjusted damages.

British Railway Traffic and Electric Company, Limited v The CRC Company Limited and the London County Council [1922] 2 KB 260; [1922] 91 LJCL 824; (1922) 126 LTR 602; (1921-22) XXXVIII TLR 190 HC KBD Failed action for slander of title where was slander but no malice.

British Railways Board and others, Harrison v [1981] 3 All ER 679 HC QBD Rescued person may (as here) owe duty of care towards rescuer who may therefore recover damages for injuries suffered in course of rescue.

British Railways Board and others, Thomas and another v [1976] 3 All ER 15; [1976] QB 913; (1976) 120 SJ 334; [1976] 2 WLR 761 CA Juxtaposition of railway/footpath imposed duty of care on Board to provide stile but local authority liable for repair.

British Railways Board v Herrington [1972] 1 All ER 749; [1972] AC 877; (1972) 116 SJ 178; [1972] 2 WLR 537 HL Occupier owes duty of care to trespasser to take reasonable acts to prevent injury.

British Railways Board, Chadwick v (1967) 111 SJ 562 HC QBD Administratix of rescuer's estate allowed recover damages for shock suffered by rescuer at scene of accident occasioned by defendant's negligence.

British Railways Board, Davies v (1984) 134 NLJ 888 HC QBD On duty of occupier towards (child) trespasser.

British Railways Board, Geddes v (1968) 112 SJ 194 CA Deceased two-thirds liable for rail accident/engine driver one-third liable for not sounding long whistle in circumstances.

British Railways Board, Gravesham Borough Council and others v [1978] 3 All ER 853 HC ChD Changing of public ferry service actionable by party suffering direct loss as obstruction/hindrance of ferry public nuisance.

British Railways Board, Greenhalgh v [1969] 2 QB 286; (1969) 113 SJ 108; [1969] 2 WLR 892 CA Non-liability under Railways Clauses Consolidation Act 1845/Occupiers' Liability Act 1957 for injury sustained by person using disrepaired public right of way.

British Telecommunications plc, Yorkshire Electricity Board v (1970) 130 SJ 613; [1986] 1 WLR 1029 HL Cause of action where owning undertakers' appartus damaged by operating undertakers did not run from date of damage but date owning undertakers suffered expense of repair.

British Thomson Houston Company (Limited), Maxwell v; Blackwell and Co, Third Parties (1901-02) XVIII TLR 278 CA Contractor liable for negligence of sub-contractor.

British Timken, Ltd, Sidwell v (1962) 106 SJ 243 CA Employers not liable for injury occasioned to plaintiff workman as direct result of another workman's prank.

British Titan Products Co, Ltd, Chipchase v [1956] 1 All ER 613 CA Negligent management of factory as did not conform with Building (Safety, Health and Welfare) Regulations 1948 though these inapplicable.

British Transport Commission v Gourley [1955] 3 All ER 796; [1956] AC 185; (1955) 105 LJ 808; [1956] 2 WLR 41 HL Income tax and surtax factors to be considered when awarding damages.

British Transport Commission v Maxine and Co, Ltd (1963) 107 SJ 1025 CA Employers not vicariously liable for negligence of worker who had not been acting in connection with his work.

British Transport Commission, Berry v [1960] 3 All ER 322; (1960) 110 LJ 654; [1961] 1 QB 149; (1960) 104 SJ 826 HC QBD On injury to fair fame as element of malicious prosecution.

British Transport Commission, Berry v [1961] 3 All ER 65; [1955] Crim LR 587; (1961) 111 LJ 548; [1962] 1 QB 306 CA Valid malicious prosecution claim where special damages sought are real costs (less costs awarded by quarter sessions).

British Transport Commission, Chadwick v [1967] 2 All ER 945; [1967] 1 WLR 912 HC QBD Damages for nervous shock to rescuer at accident scene.

British Transport Commission, Conway v (1962) 106 SJ 78 HC QBD On duty of care owed by driver of train.

British Transport Commission, Hare and another v [1956] 1 All ER 578; (1956) 106 LJ 185; (1956) 100 SJ 189; [1956] 1 WLR 250 HC QBD Guards door need not be closed when train starts but was negligent not to have closed sixty yards after starting.

British Transport Commission, Hazell v (1958) 108 LJ 74; (1958) 102 SJ 124 HC QBD Special precautions at rail accommodation crossing to be taken by those seeking to traverse same, not rail authority.

British Transport Commission, Hicks v [1958] 1 WLR 493 CA Shunter's/railway company's failure to take reasonable care of self/shunter meant both equally liable in negligence for injury of shunter.

British Transport Commission, Judson v [1954] 1 All ER 624 CA Wilful violation of company rules meant injury could not be attributed to employer's negligence.

British Transport Commission, Kemshead v (1956) 106 LJ 601; (1958) 102 SJ 122 CA Foggy conditions put onus on people traversing accommodation crossing, not rail authority, to take special care.

British Transport Commission, McDonald v [1955] 3 All ER 789; (1955) 99 SJ 912; [1955] 1 WLR 1323 HC QBD If equipment provided dangerous burden on provider to show took reasonable care of victim's safety.

British Transport Commission, O'Connor v [1958] 1 All ER 558; (1958) 108 LJ 232; (1958) 102 SJ 214 CA Injury of child on train not negligence of train owner as reasonable care of child responsibility of accompanying adult.

British Transport Commission, Trznadel v [1957] 3 All ER 196 CA On engine-drivers' responsibilities to railway employees on track.

British Transport Commission, Videan and another v [1963] 2 All ER 860; (1963) 113 LJ 529; [1963] 2 QB 650; (1963) 107 SJ 458; [1963] 3 WLR 374 CA Child trespasser could not recover damages for negligence; stationmaster on tracks was reasonably foreseeable so duty of care/ damages.

British Union for the Abolition of Vivisection, Tudor-Hart v [1937] 4 All ER 475; [1938] 2 KB 329; [1938] 107 LJCL 501; (1938) 158 LTR 162; (1937) 81 SJ 1020; (1937-38) LIV TLR 154 CA Cannot apply for particulars of facts as is application for evidence.

British Vacuum Cleaner Company (Limited) v New Vacuum Cleaner Company (Limited) [1907] 2 Ch 312; (1907-08) XCVII LTR 201; (1906-07) XXIII TLR 587 HC ChD 'Vacuum cleaner' was descriptive term not fancy term: same principles applicable to use of similar company names as apply to passing off.

British Waterways Board, Burnett v [1972] 2 All ER 1353; (1972) 116 SJ 783; [1972] 1 WLR 1329 HC QBD Employee does not freely do acts required by employer so no defence of volenti non fit injuria as actions not voluntary.

British Waterways Board, Burnett v [1973] 2 All ER 631; (1973) 123 NLJ 179t; (1973) 117 SJ 203; [1973] 1 WLR 700 CA Exclusion of liability clause inapplicable if person has no choice in accepting/rejecting it; volenti non fit injuria only if fully and freely consent to risk waiver.

Broad, R v [1914-17] All ER 90; [1915] AC 1110; (1914-15) XXXI TLR 599 PC Bye-law precluding recovery for negligence was ultra vires.

Broadbent v Mayor, Aldermen and Burgesses of the Borough of Burlington [1935] LJNCCR 258 CyCt Local authority not liable in negligence for injuries occasioned through sewer explosion from cause not previously known of.

Broadhurst, Malcolm and another v [1970] 3 All ER 508 HC QBD Reasonably foreseeable that unstable wife would be affected by negligent injury to husband; no damages for loss of wages by wife.

Broadley v Guy Clapham and Co [1994] 4 All ER 439; [1993] TLR 375 CA Limitation period in action for negligent surgical operation runs from date when victim broadly knows or could have known with the help of medical advice that injury resulted from surgery.

Broadway Approvals Ltd and another v Odhams Press Ltd and another (1964) 114 LJ 623; [1964] 2 QB 683; (1964) 108 SJ 564; [1964] 3 WLR 243 HC QBD Cannot be fair comment unless factual basis of comment is basically true.

Broadway Approvals, Ltd and another v Odhams Press, Ltd and another [1965] 2 All ER 523; (1965) 115 LJ 416; (1965) 109 SJ 294; [1965] 1 WLR 805 CA Newpaper article need not be profiting from wrongdoing (so no automatic punitive damges); non-/apology/retraction not per se evidence of malice; knowledge of one area of company need not be imputed to another; editing of article not malice but colouring article could be.

Brock v Richards [1951] 1 KB 529; (1951) 95 SJ 75; [1951] 1 TLR 69; (1951) WN (I) 22 CA Not negligent to allow non-vicious horse which had tendency to wander but posed no particular threat to stray onto highway.

Brocklebank, Manton v [1923] 1 KB 406; [1923] 92 LJCL 624 (also CA); (1922-23) 67 SJ 213; (1922-23) XXXIX TLR 112; (1922) WN (I) 341 HC KBD Liability of owner of mare (here ferae naturae) in negligence/trespass for injury caused to another's animal by mare.

Brocklebank, Manton v [1923] All ER 416; [1923] 2 KB 212; (1923) CC Rep XII 28; [1923] 92 LJCL 624 (also HC KBD); (1923) 129 LTR 135; (1922-23) 67 SJ 455; (1922-23) XXXIX TLR 344; (1923) WN (I) 107 CA Mare not dangerous animal: absent owner negligence not liable for loss occasioned by kicking.

Bromilow v Howard (1959) 109 LJ ccr268 CyCt Failed claim in detinue by owner of dog who wandered against buyer who purchased dog as stray.

Bromley Magistrates' Court, ex parte Waitrose Ltd, R v [1980] 3 All ER 464 HC QBD Faulty application within 21 days to state case may be amended within reasonable time.

Bromley Urban District Council, Davis v (1903) 67 JP 275 CA Punitive damages appropriate for trespass by local authority.

Bromley v Mercer [1922] 2 KB 126; [1922] 91 LJCL 577; (1922) 127 LTR 282; (1921-22) XXXVIII TLR 496; (1922) WN (I) 112 CA Non-liability to non-user of highway for injury suffered via wall which was public nuisance on highway.

Brook v Hoar [1967] 3 All ER 395; (1967) 117 NLJ 887t; (1967) 111 SJ 634; [1967] 1 WLR 1336 HC QBD Infant in position of lodger in parent's house not in parent's custody and control.

Brooke House Motors Ltd, Wickham Holdings Ltd v [1967] 1 WLR 295 CA Finance company could only recover outstanding amount due under hire-purchase agreement where hirer wrongfully sold goods hired.

Brown and another, Kennett v [1988] 2 All ER 600; (1988) 132 SJ 752; [1988] 1 WLR 582 CA
Claimant need not seek disapplication of limitation period unless and until other party raises it.

Brown and another, Thompson v (1981) 131 NLJ 524; (1981) 125 SJ 377; [1981] 1 WLR 744 HL
On allowing extension to claim where if was not allowed plaintff would have guaranteed claim of
success against solicitors.

Brown and others, Brice and others v [1984] 1 All ER 997; (1984) 134 NLJ 204 HC QBD
Tortfeasor liable for nervous shock and its consequences even where not those normal person
would suffer.

Brown and Root (UK) Ltd and another, Castanho v [1980] 1 All ER 689 HC QBD Court would
strike out discontinuance as abuse of process where was done in hope of getting higher damages
abroad.

Brown and Root (UK) Ltd and another, Castanho v (1980) 124 SJ 375 CA Successful appeal
against striking out of discontinuance as abuse of process (where was done in hope of getting
higher damages abroad).

Brown and Root (UK) Ltd and another, Castanho v [1981] 1 All ER 143; (1980) 124 SJ 884 HL
No discontinuance if is abuse of process; injunction restraining foreign action available unless
foreign court better forum for action.

Brown Construction (Ebbw Vale) Ltd and others, Thompson v [1981] 2 All ER 296 HL Potential
negligence claim against solicitor not ground for refusing to disapply limitation in personal
injury/fatal accident action.

Brown v Harrison (1947) 97 LJ 361; (1947) 177 LTR 281; (1947) LXIII TLR 484; (1947) WN
(I) 191 CA Owner of dying tree liable for injury sustained by person on highway on whom fell
as ought to have realised and remedied danger tree posed.

Brown v KMR Services Ltd [1995] 4 All ER 598 CA Underwriting agent owes investor duty to
provide proper information on character and risk of business underwritten; loss arising from failure
to do so is measured by probable happening if proper advice given; liability is for foreseeable loss
irrespective of scale; advice not ongoing: set-off against profits from earlier advice not possible.

Brown v KMR Services Ltd; Daniels (Sword) v Pitel and others [1994] 4 All ER 385 HC QBD
Failure of agent to advise client a breach of contract and a breach of duty of care.

Brown v Lambeth Borough Council (1915) CC Rep IV 86; (1915-16) XXXII TLR 61 HC KBD
Council not liable in negligence for collision of taxi with unlit refuge (which was normally lit) as
fact that unlit not shown to be due to council's negligence.

Brown v New Empress Saloons Limited (1937) 156 LTR 427; (1937) WN (I) 156 CA On practice
as regards awarding costs as element of damages in personal injuries action.

Brown v Rolls Royce, Ltd [1960] 1 All ER 577; (1960) 110 LJ 220 HL Burden of proof on person
claiming negligence applies to entirety of evidence, not the various elements thereof.

Brown v T and EC Cotterill (1934-35) LI TLR 21 HC KBD Monumental masons liable for injury
suffered by girl when negligently erected tombstone fell on her.

Brown, Citizen's Life Assurance Company, Limited v [1904-07] All ER 925; [1904] AC 423;
[1904] 73 LJPC 102; (1904) XC LTR 739; (1903-04) XX TLR 497; (1904-05) 53 WR 176 PC
Corporation liable for (unauthorised) malicious libel by its servant acting in course of
employment.

Brown, Durant, and Co, King v [1913] 2 Ch 416; (1913) 48 LJ 471; (1913) 82 LJCh 548 HC ChD
Commoner cannot sue other commoner/stranger for simple trespass (but can sue for interference
with his rights).

Brown, Ellwood v [1937] LJNCCR 153 CyCt Recovery of damages for harbouring of bugs but not
for invasion of same (where origin of invading bugs unproved).

Brown, Gollop v (1952) 102 LJ 360 CyCt Failed action in detinue by father against daughter for
return of piano originally given to her as birthday present.

Brown-Thomson v Harrods Limited (1924-25) 69 SJ 710 HC KBD Though store-owners may have
been prima facie negligent in allowing dogs to be chained at store entrance, person bitten by dog
at entrance might nonetheless be contributorily negligent.

Buckle v Holmes [1926] All ER 90; (1926) 90 JP 109; [1926] 2 KB 125; (1926) 61 LJ 324; [1926] 95 LJCL 547; (1926) 134 LTR 743; (1925-26) 70 SJ 464; (1925-26) XLII TLR 369; (1925) WN (I) 295 CA Cat-owner not liable for cat trespass unless aware of peculiar tendency of cat to cause damage; cats and dogs treated the same in law of trespass.

Buckles, Young v [1952] 1 KB 220 CA Recoverability of professional charges in excess of that for which building licence allowed (Defence (General) Regulations 1939, r 56(4) applied).

Buckley, Osborne, Garrett and Co, Ltd, and Wyrovoys Products, Ltd, Watson v [1940] 1 All ER 174; (1940) 89 LJ 45 HC KBD Donoghue v Stevenson applied to goods distributors.

Buckner v Ashby and Horner, Limited (1941) 105 JP 107; [1941] 1 KB 321; [1941] 110 LJ 460; (1941) 85 SJ 106; (1940-41) LVII TLR 238; (1941) WN (I) 11 HC KBD Contractor not liable for post-construction injury following approval by local authority that work had been done to its satisfaction.

Buckner v Ashby and Horner, Limited (1941) 105 JP 220; (1941) 85 SJ 200; (1940-41) LVII TLR 414; (1941) WN (I) 52 CA Contractor not liable for post-construction injury following approval by local authority that work had been done to its satisfaction.

Budd and others, Lloyds Bank Ltd (Administrators of the Estate of Peter Lewis Hughes, deceased) v [1982] RTR 80 CA Was negligent to drive defective lorry onto fog-covered motorway but person who occasioned greatest damage in pile-up was most liable as had been driving excessively fast in fog.

Budd v Anderson and others (1941) 91 LJ 294; (1941) 85 SJ 405; (1942-43) LIX TLR 341 HC KBD On procedural irregularities in detention under wartime detention legislation (Defence (General) Regulations 1939, reg 18B).

Budejovicky Budvar Narodni Podnik and others, Anheuser-Busch Inc v (1984) 128 SJ 398 CA 'Budweiser' beer found to have dual reputation in United Kingdom; sales of US 'Budweiser' on US military bases in UK did not create necessary goodwill in market at large to support passing off action.

Buesnel v Mendelson and another (Eastern Counties Omnibus Co Ltd and another (third parties)) (1959) 109 LJ ccr141 CyCt Person overtaking on inside of bus liable in damages for negligent injury occasioned to passenger on motorcycle waved forward by bus driver at junction.

Building and Civil Engineering Holidays Scheme Management Ltd v Post Office [1966] 1 QB 247; (1964) 108 SJ 939; [1965] 2 WLR 72 CA Damages for future loss arising from conversion.

Building and Civil Engineering Holidays Scheme Management Ltd v Post Office [1964] 2 QB 430; [1964] 2 WLR 967 HC QBD On damages available for conversion of chattel.

Bull (AH) and Company v West African Shipping Agency and Lighterage Company [1927] AC 686; (1927) 137 LTR 498 PC Party hiring property liable for negligence of persons under their control responsible for property.

Bull v The Mayor, &c, of Shoreditch (1903) 67 JP 37; (1902-03) XIX TLR 64 CA Local authority liable for personal injuries driver suffered when collided with earth pile (of which authority knew) in course of avoiding part of road made by local authority but unfit for public traffic.

Bull v The Mayor, &c, of Shoreditch (1901-02) XVIII TLR 171 CA Was evidence of misfeasance for jury in respect of personal injuries driver suffered when collided with earth pile (of which authority knew) in course of avoiding part of road made by local authority but unfit for public traffic.

Bull v Vasquez (1946) 96 LJ 218 HC KBD MP on Parliamentary leave while in Army could sue for slander of self in professional guise of army officer; appropriate damages.

Bull v Vasquez and another [1947] 1 All ER 334; [1947] 116 LJR 551 CA MP on Parliamentary leave while in Army could sue for slander of self in professional guise of army officer; appropriate damages.

Bull, Mayor, &c, of Shoreditch v (1904) 68 JP 415; (1904) XC LTR 210; (1903-04) XX TLR 254 HL Approval of decision whereby local authority found liable for personal injuries driver suffered when collided with earth pile (of which authority knew) in course of avoiding part of road made by local authority but unfit for public traffic.

Bullard v Croydon Hospital Group Management Committee and another [1953] 1 All ER 596; (1953) 117 JP 182; (1953) 103 LJ 139; [1953] 1 QB 511; (1953) 97 SJ 155 HC QBD Hospital group management committee could be liable in negligence.

Bullen (AH) v The Swan Electric Engraving Company (1905-06) XXII TLR 275 HC KBD Bailees not liable for loss of goods over which took same degree of care that reasonable person would take of own goods.

Bullen v The Swan Electric Engraving Company (1906-07) XXIII TLR 258 CA Bailees not liable for loss of goods over which took same degree of care that reasonable person would take of own goods.

Bullock Bros (Electrical), Ltd and another, Holdack v; Martens (third party) (1964) 108 SJ 861 HC QBD Overtaker one-third liable for not sounding horn as overtook; person being overtaken two-thirds liable for not seeing overtaker/for changing course while being overtaken.

Bullock Brothers (Electrical), Ltd, and another (Martens Third Party), Holdack v (1965) 109 SJ 238 CA Was reasonable for trial judge to hold that overtaker ought to have sounded horn though was no general requirement that had to do so.

Bullock v Reeve (1901) 84 LTR 55; [1901] 70 LJK/QB 42; (1900-01) 49 WR 93 HC QBD House owner not liable to abate nuisance arising from defective drainage which by virtue of deviation from drainage plan sanctioned by Sewage Commissioners was a sewer, not a drain.

Bulmer (HP) Ltd and another v J Bollinger SA and others [1974] Ch 401; (1977) 127 NLJ 914t; [1974] 3 WLR 202 CA Article 177 reference to European Court of Justice in course of passing off action (on EEC wine/champagne legislation).

Bulmer and Allington, Parry and others v (1913) CC Rep II 108 CyCt No damages for non-repair of fences voluntarily erected and maintained by owner of land adjoining common.

Bulmer Rayon Company, Limited, Freshwater and another v [1933] Ch 162 (also CA); (1933) 102 LJCh 102 (also CA) HC ChD Non-merger of causes of action of successive not joint tortfeasors.

Bulmer Rayon Company, Limited, Freshwater and another v [1933] Ch 162 (also HC ChD); (1933) 102 LJCh 102 (also HC ChD); (1933) 148 LTR 251; (1932) WN (I) 211 CA Non-merger of causes of action of successive not joint tortfeasors.

Bulmer Rayon Company, Limited v Freshwater and another [1933] AC 661 HL Non-merger of causes of action.

Bunce, Green v [1936] LJNCCR 349 CyCt Lorry driver negligent where failed to apply brakes when swerving to avoid pedestrian and so ended up driving onto pavement, there striking the plaintiff.

Bundy, Lloyds Bank Ltd v [1975] QB 326; [1974] 3 WLR 501 CA Bank owed fiduciary duty of care to old customer and had breached same by means of undue influence.

Bunker v Charles Brand and Son, Ltd [1969] 2 All ER 59; (1969) 119 NLJ 412; [1969] 2 QB 480; [1969] 2 WLR 1392 HC QBD Tunnel diggers were 'occupiers' of tunnel and digging machine and owed occupier's duty of care (even though victim aware of injury).

Bunn, Thomas v; Wilson v Graham; Lea v British Aerospace plc [1991] 1 AC 362; (1990) 140 NLJ 1789; [1990] TLR 783; [1991] 2 WLR 27 HL Interest on personal injury damages rightly ran from date of judgment in which damages payable gauged.

Bunnell, Larking v (1912) CC Rep I 23 CyCt Person bringing article dangerous in itself (here gas) into premises not liable where accident occurs that does not arise from said person not exercising reasonable care.

Bunting, Compton v (1939) 83 SJ 398 HC ChD Noise emanating from kindergarten/preparatory school music room deemed not to be such a nuisance as merited injunctive relief.

Burberrys v JC Cording and Co (Limited) (1909) 100 LTR 985; (1908-09) XXV TLR 576 HC ChD Failed injunction to prevent firm using name that was at once descriptive and distinctive.

Burchill and another, Berkoff v [1996] 4 All ER 1008; (1996) TLR 9/8/96 CA To state of actor that he was 'hideous-looking' could be defamatory.

Burden and others (No 2), Karak Rubber Co Ltd v (1971) 115 SJ 888; [1972] 1 WLR 602 HC ChD On duty of care owed by bankers to customers (here not discharged).

Burdett v Horne (Elizabeth) and Horne (Frederick Walters) (1910-11) XXVII TLR 402 HC KBD Husband liable for wife's torts.

Burdett v Horne and another (1911-12) XXVIII TLR 83 CA Husband liable for wife's torts.

Burge, Warren and Ridgley, Limited, Corbett v (1931-32) XLVIII TLR 626 HC KBD Failed action in tort for malicious issue of civil process (no malice proven).

Burgoyne v Phillips [1983] Crim LR 265; (1983) 147 JP 375; [1983] RTR 49; [1982] TLR 559 HC QBD On what constitutes 'driving' a car.

Burke v Purdie [1935] LJNCCR 303 CyCt Innkeeper negligent in leaving guest's car-keys on open access in reception office and so liable for damage occasioned when car taken for 'joy-ride'.

Burke, McGinley v (1973) 117 SJ 488; [1973] 1 WLR 990 HC QBD Was not proper for plaintiff in personal injuries action to see medical report prepared for defendant but not vice versa.

Burley (C), Limited v Edward Lloyd, Limited (1928-29) XLV TLR 626 HC KBD Milton Creek Conservancy Act 1899, s 78 did not empower licensee to erect obstruction in creek.

Burley v Hibell (1916) CC Rep V HC KBD Where car collides into car that has broken down the driver of the latter car (even if was negligent) may recover damages from driver of former if collision could reasonably have been avoided.

Burn, Hargrove v (1929-30) XLVI TLR 59 HC KBD On law of negligence as applied to traffic accident actions.

Burnett and Dunbar and another, Lewys v [1945] 2 All ER 555; (1945) 109 JP 253; (1945) 173 LTR 307; (1945) 89 SJ 415; (1944-45) LXI TLR 527 HC KBD Persons giving free lift negligent for not warning dead passenger of what they knew; highway authority liable in nuisance for negligent raising of road beneath bridge.

Burnett and Hallamshire Fuel, Ltd v Sheffield Telegraph and Star, Ltd [1960] 2 All ER 157; (1960) 104 SJ 388 HC QBD Privilege for fair and accurate reporting of judicial proceedings attaches to account of advocate's orations therein.

Burnett v British Waterways Board [1973] 2 All ER 631; (1973) 123 NLJ 179t; (1973) 117 SJ 203; [1973] 1 WLR 700 CA Exclusion of liability clause inapplicable if person has no choice in accepting/rejecting it; volenti non fit injuria only if fully and freely consent to risk waiver.

Burnett v British Waterways Board [1972] 2 All ER 1353; (1972) 116 SJ 783; [1972] 1 WLR 1329 HC QBD Employee does not freely do acts required by employer so no defence of volenti non fit injuria as actions not voluntary.

Burnett, Hood and Hampton v Warden [1935] LJNCCR 245 CyCt That medical treatment given in error did not mean administration of same was perforce negligent.

Burnett, Housecroft v [1986] 1 All ER 332; (1985) 135 NLJ 728 HC QBD £75,000 appropriate for pain/suffering/loss of tetraplegic; no damages in respect of national health care nursing; sham contract for services will not yield extra damages; awards for non-economic loss altered only if clearly too high/low.

Burnham v Boyer and Brown [1936] 2 All ER 1165; (1936) 82 LJ 133 HC KBD Under Law Reform (Married Women and Tortfeasors) Act 1965, s 6 contribution available from joint tortfeasor added as third party.

Burnison v Bangor Corporation (1931) 72 LJ 397 CA On liability of waterworks company in negligence for mains escape.

Burns and others v Associated Newspapers, Limited (1925) 89 JP 205; (1925-26) XLII TLR 37 HC ChD Might be libellous to call person a Communist but not statement as to personal character under Municipal Elections (Corrupt and Illegal Practices) Act 1911, s 1(1).

Burns v Ellicott (1969) 113 SJ 490 HC QBD On responsibility of driver when overtaking horserider on horse.

Burnside and another v Emerson and another (1969) 133 JP 66; (1968) 112 SJ 565; [1968] 1 WLR 1490 CA Highway authority in part liable for injury arising from inadequate maintenance of highway.

Burr v Smith [1908-10] All ER 443; [1909] 2 KB 306; [1909] 78 LJKB 889; (1909-10) 101 LTR 194; (1908-09) 53 SJ 502; (1908-09) XXV TLR 542; (1909) WN (I) 115 CA Official receiver's report absolutely privileged.

Butler (or Black) v Fife Coal Company (Limited) (1911-12) XXVIII TLR 150 HL Mineowners liable to widowed miner for negligence as regards appointing competent manager.

Butler and Co (Limited) v Quilter (1900-01) XVII TLR 159 HC QBD Innkeeper by proving was not negligent does not obviate his liability for loss of goods of guest.

Butler v Standard Telephones and Cables, Ltd; McCarthy v Standard Telephones and Cables, Ltd [1940] 1 All ER 121; [1940] 1 KB 399; [1940] 109 LJCL 238; (1940) 163 LTR 145; (1940) 84 SJ 189; (1939-40) LVI TLR 273; (1940) WN (I) 26 HC KBD Tree roots spreading into neighbour's property were deemed nuisance.

Butler, RB Policies at Lloyd's v [1949] 2 All ER 226; [1950] 1 KB 76; (1949) 99 LJ 373; (1949) LXV TLR 436; (1949) WN (I) 299 HC KBD Time for detinue action ran from date of theft though did not then know thief's identity.

Butte Mining plc (No 2), Ernst and Young (a firm) v; Butte Mining plc v Ernst and Young (a firm) and others [1997] 2 All ER 471 HC ChD Counterclaim whereby was sought to bring negligence action struck out.

Buttercup Margarine Co (Lim), Ewing (trading as the Buttercup Dairy Co) v (1916-17) 61 SJ 369; (1917) WN (I) 89 HC ChD Injunction granted to restrain use of trade name in circumstances where use in said way would give rise to confusion.

Buttercup Margarine Company, Limited, Ewing v [1917] 2 Ch 1; (1917) 52 LJ 172; (1917-18) 117 LTR 67; (1916-17) 61 SJ 443; (1917) WN (I) 153 CA Injunction granted to restrain use of trade name in circumstances where use in said way would give rise to confusion.

Butters Bros and Co, Farr v [1932] All ER 339; [1932] 2 KB 606; (1932) 74 LJ 144; (1932) 101 LJCL 768; (1932) 147 LTR 427; (1932) WN (I) 171 CA Manufacturer not liable for defect in product that could be and was discovered before use.

Bux v Slough Metals [1974] 1 All ER 262 CA Correspondence between common law and statutory duty of care a question of fact in each case.

Buxton and another v Jayne and others (1960) 104 SJ 602 CA Leave granted to bring action against local authority officer for not exercising reasonable care when deciding to have one plaintiff removed to mental hospital against her will.

Buxton, Champagne Heidsieck et Cie Monopole Societe Anonyme v [1930] 1 Ch 330; (1930) 69 LJ 43; (1930) 99 LJCh 149; (1930) 142 LTR 324 HC ChD Failed action for passing off where defendant sold plaintiff's French wine under plaintiff's label in England.

Byng, Timothy Whites Ltd v [1934] LJNCCR 47 CyCt Animal owners under positive duty to restrain their animals trespassing on another's property.

Byrne and another v Kinematograph Renters Society, Ltd and others [1958] 2 All ER 579 HC ChD No conspiracy as no trespass when inspectors from trade protection society entered cinema to monitor operation thereof.

Byrne v Byrne [1937] 2 All ER 204 CA Not defamatory to say person informed police of crime.

Byrne v Deane [1937] 1 KB 818; [1937] 106 LJCL 533; (1937) 157 LTR 10; (1937) 81 SJ 236; (1936-37) LIII TLR 469; (1937) WN (I) 126 CA Allegation that were police informer not defamatory.

Bywater v Bennett and Pye [1934] LJNCCR 117 CyCt House-owner (but not estate agent) liable in negligence towards person injured whilst being shown around unoccupied house by estate agent.

C and A Modes, Gibson v (1977) 127 NLJ 416b CA Failed negligence action against store-owners by woman who injured self in not reasonably foreseeable mannner which had not previously occurred (tripped over up-turning tile).

C and T Harris (Calne), Limited v Harris (1934) 78 SJ 13; (1933-34) L TLR 123 HC ChD Failed action to prevent person using own name where was no real risk of confusion/passing off.

C and T Harris (Calne), Limited v Harris (1933-34) L TLR 338 CA Failed action to prevent person using own name where was no real risk of confusion/passing off.

C Burley, Limited v Stepney Borough Council (1947) 176 LTR 535 HC KBD No implied warranty that goods to be carried could safely be carried.

C Czarnikow Ltd v Koufos [1966] 2 WLR 1397 CA Damages recoverable for reasonably foreseeable damage which occurs.

C De Trey and Co (Limited), The Dental Manufacturing Company (Limited) v (1911-12) XXVIII TLR 272 HC KBD Sole agent could not maintain passing off action for loss of profits through sale of profits under similar get-up of product for which is sole agent.

C De Trey and Co, Dental Manufacturing Company, Limited v [1912] 3 KB 76; (1912) 81 LJKB 1162; (1912-13) 107 LTR 111; (1911-12) XXVIII TLR 498; (1912) WN (I) 190 CA Sole agent could not maintain passing off action for loss of profits where had not sold item under own get-up.

C Gibbs and Co, Slazengers (Limited) v (1916-17) XXXIII TLR 35 HC ChD Given that First World War in progress plaintiff firm could sue for libel where was alleged to be German firm.

C v Hackney London Borough Council [1995] 2 FCR 306; [1996] 1 FLR 427; [1995] TLR 580 CA Res judicata did not apply where child seeking damages for circumstances that led mother to bring earlier successful action at which child not represented.

C v Mirror Group Newspapers and others [1996] 4 All ER 511; [1997] 1 FCR 556; [1996] 2 FLR 532; (1996) 146 NLJ 1093; (1996) TLR 15/7/96; [1997] 1 WLR 131 CA Over five years after newspaper article published woman not allowed/allowed bring defamation/malicious falsehood claim.

C, N v [1997] 2 FCR 600 CA Striking out of negligence action against valuer (regarding valuation of family home as part of divorce proceedings) where issue of valuation had been considered in the ancillary relief proceedings.

CA Daw and Son, Ltd and others, Haseldine v [1941] 1 All ER 525; (1941) 91 LJ 181; (1942) 92 LJ 60; (1941) 85 SJ 265; (1940-41) LVII TLR 431 HC KBD Flatowner liable for negligence of agent contractors; owner owed duty to warn licensee of dangers of which actually knew (did not know here); defence of having employed competent independent contractor not open as only limited maintenance contract; contractor liable for defective repairs.

CA Daw and Son, Ltd, and others, Haseldine v [1941] 3 All ER 156; [1941] 2 KB 343; (1941) 91 LJ 359; [1942] 111 LJ 45; (1941) 165 LTR 185; (1941-42) LVIII TLR 1 CA Flatowner's employment of competent contractors relieved liability in negligence; contractors liable to injury occasioned by negligent repairs.

Cackett v Earl (1976) 126 NLJ 1090t HC QBD State benefits deductible from expenses being awarded on foot of negligence claim arising from road accident.

Cadam and others v Beaverbrook Newspapers, Ltd [1959] 1 All ER 453; (1959) 109 LJ 184; [1959] 1 QB 413; (1959) 103 SJ 177 CA Just stating that writ issued/particulars of writ might be justifiable; on pleading.

Cadbury Schweppes Pty Ltd and others v Pub Squash Co Pty Ltd [1981] 1 All ER 213; (1980) 130 NLJ 1095; (1981) 125 SJ 96; [1981] 1 WLR 193 PC Passing off extends to distinctive ads. to which goodwill attached.

Cader (Mahomed Abdul) v Kaufman and another (1928) 66 LJ 425; (1928) WN (I) 264 PC Failed petition for special leave to appeal in action concerning the extent of privilege enjoyed when speaking in the Ceylonese Legislative Council.

Caffery, Dallison v [1964] Crim LR 538; (1964) 128 JP 379; [1965] 1 QB 348; (1964) 108 SJ 560; [1964] 3 WLR 385 CA No false imprisonment where policeman held reasonable belief detainee had committed offence and reasonable grounds for delaying release; not malicious prosecution as had been reasonable cause for same.

Cain (Administrator of the estate of Jill M Cain (deceased)) v Wilcock [1968] 3 All ER 817; (1969) 119 NLJ 12; (1968) 112 SJ 844; [1968] 1 WLR 1961 CA On damages for (infant's) loss of expectation of life.

Caldecutt v Piesse (1932) 76 SJ 799; (1932-33) XLIX TLR 26 HC KBD On duty owed in respect of guests' property by (non-innkeeper) person who keeps guest house for reward.

Caledonian Railway Company, Corporation of Greenock v; Corporation of Greenock v Glasgow and South-Western Railway Company [1917] AC 556; (1917) 81 JP 269 HL Liable for flooding resulting from interference with course of stream.

Callan and others, Excelsior Wire Rope Company, Limited v [1930] All ER 1; [1930] AC 404; (1930) 94 JP 174; (1930) 69 LJ 218; (1930) 99 LJCL 380; (1930) 142 LTR 531; (1930) WN (I) 55 HL Liable in negligence for injury to child trespasser where knew was probable that children would be near when dangerous machine operated.

Callinicos, Karavias v (1917) WN (I) 323 CA Successful action for damages for personal injuries suffered as result of negligence of defendant when giving plaintiff a free ride in his car.

Calliope (Owners), Carsholm (Owners) v; The Calliope [1970] 2 WLR 991 HC PDAD Finding of negligence on one hand and intervening negligence on other in shipping collision case.

Callow v Tillstone (1900-01) LXXXIII LTR 411 HC QBD Negligent certification by vet that unsound meat is fit for consumption can ground conviction for aiding and abetting in sale of unsound meat.

Caluori, Klein v [1971] 2 All ER 701; (1971) 121 NLJ 153; [1971] RTR 354; (1971) 115 SJ 228; [1971] 1 WLR 619 HC QBD Owner not vicariously liable where person who borrowed car without permission returning it under owner's instructions.

Calveley and others v Chief Constable of the Merseyside Police; Worrall and others v Same; Park v Chief Constable of the Greater Manchester Police (1988) 138 NLJ 267; [1989] QB 136; (1988) 132 SJ 1244; [1988] 3 WLR 1020 CA No common law duty of care owed by investigating officer (in disciplinary action against police officers) towards officers being investigated.

Calveley and others v Chief Constable of the Merseyside Police and other appeals [1989] 1 All ER 1025; [1989] AC 1228; (1989) 139 NLJ 469; (1989) 133 SJ 456; [1989] 2 WLR 624 HL Misfeasance in public office requires that public officer performs act in bad faith/without reasonable cause in respect of which his office shields him.

Calvert and another v Pick and another [1954] 1 All ER 566; (1954) 104 LJ 170; (1954) 98 SJ 147 HC QBD Court will not adjudicate on matter that is really settled between various parties.

Calvert, Anderson v (1907-08) XXIV TLR 399 CA On considerations for jury when assessing damages for libel.

Calvet v Tomkies and others [1963] 3 All ER 610; (1963) 113 LJ 722; (1963) 107 SJ 791; [1963] 1 WLR 1397 CA Evidence of actual loss suffered not admitted as general pecuniary loss claimed.

Cambay Prince Steamship Co, Ltd, Margarine Union GmbH v [1967] 3 All ER 775; [1969] 1 QB 219; (1967) 111 SJ 943; [1967] 3 WLR 1569 HC QBD Shipowner does not duty of care to party not owning goods when tort committed.

Cambridge Newspapers Ltd, Pedley v (1964) 108 SJ 375; [1964] 1 WLR 988 CA General damages payable for what were technically three actions in respect of three cases of innuendo.

Cambridge Water Co Ltd v Eastern Counties Leather plc [1994] 1 All ER 53; [1994] 2 AC 264; [1994] 2 WLR 53 CA Foreseeability of relevant damage necessary before strict liability for escape likely to do mischief.

Cambridge Water Co Ltd v Eastern Counties Leather plc [1994] 1 All ER 53; [1994] 2 AC 264; (1994) 144 NLJ 15; (1994) 138 SJ LB 24; [1993] TLR 641; [1994] 2 WLR 53 HL Foreseeability of relevant damage necessary before strict liability for escape likely to do mischief.

Camden and Islington Area Health Authority, Choo (Lim Poh) v [1979] 1 All ER 332; (1978) 128 NLJ 63t; [1979] QB 196; [1978] 3 WLR 895 HC QBD Damages to include lost earnings; not to be adjusted for inflation.

Camden and Islington Area Health Authority, Choo (Lim Poh) v [1979] 1 All ER 332; (1978) 128 NLJ 933; (1978) 122 SJ 509; [1979] QB 196; [1978] 3 WLR 895 CA Damages to include lost earnings; not to be adjusted for inflation.

Camden and Islington Area Health Authority, Choo (Lim Poh) v [1979] 2 All ER 910; [1980] AC 174; (1979) 129 (2) NLJ 656; (1979) 123 SJ 457; [1979] 3 WLR 44 HL Damages for loss of earnings available but to be reduced by damages for cost of future care.

Camden and Islington Area Health Authority, Connolly v [1981] 3 All ER 250; (1981) 131 NLJ 802 HC QBD Young child can claim damages for loss of earnings in lost years.

Camden and Islington Area Health Authority, Lim v (1978) 122 SJ 82 HC QBD On making allowances for inflation when awarding personal injury damages.

Campion, Bognor Regis Urban District Council v [1972] 2 All ER 61; (1972) 122 NLJ 377; [1972] 2 QB 169 HC QBD Local government authority can sue in libel to preserve its reputation.

Campling and another, Astaire v [1965] 3 All ER 666; (1965) 109 SJ 854; [1966] 1 WLR 34 CA Innuendo cannot make a true and innocent statement libellous.

Campling and others, Astaire v (1965) 109 SJ 703 HC QBD Suggested innuendoes would not occur to reasonable reader so claims of libel based on same to be struck out.

Canada Steamship Lines, Ltd v R [1952] 1 All ER 305; [1952] AC 192; [1952] 1 TLR 261 PC Exemption from negligence clause to be clearly worded; if generally worded and covers negligence other basis for action may obviate exemption from negligence suit.

Canadian Government Merchant Marine, Limited, Gosse Millard, Limited v (1928-29) XLV TLR 63 HL Recovery of damages where negligence of crew resulted in damage to goods.

Canadian Government Merchant Marine, Limited, Gosse Millard, Limited v (1926-27) XLIII TLR 544 HC KBD Recovery of damages for damage to goods where shipowner did not show that neither they nor their servants had been negligent.

Canadian Northern Railway Company, McMillan v [1923] AC 120; (1923) 128 LTR 293; (1922) WN (I) 312 PC Action brought by Ontario resident in Saskatchewan could not be maintained as cause of action could be 'justified' in Ontario.

Canadian Pacific Rail Co v R [1931] All ER 113; (1931) 100 LJPC 129 PC No trespass where was evidence of longtime occupation of land.

Canadian Pacific Railway Company v Frechette [1915] AC 871; [1915] 84 LJPC 161; (1915-16) 113 LTR 1116; (1914-15) XXXI TLR 529 PC Quebecois could not recover damages where real cause of accident was own negligence (despite contributory negligence of party sued).

Canadian Pacific Railway Company v Parke and another (1899-1900) LXXXI LTR 127 PC That Crown authorised diversion of water from natural path did not mean could not be liable under common law in performance of same.

Canadian Pacific Steamship Co, Moore v [1945] 1 All ER 128; (1946) 96 LJ 185 Assizes Statutory duty to record entry in ship's log and absence of malice meant qualified privilege.

Canadian Pacific Steamships, Ltd, Norton v [1961] 2 All ER 785; (1961) 111 LJ 484; (1961) 105 SJ 442 CA Shipowners not liable for negligence of porter not in any way connected to them other than carrying ship luggage.

Canadian Pacific Wine Co v Tuley and others [1921] LJPC 233 PC Police not rendered trespassers by seizing goods absent search warrant in course of lawful search/seizure.

Canary Wharf Ltd, Hunter and others v; Hunter and others v London Docklands Development Corp [1996] 1 All ER 482; (1995) 145 NLJ 1645; (1995) 139 SJ LB 214; [1995] TLR 514; [1996] 2 WLR 348 CA Television interference following erection of tall building not an actionable interference with use and enjoyment of land; excessive dust and physical damage gives rise to action in negligence.

Canary Wharf Ltd, Hunter and others v; Hunter and others v London Docklands Development Corporation [1997] 2 All ER 426; (1997) 147 NLJ 634; (1997) 141 SJ LB 108; [1997] TLR 219; [1997] 2 WLR 684 HL Television interference following erection of tall building not an actionable interference with use and enjoyment of land; licensee could not sue for nuisance.

Candler v Crane, Christmas and Co [1951] 1 All ER 426; [1951] 2 KB 164; (1951) 95 SJ 171; [1951] 1 TLR 371; (1951) WN (I) 113 CA Absent contractual/fiduciary relationship accountant did not owe duty of care to third party.

Candlewood Navigation Corp Ltd v Mitsui OSK Lines Ltd and another; The Mineral Transportes, The Ibaraki Maru [1985] 2 All ER 935; [1986] AC 1; (1985) 135 NLJ 677; (1985) 129 SJ 507; [1985] 3 WLR 381 PC Non-owner of chattel cannot sue damager of chattel for economic loss.

Cannock Chase District Council, Ward v [1986] Ch 546; (1986) 130 SJ 316; [1986] 2 WLR 660 HC ChD On damages available upon damage to house resulting from council's disrepair of neighbouring buildings/vandalism consequent upon neglect.

Canter v Gardner (J) and Co, Ltd and another [1940] 1 All ER 325; (1940) 89 LJ 69; (1940) 84 SJ 289; (1939-40) LVI TLR 305 HC KBD Main contractors were not negligent and did not know of danger; sub-contractors not liable where had left place in safe shape.

Canterbury City Council and others [1980] 1 All ER 928, Dodd Properties(Kent) Ltd and another v (1980) 130 NLJ 66; (1980) 124 SJ 84; [1980] 1 WLR 433 CA Damages for building repairs are compensatory; cost of repairs that on date of action.

Canterbury City Council and others, Dodd Properties (Kent) Ltd and another v [1979] 2 All ER 118 HC QBD Generally damages measured by reference to date of damage; entitled to reasonable damages for reasonable repairs.

Canvey Island Commissioners v Preedy [1922] 1 Ch 179; (1922) 86 JP 21; [1922] 91 LJCh 203; (1922) 126 LTR 445; (1921) WN (I) 363 HC ChD Damages for trespass upon foreshore.

Caparo Industries plc v Dickman and others [1990] 1 All ER 568; [1990] 2 AC 605; (1990) 140 NLJ 248; (1990) 134 SJ 494; [1990] TLR 105; [1990] 2 WLR 358 HL Court will impose duty of care in light of existing case-law; special proximity required before duty of care arises; company auditor owes no duty of care to general public.

Caparo Industries plc v Dickman and others [1989] 1 All ER 798; (1988) 138 NLJ 289; [1989] QB 653; (1989) 133 SJ 221; [1989] 2 WLR 316 CA Auditor owes duty of care to existing shareholders but not potential shareholders/takeover bidders.

Cape Town Tramway Companies, Eastern and South African Telegraph Company v [1900-03] All ER 1316; [1902] 71 LJPC 122; (1902) LXXXVI LTR 457; (1901-02) 50 WR 657 PC Non-liability for escape of electricity.

Capel, Bartley v (1932) 74 LJ ccr78 CyCt Erection of fence was a trespass; unlawful exercise of right of way a trespass.

Capel, Cave v [1953] 1 WLR 1185 HC QBD Trespass to person and goods were one where trespass occurred while bailiff (mistakenly) seizing caravan in which person residing.

Capital and Counties Bank, Limited v Gordon; London, City and Midland Bank, Limited v Gordon (1903) WN (I) 92 HL On liability of banks for conversion of cheques.

Capital and Counties plc v Hampshire County Council and others; Digital Equipment Co Ltd v Hampshire County Council and others [1996] 4 All ER 336; (1996) TLR 26/4/96; [1996] 1 WLR 1553 HC QBD Fire brigade liable in negligence for turning off fire sprinklers thereby causing fire to spread/worsen (as was reasonably foreseeable).

Capital and Counties plc v Hampshire County Council; Digital Equipment Co Ltd v Same; John Munroe (Acrylics) Ltd v London Fire and Civil Defence Authority and others; Church of Jesus Christ of Latter-Day Saints (Great Britain) v West Yorkshire Fire and Civil Defence Authority [1997] 2 All ER 865; [1997] 2 Cr App R (S) 599; (1997) 147 NLJ 598; (1997) 141 SJ LB 92; [1997] TLR 141; [1997] 3 WLR 331 CA On common law liability of fire brigades as regards attending of fires.

Capital Finance Company Ltd v Bray [1964] 1 All ER 603; [1964] 1 WLR 323 CA No detinue where (absent contractual obligation) do not bring owner's goods to owner.

Capps v Miller [1989] 2 All ER 333; [1989] RTR 312; (1989) 133 SJ 1134; [1989] 1 WLR 839 CA Improperly fastening crash helmet contributory negligence meriting 10% reduction in damages.

Carberry (formerly an infant but now of full age) v Davies and another [1968] 2 All ER 817; (1968) 118 NLJ 372t; [1968] 1 WLR 1103 CA Owner liable if driver acting on behalf and under authority of owner.

Cardiff Channel Dry Docks and Pontoon Co, Ltd, Owners of the Steamship Pass of Ballater v [1942] 2 All ER 79 HC PDAD Very strict duty of care on party bringing dangerous substances into place: defence that gave task of policing safety to independent contractor not good.

Cardiff Corporation, Williams v [1950] 1 All ER 250; (1950) 114 JP 126; [1950] 1 KB 514; (1950) 94 SJ 161; [1950] 66 (1) TLR 243; (1950) WN (I) 44 CA Broken glass/tins on property where child playing a trap rendering occupier liable for injuries child sustained.

Carey and others, Southern Water Authority v [1985] 2 All ER 1077 HC QBD Tortious liability excluded by contractual arrangements; breach of duty of care by secondary defendants to primary defendants did not entitle latter to recover damages by indemnity.

Carey v Mayor, etc, of Bermondsey (1903) 67 JP 111 HC KBD Personal injury action not allowed where brought over six months after injury occurred.

Carey v Metropolitan Borough of Bermondsey (1903) 67 JP 447; (1903-04) XX TLR 2 CA Personal injury action not allowed where brought over six months after injury occurred.

Carlin Music Corpn, Subiddu Music Ltd and Mechanical-Copyright Protection Society Ltd v Collins (1980) 130 NLJ 218c CA Copyright Protection Society could seek to have unlawful dealings in copyright injuncted as was unlawful interference with its business in that it obtained portion of all licence fees paid.

Carlisle City Council, Ben Stansfield (Carlisle) v (1982) 126 SJ 805 CA Damages for tenants who could not use portion of (and eventually had to quit) leased building in negligent disrepair.

Carlisle Rural District Council, Irving v (1907) 71 JP 212 HC KBD Council found guilty of non-feasance (not misfeasance) of ditch.

Carlswood Glassworks, Ltd, and another, Kaiser (an infant) v (1965) 109 SJ 537 CA On need for recent medical report when deciding on damages for personal injuries.

Carlton Bank, Limited, Cornford v (1899-1900) LXXXI LTR 415; [1900] 1 QB 22; (1899-1900) XVI TLR 12 CA Corporation can be sued for malicious prosecution.

Carmarthenshire County Council v Lewis [1955] AC 549; (1955) 119 JP 230; (1955) 105 LJ 136; (1955) 99 SJ 167; [1955] 2 WLR 517 HL Is duty to prevent children (unlike animals) from straying onto highway and so imperilling others.

Carmarthenshire County Council, Davies v [1971] RTR 112 CA Council (80%) liable and driver (20%) liable for collision at sunset with lamp left in dangerous position on road after road-widening.

Carmarthenshire County Council, Lewis v [1953] 2 All ER 1403; (1954) 118 JP 51; (1953) 103 LJ 797; (1953) 97 SJ 831; [1953] 1 WLR 1439 CA Teacher owed duty of care to child straying onto highway/person foreseeably injured as result.

Carmarthenshire County Council, Lewis v (1953) 117 JP 231 Assizes Teacher owed duty of care to child straying onto highway/person foreseeably injured as result.

Carnarvon County Council, Morris v (1910) 74 JP 201 (also CA); [1910] 1 KB 159; (1909) 44 LJ 783; (1910) 79 LJKB 169; (1909-10) 101 LTR 914; (1909-10) XXVI TLR 137; (1909) WN (I) 263 HC KBD Local education authority liable for negligent injury suffered by child going through door on teacher's instruction.

Carnarvon County Council, Morris v (1910) 74 JP 201 (also HC KBD); [1910] 1 KB 840; (1910) 45 LJ 268; (1910) 79 LJKB 670; (1910) 102 LTR 524; (1909-10) 54 SJ 443; (1909-10) XXVI TLR 391; (1910) WN (I) 94 CA Local education authority liable for negligent injury suffered by child going through door on teacher's instruction.

Carpenter v Finsbury Borough Council (1920) 84 JP 107; [1920] 2 KB 195; [1920] 89 LJCL 554; (1920) 123 LTR 299; (1919-20) 64 SJ 426; (1920) WN (I) 124 HC KBD Where claim injury due to inadequate street-lighting must examine adequacy of same — cannot accept lighting authority's verdict that was adequate.

Carpenters' Company of the City of London v British Mutual Banking Company, Limited (1937) 81 SJ 118; (1936-37) LIII TLR 270 HC KBD Bank negligent in accepting cheques fraudulently indorsed and lodging same to fraudster's account.

Carpenters' Company v British Mutual Banking Company, Limited [1938] 1 KB 511; (1937) 81 SJ 701; (1936-37) LIII TLR 1040; (1937) WN (I) 329 CA Bank liable in conversion for accepting cheques fraudulently indorsed and lodging to fraudster's account.

Carr and Marples Ridgeway and Partners Ltd, Ryan v (1971) 115 SJ 206 HC QBD Person who sued another in time, only to discover out of time from particulars that ought to be suing third party had limitation period extended by court.

Carr v Hackney London Borough Council [1995] TLR 153 HC QBD Could avoid issuance of nuisance order against self by showing that were not responsibility for relevant nuisance.

Carr v James Broderick and Company, Limited (1941-42) LVIII TLR 373 HC KBD On availability of damages for conversion where owner of hire-purchase property wrongfully retakes possession of same.

Cassell and Co Ltd and another, Broome v; Same v Same [1971] 1 All ER 262 HC QBD If claiming exemplary damages must give warning and basis.

Cassell and Co Ltd and another, Broome v [1971] 2 All ER 187; [1971] 2 QB 354; (1971) 115 SJ 289; [1971] 2 WLR 853 CA Rookes v Barnard was per incuriam; exemplary damages available in libel; behaviour fell in second category of Rookes v Barnard; one sum of damages where joint tortfeasors.

Cassell and Co Ltd v Broome and another [1972] 1 All ER 801; [1972] AC 1027; (1972) 122 NLJ 195t; (1972) 116 SJ 199; [1972] 2 WLR 645 HL Rookes v Barnard guidance on exemplary damages applicable to defamation cases; practice when awarding damages.

Cassell and Co, Ltd Liebrich v [1956] 1 All ER 577, (1956) 100 SJ 188; [1956] 1 WLR 249 HC QBD On statements in open court.

Cassidy v Daily Mirror Newspapers, Limited [1929] 2 KB 331 HC KBD Liable for defamatory meaning of one's words though unintended.

Cassidy v Daily Mirror Newspapers, Ltd [1929] All ER 117; (1929) 67 LJ 399; (1929) 98 LJCL 595; (1929) 141 LTR 404; (1929) 73 SJ 348; (1928-29) XLV TLR 485 CA Are liable for defamatory meaning of one's words whether intended defamation or not.

Cassidy v Ministry of Health (Fahrni, Third Party) [1951] 1 All ER 574; [1951] 2 KB 343; (1951) 101 LJ 121; (1951) 95 SJ 253; [1951] 1 TLR 539; (1951) WN (I) 147 CA On liability of hospital authorities for negligence of medical staff.

Casson and others, Brimelow v [1923] All ER 40; [1924] 1 Ch 302 HC ChD Justified interference with contractual rights by trade associations.

Casson Beckman Rutley and Co, Arenson v [1975] 3 All ER 901; [1977] AC 405; (1975) 125 NLJ 1191t; (1975) 119 SJ 810; [1975] 3 WLR 815 HL No immunity for surveyor's negligent valuation of shares unless done judicially.

Casson Beckman Rutley and Co, Arenson v (1972) 122 NLJ 330; (1972) 116 SJ 298 HC ChD Surveyor's valuation of shares immune from suit as discharged in quasi-arbitral manner.

Castanho v Brown and Root (UK) Ltd and another [1980] 1 All ER 689 HC QBD Court would strike out discontinuance as abuse of process where was done in hope of getting higher damages abroad.

Castanho v Brown and Root (UK) Ltd and another (1980) 124 SJ 375 CA Successful appeal against striking out of discontinuance as abuse of process (where was done in hope of getting higher damages abroad).

Castanho v Brown and Root (UK) Ltd and another [1981] 1 All ER 143; (1980) 124 SJ 884 HL No discontinuance if is abuse of process; injunction restraining foreign action available unless foreign court better forum for action.

Castle v St Augustine's Links, Limited, and another (1921-22) XXXVIII TLR 615 HC KBD Golf tee and hole found to be public nuisance where were situated.

Castree v ER Squibb and Sons Ltd and another (1980) 124 SJ 743; [1980] 1 WLR 1248 CA Was actionable tort where machine though manufactured abroad was placed on market in England without warning as to special dangers.

Caswell v Powell Duffryn Associated Collieries Limited [1939] 108 LJCL 779; (1939) 161 LTR 374 HL On contributory negligence as defence to action for breach of statutory workplace health and safety duty.

Catchpole v Minster (1913) CC Rep II 113; (1913-14) 109 LTR 953; (1913-14) XXX TLR 111 HC KBD Nighttime driving of sheep on highway not per se negligent.

Cater, Cheater v [1917] 2 KB 516; (1917-18) 117 LTR 335 HC KBD Lessor under Rylands v Fletcher-style liability for death of horse eating yew branches overhanging lessee's property.

Cater, Cheater v [1918] 1 KB 247; (1918) 118 LTR 203; (1917) WN (I) 365 CA Lessor not liable for death of horse eating yew branches overhanging lessee's property as lessee took property with yew trees already overhanging.

Cates, Shaw v [1909] 1 Ch 389 HC ChD Trustees not liable in negligence for failure to periodically examine state of mortgaged property.

Chappell v Mayor, etc of Dagenham (1948) 98 LJ 329; (1948) WN (I) 274 HC KBD Non-liability of local authority for non-feasance of highway.

Chaproniere v Mason (1904-05) XXI TLR 633 CA Presence of stone in bath bun was prima facie evidence of negligent manufacture.

Charing Cross, Euston and Hampstead Rail Co, Roberts v [1900-03] All ER 157 HC ChD Negligence action well-founded despite availability of statutory compensation in respect of cause of action.

Charing Cross, West End, and City Electricity Supply Co, Ltd v London Hydraulic Power Co (1913) 77 JP 378; [1913] 3 KB 442; [1914] 83 LJKB 116; (1913-14) 109 LTR 635; (1912-13) XXIX TLR 649 HC KBD Liability for nuisance (though no negligence) for injury sustained through escape of dangerous thing from property over which enjoyed licence.

Charing Cross, West End, and City Electricity Supply Co, Ltd v London Hydraulic Power Co [1914-15] All ER 85; (1914) 78 JP 305; [1914] 3 KB 772; (1914) 49 LJ 244; [1914] 83 LJKB 1352; (1914-15) 111 LTR 198; (1913-14) 58 SJ 577; (1913-14) XXX TLR 441; (1914) WN (I) 170 CA Liability for nuisance (though no negligence) for injury sustained through escape of dangerous thing.

Charles Arckoll Ltd, Tyler Mouldings Ltd v (1982) 132 NLJ 534 HC QBD On damages available to company for losses occasioned through fire started by another company.

Charles Bayer and Co, Weingarten Brothers v (1903) LXXXVIII LTR 168; (1902-03) XIX TLR 239 HC ChD Injunction granted prohibiting sale of goods not made by plaintiff under plaintiff's distinctive trade-name where was possibility of confusion among buyers.

Charles Bayer and Company, Weingarten Brothers v (1903-04) LXXXIX LTR 56; (1902-03) XIX TLR 604 CA Reversal of injunction granted by HC KBD prohibiting sale of goods not made by plaintiff under plaintiff's distinctive trade-name where was possibility of confusion among buyers.

Charles Brand and Son, Ltd, Bunker v [1969] 2 All ER 59; (1969) 119 NLJ 412; [1969] 2 QB 480; [1969] 2 WLR 1392 HC QBD Tunnel diggers were 'occupiers' of tunnel and digging machine and owed occupier's duty of care (even though victim aware of injury).

Charles John Leslie and Wife, William Cuenod and Company v (1908-09) 53 SJ 14; (1908-09) XXV TLR 2 HC KBD Husband liable for torts of judicially separated wife committed during coverture.

Charles, Thurston v (1904-05) XXI TLR 659 HC KBD Substantial damages available for wrongful conversion/detention where published another's private correspondence but privilege in communication not destroyed so no libel.

Charleston and another v News Group Newspapers Ltd [1994] TLR 16 CA Photos, headlines and connected articles could not be severed so as to find one element defamatory.

Charleston and another v News Group Newspapers Ltd and another [1995] 2 All ER 313; [1995] 2 AC 65; (1995) 145 NLJ 490; (1995) 139 SJ LB 100; [1995] TLR 171; [1995] 2 WLR 450 HL Photos, headlines and connected articles may not be severed so as to find one element defamatory.

Charlton v Forrest Printing Ink Co Ltd (1978) 122 SJ 730 HC QBD Employer failed to discharge duty of care in respect of employees responsible for collecting wages from bank.

Charman and others, Plummer v [1962] 3 All ER 823; (1962) 112 LJ 800; (1962) 106 SJ 631 CA On amendment of claim to include qualified privilege plea.

Charnwood Borough Council, Dennis v (1982) 132 NLJ 349 HC QBD Local authority owes duty of care in ensuring plans comply with building regulations; time ran from date local authority failure became apparent.

Charnwood Borough Council, Dennis and another v [1982] 3 All ER 486; [1983] QB 409; (1982) 126 SJ 730; [1982] TLR 440; [1982] 3 WLR 1064 CA Local authority owes duty of care in ensuring plans comply with building regulations; time runs from date damage occurs/local authority failure becomes apparent.

Chartered Bank of India, Australia and China, Lloyds Bank, Ltd v [1928] All ER 285 CA Negligent dealing with cheques resulting in conversion.

Chesneau v Interhome Ltd (1984) 134 NLJ 341c CA Excess accommodation costs plus damages for distress of holidaymaker who had to find own accommodation abroad when booked accommodation proved to be of lower quality than promised.

Chess (a firm), John Jacques and Son, Ltd v [1939] 3 All ER 227; (1939) 83 SJ 585; (1939-40) LVI TLR 543 HC ChD Though brand name not firmly established as unique to party's goods use of word 'genuine' by another party before that brand name was passing off.

Chess, John Jacques and Son, Ltd v (1940) 89 LJ 195; (1940) 84 SJ 302 CA Where brand name not firmly established as unique to party's goods use of word 'genuine' by another party before that brand name was not passing off.

Chessum, Kirby v (1913-14) XXX TLR 15 HC KBD Commissioners of Works not liable to indemnify contractor who committed trespass unauthorised by former in course of its work.

Chessum, Kirby v (1915) 79 JP 81; (1913-14) XXX TLR 660 CA Commissioners of Works liable to indemnify contractor who in course of work committed trespass authorised by former's architect.

Chester Corporation, Youde v [1934] LJNCCR 44 CyCt Matter at issue deemed to be res judicata in second negligence action arising from road traffic incident; could not plead were not at all negligent and that other was contributorily negligent.

Chester, Dixon v (1906) 70 JP 380 HC KBD Surveyor empowered under Highway Act 1835, s 73 to seek order requiring that highway be cleared of timber which is nuisance.

Chester, Young v [1973] RTR 319 HC QBD Seeking to start car broken down on carriageway with self-starter (which dimmed/extinguished lights) was negligent in that obviated warning to others of presence but so was other's driving too fast with dimmed lights.

Chester, Young v [1974] RTR 70 CA Seeking to start car broken down on carriageway with self-starter (which dimmed/extinguished lights) was negligent in that obviated warning to others of presence.

Chesworth v Farrar and another [1966] 2 All ER 107; (1965-66) 116 NLJ 809; [1967] 1 QB 407; (1966) 110 SJ 307; [1966] 2 WLR 1073 HC QBD Action for failure of bailee to take proper care lies in tort.

Chichester Constable and others, Eddis and another v [1969] 2 Ch 345; [1969] 3 WLR 48 CA Limitation period in conversion action ran from time fraud discovered.

Chichester-Constable and others, Eddis v [1969] 1 All ER 546; (1969) 119 NLJ 224 HC ChD Limitation period did not begin to run where right of action was fraudulently concealed.

Chief Constable of Derbyshire, Hellewell v [1995] TLR 9 HC QBD Was not breach of confidence for police to publicly use photograph of suspect as part of bona fide crime prevention scheme.

Chief Constable of Hampshire Constabulary, Cumber v [1995] TLR 32 CA Award of exemplary damages but no compensatory damages for false imprisonment was irrational.

Chief Constable of Lancashire Constabulary, Hyland v (1996) TLR 7/2/96 CA Could not bring action for false imprisonment where had been remanded into custody.

Chief Constable of North Wales and another, Davidson v [1994] 2 All ER 597; [1993] TLR 229 CA Evidence of store detective not directing, procuring, expressly requesting or encouraging arrest by police so not basis for false imprisonment.

Chief Constable of Northamptonshire, Rigby and another v [1985] 2 All ER 985; (1985) 129 SJ 832; [1985] 1 WLR 1242 HC QBD Bona fide policy decision unimpeachable; necessity a defence to trespass if defendant's negligence did not give rise to necessity; negligent to fire CS canister when no fire equipment.

Chief Constable of Northumbria Police Force, Swinney and others v [1996] 3 All ER 449; (1996) 146 NLJ 878; [1997] QB 464; (1996) TLR 28/3/96; [1996] 3 WLR 968 CA Could be that police owe duty of care to informant not to negligently disclose information concerning informant.

Chief Constable of South Yorkshire Police, Alcock and others v [1992] 1 AC 310 (also HC QBD/HL); [1991] TLR 226 CA Damages unavailable for nervous shock caused by injury/risk thereof to another when person shocked watched event on live television/heard it on radio.

Clark (In re) v Forbes Stuart (Thames Street) Ltd (Intended Action) (1964) 114 LJ 388; (1964) 108 SJ 422; [1964] 1 WLR 836 CA Extension of time limit allowed where identity of occupier became known after limitation period expired.

Clark (Sanders) v Grosvenor Mansions Company (Limited) and Guglielmo d'Allesandri (1899-1900) XVI TLR 428 HC ChD Turning premises under residential premises into restaurant was not reasonable user: liable for nuisance by heat and smell to residential occupier.

Clark and another v Kirby-Smith (1964) 114 LJ 604; (1964) 108 SJ 462; [1964] 3 WLR 239; [1964] Ch 506 HC ChD Negligent solicitor liable to client in contract not tort.

Clark and another v Woor [1965] 2 All ER 353; (1965) 109 SJ 251; [1965] 1 WLR 650 HC QBD Action not barred where concealment by fraud led to late discovery of damage; damages measured from date of discovery.

Clark and Wife v Brims [1947] 1 All ER 242; [1947] KB 497; (1947) 97 LJ 81; [1947] 116 LJR 853; (1947) 91 SJ 161; (1947) LXIII TLR 148; (1947) WN (I) 65 HC KBD Cannot sue for negligence in performing statutory duty under Road Transport Lighting Act 1927, s 1.

Clark v Lloyd's Bank Limited (1910) 74 JP 429; (1910) 45 LJ 537; [1910] 79 LJCh 645; (1910-11) 103 LTR 211; (1909-10) 54 SJ 704 HC ChD Injunction refused to hotel owner seeking to stop builder from carrying on noisy early morning construction work beside hotel.

Clark v London General Omnibus Company Limited (1905) XCII LTR 691; (1904-05) XXI TLR 505 HC KBD Father could recover funeral costs from defendants whose negligence had resulted in death of daughter who lived with father.

Clark v London General Omnibus Company (Limited) (1906) 41 LJ 492; [1906] 75 LJKB 907; (1906-07) XCV LTR 435; (1905-06) 50 SJ 631; (1905-06) XXII TLR 691 CA Funeral expenses of unmarried daughter living with father irrecoverable as fatal accident damages by father.

Clark v McLennan and another [1983] 1 All ER 416 HC QBD Burden of proof switches to doctor if pursues unorthodox treatment.

Clark v Monmouthshire County Council and others (1954) 118 JP 244 CA Schoolmasters not liable for unintended personal injury arising from scuffle between boys, one of whom had knife, as did not involve failure by teachers to maintain reasonable control over boys.

Clark, Islip et al, Warner v (1984) 134 NLJ 763c CA Exemplary damages available where breach of contract proved as liability in tort thereby set up.

Clark, R v [1963] 3 All ER 884; (1964) 48 Cr App R 69; [1964] Crim LR 45; (1964) 114 LJ 8; (1963) 107 SJ 983; [1963] 3 WLR 1067 CCA Obstruction and unreasonable user of street needed in nuisance via obstruction of highway.

Clark, Rawson v (1981) 131 NLJ 1214c CA Non-liability of person for non-negligent behaviour which aggravated and accentuated existing injury that arose from negligence of another.

Clarke (Loftus Otway) v Chowdhry (Brojendra Kissore Roy); The Same v Chowdhurani (Srimati Biseswari Debi) (1911-12) XXVIII TLR 486 PC Forced search of cutcherry where was no one to admit searchers was justified under Code of Civil Procedure.

Clarke and another v Bethnal Green Borough Council (1939) 103 JP 160; (1939) 83 SJ 218; (1938-39) LV TLR 519 HC KBD Local authority found not liable for personal injuries suffered by individual in public swimming pool.

Clarke and another, Affutu-Nartoy v [1984] TLR 47 HC QBD Was negligent for schoolteacher to participate in rugby football game with students (injuring student through tackle in the process).

Clarke and Co, Ltd and others, Barber and another v (1939) 83 SJ 925 HC KBD Failed action by infant against workman on/occupiers of land for injury suffered when dangerously standing gate fell on infant.

Clarke Chapman and Co, Ltd, Rowden v [1967] 3 All ER 608 HC QBD On personal injury damages (loss of fingers/earnings).

Clarke Pixley (a firm), Al Saudi Banque and others v [1990] Ch 313; (1989) 139 NLJ 1341; [1990] 2 WLR 344 HC ChD Auditor does not owe duty of care towards potential creditors of company whose accounts auditor audits and certifies.

Clarke v Adams (1950) 94 SJ 599 HC KBD Recovery of damages from physiotherapist for inadequate warning to client as to risk posed by certain equipment being used.

Clarke v Bruce Lance and Co (a firm) and others (1987) 137 NLJ 1064; (1987) 131 SJ 1698; [1988] 1 WLR 881 CA Solicitor had not owed duty of care to beneficiary to advise testator when amending will of effect amendment would have on beneficiary.

Clarke v Martlew and another (1972) 122 NLJ 586t; [1973] QB 58; (1972) 116 SJ 618; [1972] 3 WLR 653 CA On mutual exchange of results of medical test to which plaintiff acceded at defendant's request.

Clarke v Mayor, Aldermen, and Burgesses of the Borough of St Helens (1915) 79 JP 529; [1916] 85 LJKB 17; (1915-16) 113 LTR 681; (1914-15) 59 SJ 509 CA Public authority limitation deemed inapplicable to action where public authority whose employee had been driving car which caused injury had not been acting in course of duty.

Clarke v Rotax Aircraft Equipment Ltd [1975] 3 All ER 794; [1975] 1 WLR 1570 CA No interest on damages for loss of earning capacity.

Clarke v Winchurch and others (1968) 112 SJ 909; [1969] 1 WLR 69 CA On duty of care owed by one driver signalling to another.

Clarke, Baker and Co, Ltd, Seccombe v (1953) 103 LJ ccr624 CyCt Innkeeper not liable for loss of/damage to goods of guest unless innkeeper has been negligent.

Clarke, Davies v (1953) 103 LJ ccr141 CyCt Innkeeper liable for loss of bulk of various articles from car parked in inn yard that opened onto road.

Clarke, Mason and others v (1955) 105 LJ 232 HL Successful action inter alia for trespass arising from breach of covenant regarding hunting/shooting.

Clarke, Tuey v [1940] LJNCCR 31 CyCt Driver liable in negligence for colliding with cyclist during black-out even though cyclist did not have required red rear-light as driver not going at such speed that could pull up to avoid collision.

Clarkson v Modern Foundries Ltd (1957) 101 SJ 960; [1957] 1 WLR 1210 HC QBD Recovery for entire injury where undistinguishable part of injury occurred outside limitation period.

Claudius Ash, Son and Co (Lim) v Invicta Manufacturing Co (Lim) (1910-11) 55 SJ 348 HC ChD Injunction will be granted to restrain manufacturer from marketing goods under name that is not own/is that of rival manufacturer.

Clay Cross Co, Ltd, Slater v [1956] 2 All ER 625; (1956) 106 LJ 442; [1956] 2 QB 264; (1956) 100 SJ 450; [1956] 3 WLR 232 CA Volenti non fit injuria inapplicable as did not accept negligence of other; invitor/licensor owes duty to take reasonable care to prevent injury to person lawfully present on property.

Clay v Crump (AJ) and Sons Ltd and others (1963) 107 SJ 664; [1964] 1 QB 533; [1963] 3 WLR 866 CA On architect's duty of care to construction worker.

Clayton and others, Strangeways-Lesmere v [1936] 1 All ER 484; [1936] 2 KB 11; [1936] 105 LJCL 385; (1936) 154 LTR 463; (1936) 80 SJ 306; (1935-36) LII TLR 374; (1936) WN (I) 85 HC KBD Hospital not liable/liable for duly qualified nurse acting in professional/administrative capacity.

Clayton v Le Roy and Fils (1910-11) XXVII TLR 206 HC KBD Whether sale of goods in auction room constituted conversion.

Clayton v Le Roy and Fils [1911-13] All ER 284; (1911) 75 JP 521; (1911-12) 105 LTR 430; (1910-11) XXVII TLR 479 CA Whether sale of goods in auction room constituted conversion.

Clayton v Pontypridd Urban District Council (1918) 82 JP 246; [1918] 87 LJCL 645 HC KBD Negligence action failed where not brought in time against company acting under express and implied statutory duty to supply electricity.

Clayton v Sale Urban District Council [1925] All ER 279; (1926) 90 JP 5; [1926] 1 KB 415; (1925) 60 LJ 962; [1926] 95 LJCL 178; (1926) 134 LTR 147; (1925-26) XLII TLR 72; (1925) WN (I) 278 HC KBD Riparian owner must abate nuisance caused by flooding which has broken flood bank.

Clough and others v Clough and others (1968) 118 NLJ 372t; [1968] 1 WLR 525 CA Court exercised discretion to dismiss negligence action for want of prosecution (three years since entry of appearance yet no sign of statement of claim).

Clough v Bussan and another; West Yorkshire Police Authority (Third Party) [1990] RTR 178 HC QBD Police who had been notified of defective traffic lights did not owe duty of care to driver involved in collision thereafter (as result of malfunction).

Clowes, The Columbus Company, Limited v [1903] 1 KB 244; [1903] 72 LJKB 330 HC KBD Nominal damages for negligence where suffered no loss.

Clubb v Wimpey and Co, Ltd [1936] 1 All ER 69 HC KBD Defendant's agent merely signing charge-sheet upon handing into custody was false imprisonment.

Cluer v Chiltern Works (Engineering) Ltd (1975) 119 SJ 85 HC QBD On whether plaintiff entitled to require disclosure of medical report as pre-requisite to submitting to joint medical examination.

Cluney, Sam v [1956] Crim LR 271t HC QBD Damages for malicious prosecution by police officers whom jury found not to have seen defendant engaged in grossly indecent behaviour in public toilets.

Clwyd County Council and another, Pritchard v [1992] TLR 353 CA Presence of flood-water on road not per se evidence of non-feasance.

Clyde Helicopters Ltd, Fellowes (or Herd) and another v [1997] 1 All ER 775; [1997] AC 534; (1997) 141 SJ LB 64 HL Liability of helicopter company towards dependants of police officer killed while being conveyed in helicopter by negligent company pilot was governed by the Warsaw Convention as amended/implemented.

Co-partnership Farms v Harvey-Smith [1918] 2 KB 405; (1918) 53 LJ 191; [1919] 88 LJCL 472; (1918) 118 LTR 541; (1917-18) XXXIV TLR 414; (1918) WN (I) 175 HC KBD Statements before local military tribunal absolutely privileged.

Coachcraft, Ltd v Lancegay Safety Glass (1934), Ltd [1938] LJNCCR 380 CyCt Bailees had to prove damage occurring to bailed goods while in their care did not result from their negligence.

Coad v Cornwall and Isles of Scilly Health Authority (1996) 140 SJ LB 168; (1996) TLR 30/7/96; [1997] 1 WLR 189 CA Subjective test required in application of Limitation Act 1980, s 33(3)(a).

Coates v Rawtenstall Borough Council [1937] 1 All ER 333 Assizes Ordinary duty of care owed to child licensee.

Coates v Rawtenstall Borough Council (1937) 101 JP 483; (1937) 81 SJ 627 CA Local authority liable for injury to child licensee arising from negligent state in which playground maintained.

Coates v Wembley Stadium, Ltd and another (1940) 84 SJ 370 HC KBD Damages for excessive use of force in eviction from premises licensee who through his conduct converted himself into a trespasser.

Coates, Turner v [1916-17] All ER 264; [1917] 1 KB 670; [1917] 86 LJCL 321; (1916-17) 115 LTR 766; (1916-17) XXXIII TLR 79 HC KBD Owner liable in negligence for injuries arising from putting uncontrolled/unbroken colt on road.

Cobb and others, Williams-Ellis v (1935) 152 LTR 133 CA On providing adequate of evidence of public user so as to prove that certain land was public higway and so no trespass had been committed.

Cobstone Investments Ltd v Maxim [1985] QB 140 CA On what constitutes an adjoining occupier' (capable of complaining of nuisance of/annoyance by neighbour) for purposes of Rent Act 1977.

Cockburn and another v Smith and others [1924] 93 LJCL 764; (1924) 131 LTR 334 CA On liability of landlord for maintenance of roof of property which has let but in respect of which has not let roof.

Cocking and Sons, Ltd, Bird v [1951] 2 TLR 1260 CA On gauging personal injury damages: relevancy of awards in similar cases/relevancy of age.

Codd and another, Gorely and another v [1966] 3 All ER 891; (1965-66) 116 NLJ 1658; (1966) 110 SJ 965; [1967] 1 WLR 19 Assizes No offence/negligence if father having taken reasonable care allows child unsupervised use of air gun in non-public place.

Coleman Brothers, Pearson v [1948] 2 All ER 274; [1948] 2 KB 359; (1948) 98 LJ 371; [1948] 117 LJR 1781; (1948) WN (I) 270 CA Liability to child invitee disobeying danger sign.

Colenutt, Osborne v (1919) CC Rep VIII 25 CyCt Pedestrian with poor sight who fell through open cellar door that opened onto pavement able to recover damages for injury sustained where normally sighted person would have seen danger and avoided injury.

Coles, MacIntyre v [1966] 1 All ER 723; (1966) 130 JP 189; (1965-66) 116 NLJ 611; (1966) 110 SJ 315; [1966] 1 WLR 831 CA On yielding at junctions (and consequent negligence).

Coles v Reading and District Hospital Management Committee and another (1963) 107 SJ 115 HC QBD Cottage hospital and doctor negligent in not taking adequate care to guard against tetanus infection which led to death of accident victim whose estate brought instant action.

Coleshill v Lord Mayor, Aldermen and Citizens of the City of Manchester [1928] 1 KB 776; (1928) 65 LJ 95; (1928) 97 LJCL 229; (1928) 138 LTR 537 CA Non-liability towards licensee falling into trench which was not hidden danger/trap.

Coley v Meteor Garage (Moseley), Ltd [1941] LJNCCR 201 CyCt Garage with whom car bailed during winter not liable in negligence for not having drained radiator/for collapse of garage roof under weight of freak snow onto car.

Colledge v Bass Mitchells and Butlers Ltd [1988] 1 All ER 536 CA Redundancy payment stemming from personal injury can be deducted from damages.

Collett-Ward, Metcalfe v (1977) 127 NLJ 964b CA On what constitutes false imprisonment: aggravated damages awarded for same.

Collier v Anglian Water Authority [1983] TLR 223 CA Water authority liable as occupiers of promenade for injury suffered by member of public when tripped on irregular paving.

Collingwood v Home and Colonial Stores, Ltd [1936] 3 All ER 200; (1936) 155 LTR 550; (1936) 80 SJ 853; (1936-37) LIII TLR 53; (1936) WN (I) 305 CA Rylands v Fletcher inapplicable to domestic use of electricity.

Collingwood v Home and Colonial Stores, Ltd [1936] 1 All ER 74; (1936) 81 LJ 130; (1936) 80 SJ 167 HC KBD Absent negligence in electric fitting/maintenance no Rylands v Fletcher-style liability for escape of water resulting from electrical fault-caused fire; hoarding impeding access a nuisance (despite increase in trade while hoarding present).

Collins v Cooper (1902-03) XIX TLR 118 CA Bona fide statements made in course of detecting crime were privileged but re-trial ordered on issue whether statements at issue were bona fide.

Collins v Henry Whiteway and Company, Limited [1927] 2 KB 378; (1927) 63 LJ 537; [1927] 96 LJCL 790; (1927) 137 LTR 297; (1926-27) XLIII TLR 532; (1927) WN (I) 163 HC KBD Communications with Court of Referees not absolutely privileged.

Collins v Hertfordshire County Council and another [1947] 1 All ER 633; (1947) 111 JP 272; [1947] KB 598; [1947] 116 LJR 789; (1947) 176 LTR 456; (1947) LXIII TLR 317; (1947) WN (I) 127 HC KBD County council negligent in operation of county council hospital/not responsible for negligence of part-time surgeon employed; amendment to statement of claim allowed as not new cause of action.

Collins v Jones (1955) 105 LJ 264; [1955] 1 QB 564; (1955) 99 SJ 258; [1955] 2 WLR 813 CA Order for particulars of letter granted to enable plaintiff to make out libel claim with some certainty.

Collins v Wilcock (1984) 79 Cr App R 229; [1984] Crim LR 481; (1984) 148 JP 692; (1984) 128 SJ 660; [1984] TLR 250; [1984] 1 WLR 1172 HC QBD Constable's taking hold of person whom merely wanted to speak to was battery so assault on same not assault on constable in execution of duty.

Collins, Carlin Music Corpn, Subiddu Music Ltd and Mechanical-Copyright Protection Society Ltd v (1980) 130 NLJ 218c CA Copyright Protection Society could seek to have unlawful dealings in copyright injuncted as was unlawful interference with its business in that it obtained portion of all licence fees paid.

Collins, Dominion Natural Gas Co v; Same v Perkins and others [1908-10] All ER 61; [1909] AC 640; [1910] 79 LJPC 13; (1909-10) 101 LTR 359; (1908-09) XXV TLR 831 PC Heavy duty of care imposed on supplier of dangerous substance.

Connolly and others, Manchester Corporation v (1970) 114 SJ 108 CA Vice Chancellor ought not to have granted order for possession at interlocutory hearing.

Connolly v Camden and Islington Area Health Authority [1981] 3 All ER 250; (1981) 131 NLJ 802 HC QBD Young child can claim damages for loss of earnings in lost years.

Connolly v Smith [1956] Crim LR 834; (1956) 106 LJ 570 Ct of Passage Local health authority officer who acted in good faith not liable in damages for false imprisonment of person whom removed to mental hospital.

Conrad v Inner London Education Authority (1965-66) 116 NLJ 1630t; (1967) 111 SJ 684 CA Judo teacher not liable in negligence for injury suffered by first-time judo participant acting on his instructions.

Conry v Simpson and others [1983] 3 All ER 369 CA Court of Appeal will not interfere with judge's disapplying of limitation unless very wrong.

Conservators of the River Thames and Easton Gibb and Son, Queens of the River Steamship Company v (1905-06) XXII TLR 419 HC KBD Conservators of River Thames not liable in negligence where had taken reasonable care not to expose steamship to navigation danger.

Conservators of the River Thames, Palmer v (1901-02) LXXXV LTR 537; (1901-02) 46 SJ 84 HC ChD Unauthorised dredging under River Thames Conservancy Act 1894 constituted trespass.

Consett Urban District Council v Crawford (1903) 67 JP 309; (1902-03) 47 SJ 549; (1902-03) XIX TLR 508; (1902-03) 51 WR 669 HC KBD Urban council members had no right to enter premises to check whether nuisance abated unless owner permitted same or magistrate ordered it (Public Health Act 1875, s 102).

Constable and Co, Goldschmidt v [1937] 4 All ER 293; (1937) 81 SJ 863 CA Details of justification to accompany delivery of defence.

Constable v Jagger (1972) 122 NLJ 268 CA On whether statements in police inquiry privileged.

Constance and another, Serville v [1954] 1 All ER 662; (1954) 104 LJ 186; (1954) 98 SJ 179; [1954] 1 WLR 487 HC ChD No chance of confusion meant no recovery for passing-off.

Conti Commodity Services Ltd, Stafford and another v [1981] 1 All ER 691 HC QBD Commodities broker's error of judgment may not be negligence and consequent losses not per se evidence of negligence.

Control Risks Ltd and others v New English Library Ltd and another [1989] 3 All ER 577; (1989) 139 NLJ 1008; [1990] 1 WLR 183 CA On fair comment.

Conway Corporation, Wood v [1914-15] All ER 1097; [1914] 2 Ch 47; (1914) 78 JP 249; [1914] 83 LJCh 498; (1914) 110 LTR 917 CA Injunction not damages deemed proper remedy for continuing nuisance.

Conway v British Transport Commission (1962) 106 SJ 78 HC QBD On duty of care owed by driver of train.

Conway v George Wimpey and Co, Ltd [1951] 1 All ER 363; [1951] 1 TLR 587 CA No duty of care to trespasser.

Cook and another, Demer v (1901-07) XX Cox CC 444; (1903) 67 JP 206; (1903) LXXXVIII LTR 629; (1902-03) 47 SJ 368; (1902-03) XIX TLR 327 HC KBD Action for false imprisonment lay against prison governor not clerk of the peace.

Cook v Alexander and others [1973] 3 All ER 1037; (1973) 123 NLJ 747t; [1974] QB 279; (1973) 117 SJ 618; [1973] 3 WLR 617 CA Fair representation of Parliamentary proceedings enjoys qualified privilege.

Cook v JL Kier and Co Ltd [1970] 2 All ER 513; (1970) 120 NLJ 248t; (1970) 114 SJ 207; [1970] 1 WLR 774 CA Appropriate damages for severe brain injury.

Cook v S [1966] 1 All ER 248; (1966) 110 SJ 964; (1965-66) 116 NLJ 416; [1966] 1 WLR 635 HC QBD Damage flowing from solicitor's negligence not broken by counsel's mistaken advice.

Cook v S [1967] 1 All ER 299 CA Negligent solicitor sued in contract not liable for mental distress occasioned by negligence.

Cook v Swinfen (1965) 109 SJ 972 HC QBD Damages for loss of chances in divorce suit/of receiving maintenance as result of solicitor's negligence.

Corelli v Wall (1905-06) XXII TLR 532 HC ChD Interim injunction on publication of picture postcards refused as alleged libel insufficiently made out.

Cork v Kirby Maclean, Ltd [1952] 2 All ER 402; [1952] 2 TLR 217 CA Half-damages where employers negligent to employee who did not disclose was epileptic.

Corke (on relation of Bromley Rural District Council), Attorney-General v [1932] All ER 711; [1933] Ch 89; (1933) 102 LJCh 30; (1933) 148 LTR 95; (1932) 76 SJ 593; (1931-32) XLVIII TLR 650; (1932) WN (I) 217 HC ChD Injunction can issue to stop person allowing licensee on property where licensee causing nuisance on neighbouring property.

Cornford v Carlton Bank, Limited (1899-1900) LXXXI LTR 415; [1900] 1 QB 22; (1899-1900) XVI TLR 12 CA Corporation can be sued for malicious prosecution.

Cornish v Kearley and Tonge Ltd (1983) 133 NLJ 870 HC QBD Extension of limitation allowed where had reasonable excuse for delay/had acted with reasonable speed/no undue injustice would result to defendant.

Cornwall and Isles of Scilly Health Authority, Coad v (1996) 140 SJ LB 168; (1996) TLR 30/7/96; [1997] 1 WLR 189 CA Subjective test required in application of Limitation Act 1980, s 33(3)(a).

Cornwall Legh, The PLP Motor Carrying Co, Ltd v (1929) 68 LJ 44 CyCt Owner of tree overhanging highway must know of situation before can be liable for damage occasioned by same.

Cornwell v Myskow and others (1987) 131 SJ 476; [1987] 1 WLR 630 CA On evidence admissible as to reputation.

Corporacion Nacional del Cobre de Chile v Sogemin Metals Ltd and others [1997] 2 All ER 917 HC ChD Contributory negligence not defence to conspiracy claim (arising from alleged bribery).

Corporation of City of Glasgow, Percy (Pauper) v [1922] 2 AC 299; (1922) 86 JP 201; (1922) 127 LTR 501; (1922) WN (I) 181 HL Glasgow City Corporation tramway officials acting in excess of duties might have committed false imprisonment.

Corporation of Glasgow v Muir and others [1943] 2 All ER 44; (1944) 94 LJ 108 HL Occupier not liable to invitee for unforeseeable danger.

Corporation of Glasgow v Riddell (1911) 104 LTR 354 HL Corporation not liable for slander made by tax collector acting outside scope of his employment.

Corporation of Greenock v Caledonian Railway Company; Corporation of Greenock v Glasgow and South-Western Railway Company [1917] AC 556; (1917) 81 JP 269 HL Liable for flooding resulting from interference with course of stream.

Corporation of Liverpool, Maguire v (1905) 69 JP 153; [1905] 1 KB 767; (1905) XCII LTR 374; (1904-05) 53 WR 449 CA Liverpool Corporation not liable for non-feasance of roads.

Corporation of Lowestoft, Lambert v [1901] 1 KB 590; [1901] 70 LJK/QB 333; (1901) LXXXIV LTR 237; (1900-01) 45 SJ 295; (1900-01) XVII TLR 273; (1900-01) 49 WR 316 HC KBD Absent negligence sanitary authority not liable for injury sustained my member of public as result of disrepaired sewer.

Corporation of the City of Glasgow v Taylor [1922] 1 AC 44; (1922) 86 JP 89; (1921) 56 LJ 435; [1922] 91 LJPC 49; (1922) 126 LTR 262; (1921-22) XXXVIII TLR 102; (1921) WN (I) 333 HL Corporation possibly negligent for not taking appropriate steps to preempt children eating attractive poisonous berries in public park.

Corporation of Trinity House, Christie v (1918-19) XXXV TLR 480 HC KBD Owner of wrecked ship entitled to damages from Trinity House Corporation which had blown up ship without jurisdiction for doing so.

Corstar (Owners) v Eurymedon (Owners), The Eurymedon [1938] 1 All ER 122 CA Negligent act causing negligent mistake by other makes both responsible for result.

Corston, Kelley v [1997] 2 Cr App R (S) 1276; (1997) 147 NLJ 1276; [1997] TLR 466 CA On extent of immunity from suit enjoyed by barrister in case concluded by way of settlement of action.

Cory Brothers and Co (Limited) and others, Attorney-General v; Kennard and others v Cory Brothers and Co (Limited) (1919) 83 JP 221; [1919] 88 LJCh 410; (1918-19) XXXV TLR 570 CA Non-liability for landslide occasioned by dumping of colliery waste on mountainside.

Cory Brothers and Co (Limited) and others, Attorney-General v; Kennard and others v Cory Brothers and Co (Limited) (1917-18) XXXIV TLR 621 HC ChD Liability for landslide occasioned by dumping of colliery waste on mountainside.

Cory Brothers and Co, Limited, Kennard and others v [1922] 1 Ch 265; (1921-22) XXXVIII TLR 213 HC ChD Order given on foot of earlier action to maintain remedial works.

Cory Brothers and Co, Limited, Kennard and others v [1922] 2 Ch 1; (1922) 127 LTR 137; (1921-22) XXXVIII TLR 489; (1922) WN (I) 122 CA Order given on foot of earlier action to maintain remedial works approved.

Cory Brothers and Company, Limited, and Others, Attorney-General and Others v; Kennard and Others v Cory Brothers and Company, Limited [1921] 1 AC 521; (1921) 85 JP 129; [1921] 90 LJCh 221; (1921) 125 LTR 98; (1920-21) XXXVII TLR 343 HL Liability under Rylands v Fletcher and in negligence for landslide occasioned by dumping of colliery waste on mountainside.

Cory, Dovey and others v (1901-02) LXXXV LTR 257 HL Non-liability of director in negligence for acting in good faith on the false statements of company officers.

Cosgrove v Horsfall (1946) 175 LTR 334; (1945-46) LXII TLR 140 CA Negligent driver of omnibus not protected from liability by exemption clause in free bus pass agreement between London Passenger Transport Board and plaintiff.

Cosgrove, Scarborough and Wife v [1905] 2 KB 805; (1904-05) XXI TLR 754; (1905-06) 54 WR 100 CA Boarding-house keeper owes duty to take reasonable care of guest's property in house.

Cosgrove, Scarborough and Wife v (1904-05) XXI TLR 570 HC KBD Boarding-house keeper owes no duty to take reasonable care of guest's property in house.

Costa Brava Wine Co, Ltd (No 2), Bollinger (J) and others v [1961] 1 All ER 561; [1960] Ch 262; (1961) 111 LJ 155; (1959) 103 SJ 1028 HC ChD Goodwill could vest in geographical name and be protected from passing off.

Costa Brava Wine Company, Ltd, Bollinger (J) and others v [1959] 3 All ER 800; (1959) 109 LJ 735; (1961) 105 SJ 180; [1959] 3 WLR 966 HC ChD Goodwill attaching to geographical name could be protected by class of people producing goods in that area.

Costa v Georghiou (1984) 134 NLJ 82c HC QBD Failed attempt to have extension limitation disapplied in light of concealed fraud claim.

Costaki and another, Thompson-Schwab and another v [1956] 1 All ER 652; [1956] Crim LR 274; (1956) 106 LJ 201; (1956) 100 SJ 246; [1956] 1 WLR 335 CA Use of neighbouring premises for prostitution a nuisance.

Cotton v Derbyshire Dales District Council [1994] TLR 335 CA Occupier not liable for not posting sign warning of obvious dangers at cliffside.

Cotton v Wallis [1955] 3 All ER 373; (1955) 105 LJ 712; [1955] 1 WLR 1168 CA Low price of building merited architect's certification at lower standard than otherwise.

Coulsdon and Purley Urban District Council, Hawkins v [1953] 2 All ER 364; (1953) 117 JP 360; (1953) 103 LJ 414; [1954] 1 QB 319; (1953) 97 SJ 473; [1953] 1 WLR 882 HC QBD Licensee did not accept at night risks which were obvious by day; occupier owed duty to remedy risks which reasonable man would have recognised.

Coulsdon and Purley Urban District Council, Hawkins v [1954] 1 All ER 97; (1954) 118 JP 101; (1954) 104 LJ 25; (1954) 98 SJ 44; [1954] 2 WLR 122 CA Licensors liable in negligence where knew of physical circumstances constituting trap.

Coulson, Cox v [1916] 2 KB 177; [1916] 85 LJKB 1081; (1916) 114 LTR 599; (1914-15) XXXI TLR 390 HC KBD Duty owed by theatre owner to member of audience injured during play.

Coulson, Cox v (1916) CC Rep V 39; (1916) 51 LJ 205; (1915-16) 60 SJ 402; (1915-16) XXXII TLR 406; (1916) WN (I) 173 CA Duty owed by theatre owner to member of audience injured during play.

Council of the City of Manchester, Sharpe v (1978) 128 NLJ 312b CA Successful action in negligence/nuisance where council dealt inadequately with cockroach infestation in council flat.

County Council of the Parts of Lindsey, Lincolnshire v Marshall (Mary), wife of Lewis Alexander Marshall [1936] 2 All ER 1076; [1937] AC 97; (1936) 100 JP 411; [1936] 105 LJCL 614; (1936) 155 LTR 297; (1936) 80 SJ 702; (1935-36) LII TLR 661; (1936) WN (I) 244 HL Negligent admission of/failure to warn nursing home patient in maternity hospital where faced peculiar risk of fever.

County Personnel (Employment Agency) Ltd v Alan R Pulver and Co (a firm) [1987] 1 All ER 289; (1986) 136 NLJ 1138; (1987) 131 SJ 474; [1987] 1 WLR 916 CA Strange lease clause to put solicitor on guard/lead him to to draw client's attention to clause; general measure of damages proper if diminution in value principle inappropriate.

Courage and Co, Ltd v Meakers Garages, Ltd (1948) 98 LJ 163 HC ChD Successful action for damage occasioned by collapse of building maintained in disrepair.

Courtaulds Ltd, Dexter v [1984] 1 All ER 70; (1984) 128 SJ 81; [1983] TLR 688; [1984] 1 WLR 372 CA Half-rate interest on special damages in ordinary personal injuries case is proper.

Courtier, Wellaway v [1916-17] All ER 340; (1917) CC Rep VI 94; [1918] 1 KB 200; (1917) 52 LJ 451; [1918] 87 LJCL 299; (1918) 118 LTR 256; (1917-18) 62 SJ 161; (1917-18) XXXIV TLR 115; (1917) WN (I) 368 HC KBD Crop-purchaser can maintain action in trespass.

Coussens, IBL Ltd v [1991] 2 All ER 133; [1990] TLR 538 CA Damages for conversion not gauged by reference to date of judgment or conversion but what is fair compensation to owner for loss.

Coventry, Rose v (1965) 109 SJ 256 CA On appropriate personal injury damages where victim had toes amputated/leg length reduced/was less mobile than previously.

Cowan and another, Bach and Johnson, Ltd v (1969) 113 SJ 38 HC ChD Passing off injunction granted to owners of name 'Pembridge Gardens Hotel' against owners of name 'Pembridge Hotel'.

Cowan v Blackwill Motor Caravan Conversions Ltd (trading as Matador Service Station) [1978] RTR 421 CA Garage owners not liable in negligence for theft of car bailed with them where took all security measures ordinary driver would take on leaving car in street.

Cowan, Hope Brothers, Limited v [1913] 2 Ch 312 HC ChD Was not trespass for lessee to put flower boxes on outside of outer wall of leased office.

Cowan, Matthews v (1915) CC Rep IV 84 CyCt Non-recovery of damages in trespass for liability suffered by straying cattle where person owning land onto which cattle strayed had not discharged duty of fencing out said cattle.

Cowper and others v Milburn and others (1907-08) 52 SJ 316 HL Interference with ancient lights deemed not, in circumstances, to be a nuisance.

Cox v Coulson [1916] 2 KB 177; [1916] 85 LJKB 1081; (1916) 114 LTR 599; (1914-15) XXXI TLR 390 HC KBD Duty owed by theatre owner to member of audience injured during play.

Cox v Coulson (1916) CC Rep V 39; (1916) 51 LJ 205; (1915-16) 60 SJ 402; (1915-16) XXXII TLR 406; (1916) WN (I) 173 CA Duty owed by theatre owner to member of audience injured during play.

Cox v Dixon (1984) 134 NLJ 236 HC QBD One-third reduction in damages for driver (injured in collision with speeding police car) who knew the area/should have known that people might speed at night.

Cox v English, Scottish and Australian Bank [1904-07] All ER 1624; [1905] AC 168; [1905] 74 LJPC 62; (1905) XCII LTR 483 PC Whether reasonable and probable cause a matter for judge.

Cox, Fielden v (1905-06) XXII TLR 411 HC ChD Trespass injunction against insect-catchers refused given trivial nature of trespasses.

Cox, Frank v (1967) 111 SJ 670 CA Pedestrian struck by motorist crossing road when lights for motor traffic were red was not contributorily negligent; on awarding personal injury damages to the elderly.

Coxhead and others, Butland v (1968) 112 SJ 465 HC QBD Not negligent not to place lamp on road indicating presence of broken-down lorry.

Cozens v North Devon Hospital Management Committee and another; Hunter v Turners (Soham), Ltd [1966] 2 All ER 276; [1966] 2 QB 318; (1966) 110 SJ 273; [1966] 2 WLR 1134 HC QBD On (extension of) limitation.

Cremdean Properties Ltd et anor v Nash et al (1978) 128 NLJ 514c CA Failed appeal against finding that exclusion clause in tender that particulars therein might not be (as were not in fact) entirely correct.

Cremin and others, Thomson v [1953] 2 All ER 1185; (1956) 100 SJ 73; [1956] 1 WLR 103 HL Invitor's duty to invitee vests in invitor personally and cannot be arrogated to a third party; stevedores unloading ship not under duty to inspect it for safety purposes.

Crescent and Star Publications Ltd and Aziz, Jang Publications Ltd and Rahman v (1981) 131 NLJ 482c CA £20,000 damages not inappropriate for serious (political) libel.

Cressey v Murray (CP) and Co, Ltd and another (1965) 109 SJ 294 CA Increase in personal injury damages for person who suffered double vision as result of road accident.

Cresswell v Sirl (1947) WN (I) 310 HC KBD On criminal liability for shooting of trespassing dog.

Cresswell v Sirl (1948) 112 JP 69; [1948] 1 KB 241; (1947) 97 LJ 648; [1948] 117 LJR 654; (1947) 91 SJ 653; (1947) LXIII TLR 620 CA On test of criminal liability for shooting of trespassing dog.

Cressy v South Metropolitan Gas Co (1906) 70 JP 405 HC KBD Gas company which opened up street not liable for injury caused through local authority servant's negligent repair of street.

Crest Homes Ltd v Ascott (1975) 125 NLJ 186t CA No injunction to restrain publication of truth (albeit that publication done in eccentric manner).

Cripps and Lee Ltd and others, Revlon Inc and others v (1980) 130 NLJ 418c CA Failed action in which company sought injunction to restrain sale in the United Kingdom of products it marketed in the United States.

Cripwell, Cunningham v (1914) CC Rep III 85 CA May be custom requiring owner of adjoining fields to maintain fence so as to prevent damage by animals.

Crisp v Daily Herald (1929) and others (1959) 103 SJ 918 CA Impecuniosity no excuse for (twelve year) delay: libel action struck out.

Criterion Film Productions, Ltd and another, Russell v [1936] 3 All ER 627; (1936) 80 SJ 1036; (1936-37) LIII TLR 117 HC KBD Film production company, not cameraman, liable for injury effected through over-lighting of film scene.

Crocker and others, Addis v [1959] 2 All ER 773; (1959) 109 LJ 604; [1960] 1 QB 87; (1959) 103 SJ 636 HC QBD Proceedings before solicitors' disciplinary committee are judicial: normal privilege of judicial proceedings applies.

Crocker and others, Addis v (1960) 110 LJ 476; [1961] 1 QB 11; (1960) 104 SJ 584 CA Proceedings before solicitors' disciplinary committee similar to judicial trial and therefore absolutely privileged.

Crocker and others, Groom v (1937) 84 LJ 158; (1937) 157 LTR 308 HC KBD Failure of solicitor to act equally on behalf of both insurer/insured; damages for breach of duty and for libel.

Crocker and others, Groom v [1938] 2 All ER 394; [1939] 1 KB 194; (1938) 85 LJ 308; (1938) 158 LTR 477; (1937-38) LIV TLR 861 CA Failure of solicitor to act equally on behalf of both insurer/insured; malice on ostensibly privileged occasion; nominal damages as action in contract (not tort) and no evidence of actual damage.

Crocker v British Coal Corporation [1995] TLR 389 HC QBD Burden of proof on plaintiff seeking to show personal injuries action not outside relevant limitation period under the Limitation Act 1980, s 11.

Crofter Hand Woven Harris Tweed Company, Limited and Others v Veitch and Another [1942] 1 All ER 142; [1942] 111 LJ 17; (1943) 93 LJ 125; (1942) 166 LTR 172 HL On elements of conspiracy to injure.

Croggon and Co, Ltd and another, Johnson v [1954] 1 All ER 121 HC QBD Ex turpi causa non oritur actio precluded relief in negligence; could not recover as invitee as had general licence to use equipment but selected defective equipment.

Croke and another v Wiseman and another [1981] 3 All ER 852; (1981) 125 SJ 726; [1982] 1 WLR 71 CA Appropriate damages for permanent incapacitation of twenty-one month old infant.

Croke v Brent and Harrow Area Health Authority (1981) 131 NLJ 1237 CA Assessing damages for serious injuries suffered by infant through negligent treatment upon admission to hospital with croup.

Crook and another, Gros and another v (1969) 113 SJ 408 HC QBD Publisher liable for malicious libel published by writer-agent.

Cross v Kirklees [1997] TLR 370 CA Presence of snow/ice on highway did not mean (and here was not the case) that highway authority was in breach of its duty of care as regards maintenance of highway.

Cross v Rix (1912) CC Rep I 97 HC KBD New trial necessary where person non-suited (in light of provisions of Public Authorities Protection Act) without person consenting to same/having evidence heard.

Crossan v Bracewell (Ward) (1986) 136 NLJ 849 HC QBD Solicitor liable in negligence to client whom defended on reckless driving charge without first checking if latter's insurers would meet costs.

Crossgrove and another v Barkers Traffic Services Ltd and others (1966) 110 SJ 892 HC QBD On appropriate damages for head injuries where was uncertain whether would worsen over time.

Crossley v Rawlinson [1981] 3 All ER 674; (1981) 131 NLJ 1093; [1982] RTR 442; (1981) 125 SJ 865; [1982] 1 WLR 369 HC QBD Non-liability of driver of burning vehicle for injury suffered by AA man running towards vehicle.

Croston v Vaughan [1937] 4 All ER 249; (1938) 102 JP 11; [1938] 1 KB 540; [1938] 107 LJCL 182; (1938) 158 LTR 221; (1937) 81 SJ 882; (1937-38) LIV TLR 54; (1937) WN (I) 361 CA Stop light plus hand-signal needed when stopping; observation of Highway Code not absolute defence to negligence; apportionment of damages best done by trial judge/rarely amended by CA.

Crosville Motor Services, Ltd and another (Murphie, Third Party), Ormrod and another v [1953] 1 All ER 711; (1953) 97 SJ 154; [1953] 1 WLR 409 HC QBD Car owner vicariously liable for negligence of driver acting at owner's behest.

Crosville Motor Services, Ltd and another (Murphie, Third Party), Ormrod and another v [1953] 2 All ER 753; (1953) 103 LJ 539; (1953) 97 SJ 570; [1953] 1 WLR 1120 CA Car owner vicariously liable for negligence of friend when driving car entirely/partly for owner.

Crow v Wood [1970] 3 All ER 425; [1971] 1 QB 77; (1970) 114 SJ 474; [1970] 3 WLR 516 CA Party failing in duty to maintain walls cannot complain of cattle trespass by neighbour's sheep.

Crown River Cruises Ltd v Kimbolton Fireworks Ltd and another (1996) TLR 6/3/96 HC QBD Could claim in nuisance for damage to moored river barge.

Crowne v Warden and Co Ltd and others (1968) 112 SJ 824 CA Was just possible that newspaper headline and bold introduction could be defamatory though overall article was not.

Croydon Corporation and another, Moul v [1918-19] All ER 971; (1918) 82 JP 283; (1918) 53 LJ 227; (1918-19) 119 LTR 318; (1917-18) XXXIV TLR 473; (1918) WN (I) 194 HC KBD Highway authority not liable for nonfeasance.

Croydon Corporation, Read and another v (1939) 103 JP 25; (1938-39) LV TLR 212 HC KBD Infant who had contracted typhoid could sue local authority for negligence as regards provision of clean water.

Croydon Hospital Group Management Committee and another, Bullard v [1953] 1 All ER 596; (1953) 117 JP 182; (1953) 103 LJ 139; [1953] 1 QB 511; (1953) 97 SJ 155 HC QBD Hospital group management committee could be liable in negligence.

Crozier and another, Barnet v [1987] 1 All ER 1041; (1987) 131 SJ 298; [1987] 1 WLR 272 CA Statement of court in settlement of one libel claim permissible if no real risk of prejudice to later libel claim.

Cruikshank, Mee v (1901-07) XX Cox CC 210; (1902) LXXXVI LTR 708; (1901-02) XVIII TLR 271 HC KBD Prison governor liable for illegal detention of acquitted person by prison warders.

Cruikshank, Shiels v (1953) 103 LJ 232; (1953) 97 SJ 208; [1953] 1 WLR 533 HL Widow's own income not relevant when determining damages available after husband's death resulting from another's negligence.

Cruise v Terrell [1922] 91 LJCL 499; (1922) 126 LTR 750 CA Actual damages may be claimed in trespass action by statutory tenant against landlord who re-takes possession of premises.

Crump (AJ) and Sons Ltd and others, Clay v (1963) 107 SJ 664; [1964] 1 QB 533; [1963] 3 WLR 866 CA On architect's duty of care to construction worker.

Crump v Torfaen Borough Council (1981) 125 SJ 641 HC QBD Where building would certainly endanger others — though did not have to be about to fall in — a cause of action arose.

Cryan v Hotel Rembrandt, Limited (1925) 133 LTR 395; (1924-25) XLI TLR 287 HC KBD Innkeeper liable for loss of coat deposited by dinner-guest and lost through negligence of innkeeper/his servants.

Cubitt v Gamble (1918-19) 63 SJ 287; (1918-19) XXXV TLR 223 HC KBD Person seeking debt execution after tender of amount of debt is guilty of trespass.

Cuckmere Brick Co Ltd and another v Mutual Finance Ltd; Mutual Finance Ltd v Cuckmere Brick Co Ltd and others [1971] 2 All ER 633 CA Mortgagee under duty to mortgagor to obtain real market price of property.

Cuenod v Leslie [1909] 1 KB 880; (1909) 44 LJ 166; [1909] 78 LJKB 695; (1909) C LTR 675; (1908-09) 53 SJ 340; (1908-09) XXV TLR 374; (1909) WN (I) 65 CA Husband not liable for torts of judicially separated wife committed during coverture.

Cuff and another v London and County Land and Building Co (1912) 81 LJCh 426 (also CA); (1911-12) 56 SJ 273 HC ChD Injunction refused to require company to give allegedly negligent auditors access to company's books.

Cuff v London and County Land and Building Company Limited (1912) 81 LJCh 426 (also HC ChD); (1912) 106 LTR 285 CA Injunction refused to require company to give allegedly negligent auditors access to company's books.

Culford Metal Industries Ltd v Export Credit Guarantees Department (1981) 131 NLJ 603 HC QBD Specialist government department liable for negligent advice to first-time exporter.

Culkin v McFie and Sons, Ltd [1939] 3 All ER 613; (1939) 88 LJ 86 HC KBD Lorry carrying leaking sugar bags an allurement to/concealed danger for children.

Cullen (suing by her mother) and Cullen v Manchester Corporation [1940] LJNCCR 255 CyCt Defendants not liable to plaintiff licensees for injury occurring from danger of which defendants had hitherto been unaware.

Cumber v Chief Constable of Hampshire Constabulary [1995] TLR 32 CA Award of exemplary damages but no compensatory damages for false imprisonment was irrational.

Cummings (or McWilliams) v Sir William Arrol and Co, Ltd and another [1962] 1 All ER 623; (1962) 106 SJ 218 HL Not liable in negligence where injury would have occurred even if breach had not.

Cummings v Grainger (1975) 125 NLJ 256t; (1975) 119 SJ 425; [1975] 1 WLR 1330 HC QBD Successful action for damages under Animals Act 1975 from owner-keeper of particularly fierce Alsatian dog.

Cummings v Grainger (1977) 141 JP 95; (1976) 126 NLJ 665t; [1977] QB 397; (1976) 120 SJ 453; [1976] 3 WLR 842 CA Person with untrained guard dog not liable for injuries suffered by trespasser (who in any event entered guarded place knowing of dog and so assumed risk of injury).

Cunard and another v Antifyre, Ltd [1932] All ER 558; [1933] 1 KB 551; (1934) 103 LJCL 321; (1933) 148 LTR 287; (1932-33) XLIX TLR 184 HC KBD Negligence for failure to take steps in relation to overhanging guttering that reasonable man would do in the circumstances.

Cunard Steamship Co, Hook v (1953) 117 JP 226; (1953) 103 LJ 265; (1953) 97 SJ 334; [1953] 1 WLR 682 HC QBD Master of ship where could reasonably believe is necessary and does believe it to be necessary could detain any person on board ship so as to preserve order/discipline.

Cunard White Star, Ltd, Bishop v; Appleby v Cunard White Star, Ltd; The Queen Mary [1950] 2 All ER 22 HC PDAD On assessment of fatal accident/negligence damages.

Cunliffe v Bankes [1945] 1 All ER 459; (1946) 96 LJ 213 Assizes All reasonable steps taken to gauging safety of tree: no negligence and no nuisance (did not cause defect; did not arise through own act and failed to remedy in reasonable time).

Cunningham and others v Reading Football Club Ltd (1991) 141 NLJ 425i; [1991] TLR 153 HC QBD Football club liable as occupiers for not so maintaining concrete that it could not be torn up and hurled at police (as occurred).

Cyril Lord Carpets, Ltd, Wieland v [1969] 3 All ER 1006 HC QBD Damages available for second injury on foot of original negligence.

D and F Estates Ltd and others v Church Commissioners for England and others [1988] 2 All ER 992; [1989] AC 177; (1988) 138 NLJ 210; (1988) 132 SJ 1092; [1988] 3 WLR 368 HL Minus contractual obligation pure economic loss irrecoverable; builders not liable for negligence of competent sub-contractor.

D and L Caterers, Limited, and another v D'Ajou [1945] 1 KB 210; [1945] 114 LJ 262; (1945) 172 LTR 223; (1945) WN (I) 36 HC KBD Limited company can sue for slander though no proof of actual damage but words an aspersion on its conducting of business.

D and L Caterers, Ltd and Jackson v D'Ajou [1945] 1 All ER 563; [1945] KB 364; (1946) 96 LJ 199; [1945] 114 LJ 386; (1945) 173 LTR 21; (1944-45) LXI TLR 343; (1945) WN (I) 88 CA Limited company can sue for slander though no proof of actual damage: damage implied to ground action; on cross-examination over credit in defamation suit.

D Buckman, Ltd and another, Leibo v [1952] 2 All ER 1057; (1952) 96 SJ 865; [1952] 2 TLR 969; (1952) WN (I) 547 CA Unless reasonable and probable cause is malicious prosecution.

D Murphy and Son, Ltd, Pope and others v [1960] 2 All ER 873; (1960) 110 LJ 542; [1961] 1 QB 222; (1960) 104 SJ 427 HC QBD Loss of earning capacity to be gauged by pre-injury life expectancy.

D'Ajou, D and L Caterers, Limited, and another v [1945] 1 KB 210; [1945] 114 LJ 262; (1945) 172 LTR 223; (1945) WN (I) 36 HC KBD Limited company can sue for slander though no proof of actual damage but words an aspersion on its conducting of business.

D'Ajou, D and L Caterers, Ltd and Jackson v [1945] 1 All ER 563; [1945] KB 364; (1946) 96 LJ 199; [1945] 114 LJ 386; (1945) 173 LTR 21; (1944-45) LXI TLR 343; (1945) WN (I) 88 CA Limited company can sue for slander though no proof of actual damage: damage implied to ground action; on cross-examination over credit in defamation suit.

D'Arcy v Prison Commissioners [1956] Crim LR 56t HC QBD Successful negligence action against Prison Commissioners for injuries suffered by prisoner during attack by fellow-prisoners.

D'Rosario, Ghosh v (1962) 106 SJ 352 CA Stay of slander action required where after commencement of action defendant appointed to High Commission staff and thereby acquired diplomatic immunity.

D'Urso v Sanson [1939] 4 All ER 26; (1939) 88 LJ 252; (1939) 83 SJ 850 HC KBD Watchman returning inside burning building acted in course of employment: no volenti non fit injuria.

Daborn v Bath Tramways Motor Co, Ltd and Trevor Smithey [1946] 2 All ER 333 CA Non-negligence of driver of left-hand drive ambulance to which warning sign affixed/after correct hand-signals given.

Daily Herald, Crisp v (1929) and others (1959) 103 SJ 918 CA Impecuniosity no excuse for (twelve year) delay: libel action struck out.

Daily Mirror Newspapers Ltd v Exclusive News Agency (1937) 81 SJ 924 HC KBD Newspaper had right of indemnity against news agency which supplied it with mistakenly identified photograph that resulted in successful libel action being brought against the newspaper.

Daily Mirror Newspapers, Limited, Cassidy v [1929] 2 KB 331 HC KBD Liable for defamatory meaning of one's words though unintended.

Daily Mirror Newspapers, Ltd v Gardner and others [1968] 2 All ER 163; [1968] 2 QB 762; [1968] 2 WLR 1239 CA Interlocutory injunction available; that did not know terms of contract/did not bring about direct pressure no defence; restrictive trade practice prima facie evidence of wrongful interference.

Daily Mirror Newspapers, Ltd, Cassidy v [1929] All ER 117; (1929) 67 LJ 399; (1929) 98 LJCL 595; (1929) 141 LTR 404; (1929) 73 SJ 348; (1928-29) XLV TLR 485 CA Are liable for defamatory meaning of one's words whether intended defamation or not.

Daily Sketch and Sunday Graphic, Limited, Marengo v [1948] 117 LJR 787; (1948) LXIV TLR 160; (1948) WN (I) 92 HL On form of passing-off injunction.

Daly v Liverpool Corporation [1939] 2 All ER 142; (1939) 87 LJ 236 HC KBD On dual task of public vehicle driver to keep to schedule and avoid accidents; on driver's duty of care to elderly pedestrians.

Damant, Anglo-Saxon Petroleum Co, Ltd and others v; Anglo-Saxon Petroleum Co, Ltd and others v Regem [1947] 2 All ER 465; [1947] KB 794; (1947) WN (I) 197 CA Action for negligence of salvor lies in tort; salvor owes duty to take reasonable care to ensure possible plaintiff not injured.

Damiens v Modern Society (Limited) and another (1910-11) XXVII TLR 164 HC KBD Damages ought not to have been severed in respect of joint defendants.

Damon, Hunt v (1929-30) XLVI TLR 579 HC KBD Wrongfully expelling child from school is not per se a tort.

Daniel and Others, Legal and General Assurance Society Ltd v (1967) 117 NLJ 113t CA Successful passing off action by Legal and General Assurance Society against the 'Legal and General Enquiry Bureau'.

Daniel v Rickett, Cockerell and Co Limited, and another [1938] 2 All ER 631; [1938] 2 KB 322; (1938) 85 LJ 380; [1938] 107 LJCL 589; (1938) 82 SJ 353; (1937-38) LIV TLR 756; (1938) WN (I) 190 HC KBD Absent adequate warning to passers-by coal deliverer and householder were jointly liable for injury suffered by person falling as result of coal cellar access to pavement being open.

Daniel Wilhelmus Hattingh and Others, Greyvensteyn (Samuel Jacobus) v [1911] AC 355; (1911) 80 LJPC 158; (1910-11) XXVII TLR 358 PC Not liable for results of driving locusts from one's property in act of self-protection.

Daniels and Wife v R White and Sons Limited and another (1939) 160 LTR 128 HC KBD Failed/successful negligence action against vendor/producer for selling lemonade not fit for human consumption.

Daniels, Lincoln v [1960] 3 All ER 205; (1960) 104 SJ 625 HC QBD Complaints to Bar Council about barrister have qualified privilege.

Daniels, Lincoln v [1961] 3 All ER 740; [1955] Crim LR 647; (1961) 111 LJ 660; [1962] 1 QB 237 CA No absolute privilege letters of complaint to Bar Council where letters did not lead to disciplinary action.

Daniels, Lincoln v [1960] 3 All ER 205; (1960) 110 LJ 655 HC QBD Complaints to Bar Council about barrister have qualified privilege.

Daniels, Lincoln v [1961] 3 All ER 740; [1955] Crim LR 647 CA No absolute privilege letters of complaint to Bar Council where letters did not lead to disciplinary action.

Dann v Hamilton [1939] 1 All ER 59; [1939] 1 KB 509; (1939) 87 LJ 46; [1939] 108 LJCL 255; (1939) 160 LTR 433; (1939) 83 SJ 155; (1938-39) LV TLR 297 HC KBD Travelling in car with drunk driver does not raise volenti non fit injuria defence.

Danquah, Wuta-Ofei v [1961] 3 All ER 596; [1955] Crim LR 806 PC Little evidence needed for person to establish possession against other who never enjoyed title to land.

Daphne v Bailey (1919) CC Rep VIII 66 CyCt Landlord who after giving tenant notice to quit forcibly entered premises and threw tenant's furniture into street held to be liable in damages for trespass.

Darbishire v Warran [1963] 3 All ER 310; (1963) 107 SJ 631; [1963] 1 WLR 1067 CA Damages greater than cost of replacing damaged chattel irrecoverable.

Darby, Hamps v [1948] 2 KB 311; (1948) 98 LJ 427; [1949] 118 LJR 487; (1948) LXIV TLR 440; (1948) WN (I) 313 CA Liability of farmer for shooting and killing pigeons without first trying to scare them off.

Darby, Hamps v (1948) 98 LJ 303 CyCt On liability of farmer for shooting and killing pigeons without first trying to scare them off.

Darling Brothers and Gaselee and Son, Page and Co v; The Millwall [1905] 74 LJP 13 HC PDAD Tow owners liable to tug owners.

Darling v Attorney-General and another [1950] 2 All ER 793; (1950) 100 LJ 483 Assizes Ministries doing work on private land owe occupier duty not to endanger/cause damage to him (even if entrust work to contractor).

Darling, Gaselee v; The Millwall [1904-07] All ER 1387 CA Tow owners liable to tug owners.

Darngavil Coal Company Limited v McKinlay (1923) 87 JP 66; (1923) 128 LTR 772; (1922-23) 67 SJ 276; (1923) WN (I) 35 HL Action in negligence in respect of injury arising from dangerous gate allowed go to trial.

Dartford District Council and another, Hoadley v [1979] RTR 359; (1979) 123 SJ 129 CA No reduction in damages for person not wearing seat belt where no requirement that vehicle have seat belts and it did not in fact have seat belts.

Darton Urban District Council, Newsome v (1938) 102 JP 75; (1938) 158 LTR 149; (1937) 81 SJ 1042; (1937-38) LIV TLR 286 HC KBD Highway authority liable in nuisance/negligence for misfeasance (subsidence in trench had caused to be dug which led to injury to cyclist).

Darton Urban District Council, Newsome v (1938) 102 JP 409; (1938) 82 SJ 520; (1937-38) LIV TLR 945 CA Highway and sanitary authority liable as latter in nuisance/negligence for misfeasance (subsidence in trench had caused to be dug which led to injury to cyclist).

Dauncey v Holloway [1901] 2 KB 441; [1901] 70 LJK/QB 695; (1901) LXXXIV LTR 649; (1900-01) 45 SJ 501; (1900-01) XVII TLR 493; (1900-01) 49 WR 546 CA Words spoken of solicitor not actionable absent special damage as did not reflect on same as solicitor.

Davey v Harrow Corporation [1957] 2 All ER 305; (1957) 107 LJ 344; [1958] 1 QB 61; (1957) 101 SJ 405 CA Nuisance to owner of adjoining property if planted/self-sown trees on one's property cause of damage on other's.

Davey, Booth and another v (1988) 138 NLJ 104 CA Conveyancing solicitor not liable in negligence where had read out draft contract to clients and given them copy to peruse.

David Brown Tractors (Retail) Ltd (Rustons Engineering Co Ltd, third party), Howe and others v [1991] 4 All ER 30 CA Amendment of writ where limitation period applies; application to dispply limitation period to be made at same time/beforehand.

David Syme and Co Ltd, Lloyd (Clive Herbert) v [1986] AC 350; (1986) 130 SJ 14; [1986] 2 WLR 69 PC Failure of defence of comment in respect of (defamatory) newspaper article where writer of same did not hold views made therein.

David Taylor and Son Ltd v Bowden Transport Ltd (1965-66) 116 NLJ 726 HC QBD Carriers deemed negligent where their driver left van containing cargo unattended for several minutes in empty street early one morning.

Davids v Turner (1946) 96 LJ 56 HC KBD Failed personal injury action brought by licensee (who fell down stairs) where was no trap/hidden danger — plaintiff in fact knew of danger and failed to take reasonable precautions.

Davidson v Barclay's Bank Limited (1941) 164 LTR 25; (1940) 84 SJ 117; (1939-40) LVI TLR 343 HC KBD Making defamatory of another in genuinely mistaken belief that under duty to make statement not privileged despite mistake.

Davidson v Chief Constable of North Wales and another [1994] 2 All ER 597; [1993] TLR 229 CA Evidence of store detective not directing, procuring, expressly requesting or encouraging arrest by police so not basis for false imprisonment.

Davidson v Leggett (1969) 113 SJ 409 CA Parties to collision between two overtaking vehicles coming from opposite directions were equally responsible for accident.

Davie v New Merton Board Mills, Ltd and others [1958] 1 All ER 67; [1958] 1 QB 210 CA Master not liable to servant for defects in manufacture of tools if takes reasonable care to provide safe tools.

Davie v New Merton Board Mills, Ltd and others [1957] 2 All ER 38; [1957] 2 QB 368; (1957) 101 SJ 321 HC QBD Manufacturers and employers liable in negligence for injury to worker by defective tool.

Davie v New Merton Mills Ltd and Another [1959] AC 604; [1959] 2 WLR 331 HL Employers not liable for injury to worker from latent defect in quality tool which could not have discovered.

Davies (Joseph Owen) v Eli Lilly and Co and others [1987] 3 All ER 94; (1987) 131 SJ 842 CA Court may impose costs on persons not party to case at (or sometimes before) end of trial.

Davies (Joseph Owen) v Eli Lilly and Co and others (1987) 131 SJ 807 HC QBD On division of costs in multiple personal injuries action.

Davies and another v Powell Duffryn Associated Collieries, Ltd [1942] 1 All ER 657; [1942] AC 601; [1942] 111 LJ 418; (1943) 93 LJ 115; (1942) 167 LTR 74; (1942) 86 SJ 294; (1941-42) LVIII TLR 240; (1942) WN (I) 175 HL Damages obtained under Law Reform (Miscellaneous Provisions) Act 1934 relevant when determining damages under Fatal Accidents Act 1846.

Davies and another, Carberry (formerly an infant but now of full age) v [1968] 2 All ER 817; (1968) 118 NLJ 372t; [1968] 1 WLR 1103 CA Owner liable if driver acting on behalf and under authority of owner.

Davies and Camden and Islington Area Health Authority, Yeomans v (1981) 131 NLJ 210 HC QBD Damages following negligently performed vasectomy operation.

Davies and others, Egger v (1964) 108 SJ 619 CA Malice of joint defendant in publishing item does not taint others with malice: most be individually motivated by malice to lose qualified privilege.

Davies Brothers (Haulage), Ltd and another, Rothwell v [1963] Crim LR 577; (1963) 107 SJ 436 CA Heavy goods vehicle driver 25% liable/car driver 75% liable for collision which occurred where latter distracted former while driving.

Davies v British Railways Board (1984) 134 NLJ 888 HC QBD On duty of occupier towards (child) trespasser.

Davies v Carmarthenshire County Council [1971] RTR 112 CA Council (80%) liable and driver (20%) liable for collision at sunset with lamp left in dangerous position on road after road-widening.

Davies v Clarke (1953) 103 LJ ccr141 CyCt Innkeeper liable for loss of bulk of various articles from car parked in inn yard that opened onto road.

Davies v Fortior, Ltd [1952] 1 All ER 1359; (1952) 96 SJ 376; (1952) WN (I) 291 HC QBD Comment by dead workman directly after accident admissible as res gestae.

Davies v Gellygaer Urban District Council (1954) 104 LJ ccr140 CyCt Council deemed not to have been negligent where child injured self on broken glass bottle in council-maintained pool.

Davies v Hood and others (1903) LXXXVIII LTR 19; (1902-03) XIX TLR 158 HC KBD Personal representative of dead solicitor liable for negligent acts of latter when alive and on retainer.

Davies v Journeaux [1976] RTR 111 CA Motorist who hit young girl whom had glimpsed before she ran across road not failing to keep proper look-out as were other legitimate distractions nor was he negligent in not sounding horn.

Davies v Liverpool Corporation [1949] 2 All ER 175; (1949) 113 JP 381; (1949) 99 LJ 301; (1949) WN (I) 268 CA Conductor liable in negligence for not policing dismounting of passengers from tram.

Davies v New Merton Board Mills, Ltd [1956] 1 All ER 379; (1956) 100 SJ 170 HC QBD On pleading act of third party as defence to negligence.

Davies v Rustproof Metal Window Co, Ltd [1943] 1 All ER 248; (1942-43) LIX TLR 151 CA Cannot pay money into court denying liability, then admit liability in defence.

Davies v Swan Motor Co (Swansea), Ltd (Swansea Corporation and James, Third Parties) [1949] 1 All ER 620; [1949] 2 KB 291; (1949) LXV TLR 278; (1949) WN (I) 192 CA Lack of proper care (not breach of duty) necessary to show contributory negligence to own death.

Davies v Tenby Corporation (1974) 124 NLJ 412; (1974) 118 SJ 549 CA Council (75%) liable for paralysis suffered by person who dived from defective diving board put up by corporation.

Davies v Thomas and others [1920] All ER 438; [1920] 2 Ch 189; (1919-20) XXXVI TLR 571 CA No injunction restraining implementation of legally void rule as persons concerned not acting in unlawful conspiracy.

Davies, Deen v [1935] All ER 9; [1935] 2 KB 282; [1935] LJNCCA 202; (1935) 153 LTR 90; (1935) 79 SJ 381; (1934-35) LI TLR 398 CA Recovery for natural and probable injuries occasioned upon negligently tethered horse escaping.

Davies, Mathias v (1970) 114 SJ 268 CA On appropriate remedy for nuisance.

Davies, Tysoe v [1983] Crim LR 684; [1984] RTR 88; [1983] TLR 434 HC QBD Were (80%) to blame for accident arising directly from driving with thick clouds of smoke coming from exhaust; person with whom collided (20%) liable for not keeping proper look-out notwithstanding smoke.

Davis and another v Radcliffe and others [1990] 2 All ER 536; (1990) 134 SJ 862/1078; [1990] TLR 285; [1990] 1 WLR 821 PC Government bank regulators do not owe duty of care to depositors in failed licensed banks.

Davis and another v Rubin and another (1968) 112 SJ 51 CA Re-trial of libel action ordered where damages awarded were excessive.

Davis v Bromley Urban District Council (1903) 67 JP 275 CA Punitive damages appropriate for trespass by local authority.

Davis v Foots (1939) 83 SJ 780 CA Landlord liable for gassing of honey-mooners following negligent removal of gas fire at behest of same.

Davis v London County Council (1913-14) XXX TLR 275 HC KBD Once competent professionals employed local education authority not liable for negligence of persons whom it agrees to allow conduct medical operations on children.

Davis v London Express Newspaper, Limited (1939) 83 SJ 96; (1938-39) LV TLR 207 HC KBD Absent malice person to whom letter critical of company written could not sue newspaper which obtained copy of letter and showed it to company officer.

Davis v Marrable (1913) 48 LJ 405 HC ChD On extent of right to ancient light.

Davis v Soltenpur (1983) 133 NLJ 720; [1983] TLR 104 HC QBD Limitation period applied in favour of defendant where plaintiff still had option of bring action against solicitors.

Davis v St Mary's Demolition and Excavation Co, Ltd [1954] 1 All ER 578; (1954) 98 SJ 217; [1954] 1 WLR 592 HC QBD Liability to child trespasser as neighbour where child trespass frequent.

Davis v Town Properties Investment Corporation [1903] 72 LJCh 389 CA Assignee of reversion not liable for breach of covenant with lessee (through nuisance).

Davis, Gunter v (1924) WN (I) 288 HC KBD Order for ejectment of trespasser (costs to landlord).

Davis, Harvest Trucking Ltd v [1991] TLR 147 HC QBD On duty of care owed by insurance intermediary.

Davis, Mitchell v (1920-21) XXXVII TLR 68 HC KBD Bailment relationship continues with tradesman who has been sent goods even after he has completed repairs unless otherwise agree.

Davison, Todd (by his next best friend Anne Todd) v [1971] 1 All ER 449; (1971) 115 SJ 144; [1971] 1 WLR 267 Assizes Infant's right of action expires if reasonable parents would have brought action.

Davy v Spelthorne Borough Council [1984] AC 262; [1983] TLR 604 HL Could bring action against local council for alleged negligent advice from council which led person subject to enforcement notice not to challenge that notice.

Daw, Turley v (1906) XCIV LTR 216 HC KBD Judgment debtor cannot during duration of committal order bring action aainst County court bailiff for non-service of judgment summons.

Dawes, Kelly and another v [1990] TLR 623 HC QBD Personal injury damages payable by way of index-linked annuity earned by investment of total amount of damages.

Dawrant v Nutt [1960] 3 All ER 681; (1960) 110 LJ 830; (1961) 105 SJ 129 Assizes Highway user owes duty of care to other highway users to take reasonable care: absence of front lights a breach of duty.

Dawson and Co v Bingley Urban District Council [1911-13] All ER 596 CA Liability for misfeasance.

Dawson and Co, Griffiths v [1993] 2 FCR 515; [1993] 2 FLR 315; [1993] TLR 201 HC QBD Solicitor negligent as failed to stop divorce decree being made absolute before financial situation resolved so causing wife to lose out financially.

Dawson and others, Beevis v [1956] 3 All ER 837; [1957] 1 QB 195; (1956) 100 SJ 874; [1956] 3 WLR 1016 CA Various errors justifying re-hearing before judge alone; court may allow plaintiff to delay evidence until defence presents alleged justification.

Dawson Bentley and Co, Ltd, Marren v [1961] 2 All ER 270; (1961) 111 LJ 342; [1961] 2 QB 135; (1961) 105 SJ 383 HC QBD Day of tort not to be included when calculating limitation period.

Dawson v Spaul (1934-35) LI TLR 247 HC KBD Adjudication in personal injuries action ordered in interest of defendant despite death of plaintiff.

Day v Smith (1983) 133 NLJ 726 HC QBD Person driving several feet over central dividing line liable in negligence for fatal road traffic accident which occurred.

Day v Tidball (1929) 68 LJ ccr24 CyCt Damages available from CyCt in action for trespass following order by court of summary jurisdiction pursuant to the Small Tenements Recovery Act 1838.

Day, Bros (Pinker) v (1929) 68 LJ ccr52 CyCt Domestic horse-owner not liable for damage occasioned by horse after strayed (by way of defective fence) onto highway.

DC Thompson and Co, Ltd v Deakin and others [1952] 2 All ER 361 CA Cannot procure breach of contract where act procure is not unlawful.

DDSA Pharmaceuticals Ltd v Times Newspapers Ltd and another [1972] 3 All ER 417; (1972) 122 NLJ 609t; [1973] QB 21; (1972) 116 SJ 585; [1972] 3 WLR 582 CA Particulars in pleadings in libel actions.

De Beck and others, Haynes v (1914-15) XXXI TLR 115 HC KBD Wholesale newspaper distributors not liable where distributed newspapers which did not know (and were not negligent in not knowing) were defamatory.

De Beers Abrasive Products Ltd and others v International General Electric Co of New York Ltd and another [1975] 2 All ER 599; (1975) 119 SJ 439; [1975] 1 WLR 972 HC ChD Slander of goods where reasonable person would believe alleged 'puff' was truth.

De Bernales and others, Apley Estates Co and others v [1946] 2 All ER 338; (1947) 91 SJ 12 HC ChD Agreement with one joint tortfeasor not accord and satisfaction unless so intended.

De Bernales and others, Apley Estates Co and others v [1947] 1 All ER 213; [1947] Ch 217; [1947] 116 LJR 705; (1947) 176 LTR 182; (1947) LXIII TLR 71; (1947) WN (I) 13 CA Agreeing not to sue one joint tortfeasor does not release others.

De Buse and others v McCarthy and Stepney Borough Council [1942] 1 All ER 19; (1942) 106 JP 73; [1942] 1 KB 156; [1942] 111 LJ 170; (1943) 93 LJ 125; (1942) 166 LTR 52; (1941) 85 SJ 468; (1941-42) LVIII TLR 83; (1941) WN (I) 231 CA Council committee report to borough council published to ratepayers not privileged as no common interest/duty.

De Buse and others v McCarthy and others (1941) 105 JP 360; (1941) 165 LTR 255; (1941) 85 SJ 369; (1940-41) LVII TLR 596 HC KBD Publication of elements of allegedly libellous council committee report by distributing notice containing report to council-controlled public libraries was privileged.

De Coppett v Barnett and others (1900-01) XVII TLR 273 CA Sheriff not protected from action for trespass where substantial grievance had resulted to plaintiff as result of sheriff's actions.

De Freville v Dill [1927] 96 LJCL 1056; (1926-27) XLIII TLR 702 HC KBD Successful action for negligent committal of plaintiff to mental hospital.

De Havilland and another, Green v (1968) 112 SJ 766 HC QBD On rôle of jury in malicious prosecution action.

De Jetley Marks v Greenwood (Lord) and others [1936] 1 All ER 863 HC KBD Must be breach of contract before can sue for conspiracy to cause breach of contract.

De Jong v London and North Western Railway (1914) CC Rep III 13 CyCt Good case for negligence where entrust livestock to rail company and are delivered in damaged condition following delay/where is evidence that inadequate care taken of livestock.

De Keyser's Royal Hotel (Limited) v Spicer Brothers (Limited) and Minter (1913-14) XXX TLR 257 HC ChD Was nuisance for builders to do pile-driving at night which kept persons in adjoining premises awake.

De L'Isle (Viscount) v Times Newspapers Ltd [1987] 3 All ER 499; (1988) 132 SJ 54; [1988] 1 WLR 49 CA Finding of fact and not a discretion whether trial by judge preferable to trial by jury where many documents/accounts.

De Lecavalier v City of Montreal [1930] AC 152; (1930) 99 LJPC 53; (1930) 142 LTR 124 PC Party had no interest on which to ground nuisance action.

De Martell v Merton and Sutton Health Authority [1992] 3 All ER 820; [1992] 2 FCR 832; [1992] 3 WLR 637 (also CA) HC QBD Cause of action for injury to plaintiff at birth runs from date of birth as before that no legal personality.

De Normanville v Hereford Times Limited (1936) 80 SJ 423 CA Newspaper report deemed a fair and accurate report (slightly inaccurate paraphrasing) of what transpired at public meeting.

De Normanville v Hereford Times Limited (1935) 79 SJ 796 HC KBD Newspaper report deemed a fair and accurate report (slightly inaccurate paraphrasing) of what transpired at public meeting.

De Parrell v Walker (1932) 76 SJ 850; (1932-33) XLIX TLR 37 HC KBD Employer of clock-winder who stole property from house to which sent deemed negligent in hiring criminal person as clockwinder.

De Placido, Haggar v [1972] 2 All ER 1029; (1972) 116 SJ 396; [1972] 1 WLR 716 CrCt Victim may recover costs/losses of third parties to whom has legal liability for reasonable costs/losses they suffered (even if family members).

De Stempel v Dunkels [1937] 2 All ER 215; (1937) 156 LTR 418; (1936-37) LIII TLR 451; (1937) WN (I) 117 HC KBD Statement that person 'a Jew hater' did not refer to person in business conduct — absent special damage could not recover damages.

De Stempel v Dunkels [1938] 1 All ER 238; (1938) 158 LTR 85; (1938) 82 SJ 51; (1937-38) LIV TLR 289 CA Calling person a 'Jew-hater' is defamatory; words said in relation to other's business could be sued on though no proof of special damage.

De Vere Hotels, Ltd, Chamier v (1928) 72 SJ 155 HC KBD Hotel owner's not liable for theft of guest's jewellery where guest had been negligent in leaving same in unlocked drawer while out.

De Vries and another, Bryanston Finance Ltd and others v [1975] 2 All ER 609; (1975) 125 NLJ 231; [1975] QB 703; (1975) 119 SJ 287 [1975] 2 WLR 718 CA Qualified privilege between businessman/typist/photocopier if main purpose was usual course of business; not pleading justification does not mean words false; in action against two joint tortfeasors judgment against one bar to action against other.

Deakin and others, DC Thompson and Co, Ltd v [1952] 2 All ER 361 CA Cannot procure breach of contract where act procured is not unlawful.

Deal Corporation, Turner and another v (1967) 111 SJ 685 HC QBD Successful action in nuisance for damage to property in course of road-widening.

Dean and another, Martin v (1971) 121 NLJ 904; [1971] 3 All ER 279; [1971] 2 QB 208; [1971] RTR 280; (1971) 115 SJ 369; [1971] 2 WLR 1159 HC QBD Judgment debt (arising from negligence action) available against motor bicycle-owner as well as bicycle-driver.

Dean, Monmouthshire County Council v (1962) 112 LJ 787 CyCt Failed claim that person whom claimed to have inadequately drained bank was liable in nuisance/for obstruction where bank became waterlogged and slipped onto road.

Deane, Byrne v [1937] 1 KB 818; [1937] 106 LJCL 533; (1937) 157 LTR 10; (1937) 81 SJ 236; (1936-37) LIII TLR 469; (1937) WN (I) 126 CA Allegation that were police informer not defamatory.

Deane-Freeman, Reeves v (1953) 103 LJ 121; [1953] 1 QB 459; (1953) 97 SJ 132 CA One-year public authority limitation on tort actions applies to soldier driving military truck in course of duty.

Deane-Freeman, Reeves v (1952) 102 LJ 457; (1952) 96 SJ 531; [1952] 2 TLR 361; (1952) WN (I) 415 HC QBD One-year public authority limitation on tort actions applies to soldier driving military truck in course of duty.

Dee Conservancy Board and others v McConnell and another (1928) 97 LJCL 487; (1928) WN (I) 60 CA Abandonment of wreck sunk through negligence did not preclude liability for expenses of removing same.

Deeming v British Steel Corporation (1979) 123 SJ 303 CA Delay that did not affect value of evidence to be given in personal injuries action did not justify striking out of personal injuries claim.

Dennis v Charnwood Borough Council (1982) 132 NLJ 349 HC QBD Local authority owes duty of care in ensuring plans comply with building regulations; time ran from date local authority failure became apparent.

Dennis v London Co-operative Society, Ltd [1939] LJNCCR 39 CyCt Defendants liable for injury suffered by plaintiff who slipped on piece of fat swept by defendants into street.

Dennis v London Passenger Transport Board (1948) LXIV TLR 269 HC KBD Wages paid during absence from work repayable from peronal injury damages awarded.

Dennison, Jones and another v [1971] RTR 174 CA Presumption that epileptic involved in collision after blacked out obviated by his proving that did not know/could not reasonably have known was prone to black-outs.

Denny v Supplies and Transport Co Ld, and others [1950] 2 KB 374; (1950) 94 SJ 403; [1950] 66 (1) TLR 1168; (1950) WN (I) 294 CA Liability of stevedores for injury sustained by wharfingers' employee in unloading dangerously loaded barge.

Dental Manufacturing Company, Limited v C De Trey and Co [1912] 3 KB 76; (1912) 81 LJKB 1162; (1912-13) 107 LTR 111; (1911-12) XXVIII TLR 498; (1912) WN (I) 190 CA Sole agent could not maintain passing off action for loss of profits where had not sold item under own get-up.

Denton v South West Thames Regional Health Authority (1981) 131 NLJ 240 HC QBD Damages for nurse who suffered injuries as result of collapse of hospital bed.

Dents (Lim), Horner v (1917) CC Rep VI 2 CyCt Nominal damages for unauthorised removal of company name from watch by company whose name had featured on watch/to whom watch entrusted for repair.

Department of Employment, Jones v [1988] 1 All ER 725; (1987) 137 NLJ 1182; [1989] QB 1; (1988) 132 SJ 128; [1988] 2 WLR 493 CA By statute adjudication officers cannot be sued for negligence; misfeasance, judicial review, statutory appeal only means of challenging decision.

Department of Health and Social Security v Kinnear and others [1984] TLR 433 HC QBD Actions against Government Department for negligent advice regarding giving of whooping cough inoculations allowed to proceed.

Department of the Environment v James and others (1972) 116 SJ 712 HC ChD Court would not delay recovery of possession of property occupied by trespassers.

Department of the Environment v Thomas Bates and Son (New Towns Commission, third party) [1990] 2 All ER 943; [1991] 1 AC 499; (1990) 134 SJ 1077; [1990] TLR 561; [1990] 3 WLR 457 HL Damages unavailable for pure economic loss, for defects that do not damage building/ endanger health.

Department of the Environment v Thomas Bates and Son Ltd (New Towns Commission, third party) [1989] 1 All ER 1075; (1989) 139 NLJ 39 CA No tortious duty on builder to remedy defects in building unless pose threat of imminent physical injury.

Department of Transport v Chris Smaller (Transport) Ltd [1989] AC 1197; (1989) 139 NLJ 363; (1989) 133 SJ 361; [1989] 2 WLR 578 HL Pre-writ delay not punishable where within limitation period; post-writ delay ought not to be punished where does not unduly prejudice other.

Department of Transport v North West Water Authority [1983] 3 All ER 273; [1984] AC 336 (also HC QBD); (1983) 133 NLJ 1016; [1983] TLR 611; [1983] 3 WLR 707 HL Absent negligence no liability for nuisance caused performing statutory duty.

Department of Transport v North West Water Authority [1983] 1 All ER 892; [1984] AC 336 (also HL); [1982] TLR 617; [1983] 3 WLR 105 HC QBD Inapplicability of defence of statutory authority in public nuisance action against water authority.

Deputy Governor of Parkhurst Prison and others, ex parte Hague, R v [1990] 3 All ER 687; [1992] 1 AC 58 (also HC QBD/HL); (1990) 140 NLJ 1036; [1990] 3 WLR 1210 CA Administrative decisions by prison authorities not subject to private law remedies; intentional unreasonable detention of prisoner beyond term of imprisonment or in conditions detrimental to health is false imprisonment.

Deputy Governor of Parkhurst Prison and others, Hague v; Weldon v Home Office [1991] 3 All ER 733; [1992] 1 AC 58 (also HC QBD/CA); (1991) 141 NLJ 1185; [1991] 3 WLR 340 HL Party cannot launch private law claim for breach of statutory duty unless legislature intended it so; prisoner lawfully imprisoned cannot sue for false imprisonment in respect of residual liberty.

Devitt and others, Australian Steam Shipping Co (Limited) v (1916-17) XXXIII TLR 178 HC KBD Failed action by persons who commissioned steamship against management committee of Lloyd's Register for certifying ship as being of certain class when apparently was not.

Devitt, Dickson and Co (Limited) v (1915-16) XXXII TLR 547 HC KBD Party seeking insurance not under duty to see broker properly carried out insurance sought: could recover for broker's negligence in doing same.

Devlin v F (a juvenile) [1982] 2 All ER 450 HC QBD One-judge Divisional Court can deal with time extension application; interests of justice/defendant justify extension.

Devon County Council, Nicholls and Son v (1922) CC Rep XI 19 CyCt Licensee not liable in negligence for failure to fence in quarry (where such failure resulted in loss of straying cattle).

Devon County Council, Shepphard v (1980) 130 NLJ 14 CA Reversal of trial judge's finding that council were liable in negligence where school bus was driven over foot of boy who had jumped off the bus.

Devonshire and Smith v Jenkins (1979) 129 (1) NLJ 198c CA Aggravated, not exemplary damages for harassment/nuisance.

Dews v National Coal Board [1986] 2 All ER 769; [1987] QB 81; [1986] 3 WLR 227 CA Missed compulsory pension contributions not to be included in damages.

Dews v National Coal Board [1988] AC 1; (1987) 137 NLJ 545; [1987] 3 WLR 38 HL Missed compulsory pension contributions not to be included in damages.

Dexter v Courtaulds Ltd [1984] 1 All ER 70; (1984) 128 SJ 81; [1983] TLR 688; [1984] 1 WLR 372 CA Half-rate interest on special damages in ordinary personal injuries case is proper.

Deyong v Shenburn [1946] 1 All ER 226; [1946] KB 227 CA No implied term in producer/actor agreement and no common law duty to protect latter's personal property in theatre.

Dhillon and another, Bellingham v [1973] 1 All ER 20; [1973] QB 304; (1972) 116 SJ 566; [1972] 3 WLR 730 HC QBD Projected profits less actual profits yields amount of damages in contract/tort for loss of profits.

Diabetic Society Ltd and others, British Diabetic Association v [1995] 4 All ER 812 HC ChD Passing-off includes (unintentional) deception by one fund-raising charity that enables it to appropriate goodwill of and donations to another.

Diamond and others (McGrigor Donald (a firm), third party, Possfund Custodian Trustee Ltd and another v; Parr and others v Diamond and others (McGrigor Donald (a firm), third party) [1996] 2 All ER 774; [1996] 1 WLR 1351 HC ChD Issuers of company share prospectus may owe duty of care to subsequent purchasers of shares.

Diamond v Minter and others (1939-40) XXXI Cox CC 468; (1941) 91 LJ 142 HC KBD Unmerited arrest as were not person named in warrant; police officer cannot without warrant arrest person whom reasonably suspects committed criminal act abroad.

Dibben v Holloway (1929) 68 LJ ccr8 CyCt Building-owner not in possession of same could recover damages in trespass for loss sustained through person without authority affixing radio wires to building.

Dick, Kerr and Co Limited, T Tilling, Limited v (1905) 69 JP 172; (1904-05) 53 WR 380 HC KBD Recovery of damages for injury to omnibuses effected by contractors doing council works.

Dickens v Kay-Green (1961) 105 SJ 949 CA Driver who strayed onto wrong side of road during heavy fog deemed to be negligent.

Dickens v London Passenger Transport Board [1935] LJNCCR 171 CyCt London Passenger Transport Board enjoyed the protection afforded public authorities by the Public Authorities Protection Act 1893.

Dickie, Ash v [1936] 105 LJCh 337; (1936) 154 LTR 641; (1936) 80 SJ 364; (1935-36) LII TLR 534; (1936) WN (I) 157 CA Post-copyright infringement: on assessing damage sustained.

Dickinson v Ead and others (1914-15) XXIV Cox CC 308; (1914) 78 JP 326; (1914-15) 111 LTR 378; (1913-14) XXX TLR 496 HC KBD Genuine (and reasonable) belief that were allowed onto land meant was no trespass.

Distillers Co (Biochemicals) Ltd, S and another v; J and others v Distillers Co (Biochemicals) Ltd and others [1969] 3 All ER 1412; (1969) 113 SJ 672; [1970] 1 WLR 114 HC QBD Appropriate personal injury damages to thalidomide children.

District Messenger and Theatre Ticket Company (Limited), Long v (1915-16) XXXII TLR 596 HC KBD Courier firm's notice of conditions (wherein exempted liability) inapplicable where took delivery of parcel without asking questions as to contents of same.

Dixon v Chester (1906) 70 JP 380 HC KBD Surveyor empowered under Highway Act 1835, s 73 to seek order requiring that highway be cleared of timber which is nuisance.

Dixon, Cox v (1984) 134 NLJ 236 HC QBD One-third reduction in damages for driver (injured in collision with speeding police car) who knew the area/should have known that people might speed at night.

Dixons (Scholar Green) Ltd v JL Cooper Ltd [1970] RTR 222; (1970) 114 SJ 319 CA On assessing appropriate damages for loss of use of vehicle.

DJ Freeman and Co, Carradine Properties Ltd v (1982) 132 NLJ 534; [1982] TLR 83 CA Solicitors not negligent where when dealing with client with insurance expertise in insurance case did not ask latter if had particular policy under which was covered for loss at issue.

Dobbie v Medway Health Authority [1994] 4 All ER 450; (1994) 144 NLJ 760t; (1994) 144 NLJ 828; [1994] TLR 278; [1994] 1 WLR 1234 CA Limitation period in personal injury claim runs from date when victim knew injury resulted from action of another even if unaware legal remedy available.

Dobbin v Waldorf Toilet Saloons, Ltd [1937] 1 All ER 331 Assizes Negligent permanent waving of bleached/dyed hair by hairdresser.

Dobson and another v Horsley and another [1915] 1 KB 634; [1915] 84 LJKB 399; (1915) 112 LTR 101 CA Landlord not liable for injury suffered by child falling through defective railing (not trap/concealed danger).

Dobson v Horsley and another (1913-14) XXX TLR 148 HC KBD Landlord not liable for injury suffered by child falling through defective railing.

Dobson v North Tyneside Health Authority and Newcastle Health Authority [1997] 2 FCR 651; (1996) 140 SJ LB 165 CA Failed action for conversion of corpse.

Docker, Seligman v [1949] Ch 53; (1948) WN (I) 425 HC ChD Presence of large numbers of wild pheasants on rented land not due to unreasonable act of landlord-defendant who was not under a duty to reduce ther number/rid land of their presence.

Dodd Properties (Kent) Ltd and another v Canterbury City Council and others [1979] 2 All ER 118 HC QBD Generally damages measured by reference to date of damage; entitled to reasonable damages for reasonable repairs.

Dodd Properties(Kent) Ltd and another v Canterbury City Council and others [1980] 1 All ER 928 (1980) 130 NLJ 66; (1980) 124 SJ 84; [1980] 1 WLR 433 CA Damages for building repairs are compensatory; cost of repairs that on date of action.

Dodd, Central Asbestos Co Ltd v [1972] 2 All ER 1135; [1973] AC 518; [1972] 3 WLR 333 HL Time from which limitation runs where contracting of disease concerned.

Dodds and another v Dodds (1977) 121 SJ 619 HC QBD One dependant could claim fatal accident injuries from another dependant whose negligence led to fatal accident; multiplier to be fixed at date of trial.

Dodds, Dodds and another v (1977) 121 SJ 619 HC QBD One dependant could claim fatal accident injuries from another dependant whose negligence led to fatal accident; multiplier to be fixed at date of trial.

Dogma Properties Ltd v Gale (1984) 134 NLJ 453 HC QBD Successful suit against solicitor employed to act for person seeking to purchase property who through solicitor's negligence succeeded only in getting possession, not title to the premises.

Doherty v London Co-operative Society, Ltd (1965-66) 116 NLJ 388; (1966) 110 SJ 74 HC QBD Shop-owner not liable for injury suffered by customer who tripped over obstruction between three to four feet high.

Drane v Evangelou and others [1978] 2 All ER 437; [1978] 1 WLR 455 CA Judge can raise issue of trespass though not pleaded; exemplary damages need not be pleaded.

Dransfield v British Insulated Cables, Ltd [1937] 4 All ER 382; (1937) 84 LJ 360; (1938) 82 SJ 95; (1937-38) LIV TLR 11 HC KBD Manufacturers escaped liability for death resulting from use of defective product as was chance of intermediate inspection.

Draper and another v Hodder [1972] 2 All ER 210; (1972) 122 NLJ 128t; [1972] 2 QB 556; (1972) 116 SJ 178; [1972] 2 WLR 992 CA Can be liable in negligence for reasonably foreseeable injury caused by tame animal.

Draper v Trist and others [1939] 3 All ER 513 CA On damages for passing-off.

Dreamland (Margate), Ltd, Humphreys v [1930] All ER 327; (1931) 100 LJCL 137; (1931) 144 LTR 529; (1930) 74 SJ 862 HL Person having right to possession of land/right to exclude people therefrom liable in negligence for injuries sustained thereon, not landowner.

Dreamland, Margate, Limited, Sheehan v (1923-24) XL TLR 155 CA Non-liability of freeholder (invitor) to invitee for injury caused in sideshow which was not inherently dangerous and in respect of which neither invitees nor their servants had been negligent.

Drennan, Brewster v [1945] 2 All ER 705; (1946) 96 LJ 271; (1946) 174 LTR 62 CA Successful claim against innkeeper for theft of guest's fur cape from unlocked bedroom.

Dribbell and another v Robinson (1949) 99 LJ 233 CyCt Landlord liable for injury suffered by child when facia board which landlord knew to be in disrepair but had not repaired collapsed onto highway.

Drinkwater and another v Kimber [1951] 2 All ER 713; (1951) 101 LJ 511; (1951) 95 SJ 547; [1951] 2 TLR 630; (1951) WN (I) 496 HC KBD Cannot recover for damage from person contributorily negligent where suffer financial loss but no physical injury.

Drinkwater and another v Kimber [1952] 2 QB 281; [1952] 1 TLR 1486 CA Cannot recover for damage from person contributorily negligent where suffer financial loss but no physical injury.

Drinkwater v Joseph Lucas (Electrical) Ltd [1970] 3 All ER 769 CA Where all reasonable steps taken to discover cause of illness failure to discover justified diasapplying limitation.

Driver v William Willett Ltd and another [1969] 1 All ER 665; (1969) 119 NLJ 248 Assizes On deciding whether sufficient closeness of relationship to give rise to duty of care.

Drummond-Jackson v British Medical Association and others (1970) 114 SJ 152; [1970] 1 WLR 688 CA Statements of claim only struck out where glaringly necessary which was not the case here.

Drury Lane Theatre, Ltd and another, Hayward v [1916-17] All ER 405; [1918] 87 LJCL 18; (1917-18) 117 LTR 523; (1916-17) 61 SJ 665 CA Person voluntarily under another's control allowed recover as invitee for negligent acts of that other's servant.

Drury v Camden London Brough Council [1972] RTR 391 HC QBD Council (50%) liable in negligence/nuisance for leaving unlit skip projecting into highway; driver equally liable for failing to maintain proper vigilance.

Drury v North Eastern Railway Company [1901] 2 KB 322; [1901] 70 LJK/QB 830; (1901) LXXXIV LTR 658 HC KBD Not evidence of negligence that seated passenger's finger crushed when door closed by railway employee (who owes no special duty of care to seated passenger).

Dryden v Surrey County Council and Stewart [1936] 2 All ER 535; (1936) 82 LJ 9; (1936) 80 SJ 656 HC KBD Nurses' negligence; bases for action against two defendants being different counsel for one could cross-examine witness for other.

Drymond, Clifford v [1976] RTR 134; (1976) 120 SJ 149 CA Pedestrian on zebra crossing contributorily negligent (20%) in failing to keep an eye on oncoming traffic whilst crossing.

Dublin United Tramways v Fitzgerald (1902-03) XIX TLR 78 HL Tramway company liable for injury sustained as result of their failure to keep portion of road for which were responsible in safe condition (Tramways Act 1870, s 28).

Duckworth and Co, The Apollinaris Company (Limited) and another v (1905-06) XXII TLR 638 HC ChD Failed action for passing off where merely sold product as having properties akin to that of another and did not enable purchasers to do something they ought not to do.

Duckworth and Co, The Apollinaris Company (Limited) and another v (1905-06) XXII TLR 744 CA Failed action for passing off where merely sold product as having properties akin to that of another and did not enable purchasers to do something they ought not to do.

Duerdin-Dutton and another, RDC (Berkhamstead) v [1964] Crim LR 307t HC QBD Oral evidence unnecessary to prove facts accepted by defendant's solicitor.

Duffy v Thanet District Council and another (1984) 134 NLJ 680 HC QBD Employers vicariously liable for act done by worker which was stupid and unauthorised but nonetheless done in course of his employment.

Duke, Sampson v; Same v Huxtable (1913) CC Rep II 74 CyCt Persons who illegally seized goods of wife of debtor against whom had obtained judgment were liable in trespass.

Duke-Cohan and Co, Morris v (1975) 125 NLJ 1222; (1975) 119 SJ 826 HC QBD Successful action in negligence against conveyancing solicitors who advised exchange of contracts without taking usual safeguards.

Dulieu v White and Sons [1900-03] All ER 353; [1901] 2 KB 669; [1901] 70 LJK/QB 837; (1901-02) LXXXV LTR 126; (1900-01) 45 SJ 578; (1900-01) XVII TLR 555; (1901-02) 50 WR 76 HC KBD Damages recoverable where nervous shock followed by physical injury.

Dulverton Rural District Council v Tracy (1921) 85 JP 217 HL Damages for nuisance occasioned through killing of fish by piping sewage into river.

Dumbell v Roberts and others [1944] 1 All ER 326; (1944) 108 JP 139; (1945) 95 LJ 112; [1944] 113 LJ 185; (1944) 170 LTR 227; (1943-44) LX TLR 231 CA On special powers of arrest.

Dumbreck, R Addie and Sons (Collieries), Ltd v [1929] All ER 1; [1929] AC 358; (1929) 67 LJ 254; (1929) 98 LJPC 119; (1929) 140 LTR 650; (1928-29) XLV TLR 267; (1929) WN (I) 57 HL Absent malicious intent occupier not liable in negligence to trespasser, even child trespasser.

Dumphy v Montreal Light, Heat and Power Company [1907] AC 454; [1907] 76 LJPC 71; (1907-08) XCVII LTR 499; (1906-07) XXIII TLR 770 PC Defendants not liable for deciding to erect overhead (not underground) electric wires in pursuance of statutory duty.

Dun and others, Macintosh and another v [1908-10] All ER 664; [1908] AC 390; (1908) 77 LJPC 113; (1908-09) XCIX LTR 64; (1907-08) XXIV TLR 705 PC No qualified privilege in publication out of complete self-interest.

Duncan and Co, Concaris v (1909) WN (I) 51 HC ChD Failed action for damages for alleged trade libel.

Duncan and others, Woods v; Duncan and another v Hambrook and others; Duncan and another v Cammell Laird and Co, Ltd [1946] 1 All ER 420; [1946] AC 401; [1947] 116 LJR 120; (1946) 174 LTR 286; (1945-46) LXII TLR 283 HL Resolution of negligence action; on res ipsa loquitur.

Duncan v Cammell Laird and Co, Ltd; Craven v Cammell Laird and Co, Ltd [1944] 2 All ER 159 CA Resolution of negligence suit.

Duncan v Cammell Laird and Co, Ltd; Craven v Same; Duncan v Wailes Dove Bitumastic, Ltd; Craven v Same [1943] 2 All ER 621 HC KBD Making an undangerous thing dangerous did not create liability unless reasonable man would have appreciated new danger; contractor liable for danger-causing acts of competent sub-contractor.

Duncan v Lambeth London Borough Council [1968] 1 All ER 84; [1968] 1 QB 747; (1967) 111 SJ 909; [1968] 2 WLR 88 HC QBD Limitation period had not expired where had been infant when cause of action accrued and not properly in custody of a parent who could have bought action.

Duncan, Hordern Richmond, Ltd v [1947] 1 All ER 427; [1947] KB 545; [1947] 116 LJR 1024 HC KBD Third party recovery from person acting in public duty over one year after cause of action.

Duncan, Martindale v (1973) 123 NLJ 129t; [1973] RTR 532; (1973) 117 SJ 168; [1973] 1 WLR 574 CA No violation of onus to mitigate damages where postponed repairs to car until had sorted out insurance claim.

Dunkels, De Stempel v [1937] 2 All ER 215; (1937) 156 LTR 418; (1936-37) LIII TLR 451; (1937) WN (I) 117 HC KBD Statement that person 'a Jew hater' did not refer to person in business conduct — absent special damage could not recover damages.

Dunkels, De Stempel v [1938] 1 All ER 238; (1938) 158 LTR 85; (1938) 82 SJ 51; (1937-38) LIV TLR 289 CA Calling person a 'Jew-hater' is defamatory; words said in relation to other's business could be sued on though no proof of special damage.

Dunlop Rubber Co Ltd and ICI Ltd, Wright v; Cassidy v Same (1971) 121 NLJ 361 HC QBD Factory owners liable for negligent exposure of workers to carcinogen (liable from moment discovered its effects); manufacturers of chemical liable in negligence for not withdrawing it from sale.

Dunlop Rubber Company, Limited, GWK, Limited, and others v (1925-26) XLII TLR 376 HC KBD Substituting own tyres for those on display car (which car company and rival tyre company had come to agreement on regarding display) was interference with contractual rights for which car company/rival tyre company entitled to damages.

Dunlop Rubber Company, Limited, GWK, Limited, and others v (1925-26) XLII TLR 593 CA Appeal withdrawn from decision that substituting own tyres for those on display car (which car company and rival tyre company had come to agreement on regarding display) was interference with contractual rights for which car company/rival tyre company entitled to damages.

Dunlop v Woollahra Municipal Council [1981] 1 All ER 1202; [1982] AC 158; (1981) 125 SJ 199; [1981] 2 WLR 693 PC Can only recover for illegal act not null act; absent malice passing of null act not misfeasance and misfeasance essential to abuse of public office.

Dunn v Fairs, Blissard, Barnes and Stowe (1961) 105 SJ 932 HC QBD Solicitor not negligent in purchasing annuity for old unwell client.

Dunn, Mallett and another v [1949] 1 All ER 973; [1949] 2 KB 180; [1949] 118 LJR 1650; (1949) LXV TLR 307; (1949) WN (I) 206 HC KBD Husband could sue for medicine/household expenses though wife contributorily negligent.

Dunne and others v North Western Gas Board and another [1963] 3 All ER 916; (1964) 114 LJ 56; [1964] 2 QB 806; (1963) 107 SJ 890; [1964] 2 WLR 164 CA Not liable under Rylands v Fletcher if do what statute requires non-negligently.

Dunster v Abbott [1953] 2 All ER 1572; (1953) 103 LJ 828; (1954) 98 SJ 8 CA Person canvassing for business a licensee: here duty of care to licensee not breached as bridge over ditch not concealed danger/no negligence as regards nighttime lighting.

Dunt v London and North Eastern Railway Co (1942) 86 SJ 203 HC KBD Rail company liable for fire occasioned by sparks flying from engine: on liability of rail companies for flying sparks.

Dunton v Dover District Council (1977) 127 NLJ 538t HC QBD Injunction restricting opening hours of children's playground noise from hitherto unrestricted use of which had been a nuisance.

Durkin (Civil Engineering Contractors) Ltd, James v [1983] TLR 383 HC QBD Damages in successful negligence claim by estate of deceased driver reduced by 50% in light of contributory negligence of deceased.

Durrant v Smithfield and Argentine Meat Co Ltd (1956) 106 LJ ccr124 CyCt Was detinue where property in meat had passed to plaintiffs but meat was being retained by defendants.

Dutton v Bognor Regis United Building Co Ltd and another [1972] 1 All ER 462; (1972) 136 JP 201; (1971) 121 NLJ 617; [1972] 1 QB 373; (1972) 116 SJ 16; [1972] 2 WLR 299 CA Council in exercising building byelaws powers has duty to exercise diligently; can be liable for negligent exercise to purchaser/even if builder not liable (and builder may be liable even if owns premises).

Dutton v Bognor Regis Urban District Council [1971] 2 All ER 1003; (1971) 121 NLJ 1146t HC QBD Council owes duty of care through building inspector to later purchaser.

DW Moore and Co Ltd and others v Ferrier and others [1988] 1 All ER 400; (1987) 137 NLJ 1013; (1988) 132 SJ 227; [1988] 1 WLR 267 CA Client suffers damage from negligently drafted contract when contract executed not when defect discovered.

Dwyer and another v Mansfield [1946] 2 All ER 247; [1946] KB 437; [1947] 116 LJR 894; (1946) 175 LTR 61; (1946) 90 SJ 443; (1945-46) LXII TLR 401; (1946) WN (I) 93 HC KBD Shopping queue not proved to be nuisance — even if it was had failed to prove defendant caused it/was responsible therefor.

Edelston, Gottliffe v [1930] 2 KB 378; (1930) 99 LJCL 547; (1930) 143 LTR 595; (1930) 74 SJ 567; (1929-30) XLVI TLR 544; (1930) WN (I) 168 HC KBD Right of action for tort by woman against man ended upon marriage of former to latter.

Edenwest Ltd, Gillette UK Ltd and another v [1994] TLR 135 HC ChD Defendant who did not behave dishonestly could nonetheless be liable in damages in passing off action.

Edge (W) and Sons (Limited) v Niccolls (W) and Sons (Limited) (1909-10) XXVI TLR 588 HC ChD Injunction granted restraining use of particular get-up which had come to be identified with plaintiff's product.

Edge (W) and Sons (Limited) v Niccolls (W) and Sons (Limited) [1911] 1 Ch 5; (1910) 45 LJ 805; (1911) 80 LJCh 154; (1910-11) 103 LTR 579; (1910-11) XXVII TLR 101; (1910) WN (I) 250 CA Injunction restraining use of particular get-up which had come to be identified with plaintiff's product refused as general confusion unlikely.

Edgerley, Newton v [1959] 3 All ER 337; (1959) 109 LJ 588; (1959) 103 SJ 919; [1959] 1 WLR 1031 HC QBD Parent negligent in buying gun for child/not giving proper instruction on use before others.

Edinburgh Corporation and others, Evans v [1916-17] All ER 1010; [1916] 85 LJPC 200; (1915-16) XXXII TLR 396 HL No duty of care on person owning premises adjoining highway with door opening thereon not to open/have said door.

Edinburgh Corporation, Hanley v (1913) 77 JP 233 HL Successful claim against corporation for not properly draining burgh.

Edinburgh Water Trustees v Sommerville and Son (1906-07) XCV LTR 217 HL Absent negligence water company not liable for accidental pollution of compensation water.

Edmeades v Thames Board Mills Ltd (1969) 119 NLJ 105t; [1969] 2 QB 67; [1969] 2 WLR 668 CA Proceedings stayed to allow for new medical evidence required by new claims.

Edmeads, Thompson v (1978) 128 NLJ 514b CA Valid disregard of three year limitation in personal injuries action where source of delay was negligence on part of plaintiff's solicitors.

Edmondson v Birch and Co, Ltd [1904-07] All ER 996; [1907] 76 LJCh 347; [1907] 1 KB 371; (1907) XCVI LTR 415; (1906-07) XXIII TLR 234; (1907) WN (I) 18 CA Publication of defamatory material in privileged communication to telegram clerks did not lift privilege.

Edmondson v Rundle and others (1902-03) XIX TLR 356 HC KBD Failed action for wrongful arrest/imprisonment of soldier by superior officer during wartime: not a matter for civil courts.

Edmonton Corporation, Franklin v (1965) 109 SJ 876 HC QBD Council one-third liable in negligence for manner in which operated defective vehicle record system.

Edward Ash, Ltd, Sparks v [1943] 1 All ER 1; (1943) 107 JP 45; (1944) 94 LJ 108; (1942) 86 SJ 322; (1942-43) LIX TLR CA Contributory negligence defence open in breach of statutory duty action.

Edward Box and Co, Limited, Young v [1951] 1 TLR 789 CA Person allowed by foreman to be carried in defendant's lorry by their employee was licensee not trespasser.

Edward Lloyd (Limited), Mangena v (1908-09) XCIX LTR 824; (1908-09) XXV TLR 26 CA Headline of report based on Parliamentary blue-book fell outside privilege afforded by Parliamentary Papers Act 1840.

Edward Lloyd (Limited), Mangena v (1908) XCVIII LTR 640; (1907-08) XXIV TLR 610 HC KBD Good faith/non-malicious report based on Parliamentary blue-book enjoyed privilege afforded by Parliamentary Papers Act 1840.

Edward Lloyd, Limited, Burley (C), Limited v (1928-29) XLV TLR 626 HC KBD Milton Creek Conservancy Act 1899, s 78 did not empower licensee to erect obstruction in creek.

Edward Lloyd, Ltd, Clelland v [1937] 2 All ER 605; (1936-37) LIII TLR 644 HC KBD Occupier not liable for negligence of independent contractor over whom has no control.

Edward Wong Finance Co Ltd v Johnson Stokes and Master (a firm) [1984] AC 296; (1983) 127 SJ 784; [1984] 2 WLR 1 PC Was negligent (even though conformed with general practice) for solicitor to place mortgagee's money in hands of vendor's solicitor without making provision for relief in case of embezzlement which later occurred.

Edwards (Job), Limited v Birmingham Canal Navigations, Limited (1923-24) 68 SJ 501; (1923-24) XL TLR 88 CA Persons not causing/continuing nuisance or negligent in relation thereto not liable to fund protective measures taken by another on foot of nuisance.

Edwards and Another (Paupers) v Porter [1925] AC 1; (1924) 59 LJ 711; [1925] 94 LJCL 65; (1925) 132 LTR 496; (1924-25) 69 SJ 87; (1924-25) XLI TLR 57; (1924) WN (I) 279 HL Liability of husband for tortious act of wife during coverture.

Edwards and Another v Porter and Wife [1923] 1 KB 268; (1923) 58 LJ 34; [1923] 92 LJCL 720 (also CA); (1922-23) XXXIX TLR 124; (1923) WN (I) 9 HC KBD Non-liability of husband for false representation by wife during coverture.

Edwards and another v Porter and Wife; McNeall v Hawes [1923] 2 KB 538; [1923] 92 LJCL 720; (1923) 129 LTR 170; (1922-23) 67 SJ 482; (1922-23) XXXIX TLR 358/362; (1923) WN (I) 170 CA Non-liability of husband for tortious act of wife during coverture.

Edwards and another, Saunders and another v [1987] 2 All ER 651 CA In tortious claim arising from fraudulent contract court will look to conduct/culpability of parties in deciding whether to notice illegality; global damages for inconvenience/disappointment should not have interest added.

Edwards and others, Rost v [1990] 2 All ER 641; [1990] 2 QB 460; [1990] TLR 120; [1990] 2 WLR 1280 HC QBD Reasons for selection/de-selection from Parliamentary committee/ member's letter to Speaker privileged; register of Member's Interests not privileged.

Edwards v Bendall (1953) 103 LJ ccr351 CyCt Liquidator liable in conversion for sale of company property already purchased by another from Official Receiver.

Edwards v Lee (1991) 141 NLJ 1517 HC QBD Solicitor is liable in negligence if does not reveal that client (for whom is giving business reference) has been charged with a dishonesty offence.

Edwards v Metropolitan Water Board (1922) 86 JP 33 (also HC KBD); [1922] 1 KB 291 (also HC KBD); (1921) 56 LJ 472; [1922] 91 LJCL 210 (also HC KBD); (1921-22) 66 SJ 195; (1921-22) XXXVIII TLR 153; (1921) WN (I) 354 CA Journey out and back was on behalf of public authority so public authority limitation applied.

Edwards v Metropolitan Water Board (1922) 86 JP 33 (also CA); [1922] 1 KB 291 (also CA); [1922] 91 LJCL 210 (also CA) HC KBD Journey out and back was on behalf of public authority so public authority limitation applied.

Edwards v Railway Executive [1952] 2 All ER 430; [1952] AC 737; (1952) 102 LJ 470; (1952) 96 SJ 493; [1952] 2 TLR 237; (1952) WN (I) 383 HL Railway Executive not liable for injuries suffered by boy trespassing on railway line.

Edwards v Taylor (1922-23) 67 SJ 248 HC KBD Husband not liable where wife fraudulently represents that she is authorised to act for him.

Edwards v West Herts Group Hospital Management Committee [1957] 1 All ER 541; (1957) 121 JP 212; (1957) 107 LJ 169 CA Hospital committee not liable as invitor/master or via implied term in employment contract with house physician for personal belongings stolen from staff hostel.

Edwards, Gilson v (1928) 66 LJ ccr25 CyCt Can be sued in tort for assault notwithstanding certificate of conviction (following summary trial) for inflicting grievous bodily harm.

Edwards, Patel v [1970] RTR 425 CA On respective liabilities of cyclist pulling to right in front of stationary car and motor-cyclist overtaking car and colliding with cyclist.

Edwin Evans (a firm), Hamlin and another v (1996) 140 SJ LB 167; (1996) TLR 12/7/96 CA Limitation period ran from time house-buyers knew of valuer's negligence vis-à-vis dry rot.

Edwin Evans and Sons, Yianni v [1981] 3 All ER 592; (1981) 131 NLJ 1074; [1982] QB 438; (1981) 125 SJ 694; [1981] 3 WLR 843 HC QBD House purchaser's relying on negligent surveyor's valuation of house (for building society) were owed duty of care by surveyor.

Edwin Hill and Partners (a firm) v First National Finance Corp plc [1988] 3 All ER 801; (1988) 132 SJ 1389; [1989] 1 WLR 225 CA Defendant with equal/superior right interfering with plaintiff's contractual rights via agreement with third party not liable for interference with contractual relations.

EE Bevan, Ltd v Harfoot [1945] LJNCCR 136 CyCt On liability for wilful trespass.

EE Caledonia Ltd v Orbit Valve Co Europe [1993] 4 All ER 165; [1994] 1 WLR 221 HC QBD Unless contrary provision indemnity clause not to be taken as applying to party's own negligence. Concurrent causes of event are each causes unless event would have occurred anyway.

EE Caledonia Ltd, McFarlane v [1994] 2 All ER 1; (1993) 143 NLJ 1367; [1993] TLR 476 CA Bystander/witness of awful events ineligible for damages for nervous shock unless proximate to events and victim.

Eels and another, Hussey and another v [1990] 1 All ER 449; (1990) 140 NLJ 53 CA Profits made through resale of defective property after negligent misrepresentation not to be set off against damages for latter unless various steps part of a single transaction.

EG Stanley Brinsmead and Waddington and Sons (Limited), John Brinsmead and Sons (Limited) v (1912-13) 57 SJ 322; (1912-13) XXIX TLR 237 HC ChD Court would not injunct person from using own name on pianos he made even though might be connected with other well-known piano firm.

EG Stanley Brinsmead and Waddington and Sons (Limited), John Brinsmead and Sons (Limited) v (1912-13) 57 SJ 716; (1912-13) XXIX TLR 706 CA Court would not injunct person from using own name on pianos he made even though might be connected with other well-known piano firm.

EG Thomson (Shipping) Ltd and others (No 2), RA Lister and Co Ltd and others v; The Benarty (No 2) [1987] 3 All ER 1032; [1987] 1 WLR 1614 HC QBD Claim against co-defendant possible even if latter's action stayed and claim not procedurally enforceable.

Egdell and others, W v [1990] Ch 359 (also CA); (1989) 133 SJ 570; [1989] 2 WLR 689 HC ChD On duty of confidentiality owed (and liability for breach of same) by psychiatrist to mental patient at whose instruction prepare mental health report.

Egdell, W v [1990] Ch 359 (also HC ChD); (1990) 134 SJ 286; [1990] 2 WLR 471 CA On duty of confidentiality owed (and liability for breach of same) by psychiatrist to mental patient at whose instruction prepare mental health report.

Egerton v Harding and another [1974] 3 All ER 689; [1975] QB 62; (1974) 118 SJ 565; [1974] 3 WLR 437 CA Duty to fence against common arose from immemorial custom.

Egerton v Home Office [1978] Crim LR 494 HC QBD Failed action in negligence against Home Office for injuries suffered by sex offender at hands of fellow prisoners in prison.

Egerton, Leanse v [1943] 1 All ER 489; [1943] KB 323; (1944) 94 LJ 109; [1943] 112 LJ 273; (1943) 168 LTR 218; (1942-43) LIX TLR 191; (1943) WN (I) 56 HC KBD Occupier liable for continuing nuisance occasioned by air raid.

Egger v Chelmsford and others (1964) 108 SJ 218 HC QBD On whether malice by several defendants obviates privilege enjoyed by all defendants.

Egger v Davies and others (1964) 108 SJ 619 CA Malice of joint defendant in publishing item does not taint others with malice: most be individually motivated by malice to lose qualified privilege.

Egger v Viscount Chelmsford and others [1964] 3 All ER 406; (1964) 114 LJ 720; [1965] 1 QB 248; [1964] 3 WLR 714 CA Innocent committee members and (independently) their secretary protected by qualified privilege which other committee members lost through malice.

Eggington v Reader [1936] 1 All ER 7 HC KBD Driver an independent contractor (despite company's contribution to petrol costs) so company not liable for driver's negligence.

Eggott (GW) and Son, Ltd v Normanton (CH) and Son, Ltd [1928] All ER 468 HC KBD Permanent employer allowed claim for negligence of servant temporarily in employment of bailee.

Ehrmann Brothers, Hunt, Roope, Teage and Co v [1910] 2 Ch 198; [1910] 79 LJCh 533; (1910-11) 103 LTR 91 HC ChD Failed action for passing off: on what constitutes passing off.

Eichholz, Malzy v [1916] 85 LJKB 1132 CA Lessor not liable for nuisance occasioned by one lessee to another towards whom lessor had covenanted quiet enjoyment of property..

Eisovitch, Schneider v; Same v Same [1960] 1 All ER 169; (1960) 110 LJ 137; [1960] 2 QB 430; (1960) 104 SJ 89 HC QBD Damages available for reasonable services arising from tort even if freely given without request; damages available for nervous shock sustained after recover consciousness.

Ellicott, Burns v (1969) 113 SJ 490 HC QBD On responsibility of driver when overtaking horserider on horse.

Elliot v Chiew (1966) 110 SJ 724 CA Owner of-passenger in car could not claim damages where friend-driver involved in non-negligent single car accident which resulted in injury to driver.

Elliott and another v London County Freehold and Leasehold Properties, Ltd [1936] LJNCCR 117 CyCt Flat-owners not liable to under-lessees of flat for nuisance (emission into house of smoke/soot) occasioned by under-lessees lighting fire in flat.

Elliott and another, Agar v (1970) 114 SJ 887 CA On farm labour rendered quadraplegic in car collision.

Elliott and Jeffery and others, Anglo-Celtic Shipping Company, Limited v (1925-26) XLII TLR 297 HC KBD Manufacturer liable for injuries sustained through use of product dangerous in itself and in respect of using which did not give proper warning.

Elliott v Chief Constable of Wiltshire and others (1996) TLR 5/12/96 HC ChD Could bring action against police officer for misfeance in public office where officer had revealed criminal past of person seeking relief with intent of injuring same.

Elliott v CP Roberts and Co (Limited) (1915-16) XXXII TLR 71 HC KBD Contractor liable to other contractor's workers on-site as licensor to licensee.

Elliott v CP Roberts and Co, Limited (1917) 81 JP 20; [1916] 2 KB 518; [1916] 85 LJKB 1689; (1916-17) 115 LTR 255; (1915-16) XXXII TLR 478 CA Contractor liable to other contractor's workers on-site as invitor to invitee.

Elliott v Yates and another (1899-1900) 44 SJ 591 CA Was lawful to levy distress after financial year ended for taxes that became owing during the last financial year.

Ellis (JW) and Co, Ltd, Dornan v [1962] 1 All ER 303; [1962] 1 QB 583; (1961) 105 SJ 1083 CA Leave to amend claim outside limitation period as raised no new ground of recovery.

Ellis and another v Raine [1939] 108 LJCL 292; (1939) 161 LTR 234; (1939) 83 SJ 152; (1938-39) LV TLR 344 CA Re-trial ordered where despite direction from judge jury in action brought by parents of child killed through negligence awarded damages under Fatal Accidents Act 1846 but not under Law Reform (Miscellaneous Provisions) Act 1934.

Ellis and other appeals, Firman v [1978] 2 All ER 851; [1978] QB 886; (1978) 122 SJ 147; [1978] 3 WLR 1 CA Court's discretion to disapply limitation is unfettered.

Ellis v Banyard [1911-13] All ER 303; (1912) 106 LTR 51; (1911-12) 56 SJ 139; (1911-12) XXVIII TLR 122 CA No duty to fence in cattle (tame animals) — and even if was duty no recovery as no negligence shown.

Ellis v Banyard (1911) 104 LTR 460; (1910-11) 55 SJ 500; (1910-11) XXVII TLR 417 HC KBD Where field gate open and escaping cattle caused injury to passer-by owner (one judge) was negligent, victim (other judge) still had to prove negligence of owner.

Ellis v Fulham Borough Council [1937] 1 All ER 698; (1937) 101 JP 198; (1937) 83 LJ 150; (1937) 156 LTR 220; (1937) 81 SJ 140; (1936-37) LIII TLR 387 HC KBD Child using public paddle pool an invitee — glass hidden in sand in pool a concealed danger for which council liable.

Ellis v Fulham Borough Council (1937) 101 JP 469; [1938] 1 KB 212; (1937) 84 LJ 47; [1938] 107 LJCL 84; (1937) 157 LTR 380; (1936-37) LIII TLR 884 CA Child using public paddle pool an invitee — glass hidden in sand in pool a concealed danger for which council liable.

Ellis v Home Office [1953] 2 All ER 149; (1953) 103 LJ 380; [1953] 2 QB 135; (1953) 97 SJ 436; [1953] 3 WLR 105 CA No breach of Home Office's duty to take reasonable care of prisoners by giving mental deficient free access to other prisoners.

Ellis v John Stenning and Son [1932] All ER 597; [1932] 2 Ch 81; (1932) 76 SJ 232 HC ChD Damages for conversion: action for conversion does not deny owner's title unless/until judgment fully satisfied.

Ellis v Johnstone [1963] 1 All ER 286; (1963) 113 LJ 120; [1963] 2 QB 8; (1962) 106 SJ 1030; [1963] 2 WLR 176 CA No customary/special duty on dog owner to prevent dog straying onto highway.

Essex Goodman and Suggitt (a firm) and others, Secretary of State for the Environment v [1986] 2 All ER 69; (1970) 130 SJ 574; [1986] 1 WLR 1432 HC QBD Time runs from date acted on surveyor's report; no action for damage after that date.

Essex Rivers Catchment Board, Hunwick v [1952] 1 All ER 765; (1952) 116 JP 217 Assizes Duty to maintain sea-wall as sea-wall, not walkway.

Essex Transport and Trading Company Limited, Compania Mexicana de Petroleo 'El Aguila' v (1929) 141 LTR 106 CA On respective liabilities of shipowners/stevedores in negligence where injury sustained through negligent loading of dangerous subsances.

Esso Petroleum Co Ltd v Mardon [1976] 2 All ER 5; (1976) 126 NLJ 265t; [1976] QB 801; (1976) 120 SJ 131; [1976] 2 WLR 583 CA Forecast by party of expertise to induce another into contracting is warranty; such party owes duty of care for negligent statements; damages are all losses suffered in light of contract.

Esso Petroleum Co Ltd v Mardon [1975] 1 All ER 203; (1974) 124 NLJ 828t; [1975] QB 819; [1975] 2 WLR 147 HC QBD Duty of care if company in pre-contract talks represents certain state of affairs to induce other to sign contract.

Esso Petroleum Co, Ltd and another v Southport Corporation [1955] 3 All ER 864; [1956] AC 218; (1956) 120 JP 54; (1955) 105 LJ 824; (1956) 100 SJ 32; [1956] 2 WLR 81 HL Shipmaster not negligent so owners not vicariously so; on pleadings.

Esso Petroleum Co, Ltd and another, Southport Corporation v [1953] 2 All ER 1204; (1954) 118 JP 1; (1953) 103 LJ 750; (1953) 97 SJ 764; [1953] 3 WLR 773 HC QBD Private nuisance need not emanate from neighbour's property; public nuisance on public navigable river akin to that on highway; need to prove negligence to establish nuisance.

Esso Petroleum Co, Ltd and another, Southport Corporation v [1954] 2 All ER 561; (1954) 118 JP 411; [1954] 2 QB 182; (1954) 98 SJ 472; [1954] 3 WLR 200 CA No trespass/nuisance where act from necessity (unless negligence present); ship-stranding sufficiently abnormal to raise res ipsa loquitur unless show not negligent.

Esso Petroleum Co, Ltd, Halsey v [1961] 2 All ER 145; (1961) 111 LJ 290; (1961) 105 SJ 209 HC QBD Oil smuts damaging clothes a private/Rylands v Fletcher-style nuisance; smuts damaging car on highway a public/Rylands v Fletcher-style nuisance; odour from oil depot a nuisance by smell (though no evidence of injury); din from boilers a private nuisance as adversely affected enjoyment of ordinary comforts; din from tankers on highway at night a public nuisance/a private nuisance as connected with use of (though not occurring on) private property.

Etheridge v Pink (1932) 74 LJ ccr70 CyCt On relief available for nuisance by noise/vibration.

European American Banking Corp, UBAF Ltd v [1984] 2 All ER 226; [1984] QB 713; (1984) 128 SJ 243; [1984] 2 WLR 508 CA Cause of action following entry into contract on foot of fraudulent misrepresentation might run from later date than that of entry into contract.

Euroways Express Coaches Ltd and others, Whitmore and another v [1984] TLR 290 HC QBD Damages recoverable for shock of being in hospital with/seeing hurt spouse (albeit that were not affected medically/in psychiatric manner by the shock).

Eurymedon (Owners), The Eurymedon, Corstar (Owners) v [1938] 1 All ER 122 CA Negligent act causing negligent mistake by other makes both responsible for result.

Eustace v Ayre [1947] LJNCCR 106 CyCt Could recover damages for having to destroy bull after bull broke its leg chasing cow that strayed/trespassed onto/on field where bull kept.

Evangelization Society (Incorporated) Trust, Smith v [1933] Ch 515 (also HC ChD); (1933) 102 LJCh 275 (also HC ChD); (1932-33) XLIX TLR 262; (1933) WN (I) 66 CA On nuisance by way of obstruction of ancient light.

Evangelization Society (Incorporated) Trust, Smith v [1933] Ch 515 (also CA); (1933) 102 LJCh 275 (also CA); (1932-33) XLIX TLR 32 HC ChD On nuisance by way of obstruction of ancient light.

Evangelou and others, Drane v [1978] 2 All ER 437; [1978] 1 WLR 455 CA Judge can raise issue of trespass though not pleaded; exemplary damages need not be pleaded.

Evans (Pauper) v Lord Provost, Magistrates, and Council of the City of Edinburgh [1916] 2 AC 45; (1916) 114 LTR 911 HL Door opening outwards onto street not of itself negligence nor was it obstruction of highway.

Evans and another, Miller v; Pouleuf (Third Party) [1975] RTR 70 CA Driver not contributorily negligent in assuming oncoming traffic travelling at such speed that could stop when lights changed.

Evans and others, Fraser v (1968) 118 NLJ 956t; (1968) 112 SJ 805 CA Refusal of injunction restraining publication of article which party publishing intended to justify.

Evans and others, Lion Laboratories Ltd v [1985] QB 526; (1984) 128 SJ 533; [1984] TLR 185; [1984] 3 WLR 539 CA Court authorised disclosure of documents despite their being published in breach of confidence where public interest in disclosure demanded it.

Evans v Edinburgh Corporation and others [1916-17] All ER 1010; [1916] 85 LJPC 200; (1915-16) XXXII TLR 396 HL No duty of care on person owning premises adjoining highway with door opening thereon not to open/have said door.

Evans v London Hospital Medical College and others [1981] 1 All ER 715; (1981) 131 NLJ 291 HC QBD Immunity from action for conduct/statement part of (albeit preceding) action.

Evans v Mayor, &c, of Liverpool (1905) 69 JP 263; (1904-05) XXI TLR 558 HC KBD Local authority not liable for negligent early discharge of patient by visiting physician whom they employed.

Evans v Triplex Safety Glass Co, Ltd [1936] 1 All ER 283 HC KBD Delay between buying car/windscreen smashing; chance to examine windscreen; possible cause other than manufacturer's negligence meant manufacturer not liable in negligence for occurrence.

Evans, Griffiths v [1953] 2 All ER 1364; (1953) 103 LJ 797; (1953) 97 SJ 812; [1953] 1 WLR 1424 CA Solicitor not negligent in not advising on common law rights when specifically consulted about statutory rights.

Evans, Heddon v (1918-19) XXXV TLR 642 HC KBD On tortious liability of military officer for his actions.

Evatt, Mutual Life and Citizens' Assurance Co Ltd and another v [1971] 1 All ER 150; [1971] AC 793; (1970) 120 NLJ 1090; [1971] 2 WLR 23 PC Absent contract advisor owes duty to be honest in making statements unless fiduciary/styled as expert.

Evans, Griffiths v [1953] 2 All ER 1364; [1953] 1 WLR 1424 CA Solicitor not negligent in not advising on common law rights when specifically consulted about statutory rights.

Everett v Griffiths and another [1920] 3 KB 163; [1921] LJCL 737 HL Failed action for negligent certification of person as insane.

Everett v Griffiths and another (1919-20) 64 SJ 445 CA Failed action for negligent certification of person as insane.

Everett v Ribbands and another [1952] 1 All ER 823; (1952) 116 JP 221; [1952] 2 QB 198; (1952) 96 SJ 229; [1952] 1 TLR 933; (1952) WN (I) 166 CA Where case could have gone either way is not malicious prosecution.

Everett v Ribbands and another [1951] 2 All ER 818; (1951) 115 JP 582; [1952] 1 KB 113; (1951) 101 LJ 609; (1951) 95 SJ 698; [1951] 2 TLR 829; (1951) WN (I) 554 HC KBD Cannot sue for false imprisonment after binding over order in respect of one.

Everitt (Pauper) v Griffiths and Ankelsaria (1921) 85 JP 149 HL Failed negligence action against chairman of board of guardians/medical doctor for wrongful committal of person to lunatic asylum.

EW and WJ Moore Ltd (a firm), Sterman v [1970] 1 All ER 581 CA Limit disapplied (where just) to allow amendment of writ.

Ewing (trading as the Buttercup Dairy Co) v Buttercup Margarine Co (Lim) (1916-17) 61 SJ 369; (1917) WN (I) 89 HC ChD Injunction granted to restrain use of trade name in circumstances where use in said way would give rise to confusion.

Ewing v Buttercup Margarine Company, Limited [1917] 2 Ch 1; (1917) 52 LJ 172; (1917-18) 117 LTR 67; (1916-17) 61 SJ 443; (1917) WN (I) 153 CA Injunction granted to restrain use of trade name in circumstances where use in said way would give rise to confusion.

Faccenda Chicken Ltd v Fowler and others; Fowler v Faccenda Chicken Ltd [1986] 3 WLR 288 CA On duty owed by employee towards former employer in respect of confidential information learned during course of employment.

Facey, Helm v (1981) 131 NLJ 291 HC ChD Refusal of injunction against trespasser whose continued occupation of premises raised the sale price of those premises.

Fagan v Green and Edwards Limited (1926) 134 LTR 191; (1925) WN (I) 266 HC KBD Non-liability of (non-common) carrier-bailees for loss of goods through fire caused by own servant's negligence as had exempted selves from liability in contract.

Fairman (Pauper) v Perpetual Investment Building Society [1923] AC 74; (1923) 87 JP 21; (1922) 57 LJ 392; [1923] 92 LJCL 50; (1923) 128 LTR 386; (1922-23) XXXIX TLR 54; (1922) WN (I) 304 HL Landlord not liable in negligence for injury suffered as consequence of common staircase being in poor repair.

Fairrie, Rook v [1941] 1 All ER 297; [1941] 1 KB 507; (1942) 92 LJ 61; [1941] 110 LJ 319; (1941) 165 LTR 23; (1941) 85 SJ 297; (1940-41) LVII TLR 297; (1941) WN (I) 37 CA Judge (unlike jury) can condemn otherwise than by heavy damages.

Fairs, Blissard, Barnes and Stowe, Dunn v (1961) 105 SJ 932 HC QBD Solicitor not negligent in purchasing annuity for old unwell client.

Faithfull v Kesteven [1908-10] All ER 292; (1910-11) 103 LTR 56 CA Must show more than error of judgment on solicitor's part to recover in negligence.

Falconfilms NV and others (Hospital Ruber Internacional and another, third parties), Kinnear and others v [1994] 3 All ER 42 HC QBD Foreign third party to be joined where no alternative or better forum available to those seeking remedy.

Falkman Ltd and others, Schering Chemicals Ltd v [1982] QB 1; [1981] 2 WLR 848 CA Injunction granted restraining broadcasting of documentary in which chemical company employee spoke about matters in pending litigation: granted because would breach duty of confidence not because would be contempt of court (it would not).

Faraonio (Karan), Thompson (Christopher Bernard) v (1979) 123 SJ 301; [1979] 1 WLR 1157 PC On awarding of interest on personal injuries damages (none on portion of damages concerning post-judgment losses).

Fardon v Harcourt-Rivington [1932] All ER 81; (1932) 146 LTR 391; (1932) 76 SJ 81; (1931-32) XLVIII TLR 215 HL Owner not negligent where non-vicious dog smashed car window from inside injuring pedestrian.

Fardon v Harcourt-Rivington (1930-31) XLVII TLR 25 CA Owner not negligent where non-vicious dog smashed car window from inside injuring pedestrian.

Farmar and Moody (a firm), Buckland v (1978) 128 NLJ 365t CA Failed action for alleged negligence on part of firm of solicitors.

Farmer v Hyde [1937] 1 All ER 773; [1937] 1 KB 728; (1937) 83 LJ 167; [1937] 106 LJCL 292; (1937) 156 LTR 403; (1937) 81 SJ 216; (1936-37) LIII TLR 445; (1937) WN (I) 99 CA Fair/accurate publication of interrupter's application was privileged.

Farmer v Morning Post Ltd (1936) 80 SJ 345 CA Possible that words of non-party to action who intervened in court (said intervention being reported) were part of judicial proceedings but converse also possible so ensuing libel action not per se frivolous/vexatious.

Farmer v Wilson (1899-1901) XIX Cox CC 502; (1900) 35 LJ 245; [1900] 69 LJCL 496; (1900) LXXXII LTR 566; (1899-1900) XVI TLR 309 HC QBD Was besetting of persons on board ship (irrespective of whether contract permitting persons to be there was legal or not).

Farr v Butters Bros and Co [1932] All ER 339; [1932] 2 KB 606; (1932) 74 LJ 144; (1932) 101 LJCL 768; (1932) 147 LTR 427; (1932) WN (I) 171 CA Manufacturer not liable for defect in product that could be and was discovered before use.

Farrar and another, Chesworth v [1966] 2 All ER 107; (1965-66) 116 NLJ 809; [1967] 1 QB 407; (1966) 110 SJ 307; [1966] 2 WLR 1073 HC QBD Action for failure of bailee to take proper care lies in tort.

Farrell v Secretary of State for Defence [1980] 1 All ER 166; (1980) 70 Cr App R 224; (1980) 124 SJ 133; [1980] 1 WLR 172 HL Defence of reasonable force under Criminal Law Act (NI) 1967, s 3, open to those in immediate situation requiring force.

Farrugia v Great Western Railway Co [1947] 2 All ER 565 CA Person creating risk on highway owes duty of care to others thereon/nearby even if other trespasser or presence otherwise unlawful.

Faull (Richley, Third Party), Richley v [1965] 3 All ER 109; (1965) 129 JP 498; (1965) 115 LJ 609; (1965) 109 SJ 937; [1965] 1 WLR 1454 HC QBD Severe unexcused skid is per se evidence of negligent driving.

Fayed and others (No 5), Lonrho plc and others v [1994] 1 All ER 188; (1993) 143 NLJ 1571; [1993] TLR 422; [1993] 1 WLR 1489 CA Tortious conspiracy consists of two or more persons doing acts lawful in themselves with intent to causing injury to another who is thereby injured; damages for injury to reputation/business reputation/feelings available only if defamation.

Fayed and others, Lonrho plc v [1989] 2 All ER 65; (1989) 139 NLJ 539; [1990] 2 QB 479; [1989] 3 WLR 631 CA Interference with trade/business must be intended to hurt plaintiff but not necessarily as principal aim.

Fayed and others, Lonrho plc v [1988] 3 All ER 464; (1988) 138 NLJ 225; [1990] 1 QB 490; (1989) 133 SJ 220; [1989] 2 WLR 356 HC QBD Interference with take-over bid not an interference with business interest; if cannot claim for tort cannot claim for conspiracy to commit tort.

Fayed v Al-Tajir [1988] QB 712; (1987) 131 SJ 744; [1987] 3 WLR 102 CA Intra-embassy memorandum was absolutely privleged.

Fazeley Town Council, Tamworth Borough Council v (1978) 122 SJ 699 HC ChD Injunction to prevent operation of new market on same day as franchise market on basis that holding former constitued nuisance.

Feay v Barnwell [1938] 1 All ER 31 HC KBD Appropriate damages where overlapping of damages under Fatal Accidents Acts and Law Reform (Miscellaneous Provisions) Act 1934.

Felixstowe Dock and Railway Co, Berriello v (1989) 133 SJ 918; [1989] 1 WLR 695 CA Amount paid from seaman's fund not deductible from loss of earning damages.

Fellick, Knight v [1977] RTR 316 CA Motorist found not negligent where (on dark morning as was following other car) struck workman who must have stepped/fallen off pavement leaving no scope for evasive action by motorist.

Fellowes (or Herd) and another v Clyde Helicopters Ltd [1997] 1 All ER 775; [1997] AC 534; (1997) 141 SJ LB 64 HL Liability of helicopter company towards dependants of police officer killed while being conveyed in helicopter by negligent company pilot was governed by the Warsaw Convention as amended/implemented.

Fellowes v Rother District Council [1983] 1 All ER 513 HC QBD Grounds on which public body liable in negligence for acts ostensibly done pursuant to statutory authority.

Fellus v National Westminster Bank Ltd [1983] TLR 448 HC QBD Test of what constitutes 'undue negligence' a subjective test.

Fels v Thomas Hedley and Co (Limited) (1902-03) XIX TLR 340 HC ChD Use of word 'naphtha' in description of soap not so closely identified with plaintiff's products as to merit passing off injunction.

Fels v Thomas Hedley and Co (Limited) (1903-04) XX TLR 69 CA Use of word 'naphtha' in description of soap not so closely identified with plaintiff's products as to merit passing off injunction.

Felton and others, Turner (an infant) v [1940] LJNCCR 300 CyCt Absent reasonable basis for questioning person going to police station for questioning in belief that was required to go could claim damages from police for false imprisonment.

Feltrim, Arbuthnott v; Deeny v Gooda Walker; Henderson v Syndicates (Merrett) [1993] TLR 667 CA On extent of duty of care owed by managing/members' agents at Lloyd's towards names.

Femis-Bank (Anguilla) Ltd and others v Lazar and another [1991] 2 All ER 865; [1991] Ch 391; [1991] TLR 69; [1991] 3 WLR 80 HC ChD Injunction pending trial which would interfere with freedom of speech only exceptionally available.

Fender and another (Sun Insurance Office Ltd, third party), Vandyke v [1970] 2 All ER 335; (1970) 120 NLJ 250t; [1970] 2 QB 292; [1970] RTR 236; [1970] 2 WLR 929 CA Employers liable for negligence of/not eligible for indemnity from employee acting as agent in using their car to drive fellow employee to work at their request.

Fender and another, Vandyke v (1970) 134 JP 487; [1969] 2 QB 581 HC QBD Lender of car liable to injured party for negligence of borrower acting as lender's agent.

Fenton Textile Association, Limited v Thomas [1927] 96 LJCL 1016; (1927) 137 LTR 241; (1928-29) XLV TLR 264 CA Liability of solicitors for conversion of client's funds.

Fenton Textile Association, Limited v Thomas and Clark (1928-29) XLV TLR 113 HC KBD Liability of solicitors for conversion of client's funds.

Ferguson and another, Osman and another v [1993] 4 All ER 344 CA Police not liable for crimes committed by criminal whom they could have but failed to apprehend.

Ferguson and others, British Industrial Plastics, Ltd and others v [1940] 1 All ER 479; (1940) 162 LTR 313 HL That party 'inducing' acted in good faith precluded liability for inducing breach of contract.

Ferguson v Welsh and others [1987] 3 All ER 777; (1987) 137 NLJ 1037; (1987) 131 SJ 1552; [1987] 1 WLR 1553 HL Usually occupier not liable to contractor's employees but exceptionally may be.

Ferguson, British Industrial Plastics, Ltd v [1938] 4 All ER 504; (1939) 160 LTR 95 CA Not liable for inducing breach of contract where in good faith believed were not so doing.

Fern v London County Council [1938] LJNCCR 76 CyCt Owners of public recreation ground liable in negligence for injury suffered by person onto whom previously broken branch fell on them while they were sitting on a bench.

Fernie (or Allam) and others, Western Scottish Motor Traction Company, Limited v [1943] 2 All ER 742; (1944) 94 LJ 109; (1943) 87 SJ 399; (1943-44) LX TLR 34; (1943) WN (I) 223 HL Omnibus operators liable for negligence of driver who rounded corner so quickly that a passenger was thrown from the bus and killed.

Ferrier and others, DW Moore and Co Ltd and others v [1988] 1 All ER 400; (1987) 137 NLJ 1013; (1988) 132 SJ 227; [1988] 1 WLR 267 CA Client suffers damage from negligently drafted contract when contract executed not when defect discovered.

Fettes v Robertson (1920-21) XXXVII TLR 581 CA Statute of Limitations successfully pleaded where written promise to pay had not been unqualified.

Ffrench, Minister of Pensions v (1945-46) LXII TLR 227 HC KBD On meaning of 'injurious act' under Personal Injuries (Emergency Provisions) Act 1939, s 8(1).

Fibreglass, Ltd, Green v [1958] 2 All ER 521; (1958) 108 LJ 473; [1958] 2 QB 245; (1958) 102 SJ 472 HC QBD Occupier not liable for negligence of competent contractor employed to do work requiring expert knowledge.

Field, Pacy and another v (1937) 81 SJ 160 HC KBD Dog-owner who knew of dog's propensity to bite small boys liable for damages towards plaintiff boy bitten by dog and to father of boy.

Fielden v Cox (1905-06) XXII TLR 411 HC ChD Trespass injunction against insect-catchers refused given trivial nature of trespasses.

Fielding and another v Variety Incorporated [1967] 2 All ER 497; [1967] 2 QB 841; (1967) 111 SJ 257; [1967] 3 WLR 415 CA Absent peculiar damage only damages for financial loss for injurious falsehood; not so with libel.

Fielding v Moiseiwitsch (1946) 174 LTR 265 HC KBD Was breach of contract for pianist not to perform as had contracted; not defamatory for organiser to truthfully state what had occurred — such statement was in any event privileged.

Fielding v Moiseiwitsch (1946) 175 LTR 265 CA Was breach of contract for pianist not to perform as had contracted; not defamatory for organiser to truthfully state what had occurred — such statement was in any event privileged.

Fife Coal Company (Limited), Butler (or Black) v (1911-12) XXVIII TLR 150 HL Mineowners liable to widowed miner for negligence as regards appointing competent manager.

Filgate (Macartney) v Bishop and Sons (1964) 108 SJ 897 HC QBD Failed attempt by negligent bailee to rely on liability exemption clause following theft of bailed goods.

Film Laboratories, Ltd, Western Engraving Co v [1936] 1 All ER 106; (1936) 80 SJ 165 CA Bringing large quantities of water into factory premises a non-natural user upon escape of which Rylands v Fletcher-style liability arose.

Finlayson v Taylor (1983) 133 NLJ 720 HC QBD Person ostensibly in position of bailee but manifesting intention to keep goods against owner's wishes was liable in detinue.

Financial News (Lim) and others, Lyons v (1908-09) 53 SJ 671 CA Order as to form of particulars whereby sought to plead truthfulness of some of what stated and that rest was fair comment.

Financial News, Ltd, Maisel v [1914-15] All ER 671; [1915] 3 KB 336; (1915) 50 LJ 335; [1915] 84 LJKB 2148; (1915-16) 113 LTR 772; (1914-15) 59 SJ 596; (1914-15) XXXI TLR 510; (1915) WN (I) 264 CA Post-libel incidents can be relied on to justify libel.

Financial Times (Limited), Maisel v [1915] 84 LJKB 2145; (1915) 112 LTR 953; (1914-15) 59 SJ 248; (1914-15) XXXI TLR 192 HL Post-libel incidents can be relied on to justify libel.

Finch and another, Moorgate Mercantile Co, Ltd v [1962] 2 All ER 467; (1962) 112 LJ 402; [1962] 1 QB 701; (1962) 106 SJ 284 CA Not paying instalment breached hire-purchase agreement: owners could bring conversion action; placing uncustomed goods in car then forfeited to customs a conversion as forfeiture natural/probable result of acts.

Fink, Szalatnay-Stacho v [1946] 2 All ER 231; [1947] KB 1; [1946] 115 LJ 455; (1946) 175 LTR 336; (1946) 90 SJ 442; (1945-46) LXII TLR 573; (1946) WN (I) 134 CA On absolute privilege of communications of Czech wartime government-in-exile.

Fink, Szalatnay-Stacho v [1946] 1 All ER 303; (1946) 174 LTR 191; (1945-46) LXII TLR 146; (1946) WN (I) 18 HC KBD On absolute privilege of communications of Czech wartime government-in-exile.

Finlay and Co, Ltd v City Business Properties, Ltd [1943] LJNCCR 14 CyCt Landlords liable for damage occurring when water pipe burst during frosty weather (term in lease excluding liability for damage due to weather held not to protect them).

Finlayson v Taylor [1983] TLR 259 HC QBD Landlord liable in detinue/conversion for seeking to exercise lien over goods bailed with him by tenant where latter owed arrears of rent.

Finsbury Borough Council, Carpenter v (1920) 84 JP 107; [1920] 2 KB 195; [1920] 89 LJCL 554; (1920) 123 LTR 299; (1919-20) 64 SJ 426; (1920) WN (I) 124 HC KBD Where claim injury due to inadequate street-lighting must examine adequacy of same — cannot accept lighting authority's verdict that was adequate.

Finzi, Lertora v [1973] RTR 161 HC QBD Failed attempt to prove injured driver contributorily negligent as regards injuries suffered when not wearing seat belt.

Firestone Tire and Rubber Company (SS) Ltd v Singapore Harbour Board (1952) 96 SJ 448; [1952] 1 TLR 1625 PC Failure of action against harbour board where not brought within six-month limitation prescribed by public authority protection ordinance.

Firman v Ellis (1977) 121 SJ 606 HC QBD On extent of discretion of court to disapply limitation period.

Firman v Ellis and other appeals [1978] 2 All ER 851; [1978] QB 886; (1978) 122 SJ 147; [1978] 3 WLR 1 CA Court's discretion to disapply limitation is unfettered.

First Interstate Bank of California v Cohen Arnold and Co [1995] TLR 664 CA Damages recoverable from negligent tortfeasor whose actions resulted in plaintiff losing very real commercial opportunity.

First National Commercial Bank plc v Humberts [1995] 2 All ER 673; (1995) 145 NLJ 345; [1995] TLR 29 CA Cause of action where loan made following negligent advice runs from date of loss.

First National Commercial Bank plc v Loxleys (1997) 141 SJ LB 6; (1996) TLR 14/11/96 CA Disclaimer (on standard conveyancing form) had to be proved to be subjectively reasonable in each case.

First National Finance Corp plc, Edwin Hill and Partners (a firm) v [1988] 3 All ER 801; (1988) 132 SJ 1389; [1989] 1 WLR 225 CA Defendant with equal/superior right interfering with plaintiff's contractual rights via agreement with third party not liable for interference with contractual relations.

Foot and others, Kemsley v [1952] 1 All ER 501; [1952] AC 345; (1952) 102 LJ 136; (1952) 96 SJ 165; [1952] 1 TLR 532; (1952) WN (I) 111 HL Fair comment basis open though factual basis thereof not fully stated.

Foots, Davis v (1939) 83 SJ 780 CA Landlord liable for gassing of honeymooners following negligent removal of gas fire at behest of same.

Forangirene (Rederiet), Henaghan v [1936] 2 All ER 1426 Assizes Stevedore an invitee.

Forbes Stuart (Thames Street) Ltd (Intended Action), Clark (In re) v (1964) 114 LJ 388; (1964) 108 SJ 422; [1964] 1 WLR 836 CA Extension of time limit allowed where identity of occupier became known after limitation period expired.

Forbes v Kemsley Newspapers, Limited [1951] 2 TLR 656 HC ChD On propietorial rights of journalist in pseudonym under which writes.

Forbes v Wandsworth Health Authority [1996] 4 All ER 881; (1996) 146 NLJ 477; [1997] QB 402; (1996) 140 SJ LB 85; (1996) TLR 21/3/96; [1996] 3 WLR 1108 CA On when possess adequate knowledge for limitation period to commence running.

Forbes, Abbott, and Lennard Limited v Great Western Railway Company (1928) 138 LTR 286 CA Chelsea Dock-owners not liable for negligence of their servants by virtue of exemption clause in their by-laws.

Forbes, Abbott, and Lennard, Limited v Great Western Railway Company [1927] 96 LJCL 995; (1926-27) XLIII TLR 769 HC KBD Chelsea Dock-owners liable for negligence of their servants notwithstanding attempt to exempt liability by way of exemption clause.

Ford and another v White and Co (a firm) (1964) 114 LJ 554; (1964) 108 SJ 542; [1964] 1 WLR 885 HC ChD On quantifying damages available where property purchased on foot of solicitor's negligent advice.

Ford Motor Co, Ltd and another, Turner v [1965] 2 All ER 583; (1965) 115 LJ 448; (1965) 109 SJ 354; [1965] 1 WLR 948 CA Defendant allowed amend claim to allege negligence of plaintiff in not protecting self with equipment given by employers though plaintiff time-barred from claim against employers upon amendment.

Ford v Scarth (1951) 101 LJ 289 CyCt Failed action in trespass by aged aunt who took in niece and her family as tenants/occupiers and then sought to evict them when she decided to sell the house.

Ford, Rose v [1937] AC 826; (1937) 84 LJ 29; [1937] 106 LJCL 576; (1937) 157 LTR 174; (1936-37) LIII TLR 873; (1937) WN (I) 275 HL Deceased's personal representative could claim damages for loss of life expectancy.

Ford, Rose v [1936] 1 KB 90; (1935) 80 LJ 273; [1936] 105 LJCL 21; (1936) 154 LTR 77; (1935) 79 SJ 816; (1935-36) LII TLR 7; (1935) WN (I) 168 CA On availability of personal injury damages to deceased victim's personal representative (claiming on behalf of deceased's estate).

Fordham, Polley v (1903-04) XX TLR 435 HC KBD Action brought within six months of illegal distress allowed — distress was act complained of not the (quashed) conviction from which distress warrant arose.

Forest Rock Granite Company (Leicestershire) (Limited), Miles v (1917-18) 62 SJ 634; (1917-18) XXXIV TLR 500 CA Quarry owner to contain effects of explosions on own land — where fails to do so is liable for acts regardless of negligence.

Forrest Printing Ink Co Ltd, Charlton v (1978) 122 SJ 730 HC QBD Employer failed to discharge duty of care in respect of employees responsible for collecting wages from bank.

Forrest v Sharp (1963) 107 SJ 536 HC QBD On relevancy of injured person's awareness of affliction to level of damages awarded.

Forster v Outred and Co (a firm) [1982] 2 All ER 753; [1982] 1 WLR 86 CA Once solicitor's negligent advice acted on to one's detriment time for economic loss action runs.

Forsyth v Manchester Corporation (1912) 76 JP 465; (1912-13) XXIX TLR 15 CA Corporation not liable for negligence of gas inspector which resulted in injury to infant.

Forsyth v Manchester Corporation (1912) 76 JP 246 Assizes Corporation not liable for negligence of gas inspector which resulted in injury to infant.

Fortior, Ltd, Davies v [1952] 1 All ER 1359; (1952) 96 SJ 376; (1952) WN (I) 291 HC QBD Comment by dead workman directly after accident admissible as res gestae.

Forward v Hendricks [1997] 2 All ER 395 CA On whether/when limitation period may be disregarded in personal injury actions (Limitation Act 1980, s 33(1)).

Fosbrooke-Hobbes v Airwork, Limited, and another (1937) 81 SJ 80; (1936-37) LIII TLR 254; (1937) WN (I) 48 HC KBD Carrier but not charterer liable to widow suing for fatal accident damages after pilot husband killed in aeroplane accident; res ipsa loquitur arose where emerged that accident caused by pilot's negligence.

Foskett (an infant) v Mistry [1984] RTR 1 CA Plaintiff infant who ran from hill onto road (75%) contributorily negligent as regarded resulting accident; driver who ought to have seen boy and recognised danger posed (25% negligent).

Foster v Bush House, Ltd (1952) 96 SJ 763 CA Waitress deemed, in instant circumstances, not to have been negligent in tripping and spilling soup down rear of guest diner's dress.

Foster v Gillingham Corporation [1942] 1 All ER 304; (1942) 106 JP 131; [1942] 111 LJ 364; (1943) 93 LJ 108 CA Failure to light barrier placed across road was negligence.

Foster v Tyne and Wear County Council [1986] 1 All ER 567 CA Half the value of social security benefits paid for five years after cause of action deductible from award for loss of earning capacity.

Foster Wheeler Ltd and another, Sims v; Plibrico Ltd (Third Party) [1966] 1 WLR 769 CA On liability of joint tortfeasors for damages in presence of warranty contract.

Foster, The Mayor, &c, of Chichester v (1905-06) XCIII LTR 750; (1905-06) XXII TLR 18; (1905-06) 54 WR 199 HC KBD Recovery of damages from driver of traction engine who in driving along road crushed water mains leading to waterworks.

Fothergill, Mitchell v (1917) CC Rep VI 58 CyCt Occupier of house liable for injury sustained by passer-by when coping which occupier knew to be in disrepair fell onto passer-by.

Foulger v Arding [1901] 70 LJK/QB 580 HC KBD On covenant in lease necessary to render tenant liable for expense of abating nuisance occasioned by structural defect in leased premises.

Foulger v Arding [1902] 71 LJCL 499 CA On covenant in lease necessary to render tenant liable for expense of abating nuisance occasioned by structural defect in leased premises.

Fowler and another v Grace (1970) 120 NLJ 200t; (1970) 114 SJ 193 CA On appropriate damages for person paralysed in all her limbs as a result of a motor accident.

Fowler and others, Faccenda Chicken Ltd v; Fowler v Faccenda Chicken Ltd [1986] 3 WLR 288 CA On duty owed by employee towards former employer in respect of confidential information learned during course of employment.

Fowler v AW Hawksley, Ltd (1951) 95 SJ 788 CA On appropriate damages for personal injuries to already disabled man.

Fowler v Lanning [1959] 1 All ER 290; (1959) 109 LJ 201; [1959] 1 QB 426; (1959) 103 SJ 157 HC QBD No trespass to person if injury was not negligent and was unintended (though foreseeable): here not proved.

Fowles v Bedfordshire County Council [1995] TLR 294 CA Local authority negligent in manner in which allowed gym classes at youth centre to be conducted.

Fowles v The Eastern and Australian Steamship Company (Limited) (1916-17) 115 LTR 354; (1915-16) XXXII TLR 663 PC Queensland government not liable for negligence of shipping pilots it provided.

Fowles, Watson v [1967] 3 All ER 721 CA Damages awarded as one sum: need not be divided under headings; actuarial approach undesirable.

Fowley Marine (Emsworth) Ltd v Gafford [1967] 2 All ER 472; [1967] 2 QB 808 HC QBD Quality claims to ownership plus paper title could not sustain trespass action; failure to prove sixty years' adverse possession meant did not displace Crown title to tidal creek.

Fowley Marine (Emsworth), Ltd v Gafford [1968] 1 All ER 979; (1968) 118 NLJ 110t; [1968] 2 QB 618; [1968] 2 WLR 842 CA Quality of claims to ownership plus paper title could sustain trespass action.

Fox and Son v Morrish, Grant, and Co (1918-19) 63 SJ 193; (1918-19) XXXV TLR 126 HC KBD Accountant owes duty of care to check cash and bank balances where is retained to check account books.

Fox v Newcastle-upon-Tyne Corporation [1941] 3 All ER 563; (1941) 105 JP 404; [1941] 2 KB 120; (1941) 91 LJ 270; (1942) 92 LJ 59; (1941) 165 LTR 90; (1940-41) LVII TLR 602 CA Local authority not liable in negligence for injury sustained by cyclist through collision with inadequately lit air-raid shelter during black-out conditions.

Fox v Newcastle-upon-Tyne Corporation [1941] LJNCCR 165 CyCt Negligent for corporation not to have taken steps to make air-raid shelter more visible.

Fox, Benning v (1925) 60 LJ 1055 CyCt Sane, heroic act to remove danger to public safety caused by another's negligence was not contributory negligence disentitling hero of relief in damages.

Fox, Walkley v (1914) CC Rep III 66 CyCt Prescription Act 1832 deemed inapplicable insofar as Dean Forest Re-afforestation Act 1668 applied so person acquired no right of user after forty years.

Foxley and another v Olton [1964] 3 All ER 248; [1965] 2 QB 306; (1964) 108 SJ 522; [1964] 3 WLR 1155 HC QBD On deduction/non-deduction of unemployment benefit/national assistance grants.

France v Parkinson [1954] 1 All ER 739; (1954) 104 LJ 234; (1954) 98 SJ 214; [1954] 1 WLR 581 CA Absent contrary evidence equal negligence/liability for collision at equal crossroads.

Francis Day and Hunter, Limited v Twentieth Century Fox Corporation, Limited, and others (1939) 83 SJ 796; (1939-40) LVI TLR 9 PC For there to be passing off the work passed off must be similar to that which it is passing off.

Francis Shaw and Co Ltd, McGee v [1973] RTR 409 HC QBD Person choosing not to wear seat belt one-third liable for injuries suffered in accident; no damages for being/not being prevented because of injury with chance to work abroad.

Francis, Anderson v (1906) WN (I) 160 HC ChD Injunction to restrain erection of building in such form as would cause nuisance through interference with ancient windows.

Francis, Newman v (1953) 117 JP 214 HC QBD Private individual could not rest cause of action on breach of parks bye-law.

Frangoulis, Ichard and another v [1977] 2 All ER 461; (1977) 121 SJ 287; [1977] 1 WLR 556 HC QBD Loss of enjoyment of holiday recoverable as general damages in personal injuries action, not as specific head.

Frank Smythson, Ltd v GA Cramp and Sons, Ltd and The Surrey Manufacturing Co [1943] 1 All ER 322; (1943) 168 LTR 257 CA Copyright owner's letter to persons publishing matter in which copyright infringed was privileged.

Frank v Cox (1967) 111 SJ 670 CA Pedestrian struck by motorist crossing road when lights for motor traffic were red was not contributorily negligent; on awarding personal injury damages to the elderly.

Frank v Seifert, Sedley and Co (1964) 108 SJ 523 HC QBD Failed action for negligence against solicitors in relation to their conduct in failed land deal (mistakenly revealed re-sale price of premises to original vendor in course of dealings)..

Franklin v Bristol Tramways and Carriage Co, Ltd [1941] 1 All ER 188; [1941] 1 KB 255; (1942) 92 LJ 59; [1941] 110 LJ 248 CA Contributory negligence where pedestrian (in black-out conditions) did not keep look-out for overtaking traffic.

Franklin v Edmonton Corporation (1965) 109 SJ 876 HC QBD Council one-third liable in negligence for manner in which operated defective vehicle record system.

Franklin, Aldridge v (1953) 103 LJ ccr496 CyCt Deemed to be no negligence insofar as loss of coat bailed at cloakroom was concerned.

Franks v Westminster Press Ltd [1990] TLR 275 HC QBD Absent express waiver complaint to Press Council did not involve waiving right to sue for libel over relevant article.

Franks, Gillette Safety Razor Company and Gillette Safety Razor, Limited v (1923-24) XL TLR 606 HC ChD Injunction granted to restrain sale of second-hand Gillette razor blades as new blades.

Freeson, Beach and another v [1971] 2 All ER 854; [1972] 1 QB 14; (1971) 115 SJ 145; [1971] 2 WLR 805 HC QBD Publication of defamatory letter on foot of one's duties as MP enjoys qualified privilege.

French v Hills Plymouth Company and others; Same v Same (1907-08) XXIV TLR 644 HC KBD Rail company's licence to cross line did not include licence to cross when train there.

French v Sunshine Holiday Camp (Hayling Island), Ltd (1963) 107 SJ 595 HC ChD Holiday camp liable towards child who fell from wall (from which had been ordered down) and through glass: accident reasonably foreseeable/child not contributorily negligent.

Frensham (George), Ltd v Shorn (M) and Sons, Ltd and another (1950) 94 SJ 553; (1950) WN (I) 406 HC KBD Landlords negligent in leaving central-heating boiler unlit during period of cold weather without even warning tenants.

Freshwater and another v Bulmer Rayon Company, Limited [1933] Ch 162 (also HC ChD); (1933) 102 LJCh 102 (also HC ChD); (1933) 148 LTR 251; (1932) WN (I) 211 CA Non-merger of causes of action of successive not joint tortfeasors.

Freshwater and another v Bulmer Rayon Company, Limited [1933] Ch 162 (also CA); (1933) 102 LJCh 102 (also CA) HC ChD Non-merger of causes of action of successive not joint tortfeasors.

Freshwater and Another, Bulmer Rayon Company, Limited v [1933] AC 661 HL Non-merger of causes of action.

Friend, Kirby v [1945] LJNCCR 90 CyCt Owner of property liable for injury suffered by way of defective coal-plate by person lawfully using highway onto which plate extended.

Friern Hospital Management Committee, Bolam v [1957] 2 All ER 118; (1957) 107 LJ 315; (1957) 101 SJ 357 HC QBD Doctor not negligent if susbscribes to one of two conflicting views held by responsible bodies of medics; doctor negligent in not giving warning to mentally ill person of what he believes to be minimal dangers of treatment; must show failure to warn not negligent and would not have consented if warned.

Frisby v Theodore Goddard and Co [1984] TLR 127 CA On concealment of right of action as ground for striking out claim.

Froom and others v Butcher [1975] 3 All ER 520; [1976] QB 286; [1975] RTR 518; (1975) 119 SJ 613; [1975] 3 WLR 379 CA Is contributory negligence where car passenger does not wear seat belt.

Froom and others v Butcher [1974] 3 All ER 517; (1975) 125 NLJ 843t; [1974] RTR 528; (1974) 118 SJ 758; [1974] 1 WLR 1297 HC QBD No negligence if person acting on reasonably held belief drove without seat belt.

Frost and others v Chief Constable of South Yorkshire [1995] TLR 379 HC QBD On recovery of damages for nervous shock by professional rescuers.

Frost and others v Chief Constable of the South Yorkshire Police and others; Duncan v British Coal Corp [1997] 1 All ER 540 CA On liability of employer for psychiatric injury suffered by employee in course of rescue operation.

Frost v London Joint Stock Bank, Limited (1905-06) XXII TLR 760 CA Return of cheque to person seeking payment on same with note attached stating 'Reason assigned: not stated' not per se libellous.

Frost v The King Edward VII Welsh National Memorial Assocciation for Prevention, Treatment and Abolition of Tuberculosis [1918] 2 Ch 180; (1918) 82 JP 249; (1918) 53 LJ 227; [1918] 87 LJCh 561; (1918-19) 119 LTR 220; (1918) WN (I) 185 HC ChD Operation of tuberculosis hospital deemed not to cause nuisance by virtue of noise/offensiveness/threat of infection.

Fry (JS) and Sons, Limited, Tolley v [1930] 1 KB 467; (1929) 68 LJ 429; (1930) 99 LJCL 149; (1930) 142 LTR 270; (1929) 73 SJ 818; (1929-30) XLVI TLR 108; (1929) WN (I) 272 CA Something innocently stated could not through circumstance of publication be defamatory.

Fry (JS) and Sons, Ltd, Tolley v [1931] All ER 131; [1931] AC 333; (1931) 71 LJ 277; (1931) 100 LJCL 328; (1931) 145 LTR 1; (1931) 75 SJ 220; (1930-31) XLVII TLR 351; (1931) WN (I) 87 HL Something innocently stated may through circumstance of publication be defamatory.

Gage and another v King [1960] 3 All ER 62; (1960) 110 LJ 541 HC QBD Party legally liable for expenses entitled to recover.

Gahan v Szerelmey (UK) Ltd and another [1996] 1 WLR 439 CA Non-dismissal of personal injuries action for want of prosecution where defendant's having money during period of delay which would otherwise have paid as compensation meant could not plead undue prejudice arising from delay.

Gaisford and another v Ministry of Agriculture, Fisheries and Food (1996) TLR 18/7/96 HC QBD Ministry of Agriculture, Fisheries and Food did not owe duty of care towards purchasers of imported animals to discover between importation and expiry of quarantine period whether animals were suffering from disease.

Gale and another v Rhymney and Aber Valleys Gas and Water Company (1903) 67 JP 430 CA Water company guilty of trespass where unlawfully cut houseowner's connection with water mains.

Gale and Power, Eagle Star Insurance Co, Ltd v (1955) 105 LJ 458 HC QBD Successful action in negligence against surveyor for making negligent report on basis of which plaintiff had advanced loan.

Gale, Dogma Properties Ltd v (1984) 134 NLJ 453 HC QBD Successful suit against solicitor employed to act for person seeking to purchase property who through solicitor's negligence succeeded only in getting possession, not title to the premises.

Galoo Ltd (in liq) and others v Bright Grahame Murray (a firm) and another [1995] 1 All ER 16; [1994] 1 WLR 1360 CA No duty of care on auditor towards potential shareholder or lender who relies on audited accounts.

Gamage (AW) (Limited) and Benetfink and Co (Limited), Spalding (AG) and Brothers v (1912-13) XXIX TLR 541 HC ChD Passing off where sold goods of inferior quality made by particular trader as goods of higher quality made by same.

Gamage (AW), Ltd, Spalding (AG) Brothers v [1914-15] All ER 147; [1915] 84 LJCh 449; (1915-16) 113 LTR 198; (1914-15) XXXI TLR 328; (1915) WN (I) 151 HL Passing off where sold goods of inferior quality made by particular trader as goods of higher quality made by same.

Gamble, Cubitt v (1918-19) 63 SJ 287; (1918-19) XXXV TLR 223 HC KBD Person seeking debt execution after tender of amount of debt is guilty of trespass.

Gambling v Benham [1940] 1 All ER 275; (1940) 84 SJ 132 CA On appropriate damages for loss of life expectancy (of infant).

Gambling, Benham v [1941] 1 All ER 7; [1941] AC 157; (1941) 91 LJ 26; (1942) 92 LJ 61; [1941] 110 LJ 49; (1941) 164 LTR 290; (1940) 84 SJ 703; (1940-41) LVII TLR 177 HL On appropriate damages for road death: damages not gauged on actuarial basis.

Gammell v Wilson and another [1980] 2 All ER 557; [1982] AC 27 (also HL); (1980) 130 NLJ 510; (1980) 124 SJ 329; [1980] 3 WLR 591 CA Estate can sue for lost earnings in lost years; gravestone is funeral expense; sum for loss of life expectation changeable/not constantly reviewable.

Gammell v Wilson and others; Furness and another v B and S Massey Ltd [1981] 1 All ER 578; [1982] AC 27 (also CA); (1981) 131 NLJ 197; (1981) 125 SJ 116; [1981] 2 WLR 248 HL Estate of deceased can recover damages for deceased's loss of earnings in lost years.

Gapp (FW) and Company, Limited, and Gapp, Baxter v [1939] 2 KB 271; [1939] 108 LJCL 522; (1939) 83 SJ 436; (1938-39) LV TLR 739; (1939) WN (I) 201 CA On appropriate damages for negligent evaluation of property.

Garbett v Hazell, Watson and Viney, Ltd and others [1943] 2 All ER 359 CA Print and photographs laid out in such a manner that there was a defamatory innuendo.

Garbutt and others, Green v (1911-12) XXVIII TLR 575 CA Person bringing false imprisonment action on foot of detention for alleged felony allowed seek details of alleged felony plus basis for suspecting him but not identity of persons who informed on him.

Gardiner v Moore and others [1966] 1 All ER 365; [1969] 1 QB 55; [1966] 3 WLR 786 HC QBD No implied term in settlement with two of three joint tortfeasors that would not sue other.

Gardner (J) and Co, Ltd and another, Canter v [1940] 1 All ER 325; (1940) 89 LJ 69; (1940) 84 SJ 289; (1939-40) LVI TLR 305 HC KBD Main contractors were not negligent and did not know of danger; sub-contractors not liable where had left place in safe shape.

Gardner (JA) v Fishel (JH) (1977) 127 NLJ 1152 CA On relevancy of law reports to assessment of appropriate damages in negligence action.

Gardner and another v Marsh and Parsons (a firm) and another [1997] 3 All ER 871; (1996) 140 SJ LB 262; (1996) TLR 2/12/97; [1997] 1 WLR 489 CA Damages available where purchased property in reliance on negligent surveyor's report where difference in cost of property and cost ought to have been were defects known when purchasing.

Gardner and others, Daily Mirror Newspapers, Ltd v [1968] 2 All ER 163; [1968] 2 QB 762; [1968] 2 WLR 1239 CA Interlocutory injunction available; that did not know terms of contract/did not bring about direct pressure no defence; restrictive trade practice prima facie evidence of wrongful interference.

Gardner Steel Ltd v Sheffield Brothers (Profiles) Ltd [1978] 3 All ER 399 CA Interest on summary judgment possible.

Gardner v Dyson [1967] 3 All ER 762; (1967) 117 NLJ 1087t; (1967) 111 SJ 793; [1967] 1 WLR 1497 CA Appropriate damages upon loss of eye.

Gardner, Lewis v (1981) 131 NLJ 1134 HC QBD On appropriate damages for motor cycle pillion passenger who suffered brain damage in road traffic accident.

Garford and others, Carroll v (1968) 112 SJ 948 HC QBD Licensees/dog-owner not liable for injury suffered by third party who tripped over generally well-behaved dog that had been brought into pub.

Garland and others, West Wiltshire District Council v; Cond and others (third parties) [1993] Ch 409; [1993] TLR 112; [1993] 3 WLR 626 HC ChD On duty of care owed by district auditors when auditing local authority accounts.

Garland and others, West Wiltshire District Council v; Cond and others (third parties) [1995] Ch 297; (1995) 139 SJ LB 18; [1994] TLR 622; [1995] 2 WLR 439 CA On duty of care owed by district auditors when auditing local authority accounts.

Garston Haulage Co, Ltd, Ware v [1943] 2 All ER 558; [1944] KB 30; (1944) 94 LJ 109; [1944] 113 LJ 45; (1944) 170 LTR 155; (1943-44) LX TLR 77 CA Unlit motor vehicle on unlit nighttime road a nuisance.

Garston Warehousing Co Ltd v OF Smart (Liverpool) Ltd [1973] RTR 377 CA Van driver driving too fast on wet November morning and ignoring warnings from another driver was two-thirds liable for resultant collision at city crossroads.

Garton Sons and Co Ltd, Rankine v [1979] 2 All ER 1185; (1979) 123 SJ 305 CA RSC Judgment available if admission of negligence and liability, not former alone.

Gas Light and Coke Co, Ltd, Kimber v [1918-19] All ER 123; (1918) 82 JP 125; [1918] 1 KB 439; [1918] 87 LJCL 651; (1918) 118 LTR 562; (1917-18) 62 SJ 329; (1917-18) XXXIV TLR 260 CA Person creating danger has duty to warn person unaware of hazard actually/in danger of exposing themselves thereto from doing so.

Gas, Anders v (1960) 110 LJ 350; (1960) 104 SJ 211 HC QBD On defence of fair comment.

Gaselee v Darling; The Millwall [1904-07] All ER 1387 CA Tow owners liable to tug owners.

Gaskill v Preston [1981] 3 All ER 427; (1981) 131 NLJ 501 HC QBD Family income supplement payments deductible from road traffic accident damages.

Gasquet, Metcalfe and Walton, Webber v (1982) 132 NLJ 665 HC ChD Recovery of damages for negligence of solicitors vis-à-vis safeguarding plaintiff's property rights during divorce action.

Gates v R Bill and Son [1902] 2 KB 38; [1902] 71 LJCL 702; (1902-03) LXXXVII LTR 288; (1901-02) 46 SJ 498; (1901-02) 50 WR 546 CA Unlicensed proprietor of taxi cab could be sued for negligence of driver.

Gates, Stein v [1935] LJNCCA 171; (1935) 79 SJ 252 CA Re-trial ordered as to whether had been negligent not to take special precautions for protection of frequent (unsighted) customer from peril of falling through open trap-door which had been adequately signposted for sighted persons.

Gates, Stein v [1934] LJNCCR 343 CyCt Hotel licensee not liable in negligence towards blind invitee who fell through cellar door on former's premises while door open for goods delivery.

Gauler, Pirie v (1930) 70 LJ ccr2 CyCt Dog-owner not liable in damages to owner of another dog where latter dog injured by former.

Gawthrop v Boulton and others [1978] 3 All ER 615; (1978) 122 SJ 297 HC ChD Limitation period continues to run to defendant's advantage to date added as party.

Gayler and Pope, Ltd v B Davies and Son, Ltd [1924] All ER 94; [1924] 2 KB 75; (1924) 59 LJ 282; [1924] 93 LJCL 702; (1924) 131 LTR 507; (1923-24) 68 SJ 685; (1923-24) XL TLR 591; (1924) WN (I) 158 HC KBD Owner liable for damage by stray horse where was negligent — not for trespass of horse per se.

Gaynor v Allen [1959] 2 All ER 644; [1959] Crim LR 786; (1959) 123 JP 413; (1959) 109 LJ 441; [1959] 2 QB 403; (1959) 103 SJ 677 HC QBD Police motorcyclist owes duty of care in negligence though driving at speed in course of duty.

GB Chapman Ltd, Sylvester v [1935] LJNCCA 261; (1935) 79 SJ 777 CA Circus not liable for injuries to groom who took it upon himself to extinguish cigarette in leopard cage and was mauled in the process.

Geddes v British Railways Board (1968) 112 SJ 194 CA Deceased two-thirds liable for rail accident/engine driver one-third liable for not sounding long whistle in circumstances.

Gee Cars, Ltd, Grey v (1940) 84 SJ 538 HC KBD Car hire firm not liable in negligence for loss occasioned to client by way of dishonest company chauffeur.

Geel (Jacob), Winnipeg Electric Company v [1932] AC 690; (1932) 101 LJPC 187; (1933) 148 LTR 24; (1931-32) XLVIII TLR 657 PC Matter for jury whether motor vehicle owner has negatived presumption of negligence under Manitoban law where motor vehicle injures another.

Geeves v London General Omnibus Company (Limited) (1900-01) XVII TLR 249 CA On appropriate direction as regards negligence/contributory negligence where passenger who consented to bus starting was injured when bus started.

Gellygaer Urban District Council, Davies v (1954) 104 LJ ccr140 CyCt Council deemed not to have been negligent where child injured self on broken glass bottle in council-maintained pool.

Gelston v King (1918) CC Rep VII 66 CyCt Successful damages for conversion of swarm of bees hived by person who refused to return them to person who formerly hived swarm for one day.

Gelston, Powell v [1916-17] All ER 953; [1916] 2 KB 615; [1916] 85 LJKB 1783; (1916-17) 115 LTR 379; (1915-16) 60 SJ 696; (1915-16) XXXII TLR 703; (1916) WN (I) 323 HC KBD Opening of confidential letter defamatory of another by third party not libel as writer had been assured of confidentiality.

General Accident, Fire and Life Assurance Corporation v Tanter (1984) 134 NLJ 35/82 HC QBD Broker owed duty of care to underwriter to whom gave signing down indication.

General and Finance Facilities Ltd v Cooks Cars (Romford) Ltd (1963) 113 LJ 432; [1963] 1 WLR 644 CA Master's decision in detinue action ought to separately itemise value of item in detinue and damages awarded.

General Cleaning Contractors, Ltd and others, Christmas v [1952] 1 All ER 39; [1952] 1 KB 141; (1951) 101 LJ 706; (1951) 95 SJ 802; [1951] 2 TLR 1218 CA Occupier need not warn invitee of something that is ordinarily safe though could be dangerous to invitee.

General Cleaning Contractors, Ltd, Christmas v (1951) 95 SJ 452; (1951) WN (I) 294 HC KBD Occupier and employer of invitee (window-cleaner) liable in negligence for injury to latter while at work..

General Council and Register of Osteopaths Ltd and another v Register of Osteotherapists and Naturopaths Ltd and another (1968) 112 SJ 443 HC ChD Successful passing off action for proprietors of name 'MRO' for osteopaths against persons using name 'MRO' followed by 'registered osteotherapist'.

General Medical Council, McCandless (David Noel) v (1996) 140 SJ LB 28; [1995] TLR 668; [1996] 1 WLR 167 PC Gravely negligent treatment of patients could constitute serious professional misconduct.

Georgius v Oxford University Press (Delegates) and others [1949] 1 All ER 342; [1949] 1 KB 729; [1949] 118 LJR 454; (1949) LXV TLR 101; (1949) WN (I) 47 CA Non-interference with non-allowance of interrogatory seeking source of information in libel.

Gerhold v Baker (1918) 53 LJ 417; (1918-19) 63 SJ 135; (1918-19) XXXV TLR 102; (1918) WN (I) 368 CA Third-party letter to Appeal Tribunal over appeal against military service enjoyed qualified privilege (and absent malice could not be libellous).

Gerrard v Birkenhead Corporation [1937] LJNCCR 325 CyCt Day of accident not included when calculating limitation period for purpose of the Public Authorities Protection Act 1893.

Gerson and another, Chatterton v [1981] 1 All ER 257; (1981) 131 NLJ 238; [1981] QB 432; (1980) 124 SJ 885; [1980] 3 WLR 1003 HC QBD Trespass to person requires lack of real consent; no such lack where general explanation of operation/risks by doctor (which obliged to give).

Ghani and others v Jones [1969] 3 All ER 720; [1969] Crim LR 605; (1970) 134 JP 166; (1969) 113 SJ 775 HC QBD Police cannot retain non-evidential items of persons unconnected to crime.

Ghani and others v Jones [1969] 3 All ER 1700; [1970] Crim LR 36t; (1969) 113 SJ 854; [1969] 3 WLR 1158 CA Police cannot retain non-evidential items of persons unconnected to crime.

Ghosh v D'Rosario (1962) 106 SJ 352 CA Stay of slander action required where after commencement of action defendant appointed to High Commission staff and thereby acquired diplomatic immunity.

Ghosh, High Commissioner for India and others v (1959) 109 LJ 683; (1959) 103 SJ 939 CA Striking out of counter-claim for slander against High Commissioner/Union of India (sovereign immunity not waived by plaintiffs bringing action for money lent against defendants).

Gibaud v Great Eastern Rail Co [1921] All ER 35; [1921] 2 KB 426; (1921) CC Rep X 21; (1921) 56 LJ 92; [1921] LJCL 535; (1921) 125 LTR 76; (1920-21) 65 SJ 454; (1920-21) XXXVII TLR 422; (1921) WN (I) 80 CA Exemption clause disclaiming liability for loss effected 'in any way possible' included own negligence.

Gibaud v Great Eastern Rail Co [1920] 3 KB 689; [1921] LJCL 194; (1919-20) XXXVI TLR 884 HC KBD Exemption clause disclaiming liability for loss effected 'in any way possible' included own negligence.

Gibbs v Barking Corporation [1936] 1 All ER 115 CA Education authority liable for injury to boy during PT class whom teacher did not assist.

Gibby v East Grinstead Gas and Water Company (1944) 170 LTR 250 CA Person walking on unfenced gantry at night without light was guilty of contributory negligence.

Gibson and others, Bank of England v [1994] TLR 253 HC QBD Standard of proof in action for wrongful appropriation of money is the civil standard.

Gibson v C and A Modes (1977) 127 NLJ 416b CA Failed negligence action against store-owners by woman who injured self in not reasonably foreseeable mannner which had not previously occurred (tripped over up-turning tile).

Gibson, Swingcastle Ltd v [1990] 3 All ER 463; (1990) 140 NLJ 818; [1990] 1 WLR 1223 CA Negligent surveyor liable to mortgagee for all loss where mortgagee seeks to sell property following mortgagor's default on repayment.

Giddins, Snow v (1969) 113 SJ 229 CA Pedestrian deemed 25% negligent where in accident occasioned when crossed road at point where was no pedestrian crossing/central refuge.

Giddy, Smith v [1904-07] All ER 289; [1904] 2 KB 448; (1904) 39 LJ 346; [1904] 73 LJCL 894; (1904-05) XCI LTR 296; (1903-04) 48 SJ 589; (1903-04) XX TLR 596; (1904) WN (I) 130; (1904-05) 53 WR 207 HC KBD Can lop overhanging branches causing nuisance and claim for damage effected thereby.

Giffen Couch and Archer (a firm), National Home Loans Corp plc v [1997] 3 All ER 808 CA On extent of duty of care owed by solicitor to lender where is acting for borrower and lender in loan transaction.

Gilbey v Great Northern Railway Company (1919-20) XXXVI TLR 562 HC KBD Rail company not liable in negligence for stage props carried by passenger as personal luggage though were not personal luggage.

Goldsmith and another v Bhoyrul and others (1997) 141 SJ LB 151; [1997] TLR 319 HC QBD Political party per se could not bring libel action.

Goldsmith and another v Pressdram Ltd and others [1988] 1 WLR 64 CA Refusal of application for trial of libel action by jury.

Goldsmith v Pressdram Ltd (1976) 126 NLJ 888t; (1976) 120 SJ 606 HC QBD On availability of injunction from stating what was claimed to be a libel.

Goldsmith v Sperrings Ltd [1977] 2 All ER 566; (1977) 121 SJ 304; [1977] 1 WLR 478 CA Abuse of process where action really brought to serve secondary purpose unavailable in law.

Goldston v Bradshaw [1934] LJNCCR 355 CyCt Absent negligence/intent on part of pig drover/his employer could not recover damages from same for damage occasioned by straying pig.

Goldstone v Cheshire Lines Committee [1938] LJNCCR 130 CyCt Rail company liable for injury suffered by person alighting from unlit carriage onto insufficiently lit platform.

Goldthorpe, Chambers v (1899-1900) 44 SJ 229; (1899-1900) XVI TLR 180 HC QBD Architect acting as arbitrator between builder and builder's client could not be guilty of negligence absent fraud/dishonesty.

Goldthorpe, Chambers v (1900-01) 45 SJ 325; (1901) WN (I) 51; (1900-01) 49 WR 401 CA Architect acting as arbitrator between builder and builder's client could not be guilty of negligence.

Gollop v Brown (1952) 102 LJ 360 CyCt Failed action in detinue by father against daughter for return of piano originally given to her as birthday present.

Gomberg v Smith [1962] 1 All ER 725; (1962) 112 LJ 205; [1963] 1 QB 25; (1962) 106 SJ 95 CA Non-escape but bringing of animal onto highway meant owner liable in negligence for injury through collision.

Good, Mint and another v [1950] 2 All ER 1159; [1951] 1 KB 517; (1950) 100 LJ 691; (1950) 94 SJ 822; [1950] 66 (2) TLR 1110; (1950) WN (I) 555 CA Landlord liable (absent contrary agreement) to maintain premises (here walls adjoining highway) in safe condition.

Goodbody v Poplar Borough Council (1915) 79 JP 218; [1915] 84 LJKB 1230 HC KBD Non-liability under Rylands v Fletcher principles for thing (electric/fuse box) made dangerous by presence of another thing (gas) over which had no control.

Goodchild v Greatness Timber Co, Ltd [1968] 2 All ER 25; [1968] 2 QB 372; (1968) 112 SJ 192; [1968] 2 WLR 1283 CA Evidence unnecessary to decide if limitation applied.

Gooding and Son, Stearn v (1912) CC Rep I 77 CyCt Painters in meadow who left paints in such a way that animals could (and did) gain access to them and (as happened) get sick were liable in negligence.

Goodrich, Bryant v (1966) 110 SJ 108 CA Damages for negligent advice of solicitor in divorce case.

Goodway and London Association of Accountants, Limited, Society of Accountants and Auditors v [1907] 1 Ch 489; (1907) XCVI LTR 326; (1907) WN (I) 45 HC ChD Injunction to prevent improper use of term 'incorporated acountant' and to stop defendant society advertising its members as being able to use such a title.

Goodwill v British Pregnancy Advisory Service [1996] 2 All ER 161; [1996] 2 FCR 680; [1996] 2 FLR 55; (1996) 146 NLJ 173; (1996) 140 SJ LB 37; (1996) TLR 29/1/96; [1996] 1 WLR 1397 CA Must be known/deducible that advice will be acted on by third party before duty of care in respect of same will arise.

Goodwin, Waterfield v (1955) 105 LJ ccr332 CyCt Successful action in nuisance against neighbours (in semi-detached house) whose music lessons/practising of music/fondness for gramophone and radio music created a nuisance by noise.

Goody v Baring [1956] 2 All ER 11; (1956) 106 LJ 266; (1956) 100 SJ 320; [1956] 1 WLR 448 HC ChD Solicitor failed in duty to make proper inquiries on client's behalf.

Goody v Odhams Press, Ltd [1966] 3 All ER 369; [1967] 1 QB 333; (1966) 110 SJ 793; [1966] 3 WLR 460 CA Evidence of relevant previous convictions admissible to show plaintiff's generally bad reputation; can be partial justification of article if part severable.

Gordon Doctors and Walton (a firm), Lynne and another v (1991) 135 SJ LB 29 HC QBD Failed action to recoup from allegedly negligent solicitors purported loss personal representatives suffered through solicitors not taking out life assurance for deceased mortgagor.

Gordon Lennox and another, Trawnik and another v [1985] 2 All ER 368; (1985) 129 SJ 225; [1984] TLR 723; [1985] 1 WLR 532 CA Crown cannot be sued in tort.

Gordon v London, City and Midland Bank, Limited; Gordon v Capital and Counties Bank, Limited [1902] 1 KB 242; (1901-02) 50 WR 276 CA Liability of banks for conversion of cheques.

Gordon, Capital and Counties Bank, Limited v; London, City and Midland Bank, Limited v Gordon (1903) WN (I) 92 HL On liability of banks for conversion of cheques.

Gordon, Wellingborough Council v (1991) 155 JP 494; [1990] TLR 713 HC QBD Prosecution arising from noise at Friday night birthday party to which all neighbours invited, most attended and none complained, an extreme reaction: nonetheless was no 'reasonable excuse' for noise (Control of Pollution Act 1974, s 58).

Gore Wood and Co, Westway Homes Ltd v [1991] TLR 331 CA How solicitor behaved and not what solicitor thought relevant to determination of whether solicitor behaved negligently.

Gorely and another v Codd and another [1966] 3 All ER 891; (1965-66) 116 NLJ 1658; (1966) 110 SJ 965; [1967] 1 WLR 19 Assizes No offence/negligence if father having taken reasonable care allows child unsupervised use of air gun in non-public place.

Gosforth, Ltd, Bee-Line Safety Coaches, Ltd v [1940] LJNCCR 330 CyCt Failed claim against persons who admitted negligence in collision involving lorry already involved in another collision where lorry-owners sought special damages for loss of use of lorry while in for repairs but failed to prove duration of repairs extended by second collision.

Gosling v Islington Corporation [1938] LJNCCR 427 CyCt Sand bin by highway was an allurement/trap and defendants were negligent in not making sure that bin was kept locked.

Gosport Corporation, Southern Railway Company v (1926) 135 LTR 630 CA Corporation liable for negligent damage to bridge effected by temporary servant in charge of steam-roller which corporation had hired.

Gosse Millard, Limited v Canadian Government Merchant Marine, Limited (1928-29) XLV TLR 63 HL Recovery of damages where negligence of crew resulted in damage to goods.

Gosse Millard, Limited v Canadian Government Merchant Marine, Limited (1926-27) XLIII TLR 544 HC KBD Recovery of damages for damage to goods where shipowner did not show that neither they nor their servants had been negligent.

Gottliffe v Edelston [1930] 2 KB 378; (1930) 99 LJCL 547; (1930) 143 LTR 595; (1930) 74 SJ 567; (1929-30) XLVI TLR 544; (1930) WN (I) 168 HC KBD Right of action for tort by woman against man ended upon marriage of former to latter.

Gough v National Coal Board [1953] 2 All ER 1283; [1954] 1 QB 191; (1953) 97 SJ 811; [1953] 3 WLR 900 CA Child playing on land a licensee under general licence — not trespasser just because did something not supposed to do; slow-moving trucks an allurement; licensor negligently failed to take reasonable care to protect child.

Gough v Thorne [1966] 3 All ER 398; (1966) 110 SJ 529; [1966] 1 WLR 1387 CA Driver waving child to cross negligent if child struck despite failing to check for overtaking traffic.

Gould v Birkenhead Corporation (1910) 74 JP 105 HC KBD Nonsuit unjustified where was evidence that malfeasance of defendants' servants resulted in injury to plaintiff.

Gould v McAuliffe [1941] 1 All ER 515; (1941) 91 LJ 191; (1942) 92 LJ 60; (1941) 85 SJ 215; (1940-41) LVII TLR 369 HC KBD Customer looking for outside pub lavatory could recover for animal injury though trespasser.

Gould, Shotter v (1928) 66 LJ ccr8 CyCt Not defence in personal injuries action brought by motor cycle pillion passenger against car driver following accident that motor cycle driver had been contributorily negligent.

Gourley, British Transport Commission v [1955] 3 All ER 796; [1956] AC 185; (1955) 105 LJ 808; [1956] 2 WLR 41 HL Income tax and surtax factors to be considered when awarding damages.

Government of Malaysia and another Keow (Chin) v (1967) 111 SJ 333; [1967] 1 WLR 813 PC Expert evidence unnecessary for/that doctor followed same practice each day as that challenged in instant case had no bearing on finding of negligent medical practice.

Government of Malaysia v Ning (Lee Hock) [1974] AC 76; (1973) 117 SJ 617; [1973] 3 WLR 334 PC Special public authority limitation period did not apply in respect of action based on private contract.

Governors of Rydal School, Povey v [1970] 1 All ER 841 Assizes Appropriate damages for tetraplegia.

Governors of the Peabody Donation Fund v Sir Lindsay Parkinson and Co Ltd and others [1983] 3 All ER 417; [1985] AC 210 (also HL); (1983) 127 SJ 749; [1983] 3 WLR 754 CA Local authority not under duty to force compliance with building requirements.

Governors of the Peabody Donation Fund v Sir Lindsay Parkinson and Co Ltd and others [1985] AC 210 (also CA); (1984) 128 SJ 753; [1984] 3 WLR 953 HL Local authority not under duty to force compliance with building requirements.

Governors of Wellingborough School and Fryer, Langham v (1932) 96 JP 236; (1932) 73 LJ 361; (1932) 101 LJCL 513; (1932) 147 LTR 91 CA Not negligent/no res ipsa loquitur where school pupil struck by golf ball that other pupil hit from door into schoolground.

Grabowski, Suchcicka v (1973) 117 SJ 58 CA On personal injuries damages (and interest awardable thereon) for foreigner injured in collision (exchange rate being particularly difficult to calculate).

Grace, Fowler and another v (1970) 120 NLJ 200t; (1970) 114 SJ 193 CA On appropriate damages for person paralysed in all her limbs as a result of a motor accident.

Graham and Bolangaro, Stores and Stores v (1949) 99 LJ 108 CyCt Damages from police for false imprisonment (continued detention in police station after police believed detained suspect to be innocent of alleged offence).

Graham Pearce and Co (a firm), Acton v [1997] 3 All ER 909 HC ChD Solicitors deemed not to be immune from suit in negligence; award of damages where solicitor's negligence meant had lost chance either not to be prosecuted or (if prosecuted) acquitted.

Graham, North Central Wagon and Finance Co, Ltd v [1950] 1 All ER 780; [1950] 2 KB 7 CA Hirer could sue in conversion for breach of hire-purchase agreement as under particular agreement breach placed property immediately in hirer's possession.

Graham, Wilson v [1990] TLR 485 HC QBD Commercial interest available on damages from when judgment on liability entered.

Grahame-White Aviation Company Limited, Meering v [1918-23] All ER 292; (1920) 122 LTR 44 CA On imprisonment by private prosecutor/police.

Grainger, Cummings v (1977) 141 JP 95; (1976) 126 NLJ 665t; [1977] QB 397; (1976) 120 SJ 453; [1976] 3 WLR 842 CA Person with untrained guard dog not liable for injuries suffered by trespasser (who in any event entered guarded place knowing of dog and so assumed risk of injury).

Grainger, Cummings v (1975) 125 NLJ 256t; (1975) 119 SJ 425; [1975] 1 WLR 1330 HC QBD Successful action for damages under Animals Act 1975 from owner-keeper of particularly fierce Alsatian dog.

Gran Gelato Ltd v Richcliff (Group) Ltd and others [1992] 1 All ER 865; [1992] Ch 560; (1992) 142 NLJ 51; [1992] 2 WLR 867 HC ChD Normally conveyancing solicitor for seller does not owe duty to buyer because action already lies against seller; in concurrent claims for negligence/misrepresentation contributory negligence can apply to both claims.

Grand Trunk Railway Co v Barnett [1911-13] All ER 1624 PC No liability for injury to trespasser occurring through one's negligence.

Grand Trunk Railway Company of Canada v Barnett (Walter C) [1911] AC 361; (1911) 80 LJPC 117; (1911) 104 LTR 362; (1910-11) XXVII TLR 359 PC Non-recovery for negligence where no breach of duty/cause of action shown.

Grand Trunk Railway Company of Canada v Robinson (Arthur) [1915] AC 740; [1915] 84 LJPC 194; (1915-16) 113 LTR 350; (1914-15) XXXI TLR 395; (1915) WN (I) 173 PC Valid exemption clause in half-fare travel contract.

Grange Motors (Cwmbran) Ltd v Spencer and another [1969] 1 All ER 340; (1969) 119 NLJ 154t; (1968) 112 SJ 908; [1969] 1 WLR 53 CA On duty of care owed by one driver signalling to another.

Grant v Australian Knitting Mills [1935] All ER 209; (1935) 80 LJ 378; [1936] 105 LJPC 6; (1935) 79 SJ 815; (1935-36) LII TLR 38 PC Where product reached consumer in same state that left manufacturer, latter liable for injury caused by latent defect undiscoverable by reasonable scrutiny.

Grant v Derwent (1929) 93 JP 113; (1929) 67 LJ 12; (1929) 98 LJCh 70; (1929) 140 LTR 330 CA Council's trespass in laying sewage pipe did not render person who requested council to connect house to sewer liable for trespass.

Grant v Derwent (1929) 93 JP 1; (1928) 97 LJCh 434 HC ChD Council not liable for trespass in laying sewage pipe as plaintiff's rights over soil subject to those of council in respect of sewer.

Grant v Sun Shipping Co, Ltd and others [1948] 2 All ER 238; [1948] AC 549 HL Stevedore could recover damages from shipowner/repairers where repairers negligently left hatch open.

Grant, Wandsworth, Wimbledon and Epsom District Gas Company v (1926) 62 LJ ccr70 CyCt Failed action in trespass against gas company which laid gas mains along road without agreement of soil-owner.

Granville, Ad-Lib Club Ltd v [1971] 2 All ER 300; (1971) 121 NLJ 13t; (1971) 115 SJ 74 HC ChD Passing-off action grounded in goodwill which can attach to defunct business.

Grappelli and another v Derek Block (Holdings) Ltd and another [1981] 2 All ER 272; (1981) 125 SJ 169; [1981] 1 WLR 822 CA Material to be libellous must be so upon publication; if plea of innuendo in limited publication must identify those understanding innuendo.

Grattan-Storey, Gussman v (1968) 112 SJ 884 CA Valid finding that person was better to drive on and possibly kill pheasant than to stop and so (negligently) endanger following traffic.

Gravelworks, Ltd, Rouse v [1940] 109 LJCL 408; (1940) 84 SJ 112; (1940) WN (I) 12 CA Failed trespass action where water blown from pond formed after natural user (quarrying) caused erosion to neighbour's land.

Graves v Pocket Publications, Limited (1937-38) LIV TLR 952 HC ChD Damages for conversion in context of copyright infringement.

Gravesham Borough Council and others v British Railways Board [1978] 3 All ER 853 HC ChD Changing of public ferry service actionable by party suffering direct loss as obstruction/hindrance of ferry public nuisance.

Gray and Walker (a firm) and others, Harper v [1985] 2 All ER 507; [1985] 1 WLR 1196 HC QBD Contribution notice remained valid after discontinuance of action against joint defendants as liability undetermined.

Gray v Jones [1939] 1 All ER 798; (1939) 87 LJ 199; (1939) 160 LTR 361; (1939) 83 SJ 278; (1938-39) LV TLR 437 HC KBD To say that person a convict, if untrue, is defamatory.

Gray v Mid-Herts Group Hospital Management Committee (1974) 124 NLJ 367t; (1974) 118 SJ 501 HC QBD On appropriate damages for injuries suffered by child as result of negligent hospital operation.

Gray, Gilling v (1910-11) XXVII TLR 39 HC ChD Injunction against causing noise by sawing and planing where constituted nuisance plus damages for past nuisance.

Great Central Railway Company v Bates [1921] 3 KB 578; (1921) CC Rep X 61; [1921] LJCL 1269; (1920-21) 65 SJ 768; (1920-21) XXXVII TLR 948 HC KBD No duty to policeman entering premises to ascertain whether everything all right.

Great Central Railway Company v Hewlett [1916-17] All ER 1027; [1916] 2 AC 511; (1916) 51 LJ 418; [1916] 85 LJKB 1705; (1916-17) 115 LTR 349; (1915-16) XXXII TLR 707 HL Railway company not under duty to warn public of presence of post authorised by statute and maintainable by them.

Great Central Railway Company, Hewlett v (1915-16) 60 SJ 428; (1915-16) XXXII TLR 373; (1916) WN (I) 144 CA Railway company deemed in circumstances to be under duty to warn public of presence of post authorised by statute and maintainable by them.

Great Central Railway v Doncaster Rural District Council (1918) 82 JP 33; [1918] 87 LJCh 80; (1918) 118 LTR 19; (1917-18) 62 SJ 212 HC ChD Delayed injunction granted to restrain use of tip causing nuisance by smell.

Great Eastern Rail Co, Gibaud v [1921] All ER 35; [1921] 2 KB 426; (1921) CC Rep X 21; (1921) 56 LJ 92; [1921] LJCL 535; (1921) 125 LTR 76; (1920-21) 65 SJ 454; (1920-21) XXXVII TLR 422; (1921) WN (I) 80 CA Exemption clause disclaiming liability for loss effected 'in any way possible' included own negligence.

Great Eastern Rail Co, Gibaud v [1920] 3 KB 689; [1921] LJCL 194; (1919-20) XXXVI TLR 884 HC KBD Exemption clause disclaiming liability for loss effected 'in any way possible' included own negligence.

Great Eastern Railway Company, Lambert v (1911-13) XXII Cox CC 165; [1909] 2 KB 776; (1909) 73 JP 445; (1908-09) XXV TLR 734; (1909) WN (I) 186 CA Railway company liable in damages for false imprisonment by their special constables.

Great Northern Railway Company v Woods (1917) CC Rep VI 50 CyCt Rail company liable in negligence for carriage of sheep in overcrowded conditions.

Great Northern Railway Company, Gilbey v (1919-20) XXXVI TLR 562 HC KBD Rail company not liable in negligence for stage props carried by passenger as personal luggage though were not personal luggage.

Great Northern Railway Company, Maxey Drainage Board v (1912) 76 JP 236 HC KBD Landowner entitled to do what is necessary and reasonable to protect land from expected flooding.

Great Western Rail Co and another, Smith v [1926] All ER 242; (1926) 135 LTR 112; (1925-26) XLII TLR 391 HC KBD Railway company not liable for continuance of nuisance where took all reasonable steps regarding same; party consigning leaking oil tank to rail carriers which resulted in injury to third party liable in nuisance.

Great Western Rail Co, Jenkins v [1911-13] All ER 216; [1912] 1 KB 525; (1911) 46 LJ 804; (1912) 81 LJKB 378 (1911-12) 105 LTR 882 CA Not liable in respect of injury to child wandering from where had licence to play.

Great Western Rail Co, McDowall v [1900-03] All ER 593; [1903] 2 KB 331; (1903) 38 LJ 316; [1903] 72 LJKB 652; (1903) LXXXVIII LTR 825; (1902-03) 47 SJ 603; (1902-03) XIX TLR 552; (1903) WN (I) 117 CA Railway company not liable for unforeseen acts of trespassers where took all reasonable precautions.

Great Western Railway Co, Farrugia v [1947] 2 All ER 565 CA Person creating risk on highway owes duty of care to others thereon/nearby even if other trespasser or presence otherwise unlawful.

Great Western Railway Co, Liddiatt v [1946] LJNCCR 22 CyCt Rail company liable for negligent operation of accommodation crossing.

Great Western Railway Co, McDowall v [1902] 1 KB 618; [1902] 71 LJCL 330; (1902) LXXXVI LTR 558; (1901-02) XVIII TLR 340 HC KBD Railway company liable for acts of trespassers where did not take all reasonable precautions.

Great Western Railway Company v Donald Macpherson and Co (Lim) (1918) CC Rep VII 19 CyCt Consignor liable to common carrier for loss occasioned by leakage from consigned goods onto other goods carried even though was no evidence of negligence on part of consignor.

Great Western Railway Company, Forbes, Abbott, and Lennard Limited v (1928) 138 LTR 286 CA Chelsea Dock-owners not liable for negligence of their servants by virtue of exemption clause in their by-laws.

Great Western Railway Company, Forbes, Abbott, and Lennard, Limited v [1927] 96 LJCL 995; (1926-27) XLIII TLR 769 HC KBD Chelsea Dock-owners liable for negligence of their servants notwithstanding attempt to exempt liability by way of exemption clause.

Great Western Railway Company, Hyett v [1947] 2 All ER 264; [1948] 1 KB 345; [1947] 116 LJR 1243; (1947) 177 LTR 178; (1947) 91 SJ 434; (1947) LXIII TLR 411; (1947) WN (I) 220 CA Invitors owed duty of reasonable care to protect invitee; invitee injured while seeking to extinguish fire on invitor's premises could recover damages.

Great Western Railway Company, Johnston v (1904) 39 LJ 224; [1904] 73 LJCL 568; (1904-05) XCI LTR 157; (1903-04) 48 SJ 435 CA On appropriate damages for personal injuries resulting in loss of earning capacity.

Great Western Railway Company, Jones v [1924-35] All ER 462; (1931) 144 LTR 194; (1930-31) XLVII TLR 39 HL Fatal accident damages allowed in respect of accident to which no witnesses in action to which defence submitted was no case to answer.

Great Western Railway Company, Liddiatt v [1946] KB 545; [1946] LJNCCR 94; (1946) 175 LTR 224; (1946) 90 SJ 369; (1945-46) LXII TLR 345 CA Closeness of accommodation crossing to level crossing traversed by public carriageway did not place special duty of care on railway company.

Great Western Railway Company, Lory v [1942] 1 All ER 230; (1943) 93 LJ 116; (1942) WN (I) 73 HC KBD Charitable/voluntary pensions deductible from fatal accident damages.

Great Western Railway Company, Norman v [1914-17] All ER 205; (1914) CC Rep III 102; [1915] 1 KB 584; (1914) 49 LJ 638; [1915] 84 LJKB 598; (1914) 110 LTR 306; (1914-15) XXXI TLR 53; (1914) WN (I) 415 CA Duty of railway company to invitees same as that of shopkeeper to invitees.

Great Western Railway Company, Norman v [1914] 2 KB 153; [1914] 83 LJKB 669; (1913-14) XXX TLR 241; (1914) WN (I) 15 HC KBD Duty of railway company to invitees.

Great Western Railway Company, Ormiston v [1917] 86 LJCL 759; (1917) 116 LTR 479; (1916-17) XXXIII TLR 171 HC KBD Railway company servant cannot arrest passenger for travelling without proper fare unless passenger refuses to show ticket and disclose name and address but what servant says in course of arrest can only be slanderous if is special damage.

Great Western Railway Company, Trinder v (1918-19) XXXV TLR 291 HC KBD Bus company not liable for injury to passenger on upper level hit by tree which had been cut back by company and where driver not negligent/company unaware was overhanging tree.

Great Western Railway Company, Trubyfield and another v [1937] 4 All ER 614; (1937) 84 LJ 420; (1938) 158 LTR 135; (1937) 81 SJ 1002; (1937-38) LIV TLR 221; (1938) WN (I) 12 HC KBD On appropriate fatal accident damages to administrator of infant daughter's estate where daughter killed through negligence of rail company's driver.

Great Western Railway Company, United Machine Tool Company v (1913-14) XXX TLR 312 HC KBD Damages for apparently negligent damage to goods while being consigned by railway.

Great Western Railway Company, Vosper v (1927) 64 LJ 93; (1928) 97 LJCL 51; (1927) 137 LTR 520; (1927) 71 SJ 605; (1926-27) XLIII TLR 738; (1927) WN (I) 237 HC KBD Recovery of damages for loss of passenger's luggage which rail company failed to prove was through passenger's negligence.

Great Western Railway, Knight v [1942] 2 All ER 286; [1943] KB 105; [1943] 112 LJ 321; (1943) 93 LJ 109; (1942) 167 LTR 71; (1942) 86 SJ 331; (1941-42) LVIII TLR 352 HC KBD Is no duty upon train drivers to keep to speed such that can stop within limits of sight.

Greater London Council and another, H and N Emanuel Ltd v [1971] 2 All ER 835; (1971) 121 NLJ 226; (1971) 115 SJ 226 CA Occupier liable for negligent escape of fire by anyone on land with consent save strangers (or those with consent who act as strangers).

Greater London Council and another, H and N Emanuel Ltd v (1970) 120 NLJ 707t; (1970) 114 SJ 653 HC QBD Occupier liable for negligent escape of fire by non-stranger on land.

Greater London Council and another, Tate and Lyle Food and Distribution Ltd v [1981] 3 All ER 716 HC QBD On damages for waste of managerial time in resolving problem created by negligent act; on awarding interest on damages in commercial cases.

Greater London Council and another, Tate and Lyle Industries Ltd and another v [1983] 1 All ER 1159; [1983] 2 AC 509; (1983) 127 SJ 257 HL Inapplicability of defence of statutory authority in public nuisance action.

Greater Nottingham Co-operative Society Ltd v Cementation Piling and Foundations Ltd and others [1988] 2 All ER 971; (1988) 138 NLJ 112; [1989] QB 71; (1988) 132 SJ 754; [1988] 3 WLR 396 CA Minus contractual obligation economic loss generally irrecoverable.

Greatness Timber Co, Ltd, Goodchild v [1968] 2 All ER 25; [1968] 2 QB 372; (1968) 112 SJ 192; [1968] 2 WLR 1283 CA Evidence unnecessary to decide if limitation applied.

Greaves and Co (Contractors) Ltd v Baynham Meikle and Partners [1975] 3 All ER 99 CA Standards expected of professional depend on case — special cases may create special duty.

Grech v Odhams Press Ltd and another; Addis v Odhams Press Ltd and another [1958] 2 All ER 462; (1958) 108 LJ 424; [1958] 2 QB 275; (1958) 102 SJ 453 CA Reporting of untrue words can be fair comment.

Grech v Odhams Press Ltd and another; Addis v Same [1957] 3 All ER 556; [1958] 1 QB 310; (1957) 101 SJ 921 HC QBD Reporting of untrue words can be fair comment.

Green and another v Hills (1969) 113 SJ 385 HC QBD Not negligent for epileptic subject to automatism to go out unaccompanied.

Green and another v The Jockey Club (1975) 119 SJ 258 HC QBD Horse trainer (as possessor of chattel-horse) could sue Jockey Club for negligent injury to horse whilst latter being drug-tested.

Green and Edwards Limited, Fagan v (1926) 134 LTR 191; (1925) WN (I) 266 HC KBD Non-liability of (non-common) carrier-bailees for loss of goods through fire caused by own servant's negligence as had exempted selves from liability in contract.

Green and others (No 3), Midland Bank Trust Co Ltd and another v [1979] 2 All ER 193; (1979) 123 SJ 306; [1979] 2 WLR 594 HC ChD Husband and wife can be liable for tortious conspiracy.

Green and Sons (a firm), Scott v (1969) 119 NLJ 81t; (1969) 113 SJ 73; [1969] 1 WLR 301 CA Liable (under Highways Act 1959, s 154(5)) for not keeping flagstone in good repair only if negligence/nuisance element present.

Green v Bunce [1936] LJNCCR 349 CyCt Lorry driver negligent where failed to apply brakes when swerving to avoid pedestrian and so ended up driving onto pavement, there striking the plaintiff.

Green v De Havilland and another (1968) 112 SJ 766 HC QBD On rôle of jury in malicious prosecution action.

Green v Fibreglass, Ltd [1958] 2 All ER 521; (1958) 108 LJ 473; [1958] 2 QB 245; (1958) 102 SJ 472 HC QBD Occupier not liable for negligence of competent contractor employed to do work requiring expert knowledge.

Green v Garbutt and others (1911-12) XXVIII TLR 575 CA Person bringing false imprisonment action on foot of detention for alleged felony allowed seek details of alleged felony plus basis for suspecting him but not identity of persons who informed on him.

Green v Green (1924) CC Rep XIII 50 CyCt Husband could not bring action of ejectment against wife.

Green v Matthews and Co (1929-30) XLVI TLR 206 HC ChD Cannot claim right to pollute stream/waterway whether by prescription/under lost grant.

Green v Simmonds (1926) 62 LJ ccr74 CyCt Was assault where person injured self in course of reaction to stated intention of another to strike same.

Greene v Chelsea Borough Council [1954] 2 All ER 318; (1954) 118 JP 346; [1954] 2 QB 127; (1954) 98 SJ 389; [1954] 3 WLR 12 CA Requisitioning authority owed duty to residents as licensees; negligent for failing to remedy foreseeable danger.

Greenhalgh v British Railways Board [1969] 2 QB 286; (1969) 113 SJ 108; [1969] 2 WLR 892 CA Non-liability under Railways Clauses Consolidation Act 1845/Occupiers' Liability Act 1957 for injury sustained by person using disrepaired public right of way.

Greenhalgh v Mallard [1947] 2 All ER 255 CA Res judicata where having pleaded unlawful purpose or unlawful means later bring action pleading unlawful purpose and unlawful means.

Greenlands (Limited) v Wilmshurst and others (1912-13) XXIX TLR 64 HC KBD Statements of person acting as confidential agent of member of trade association not privileged.

Greenlands, Limited v Wilmshurst and the London Association for Protection of Trade and another [1913] 3 KB 507; (1913) 48 LJ 471; [1914] 83 LJKB 1; (1913-14) 109 LTR 487; (1912-13) 57 SJ 740; (1912-13) XXIX TLR 685 CA Statements of person acting as confidential agent of member of trade association not privileged.

Greenlands, Limited, London Association for Protection of Trade and another v [1916-17] All ER 452; [1916] 2 AC 15; (1916) 51 LJ 77; [1916] 85 LJKB 698; (1916) 114 LTR 434; (1915-16) 60 SJ 272; (1915-16) XXXII TLR 281; (1916) WN (I) 45 HL On privilege attaching to communication by trade protection society on foot of bona fide enquiry by trader as to creditworthiness of another trader.

Greenslade and another v Swaffer and others; Same v World's Press News Publishing Co, Ltd and another [1955] 3 All ER 200; (1955) 105 LJ 536; (1955) 99 SJ 725; [1955] 1 WLR 1109 CA On facts to support innuendo (and striking out where not there).

Greenwell and another v Howell and another [1900] 69 LJCL 461; (1899-1900) XVI TLR 235 CA County surveyor/deputy clerk committing trespass for purpose of bringing test action protected by provisions of Public Authorities Protection Act 1893.

Greenwell v Prison Commissioners (1951) 101 LJ 486 CyCt Prison Commissioners liable in negligence for damage occasioned by Borstal inmates to third person's property in course of escape.

Greenwell v Welch (1904-05) 49 SJ 538 HC KBD Not allowed to treat as distress what have dealt with as trespass.

Greenwood (Lord) and others, De Jetley Marks v [1936] 1 All ER 863 HC KBD Must be breach of contract before can sue for conspiracy to cause breach of contract.

Greenwood v Atherton (1939) 103 JP 41; [1939] 1 KB 388; [1939] 108 LJCL 165; (1939) 160 LTR 37; (1938-39) LV TLR 222; (1938) WN (I) 410 CA Public authority limitation applied to managers of non-provided public elementary school (and here barred out-of-time action for negligence).

Greenwood v Atherton (1938) 85 LJ 328 HC KBD Public authority limitation applied to managers of non-provided public elementary school (and here barred out-of-time action for negligence).

Greenwood v Central Service Company, Limited and another [1940] 2 KB 447; (1940) 163 LTR 414 CA Non-liability of council for injury sustained in street 'blacked out' pursuant to emergency legislation.

Greenwood, Yardy v [1935] LJNCCA 218; (1935) 79 SJ 363 CA Inappropriate staying of action for assault so that prosecution for causing grievous bodily harm with intent/causing grievous bodily harm might be brought.

Gregory and another, Prince and another v [1959] 1 All ER 133; (1959) 103 SJ 130 CA Owner/occupier not liable for accident occurring through children playing with lime mortar left outside premises pending repairs.

Gregory v Kelly (1978) 128 NLJ 488t; [1978] RTR 426 HC QBD Plaintiff-passenger/defendant-driver 40%/60% liable for injuries/losses arising from collision when travelling in car (plaintiff without seat belt) in car without footbrake: defendant precluded statutorily from pleading volenti non fit injuria.

Gregory v Tarlo (1964) 108 SJ 219 HC QBD Damages awarded against solicitor for failure to prosecute client's claim within statutorily allowed period.

Gregory, Henty v (1915) CC Rep IV 67 CyCt Damages recoverable from owner of shipwreck for loss suffered through damage to groynes on foreshore by shipwreck.

Grenier, Prefontaine v [1907] AC 101; [1907] 76 LJPC 4; (1906-07) XCV LTR 623; (1906-07) XXIII TLR 27 PC President of banking company not deemed negligent for having trusted cashier (lead executive officer after directors).

Grenville Hotel, (Bude) Limited, Behrens v (1924-25) 69 SJ 346 HC KBD Hoteliers liable for loss of case of jewellery clearly left with them for safe keeping.

Grey v Gee Cars, Ltd (1940) 84 SJ 538 HC KBD Car hire firm not liable in negligence for loss occasioned to client by way of dishonest company chauffeur.

Greyvensteyn (Samuel Jacobus) v Daniel Wilhelmus Hattingh and Others [1911] AC 355; (1911) 80 LJPC 158; (1910-11) XXVII TLR 358 PC Not liable for results of driving locusts from one's property in act of self-protection.

Grove v Eastern Gas Board [1951] 2 KB 586; (1951) WN (I) 312 HC KBD Forcible entry by Gas Board officials to inspect supply pipes/gas meter and empty coins from meter not trespass.

Grove v Eastern Gas Board [1952] 1 KB 77; (1951) 101 LJ 331; (1951) 95 SJ 789; (1951) WN (I) 615 CA Forcible entry by Gas Board officials to inspect supply pipes/gas meter and empty coins from meter not trespass.

Groves v Western Mansions (Limited) (1917) CC Rep VI 5; (1916-17) XXXIII TLR 76 HC KBD Tenant's wife injuring self on broken stairs failed in negligence action against landlord as could not prove was concealed trap.

Grubb v Bristol United Press, Ltd [1962] 2 All ER 380; (1962) 112 LJ 369; [1963] 1 QB 309; (1962) 106 SJ 262 CA On innuendo in libel cases.

Grundy and another, Boots, Cash Chemists (Lancashire) (Limited), and others v (1900) 35 LJ 413; (1900) LXXXII LTR 769; (1899-1900) XVI TLR 457; (1900) WN (I) 142 HC QBD Cannot bring action against persons combining to induce other persons not to trade with third party.

Grunnell v Welch [1905] 2 KB 650; (1905-06) 54 WR 216 HC KBD Trespass ab initio in proceeding under first trespass warrant.

Grunnell v Welch (1905-06) 54 WR 581 CA Trespass ab initio in proceeding under first trespass warrant.

Grünhalle Lager International and another, Löwenbräu München and another v (1974) 118 SJ 50 HC ChD Interlocutory injunction to Löwenbräu München beer to restrain sales of Grünhalle Löwenbräu pending full passing off action.

Guardian Assurance plc and others, Spring v [1992] TLR 46 HC QBD Employer furnishing reference to prospective employer for employee liable for breach of duty of care to latter.

Guardian Assurance plc and others, Spring v [1994] 3 All ER 129; [1995] 2 AC 296; (1994) 144 NLJ 971; (1994) 138 SJ LB 183; [1994] TLR 381; [1994] 3 WLR 354 HL Employer under duty of care not to make negligent mis-statement when giving character reference; reasonable care requirement of employer may be implied term of contract.

Guardian Assurance plc and others, Spring v [1993] 2 All ER 273; [1992] TLR 628 CA Test for malice in malicious falsehood same as that in libel and slander; referee owes no duty of care in negligence to subject of reference when preparing or giving reference.

Guardian Newspapers Ltd, Bennett and others v [1995] TLR 719 HC QBD Were not allowed greater leeway in criticisms of public figures before what said could be construed as libellous.

Guardian Newspapers Ltd, Bennett and others v [1997] TLR 104 CA On relevant considerations when determining distress occasioned by libel.

Guardians of City of London, Guardians of Southwark Union v [1906] 2 KB 112 CA Husband ordering drunken (and later adulterous) wife from home was in desertion for purposes of Poor Removal Act, s 3.

Guildford Gas Light and Coke Co, Buckland v [1948] 2 All ER 1086; (1949) 113 JP 44; [1949] 1 KB 410; (1948) WN (I) 488 HC KBD Electricity company liable for child's electrocution where allowed tree grow too closely to and obscure electric wires even if child was trespasser.

Guilfoyle v Port of London Authority [1931] All ER 365; (1931) 95 JP 217; (1932) 101 LJCL 91; (1931-32) XLVIII TLR 55 HC KBD Port Authority liable for misfeasance/nonfeasance of bridge.

Guinnear v LPT Board (1948) 98 LJ 217 HC KBD Fifty percent of damages otherwise available to plaintiff who was negligent in boarding a moving bus whose driver in turn was negligent for moving on without proper regard for plaintiff's safety.

Gulf Oil (GB) Ltd v Page and others [1987] 3 All ER 14; [1987] Ch 327; (1987) 137 NLJ 409; (1987) 131 SJ 695 CA Where conspiracy to injure injunction is available to restrain publication, even one it is later hoped to justify.

Gulf Oil Refining Ltd and another, Thomas v (1979) 123 SJ 787 HC QBD Landowner may abstract water from under own land for whatever reason.

Gulf Oil Refining Ltd, Allen v [1981] 1 All ER 353; [1981] AC 1001; (1981) 131 NLJ 140; (1981) 125 SJ 101; [1981] 2 WLR 188 HL Statutory immunity for activities at oil refinery of which nuisance inevitable consequence.

Hadmor Productions Ltd and others v Hamilton and another (1982) 132 NLJ 348; [1982] 2 WLR 322 HL While trade union might be guilty of unlawful interference (via intimidation) with contract between television companies was immune from liability as acting in connection with trade dispute.

Hadmor Productions Ltd and others v Hamilton and others (1981) 131 NLJ 445; [1981] 3 WLR 139 CA Trade union liable for unlawful interference with contract between television companies where was not acting in connection with trade dispute.

Hadow and others, Fraser-Armstrong v [1994] TLR 35 CA Not proper to seek to defend self by way of libel action (through reliance upon qualified privilege) from criticisms that were in fact true.

Hadwell v Righton (1907) 71 JP 499; [1907] 2 KB 345; [1907] 76 LJKB 891; (1906-07) XXIII TLR 548 HC KBD Owner of fowl not liable for injury caused by same while trespassing on highway footpath as was too remote.

Haggar v De Placido [1972] 2 All ER 1029; (1972) 116 SJ 396; [1972] 1 WLR 716 CrCt Victim may recover costs/losses of third parties to whom has legal liability for reasonable costs/losses they suffered (even if family members).

Hague v Deputy Governor of Parkhurst Prison and others; Weldon v Home Office [1991] 3 All ER 733; [1992] 1 AC 58 (also HC QBD/CA); (1991) 141 NLJ 1185; [1991] 3 WLR 340 HL Party cannot launch private law claim for breach of statutory duty unless legislature intended it so; prisoner lawfully imprisoned cannot sue for false imprisonment in respect of residual liberty.

Hague v Doncaster Rural District Council (1909) 73 JP 69; (1909) C LTR 121; (1908-09) 53 SJ 135; (1908-09) XXV TLR 130 HC KBD Public authority limitation applicable but as action concerned ongoing damage (pollution of stream) was of no effect.

Haigh v Deudraeth Rural District Council [1945] 2 All ER 661; (1946) 110 JP 97; (1946) 96 LJ 213; (1946) 174 LTR 243; (1945) 89 SJ 579 HC ChD Injunction against local authority (having same liability as private individual) to prevent escape of sewage into river.

Haimes v Watson [1981] RTR 90 CA Horse rider not negligent where collision occurred after horse shied.

Haines v Minister of Pensions (1944-45) LXI TLR 181 HC KBD On recovery for nervous debility arising from civil defence duties.

Haines, Allason v (1995) 145 NLJ 1576; [1995] TLR 438 HC QBD Member of Parliament's libel action to be stayed if Member's privilege precludes defendants from putting forward their preferred defence.

Haiste Ltd, Birse Construction Ltd v; Watson and others (third parties) [1995] TLR 666; [1996] 1 WLR 675 CA Physical faults in reservoir/cost of building new reservoir (losses suffered by two parties respectively) not 'the same damage' so defendant engineers could not recover contribution from third party engineer under Civil Liability (Contribution) Act 1978, s 1(1).

Hajjar and others (No 2), Allied Arab Bank Ltd v [1988] QB 944; (1988) 132 SJ 1148; [1988] 3 WLR 533 HC QBD Tort of conspiracy only occurs if injury to victim was directly intended by conspirators — if (as here) was side-effect of alleged conspiracy principally intended to benefit others (not injure victim) tort of conspiracy does not arise.

Hale v Hants and Dorset Motor Services, Ltd and another (1948) 112 JP 47 CA On liability of highway authority/omnibus driver for injury to upstairs passenger on omnibus struck by overhanging branches of tree.

Hale v Jennings Brothers [1938] 1 All ER 579; (1938) 85 LJ 157; (1938) 82 SJ 193 CA Rylands v Fletcher applied in case of defective chair-o-plane.

Hale v Jennings Brothers [1937] LJNCCR 228 CyCt Fairground operators not liable in negligence/ nuisance for injuries suffered by woman when 'chair-o-plane' (which became detached as result of its occupant's recklessness) struck her, there being no latent defect in the 'chair-o-plane' machine which was not dangerous in itself and where machine not operated negligently.

Hale, Sigley v [1938] 3 All ER 87; (1937-38) LIV TLR 967 CA No payment into court possible in case of joint tortfeasors.

Hales v Kerr [1908] 2 KB 601; [1908] 77 LJCL 870; (1908-09) XCIX LTR 364; (1907-08) XXIV TLR 779 HC KBD Evidence that pointed to continued negligent practice admissible to prove negligence.

Hales, Re Wykeham Terrace, Brighton, ex parte Territorial Auxiliary and Volunteer Reserve Association for the South East Territorial Association v (1969) 113 SJ 921 HC ChD Refusal to restrain trespass by way of ex parte application.

Haley v London Electricity Board [1963] 3 All ER 1003; (1964) 128 JP 162; (1964) 114 LJ 24; [1964] 2 QB 121; (1963) 107 SJ 1001; [1964] 2 WLR 444 CA Corporation doing streetworks owed no special duty of care to the blind.

Haley v London Electricity Board (1965) 109 SJ 295 CA On appropriate damages for blind person rendered deaf through negligence of another.

Haley v London Electricity Board (1963) 107 SJ 416 HC QBD Corporation doing streetworks owed no special duty of care to the blind.

Haley v London Electricity Board [1964] 3 All ER 185; [1965] AC 778; (1965) 129 JP 14; (1964) 114 LJ 585; (1964) 108 SJ 637; [1964] 3 WLR 479 HL Persons doing street works owed duty of care to blind users of highway.

Haley v London Electricity Board (1964) 108 SJ 1013 HC QBD On appropriate damages for blind person essentially rendered deaf by negligence of another.

Halford v Brookes and another [1991] 3 All ER 559; (1991) 141 NLJ 1367g; [1991] 1 WLR 428 CA Legal advice unnecessary for there to be knowledge of facts causing limitation period to run; ignorance of law relevant when deciding to disapply limitation period.

Halifax Corporation, Baldwin's, Limited v (1916) 80 JP 357; [1916] 85 LJKB 1769 HC KBD Lack of care in technical design of road was misfeasance for which liable in damages to party injured in consequence.

Hall and another, Lawrence v (1928) 72 SJ 87 HC KBD Letter by club secretary written in context of leasing of premises and in which it was implied (according to the plaintiff-solicitor) that he was incompetent was privileged/not motivated by malice.

Hall and Co, Ltd v Pearlberg [1956] 1 All ER 297; (1956) 100 SJ 187; [1956] 1 WLR 244 HC QBD On income/profits taxes when gauging damages.

Hall and others, Percy and another v [1996] 4 All ER 523; (1996) TLR 31/5/96; [1997] 3 WLR 573 CA Bona fide actions under bye-law later deemed invalid did not render persons effecting those actions liable in tort.

Hall and Pickles Ltd, Hart v; George Reyner and Co Ltd (second defendants and third parties) [1968] 3 All ER 291; (1968) 118 NLJ 980 [1969] 1 QB 405; [1968] 3 WLR 744 CA Dismissal of action against one joint tortfeasor does not mean not liable to other joint tortfeasors.

Hall and Wife v Lees and others (1903-04) 48 SJ 638 CA Nursing association not liable for negligence of trained nurses it supplied as agreement was to provide nurse and it exercised reasonable care in doing so.

Hall v Avon Area Health Authority (Teaching) (1980) 124 SJ 293; [1980] 1 WLR 481 CA Request that medical examination by doctor nominated by other party to action be conducted in presence of own doctor not reasonable/granted.

Hall v Barrow-in-Furness Corporation [1937] LJNCCR 157 CyCt Corporation not liable in negligence for damage to window by stone thrown up by car passing area on road where corporation had recently been doing roadworks.

Hall v Beckenham Corporation [1949] 1 All ER 423; (1949) 113 JP 179; [1949] 1 KB 716; [1949] 118 LJR 965; (1949) LXV TLR 146; (1949) WN (I) 74 HC KBD Local authority not liable for nuisance of persons flying model aeroplanes in public park.

Hall v Kingston and St Andrew Corporation [1941] 2 All ER 1; [1941] AC 284; (1940-41) LVII TLR 397 PC Corporation liable for servant's negligence.

Hall v Meyrick [1957] 1 All ER 208; (1957) 107 LJ 74; [1957] 2 QB 455; (1957) 101 SJ 229; [1957] 2 WLR 458 HC QBD Solicitor's negligent failure to advise parties that marriage revoked earlier wills he drafted for them meant liable for damages suffered upon intestacy.

Harris v Perry and Co [1903] 2 KB 219; [1903] 72 LJKB 725; (1903-04) LXXXIX LTR 174; (1902-03) XIX TLR 537 CA Contractor liable for servant's failure to take reasonable care of person travelling on engine.

Harris v Thompson [1938] LJNCCR 69 CyCt Person driving uninsured vehicle could recover damages in negligence against person with whom collided even though should not have been driving uninsured vehicle on road (as was not causative factor).

Harris v Warren and Phillips (1918) 53 LJ 213; [1918] 87 LJCh 491; (1918-19) 119 LTR 217; (1917-18) 62 SJ 568; (1917-18) XXXIV TLR 440; (1918) WN (I) 173 HC ChD Failed passing off action against persons who had acquired copyright over old song newly publishing same.

Harris, C and T Harris (Calne), Limited v (1934) 78 SJ 13; (1933-34) L TLR 123 HC ChD Failed action to prevent person using own name where was no real risk of confusion/passing off.

Harris, C and T Harris (Calne), Limited v (1933-34) L TLR 338 CA Failed action to prevent person using own name where was no real risk of confusion/passing off.

Harris, Gillingham v (1949) 99 LJ 416 CyCt Person using major road enjoys no 'right of the road'.

Harris, Harris (an infant) v (1972) 122 NLJ 1061; (1972) 116 SJ 904 CA On awarding damages for loss of marriage prospects as result of injuries suffered through another's negligence.

Harris (an infant) v Harris (1972) 122 NLJ 1061; (1972) 116 SJ 904 CA On awarding damages for loss of marriage prospects as result of injuries suffered through another's negligence.

Harris, Hill v [1965] 2 All ER 359; [1965] 2 QB 601; [1965] 2 WLR 1331 CA Sub-lessee's solicitor negligent if fails to inspect head lease for covenants.

Harris, Lowther v (1926-27) XLIII TLR 24 HC KBD Successful action for conversion of tapestries by antique dealer; not estopped from recovering damages for conversion of tapestry which never represented agent had authority to sell.

Harris, Newman and Co v Hayles (Cuthbert) (1914) CC Rep III 90 CyCt High Bailiff held to be negligent as regards execution of court judgment.

Harris, Smith v [1939] 3 All ER 960; (1939) 83 SJ 730 CA Equal blame apportioned between motorcyclists involved in collision.

Harrison and another, Cunningham v [1973] 3 All ER 463; (1973) 123 NLJ 542t; [1973] QB 942; (1973) 117 SJ 547; [1973] 3 WLR 97 CA Damages not reduced by ex-gratia payments from employer; damages for nursing/attendants/accommodation to be reasonable.

Harrison v British Railways Board and others [1981] 3 All ER 679 HC QBD Rescued person may (as here) owe duty of care towards rescuer who may therefore recover damages for injuries suffered in course of rescue.

Harrison v Jackson [1947] LJNCCR 242 CyCt Person who failed to take reasonable care when having cattle driven across highway liable in negligence for motor collision which occurred.

Harrison v Stepney Borough Council (1942) 86 SJ 234 HC KBD Council which had taken adequate steps to prevent accident arising not liable for injury suffered by person who slipped on soap at public baths.

Harrison v Surrey County Council and others [1994] 2 FCR 1269; [1994] TLR 43 HC QBD Local authority liable for negligent misstatement of employee as to reliability of registered child-minder about whom employee knew there were doubts.

Harrison v Vincent and others [1982] RTR 8 CA Ordinary standard of care applied where defect in sports motor vehicle was workshop defect; volenti non fit injuria inapplicable where person claimed as being subject to doctrine unaware of facts presenting risk.

Harrison v Ward [1939] LJNCCR 160 CyCt Doctor liable for increased suffering caused to patient by his negligent treatment of same.

Harrison, Brown v (1947) 97 LJ 361; (1947) 177 LTR 281; (1947) LXIII TLR 484; (1947) WN (I) 191 CA Owner of dying tree liable for injury sustained by person on highway on whom fell as ought to have realised and remedied danger tree posed.

Harrison, Hambridge v (1973) 117 SJ 343 CA On appropriate personal injury damages for person who endured personality change/unhappiness with way of life; agreed medical reports must be 'agreed' — court must not have to choose between them.

Harrison, Lockhart v [1928] All ER 149; (1928) 139 LTR 521 HL Jury decision that words which need not be defamatory are not defamatory is valid — could be set aside if flew in face of reason.

Harrison, Noble v [1926] All ER 284; (1926) 90 JP 188; [1926] 2 KB 332; [1926] 95 LJCL 813; (1926) 135 LTR 325; (1925-26) 70 SJ 691; (1925-26) XLII TLR 518; (1926) WN (I) 171 HC KBD Overhanging tree not dangerous object/nuisance: no liability if falls and injures person on highway if neither knew/ought to have known might happen.

Harrison, Swindle and others v [1997] TLR 197 CA On damages recoverable by person who suffered loss as result of negligence of solicitors in context of mortgage-bridging loan-property purchase transaction.

Harrisons of Thurnscoe Ltd and others, Hole and Son (Sayers Common) Ltd and another v (1972) 116 SJ 922 HC QBD On appropriate damages following accident which demolished cottage.

Harriss and Harriss (a firm), London Congregational Union Inc v [1988] 1 All ER 15 CA Cause of action runs from time defect causes damage; plaintiff to show cause of action lies in limitation period.

Harriss and Harriss (a firm), London Congregational Union Inc v [1985] 1 All ER 335 HC QBD Cause of action ran from time defect caused damage.

Harrodian School, Harrods Ltd v (1996) TLR 3/4/96 CA Failed passing off action by Harrods' department store against private preparatory school called 'The Harrodian School'.

Harrods Limited, Brown-Thomson v (1924-25) 69 SJ 710 HC KBD Though store-owners may have been prima facie negligent in allowing dogs to be chained at store entrance, person bitten by dog at entrance might nonetheless be contributorily negligent.

Harrods Ltd v Harrodian School (1996) TLR 3/4/96 CA Failed passing off action by Harrods' department store against private preparatory school called 'The Harrodian School'.

Harrods, Ltd, Fisher v (1965-66) 116 NLJ 919; (1966) 110 SJ 133 HC QBD Store liable for not exercising adequate care in marketing goods produced by unknown manufacturer.

Harrow Corporation, Davey v [1957] 2 All ER 305; (1957) 107 LJ 344; [1958] 1 QB 61; (1957) 101 SJ 405 CA Nuisance to owner of adjoining property if planted/self-sown trees on one's property cause of damage on other's.

Harrow London Borough Council, P and others v [1993] 2 FCR 341; [1993] 1 FLR 723; [1992] TLR 215 HC QBD Local authority not guilty of breaching statutory duty where placed children (in care/control of parents) with special educational needs in state-approved boarding school where were sexually abused by headmaster.

Harry and Co v Tuck (1912) CC Rep I 60 CyCt Dog-owner not liable for injury occasioned by dog absent interference by owner.

Hart and another v Rogers (1916) 114 LTR 329 HC KBD Landlord of house let in flats owed duty to keep roof in good repair.

Hart v Hall and Pickles Ltd; George Reyner and Co Ltd (second defendants and third parties) [1968] 3 All ER 291; (1968) 118 NLJ 980 [1969] 1 QB 405; [1968] 3 WLR 744 CA Dismissal of action against one joint tortfeasor does not mean not liable to other joint tortfeasors.

Hart v Liverpool Corporation (1949) 99 LJ 594; (1949) LXV TLR 677 CA Tenant coming back to flat by different approach to normal was nonetheless invitee and hole into which fell was unusual danger so landlord liable.

Hart v St Marylebone Borough Council (1912) 76 JP 257 HC KBD Recovery of cost of repairs necessitated by subsidence in road as result of negligent inattention of council to sewer repair.

Harte and others, Portland Managements Ltd v [1976] 1 All ER 225 CA Trespasser in possession to confess/avoid trespass if absolute owner proves title/intent to regain possession; Court of Appeal can order new trial even if defendant had adduced no evidence at original hearing.

Hartin v London County Council (1926-30) XXVIII Cox CC 618; (1929) 93 JP 160; (1929) 141 LTR 120 HC KBD Special public authority limitation period inapplicable to malicious prosecution action as criminal prosecution not a public duty under Public Authorities Protection Act 1893.

Harwood (G) and Son, Haynes v [1934] All ER 103; [1935] 1 KB 146; (1934) 77 LJ 340; (1934) 78 LJ 323; (1935) 152 LTR 121; (1934) 78 SJ 801; (1934-35) LI TLR 100; (1934) WN (I) 208 CA Natural result of one's negligence cannot be novus actus interveniens; person leaving horses in street owes duty of care to safeguard persons using highway (including police officer chasing after bolting horse): no volenti non fit injuria by highway users.

Harwood Cash and Co (Limited), The Fine Cotton Spinners' and Doublers' Association (Limited) and John Cash and Sons (Limited) v [1907] 2 Ch 184; (1907-08) XCVII LTR 45; (1906-07) XXIII TLR 537; (1907) WN (I) 127 HC ChD Injunction granted to prevent new company using name of existing company.

Harwood, Haynes v [1934] 2 KB 240; (1934) 103 LJCL 410; (1934) 151 LTR 135; (1934) 78 SJ 384; (1933-34) L TLR 371; (1934) WN (I) 106 HC KBD Natural result of one's negligence cannot be novus actus interveniens; person leaving horses in street owes duty of care to safeguard persons using highway (including police officer chasing after bolting horse).

Hase v The London General Omnibus Company (Limited) (1906-07) XXIII TLR 616 HC KBD Not negligent of bus driver to turn bus close to kerb and so occasion injury to upstairs passenger struck by small obstruction avoidable by wider turn.

Haseldine v CA Daw and Son, Ltd and others [1941] 1 All ER 525; (1941) 91 LJ 181; (1942) 92 LJ 60; (1941) 85 SJ 265; (1940-41) LVII TLR 431 HC KBD Flatowner liable for negligence of agent contractors; owner owed duty to warn licensee of dangers of which actually knew (did not know here); defence of having employed competent independent contractor not open as only limited maintenance contract; contractor liable for defective repairs.

Haseldine v CA Daw and Son, Ltd, and others [1941] 3 All ER 156; [1941] 2 KB 343; (1941) 91 LJ 359; [1942] 111 LJ 45; (1941) 165 LTR 185; (1941-42) LVIII TLR 1 CA Flatowner's employment of competent contractors relieved liability in negligence; contractors liable to injury occasioned by negligent repairs.

Haslam, Turner v [1939] LJNCCR 267 CyCt Visitor to hotel (licensee) could recover damages from occupier where injured self on (what constituted trap) an unlit accessible flight of stairs which knew to be customarily either lit/inaccessible.

Hassall v Secretary of State for Social Security; Pether v Secretary of State for Social Security [1995] 3 All ER 909; [1995] RTR 316; [1994] TLR 667 CA Secretary of State can deduct full amount of post-accident benefits from sums awarded as personal injuries damages.

Hasselblad (GB) Ltd v Orbinson [1985] 1 All ER 173; [1985] QB 475; (1985) 129 SJ 32; [1985] 2 WLR 1 CA On privilege attaching to letter sent voluntarily to European Commission in course of essentially administrative proceedings.

Haste v Sandell Perkins Ltd [1984] 2 All ER 615; (1984) 134 NLJ 681; [1984] QB 735; (1984) 128 SJ 334; [1984] 3 WLR 73 HC QBD When benefits to be deducted from damages fully defined in Law Reform (Personal Injuries) Act 1948.

Haste, Westminster City Council v [1950] 66 (1) TLR 1083 HC ChD Company receiver personally liable in tort for non-payment of rates owed by company.

Hastings Corporation and others, Attorney-General v; Parsons and others v Same (1950) 94 SJ 225 CA Motor racing in residential area was actionable private, not public nuisance.

Hattam v National Coal Board (1978) 128 NLJ 1149t; (1978) 122 SJ 777 CA Staying of action where all evidence lost/plaintiff had received full industrial benefits since suffered workplace injury.

Havana Cigar and Tobacco Factories, Limited v Oddenino [1923] 2 Ch 243; (1923) 58 LJ 238; [1924] 93 81 (also CA); (1922-23) 67 SJ 640; (1923) WN (I) 171 HC ChD Corona cigar manufacturers could bring passing off action where person sold cigar not of their make (but of Corona size and shape) as a Corona cigar: on elements of said passing off.

Havana Cigar and Tobacco Factories, Limited v Oddenino [1924] 1 Ch 179; [1924] 93 81 (also HC ChD); (1923) 58 LJ 568; (1924) 130 LTR 428; (1923-24) XL TLR 102 CA Corona cigar manufacturers could bring passing off action where person sold cigar not of their make (but of Corona size and shape) as a Corona cigar: on elements of said passing off.

Hawes, McNeall v (1923) 58 LJ 160; [1923] 92 LJCL 729 (also HC KBD); (1922-23) 67 SJ 483; (1922-23) XXXIX TLR 362; (1923) WN (I) 170 CA Non-liability of husband for tortious act of wife during coverture.

Hawes, McNeall v [1923] 1 KB 273; [1923] 92 LJCL 729 (also CA); (1922-23) 67 SJ 316; (1922-23) XXXIX TLR 167; (1923) WN (I) 14 HC KBD Liability of husband for tortious act of wife during coverture.

Hawker v Stourfield Park Hotel Company (1900) WN (I) 51 HC ChD Can restrain making of untrue statement even if not libellous/defamatory if statement operates to injure another.

Hawkes v Torquay Corporation (1938) 86 LJ 294 HC KBD Public Authorities Protection Act provisions did not apply to pavilion built and operated by local authority.

Hawkins and Co, King v (1982) 132 NLJ 322 HC QBD On damages available from solicitor-conveyancers to person who received smaller piece of land of different quality to that anticipated through their negligence.

Hawkins v Coulsdon and Purley Urban District Council [1953] 2 All ER 364; (1953) 117 JP 360; (1953) 103 LJ 414; [1954] 1 QB 319; (1953) 97 SJ 473; [1953] 1 WLR 882 HC QBD Licensee did not accept at night risks which were obvious by day; occupier owed duty to remedy risks which reasonable man would have recognised.

Hawkins v Coulsdon and Purley Urban District Council [1954] 1 All ER 97; (1954) 118 JP 101; (1954) 104 LJ 25; (1954) 98 SJ 44; [1954] 2 WLR 122 CA Licensors liable in negligence where knew of physical circumstances constituting trap.

Hawkins v Express Dairy Co Ltd and Others (1940) 163 LTR 147; (1940) 84 SJ 393 HC KBD Could when assessing damages take into account misbehaviour admitted by person who was victim of libel.

Hawkins v Ian Ross (Castings) Ltd [1970] 1 All ER 180 HC QBD No reduction of damages though contributorily negligent.

Hawkins v New Mendip Engineering, Ltd [1966] 3 All ER 228; (1965-66) 116 NLJ 1377; [1966] 1 WLR 1341 CA Possibility of serious supervening illness a legitimate factor when assessing damages.

Hawley and another v Alexander and Wife (1930) 74 SJ 247 HC KBD Parents of young teenage son liable in negligence for personal injuries occasioned consequent upon their allowing son to use air-gun without adequate supervision.

Hay (or Bourhill) v Young [1942] 2 All ER 396; [1942] 111 LJ 97; (1943) 93 LJ 108; (1942) 167 LTR 261; (1942) 86 SJ 349; [1943] AC 92 HL Tortfeasor in motor vehicle collision not liable to bystander for nervous shock as not reasonably foreseeable.

Haydon v Kent County Council (1978) 142 JP 349; [1978] QB 343; (1977) 121 SJ 849; [1978] 2 WLR 485 CA Failed attempt by pedestrian injured by slipping on snowy path to prove highway authority had been negligent in giving priority to salting/sanding/gritting of highway rather than of paths.

Hayes and another, Birkett v [1982] 2 All ER 710; (1982) 126 SJ 399; [1982] TLR 157; [1982] 1 WLR 816 CA Interest usual when awarding general damages for pain/suffering/loss of amenities.

Hayes v Bowman [1989] 1 WLR 456 CA Court could (but did not here) strike out personal injuries action where want of prosecution led to increase in (loss of earnings) damages available.

Hayles (Cuthbert), Harris, Newman and Co v (1914) CC Rep III 90 CyCt High Bailiff held to be negligent as regards execution of court judgment.

Hayman and another, Lincoln v [1982] 2 All ER 819; [1982] RTR 336; (1982) 126 SJ 174; [1982] 1 WLR 488 CA Supplementary benefits to be deducted from special damages.

Haymarket Magazines Ltd, Box Television Ltd v (1997) 141 SJ LB 47; [1997] TLR 111 HC ChD Failed passing off action by owners of 'The Box' cable channel to restrain publication of unrelated magazine entitled 'The Box'.

Haynes (Claremont), Smith and another v [1991] TLR 409 HC QBD Solicitor liable in negligence to intended beneficiaries of will which ought to have prepared swiftly (given perilous health of deceased when orally communicated terms of intended but never-drafted will).

Herschthal v Stewart and Arden, Limited [1939] 4 All ER 123; [1940] 1 KB 155; (1939) 88 LJ 299; [1940] 109 LJCL 328; (1939) 161 LTR 331; (1940) 84 SJ 79; (1939-40) LVI TLR 48; (1939) WN (I) 371 HC KBD Interpretation of Donoghue v Stevenson: on intermediate examination of item.

Hertfordshire County Council and another, Collins v [1947] 1 All ER 633; (1947) 111 JP 272; [1947] KB 598; [1947] 116 LJR 789; (1947) 176 LTR 456; (1947) LXIII TLR 317; (1947) WN (I) 127 HC KBD County council negligent in operation of county council hospital/not responsible for negligence of part-time surgeon employed; amendment to statement of claim allowed as not new cause of action.

Hertfordshire County Council, Shrimpton (Florence M) (an infant by her father and next friend), Pauper, v (1911) 75 JP 201; (1911) 104 LTR 145; (1910-11) 55 SJ 270; (1910-11) XXVII TLR 251 HL Education authority liable for personal injury suffered by child on school transportation (though child not supposed to be using same).

Hertfordshire County Council, Shrimpton v (1910) 74 JP 305 CA Education authority not liable for personal injury suffered by child on school transportation (where child not supposed to be using same).

Hertfordshire County Council, Ward v (1969) 133 JP 514; (1969) 119 NLJ 272t; (1969) 113 SJ 343; [1969] 1 WLR 790 HC QBD Local education authority liable at common law for failure to adequately protect schoolchildren from reasonably foreseeable risk when playing in schoolyard before school hours.

Hertfordshire County Council, Ward v (1970) 134 JP 261; (1970) 120 NLJ 13t; (1970) 114 SJ 87; [1970] 1 WLR 356 CA Local education authority not liable at common law for injury suffered by child playing in schoolyard before school began — not inherently dangerous area/providing warder would not have prevented accident.

Hertfordshire County Council, Watt v [1954] 2 All ER 368; (1954) 118 JP 377; (1954) 98 SJ 372; [1954] 1 WLR 835 CA Not liable in negligence to fireman for injury resulting from risk that ought reasonably be assumed by fireman.

Hertfordshire County Council, Watt v [1954] 1 All ER 141; (1954) 118 JP 97; (1954) 104 LJ 376; [1954] 1 WLR 208 HC QBD Fireman has heavier burden to discharge in proving what asked to do shows employer not taking reasonable care of him.

Hesketh v Birmingham Corporation (1924) 88 JP 77; [1924] 1 KB 260; [1924] 93 LJCL 461; (1924) 130 LTR 476 CA Local authority not liable in nuisance for discharging sewer water into stream/not liable for non-feasance of drainage system.

Hesketh v Liverpool Corporation [1940] 4 All ER 429 Assizes Pilot in crash-landing not negligent simply for clipping trees he knew were there.

Hesketh v Nicholson (1940) 84 SJ 646 HC KBD Solicitor liable for failure to advise client of provisions of Public Authorities Protection Act as regards negligence action against public authority.

Heslop, Watson v [1971] RTR 308; (1971) 115 SJ 308 CA Negligent to park car in narrow, busy road at night; negligent not to have slowed down as soon as dazzled by oncoming lights.

Hesperides Hotels Ltd and another v Muftizade (1978) 142 JP 541; (1978) 122 SJ 507 HL Court could not hear action regarding conspiracy to trespass on property in foreign country but could hear action for trespass to chattels in that property.

Hett, Stubbs and Kemp (a firm), Midland Bank Trust Co Ltd and another v [1978] 3 All ER 571; [1979] Ch 384; (1978) 128 NLJ 33t; (1977) 121 SJ 830; [1978] 3 WLR 167 HC ChD Solicitor always liable in tort for failure to exercise reasonable care and skill.

Hevican v Ruane [1991] 3 All ER 65; (1991) 141 NLJ 235 HC QBD Damages for nervous shock after son's injury despite third party relaying of news as each stage in relay foreseeable; damages available for unforeseeably severe nervous shock if nervous shock foreseeable.

Hewer v Bryant [1969] 3 All ER 578; (1969) 119 NLJ 600t; [1970] 1 QB 357; (1969) 113 SJ 525; [1969] 3 WLR 425 CA 15 year old trainee on farm away from home not in parent's custody: action not barred.

Hewer v Bryant (1968) 118 NLJ 684t; [1969] 1 QB 415; (1968) 112 SJ 762; [1968] 3 WLR 910 HC QBD 15 year old trainee on farm away from home was in parent's custody: action barred.

Hewitson and another, O'Connor v [1979] Crim LR 46 CA Valid refusal of aggravated/exemplary damages to prisoner assaulted by police officer given behaviour of prisoner leading up to assault.

Hewitson v Steele and Co (1912) CC Rep I 75 CyCt Damages unavailable for skin disease occasioned by negligent cut to neck with scissors by hairdresser's aid (not direct/natural result of injury).

Hewitt v Bonvin and another [1940] 1 KB 189; [1940] 109 LJCL 223; (1939) 161 LTR 360; (1939) 83 SJ 869; (1939-40) LVI TLR 43 CA Father not liable for negligent driving of son who was neither his servant nor agent.

Hewlett v Great Central Railway Company (1915-16) 60 SJ 428; (1915-16) XXXII TLR 373; (1916) WN (I) 144 CA Railway company deemed in circumstances to be under duty to warn public of presence of post authorised by statute and maintainable by them.

Hewlett v London County Council (1908) 72 JP 136; (1907-08) XXIV TLR 331 HC KBD Defendants could plead public authority limitation despite plaintiff's claim that action brought out of time because defendants indicated wanted out of court settlement.

Hewlett, Great Central Railway Company v [1916-17] All ER 1027; [1916] 2 AC 511; (1916) 51 LJ 418; [1916] 85 LJKB 1705; (1916-17) 115 LTR 349; (1915-16) XXXII TLR 707 HL Railway company not under duty to warn public of presence of post authorised by statute and maintainable by them.

Hewson v Downes and another [1970] 1 QB 73; (1969) 119 NLJ 274t; (1969) 113 SJ 309; [1969] 2 WLR 1169 HC QBD State pension relevant to level of damages awarded to person who suffered injuries in motor car accident.

Hextall Erskine and Co (a firm), British Racing Drivers' Club Ltd and another v [1996] 3 All ER 667 HC ChD Solicitors liable for negligent advice (failed to advise directors that members required to approve certain transaction which was later rescinded by members thereby occasioning loss).

Heyman, Abbott v (1925) 60 LJ 1055 CyCt Successful action for damages for nuisances occasioned by removal of door, said removal interfering with exercise of right of way.

HG Swindells (trading as West View Garage Co), Macrae v (1954) 98 SJ 233; [1954] 1 WLR 597 HC QBD Could recover cost of hiring car where car loaned for period that own car being repaired following garage's negligence was lost through own negligence.

Hibell, Burley v (1916) CC Rep V HC KBD Where car collides into car that has broken down the driver of the latter car (even if was negligent) may recover damages from driver of former if collision could reasonably have been avoided.

Hickman, Vincent v [1936] LJNCCR 320 CyCt Dangerous parking of car in contravention of Road Traffic Act 1930, s 50, meant were guilty of breach of statutory duty for which person injured in consequence could recover damages.

Hicks and another v Chief Constable of the South Yorkshire Police; Wafer v Chief Constable of the South Yorkshire Police [1992] 1 All ER 690 CA Horror and fear not heads of damages unless result in real psychiatric damage; no damages for pain and suffering if part of death.

Hicks Anderson and Co (a firm), James McNaughton Paper Group Ltd v [1991] 1 All ER 134; (1990) 140 NLJ 1311; [1991] 2 QB 113; [1990] TLR 630; [1991] 2 WLR 641 CA Purpose of statement, relationship between maker/giver and other party, knowledge of maker/giver, size of class to which other party belongs are factors when deciding if duty of care on maker/giver of statement to unintended third party recipient.

Hicks v British Transport Commission [1958] 1 WLR 493 CA Shunter's/railway company's failure to take reasonable care of self/shunter meant both equally liable in negligence for injury of shunter.

Hicks v Meaker and Brown (1952) 102 LJ 725 CyCt Failed action in negligence in respect of damage arising from allegedly negligent disrepair of houses.

Hicks v Pier House Management Ltd (1984) 134 NLJ 657 HC QBD Employers of flat porter vicariously liable for theft by latter from flat of tenant who entrusted porter with keys while away from flat.

Hicks, Arnold and Co and another v Bloch (1964) 108 SJ 336 HC QBD Damages for trespass on firm/assault on solicitor and injunction restraining future trespass.

Hicks, Moresk Cleaners Ltd v (1965-66) 116 NLJ 1546 Assizes Architect negligent in delegating his design responsibilities to builders.

Higgins and another v North West Metropolitan Regional Hospital Board and another [1954] 1 All ER 414; (1954) 104 LJ 122; (1954) 98 SJ 147; [1954] 1 WLR 411 HC QBD Hospital specialist acting for local authority enjoys one year limitation under Limitation Act 1939, s 21(1).

Higgins v Arfon Borough Council [1975] 2 All ER 589; [1975] 1 WLR 524 HC QBD Cause of action ran from date of damage not discovery.

Higgins v Betts [1905] 2 Ch 210; (1905) XCII LTR 850; (1904-05) 49 SJ 535; (1904-05) XXI TLR 552; (1904-05) 53 WR 549 HC ChD Considerable deprivation of light rendering occupation of premises difficult is nuisance.

Higgins v Searle (1909) 73 JP 185; (1909) C LTR 280; (1908-09) XXV TLR 301 CA Owner of sow that strayed onto road which frightened horse which in turn caused motor accident found not to be negligent.

Higgins v Searle (1908) 72 JP 449 HC KBD Owner of sow that strayed onto road which frightened horse which in turn caused motor accident could be negligent.

Higgs and Hill Limited, Fishenden v (1935) 153 LTR 128 CA Interference with ancient lights sufficiently grave as to constitute nuisance.

High Commissioner for India and others v Ghosh (1959) 109 LJ 683; (1959) 103 SJ 939 CA Striking out of counter-claim for slander against High Commissioner/Union of India (sovereign immunity not waived by plaintiffs bringing action for money lent against defendants).

High Wycombe Borough Council and another, RG Stanners Ltd v (1968) 118 NLJ 614t; (1968) 112 SJ 766 HC QBD Both contractors and local authority for whom working liable for theft from warehouse effected via lean-to which council had been supposed to remove at which time warehouse was to be secured.

Higham v Stena Sealink Ltd [1996] 3 All ER 660; [1996] 1 WLR 1107 CA Cannot disregard two year limitation on personal injury actions by ferry passenger.

Highway Ironfounders (West Bromwich), Ltd, Richards v [1955] 3 All ER 205; [1955] 1 WLR 1049 CA No damages for loss of chance to provide for dependants.

Hilder v Associated Portland Cement Manufacturers, Ltd [1961] 3 All ER 709; [1955] Crim LR 725; (1961) 111 LJ 757 HC QBD Not wearing crash helmet not negligent; occupier of green on which children played owed duty to take reasonable steps to prevent injury.

Hilditch, Price v [1930] 1 Ch 500; (1930) 99 LJCh 299; (1930) WN (I) 44 HC ChD Failed action for injunction to restrain obstruction of ancient light: right to light not determined by reference to past purpose for which place used.

Hill (Gary) v Chief Constable of the South Yorkshire Police [1990] 1 All ER 1046 (1990) 134 SJ 197 CA Jury trial necessary if judge satisfied that false imprisonment claim arises; guilty plea/verdict does not preclude claim of false imprisonment.

Hill Samuel Bank Ltd and others, Morgan Crucible Co plc v [1991] 1 All ER 148; [1991] Ch 295 (also HC ChD); (1990) 140 NLJ 1605; [1990] TLR 699; [1991] 2 WLR 655 CA Duty of care on directors of/financial advisers to company not to make misleading statements to known bidder.

Hill Samuel Bank Ltd and others, Morgan Crucible Co plc v [1990] 3 All ER 330; [1991] Ch 295 (also CA); (1990) 140 NLJ 1271 HC ChD Directors of/financial advisers to company owe no duty of care to known take-over bidder in preparation of documents prepared to contest bid.

Hill v Archbold [1967] 2 WLR 1180 HC QBD Master (union) could support servant (officials) in libel action brought against latter arising from their employment.

Hill v Chief Constable of West Yorkshire [1987] 1 All ER 1173; (1987) 137 NLJ 222; [1988] QB 60; (1987) 131 SJ 626; [1987] 2 WLR 1126 CA Police do not owe public duty of care to catch unknown criminal.

Hillyer v The Governors of St Bartholmew's Hospital (1909) 73 JP 501; [1909] 2 KB 820; (1909) 44 LJ 483; [1909] 78 LJKB 958; (1909-10) 101 LTR 368; (1908-09) 53 SJ 714; (1909) WN (I) 188 CA Hospital governors not liable for injury allegedly sustained by plaintiff at hands of hospital workers.

Hilt, Whiteley, Limited v [1918] 2 KB 115; (1918) CC Rep VII 37; (1917-18) XXXIV TLR 402 HC KBD Third party buying hire-purchase item from hirer thereby repudiating hire-purchase of same could be successfully sued in detinue/conversion.

Hilt, Whiteley, Limited v [1918] 2 KB 808; (1917-18) XXXIV TLR 592 CA Third party buying hire-purchase item from hirer thereby repudiating hire-purchase of same acquired interest of hirer.

Hilton v Sutton Steam Laundry [1946] 115 LJ 33; (1946) 174 LTR 31 CA Out of time action disallowed.

Hilton v Westminster Bank, Limited (1925-26) XLII TLR 423 CA Bank were negligent to pay on cheque which customer asked to be stopped quoting wrong number but giving details which enabled bank to know which cheque wanted to be stopped.

Hilton, Westminster Bank, Limited v (1925-26) 70 SJ 1196; (1926-27) XLIII TLR 124; (1926) WN (I) 332 HL Bank not negligent in not stopping particular cheque where number of cheque were instructed to stop was not number of cheque customer wanted stopped.

Hinchcliffe, Glick v (1967) 111 SJ 927 CA Judge's words at end of criminal prosecution did enjoy absolute privilege.

Hindley v Pemberton (1957) 107 LJ ccr620 CyCt On trespass by person acting under licence.

Hindmarsh v Henry and Leigh Slater, Ltd (1965-66) 116 NLJ 868t; (1966) 110 SJ 429 CA On appropriate personal injury damages for person left with physical deformity/personality change but who could not understand consequences of his injuries.

Hinds v London Transport Executive (1978) 128 NLJ 1150t; [1979] RTR 103 CA Expert evidence as to causation unnecessary where could be determined on common sense basis.

Hines (Edith) v Tousley and another (1926) 61 LJ ccr14 CyCt Owner of normally well-behaved dog liable for damage caused by dog.

Hines v Tousley (Newell, third party) (1926) 61 LJ 491 CA Owner of normally well-behaved dog not liable for damage caused by dog.

Hines v Winnick [1947] 2 All ER 517; [1947] Ch 708; [1948] 117 LJR 187; (1947) 91 SJ 560; (1947) LXIII TLR 520; (1947) WN (I) 244 HC ChD Stage name of musician protected in passing off action.

Hinton, Oliver v (1899-1900) LXXXI LTR 212 CA Grossly careless purchaser not allowed deprive prior innocent mortgagee of her priority.

Hinz v Berry [1970] 1 All ER 1074; (1970) 120 NLJ 81t; [1970] 2 QB 40; (1970) 114 SJ 111; [1970] 2 WLR 684 CA Appropriate damages for nervous shock.

Hirsch and another v Somervell and others (1946) 90 SJ 394; (1945-46) LXII TLR 592 CA Successful appeal against striking out of false imprisonment/trespass action against successive Home Secretaries.

Hirsch and others v Somervell and others (1946) 90 SJ 369 HC ChD Striking out of false imprisonment/trespass action against successive Home Secretaries.

Hirst, Kidd and Rennie, Ltd, and another, Mitchell and another v [1936] 3 All ER 872; (1936) 82 LJ 425 HC KBD Damages for unfair/inaccurate reporting of court proceedings; judge sitting alone may apportion damages between tortfeasors.

His Majesty's Postmaster-General v Liverpool Corporation (1922) 86 JP 157; (1922) CC Rep XI 51 CA Not liable to pay for repairs caused to telegraph line where damage prompted by original negligence of Postmaster-General or those for whose acts was answerable.

HM Postmaster General v Blackpool and Fleetwood Tramroad Company, Ltd (1918) CC Rep VII 3 CyCt Tram company not liable for damage occasioned to telephone cable by escape of electricity from tram lines absent proof of negligence/non-compliance with relevant regulations.

Hoadley v Dartford District Council and another [1979] RTR 359; (1979) 123 SJ 129 CA No reduction in damages for person not wearing seat belt where no requirement that vehicle have seat belts and it did not in fact have seat belts.

Hoar, Brook v [1967] 3 All ER 395; (1967) 117 NLJ 887t; (1967) 111 SJ 634; [1967] 1 WLR 1336 HC QBD Infant in position of lodger in parent's house not in parent's custody and control.

Hoare and Co, Ltd v Sir Robert McAlpine, Sons and Co [1922] All ER 759; [1923] 1 Ch 167; [1923] 92 LJCh 81; (1923) 128 LTR 526; (1922-23) 67 SJ 146; (1922-23) XXXIX TLR 97; (1922) WN (I) 329 HC ChD Rylands v Fletcher applied to nuisance by vibration.

Hoare v Tom Pettifer Ltd et al (1984) 134 NLJ 284c CA Extension of time allowed that service of writ might be acknowledged.

Hobbs v Tinling (CT) and Co, Ltd; Hobbs v Nottingham Journal, Ltd [1929] All ER 33; (1929) 67 LJ 290; (1929) 98 LJCL 421; (1929) WN (I) 89 CA On libel; on mitigation of damages where are of bad character.

Hobbs v Tinling (CT) and Company, Limited; Hobbs v Nottingham Journal, Limited [1929] 2 KB 1 HC KBD On procedure in libel action; on mitigation of damages where are of bad character.

Hobbs, Hummingbird Motors Ltd v [1986] RTR 276 CA No misrepresentation/breach of warranty where sold second-hand car to another in bona fide but mistaken belief that odometer reading correct.

Hobson v Bartram and Sons, Ltd [1950] 1 All ER 412 CA That person is under one's control need not mean are one's agents for all purposes.

Hocking v Bell (1948) WN (I) 21 PC Successful action against negligent surgeon.

Hodder, Draper and another v [1972] 2 All ER 210; (1972) 122 NLJ 128t; [1972] 2 QB 556; (1972) 116 SJ 178; [1972] 2 WLR 992 CA Can be liable in negligence for reasonably foreseeable injury caused by tame animal.

Hodges v Harland and Wolff, Ltd [1965] 1 All ER 1086 CA Exceptional action in which trial by jury justified.

Hodges, Heath's Garage (Lim) and another v (1915) CC Rep IV 67 CyCt Owner of land adjoining adjoining highway liable in negligence for failure to fence in animals.

Hodges, Heath's Garage, Limited v [1916-17] All ER 358; (1916) 80 JP 321; [1916] 2 KB 370; (1916) 51 LJ 295; [1916] 85 LJKB 1289; (1916-17) 115 LTR 129; (1915-16) 60 SJ 554; (1915-16) XXXII TLR 570; (1916) WN (I) 229 CA Non-liability of sheep-owner for injury caused through sheep straying onto highway.

Hodges, Heath's Garages, Ltd v (1916) 80 JP 281; [1916] 1 KB 206; [1916] 85 LJKB 485; (1916) 114 LTR 507; (1915-16) 60 SJ 458; (1915-16) XXXII TLR 134; (1915) WN (I) 390 HC KBD Non-liability in nuisance/negligence of landowner adjoining highway to fence in tame animals.

Hodgkinson and Corby Ltd and another v Wards Mobility Services Ltd [1994] TLR 446; [1994] 1 WLR 1564 HC ChD Must be deception for there to be passing off (no deception here so no passing off).

Hodgson v British Arc Welding Company, Limited and Others (1946) 174 LTR 379 HC KBD Shipwrights not sub-contractors liable for injury to sub-contractor's employee.

Hodgson v Trapp and another [1988] 3 All ER 870; [1989] AC 807; [1988] 1 FLR 69; (1988) 138 NLJ 327; (1988) 132 SJ 1672; [1988] 3 WLR 1281 HL Attendance/mobility allowances deductible from personal injuries awards; damages multiplier not to be increased to allow for tax.

Hodgson's Kingston Brewery Company (Limited), Wilson and another v (1916) 80 JP 39; [1916] 85 LJKB 270; (1915-16) 113 LTR 1112; (1915-16) 60 SJ 142; (1915-16) XXXII TLR 60; (1915) WN (I) 352 HC KBD Brewery/tenant of tied pub not liable for injury suffered by independent deliverer who elected to deliver beer by particular route.

Hodkinson v Henry Wallwork and Co, Ltd [1955] 3 All ER 236 CA Contributory negligence of ninety per cent despite employer's breach of statutory duty where did something unauthorised.

Hodson-Pressinger and Betts, Sampson v [1981] 3 All ER 710; (1981) 131 NLJ 1212; (1981) 125 SJ 623 CA Damages for nuisance by noise through use of terrazza.

Hoffman v Sofaer (1982) 126 SJ 611; [1982] 1 WLR 1350 HC QBD Appropriate that United States resident suffering personal injury while in Britain be awarded damages in dollars.

Hogg, Islander Trucking Ltd (in liq) v; Robinson and Gardner Mountain (Marine) Ltd and others [1990] 1 All ER 826 HC QBD Injury caused upon procuring of voidable insurance contract.

Holdack v Bullock Bros (Electrical), Ltd and another; Martens (third party) (1964) 108 SJ 861 HC QBD Overtaker one-third liable for not sounding horn as overtook; person being overtaken two-thirds liable for not seeing overtaker/for changing course while being overtaken.

Holdack v Bullock Brothers (Electrical), Ltd, and another (Martens Third Party) (1965) 109 SJ 238 CA Was reasonable for trial judge to hold that overtaker ought to have sounded horn though was no general requirement that had to do so.

Holden v White [1982] 2 All ER 328; (1981) 131 NLJ 476; [1982] QB 679; (1982) 126 SJ 230; [1982] TLR 165; [1982] 2 WLR 1030 CA Not visitor if using public/private right of way.

Holder, Erith Corporation v [1949] 2 KB 46 CA House-owner rendered trespasser in own home by virtue of emergency (requisitioning) legislation.

Holdsworth (TW), Limited v Associated Newspapers, Limited [1938] 107 LJCL 69; (1937) 157 LTR 274; (1937) 81 SJ 685; (1936-37) LIII TLR 1029 CA On whether newspaper comments to effect that employer refusing to implement wages award/pact were libellous.

Hole and Son (Sayers Common) Ltd and another v Harrisons of Thurnscoe Ltd and others (1972) 116 SJ 922 HC QBD On appropriate damages following accident which demolished cottage.

Hole, Sadgrove v [1901] 2 KB 1; [1901] 70 LJK/QB 455; (1901) LXXXIV LTR 647; (1900-01) 45 SJ 342; (1900-01) XVII TLR 332; (1900-01) 49 WR 473 CA Absent malice communication by way of postcard was privileged.

Holgate v Bleazard [1916-17] All ER 817; (1917) CC Rep VI 13; [1917] 1 KB 443; [1917] 86 LJCL 270; (1916-17) 115 LTR 788; (1916-17) XXXIII TLR 116; (1916) WN (I) 432 HC KBD Animal-owner liable for damage caused by escaping animal (horses).

Holland and Hannen and Cubitts (Scotland) Ltd, McKew v [1969] 3 All ER 1621 HL Careless act broke causation between first injury and later injury.

Holland and Hannen and Cubitts (Southern) Ltd, and another, Braniff v [1969] 3 All ER 959; [1969] 1 WLR 1533 CA Weldon v Neal principles still generally applicable.

Holland, Hannen and Cubitts (Southern), Ltd, Savory v [1964] 3 All ER 18; [1964] 1 WLR 1158 CA Occupier owed duty of reasonable care to servant but not breached here.

Hollands and another, Kubach and another v; Frederick Allen and Sons (Poplar), Limited (Third Party) (1937) 84 LJ 157; (1937) 81 SJ 766; (1936-37) LIII TLR 1024 HC KBD Negligent suppliers of chemicals to school who were successfully sued by student injured through their negligence could not in turn recover against wholesale suppliers.

Holliday and Greenwood (Limited) and another, Padbury v (1911-12) XXVIII TLR 494 CA Main contractor not liable for injury to third party through negligence of sub-contractor's servant.

Holliday v National Telephone Company (1899-1900) LXXXI LTR 252 CA Employer of independent contractor liable for injury caused through latter's work.

Holling and another v Yorkshire Traction Co, Ltd and others [1948] 2 All ER 662 Assizes Blowing of smoke across road so that view obscured a nuisance.

Hollins and another, Worsley v (1991) 141 NLJ 425t; [1991] RTR 252; [1991] TLR 153 CA Full service undertaken/MoT certificate issued six weeks/one month before collision negatived presumption of res ipsa loquitur.

Holloway v Lord Mayor, etc of Birmingham (1905) 69 JP 358 HC KBD Absent evidence of defective construction highway authority could not be found guilty of misfeasance.

Holloway, Dauncey v [1901] 2 KB 441; [1901] 70 LJK/QB 695; (1901) LXXXIV LTR 649; (1900-01) 45 SJ 501; (1900-01) XVII TLR 493; (1900-01) 49 WR 546 CA Words spoken of solicitor not actionable absent special damage as did not reflect on same as solicitor.

Holloway, Dibben v (1929) 68 LJ ccr8 CyCt Building-owner not in possession of same could recover damages in trespass for loss sustained through person without authority affixing radio wires to building.

Holloway, Lane v [1967] 3 All ER 129; (1967) 117 NLJ 731t; [1968] 1 QB 379; (1967) 111 SJ 655; [1967] 3 WLR 1003 CA Disproportionate reaction to provocative conduct precludes ex turpi causa non oritur actio; provocation not ground for reducing damages.

Hollywood Silver Fox Farm, Limited v Emmett [1936] 1 All ER 825; [1936] 2 KB 468; (1936) 81 LJ 331; [1936] 105 LJCL 829; (1936) 155 LTR 288; (1936) 80 SJ 488; (1935-36) LII TLR 611 HC KBD Lawful act but extraordinary user of own land rendered liable in nuisance (firing of gun to frighten neighbour's silver foxes).

Holman v George Elliot and Co, Limited (1943-44) LX TLR 394 HC KBD Validity of fatal accident writ extended in time where had been issued in time but not served in time.

Holmes and another v H Kennard and Son (1984) 128 SJ 854 CA Solicitors negligent in manner in which approached land purchase.

Holmes and another v H Kennard and Son (a firm) (1983) 127 SJ 172 HC ChD Solicitors not negligent in manner in which approached land purchase.

Holmes and another, Sutcliffe v [1946] 2 All ER 599; [1947] KB 147; [1947] 116 LJR 415; (1946) 175 LTR 487; (1945-46) LXII TLR 733; (1947) WN (I) 7 CA Sheep trespass: could not claim other party liable to fence as no evidence of same; could not claim due to third party's non-fencing as had known of third party's failure and should have guarded against it.

Holmes and Hills, Raintree Ltd v (1984) 134 NLJ 522 HC QBD Solicitor liable in negligence for failing to check expiry date of planning permission on land in respect of purchase of which they were advising client.

Holmes and Ward v Hargreaves and Audsley (1923) CC Rep XII 35 CyCt Constables liable to pay damages for false imprisonment for detaining persons merely suspected of committing offence under the Vagrancy Act 1824.

Holmes v Ashford and others [1950] 2 All ER 76; (1950) 94 SJ 337; (1950) WN (I) 269 CA Manufacturers having warned commercial buyer of dangers did not owe duty to final recipient.

Holmes v Ashford and others (1950) 94 SJ 226; (1950) WN (I) 117 HC KBD Manufacturers and commercial buyer of hair-dye, use of which involved certain dangers did not meet duty of care owed to final recipient.

Holmes, Buckle v [1926] All ER 90; (1926) 90 JP 109; [1926] 2 KB 125; (1926) 61 LJ 324; [1926] 95 LJCL 547; (1926) 134 LTR 743; (1925-26) 70 SJ 464; (1925-26) XLII TLR 369; (1925) WN (I) 295 CA Cat-owner not liable for cat trespass unless aware of peculiar tendency of cat to cause damage; cats and dogs treated the same in law of trespass.

Holmes, Buckle v [1925] All ER 676; (1926) 90 JP 47; (1925) 60 LJ 1029; [1926] 95 LJCL 158 (also CA); (1926) 134 LTR 284; (1925-26) 70 SJ 284; (1925-26) XLII TLR 147 HC KBD Cat-owner not liable for damage caused by trespassing cat unless aware of peculiar tendency of cat to cause damage.

Holmes, Mulligan v; Yorkshire Bank Ltd v Holmes [1971] RTR 179 CA Driver (80%) liable and pedestrians at studded crossing (20%) liable for collision where former driving too fast/latter not maintaining proper look-out.

Holsey, Sheringham Urban District Council v (1903-04) XX TLR 402 HC ChD District council could sue for damages where post was removed and public path used as carriageway.

Holst and Co, Ltd, and others, Walsh v [1958] 3 All ER 33; (1958) 108 LJ 537; (1958) 102 SJ 545 CA Brick falling from construction site and hitting passer-by raised res ipsa loquitur (but was defeated here).

Homberger and Co, Yeatman and others v (1912-13) 107 LTR 742; (1912-13) XXIX TLR 26 CA Not to repeat action not satisfactory response to passing off complaint: must seek to redress damage done.

Home and Colonial Stores, Limited, Colls v [1904] AC 179 HL Must be considerable interference with light to succeed in action for obstruction of ancient lights.

Home and Colonial Stores, Ltd, Collingwood v [1936] 3 All ER 200; (1936) 155 LTR 550; (1936) 80 SJ 853; (1936-37) LIII TLR 53; (1936) WN (I) 305 CA Rylands v Fletcher inapplicable to domestic use of electricity.

Home and Colonial Stores, Ltd, Collingwood v [1936] 1 All ER 74; (1936) 81 LJ 130; (1936) 80 SJ 167 HC KBD Absent negligence in electric fitting/maintenance no Rylands v Fletcher-style liability for escape of water resulting from electrical fault-caused fire; hoarding impeding access a nuisance (despite increase in trade while hoarding present).

Home Brewery plc v William Davis and Co (Leicester) Ltd [1987] 1 All ER 637; [1987] QB 339; (1987) 131 SJ 102; [1987] 2 WLR 117 HC QBD Lower land occupier taking steps to prevent water flowing from higher land liable in nuisance to higher land occupier if steps unreasonable and cause damage.

Home Flats, Ltd, Andrews v [1945] 2 All ER 698 CA Landlord liable as bailee for reward for operating negligent system of safeguarding bailed goods.

Home Office, Knight v [1990] 3 All ER 237; (1990) 140 NLJ 210 HC QBD On standard of care owed towards mentally unwell prisoner held in prison hospital pending admission to secure hospital.

Home Office and another, Olotu v [1997] 1 All ER 385; (1996) TLR 11/12/96; [1997] 1 WLR 328 CA Person committed to CrCt for trial could not sue Home Secretary/Crown Prosecution Service for false imprisonment/breach of statutory duty where was detained beyond time stipulated.

Home Office v Dorset Yacht Co Ltd [1970] 2 All ER 294 [1970] AC 1004; (1970) 120 NLJ 458t; (1970) 114 SJ 375; [1970] 2 WLR 1140 HL Home Office/its officers do not enjoy immunity from negligence; borstal officers liable for damage to third party vessel caused by persons escaping on foot of their negligence.

Home Office, Barbara v (1984) 134 NLJ 888 HC QBD Trespass by Government (prison) officials punished by way of damages/aggravated damages but not exemplary damages.

Home Office, Dorset Yacht Co Ltd v [1969] 2 All ER 564; [1969] 2 QB 412; (1969) 113 SJ 227; [1969] 2 WLR 1008 CA Home Office/its officers liable for damage to third party vessel caused by persons escaping on foot of their negligence.

Home Office, Dorset Yacht Co Ltd v (1969) 113 SJ 57 HC QBD Home Office/its officers might be liable for damage to third party vessel caused by persons escaping on foot of their negligence.

Home Office, Egerton v [1978] Crim LR 494 HC QBD Failed action in negligence against Home Office for injuries suffered by sex offender at hands of fellow prisoners in prison.

Home Office, Ellis v [1953] 2 All ER 149; (1953) 103 LJ 380; [1953] 2 QB 135; (1953) 97 SJ 436; [1953] 3 WLR 105 CA No breach of Home Office's duty to take reasonable care of prisoners by giving mental deficient free access to other prisoners.

Home Office, Freeman v [1984] 1 All ER 1036; (1984) 128 SJ 298; [1984] TLR 132; [1984] 2 WLR 802 CA Doctrine of informed consent not part of English law.

Home Office, Racz v [1994] 1 All ER 97; [1994] 2 AC 45; (1994) 144 NLJ 89; (1994) 138 SJ LB 12; [1993] TLR 660; [1994] 2 WLR 23 HL Home Office vicariously liable for misfeasance in public office by prison officers; that a tort similar to libel, slander, malicious prosecution or false imprisonment irrelevant to determining if presumption against jury trial applies.

Home Office, Racz v [1992] TLR 559 HC QBD Home Office not vicariously liable for misfeasance in public office by prison officers acting outside scope of employment.

Home Office, Racz v [1992] TLR 624 CA Home Office not vicariously liable for misfeasance in public office by prison officers acting outside scope of employment.

Home Office, Weldon v [1990] 3 All ER 672; [1992] 1 AC 58 (also HC QBD/HL); [1990] TLR 269; [1990] 3 WLR 465 CA Intentional unreasonable deprivation by prison authorities of residual liberty of prisoner is false imprisonment.

Homewood and another v Spiller (Hodder, third party) [1963] Crim LR 52; (1962) 106 SJ 900 CA Dotted white lines on approach to junction did not alter duty of care owed by motorists.

Honeywill and Stein, Ltd v Larkin Bros (London's Commercial Photographers), Ltd [1933] All ER 77; [1934] 1 KB 191; (1933) 76 LJ 289; (1934) 103 LJCL 74; (1934) 150 LTR 71; (1933-34) L TLR 56; (1933) WN (I) 240 CA Cannot absolve oneself from duty by appointing independent contractor.

Hood and others, Davies v (1903) LXXXVIII LTR 19; (1902-03) XIX TLR 158 HC KBD Personal representative of dead solicitor liable for negligent acts of latter when alive and on retainer.

Hoogstraten, Inland Revenue Commissioners v (1984) 128 SJ 484; [1984] TLR 207 CA Three month period given to party within which to sue court officer-sequestrator for alleged negligent management of sequestrated property.

Hook v Cunard Steamship Co (1953) 117 JP 226; (1953) 103 LJ 265; (1953) 97 SJ 334; [1953] 1 WLR 682 HC QBD Master of ship where could reasonably believe is necessary and does believe it to be necessary could detain any person on board ship so as to preserve order/discipline.

Hooper v Furness Railway Company (1906-07) XXIII TLR 451 HC KBD Inadequate notice of exemption clause on ticket meant passenger could recover personal injury damages.

Hooper, Carroll v [1964] 1 All ER 845; (1964) 114 LJ 272; (1964) 108 SJ 120; [1964] 1 WLR 345 HC QBD Service disablement pension not relevant when gauging appropriate personal injury damages.

Hope Brothers, Limited v Cowan [1913] 2 Ch 312 HC ChD Was not trespass for lessee to put flower boxes on outside of outer wall of leased office.

Hope v I'Anson and Weatherby (1901-02) XVIII TLR 201 CA Jockey Club decisions did not enjoy judicial privilege nor did person party to action submit to decision being published as though it were Court decision.

Hope v Osborne [1913] 2 Ch 349; (1913) 77 JP 317; (1913) 48 LJ 393; (1913) 82 LJCh 457; (1913-14) 109 LTR 41; (1912-13) XXIX TLR 606; (1913) WN (I) 201 HC ChD Liable in damages for excessive trespass in entering onto another's land to remove nuisance.

Hope v Sir WC Leng and Co (Sheffield Telegraph) (Limited) (1906-07) XXIII TLR 243 CA On determining whether newspaper report of court proceedings is fair and accurate.

Hopkins v Mackenzie (1994) 138 SJ LB 222; [1994] TLR 546 CA Period of limitation in negligence action against solicitor (whose negligence resulted in loss of right of claim) ran from date of striking out.

Hopkins v R and S Jenkins (1919) CC Rep VIII 74 CyCt On liability of owners of cattle with right of common in two areas for damage occasioned when strayed from public highway between two areas into another's land.

Hopkinson, Andrews v [1956] 3 All ER 422; [1957] 1 QB 229; [1956] 3 WLR 732 Assizes Non-purchaser could rely on warranty that induced hire-purchase arrangement; damages for personal injuries for breach of warranty that was safe car; damages for negligence in delivering unsafe car when defects reasonably discoverable by supplier.

Hopwood Homes Ltd v Kennerdine [1975] RTR 82 CA Driver not contributorily negligent in assuming oncoming traffic travelling at such speed that could stop when lights changed.

Hopwood v Muirson [1945] 1 All ER 453; [1945] KB 313; (1946) 96 LJ 199; [1945] 114 LJ 267; (1945) 172 LTR 231; (1945) 89 SJ 224; (1944-45) LXI TLR 312; (1945) WN (I) 78 CA Words spoken of solicitor not slander of him in professional rôle as reflected on him personally.

Hordern Richmond, Ltd v Duncan [1947] 1 All ER 427; [1947] KB 545; [1947] 116 LJR 1024 HC KBD Third party recovery from person acting in public duty over one year after cause of action.

Horlick's Malted Milk Company v Summerskill (1916) 51 LJ 129; [1917] 86 LJCh 175; (1916-17) 61 SJ 114; (1916-17) XXXIII TLR 83 HL Term 'malted milk' a descriptive term use of which by rival sellers of malted milk was not passing off.

Horlick's Malted Milk Company v Summerskill [1916] 85 LJP 338; (1916) 114 LTR 484; (1915-16) 60 SJ 320; (1915-16) XXXII TLR 311 CA Term 'malted milk' a descriptive term use of which by rival sellers of malted milk was not passing off.

Horlick's Malted Milk Company v Summerskill (W) (1915-16) XXXII TLR 63 HC ChD Term 'malted milk' a descriptive term use of which by rival sellers of malted milk was not passing off.

Hornby v Gillam (1912) CC Rep I 23 CyCt Seller of property who entered onto same after conveyance/sale complete was trespasser.

Hotson v East Berkshire Area Health Authority [1987] AC 750 (also CA); (1987) 137 NLJ 638; [1987] 3 WLR 232 HL Tortious damages available for lost chance of recovery if can prove causation (which here failed to do).

Hotson v Fitzgerald and others (1985) 129 SJ 558; [1985] 1 WLR 1036 HC QBD On recovery of damages where claiming that but for medical negligence would not have suffered injury to extent which did.

Hough v London Express Newspaper, Ltd [1940] 3 All ER 31; [1940] 2 KB 507; (1940) 89 LJ 270; [1940] 109 LJCL 524; (1940) 163 LTR 162; (1940) 84 SJ 573; (1939-40) LVI TLR 758 CA That reasonable people would believe article as referring to plaintiff was defamatory.

Houghland v Low (RR) (Luxury Coaches), Ltd [1962] 2 All ER 159; (1962) 112 LJ 353; [1962] 1 QB 694; (1962) 106 SJ 243; [1962] 2 WLR 1015 CA Non-return of item establishes prima facie case of detinue/negligence which defendant must counter.

Hounslow London Borough Council, Berryman v (1996) TLR 18/12/96 CA Failed action against landlord for personal injuries for spinal injuries suffered through having to use stairs where lift was not functioning.

Housecroft v Burnett [1986] 1 All ER 332; (1985) 135 NLJ 728 HC QBD £75,000 appropriate for pain/suffering/loss of tetraplegic; no damages in respect of national health care nursing; sham contract for services will not yield extra damages; awards for non-economic loss altered only if clearly too high/low.

Hove Corporation and others, Kinney and another v (1950) 94 SJ 551 HC ChD Use of public park by circus deemed not to be a nuisance.

Howard and Seddon Partnership (a firm), Lancashire and Cheshire Association of Baptist Churches Inc v [1993] 3 All ER 467 HC QBD Tortious duty of care may arise in contractual professional relationship; architect's plans not representation on technical qualities of building; architect not liable for economic loss.

Howard and Wife v Walker and Lake (Trustees) and Crisp [1947] KB 860; [1947] 116 LJR 1366; (1947) 177 LTR 326; (1947) 91 SJ 494; (1947) LXIII TLR 518; (1947) WN (I) 216 HC KBD Landlord not liable to invitee of tenant injured while on tenanted property.

Howard Cundey (trading as Henry Poole and Co) v Lerwill and Pike (1908-09) XCIX LTR 273; (1907-08) XXIV TLR 584 HC ChD No injunction to restrain longtime employee who left to run own business from using connection with earlier firm to advertise own worth.

Howard E Perry and Co Ltd v British Railways Board [1980] 2 All ER 579; [1980] 1 WLR 1375 HC ChD Indefinite interference with property rights is wrongful interference; delivery-up order available if damages inappropriate.

Howard Marine and Dredging Co Ltd v A Ogden and Sons (Excavations) Ltd [1978] 2 All ER 1134; [1978] QB 574; (1978) 122 SJ 48; [1978] 2 WLR 515 CA Misrepresentation acted upon actionable unless misrepresentor has reasonable belief statement true; barge owners/charterers under duty of care when giving advice on specialist matter.

Howard v Bemrose [1973] RTR 32 CA Parties to accident to which there was no witness properly blamed equally given the circumstances.

Howard v Furness Houlder Argentine Lines, Ltd and A and R Brown, Ltd [1936] 2 All ER 781; (1936) 80 SJ 554 HC KBD Negligence where supply/fixing of non-dangerous article made it dangerous; Rylands v Fletcher inapplicable as no escape/no unnatural user.

Howard v Pickfords, Ltd (1935) 79 SJ 69 HC KBD Driver not negligent where child sitting on running board of van without permission was injured when driver began driving.

Howard v SW Farmer and Son, Ltd [1938] 2 All ER 296; (1938) 85 LJ 292; (1938) 82 SJ 351 CA Workman unsuccessful in negligence suit as he was careless in uncompleted building.

Howard, Bailey v [1938] 4 All ER 827; [1939] 1 KB 453; (1939) 87 LJ 9; [1939] 108 LJCL 182; (1939) 160 LTR 87; (1938) 82 SJ 1030; (1938-39) LV TLR 249; (1939) WN (I) 17 CA On appropriate damages for loss of life expectancy (of child).

Howard, Bromilow v (1959) 109 LJ ccr268 CyCt Failed claim in detinue by owner of dog who wandered against buyer who purchased dog as stray.

Howard, Henniker v (1904) XC LTR 157 HC KBD Maintenance of bank, fence and ditch for almost fifty years held not rebut presumption of ownership in respect of another.

Howard-Williams v Bearman and Associated Newspapers, Ltd (1962) 106 SJ 1009 CA Party allowed plead partial justification.

Howatt, Cooper v (1921-22) XXXVIII TLR 721 HC KBD Whether defendant in personal injuries action found to be contributorily negligent (not substantive issue) but not negligent was 'wholly successful defendant'.

Howe and others v David Brown Tractors (Retail) Ltd (Rustons Engineering Co Ltd, third party) [1991] 4 All ER 30 CA Amendment of writ where limitation period applies; application to disapply limitation period to be made at same time/beforehand.

Howe v Oliver; Haynes Third Party (1907-08) XXIV TLR 781 HC KBD Could not bring action against second partner in respect of same cause of action subject of settlement with one partner.

Howe, Worsfold v [1980] 1 All ER 1028; (1980) 130 NLJ 140; [1980] RTR 131; (1980) 124 SJ 646; [1980] 1 WLR 1175 CA Contributory negligence where collision between motorcyclist on main road and driver edging from lesser road.

Howell and another, Greenwell and another v [1900] 69 LJCL 461; (1899-1900) XVI TLR 235 CA County surveyor/deputy clerk committing trespass for purpose of bringing test action protected by provisions of Public uthorities Protection Act 1893.

Howell v West Midland Passenger Executive (1973) 123 NLJ 13t CA Limitation period disapplied where unaware of rights until shortly before instigated action.

Howgate v Bagnall and another [1951] 1 KB 265; (1950) 94 SJ 725; [1950] 66 (2) TLR 997 HC KBD Injuries sustained through crash landing of aircraft not war injuries: damages available.

Hubbard and others v Pitt and others [1975] 3 All ER 1 CA Watching and besetting with view to securing certain behaviour might be nuisance.

Hucks v Cole and another (1968) 118 NLJ 469t; (1968) 112 SJ 483 CA On heavy burden of proof plaintiff must discharge when alleging negligence against medical practitioner.

Huddart, Boord and Son v (1903-04) LXXXIX LTR 718; (1903-04) 48 SJ 143 HC ChD Injunction granted to restrain passing off sloe gin as established brand of sloe gin.

Hudston v Viney [1921] 1 Ch 98 HC ChD Negligence of mortgagees not of such a degree as to relieve them/purchaser from them of the protection of their legal estate.

Hue v Whiteley (1928) 66 LJ 304; (1929) 98 LJCh 227; (1929) 140 LTR 531; (1928) WN (I) 257 HC ChD On inferring right of way from traditional user of pathway/roadway (in action for injunction to restrain alleged trespass).

Huggett v Miers [1908-10] All ER 184; [1908] 2 KB 278; (1908) 43 LJ 282; [1908] 77 LJCL 710; (1908-09) XCIX LTR 326; (1908) WN (I) 115 CA Landlord did not owe higher duty of care to invitee of tenant than tenant owed.

Hughes and another (Jones, third party), Slater v; Hughes v Slater and another; Slater v Hughes and another (Slater and another, third parties) [1971] 3 All ER 1287; [1971] RTR 491; (1971) 115 SJ 428; [1971] 1 WLR 1438 CA Date from which interest payable.

Hughes and another v Sheppard and others; Morley and others v Same (1940) 104 JP 357; (1940) 163 LTR 177; (1939-40) LVI TLR 810 HC KBD Not negligent/nuisance for council workers to mark where were painting lines on road with cans and flags — even if was nuisance only negligent driver who failed to see same and collided with another vehicle liable in actions arising from accident.

Hughes and another, Billingham v [1949] 1 All ER 684; [1949] 1 KB 643; (1949) LXV TLR 246; (1949) WN (I) 135 CA Damages for loss of future earnings are for gross earnings.

Hughes of Beaconsfield Ltd and another, West v [1971] RTR 298 HC QBD On liabilities of van driver and following car for injuries to cyclist whom former knocked down and latter ran over (latter act not novus actus interveniens).

Hughes v Bailly (1919-20) XXXVI TLR 398 HC KBD Hotel proprietor not liable for theft by visitor whom boarded out with another where could not reasonably have discovered criminal propensity of visitor.

Hughes v Cassares (1967) 111 SJ 637 HC QBD Not assault for police officer to push person aside when in course of moving struggling arrestee to police vehicle.

Hughes v Lord Advocate [1963] 1 All ER 705; [1963] AC 837; (1963) 113 LJ 232; (1963) 107 SJ 232; [1963] 2 WLR 779 HL Act akin to reasonably foreseeable act need not itself be reasonably foreseeable for liability in negligence to arise.

Hughes v McKeown (1985) 129 SJ 543; [1985] 1 WLR 963 HC QBD On determining personal injury damages for young woman who because of injury has limited future earning ability and no chance of marriage.

Hughes v National Union of Mineworkers and others [1991] 4 All ER 278; [1991] TLR 301 HC QBD Generally senior police officers not liable to junior police officers for exposure of latter to undue risk.

Hughes v Waltham Forest Health Authority [1990] TLR 714 CA That surgical decision erroneous or that other surgeons critical of decision did not preclude finding that surgeons being sued not negligent.

Hughes, Speake v [1904] 1 KB 138; [1904] 73 LJCL 172; (1903-04) LXXXIX LTR 576 CA Damage allegedly arising from slander (loss of damage) too remote for recovery of damages.

Hull and Barnsley Rail Co, Pyman Steamship Co, Ltd v [1914-15] All ER 292; (1915) 112 LTR 1103; (1914-15) XXXI TLR 243 CA Effective exemption of liability clause.

Hull and Barnsley Railway Company, Pyman Steamship Company v (1914-15) 111 LTR 41; (1913-14) XXX TLR 430 HC KBD Effective exemption of liability clause.

Hull and Netherlands Steamship Company, Limited, Verschures Creameries, Limited v [1921] 2 KB 608; [1922] 91 LJCL 39; (1921) 125 LTR 165 CA Owner having sought and received judgment against customer could not later seek damages from negligent forwarding agent.

Hulton Press, Limited, Thaarup v (1943) 169 LTR 309; (1943) WN (I) 184 CA Re-trial ordered where trial judge in libel action found word 'pansy' to be incapable of defamatory meaning.

Hultquist v Universal Pattern and Precision Engineering Co, Ltd [1960] 2 All ER 266; [1960] 2 QB 467; (1960) 104 SJ 427 CA Appropriate personal injury damages.

Humberside County Council, Paterson and another v [1995] TLR 224 HC QBD Tree-owner liable in nuisance/negligence for subsidence consequent upon drying out of soil by trees.

Humberts (a firm) and others, Beaumont and another v [1990] TLR 543 CA Surveyor held not to have been negligent in his assessment of the reinstatement worth of a three hundred year old house.

Humberts, First National Commercial Bank plc v [1995] 2 All ER 673; (1995) 145 NLJ 345; [1995] TLR 29 CA Cause of action where loan made following negligent advice runs from date of loss.

Hummingbird Motors Ltd v Hobbs [1986] RTR 276 CA No misrepresentation/breach of warranty where sold second-hand car to another in bona fide but mistaken belief that odometer reading correct.

Humphery v Bowers (1928-29) XLV TLR 297 HC KBD Failed action in negligence against surveyor provided by Lloyd's Register who certified defective yacht as being in good state.

Humphrey and another v Leigh and another [1971] RTR 363 CA Driver on main road not required to take precaution of taking foot from accelerator and placing above brake as approached/passed side-road.

Humphrey, Williams v (1975) 125 NLJ 230/262 HC QBD Person liable for injuries suffered by another whom mischeviously pushed into swimming pool.

Humphreys v Dreamland (Margate), Ltd [1930] All ER 327; (1931) 100 LJCL 137; (1931) 144 LTR 529; (1930) 74 SJ 862 HL Person having right to possession of land/right to exclude people therefrom liable in negligence for injuries sustained thereon, not landowner.

Hungate Builders Ltd and others, Saper v; King v Hungate Builders Ltd and others [1972] RTR 380 HC QBD Presence of poorly lit skip negligent/a nuisance but person who drove into it found contributorily negligent (40%).

Hunt and another, Pitts v [1990] 3 All ER 344; [1991] 1 QB 24; [1990] RTR 290; [1990] TLR 312; [1990] 3 WLR 542 CA Person injured by unlawful acts he encouraged other to undertake barred from recovering damages by virtue of ex turpi causa maxim, public policy and absence of duty of care.

Hurlock v Inglis (1963) 107 SJ 1023 HC QBD Person driving at high speed was negligent in assumption that when overtaking another that other would properly observe rules of the road.

Hurlstone v London Electric Railway Company and another (1913-14) XXX TLR 398 CA Railway company not liable for negligence of building contractors.

Hurlstone v London Electric Railway Company and another (1912-13) XXIX TLR 514 HC KBD Railway company liable for negligence of building contractors.

Hurst and another v Hampshire County Council [1997] 2 Cr App R (S) 1025; (1997) 147 NLJ 1025; (1997) 141 SJ LB 152; [1997] TLR 339 CA Highway authority liable for damage to house occasioned by roots of tree standing on verge of adjacent highway dedicated to the public.

Hurst and others, Maher v (1969) 113 SJ 167 CA Lorry driver/owners, not roadworkers liable for injury which occurred when lorry driver drove too fast through area of roadworks.

Hurst v Picture Theatres, Limited [1915] 1 KB 1; (1914) 49 LJ 439; [1914] 83 LJKB 1837; (1914-15) 111 LTR 972; (1913-14) XXX TLR 642 CA Recovery for assault/false imprisonment by theatre audience member mistakenly ejected from seat having paid for ticket.

Hurst v Picture Theatres, Limited (1913-14) XXX TLR 98 HC KBD Recovery for assault/false imprisonment by theatre audience member mistakenly ejected from seat having paid for ticket.

Hurt v Murphy [1971] RTR 186 HC QBD Speeding driver/unvigilant pedestrian 80%/20% liable for collision at pedestrian crossing; husband's damages for loss of wife's services based on costs of keeping a daily help.

Hussain v New Taplow Paper Mills Ltd [1987] 1 All ER 417; [1987] 1 WLR 336 CA Long-term sickness benefit an earning which if not paid for are deductible from damages.

Hussain v New Taplow Paper Mills Ltd [1988] 1 All ER 541; [1988] AC 514; (1988) 138 NLJ 45; [1988] 2 WLR 266 HL Long-term sickness benefit deductible from personal injury damages.

Hussey and another v Eels and another [1990] 1 All ER 449; (1990) 140 NLJ 53 CA Profits made through resale of defective property after negligent misrepresentation not to be set off against damages for latter unless various steps part of a single transaction.

Hussien (Shaaban Bin) and others v Kam (Chong Fook) and another [1969] 3 All ER 1626; [1970] AC 942; [1970] Crim LR 219; (1970) 114 SJ 55; [1970] 2 WLR 441 PC 'Reasonable suspicion' is not 'prima facie proof'; reasonable suspicion once lies compund circumstantial evidence.

Hutchins and others, Woodward and others v (1977) 121 SJ 409; [1977] 1 WLR 760 CA Refusal to grant injunction restraining disclosure of confidential information obtained in course of employment.

Hutchins v Maunder (1920-21) XXXVII TLR 72 HC KBD Placing car on highway in condition where by virtue of defective steering it posed danger to other highway users was negligent even though unaware of defect.

Hutchins, Montgomery v (1906) XCIV LTR 207 HC KBD On appropriate amages for conversion of goods under sale of goods contract.

Hutchinson and Co (Publishers), Limited, Ash v [1936] 105 LJCh 303; (1936) 155 LTR 46; (1935-36) LII TLR 429 CA Action for conversion following on infringement of copyright.

Hutchinson and Company (Publishers), Limited, and others, Ash and another v [1936] Ch 489 CA On post-infringement of copyright damages for conversion.

Hutchinson v London and North Eastern Railway Company [1942] 1 KB 481 CA Breach of statutory duty in not providing look-out for oncoming train while workmen on line.

Hutchinson, Ridgway v (1923) 58 LJ 296 HC ChD Failed passing-off action by proprietors of 'Adventure' magazine against the proprietors of 'Hutchinson's Adventure-Story Magazine'.

Huth v Huth [1914-15] All ER 242; [1915] 3 KB 32; (1915) 50 LJ 195; [1915] 84 LJKB 1307; (1915-16) 113 LTR 145; (1914-15) XXXI TLR 350; (1915) WN (I) 154 CA No libel where unsealed letter sent through post and inadvertently read by addressee's butler.

Hutt, Oram v (1914) 78 JP 51; (1913) 48 LJ 659; [1914] 83 LJCh 161; (1914) 110 LTR 187; (1913-14) 58 SJ 80; (1913-14) XXX TLR 55 CA Trade union acted ultra vires when paid for legal costs of general secretary in slander action — money to be repaid with interest.

Ilford Urban District Council, Jackson, Third Party, Ilford Gas Company v (1903) 67 JP 365 CA Contractor not liable to indemnify council for damage to gas pipe which jury found was not effected by manner in which contractor did work.

Ilford Urban District Council, Torrance v (1909) 73 JP 225; (1908-09) XXV TLR 355 CA Council were negligent in manner in which left stones on road but driver could not recover damages as had seen stones, appreciated risk and taken risk anyway.

Ilford Urban District Council, Torrance v (1908) 72 JP 526; (1908-09) XCIX LTR 847 HC KBD Council were perhaps negligent in manner in which left stones on road but damage which occurred not proved to be natural and direct consequence of that action.

Ilfracombe Urban District Council, Dyer v [1956] 1 All ER 581; (1956) 120 JP 220; (1956) 100 SJ 169; [1956] 1 WLR 218 CA Licensor not liable for allurement not concealing hidden danger.

Ilkiw v Samuels and others (1963) 107 SJ 680; [1963] 1 WLR 991 CA Employers liable for negligence of employee who acting within scope of responsibility behaved in unauthorised way; appropriate damages for personal injuries.

Illustrated Newspapers, Limited v Publicity Services (London), Limited [1938] Ch 414; [1938] 107 LJCh 154; (1938) 158 LTR 195; (1938) 82 SJ 76; (1937-38) LIV TLR 364; (1938) WN (I) 59 HC ChD Injunction to restrain placing of unauthorised supplement in certain publication of plaintiff as were passing off former as being part of latter.

Imperial Bank of Canada v Bank of Hamilton (1902-03) LXXXVII LTR 457; (1902-03) 51 WR 289 PC Not negligent for bank to cash certified cheque which did not on face of it seem suspect.

Imperial Chemical Industries Ltd v Shatwell [1964] 3 WLR 329 HL Volenti non fit injuria held to arise where workman injured after behaving with co-workman in manner contrary to employer's instructions/to law; on causation.

Imperial London Hotels, Ltd, Silverman v [1927] All ER 712; (1927) 137 LTR 57; (1926-27) XLIII TLR 260 HC KBD Breach of implied term of contract (and negligent) allowing invitee into premises knowing of a danger (and failing to address danger).

Imperial Tobacco Co (of Great Britain and Ireland), Ltd, Kelsen v [1957] 2 All ER 343; (1957) 107 LJ 377; [1957] 2 QB 334; (1957) 101 SJ 446 HC QBD Incursion by advertisements into air space above shop a trespass against which injunction granted; three year non-objection to sign did not raise estoppel as other party had not acted to detriment on representation of intention not to object (which in itself could not create estoppel).

Imperial Tobacco Company of Great Britain and Ireland v Pasquali; Re Imperial Tobacco Company's Trade Marks [1918] 2 Ch 207 CA Using word 'Regiment' in respect of one's products where rival company's trade mark is 'Regimental' is not breach unless inter alia is real risk of passing off.

Imperial Tobacco Company of India v Albert Bonnan and Bonnan and Co (1924) 131 LTR 642 PC Not passing off to sell manufacturer's cigarettes as such even though had previously sold same cigarettes under particular trade mark.

In the Estate of Park; Park v Park [1953] 2 All ER 408 HC PDAD No estoppel from re-pleading matters where issue in later case not the same; marriage a readily comprehensible arrangement: capacity necessary to enter marriage set quite low.

Inco Alloys Ltd and another, Nitrigin Eireann Teoranta and another v [1992] 1 All ER 854; (1991) 135 SJ LB 213; [1991] TLR 489; [1992] 1 WLR 498 HC QBD Cause of action arises in negligence not when economic loss occurs but when when physical damage occurs on foot of negligence.

Incorporated Central Council of the Girls' Friendly Society, Morgan v [1936] 1 All ER 404; (1936) 81 LJ 187; (1936) 80 SJ 323 HC KBD Independent contractors but not landlord liable in negligence to licensee falling down lift shaft when lift gate left open.

Ind Coope and Allsopp, Limited, Heap v (1940) 84 SJ 536; (1939-40) LVI TLR 948 CA Appropriate that personal injuries action be brought against landlord as despite lease requiring tenant to do internal repairs landlord did all repairs (claimant's action arose through injury suffered by way of defective outside repairs).

International Harvester Co Ltd of GB, Coddington v (1969) 119 NLJ 249t HC QBD Employers not vicariously liable for act of worker which resulted in train if events causing injury to another worker/the plaintiff.

Interoven Stove Co Ltd v British Broadcasting Corporation (1935) 79 SJ 921 HC KBD Failed action for alleged slander of goods in course of radio broadcast: on elements of 'slander of goods'.

Invercargill City Council v Hamlin [1996] 1 All ER 756; [1996] AC 624; (1996) 146 NLJ 246; (1996) 140 SJ LB 86; (1996) TLR 15/2/96; [1996] 2 WLR 367 PC New Zealand Court of Appeal may take into account local considerations when adjudicating on developing areas of common law; cause of action for latent damage ought generally to run from when economic (and not property) damage occurs.

Inverugie Investments Ltd v Hackett [1995] 3 All ER 841; [1995] 1 WLR 713 PC Hirer of goods or letter of property may recover damages for wrongful use arising from trespass regardless of actual loss suffered.

Investors in Industry Commercial Properties Ltd v South Bedfordshire District Council (Ellison and Partners (a firm) and others, third parties) [1986] 1 All ER 787; (1986) 136 NLJ 118; [1986] QB 1034; (1986) 130 SJ 71; [1986] 2 WLR 937 CA Local authority does not owe duty to building owner to ensure building accords with building regulations; professional not responsible for work of specialist consultant unless as professional foresees problem therewith.

Invicta Manufacturing Co (Lim), Claudius Ash, Son and Co (Lim) v (1910-11) 55 SJ 348 HC ChD Injunction will be granted to restrain manufacturer from marketing goods under name that is not own/is that of rival manufacturer.

IPC Magazines Ltd and another, Khashoggi v [1986] 3 All ER 577; (1986) 136 NLJ 1111; (1970) 130 SJ 862; [1986] 1 WLR 1412 CA Interlocutory injunction unavailable regarding unproveable claims if justification to be pleaded regarding connected claims.

Irish Linen Manufacturing Co v Lowe (1956) 106 LJ ccr828 CyCt Failed action in negligence where water escaped from one premises into another.

Iron Trade Mutual Insurance Co Ltd and others v JK Buckenham Ltd [1990] 1 All ER 808 HC QBD Injury caused upon procuring of voidable reinsurance policies; actions in contract/tort to be treated separately under Limitation Act even if same time limits; issue whether latent damage action is time-barred to be decided at trial/as preliminary issue, not in strike-out proceedings.

Ironbridge Metal Works, Ltd, and others, Merrington v [1952] 2 All ER 1101; (1953) 117 JP 23 Assizes Liability to firemen does not rest on how are there; owner not liable as invitor as fireman would probably have risked danger even if told; owner liable to firemen for keeping building in condition dangerous to them; volenti non fit injuria if fully appreciate risk and freely assume that risk.

Ironfield v Eastern Gas Board [1964] 1 All ER 544; (1964) 108 SJ 691; [1964] 1 WLR 1125 HC QBD Excess insurance and 'no claims bonus' recoverable as special damages.

Irving v Carlisle Rural District Council (1907) 71 JP 212 HC KBD Council found guilty of non-feasance (not misfeasance) of ditch.

Irving v London County Council (1965) 109 SJ 157 HC QBD Occupiers not required to light common staircase at all times without special cause.

Isaac Walton and Co v The Vanguard Motorbus Co (Limited); Gibbons v The Vanguard Motorbus Co (Limited) (1908) 72 JP 505; (1908-09) 53 SJ 82; (1908-09) XXV TLR 13 HC KBD Bus striking permanent structure (in first case) could be due to negligence of driver (and in second case) was negligent use of nuisance placed on highway.

Isaacs (M) and Sons, Limited, and others v Cook [1925] 2 KB 391; (1925) 60 LJ 739; [1925] 94 LJCL 886; (1926) 134 LTR 286; (1924-25) 69 SJ 810; (1924-25) XLI TLR 647; (1925) WN (I) 226 HC KBD British High Commissioner to Australia's official communications to Australian Prime Minister (and vice versa) privileged; State document on business concerns could be privileged.

Isaacs and others, O'Connor v [1956] 2 All ER 417; [1956] Crim LR 482; (1956) 106 LJ 392; (1956) 100 SJ 432; [1956] 3 WLR 172 CA Failed action against justices for committal to prison on foot of maintenance order made without jurisdiction; application of public authority limitation.

J and J Cash, Ltd v Cash (1901) 36 LJ 122; (1901) LXXXIV LTR 349; (1901) WN (I) 46 HC ChD Restraint ordered on trading in own name.

J and P Coates (UK) Ltd, Brooks v [1984] 1 All ER 702 HC QBD Limitation lifted as plaintiff blameless and would suffer greater prejudice if action barred than defendants would in meeting claim after long delay.

J Birby and Sons, Ltd, Birchall v [1953] 1 All ER 163 Assizes Res ipsa loquitur where rope in warehouse snapped and bags fell injuring person; proof that rope maliciously cut discharged res ipsa loquitur.

J Bollinger SA and others, Bulmer (HP) Ltd and another v [1974] Ch 401; (1977) 127 NLJ 914t; [1974] 3 WLR 202 CA Article 177 reference to European Court of Justice in course of passing off action (on EEC wine/champagne legislation).

J Goldberg and Sons v The Corporation of Liverpool (1900) LXXXII LTR 362; (1899-1900) XVI TLR 320 CA Bona fide placing of pole and fuse-box at entrance to plaintiffs' premises was authorised by statute/was not nuisance.

J Hampson and Co, Roberts and another v [1989] 2 All ER 504; (1988) 138 NLJ 166; (1989) 133 SJ 1234; [1990] 1 WLR 94 HC QBD Building society surveyor liable in damages to purchaser of house for negligent survey of same.

J Jobson and Son, Park v [1944] LJNCCR 153 CyCt Person who was author of own troubles in that created situation whereby cattle could trespass on own property could not recover damages from cattle owner when cattle so trespassed.

J Jobson and Son, Park v [1945] 1 All ER 222; (1946) 96 LJ 213 CA No duty on allotment holder to keep allotment fenced; no liability on one allotment holder with defective fence to others as no evidence of animal trespass through particular part of fence.

J Lionel Barber and Co (Limited) v Deutsche Bank (Berlin) London Agency (1916-17) XXXIII TLR 543 CA No damages for libel on privileged occasion as was no express malice proved.

J Lionel Barber and Co, Ltd v Deutsche Bank (Berlin) London Agency, et e contra [1918-19] All ER 407; (1919) 120 LTR 288 HL No re-trial where post misdirection (on damages only) plaintiffs offer to reduce damages to remedy injustice.

J Lyons and Co, Ltd, Clinton v [1911-13] All ER 577; [1912] 3 KB 198; (1912) 81 LJKB 923; (1912) 106 LTR 988; (1911-12) XXVIII TLR 462 HC KBD No liability for injuries caused by cat unnaturally vicious because had kittens.

J Lyons and Co, Ltd, Read (Norah) v [1944] 2 All ER 98; [1945] KB 216; (1944) 170 LTR 418; (1944) 88 SJ 298; (1943-44) LX TLR 363 HC KBD High explosives manufacturer subject to strict liability (Rylands v Fletcher applies — non-natural user); no volenti non fit injuria as victim was employed against her will.

J Lyons and Co, Ltd, Read (Norah) v [1945] 1 All ER 106; (1946) 96 LJ 213; (1947) 91 SJ 54; (1944-45) LXI TLR 148 CA Rylands v Fletcher inapplicable to explosion in high explosives manufacturers and no volenti non fit injuria.

J Lyons and Co, Ltd, Read v [1946] 2 All ER 471; [1947] AC 156; [1947] 116 LJR 39; (1946) 175 LTR 413; (1945-46) LXII TLR 646 HL Manufacturer of explosive shells not absolutely liable for personal injuries caused; unwilling worker an invitee to whom strict but not absolute liability; notion of 'escape' in Rylands v Fletcher.

J Ralph Moss Ltd, Osman v (1970) 120 NLJ 177t CA Recovery of damages from insurance broker who advised plaintiff to insure car with company that collapsed thereby rendering plaintiff uninsured.

J Sargent (Garages) Ltd v Motor Auctions (West Bromwich) Ltd and another [1977] RTR 121 CA Person giving car/log book to another who wrongfully sold it not estopped — even if negligent — from denying latter's authority to sell; damages set at price plaintiffs had expected to sell (what was a special) car.

J Spurling, Ltd and others, Philco Radio and Television Corporation of Great Britain, Ltd v [1949] 2 All ER 129; (1949) 99 LJ 289; (1949) LXV TLR 388 HC KBD Strict liability where bring dangerous material into premises.

J Spurling, Ltd v Bradshaw [1956] 2 All ER 121; (1956) 106 LJ 281; (1956) 100 SJ 317; [1956] 1 WLR 461 CA Exemption clause in bailment contract applied in negligence suit.

J Townend and Sons (Hull) Ltd and others, Erven Warnink BV and others v [1979] 2 All ER 927; [1979] AC 731; (1979) 129 (1) NLJ 631; (1979) 123 SJ 472; [1979] 3 WLR 68 HL Passing-off relief if goodwill in descriptive name of product (whether because of ingredients/place of origin).

J Trevor and Sons (a firm) v Solomon (1978) 128 NLJ 134t CA Refusal of injunction preventing person from stating what he considered to be the truth.

J v R and another (1984) 128 SJ 333 HC QBD Plaintiff allowed make statement in open court following acceptance of money paid into court by defendants in full satisfaction of plaintiff's libel claim.

JA Scott (Limited), Dickson v (1914) 49 LJ 112; (1913-14) XXX TLR 256 CA Occupier owes duty to man whom allows onto land in darkness to alert/save same as to/from danger posed by hatchway.

Jackman v Corbett [1988] QB 154; (1987) 131 SJ 808; [1987] 3 WLR 586 CA Half of invalidity benefit in five-year period from date when cause of action arose was deductible from personal injury damages.

Jackson and another, Adler v [1954] 3 All ER 397 CA Company's exemption clauses did not protect servants of company.

Jackson and another, Miller and another v [1977] 3 All ER 338; (1977) 127 NLJ 568t; [1977] QB 966; (1977) 121 SJ 287; [1977] 3 WLR 20 CA Cricket balls emanating from village cricket ground a negligent act.

Jackson v L Obertling, Ltd (1925) 60 LJ 521 CyCt Damages recoverable for nuisance occasioned by broken pavement light (said light not being part of highway repairable by highway authority).

Jackson v London County Council and Chappell (1912) 76 JP 37; (1911-12) XXVIII TLR 66 HC KBD Education authority/building contractor may have been negligent to leave sand mixture in school yard which one child threw at another, causing injury.

Jackson v London County Council and Chappell (1912) 76 JP 217; (1911-12) XXVIII TLR 359 CA Education authority/building contractor may have been negligent to leave sand mixture in school yard which one child threw at another, causing injury.

Jackson v Mirror Group Newspapers Ltd and another [1994] TLR 174 CA Stay of action merited unless plaintiff to libel action underwent medical test; defendants' medic could seek discovery of medical records from plaintiff's doctor.

Jackson v Wimbledon Urban District Council (1904-05) XXI TLR 479 CA Nuisance arising from pipe bringing sewage from house to main sewer was a matter for local authority to remedy.

Jackson, Ashover Fluor Spar Mines, Limited v (1911) WN (I) 163 HC ChD On assessment of damages for trespass on mine.

Jackson, Harrison v [1947] LJNCCR 242 CyCt Person who failed to take reasonable care when having cattle driven across highway liable in negligence for motor collision which occurred.

Jackson, O'Connell v [1971] 3 All ER 129; (1971) 121 NLJ 618t; [1972] 1 QB 270; [1972] RTR 51; (1971) 115 SJ 742; [1971] 3 WLR 463 CA Person contributing to injury but not to accident is contributorily negligent.

Jackson, Pitt v [1939] 1 All ER 129; (1939) 87 LJ 64; (1939) 83 SJ 216 HC KBD Polished linoleum not a trap for which liable to licensee slipping thereon.

Jackson, Valentine v [1972] 1 WLR 528 HC QBD Police officer to have suspicion that crime committed/about to be committed before may insist on entering licensed premises under Licensing Act 1964, s 186(1).

Jacob, Walton v (1938) 82 SJ 586 HC KBD On assessing apppropriate damages for loss of expectation of life for healthy twenty-one year old man killed in negligent road traffic collision.

Jacobi and another, Jay's, Ltd v [1933] All ER 690; [1933] Ch 411; (1933) 102 LJCh 130; (1933) 149 LTR 90; (1933) 77 SJ 176; (1933) WN (I) 54 HC ChD No passing off where traded under own name (even if caused some confusion) absent intent to confuse consumers that were another.

Jacobs and another v London County Council [1949] 1 All ER 790; [1949] 1 KB 685; (1949) 99 LJ 219; (1949) WN (I) 179 CA Person on forecourt not open to public a licensee; no nuisance adjoining highway proved as was not using highway when encountered 'nuisance'.

Jacobs v London County Council [1950] 1 All ER 737; [1950] AC 361; (1950) 114 JP 204; (1950) 100 LJ 175; (1950) 94 SJ 318; [1950] 66 (1) TLR 659; (1950) WN (I) 170 HL Person on forecourt not open to public a licensee; no nuisance adjoining highway proved as was not using highway when encountered 'nuisance'.

Jacobs v London County Council and Smith, Gard & Co, Ltd (1949) 99 LJ 52 CyCt Council liable in negligence/nuisance for injury suffered by individual when crossing forecourt in some disrepair.

Jacoby v Prison Commissioners [1940] 2 All ER 499 HC KBD Special public authority time limitation applicable in suit against prison commissioners.

Jacoby v Prison Commissioners [1940] 3 All ER 506 CA Special public authority time limitation applicable in suit against prison commissioners.

Jaeger (Professor Dr G) v The Jaeger Company, Limited (1926-27) XLIII TLR 220 HC ChD Injunction to prevent use of trade name where was danger of confusion resulting.

Jag Shakti (Owners), Chabbra Corporation Pte Ltd v; The Jag Shakti [1986] AC 337; [1986] 2 WLR 87 PC Appropriate damages to bearers of bills of lading from shipowners for conversion effected by shipowner's wrongful delivery of cargo to buyers.

Jaggard v Sawyer and another [1995] 2 All ER 189 CA Court may award 'once and for all' damages insead of injunction to restrain trespass or breach of covenant; oppression to be judged as facts stand on date injunction sought.

Jagger, Constable v (1972) 122 NLJ 268 CA On whether statements in police inquiry privileged.

Jakeman and Turner, Jakeman v [1963] 3 All ER 889; (1964) 114 LJ 10; (1963) 107 SJ 438; [1964] 2 WLR 90 HC PDAD Re-hearing on damages as not originally argued because of solicitor's negligence; solicitor personally liable for costs of first hearing.

Jakeman v Jakeman and Turner [1963] 3 All ER 889; (1964) 114 LJ 10; (1963) 107 SJ 438; [1964] 2 WLR 90 HC PDAD Re-hearing on damages as not originally argued because of solicitor's negligence; solicitor personally liable for costs of first hearing.

Jambo Holdings Ltd and others, Allen and others v [1980] 2 All ER 502; (1980) 124 SJ 742 CA Mareva injunction available in personal injuries action.

James and Charles Dodd, Mainz v (1978) 128 NLJ 978t HC QBD Damages for negligence of solicitor whose inaction resulted in plaintiff's actions being struck out for want of prosecution.

James and others, Department of the Environment v (1972) 116 SJ 712 HC ChD Court would not delay recovery of possession of property occupied by trespassers.

James Archdale and Co, Ltd v Comservices, Ltd [1954] 1 All ER 210; (1954) 98 SJ 143; [1954] 1 WLR 459 CA Non-applicability of principle that generally worded exception clause does not apply to own/servant's negligence.

James Beattie, Limited, Hortons' Estate, Limited v [1927] 1 Ch 75; (1925-26) XLII TLR 701 HC ChD Particular obstruction of ancient light was actionable nuisance.

James Broderick and Company, Limited, Carr v (1941-42) LVIII TLR 373 HC KBD On availability of damages for conversion where owner of hire-purchase property wrongfully retakes possession of same.

James Brothers and Sons, Limited, Baker v [1921] 2 KB 674 HC KBD Recovery by servant for injury suffered by means of defective company car (despite awareness of defect).

James Crowe (Cases) Ltd, Hill v [1978] 1 All ER 812; (1977) 127 NLJ 637 HC QBD Manufacturer vicariously liable for workmen's negligence despite good work system/proper supervision.

James McNaughton Paper Group Ltd v Hicks Anderson and Co (a firm) [1991] 1 All ER 134; (1990) 140 NLJ 1311; [1991] 2 QB 113; [1990] TLR 630; [1991] 2 WLR 641 CA Purpose of statement, relationship between maker/giver and other party, knowledge of maker/giver, size of class to which other party belongs are factors when deciding if duty of care on maker/giver of statement to unintended third party recipient.

James v Audigier (1932) 74 LJ 407; (1932-33) XLIX TLR 36; (1932) WN (I) 250 CA Dismissal of appeal over questions that were asked in running-down case over earlier accident in which defendant involved.

James v Audigier (1931-32) XLVIII TLR 600; (1932) WN (I) 181 HC KBD On appropriate questions which may be put to driver in 'running down' case.

James v Durkin (Civil Engineering Contractors) Ltd [1983] TLR 383 HC QBD Damages in successful negligence claim by estate of deceased driver reduced by 50% in light of contributory negligence of deceased.

James v Hepworth and Grandage Ltd [1967] 3 WLR 178 CA Company not negligent where had advertised availability of safety equipment to employees even though injured employee illiterate; non-provision of safety equipment even if negligent was not cause of injury.

James v Parsons (1974) 124 NLJ 1029t; [1975] RTR 20; (1974) 118 SJ 777 HC QBD Front seat passenger without seat belt not guilty of contributory negligence as regards injuries suffered in accident absent warning from driver of need to wear belt.

James v Woodall Duckham Construction Co Ltd [1969] 2 All ER 794; (1969) 113 SJ 225; [1969] 1 WLR 903 CA Damages for loss of earnings reduced where delay deferred return to work.

James, Gunter v (1908) 72 JP 448; (1907-08) XXIV TLR 868 HC KBD Owner of traction-engine (a dangerous spark-emitting machine) liable for damage caused to crops when engine driven along road though no negligent user.

James, Ward v [1965] 1 All ER 563; (1965) 115 LJ 228; (1965) 109 SJ 111; [1965] 2 WLR 455 CA On damages/when jury trial appropriate in personal cases.

Jang Publications Ltd and Rahman v Crescent and Star Publications Ltd and Aziz (1981) 131 NLJ 482c CA £20,000 damages not inappropriate for serious (political) libel.

Janney v Gentry (1966) 110 SJ 408 HC QBD Allowance made when awarding personal injury damages for civil service pension of which plaintiff in receipt.

Janvier v Sweeney and another (1919) 121 LTR 179; (1918-19) XXXV TLR 226 HC KBD Is good cause of action where make statement with intent to injure another who is injured thereby.

Janvier v Sweeney and Barker [1919] 88 LJCL 1231; (1918-19) 63 SJ 430; (1918-19) XXXV TLR 360 CA Is good cause of action where make statement with intent to injure another who is injured thereby.

Jarvis v Smith (1957) 107 LJ ccr476 CyCt RSPCA inspector did not trespass on land when entered on same when investigating allegations but did commit trespass when removed carcase from land.

Jarvis v T Richards and Co (1980) 124 SJ 793 HC ChD On appropriate damages where negligence of solicitor in property transaction resulted in plaintiff having no place to live.

Jarvis v Williams [1955] 1 All ER 108; (1955) 105 LJ 40; (1955) 99 SJ 73; [1955] 1 WLR 71 CA Seller seeking to recover property legally passed to buyer's agent could not sue in detinue upon non-return of property.

Jauffur v Akhbar and another [1984] TLR 51 HC QBD On duty of care owed by parent vis-à-vis warning/supervising children regarding/in use of lighted candles.

Jaundrill v Gillett (1996) TLR 30/1/96 CA Horse-owner not liable to driver injured in collision with horses that were on public highway following malicious release by third party onto same.

Jay's, Ltd v Jacobi and another [1933] All ER 690; [1933] Ch 411; (1933) 102 LJCh 130; (1933) 149 LTR 90; (1933) 77 SJ 176; (1933) WN (I) 54 HC ChD No passing off where traded under own name (even if caused some confusion) absent intent to confuse consumers that were another.

Jayanbee Joinery, Ltd, Weait and another v [1962] 2 All ER 568 CA Can amend defence to show not liable if evidence so showing first emerges after limitation.

Jayne and others, Buxton and another v (1960) 104 SJ 602 CA Leave granted to bring action against local authority officer for not exercising reasonable care when deciding to have one plaintiff removed to mental hospital against her will.

Jayson v Midland Bank, Ltd (1967) 111 SJ 719 HC QBD Issue whether bank's writing 'refer to drawer' on cheque was libellous left to jury.

Jaytex Ltd, Infabrics Ltd and others v (1980) 124 SJ 309 CA On assessing damages for conversion arising from breach of copyright.

Jaytex Ltd, Infabrics Ltd and others v (1981) 125 SJ 257 HL On assessing damages for conversion arising from breach of copyright.

JC Cording and Co (Limited), Burberrys v (1909) 100 LTR 985; (1908-09) XXV TLR 576 HC ChD Failed injunction to prevent firm using name that was at once descriptive and distinctive.

JE Binstock Miller and Co, Simple Simon Catering Ltd v (1973) 117 SJ 529 CA On appropriate damages for negligence of solicitor in drawing up underlease (as result of which suffered loss).

JE Evans and Co (Cardiff), Ltd and another, National Coal Board v [1951] 2 All ER 310; [1951] 2 KB 861; (1951) 101 LJ 345; (1951) 95 SJ 399; [1951] 2 TLR 415; (1951) WN (I) 354 CA No trespass in action where plaintiffs partly to blame for occurrence and defendants blameless.

JEB Fasteners Ltd v Marks Bloom and Co [1981] 3 All ER 289; (1981) 131 NLJ 447 HC QBD Auditors owed duty of care to person with whom had no contractual relationship but who relied on audited accounts in deciding whether to purchase company.

JEB Fasteners Ltd v Marks Bloom and Co (a firm) [1983] 1 All ER 583; [1982] TLR 403 CA Auditor not liable to third party for negligent audits unless induce (not encourage) latter to invest in company.

Jebara, Ottoman Bank v [1928] AC 269 HL Failed action for alleged conversion on foot of sale of goods contract.

Jeeves v Sutton [1934] LJNCCR 288 CyCt Was trespass for owner of premises not to allow statutory tenant return to premises.

Jefferey v London County Council (1955) 119 JP 45 HC QBD School not liable for fatal after-hours playground injury to child waiting to be collected.

Jefferies and A and R Atkey and Co, Limited v Derbyshire Farmers, Limited (1919-20) XXXVI TLR 825 HC KBD Defendant deliverers liable for fire caused as consequence of their servant's acting in breach of their contract with plaintiffs (despite damage being directly caused by servant acting outside his authority).

Jefferson and others v Derbyshire Farmers, Limited [1921] 2 KB 281; [1921] LJCL 1361; (1921) 124 LTR 775 CA Master liable for negligence of servant in respect of dangerous object regarding which failed to take extra care.

Jeffery v Smith (1970) 120 NLJ 272t; [1970] RTR 279; (1970) 114 SJ 268 CA On appropriate damages in negligence for loss to husband of services of wife killed in motor accident.

Jeffery, Warwick and another v (1983) 133 NLJ 912 HC QBD On awarding of damages following road traffic accident in actions under Fatal Accidents Act 1976/Law Reform (Miscellaneous Provisions) Act 1934 in actions brought by ex-wife (who bore children by deceased) and co-habitee (who bore one child by deceased).

Jefford and another v McGee [1970] 1 All ER 1202; (1970) 114 SJ 206 CA On interest on fatal accident damages.

Jeffrey v Fisher (1982) 132 NLJ 490 CA Colleague struck by another who was driving stolen bus found not to have been contributorily negligent.

Jeffrey v Sherry [1947] LJNCCR 29 CyCt Rooms held to have been lawfully sub-let by tenant so was no trespass.

Jenkins v Great Western Rail Co [1911-13] All ER 216; [1912] 1 KB 525; (1911) 46 LJ 804; (1912) 81 LJKB 378 (1911-12) 105 LTR 882 CA Not liable in respect of injury to child wandering from where had licence to play.

Jenkins, Coop v (1982) 132 NLJ 141 HC QBD Licensee liable in negligence for injuries sustained by bar-manageress who fell through trapdoor left open by barman.

Jenkins, Devonshire and Smith v (1979) 129 (1) NLJ 198c CA Aggravated, not exemplary damages for harassment/nuisance.

Jenner v South-Eastern Railway Company (1911) 75 JP 419; (1911-12) 105 LTR 131; (1910-11) 55 SJ 553; (1910-11) XXVII TLR 445 HC KBD Circumstances justified jury finding that there was inadequate care taken to protect vehicles using level crossing.

Jennings Brothers, Hale v [1938] 1 All ER 579; (1938) 85 LJ 157; (1938) 82 SJ 193 CA Rylands v Fletcher applied in case of defective chair-o-plane.

Jennings Brothers, Hale v [1937] LJNCCR 228 CyCt Fairground operators not liable in negligence/ nuisance for injuries suffered by woman when 'chair-o-plane' (which became detached as result of its occupant's recklessness) struck her, there being no latent defect in the 'chair-o-plane' machine which was not dangerous in itself and where machine not operated negligently.

Jennings v British Railways Board (1984) 134 NLJ 584 HC QBD Defendant liable for accident occasioned to plaintiff as result of former's inadequate cleaning system in certain area.

Jennings v Cole [1949] 2 All ER 191 HC KBD Neighbour doing agreed task in neighbour's house which materially benefited latter an invitee.

Jennings v Norman Collison (Contractors) Ltd [1970] 1 All ER 1121 CA Contributory negligence re-appraised where factual error by trial judge.

Jensen and others, Pavlides v [1956] 3 WLR 224 HC ChD Negligence claim against directors for alleged non-fraudulent sale of company assets at under-value was unmaintainable.

Jepps v LMS Railway Co [1944] LJNCCR 129 CyCt Was negligent for train to be pulled up at station in such a way that passenger could not but injure self in alighting from his carriage.

Jeremiah Ambler and Sons, Limited v Bradford Corporation [1902] 2 Ch 585 CA Public Authority Protection Act 1893, s 1(b) — judgment for defendant in action for negligent discharge of statutory function carries costs between solicitor and client — applies to performing duties under provisional electric lights regulation (but does not apply to appeals).

Jerome v Bentley and Co [1952] 2 All ER 114; (1952) 102 LJ 343; (1952) 96 SJ 462; [1952] 2 TLR 58 HC QBD Liability for conversion where bought item from person not authorised as/could not be presumed to be agent for sale.

Jerram v Southampton County Council and another (1927) 64 LJ ccr38 CyCt Failed action for negligence/nuisance against local councils for person who injured self in drain-grating.

Jerred and others v T Roddam Dent and Son, Ltd (Glen Line, Ltd Third Party) [1948] 2 All ER 104 Assizes Duty of invitor to invitee did not extend to third party.

Jewelowski v Propp [1944] 1 All ER 483; (1944) 171 LTR 234; (1943-44) LX TLR 559 HC KBD No duty to mitigate damages in fraudulent misrepresentation action.

Jewish Colonial Trust, Ose Gesellschaft, &c v (1926-27) XLIII TLR 398 HC KBD Failed action for negligence where cheque was lost and amount was debited from account when cheque later used fraudulently.

Jeyaretnam (Joshua Benjamin) v Tong (Goh Chok) (1989) 133 SJ 1032; [1989] 1 WLR 1109 PC Comments of politician at press conference deemed to be fair comments and not defamatory.

JH Cobden Ltd and another, Pritchard v [1987] 1 All ER 300; [1988] Fam 22; [1987] 2 FLR 30; (1970) 130 SJ 715; [1987] 2 WLR 627 CA Date of trial date on which to assess actual/future loss of earnings; divorce costs cannot be included in damages as not a loss.

JH Coles Proprietary Limited (in liquidation) v Need (John Francis) (1934) 150 LTR 166 PC Injunction granted to restrain use of another's trade names after that other's licence to do so had been revoked.

JH Dewhurst, Ltd v Ratcliffe (1951) 101 LJ 361 CyCt Failed application in nuisance against hedge owner by motorist who on brushing against hedge collided with tree stump hidden by hedge.

JJ Saunders Ltd and others, Wheeler and another v [1995] 2 All ER 697; [1996] Ch 19; [1995] TLR 3; [1995] 3 WLR 466 CA Planning consent does not preclude action for nuisance.

JK Buckenham Ltd, Iron Trade Mutual Insurance Co Ltd and others v [1990] 1 All ER 808 HC QBD Injury caused upon procuring of voidable reinsurance policies; actions in contract/tort to be treated separately under Limitation Act even if same time limits; issue whether latent damage action is time-barred to be decided at trial/as preliminary issue, not in strike-out proceedings.

JL Cooper Ltd, Dixons (Scholar Green) Ltd v [1970] RTR 222; (1970) 114 SJ 319 CA On assessing appropriate damages for loss of use of vehicle.

JL Kier and Co Ltd, Cook v [1970] 2 All ER 513; (1970) 120 NLJ 248t; (1970) 114 SJ 207; [1970] 1 WLR 774 CA Appropriate damages for severe brain injury.

Job Edwards, Limited v The Company of Proprietors of the Birmingham Navigations [1924] 1 KB 341; [1924] 93 LJCL 261; (1924) 130 LTR 522 CA Non-liability of landowner for failure to abate fire.

Jobling v Associated Dairies Ltd [1980] 3 All ER 769; [1981] QB 389; (1980) 124 SJ 631; [1980] 3 WLR 704 CA Tortious liability falls if tortious injury overtaken by supervening illness.

Jobling v Associated Dairies Ltd [1981] 2 All ER 752; [1982] AC 794; (1981) 125 SJ 481; [1981] 3 WLR 155 HL Supervening illness to be taken into account when assessing liability of tortfeasor for injury.

John Bright (Outfitters) Limited, John Bright and Brothers, Limited v (1922-23) 67 SJ 112 CA Refusal of 'passing off' injunction where was good faith use of same name/no competition between the two firms/defendants prepared to make it clear their business was not that of plaintiffs.

John Bright and Brothers, Limited v John Bright (Outfitters) Limited (1922-23) 67 SJ 112 CA Refusal of 'passing off' injunction where was good faith use of same name/no competition between the two firms/defendants prepared to make it clear their business was not that of plaintiffs.

John Brinsmead and Sons (Limited) v EG Stanley Brinsmead and Waddington and Sons (Limited) (1912-13) 57 SJ 322; (1912-13) XXIX TLR 237 HC ChD Court would not injunct person from using own name on pianos he made even though might be connected with other well-known piano firm.

John Brinsmead and Sons (Limited) v EG Stanley Brinsmead and Waddington and Sons (Limited) (1912-13) 57 SJ 716; (1912-13) XXIX TLR 706 CA Court would not injunct person from using own name on pianos he made even though might be connected with other well-known piano firm.

John Crilley and Son, Chubb Cash Ltd v (1983) 127 SJ 153; [1983] 1 WLR 599 CA Damages for conversion were market value of goods (gauged by reference to price raised for goods at wrongful auction of same).

John Gardner (London), Limited, Hornsey v [1934] LJNCCR 293 CyCt Liable towards customer-invitee in restaurant who fell through open trap-door having being given inadequate warning about its being opened.

John Gardner (London), Limited, Hornsey v [1935] LJNCCA 97 CA Liable towards customer-invitee in restaurant who fell through open trap-door having being given inadequate warning about its being opened.

John H Andrew and Co (Limited) v Kuehnrich (1912-13) XXIX TLR 771 CA Person using un/registered trade mark can oppose registration of similar mark likely to cause confusion.

John Harper and Co Ltd, Harper v (1979) 129 (1) NLJ 198c CA £700 damages for sixty year old who through negligence of another suffered an inguinal hernia.

John I Thornycroft and Co, Ltd and others, Williamson v; Goulding and another v John I Thornycroft and Co, Ltd and others [1940] 4 All ER 61 CA In assessing damages for negligence which caused death all occurrences before date of trial are relevant.

John I Thornycroft and Company, Limited, Britannia Hygienic Laundry Company, Limited v [1925] 94 LJCL 858; (1924-25) XLI TLR 667; (1925) WN (I) 227 HC KBD Costs incurred as defendants in earlier action prompted by present defendant's negligence/breach of contract were recoverable by plaintiffs here.

John I Thornycroft and Company, Limited, Britannia Hygienic Laundry Company, Limited v [1926] 95 LJCL 237; (1926) 135 LTR 83; (1923-24) 68 SJ 102; (1925-26) XLII TLR 198; (1926) WN (I) 16 CA Costs incurred as defendants in earlier action prompted irrecoverable by plaintiffs as did not prove negligence of instant defendants.

John Jacques and Son, Ltd v 'Chess' (1940) 89 LJ 195; (1940) 84 SJ 302 CA Where brand name not firmly established as unique to party's goods use of word 'genuine' by another party before that brand name was not passing off.

John Jacques and Son, Ltd v 'Chess' (a firm) [1939] 3 All ER 227; (1939) 83 SJ 585; (1939-40) LVI TLR 543 HC ChD Though brand name not firmly established as unique to party's goods use of word 'genuine' by another party before that brand name was passing off.

Johnson v Cartledge and Matthews (Matthews, Third Party) [1939] 3 All ER 654 Assizes Damage in two actions was different so no res judicata; cannot be tortfeasor if were not negligent.

Johnson v Chief Constable of Surrey [1992] TLR 551 CA On deciding whether to allow action to be brought after is statute barred.

Johnson v Croggon and Co, Ltd and another [1954] 1 All ER 121 HC QBD Ex turpi causa non oritur actio precluded relief in negligence; could not recover as invitee as had general licence to use equipment but selected defective equipment.

Johnson v Hill [1945] 2 All ER 272; (1945) 173 LTR 38; (1944-45) LXI TLR 398 CA Crown pension relevant when determining fatal accident damages.

Johnson v Martin (1950) 100 LJ 541 CyCt Failed action in nuisance against bee-keeper by person who had along with her goats been injured by the defendant's bees (one goat dying).

Johnson v Rea Ltd [1961] 3 All ER 816; [1962] 1 QB 373 CA Persons creating hazard owe duty to take reasonable steps to protect others from hazard.

Johnson-Smith, Church of Scientology of California v [1972] 1 All ER 378; [1972] 1 QB 522; (1971) 115 SJ 658; [1971] 3 WLR 434 HC QBD Parliamentary proceedings completely and absolutely privileged.

Johnston v Braham and Campbell, Limited [1917] 1 KB 586 CA Liability of agent for negligent statement to principal.

Johnston v Great Western Railway Company (1904) 39 LJ 224; [1904] 73 LJCL 568; (1904-05) XCI LTR 157; (1903-04) 48 SJ 435 CA On appropriate damages for personal injuries resulting in loss of earning capacity.

Johnstone and another, Roberts v [1989] QB 878; (1988) 132 SJ 1672; [1988] 3 WLR 1247 CA On personal injury damages for nursing care/new accommodation requirements.

Johnstone v Pedlar [1921] 2 AC 262; (1921-25) XXVII Cox CC 68; (1921) 125 LTR 809; (1920-21) XXXVII TLR 870; (1921) WN (I) 229 HL Not good defence to action by friendly alien to recover property wrongfully seized/detained by police that seizure/detention ratified by Crown.

Johnstone v Simmons [1937] LJNCCR 289 CyCt Person liable for collapse of wall where if did not know of dangerous condition of wall she ought to have known of it.

Johnstone, Ellis v [1963] 1 All ER 286; (1963) 113 LJ 120; [1963] 2 QB 8; (1962) 106 SJ 1030; [1963] 2 WLR 176 CA No customary/special duty on dog owner to prevent dog straying onto highway.

Johnstone, McNeill and another v [1958] 3 All ER 16; (1958) 108 LJ 570; (1958) 102 SJ 602 HC QBD Husband allowed recover portion of expenses incurred through month's leave of absence from work to be near wife.

Joint Committee of the River Ribble v Halliwell; Same v Shorrock (1899-1900) LXXXI LTR 38 CA Failed action for nuisance arising from alleged placing of putrid solid matter in river.

Jolliffe v Willmett and Co and another [1971] 1 All ER 478; (1970) 120 NLJ 707t; (1970) 114 SJ 619 HC QBD Person entering home of separated spouse (not family home) with permission of other spouse is trespasser; employer not responsible for torts of independent contractor unless commssioned tort/negligence in choosing same led to tort.

Jolly v Kine [1907] AC 1; [1907] 76 LJCh 1; (1906-07) XCV LTR 656; (1906-07) 51 SJ 11; (1906-07) XXIII TLR 1 HL Obstruction of ancient lights a nuisance though room still well-lit.

Jolly, Kine v [1905] 1 Ch 480; (1905) XCII LTR 209; (1904-05) 49 SJ 164; (1904-05) XXI TLR 128; (1904-05) 53 WR 462 CA Obstruction of ancient lights a nuisance.

Jones (Isgoed) v Llanrwst Urban District Council (1911) 75 JP 68; (1910-11) 103 LTR 751 HC ChD Injunction granted to restrain nuisance/trespass occasioned by local authority's discharge of sewage into boundary river.

Jones (Morgan), Paddick v (1931) 72 LJ ccr31 CyCt Person liable in damages for injuries to pigeons occasioned by his cat which he had known to be vicious.

Jones (Mrs JP) or M'Ewan et é contra, Watson (Sir Patrick H) v; Watson (Sir Patrick H) v Jones (James) [1905] AC 480; [1905] 74 LJPC 151; (1905-06) XCIII LTR 489; (1905) WN (I) 130 HL Witness privilege in witness box against later slander action extends to communications to solicitor/client in preparing for trial.

Jones v Bennett (1975) 125 NLJ 870t HC QBD Failed application for extension of limitation where although applicant was illiterate she had been in possesssion of the relevant facts.

Jones v Department of Employment [1988] 1 All ER 725; (1987) 137 NLJ 1182; [1989] QB 1; (1988) 132 SJ 128; [1988] 2 WLR 493 CA By statute adjudication officers cannot be sued for negligence; misfeasance, judicial review, statutory appeal only means of challenging decision.

Jones v E Hulton and Co [1908-10] All ER 29; [1909] 2 KB 444; [1909] 78 LJKB 937; (1909-10) 101 LTR 330; (1908-09) XXV TLR 597; (1909) WN (I) 133 CA No defence to libel that was unintentional.

Jones v Great Western Railway Company [1924-35] All ER 462; (1931) 144 LTR 194; (1930-31) XLVII TLR 39 HL Fatal accident damages allowed in respect of accident to which no witnesses in action to which defence submitted was no case to answer.

Jones v Griffith [1969] 2 All ER 1015; (1969) 113 SJ 309; [1969] 1 WLR 795 CA Appropriate damages where epilepsy induced by accident.

Jones v Hall (1981) 131 NLJ 856 HC QBD Succesful action for damages in negligence for injuries suffered by person kicked by another's horse.

Jones v Jones [1985] QB 704; (1984) 128 SJ 470; [1984] TLR 415; [1984] 3 WLR 862 CA Person inflicting personal injuries liable for costs incurred by break-up of injured party's marriage (caused directly by injuries inflicted).

Jones v Jones and another [1970] 3 All ER 47; [1971] 1 WLR 396 CA Solicitor jeopardising client's claim to interest on damages through late issue of writ open to negligence action.

Jones v Jones and Wife [1914-17] All ER 560; [1916] 2 AC 481; (1916) 51 LJ 409; [1916] 85 LJKB 1519; (1916-17) 115 LTR 432; (1916-17) 61 SJ 8; (1915-16) XXXII TLR 705; (1916) WN (I) 312 HL Allegation of immorality against schoolteacher not of itself actionable.

Jones v Jones and Wife (1915) 50 LJ 133; [1915] 84 LJKB 1140; (1915-16) 113 LTR 336; (1914-15) XXXI TLR 245; (1915) WN (I) 115 HC KBD Allegation of immorality against schoolteacher actionable without proof of special damage.

Jones v Jones and Wife [1916] 1 KB 351; (1915) 50 LJ 630; [1916] 85 LJKB 388; (1916) 114 LTR 253; (1915-16) 60 SJ 140; (1915-16) XXXII TLR 171; (1915) WN (I) 408 CA Allegation of adultery against schoolmaster not slander unless reflects on same as professional.

Jones v Lawrence [1969] 3 All ER 267 Assizes Normal carelessness of 7 year old not negligence; damages for loss of grammar school place/concentration.

Jones v Livox Quarries Ld; Same v Same [1952] 2 QB 608 CA Person injured by travelling on towbar of vehicle despite contrary instructions was contributorily negligent towards injuries suffered.

Jones v Oceanic Steam Navigation Company, Limited (1924-25) 69 SJ 106; (1923-24) XL TLR 847 HC KBD Construction of contract of passage (failed attempt at precluding liability for injuries to passenger).

Jones v Price (1965) 115 LJ 512; [1965] 2 QB 618; [1965] 3 WLR 296 CA Absent agreement to do so was no obligation on landowner to fence property so as to stop neighbour's cattle straying.

Jones v Pritchard [1908] 1 Ch 630; (1908) XCVIII LTR 386 HC ChD Person enjoying easements as regards user of common wall not liable for nuisance arising from user so long as is not negligent/careless and uses it for purposes envisioned.

Jones v Rew [1908-10] All ER 955; (1910) 74 JP 321 (also HC KBD); (1910) 79 LJKB 1030; (1910-11) 103 LTR 165 CA Urban sanitary authority liable in nuisance for state of carriage plate (not party who sometimes cleaned it out).

Jones v Rew (1910) 74 JP 321 (also CA) HC KBD Party who sometimes cleaned out carriage plate, not sanitary authority, liable in nuisance for state of same.

Jones v Staveley Iron and Chemical Co Ld [1955] 1 QB 474 CA Test for negligence versus that for contributory negligence.

Jones v Swansea City Council (1989) 139 NLJ 503; (1990) 134 SJ 341; [1990] 1 WLR 54 CA Could be misfeasance in public office for council to refuse change of user of leasehold premises because of ill-will towards lessee's husband, a member of a minority political party on the local authority.

Kralj and another v McGrath and another [1986] 1 All ER 54; (1985) 135 NLJ 913 HC QBD Aggravated damages not appropriate for medical negligence though compensatory damages may be raised; damages for nervous shock, not grief; financial loss in replacing dead child recoverable.

Kubach and another v Hollands and another; Frederick Allen and Sons (Poplar), Limited (Third Party) (1937) 84 LJ 157; (1937) 81 SJ 766; (1936-37) LIII TLR 1024 HC KBD Negligent suppliers of chemicals to school who were successfully sued by student injured through their negligence could not in turn recover against wholesale suppliers.

Kuehnrich, John H Andrew and Co (Limited) v (1912-13) XXIX TLR 771 CA Person using un/registered trade mark can oppose registration of similar mark likely to cause confusion.

Kum (Chan Cheng), Wah Tat Bank Ltd and another v [1975] 2 All ER 257; [1975] AC 507; (1975) 125 NLJ 133; (1975) 119 SJ 151; [1975] 2 WLR 475 PC Joint tortfeasor not sued to judgment could be sued again.

Kuys (Laurentius Cornelius) and another, New Zealand Netherlands Society 'Oranje' Incorporated v (1973) 117 SJ 565; [1973] 1 WLR 1126 PC Person in fiduciary position in a society held to owe no fiduciary duty to society as regards newspaper person published himself: granted injunction against society publishing newspaper under same name.

Kynoch Limited v Rowlands [1911-13] All ER 1258; [1912] 1 Ch 527 (also HC ChD); (1912) 81 LJCh 340 (also HC ChD); (1912) 106 LTR 316 CA Trespass found where was inadequate evidence of discontinuance of possession.

Kynoch, Limited v Rowlands [1912] 1 Ch 527 (also CA); [1912] 81 LJCh 340 (also CA); (1910-11) 55 SJ 617 HC ChD Trespass found where was inadequate evidence of discontinuance of possession.

L Goodall and Sons, Ltd and Another, Sims v (1965-66) 116 NLJ 472t HC QBD Contractors who left gas cylinder on site not liable in negligence for subsequent injury to member of public who sought to put out fire caused when cylinder exploded.

L Homberger and Co, Yeatman v (1912-13) 107 LTR 43; (1911-12) 56 SJ 614 HC ChD Injunction granted to restrain passing off in price circular of one wine as another.

L Obertling, Ltd, Jackson v (1925) 60 LJ 521 CyCt Damages recoverable for nuisance occasioned by broken pavement light (said light not being part of highway repairable by highway authority).

La Morta, Shapiro v [1923] All ER 378; (1923) 58 LJ 513; (1924) 130 LTR 622; (1923-24) 68 SJ 522; (1923-24) XL TLR 201 CA Must prove damage/malice and can only recover damages for actual damage in action for malicious falsehood affecting business/property.

La Morta, Shapiro v (1923-24) 68 SJ 142; (1923-24) XL TLR 39; (1923) WN (I) 290 HC KBD Must prove malice and can only recover damages for actual damage in action for malicious falsehood (failed to do so here).

La Radiotechnique v Weinbaum (1927) 64 LJ 121; (1928) 97 LJCh 17; (1927) 71 SJ 824; (1927) WN (I) 211 HC ChD On when HC will order particulars of defence.

La Société Anonyme de Remorquage Hélice v Bennetts [1911] 1 KB 243 HC KBD Damages not recoverable despite presence of negligence for results which did not directly flow from same.

Labouchere Dakhyl v [1908] 2 KB 325; [1908] 77 LJCL 728; (1907) XCVI LTR 399; (1906-07) XXIII TLR 364 HL On defence of fair comment.

Ladbroke and Co v Todd (1914-15) 111 LTR 43 HC KBD Is negligent for banker without making inquiries to open account for person presenting cheque marked 'Account payee only'.

Lagan Navigation Company v Lambeg Bleaching, Dyeing and Finishing Company, Limited [1926] All ER 230; [1927] AC 226; (1927) 91 JP 46; (1927) 96 LJPC 25; (1927) 136 LTR 417 HL No nuisance but had there been court disdained private abatement thereof.

Laing and others, Jungnickel v (1967) 111 SJ 19 CA To reduce one's driving speed without warning was not negligent.

Laing, R v [1995] Crim LR 395 CA Could not be guilty of burglary where were not trespasser when entered building.

Lait v AA King (Contractors) Ltd, London Electricity Board and Pitchers (1975) 125 NLJ 432 HC QBD Person who damaged electric cable plates but did not tell Electricity Board was liable along with later worker's employer for injury that followed from damage (Electricity Board not liable).

Larking v Bunnell (1912) CC Rep I 23 CyCt Person bringing article dangerous in itself (here gas) into premises not liable where accident occurs that does not arise from said person not exercising reasonable care.

Larner v Larner [1904-07] All ER 1022; [1905] 2 KB 539; (1905) 40 LJ 544; (1905-06) XCIII LTR 537; (1904-05) XXI TLR 637; (1905) WN (I) 116; (1905-06) 54 WR 62 HC KBD Wife can bring detinue action against husband.

Larrinaga Steamship Company Ltd, Navarro v; The Niceto de Larrinaga (1965) 109 SJ 633; [1965] 3 WLR 573 HC PDAD Two year limitation on fatal accident claims under Maritime Conventions Act 1911 inapplicable to vessel in which travelling when cause of claim arose.

Lasczyk v National Coal Board [1954] 3 All ER 205 Assizes Guilty of contributory negligence where acting under supervisor's instructions but contrary to training officer's ordinance.

Laskey and another, Malone v [1904-07] All ER 304; [1907] 2 KB 141; (1907-08) XCVII LTR 324; (1906-07) 51 SJ 356; (1906-07) XXIII TLR 399 CA Licensee not allowed recover for private nuisance (vibration).

Lasseter, Lawrence (Lim) v (1924) CC Rep XIII 2 CyCt Successful claim against party guilty of purchase-conversion of furniture which had comprised security for loan to vendor of furniture.

Latchford v Beirne (1981) 131 NLJ 856 HC QBD Receiver did not owe duty of care to individual creditors.

Latchford v Spedeworth International Ltd (1984) 134 NLJ 36; [1983] TLR 587 HC QBD Successful negligence claim by hot-rod racer for injury suffered where tyres on track after another's collision with tyre fence forced him into collision with concrete flower bed.

Lathall v Joyce (A) and Son and others [1939] 3 All ER 854; (1938-39) LV TLR 994 HC KBD Non-recovery for attack by domestic animal not reasonably to be expected.

Latham v Richard Johnson and Nephew, Ltd [1911-13] All ER 117; (1913) 77 JP 137; [1913] 1 KB 398; (1912) 47 LJ 748; [1913] 82 LJKB 258; (1913) 108 LTR 4; (1912-13) 57 SJ 127; (1912-13) XXIX TLR 124; (1912) WN (I) 290 CA Occupier of land on which stones owed no special duty of care to children playing thereon — implied term in licence that children to be accompanied by adults.

Laughton and others, Merkur Island Shipping Corp v [1983] 1 All ER 334; (1983) 133 NLJ 186; [1983] 2 WLR 45 CA Elements of 'inducement to commit breach of contract'; immunity from action in tort if purpose of secondary action to frustrate contract between picketed employer and employer facing secondary action.

Launchbury and others v Morgan and others [1971] 1 All ER 642; (1971) 121 NLJ 83t; [1971] 2 QB 245; [1971] RTR 97; (1971) 115 SJ 96; [1971] 2 WLR 602 CA Owner vicariously liable for negligence of third party driving car.

Laurence and another v Lexcourt Holdings Ltd [1978] 2 All ER 810; [1978] 1 WLR 1128 HC ChD Common mistake/misrepresentation where incorrectly state premises have unrestricted planning permission for office use; reasonable delay/inaction not acquiescence.

Laurie v Raglan Building Co, Ltd [1941] 3 All ER 332; [1942] 1 KB 152; (1941) 91 LJ 422; (1942) 92 LJ 60; [1942] 111 LJ 292; (1942) 166 LTR 63; (1942) 86 SJ 69 CA Skid requires driver (or here driver's employers) to show were not negligent.

Lavender, Limited and another, Becker v (1946) 90 SJ 502; (1945-46) LXII TLR 504; (1946) WN (I) 135 HC KBD Bailee for reward liable where did not take as much care of bailed property as would of own.

Lavery, Owen v (1899-1900) XVI TLR 375 CA Bringing bankruptcy proceedings from ulterior motive different to that envisaged by bankruptcy legislation was malicious prosecution.

Lavis v Kent County Council [1994] TLR 600 HC QBD County council deemed not to have been negligent in non-erection of road signs in certain place.

Law Debenture Trust Corp plc v Ural Caspian Oil Corp Ltd and others [1995] 1 All ER 157; [1995] Ch 152; [1994] 3 WLR 1221 CA Tort of procuring violation of right extends not only to contractual rights but to right to relief.

Law Society, Wood v (1993) 143 NLJ 1475 HC QBD Law Society does not owe duty of care to protect client from loss occasioned by solicitor whom are investigating on foot of client's complaint.

Law v Llewellyn [1904-07] All ER 536; (1906) 70 JP 220; [1906] 1 KB 487; (1906) 41 LJ 137; [1906] 75 LJKB 320; (1906) XCIV LTR 359; (1905-06) 50 SJ 289; (1906) WN (I) 50; (1905-06) 54 WR 368 CA Magistrate absolutely privileged in respect of defamatory statements made in course of acting as magistrate.

Law v Railway Executive and another (1949) LXV TLR 288 HC KBD Railway company/local authority liable in negligence for injury suffered by person colliding with wall and pavement the former had put in place of level crossing gates.

Law, The City of Birmingham Tramways Company Limited v (1910) 74 JP 355; [1910] 2 KB 965; (1911) 80 LJCL 80; (1910-11) 103 LTR 44 HC KBD Lessees of tramway could recover compensation paid from party who had contracted with lessor to relay tramway/indemnify lessor for related claims.

Lawrence (CS) and Partners (a firm) and others (PJ Crook and Co (a firm), third party), Rath and another v [1991] 3 All ER 679 CA Delay in issuing writ not inordinate delay but wilful delay following writ may be.

Lawrence (Lim) v Lasseter (1924) CC Rep XIII 2 CyCt Successful claim against party guilty of purchase-conversion of furniture which had comprised security for loan to vendor of furniture.

Lawrence v Hall and another (1928) 72 SJ 87 HC KBD Letter by club secretary written in context of leasing of premises and in which it was implied (according to the plaintiff-solicitor) that he was incompetent was privileged/not motivated by malice.

Lawrence v WM Palmer (Excavations), Ltd, and another (1965) 109 SJ 358 HC QBD Two-third/ one-third apportionment of liability between driver/deaf pedestrian for accident at pedestrian crossing.

Lawrence, Jones v [1969] 3 All ER 267 Assizes Normal carelessness of 7 year old not negligence; damages for loss of grammar school place/concentration.

Lawrence, Messer and Co, Malyon v (1969) 119 NLJ 38; (1968) 112 SJ 623 HC QBD Recovery of damages from solictors which would have recovered in action in Germany had not negligence of solicitors led to action being time-barred.

Laws and others v Florinplace Ltd and another [1981] 1 All ER 659 HC ChD Injunction possible for nuisance not involving physical emanation.

Lawson and another, Moore v (1914-15) XXXI TLR 418 CA Court will not strike out claim statement in libel action on basis that words cannot be defamatory — whether are defamatory a matter for trial judge.

Lawson v Tuddenham [1945] LJNCCR 141 CyCt Failed claim in nuisance/trespass arising from allegedly excessive user of right of way.

Lawton, Waller v (1981) 131 NLJ 1134 HC QBD On appropriate damages for person who suffered inter alia serious brain damage when struck by motor vehicle.

Lazar and another, Femis-Bank (Anguilla) Ltd and others v [1991] 2 All ER 865; [1991] Ch 391; [1991] TLR 69; [1991] 3 WLR 80 HC ChD Injunction pending trial which would interfere with freedom of speech only exceptionally available.

Le Fleming, Lancaster v (1920) CC Rep IX 86 CyCt Lord of Manor liable in negligence for failure to fence off quarry (with result that cow was lost).

Le Jean, Limited, Sales Affiliates, Limited v [1947] Ch 295; (1947) 97 LJ 106; [1947] 116 LJR 729; (1947) 176 LTR 251; (1947) 91 SJ 100 HC ChD Injunction to prevent giving 'Jamal' hair-wave without using 'Jamal' products: absent actual sale of goods passing-off can be proved by evidence from trade witness.

Le Roy and Fils, Clayton v [1911-13] All ER 284; (1911) 75 JP 521; (1911-12) 105 LTR 430; (1910-11) XXVII TLR 479 CA Whether sale of goods in auction room constituted conversion.

Le Roy and Fils, Clayton v (1910-11) XXVII TLR 206 HC KBD Whether sale of goods in auction room constituted conversion.

Leach v British Oxygen Co, Ltd (1965) 109 SJ 157 CA Employers not liable for injury which occurred to workman directed to do certain task.

Leach v Standard Telephones and Cables, Ltd [1966] 2 All ER 523 HC QBD Employer contributorily negligent towards employee's breach of employee duty under Factory Act 1961.

Leachinsky v Christie [1945] 2 All ER 395; (1946) 110 JP 23; [1946] KB 124; (1946) 96 LJ 185; [1946] 115 LJ 241; (1946) 174 LTR 13; (1944-45) LXI TLR 584 CA Cannot be arrested for misdemeanour because suspected of felony; on special powers of arrest.

Leachinsky, Christie and another v [1947] 1 All ER 567; [1947] AC 573; (1947) 111 JP 224; (1947) 97 LJ 165; [1947] 116 LJR 757; (1947) 176 LTR 443; (1947) LXIII TLR 231 HL False imprisonment where arrested without warrant and not told why/not obvious why/inobvious why and do not resist.

League Against Cruel Sports Ltd v Scott and others [1985] 2 All ER 489; [1986] QB 240; (1985) 129 SJ 543 HC QBD Master of hounds liable for hounds' trespass where knew real risk of entry/negligently failed to prevent trespass; master liable for persons over whom has control; intent/negligence judged by conduct.

Leake v Wootton and Kelley (trading as the Stoneleigh Quarry Company) (1923) CC Rep XII 68 CyCt Failed action against quarrying company for damages after cattle got sick drinking water polluted (but only inter alia) by local quarry.

Leakey and others v National Trust for Places of Historic Interest or Natural Beauty [1980] 1 All ER 17; (1979) 129 (2) NLJ 781; [1980] QB 485; (1979) 123 SJ 606; [1980] 2 WLR 65 CA Must take reasonable steps to prevent natural/man-made features on one's land causing damage/becoming danger to another.

Leakey and others v National Trust for Places of Historic Interest or Natural Beauty [1978] 3 All ER 234; (1978) 128 NLJ 242t; [1978] QB 849; (1978) 122 SJ 231; [1978] 2 WLR 774 HC QBD Occupier must take reasonable steps to remove occurrence on land which is hazard for neighbour.

Lean v Alston [1947] 1 All ER 261 CA Third party recovery from deceased's estate posible though deceased not party to negligence action.

Leanse v Egerton [1943] 1 All ER 489; [1943] KB 323; (1944) 94 LJ 109; [1943] 112 LJ 273; (1943) 168 LTR 218; (1942-43) LIX TLR 191; (1943) WN (I) 56 HC KBD Occupier liable for continuing nuisance occasioned by air raid.

Leathem, Quinn v [1900-03] All ER 1; (1901) WN (I) 170 HL Damages available for conspiracy to induce breaches of contract by employees/customers.

Leather v Kirby [1965] 3 All ER 927; (1965-66) 116 NLJ 275; [1965] 1 WLR 1489 HL On claim compromises by persons under disability.

Leather, Kirby v [1965] 2 All ER 41; [1965] 2 QB 367; (1965) 109 SJ 357; [1965] 2 WLR 1318 CA Incapability of managing own affairs means 'of unsound mind'; adult being looked after by mother is not in her custody.

Leaver v Pontypridd Urban District Council (1911) 75 JP 25 CA Not enough evidence of negligence for matter to go to jury where tram driver did not stop tram when confronted by obstruction.

Leaver v Pontypridd Urban District Council (1910) 74 JP 199 HC KBD Was sufficient evidence of negligence for matter to go to jury where tram driver did not stop tram when confronted by obstruction.

Leaver v Pontypridd Urban District Council (1912) 76 JP 31; (1911-12) 56 SJ 32 HL Was evidence of negligence such that matter should go to jury where tram driver did not stop tram when confronted by obstruction.

Lecouturier and others v Rey and another; Lecouturier and others v Rey and others [1910] AC 262; (1910) 45 LJ 205; (1909-10) 54 SJ 375; (1909-10) XXVI TLR 368; (1910) WN (I) 79 HL Foreign manufacturer could succeed in passing off action where locus of passing off was England as had acquired reputation there.

Lecouturier, Rey v [1908] 2 Ch 715; [1909] 78 LJCh 181; (1908) XCVIII LTR 197 CA Foreign manufacturer could succeed in passing off action where locus of passing off was England as had acquired reputation there.

Ledingham and others v Bermejo Estancia Co, Ltd; Agar and others v Same [1947] 1 All ER 749 HC KBD Contract valid as legal relationship desired/was consideration; limitation ran once ability to pay under contract ceased.

Lee and Another v Walkers (a firm) and Another (1940) 162 LTR 89; (1939) 83 SJ 925 HC KBD Owner not liable for injury caused by dog whom knew to pose a risk where person injured by dog brought injury upon themself through their own interference.

Lee Conservancy Board v Leyton Urban District Council (1906-07) XCV LTR 487 HC KBD Single act of negligence in allowing sewage into river did not render council guilty of offence under Lee Conservancy Act 1868.

Lee Cooper, Ltd v CH Jeakins and Sons, Ltd [1965] 1 All ER 280; (1965) 115 LJ 126; [1967] 2 QB 1; (1965) 109 SJ 794; [1965] 3 WLR 753 HC QBD Bailees owed duty of care to non-bailor owners.

Lee Kar Choo (trading as Yeen Thye Co) v Lee Lian Choon (trading as Chuan Lee Co) [1966] 3 All ER 1000; [1967] AC 602; (1966) 110 SJ 946; [1966] 3 WLR 1175 PC That no trade mark violations does not mean no passing-off; injunction/ancillary relief available where contrive to implement passing off.

Lee Lian Choon (trading as Chuan Lee Co), Lee Kar Choo (trading as Yeen Thye Co) v [1966] 3 All ER 1000; [1967] AC 602; (1966) 110 SJ 946; [1966] 3 WLR 1175 PC That no trade mark violations does not mean no passing-off; injunction/ancillary relief available where contrive to implement passing off.

Lee v Lever [1974] RTR 35 CA Parties equally liable where negligent driver collided with unlit car left parked at night on well-lit clearway.

Lee v Luper [1936] 3 All ER 817; (1937) 81 SJ 15 HC KBD Publican not liable to invitee sustaining injury in private area of pub.

Lee v Sheard [1955] 3 All ER 777; (1955) 105 LJ 809; [1956] 1 QB 192; (1955) 99 SJ 888; [1955] 3 WLR 951 CA Reduction in share of company profits by third party consequent upon tort recoverable from tortfeasor.

Lee, Edwards v (1991) 141 NLJ 1517 HC QBD Solicitor is liable in negligence if does not reveal that client (for whom is giving business reference) has been charged with a dishonesty offence.

Lee, Jones and another v [1911-13] All ER 313; (1912) 76 JP 137; (1912) 106 LTR 123; (1911-12) 56 SJ 125; (1911-12) XXVIII TLR 92 HC KBD Landowner not liable for damage caused by horse straying — no duty to fence in.

Lee, Ramsden v [1992] 2 All ER 204 CA Court should have regard to all circumstances before disapplying limitation period.

Lee-Leviten and another, Marlton (an infant) and another v [1968] 2 All ER 874 CA Inexcusable delay excused as no prejudice, action certain of success, plaintiff's infancy, payment into court.

Leech Brain and Co, Ltd and another, Smith v [1961] 3 All ER 1159; (1962) 112 LJ 89; [1962] 2 QB 405; (1962) 106 SJ 77 HC QBD Person committing tort must take victim as found — here liable for cancer resulting from burn to malignancy.

Leeds Corporation, Bedford v (1913) 77 JP 430 HC ChD Action to restrain nuisance occasioned by holding of yearly feast (action successful in part).

Leeds Western Health Authority and another, Saunders v (1985) 129 SJ 225 HC QBD Successful negligence action (based on res ipsa loquitur) by normal party who went into hospital for routine operation and emerged a partially sighted, mentally retarded spastic quadraplegic.

Leeman v Montagu [1936] 2 All ER 1677; (1936) 80 SJ 691 HC KBD Noise from poultry farm a nuisance.

Leeming, Freeborn v (1926) 90 JP 179; [1926] 1 KB 160 (also CA); (1925) 60 LJ 637/823; [1926] 95 LJCL 114 (also CA); (1924-25) 69 SJ 663/692; (1928-29) XLV TLR 567 HC KBD Six month limitation against public authority ran from moment patient stopped being in doctor's care.

Leeming, Freeborn v (1926) 90 JP 53; [1926] 1 KB 160 (also HC KBD); (1925) 60 LJ 1007; [1926] 95 LJCL 114 (also HC KBD); (1926) 134 LTR 117; (1925-26) 70 SJ 264; (1925-26) XLII TLR 119; (1925) WN (I) 273 CA Six month limitation against public authority ran from moment patient stopped being in doctor's care.

Lees and others, Hall and Wife v (1903-04) 48 SJ 638 CA Nursing association not liable for negligence of trained nurses it supplied as agreement was to provide nurse and it exercised reasonable care in doing so.

Leetham v Rank (1912-13) 57 SJ 111 CA Must prove actual loss of customers to succeed in defamation action where allege that have suffered injury as result of malicious falsehoods that are not actionable of themselves.

Lefever, Wright v (1902-03) 47 SJ 109; (1902-03) 51 WR 149 CA House-owner liable to person-invitee injured at house when (after getting key from house-agent) went to look over same with view to renting it.

Legal and General Assurance Society Ltd v Daniel and Others (1967) 117 NLJ 113t CA Successful passing off action by Legal and General Assurance Society against the 'Legal and General Enquiry Bureau'.

Leggett, Davidson v (1969) 113 SJ 409 CA Parties to collision between two overtaking vehicles coming from opposite directions were equally responsible for accident.

Leibo v D Buckman, Ltd and another [1952] 2 All ER 1057; (1952) 96 SJ 865; [1952] 2 TLR 969; (1952) WN (I) 547 CA Unless reasonable and probable cause is malicious prosecution.

Leicester Corporation, Lofthouse v (1948) LXIV TLR 604 CA On reversal of decisions of trial judge in Fatal Accident/running down actions (here unreversed).

Leigh and another, Humphrey and another v [1971] RTR 363 CA Driver on main road not required to take precaution of taking foot from accelerator and placing above brake as approached/passed side-road.

Leigh and Sillavan Ltd v Aliakmon Shipping Co Ltd; The Aliakmon [1985] 2 All ER 44; [1985] QB 350; (1985) 129 SJ 69; [1984] TLR 710; [1985] 2 WLR 289 CA Duty of care but no liability because would create vague liability to vague class; despite foreseeability circumstances did not justify recovery for economic loss; negligence that of stevedores not shipowners.

Leigh and Sillivan Ltd v Aliakmon Shipping Co Ltd; The Aliakmon [1986] 2 All ER 145; [1986] AC 785; (1986) 136 NLJ 415; (1986) 130 SJ 357; [1986] 2 WLR 902 HL Buyer of goods cannot claim for loss or damage from negligence unless owns/has title to property.

Leigh Rugby Club, Ltd, Simms v [1969] 2 All ER 923; (1969) 119 NLJ 649 Assizes Rugby player accepts risks of rugby/pitch conforming to Rugby League specifications; occupier not liable for foreseeable but unlikely events.

Leigh v Gladstone and others (1909-10) XXVI TLR 139 HC KBD Depends on circumstances whether force-feeding of prisoners constituted trespass to the person (here was not); medical officer's reports to prison governor are not privileged.

Leighton, Wilkins v [1932] All ER 55; [1932] 2 Ch 106; (1932) 73 LJ 255; (1932) 101 LJCh 385; (1932) 147 LTR 495; (1932) 76 SJ 232; (1932) WN (I) 68 HC ChD Occupier not liable for nuisance unless created it or knowingly allows it to continue when could abate it.

Leiper and others, O'Boyle and another v (1990) 134 SJ 316 CA Settlement in full and final settlement of all claims treated as precisely that.

Lennon (Limited), British Chartered Company of South Africa v [1916] 85 LJPC 111; (1915-16) 113 LTR 935; (1914-15) XXXI TLR 585 PC Recovery of damages for loss suffered through use of cattle dip marketed as particular concentrate but actually stronger.

Leonard D Ford and Teller Limited, Marchant Manufacturing Company Limited v (1936) 154 LTR 430 HC KBD Rylands v Fletcher inapplicable to situation where some water in water boiler installed on second floor of commercial premises leaked into ground floor: failed negligence action.

Leonard v London Corporation [1940] LJNCCR 267 CyCt Non-liability on basis of principle of volenti non fit injuria in respect of injury suffered by invitee.

Leonard, Eagus v (1962) 106 SJ 918 CA On rôle of agreed medical reports in assessment of personal injuries damages.

Lertora v Finzi [1973] RTR 161 HC QBD Failed attempt to prove injured driver contributorily negligent as regards injuries suffered when not wearing seat belt.

Lewis and others, Lambert and another v; Lexmead (Basingstoke) Ltd (Third Party); B Dixon Bate Ltd (Fourth Party) [1979] RTR 61 HC QBD Owner and manufacturers of defective coupling were liable in negligence for damage caused thereby; retailer of coupling not liable.

Lewis and others, Lexmead (Basingstoke) Ltd v [1982] AC 225 (also CA); (1981) 131 NLJ 422; [1981] RTR 346; (1981) 125 SJ 310; [1981] 2 WLR 713 HL Warranty expired once person to whom item supplied behaved in negligent manner.

Lewis and others, Ward v [1955] 1 All ER 55; [1955] 1 WLR 9 CA No connection between alleged slander and special damage meant could be no conspiracy to slander.

Lewis and others; Lexmead (Basingstoke) Ltd (Third Party), Lambert and another v; Dixon Bate Ltd (Fourth Party) [1980] RTR 152 CA Owner/retailers of defective coupling were liable in negligence for damage caused thereby; manufacturer of coupling not liable.

Lewis Hillman Ltd and another, Gross v [1969] 3 WLR 787 CA Misrepresentation only fraudulent if intended to be so.

Lewis Trusts v Bambers Stores Ltd [1983] TLR 125 CA Award of damages for conversion under the Copyright Act Act 1956, s 18.

Lewis v Carmarthenshire County Council [1953] 2 All ER 1403; (1954) 118 JP 51; (1953) 103 LJ 797; (1953) 97 SJ 831; [1953] 1 WLR 1439 CA Teacher owed duty of care to child straying onto highway/person foreseeably injured as result.

Lewis v Carmarthenshire County Council (1953) 117 JP 231 Assizes Teacher owed duty of care to child straying onto highway/person foreseeably injured as result.

Lewis v Daily Telegraph, Ltd; Rubber Improvement, Ltd v Same; Lewis v Associated Newspapers, Ltd; Rubber Improvement, Ltd v Same (1962) 106 SJ 307 CA Re-trial ordered where was inadequate direction as to innuendo: to wrongly say person subject of Serious Fraud investigation was defamatory but not in same league as saying were guilty of fraud.

Lewis v Gardner (1981) 131 NLJ 1134 HC QBD On appropriate damages for motor cycle pillion passenger who suffered brain damage in road traffic accident.

Lewis v Gunter-Jones (1949) LXV TLR 181 CA Failed action for trespass under Small Tenements Recovery Act 1838, s 3.

Lewis v Ronald [1908-10] All ER 782; (1909-10) 101 LTR 534; (1909-10) XXVI TLR 30 HC KBD Landlord not liable for injuries suffered by person visiting premises in area which landlord had contracted to light for tenants but had not done so.

Lewis v Ursell [1983] TLR 282 HC QBD Collision of motor car with gateway an accident that occurred owing to presence of that vehicle on road within meaning of the Road Traffic Act 1972, s 8(2).

Lewis, Carmarthenshire County Council v [1955] AC 549; (1955) 119 JP 230; (1955) 105 LJ 136; (1955) 99 SJ 167; [1955] 2 WLR 517 HL Is duty to prevent children (unlike animals) from straying onto highway and so imperilling others.

Lewis, Childs v (1923-24) XL TLR 870 HC KBD Damages allowed for resignation from board of directors following on false imprisonment by police.

Lewis, Nationwide Building Society v [1997] 3 All ER 498 HC ChD Estopped from denying liability as partner for negligence of other solicitor-partner where relationship really one of master and servant, not partnership but had been held out to plaintiff as partnership.

Lewis, Smith v (1916-17) XXXIII TLR 195 HC KBD Need not plead express malice where in defence to claim that publication was malicious privilege is pleaded.

Lewis, Thomas v [1937] 1 All ER 137; (1937) 81 SJ 98 HC ChD Quarry owner not liable/liable for damage to own land rented to farmer/to farmer's own land adjoining rented land for nuisance arising from quarrying.

Lewisham Borough Council, Bint v (1946) 110 JP 103; (1946) 174 LTR 128; (1946) 90 SJ 80; (1945-46) LXII TLR 238; (1946) WN (I) 12 HC KBD Local authority not negligent in not repairing fence adjacent to railway (adjoining railway fence having being fixed by railway company).

Liebrich v Cassell and Co, Ltd [1956] 1 All ER 577 (1956) 100 SJ 188; [1956] 1 WLR 249 HC QBD On statements in open court.

Liff v Peasley and another [1980] 1 All ER 623; (1980) 124 SJ 360; [1980] 1 WLR 781 CA No extension of limitation period where strong case against defendant/involvement of Motor Insurers' Bureau.

Liffen v Watson [1940] 2 All ER 213; [1940] 1 KB 556; (1940) 89 LJ 183; [1940] 109 LJCL 367; (1940) 84 SJ 368; (1939-40) LVI TLR 442; (1940) WN (I) 100 CA Damages for traumatic neurosis and for loss of board and lodging at place of employment.

Liffen v Watson (1939) 161 LTR 351; (1939) 83 SJ 871 HC KBD Taxi-driver was negligent where could not explain why had braked and skidded when knew was likely to skid when so braked.

Lilley, Morris Motors Ltd v [1959] 1 WLR 1184 HC ChD Injunction available to stop person selling manufacturer's cars as new where were not (interfered with goodwill of manufacturer).

Lim v Camden and Islington Area Health Authority (1978) 122 SJ 82 HC QBD On making allowances for inflation when awarding personal injury damages.

Limmer and Trinidad Lake Asphalt Co, Ltd and another, Jordan v [1946] 1 All ER 527; [1946] KB 356; (1946) 175 LTR 89; (1945-46) LXII TLR 302; (1946) WN (I) 76 HC KBD Income tax not to be deduced from future earnings when assessing personal injury damages.

Lincoln v Daniels [1960] 3 All ER 205; (1960) 104 SJ 625 HC QBD Complaints to Bar Council about barrister have qualified privilege.

Lincoln v Daniels [1961] 3 All ER 740; [1955] Crim LR 647; (1961) 111 LJ 660; [1962] 1 QB 237 CA No absolute privilege letters of complaint to Bar Council where letters did not lead to disciplinary action.

Lincoln v Daniels [1960] 3 All ER 205; (1960) 110 LJ 655 HC QBD Complaints to Bar Council about barrister have qualified privilege.

Lincoln v Hayman and another [1982] 2 All ER 819; [1982] RTR 336; (1982) 126 SJ 174; [1982] 1 WLR 488 CA Supplementary benefits to be deducted from special damages.

Lind v Mitchell (1928-29) XLV TLR 54 CA Recovery of damages where negligence of ship's master resulted in loss of ship.

Lindsay, Bradburn v; Bradburn and another v Lindsay [1983] 2 All ER 408 HC ChD Neglected house owner has duty to prevent damage to neighbour's house; right of entry to abate nuisance does not vitiate liability for nuisance.

Lindsey County Council, Marshall v (1935) 99 JP 185; (1935) 152 LTR 421; (1935) 79 SJ 251; (1934-35) LI TLR 279; (1935) WN (I) 32 CA Negligent admission of/failure to warn nursing home patient in maternity hospital where faced peculiar risk of fever.

Lindsey County Council, Marshall v [1935] 1 KB 516 HC KBD Admission of/failure to warn nursing home patient in maternity hospital where faced peculiar risk of fever was not negligent.

Linklater v Daily Telegraph (1964) 108 SJ 992 HC QBD Left to jury as to whether calling half-Czech/half-Briton a 'Czech' was defamatory (though trial judge personally considered was not).

Linom, Walker v [1907] 2 Ch 104; [1907] 76 LJCh 500; (1907-08) XCVII LTR 92; (1906-07) 51 SJ 483 HC ChD Legal estate of negligent trustees second to equitable interest of purchaser of property who through negligence of trustees bought property without notice of settlement.

Linotype Company Limited v British Empire Type-Setting Machine Company Limited (1899-1900) LXXXI LTR 331 HL On libel of tradesman in his conduct of trade.

Linsberg and Leies, R v (1905) 69 JP 107 HC KBD False imprisonment absent assault/battery/belief that had legal authority so to do an indictable crime.

Linskills (a firm) and another, Smith v [1995] 3 All ER 226 HC QBD Challenge to outcome of criminal trial via negligence action against defence solicitors an abuse of process unless new evidence impugns criminal verdict.

Linskills (a firm), Smith v (1996) 146 NLJ 209; (1996) TLR 7/2/96 CA Convict's negligence suit against solicitor who defended him in criminal action a collateral attack on criminal action and so unpermitted.

Lintsbrook Development Ltd, Balls and another v (1976) 120 SJ 29 HC ChD Action dismissed for delay (albeit that delay nonetheless meant action being brought inside limitation period).

Lion Laboratories Ltd v Evans and others [1985] QB 526; (1984) 128 SJ 533; [1984] TLR 185; [1984] 3 WLR 539 CA Court authorised disclosure of documents despite their being published in breach of confidence where public interest in disclosure demanded it.

Lionel Barber and Company, Limited v Deutsche Bank (Berlin) London Agency et e Contra [1919] AC 304; (1918) 53 LJ 436l [1919] 88 LJCL 194; (1918-19) XXXV TLR 120; (1918) WN (I) 373 HL Libel re-trial order quashed where plaintiffs agreed to reduce damages awarded.

Lipkin Gorman v Karpnale Ltd and another (1986) 136 NLJ 659; [1987] 1 WLR 987 HC QBD On recovery for conversion/negligence where gambling club/bank accepted draft which was not gambler's to present/breached duty to customer to ascertain from where gambler obtaining funds (but where gambler's business partners were contributorily negligent in not inquiring into gambler's affairs once had notice of spending irregularities).

Lipkin Gorman v Karpnale Ltd and another [1989] 1 WLR 1340 CA On liability in conversion/ negligence where gambling club/bank accepted draft which was not gambler's to present/did not ascertain from where gambler obtaining funds.

Lipkin Gorman v Karpnale Ltd and another [1992] 1 All ER 512; [1991] 3 WLR 10 HL On liability in conversion/negligence where gambling club/bank accepted draft which was not gambler's to present/did not ascertain from where gambler obtaining funds.

Lipman v George Pulman and Sons Limited (1904) 39 LJ 369; (1904-05) XCI LTR 132; (1904) WN (I) 139 HC ChD On damages recoverable where seeking same in addition to injunction to prevent nuisance by noise/vibration.

Lippitt v Jones (1930) 70 LJ ccr30 CyCt Shop-owner liable under principle in Rylands v Fletcher/in nuisance for injury occasioned to person when shop sunblind collapsed on them.

Lister v Romford Ice and Cold Storage Co, Ltd [1957] 1 All ER 125; (1957) 121 JP 98 HL Master could recover damages (including costs of action) paid by them on foot of servant's negligence.

Lister, Romford Ice and Cold Storage Co Ld v [1955] 3 All ER 460; [1955] 3 WLR 631 CA Damages available to master for servant's failure in duty of care unaffected by being vicariously liable joint tortfeasor.

Litchfield-Speer and another v Queen Anne's Gate Syndicate (No 2), Ltd [1918-19] All ER 1075 HC ChD On restraint of anticipated nuisance.

Littler v BBC and another (1966) 110 SJ 585 HC QBD Fair comment plea allowed despite looseness as to factual basis on which grounded.

Littler v GL Moore (Contractors) Ltd (1967) 111 SJ 637; [1967] 1 WLR 1241 Assizes Damages available for possible future loss in quality of vision.

Littler, London Artists, Ltd v [1969] 2 All ER 193; [1969] 2 QB 375; (1969) 113 SJ 37; [1969] 2 WLR 409 CA Untrue claim of plot regarding matter of public interest not fair comment.

Littler, London Artists, Ltd v [1968] 1 All ER 1075; (1968) 118 NLJ 1196t; (1968) 112 SJ 194; [1968] 1 WLR 607 HC QBD Where no public interest (or private duty compelling publication) is no qualified privilege.

Littlewood v George Wimpey and Co, Ltd British Overseas Airways Corporation (second defendants and third parties) [1953] 2 All ER 915; (1953) 117 JP 484; (1953) 103 LJ 589; [1953] 2 QB 501; (1953) 97 SJ 587; [1953] 3 WLR 553 CA Cannot seek contribution from party sued and found not to be liable; time runs for recovery of contribution from date when judgment given against one.

Littlewood v George Wimpey and Co, Ltd; British Overseas Airways Corporation (second defendants and third parties) [1953] 1 All ER 583; (1953) 103 LJ 138; (1953) 97 SJ 152; [1953] 1 WLR 426 HC QBD Corporation a public authority doing public duty so special limitation under Limitation Act 1939, s 2(1) applied and could not be sued: as not sued was not liable for contribution.

Littlewoods Organisation Ltd (Chief Constable, Fife Constabulary, third party) and conjoined appeal, Smith and others v [1987] 1 All ER 710; [1987] AC 241; [1987] 2 WLR 480 HL Generally/exceptionally is/can be duty of care to ensure property not a danger to neighbouring property.

London and County Land and Building Co, Cuff and another v (1912) 81 LJCh 426 (also CA); (1911-12) 56 SJ 273 HC ChD Injunction refused to require company to give allegedly negligent auditors access to company's books.

London and County Land and Building Company Limited, Cuff v (1912) 81 LJCh 426 (also HC ChD); (1912) 106 LTR 285 CA Injunction refused to require company to give allegedly negligent auditors access to company's books.

London and North Eastern Railway Co, Dunt v (1942) 86 SJ 203 HC KBD Rail company liable for fire occasioned by sparks flying from engine: on liability of rail companies for flying sparks.

London and North Eastern Railway Co, Schlarb v [1936] 1 All ER 71; (1936) 80 SJ 168 HC KBD Negligence to wards first-time user of station on foggy night despite white line marking edge of platform off which fell.

London and North Eastern Railway Company (Coote and Warren, Limited, Third Parties), Henson v (1945-46) LXII TLR 369 CA Exemption clause ineffective where person purportedly subject thereto had not been given adequate notice of same.

London and North Eastern Railway Company, Hallett v (1915) CC Rep IV 4; [1940] LJNCCR 334 CyCt On duty on rail company/passenger regarding ensuring/checking was safe to alight from train which pulled up at station in black-out conditions.

London and North Eastern Railway Company, Hutchinson v [1942] 1 KB 481 CA Breach of statutory duty in not providing look-out for oncoming train while workmen on line.

London and North Eastern Ry Co, Avery v; Harris v London and North Eastern Ry Co; Bonner v London and North Eastern Ry Co; Watson v London and North Eastern Ry Co [1938] 2 All ER 592; (1938) 85 LJ 360 HL Relevant classes of dependants can recover maximum amounts allowed under Employers' Liability Act 1880 and Workmen's Compensation Act 1925 respectively.

London and North Eastern Ry Co, Avery v; Harris v London and North Eastern Ry Co; Bonner v London and North Eastern Ry Co; Watson v London and North Eastern Ry Co (1937) 83 LJ 378; [1937] 2 KB 515 CA Relevant classes of dependants can recover maximum amounts allowed under Employers' Liability Act 1880 and Workmen's Compensation Act 1925 respectively.

London and North Eastern Ry Co, Easson v [1944] 2 All ER 425; [1944] KB 421; (1945) 95 LJ 113; [1944] 113 LJ 449; (1944) 170 LTR 234; (1944) 88 SJ 143; (1943-44) LX TLR 280; (1944) WN (I) 89 CA No res ipsa loquitur that if train door opens in transit railway company negligent.

London and North Western Railway, De Jong v (1914) CC Rep III 13 CyCt Good case for negligence where entrust livestock to rail company and are delivered in damaged condition following delay/where is evidence that inadequate care taken of livestock.

London and North-Western Railway Co, Mayor, &c, of Westminster v (1905-06) 54 WR 129 HL Injunction to restrain trespass by local authority in erection of public toilets.

London and North-Western Railway Company, Atherton v (1905-06) XCIII LTR 464; (1904-05) XXI TLR 671 CA Was fair to find rail company negligent for not erecting screen to protect passengers (passing along exit company provided) from sparks from engine.

London and North-Western Railway Company, Manning v (1906-07) XXIII TLR 222 CA Evidence of height of train from platform in nearby stations admitted to defeat negligence claim by plaintiff claiming distance between train and platform resulted in her injuring herself.

London and North-Western Railway v Westminster Corporation [1904] 73 LJCh 386; (1903-04) 48 SJ 330; (1903-04) 52 WR 596 CA Injunction to restrain trespass by local authority in erection of public toilets.

London and North-Western Railway v Westminster Corporation [1902] 71 LJCh 34; (1901-02) 50 WR 268 HC ChD Injunction to restrain trespass by local authority in erection of public toilets.

London and Northern Bank (Limited) v George Newnes (Limited) (1899-1900) XVI TLR 433 CA In action for allegedly libellous statement that particular bank was in liquidation court ordered that particulars be given on where was run on bank and for how long.

London and South of England Building Society v Stone [1983] 3 All ER 105; (1983) 127 SJ 446; [1983] TLR 407; [1983] 1 WLR 1242 CA Damages for financial burden suffered/not difference between amount lent and amount would have lent on proper valuation; cannot claim for costs arising from unreasonable non-mitigation.

London and South of England Building Society v Stone (1982) 132 NLJ 218 HC QBD Damages awarded in successful negligence action against surveyor was difference between valuation price and true worth at time of survey.

London and South Western Bank, Limited, Bavins, Junr and Sims v [1900] 69 LJCL 164; (1899-1900) LXXXI LTR 655; [1900] 1 QB 270; (1899-1900) 48 WR 210 CA Party allowed recover money had and received by way of stolen money order.

London and South Western Railway Co, Wilden v (1919) CC Rep VIII 18 CyCt Rail company not liable where tunnel under rail unlit and person negligently continued to drive under same (albeit that tunnel being unlit was itself negligent).

London Artists, Ltd v Littler [1969] 2 All ER 193; [1969] 2 QB 375; (1969) 113 SJ 37; [1969] 2 WLR 409 CA Untrue claim of plot regarding matter of public interest not fair comment.

London Artists, Ltd v Littler [1968] 1 All ER 1075; (1968) 118 NLJ 1196t; (1968) 112 SJ 194; [1968] 1 WLR 607 HC QBD Where no public interest (or private duty compelling publication) is no qualified privilege.

London Association for Protection of Trade and another v Greenlands, Limited [1916-17] All ER 452; [1916] 2 AC 15; (1916) 51 LJ 77; [1916] 85 LJKB 698; (1916) 114 LTR 434; (1915-16) 60 SJ 272; (1915-16) XXXII TLR 281; (1916) WN (I) 45 HL On privilege attaching to communication by trade protection society on foot of bona fide enquiry by trader as to creditworthiness of another trader.

London Association for the Protection of Trade, Elkington v (1911-12) XXVIII TLR 117 HC KBD Insolvency inquiries published in trade society's confidential newsletter not privileged.

London Borough Council of Lewisham v Leslie and Co Ltd (1979) 129 (2) NLJ 1179c CA Possible concealed fraud would justify action to determine whether breach of contract action out of time.

London Borough Council of Newman, Ephraim v (1993) 137 SJ LB 13 CA On extent of duty of care owed by local authority to unintentionally homeless person whom they advise about availability of certain property.

London Borough of Brent, Masters v [1978] 2 All ER 664; (1978) 128 NLJ 34t; [1978] QB 841; (1978) 122 SJ 300; [1978] 2 WLR 768 HC QBD Damages recoverable for nuisance begun before acquired proprietary title.

London Borough of Bromley, Barnes v (1984) 134 NLJ 312; [1983] TLR 678 HC QBD Teacher one-third negligent for injuries he suffered in use of defective school equipment.

London Borough of Camden and another, Lamb and another v [1981] 2 All ER 408; (1981) 131 NLJ 474; [1981] QB 625; [1981] 2 WLR 1038 CA Liability of tortfeasor for acts caused by novus actus interveniens.

London Borough of Camden, Ryan v [1982] TLR 640 CA Local authority not liable in negligence for injury suffered by child who touched uninsulated heating pipe as could reasonably expect parents to safeguard children from doing same.

London Borough of Hammersmith v Magnum Automated Forecourts Ltd [1978] 1 All ER 401; (1978) 142 JP 130; (1977) 127 NLJ 691t; (1977) 121 SJ 529; [1978] 1 WLR 50 CA High Court action (for injunction) permissible despite right to bring summary action for nuisance.

London Borough of Merton, Anns and others v [1977] 2 All ER 492; [1978] AC 728; (1977) 141 JP 526; (1977) 127 NLJ 614t; (1977) 121 SJ 377; [1977] 2 WLR 1024 HL That act done under statute need not mean no breach of common law duty of care; duty of care to supervise builder owed to building owner/occupiers; where breach of duty time runs from date damage caused by negligence.

London Borough of Newham and others, M and another v [1993] 2 FLR 575 HC QBD On how far witness immunity from suit extends; parent could not sue local authority for in-/action towards child or local authority psychiatrist/social worker for how performed duties.

512

London County Council, Davis v (1913-14) XXX TLR 275 HC KBD Once competent professionals employed local education authority not liable for negligence of persons whom it agrees to allow conduct medical operations on children.

London County Council, Fern v [1938] LJNCCR 76 CyCt Owners of public recreation ground liable in negligence for injury suffered by person onto whom previously broken branch fell on them while they were sitting on a bench.

London County Council, Giles v (1904) 68 JP 10 HC KBD Council not liable for injury done to man by unconcealed, non-lurking danger present on public cricket ground on which man elects to play.

London County Council, Hartin v (1926-30) XXVIII Cox CC 618; (1929) 93 JP 160; (1929) 141 LTR 120 HC KBD Special public authority limitation period inapplicable to malicious prosecution action as criminal prosecution not a public duty under Public Authorities Protection Act 1893.

London County Council, Hewlett v (1908) 72 JP 136; (1907-08) XXIV TLR 331 HC KBD Defendants could plead public authority limitation despite plaintiff's claim that action brought out of time because defendants indicated wanted out of court settlement.

London County Council, Irving v (1965) 109 SJ 157 HC QBD Occupiers not required to light common staircase at all times without special cause.

London County Council, Jacobs and another v [1949] 1 All ER 790; [1949] 1 KB 685; (1949) 99 LJ 219; (1949) WN (I) 179 CA Person on forecourt not open to public a licensee; no nuisance adjoining highway proved as was not using highway when encountered 'nuisance'.

London County Council and Smith, Gard & Co, Ltd, Jacobs v (1949) 99 LJ 52 CyCt Council liable in negligence/nuisance for injury suffered by individual when crossing forecourt in some disrepair.

London County Council, Jacobs v [1950] 1 All ER 737; [1950] AC 361; (1950) 114 JP 204; (1950) 100 LJ 175; (1950) 94 SJ 318; [1950] 66 (1) TLR 659; (1950) WN (I) 170 HL Person on forecourt not open to public a licensee; no nuisance adjoining highway proved as was not using highway when encountered 'nuisance'.

London County Council, Jefferey v (1955) 119 JP 45 HC QBD School not liable for fatal after-hours playground injury to child waiting to be collected.

London County Council, Jones and another v (1931-32) XLVIII TLR 368 HC KBD Failed action against council where its servant had ordered boy on instruction course to take part in rough game whereby boy suffered injury.

London County Council, Jones and another v (1932) 96 JP 371; (1931-32) XLVIII TLR 577 CA Failed action against council where its servant had ordered boy on instruction course to take part in rough game whereby boy suffered injury.

London County Council, Martin v [1947] 1 All ER 783; (1947) 111 JP 310; [1947] KB 628; (1947) 97 LJ 221; [1947] 116 LJR 1231; (1947) 177 LTR 38; (1947) 91 SJ 264; (1947) LXIII TLR 284; (1947) WN (I) 146 HC KBD Local authority running hospital not gratuitous bailee of patient's property/could not assume property bailed of no value; purchase tax relevant in deciding level of damages.

London County Council, Parker v (1904) 68 JP 239; [1904] 2 KB 501; [1904] 73 LJCL 561; (1904) XC LTR 415; (1903-04) XX TLR 271; (1903-04) 52 WR 476 HC KBD Special public authority limitation period under Public Authorities Protection Act 1893 applies to county council as tramway owner.

London County Council, Ralph v (1947) 111 JP 246; (1947) 91 SJ 221; (1947) LXIII TLR 239 HC KBD Council liable in negligence for injury suffered by child in course of supervised game in assembly hall (council failed to take steps that reasonably cautious father would have taken).

London County Council, Ralph v (1947) 111 JP 548; (1947) LXIII TLR 546 CA Council liable in negligence for injury suffered by child in course of supervised game in assembly hall (council failed to take steps that reasonably cautious father would have taken).

London County Council, Rich and another v [1953] 2 All ER 376; (1953) 117 JP 353; (1953) 97 SJ 472; [1953] 1 WLR 895 CA School owes duty of responsible parent towards pupils.

London County Council, Richardson v (1957) 107 LJ 328 CA Failed appeal against refusal of leave to bring action in which (inter alia) claimed that negligence of public authorities led to purportedly unlawful detention pursuant to the Mental Deficiency Act 1913.

London County Council, S and R Steamships Ltd v (1938) 82 SJ 353 HC KBD Successful action in negligence by shipowner against local authority for loss occasioned on foot of latter's negligent operation of bridge.

London County Council, Shaw v; Jacobs v London County Council [1924-35] All ER 696; (1935) 99 JP 10; [1935] 1 KB 67 CA Limitation period does not run for infant until reaches age of twenty-one.

London County Council, Ward v [1938] 2 All ER 341; (1938) 85 LJ 310; (1938) 82 SJ 274 HC KBD Fire engine driver bound by traffic light regulations.

London County Council, Whittaker v (1915) 79 JP 437; [1915] 2 KB 676; (1915-16) 113 LTR 544; (1915) WN (I) 212 HC KBD Recovery of damages for injuries sustained when wrongfully ejected physically from tramway.

London County Freehold and Leasehold Properties, Ltd, Elliott and another v [1936] LJNCCR 117 CyCt Flat-owners not liable to under-lessees of flat for nuisance (emission into house of smoke/soot) occasioned by under-lessees lighting fire in flat.

London County Westminster and Parr's Bank, Limited, Souchette, Limited, v (1919-20) XXXVI TLR 195 HC KBD Negligent cashing by bank of one of five cheques.

London County, Westminster and Parr's Bank (Lim), Ross v (1918-19) 63 SJ 411; (1919) WN (I) 87 HC KBD Bank negligent in accepting (stolen) cheques and paying them into account.

London District Auditor and others, Pentecost and another v (1951) 115 JP 421; (1951) 95 SJ 432; [1951] 2 TLR 497 HC KBD On what constitutes negligence under Local Government Act 1933, s 228(1)/negligence generally.

London Electric Railway Company and another, Hurlstone v (1913-14) XXX TLR 398 CA Railway company not liable for negligence of building contractors.

London Electric Railway Company and another, Hurlstone v (1912-13) XXIX TLR 514 HC KBD Railway company liable for negligence of building contractors.

London Electric Supply Corporation, Ltd v Alexander [1942] LJNCCR 49 CyCt Failed action in negligence/trespass against driver who struck lamp post after swerved to avoid dog on road.

London Electricity Board, Haley v [1963] 3 All ER 1003; (1964) 128 JP 162; (1964) 114 LJ 24; [1964] 2 QB 121; (1963) 107 SJ 1001; [1964] 2 WLR 444 CA Corporation doing streetworks owed no special duty of care to the blind.

London Electricity Board, Haley v (1965) 109 SJ 295 CA On appropriate damages for blind person rendered deaf through negligence of another.

London Electricity Board, Haley v (1963) 107 SJ 416 HC QBD Corporation doing streetworks owed no special duty of care to the blind.

London Electricity Board, Haley v [1964] 3 All ER 185; [1965] AC 778; (1965) 129 JP 14; (1964) 114 LJ 585; (1964) 108 SJ 637; [1964] 3 WLR 479 HL Persons doing street works owed duty of care to blind users of highway.

London Electricity Board, Haley v (1964) 108 SJ 1013 HC QBD On appropriate damages for blind person essentially rendered deaf by negligence of another.

London Express Newsaper, Limited, Shaw v (1924-25) XLI TLR 475 HC KBD Newspaper article giving true account of murder in which person coincidentally had name of another who might be mistaken as person in article deemed non-libellous.

London Express Newspaper, Limited, Davis v (1939) 83 SJ 96; (1938-39) LV TLR 207 HC KBD Absent malice person to whom letter critical of company written could not sue newspaper which obtained copy of letter and showed it to company officer.

London Express Newspaper, Limited, Knupffer v [1944] 1 All ER 495; [1944] AC 116; (1945) 95 LJ 112; [1944] 113 LJ 251; (1944) 170 LTR 362; (1944) 88 SJ 143; (1943-44) LX TLR 310; (1944) WN (I) 111 HL Cannot claim individually libelled by class/group libel unless can show words refer to one as individual.

London Express Newspaper, Limited, Newstead v [1939] 3 All ER 263; [1939] 2 KB 317; [1939] 108 LJCL 618; (1939) 161 LTR 236; (1939) 83 SJ 548; (1938-39) LV TLR 679; (1939) WN (I) 184 HC KBD Words true of one person can be libel of another.

London Express Newspaper, Ltd and another, Childs v (1941) 85 SJ 179 HC KBD Plea of innuendo deemed to fail in case where defence of fair comment would in any event have succeeded.

London Express Newspaper, Ltd, Hough v [1940] 3 All ER 31; [1940] 2 KB 507; (1940) 89 LJ 270; [1940] 109 LJCL 524; (1940) 163 LTR 162; (1940) 84 SJ 573; (1939-40) LVI TLR 758 CA That reasonable people would believe article as referring to plaintiff was defamatory.

London Express Newspaper, Ltd, Newstead v [1939] 4 All ER 319; [1940] 1 KB 377; (1939) 88 LJ 314; [1940] 109 LJCL 166; (1940) 162 LTR 17; (1939) 83 SJ 942; (1939-40) LVI TLR 130; (1939) WN (I) 406 CA Words true of one person can be libel of another.

London Fire and Civil Defence Authority and others, John Munroe (Acrylics) Ltd v [1996] 4 All ER 318; (1996) TLR 22/5/96; [1996] 3 WLR 988 HC QBD On extent of liability in negligence of fire brigade vis-à-vis person whose property goes on fire (no duty of care owed in instant case).

London Fire and Civil Defence Authority, Smoker v [1991] 2 WLR 422 HC QBD Damages for loss of earnings not to be reduced by amount of disablement pension.

London Fire and Civil Defence Authority, Smoker v; Wood v British Coal Corp [1991] 2 All ER 449; [1991] 2 WLR 1052 HL Damages for loss of earnings not to be reduced by amount of disablement pension.

London General Omnibus Co, White and another v (1914) 49 LJ 114; (1913-14) 58 SJ 339; (1914) WN (I) 78 HC ChD Nuisance by noise/smell from garage not permanent injury to reversion.

London General Omnibus Co, Wing v [1908-10] All ER 496; (1909) 73 JP 429; [1909] 2 KB 652; [1909] 78 LJKB 1063; (1909-10) 101 LTR 411; (1908-09) 53 SJ 713; (1908-09) XXV TLR 729 CA Skidding not per se evidence of negligent driving; on res ipsa loquitur; Rylands v Fletcher applies to unnatural user of highway for traffic.

London General Omnibus Company (Limited), Geeves v (1900-01) XVII TLR 249 CA On appropriate direction as regards negligence/contributory negligence where passenger who consented to bus starting was injured when bus started.

London General Omnibus Company (Limited), Parker v (1909) 73 JP 283; (1909) C LTR 409; (1908-09) XXV TLR 429 HC KBD Personal injury victim failed in action against bus company whose driver/placing bus on road was negligent/may or may not have been nuisance.

London General Omnibus Company (Limited), Parker v (1910) 74 JP 20; (1909-10) 101 LTR 623; (1908-09) 53 SJ 867; (1909-10) XXVI TLR 18 CA Personal injury victim failed in action against bus company whose driver/placing bus on road was negligent/may or may not have been nuisance.

London General Omnibus Company (Limited), Robinson v (1910) 74 JP 161; (1909-10) XXVI TLR 233 HC ChD Over-use of streets for maintenance/repair/turning of buses was nuisance.

London General Omnibus Company Limited, Clark v (1905) XCII LTR 691; (1904-05) XXI TLR 505 HC KBD Father could recover funeral costs from defendants whose negligence had resulted in death of daughter who lived with father.

London General Omnibus Company Limited, Wing v (1909) 73 JP 170; (1909) C LTR 301; (1908-09) 53 SJ 287 HC KBD Recovery of damages for personal injuries sustained by passenger when bus skidded (not proved that passenger knew of/had accepted risk of skidding).

London General Omnibus Company, Barnes Urban District Council v (1909) 73 JP 68 HC KBD Bus driver is on face of it negligent where collides in daylight with lamp post (but can prove otherwise to be the case).

London General Omnibus Company, Limited v Tilbury Contracting and Dredging Company (1906), Limited (1907) 71 JP 534 HC ChD Successful action for damage to building effected by negligent laying of sewers.

London Graving Dock Co, Ltd v Horton [1951] 2 All ER 1; [1951] AC 737; (1951) 101 LJ 301; (1951) 95 SJ 465; [1951] 1 TLR 949; (1951) WN (I) 278 HL Contractor had to show safe system of work/defendant accepted risk — this a question of fact.

London Graving Dock Co, Ltd, Horton v [1949] 2 All ER 169; [1949] 2 KB 584; (1949) 99 LJ 356; [1949] 118 LJR 1639; (1949) LXV TLR 386; (1949) WN (I) 281 HC KBD Invitor's duty to warn of unusual dangers means dangers unusual to invitee.

London Graving Dock Company, Ltd, Horton v [1950] 1 All ER 180; [1950] 1 KB 421; (1950) 100 LJ 20; (1950) 94 SJ 14; (1950) 66 (1) TLR 246; (1950) WN (I) 33 CA An 'unusual danger' is an abnormal danger (albeit one of which victim knew).

London Guarantee and Accident Company, Limited, and Others, Northwestern Utilities, Limited v [1935] All ER 196; [1936] AC 108; (1935) 80 LJ 378; [1936] 105 LJPC 18; (1936) 154 LTR 89; (1935) 79 SJ 902; (1935-36) LII TLR 93; (1935) WN (I) 176 PC Gas company under duty of care to protect general public from effects of City works close by mains.

London Hospital Medical College and others, Evans v [1981] 1 All ER 715; (1981) 131 NLJ 291 HC QBD Immunity from action for conduct/statement part of (albeit preceding) action.

London Hydraulic Power Co, Charing Cross, West End, and City Electricity Supply Co, Ltd v [1914-15] All ER 85; (1914) 78 JP 305; [1914] 3 KB 772; (1914) 49 LJ 244; [1914] 83 LJKB 1352; (1914-15) 111 LTR 198; (1913-14) 58 SJ 577; (1913-14) XXX TLR 441; (1914) WN (I) 170 CA Liability for nuisance (though no negligence) for injury sustained through escape of dangerous thing.

London Hydraulic Power Co, Charing Cross, West End, and City Electricity Supply Co, Ltd v (1913) 77 JP 378; [1913] 3 KB 442; [1914] 83 LJKB 116; (1913-14) 109 LTR 635; (1912-13) XXIX TLR 649 HC KBD Liability for nuisance (though no negligence) for injury sustained through escape of dangerous thing from property over which enjoyed licence.

London Jewellers, Limited v Sutton; Same v Robertsons (London), Limited (1934) 77 LJ 94; (1933-34) L TLR 193; (1934) WN (I) 21 HC KBD Pawnbrokers with whom fraudulently obtained goods were pawned liable to true owners of jewellery in detinue.

London Joint Stock Bank, Limited v Macmillan and Arthur [1918] AC 777; (1918) 53 LJ 242; [1919] 88 LJCL 55; (1918-19) 119 LTR 387; (1917-18) XXXIV TLR 509 HL Customer required to bear loss occasioned through own negligent completion of cheque.

London Joint Stock Bank, Limited, Frost v (1905-06) XXII TLR 760 CA Return of cheque to person seeking payment on same with note attached stating 'Reason assigned: not stated' not per se libellous.

London Joint Stock Bank, Limited, Macmillan and another v [1917] 2 KB 439; (1917-18) 117 LTR 202; (1916-17) XXXIII TLR 398; (1917) WN (I) 181 CA Customer not required to bear loss occasioned through own negligent completion of cheque.

London Joint Stock Bank, Macmillan and another v (1916-17) XXXIII TLR 140 HC KBD Customer not required to bear loss occasioned through own negligent completion of cheque.

London Midland and Scottish Railway Co, Williams and Hill v (1946) 96 LJ 134 HC KBD Intent not necessary to be guilty of libel.

London Midland and Scottish Railway Company v The Ribble Hat Works Limited (1936) 80 SJ 1038 HC ChD Was negligent/nuisance for defendants to place red/green neon sign adjacent to rail lights and so render those light signals more difficult to view.

London Midland and Scottish Railway Company, Sugar v (1941) 105 JP 100; (1941) 164 LTR 311; (1941) 85 SJ 32; (1940-41) LVII TLR 197 HC KBD Exemption clause inapplicable where had been blocked out by date stamp.

London Passenger Transport Board, Batting v [1941] 1 All ER 228 CA No leave to amend outside time under old limitation statute though new limitation statute had come into force since action started.

London Passenger Transport Board, Brookes v [1947] 1 All ER 506 HC KBD Board negligent for not closing door before train left station.

London Passenger Transport Board, Dennis v (1948) LXIV TLR 269 HC KBD Wages paid during absence from work repayable from personal injury damages awarded.

London Passenger Transport Board, Dickens v [1935] LJNCCR 171 CyCt London Passenger Transport Board enjoyed the protection afforded public authorities by the Public Authorities Protection Act 1893.

Long and Co, Ruoff v (1915) CC Rep IV 94; (1916) 80 JP 158; [1916] 1 KB 148; (1915) 50 LJ 546; [1916] 85 LJKB 364; (1916) 114 LTR 186; (1915-16) 60 SJ 323; (1915-16) XXXII TLR 82 HC KBD Non-liability of person leaving lorry on highway for unexpected act of third party.

Long v District Messenger and Theatre Ticket Company (Limited) (1915-16) XXXII TLR 596 HC KBD Courier firm's notice of conditions (wherein exempted liability) inapplicable where took delivery of parcel without asking questions as to contents of same.

Long v Hepworth [1968] 3 All ER 248; (1968) 118 NLJ 516t; (1968) 112 SJ 485; [1968] 1 WLR 1299 HC QBD Wilful trespass to person is a breach of duty precluding extension of time limit under Limitation Act 1939.

Longcroft and others, Al-Nakib Investments (Jersey) Ltd and another v [1990] 3 All ER 321; (1990) 140 NLJ 741; [1990] 1 WLR 1390 HC ChD Duty of care owed by company directors to persons subscribing for shares in reliance on prospectus does not extend to persons buying shares on stock market in reliance on prospectus.

Longdon-Griffiths v Smith and others [1950] 2 All ER 662; [1951] 1 KB 295; (1950) 100 LJ 413; (1950) 94 SJ 580; [1950] 66 (2) TLR 627; (1950) WN (I) 448 HC KBD Libel action to be directed at Friendly Society per se not its trustees; special damages available where libel led to losing job; that one of four parties acted maliciously did not affect qualified privilege of others.

Longhurst (E) and Sons, Ltd, Baker v [1932] All ER 102; [1933] 2 KB 461; (1933) 102 LJCL 573; (1933) 149 LTR 264 CA Person driving at night must be able to stop within limits of vision.

Longhurst v Metropolitan Water Board (1947) 111 JP 212; [1947] 116 LJR 612 HC KBD Water board liable for injury suffered through its negligence in repair of leak.

Longhurst v Metropolitan Water Board [1948] 2 All ER 834; (1948) 112 JP 470 HL Where act under statutory authority no nuisance absent negligence (and here no negligence).

Longhurst v Metropolitan Water Board (1947) 111 JP 477; (1947) 91 SJ 653 CA Water Board owed qualified duty of care to public when effecting repairs under the Waterworks Clauses Act 1847 — here not violated.

Longmans Green and Co, Ltd, and another, Montereale v (1965) 109 SJ 215 HC QBD No qualified privilege in relation to commentary on foreign judicial proceedings.

Longsdon, Watt v [1929] All ER 284; [1930] 1 KB 130; (1929) 68 LJ 76; (1929) 98 LJCL 711; (1930) 142 LTR 4; (1929) 73 SJ 544; (1928-29) XLV TLR 619 CA Absent common interest must be duty on maker's side and interest meriting protection on recipient's side for occasion of statement to be privileged.

Longsdon, Watt v (1928-29) XLV TLR 419 HC KBD Absent common interest bona fide voluntary revelation of information believed to be true and pertaining to interest meriting protection on recipient's side is privileged.

Longton v Committee of Visitors of Winwick Asylum (1911) 75 JP 348 HC KBD Damages for injury suffered through flooding caused by other's negligence.

Longton v Committee of Visitors of Winwick Asylum (1912) 76 JP 113 CA Out-of-court settlement of appeal from action in which damages awarded for injury suffered through flooding caused by other's negligence.

Lonrho Ltd and another v Shell Petroleum Co Ltd and another (No 2) (1981) 131 NLJ 632; [1981] 3 WLR 33 HL Oil supplies to Zimbabwe-Rhodesia in violation of Southern Rhodesia (Petroleum) Order 1965 did not give rise to tortious liability to injured party.

Lonrho Ltd and others v Shell Petroleum Co Ltd and others [1981] 2 All ER 456; [1982] AC 173; (1981) 125 SJ 429; [1980] 1 WLR 627 HL Breach of sanctions order not breach of statutory duty; conspiracy if do not intend to injure another nor protect oneself.

Lonrho plc and others v Fayed and others (No 5) [1994] 1 All ER 188; (1993) 143 NLJ 1571; [1993] TLR 422; [1993] 1 WLR 1489 CA Tortious conspiracy consists of two or more persons doing acts lawful in themselves with intent to causing injury to another who is thereby injured; damages for injury to reputation/business reputation/feelings available only if defamation.

Lonrho plc v Fayed and others [1989] 2 All ER 65; (1989) 139 NLJ 539; [1990] 2 QB 479; [1989] 3 WLR 631 CA Interference with trade/business must be intended to hurt plaintiff but not necessarily as principal aim.

Lonrho plc v Fayed and others [1988] 3 All ER 464; (1988) 138 NLJ 225; [1990] 1 QB 490; (1989) 133 SJ 220; [1989] 2 WLR 356 HC QBD Interference with take-over bid not an interference with business interest; if cannot claim for tort cannot claim for conspiracy to commit tort.

Lonrho plc v Tebbit and another [1992] 4 All ER 280 CA Private action for negligence may arise if Secretary of State fails to release firm from undertaking to Secretary regarding purchase of shares.

Lonrho plc v Tebbit and another [1991] 4 All ER 973; (1991) 141 NLJ 1295 HC ChD Striking-out application not appropriate forum for deciding legal points in new field of law; duty of care may arise in respect of discharge of statutory powers implementing, but not deciding policy even where purely economic loss; action against minister rather than judicial review permissible.

Lord Advocate, Hughes v [1963] 1 All ER 705; [1963] AC 837; (1963) 113 LJ 232; (1963) 107 SJ 232; [1963] 2 WLR 779 HL Act akin to reasonably foreseeable act need not itself be reasonably foreseeable for liability in negligence to arise.

Lord and another v Pacific Steam Navigation Co, Ltd; The Oropesa [1943] 1 All ER 211; (1944) 94 LJ 108; [1943] 112 LJ 91 CA Capsizing of lifeboat direct result of negligently caused collision between two boats.

Lord and another, Blackshaw v [1983] 2 All ER 311; [1984] QB 1; (1983) 127 SJ 289; [1983] TLR 118; [1983] 3 WLR 283 CA Not everything said by government official in course of employment is privileged under Defamation Act 1952, s 7(1); public to have legitimate interest in report and publisher to have like duty in publishing for qualified privilege to arise; test for varying jury's award of damages stricter than for judge.

Lord Bernstein of Leigh v Skyviews and General Ltd [1977] 2 All ER 902; (1977) 127 NLJ 242t; [1978] QB 479; (1977) 121 SJ 157; [1977] 3 WLR 136 HC QBD Rights of owner in land extend to airspace over it necessary for reasonable use/enjoyment; aerial trespass action against aerial photographer barred by Civil Aviation Act 1949, s 40(1).

Lord Mayor, Aldermen and Citizens of the City of Manchester v Markland [1935] All ER 667; [1936] AC 360; (1935) 99 JP 343; (1935) 153 LTR 302; (1934-35) LI TLR 527 HL Corporation found liable in negligence for failure to attend to water leak which made road dangerous resulting in accident.

Lord Mayor, Aldermen and Citizens of the City of Manchester, Coleshill v [1928] 1 KB 776; (1928) 65 LJ 95; (1928) 97 LJCL 229; (1928) 138 LTR 537 CA Non-liability towards licensee falling into trench which was not hidden danger/trap.

Lord Mayor, etc of Birmingham, Holloway v (1905) 69 JP 358 HC KBD Absent evidence of defective construction highway authority could not be found guilty of misfeasance.

Lord Provost, Magistrates, and Council of the City of Edinburgh, Evans (Pauper) v [1916] 2 AC 45; (1916) 114 LTR 911 HL Door opening outwards onto street not of itself negligence nor was it obstruction of highway.

Lord v Sunday Telegraph Ltd [1970] 3 All ER 504; (1970) 120 NLJ 1066; [1971] 1 QB 235; (1970) 114 SJ 706; [1970] 3 WLR 754 CA Need not seperate comments from facts but must explain basic facts if relying on fair comment.

Lory v Great Western Railway Company [1942] 1 All ER 230; (1943) 93 LJ 116; (1942) WN (I) 73 HC KBD Charitable/voluntary pensions deductible from fatal accident damages.

Losner v Michael Cohen and Co (1975) 119 SJ 340 CA Damages against solicitor for failing to ensure proper defendants joined to action under Dogs Act 1871, s 2.

Lothian, Rickards v [1911-13] All ER 71; [1913] AC 263; (1913) 82 LJPC 42; (1912-13) XXIX TLR 281; (1913) 108 LTR 225 PC Not liable in negligence/nuisance for damage resulting from third party malicious act in relation to reasonable user.

Loudon v Ryder [1953] 1 All ER 741; [1953] 2 QB 202; (1953) 97 SJ 170; [1953] 2 WLR 537 CA On exemplary damages for trespass/assault.

Loudon v Ryder (No 2) [1953] Ch 423; (1953) 97 SJ 299; [1953] 2 WLR 863 HC ChD In action for slander of title statements made though false were made absent malice and in belief that were true so no damages/injunction for same.

Lubovsky v Snelling (1944) 170 LTR 2; (1943-44) LX TLR 52 CA Where party accepts liability and parties agree to go to court on matter of damages only expiry of limitation period cannot be pleaded as defence.

Lucas-Box v News Group Newspapers Ltd; Lucas-Box v Associated Newspapers Group plc and others [1986] 1 All ER 177; (1986) 130 SJ 111; [1986] 1 WLR 147 CA Party to specify meaning intends to justify before starting justification.

Lucile (Limited), Barnes v (1906-07) XXIII TLR 389 HC KBD Owner of dog liable for injuries it causes by biting where knows dog to be even occasionally vicious towards humans.

Lucy v Bawden [1914] 2 KB 318; [1914] 83 LJKB 523; (1914) 110 LTR 580; (1913-14) XXX TLR 321; (1914) WN (I) 79 HC KBD Owner not to expose tenant's wife to unexpected danger without warning.

Lucy v WT Henleys Telegraph Works Co Ltd (ICI Ltd, Third Party) [1969] 3 All ER 456 HC QBD If direct action would fail because of Limitation Act cannot be added as defendant to related action.

Lucy v WT Henleys Telegraph Works Co Ltd (ICI Ltd, Third Party); Wild v Siemens Brothers and Co Ltd [1969] 3 All ER 456; [1970] 1 QB 393; (1969) 113 SJ 641; [1969] 3 WLR 588 CA Could not add third party to action where that was precluded by Limitation Act 1963.

Ludditt and others v Ginger Coote Airways, Limited (1947) LXIII TLR 157 PC Contract exempting liability of carrier of passengers for own negligence was valid.

Ludgate v Lovett [1969] 2 All ER 1275; (1969) 119 NLJ 414t; (1969) 113 SJ 369; [1969] 1 WLR 1016 CA No evidence capable of rebutting res ipsa loquitur.

Ludlam v Peel (WE) and Sons (1939) 83 SJ 832 CA Competent drover who took reasonable care not liable for collision between motor vehicle and cow being driven along road.

Luff, Williams and another v (1978) 122 SJ 164 HC QBD Duty of care owed towards child en ventre sa mère injured in road traffic collision.

Luker v Chapman (1970) 114 SJ 788 HC QBD Personal injury damages reduced by amount plaintiff would have earned at alternative post-employment he was offered had he not instead elected to become a teacher.

Lupdine Ltd and another (Thurgar Bolle Ltd, third party), Aswan Engineering Establishment Co v [1987] 1 All ER 135; [1987] 1 WLR 1 CA Manufacturer's duty of care extends to foreseeable occurrences.

Luper, Lee v [1936] 3 All ER 817; (1937) 81 SJ 15 HC KBD Publican not liable to invitee sustaining injury in private area of pub.

Luton Corporation, Hill v [1951] 1 All ER 1028; (1951) 115 JP 340; [1951] 2 KB 387; [1951] 1 TLR 853; (1951) WN (I) 269 HC KBD Defective writ served in time and amended out of time allowed to stand.

Luxmoore-May and another v Messenger May Baverstock (1988) 138 NLJ 341 HC QBD On duty owed to client by provincial auctioneer to establish value of auctioned item before auction.

Luxmoore-May and another v Messenger May Baverstock (a firm) [1990] 1 All ER 1067; (1990) 140 NLJ 89; [1990] 1 WLR 1009 CA Duty of care expected of provincial auctioneer similar to that of general medical practitioner.

Lybert v Warrington Health Authority [1995] TLR 290 CA On appropriate warning pre-sterilisation operation as to possibility of pregnancy post-sterilisation operation (here warning inadequate).

Lyes v Middlesex County Council (1963) 113 LJ 348 HC QBD Education authority liable in negligence for injury to pupil who slipped and put hand through glass in door.

Lyle-Samuel v Odhams, Ltd [1918-19] All ER 779; [1920] 1 KB 135; (1919) 54 LJ 338; [1919] 88 LJCL 1161; (1920) 122 LTR 57; (1918-19) 63 SJ 748; (1918-19) XXXV TLR 711 CA Absent special circumstances person sued for defamation not obliged to reveal source.

Lyles v Southend-on-Sea Corporation (1905) 69 JP 193; [1905] 2 KB 1; (1905) 40 LJ 282; (1905) XCII LTR 586; (1904-05) XXI TLR 389; (1905) WN (I) 63 CA Six-month public authority limitation applied in negligence action against municpal corporation acting as tramway operator.

Lyne v Nicholls (1906-07) XXIII TLR 86 HC ChD Absent proof of actual damage disparagement of competitor's goods (rather than advertising puff) was not libel but otherwise would be.

Lynne and another v Gordon Doctors and Walton (a firm) (1991) 135 SJ LB 29 HC QBD Failed action to recoup from allegedly negligent solicitors purported loss personal representatives suffered through solicitors not taking out life assurance for deceased mortgagor.

Lyon and Lyon v Daily Telegraph, Ltd [1943] 1 All ER 586; (1943) 168 LTR 251; (1942-43) LIX TLR 193 HC KBD Impossible to determine fair comment where writer of libel unknown; defamation in professional capacity.

Lyon and Lyon v Daily Telegraph, Ltd [1943] 2 All ER 316; [1943] KB 746; [1943] 112 LJ 547; (1944) 94 LJ 108; (1943) 169 LTR 274; (1943) 87 SJ 309; (1942-43) LIX TLR 402; (1943) WN (I) 191 CA Fair comment defence open despite factual error as publication was on matter of public interest and there was no malice involved.

Lyons v Financial News (Lim) and others (1908-09) 53 SJ 671 CA Order as to form of particulars whereby sought to plead truthfulness of some of what stated and that rest was fair comment.

Lyons, Son and Co v Gulliver and The Capital Syndicate (Limited) (1912-13) 57 SJ 444; (1912-13) XXIX TLR 428 HC ChD Theatre owners liable in nuisance for obstruction on highway caused by persons queuing outside premises.

Lyons, Sons and Co v Gulliver and The Capital Syndicate (Limited) [1911-13] All ER 537; [1914] 1 Ch 631; (1914) 78 JP 98; [1914] 83 LJCh 281; (1914) 110 LTR 284; (1913-14) 58 SJ 97; (1913-14) XXX TLR 75 CA Theatre owners liable in nuisance for obstruction on highway caused by persons queuing outside premises.

Lyster, Oakley v [1930] All ER 234; [1931] 1 KB 148; (1931) 144 LTR 363 CA Cannot convert another's property unless in dealing with same intend to deny owner's rights/assert right inconsistent with that of owner.

Löwenbräu München and another v Grünhalle Lager International and another (1974) 118 SJ 50 HC ChD Interlocutory injunction to Löwenbräu München beer to restrain sales of Grünhalle Löwenbräu pending full passing off action.

M (a minor) and another v Newham London Borough Council and others; X and others (minors) v Bedfordshire County Council [1994] 4 All ER 602; [1995] 2 AC 633 (also HL); [1994] 2 FCR 1313; [1994] 1 FLR 431 (also HC QBD); (1994) 144 NLJ 357; [1994] TLR 119; [1994] 2 WLR 554 CA Those discharging public law task of child-care owe no private law duty of care for in-/action; psychiatrist/social worker owes duty of care to local authority/health authority, not to mother or child.

M and another v London Borough of Newham and others [1993] 2 FLR 575 HC QBD On how far witness immunity from suit extends; parent could not sue local authority for in-/action towards child or local authority psychiatrist/social worker for how performed duties.

M Jones and Son, Lomas v [1944] KB 4; [1944] 113 LJ 193; (1944) 170 LTR 139; (1943-44) LX TLR 28; (1943) WN (I) 225 CA Farmer voluntarily aiding in delivery of heifer could recover damages for injury sustained through deliverer's negligence.

M Julius Melchior and Co (a firm), Somasundaram v [1989] 1 All ER 129; (1988) 138 NLJ 253; (1988) 132 SJ 1732; [1988] 1 WLR 1394 CA Action for negligence against barrister/solicitor struck off if really attack on court of competent jurisdiction.

M'Nair v Baker (1903-04) XX TLR 95 HC KBD Club-house not a private house so smoke nuisance a contravention of Public Health (London) Act 1891, s 24.

M, R v; R v W (1968) 118 NLJ 1004t CA On respective liabilities of solicitor/surveyor towards client seeking to buy house.

Maberley (Alan) v Henry W Peabody and Co of London, Ltd, Rowland Smith Motors, Ltd and Rowland Smith [1946] 2 All ER 192 HC KBD Nuisance to wall caused by neighbour piling clay against it and pouring chemicals on clay merited injunction though damage to date of action slight.

MacDonald, Barry v (1966) 110 SJ 56 HC QBD Not negligent to drive within few feet of nearside of road.

Macrae v HG Swindells (trading as West View Garage Co) (1954) 98 SJ 233; [1954] 1 WLR 597 HC QBD Could recover cost of hiring car where car loaned for period that own car being repaired following garage's negligence was lost through own negligence.

Madden v Quirk [1989] RTR 304; (1989) 133 SJ 752; [1989] 1 WLR 702 HC QBD Apportionment of liability as regards truck driver whose dangerous driving resulted in injury to person whom had been carrying in open rear.

Madders, Wood v [1935] LJNCCR 253 CyCt Cow-owner liable for injury ocasioned by cow straying from unfenced/poorly fenced field onto adjacent highway.

Magnesium Castings and Products, Ltd, Olsen v [1947] 1 All ER 333 CA Employer must show (if so claiming) that workman accepted workmen's compensation in lieu of common law entitlements.

Magnet Bowling, Ltd and another, AMF International, Ltd v [1968] 2 All ER 789; (1968) 112 SJ 522; [1968] 1 WLR 1028 HC QBD Application of occupier's liability/negligence principles.

Magnum Automated Forecourts Ltd, London Borough of Hammersmith v [1978] 1 All ER 401; (1978) 142 JP 130; (1977) 127 NLJ 691t; (1977) 121 SJ 529; [1978] 1 WLR 50 CA High Court action (for injunction) permissible despite right to bring summary action for nuisance.

Maguire v Corporation of Liverpool (1905) 69 JP 153; [1905] 1 KB 767; (1905) XCII LTR 374; (1904-05) 53 WR 449 CA Liverpool Corporation not liable for non-feasance of roads.

Maher v Hurst and others (1969) 113 SJ 167 CA Lorry driver/owners, not roadworkers liable for injury which occurred when lorry driver drove through fast through area of roadworks.

Mahon v Osborne [1939] 1 All ER 535; [1939] 2 KB 14; [1939] 108 LJCL 567; (1939) 160 LTR 329; (1939) 83 SJ 134 CA Res ipsa loquitur cannot arise in relation to complex surgery; whether leaving swab in patient negligent depends on circumstances.

Mahoney v Purnell and others [1997] 1 FLR 612 HC QBD Agreement between father-in-law and son-in-law set aside as was markedly disadvantageous to former; solicitor liable in negligence for not adequately drawing the father-in-law's attention to disadvantageous nature of transaction.

Mainz v James and Charles Dodd (1978) 128 NLJ 978t HC QBD Damages for negligence of solicitor whose inaction resulted in plaintiff's actions being struck out for want of prosecution.

Maisel v Financial News, Ltd [1914-15] All ER 671; [1915] 3 KB 336; (1915) 50 LJ 335; [1915] 84 LJKB 2148; (1915-16) 113 LTR 772; (1914-15) 59 SJ 596; (1914-15) XXXI TLR 510; (1915) WN (I) 264 CA Post-libel incidents can be relied on to justify libel.

Maisel v Financial Times (Limited) [1915] 84 LJKB 2145; (1915) 112 LTR 953; (1914-15) 59 SJ 248; (1914-15) XXXI TLR 192 HL Post-libel incidents can be relied on to justify libel.

Maison Talbot, the Earl of Shrewsbury and Talbot, and DM Weigel, The Dunlop Pneumatic Tyre Company (Limited) v; Clipper Pneumatic Tyre Company v Same (1903-04) 48 SJ 156; (1903-04) XX TLR 88 HC KBD Injunction to restrain slander of title before actual damage transpires is available.

Maitland v Raisbeck [1944] 2 All ER 272; [1944] KB 689; (1945) 95 LJ 112; [1944] 113 LJ 549; (1944) 171 LTR 118; (1944) 88 SJ 359; (1943-44) LX TLR 521; (1944) WN (I) 195 CA That rear light of lorry not on did not necessarily make lorry a nuisance.

Maitland v Raisbeck and RT and J Hewitt, Ltd [1944] LJNCCR 26 CyCt That rear light of lorry not on did not necessarily make lorry a nuisance.

Makinson, Horridge v (1915) 79 JP 484; [1915] 84 LJKB 1294; (1915-16) 113 LTR 498; (1914-15) XXXI TLR 389; (1915) WN (I) 180 HC KBD Frontager not liable for nuisance on highway for which highway authority responsible.

Malcolm and another v Broadhurst [1970] 3 All ER 508 HC QBD Reasonably foreseeable that unstable wife would be affected by negligent injury to husband; no damages for loss of wages by wife.

Malfroot and another v Noxall, Limited (1935) 79 SJ 610; (1934-35) LI TLR 551 HC KBD Fitter of side-car to motor-cycle liable in contract and tort to owner of same and in tort to passenger in same for negligent fitting which resulted in car becoming detached from cycle during use and consequent injury.

Mallard, Greenhalgh v [1947] 2 All ER 255 CA Res judicata where having pleaded unlawful purpose or unlawful means later bring action pleading unlawful purpose and unlawful means.

Mallett and another v Dunn [1949] 1 All ER 973; [1949] 2 KB 180; [1949] 118 LJR 1650; (1949) LXV TLR 307; (1949) WN (I) 206 HC KBD Husband could sue for medicine/household expenses though wife contributorily negligent.

Mallinson and Bowie, Hammond v [1939] LJNCCR 357 CyCt Agister (not owner) liable for trespass by agisted sheep.

Mallock v Mason and Mason [1938] LJNCCR 387 CyCt Barking at night from premises used for breeding of dogs held to be a nuisance.

Malone v Laskey and another [1904-07] All ER 304; [1907] 2 KB 141; (1907-08) XCVII LTR 324; (1906-07) 51 SJ 356; (1906-07) XXIII TLR 399 CA Licensee not allowed recover for private nuisance (vibration).

Maloney, Curtis v (1950) 94 SJ 761 CA Application of the Bankruptcy and Deeds of Arrangement Act 1913, s 15.

Maloney, Curtis v; R Cheke and Co and another; Third Parties (1950) 94 SJ 437; (1950) WN (I) 307 HC QBD Application of the Bankruptcy and Deeds of Arrangement Act 1913, s 15.

Malyon v Lawrence, Messer and Co (1969) 119 NLJ 38; (1968) 112 SJ 623 HC QBD Recovery of damages from solicitors which would have recovered in action in Germany had not negligence of solicitors led to action being time-barred.

Malz v Rosen [1966] 2 All ER 10; (1965-66) 116 NLJ 753; (1966) 110 SJ 332; [1966] 1 WLR 1008 HC QBD Not malicious prosecution if acting on advice of responsible police officer.

Malzy v Eichholz [1916] 85 LJKB 1132 CA Lessor not liable for nuisance occasioned by one lessee to another towards whom lessor had covenanted quiet enjoyment of property..

Manchester and Liverpool District Banking Company Limited, Walker and another v (1913) 108 LTR 728; (1912-13) 57 SJ 478 HC KBD Customer could recover amounts bank paid out on foot of forged cheques though customer had not checked pass-book when from time to time was returned to him.

Manchester City Council, Smith v (1974) 118 SJ 597 CA Real prospects of getting new job to be considered when determining personal injury damages.

Manchester Corporation v Connolly and others (1970) 114 SJ 108 CA Vice Chancellor ought not to have granted order for possession at interlocutory hearing.

Manchester Corporation, Cullen (suing by her mother) and Cullen v [1940] LJNCCR 255 CyCt Defendants not liable to plaintiff licensees for injury occurring from danger of which defendants had hitherto been unaware.

Manchester Corporation, Forsyth v (1912) 76 JP 465; (1912-13) XXIX TLR 15 CA Corporation not liable for negligence of gas inspector which resulted in injury to infant.

Manchester Corporation, Forsyth v (1912) 76 JP 246 Assizes Corporation not liable for negligence of gas inspector which resulted in injury to infant.

Manchester Corporation, Markland v (1934) 98 JP 117; [1934] 1 KB 566; (1934) 77 LJ 125; (1934) 103 LJCL 265; (1934) 150 LTR 405; (1934) 78 SJ 103; (1933-34) L TLR 215 CA Corporation found liable in negligence for failure to attend to water leak which made road dangerous resulting in accident.

Manchester Corporation, McClelland v [1911-13] All ER 562; (1912) 76 JP 21; (1912) 81 LJKB 98; (1911-12) 105 LTR 707; (1911-12) XXVIII TLR 21 HC KBD Liability for misfeasance not nonfeasance.

Manchester Corporation, Priest v [1915] 84 LJKB 1734 HC KBD Sale of land for tipping purposes did not authorise tipping in such a way as to occasion nuisance.

Mangena v Edward Lloyd (Limited) (1908-09) XCIX LTR 824; (1908-09) XXV TLR 26 CA Headline of report based on Parliamentary blue-book fell outside privilege afforded by Parliamentary Papers Act 1840.

Mangena v Edward Lloyd (Limited) (1908) XCVIII LTR 640; (1907-08) XXIV TLR 610 HC KBD Good faith/non-malicious report based on Parliamentary blue-book enjoyed privilege afforded by Parliamentary Papers Act 1840.

Mapey v Baker (1909) 73 JP 289; (1908-09) 53 SJ 429 CA Slanderous words uttered of rate collector at meeting of Board of Guardians were uttered on privileged occasion.

Mapp v News Group Newspapers Ltd [1997] 2 Cr App R (S) 562; (1997) 147 NLJ 562; [1997] TLR 124 CA On determining whether words complained of are capable of bearing alleged defamatory meaning.

Mara (Kenderaan Bas), Tew (Yew Bon) alias Tiew (Yong Boon) and another v [1983] 1 AC 553; (1982) 126 SJ 729; [1982] TLR 458; [1982] 3 WLR 1026 PC Enactment of special limitation period for public authorities (could but) did not operate retroactively to defeat limitation plea benefiting defendants.

Marc Rich and Co AG and others v Bishop Rock Marine Co Ltd and others 'The Nicholas H' [1995] 3 All ER 307; [1996] 1 AC 211; (1995) 145 NLJ 1033; (1995) 139 SJ LB 165; [1995] TLR 398; [1995] 3 WLR 227 HL Classification society does not owe duty of care to cargo owners who suffer loss.

Marc Rich and Co AG and others v Bishop Rock Marine Co Ltd and others 'The Nicholas H' [1994] 3 All ER 686; [1994] TLR 101; [1994] 1 WLR 1071 CA No distinction in law between cases where negligence causes physical damage and where causes economic loss; classification society valuers not under duty of care to shipowners.

Marchant Manufacturing Company Limited v Leonard D Ford and Teller Limited (1936) 154 LTR 430 HC KBD Rylands v Fletcher inapplicable to situation where some water in water boiler installed on second floor of commercial premises leaked into ground floor: failed negligence action.

Mardon, Esso Petroleum Co Ltd v [1976] 2 All ER 5; (1976) 126 NLJ 265t; [1976] QB 801; (1976) 120 SJ 131; [1976] 2 WLR 583 CA Forecast by party of expertise to induce another into contracting is warranty; such party owes duty of care for negligent statements; damages are all losses suffered in light of contract.

Mardon, Esso Petroleum Co Ltd v [1975] 1 All ER 203; (1974) 124 NLJ 828t; [1975] QB 819; [1975] 2 WLR 147 HC QBD Duty of care if company in pre-contract talks represents certain state of affairs to induce other to sign contract.

Marengo v Daily Sketch and Sunday Graphic, Limited [1948] 117 LJR 787; (1948) LXIV TLR 160; (1948) WN (I) 92 HL On form of passing-off injunction.

Marengo v Daily Sketch and Sunday Graphic, Limited (1946) 96 LJ 317 CA Failed passing off action by cartoonist with name highly similar to that being used by another cartoonist.

Marfani and Co Ltd v Midland Bank Ltd (1968) 112 SJ 396 CA Bank not negligent (though barely so) in allowing person to open new bank account with stolen cheque, then withdraw proceeds.

Margarine Union GmbH v Cambay Prince Steamship Co, Ltd [1967] 3 All ER 775; [1969] 1 QB 219; (1967) 111 SJ 943; [1967] 3 WLR 1569 HC QBD Shipowner does not owe duty of care to party not owning goods when tort committed.

Margereson v JW Roberts Ltd; Hancock v Same (1996) TLR 17/4/96 CA Factory owners liable for deaths occurring to individuals as result of foreseeable pulmonary damage arising from dead persons having played as children in asbestos-laden atmosphere adjacent to factory.

Margolis, Wardley v (1981) 131 NLJ 447 HC QBD Damages from solicitor who negligently allowed personal injuries action with every chance of success to lapse.

Marine Board of Table Cape, Van Diemen's Land Company v [1904-07] All ER 1427; [1906] AC 92; [1906] 75 LJPC 28; (1905-06) XCIII LTR 709; (1905-06) XXII TLR 114; (1905-06) 54 WR 498 PC Pre-Crown grant occupation/user of land granted admissible to show land included in grant.

Maritime Agencies (Southampton), Ltd, Trucks and Spares, Ltd v [1951] 2 All ER 982 CA Bills of lading proper proof of title justifying interim delivery order.

Market Harborough Industrial Co-operative Society Ld, Baker v; Wallace v Richards (Leicester) Ld (1953) 97 SJ 861; [1953] 1 WLR 1472 CA Absent other evidence is presumption of equal blame where two vehicles collide in middle of straight road when dark.

Marriott v East Grinstead Gas and Water Company [1909] 1 Ch 70 HC ChD Owner of soil under which water board laying unauthorised pipes can sue for trespass/seek injunction (without joining Attorney-General).

Marsay, Bainbridge v [1937] LJNCCR 218 CyCt Successful action in negligence where cow had been negligently driven onto road into path of oncoming motor cycle.

Marsden and another, Morriss v [1952] 1 All ER 925; (1952) 102 LJ 219; (1952) 96 SJ 281; [1952] 1 TLR 947; (1952) WN (I) 188 HC QBD Knowledge of nature/quality though not wronfulness of act opens one to tortious liability.

Marsh and Parsons (a firm) and another, Gardner and another v [1997] 3 All ER 871; (1996) 140 SJ LB 262; (1996) TLR 2/12/97; [1997] 1 WLR 489 CA Damages available where purchased property in reliance on negligent surveyor's report were difference in cost of property and cost ought to have been were defects known when purchasing.

Marshal Shipping Company v Board of Trade [1923] 2 KB 343; (1923) WN (I) 115 CA Liability of Board of Trade for acts of Shipping Controller.

Marshall (Mary), wife of Lewis Alexander Marshall, County Council of the Parts of Lindsey, Lincolnshire v [1936] 2 All ER 1076; [1937] AC 97; (1936) 100 JP 411; [1936] 105 LJCL 614; (1936) 155 LTR 297; (1936) 80 SJ 702; (1935-36) LII TLR 661; (1936) WN (I) 244 HL Negligent admission of/failure to warn nursing home patient in maternity hospital where faced peculiar risk of fever.

Marshall and another, The Colonial Bank of Australasia (Limited) v [1906] 75 LJPC 76; (1905-06) XXII TLR 746 PC Leaving spaces on cheque that forger might use not negligence on part of customers so were not estopped from denying amended cheques were their cheques.

Marshall v Cellactite and British Uralite Limited and another (1947) LXIII TLR 456 CA Non-liability of factory owner for injury to contractors' employee injured through use of factory owner's defective equipment which contractors had elected to use and chosen themselves.

Marshall v Lindsey County Council (1935) 99 JP 185; (1935) 152 LTR 421; (1935) 79 SJ 251; (1934-35) LI TLR 279; (1935) WN (I) 32 CA Negligent admission of/failure to warn nursing home patient in maternity hospital where faced peculiar risk of fever.

Marshall v Lindsey County Council [1935] 1 KB 516 HC KBD Admission of/failure to warn nursing home patient in maternity hospital where faced peculiar risk of fever was not negligent.

Marshall v London Passenger Transport Board [1936] 3 All ER 83; (1936) 82 LJ 296; (1936) 80 SJ 893 CA Amendment of pleadings introducing new cause of action precluded by Public Authorities Protection Act 1893, s 1.

Marshall v Osmond and another [1982] 2 All ER 610; [1982] Crim LR 441; [1982] QB 857; [1983] RTR 111; (1982) 126 SJ 210; [1982] TLR 38; [1982] 3 WLR 120 HC QBD Police do not owe normal duty of care to person suspected of crime who is unintentionally injured in course of hot pursuit.

Marshall v Osmond and another [1983] 2 All ER 225; [1983] QB 1034; [1983] RTR 475; (1983) 127 SJ 309; [1983] TLR 190; [1983] 3 WLR 13 CA Police owe normal duty of care to person suspected of crime who is unintentionally injured in course of hot pursuit.

Marshall: Cotton, Third Party, McGlynn v [1944] LJNCCR 96 CyCt Occupier only liable in nuisance for injury occurring on foot of defect in premises if knew of defect and did nothing to fix it/was too slow in fixing it.

Marti v Smith and Home Office (1981) 131 NLJ 1028 HC QBD Failed negligence action against Home Office by person injured by actions of person who escaped from 'open' Borstal.

Martin and Co (Contractors) Ltd, Spartan Steel and Alloys Ltd v [1972] 3 All ER 557; (1972) 122 NLJ 585t; [1973] QB 27; (1972) 116 SJ 648; [1972] 3 WLR 502 CA Liability for physical damage but not non-consequential economic loss: no doctrine of 'parasitic damages'.

Martin and the Corporation of Kingston-upon-Hull, Smith v (1911) 75 JP 433; [1911] 2 KB 775; (1911) 80 LJCL 1256; (1910-11) XXVII TLR 468 CA Local authority liable for (non-teaching) act of teacher (who was also liable) resulting in injury to student.

Martin and the Mayor, &c, of Kingston-upon-Hull, Smith v (1911) 75 JP 135; (1911-12) 105 LT
281; (1910-11) XXVII TLR 165 HC KBD Non-liability of local authority for (non-teaching) ac
of teacher (who was personally liable) resulting in injury to student.

Martin Mears and Co, McNamara v (1983) 127 SJ 69 HC QBD On appropriate damages from
negligent solicitor who requested/advised client to accept lower divorce settlement than should have

Martin v Dean and another (1971) 121 NLJ 904; [1971] 3 All ER 279; [1971] 2 QB 208; [1971
RTR 280; (1971) 115 SJ 369; [1971] 2 WLR 1159 HC QBD Judgment debt (arising from
negligence action) available against motor bicycle-owner as well as bicycle-driver.

Martin v London County Council [1947] 1 All ER 783; (1947) 111 JP 310; [1947] KB 628; (1947
97 LJ 221; [1947] 116 LJR 1231; (1947) 177 LTR 38; (1947) 91 SJ 264; (1947) LXIII TLR
284; (1947) WN (I) 146 HC KBD Local authority running hospital not gratuitous bailee o
patient's property/could not assume property bailed of no value; purchase tax relevant in deciding
level of damages.

Martin v Middlesbrough Corporation (1965) 109 SJ 576 CA Corporation liable for injury caused
to pupil who fell on piece of glass in school playground.

Martin v Nolan and another [1944] 2 All ER 342; (1943-44) LX TLR 558 HC KBD Conviction
and breach of recognisance two offences so Borstal training merited: issue arose in course of
successful libel action.

Martin v Stanborough (1924) CC Rep XIII 85; (1924) 59 LJ 680; (1924-25) 69 SJ 104; (1924-25)
XLI TLR 1 CA Was negligence to leave parked car with defective brakes on steep hill with only
a piece of wood to stop it rolling forwards.

Martin v Stanborough (1923-24) 68 SJ 739; (1923-24) XL TLR 557 HC KBD Was prima facie
evidence of negligence to leave parked car with defective brakes on steep hill with only a piece of
wood to stop it rolling forwards.

Martin v Stirk (1969) 113 SJ 527 HC QBD On personal injuries damages for person rendered
quadriplegic by another's negligence and who had awareness of her injuries.

Martin v Watson [1994] 2 All ER 606; (1994) 144 NLJ 463; [1994] QB 425; (1994) 138 SJ LB
55; [1994] TLR 45; [1994] 2 WLR 500 CA That a defendant is not technically the prosecutor
precludes finding of malicious prosecution where a prosecution undertaken was a natural and
intended consequence of false and malicious actions by defendant.

Martin v Watson [1995] 3 All ER 559; [1996] 1 AC 74; (1995) 145 NLJ 1093; (1995) 139 SJ LB
190; [1995] TLR 408; [1995] 3 WLR 318 HL That a defendant is not technically the prosecutor
does not preclude a finding of malicious prosecution where a prosecution undertaken was a
natural and intended consequence of false and malicious actions by defendant.

Martin, Johnson v (1950) 100 LJ 541 CyCt Failed action in nuisance against bee-keeper by person
who had along with her goats been injured by the defendant's bees (one goat dying).

Martin, Pitcher v (1937) 81 SJ 670; (1936-37) LIII TLR 903 HC KBD Dog owner liable in
negligence/nuisance for injury caused to person after leashed dog escaped owner's control and ran
after cat.

Martin, Pratt v (1911-13) XXII Cox CC 442; (1911) 75 JP 328; [1911] 2 KB 90; (1911) 80 LJCL
711; (1911-12) 105 LTR 49; (1910-11) XXVII TLR 377; (1911) WN (I) 102 HC KBD Not
trespass to send one's dog across another's land to search for game.

Martindale v Duncan (1973) 123 NLJ 129t; [1973] RTR 532; (1973) 117 SJ 168; [1973] 1 WLR
574 CA No violation of onus to mitigate damages where postponed repairs to car until had sorted
out insurance claim.

Martine v South East Kent Health Authority [1993] TLR 119 CA No action lay in negligence
against health authority in respect of its investigation regarding standards at nursing home.

Martins Bank, Ltd and another, Woods v (1958) 108 LJ 665 HC QBD Bank and manager liable
for negligent advice regarding investments given by manager to plaintiff.

Martlew and another, Clarke v (1972) 122 NLJ 586t; [1973] QB 58; (1972) 116 SJ 618; [1972]
3 WLR 653 CA On mutual exchange of results of medical test to which plaintiff acceded at
defendant's request.

Matthews v Cowan (1915) CC Rep IV 84 CyCt Non-recovery of damages in trespass for liability suffered by straying cattle where person owning land onto which cattle strayed had not discharged duty of fencing out said cattle.

Matthews v Smallwood [1910] 1 Ch 777 HC ChD No relief against forfeiture for negligent trustees (Conveyancing and Law of Property Act 1892, s 4).

Matthews, Shears v [1948] 2 All ER 1064; (1949) 113 JP 36; (1949) LXV TLR 194; (1948) WN (I) 472 HC KBD Highway Act 1835, s 78, covers negligence directly connected to driving.

Mattocks v Mann [1993] RTR 13; [1992] TLR 303 CA All reasonable car-hire costs available to person whose car was negligently damaged by another and had to be repaired: damages available for period after repairs effected but before received insurance money to pay for same.

Matusevitch, Telnikoff v [1990] 3 All ER 865; [1991] 1 QB 102; (1990) 134 SJ 1078; [1990] TLR 423; [1990] 3 WLR 725 CA Court may look to broader context in deciding if material libellous; plea of fair comment raises presumption that comment an honest expression of opinion unless counter-claim of malicious publication.

Matusevitch, Telnikoff v [1991] 4 All ER 817; [1992] 2 AC 343; (1991) 141 NLJ 1590; [1991] TLR 513; [1991] 3 WLR 952 HL Letter in reply to article to be looked at in isolation when jury deciding if fair comment/libel; fair comment must be objectively fair.

Maudsley v Palumbo and others [1995] TLR 690 HC ChD On what constitutes breach of confidence in respect of which damages are available.

Maulding v Stott and Daily Mirror Newspapers Ltd (1978) 128 NLJ 464t CA Exemplary damages could be sought where newspaper committing libel did so in belief that any damages might have to pay would be less than increased profits made by publishing article.

Maunder, Hutchins v (1920-21) XXXVII TLR 72 HC KBD Placing car on highway in condition where by virtue of defective steering it posed danger to other highway users was negligent even though unaware of defect.

Maurice, Thake and another v [1986] 1 All ER 497; (1986) 136 NLJ 92; [1986] QB 644; [1986] 2 WLR 337 CA Absent express guarantee no guarantee that medical operation will be success; failure to warn of possible future pregnancies a failure of duty of care; damages for distress/pain/ suffering caused by pregnancy/birth available.

Maurice, Thake and another v [1984] 2 All ER 513; (1985) 129 SJ 86/894; [1984] TLR 225; [1985] 2 WLR 215 HC QBD Absent warning a guarantee of successful vasectomy arose; failure to warn of possible future pregnancies a warranty of completely successful vasectomy; damages for costs of birth and of rearing child ordered.

Maxey Drainage Board v Great Northern Railway Company (1912) 76 JP 236 HC KBD Landowner entitled to do what is necessary and reasonable to protect land from expected flooding.

Maxfield v Llewellyn and others [1961] 3 All ER 95; (1961) 105 SJ 550 CA Where assessing contributions of joint tortfeasors court not to look to persons who may be contributorily negligent but not so found/party to action.

Maxim's Ltd and another v Dye [1978] 2 All ER 55; (1977) 127 NLJ 715t; (1977) 121 SJ 727; [1977] 1 WLR 1155 HC ChD Passing-off relief available to business in other jurisdiction but goodwill in England.

Maxim, Cobstone Investments Ltd v [1985] QB 140 CA On what constitutes an 'adjoining occupier' (capable of complaining of nuisance of/annoyance by neighbour) for purposes of Rent Act 1977.

Maxine and Co, Ltd, British Transport Commission v (1963) 107 SJ 1025 CA Employers not vicariously liable for negligence of worker who had not been acting in connection with his work.

Maxwell v British Thomson Houston Company (Limited); Blackwell and Co, Third Parties (1901-02) XVIII TLR 278 CA Contractor liable for negligence of sub-contractor.

Maxwells of Emsworth, Ltd and another, Moore v [1968] 2 All ER 779; (1968) 118 NLJ 373t; (1968) 112 SJ 424; [1968] 1 WLR 1077 CA Negligence presumption rebutted if show took all reasonable steps to avoid cause of action.

Mayfair Hotel Co, Ltd, Vanderpant v [1929] All ER 296; [1930] 1 Ch 138; (1929) 68 LJ 256; (1930) 99 LJCh 84; (1930) 94 JP 23; (1930) 142 LTR 198; (1929) WN (I) 221 HC ChD Interests of public regarding public highway greater than that of occupier adjoining same but person seeking to restrain latter must show special/direct interest in so doing; on judging when noise a nuisance.

Maynard and another v Rogers [1970] RTR 392 HC QBD Person stepping on to uncontrolled pedestrian crossing without looking in either direction was contributorily negligent but driver also negligent in not yielding to person on uncontrolled pedestrian crossing.

Maynard v West Midlands Regional Health Authority [1985] 1 All ER 635; (1983) 133 NLJ 641; (1984) 128 SJ 317; [1983] TLR 316; [1984] 1 WLR 634 HL Doctor not proved negligent simply because was reputable body of opinion that disagreed with action he took as well as body of opinion that agreed with action he took.

Mayoh and Co and another, Hartley v [1953] 2 All ER 525; (1953) 117 JP 369 Assizes Fireman an invitee; presumed fireman has ordinary knowledge of shutting off electricity — here occupier negligent as failed to warn fireman of peculiarity of electrical system (and previously to test system); electricity supply board contributorily negligent for electrocution arising in part from defective installation.

Mayoh and Co and another, Hartley v (1954) 118 JP 178; [1954] 1 QB 383; (1954) 98 SJ 107; [1954] 1 WLR 355 CA Fireman an invitee; presumed fireman has ordinary knowledge of shutting off electricity — here occupier negligent as failed to warn fireman of peculiarity of electrical system (and previously to test system).

Mayor and Corporation of Hawthorn v Kannuluik [1904-07] All ER 1422; (1905-06) XCIII LTR 644 PC Liability of authority for negligent operation of drain.

Mayor of Hastings and other, Woodward and another v [1944] 2 All ER 565; (1945) 109 JP 41; [1945] KB 174; [1945] 114 LJ 211 (also HC KBD); (1945) 172 LTR 16; (1944-45) LXI TLR 94; (1944) WN (1) 239 CA Grammar school governors not public authority/were liable for caretaker's negligence.

Mayor of Hastings and others, Woodward and another v [1944] 2 All ER 119; (1944) 108 JP 247; [1944] KB 671; (1945) 95 LJ 111; [1945] 114 LJ 211 (also CA); (1944) 171 LTR 231; (1943-44) LX TLR 404 HC KBD Suing school governors subject to public authority limitation.

Mayor, &c, of Bolton, Schofield v (1909-10) 54 SJ 213; (1909-10) XXVI TLR 230 CA Persons allowing children to play in field not liable in negligence where left gate to railway line open, child went onto line and was injured.

Mayor, &c, of Liverpool, Evans v (1905) 69 JP 263; (1904-05) XXI TLR 558 HC KBD Local authority not liable for negligent early discharge of patient by visiting physician whom they employed.

Mayor, &c, of Rochdale, Hartley v [1908] 2 KB 594; (1908-09) XCIX LTR 275; (1907-08) XXIV TLR 625 HC KBD Local authority's failure to remedy subsidence of road caused by water leak did not preclude water company's liability for person injured as result of same.

Mayor, &c, of Shoreditch v Bull (1904) 68 JP 415; (1904) XC LTR 210; (1903-04) XX TLR 254 HL Approval of decision whereby local authority found liable for personal injuries driver suffered when collided with earth pile (of which authority knew) in course of avoiding part of road made by local authority but unfit for public traffic.

Mayor, &c, of Westminster v London and North-Western Railway Co (1905-06) 54 WR 129 HL Injunction to restrain trespass by local authority in erection of public toilets.

Mayor, Aldermen and Burgesses of Bethnal Green, Baker (Annie Amelia) v [1944] 2 All ER 301; (1945) 95 LJ 111 HC KBD State of staircase made it a concealed danger; stairway not air-raid cause of injury so not a'war injury'.

Mayor, Aldermen and Burgesses of Bethnal Green, Baker (Annie Amelia) v [1945] 1 All ER 135; (1945) 109 JP 72 CA Injury in air-raid shelter due to poorly maintained staircase was negligent personal injury, not 'war injury'.

Mayor, Aldermen and Burgesses of the Borough of Burlington, Broadbent v [1935] LJNCCR 258 CyCt Local authority not liable in negligence for injuries occasioned through sewer explosion from cause not previously known of.

Mayor, Aldermen and Burgesses of the Borough of Glossop, Sheppard v (1921) 85 JP 205; [1921] 3 KB 132 CA Non-liability of local authority for not lighting area around retaining wall which had been source of injury to person.

Mayor, Aldermen and Burgesses of the Borough of Luton, Morris v [1946] 1 All ER 1; (1946) 110 JP 102; [1946] KB 114; [1946] 115 LJ 202; (1946) 174 LTR 26; (1946) 90 SJ 91; (1945-46) LXII TLR 145; (1945) WN (I) 239 CA No rule that party driving in dark must be able to stop within limits of sight or is negligent.

Mayor, Aldermen, and Burgesses of Halifax, Riley v (1907) 71 JP 428; (1907-08) XCVII LTR 278; (1906-07) XXIII TLR 613 HC ChD Damages for trespass rather than injunction to stop same merited in the circumstances.

Mayor, Aldermen, and Burgesses of the Borough of St Helens, Clarke v (1915) 79 JP 529; [1916] 85 LJKB 17; (1915-16) 113 LTR 681; (1914-15) 59 SJ 509 CA Public authority limitation deemed inapplicable to action where public authority whose employee had been driving car which caused injury had not been acting in course of duty.

Mayor, Aldermen, and Citizens of Manchester, Midwood and Co Limited v [1904-07] All ER 1364; (1905) 69 JP 348; [1905] 2 KB 597; (1905-06) XCIII LTR 525; (1904-05) XXI TLR 667; (1905-06) 54 WR 37 CA Corporation liable in nuisance for escape of electricity causing explosion.

Mayor, Commonalty, and Citizens of the City of London, Phelps v [1916] 2 Ch 255; (1916) 114 LTR 1200 HC ChD On construction of lease defendants found not to have committed trespass in their actions.

Mayor, Councillors, and Citizens of Hawthorn v Kannuluik [1906] AC 105; (1905-06) 54 WR 285 PC Municipal authority liable in negligence for flooding from drain which when constructed was adequate for purpose for which used.

Mayor, etc of Dagenham, Chappell v (1948) 98 LJ 329; (1948) WN (I) 274 HC KBD Non-liability of local authority for non-feasance of highway.

Mayor, etc, of Bermondsey, Carey v (1903) 67 JP 111 HC KBD Personal injury action not allowed where brought over six months after injury occurred.

Mazure, Stubbs, Ltd v [1918-19] All ER 1081; [1920] AC 66; (1919) 54 LJ 344; [1919] 88 LJPC 135; (1920) 122 LTR 5; (1918-19) XXXV TLR 697; (1919) WN (I) 234 HL Wrongful publication of name in Stubbs' Gazette deemed defamatory despite qualifier published at head of relevant section.

McAlister (or Donoghue) (Pauper) v Stevenson [1932] All ER 1; [1932] AC 562; (1932) 73 LJ 428; (1932) 101 LJPC 119; (1932) 147 LTR 281; (1932) 76 SJ 396; (1931-32) XLVIII TLR 494; (1932) WN (I) 139 HL Manufacturer owes duty of reasonable care to ultimate consumer to ensure item does not endanger health where intermediate examination not possible.

McAll v Brooks [1984] RTR 99; [1983] TLR 115 CA Person unaware of any possible illegality in car-replacement agreement with insurance company could recoup reasonable costs of replacement from person responsible for collision which necessitated replacement.

McAlpine (since deceased) and others, The Grand Trunk Railway Company of Canada v [1914] 83 LJPC 44; (1913-14) 109 LTR 693; (1912-13) XXIX TLR 679 PC Rail company liable for injury at level crossing only if proved that failing to give warning of approach/ring bell led to accident.

McArdle v Andmac Roofing Co and others [1967] 1 All ER 583; (1967) 111 SJ 37; [1967] 1 WLR 356 CA Main contractor liable for (acts of sub-contractors leading to) foreseeable injury of workman.

McArdle v Andmac Roofing Co and others [1966] 3 All ER 241; (1965-66) 116 NLJ 1404 Assizes Two sub-contractors owed duty of care to worker and were liable in negligence for leaving matter to others.

McArthur v The Dominion Cartridge Company (Limited) [1905] 74 LJPC 30; (1904-05) XXI TLR 47; (1904-05) 53 WR 305 PC Circumstances of injury to workman in ammunition factory could ground successful negligence.

McAuley v Bristol City Council [1992] 1 All ER 749 CA Council right to enter house entailed right to enter garden so duty of care to carry out repairs in garden.

McGee v Francis Shaw and Co Ltd [1973] RTR 409 HC QBD Person choosing not to wear seat belt one-third liable for injuries suffered in accident; no damages for being/not being presented because of injury with chance to work abroad.

McGee, Jefford and another v [1970] 1 All ER 1202; (1970) 114 SJ 206 CA On interest on fatal accident damages.

McGeown v Northern Ireland Housing Executive [1994] 3 All ER 53; [1995] 1 AC 233; (1994) 144 NLJ 901; (1994) 138 SJ LB 156; [1994] TLR 343; [1994] 3 WLR 187 HL Owner of land over which public right of way not liable for negligent nonfeasance; person exercising public right of way not licensee or invitee.

McGhee v National Coal Board [1972] 3 All ER 1008 HL If breach of duty causes/contributes to injury are liable in negligence.

McGinlay (or Titchener) v British Railways Board [1983] 3 All ER 770; (1984) 134 NLJ 36; (1983) 127 SJ 825; [1983] 1 WLR 1427 HL Occupier owes reasonable care to person on premises; reasonableness depends on case.

McGinley v Burke (1973) 117 SJ 488; [1973] 1 WLR 990 HC QBD Was not proper for plaintiff in personal injuries action to see medical report prepared for defendant but not vice versa.

McGlynn v Marshall: Cotton, Third Party [1944] LJNCCR 96 CyCt Occupier only liable in nuisance for injury occurring on foot of defect in premises if knew of defect and did nothing to fix it/was too slow in fixing it.

McGowan v Stott (1930) 143 LTR 217 CA Re-trial ordered where facts required defendant to explain them.

McGrath and another, Kralj and another v [1986] 1 All ER 54; (1985) 135 NLJ 913 HC QBD Aggravated damages not appropriate for medical negligence though compensatory damages may be raised; damages for nervous shock, not grief; financial loss in replacing dead child recoverable.

McIntyre v Coles [1966] 1 All ER 723 [1966] 1 WLR 831 CA On yielding at junctions (and consequent negligence).

McIsaac v Vos (1983) 133 NLJ 185 HC QBD On appropriate damages for previously outgoing girl who was physically and mentally scarred in serious road traffic accident.

McIver, Glinski v [1962] 1 All ER 696; [1962] Crim LR 392t; [1962] AC 726; (1962) 112 LJ 220; (1962) 106 SJ 261 HL Whether honest belief in guilt an issue only if doubt; defendant's task in prosecution engendering action was whether reasonable/probable basis for prosecution; if no such basis may be malice but not vice versa.

McIver, Glinski v [1960] Crim LR 428t CA Successful appeal against finding that police officer undertook malicious prosecution: was reasonable and probable cause for prosecution.

McIver, Glinski v [1959] Crim LR 56t HC QBD Successful action against police officer for malicious prosecution.

McKay and another v Essex Area Health Authority and another [1982] 2 All ER 771; (1982) 132 NLJ 466; [1982] QB 1166; [1982] TLR 90; [1982] 2 WLR 890 CA Sole duty to foetus is duty not to injure it.

McKenna v Scottish Omnibuses Ltd and Northumberland County Council (1984) 134 NLJ 681 HC QBD Bus company, not highway authority liable for personal injuries suffered when bus slid on black ice (winter hazard of which driver should have known/which highway authority not here under duty to remove).

McKenzie, Vaughan v [1968] 1 All ER 1154; [1968] Crim LR 265; (1968) 118 NLJ 204t; [1969] 1 QB 557; (1968) 112 SJ 212; [1968] 2 WLR 1133 HC QBD Not assault on bailiff in execution of duty where assault occurred when resident sought to impede bailiff's entry (bailiff in so entering was trespassing).

McKeown, Hughes v (1985) 129 SJ 543; [1985] 1 WLR 963 HC QBD On determining personal injury damages for young woman who because of injury has limited future earning ability and no chance of marriage.

McKew v Holland and Hannen and Cubitts (Scotland) Ltd [1969] 3 All ER 1621 HL Careless act broke causation between first injury and later injury.

McNeall v Hawes (1923) 58 LJ 160; [1923] 92 LJCL 729 (also HC KBD); (1922-23) 67 SJ 483; (1922-23) XXXIX TLR 362; (1923) WN (I) 170 CA Non-liability of husband for tortious act of wife during coverture.

McNeall v Hawes [1923] 1 KB 273; [1923] 92 LJCL 729 (also CA); (1922-23) 67 SJ 316; (1922-23) XXXIX TLR 167; (1923) WN (I) 14 HC KBD Liability of husband for tortious act of wife during coverture.

McNealy v Pennine Insurance Co Ltd and others [1978] RTR 285 CA Brokers liable where their breach of duty of care owed towards client resulted in latter not being covered by insurance policy.

McNeil, Rands v (1954) 104 LJ 840; [1955] 1 QB 253; (1954) 98 SJ 851 CA No liability for injury to farm worker entering pen in which dangerous bull kept loose (had not escaped so no strict liability).

McNeill and another v Johnstone [1958] 3 All ER 16; (1958) 108 LJ 570; (1958) 102 SJ 602 HC QBD Husband allowed recover portion of expenses incurred through month's leave of absence from work to be near wife.

McNiven, Donaldson v [1952] 2 All ER 691; (1952) 102 LJ 594; (1952) 96 SJ 747; (1952) WN (I) 466 CA Parent not liable for negligent firing of air rifle by son.

McNiven, Donaldson v [1952] 1 All ER 1213 Assizes Parent not liable for negligent firing of air rifle by son.

McNulty, Thomson (DC) and Co v (1927) 71 SJ 744 HL Failed libel action where was not shown that newspaper article in question referred to respondent to appeal.

McPhail v Unknown (Persons); Bristol Corporation v Ross and another (1973) 117 SJ 448 CA On non-availability of suspension of possession order where latter made against squatter-trespassers.

McPhail, Cutler and another v [1962] 2 All ER 474; (1962) 112 LJ 370; [1962] 2 QB 292; (1962) 106 SJ 391 HC QBD Complete release of joint tortfeasors not covenant not to sue so ended all rights of action.

McQuaker v Goddard [1940] 1 All ER 471; [1940] 1 KB 687; (1940) 89 LJ 119; [1940] 109 LJCL 673; (1940) 162 LTR 232; (1940) 84 SJ 203; (1939-40) LVI TLR 409; (1940) WN (I) 80 CA Camel a domestic animal; camel-owner not negligent in fencing provided.

McQuire v Western Morning News Co [1900-03] All ER 673; [1903] 2 KB 100; [1903] 72 LJKB 612; (1903) LXXXVIII LTR 757; (1902-03) XIX TLR 471; (1903) WN (I) 98; (1902-03) 51 WR 689 CA Criticism of play must be reasonably describable as criticism; matter for judge whether something goes beyond fair criticism.

McVittie v Turner [1916] 85 LJKB 23; (1915-16) 113 LTR 982; (1915-16) 60 SJ 238 CA Secondary motives of police officer entering theatre pursuant to Cinematograph Act 1909 for valid purpose did not render entry a trespass.

Mead and others, Osborne v (1928) 66 LJ ccr18 CyCt Where unlawfully place chattels on another's land that other is allowed to remove same.

Meadows, O'Brien v (1965) 109 SJ 316 CA On appropriate personal injury damages for person who suffered venous thrombosis after accident arising from another's negligent driving.

Meah v McCreamer [1985] 1 All ER 367; (1985) 135 NLJ 80; [1984] TLR 426 HC QBD Damages for imprisonment for offences committed following on personality change occasioned by negligence of defendant.

Meah v McCreamer and others (No 2) [1986] 1 All ER 943; (1986) 136 NLJ 235; (1985) 135 NLJ 80 HC QBD Damages unavailable to meet cost of damages paid to third party for acts arising from earlier negligent action.

Meah, W v; D v Meah and another [1986] 1 All ER 935; (1986) 136 NLJ 165 HC QBD Damages for trespass primarily compensatory.

Meaker and Brown, Hicks v (1952) 102 LJ 725 CyCt Failed action in negligence in respect of damage arising from allegedly negligent disrepair of houses.

Meakers Garages, Ltd, Courage and Co, Ltd v (1948) 98 LJ 163 HC ChD Successful action for damage occasioned by collapse of building maintained in disrepair.

Mecca, Ltd, Morecambe and Heysham Corporation v (1966) 110 SJ 70 HC ChD Failed passing off action brought by organisers of 'Miss Great Britain' contest against organisers of 'Miss Britain' contest.

Medici and another, Balsamo v [1984] 2 All ER 304; (1984) 128 SJ 500; [1984] 1 WLR 951 HC ChD Cannot pursue one defendant in contract and other in tort for connected cause; no action aginst third party whose negligence did not affect cause of contractual action.

Medley and others, Schnitzler v (1963) 107 SJ 810 CA On elements/proving of slander of title.

Medway (Chatham) Dock Co Ltd and others, Gillingham Borough Council v [1992] 3 All ER 923; [1993] QB 343; [1991] TLR 440; [1992] 3 WLR 449 HC QBD Nuisance to be decided by reference to neighbourhood despite change of use following planning permission.

Medway and Gravesend Hospital Management Committee and another, Whichello v (1964) 108 SJ 55 HC QBD Decision not to take step which might have proved more fruitful approach to treating patient was not actually negligent.

Medway Health Authority, Dobbie v [1994] 4 All ER 450; (1994) 144 NLJ 760t; (1994) 144 NLJ 828; [1994] TLR 278; [1994] 1 WLR 1234 CA Limitation period in personal injury claim runs from date when victim knew injury resulted from action of another even if unaware legal remedy available.

Mee v Cruikshank (1901-07) XX Cox CC 210; (1902) LXXXVI LTR 708; (1901-02) XVIII TLR 271 HC KBD Prison governor liable for illegal detention of acquitted person by prison warders.

Meekins v Henson and others [1962] 1 All ER 899; (1962) 112 LJ 290; [1964] 1 QB 472; (1962) 106 SJ 571 HC QBD Qualified privilege for three partners, one liable in libel action as was motivated by malice.

Meering v Grahame-White Aviation Company Limited [1918-23] All ER 292; (1920) 122 LTR 44 CA On imprisonment by private prosecutor/police.

Mellish and Harkavy, Neushul v (1966) 110 SJ 792 HC QBD On duty owed by solicitor to client when acting for two parties (here failed to meet duty of care).

Mellish and Harkavy, Neushul v (1967) 111 SJ 399 CA On duty owed by solicitor to client when acting for two parties (here failed to meet duty of care).

Mellor and others, Pridgeon v (1911-12) XXVIII TLR 261 HC KBD Treasury solicitor and aides not liable in trespass for seizure on foot of writ issued as result of judicial proceedings.

Melton v Walker and Stanger (1981) 131 NLJ 1238; (1981) 125 SJ 861 HC ChD Date of cause of action ran from date negligently drafted document was signed.

Mendelovitch v Eastern Cinemas (GCF) Ltd [1940] LJNCCR 158 CyCt Cinema-owners not liable in negligence for injury suffered by patron-invitee who slipped on floor despite all reasonable efforts being taken by cinema to prevent any such occurrence.

Mendelson and another (Eastern Counties Omnibus Co Ltd and another (third parties)), Buesnel v (1959) 109 LJ ccr141 CyCt Person overtaking on inside of bus liable in damages for negligent injury occasioned to passenger on motorcycle waved forward by bus driver at junction.

Mercer v South Eastern and Chatham Rail Co's Managing Committee [1922] All ER; [1922] 2 KB 549; [1923] 92 LJCL 25; (1922) 127 LTR 723; (1921-22) XXXVIII TLR 431 HC KBD Gate usually locked when train approaching left open: victim could recover damages in negligence for injuries consequently suffered.

Mercer, Bromley v [1922] 2 KB 126; [1922] 91 LJCL 577; (1922) 127 LTR 282; (1921-22) XXXVIII TLR 496; (1922) WN (I) 112 CA Non-liability to non-user of highway for injury suffered via wall which was public nuisance on highway.

Merchants' Fire Office (Lim) v Armstrong and others (1901) 36 LJ 403; (1900-01) 45 SJ 706 CA Negligent company directors liable to repay to company amount paid out negligently.

Mercouris and another, Alexander and another v [1979] 3 All ER 305 CA Defective Premises Act 1972 does not apply to work commenced before Act.

Merkur Island Shipping Corp v Laughton and others [1983] 1 All ER 334; (1983) 133 NLJ 186; [1983] 2 WLR 45 CA Elements of 'inducement to commit breach of contract'; immunity from action in tort if purpose of secondary action to frustrate contract between picketed employer and employer facing secondary action.

Messenger May Baverstock, Luxmoore-May and another v (1988) 138 NLJ 341 HC QBD On duty owed to client by provincial auctioneer to establish value of auctioned item before auction.

Metall und Rohstoff AG v Donaldson Lufkin and Jenrette Inc and another [1990] 1 QB 391 (also HC QBD); (1989) 133 SJ 1200; [1989] 3 WLR 563 CA Conspiracy does not require that sole/principal aim be to injure other party; to commit tort of abuse of legal process sole/principal aim of one's actions must be said abuse.

Metall und Rohstoff AG v Donaldson Lufkin and Jenrette Inc and another [1988] 3 All ER 116; [1990] 1 QB 391 (also CA); (1988) 132 SJ 1149; [1988] 3 WLR 548 HC QBD Conspiracy does not require that sole/principal aim be to injure other party.

Metals and Ropes Co Ltd v Tattersall [1966] 3 All ER 401; (1965-66) 116 NLJ 1460; [1966] 1 WLR 1500 CA Where do not yield up delivery but regard property in items in one's control to rest with other must communicate this to other.

Metcalfe v Collett-Ward (1977) 127 NLJ 964b CA On what constitutes false imprisonment: aggravated damages awarded for same.

Meteor Garage (Moseley), Ltd, Coley v [1941] LJNCCR 201 CyCt Garage with whom car bailed during winter not liable in negligence for not having drained radiator/for collapse of garage roof under weight of freak snow onto car.

Metro-Goldwyn-Mayer Pictures Ltd, Turner v (1947) 97 LJ 389; (1947) 91 SJ 495 HC KBD Was libellous to suggest in writing that critic deliberately sought to damage the industry which provided the matter (film) that critic analysed.

Metro-Goldwyn-Mayer Pictures, Limited, Turner v (1950) 100 LJ 93; [1950] 66 (1) TLR 342; (1950) WN (I) 83 HL On malice; on trial procedure at libel/slander trials.

Metro-Goldwyn-Mayer Pictures, Limited, Youssoupoff v (1934) 78 SJ 617; (1933-34) L TLR 581 CA Defamation via ('talking') cinema film is libel; allegation that woman has been seduced is defamatory of her; on appropriate damages for libel.

Metro-Goldwyn-Mayer Pictures, Ltd, Turner (otherwise Robertson) v [1950] 1 All ER 449; (1950) 94 SJ 145 HL That motivated by financial interest need not mean malicious; opinion need only be genuine not right — here honest views absent malice so qualified privilege remained.

Metro-Goldwyn-Mayer Pictures, Ltd, Turner v (1948) 98 LJ 441 CA Potentially libellous to suggest in writing that critic deliberately sought to damage the industry which provided the matter (film) that critic analysed but no malice proved on part of maker of statement.

Metropolitan Borough of Bermondsey, Carey v (1903) 67 JP 447; (1903-04) XX TLR 2 CA Personal injury action not allowed where brought over six months after injury occurred.

Metropolitan District Railway Company, King (J) and King (WH) v (1908) 72 JP 294; (1908-09) XCIX LTR 278 HC KBD On statutory protection afforded special constable (employed by rail company) in effecting arrest.

Metropolitan Police Commissioner and others, Bishop v (1989) 133 SJ 1626 CA Plaintiff's conduct relevant to setting exemplary damages payable by defendant guilty of malicious prosecution.

Metropolitan Police Commissioner, Carter v (1975) 125 NLJ 87t CA Failed action for false imprisonment by woman removed to place of safety by police constable who believed her to be mentally unwell (Mental Health Act 1959, s 136(1)).

Metropolitan Police Commissioner, White and another v [1982] TLR 221 HC QBD Exemplary damages from Police Commissioner for false imprisonment/assault/malicious prosecution by police officers.

Metropolitan Police District Receiver v Tatum (1948) 112 JP 209; (1948) WN (I) 152 HC KBD Police receiver allowed recover off-work sums paid for/to officer injured through defendant's negligence.

Metropolitan Police District Receiver, McCafferty v [1977] 2 All ER 756; (1977) 121 SJ 678; [1977] 1 WLR 1073 CA Express/non-express reasons for delay in bringing action of relevance in deciding if limitation not to apply.

Metropolitan Police District Receiver, Parnell v [1976] RTR 201 CA No evidence proving that minibus driver had been travelling too close to preceding vehicle/had not seen in time that preceding vehicle stopping.

Midland Bank, Ltd, Jayson v (1967) 111 SJ 719 HC QBD Issue whether bank's writing 'refer to drawer' on cheque was libellous left to jury.

Midland Great Western Railway of Ireland, Cooke v [1908-10] All ER 16; [1909] AC 229; [1909] 78 LJPC 76; (1909) C LTR 626; (1908-09) 53 SJ 319; (1908-09) XXV TLR 375; (1909) WN (I) 56 HL Liable in negligence for injury to child through allurement.

Midland Railway Company, Anthony v (1909) C LTR 117; (1908-09) XXV TLR 98 HC KBD Passenger injured by stepping from train which overshot platform before could be warned could not recover damages in negligence.

Midland Railway Company, Brackley v [1916] 85 LJKB 1596; (1916) 114 LTR 1150 CA Rail company not liable for inadequate maintenance of railway footbridge/hidden danger it posed where bridge had been dedicated to public.

Midland Silicones Ltd v Scruttons Ltd (1959) 109 LJ 362; [1959] 2 QB 171; (1959) 103 SJ 415 HC QBD Non-party (and non-agent) cannot benefit from terms of contract.

Midland Silicones, Ltd v Scruttons, Ltd [1960] 2 All ER 737; [1961] 1 QB 106 CA Non-party (and non-agent) cannot benefit from terms of contract.

Midwood and Co Limited v Mayor, Aldermen, and Citizens of Manchester [1904-07] All ER 1364; (1905) 69 JP 348; [1905] 2 KB 597; (1905-06) XCIII LTR 525; (1904-05) XXI TLR 667; (1905-06) 54 WR 37 CA Corporation liable in nuisance for escape of electricity causing explosion.

Miers, Huggett v [1908-10] All ER 184; [1908] 2 KB 278; (1908) 43 LJ 282; [1908] 77 LJCL 710; (1908-09) XCIX LTR 326; (1908) WN (I) 115 CA Landlord did not owe higher duty of care to invitee of tenant than tenant owed.

Milburn and others, Cowper and others v (1907-08) 52 SJ 316 HL Interference with ancient lights deemed not, in circumstances, to be a nuisance.

Miles v Forest Rock Granite Company (Leicestershire) (Limited) (1917-18) 62 SJ 634; (1917-18) XXXIV TLR 500 CA Quarry owner to contain effects of explosions on own land — where fails to do so is liable for acts regardless of negligence.

Millar's Karri and Jarrah Forests (Limited) and another, Alcott v (1904-05) XCI LTR 722; (1904-05) 49 SJ 32; (1904-05) XXI TLR 30 CA On trade libel.

Miller and another v Jackson and another [1977] 3 All ER 338; (1977) 127 NLJ 568t; [1977] QB 966; (1977) 121 SJ 287; [1977] 3 WLR 20 CA Cricket balls emanating from village cricket ground a negligent act.

Miller and Co, B v [1996] 3 FCR 435; [1996] 2 FLR 23 HC QBD Not collateral attack on order of competent court for plaintiff to bring negligence action against solicitors who advised her in ancillary relief/consent order proceedings.

Miller and others v Ismay Distributors, Ltd [1939] LJNCCR 112 CyCt Mother of child injured by defectively constructed electric washing machine allowed recover damages for shock from manufacturer.

Miller v Evans and another; Pouleuf (Third Party) [1975] RTR 70 CA Driver not contributorily negligent in assuming oncoming traffic travelling at such speed that could stop when lights changed.

Miller v Liverpool Co-operative Society, Ltd, and others [1940] 4 All ER 367 Assizes Passenger/licensee recovering against both parties in motor vehicle collision.

Miller, Capps v [1989] 2 All ER 333; [1989] RTR 312; (1989) 133 SJ 1134; [1989] 1 WLR 839 CA Improperly fastening crash helmet contributory negligence meriting 10% reduction in damages.

Miller, McCready v [1979] RTR 186 CA On duty of care owed by minicab driver towards passengers.

Miller, Parker v (1925-26) XLII TLR 408 CA That car ran down hill when unattended was per se evidence of negligence for which person enjoying right of control over car was liable.

Millikin v Smith (1951) 95 SJ 560 CA On procedure as regards assessment of damages in personal injury actions.

Ministry of Defence, Mulcahy v (1996) 146 NLJ 334; [1996] QB 732; [1996] 2 WLR CA Ministry of Defence did not have to provide safe place of work/fellow soldiers do not owe each other duty of care in tort in battlefront conditions.

Ministry of Defence, Murray v [1988] 2 All ER 521; (1988) 138 NLJ 164; (1988) 132 SJ 852; [1988] 1 WLR 692 HL Arrest can begin before formal words of arrest spoken; formal words usually to be said at moment of arrest.

Ministry of Defence, Pritchard v [1995] TLR 26 HC QBD Failed claim in false imprisonment by individual who claimed was compelled to remain in Army (but such a claim could be successful).

Ministry of Defence, Trawnik and another v [1984] 2 All ER 791; (1984) 128 SJ 665; [1984] TLR 198/265 HC ChD General claim in tort/seeking declaration of rights may be possible against Crown.

Ministry of Defence, Willson v [1991] 1 All ER 638 HC QBD 'Chance of serious deterioration': 'chance' means something more than fanciful/'serious deterioration' more than ongoing deterioration and greater than ordinary deterioration.

Ministry of Health (Fahrni, Third Party), Cassidy v [1951] 1 All ER 574; [1951] 2 KB 343; (1951) 101 LJ 121; (1951) 95 SJ 253; [1951] 1 TLR 539; (1951) WN (I) 147 CA On liability of hospital authorities for negligence of medical staff.

Ministry of Health and others, Roe v; Woolley v Same [1954] 2 All ER 131; (1954) 104 LJ 313; [1954] 2 QB 66; (1954) 98 SJ 319; [1954] 2 WLR 915 CA Hospital liable for negligence of anaesthesist here — no negligence here as standard of care was that to be expected of reasonably competent anaesthesist.

Ministry of Housing and Local Government v Sharp and another [1970] 1 All ER 1009; (1969) 133 JP 595; [1970] 2 QB 223; [1970] 2 WLR 802 CA Need not be voluntary taking of responsibility to be tortiously liable for misstatement.

Ministry of Housing and Local Government v Sharp and another [1969] 3 WLR 1020 HC QBD Local land charges registrar owed duty of care to ensure search certificate included all entries in local land charges register (and were vicariously liable for negligence of employee).

Ministry of Transport, Bright v (1970) 120 NLJ 549t; [1970] RTR 401; (1970) 114 SJ 475 HC QBD Ministry of Transport negligent in manner in which had removed white lines from road.

Ministry of Transport, Bright v [1971] RTR 253 CA Ministry of Transport vicariously liable for negligent manner in which council workers removed traffic lines from road.

Minories Finance Ltd v Arthur Young (a firm) (Bank of England, third party); Johnson Matthey plc v Arthur Young (a firm) (Bank of England, third party) [1989] 2 All ER 105 HC QBD Bank of England not under duty of care to commercial banks/depositors when policing commercial banks.

Minster, Catchpole v (1913) CC Rep II 113; (1913-14) 109 LTR 953; (1913-14) XXX TLR 111 HC KBD Nighttime driving of sheep on highway not per se negligent.

Mint and another v Good [1950] 2 All ER 1159; [1951] 1 KB 517; (1950) 100 LJ 691; (1950) 94 SJ 822; [1950] 66 (2) TLR 1110; (1950) WN (I) 555 CA Landlord liable (absent contrary agreement) to maintain premises (here walls adjoining highway) in safe condition.

Minter and others, Diamond v (1939-40) XXXI Cox CC 468; (1941) 91 LJ 142 HC KBD Unmerited arrest as were not person named in warrant; police officer cannot without warrant arrest person whom reasonably suspects committed criminal act abroad.

Minter v Priest [1930] All ER 431; [1930] AC 558; (1930) 69 LJ 250; (1930) 99 LJCL 391; (1930) 143 LTR 57; (1930) 74 SJ 200; (1929-30) XLVI TLR 301; (1930) WN (I) 83 HL Whether occasion privileged a matter for judge; no absolute privilege as solicitor not acting for party and qualified privilege attaching to occasion defeated by solicitor's malice.

Minter v Priest [1929] 1 KB 655; (1929) 67 LJ 378; (1929) 141 LTR 140 HC KBD On professional privilege in defamation actions.

Minter v Priest (1929) 98 LJCL 661; (1929) 73 SJ 529; (1928-29) XLV TLR 393; (1929) WN (I) 94 CA Privilege attaches to communications between solicitor and prospective client regarding possible retainer of former by latter.

Moan v Reed Brothers (Engineers), Ltd (1962) 106 SJ 283 CA Judgment set aside where was based on negligence that had not in fact been pleaded.

Modern Foundries Ltd, Clarkson v (1957) 101 SJ 960; [1957] 1 WLR 1210 HC QBD Recovery for entire injury where undistinguishable part of injury occurred outside limitation period.

Modern Society (Limited) and another, Damiens v (1910-11) XXVII TLR 164 HC KBD Damages ought not to have been severed in respect of joint defendants.

Moeliker v A Reyrolle and Co Ltd [1977] 1 All ER 9; [1977] 1 WLR 132 CA Damages for loss of earning capacity to employed only if real prospect of job loss; how to measure loss of earning capacity.

Moffatt and others, Watkins v (1967) 111 SJ 719 CA Person who emerged from side road and drove onto main road at speed was guilty of negligence.

Moffatt and others, Watkins v [1970] RTR 205 CA Driver on main road not contributorily negligent where collided with driver suddenly emerging from side road without paying heed to warning signs.

Moi (Chong Kew), Tan Chye Choo and others v [1970] 1 All ER 266; (1969) 113 SJ 1000; [1970] 1 WLR 147 PC No right of action where defect in vehicle not result of negligence.

Moir, Wallersteiner v; Moir v Wallersteiner and others [1974] 3 All ER 217; (1974) 124 NLJ 525t; [1974] 1 WLR 991 CA Libel action used to gag party an abuse of process; consideration of sub judice company affairs at company meeting not contempt.

Moiseiwitsch, Fielding v (1946) 174 LTR 265 HC KBD Was breach of contract for pianist not to perform as had contracted; not defamatory for organiser to truthfully state what had occurred — such statement was in any event privileged.

Moiseiwitsch, Fielding v (1946) 175 LTR 265 CA Was breach of contract for pianist not to perform as had contracted; not defamatory for organiser to truthfully state what had occurred — such statement was in any event privileged.

Mole Valley District Council and another, Potter and others v [1982] TLR 486 HC QBD Flooding resulting from road works a public/private nuisance for which county council responsible.

Molloy v The Mutual Reserve Life Insurance Company (1906) XCIV LTR 756; (1905-06) XXII TLR 525 CA Action to recover money paid out on foot of misrepresentation defeated by Statute of Limitations.

Moloney v Lambeth Borough Council (1966) 110 SJ 406 HC QBD Occupier liable where staircase railing had gaps so wide that child whom could expect to use staircase fell through gaps and injured self.

Monk v Warbey and others (1934) 151 LTR 100; (1933-34) L TLR 263 HC KBD Owner of car liable towards person injured by car when driven by individual accompanying person to whom car loaned.

Monk v Warbey and others (1935) 152 LTR 194; (1934-35) LI TLR 77 CA Owner of car liable towards person injured by car when driven by individual accompanying person to whom car loaned.

Monmouthshire County Council and others, Clark v (1954) 118 JP 244 CA Schoolmasters not liable for unintended personal injury arising from scuffle between boys, one of whom had knife, as did not involve failure by teachers to maintain reasonable control over boys.

Monmouthshire County Council v Dean (1962) 112 LJ 787 CyCt Failed claim that person whom claimed to have inadequately drained bank was liable in nuisance/for obstruction where bank became waterlogged and slipped onto road.

Montagu v Bird and Bird (a firm) (1973) 117 SJ 448 HC ChD Refusal to strike out professional negligence claim in which plaintiff seeking damages to compensate him for position he would have been in had he not been allegedly negligent advice.

Montagu, Leeman v [1936] 2 All ER 1677; (1936) 80 SJ 691 HC KBD Noise from poultry farm a nuisance.

Montereale v Longmans Green and Co, Ltd, and another (1965) 109 SJ 215 HC QBD No qualified privilege in relation to commentary on foreign judicial proceedings.

More v Weaver (1928) 72 SJ 319; (1928) WN (I) 158 HC KBD Absolute privilege attaches to communications between solicitor-client in matters pertinent to that relationship.

Morecambe and Heysham Corporation v Mecca, Ltd (1966) 110 SJ 70 HC ChD Failed passing off action brought by organisers of 'Miss Great Britain' contest against organisers of 'Miss Britain' contest.

Moresk Cleaners Ltd v Hicks (1965-66) 116 NLJ 1546 Assizes Architect negligent in delegating his design responsibilities to builders.

Morey v Woodfield [1963] 3 All ER 533; (1963) 107 SJ 651; [1964] 1 WLR 16 CA On appeals concerning personal injury damages.

Morgan (Charles) v Khyatt (Najlo A) (1964) 108 SJ 236; [1964] 1 WLR 475 PC Was nuisance where roots of trees on one person's property ran onto another's and caused structural damage.

Morgan and another v Wallis (1916-17) XXXIII TLR 495 HC KBD Qualified privilege where solicitor in dictating bill of costs included without malice as a point of information a statement that was in fact defamatory.

Morgan and others, Launchbury and others v [1971] 1 All ER 642; (1971) 121 NLJ 83t; [1971] 2 QB 245; [1971] RTR 97; (1971) 115 SJ 96; [1971] 2 WLR 602 CA Owner vicariously liable for negligence of third party driving car.

Morgan Crucible Co plc v Hill Samuel Bank Ltd and others [1991] 1 All ER 148; [1991] Ch 295 (also HC ChD); (1990) 140 NLJ 1605; [1990] TLR 699; [1991] 2 WLR 655 CA Duty of care on directors of/financial advisers to company not to make misleading statements to known bidder.

Morgan Crucible Co plc v Hill Samuel Bank Ltd and others [1990] 3 All ER 330; [1991] Ch 295 (also CA); (1990) 140 NLJ 1271 HC ChD Directors of/financial advisers to company owe no duty of care to known take-over bidder in preparation of documents prepared to contest bid.

Morgan v Ashmore, Benson, Pease and Co, Ltd and another [1953] 1 All ER 328; (1953) 97 SJ 152; [1953] 1 WLR 418 HC QBD Can recover from joint tortfeasor if could have been successfuly sued in past.

Morgan v Aylen [1942] 1 All ER 489; (1943) 93 LJ 115 HC KBD Running in front of motor vehicle to save child not contributory negligence.

Morgan v Incorporated Central Council of the Girls' Friendly Society [1936] 1 All ER 404; (1936) 81 LJ 187; (1936) 80 SJ 323 HC KBD Independent contractors but not landlord liable in negligence to licensee falling down lift shaft when lift gate left open.

Morgan v Odhams Press Ltd and another [1971] 2 All ER 1156; (1971) 115 SJ 587; [1971] 1 WLR 1239 HL Article need not clearly point to certain person to be defamatory (though traditional test applies); misdirection on damages where failed to mention low circulation; imprecise, sensationalist article; some persons misled could be told truth by plaintiff; that no apology needed where defendant alleges never impugned plaintiff.

Morgan v Odhams Press Ltd and another [1970] 2 All ER 544; (1970) 120 NLJ 200t; (1970) 114 SJ 193; [1970] 1 WLR 820 CA Libel action to be grounded in actual words; no libel if no one would have understood referred to plaintiff; CA decision that case arguable does not mean libel case must be left to jury.

Morgan v Scoulding [1938] 1 All ER 28; [1938] 1 KB 786; [1938] 107 LJCL 299; (1938) 158 LTR 230; (1937) 81 SJ 1041; (1937-38) LIV TLR 253; (1938) WN (I) 13 HC KBD Cause of action in motor collision is collision so that die instantly does not mean no cause of action.

Morgan, Arnold v [1908-10] All ER 392 HC KBD magistrates' jurisdiction to hear trespass action ended upon public right of way being established.

Morgan, Broom v (1952) 102 LJ 665; (1952) 96 SJ 803; [1952] 2 TLR 904; (1952) WN (I) 531 HC QBD Wife could sue husband's employers for tort husband did to her in course of his employment.

Morgan, Broom v [1953] 1 QB 597; (1953) 97 SJ 247; [1953] 2 WLR 737 CA Wife could sue husband's employers for tort husband did to her in course of his employment.

Morgan, Saxby v [1997] TLR 242 CA On when limitation period starts to run in personal injury claim.

Moriarty v McCarthy [1978] 2 All ER 213; (1977) 127 NLJ 1049t; (1977) 121 SJ 745; [1978] 1 WLR 155 HC QBD Marriage/children consideration in deciding young woman's loss of future earnings; if no marriage prospects loss of husband's financial support heading for damages.

Morison v London County and Westminster Bank Limited (1914-15) 111 LTR 114 CA On negligence of bank in paying money from account on foot of fraudulently prepared crossed/uncrossed cheques.

Morland and Co Ltd, Wood v (1971) 115 SJ 569 HC QBD Occupiers not liable for not sweeping away snow on which persons exiting premises slipped as could have done nothing to render situation less dangerous.

Morley v Staffordshire County Council [1939] 4 All ER 93; (1939) 83 SJ 848 CA Allurement did not make liable for injury caused by obvious danger.

Morning Post Ltd, Farmer v (1936) 80 SJ 345 CA Possible that words of non-party to action who intervened in court (said intervention being reported) were part of judicial proceedings but converse also possible so ensuing libel action not per se frivolous/vexatious.

Morning Star Newspaper Co-operative Society Ltd v Express Newspapers Ltd (1978) 128 NLJ 1100t HC ChD Failed action by The Morning Star newspaper for interim injunction to restrain launch of The Daily Star newspaper as was slim chance of confusion between the two.

Morrell v Owen and others [1993] TLR 645 HC QBD On extent of duty of care owed by sports organisers towards persons taking part in disabled persons sports event.

Morrell v Thomson (International) [1989] 3 All ER 733; (1989) 139 NLJ 1007 CA On pleading justification.

Morris and another v Redland Bricks Ltd [1967] 1 WLR 967 CA On when injunction/damages appropriate remedy for nuisance.

Morris and another v Sandess Universal Products [1954] 1 All ER 47; (1954) 104 LJ 9; (1954) 98 SJ 10 CA Test whether defamatory is would reasonable jury find defamatory.

Morris and another, Levine and another v [1970] 1 All ER 144; (1970) 134 JP 158; (1969) 119 NLJ 947t; (1969) 113 SJ 798; [1970] RTR 93; [1970] 1 WLR 71 CA In choosing road signs Ministry owes duty not to unduly endanger motorists.

Morris Motors Ltd v Lilley [1959] 1 WLR 1184 HC ChD Injunction available to stop person selling manufacturer's cars as new where were not (interfered with goodwill of manufacturer).

Morris Motors Ltd v Phelan [1960] 1 WLR 352 HC ChD On appropriate form of injunction for passing off.

Morris v Beardmore [1980] 2 All ER 753; [1981] AC 446; (1980) 71 Cr App R 256 (also HC QBD); [1979] Crim LR 394; (1980) 144 JP 331; (1980) 130 NLJ 707; [1980] RTR 321; (1980) 124 SJ 512; [1980] 3 WLR 283 HL Request to take breath test invalid where police officer trespassing on property of person requested at time of request.

Morris v Beardmore (1980) 71 Cr App R 256 (also HL); [1979] RTR 393; (1979) 123 SJ 300; [1979] 3 WLR 93 HC QBD Request to take breath test valid though police officer trespassing on property of person requested at time of request.

Morris v Carnarvon County Council (1910) 74 JP 201 (also CA); [1910] 1 KB 159; (1909) 44 LJ 783; (1910) 79 LJKB 169; (1909-10) 101 LTR 914; (1909-10) XXVI TLR 137; (1909) WN (I) 263 HC KBD Local education authority liable for negligent injury suffered by child going through door on teacher's instruction.

Morris v Carnarvon County Council (1910) 74 JP 201 (also HC KBD); [1910] 1 KB 840; (1910) 45 LJ 268; (1910) 79 LJKB 670; (1910) 102 LTR 524; (1909-10) 54 SJ 443; (1909-10) XXVI TLR 391; (1910) WN (I) 94 CA Local education authority liable for negligent injury suffered by child going through door on teacher's instruction.

Morris v Curtis [1947] LJNCCR 284 CyCt Absent proof that third party had left field gate open cattle owner was liable for damage occasioned to vegetable plot onto which cattle strayed/trespassed by way of open gate.

Morris v Duke-Cohan and Co (1975) 125 NLJ 1222; (1975) 119 SJ 826 HC QBD Successful action in negligence against conveyancing solicitors who advised exchange of contracts without taking usual safeguards.

Morris v Johnson Matthey and Co Ltd (1968) 112 SJ 32 CA On appropriate damages for fifty-two year old craftsman who suffered permanent injury to his hand.

Morris v Mayor, Aldermen and Burgesses of the Borough of Luton [1946] 1 All ER 1; (1946) 110 JP 102; [1946] KB 114; [1946] 115 LJ 202; (1946) 174 LTR 26; (1946) 90 SJ 91; (1945-46) LXII TLR 145; (1945) WN (I) 239 CA No rule that party driving in dark must be able to stop within limits of sight or is negligent.

Morris v Murray and another [1990] 3 All ER 801; (1990) 140 NLJ 1459; [1991] 2 QB 6; (1990) 134 SJ 1300; [1990] TLR 610; [1991] 2 WLR 195 CA Person electing to fly with drunken pilot taken to waive rights to damages for negligence by virtue of volenti non fit injuria maxim.

Morris v West Hartlepool Steam Navigation Co, Ltd [1956] 1 All ER 385; (1956) 100 SJ 129 HL Non-closure of hatch of hold through which party fell was negligent.

Morris v Winsbury-White [1937] 4 All ER 494 HC KBD Visiting surgeon not liable for negligence of resident surgeons/nurses (did not act as agents); post-operation finding of tube in patient's body not res ipsa loquitur.

Morris, Tolley v [1979] 1 All ER 71; (1978) 128 NLJ 712t; (1978) 122 SJ 436; [1979] 1 WLR 205 CA Court would not dismiss for inaction suit of infant plaintiff brought in extended limitation period.

Morris, Tolley v (1979) 129 (1) NLJ 518; (1979) 123 SJ 353; [1979] 1 WLR 592 HL Non-dismissal for inaction of suit of infant plaintiff brought in extended limitation period.

Morris, Wheeler v [1914-15] All ER 1196; (1915) CC Rep IV 53; (1915) 50 LJ 335; [1915] 84 LJKB 1435; (1915-16) 113 LTR 644 CA Shopowner not liable for injury to party caused by two men pulling on external sun-blind as was not reasonably foreseeable/had taken all reasonable steps.

Morris, Wheeler v [1915] 84 LJKB 269; (1915) 112 LTR 412 HC KBD Shopowner could be liable for injury to party caused by two men pulling on external sun-blind in respect of which inadequate precautions taken.

Morrish, Grant, and Co, Fox and Son v (1918-19) 63 SJ 193; (1918-19) XXXV TLR 126 HC KBD Accountant owes duty of care to check cash and bank balances where is retained to check account books.

Morrison v Sheffield Corporation (1917) 81 JP 277; [1917] 86 LJCL 1456; (1917-18) 117 LTR 520; (1916-17) 61 SJ 611; (1916-17) XXXIII TLR 492 CA Owners of spiked fence were negligent not to have taken special measures to avoid injury to public during black-out conditions.

Morriss v Baines and Co Limited (1933) 148 LTR 428 HC KBD Plaintiff awarded less than amount paid into court could not be ordered to pay back amount in excess of award where had already withdrawn payment from bank.

Morriss v Marsden and another [1952] 1 All ER 925; (1952) 102 LJ 219; (1952) 96 SJ 281; [1952] 1 TLR 947; (1952) WN (I) 188 HC QBD Knowledge of nature/quality though not wrongfulness of act opens one to tortious liability.

Morriss v Winter and another (1926-30) XXVIII Cox CC 687; [1930] 1 KB 243; (1930) 142 LTR 67; (1928-29) XLV TLR 643 HC KBD No right to early discharge where earn remission marks so no false imprisonment therafter.

Mortgage Express Ltd v Bowerman and Partners (a firm) [1994] TLR 285 HC ChD On extent of duty of care owed by solicitor to parties to loan transaction where is acting for both sides.

Mortgage Express Ltd v Bowerman and Partners (a firm) [1995] TLR 450 CA On extent of duty of care owed by solicitor to parties to loan transaction where is acting for both sides.

Mortimore, Spry v [1946] LJNCCR 83 CyCt Owner of ponies pasturing on common not liable for trespass by ponies (by way of public highway) onto private property adjoining common.

Morts Dock and Engineering Co, Ltd, Overseas Tankship (UK), Ltd v [1961] 1 All ER 404; (1961) 111 LJ 104; (1961) 105 SJ 85 PC Non-foreseeability (by reasonable man) precluded liability in negligence.

Moser v Enfield and Haringey Area Health Authority (1983) 133 NLJ 105 HC QBD On appropriate damages for negligently performed minor operation that rendered infant boy brain-damaged quadriplegic.

Moss and another, Smith v [1940] 1 All ER 469; [1940] 1 KB 424; (1940) 89 LJ 107; [1940] 109 LJCL 271; (1940) 162 LTR 267; (1940) 84 SJ 115; (1939-40) LVI TLR 305; (1940) WN (I) 22 HC KBD Wife could recover for husband's tort against her where he had acted as mother's agent.

Moss v Christchurch Rural District Council; Rogers v Same [1925] 2 KB 750; [1926] 95 LJCL 81 HC KBD Damages recoverable where house damaged by fire/nuisance were cash difference between value of house pre-/post-fire.

Moss, Archer v; Applegate v Moss [1971] 1 All ER 747; [1971] 1 QB 406; (1970) 114 SJ 971; [1971] 2 WLR 541 CA Fraud in Limitation Act is equitable fraud; assessment of damages for breach of warranty.

Mothercare Ltd v Robson Books Ltd (1979) 129 (1) NLJ 317 HC ChD Injunction granted to Mothercare Ltd to restrain Robson Books from publishing book entitled 'Mother Care' (or other similarly deceptive name).

Mothew (t/a Stapley and Co), Bristol and West Building Society v [1996] 4 All ER 698; (1996) TLR 2/8/96; [1997] 2 WLR 436 CA Liability of solicitor towards lender for defective advice given during mortgage deal in which acted for lender and borrower.

Motor Auctions (West Bromwich) Ltd and another, J Sargent (Garages) Ltd v [1977] RTR 121 CA Person giving car/log book to another who wrongfully sold it not estopped — even if negligent — from denying latter's authority to sell; damages set at price plaintiffs had expected to sell (what was a special) car.

Motor Manufacturers' and Traders' Mutual Insurance Co, Ltd, Motor Manufacturers' and Trading Society, Ltd v [1925] All ER 616; [1925] Ch 675 (also HC ChD); (1925) 133 LTR 330 CA On granting injunctions to stop passing off (here injunction refused).

Motor Manufacturers' and Traders' Mutual Insurance Company, Limited, The Society of Motor Manufacturers and Traders, Limited v [1925] Ch 675 (also CA); (1924-25) 69 SJ 428 HC ChD On granting injunctions to stop passing off (here injunction refused).

Motor Manufacturers' and Trading Society, Ltd v Motor Manufacturers' and Traders' Mutual Insurance Co, Ltd [1925] All ER 616; [1925] Ch 675 (also HC ChD); (1925) 133 LTR 330 CA On granting injunctions to stop passing off (here injunction refused).

Motor Surveys Limited, Joyce v [1948] Ch 252; [1948] 117 LJR 935; (1948) WN (I) 84 HC ChD False statements made with intent of ending person's business were malicious.

Motor Trade Association and others, Ware and De Freville, Ltd v [1920] All ER 387; [1921] LJCL 949 CA Absent special circumstances statement that intend to do lawful act cannot be defamatory.

Motor-Car Co (1905) Lim and Ford, Clerk v (1904-05) 49 SJ 418 HC ChD Injunction granted where had been unauthorised use of plaintiff's name in connection with defendant's business.

Mott and another v The Mayor, Aldermen and Councillors of the Metropolitan Borough of Stepney [1935] LJNCCR 30 CyCt That council lamp bracket fell was of itself evidence of negligence on part of council.

Mottershead, Hartland v (1956) 106 LJ ccr269 CyCt Damages plus liberty to apply for injunction to elderly plaintiff whose neighbours were guilty of nuisance by noise by way of piano playing/playing the radio.

Mottram v South Lancashire Transport Co [1942] 2 All ER 452; (1943) 93 LJ 109; (1942) 86 SJ 321 CA Bus conductress not negligent in not policing dismounting of passengers.

Moul v Croydon Corporation and another [1918-19] All ER 971; (1918) 82 JP 283; (1918) 53 LJ 227; (1918-19) 119 LTR 318; (1917-18) XXXIV TLR 473; (1918) WN (I) 194 HC KBD Highway authority not liable for nonfeasance.

Moul v Shepcott (1924-25) 69 SJ 680 HC ChD Court would not in quia timet action grant interlocutory injunction to restrain apprehended nuisance where subjects of proposed order did not consent to it.

Moul v Thomas Tilling, Lim and another [1919] 88 LJCL 505 HC ChD Non-liability of highway authority for non-feasance.

Mulready v H (J) and W Bell, Ltd and another [1952] 2 All ER 663 Assizes Non-employers not liable in negligence for not safeguarding worker.

Multinational Gas and Petrochemical Co v Multinational Gas and Petrochemical Services Ltd and others [1983] Ch 258 CA Company could not sue directors for negligence where shareholders had ratified actions of directors.

Multinational Gas and Petrochemical Services Ltd and others, Multinational Gas and Petrochemical Co v [1983] Ch 258 CA Company could not sue directors for negligence where shareholders had ratified actions of directors.

Mulvaine v Joseph and others (1968) 118 NLJ 1078t; (1968) 112 SJ 927 HC QBD Damages from taxi-driver for professional golfer injured in taxi-cab accident caused by negligence of taxi-driver.

Mumford v Naylor (1951) 95 SJ 383; [1951] 1 TLR 1068; (1951) WN (I) 241 HC KBD Person injured crossing private forecourt to front of shop could recover damages as licensee from shop-owner where injured self in hole/concealed trap of which shopowner knew.

Mumford v Naylor (1951) 95 SJ 742; (1951) WN (I) 579 CA On what constitutes a concealed trap — such a trap found not to exist here.

Mungovin, Roebuck v [1994] 2 AC 224; (1994) 138 SJ LB 59; [1994] 2 WLR 290 HL Appropriate that personal injuries claim be struck out where plaintiff guilty of great delay even though defendant's behaviour not entirely blameless.

Munro v Porthkerry Park Holiday Estates Ltd [1984] TLR 138 HC QBD On duty of care owed by licensee towards customer who has consumed large quantity of alcohol.

Munro v Willmott [1948] 2 All ER 983; [1949] 1 KB 295; (1948) 98 LJ 657; [1949] 118 LJR 471; (1948) LXIV TLR 627; (1948) WN (I) 459 HC KBD Appropriate damages for conversion/detinue.

Murdoch Magazines (UK) Ltd and another, Keays v [1991] 4 All ER 491; (1991) 141 NLJ 893; [1991] 1 WLR 1184 CA Court may order preliminary hearing in libel action to determine if words used can be libellous/import meaning suggested by defendant.

Murphy v Bradford Metropolitan Council [1991] TLR 66 CA Local authority liable for breach of duty of care to ensure cleared, salted school path was not slippy.

Murphy v Brentwood District Council [1990] 2 All ER 269; [1991] 1 AC 398 (also HL); (1990) 134 SJ 458; [1990] 2 WLR 944 CA Statutory duty on council to ensure houses properly built meant duty of care on council even though consulting engineers negligent; damages owed are those necessary to put house in safe condition or enable occupier to move to safe house.

Murphy v Brentwood District Council [1990] 2 All ER 908; [1991] 1 AC 398 (also CA); (1990) 140 NLJ 1111; (1990) 134 SJ 1076; [1990] TLR 558; [1990] 3 WLR 414 HL Local authority does not owe duty of care for pure economic loss to building owner/occupier when discharging statutory functions.

Murphy v Stone Wallwork (Charlton) Ltd [1969] 2 All ER 949; (1969) 119 NLJ 600t HL Lords may allow fresh evidence pointing to mistaken assessment of damages.

Murphy v William Henderson Sons, Ltd; McBride v Same (1963) 107 SJ 534 CA Occupiers liable in negligence for having fire doors open or for not closing them as soon as possible after became aware of fire.

Murphy, Hurt v [1971] RTR 186 HC QBD Speeding driver/unvigilant pedestrian 80%/20% liable for collision at pedestrian crossing; husband's damages for loss of wife's services based on costs of keeping a daily help.

Murphy, Kitcat v (1969) 113 SJ 385 HC QBD On appropriate damages for personal injuries that resulted in quadriplegia.

Murphy, Reynolds v (1965) 109 SJ 255 HC QBD On need for swift conclusion to personal injuries actions.

Murray (CP) and Co, Ltd and another, Cressey v (1965) 109 SJ 294 CA Increase in personal injury damages for person who suffered double vision as result of road accident.

Murray and another v Harringay Arena, Ltd [1951] 2 All ER 320; [1951] 2 KB 529; (1951) 101 LJ 48; (1951) 95 SJ 529; (1951) WN (I) 356 CA No negligence/breach of implied contract/ inadequacy of safety measures/unusual danger in spectator being hit by puck at ice hockey match.

Murray and another v Harringay Arena, Ltd (1951) 95 SJ 123; (1951) WN (I) 38 HC KBD No negligence on part of event-holders where spectator was hit by puck at ice hockey match.

Murray and another, Morris v [1990] 3 All ER 801; (1990) 140 NLJ 1459; [1991] 2 QB 6; (1990) 134 SJ 1300; [1990] TLR 610; [1991] 2 WLR 195 CA Person electing to fly with drunken pilot taken to waive rights to damages for negligence by virtue of volenti non fit injuria maxim.

Murray and Co, Watson v [1955] 1 All ER 350 HC QBD Sheriff committed trespass in taking exclusive possession of party's store/in preparing to hold sale in store; were liable in negligence for goods stolen from store.

Murray v Lloyd and others [1990] 2 All ER 92; (1989) 139 NLJ 938; [1989] 1 WLR 1060 HC ChD Damages where solicitor's negligence led to client's failure to become statutory tenant are amount needed for client to become statutory tenant in similar property elsewhere.

Murray v Ministry of Defence [1988] 2 All ER 521; (1988) 138 NLJ 164; (1988) 132 SJ 852; [1988] 1 WLR 692 HL Arrest can begin before formal words of arrest spoken; formal words usually to be said at moment of arrest.

Murray v Park Bros (Liverpool), Ltd and others (1959) 109 LJ 460 HC QBD Apportionment of liabilities for accident ultimately arising from negligent parking of van.

Musgrave and Porter, Peacock and Hoskyn v [1956] Crim LR 414t HC QBD Detention by police of persons whom police reasonably believed to have committed offence was not false imprisonment.

Musgrove v Pandelis [1918-19] All ER 589; [1919] 1 KB 314; (1919) 54 LJ 106; [1919] 88 LJCL 915 (also CA); (1918-19) 63 SJ 353; (1918-19) XXXV TLR 202; (1919) WN (I) 27 HC KBD Liability for fire negligently started.

Musgrove v Pandelis and others [1919] 88 LJCL 915 (also HC KBD); (1919) 120 LTR 601; (1918-19) XXXV TLR 299; (1919) WN (I) 79 CA Liability for fire negligently started.

Musial, Scott v [1959] 3 All ER 193; [1959] 2 QB 429; [1959] 3 WLR 437 CA Only interfere with jury awards where out of all proportion to injuries.

Mutual Finance Ltd, Cuckmere Brick Co Ltd and another v; Mutual Finance Ltd v Cuckmere Brick Co Ltd and others [1971] 2 All ER 633 CA Mortgagee under duty to mortgagor to obtain real market price of property.

Mutual Life and Citizens' Assurance Co Ltd and another v Evatt [1971] 1 All ER 150; [1971] AC 793; (1970) 120 NLJ 1090; [1971] 2 WLR 23 PC Absent contract advisor owes duty to be honest in making statements unless fiduciary/styled as expert.

Mutual Reinsurance Co Ltd v Peat Marwick Mitchell and Co and another (1996) TLR 15/10/96 CA Accountants appointed as company auditors pursuant to Bermudan law/company bylaws could not later be sued for negligence by the company.

Mycroft v Sleight [1918-23] All ER 509; [1921] LJCL 883; (1921) 125 LTR 622; (1920-21) XXXVII TLR 646; (1921) WN (I) 175 HC KBD Defamatory words not spoken of person in relation to profession inactionable absent special damage.

Myers v Bradford Corporation (1914) CC Rep III 102; (1915) 79 JP 130; [1915] 1 KB 417; (1914) 49 LJ 638; [1915] 84 LJKB 306; (1915) 112 LTR 206; (1914-15) 59 SJ 57; (1914-15) XXXI TLR 44; (1914) WN (I) 400 CA Public Authorities Protection Act 1893 limitation period deemed inapplicable to instant action against public authority for negligence.

Myers v Bradford Corporation (1914) 78 JP 177; (1914) 110 LTR 254; (1913-14) XXX TLR 181 HC KBD Equally divided court as to whether Public Authorities Protection Act 1893 limitation period applicable to instant action.

Myers, Bradford Corporation v [1916] 1 AC 242; (1916) CC Rep V 4; (1916) 80 JP 121; (1915) 50 LJ 555; [1916] 85 LJKB 146; (1916) 114 LTR 83; (1915-16) 60 SJ 74; (1915-16) XXXII TLR 113; (1915) WN (I) 367 HL Public Authorities Protection Act 1893 limitation period deemed inapplicable to instant action against public authority for negligence.

Myskow and others, Cornwell v (1987) 131 SJ 476; [1987] 1 WLR 630 CA On evidence admissible as to reputation.

National Coal Board, Gough v [1953] 2 All ER 1283; [1954] 1 QB 191; (1953) 97 SJ 811; [1953] 3 WLR 900 CA Child playing on land a licensee under general licence — not trespasser just because did something not supposed to do; slow-moving trucks an allurement; licensor negligently failed to take reasonable care to protect child.

National Coal Board, Hattam v (1978) 128 NLJ 1149t; (1978) 122 SJ 777 CA Staying of action where all evidence lost/plaintiff had received full industrial benefits since suffered workplace injury.

National Coal Board, Lasczyk v [1954] 3 All ER 205 Assizes Guilty of contributory negligence where acting under supervisor's instructions but contrary to training officer's ordinance.

National Coal Board, McGhee v [1972] 3 All ER 1008 HL If breach of duty causes/contributes to injury are liable in negligence.

National Coal Board, Rushton v [1953] 1 All ER 314; [1953] 1 QB 495; (1953) 97 SJ 94; [1953] 1 WLR 292 CA Appropriate damages in personal injury cases.

National Coal Board, Starr v (1976) 126 NLJ 1120t; (1976) 120 SJ 721; [1977] 1 WLR 63 CA Must submit to medical examination by doctor of defendant's choosing unless have reasonable reason not to do so which reveal to court.

National Coal Board, Storey v [1983] 1 All ER 375 HC QBD Company officials engaging in dangerous practice of which employees warned not condoning practice: no negligence.

National Home Loans Corp plc v Giffen Couch and Archer (a firm) [1997] 3 All ER 808 CA On extent of duty of care owed by solicitor to lender where is acting for borrower and lender in loan transaction.

National Mutual Life Nominees Ltd, Deloitte Haskins and Sells v [1993] 2 All ER 1015; [1993] AC 774; (1993) 143 NLJ 883; [1993] 3 WLR 347 PC Auditors owe duty of care in preparing reports but question of insolvency subjective matter for individual auditor.

National Provincial Bank Limited and Elevenist Syndicate, Matania v [1937] 106 LJCL 113; (1936) 155 LTR 74 CA Independent contractors found liable for nuisance by noise/dust effected through their work.

National Provincial Bank, Limited, Penmount Estates, Limited v; Stanley Moss and Pilcher (third party) (1945) 173 LTR 344 HC KBD Action for conversion/negligence where bank credited amount of cashed cheque to wrong bank account.

National Smelting Co, Ltd, Quintas v [1961] 1 All ER 630 CA Master liable in negligence/plaintiff contributorily so for injury caused in factory by article not machinery under Factories Act 1937, s 14.

National Telephone Co, Ltd, Sewell v [1904-07] All ER 457; [1907] 76 LJCL 196; (1907) XCVI LTR 483; (1906-07) 51 SJ 207; (1906-07) XXIII TLR 226 CA False imprisonment not proven through signing of charge-sheet while party in police custody.

National Telephone Company, Holliday v (1899-1900) LXXXI LTR 252 CA Employer of independent contractor liable for injury caused through latter's work.

(1) National Trust Company, Limited and Others, Eastern Construction Company, Limited v; (2) Therese Schmidt and Others; Attorney-General for the Province of Ontario (Intervenant) [1914] AC 197; [1914] 83 LJPC 122; (1914) 110 LTR 321 PC Not liable for trespass by person with whom have contract but who is not servant/agent; Crown patentee/licensee a bailee for Crown of trees wrongfully felled so could not sue fellers for trover/detinue.

National Trust for Places of Historic Interest or Natural Beauty, Leakey and others v [1980] 1 All ER 17; (1979) 129 (2) NLJ 781; [1980] QB 485; (1979) 123 SJ 606; [1980] 2 WLR 65 CA Must take reasonable steps to prevent natural/man-made features on one's land causing damage/becoming danger to another.

National Trust for Places of Historic Interest or Natural Beauty, Leakey and others v [1978] 3 All ER 234; (1978) 128 NLJ 242t; [1978] QB 849; (1978) 122 SJ 231; [1978] 2 WLR 774 HC QBD Occupier must take reasonable steps to remove occurrence on land which is hazard for neighbour.

National Union of General and Municipal Workers v Gillian and others [1945] 2 All ER 593 (also HC KBD); [1946] KB 81; (1946) 96 LJ 199; [1946] 115 LJ 43; (1945) 89 SJ 543 (also HC KBD); (1945-46) LXII TLR 46; (1945) WN (I) 214 CA Trade union can sue for libel of its name.

National Union of General and Municipal Workers v Gillian and others [1945] 2 All ER 593 (also CA); (1945) 89 SJ 543 (also CA); (1945) WN (I) 194 HC KBD Trade union can sue for libel of its name.

National Union of Mineworkers (South Wales Area) and others, Thomas and others v [1985] 2 All ER 1 HC ChD Peaceful/responsible picketing not watching or besetting/nuisance even if secondary picketing.

National Union of Mineworkers and others, Hughes v [1991] 4 All ER 278; [1991] TLR 301 HC QBD Generally senior police officers not liable to junior police officers for exposure of latter to undue risk.

National Westminster Bank Ltd v Barclays Bank International Ltd and another [1974] 3 All ER 834; (1974) 124 NLJ 767t; (1974) 118 SJ 627; [1975] 2 WLR 12 HC QBD Bank not negligent in honouring forged cheque; by honouring forged cheque bank did not represent it as genuine so were not estopped by representation (or by negligence) from seeking repayment of cheque.

National Westminster Bank Ltd, Fellus v [1983] TLR 448 HC QBD Test of what constitutes 'undue negligence' a subjective test.

National Westminster Bank Ltd, John Trenberth Ltd v (1979) 129 (1) NLJ 566; (1979) 123 SJ 388 HC ChD Injunction granted to restrain trespass (even though the damage caused by the trespass was not great).

National Westminster Bank Ltd, Wealden Woodlands (Kent) Ltd v [1983] TLR 182 CA Company not estopped (by not itself noticing same) from bringing action against bank for clearance of forged cheques drawn on its account.

National Westminster Bank plc v Powney and others [1990] 2 All ER 416 CA Application for leave to execute judgment not an action.

Nationwide Anglia Building Society, Beaton and another v [1990] TLR 645 HC QBD Building society liable for negligence of employee-surveyor despite clause in prescribed form given to every mortgagee stating that the price charged for property did not necessarily indicate its true worth.

Nationwide Building Society v Lewis [1997] 3 All ER 498 HC ChD Estopped from denying liability as partner for negligence of other solicitor-partner where relationship really one of master and servant, not partnership but had been held out to plaintiff as partnership.

Natural Life Health Foods Ltd and another, Williams and another v (1996) 140 SJ LB 43; [1997] TLR 24 HC QBD Company director found liable for tortious acts of company.

Naum, Richards v (1970) 114 SJ 809 CA Libel action struck out for want of prosecution.

Naum, Richards v [1966] 3 All ER 812; [1967] 1 QB 620; (1966) 110 SJ 794; [1966] 3 WLR 1113 CA Facts to be determined before preliminary point could be decided.

Navan, Norwood v [1981] RTR 457 CA Husband/car owner not vicariously liable for wife/provisional licence holder's unsupervised driving as she was not acting as his agent/servant.

Navarro v Larrinaga Steamship Company Ltd; The Niceto de Larrinaga (1965) 109 SJ 633; [1965] 3 WLR 573 HC PDAD Two year limitation on fatal accident claims under Maritime Conventions Act 1911 inapplicable to vessel in which travelling when cause of claim arose.

Naylor Brothers, Ltd, Roberts v [1959] 2 All ER 409; (1959) 103 SJ 491 HC QBD Disablement gratuity deductible from loss of earnings.

Naylor v Yorkshire Electricity Board [1966] 3 All ER 327; (1965-66) 116 NLJ 1032t/1432; [1967] 1 QB 244; (1966) 110 SJ 528; [1966] 3 WLR 654 CA Appropriate damages for loss of life of young, engaged man.

Naylor, Adams v [1944] 2 All ER 21; (1945) 95 LJ 111; [1944] 113 LJ 499; (1944) 171 LTR 105; (1944) 88 SJ 325 CA No duty of care to trespassers.

Naylor, Adams v [1944] 2 All ER 21 Assizes No duty of care to trespassers.

Naylor, Mumford v (1951) 95 SJ 383; [1951] 1 TLR 1068; (1951) WN (I) 241 HC KBD Person injured crossing private forecourt to front of shop could recover damages as licensee from shop-owner where injured self in hole/concealed trap of which shopowner knew.

Naylor, Mumford v (1951) 95 SJ 742; (1951) WN (I) 579 CA On what constitutes a concealed trap — such a trap found not to exist here.

Nayoh and Co and another, Hartley v [1954] 1 All ER 375 CA Electricity board in breach of regulations but company partly negligent to fireman in not familiar with own mains.

Neal v Bingle [1997] TLR 409 CA Could claim in damages social security payments that would have received but for personal injury in respect of which bringing claim.

Need (John Francis), JH Coles Proprietary Limited (in liquidation) v (1934) 150 LTR 166 PC Injunction granted to restrain use of another's trade names after that other's licence to do so had been revoked.

Needham, Williams v [1972] RTR 387 HC QBD Driver partly liable for collision as did not take precautionary steps when saw pedestrian who had not looked in his direction about to cross road.

Neil and another, Kiam v [1994] TLR 647 CA Pre-trial settlement offer could not be presented to jury post-trial (by offeror) in effort to mitigate damages to be awarded by jury.

Neill and another, Kiam v (1996) TLR 22/7/96 CA £45,000 damages merited for irresponsible libel.

Nelson Corpn and Fryer and Co (Nelson), Ltd, Bank View Mill, Ltd and others v [1942] 2 All ER 477 Assizes Corporation in occupation and control knowing of obstruction and with chance to remove liable in nuisance; flooding slightly due to weir: nominal damages against weir-owner.

Nelson Corporation and Fryer and Co (Nelson), Ltd, Bank View Mill, Ltd and others v [1943] 1 All ER 299; [1943] KB 337; [1943] 112 LJ 306; (1943) 168 LTR 244 CA Corporation not in occupation so not liable for nuisance.

Nelson Holdings Ltd v British Gas plc and others [1997] TLR 122 HC QBD Generally no duty of care owed by fire authority to owner of burning property.

Nelson v Cookson and another [1939] 4 All ER 30; (1939) 103 JP 363; [1940] 1 KB 100; (1939) 88 LJ 241; [1940] 109 LJCL 154; (1939) 161 LTR 346; (1939) 83 SJ 871; (1939-40) LVI TLR 2; (1939) WN (I) 350 HC KBD Public authority limitation period applied in respect of county hospital assistant medical officers.

Nelson, Murdoch and Co v Wood (1921) CC Rep X 76; (1922) 126 LTR 745; (1921-22) XXXVIII TLR 23 HC KBD Improper sale of hire-purchase piano not per se a repudiation of hire-purchase contract and as finance company had not accepted repudiation/terminated contract transfer of piano was not conversion.

Nesbit and another v Pearson and another (1915) CC Rep IV 69 CyCt Child could recover damages from shopkeeper for injury suffered consequent upon being sold fireworks (parents who ordered child to return fireworks to store — injuries being suffered while child returning — could not).

Nettleship v Weston [1971] 3 All ER 581; (1971) 121 NLJ 592t; [1971] 2 QB 691; [1971] RTR 425; (1971) 115 SJ 624; [1971] 3 WLR 370 CA Learner-/drivers owe duty to drive with reasonable care/skill; instructor contributorily negligent where learner in accident; volenti non fit injuria only where unqualified express/implied renunciation of any right to claim.

Neushul v Mellish and Harkavy (1966) 110 SJ 792 HC QBD On duty owed by solicitor to client when acting for two parties (here failed to meet duty of care).

Neushul v Mellish and Harkavy (1967) 111 SJ 399 CA On duty owed by solicitor to client when acting for two parties (here failed to meet duty of care).

New Empress Saloons Limited, Brown v (1937) 156 LTR 427; (1937) WN (I) 156 CA On practice as regards awarding costs as element of damages in personal injuries action.

New English Library Ltd and another, Control Risks Ltd and others v [1989] 3 All ER 577; (1989) 139 NLJ 1008; [1990] 1 WLR 183 CA On fair comment.

New Mendip Engineering, Ltd, Hawkins v [1966] 3 All ER 228; (1965-66) 116 NLJ 1377; [1966] 1 WLR 1341 CA Possibility of serious supervening illness a legitimate factor when assessing damages.

New Merton Board Mills, Ltd and others, Davie v [1958] 1 All ER 67; [1958] 1 QB 210 CA Master not liable to servant for defects in manufacture of tools if takes reasonable care to provide safe tools.

New Merton Board Mills, Ltd and others, Davie v [1957] 2 All ER 38; [1957] 2 QB 368; (1957) 101 SJ 321 HC QBD Manufacturers and employers liable in negligence for injury to worker by defective tool.

New Merton Board Mills, Ltd, Davie v [1956] 1 All ER 379; (1956) 100 SJ 170 HC QBD On pleading act of third party as defence to negligence.

New Merton Board Mills, Ltd, Wheeler and another v [1933] All ER 28 CA Cannot be volenti non fit injuria in action for breach of statutory duty.

New Merton Mills Ltd and Another, Davie v [1959] AC 604; [1959] 2 WLR 331 HL Employers not liable for injury to worker from latent defect in quality tool which could not have discovered.

New Motor and General Rubber Company, Limited, Warwick Tyre Company, Limited v [1910] 1 Ch 248; (1910) 45 LJ 36; [1910] 79 LJCh 177; (1909-10) 101 LTR 889; (1910) WN (I) 8 HC ChD Injunction to stop use of name 'Warwick' in respect of motor tyres as calculated to deceive consumers that defendant's tyres produced by plaintiffs.

New South Wales Branch of the British Medical Association, Thompson v [1924] AC 764; [1924] 93, 1203; (1924) 131 LTR 162 PC Expulsion rule of Medical Association was to promote trade, not restrain it; Medical Association meeting's resolving to expel member a privileged occasion.

New Taplow Paper Mills Ltd, Hussain v [1987] 1 All ER 417; [1987] 1 WLR 336 CA Long-term sickness benefit an earning which if not paid for are deductible from damages.

New Taplow Paper Mills Ltd, Hussain v [1988] 1 All ER 541; [1988] AC 514; (1988) 138 NLJ 45; [1988] 2 WLR 266 HL Long-term sickness benefit deductible from personal injury damages.

New Vacuum Cleaner Company (Limited), British Vacuum Cleaner Company (Limited) v [1907] 2 Ch 312; (1907-08) XCVII LTR 201; (1906-07) XXIII TLR 587 HC ChD 'Vacuum cleaner' was descriptive term not fancy term: same principles applicable to use of similar company names as apply to passing off.

New Zealand Netherlands Society 'Oranje' Incorporated v Kuys (Laurentius Cornelius) and another (1973) 117 SJ 565; [1973] 1 WLR 1126 PC Person in fiduciary position in a society held to owe no fiduciary duty to society as regards newspaper person published himself: granted injunction against society publishing newspaper under same name.

Newall v Tunstall [1970] 3 All ER 465; (1971) 115 SJ 14 Assizes No interest where order made not order against defendant.

Newalls Insulation Co, Ltd and another, Beckett v [1953] 1 All ER 250; (1953) 97 SJ 8; [1953] 1 WLR 8 CA Heightened standard of care required where one's task poses heightened risk to others.

Newberry v Bristol Tramway and Carriage Company (Limited) (1912-13) 107 LTR 801; (1912-13) 57 SJ 172; (1912-13) XXIX TLR 177 CA Tram company not liable for freak injury to passenger where had adopted best practice to avoid injury.

Newberry, Revill v [1996] 1 All ER 291; (1996) 146 NLJ 50; [1996] QB 567; (1995) 139 SJ LB 244; [1995] TLR 563; [1996] 2 WLR 239 CA Duty of care to trespassers extends to trespassers engaged in criminal enterprise.

Newbrook v LM and S and GW Joint Railway Companies (1924) CC Rep XIII 10 CyCt On extent of liability of rail company in negligence for damage occasioned by sparks flying from engine.

Newcastle Chronicle and Journal Ltd and another, Fullam v [1977] 3 All ER 32; (1977) 127 NLJ 540t; (1977) 121 SJ 376; [1977] 1 WLR 651 CA Where legal innuendo must specify facts raising innuendo/persons understanding it — here latter rare and exceptional so action struck out.

Newcastle Health Authority, Harris v [1989] 2 All ER 273; (1989) 133 SJ 47; [1989] 1 WLR 96 CA Pre-trial disclosure available unless obvious that limitation defence will succeed.

Newcastle-under-Lyme Corporation v Wolstanton Ltd (1947) 111 JP 102 CA Damages for nuisance occasioned by mining company to corporation's gas mains/pipes.

Newcastle-under-Lyme Corporation v Wolstanton, Limited [1947] Ch 92; (1946) 110 JP 376; (1946) 90 SJ 419 HC ChD Damages for nuisance occasioned by mining company to corporation's gas mains/pipes.

Newcastle-upon-Tyne Corporation, Dormer and others v [1940] 2 All ER 521; (1940) 104 JP 316; [1940] 2 KB 204; (1940) 89 LJ 239; [1940] 109 LJCL 708 (also HC KBD); (1940) 163 LTR 266; (1939-40) LVI TLR 673; (1940) WN (I) 186 CA Safety railings could be erected at side of pavement despite being public/private nuisance.

Newcastle-upon-Tyne Corporation, Fox v [1941] 3 All ER 563; (1941) 105 JP 404; [1941] 2 KB 120; (1941) 91 LJ 270; (1942) 92 LJ 59; (1941) 165 LTR 90; (1940-41) LVII TLR 602 CA Local authority not liable in negligence for injury sustained by cyclist through collision with inadequately lit air-raid shelter during black-out conditions.

Newcastle-upon-Tyne Corporation, Fox v [1941] LJNCCR 165 CyCt Negligent for corporation not to have taken steps to make air-raid shelter more visible.

Newcombe v Yewen and the Croydon Rural District Council (1912-13) XXIX TLR 299 HC KBD Council could reach indemnity agreement with contractor.

Newell v Starkie (1919) 83 JP 113; [1920] 89 LJPC 1 HL Absent proof of malice (of which was none) action against Education Commissioner out of time under Public Authorities Protection Act 1893.

Newham London Borough Council and others, M (a minor) and another v; X and others (minors) v Bedfordshire County Council [1994] 4 All ER 602; [1995] 2 AC 633 (also HL); [1994] 2 FCR 1313; [1994] 1 FLR 431 (also HC QBD); (1994) 144 NLJ 357; [1994] TLR 119; [1994] 2 WLR 554 CA Those discharging public law task of child-care owe no private law duty of care for in-/action; psychiatrist/social worker owes duty of care to local authority/health authority, not to mother or child.

Newland v Boardwell; MacDonald v Platt [1983] 3 All ER 179; [1984] RTR 188 CA Admission of liability but denial of liability an abuse of process.

Newman v Bennett [1981] QB 726 HC QBD Right of common pur vicinage gives right to graze on adjoining land and is not therefore a mere defence to trespass.

Newman v Bourne and Hollingsworth (1914-15) XXXI TLR 209 HC KBD Shop liable in negligence where through fault of shop employee lost property handed in went missing.

Newman v Francis (1953) 117 JP 214 HC QBD Private individual could not rest cause of action on breach of parks bye-law.

Newman v Real Estate Debenture Corporation, Ltd, and Flower Decorations, Ltd [1940] 1 All ER 131 HC KBD Alteration of premises/business conducted in premises in respect of which covenant that were only for residential purposes was a nuisance.

Newport Corporation, Smerkinich v (1912) 76 JP 454 HC KBD Failed action for negligence by student who lost thumb in saw at technical institute classes: volenti non fit injuria applicable.

News Group Newspapers Ltd and another, Charleston and another v [1995] 2 All ER 313; [1995] 2 AC 65; (1995) 145 NLJ 490; (1995) 139 SJ LB 100; [1995] TLR 171; [1995] 2 WLR 450 HL Photos, headlines and connected articles may not be severed so as to find one element defamatory.

News Group Newspapers Ltd, Attorney General v [1986] 2 All ER 833; (1986) 136 NLJ 584; [1987] QB 1; (1986) 130 SJ 408; [1986] 3 WLR 365 CA Injunction generally unavailable if justification to be pleaded as defence unless serious risk of prejudice to trial.

News Group Newspapers Ltd, Charleston and another v [1994] TLR 16 CA Photos, headlines and connected articles could not be severed so as to find one element defamatory.

News Group Newspapers Ltd, Lucas-Box v; Lucas-Box v Associated Newspapers Group plc and others [1986] 1 All ER 177; (1986) 130 SJ 111; [1986] 1 WLR 147 CA Party to specify meaning intends to justify before starting justification.

News Group Newspapers Ltd, Mapp v [1997] 2 Cr App R (S) 562; (1997) 147 NLJ 562; [1997] TLR 124 CA On determining whether words complained of are capable of bearing alleged defamatory meaning.

News Group Newspapers Ltd, Riches and others v [1985] 2 All ER 845; (1985) 135 NLJ 391; [1986] QB 256; (1985) 129 SJ 401; [1985] 3 WLR 432 CA Exemplary damages to be shared among joint plaintiffs rather than separately awarded to each plaintiff.

News of the World Ltd and another, Moore v [1972] 1 All ER 915; [1972] 2 WLR 419 CA Must plead justification if going to raise it.

News of the World, Limited v Allen Fairhead and Sons, Limited [1931] 2 Ch 402; (1931) 100 LJCh 394; (1932) 146 LTR 11 HC ChD On gauging degree of nuisance (if nuisance there is) where ancient light reduced by new construction.

Newsome v Darton Urban District Council (1938) 102 JP 75; (1938) 158 LTR 149; (1937) 81 SJ 1042; (1937-38) LIV TLR 286 HC KBD Highway authority liable in nuisance/negligence for misfeasance (subsidence in trench had caused to be dug which led to injury to cyclist).

564

Nicholson, Hesketh v (1940) 84 SJ 646 HC KBD Solicitor liable for failure to advise client of provisions of Public Authorities Protection Act as regards negligence action against public authority.

Night Riders (a firm) and others, Rogers v [1983] RTR 324 CA Mini-cab firm liable for negligent maintenance of car by driver (whether latter an employee/independent contractor).

Ning (Lee Hock), Government of Malaysia v [1974] AC 76; (1973) 117 SJ 617; [1973] 3 WLR 334 PC Special public authority limitation period did not apply in respect of action based on private contract.

Nissan v Attorney-General [1968] 1 QB 286 (also CA); (1967) 111 SJ 195; [1967] 3 WLR 109 HC QBD That acts complained of were 'acts of state' not defence in tort action.

Nissan v Attorney-General [1968] 1 QB 286 (also HC QBD); (1967) 117 NLJ 834t; (1967) 111 SJ 544; [1967] 3 WLR 1044 CA That acts complained of were 'acts of state' not defence in tort action.

Nissan, Attorney-General v [1969] 1 All ER 629; [1970] AC 179; (1969) 119 NLJ 250; (1969) 113 SJ 207; [1969] 2 WLR 926 HL That acts complained of were 'acts of state' not defence in tort action.

Nitrigin Eireann Teoranta and another v Inco Alloys Ltd and another [1992] 1 All ER 854; (1991) 135 SJ LB 213; [1991] TLR 489; [1992] 1 WLR 498 HC QBD Cause of action arises in negligence not when economic loss occurs but when when physical damage occurs on foot of negligence.

Noakes, Ellis v [1930] All ER 382; [1932] 2 Ch 98 CA Liability for conversion of timber which conveyance expressly did not include (even though timber not removed by date specified in conveyance).

Noble v Harrison [1926] All ER 284; (1926) 90 JP 188; [1926] 2 KB 332; [1926] 95 LJCL 813; (1926) 135 LTR 325; (1925-26) 70 SJ 691; (1925-26) XLII TLR 518; (1926) WN (I) 171 HC KBD Overhanging tree not dangerous object/nuisance: no liability if falls and injures person on highway if neither knew/ought to have known might happen.

Noel T James, Ltd v Central Electricity Authority (1958) 108 LJ 250 HC QBD Successful claim in negligence against Electricity Board on foot of damage occasioned to plaintiff's property when fire escaped from Board's premises.

Nolan and another, Martin v [1944] 2 All ER 342; (1943-44) LX TLR 558 HC KBD Conviction and breach of recognisance two offences so Borstal training merited: issue arose in course of successful libel action.

Nolan v Merseyside County Council and Northwest Water Authority (1983) 133 NLJ 616c CA On recovery of contribution from joint tortfeasor.

Nore v Meyer (1911-12) 56 SJ 109 HC ChD Trustees who advanced money on property without making full inquiry as to property concerned were not (by virtue of the Trustee Act 1893) liable for their actions in negligence.

Norfolk (Duke) and others, Russell v [1948] 1 All ER 488; (1948) LXIV TLR 263 HC KBD No implied term in Jockey Club contract to hold inquiry before withdrawing licence; where common interest and agree to publish is qualified privilege unless malice.

Norman Collison (Contractors) Ltd, Jennings v [1970] 1 All ER 1121 CA Contributory negligence re-appraised where factual error by trial judge.

Norman Kark Publications, Ltd v Odhams Press, Ltd [1962] 1 All ER 636; (1962) 112 LJ 239; (1962) 106 SJ 195 HC ChD Must show proprietary right in goodwill of name and likely confusion to succeed.

Norman v Great Western Railway Company [1914-17] All ER 205; (1914) CC Rep III 102; [1915] 1 KB 584; (1914) 49 LJ 638; [1915] 84 LJKB 598; (1914) 110 LTR 306; (1914-15) XXXI TLR 53; (1914) WN (I) 415 CA Duty of railway company to invitees same as that of shopkeeper to invitees.

Norman v Great Western Railway Company [1914] 2 KB 153; [1914] 83 LJKB 669; (1913-14) XXX TLR 241; (1914) WN (I) 15 HC KBD Duty of railway company to invitees.

Norton-Radstock Urban District Council, Radstock Co-operative and Industrial Society, Ltd v [1968] 2 All ER 59; [1968] Ch 605; (1968) 132 JP 238; (1968) 112 SJ 135; [1968] 2 WLR 1214 CA Something that does not begin as nuisance cannot become so just through passage of time.

Norton-Radstock Urban District Council, Radstock Co-operative and Industrial Society, Ltd v [1967] 2 All ER 812; [1967] Ch 1094; (1967) 131 JP 387; [1967] 3 WLR 588 HC ChD Obstruction which does not begin as nuisance cannot become nuisance just by virtue of time.

Norwest Holst Southern Ltd, Simpson v [1980] 2 All ER 471; (1980) 130 NLJ 391; (1980) 124 SJ 313; [1980] 1 WLR 968 CA Bona fide failure to discover identity of defendant justified disapplying limitation.

Norwich City Council v Harvey and another (1989) 133 SJ 694; [1989] 1 WLR 828 CA Sub-contractor/sub-contractor's employee deemed not to owe duty of care to building employer for damage occasioned by carelessness of sub-contractor's employee.

Norwood v Navan [1981] RTR 457 CA Husband-car owner not vicariously liable for wife-provisional licence holder's unsupervised driving as she was not acting as his agent/servant.

Nottingham City Council, Nottingham Health Authority v (1988) 132 SJ 899; [1988] 1 WLR 903 CA Are only precluded from seeking recovery from joint defendants if they have been sued to judgment and deemed not liable.

Nottingham Corporation and another, Custins v [1970] RTR 365 CA Bus-driver not negligent where bus skidded on ice and collided with person after driver had gently pulled to a halt.

Nottingham Health Authority v Nottingham City Council (1988) 132 SJ 899; [1988] 1 WLR 903 CA Are only precluded from seeking recovery from joint defendants if they have been sued to judgment and deemed not liable.

Noxall, Limited, Malfroot and another v (1935) 79 SJ 610; (1934-35) LI TLR 551 HC KBD Fitter of side-car to motor-cycle liable in contract and tort to owner of same and in tort to passenger in same for negligent fitting which resulted in car becoming detached from cycle during use and consequent injury.

Nunn v Parkes and Co (1924) 59 LJ 806 HC KBD Only owner/occupier of property impinged upon by nuisance (here occasioning damage to chattels) could bring action in nuisance.

Nurse, Armitage v [1997] TLR 177 CA Trustee could (as here) validly exclude liability for gross negligence by way of trustee exemption clause.

Nurse, Mann v (1900-01) XVII TLR 569 HC KBD Justices' jurisdiction ousted where person charged with trespass in pursuit of game had reasonably held belief was allowed to shoot on land in issue.

Nute, Treolar v [1977] 1 All ER 230 CA Time runs from date of possession even if owner not put out by possession.

Nutt, Dawrant v [1960] 3 All ER 681; (1960) 110 LJ 830; (1961) 105 SJ 129 Assizes Highway user owes duty of care to other highway users to take reasonable care: absence of front lights a breach of duty.

Nwabudike (a minor) v London Borough of Southwark (1996) 140 SJ LB 128 HC QBD Failed claim in negligence against school which took all reasonable steps to ensure child did not run out onto road (as happened).

Nye, Restell v (1899-1900) XVI TLR 154 HC QBD House-owner could not recover from architect money paid to builder on foot of architect's negligent certification that builder's work was done.

O and G Rushton (Limited), Henry Faulder and Co (Limited) v (1902-03) XIX TLR 452 CA Injunction granted to restrain sale of jams as 'Silverpan' jams when were not made by plaintiffs.

O'Boyle and another v Leiper and others (1990) 134 SJ 316 CA Settlement in full and final settlement of all claims treated as precisely that.

O'Brian and another, McLoughlin v [1982] 2 All ER 298; [1983] 1 AC 410; (1982) 132 NLJ 664; [1982] RTR 209 (also CA); (1982) 126 SJ 347; [1982] TLR 242; [1982] 2 WLR 982 HL Damages for nervous shock if injury foreseeable result of other's negligence; reasonable foreseeability sole criterion in highway negligence cases.

Odhams Press, Ltd and others, Loughans v [1962] 1 All ER 404; (1962) 112 LJ 137; [1963] 1 QB 299; (1962) 106 SJ 262 CA Can plead innuendo by inference.

Odhams Press, Ltd, Goody v [1966] 3 All ER 369; [1967] 1 QB 333; (1966) 110 SJ 793; [1966] 3 WLR 460 CA Evidence of relevant previous convictions admissible to show plaintiff's generally bad reputation; can be partial justification of article if part severable.

Odhams Press, Ltd, Norman Kark Publications, Ltd v [1962] 1 All ER 636; (1962) 112 LJ 239; (1962) 106 SJ 195 HC ChD Must show proprietary right in goodwill of name and likely confusion to succeed.

Odhams, Ltd, Lyle-Samuel v [1918-19] All ER 779; [1920] 1 KB 135; (1919) 54 LJ 338; [1919] 88 LJCL 1161; (1920) 122 LTR 57; (1918-19) 63 SJ 748; (1918-19) XXXV TLR 711 CA Absent special circumstances person sued for defamation not obliged to reveal source.

OF Smart (Liverpool) Ltd, Garston Warehousing Co Ltd v [1973] RTR 377 CA Van driver driving too fast on wet November morning and ignoring warnings from another driver was two-thirds liable for resultant collision at city crossroads.

Office Cleaning Services, Limited v Westminster Window and General Cleaners, Limited (1946) 174 LTR 229; (1946) WN (I) 24 HL No passing off where names were 'Office Cleaning Services' and 'Office Cleaning Association'.

Office Cleaning Services, Ltd v Westminster Office Cleaning Association [1944] 2 All ER 269 CA No passing off where names were 'Office Cleaning Services' and 'Office Cleaning Association'.

Ogwo v Taylor [1987] 1 All ER 668; [1988] AC 431 (also HL); (1987) 137 NLJ 99; (1987) 131 SJ 506; [1987] 2 WLR 988 CA Negligent starter of fire liable to fireman for any foreseeable injuries suffered.

Ogwo v Taylor [1987] 3 All ER 961; [1988] AC 431 (also CA); (1987) 137 NLJ 1110; (1987) 131 SJ 1628; [1987] 3 WLR 1145 HL Negligent starter of fire owes duty of care to firemen for injuries suffered extinguishing fire.

Old Gate Estates, Ltd v Toplis and Harding and Russell [1939] 3 All ER 209; (1939) 88 LJ 11; (1939) 161 LTR 227; (1939) 83 SJ 606 HC KBD No recovery for pure economic loss.

Oldham Corporation, Fisher v [1930] All ER 96; (1931-34) XXIX Cox CC 154; (1930) 94 JP 132; (1930) 99 LJCL 569; (1930) 143 LTR 281; (1929-30) XLVI TLR 390 HC KBD Police officer acts for Crown in effecting arrest so not liable for false imprisonment.

Oldham v Sheffield Corporation (1927) 91 JP 69; (1927) 136 LTR 681; (1926-27) XLIII TLR 222 CA Liable in negligence for pplacing obstruction on private road and thereby causing invitee injury.

Oldham, Cleghorn v (1927) 63 LJ 498; (1926-27) XLIII TLR 465; (1927) WN (I) 147 HC KBD Golfer liable in negligence where struck girl acting as caddie when demonstrating golf stroke to another.

Oliver and another v Birmingham and Midland Motor Omnibus Co, Ltd [1932] All ER 820; [1933] 1 KB 35; (1932) 74 LJ 80; (1933) 102 LJCL 65; (1932) 147 LTR 317; (1931-32) XLVIII TLR 540; (1932) WN (I) 156 HC KBD Infant not so identified with grandfather with whom crossing road that grandfather's negligence precluded infant from recovering.

Oliver and others v Ashman and another [1960] 3 All ER 677; (1960) 110 LJ 830; (1961) 111 LJ 580; [1961] 1 QB 337; (1960) 104 SJ 1036 HC QBD Shortened lifespan/that most of damages will not be spent on claimant relevant in deciding level of damages.

Oliver and others v Ashman and another [1961] 3 All ER 323; [1955] Crim LR 608; [1962] 2 QB 210 CA Loss of life expectation to include loss of earnings estimate.

Oliver Blais Co, Ld, Yachuk and Another v [1949] 2 All ER 150; [1949] AC 386; (1949) LXV TLR 300; (1949) WN (I) 186 PC No contributory negligence by young child purchaser of petrol: seller thereof completely liable for later injuries suffered by child.

Oliver v Hinton (1899-1900) LXXXI LTR 212 CA Grossly careless purchaser not allowed deprive prior innocent mortgagee of her priority.

Oliver, Howe v; Haynes Third Party (1907-08) XXIV TLR 781 HC KBD Could not bring action against second partner in respect of same cause of action subject of settlement with one partner.

OLL Ltd v Secretary of State for Transport [1997] 3 All ER 897; [1997] 2 Cr App R (S) 1099; (1997) 147 NLJ 1099; [1997] TLR 407 HC QBD On duty of care owed by coastguard in answering distress call.

Ollard and Bentley and Marsland and Barber, Baker v (1983) 133 NLJ 422c; (1982) 126 SJ 593 CA Limitation period in negligence action stemming from negligent conveyance ran from date of conveyance.

Olley v Marlborough Court, Ltd [1948] 1 All ER 955; (1948) 98 LJ 273; (1948) WN (I) 192 HC KBD Bailee's failure to adequately secure bailed items was negligent.

Olley v Marlborough Court, Ltd [1949] 1 All ER 127; [1949] 1 KB 532; (1948) 98 LJ 699; [1949] 118 LJR 360; (1949) LXV TLR 95; (1949) WN (I) 17 CA Bailee's failure to adequately secure bailed items was negligent; exception clause inapplicable as not clear and not made aware thereof before taken as guest.

Olotu v Home Office and another [1997] 1 All ER 385; (1996) TLR 11/12/96; [1997] 1 WLR 328 CA Person committed to CrCt for trial could not sue Home Secretary/Crown Prosecution Service for false imprisonment/breach of statutory duty where was detained beyond time stipulated.

Olotu v Secretary of State for the Home Department and another (1996) TLR 8/5/96 CA Prison governor not liable for false imprisonment of individual kept in remand custody after prescribed time as result of Crown Prosecution Service not applying for extension of time.

Olsen v Magnesium Castings and Products, Ltd [1947] 1 All ER 333 CA Employer must show (if so claiming) that workman accepted workmen's compensation in lieu of common law entitlements.

Olton, Foxley and another v [1964] 3 All ER 248; [1965] 2 QB 306; (1964) 108 SJ 522; [1964] 3 WLR 1155 HC QBD On deduction/non-deduction of unemployment benefit/national assistance grants.

Oram v Hutt (1914) 78 JP 51; (1913) 48 LJ 659; [1914] 83 LJCh 161; (1914) 110 LTR 187; (1913-14) 58 SJ 80; (1913-14) XXX TLR 55 CA Trade union acted ultra vires when paid for legal costs of general secretary in slander action — money to be repaid with interest.

Oram v Hutt [1913] 1 Ch 259; (1913) 77 JP 110; (1912) 47 LJ 723; (1913) 82 LJCh 152 (1913) 108 LTR 410 HC ChD Trade union acted ultra vires when paid for legal costs of general secretary in slander action.

Orbinson, Hasselblad (GB) Ltd v [1985] 1 All ER 173; [1985] QB 475; (1985) 129 SJ 32; [1985] 2 WLR 1 CA On privilege attaching to letter sent voluntarily to European Commission in course of essentially administrative proceedings.

Orbit Mining and Trading Co, Ltd v Westminster Bank, Ltd (1962) 112 LJ 338; (1962) 106 SJ 373 HC QBD Bank negligent in its collection of cheques; true owner of goods may recover for conversion of same though has assisted in loss suffered through his own negligence.

Orbit Mining and Trading Co, Ltd v Westminster Bank, Ltd (1962) 106 SJ 937 CA Bank not negligent in its collection of cheques.

Orbit Valve Co Europe, EE Caledonia Ltd v [1993] 4 All ER 165; [1994] 1 WLR 221 HC QBD Unless contrary provision indemnity clause not to be taken as applying to party's own negligence. Concurrent causes of event are each causes unless event would have occurred anyway.

Orchard v Connaught Club, Limited (1930) 74 SJ 169; (1929-30) XLVI TLR 214; (1930) WN (I) 38 HC KBD Club rule precluded liability in negligence for loss of member's goods.

Orchard v South Eastern Electricity Board (1986) 136 NLJ 1112 CA Solicitor (but not barrister) may be liable for opponent's costs.

Ormiston v Great Western Railway Company [1917] 86 LJCL 759; (1917) 116 LTR 479; (1916-17) XXXIII TLR 171 HC KBD Railway company servant cannot arrest passenger for travelling without proper fare unless passenger refuses to show ticket and disclose name and address but what servant says in course of arrest can only be slanderous if is special damage.

Ormrod and another v Crosville Motor Services, Ltd and another (Murphie, Third Party) [1953] 2 All ER 753; (1953) 103 LJ 539; (1953) 97 SJ 570; [1953] 1 WLR 1120 CA Car owner vicariously liable for negligence of friend when driving car entirely/partly for owner.

Ormrod and another v Crosville Motor Services, Ltd and another (Murphie, Third Party) [1953] 1 All ER 711; (1953) 97 SJ 154; [1953] 1 WLR 409 HC QBD Car owner vicariously liable for negligence of driver acting at owner's behest.

Orum and others, South Suburban Co-operative Society, Limited v [1937] 2 KB 690; (1937) 83 LJ 410; [1937] 106 LJCL 555; (1937) 157 LTR 93; (1937) 81 SJ 497; (1936-37) LIII TLR 803; (1937) WN (I) 259 CA Writer of allegedly libellous letter to newspaper who pleads fair comment must reveal person/s from whom obtained information.

Osborn v The Metropolitan Water Board (1910) 74 JP 190; (1910) 102 LTR 217; (1909-10) XXVI TLR 283 HC KBD Metropolitan Water Board liable for inadequate maintenance of stop-cock box in pavement and consequent injury to plaintiff.

Osborn v Thomas Boulter and Son [1930] All ER 154; [1930] 2 KB 226; (1930) 99 LJCL 556; (1930) 143 LTR 460 CA Privileged communication did not lose privilege through communication to typist.

Osborne Garrett and Co, Ltd and another, Brandon and another v [1924] All ER 703; [1924] 1 KB 548; (1924) 59 LJ 76; [1924] 93 LJCL 304; (1924) 130 LTR 670; (1923-24) 68 SJ 460; (1923-24) XL TLR 235; (1924) WN (I) 33 HC KBD Wife could recover for injury suffered in course of non-negligent act to rescue husband from danger.

Osborne v Colenutt (1919) CC Rep VIII 25 CyCt Pedestrian with poor sight who fell through open cellar door that opened onto pavement able to recover damages for injury sustained where normally sighted person would have seen danger and avoided injury.

Osborne v Mead and others (1928) 66 LJ ccr18 CyCt Where unlawfully place chattels on another's land that other is allowed to remove same.

Osborne, Hope v [1913] 2 Ch 349; (1913) 77 JP 317; (1913) 48 LJ 393; (1913) 82 LJCh 457; (1913-14) 109 LTR 41; (1912-13) XXIX TLR 606; (1913) WN (I) 201 HC ChD Liable in damages for excessive trespass in entering onto another's land to remove nuisance.

Osborne, Mahon v [1939] 1 All ER 535; [1939] 2 KB 14; [1939] 108 LJCL 567; (1939) 160 LTR 329; (1939) 83 SJ 134 CA Res ipsa loquitur cannot arise in relation to complex surgery; whether leaving swab in patient negligent depends on circumstances.

Oscar Faber and Partners, Pirelli General Cable Works Ltd v [1983] 1 All ER 65; [1983] 2 AC 1; (1983) 133 NLJ 63; (1983) 127 SJ 16; [1982] TLR 623; [1983] 2 WLR 6 HL Time runs from date of physical damage in negligent design/workmanship action.

Oscar Faber and Partners, Pirelli General Cable Works Ltd v [1982] TLR 54 CA On when limitation period starts to run in negligent design/workmanship action.

Ose Gesellschaft, &c v Jewish Colonial Trust (1926-27) XLIII TLR 398 HC KBD Failed action for negligence where cheque was lost and amount was debited from account when cheque later used fraudulently.

Osman and another v Ferguson and another [1993] 4 All ER 344 CA Police not liable for crimes committed by criminal whom they could have but failed to apprehend.

Osman v J Ralph Moss Ltd (1970) 120 NLJ 177t CA Recovery of damages from insurance broker who advised plaintiff to insure car with company that collapsed thereby rendering plaintiff uninsured.

Osmond and another, Marshall v [1982] 2 All ER 610; [1982] Crim LR 441; [1982] QB 857; [1983] RTR 111; (1982) 126 SJ 210; [1982] TLR 38; [1982] 3 WLR 120 HC QBD Police do not owe normal duty of care to person suspected of crime who is unintentionally injured in course of hot pursuit.

Osmond and another, Marshall v [1983] 2 All ER 225; [1983] QB 1034; [1983] RTR 475; (1983) 127 SJ 309; [1983] TLR 190; [1983] 3 WLR 13 CA Police owe normal duty of care to person suspected of crime who is unintentionally injured in course of hot pursuit.

Osram, Kansara v [1967] 3 All ER 230 CA Appropriate damages in cases meriting small awards.

Ottawa Electric Railway Company, Letang v [1926] All ER 546; [1926] AC 725; (1926) 95 LJPC 153; (1926) 135 LTR 421; (1925-26) XLII TLR 596 PC Invitee must freely/voluntarily accept risk inherent in visiting dangerous premises for volenti non fit injuria to apply.

Page Motors Ltd v Epsom and Ewell Borough Borough Council (1980) 124 SJ 273 HC ChD Adoption of nuisance (posed by gypsies) by landowner.

Page Motors Ltd v Epsom and Ewell Borough Borough Council (1981) 125 SJ 590 CA Adoption of nuisance (posed by gypsies) by landowner.

Page Motors, Limited, Aitchison v (1936) 154 LTR 128; (1935-36) LII TLR 137 HC KBD Recovery of damages for injury suffered through negligence of bailee for reward's servant (even though latter had been acting outside scope of authority).

Page v London, Midland and Scottish Railway Company (1943) 168 LTR 168 HC KBD Construction of rail company's exemption clause in respect of negligence in carriage of luggage: clause ineffective.

Page v Smith [1995] 2 All ER 736; [1996] 1 AC 155; (1995) 145 NLJ 723; [1995] RTR 210; (1995) 139 SJ LB 173; [1995] TLR 275; [1995] 2 WLR 644 HL Negligent driver liable to primary victim for nervous shock if personal injury reasonably foreseeable as result of accident even if no physical injury.

Page v Smith [1996] 3 All ER 272; (1994) 144 NLJ 756; [1994] TLR 240; [1996] 1 WLR 855 CA Negligent driver not liable to primary victim for nervous shock though personal injury reasonably foreseeable as result of accident.

Paget, Sorrell v [1949] 2 All ER 609; [1950] 1 KB 252 CA Person impounding straying cattle had lien on same until appropriate amount paid/offered for distress damage feasant.

Paget, Sorrell v (1949) LXV TLR 595 HC KBD Person impounding straying cattle had lien on same until appropriate amount paid/offered for distress damage feasant.

Paine v Colne Valley Electricity Supply Co, Ltd and British Insulated Cables, Ltd [1938] 4 All ER 803; (1939) 83 SJ 115; (1938-39) LV TLR 181 HC KBD Manufacturer not liable in respect of dangerous article where ample chance of inspection.

Palacath Ltd v Flanagan [1985] 2 All ER 161 HC QBD Surveyor not acting in quasi-/judicial rôle not immune from negligence suit.

Paley (Princess Olga) v Weisz and others (1928-29) XLV TLR 102 HC KBD Failed action in detinue/conversion by Russian exile against defendants who purchased property confiscated by Soviets.

Paley (Princess Olga) v Weisz and others (1928-29) XLV TLR 365 CA Failed action in detinue/conversion by Russian exile against defendants who purchased property confiscated by Soviets.

Palmer v Conservators of the River Thames (1901-02) LXXXV LTR 537; (1901-02) 46 SJ 84 HC ChD Unauthorised dredging under River Thames Conservancy Act 1894 constituted trespass.

Palmer, Bray v (1953) 97 SJ 830; [1953] 1 WLR 1455 CA Re-trial merited where trial judge had been unable to fully determine facts of case and apportion blame.

Palmer, Rutter v [1922] All ER 367; [1922] 2 KB 87; (1922) 57 LJ 195; [1922] 91 LJCL 657; (1922) 127 LTR 419; (1921-22) 66 SJ 576; (1921-22) XXXVIII TLR 555 CA Clause exempting bailee from liability for negligence deemed valid.

Paludina (Owners), Singleton Abbey (Owners) v; The Paludina [1926] All ER 220 HL On novus actus interveniens.

Palumbo and others, Maudsley v [1995] TLR 690 HC ChD On what constitutes breach of confidence in respect of which damages are available.

Pamplin v Express Newspapers Ltd (1985) 129 SJ 190 CA Libel verdict not set aside where plaintiff awarded nominal damages claimed jury not directed to disregard costs issue when reaching their verdict.

Pamplin v Express Newspapers Ltd (No 2) [1988] 1 All ER 282; (1985) 129 SJ 188; [1988] 1 WLR 116 CA Defendant may produce evidence concerning general reputation and previous convictions when arguing for low damages; jury may not take costs into account when reaching verdict.

Pandelis and others, Musgrove v [1919] 88 LJCL 915 (also HC KBD); (1919) 120 LTR 601; (1918-19) XXXV TLR 299; (1919) WN (I) 79 CA Liability for fire negligently started.

Pandelis, Musgrove v [1918-19] All ER 589; [1919] 1 KB 314; (1919) 54 LJ 106; [1919] 88 LJCL 915 (also CA); (1918-19) 63 SJ 353; (1918-19) XXXV TLR 202; (1919) WN (I) 27 HC KBD Liability for fire negligently started.

Panhard Levassor Motor Co Ltd and others, Société Anonyme des Anciens Etablissements Panhard et Levassor v [1900-03] All ER 477; (1901) 36 LJ 393; [1901] 70 LJCh 738; (1901-02) LXXXV LTR 20; (1900-01) XVII TLR 680 HC ChD Foreign company can recover directly in passing off though sells through intermediary into England.

Pannett v P McGuinness and Co Ltd [1972] 3 All ER 137; [1972] 2 QB 599; (1972) 116 SJ 335; [1972] 3 WLR 386 CA Occupiers owed such duties to trespassing children as common sense/humanity demanded.

Papworth v Battersea Borough Council [1914-15] All ER 406; (1916) 80 JP 177; [1916] 1 KB 583; [1916] 85 LJKB 746; (1916) 114 LTR 340; (1915-16) 60 SJ 120 CA Trial ordered as to liability of local authority for negligently constructed road gully.

Papworth v Battersea Borough Council (1914) 78 JP 172; (1915) 79 JP 309; [1914] 2 KB 89; [1915] 84 LJKB 1881; [1914] 83 LJKB 358; (1914) 110 LTR 385; (1913-14) XXX TLR 240 HC KBD Non-liability/liability as highway/sewer authority.

Pardex Plant Engineers Ltd, Sparks and another v (1969) 113 SJ 1003 CA On appropriate damages for young girl left with permanent disfiguring scar on leg following negligent collision.

Parish v Judd [1960] 3 All ER 33; (1960) 124 JP 444; (1960) 110 LJ 701; (1960) 104 SJ 644 HC QBD Prima facie negligent to leave unlit car in unlit place on road at night (not here as lamp/reasonable care); nuisance if unlit car in unlit place on road at night is dangerous obstruction.

Parish v The Mayor, &c, of the City of London (1901-02) XVIII TLR 63 HC ChD Order for removal of public urinal which was occasioning nuisance to warehouse owner.

Park Bros (Liverpool), Ltd and others, Murray v (1959) 109 LJ 460 HC QBD Apportionment of liabilities for accident ultimately arising from negligent parking of van.

Park Court Hotel Ltd v Trans-World Hotels Ltd (1970) 120 NLJ 202t; (1970) 114 SJ 166 HC ChD Failed action by owners of 'Hotel International' (a hotel in London) to restrain party from using name 'London International Hotel' in respect of latter's hotel.

Park v J Jobson and Son [1944] LJNCCR 153 CyCt Person who was author of own troubles in that created situation whereby cattle could trespass on own property could not recover damages from cattle owner when cattle so trespassed.

Park v J Jobson and Son [1945] 1 All ER 222; (1946) 96 LJ 213 CA No duty on allotment holder to keep allotment fenced; no liability on one allotment holder with defective fence to others as no evidence of animal trespass through particular part of fence.

Park, Thompson v [1944] 2 All ER 477; [1944] KB 408; (1945) 95 LJ 112; [1944] 113 LJ 561; (1944) 170 LTR 207 CA Injunction available to stop licensee whose licence is revoked committing trespass.

Parke and another, Canadian Pacific Railway Company v (1899-1900) LXXXI LTR 127 PC That Crown authorised diversion of water from natural path did not mean could not be liable under common law in performance of same.

Parke Davis and Co Ltd, Ciba Geigy plc v [1993] TLR 202 HC ChD No interlocutory injunction merited preventing advertisement by alleged tortfeasor in pending passing off action that alleged tortfeasor's drug was as effective as but less expensive than competitor (bringing passing off action).

Parker (RJ) (Male), Rodriguez v [1966] 3 WLR 546 HC QBD On giving leave for post-limitation period amendment of writs.

Parker and Smith v Satchwell and Co (Lim) (1900-01) 45 SJ 502 HC ChD On form of injunction in passing off/patent action.

Parker v London County Council (1904) 68 JP 239; [1904] 2 KB 501; [1904] 73 LJCL 561; (1904) XC LTR 415; (1903-04) XX TLR 271; (1903-04) 52 WR 476 HC KBD Special public authority limitation period under Public Authorities Protection Act 1893 applies to county council as tramway owner.

Parker v London General Omnibus Company (Limited) (1909) 73 JP 283; (1909) C LTR 409; (1908-09) XXV TLR 429 HC KBD Personal injury victim failed in action against bus company whose driver/placing bus on road was negligent/may or may not have been nuisance.

Parker v London General Omnibus Company (Limited) (1910) 74 JP 20; (1909-10) 101 LTR 623; (1908-09) 53 SJ 867; (1909-10) XXVI TLR 18 CA Personal injury victim failed in action against bus company whose driver/placing bus on road was negligent/may or may not have been nuisance.

Parker v Miller (1925-26) XLII TLR 408 CA That car ran down hill when unattended was per se evidence of negligence for which person enjoying right of control over car was liable.

Parker v Williams (1917) CC Rep VI 50 CyCt Landlord liable in nuisance for loss occasioned by collapse into adjoining premises of gutters which previously overhung same.

Parker, Bates v [1952] 2 All ER 987 Assizes Occupier not liable to window cleaner for injuries sustained in cleaning but not through defect in property.

Parker, Bates v [1953] 2 QB 231; (1953) 97 SJ 226; [1953] 2 WLR 642 CA Invitee (window cleaner) not warned of unusual dangers by invitor who was therefore liable in negligence.

Parkes and Co, Nunn v (1924) 59 LJ 806 HC KBD Only owner/occupier of property impinged upon by nuisance (here occasioning damage to chattels) could bring action in nuisance.

Parkes and Hartry, Southsea Beach Mansions Hotel Ltd v (1918) CC Rep VII 41 CyCt Lessee/occupier liable for nuisance occasioned by way of inadequate drains.

Parkinson and another v Parkinson [1973] RTR 193 CA Not contributory negligence for pedestrians to walk on left hand side of road.

Parkinson v Liverpool Corporation [1950] 1 All ER 367; (1950) 114 JP 146; (1950) 94 SJ 161; [1950] 66 (1) TLR 262; (1950) WN (I) 43 CA Sharp braking to avoid accident resulting in passenger injury not negligent.

Parkinson v West Riding of Yorkshire County Council (1921-22) 66 SJ 488 HC KBD Council liable for misfeasance of highway where accident arose as result of state in which workmen left road overnight.

Parkinson, Craven v (1923) CC Rep XII 26 CyCt On duty of care owed by bailee towards animals left in his keeping.

Parkinson, France v [1954] 1 All ER 739; (1954) 104 LJ 234; (1954) 98 SJ 214; [1954] 1 WLR 581 CA Absent contrary evidence equal negligence/liability for collision at equal crossroads.

Parkinson, Parkinson and another v [1973] RTR 193 CA Not contributory negligence for pedestrians to walk on left hand side of road.

Parncliffe Investments, Ltd, Appah v (1964) 114 LJ 288 CA Landlord liable in negligence for not providing licensee for reward with key to mortice lock which resulted in subsequent loss through burglary.

Parnell v Metropolitan Police District Receiver [1976] RTR 201 CA No evidence proving that minibus driver had been travelling too close to preceding vehicle/had not seen in time that preceding vehicle stopping.

Parnell v Shields [1973] RTR 414 HC QBD Person deemed one-fifth liability for (fatal) injury through collision where had not been wearing seat belt.

Parry and others v Bulmer and Allington (1913) CC Rep II 108 CyCt No damages for non-repair of fences voluntarily erected and maintained by owner of land adjoining common.

Parry v Aluminium Corporation, Ltd (1940) 162 LTR 236 CA Re-trial on question of damages alone where injured employee established machine whereby was injured was dangerous/unfenced.

Parry v Cleaver [1967] 2 All ER 1168; (1967) 117 NLJ 810; [1968] 1 QB 195; (1967) 111 SJ 415; [1967] 3 WLR 739 CA Damages reduced by compulsory pension.

Parry v Cleaver [1970] AC 1; (1969) 113 SJ 147; [1969] 2 WLR 821 HL Disability pension to be ignored in assessing personal injury damages.

Parry v English Electric Co Ltd [1971] 2 All ER 1094; [1971] 1 WLR 664 CA Appopriate personal injury damages to be assessed in each case.

Parsons and Parsons, Samuel Williams and Sons (Limited) and William Christie and Co (Limited) v (1908-09) XXV TLR 569 HC KBD Wharfingers responsible for canal management liable in negligence for damage caused to barge by sluices being opened and water lowered too far.

Parsons and Parsons, Samuel Williams and Sons (Limited) and William Christie and Co (Limited) v (1909-10) 54 SJ 64; (1909-10) XXVI TLR 78 CA Wharfingers responsible for canal management not liable in negligence for damage caused to barge by sluices being opened and water lowered too far.

Parsons v FW Woolworth and Co Ltd [1980] 3 All ER 456; (1980) 124 SJ 775 HC QBD Issuing of draft case to parties within 21 days is discretionary and court may hear case where violated.

Parsons, Chadwick v (1971) 121 NLJ 177t; (1971) 115 SJ 127 HC QBD On awarding interest on damages.

Parsons, James v (1974) 124 NLJ 1029t; [1975] RTR 20; (1974) 118 SJ 777 HC QBD Front seat passenger without seat belt not guilty of contributory negligence as regards injuries suffered in accident absent warning from driver of need to wear belt.

Partridge and Wilson (a firm), Walpole and another v [1994] 1 All ER 385; [1994] QB 106; [1993] 3 WLR 1093 CA Collateral attack on final decision in earlier proceedings not necessarily abuse of process.

Pasquali, Imperial Tobacco Company of Great Britain and Ireland v; Re Imperial Tobacco Company's Trade Marks [1918] 2 Ch 207 CA Using word 'Regiment' in respect of one's products where rival company's trade mark is 'Regimental' is not breach unless inter alia is real risk of passing off.

Pasternack v Poulton [1973] 2 All ER 74; (1973) 123 NLJ 180t; [1973] RTR 334; (1973) 117 SJ 225; [1973] 1 WLR 476 HC QBD Contributory negligence if not wearing seat-belt as chance of car accident foreseeable.

Patel and others v WH Smith (Eziot) Ltd and another [1987] 1 WLR 853 CA On granting of injunction to landowner to halt trespass onto land to which holds unchallenged title.

Patel v Edwards [1970] RTR 425 CA On respective liabilities of cyclist pulling to right in front of stationary car and motor-cyclist overtaking car and colliding with cyclist.

Paterson (Annie), London, Tilbury, and Southend Railway v (1913) CC Rep II 47; (1912-13) XXIX TLR 413 HL Rail company liable in negligence for injury suffered when passenger slipped off platform on foggy evening when other passengers had already slipped off.

Paterson and another v Humberside County Council [1995] TLR 224 HC QBD Tree-owner liable in nuisance/negligence for subsidence consequent upon drying out of soil by trees.

Paterson and others, Wyman or Ferguson (Pauper) v [1900] LXIX (3) LJ 32; (1900) LXXXII LTR 473; (1899-1900) XVI TLR 270 HL Trustees liable for trust funds lost through their gross negligence.

Paterson v Norris (1913-14) XXX TLR 393 HC KBD Boarding-house keeper owes duty of care to keep door of premises closed.

Paterson, Arneil v (1931) 71 LJ 425; (1931) 100 LJPC 161; (1931) 145 LTR 393; (1931) 75 SJ 424; (1930-31) XLVII TLR 441; (1931) WN (I) 137 HL Owners jointly liable for entirety of damage where impossible to apportion respective liabilities for damage to cattle by dogs acting in concert.

Patience v Andrews and another [1983] RTR 447; [1982] TLR 574 HC QBD Damages reduced by 25% where passenger injured in collision not wearing seat-belt.

Pattenden v Beney (1934) 78 SJ 121 CA Failed claim by widow of dustman against doctor for fatal injuries suffered by dustman after collected gas containers from doctor's house.

Pattenden v Beney (1933) 77 SJ 732; (1933-34) L TLR 10 HC KBD Failed claim by widow of dustman against doctor for fatal injuries suffered by dustman after collected gas containers from doctor's house.

Paul and another v Robson and others [1914] 83 LJPC 304; (1914-15) 111 LTR 481 PC In action for interference with light and air acts complained of must be nuisance to be successful.

Paul E Schweder and Co v Walton and Hemingway (1910-11) XXVII TLR 89 HC KBD Non-recovery for losses country broker incurred on sale of shares (without consulting clients) following advice from their agent, a London stockbroker firm.

Paul v Rendell (1981) 131 NLJ 657 PC Only exceptionally will PC interfere with personal injury awards settled on by trial judge/full court and would not do so here.

Pauldens, Limited; WT French and Son, Third Party, Procter and others v [1934] LJNCCR 263 CyCt Kettle-sellers and manufacturers of kettle liable in negligence for injury occasioned to wife/child of purchaser for injuries suffered short time after purchase as result of defect in kettle.

Pavlides v Jensen and others [1956] 3 WLR 224 HC ChD Negligence claim against directors for alleged non-fraudulent sale of company assets at under-value was unmaintainable.

Paxon v Allsopp (1971) 115 SJ 446 CA Stay of action in light of ten year delay since settlement offer made.

Payne v Railway Executive [1952] 1 KB 26; (1951) 95 SJ 710; [1951] 2 TLR 929; (1951) WN (I) 547 CA Service pension not to be taken into account when assessing personal injury damages.

Payne v Railway Executive (1951) 95 SJ 268; [1951] 1 TLR 921; (1951) WN (I) 240 HC KBD Service pension not to be taken into account when assessing personal injury damages.

Payne-Crofts v Aird Bros, Ltd and British Transport Commission (1953) 103 LJ ccr832 CyCt Successful action against warehouse keepers for goods negligently converted/detained/lost.

Payton and Co (Limited) v Snelling, Lampard, and Co (Limited) (1899-1900) XVI TLR 56 CA Failed action for passing off based on get-up of goods.

Payton and Co, Limited v Snelling, Lampard and Co, Limited [1901] AC 308; [1901] 70 LJCh 644; (1901-02) LXXXV LTR 287 HL Role of judge/witnesses in passing off trial.

Payton v Brooks [1974] RTR 169 CA Valid finding by trial judge that market value of repaired car unaffected by those repairs having been necessitated by damage sustained in car accident: damages for this alleged loss not allowed.

Peacock and Hoskyn v Musgrave and Porter [1956] Crim LR 414t HC QBD Detention by police of persons whom police reasonably believed to have committed offence was not false imprisonment.

Pearce and another; Somerset County Council (Third Party), Bird v [1978] RTR 290 HC QBD On duty owed towards road users by highway authority re-surfacing road and so obliterating road markings.

Pearce and another; Somerset County Council (Third Party), Bird v (1979) 129 (2) NLJ 681; [1979] RTR 369 CA On duty owed towards road users by highway authority re-surfacing road and so obliterating road markings.

Pearce v Round Oak Steel Works Ltd [1969] 3 All ER 680; [1969] 1 WLR 595 CA Must show not negligent in acquiring/discovering defect in second hand purchase for res ipsa loquitur not to apply.

Pearce v Secretary of State for Defence and another [1988] 2 All ER 348 (also CA); [1988] AC 755 (also HC QBD/CA); (1988) 132 SJ 699; [1988] 2 WLR 1027 HL Secretary of State liable in tort for acts of Atomic Energy Authority.

Pearce v Secretary of State for Defence and another [1988] 2 All ER 348 (also HL); [1988] AC 755 (also HC QBD/HL); (1987) 137 NLJ 922; (1988) 132 SJ 127; [1988] 2 WLR 144 CA Secretary of State liable in tort for acts of Atomic Energy Authority.

Pearce v Secretary of State for Defence and another [1988] AC 755 (also CA/HL); (1987) 137 NLJ 80; (1987) 131 SJ 362; [1987] 2 WLR 782 HC QBD Secretary of State liable in tort for acts of Atomic Energy Authority.

Pearce, Hyde v [1982] 1 All ER 1029 CA No adverse possession if uncompleted conveyance would be a defence to charge of possession/if contract terminable upon vendor's demanding return of keys.

Pearks, Gunston and Tee (Limited) v Thompson, Talmey, and Co (1900-01) XVII TLR 250 HC ChD Injunction granted to prominent company trading as 'Talmey and Co' precluding new rival company from trading as 'Thompson, Talmey and Co'.

Pemberton and another v Bright and others [1960] 1 All ER 792; (1960) 124 JP 265; (1960) 110 LJ 284; (1960) 104 SJ 349 CA Blockable culvert a potential nuisance; blocked culvert a nuisance: council liable for constructing nuisance, occupiers liable for continuing it.

Pemberton, Hindley v (1957) 107 LJ ccr620 CyCt On trespass by person acting under licence.

Penmount Estates, Limited v National Provincial Bank, Limited; Stanley Moss and Pilcher (third party) (1945) 173 LTR 344 HC KBD Action for conversion/negligence where bank credited amount of cashed cheque to wrong bank account.

Penn v Bristol and West Building Society and others [1996] 2 FCR 729; [1995] 2 FLR 938; [1995] TLR 348 HC ChD Solicitors liable to wife for selling matrimonial house without realising that wife's signature on documents was forged, and to building society for mortgage loan it gave to purchaser.

Pennine Insurance Co Ltd and others, McNealy v [1978] RTR 285 CA Brokers liable where their breach of duty of care owed towards client resulted in latter not being covered by insurance policy.

Pennington and Son (a firm), Simmons v [1955] 1 All ER 240; (1955) 99 SJ 146; [1955] 1 WLR 183 CA Mistaken answer but which conformed to general conveyancing practice not negligent; damages irrecoverable for fire damage to premises unsold through solicitor's 'negligence'.

Penny v Northampton Borough Council (1974) 124 NLJ 768t; (1974) 118 SJ 628 CA Failed negligence action for damages on foot of injury suffered by child trespassing on council rubbish tip on which children often trespassed.

Penrose v Mansfield (1970) 120 NLJ 944t HC QBD Failed claim that state of mind following accident caused by another's negligence should have led to limitation period being prolonged.

Penrose v Mansfield (1971) 121 NLJ 249t; (1971) 115 SJ 309 CA Failed claim that state of mind following accident caused by another's negligence should have led to limitation period being prolonged.

Pentecost and another v London District Auditor and others (1951) 115 JP 421; (1951) 95 SJ 432; [1951] 2 TLR 497 HC KBD On what constitutes negligence under Local Government Act 1933, s 228(1)/negligence generally.

Penton v Southern Railway [1931] 2 KB 103; (1931) 100 LJCL 228; (1931) 144 LTR 614 HC KBD Exemption clause to be adequately drawn to customer's notice: was done here.

People's Refreshment House Association Ld, Watson and others v [1952] 1 KB 318; (1952) 96 SJ 150; [1952] 1 TLR 361; (1952) WN (I) 74 HC KBD Non-liability of innkeeper for damage to coach parked outside hospitium of inn with his permission but not at his invitation.

Percy (Pauper) v Corporation of City of Glasgow [1922] 2 AC 299; (1922) 86 JP 201; (1922) 127 LTR 501; (1922) WN (I) 181 HL Glasgow City Corporation tramway officials acting in excess of duties might have committed false imprisonment.

Percy and another v Hall and others [1996] 4 All ER 523; (1996) TLR 31/5/96; [1997] 3 WLR 573 CA Bona fide actions under bye-law later deemed invalid did not render persons effecting those actions liable in tort.

Percy v Director of Public Prosecutions [1995] 3 All ER 124; [1995] Crim LR 714; (1995) 159 JP 337; (1995) 139 SJ LB 34; [1994] TLR 644; [1995] 1 WLR 1382 HC QBD Civil trespass not a breach of peace unless violence a natural consequence of trespass; criminal standard of proof necessary to establish breach of peace.

Pereira v Keleman [1994] 2 FCR 635; [1995] 1 FLR 428 HC QBD Successful claim by daughters against father who had physically and sexually assaulted them.

Perel and others, Australian Bank of Commerce Limited v (1926) 135 LTR 586 PC Failed appeal by bank in action brought against bank inter alia for conversion of cheques (failed to establish course of business which had greater effect than written instructions given).

Perera (MG) v Peiris and Another [1949] AC 1; [1949] 118 LJR 426; (1948) LXIV TLR 590; (1948) WN (I) 388 PC Unsuccessful defamation suit where newspaper published extracts from Government Bribery Commission Report without malice.

Perera v Vandiyar (1953) 97 SJ 332; [1953] 1 WLR 672 CA Landlord's cutting off gas and electricity not tortious (not trespass).

Pether v Kessex Cinemas, Ltd [1937] LJNCCR 314 CyCt Cinema owners liable in negligence for injuries sustained by person falling over sign displayed by another in manner cinema owners ordained.

Peto and others, Pritchard v [1917] 2 KB 173; [1917] 86 LJCL 1292; (1917-18) 117 LTR 145 HC KBD Houseowner owed duty not to expose calling tradesman to concealed dangers of which owner knew (duty met).

Phelan, Morris Motors Ltd v [1960] 1 WLR 352 HC ChD On appropriate form of injunction for passing off.

Phelps v Kemsley (1943) 168 LTR 18 CA On nature of privilege: interested person's communication to another's doctor was privileged.

Phelps v Mayor, Commonalty, and Citizens of the City of London [1916] 2 Ch 255; (1916) 114 LTR 1200 HC ChD On construction of lease defendants found not to have committed trespass in their actions.

Philco Radio and Television Corporation of Great Britain, Ltd v J Spurling, Ltd and others [1949] 2 All ER 129; (1949) 99 LJ 289; (1949) LXV TLR 388 HC KBD Strict liability where bring dangerous material into premises.

Philco Radio and Television Corporation of Great Britain, Ltd v Spurling (J), Ltd and others [1949] 2 All ER 882; (1949) 99 LJ 637; (1949) LXV TLR 757; (1949) WN (I) 271 CA Strict liability where bringing dangerous goods onto premises.

Philcox v Civil Aviation Authority (1995) 139 SJ LB 146; [1995] TLR 332 CA Civil Aviation Authority did not owe duty of care to tell person whether maintenance of own aircraft was adequate/deficient.

Philip Conway Thomas and Co, Ashton v (1939) 83 SJ 891 HC KBD Successful claim against firm of solicitors for negligent failure to make workmen's compensation claim in time.

Philips v Ward [1956] 1 All ER 874; (1956) 106 LJ 281; (1956) 100 SJ 317; [1956] 1 WLR 471 CA Damages for negligent survey/valuation were difference between real value and value in report; damages to be measured at date of report.

Philips v William Whiteley, Ltd [1938] 1 All ER 566 HC KBD Surgeon's standard of care not expected of jeweller doing ear-piercing.

Phillimore v Watford Rural District Council [1913] 2 Ch 434; (1913) 77 JP 453; (1913-14) 109 LTR 616 HC ChD Injunction to restrain sewage farm discharging effluent into private ditch/sewer of another; damages also awarded for nuisance by smell/underground passage of sewage.

Phillips and another, Hill v (1963) 107 SJ 890 CA Driver negligent in that did not anticipate unlit obstruction (broken down trailer) but trailer owner equally negligent in manner in which left trailer on road.

Phillips v Britannia Hygienic Laundry Company, Limited [1923] 1 KB 539; (1923) CC Rep XII 28; [1923] 92 LJCL 389; (1923) 128 LTR 690; (1922-23) 67 SJ 365; (1922-23) XXXIX TLR 207; (1923) WN (I) 47 HC KBD Apportionment of liability for motor car with hidden defect.

Phillips v Britannia Hygienic Laundry Company, Limited [1924] 93 LJCL 5; (1922-23) XXXIX TLR 530 CA Regulations concerning use and construction of motor cars did not create personal remedy against repairers who returned car with latent defect which meant car did not comply with regulations.

Phillips v William Whiteley, Limited (1938) 82 SJ 196; (1937-38) LIV TLR 379 HC KBD On duty of care owed by ear-piercer.

Phillips, Brightside and Carbrook (Sheffield) Co-operative Society Ltd v (1964) 108 SJ 53; [1964] 1 WLR 185 CA Can make non-specific claim of conversion.

Phillips, Burgoyne v [1983] Crim LR 265; (1983) 147 JP 375; [1983] RTR 49; [1982] TLR 559 HC QBD On what constitutes 'driving' a car.

Phillips, Glenwood Lumber Company, Limited v [1904-07] All ER 203; [1904] AC 405; [1904] 73 LJPC 62 PC Damages for trespasser's removal of felled trees from property.

Phillips, King and another v [1952] 2 All ER 459 HC QBD Non-liability of taxi-driver tipping child with taxi for shock sustained by mother viewing incident from over two hundred feet away.

Phillips, King v [1953] 1 All ER 617; (1953) 103 LJ 153; [1953] 1 QB 429; [1953] 2 WLR 526 CA No duty of care owed by taxi-driver tipping child with taxi for shock sustained by mother viewing incident from over two hundred deet away.

Phillips, Powell v [1972] 3 All ER 864; (1973) 137 JP 31; (1972) 122 NLJ 681t; (1972) 116 SJ 713; [1973] RTR 19 CA Highway Code violation does not establish negligence.

Phillips-Higgins v Harper [1954] 2 All ER 51; [1954] 2 WLR 117 CA On when limitation runs where action concerns mistake in contract.

Phillips-Higgins v Harper [1954] 2 WLR 782 CA Affirmation of Phillips-Higgins v Harper (CA).

Phillips-Higgins v Harper [1954] 1 QB 411; (1954) 98 SJ 45 HC QBD On when limitation runs where action concerns mistake in contract.

Phipps v Rochester Corporation [1955] 1 All ER 129; (1955) 119 JP 92; (1955) 105 LJ 41; [1955] 1 QB 450; (1955) 99 SJ 45; [1955] 2 WLR 23 HC QBD Occupier not liable in negligence to child as unaccompanied by parent so trespasser/or though child licensee was unreasonable for child to be there unaccompanied.

Phipps v The New Claridge's Hotel (Limited) (1905-06) XXII TLR 49 HC KBD Person to whom goods entrusted as bailee and who loses them must disprove negligence.

Pick and another, Calvert and another v [1954] 1 All ER 566; (1954) 104 LJ 170; (1954) 98 SJ 147 HC QBD Court will not adjudicate on matter that is really settled between various parties.

Pickering, Wilson and Meeson (a Firm) v [1946] 1 All ER 394; [1946] KB 422; (1945-46) LXII TLR 223; (1946) WN (I) 51 CA Estoppel by negligence could not arise as no duty owed/bias suffered and was fraud not negligence at centre of action; estoppel applying to blank instruments given to agents does not apply to non-negotiable instruments.

Pickett v British Rail Engineering Ltd (1977) 121 SJ 814 CA Loss of earnings in lost years unavailable to plaintiff suffering work related injury/disease whose action came to court during his lifetime.

Pickett v British Rail Engineering Ltd; British Rail Engineering Ltd v Pickett [1979] 1 All ER 774; [1980] AC 136; (1978) 128 NLJ 1198t; (1978) 122 SJ 778; [1978] 3 WLR 955 HL Loss of earnings damages where life expectancy diminished are for whole of pre-injury life expectancy; interest available on inflation-adjusted damages.

Pickford (Limited), Frederick Betts (Limited) v [1906] 2 Ch 87; (1905-06) XXII TLR 315 HC ChD Use of non-party walls as party walls could be trespass.

Pickfords Limited, Betts Limited v (1906) XCIV LTR 363 HC ChD Injunction to restrain trespass occasioned by unconsented to building of party wall.

Pickfords, Ltd, Howard v (1935) 79 SJ 69 HC KBD Driver not negligent where child sitting on running board of van without permission was injured when driver began driving.

Pickles v National Coal Board (Intended Action) [1968] 2 All ER 598; [1968] 1 WLR 997 CA Limitation disapplied where all reasonable advice sought.

Picture Theatres, Limited, Hurst v [1915] 1 KB 1; (1914) 49 LJ 439; [1914] 83 LJKB 1837; (1914-15) 111 LTR 972; (1913-14) XXX TLR 642 CA Recovery for assault/false imprisonment by theatre audience member mistakenly ejected from seat having paid for ticket.

Picture Theatres, Limited, Hurst v (1913-14) XXX TLR 98 HC KBD Recovery for assault/false imprisonment by theatre audience member mistakenly ejected from seat having paid for ticket.

Pier House Management Ltd, Hicks v (1984) 134 NLJ 657 HC QBD Employers of flat porter vicariously liable for theft by latter from flat of tenant who entrusted porter with keys while away from flat.

Piesse, Caldecutt v (1932) 76 SJ 799; (1932-33) XLIX TLR 26 HC KBD On duty owed in respect of guests' property by (non-innkeeper) person who keeps guest house for reward.

Pigden, Barber v [1937] 1 All ER 115; [1937] 1 KB 664; (1937) 83 LJ 42; [1937] 106 LJCL 858; (1937) 156 LTR 245; (1937) 81 SJ 78; (1936-37) LIII TLR 246; (1937) WN (I) 8 CA Husband not liable for wife's torts unless proceedings begun before Law Reform (Married Women and Tortfeasors) Act 1935; no evidence that wife made slanderous comments as husband's agent.

Pitts v Hunt and another [1990] 3 All ER 344; [1991] 1 QB 24; [1990] RTR 290; [1990] TLR 312; [1990] 3 WLR 542 CA Person injured by unlawful acts he encouraged other to undertake barred from recovering damages by virtue of ex turpi causa maxim, public policy and absence of duty of care.

Pitts v Hunt and another [1990] 1 QB 302; [1989] RTR 365; (1990) 134 SJ 834; [1989] 3 WLR 795 HC QBD Person injured by unlawful acts he encouraged other to undertake barred from recovering damages by virtue of ex turpi causa maxim and absence of duty of care; volenti non fit injuria arose but was defeated by 100% contributory negligence/was here precluded from being relied upon by statute.

Plaistow, Thomas v [1997] TLR 280 CA 'Disability' in the Limitation Act 1980, s 33(3)(d) meant that were minor/mentally imbalanced.

Plascott v Southampton Bill-Posting Co (1921) CC Rep X 75 CyCt Is trespass for person posting bills to vandalise bills of other person authorised by occupier to post bills on same premises.

Plato Films, Ltd and others v Speidel [1961] 1 All ER 876; (1961) 111 LJ 220; (1961) 105 SJ 230 HL Can mitigate damages by introducing evidence of actual bad reputation (but not that should have bad reputation).

Plato Films, Ltd and others, Speidel v; Same v Unity Theatre Society, Ltd [1960] 2 All ER 521; (1960) 110 LJ 428; (1960) 104 SJ 602 CA In mitigation of damages can prove bad reputation in general/inexorably linked to libel.

Plovidba (Losinjska) v Transco Overseas Ltd and others [1995] TLR 419 HC QBD On duty of care owed by person putting dangerous materials into circulation to neutralise dangers from same.

Plummer Roddis, Limited, Elvin and Powell, Limited v (1934) 78 SJ 48; (1933-34) L TLR 158 HC KBD Involuntary bailees not liable in conversion for non-negligent act which results in loss of property.

Plummer v Charman and others [1962] 3 All ER 823; (1962) 112 LJ 800; (1962) 106 SJ 631 CA On amendment of claim to include qualified privilege plea.

Plummer v PW Wilkins and Son Ltd [1981] 1 All ER 91; (1980) 130 NLJ 1043; (1981) 125 SJ 399; [1981] 1 WLR 831 HC QBD Special damages to be reduced by amount of supplementary benefits.

Plunkett and another v Barclay's Bank Limited (1936) 154 LTR 465 HC KBD Marking cheque 'refer to drawer' was not defamatory of plaintiff drawer.

Plymouth and Stonehouse Gas Light and Coke Co, Atwill v [1934] LJNCCR 361 CyCt Person who lit match following gas leak and so herself caused explosion could not recover damages in nuisance (and was no negligence on part of gas suppliers proved).

Pocket Publications, Limited, Graves v (1937-38) LIV TLR 952 HC ChD Damages for conversion in context of copyright infringement.

Pointers Transport Services, Ltd, Pigney v [1957] 2 All ER 807 Assizes Wife could seek damages for husband's suicide (though felony) arising from negligent injury.

Polkinghorn and another v Lambeth Borough Council (1938) 102 JP 131; (1938) 158 LTR 127; (1938) 82 SJ 94 CA Local authority liable in negligence for collision arising from its inadequate lighting of safety island post.

Polkinghorn v Lambeth Borough Council; Leach v Same (1937-38) LIV TLR 345 HC KBD Local authority liable in negligence for collision arising from its inadequate lighting of safety island post.

Polley v Fordham (1903-04) XX TLR 435 HC KBD Action brought within six months of illegal distress allowed — distress was act complained of not the (quashed) conviction from which distress warrant arose.

Polly Peck (Holdings) plc and others v Trelford and others [1986] 2 All ER 84; [1986] QB 1000; (1986) 130 SJ 300; [1986] 2 WLR 845 CA Can place words in context of whole work if claimed part of work defamatory; where separate defamatory statements plaintiff can complain of just one; s 5 of Defamation Act inapplicable if not claiming words contain two/more charges.

Polsue and Alfieri (Limited), Rushmer v [1906] 1 Ch 234; (1905) 40 LJ 867; (1905-06) XCIII LTR 823; (1905-06) 50 SJ 126; (1905-06) XXII TLR 139; (1906) WN (I) 3; (1905-06) 54 WR 161 CA Use of printing machinery by night was nuisance (though in area where much printing took place).

Powell v Thorndike and others (1910) 102 LTR 600; (1909-10) XXVI TLR 399 HC KBD Landlords not liable for injury caused by lift which was safe for use if used as intended to be used.

Powles, Watson v (1967) 117 NLJ 758t; [1968] 1 QB 596; (1967) 111 SJ 562; [1967] 3 WLR 1364 CA On gauging damages in personal injury actions.

Powney and others, National Westminster Bank plc v [1990] 2 All ER 416 CA Application for leave to execute judgment not an action.

Poyner, Moore (an infant) v (1974) 124 NLJ 1084t; [1975] RTR 127 CA On duty of care owed by Sunday driver in residential area to children playing in area.

Prager v Times Newspapers Ltd [1988] 1 All ER 300; (1987) 137 NLJ 810; (1988) 132 SJ 55; [1988] 1 WLR 77 CA Cannot plead wider meaning of words used where if proved would not create less damnable form of statement made; can plead justification of any alternative meaning that might convince jury.

Pratt v Martin (1911-13) XXII Cox CC 442; (1911) 75 JP 328; [1911] 2 KB 90; (1911) 80 LJCL 711; (1911-12) 105 LTR 49; (1910-11) XXVII TLR 377; (1911) WN (I) 102 HC KBD Not trespass to send one's dog across another's land to search for game.

Pratt v Richards and others [1951] 1 All ER 90 HC KBD Fatal accident damages for building site injury occasioned by negligence.

Prebble (Richard William) v Television New Zealand Ltd [1995] 1 AC 321; (1994) 144 NLJ 1131; (1994) 138 SJ LB 175; [1994] TLR 393; [1994] 3 WLR 970 PC On praying in aid Parliamentary proceedings to justify alleged defamation.

Prechtel, Flower v [1934] All ER 810 CA Executors liable in tort personally/as representatives of deceased's estate.

Precision Forgings Ltd, Walkley v [1979] 2 All ER 548; (1979) 129 (1) NLJ 520; (1979) 123 SJ 354; [1979] 1 WLR 606 HL Courts will rarely disapply limitation to enable second action where earlier action begun in time but allowed lapse.

Precision Forgings Ltd, Walkley v [1979] 1 All ER 102; [1978] 1 WLR 1228 CA Plaintiff may ask for disapplication of limitation period in respect of second action even if first dismissed for want of prosecution.

Preedy, Canvey Island Commissioners v [1922] 1 Ch 179; (1922) 86 JP 21; [1922] 91 LJCh 203; (1922) 126 LTR 445; (1921) WN (I) 363 HC ChD Damages for trespass upon foreshore.

Prefontaine v Grenier [1907] AC 101; [1907] 76 LJPC 4; (1906-07) XCV LTR 623; (1906-07) XXIII TLR 27 PC President of banking company not deemed negligent for having trusted cashier (lead executive officer after directors).

Prendergast, Smith v [1984] TLR 572 CA Owner of yard liable in negligence for injury occasioned to girl walking past open gate of yard by stray dog owner allowed to wander at will in yard.

Prentice Bros, Ltd, Stearn v [1918-19] All ER 495; (1919) CC Rep VIII 13; [1919] 1 KB 394; [1919] 88 LJCL 422; (1919) 120 LTR 445; (1918-19) 63 SJ 229; (1918-19) XXXV TLR 207 HC KBD Bone merchant not liable for trespass of rats running to and from premises.

Prescott v Lancashire United Transport Co, Ltd [1953] 1 All ER 288; (1953) 117 JP 80; (1953) 97 SJ 64; [1953] 1 WLR 232 CA Conductor on stopped bus liable for not warning passenger not to alight before proper stop reached or preventing passenger alighting/bus re-starting.

Pressdram Ltd and others, Goldsmith and another v [1988] 1 WLR 64 CA Refusal of application for trial of libel action by jury.

Pressdram Ltd and others, Herbage v [1984] 2 All ER 769; (1984) 128 SJ 615; [1984] TLR 289; [1984] 1 WLR 1160 CA Damages recoverable for malicious publication of spent convictions.

Pressdram Ltd, Goldsmith v (1976) 126 NLJ 888t; (1976) 120 SJ 606 HC QBD On availability of injunction from stating what was claimed to be a libel.

Pressdram Ltd, Sutcliffe v [1990] 1 All ER 269; (1989) 139 NLJ 1453; [1991] 1 QB 152; [1990] 2 WLR 271 CA Indirect evidence of newspaper payments not adequate to determine if payments made; damages a matter for jury — may be advised of what money is worth but not awards in other cases.

Pridmore and others, The Earl of Craven v (1901-02) XVIII TLR 282 CA Neighbour's longtime repairing of fence/cutting of trees in ditch bounding rented land (actions known to tenant but not to landlord of rented land) did not rebut presumption that fence was on landlord's land.

Priest v Manchester Corporation [1915] 84 LJKB 1734 HC KBD Sale of land for tipping purposes did not authorise tipping in such a way as to occasion nuisance.

Priest, Minter v [1930] All ER 431; [1930] AC 558; (1930) 69 LJ 250; (1930) 99 LJCL 391; (1930) 143 LTR 57; (1930) 74 SJ 200; (1929-30) XLVI TLR 301; (1930) WN (I) 83 HL Whether occasion privileged a matter for judge; no absolute privilege as solicitor not acting for party and qualified privilege attaching to occasion defeated by solicitor's malice.

Priest, Minter v [1929] 1 KB 655; (1929) 67 LJ 378; (1929) 141 LTR 140 HC KBD On professional privilege in defamation actions.

Priest, Minter v (1929) 98 LJCL 661; (1929) 73 SJ 529; (1928-29) XLV TLR 393; (1929) WN (I) 94 CA Privilege attaches to communications between solicitor and prospective client regarding possible retainer of former by latter.

Prince and another v Gregory and another [1959] 1 All ER 133; (1959) 103 SJ 130 CA Owner/occupier not liable for accident occurring through children playing with lime mortar left outside premises pending repairs.

Prince of Wales Theatre (Birmingham), Limited, Peters v [1942] 2 All ER 553; (1943) 93 LJ 117; (1943) 168 LTR 241; (1943) 87 SJ 83 CA Rylands v Fletcher inapplicable where implied consent to hazard.

Principality Finance Ltd and another, Bryanston Leasings Ltd v [1977] RTR 45 HC QBD Company/receiver liable in detinue and/conversion where latter refused to assist in obtaining replacement registration books for two lost after leased cars from plaintiffs.

Pringle, Wilson v [1986] 2 All ER 440; (1986) 136 NLJ 416; [1987] QB 237; (1986) 130 SJ 468; [1986] 3 WLR 1 CA Intended hostile act not intent to injure necessary for trespass to person to occur.

Prison Commissioners, D'Arcy v [1956] Crim LR 56t HC QBD Successful negligence action against Prison Commissioners for injuries suffered by prisoner during attack by fellow-prisoners.

Prison Commissioners, Greenwell v (1951) 101 LJ 486 CyCt Prison Commissioners liable in negligence for damage occasioned by Borstal inmates to third person's property in course of escape.

Prison Commissioners, Jacoby v [1940] 2 All ER 499 HC KBD Special public authority time limitation applicable in suit against prison commissioners.

Prison Commissioners, Jacoby v [1940] 3 All ER 506 CA Special public authority time limitation applicable in suit against prison commissioners.

Pritchard v Clwyd County Council and another [1992] TLR 353 CA Presence of flood-water on road not per se evidence of non-feasance.

Pritchard v JH Cobden Ltd and another [1987] 1 All ER 300; [1988] Fam 22; [1987] 2 FLR 30; (1970) 130 SJ 715; [1987] 2 WLR 627 CA Date of trial date on which to assess actual/future loss of earnings; divorce costs cannot be included in damages as not a loss.

Pritchard v Ministry of Defence [1995] TLR 26 HC QBD Failed claim in false imprisonment by individual who claimed was compelled to remain in Army (but such a claim could be successful).

Pritchard v Peto and others [1917] 2 KB 173; [1917] 86 LJCL 1292; (1917-18) 117 LTR 145 HC KBD Houseowner owed duty not to expose calling tradesman to concealed dangers of which owner knew (duty met).

Pritchard v Post Office (1950) 114 JP 370; (1950) 94 SJ 404; (1950) WN (I) 310 CA Failed action against Post Office by non-sighted woman who suffered personal injuries after falling into open manhole adequately signposted to sighted people.

Pritchard, Jones v [1908] 1 Ch 630; (1908) XCVIII LTR 386 HC ChD Person enjoying easements as regards user of common wall not liable for nuisance arising from user so long as is not negligent/careless and uses it for purposes envisioned.

Pritty v Child (1902) 37 LJ 191; [1902] 71 LJCL 512 HC KBD Water-finder liable for reckless statement as to location of water.

Procter and others v Pauldens, Limited; WT French and Son, Third Party [1934] LJNCCR 263 CyCt Kettle-sellers and manufacturers of kettle liable in negligence for injury occasioned to wife/child of purchaser for injuries suffered short time after purchase as result of defect in kettle.

Procter, Mersey Docks and Harbour Board v [1923] All ER 134; [1923] AC 253; (1923) 58 LJ 14; [1923] 92 LJCL 479; (1923) 129 LTR 34; (1922-23) 67 SJ 400; (1922-23) XXXIX TLR 275; (1923) WN (I) 85 HL Failure of claim against Docks Board as were not negligent/acts were not cause of death.

Proctor v British Northrop Co Ltd (1937) 81 SJ 611 CA Defendants not liable for injury to child trespasser (who knew should not have been where was) where took all reasonable steps/did not lay trap.

Producers' Distributing Co, Ltd, Samuelson v [1931] All ER 74; [1932] 1 Ch 201 (also HC ChD); (1932) 101 LJCh 168 (also HC ChD); (1932) 146 LTR 37 CA Passing off of film as cinema version of written work.

Producers' Distributing Company, Limited, Samuelson v [1932] 1 Ch 201 (also CA); (1932) 101 LJCh 168 (also CA) HC ChD Passing off of film as cinema version of written work.

Prole v Allen and others [1950] 1 All ER 476 Assizes Club steward liable to club member for injury caused upon his doing his duties negligently.

Pronek v Winnipeg, Selkirk and Lake Winnipeg Railway Company [1933] AC 61; (1933) 102 LJPC 12; (1933) 148 LTR 193 PC On duty of railway company operating its cars in part on a highway.

Propp, Jewelowski v [1944] 1 All ER 483; (1944) 171 LTR 234; (1943-44) LX TLR 559 HC KBD No duty to mitigate damages in fraudulent misrepresentation action.

Prosser (A) and Son, Ltd v Levy and others [1955] 3 All ER 577; (1955) 105 LJ 760; (1955) 99 SJ 815; [1955] 1 WLR 1224 CA Trustees liable in negligence where left pipe in bad condition and water escaped for no apparent reason.

Prosser (A) and Son, Ltd v Levy and others and Barden Morris Incorporated, Ltd (1955) 105 LJ 569 HC QBD On liability for escape of water in office premises.

Prothero and Prothero, Scudder v (1966) 110 SJ 248 HC QBD Small damages for solicitors' technical breach of duty of care regarding calling of witness where had not resulted in damage to case.

Prout, Swift v (1964) 108 SJ 317 CA On appropriate personal injury damages for person whose injuries had shortened his lifespan to three years from date of accident.

Provender Millers (Winchester) Limited v Southampton County Council (1939) 161 LTR 162 HC ChD Local authority discharging statutory duty cannot transgress another's rights unless unreasonable to otherwise discharge responsibility.

Pryce and Son, Limited v Pioneer Press, Limited (1925-26) XLII TLR 29 HC KBD Printing/ publishing of another printer's imprint was libellous.

Pryce v Elwood (1964) 108 SJ 583 HC QBD No deduction for income tax for damages payable for loss of trading profits suffered by plaintiff car hirer as result of collision occasioned by defendant.

Pub Squash Co Pty Ltd, Cadbury Schweppes Pty Ltd and others v [1981] 1 All ER 213; (1980) 130 NLJ 1095; (1981) 125 SJ 96; [1981] 1 WLR 193 PC Passing off extends to distinctive ads to which goodwill attached.

Publicity Services (London), Limited, Illustrated Newspapers, Limited v [1938] Ch 414; [1938] 107 LJCh 154; (1938) 158 LTR 195; (1938) 82 SJ 76; (1937-38) LIV TLR 364; (1938) WN (I) 59 HC ChD Injunction to restrain placing of unauthorised supplement in certain publication of plaintiff as were passing off former as being part of latter.

Pui (Ng Chun) and others v Tat (Lee Chuen) and another [1988] RTR 298; (1988) 132 SJ 1244 PC Plaintiff must still prove negligence though relying on res ipsa loquitur claim; driver not to be judged by too severe a standard when acting in emergency (here driver acted reasonably).

Pulsford v Devenish [1903] 2 Ch 625 HC ChD Company liquidator found negligent in performance of his duties.

Purcell, Fitzhardinge (Lord) v (1908-09) XCIX LTR 154 HC ChD Injunction granted to restrain trespass by wildfowler going from river to foreshore in exercise of purported right.

Purdew and another v Seress-Smith (1992) 136 SJ LB 244; [1992] TLR 438 HC QBD Letter to social security adjudication officer not absolutely privileged.

Purdie, Burke v [1935] LJNCCR 303 CyCt Innkeeper negligent in leaving guest's car-keys on open access in reception office and so liable for damage occasioned when car taken for 'joy-ride'.

Purdy, Young v [1997] 1 FCR 632; [1996] 2 FLR 795 CA Solicitor not liable in damages for negligent actions of client consequent upon solicitor's breach of contract by way of termination of retainer.

Purkis v Walthamstow Borough Council [1934] All ER 64; (1934) 98 JP 244 CA Child using playground swing a licensee.

Purnell and others, Mahoney v [1997] 1 FLR 612 HC QBD Agreement between father-in-law and son-in-law set aside as was markedly disadvantageous to former; solicitor liable in negligence for not adequately drawing the father-in-law's attention to disadvantageous nature of transaction.

Purnell, Theyer v [1918] 2 KB 333; [1919] 88 LJCL 263; (1918-19) 119 LTR 285; (1918) WN (I) 174 HC KBD Recovery of damages consequent upon trespass of sheep: doctrine of scienter inapplicable.

Pusey v Peters and another (1974) 124 NLJ 1030t; (1975) 119 SJ 85 HC QBD Gas Board negligent as regards inadequate safeguards regarding ventilation upon change of gas supply to form needing more ventilation.

PW Wilkins and Son Ltd, Plummer v [1981] 1 All ER 91; (1980) 130 NLJ 1043; (1981) 125 SJ 399; [1981] 1 WLR 831 HC QBD Special damages to be reduced by amount of supplementary benefits.

Pwllbach Colliery Co, Ltd v Woodman [1914-15] All ER 124; [1915] AC 634; (1915) 50 LJ 117; [1915] 84 LJKB 874; (1915-16) 113 LTR 10; (1914-15) XXXI TLR 271; (1915) WN (1) 108 HL Authorisation to carry on business not per se authorisation to carry on nuisance (unless cannot otherwise be carried on).

Pwllbach Colliery Company Limited, Woodman v (1914-15) 111 LTR 169 CA No common law right or easement pursuant to lease of colliery to create nuisance..

PYA Quarries, Ltd, Attorney-General (on the relation of Glamorgan County Council and Pontar- dawe Rural District Council) v [1957] 1 All ER 894; [1957] 2 QB 169; [1957] 2 WLR 770 CA Nuisance a public nuisance if affects class of people in vicinity thereof; on nuisance by vibration.

Pye Ltd v BG Transport Service Ltd (1965-66) 116 NLJ 1713 HC QBD Carriers liable in negligence for loss of goods being carried when they were left unattended.

Pygram v London & Home Counties Electricity Authority [1941] LJNCCR 318 CyCt Absent warning/contributory negligence on part of victim electricity contractors liable in negligence for injury to person whom ought reasonably to have foreseen might be injured by what were doing.

Pyman Steamship Co, Ltd v Hull and Barnsley Rail Co [1914-15] All ER 292; (1915) 112 LTR 1103; (1914-15) XXXI TLR 243 CA Effective exemption of liability clause.

Pyman Steamship Company v Hull and Barnsley Railway Company (1914-15) 111 LTR 41; (1913-14) XXX TLR 430 HC KBD Effective exemption of liability clause.

Quainoo v Brent and Harrow Area Health Authority (1982) 132 NLJ 1100 HC QBD On extent of damages recoverable in respect of funeral expenses following fatal accident.

Qualcast (Wolverhampton), Ltd v Haynes [1959] 2 All ER 38 HL In negligence trial by judge only reasoning of judge on what would otherwise be left to jury is not law: no precedent to be cited.

Quebec Railway, Light, Heat and Power Company, Limited v Vandry and others [1920] AC 662; [1920] 89 LJPC 99; (1920) 123 LTR 1; (1919-20) XXXVI TLR 296 PC Party liable in negligence where failed to establish that could not have prevented relevant damage.

Queen Anne's Gate Syndicate (No 2), Ltd, Litchfield-Speer and another v [1918-19] All ER 1075 HC ChD On restraint of anticipated nuisance.

Queens of the River Steamship Company v Conservators of the River Thames and Easton Gibb and Son (1905-06) XXII TLR 419 HC KBD Conservators of River Thames not liable in negligence where had taken reasonable care not to expose steamship to navigation danger.

Railway Executive and another, Law v (1949) LXV TLR 288 HC KBD Railway company/local authority liable in negligence for injury suffered by person colliding with wall and pavement the former had put in place of level crossing gates.

Railway Executive, Adams and another v (1952) 96 SJ 361 HC QBD Loss of consortium must be entire before can recover for same.

Railway Executive, Blackman v [1953] 1 All ER 4; (1953) 97 SJ 10 HC QBD No failure to keep station safe for passengers/licensees so no liability.

Railway Executive, Blackman v [1953] 2 All ER 323; (1954) 98 SJ 61; [1954] 1 WLR 220 CA On responsibility towards invitees.

Railway Executive, Bloomstein v [1952] 2 All ER 418; (1952) 102 LJ 455; (1952) 96 SJ 496; (1952) WN (I) 378 HC QBD British Transport Commission invitor even on properties run by Railway Executive and London Transport Executive; duty of care not obviated where maintenance of machine causing accident has been entrusted to manufacturers thereof.

Railway Executive, Edwards v [1952] 2 All ER 430; [1952] AC 737; (1952) 102 LJ 470; (1952) 96 SJ 493; [1952] 2 TLR 237; (1952) WN (I) 383 HL Railway Executive not liable for injuries suffered by boy trespassing on railway line.

Railway Executive, John Lee and Son (Grantham), Limited v (1949) LXV TLR 604 CA Warehouse tenancy agreement with railway company deemed not to preclude recovery in negligence — if there was negligence — for fire in warehouse allegedly started by spark from engine.

Railway Executive, Landau v (1949) 99 LJ 233 CyCt Defendant horse-owners liable in negligence for damage occasioned by runaway horse even though horse had never previously sought to run away.

Railway Executive, Lloyds Bank Ltd v (1952) 102 LJ 273; (1952) 96 SJ 313; [1952] 1 TLR 1207 CA Railway Executive liable in negligence for inadequate precautions at level crossing.

Railway Executive, Payne v [1952] 1 KB 26; (1951) 95 SJ 710; [1951] 2 TLR 929; (1951) WN (I) 547 CA Service pension not to be taken into account when assessing personal injury damages.

Railway Executive, Payne v (1951) 95 SJ 268; [1951] 1 TLR 921; (1951) WN (I) 240 HC KBD Service pension not to be taken into account when assessing personal injury damages.

Railway Executive, Stowell v [1949] 2 All ER 193; [1949] 2 KB 519; (1949) 99 LJ 356; [1949] 118 LJR 1482; (1949) LXV TLR 387; (1949) WN (I) 288 HC KBD Person meeting train passenger an invitee at railway station: oil on platform an unusual danger.

Railway Executive, Warren v (1950) 100 LJ 344; (1950) 94 SJ 457 HC KBD Rail company liable where invitee-passenger got into unlighted train waiting on platform and injured self while looking for seat.

Raine, Ellis and another v [1939] 108 LJCL 292; (1939) 161 LTR 234; (1939) 83 SJ 152; (1938-39) LV TLR 344 CA Re-trial ordered where despite direction from judge jury in action brought by parents of child killed through negligence awarded damages under Fatal Accidents Act 1846 but not under Law Reform (Miscellaneous Provisions) Act 1934.

Rainham Chemical Works, Limited (in liquidation), and others v Belvedere Fish Guano Company [1921] All ER 48; [1921] 2 AC 465; (1921) 56 LJ 314; [1921] LJCL 1252; (1922) 126 LTR 70; (1921-22) 66 SJ wr7; (1920-21) XXXVII TLR 973; (1921) WN (I) 281 HL Occupiers and tenants liable under Rylands v Fletcher for explosion occasioned by non-natural user of land.

Rainham Chemical Works, Limited, Feldman and Partridge, Belvedere Fish Guano Company, Limited v; Ind Coope and Company, Limited v Same (1920) 84 JP 185; [1920] 2 KB 487; (1920) 55 LJ 108; [1920] 89 LJCL 631; (1920) 123 LTR 211; (1919-20) XXXVI TLR 362; (1920) WN (I) 111 CA Manufacturers and directors of company personally liable for nuisance under Rylands v Fletcher rules.

Raintree Ltd v Holmes and Hills (1984) 134 NLJ 522 HC QBD Solicitor liable in negligence for failing to check expiry date of planning permission on land in respect of purchase of which they were advising client.

Raisbeck and RT and J Hewitt, Ltd, Maitland v [1944] LJNCCR 26 CyCt That rear light of lorry not on did not necessarily make lorry a nuisance.

Raisbeck, Maitland v [1944] 2 All ER 272; [1944] KB 689; (1945) 95 LJ 112; [1944] 113 LJ 549; (1944) 171 LTR 118; (1944) 88 SJ 359; (1943-44) LX TLR 521; (1944) WN (I) 195 CA That rear light of lorry not on did not necessarily make lorry a nuisance.

Ralph v London County Council (1947) 111 JP 246; (1947) 91 SJ 221; (1947) LXIII TLR 239 HC KBD Council liable in negligence for injury suffered by child in course of supervised game in assembly hall (council failed to take steps that reasonably cautious father would have taken).

Ralph v London County Council (1947) 111 JP 548; (1947) LXIII TLR 546 CA Council liable in negligence for injury suffered by child in course of supervised game in assembly hall (council failed to take steps that reasonably cautious father would have taken).

Ralph Wood and Co, Ltd, Joseph (D), Ltd v (1951) 95 SJ 319; (1951) WN (I) 225 HC KBD On appropriate damages where had been detinue.

Ralston v Ralston [1930] All ER 336; [1930] 2 KB 238; (1930) 69 LJ 168; (1930) 99 LJCL 266; (1930) 142 LTR 487 HC KBD Tombstone alleging another woman wife of defendant could be defamatory of actual wife — as did not affect wife in trade/business no action lay under Married Women's Property Act 1882, s 12.

Ramage and others, Tarrant v [1997] TLR 434 HC QBD Shipowners must take reasonable care of crew members on ship operating in war zone.

Rambarran v Gurrucharran [1970] 1 All ER 749; (1970) 120 NLJ 128t; [1970] RTR 195; (1970) 114 SJ 244; [1970] 1 WLR 556 PC Presumption that if using other's motor vehicle are their agent/servant is rebuttable.

Ramsbottom, Roberts and others v [1980] 1 All ER 7; [1980] RTR 261; (1980) 124 SJ 313; [1980] 1 WLR 823 HC QBD Absent automatism are liable for negligent acts.

Ramsden v Lee [1992] 2 All ER 204 CA Court should have regard to all circumstances before disapplying limitation period.

Ramsey Urban District Council, Bostock v (1899-1900) XVI TLR 18 HC QBD Not malicious prosecution to bring proceedings for obstruction of highway by employee against employer.

Ramwade Ltd v WJ Emson and Co Ltd [1987] RTR 72; (1970) 130 SJ 804 CA Brokers who were negligent in not insuring client's lorry liable in damages to latter to amount that insurance company would have paid out for event that transpired.

Ranaboldo, Hennell v [1963] 3 All ER 684 CA Judge only trials desirable in personal injury cases.

Rance and another v Mid-Downs Health Authority and another [1991] 1 All ER 801; (1990) 140 NLJ 325; [1991] 1 QB 587; [1990] TLR 113; [1991] 2 WLR 159 HC QBD Child 'capable of being born alive' where if born could live and breathe via its own lungs. Failure to advise about abortion of child 'capable of being born alive' not negligent as abortion would be unlawful.

Randall v Tarrant [1955] 1 All ER 600; (1955) 105 LJ 168; (1955) 99 SJ 184; [1955] 1 WLR 255 CA Driver of moving vehicle must show not negligent where strikes obvious non-moving vehicle; trespass by driver in field adjoining highway did not mean trespass/nuisance on highway.

Rands v McNeil (1954) 104 LJ 840; [1955] 1 QB 253; (1954) 98 SJ 851 CA No liability for injury to farm worker entering pen in which dangerous bull kept loose (had not escaped so no strict liability).

Rank, Leetham v (1912-13) 57 SJ 111 CA Must prove actual loss of customers to succeed in defamation action where allege that have suffered injury as result of malicious falsehoods that are not actionable of themselves.

Rankine v Garton Sons and Co Ltd [1979] 2 All ER 1185; (1979) 123 SJ 305 CA RSC Judgment available if admission of negligence and liability, not former alone.

Rantzen v Mirror Group Newspapers (1986) Ltd and others [1993] 4 All ER 975; (1993) 143 NLJ 507; [1994] QB 670; [1993] TLR 206; [1993] 3 WLR 953 CA Awards for defamation subject to rigorous scrutiny by Court of Appeal in interests of preserving freedom of publication.

Raphael Tuck and Sons, Limited, Preston v (1925-26) XLII TLR 440 HC ChD Failed action for passing off of drawings as those of plaintiff.

Rasdi (Yang Kamsiah Bte Meor) and another, Harun (Jamil Bin) v [1984] AC 529; (1984) 128 SJ 281; [1984] 2 WLR 668 PC Malaysian Federal Court could itemise rather than award general damages for child's permanent incapacitation on foot of accident.

Ratcliffe, JH Dewhurst, Ltd v (1951) 101 LJ 361 CyCt Failed application in nuisance against hedge owner by motorist who on brushing against hedge collided with tree stump hidden by hedge.

Ratcliffe, University of Essex v (1969) 119 NLJ 1118t CA University graduand who entered university premises could be dealt with as trespasser.

Rath and another v Lawrence (CS) and Partners (a firm) and others (PJ Crook and Co (a firm), third party) [1991] 3 All ER 679 CA Delay in issuing writ not inordinate delay but wilful delay following writ may be.

Raulin v Fischer (1911) WN (I) 41 HC KBD On enforceability of foreign tribunal's decision as regards negligence of party.

Raum v British Holiday Estates, Ltd (1952) 102 LJ 416 CyCt Hotel-owners liable for personal injuries sustained by patron upon collapse of garden chair on which victim seated.

Raven, Winkworth v [1931] All ER 847; (1931) 71 LJ 119; (1931) 100 LJCL 206; (1931) 144 LTR 594; (1931) 75 SJ 120; (1930-31) XLVII TLR 254; (1931) WN (I) 42 HC KBD Responsibilities of innkeeper to guest: no liability as no negligence shown.

Ravenscroft v Transatlantic (Rederiaktib'laget) [1992] 2 All ER 470; (1991) 141 NLJ 600; [1992] TLR 169 CA Damages for nervous shock of parent over child's death only if saw/heard event or aftermath.

Ravenscroft v Transatlantic (Rederiaktib'laget) [1991] TLR 190 HC QBD Damages for nervous shock of parent over child's death though did not see/hear event or aftermath.

Rawlins v Gillingham Corporation (1932) 96 JP 153; (1932) 146 LTR 486 HC KBD Negligence action failed where brought out of time under Public Authorities Protection Act 1893.

Rawlinson, Crossley v [1981] 3 All ER 674; (1981) 131 NLJ 1093; [1982] RTR 442; (1981) 125 SJ 865; [1982] 1 WLR 369 HC QBD Non-liability of driver of burning vehicle for injury suffered by AA man running towards vehicle.

Rawson v Clark (1981) 131 NLJ 1214c CA Non-liability of person for non-negligent behaviour which aggravated and accentuated existing injury that arose from negligence of another.

Rawtenstall Borough Council, Coates v [1937] 1 All ER 333 Assizes Ordinary duty of care owed to child licensee.

Rawtenstall Borough Council, Coates v (1937) 101 JP 483; (1937) 81 SJ 627 CA Local authority liable for injury to child licensee arising from negligent state in which playground maintained.

Razzel v Snowball [1954] 3 All ER 429; (1954) 104 LJ 760; (1954) 98 SJ 787; [1954] 1 WLR 1382 CA Surgeon performing operation did so in execution of National Health Service Act 1946 so covered by Limitation Act 1939, s 2(1).

RB Policies at Lloyd's v Butler [1949] 2 All ER 226; [1950] 1 KB 76; (1949) 99 LJ 373; (1949) LXV TLR 436; (1949) WN (I) 299 HC KBD Time for detinue action ran from date of theft though did not then know thief's identity.

RDC (Berkhamstead) v Duerdin-Dutton and another [1964] Crim LR 307t HC QBD Oral evidence unnecessary to prove facts accepted by defendant's solicitor.

Re a Company's application [1989] 3 WLR 265 HC ChD Failed action for injunction to restrain employee from disclosing confidential company information to statutory financial regulatory authority.

Re an Intended Action Biss v Lewisham Group Hospital Management Committee (1975) 125 NLJ 208t CA Extension of limitation period in negligence action allowed where requirements of Limitation Act 1963, s 7 met.

Re B Johnson and Co (Builders) Ld [1955] Ch 634 CA Companies Act 1948, s 333 did not extend to common law negligence.

Re Brazilian Rubber Plantations and Estates, Limited [1911] 1 Ch 425; (1911) 80 LJCh 221 HC ChD Director's acceptance of statements in report on which based prospectus not grossly negligent.

Re Charnley Davies Ltd [1990] TLR 481 HC ChD On duty of care owed by company administrator.

Receiver for the Metropolitan Police District and Carter Paterson and Company, Limited, Betts v (1932) 96 JP 327; [1932] 2 KB 595; (1932) 74 LJ 60; (1932) 101 LJCL 588; (1932) 147 LTR 336; (1932) 76 SJ 474; (1931-32) XLVIII TLR 517; (1932) WN (I) 15i HC KBD Public authority limitation precluded police authority liability for conversion/detinue of seized goods.

Receiver of the Metropolitan Police and another, McLeod v [1971] Crim LR 364 HC QBD Damages for collision arising out of negligent driving by police officer en route to emergency.

Reckitt and Colman Products Ltd v Borden Inc and others [1990] 1 All ER 873; (1990) 134 SJ 784; [1990] TLR 101; [1990] 1 WLR 491 HL Can be misrepresentation as to whole or part of product get-up; get-up may have secondary significance of indicating not only class of product but particular brand.

Reckitt and others, Midland Bank, Ltd v [1932] All ER 90; (1931-32) XLVIII TLR 271 HL Bank liable in negligence/conversion for cashing cheques signed by solicitor whom bank had notice was operating outside authority as agent.

Red Sea Insurance Co Ltd v Bouygues SA and others [1994] 3 All ER 749; [1994] TLR 414 PC Rule that tort in other jurisdiction must be actionable there and in England to be actionable not absolute rule — lex loci delicti may take precedence over lex fori.

Redfern and another, Walsh v [1970] RTR 201 HC QBD Person on main road to give way to person on minor road if necessary to avoid accident; lorry driver not contributorily negligent where was driving at reasonable speed on main road and collided with car emerging from minor road without paying heed to warning signs.

Redland Bricks Ltd, Morris and another v [1967] 1 WLR 967 CA On when injunction/damages appropriate remedy for nuisance.

Redpath Brown and Co Ltd (No 2), McLean v (1964) 108 SJ 239 HC QBD On undesirability of lengthy period between date of accident and date of trial.

Redpath Dorman Long Ltd, Waite v [1971] 1 All ER 513 HC QBD No interest on order made under RSC Ord 22, r 5.

Redpath Dorman Long Ltd, Welsh Development Agency v [1994] 4 All ER 10; (1994) 138 SJ LB 87; [1994] TLR 190; [1994] 1 WLR 1409 CA Leave to amend unavailable after time limit on claim expires even if application for leave made before expiry; leave to amend by adding new claim not to be given unless defendant has not reasonably arguable case on limitation.

Reece, Boaks v [1956] 2 All ER 750; [1956] Crim LR 563; (1956) 100 SJ 511; [1956] 1 WLR 886 HC QBD Was not wrongful imprisonment for magistrate to remand person in custody pending preparation of medical report prior to sentencing.

Reed Brothers (Engineers), Ltd, Moan v (1962) 106 SJ 283 CA Judgment set aside where was based on negligence that had not in fact been pleaded.

Reed, Billings v [1944] 2 All ER 415; [1945] KB 11; (1945) 95 LJ 111; (1944-45) LXI TLR 27 CA On Personal Injuries (Emergency Provisions) Act 1939 ('war injuries').

Reed, Rice v [1900] 69 LJCL 33; (1899-1900) LXXXI LTR 410; [1900] 1 QB 54 CA Did not waive right to bring action against second tortfeasor by settling action with first tortfeasor.

Rees (D) v West Glamorgan County Council (1993) 143 NLJ 814 CA Status of payment to Compensation Recovery Unit controverted.

Rees v Saville [1983] RTR 332; [1983] TLR 235 CA Seller of second-hand car liable for latent defect in car to buyer who relied on apparent good condition of car and recent MOT test as proof of roadworthiness.

Rees, Stuart v (1965) 109 SJ 358 HC QBD Immaterial why person driving at night did not see person with whom collided until was too late: was guilty of negligence.

Reeve v Sadler (1903) 67 JP 63; (1903) LXXXVIII LTR 95; (1902-03) 51 WR 603 HC KBD Subject of sanitary notice cannot recoup part of expenses of work done thereunder from adjoining owner subject to another sanitary notice.

Reeve, Bullock v (1901) 84 LTR 55; [1901] 70 LJK/QB 42; (1900-01) 49 WR 93 HC QBD House owner not liable to abate nuisance arising from defective drainage which by virtue of deviation from drainage plan sanctioned by Sewage Commissioners was a sewer, not a drain.

Rew, Jones v [1908-10] All ER 955; (1910) 74 JP 321 (also HC KBD); (1910) 79 LJKB 1030; (1910-11) 103 LTR 165 CA Urban sanitary authority liable in nuisance for state of carriage plate (not party who sometimes cleaned it out).

Rew, Jones v (1910) 74 JP 321 (also CA) HC KBD Party who sometimes cleaned out carriage plate, not sanitary authority, liable in nuisance for state of same.

Rew, Pinn v (1915-16) XXXII TLR 451 HC KBD Drover (whether or not independent contractor) and cattle purchaser liable for damage caused by cow which could reasonably have foreseen would be dangerous.

Rey and another, Lecouturier and others v; Lecouturier and others v Rey and others [1910] AC 262; (1910) 45 LJ 205; (1909-10) 54 SJ 375; (1909-10) XXVI TLR 368; (1910) WN (I) 79 HL Foreign manufacturer could succeed in passing off action where locus of passing off was England as had acquired reputation there.

Rey v Lecouturier [1908] 2 Ch 715; [1909] 78 LJCh 181; (1908) XCVIII LTR 197 CA Foreign manufacturer could succeed in passing off action where locus of passing off was England as had acquired reputation there.

Reynolds (John Joseph), Attorney-General of St Christopher Nevis and Anguilla v [1980] AC 637; [1980] 2 WLR 171 PC Exemplary damages for false imprisonment pursuant to emergency legislation was justified.

Reynolds v Boston Deep Sea Fishing and Ice Company, Limited (1921-22) XXXVIII TLR 22 HC KBD Exemption clause though did not specifically mention negligence did exclude liability for same.

Reynolds v Boston Deep Sea Fishing and Ice Company, Limited (1921-22) XXXVIII TLR 429 CA Exemption clause though did not specifically mention negligence did exclude liability for same.

Reynolds v British Leyland Ltd [1991] 1 WLR 675 CA Appeal dismissed for want of prosecution (and defendants had not behaved in such a way as to warrant continuance of action).

Reynolds v Commissioner of Police for the Metropolis [1982] Crim LR 600; [1982] TLR 274 CA £12,000 damages merited in serious case of wrongful arrest/false imprisonment.

Reynolds v Murphy (1965) 109 SJ 255 HC QBD On need for swift conclusion to personal injuries actions.

Reynolds v Shipping Federation, Ltd [1923] All ER 383; [1924] 1 Ch 28; (1923-24) 68 SJ 61 HC ChD Trade union/employer agreement that only trade union members be employed deemed not to be conspiracy/unlawful combination.

Reynolds v Thomas Tilling (Limited) (1902-03) XIX TLR 539 HC KBD Interpretation of findings of jury as to negligence/contributory negligence: non-recovery for personal injuries sustained through injury partly caused by own negligence.

Reynolds v Thomas Tilling (Limited) (1903-04) XX TLR 57 CA Approval of lower court's interpretation of findings of jury as to negligence/contributory negligence: non-recovery for personal injuries sustained through injury partly caused by own negligence.

RG O'Dell, Ltd and another (Galway Third Party), Harvey v [1958] 1 All ER 657; (1958) 108 LJ 266; [1958] 2 QB 78; (1958) 102 SJ 196 HC QBD Negligent master recovering all damages from joint tortfeasor servant.

RG Stanners Ltd v High Wycombe Borough Council and another (1968) 118 NLJ 614t; (1968) 112 SJ 766 HC QBD Both contractors and local authority for whom working liable for theft from warehouse effected via lean-to which council had been supposed to remove at which time warehouse was to be secured.

RH Willis and Son v British Car Auctions Ltd (1978) 128 NLJ 186t; [1978] RTR 244; [1978] 1 WLR 438 CA Auctioneers liable to car-dealers in conversion for selling hire-purchase car on behalf of hirer who had no title to sell.

RHM Outhwaite (Underwriting Agencies Ltd) and others, Sheldon and others v [1994] 4 All ER 481 (also HC QBD); [1996] 1 AC 102 (also HC QBD/HL); [1994] TLR 359; [1994] 3 WLR 999 CA Limitation period continues to run if concealment of facts post-dates cause of action.

RHM Outhwaite (Underwriting Agencies Ltd) and others, Sheldon and others v [1994] 4 All ER 481 (also CA); [1996] 1 AC 102 (also CA/HL); [1993] TLR 632; [1994] 1 WLR 754 HC QBD Limitation period continues to run if concealment of facts post-dates cause of action.

RHM Outhwaite (Underwriting Agencies) Ltd and others, Sheldon and others v [1995] 2 All ER 558; [1996] 1 AC 102 (also CA); (1995) 145 NLJ 687; (1995) 139 SJ LB 119; [1995] TLR 258; [1995] 2 WLR 570 HL Concealment of facts postpones time running until concealment was/should have been discovered.

Rhodes (Liverpool), Ltd and others, Anderson (WB) and Sons, Ltd and others v [1967] 2 All ER 850 Assizes Employer owes duty of care to persons acting on business representations of employees.

Rhymney and Aber Valleys Gas and Water Company, Gale and another v (1903) 67 JP 430 CA Water company guilty of trespass where unlawfully cut houseowners connection with water mains.

Rialas v Mitchell (1983) 133 NLJ 378; (1984) 128 SJ 704 HC QBD On appropriate damages for infant child rendered spastic quadriplegic in road traffic accident.

Rialas v Mitchell [1984] TLR 460 CA On appropriate damages for infant child rendered spastic quadriplegic in road traffic accident.

Ribbands and another, Everett v [1952] 1 All ER 823; (1952) 116 JP 221; [1952] 2 QB 198; (1952) 96 SJ 229; [1952] 1 TLR 933; (1952) WN (I) 166 CA Where case could have gone either way is not malicious prosecution.

Ribbands and another, Everett v [1951] 2 All ER 818; (1951) 115 JP 582; [1952] 1 KB 113; (1951) 101 LJ 609; (1951) 95 SJ 698; [1951] 2 TLR 829; (1951) WN (I) 554 HC KBD Cannot sue for false imprisonment after binding over order in respect of one.

Rice v Reed [1900] 69 LJCL 33; (1899-1900) LXXXI LTR 410; [1900] 1 QB 54 CA Did not waive right to bring action against second tortfeasor by settling action with first tortfeasor.

Rich and another v London County Council [1953] 2 All ER 376; (1953) 117 JP 353; (1953) 97 SJ 472; [1953] 1 WLR 895 CA School owes duty of responsible parent towards pupils.

Rich v Circuits Management Association, Ltd (1957) 107 LJ 556 CyCt Successful reliance on exemption from negligence clause by cloakroom operators with whom lost overcoat bailed.

Richard Costain Ltd, Woollerton and Wilson Ltd v [1970] 1 All ER 483; (1969) 119 NLJ 1093t; (1970) 114 SJ 170; [1970] 1 WLR 411 HC ChD Postponed injunction granted against party guilty of trespass when swang crane to and fro.

Richard Johnson and Nephew, Ltd, Latham v [1911-13] All ER 117; (1913) 77 JP 137; [1913] 1 KB 398; (1912) 47 LJ 748; [1913] 82 LJKB 258; (1913) 108 LTR 4; (1912-13) 57 SJ 127; (1912-13) XXIX TLR 124; (1912) WN (I) 290 CA Occupier of land on which stones owed no special duty of care to children playing thereon — implied term in licence that children to be accompanied by adults.

Richards and others, Pratt v [1951] 1 All ER 90 HC KBD Fatal accident damages for building site injury occasioned by negligence.

Richards v Highway Ironfounders (West Bromwich), Ltd [1955] 3 All ER 205; [1955] 1 WLR 1049 CA No damages for loss of chance to provide for dependants.

Richards v Naum (1970) 114 SJ 809 CA Libel action struck out for want of prosecution.

Richards v Naum [1966] 3 All ER 812; [1967] 1 QB 620; (1966) 110 SJ 794; [1966] 3 WLR 1113 CA Facts to be determined before preliminary point could be decided.

Richards, Behrens v [1905] 2 Ch 614; (1905) 69 JP 381; (1905-06) XCIII LTR 623; (1904-05) 49 SJ 685; (1905-06) 54 WR 141 HC ChD Nominal damages but no injunction in respect of trespass whereby owner not injured.

Richards, Brock v [1951] 1 KB 529; (1951) 95 SJ 75; [1951] 1 TLR 69; (1951) WN (I) 22 CA Not negligent to allow non-vicious horse which had tendency to wander but posed no particular threat to stray onto highway.

Richards, Walford and others v (1975) 125 NLJ 1023t CA Limitation period disapplied in light of plaintiff's unawareness of material fact of decisive nature.

Richardson and others, Smith v (1923) CC Rep XII 2 CyCt Agisters not liable for trespass of horses onto allotments where responsibility of maintaining fence at allotments fell on certain rail company.

Richardson and Wrench Ltd, Kooragang Investments Pty Ltd v [1981] 3 All ER 65; (1981) 125 SJ 641; [1981] 3 WLR 493 PC Master not vicariously liable for unauthorised negligent acts of servant.

Richardson v London County Council (1957) 107 LJ 328 CA Failed appeal against refusal of leave to bring action in which (inter alia) claimed that negligence of public authorities led to purportedly unlawful detention pursuant to the Mental Deficiency Act 1913.

Richardson v West Lindsey District Council and others [1990] 1 All ER 296; (1989) 139 NLJ 1263; [1990] 1 WLR 522 CA Local authority does not normally owe duty of care to see that building project complies with building regulations.

Richardson's (a firm), Boynton v (1924) WN (I) 262 HC KBD No action in negligence to lie against arbitrator or quasi-arbitrator.

Richardson, Theaker v [1962] 1 All ER 229; (1962) 112 LJ 136; (1962) 106 SJ 151 CA Could be anticipated/natural and probable result of writing letter to person that would be opened by spouse.

Richardson, Woodman v (1937) 84 LJ 144; (1937) 81 SJ 70 CA Non-liability of invitor towards invitee for not reasonably foreseeable course of events (not instigated by invitor's employees) that resulted in injury to invitee.

Richcliff (Group) Ltd and others, Gran Gelato Ltd v [1992] 1 All ER 865; [1992] Ch 560; (1992) 142 NLJ 51; [1992] 2 WLR 867 HC ChD Normally conveyancing solicitor for seller does not owe duty to buyer because action already lies against seller; in concurrent claims for negligence/misrepresentation contributory negligence can apply to both claims.

Riches and others v News Group Newspapers Ltd [1985] 2 All ER 845; (1985) 135 NLJ 391; [1986] QB 256; (1985) 129 SJ 401; [1985] 3 WLR 432 CA Exemplary damages to be shared among joint plaintiffs rather than separately awarded to each plaintiff.

Riches v Director of Public Prosecutions [1973] 2 All ER 935; (1973) 117 SJ 585 CA No presumption that prosecutions initiated by DPP not malicious; court may strike action of defendant who will seek but not succeed in having limitation period disapplied.

Richley v Faull (Richley, Third Party) [1965] 3 All ER 109; (1965) 129 JP 498; (1965) 115 LJ 609; (1965) 109 SJ 937; [1965] 1 WLR 1454 HC QBD Severe unexcused skid is per se evidence of negligence.

Rickards v Bartram and others (1908-09) XXV TLR 181 HC KBD Trade union could be sued for alleged libel in its newsletter where was no ongoing/pending trade dispute when published.

Rickards v Lothian [1911-13] All ER 71; [1913] AC 263; (1913) 82 LJPC 42; (1912-13) XXIX TLR 281; (1913) 108 LTR 225 PC Not liable in negligence/nuisance for damage resulting from third party malicious act in relation to reasonable user.

Rickett, Cockerell and Co Limited, and another, Daniel v [1938] 2 All ER 631; [1938] 2 KB 322; (1938) 85 LJ 380; [1938] 107 LJCL 589; (1938) 82 SJ 353; (1937-38) LIV TLR 756; (1938) WN (I) 190 HC KBD Absent adequate warning to passers-by coal deliverer and householder were jointly liable for injury suffered by person falling as result of coal cellar access to pavement being open.

Ricketts v Erith Borough Council and another [1943] 2 All ER 629; (1944) 108 JP 22; (1944) 94 LJ 108; [1944] 113 LJ 269; (1943) 169 LTR 396 HC KBD Bow and arrow not dangerous thing so no duty on seller; absence of teacher from school playground during breaktime not negligent.

Riddell, Corporation of Glasgow v (1911) 104 LTR 354 HL Corporation not liable for slander made by tax collector acting outside scope of his employment.

Riddiford v R [1905] AC 147 PC Lands surrendered to Crown subject to existing contracts did not include conveyance to appellant who was consequently trespasser.

Riden v Billings (AC) and Sons, Ltd and others [1956] 3 All ER 357; [1957] 1 QB 46; (1956) 100 SJ 748; [1956] 3 WLR 704 CA Damages for negligence as (non-occupying) contractors creating danger owed duty of care to prevent injury.

Riden, Billings (AC) and Sons, Ltd v [1957] 3 All ER 1; [1958] AC 240; (1957) 107 LJ 521; (1957) 101 SJ 645 HL Contractors could not rely on occupier's liability (as occupier) to licensee to preclude their own liability.

Rider and another, Rider v [1973] RTR 178 CA On standard of care required of highway authority.

Rider v Metropolitan Water Board (1949) 113 JP 377 HC KBD Failed action against Water Board for personal injury sustained on foot of alterations it effected.

Rider v Rider and another [1973] RTR 178 CA On standard of care required of highway authority.

Ridge v The 'English Illustrated' Magazine (Limited) (1912-13) XXIX TLR 592 HC KBD Publishers liable (on foot of publishing story falsely ascribed to plaintiff author) in libel if perception of plaintiff would be that of ordinary pen-pusher/in passing off if facts proved and damage inevitable result.

Ridgway v Hutchinson (1923) 58 LJ 296 HC ChD Failed passing-off action by proprietors of 'Adventure' magazine against the proprietors of 'Hutchinson's Adventure-Story Magazine'.

Ridley and another, Robertson v [1989] 2 All ER 474; (1989) 133 SJ 1170; [1989] 1 WLR 872 CA That certain members responsible for conduct of club does not mean responsible for condition of premises.

Rigby and another v Chief Constable of Northamptonshire [1985] 2 All ER 985; (1985) 129 SJ 832; [1985] 1 WLR 1242 HC QBD Bona fide policy decision unimpeachable; necessity a defence to trespass if defendant's negligence did not give rise to necessity; negligent to fire CS canister when no fire equipment.

Righton, Hadwell v (1907) 71 JP 499; [1907] 2 KB 345; [1907] 76 LJKB 891; (1906-07) XXIII TLR 548 HC KBD Owner of fowl not liable for injury caused by same while trespassing on highway footpath as was too remote.

Riley v Mayor, Aldermen, and Burgesses of Halifax (1907) 71 JP 428; (1907-08) XCVII LTR 278; (1906-07) XXIII TLR 613 HC ChD Damages for trespass rather than injunction to stop same merited in the circumstances.

Rimmer v Liverpool City Council [1984] 1 All ER 930; [1985] QB 1; (1984) 128 SJ 225; [1983] TLR 762; [1984] 2 WLR 426 CA Landlord who is builder/designer owes duty of care to all affected by build/design of premises.

Rimmer, Blundell v (1970) 120 NLJ 1138; (1971) 115 SJ 15 HC QBD On payment of interest on damages payable into court.

Ripley v Arthur and Co (1902) LXXXVI LTR 495; (1900-01) 45 SJ 165 HC ChD Where as result of judgment by default defendants were estopped from denying alleged passing off attachment would not issue.

Ripley v Arthur and Co (1902) LXXXVI LTR 735 CA Where as result of judgment by default defendants were estopped from denying alleged passing off attachment would not issue.

Rippon v Port of London Authority and J Russell and Co (Port of London Authority, Third Party) [1940] 1 All ER 637 HC KBD Port authority (occupiers) and ship-repairers (notional occupiers) liable for workman's injury.

Rivers v Cutting [1982] 3 All ER 69; [1982] Crim LR 525; [1983] RTR 105; (1982) 126 SJ 362; [1982] TLR 213; [1982] 1 WLR 1146 CA Police not vicariously liable for acts of contractor employed to remove broken-down/abandoned vehicle.

Riverstone Meat Co Pty Ltd v Lancashire Shipping Co Ltd [1960] 1 QB 536; (1960) 104 SJ 50 CA Liability of shipowners for negligence of workman employed by competent repairer obtained by carrier.

Riverstone Meat Co Pty Ltd v Lancashire Shipping Co Ltd (1958) 102 SJ 656 HC QBD Non-liability of shipowners for negligence of workman employed by competent repairer obtained by carrier.

Riverstone Meat Co Pty, Ltd v Lancashire Shipping Co, Ltd (1961) 105 SJ 148 HL Non-liability of shipowners for negligence of workman employed by competent repairer obtained by carrier.

Rivlin v Bilainkin [1953] 1 All ER 534; [1953] 1 QB 485; (1953) 97 SJ 97 HC QBD Publication of document to Member of Parliament not privileged if unconnected with Parliamentary proceedings.

Rix, Chapman v (1959) 103 SJ 940 CA Doctor dealing with crisis situation not negligent in not consulting patient's own doctor.

Rix, Cross v (1912) CC Rep I 97 HC KBD New trial necessary where person non-suited (in light of provisions of Public Authorities Protection Act) without person consenting to same/having evidence heard.

RL Holdings Ltd v Robert J Wood and Partners (1978) 128 NLJ 978t HC QBD Architect liable in negligence for failing to advise client that planning permission might be legally defective and hence ineffective.

Roach v Yates [1938] 1 KB 256; [1938] 107 LJCL 170; (1937) 81 SJ 610 CA On assessment of personal injury damages for person rendered unable to look after self.

Road Haulage Executive, Harvey v [1952] 1 KB 120; (1951) 101 LJ 651; (1951) 95 SJ 759; (1951) WN (I) 588 CA Obsolesence of 'last opportunity' doctrine; non-severabilty of negligent/ contributorily negligent acts.

Robert Addie and Sons (Collieries), Limited v Dumbreck [1929] AC 358; (1929) 140 LTR 650; (1928-29) XLV TLR 267 HL Non-liability towards child killed by dangerous machine while trespassing.

Robert J Wood and another, BL Holdings Ltd v (1979) 123 SJ 570 CA Architect not negligent as regards advice gave to clients concerning planning permission application/process.

Robert J Wood and another, BL Holdings Ltd v (1978) 122 SJ 525 HC QBD Architect negligent as regards advice gave to clients concerning planning permission application/process.

Robert J Wood and Partners, RL Holdings Ltd v (1978) 128 NLJ 978t HC QBD Architect liable in negligence for failing to advise client that planning permission might be legally defective and hence ineffective.

Roberts and another v J Hampson and Co [1989] 2 All ER 504; (1988) 138 NLJ 166; (1989) 133 SJ 1234; [1990] 1 WLR 94 HC QBD Building society surveyor liable in damages to purchaser of house for negligent survey of same.

Roberts and others v Ramsbottom [1980] 1 All ER 7; [1980] RTR 261; (1980) 124 SJ 313; [1980] 1 WLR 823 HC QBD Absent automatism are liable for negligent acts.

Roberts and others, Dumbell v [1944] 1 All ER 326; (1944) 108 JP 139; (1945) 95 LJ 112; [1944] 113 LJ 185; (1944) 170 LTR 227; (1943-44) LX TLR 231 CA On special powers of arrest.

Roberts v Charing Cross, Euston and Hampstead Rail Co [1900-03] All ER 157 HC ChD Negligence action well-founded despite availability of statutory compensation in respect of cause of action.

Roberts v J and F Stone Lighting and Radio, Limited and another (1946) 96 LJ 42; (1945) 172 LTR 240; (1944-45) LXI TLR 338 HC KBD On recovery for personal injuries of difference between amount of settlement in first action and total amount claim would have been awarded in personal injuries action had subpoenaed witness (defendant in second action) given evidence in court.

Roberts v Johnstone and another [1989] QB 878; (1988) 132 SJ 1672; [1988] 3 WLR 1247 CA On personal injury damages for nursing care/new accommodation requirements.

Roberts v JW Ward and Son (1982) 126 SJ 120 CA Solicitors liable for negligent failure not to serve notice to exercise option agreement on company/not stating option purchase price.

Roberts v Naylor Brothers, Ltd [1959] 2 All ER 409; (1959) 103 SJ 491 HC QBD Disablement gratuity deductible from loss of earnings.

Roberts, Barclays Bank, Ltd v (1954) 104 LJ 617 CA Failed action in trespass following on improper execution of writ of possession.

Roberts, St Anne's Well Brewery Co v [1928] All ER 28; (1928) 92 JP 180; (1929) 140 LTR 1 CA No recovery for nuisance when retaining wall (normal use) collapsed without owner knowing of any defect.

Roberts, St Anne's Well Brewery Company v (1928) 92 JP 95 HC KBD Recovery of damages when retaining wall (normal user) collapsed without defective state being known.

Robertson and another, Kaye v [1990] TLR 232 CA Is no right to privacy.

Robertson v Ridley and another [1989] 2 All ER 474; (1989) 133 SJ 1170; [1989] 1 WLR 872 CA That certain members responsible for conduct of club does not mean responsible for condition of premises.

Robertson v The Balmain New Ferry Company (Limited) (1909-10) XXVI TLR 143 PC Use of reasonable force to impede person trying to leave wharf without making required payment was not assault.

Robertson v Turnbull (1981) 131 NLJ 1211 HL Refusal of damages (expenses/solatium) to husband whose wife suffered non-fatal injury in road accident.

Robertson, Fettes v (1920-21) XXXVII TLR 581 CA Statute of Limitations successfully pleaded where written promise to pay had not been unqualified.

Robertson, Glover v (1911-13) XXII Cox CC 692; (1912) 76 JP 135 HC KBD Non-liability for importation of sheep to England from Middle East via Marseilles.

Robinson (Archibald Nugent) v Balmain New Ferry Company, Limited [1910] AC 295; [1910] 79 LJPC 84 PC No false imprisonment where were merely using reasonable tactic to preempt forcible avoidance of payment for exit from wharf.

Robinson (Arthur), Grand Trunk Railway Company of Canada v [1915] AC 740; [1915] 84 LJPC 194; (1915-16) 113 LTR 350; (1914-15) XXXI TLR 395; (1915) WN (I) 173 PC Valid exemption clause in half-fare travel contract.

Robinson and another v Urban District Council of Beaconsfield (1911) 75 JP 353 (also CA); (1911) 80 LJCh 647 (also CA); (1910-11) XXVII TLR 319 HC ChD Local authority liable in nuisance for defective manner of sewage disposal by contractor.

Robinson and others v Unicos Property Corporation, Ltd [1962] 2 All ER 24 CA Limitation applied despite amendment to claim as was still same action.

Robinson Rentals, Ltd, Bradford v [1967] 1 All ER 267; (1967) 111 SJ 33; [1967] 1 WLR 337 Assizes Recovery where chance of injury reasonably foreseeable but particular injury not so.

Robinson v Beaconsfield Urban District Council [1911-13] All ER 997; [1911] 2 Ch 188; (1911) 75 JP 353 (also HC ChD); (1911) 80 LJCh 647 (also HC ChD); (1911-12) 105 LTR 121; (1910-11) XXVII TLR 478 CA Local authority liable in nuisance for manner of sewage disposal by contractor with whom had not contracted for disposal.

Robinson v London General Omnibus Company (Limited) (1910) 74 JP 161; (1909-10) XXVI TLR 233 HC ChD Over-use of streets for maintenance/repair/turning of buses was nuisance.

Robinson v Post Office and another (1973) 117 SJ 915 CA On appropriate personal injuries damages from employer (doctor not negligent) to worker who contracted encephalitis on foot of anti-tetanus injection.

Robinson v State of South Australia (1931) 72 LJ 24; (1929) 98 LJPC 136; (1929) 141 LTR 70 PC On liability in negligence of Government of South Australia when performing its duties under the Wheat Harvest Acts 1915-17.

Robinson v The Post Office and another [1974] 2 All ER 737; (1973) 123 NLJ 1017t; [1974] 1 WLR 1176 CA Negligent doctor's act not causing/materially contributing to existing injury not novus actus interveniens.

Robinson v Ward (1958) 108 LJ 491 HC QBD On elements of slander of office of honour.

Robinson v WH Smith and Son (1900-01) XVII TLR 235 HC KBD Dangerous employment (newspaper boys at railway station having to cross lines) put special duty of care on employers which may not have discharged.

Robinson v WH Smith and Son (1900-01) XVII TLR 423 CA Dangerous employment (newspaper boys at railway station having to cross lines) put special duty of care on employers which may not have discharged.

Robinson v Whittle [1980] 3 All ER 459; (1980) 124 SJ 807; [1980] 1 WLR 1476 HC QBD Faulty application within 21 days to state case may be amended anytime before High Court hearing; could not plead defence in respect of killing birds under Protection of Birds Act 1954, s 4(2) (a) where charged with laying poison to kill birds.

Robinson, Dribbell and another v (1949) 99 LJ 233 CyCt Landlord liable for injury suffered by child when facia board which landlord knew to be in disrepair but had not repaired collapsed onto highway.

Robinson, Elstob v [1964] 1 All ER 848; (1964) 114 LJ 358; (1964) 108 SJ 543; [1964] 1 WLR 726 HC QBD Personal injury damages not to be reduced in light of service disability pension.

Robson and another v Hallett [1967] 2 All ER 407; (1967) 51 Cr App R 307; (1967) 131 JP 333; [1967] 2 QB 939; (1967) 111 SJ 254; [1967] 3 WLR 28 HC QBD Police have implied licence to enter garden in course of duty; once licence revoked by owner have reasonable time to go before become trespasser; if breach of peace in garden police can enter to stop it.

Robson and others, Paul and another v [1914] 83 LJPC 304; (1914-15) 111 LTR 481 PC In action for interference with light and air acts complained of must be nuisance to be successful.

Robson Books Ltd, Mothercare Ltd v (1979) 129 (1) NLJ 317 HC ChD Injunction granted to Mothercare Ltd to restrain Robson Books from publishing book entitled 'Mother Care' (or other similarly deceptive name).

Rochester Corporation, Phipps v [1955] 1 All ER 129; (1955) 119 JP 92; (1955) 105 LJ 41; [1955] 1 QB 450; (1955) 99 SJ 45; [1955] 2 WLR 23 HC QBD Occupier not liable in negligence to child as unaccompanied by parent so trespasser/or though child licensee was unreasonable for child to be there unaccompanied.

Rochford Rural District Council, Nash v [1916-17] All ER 299; (1917) 81 JP 57; [1917] 86 LJCL 370; (1917) 116 LTR 129 CA Succeeding highway authority not liable for negligence of preceding highway authority.

Rochford v Essex County Council [1916] 85 LJP 281 HC PDAD Raising of footpath so that covered part of previously existing fence was trespass.

Rochman v J and E Hall, Ltd, and another [1947] 1 All ER 895 HC KBD Licensor not responsible for every danger arising from acts of unauthorised persons.

Rock v Smith's, Ltd [1936] LJNCCR 31 CyCt Sellers of piano stool deemed not to be liable for personal injuries suffered as result of latent defect in stool.

Roderick and others, Dwyer v [1983] TLR 668 CA On burden of proof as regards proving proving professional persons negligent; on need for greater speed in professional negligence actions.

Rodriguez v Parker (RJ) (Male) [1966] 3 WLR 546 HC QBD On giving leave for post-limitation period amendment of writs.

Rodriguez v Rodriguez (1989) 133 SJ 1134 CA Work incapacity benefits not deductible from benefits.

Rodriguez, International Factors Ltd v [1979] QB 351; [1978] 3 WLR 877 CA Recovery in conversion by factoring firm of amounts (originally) owed and paid to bank account of company from whom factoring firm had purchased the debts.

Roe v Minister of Health and others; Woolley v Same [1954] 2 QB 66; (1954) 98 SJ 30; [1954] 1 WLR 128 HC QBD Hospital not liable for negligence of anaesthesist.

Roe v Ministry of Health and others; Woolley v Same [1954] 2 All ER 131; (1954) 104 LJ 313; [1954] 2 QB 66; (1954) 98 SJ 319; [1954] 2 WLR 915 CA Hospital liable for negligence of anaesthesist — no negligence here as standard of care was that to be expected of reasonably competent anaesthesist.

Roe, Attorney-General (at the relation of Knottingley Urban District Council) and Knottingley Urban District Council v (1915) 79 JP 263; (1915) 112 LTR 581 HC ChD Owner of disused quarry ordered to abate nuisance created on adjacent highway through subsidence consequent upon onetime quarrying.

Roe, Attorney-General v [1914-15] All ER 1190; [1915] 1 Ch 235; [1915] 84 LJCh 322 HC ChD Party liable to fence off from highway adjoining area in which dangerous excavation work being undertaken.

Roebuck v Mungovin [1994] 2 AC 224; (1994) 138 SJ LB 59; [1994] 2 WLR 290 HL Appropriate that personal injuries claim be struck out where plaintiff guilty of great delay even though defendant's behaviour not entirely blameless.

Roff v British and French Chemical Manufacturing Company and Gibson [1918] 2 KB 677; (1918) 53 LJ 272; [1918] 87 LJCL 996; (1918-19) 119 LTR 436; (1917-18) 62 SJ 620; (1917-18) XXXIV TLR 485 CA Privileged communication did not lose privilege through communication to clerks.

Rogers (Mollie) v Kaus (Otto) (1976) 126 NLJ 544t CA Escape of grime/oil from cars not covered by Rylands v Fletcher but was negligent to allow escaped material to heap up.

Rogers v Exeter and Mid-Devon Hospitals Management Committee (1974) 124 NLJ 1186t; (1975) 119 SJ 86 HC QBD Child taken from mother and placed in cot in another room (where suffered negligently caused injuries) remained in custody of mother.

Rogers v Night Riders (a firm) and others [1983] RTR 324 CA Mini-cab firm liable for negligent maintenance of car by driver (whether latter an employee/independent contractor).

Rogers v Tarratt (1931) 72 LJ ccr43 CyCt Person failing to establish title to near-abandoned property that adjoined own held to have trespassed on near-abandoned property.

Rogers, Hart and another v (1916) 114 LTR 329 HC KBD Landlord of house let in flats owed duty to keep roof in good repair.

Rogers, Maynard and another v [1970] RTR 392 HC QBD Person stepping on to uncontrolled pedestrian crossing without looking in either direction was contributorily negligent but driver also negligent in not yielding to person on uncontrolled pedestrian crossing.

Roles v Nathan and others; Roles v Corney and others [1963] 2 All ER 908; (1963) 113 LJ 496; (1963) 107 SJ 680; [1963] 1 WLR 1117 CA Occupier not liable for death of chimney sweeps whom had warned of special risks.

Rolls Royce, Ltd, Brown v [1960] 1 All ER 577; (1960) 110 LJ 220 HL Burden of proof on person claiming negligence applies to entirety of evidence, not the various elements thereof.

Romford Football Club Ltd and others, Stretch v (1971) 115 SJ 741 HC ChD Injunction granted to restrain speedway racing near residential area as was a nuisance.

Romford Ice and Cold Storage Co Ld v Lister [1955] 3 All ER 460; [1955] 3 WLR 631 CA Damages available to master for servant's failure in duty of care unaffected by being vicariously liable joint tortfeasor.

Romford Ice and Cold Storage Co, Ltd, Lister v [1957] 1 All ER 125; (1957) 121 JP 98 HL Master could recover damages (including costs of action) paid by them on foot of servant's negligence.

Ronald, Lewis v [1908-10] All ER 782; (1909-10) 101 LTR 534; (1909-10) XXVI TLR 30 HC KBD Landlord not liable for injuries suffered by person visiting premises in area which landlord had contracted to light for tenants but had not done so.

Rondel v Worsley [1967] 3 All ER 993; [1969] 1 AC 191; (1967) 111 SJ 927; [1967] 3 WLR 1666 HL Counsel immune from negligence action for all work in conduct of/pending litigation; solicitor immune for advocacy work/in settling case.

Rondel v Worsley [1966] 3 All ER 657; [1967] 1 QB 443 (also HC QBD); (1966) 110 SJ 810; [1966] 3 WLR 950 CA Solicitor acting as advocate can be sued for negligence; barrister cannot be sued for acts done pending/in course of litigation.

Rondel v Worsley [1966] 1 All ER 467; (1965-66) 116 NLJ 501; [1966] 2 WLR 300 HC QBD Counsel not liable in negligence for acts of advocacy.

Ronex Properties Ltd v John Laing Construction Ltd and others (Clarke, Nicholls and Marcel (a firm), third parties) [1982] 3 All ER 961; [1983] QB 398; (1982) 126 SJ 727; [1982] 3 WLR 875 CA Possible limitation defence not good cause for striking out claim; claim against joint tortfeasor for contribution not extinguished in death as not in tort but a right sui generis.

Rook v Fairrie [1941] 1 All ER 297; [1941] 1 KB 507; (1942) 92 LJ 61; [1941] 110 LJ 319; (1941) 165 LTR 23; (1941) 85 SJ 297; (1940-41) LVII TLR 297; (1941) WN (I) 37 CA Judge (unlike jury) can condemn otherwise than by heavy damages.

Rookes v Barnard and others [1961] 2 All ER 825; [1963] 1 QB 623 (also CA) HC QBD Injury arising through threat to break contract with third person intimidation (if acted alone; otherwise conspiracy) — no protection under Trade Disputes Act 1906, ss 1 and 3.

Rookes v Barnard and others [1962] 2 All ER 579; [1963] 1 QB 623 (also HC QBD) CA Is a tort of intimidation but mere threat to break contract not intimidation: must be fraud/threats/violence.

Rookes v Barnard and Others [1964] 1 All ER 367; [1964] AC 1129; [1964] 2 WLR 269 HL Is a tort of intimidation which embraces threatening breach of contract: on exemplary damages for intimidation.

Rose v Buckett [1901] 2 KB 449; [1901] 70 LJK/QB 736; (1901) LXXXIV LTR 670; (1900-01) XVII TLR 544; (1901-02) 50 WR 8 CA Right of action for trespass/conversion did not pass to trustee upon plaintiff becoming bankrupt.

Rose v Coventry (1965) 109 SJ 256 CA On appropriate personal injury damages where victim had toes amputated/leg length reduced/was less mobile than previously.

Rose v Ford [1937] AC 826; (1937) 84 LJ 29; [1937] 106 LJCL 576; (1937) 157 LTR 174; (1936-37) LIII TLR 873; (1937) WN (I) 275 HL Deceased's personal representative could claim damages for loss of life expectancy.

Rose v Ford [1936] 1 KB 90; (1935) 80 LJ 273; [1936] 105 LJCL 21; (1936) 154 LTR 77; (1935) 79 SJ 816; (1935-36) LII TLR 7; (1935) WN (I) 168 CA On availability of personal injury damages to deceased victim's personal representative (claiming on behalf of deceased's estate).

Rose v George Hurry Collier, Ltd (1939) WN (I) 19 CA Failed appeal by owners of vicious mare for injuries occasioned by same while left unattended.

Rose, Bowker v (1978) 122 SJ 147 CA State mobility/attendance allowances not deductible from personal injury damages.

Rose, Bowker v (1977) 121 SJ 274 HC QBD State mobility/attendance allowances not deductible from personal injury damages.

Rosen, Malz v [1966] 2 All ER 10; (1965-66) 116 NLJ 753; (1966) 110 SJ 332; [1966] 1 WLR 1008 HC QBD Not malicious prosecution if acting on advice of responsible police officer.

Rosenbaum v The Metropolitan Water Board (1910) 74 JP 378; (1909-10) XXVI TLR 510 HC KBD Water board liable in negligence for injury caused to footpath user by way of inadequately maintained stopcock box.

Rosenbaum v The Metropolitan Water Board (1911) 75 JP 12; (1910-11) XXVII TLR 103 CA Retrial ordered as to whether water board liable in negligence for injury caused to footpath user by way of inadequately maintained stopcock box.

Rosenthal v Alderton and Sons, Ltd [1946] 1 All ER 583; [1946] KB 374; [1946] 115 LJ 215; (1946) 174 LTR 214; (1946) 90 SJ 163; (1945-46) LXII TLR 236; (1946) WN (I) 55 CA Value of goods determined at date of decision.

Ross v Caunters (a firm) [1979] 3 All ER 580; [1980] Ch 297; (1979) 129 (2) NLJ 880; (1979) 123 SJ 605; [1979] 3 WLR 605 HC ChD Solicitor drafting will owes duty of care to beneficiary; beneficiary can recover economic loss.

Ross v English Steel Corporation Limited (1945) 173 LTR 138 HC KBD Preferral of information inside six months of accident was valid.

Ross v London County, Westminster and Parr's Bank (Lim) (1918-19) 63 SJ 411; (1919) WN (I) 87 HC KBD Bank negligent in accepting (stolen) cheques and paying them into account.

Rost v Edwards and others [1990] 2 All ER 641; [1990] 2 QB 460; [1990] TLR 120; [1990] 2 WLR 1280 HC QBD Reasons for selection/de-selection from Parliamentary committee/ member's letter to Speaker privileged; register of Member's Interests not privileged.

Rotax Aircraft Equipment Ltd, Clarke v [1975] 3 All ER 794; [1975] 1 WLR 1570 CA No interest on damages for loss of earning capacity.

Rother District Council, Fellowes v [1983] 1 All ER 513 HC QBD Grounds on which public body liable in negligence for acts ostensibly done pursuant to statutory authority.

Rothermere and others v Times Newspapers Ltd and others [1973] 1 All ER 1013; (1973) 123 NLJ 250t; (1973) 117 SJ 266; [1973] 1 WLR 448 CA Prolonged examination of documents (not complexity/length of trial) can justify no jury but need not.

Rothwell v Davies Brothers (Haulage), Ltd and another [1963] Crim LR 577; (1963) 107 SJ 436 CA Heavy goods vehicle driver 25% liable/car driver 75% liable for collision which occurred where latter distracted former while driving.

Round Oak Steel Works Ltd, Pearce v [1969] 3 All ER 680; [1969] 1 WLR 595 CA Must show not negligent in acquiring/discovering defect in second hand purchase for res ipsa loquitur not to apply.

Rourke v Barton and others [1982] TLR 330 HC QBD Amount included in personal injury damages for fact that injured party was unable to aid terminally ill husband.

Rouse v Gravelworks, Ltd [1940] 109 LJCL 408; (1940) 84 SJ 112; (1940) WN (I) 12 CA Failed trespass action trespass where water blown from pond formed after natural user (quarrying) caused erosion to neighbour's land.

Rouse v Squires and others [1973] 2 All ER 903; [1973] QB 889; [1973] RTR 550; (1973) 117 SJ 431; [1973] 2 WLR 925 CA Negligent obstruction of highway contributorily negligent to later negligent collision therewith.

Rover Co, Ltd and others (Richard W Carr and Co, Ltd, Third Party), Taylor v [1966] 2 All ER 181; (1965-66) 116 NLJ 809; [1966] 1 WLR 1491 Assizes Manufacturer not liable where employer keeps defective tool (in production of which manufacturer took all reasonable steps) in use when knows it to be dangerous.

Rowden v Clarke Chapman and Co, Ltd [1967] 3 All ER 608 HC QBD On personal injury damages (loss of fingers/earnings).

Rowe v Herman and others [1997] TLR 298 CA Occupier not liable in negligence for hazard created by independent contractor who had been working for occupier and since finished and left.

Rowe, Truro Corporation v [1902] 71 LJCL 974 CA Successful claim by corporation against oyster fisherman who trespassed upon foreshore in course of trade.

Rowlands and another, Tarrant v [1979] RTR 144 HC QBD Inadequate drainage by highway authority of area where water habitually collected after rain meant authority liable for accident occasioned thereby; person causing collision by driving so fast that fails to observe pool of water and drives into same losing control of car is negligent.

Rowlands, Glazier v [1940] LJNCCR 274 CyCt Failed action in negligence against owner of horse which strayed by way of broken fence onto highway and there occasioned damage by behaving in uncustomarily wild manner.

Rowlands, Kynoch Limited v [1911-13] All ER 1258; [1912] 1 Ch 527 (also HC ChD); (1912) 81 LJCh 340 (also HC ChD); (1912) 106 LTR 316 CA Trespass found where was inadequate evidence of discontinuance of possession.

Rowlands, Kynoch, Limited v [1912] 1 Ch 527 (also CA); [1912] 81 LJCh 340 (also CA); (1910-11) 55 SJ 617 HC ChD Trespass found where was inadequate evidence of discontinuance of possession.

Rowley Regis Corporation, Bowater v (1944) 108 JP 163; (1944) WN (I) 105 CA On rarity of application of volenti non fit injuria between master and servant (here not applied).

Rowling and another v Takaro Properties Ltd [1988] 1 All ER 163; [1988] AC 473; (1988) 132 SJ 126; [1988] 2 WLR 418 PC Minister exercising statutory duty not liable for negligence despite judicial review finding that he considered irrelevant material as opinion was still reasonable.

Roxhan and others, Levene v [1970] 3 All ER 683; (1970) 120 NLJ 662t; (1970) 114 SJ 721; [1970] 1 WLR 1322 CA Separating of non-/defamatory elements of article possible but inappropriate; striking-out of claim.

Roy, The Canadian Pacific Railway Company v [1902] 71 LJPC 51; (1901-02) XVIII TLR 200; (1901-02) 50 WR 415 PC Statutorily authorised rail company not liable absent negligence for damage caused by locomotive sparks.

Royal Air Force Association and others, Kitchen v [1958] 2 All ER 241; (1958) 108 LJ 344; (1958) 102 SJ 363 CA Fraud in Limitation Act does not just cover dishonest behaviour; substantial damages where fatal accidents claim barred through negligence.

Royal Mail Steam Packet Company v George and another [1900-03] All ER 1704; (1900) LXXXII LTR 539 PC On drawing by court of inferences of fact in nuisance action.

Royster v Cavey (1945-46) LXII TLR 709; (1947) WN (I) 8 CA Cannot bring tort action against nominated defendant who owed no duty of care to plaintiff.

Royston ater Company Limited, Titchmarsh v (1899-1900) LXXXI LTR 673 HC ChD Injunction granted to halt trespass on private road.

RP Howard Ltd v Woodman Matthews and Co (1983) 133 NLJ 598 HC QBD Solicitor liable in negligence for failure to seek new tenancy for client under terms of Landlord and Tenant Act 1954, Part II.

Ruane, Hevican v [1991] 3 All ER 65; (1991) 141 NLJ 235 HC QBD Damages for nervous shock after son's injury despite third party relaying of news as each stage in relay foreseeable; damages available for unforeseeably severe nervous shock if nervous shock foreseeable.

Rubber Improvement Ltd and Another v Daily Telegraph Ltd; Same v Associated Newspapers Ltd [1964] AC 234; (1963) 107 SJ 356; [1963] 2 WLR 1063 HL Judge must rule whether words capable of bearing alternative defamatory meanings alleged; on innuendo/justification; damages here too great.

Rubin and another, Davis and another v (1968) 112 SJ 51 CA Re-trial of libel action ordered where damages awarded were excessive.

Ruislip Dog Sanatorium (Limited), Barton v (1916-17) XXXIII TLR 458 HC KBD Exception clause meant dogs' home owner not liable in negligence for illness and death of dog lodged there.

Rule, R v [1937] 2 All ER 772; (1934-39) XXX Cox CC 599; (1936-38) 26 Cr App R 87; [1937] 2 KB 375; (1937) 83 LJ 362; [1937] 106 LJCL 807; (1937) 157 LTR 48; (1936-37) LIII TLR 720; (1937) WN (I) 215 CCA Constitutent's letter to MP in Parliamentary capacity a privileged occasion.

Rundle and others, Edmondson v (1902-03) XIX TLR 356 HC KBD Failed action for wrongful arrest/imprisonment of soldier by superior officer during wartime: not a matter for civil courts.

Ruoff v Long and Co (1915) CC Rep IV 94; (1916) 80 JP 158; [1916] 1 KB 148; (1915) 50 LJ 546; [1916] 85 LJKB 364; (1916) 114 LTR 186; (1915-16) 60 SJ 323; (1915-16) XXXII TLR 82 HC KBD Non-liability of person leaving lorry on highway for unexpected act of third party.

Rushmer v Polsue and Alfieri (Limited) [1906] 1 Ch 234; (1905) 40 LJ 867; (1905-06) XCIII LTR 823; (1905-06) 50 SJ 126; (1905-06) XXII TLR 139; (1906) WN (I) 3; (1905-06) 54 WR 161 CA Use of printing machinery by night was nuisance (though in area where much printing took place).

Rushmer v Polsue and Alfieri (Limited) (1904-05) XXI TLR 183 HC ChD Use of printing machinery by night was nuisance (though in area where much printing took place).

Rushmer, Polsue and Alfieri, Ltd v [1904-07] All ER 586; [1907] AC 121; (1907) 42 LJ 180; [1907] 76 LJCh 365; (1907) XCVI LTR 510; (1906-07) 51 SJ 324; (1906-07) XXIII TLR 362; (1907) WN (I) 67 HL General circumstances of situation relevant when seeking injunction for nuisance by noise.

Rushton v National Coal Board [1953] 1 All ER 314; [1953] 1 QB 495; (1953) 97 SJ 94; [1953] 1 WLR 292 CA Appropriate damages in personal injury cases.

Rushton, Nicholls v [1992] TLR 303 CA Damages irrecoverable for nervous injury incapable of psychological definition from which suffered after road accident.

Russell and another v Barnet London Borough Council [1984] TLR 262 HC QBD Highway authority liable in nuisance for damage occasioned by tree roots to property even though did not actually own the trees.

Russell v Criterion Film Productions, Ltd and another [1936] 3 All ER 627; (1936) 80 SJ 1036; (1936-37) LIII TLR 117 HC KBD Film production company, not cameraman, liable for injury effected through over-lighting of film scene.

Russell v Norfolk (Duke) and others [1948] 1 All ER 488; (1948) LXIV TLR 263 HC KBD No implied term in Jockey Club contract to hold inquiry before withdrawing licence; where common interest and agree to publish is qualified privilege unless malice.

Russell, Stubbs, Limited v [1913] AC 386; (1913) 48 LJ 227; (1913) 82 LJPC 98; (1913) 108 LTR 529; (1912-13) XXIX TLR 409; (1913) WN (I) 103 HL Mistaken naming of party in Stubbs Gazette not libellous in light of note at head of list of names.

S v Walsall Metropolitan Borough Council [1986] 1 FLR 397; (1985) 135 NLJ 986; (1985) 129 SJ 685; [1985] 1 WLR 1150 CA Local authority not vicariously liable for negligence of foster parents.

S, Cook v [1967] 1 All ER 299 CA Negligent solicitor sued in contract not liable for mental distress occasioned by negligence.

S, Cook v [1966] 1 All ER 248; (1965-66) 116 NLJ 416; (1966) 110 SJ 964; [1966] 1 WLR 635 HC QBD Damage flowing from solicitor's negligence not broken by counsel's mistaken advice.

S, P v (1979) 129 (1) NLJ 19c CA Level of damages awarded in personal injury actions not relevant when determining appropriate level of damages for defamation.

SA (Flota Mercante Grancolombiana), Mitsui and Co Ltd and another v (1988) 132 SJ 1182; [1988] 1 WLR 1145 CA Shipowner liable in tort in respect of goods damaged on board ship only to owner of goods at time were damaged.

Sack v Jones [1925] 94 LJCh 229; (1925) 133 LTR 129 HC ChD Failure of one joint owner to give lateral support to party wall not a nuisance.

Saddler and Company and Others, Chapman or Oliver and Another v [1929] AC 584; (1929) 67 LJ 362; (1929) 98 LJPC 87; (1929) 141 LTR 305; (1928-29) XLV TLR 456; (1929) WN (I) 130 HL Stevedore firm liable to porter injured by defective sling.

Saddleworth Urban District Council v Aggregate and Sand Ltd (1970) 114 SJ 931 HC QBD Unavailability of money/reliance on expert advice not/could be reasonable excuse for non-abatement of nuisance.

Sadek and others, Jozwiak v [1954] 1 All ER 3; (1954) 104 LJ 10; (1954) 98 SJ 94 HC QBD Later public comments/anonymous telephone calls admissible to prove libel.

Sadgrove v Hole [1901] 2 KB 1; [1901] 70 LJK/QB 455; (1901) LXXXIV LTR 647; (1900-01) 45 SJ 342; (1900-01) XVII TLR 332; (1900-01) 49 WR 473 CA Absent malice communication by way of postcard was privileged.

Sadiq, Louis v (1996) TLR 22/11/96 CA Builder liable in nuisance for damage occasioned to adjoining property by works carried out by him in breach of statutory requirements.

Sadler and another, King v (1970) 114 SJ 192 HC QBD Hotel owner and Gas Board equally liable for injury to hotel guest injured by carbon monoxide gas from boiler room below hotel room.

Sadler, Cleghorn v [1945] 1 All ER 544; [1945] KB 325; (1946) 96 LJ 199; [1945] 114 LJ 508; (1945) 172 LTR 334; (1944-45) LXI TLR 318; (1945) WN (I) 84 HC KBD Firewatching not a profession so 'slanderous' words spoken of firewatcher cannot be spoken of same in professional capacity.

Sadler, Reeve v (1903) 67 JP 63; (1903) LXXXVIII LTR 95; (1902-03) 51 WR 603 HC KBD Subject of sanitary notice cannot recoup part of expenses of work done thereunder from adjoining owner subject to another sanitary notice.

Sale Urban District Council, Clayton v [1925] All ER 279; (1926) 90 JP 5; [1926] 1 KB 415; (1925) 60 LJ 962; [1926] 95 LJCL 178; (1926) 134 LTR 147; (1925-26) XLII TLR 72; (1925) WN (I) 278 HC KBD Riparian owner must abate nuisance caused by floodingwhich has broken flood bank.

Sales Affiliates, Limited v Le Jean, Limited [1947] Ch 295; (1947) 97 LJ 106; [1947] 116 LJR 729; (1947) 176 LTR 251; (1947) 91 SJ 100 HC ChD Injunction to prevent giving 'Jamal' hair-wave without using 'Jamal' products: absent actual sale of goods passing-off can be proved by evidence from trade witness.

Sales, Bebee v (1915-16) XXXII TLR 413 HC KBD Was negligent to allow son to continue using airgun after had already promised to destroy gun on foot of earlier complaint regarding son's use of same.

Salford Corporation and another, Fryer v (1937) 101 JP 263; (1937) 81 SJ 177 CA Education authority liable for reasonably foreseeable/preventable accident which occurred to girl during school cookery class.

Salih and another v Enfield Health Authority [1991] 3 All ER 400; (1991) 141 NLJ 460i CA Decision not to have another child and savings made thereby relevant when determining damages for unwanted pregnancy.

Samuel Williams and Sons, Limited, Cawood, Wharton and Company, Limited v; The Cawood III [1951] 1 TLR 924 HC PDAD Jetty owners liable for damage to lighter notwithstanding presence of exemption clause.

Samuel Williams and Sons, Ltd and another, Ashdown v [1957] 1 All ER 35; (1957) 107 LJ 42; [1957] 1 QB 409; (1956) 100 SJ 945; [1956] 3 WLR 1104 CA Exemption notice applied though plaintiff unaware of specific contents as had been adequately brought to her attention.

Samuel Williams and Sons, Ltd and another, Ashdown v [1956] 2 All ER 384; (1956) 106 LJ 378; [1956] 2 QB 580; (1956) 100 SJ 420 [1956] 3 WLR 128 HC QBD Licensor not liable to licensee where latter aware sign excluding liability exists and of its nature but not its contents; employer liable to worker for not warning her of known dangers on short cut they allow her to use.

Samuel Williams and Sons, Smith v (1972) 122 NLJ 217t HC QBD Failed action for damages on foot of road traffic accident as causation of plaintiff's injuries by defendant's negligence not proved.

Samuel, Marks v [1904] 2 KB 287; (1904) 39 LJ 213; [1904] 73 LJCL 587; (1904) XC LTR 590; (1903-04) 48 SJ 415; (1903-04) XX TLR 430; (1904) WN (I) 86; (1904-05) 53 WR 88 CA Absent special damage can still sue for slander where alleged brought blackmail action.

Samuels and others, Ilkiw v (1963) 107 SJ 680; [1963] 1 WLR 991 CA Employers liable for negligence of employee who acting within scope of responsibility behaved in unauthorised way; appropriate damages for personal injuries.

Samuelson v Producers' Distributing Co, Ltd [1931] All ER 74; [1932] 1 Ch 201 (also HC ChD); (1932) 101 LJCh 168 (also HC ChD); (1932) 146 LTR 37 CA Passing off of film as cinema version of written work.

Samuelson v Producers' Distributing Company, Limited [1932] 1 Ch 201 (also CA); (1932) 101 LJCh 168 (also CA) HC ChD Passing off of film as cinema version of written work.

Samways v Westgate Engineers, Ltd (1962) 106 SJ 937 CA Refuse collector/disposers equally negligent in not wearing gloves when collecting/not warning of particular hazard attaching to certain rubbish.

Sandell Perkins Ltd, Haste v [1984] 2 All ER 615; (1984) 134 NLJ 681; [1984] QB 735; (1984) 128 SJ 334; [1984] 3 WLR 73 HC QBD When benefits to be deducted from damages fully defined in Law Reform (Personal Injuries) Act 1948.

Sanders-Clark v Grosvenor Mansions Company, Limited and G D'Allessandri [1900] 2 Ch 373; (1900) 35 LJ 363; [1900] LXIX (1) LJ 579; (1900) LXXXII LTR 758; (1899-1900) 44 SJ 502; (1900) WN (I) 136; (1899-1900) 48 WR 570 HC ChD Reasonable use of property a relevant factor when deciding nuisance cases involving adjoining houseowners.

Sanderson and another (Keel and Block, Third Party), Boardman and another v (1961) 105 SJ 152; [1964] 1 WLR 1317 CA Were liable to father who could hear negligent injury to child for shock suffered by father in consequence.

Sanderson, Fletcher v (1976) 126 NLJ 1068t CA £6,500 damages for three year old who had to spend three weeks in hospital and suffered serious pelvic injuries after being knocked down.

Sandess Universal Products, Morris and another v [1954] 1 All ER 47; (1954) 104 LJ 9; (1954) 98 SJ 10 CA Test whether defamatory is would reasonable jury find defamatory.

Sandholme Iron Co Ltd, Hartley v [1974] 3 All ER 475; (1974) 118 SJ 702; [1974] 3 WLR 445 HC QBD Personal injury damages can be reduced by income tax savings resulting from injury.

Sandow Limited, Henry Thorne and Co Limited v (1912) 106 LTR 926 HC ChD Failed action for passing off in respect of use of term 'Health' in relation to cocoa.

Sandown Urban District Council, Webb and another v (1925) 60 LJ 606 CyCt Person did not by virtue of occasional trespass of cattle upon another's land for under twelve years acquire title to same to exclusion of owner.

Sanson, D'Urso v [1939] 4 All ER 26; (1939) 88 LJ 252; (1939) 83 SJ 850 HC KBD Watchman returning inside burning building acted in course of employment: no volenti non fit injuria.

Saper v Hungate Builders Ltd and others; King v Hungate Builders Ltd and others [1972] RTR 380 HC QBD Presence of poorly lit skip negligent/a nuisance but person who drove into it found contributorily negligent (40%).

619

Sharp, Caudle and others v; Grove v Sharp [1994] TLR 131 HC QBD That continued not to check risks involved in writing reinsurance contracts a single event from which negligence could be discerned.

Sharp, Forrest v (1963) 107 SJ 536 HC QBD On relevancy of injured person's awareness of affliction to level of damages awarded.

Sharp, Wright v (1947) 176 LTR 308 HC KBD Failed action for false imprisonment/malicious prosecution following taxi-driver's arrest/failed prosecution after taxi had been hired for robbery.

Sharpe (No 2), Cope v [1911] 2 KB 837; (1911) 80 LJCL1008; (1911) 104 LTR 718 HC KBD Trespass through genuine necessity justified.

Sharpe v Council of the City of Manchester (1978) 128 NLJ 312b CA Successful action in negligence/nuisance where council dealt inadequately with cockroach infestation in council flat.

Sharpe v Southern Rail Co [1925] All ER 372; [1925] 2 KB 311; [1925] 94 LJCL 913; (1925) 133 LTR 693; (1924-25) 69 SJ 775 CA Company though/if negligent not liable to party who was contributorily negligent.

Sharpe v Sweeting (ET) and Son, Ltd [1963] 2 All ER 455; (1963) 113 LJ 399; (1963) 107 SJ 666; [1963] 1 WLR 665 HC QBD Sufficient proximity between builder and later occupier of premises to sustain negligence action.

Sharpe, Cope v [1910] 1 KB 168; (1910) 45 LJ 8; (1910) 79 LJKB 281; (1910) 102 LTR 102; (1909-10) XXVI TLR 172; (1910-11) XXVII TLR 396; (1910) WN (I) 10 HC KBD Trespass through necessity not trespass.

Sharpe, Cope v [1911-13] All ER 1212; [1912] 1 KB 496; (1912) 47 LJ 8; (1912) 81 LJKB 346; (1912) 106 LTR 56; (1911-12) 56 SJ 187; (1911-12) XXVIII TLR 157; (1912) WN (I) 17 CA Trespass through necessity not trespass.

Sharwood (JA) and Co Limited (No 2), Pink v; Re Sidney Ord and Co's Trade Mark (1913-14) 109 LTR 594 HC ChD Failed action for passing off where plaintiff's business had ceased to trade.

Shatwell, Imperial Chemical Industries Ltd v [1964] 3 WLR 329 HL Volenti non fit injuria held to arise where workman injured after behaving with co-workman in manner contrary to employer's instructions/to law; on causation.

Shaw and others v London County Council and another (1934) 98 JP 398; (1934) 78 LJ 44; (1933-34) L TLR 489 HC KBD Six month limitation on action against public authority applicable to claims of infants.

Shaw and others v London County Council and another [1924-35] All ER 696; (1935) 99 JP 10; [1935] 1 KB 67; (1934) 78 LJ 286; [1935] 104 LJCL 84; (1934) 78 SJ 734; (1934-35) LI TLR 16; (1934) WN (I) 183 CA Six month limitation on action against public authority applicable to claims of infants.

Shaw and others, Bramwell v [1971] RTR 167 HC QBD On liabilities of speeding driver, his employer and highway authority for collision occurring on poorly maintained road.

Shaw v BG Services and Evans [1939] LJNCCR 226 CyCt Failed action in negligence against driver against whom it was alleged that should not have continued to drive van (which was eventually blown over) in windy weather.

Shaw v Cates [1909] 1 Ch 389 HC ChD Trustees not liable in negligence for failure to periodically examine state of mortgaged property.

Shaw v London Express Newsaper, Limited (1924-25) XLI TLR 475 HC KBD Newspaper article giving true account of murder in which person coincidentally had name of another who might be mistaken as person in article deemed non-libellous.

Shaw, Peters v [1965] Crim LR 429t HC QBD Nominal damages awarded against police officer who entered on to property absent permission/without warrant/when not in hot pursuit.

Shean, Price v [1939] LJNCCR 395 CyCt Declaration of title granted plus damages for cost of removing construction works improperly extending onto plaintiff's land.

Sheard, Lee v [1955] 3 All ER 777; (1955) 105 LJ 809; [1956] 1 QB 192; (1955) 99 SJ 888; [1955] 3 WLR 951 CA Reduction in share of company profits by third party consequent upon tort recoverable from tortfeasor.

Shearer and another v Shields [1914] AC 808; [1914] 83 LJPC 216 HL Malice in fact unnecessary for false imprisonment in pursuance of Glasgow Police Act 1866.

Shearman v Folland [1950] 1 All ER 976; [1950] 2 KB 43; (1950) 100 LJ 245; (1950) 94 SJ 336; [1950] 66 (1) TLR 853; (1950) WN (I) 206 CA Bed and board but not cost of hotels in which plaintiff would have stayed deducted from personal injury damages.

Shearmur, Clapham v [1940] LJNCCR 138 CyCt Failed claim in negligence against innkeeper by patron where loss suffered by patron would not have occurred but for patron's negligence.

Shears v Matthews [1948] 2 All ER 1064; (1949) 113 JP 36; (1949) LXV TLR 194; (1948) WN (I) 472 HC KBD Highway Act 1835, s 78, covers negligence directly connected to driving.

Sheath, Carter v [1990] RTR 12 CA That plaintiff failed to explain how accident occurred meant defendant could not be held to be contributorily negligent.

Sheehan v Dreamland, Margate, Limited (1923-24) XL TLR 155 CA Non-liability of freeholder (invitor) to invitee for injury caused in sideshow which was not inherently dangerous and in respect of which neither invitees nor their servants had been negligent.

Sheffield Brothers (Profiles) Ltd, Gardner Steel Ltd v [1978] 3 All ER 399 CA Interest on summary judgment possible.

Sheffield Conservative and Unionist Club (Limited) v Brighton [1916] 85 LJKB 1669; (1915-16) XXXII TLR 598 HC KBD Action for trespass unsustainable against military authority commandeering premises under emergency legislation for clerical rather than 'military' staff (Defence of the Realm (Consolidation) Regulations 1914, regulation 2).

Sheffield Corporation, Knight v [1942] 2 All ER 411; (1942) 106 JP 197; (1943) 93 LJ 108; (1942) 167 LTR 203; (1942) 86 SJ 311 HC KBD Local authority had duty to light entrance to shelter where had been in habit of so lighting; was negligent exercise of statutory authority to establish access to air raid shelter by way of unfenced hole in pavement.

Sheffield Corporation, Morrison v (1917) 81 JP 277; [1917] 86 LJCL 1456; (1917-18) 117 LTR 520; (1916-17) 61 SJ 611; (1916-17) XXXIII TLR 492 CA Owners of spiked fence were negligent not to have taken special measures to avoid injury to public during black-out conditions.

Sheffield Corporation, Norman v (1917) 52 LJ 298 CA Local authority liable for failure to take reasonable care to avoid injury being occasioned by tree guards during wartime 'black-out' conditions.

Sheffield Corporation, Oldham v (1927) 91 JP 69; (1927) 136 LTR 681; (1926-27) XLIII TLR 222 CA Liable in negligence for placing obstruction on private road and thereby causing invitee injury.

Sheffield Health Authority, Hurditch v [1989] 2 All ER 869; [1989] QB 562; (1989) 133 SJ 630; [1989] 2 WLR 827 CA Parties agreeing on need for provisional damages but disagreeing on some evidence enough basis for taxing master to make order.

Sheffield Telegraph and Star, Ltd, Burnett and Hallamshire Fuel, Ltd v [1960] 2 All ER 157; (1960) 104 SJ 388 HC QBD Privilege for fair and accurate reporting of judicial proceedings attaches to account of advocate's orations therein.

Shelbourne Hotel, Ltd, Campbell v [1939] 2 All ER 351; [1939] 2 KB 534; (1939) 87 LJ 303; [1939] 108 LJCL 607; (1939) 160 LTR 436; (1939) 83 SJ 456; (1938-39) LV TLR 938 HC KBD Hotelier negligent in not keeping passageway to communal toilet lit for guest/invitee.

Sheldon and others v RHM Outhwaite (Underwriting Agencies Ltd) and others [1994] 4 All ER 481 (also HC QBD); [1996] 1 AC 102 (also HC QBD/HL); [1994] TLR 359; [1994] 3 WLR 999 CA Limitation period continues to run if concealment of facts post-dates cause of action.

Sheldon and others v RHM Outhwaite (Underwriting Agencies Ltd) and others [1994] 4 All ER 481 (also CA); [1996] 1 AC 102 (also CA/HL); [1993] TLR 632; [1994] 1 WLR 754 HC QBD Limitation period continues to run if concealment of facts post-dates cause of action.

Sheldon and others v RHM Outhwaite (Underwriting Agencies) Ltd and others [1995] 2 All ER 558; [1996] 1 AC 102 (also CA); (1995) 145 NLJ 687; (1995) 139 SJ LB 119; [1995] TLR 258; [1995] 2 WLR 570 HL Concealment of facts postpones time running until concealment was/should have been discovered.

Shell Petroleum Co Ltd and another (No 2), Lonrho Ltd and another v (1981) 131 NLJ 632; [1981] 3 WLR 33 HL Oil supplies to Zimbabwe-Rhodesia in violation of Southern Rhodesia (Petroleum) Order 1965 did not give rise to tortious liability to injured party.

Shell Petroleum Co Ltd and others, Lonrho Ltd and others v [1981] 2 All ER 456; [1982] AC 173; (1981) 125 SJ 429; [1980] 1 WLR 627 HL Breach of sanctions order not breach of statutory duty; conspiracy if do not intend to injure another nor protect oneself.

Shelley v Paddock and another [1980] 1 All ER 1009; [1980] QB 348; (1979) 123 SJ 706; [1980] 2 WLR 647 CA Inadvertent illegality in presence of fraud precluded guilty party raising defence of illegality.

Shelley v Paddock and another [1978] 3 All ER 129; [1979] QB 120; (1978) 122 SJ 316; [1978] 2 WLR 877 HC QBD Inadvertent unlawful behaviour does not prevent recovery in tort action.

Shenburn, Deyong v [1946] 1 All ER 226; [1946] KB 227 CA No implied term in producer/actor agreement and no common law duty to protect latter's personal property in theatre.

Shepcott, Moul v (1924-25) 69 SJ 680 HC ChD Court would not in quia timet action grant interlocutory injunction to restrain apprehended nuisance where subjects of proposed order did not consent to it.

Shephard v H West and Son, Ltd, and another (1962) 106 SJ 817 CA On appropriate injuries for brain damaged accident victim who was possibly aware of her condition.

Shephard, West (H) and Son, Ltd and another v [1963] 2 All ER 625; [1964] AC 326; (1963) 113 LJ 432; (1963) 107 SJ 454; [1963] 2 WLR 1359 HL Purpose/measurement of personal injury damages.

Shepherd v Essex County Council and another (1912-13) XXIX TLR 303 HC KBD On duty owed by school teacher to pupils.

Shepherd v Hunter [1938] 2 All ER 587; (1938) 85 LJ 361; (1938) 82 SJ 375 CA Appropriate damages for loss of life expectancy (of infant).

Shepherd v West (H) and Son, Ltd, and another (1962) 106 SJ 391 HC QBD Lorry driver liable in negligence where overtook stationary bus at traffic lights changing to green and struck pedestrian.

Sheppard and others, Hughes and another v; Morley and others v Same (1940) 104 JP 357; (1940) 163 LTR 177; (1939-40) LVI TLR 810 HC KBD Not negligent/nuisance for council workers to mark where were painting lines on road with cans and flags — even if was nuisance only negligent driver who failed to see same and collided with another vehicle liable in actions arising from accident.

Sheppard and Short, Ltd, Armstrong v [1959] 2 All ER 651; (1959) 123 JP 401; (1959) 109 LJ 477; [1959] 2 QB 384 CA Oral consent to acts done defeats trespass action even though not fully aware of proprietary rights when consented.

Sheppard v Mayor, Aldermen and Burgesses of the Borough of Glossop (1921) 85 JP 205; [1921] 3 KB 132 CA Non-liability of local authority for not lighting area around retaining wall which had been source of injury to person.

Shepphard v Devon County Council (1980) 130 NLJ 14 CA Reversal of trial judge's finding that council were liable in negligence where school bus was driven over foot of boy who had jumped off the bus.

Sher Brothers, Bermingham v (1980) 130 NLJ 137; (1980) 124 SJ 117 HL Occupier does not owe duty of care to provide members of fire services with means of escape from place of fire for duration of time they seek to put out fire.

Sherbourne v Walker [1955] Crim LR 184 HC QBD Successful action for damages against policeman guilty of assault/wrongful imprisonment/malicious prosecution.

Sherburn (JA), Warboys (JH) v (1977) 127 NLJ 1151b CA On best means of assessing appropriate damages in negligence actions (by reference to medical reports not law reports).

Sheridan v Boots Co Ltd and Kensington and Chelsea and Westminster Area Health Authority (1981) 131 NLJ 479 HC QBD Failed action for negligence arising from prescription of drug which resulted in plaintiff going blind.

Shutt and another v Extract Wool and Merino Co Ltd (1969) 113 SJ 672 HC QBD On damages available for temporary loss of sexual intercourse with wife as result of personal injury.

Sibley, Thorne v (1913) CC Rep II 11 CyCt Person who had horse on trial not liable for injury horse inflicted on self (no negligence on part of said person), property not having passed to that person.

Sidaway v Bethlem Royal Hospital Governors and others [1984] 1 All ER 1018; [1984] QB 493; (1984) 128 SJ 301; [1984] TLR 97; [1984] 2 WLR 778 CA Standard expected of surgeon advising on operation is that of experienced, skilled body of medical persons.

Sidaway v Board of Governors of the Bethlem Royal Hospital and the Maudsley Hospital and another (1982) 132 NLJ 814 HC QBD On duty of care owed by surgeon to patient.

Sidaway v Board of Governors of the Bethlem Royal Hospital and the Maudsley Hospital and others [1985] 1 All ER 643; [1985] AC 871; (1985) 135 NLJ 203; (1985) 129 SJ 154; [1985] 2 WLR 480 HL On duty of care owed by surgeon to patient.

Sidney Phillips and Son (a firm), Perry v [1982] 1 All ER 1005; (1981) 131 NLJ 1135 HC QBD Damages available for cost of repairing defects (not difference between cost/value) where will occupy negligently surveyed house; occupier's delay of repairs undiscovered by negligent surveyor reasonable if no money; damages available for distress/discomfort of repairs/occupying defective house.

Sidwell v British Timken, Ltd (1962) 106 SJ 243 CA Employers not liable for injury occasioned to plaintiff workman as direct result of another workman's prank.

Sievier, Wootton v [1911-13] All ER 1001; [1913] 3 KB 499; (1913) 48 LJ 374; [1913] 82 LJKB 1242; (1913-14) 109 LTR 28; (1912-13) 57 SJ 609; (1912-13) XXIX TLR 596; (1913) WN (I) 187 CA Particulars required when justification pleaded.

Sigley v Hale [1938] 3 All ER 87; (1937-38) LIV TLR 967 CA No payment into court possible in case of joint tortfeasors.

Sigurdson (Marvin) v British Columbia Electric Railway Co Ld [1953] AC 291; (1952) WN (I) 411 PC On contributory negligence.

Silkin v Beaverbrook Newspapers, Ltd and another [1958] 2 All ER 516; (1958) 108 LJ 443; (1958) 102 SJ 491 HC QBD Fair comment on matter of public interest if opinion honestly held.

Silver and others, Mills and another v [1991] 1 All ER 449; [1990] TLR 535 CA Use with landowner's acqiuescence/tolerance does not preclude use as of right. Improvement of easement well beyond repair is trespass.

Silverman v Imperial London Hotels, Ltd [1927] All ER 712; (1927) 137 LTR 57; (1926-27) XLIII TLR 260 HC KBD Breach of implied term of contract (and negligent) allowing invitee into premises knowing of a danger (and failing to address danger).

Sim v Heinz (HJ) Co, Ltd and another [1959] 1 All ER 547; (1959) 109 LJ 200; (1959) 103 SJ 238 CA Interlocutory injunction unavailable for alleged passing off/libel.

Sim v Stretch [1936] 2 All ER 1237; (1936) 80 SJ 703; (1935-36) LII TLR 669 HL Test for defamation is whether would lower opinion of person in eyes of reasonable person/class of persons to whom statement addressed.

Sim, Stretch v (1935) 79 SJ 453 CA Was matter for jury whether allegation in telegram that gentleman had been required to borrow money from housemaid was defamatory (certainly was potentially so).

Simaan General Contracting Co v Pilkington Glass [1988] 1 All ER 791; (1988) 138 NLJ 53; [1988] QB 758; (1988) 132 SJ 463; [1988] 2 WLR 761 CA Minus express assumption of responsibility pure economic loss irrecoverable.

Simmonds, Green v (1926) 62 LJ ccr74 CyCt Was assault where person injured self in course of reaction to stated intention of another to strike same.

Simmons and Simmons (a firm), Allied Maples Group Ltd v [1995] 4 All ER 907; (1995) 145 NLJ 1646; [1995] 1 WLR 1602 CA If plaintiff's loss on foot of negligent advice rests on imagined action of another and is a substantial chance that other would have acted to confer benefit on or avoid risk to plaintiff the evaluation of that chance is for judge determining quantum.

Smith and others, Longdon-Griffiths v [1950] 2 All ER 662; [1951] 1 KB 295; (1950) 100 LJ 413; (1950) 94 SJ 580; [1950] 66 (2) TLR 627; (1950) WN (I) 448 HC KBD Libel action to be directed at Friendly Society per se not its trustees; special damages available where libel led to losing job; that one of four parties acted maliciously did not affect qualified privilege of others.

Smith and UMB Chrysler (Scotland) Ltd v South Wales Switchgear Co Ltd (1978) 122 SJ 61 HL Indemnity clause did not indemnify respondents against their own negligence/that of their servants.

Smith v Abraham, Hague and Mew, Langton and Co, Ltd [1937] LJNCCR 205 CyCt Failed action for trespass by licensee entitled to supply refreshments at dance hall against owners/tenants of same who notwithstanding licence arrangement with plaintiff obtained occasional excise licences and sold alcohol to patrons of dance hall.

Smith v Austin Lifts, Ltd and others [1959] 1 All ER 81 HL Occupiers liable to invitee for failure to take reasonable care to maintain safe premises; employers also liable in negligence.

Smith v Bray (Wickham, Third Party) (1940) 84 SJ 170; (1939-40) LVI TLR 200 HC KBD Apportionment of costs/damages in proportion to apportionment of negligence between joint tortfeasors.

Smith v British European Airways Corporation and another [1951] 2 All ER 737; [1951] 2 KB 893; (1951) 101 LJ 498; [1951] 2 TLR 608 HC KBD Death benefit deductible from fatal accident damages; on infants'/widow's right of recovery despite latter's acceptance of death benefit.

Smith v Bush; Harris v Wyre Forest District Council (1989) 139 NLJ 576 HL On duty of care owed by building society valuer towards mortgagor/mortgagee.

Smith v Central Asbestos Co Ltd [Consolidated actions] [1971] 3 All ER 204; (1971) 121 NLJ 500t; [1972] 1 QB 244; [1971] 3 WLR 206 CA Unawareness of extent of injury/right of action could justify disapplying limitation.

Smith v Eric S Bush (a firm); Harris and another v Wyre Forest District Council and another [1989] 2 All ER 514; [1990] 1 AC 831; (1989) 133 SJ 597; [1989] 2 WLR 790 HL Property valuer owes contractual/tortious duty of care to mortgagor/mortgagee; can disclaim duty but disclaimer must be reasonable.

Smith v Evangelization Society (Incorporated) Trust [1933] Ch 515 (also HC ChD); (1933) 102 LJCh 275 (also HC ChD); (1932-33) XLIX TLR 262; (1933) WN (I) 66 CA On nuisance by way of obstruction of ancient light.

Smith v Evangelization Society (Incorporated) Trust [1933] Ch 515 (also CA); (1933) 102 LJCh 275 (also CA); (1932-33) XLIX TLR 32 HC ChD On nuisance by way of obstruction of ancient light.

Smith v Giddy [1904-07] All ER 289; [1904] 2 KB 448; (1904) 39 LJ 346; [1904] 73 LJCL 894; (1904-05) XCI LTR 296; (1903-04) 48 SJ 589; (1903-04) XX TLR 596; (1904) WN (I) 130; (1904-05) 53 WR 207 HC KBD Can lop overhanging branches causing nuisance and claim for damage effected thereby.

Smith v Great Western Rail Co and another [1926] All ER 242; (1926) 135 LTR 112; (1925-26) XLII TLR 391 HC KBD Railway company not liable for continuance of nuisance where took all reasonable steps regarding same; party consigning leaking oil tank to rail carriers which resulted in injury to third party liable in nuisance.

Smith v Harris [1939] 3 All ER 960; (1939) 83 SJ 730 CA Equal blame apportioned between motorcyclists involved in collision.

Smith v Leech Brain and Co, Ltd and another [1961] 3 All ER 1159; (1962) 112 LJ 89; [1962] 2 QB 405; (1962) 106 SJ 77 HC QBD Person committing tort must take victim as found — here liable for cancer resulting from burn to malignancy.

Smith v Lewis (1916-17) XXXIII TLR 195 HC KBD Need not plead express malice where in defence to claim that publication was malicious privilege is pleaded.

Smith v Linskills (a firm) (1996) 146 NLJ 209; (1996) TLR 7/2/96 CA Convict's negligence suit against solicitor who defended him in criminal action a collateral attack on criminal action and so unpermitted.

Solomon, J Trevor and Sons (a firm) v (1978) 128 NLJ 134t CA Refusal of injunction preventing person from stating what he considered to be the truth.

Solomons v R Gertzenstein Ld and others (1954) 104 LJ 266; [1954] 1 QB 565; (1954) 98 SJ 270; [1954] 2 WLR 823 HC QBD Liability of rackrent receiver for personal injuries suffered by tenants of building that went on fire.

Solomons v R Gertzenstein Ld and others (1954) 104 LJ 442; [1954] 2 QB 243 CA Liability of rackrent receiver for personal injuries suffered by tenants of building that went on fire.

Solomons v Stepney Borough Council (1905) 69 JP 360 HC KBD Was evidence of negligence (leakage of electricity in explosive atmosphere) upon which jury could decide.

Soltenpur, Davis v (1983) 133 NLJ 720; [1983] TLR 104 HC QBD Limitation period applied in favour of defendant where plaintiff still had option of bring action against solicitors.

Somasundaram v M Julius Melchior and Co (a firm) [1989] 1 All ER 129; (1988) 138 NLJ 253; (1988) 132 SJ 1732; [1988] 1 WLR 1394 CA Action for negligence against barrister/solicitor struck off if really attack on court of competent jurisdiction.

Somerfield and others, Wheeler v [1966] 2 All ER 305; (1965-66) 116 NLJ 837; [1966] 2 QB 94; [1966] 2 WLR 1006 CA Libel damages for injury to health possible (but not here); could be that to include articles of certain section of publication might carry innuendo but not here.

Somerfield and others, Wheeler v (1965) 109 SJ 875 HC QBD Failed claim of innuendo in one article based on other articles.

Somertons of Harrow, Ltd, Mack v (1965) 109 SJ 53 HC QBD Shop-owner liable in common law/for breach of statutory duty for injury to customer who slipped on inadequately secured metal strip around store doormat.

Somervell and others, Hirsch and another v (1946) 90 SJ 394; (1945-46) LXII TLR 592 CA Successful appeal against striking out of false imprisonment/trespass action against successive Home Secretaries.

Somervell and others, Hirsch and others v (1946) 90 SJ 369 HC ChD Striking out of false imprisonment/trespass action against successive Home Secretaries.

Sommerville and Son, Edinburgh Water Trustees v (1906-07) XCV LTR 217 HL Absent negligence water company not liable for accidental pollution of compensation water.

Soo (Lee Kim), Seng (Goh Cheen) v [1925] AC 550 PC Master liable for servant's negligence though servant commits unauthorised trespass.

Sorrell v Paget [1949] 2 All ER 609; [1950] 1 KB 252 CA Person impounding straying cattle had lien on same until appropriate amount paid/offered for distress damage feasant.

Sorrell v Paget (1949) LXV TLR 595 HC KBD Person impounding straying cattle had lien on same until appropriate amount paid/offered for distress damage feasant.

Sotheby and Co, Elliott (Third Party), Kendrick v (1967) 111 SJ 470 HC QBD Successful action in detinue against innocent defendants who innocently purchased plaintiff's statuette from fraudulent third party.

Souchette, Limited, v London County Westminster and Parr's Bank, Limited (1919-20) XXXVI TLR 195 HC KBD Negligent cashing by bank of one of five cheques.

South Australia Asset Management Corporation v York Montague Ltd; United Bank of Kuwait plc v Prudential Property Services Ltd; Nykredit Mortgage Bank plc v Edward Erdman Group Ltd (formerly Edward Erdman) (an unlimited company) [1996] 3 All ER 365; [1997] AC 191; (1996) 146 NLJ 956; (1996) 140 SJ LB 156; (1996) TLR 24/6/96; [1996] 3 WLR 87 HL Damages available where relied on negligent valuation given by surveyor were for losses which mistake in valuation could foreseeably entail.

South Bedfordshire District Council (Ellison and Partners (a firm) and others, third parties), Investors in Industry Commercial Properties Ltd v [1986] 1 All ER 787; (1986) 136 NLJ 118; [1986] QB 1034; (1986) 130 SJ 71; [1986] 2 WLR 937 CA Local authority does not owe duty to building owner to ensure building accords with building regulations; professional not responsible for work of specialist consultant unless as professional foresees problem therewith.

South Durham Steel Co, Ltd and another, Braithwaite v [1958] 3 All ER 161; (1958) 102 SJ 655 HC QBD Master negligent in not providing safe place to work; licensor liable in negligence despite unintended trespass of licencee at moment of accident to escape therefrom.

South East Kent Health Authority, Martine v [1993] TLR 119 CA No action lay in negligence against health authority in respect of its investigation regarding standards at nursing home.

South Eastern and Chatham Rail Co's Managing Committee, Mercer v [1922] All ER; [1922] 2 KB 549; [1923] 92 LJCL 25; (1922) 127 LTR 723; (1921-22) XXXVIII TLR 431 HC KBD Gate usually locked when train approaching left open: victim could recover damages in negligence for injuries consequently suffered.

South Eastern Electricity Board, Orchard v (1986) 136 NLJ 1112 CA Solicitor (but not barrister) may be liable for opponent's costs.

South Eastern Gas Board, Smith v; Parsons and another v Same; Knopp v Same (1964) 108 SJ 337 HC QBD Damages awarded for negligence of Gas Board workers in failing to pre-empt explosion.

South Essex Recorders, Limited, and another, Standen v (1933-34) L TLR 365 HC KBD Newspaper observations on local authority meeting not privileged.

South Hams District Council, Aitken v [1994] 3 All ER 400; [1995] 1 AC 262; (1994) 144 NLJ 1096; (1994) 138 SJ LB 167; [1994] TLR 380; [1994] 3 WLR 333 HL Noise abatement order made under repealed legislation is effective.

South Lancashire Transport Co, Mottram v [1942] 2 All ER 452; (1943) 93 LJ 109; (1942) 86 SJ 321 CA Bus conductress not negligent in not policing dismounting of passengers.

South Manchester Health Authority, Walkin v [1995] 4 All ER 132; [1995] TLR 380; [1995] 1 WLR 1543 CA Limitation period on claims for physical injury or economic loss arising from unwanted pregnancy after failed sterilisation runs from date of personal injury i.e., date of conception.

South Metropolitan Gas Co, Cressy v (1906) 70 JP 405 HC KBD Gas company which opened up street not liable for injury caused through local authority servant's negligent repair of street.

South Suburban Co-operative Society, Limited v Orum and others [1937] 2 KB 690; (1937) 83 LJ 410; [1937] 106 LJCL 555; (1937) 157 LTR 93; (1937) 81 SJ 497; (1936-37) LIII TLR 803; (1937) WN (I) 259 CA Writer of allegedly libellous letter to newspaper who pleads fair comment must reveal person/s from whom obtained information.

South Suburban Gas Co, Crane v [1914-15] All ER 93; (1916) 80 JP 51; [1916] 1 KB 33; [1916] 85 LJKB 172; (1916) 114 LTR 71; (1915-16) 60 SJ 222; (1915-16) XXXII TLR 74 HC KBD Liability in nuisance and negligence for injury occasioned to person as result of third party intervention on foot of dangerous work by highway.

South Wales Miners' Federation and others v Glamorgan Coal Company Limited, and others [1905] AC 239; (1904-05) XXI TLR 441 HL Miners' federation could be sued for good faith direction to miners not to work on particular days.

South Wales Miners' Federation and others, Glamorgan Coal Company, Limited and others v [1903] 2 KB 545; (1903) 38 LJ 417; (1902-03) XIX TLR 701 CA Liability for procuring breach of contract.

South Wales Miners' Federation and others, Glamorgan Coal Company, Limited and others v [1903] 1 KB 118 HC KBD Is defence to combination to secure breach of contract that no malice towards other party to contract.

South Wales Switchgear Co Ltd, Smith and UMB Chrysler (Scotland) Ltd v (1978) 122 SJ 61 HL Indemnity clause did not indemnify respondents against their own negligence/that of their servants.

South Wales Transport Co, Ltd, Barkway v [1950] 1 All ER 392; (1950) 114 JP 172; (1950) 94 SJ 128; [1950] 66 (1) TLR 597; (1950) WN (I) 95 HL On res ipsa loquitur.

South Wales Transport Co, Ltd, Barkway v [1948] 2 All ER 460; [1949] 1 KB 54 CA Tyre burst causing skid raises presumption of negligence: must show tyre burst not negligent/that took reasonable care.

South West Thames Health Authority, Eastman v [1990] RTR 315; [1990] TLR 354 HC QBD Ambulance passenger's failure to wear seat-belt not negligent where not informed of need for/availability of same.

South West Thames Regional Health Authority, Denton v (1981) 131 NLJ 240 HC QBD Damages for nurse who suffered injuries as result of collapse of hospital bed.

South West Thames Regional Health Authority, Eastman v [1991] RTR 389; (1991) 135 SJ LB 99; [1991] TLR 352 CA Ambulance authority not negligent in failing to inform passenger of need for/availability of seat-belts.

South West Water Services Ltd, B (A) and others v [1992] 4 All ER 574; (1992) 142 NLJ 897; [1992] TLR 232 HC QBD Exemplary and aggravated damages available for deliberate public nuisance.

South West Water Services Ltd, B (A) and others v [1993] 1 All ER 609; (1993) 143 NLJ 235; [1993] QB 507; [1993] 2 WLR 507 CA Exemplary damages unavailable for public nuisance; water company a commercial operation not exercising executive power so exemplary damages unavailable; aggravated damages unavailable for anger and indignation.

South-Eastern Railway Company, Jenner v (1911) 75 JP 419; (1911-12) 105 LTR 131; (1910-11) 55 SJ 553; (1910-11) XXVII TLR 445 HC KBD Circumstances justified jury finding that there was inadequate care taken to protect vehicles using level crossing.

Southam v Smout [1963] Crim LR 637; [1964] 1 QB 308; (1963) 107 SJ 513; [1963] 3 WLR 606 CA Bailiff's entry by closed/unlocked door rendered lawful as person whom wanted was found in house entered: in consequence houseowner could not order bailiffs out.

Southampton Bill-Posting Co, Plascott v (1921) CC Rep X 75 CyCt Is trespass for person posting bills to vandalise bills of other person authorised by occupier to post bills on same premises.

Southampton County Council and another, Jerram v (1927) 64 LJ ccr38 CyCt Failed action for negligence/nuisance against local councils for person who injured self in drain-grating.

Southampton County Council, Provender Millers (Winchester) Limited v (1939) 161 LTR 162 HC ChD Local authority discharging statutory duty cannot transgress another's rights unless unreasonable to otherwise discharge responsibility.

Southend Health Authority, Savill v [1995] 1 WLR 1254 CA Non-exercise of discretion/dismissal of appeal (against dismissal of claim on want of prosecution basis) where notice of appeal issued five days out of time was valid.

Southend-on-Sea Corporation, Lyles v (1905) 69 JP 193; [1905] 2 KB 1; (1905) 40 LJ 282; (1905) XCII LTR 586; (1904-05) XXI TLR 389; (1905) WN (I) 63 CA Six-month public authority limitation applied in negligence action against municpal corporation acting as tramway operator.

Southern Electricity Board, Adams v [1993] TLR 512 CA On extent of duty of care owed by electricity board towards teenage trespasser — here failed to meet that duty of care.

Southern Electricity Board, Pitman v [1978] 3 All ER 901; (1979) 143 JP 156; (1978) 122 SJ 300 CA Metal plate covering new hole a new hazard justifying negligence action.

Southern Portland Cement Ltd v Cooper [1974] 1 All ER 87; [1974] AC 623; (1974) 118 SJ 99; [1974] 2 WLR 152 PC Duty of occupier towards trespassers gauged by reference to humaneness.

Southern Rail Co and Cheam UDC, Nicholson v [1935] All ER 168; [1935] 1 KB 558; (1935) 79 LJ 116; (1935) 152 LTR 349 HC KBD Owner of land adjoining highway not under duty to maintain land so as to minimise dangers arising from roadworks: highway authority liable for altering level of highway so as to create danger.

Southern Rail Co, Sharpe v [1925] All ER 372; [1925] 2 KB 311; [1925] 94 LJCL 913; (1925) 133 LTR 693; (1924-25) 69 SJ 775 CA Company though/if negligent not liable to party who was contributorily negligent.

Southern Railway Co, Swain v [1938] 3 All ER 705; [1939] 1 KB 77; (1937-38) LIV TLR 1119 HC KBD Railway company not a public authority enjoying benefit of Public Authorities Protection Act 1893, s 1.

Southern Railway Company v Gosport Corporation (1926) 135 LTR 630 CA Corporation liable for negligent damage to bridge effected by temporary servant in charge of steam-roller which corporation had hired.

Sparham-Souter and others v Town and Country developments (Essex) Ltd and another [1976] 2 All ER 65; (1976) 126 NLJ 265t; [1976] QB 858; (1976) 120 SJ 216; [1976] 2 WLR 493 CA Cause of action from time building defects discovered/ought to have been discovered.

Sparks and another v Pardex Plant Engineers Ltd (1969) 113 SJ 1003 CA On appropriate damages for young girl left with permanent disfiguring scar on leg following negligent collision.

Sparks v Edward Ash, Ltd [1943] 1 All ER 1; (1943) 107 JP 45; (1944) 94 LJ 108; (1942) 86 SJ 322; (1942-43) LIX TLR CA Contributory negligence defence open in breach of statutory duty action.

Spartan Steel and Alloys Ltd v Martin and Co (Contractors) Ltd [1972] 3 All ER 557; (1972) 122 NLJ 585t; [1973] QB 27; (1972) 116 SJ 648; [1972] 3 WLR 502 CA Liability for physical damage but not non-consequential economic loss: no doctrine of 'parasitic damages'.

Spaul, Dawson v (1934-35) LI TLR 247 HC KBD Adjudication in personal injuries action ordered in interest of defendant despite death of plaintiff.

Speake v Hughes [1904] 1 KB 138; [1904] 73 LJCL 172; (1903-04) LXXXIX LTR 576 CA Damage allegedly arising from slander (loss of damage) too remote for recovery of damages.

Spedding, Thompson v [1973] RTR 312 CA On duty/liability of various drivers where 'tailing' each other as drive along road.

Spedeworth International Ltd, Latchford v (1984) 134 NLJ 36; [1983] TLR 587 HC QBD Successful negligence claim by hot-rod racer for injury suffered where tyres on track after another's collision with tyre fence forced him into collision with concrete flower bed.

Speidel v Plato Films, Ltd and others; Same v Unity Theatre Society, Ltd [1960] 2 All ER 521; (1960) 110 LJ 428; (1960) 104 SJ 602 CA In mitigation of damages can prove bad reputation in general/inexorably linked to libel.

Speidel, Plato Films, Ltd and others v [1961] 1 All ER 876; (1961) 111 LJ 220; (1961) 105 SJ 230 HL Can mitigate damages by introducing evidence of actual bad reputation (but not that should have bad reputation).

Spelthorne Borough Council, Davy v [1984] AC 262; [1983] TLR 604 HL Could bring action against local council for alleged negligent advice from council which led person subject to enforcement notice not to challenge that notice.

Spencer and another, Grange Motors (Cwmbrian) Ltd v [1969] 1 All ER 340; (1969) 119 NLJ 154t; (1968) 112 SJ 908; [1969] 1 WLR 53 CA On duty of care owed by one driver signalling to another.

Spenser v H Sinclair and Son [1934] LJNCCR 96 CyCt Was good cause for negligence action by owner of fence damaged by person who repeatedly skidded when out driving.

Sperrings Ltd, Goldsmith v [1977] 2 All ER 566; (1977) 121 SJ 304; [1977] 1 WLR 478 CA Abuse of process where action really brought to serve secondary purpose unavailable in law.

Spicer and another v Smee [1946] 1 All ER 489; (1946) 175 LTR 163 HC KBD Owner liable for nuisance on property though not in occupation; in nuisance can be liable for acts of independent contractor; same liability for private/public nuisance.

Spicer Brothers (Limited) and Minter, De Keyser's Royal Hotel (Limited) v (1913-14) XXX TLR 257 HC ChD Was nuisance for builders to do pile-driving at night which kept persons in adjoining premises awake.

Spiers and Pond (Limited), Michael v (1909-10) 101 LTR 352; (1908-09) XXV TLR 740 HC KBD Must be special damage for statement that person on licensed premises was drunk to be slander (that might be removed as company director sometime in future too tendentious).

Spiller (Hodder, third party), Homewood and another v [1963] Crim LR 52; (1962) 106 SJ 900 CA Dotted white lines on approach to junction did not alter duty of care owed by motorists.

Spring v Guardian Assurance plc and others [1992] TLR 46 HC QBD Employer furnishing reference to prospective employer for employee liable for breach of duty of care to latter.

Spring v Guardian Assurance plc and others [1994] 3 All ER 129; [1995] 2 AC 296; (1994) 144 NLJ 971; (1994) 138 SJ LB 183; [1994] TLR 381; [1994] 3 WLR 354 HL Employer under duty of care not to make negligent mis-statement when giving character reference; reasonable care requirement of employer may be implied term of contract.

Stephen Smith and Co (Limited), Coleman and Co (Limited) v (1910-11) XXVII TLR 533 HC ChD Failure of action brought by makers of 'Wincarnis' meat wine on trade mark, get up and passing off grounds against makers of 'Carvino' meat wine.

Stephen Smith and Co (Limited), Coleman and Co (Limited) v [1911] 2 Ch 572; (1911-12) XXVIII TLR 65 CA Failure of action brought by makers of 'Wincarnis' meat wine on trade mark, get up and passing off grounds against makers of 'Carvino' meat wine.

Stephens v Anglian Water Authority [1987] 1 WLR 1381 CA Landowner abstracting water from under own land owes no duty of care to neighbours in doing so.

Stephens v Avery and others (1988) 132 SJ 822 HC ChD Lesbian did have good basis for breach of confidence action against sometime partner for disclosing details of their relationship to the press.

Stephens, Weld-Blundell v [1920] All ER 32; (1920) 55 LJ 206; [1920] 89 LJCL 705; (1920) 123 LTR 593; (1919-20) 64 SJ 529; (1919-20) XXXVI TLR 640 HL Nominal damages where ultimate cause of action was one's own behaviour/where recovery sought for consequences that were not natural/probable consequences of acts of party aginst whom claiming.

Stephens, Weld-Blundell v [1919] 1 KB 520; [1919] 88 LJCL 689 (also HC KBD); (1919) 120 LTR 494; (1918-19) 63 SJ 301; (1918-19) XXXV TLR 245 CA Nominal damages where ultimate cause of action was one's own behaviour.

Stephens, Weld-Blundell v [1918] 2 KB 742; [1919] 88 LJCL 689 (also CA); (1917-18) XXXIV TLR 564; (1918) WN (I) 254 HC KBD Non-recovery of damages where ultimate cause of action was one's own.

Stepney Borough Council, C Burley, Limited v (1947) 176 LTR 535 HC KBD No implied warranty that goods to be carried could safely be carried.

Stepney Borough Council, Harrison v (1942) 86 SJ 234 HC KBD Council which had taken adequate steps to prevent accident arising not liable for injury suffered by person who slipped on soap at public baths.

Stepney Borough Council, Solomons v (1905) 69 JP 360 HC KBD Was evidence of negligence (leakage of electricity in explosive atmosphere) upon which jury could decide.

Sterling Wharfage Co, Ltd v Peek Brothers and Winch, Ltd [1935] LJNCCA 235 CA Persons from whose property water leaked into another's premises held to be under duty to show escape of water did not result from their negligence (failed to discharge this duty).

Sterman v EW and WJ Moore Ltd (a firm) [1970] 1 All ER 581 CA Limit disapplied (where just) to allow amendment of writ.

Stern v Piper and others [1996] 3 All ER 385; [1997] QB 123; (1996) 140 SJ LB 175; (1996) TLR 30/5/96; [1996] 3 WLR 715 CA Failed plea of justification in respect of newspaper publication of claims in affirmation concerning pending court action.

Stevens and Sons, Ltd and Sweet and Maxwell, Ltd, Coke Press Limited v (1936) 82 LJ 363 HC KBD Settlement of libel action brought by owners-publishers of 'The Law Journal'/the 'All England Reports' against the owners-publishers of the 'Law Journal Reports' (on foot of certain advertising by latter).

Stevens Scanlan and Co, Bagot v [1964] 3 All ER 577; [1966] 1 QB 197; (1964) 108 SJ 604; [1964] 3 WLR 1162 HC QBD Professional's failure to exercise proper care and skill in what contracted to do gives rise to claim in contract: no corollary duty on tort.

Stevens v Kelland and others [1970] RTR 445 HC QBD On respective liabilities for collision arising from negligent parking of vehicle.

Stevens v Stevens (1906-07) 51 SJ 825 HC KBD Injunction granted to restrain forty-nine year old son from imposing self on mother and insisting on living with her.

Stevens v William Nash, Ltd [1966] 3 All ER 156; (1965-66) 116 NLJ 1203; (1966) 110 SJ 710; [1966] 1 WLR 1550 CA Generally CA will not seek to examine personal injuries.

Stevenson v Society (Nationwide Building) (1984) 128 SJ 875 HC QBD Building society valuer not liable where despite disclaimer purchaser chose to rely on valuer's report as structural report, not mere valuation.

Stone v Bolton and others [1949] 1 All ER 237 Assizes Single incident not nuisance; cricket-playing not unnatural land user (Rylands v Fletcher inapplicable); cricket-ball inadvertently striking person on highway not negligent.

Stone v Bolton and others [1949] 2 All ER 851; [1950] 1 KB 201; (1949) 99 LJ 625; (1949) LXV TLR 683; (1949) WN (I) 432 CA Cricket ball flying from ground to highway was negligent/not nuisance.

Stone v Brewis (1902-03) 47 SJ 70 CA Addressing letter to notorious person care of another's address validly found to be libellous of latter; punitive damages justified.

Stone v Taffe [1974] 3 All ER 1016; (1974) 118 SJ 863 CA Occupier liable for injury to licensee who fell down unlit staircase when leaving public house premises after-hours.

Stone Wallwork (Charlton) Ltd, Murphy v [1969] 2 All ER 949; (1969) 119 NLJ 600t HL Lords may allow fresh evidence pointing to mistaken assessment of damages.

Stone, Bolton and others v [1951] 1 All ER 1078; [1951] AC 850; (1951) 101 LJ 287; (1951) 95 SJ 333; [1951] 1 TLR 977; (1951) WN (I) 280 HL Non-liability where ball from cricket game struck person on highway as foreseeable but negligible risk.

Stone, Coote and another v (1970) 120 NLJ 1205; [1971] RTR 66; (1971) 115 SJ 79 CA Parked car on clearway not a common law nuisance.

Stone, London and South of England Building Society v [1983] 3 All ER 105; (1983) 127 SJ 446; [1983] TLR 407; [1983] 1 WLR 1242 CA Damages for financial burden suffered/not difference between amount lent and amount would have lent on proper valuation; cannot claim for costs arising from unreasonable non-mitigation.

Stone, London and South of England Building Society v (1982) 132 NLJ 218 HC QBD Damages awarded in successful negligence action against surveyor was difference between valuation price and true worth at time of survey.

Stoop, Moy v (1908-09) XXV TLR 262 HC KBD Noise from house used as children's nursery not nuisance.

Stopes et e contra, Sutherland and Others v [1924] All ER 19; [1925] AC 47; (1924) 59 LJ 757; [1925] 94 LJCL 166; (1925) 132 LTR 550; (1924-25) 69 SJ 138; (1924-25) XLI TLR 106 HL Plea seeming partly one of justification, partly one of fair comment a plea of fair comment.

Stopes v Sutherland and another (1922-23) XXXIX TLR 242 HC KBD Libel action failed where jury found words complained of though unfair were true in substance/fact.

Stopes v Sutherland and another (1923) 58 LJ 366; (1922-23) XXXIX TLR 677 CA Libel action succeeded where jury found words complained of were true in substance/fact but unfair comment.

Stores and Stores v Graham and Bolangaro (1949) 99 LJ 108 CyCt Damages from police for false imprisonment (continued detention in police station after police believed detained suspect to be innocent of alleged offence).

Storey v National Coal Board [1983] 1 All ER 375 HC QBD Company officials engaging in dangerous practice of which employees warned not condoning practice: no negligence.

Stott and Daily Mirror Newspapers Ltd, Maulding v (1978) 128 NLJ 464t CA Exemplary damages could be sought where newspaper committing libel did so in belief that any damages might have to pay would be less than increased profits made by publishing article.

Stott v Sir William Arrol and Co, Ltd [1953] 2 All ER 416; [1953] 2 QB 92; (1953) 97 SJ 439; [1953] 3 WLR 166 HC QBD One half of all injury benefits accruing to party during and post-incapacity to be considered when awarding damages.

Stott v West Yorkshire Road Car Co Ltd and another (Home Bakeries Ltd and another, third parties) [1971] 3 All ER 534; [1971] 2 QB 651; [1971] 3 WLR 282 CA Persons settling action without admitting liability can seek contribution from third parties.

Stott, McGowan v (1930) 143 LTR 217 CA Re-trial ordered where facts required defendant to explain them.

Stourfield Park Hotel Company, Hawker v (1900) WN (I) 51 HC ChD Can restrain making of untrue statement even if not libellous/defamatory if statement operates to injure another.

Stubbings v Webb and another [1993] 1 All ER 322; [1993] AC 498; [1993] 2 FCR 699 (also CA); [1993] 1 FLR 714; (1993) 143 NLJ 166; (1993) 137 SJ LB 32; [1992] TLR 619; [1993] 2 WLR 120 HL Claim for damages arising from mental ill-health following childhood rape/indecent assault an action for trespass to person and hence subject to six-year limitation period.

Stubbings v Webb and another [1991] 3 ALL ER 949; [1993] 2 FCR 699 (also HL); [1992] 1 FLR 296; [1992] QB 197; [1991] TLR 171; [1991] 3 WLR 383 CA Cause of action for personal injury on foot of sexual abuse ran from date plaintiff realised personal injury attributable to sexual abuse.

Stubbs v Anthony (1948) 98 LJ 94 CyCt Defendant liable in negligence for damage occasioned by collapse of his chimney stack onto adjoining property of another.

Stubbs, Limited v Russell [1913] AC 386; (1913) 48 LJ 227; (1913) 82 LJPC 98; (1913) 108 LTR 529; (1912-13) XXIX TLR 409; (1913) WN (I) 103 HL Mistaken naming of party in Stubbs' Gazette not libellous in light of note at head of list of names.

Stubbs, Ltd v Mazure [1918-19] All ER 1081; [1920] AC 66; (1919) 54 LJ 344; [1919] 88 LJPC 135; (1920) 122 LTR 5; (1918-19) XXXV TLR 697; (1919) WN (I) 234 HL Wrongful publication of name in Stubbs' Gazette deemed defamatory despite qualifier published at head of relevant section.

Studds (Walter John), R v (1909) 3 Cr App R 207 CCA Must specify elements of (alleged) justification to libel.

Sturge v Hackett [1962] 3 All ER 166; [1962] 1 WLR 1257 CA Occupier liable for escape of fire and in negligence for starting fire.

Sturley v Commissioner of Police of the Metropolis [1984] TLR 410 HC QBD Successful action for assault against police officers for excessively forceful form of restraint employed on middle-aged female detainee.

Suchcicka v Grabowski (1973) 117 SJ 58 CA On personal injuries damages (and interest awardable thereon) for foreigner injured in collision (exchange rate being particularly difficult to calculate).

Sudds v Hanscombe [1971] RTR 212 CA Person entering junction after lights red/green was/was not (as had behaved reasonably in circumstances) negligent.

Sudron and Coulson, Smith v (1982) 132 NLJ 415c CA Successful appeal against finding of negligence where puppy slipped through fence (reasonably designed to keep it in) and caused road accident.

Sugar v London Midland and Scottish Railway Company (1941) 105 JP 100; (1941) 164 LTR 311; (1941) 85 SJ 32; (1940-41) LVII TLR 197 HC KBD Exemption clause inapplicable where had been blocked out by date stamp.

Sully, Barnard v (1931) 72 LJ 122; (1930-31) XLVII TLR 557; (1931) WN (I) 180 HC KBD Where damage proved to have been done by another's motor car is rebuttable presumption that owner of car (or agent/servant) was driving same.

Sum (Li Ping), Tong (Chan Wai) and another v [1985] AC 446; (1985) 129 SJ 153; [1985] 2 WLR 396 PC On appropriate damages for personal injuries; on damages for loss of future earnings.

Summerskill (W), Horlick's Malted Milk Company v (1915-16) XXXII TLR 63 HC ChD Term 'malted milk' a descriptive term use of which by rival sellers of malted milk was not passing off.

Summerskill, Horlick's Malted Milk Company v (1916) 51 LJ 129; [1917] 86 LJCh 175; (1916-17) 61 SJ 114; (1916-17) XXXIII TLR 83 HL Term 'malted milk' a descriptive term use of which by rival sellers of malted milk was not passing off.

Summerskill, Horlick's Malted Milk Company v [1916] 85 LJP 338; (1916) 114 LTR 484; (1915-16) 60 SJ 320; (1915-16) XXXII TLR 311 CA Term 'malted milk' a descriptive term use of which by rival sellers of malted milk was not passing off.

Sumner and another, Wooldridge v [1962] 2 All ER 978; (1962) 112 LJ 520; [1963] 2 QB 43; (1962) 106 SJ 489 CA Sports participant not liable in negligence to viewing public injured through non-reckless errors of judgment; volenti non fit injuria not relevant.

Sun Life Assurance Co of Canada v WH Smith and Son, Ltd [1933] All ER 432; (1934) 150 LTR 211 CA Vendor liable for libel in negligently not knowing poster contained libel.

Surtees v Kingston-upon-Thames Royal Borough Council and Hughes and Hughes [1990] 1 FLR 103 HC QBD Local authority/foster-parents not negligent as regards injuries suffered by plaintiff while in foster-care.

Sutcliffe v Holmes and another [1946] 2 All ER 599; [1947] KB 147; [1947] 116 LJR 415; (1946) 175 LTR 487; (1945-46) LXII TLR 733; (1947) WN (I) 7 CA Sheep trespass: could not claim other party liable to fence as no evidence of same; could not claim due to third party's non-fencing as had known of third party's failure and should have guarded against it.

Sutcliffe v Pressdram Ltd [1990] 1 All ER 269; (1989) 139 NLJ 1453; [1991] 1 QB 152; [1990] 2 WLR 271 CA Indirect evidence of newspaper payments not adequate to determine if payments made; damages a matter for jury — may be advised of what money is worth but not awards in other cases.

Sutcliffe v Thackrah and others [1974] 1 All ER 859; [1974] AC 727; (1974) 124 NLJ 200t; (1974) 118 SJ 148; [1974] 2 WLR 295 HL Architect/valuer acting in arbitral rôle immune from action for negligence in so doing.

Sutcliffe v Thackrah and others [1973] 2 All ER 1047; (1973) 117 SJ 509; [1973] 1 WLR 888 CA Architect's giving of final certificate an arbitral act clothed with immunity from action for negligence.

Sutherland and another, Stopes v (1922-23) XXXIX TLR 242 HC KBD Libel action failed where jury found words complained of though unfair were true in substance/fact.

Sutherland and another, Stopes v (1923) 58 LJ 366; (1922-23) XXXIX TLR 677 CA Libel action succeeded where jury found words complained of were true in substance/fact but unfair comment.

Sutherland and Others v Stopes et e contra [1924] All ER 19; [1925] AC 47; (1924) 59 LJ 757; [1925] 94 LJCL 166; (1925) 132 LTR 550; (1924-25) 69 SJ 138; (1924-25) XLI TLR 106 HL Plea seeming partly one of justification, partly one of fair comment a plea of fair comment.

Sutherland Publishing Co, Ltd v Caxton Publishing Co, Ltd (No 2) [1937] 4 All ER; [1938] Ch 174; [1938] 107 LJCh 99; (1936) 154 LTR 367; (1935-36) LII TLR 230; (1937) WN (I) 393 CA On post-breach of copyright damages for conversion.

Sutherland Publishing Co, Ltd v Caxton Publishing Co, Ltd (No 2) [1937] 1 All ER 338; [1937] Ch 294; [1937] 106 LJCh 104; (1937) 156 LTR 191; (1936-37) LIII TLR 277; (1937) WN (I) 46 HC ChD Appropriate damages for conversion; three-year limitation period for conversion action subsequent to copyright infringement.

Sutherland Publishing Co, Ltd, Caxton Publishing Co, Ltd v [1938] 4 All ER 389; [1939] 108 LJCh 5; (1938) 86 LJ 383; (1939) 160 LTR 17; (1938) 82 SJ 1047; (1938-39) LV TLR 123; (1938) WN (I) 367 HL Three-year limitation on post-breach of copyright conversion action; damages available for both infringement and conversion post-breach of copyright.

Sutherland Publishing Company, Limited v Caxton Publishing Company, Limited [1936] 105 LJCh 150; (1938) 158 LTR 17; (1937-38) LIV TLR 112; (1936) WN (I) 58 CA Six-year limitation on post-breach of copyright conversion action; on gauging damages for such conversion.

Sutherland v CR Maton and Sons Ltd (1977) 127 NLJ 291 HC QBD Bungalow-builders liable to first and subsequent owners for defects in construction of house (even though buyers relied on building society inspection and did not employ own surveyor to inspect house).

Sutherland, Glasgow Corporation v (1951) 95 SJ 204; (1951) WN (I) 111 HL Tram driver who braked suddenly to avoid injury to animal and so occasioned injury to passenger who fell held not to be negligent.

Sutton and Co, Glanville v [1928] 1 KB 571; (1927) 64 LJ 455; (1928) 97 LJCL 166; (1928) 138 LTR 336; (1927) WN (I) 311 HC KBD That owner knew horse bit horses did not show owner knew horse would bite humans.

Sutton Steam Laundry, Hilton v [1946] 115 LJ 33; (1946) 174 LTR 31 CA Out of time action disallowed.

Sutton v Bootle Corporation [1947] 1 All ER 92; (1947) 111 JP 81; [1947] KB 359; (1947) 97 LJ 23; (1947) 177 LTR 168 CA Licensor only obliged to warn licensee of dangers actually known.

Sutton v Child (1916) CC Rep V 91 CyCt Absent scienter dog-owner not liable in negligence for to owner of turkey killed by dog.

Sutton, Jeeves v [1934] LJNCCR 288 CyCt Was trespass for owner of premises not to allow statutory tenant return to premises.

Sutton, London Jewellers, Limited v; Same v Robertsons (London), Limited (1934) 77 LJ 94; (1933-34) L TLR 193; (1934) WN (I) 21 HC KBD Pawnbrokers with whom fraudulently obtained goods were pawned liable to true owners of jewellery in detinue.

SW Farmer and Son, Ltd, Howard v [1938] 2 All ER 296; (1938) 85 LJ 292; (1938) 82 SJ 351 CA Workman unsuccessful in negligence suit as he was careless in uncompleted building.

Swadling v Cooper [1930] All ER 257; [1931] AC 1; (1930) 70 LJ 108; (1931) 100 LJCL 97; (1930) 143 LTR 732; (1930) 74 SJ 536; (1929-30) XLVI TLR 597; (1930) WN (I) 204 HL On direction regarding negligence in case where person knocked down in motor collision.

Swadling, Cooper v [1930] 1 KB 403; (1930) 69 LJ 9; (1930) 99 LJCL 118; (1930) 142 LTR 411; (1929-30) XLVI TLR 73; (1929) WN (I) 273 CA On direction regarding negligence in case where person knocked down in motor collision.

Swaffer and others, Greenslade and another v; Same v World's Press News Publishing Co, Ltd and another [1955] 3 All ER 200; (1955) 105 LJ 536; (1955) 99 SJ 725; [1955] 1 WLR 1109 CA On facts to support innuendo (and striking out where not there).

Swaffer v Mulcahy; Hooker v Same; Smith v Same (1933-34) L TLR 179 HC KBD Sheep/beasts of plough privileged from seizure if alternative distress possible; wrongful seizure of bailment entitles one to bring action of replevin.

Swain v Southern Railway Co [1938] 3 All ER 705; [1939] 1 KB 77; (1937-38) LIV TLR 1119 HC KBD Railway company not a public authority enjoying benefit of Public Authorities Protection Act 1893, s 1.

Swain v Southern Railway Company (1939) 160 LTR 606; (1939) 83 SJ 476; (1938-39) LV TLR 805 CA Railway company not a public authority enjoying benefit of Public Authorities Protection Act 1893, s 1.

Swan and Edgar, Bourne v (1902-03) 47 SJ 92 HC ChD On type of evidence admissible in support of passing off action.

Swan and Edgar, Ltd and another, O'Connor v (1963) 107 SJ 215 HC QBD Independent contractor (plasterer) liable for latent defect in plastering which five years after completion was responsible for injury.

Swan Hunter Group plc and others, Bryce v [1988] 1 All ER 659 HC QBD Failure to meet duty to minimise asbestos exposure raised presumption that caused asbestos-related death.

Swan Motor Co (Swansea), Ltd (Swansea Corporation and James, Third Parties), Davies v [1949] 1 All ER 620; [1949] 2 KB 291; (1949) LXV TLR 278; (1949) WN (I) 192 CA Lack of proper care (not breach of duty) necessary to show contributory negligence to own death.

Swan v Salisbury Construction Co, Ltd [1966] 2 All ER 138; (1965) 109 SJ 195; [1966] 1 WLR 204 PC Res ipsa loquitur arises when crane collapses.

Swansea City AFC Ltd and another, McCord v [1997] TLR 64 HC QBD Football player could be liable in negligence for injuries occasioned to another player during football match.

Swansea City Council v Glass [1992] 2 All ER 680 CA Cause of action to recover expenses runs from date works completed not date of first demand for payment.

Swansea City Council, Jones v (1989) 139 NLJ 503; (1990) 134 SJ 341; [1990] 1 WLR 54 CA Could be misfeasance in public office for council to refuse change of user of leasehold premises because of ill-will towards lessee's husband, a member of a minority political party on the local authority.

Swansea City Council, Jones v (1990) 134 SJ 1437; [1990] 1 WLR 1453 HL Not proven to be misfeasance in public office where council refused change of user of leasehold premises to lessee whose husband was a member of a minority political party on the local authority.

Sweeney and another, Janvier v (1919) 121 LTR 179; (1918-19) XXXV TLR 226 HC KBD Is good cause of action where make statement with intent to injure another who is injured thereby.

Sweeney and Barker, Janvier v [1919] 88 LJCL 1231; (1918-19) 63 SJ 430; (1918-19) XXXV TLR 360 CA Is good cause of action where make statement with intent to injure another who is injured thereby.

Sweeney v Coote [1907] AC 221; [1907] 76 LJPC 49; (1907) XCVI LTR 749; (1906-07) 51 SJ 444; (1906-07) XXIII TLR 448; (1907) WN (I) 92 PC Failed claim for injunction to restrain impeding one in carrying on business/job.

Sweeney, Wharton v (1961) 105 SJ 887 CA On appropriate damages for loss of eye.

Sweetapple v Minett (1976) 126 NLJ 1168b CA Smoke billowing from neighbour's fire into plaintiff's house not an actionable nuisance: people must live and let live.

Sweeting (ET) and Son, Ltd, Sharpe v [1963] 2 All ER 455; (1963) 113 LJ 399; (1963) 107 SJ 666; [1963] 1 WLR 665 HC QBD Sufficient proximity between builder and later occupier of premises to sustain negligence action.

Swift v Ellis [1939] LJNCCR 384 CyCt Failed action for trespass by sheep from common onto land adjoining common which plaintiff-owner was under duty to fence off.

Swift v Prout (1964) 108 SJ 317 CA On appropriate personal injury damages for person whose injuries had shortened his lifespan to three years from date of accident.

Swindle and others v Harrison [1997] TLR 197 CA On damages recoverable by person who suffered loss as result of negligence of solicitors in context of mortgage-bridging loan-property purchase transaction.

Swinfen, Cook v (1965) 109 SJ 972 HC QBD Damages for loss of chances in divorce suit/of receiving maintenance as result of solicitor's negligence.

Swingcastle Ltd v Alastair Gibson (a firm) [1991] 2 All ER 353; (1991) 141 NLJ 563; [1991] TLR 197; [1991] 2 WLR 1091 HL Where loan made on foot of negligent valuation only damages available are for loss of use of amount loaned.

Swingcastle Ltd v Gibson [1990] 3 All ER 463; (1990) 140 NLJ 818; [1990] 1 WLR 1223 CA Negligent surveyor liable to mortgagee for all loss where mortgagee seeks to sell property following mortgagor's default on repayment.

Swinney and others v Chief Constable of Northumbria Police Force [1996] 3 All ER 449; (1996) 146 NLJ 878; [1997] QB 464; (1996) TLR 28/3/96; [1996] 3 WLR 968 CA Could be that police owe duty of care to informant not to negligently disclose information concerning informant.

Swordheath Properties Ltd v Tabet and others [1979] 1 All ER 240; (1979) 129 (1) NLJ 40; [1979] 1 WLR 285 CA Damages for continuing trespass whether or not land would have been let; measure of damages.

Sycamore v Ley [1932] All ER 97; (1932) 74 LJ 41; (1932) 147 LTR 342 CA Not negligent to leave non-vicious dog inside car as guard-dog.

Sydney Mitchell and Co (a firm) and others, P (third party) , Ali (Saif) v [1977] 3 All ER 744; (1977) 127 NLJ 638t; [1978] QB 95; (1977) 121 SJ 336; [1977] 3 WLR 421 CA Barrister immune from negligence suits for actions during trial and pre-trial actions connected with trial.

Sydney Mitchell and Co (a firm) and others, P (third party) [1978] 3 All ER 1033, Ali (Saif) v [1980] AC 198; (1978) 128 NLJ 1196t; (1978) 122 SJ 761; [1978] 3 WLR 849 HL Only acts of counsel intrinsically connected with conduct of case in court immune from negligence suit.

Syed Hussain Bin Abdul Rahman Bin Shaikh Alkaff and others [1985] 1 WLR 1392 PC Stayed possession order valid where trespassers had conceded were such (and so not protected under Control of Rent Act) in consenting to stayed possession order.

Sykes and others v Midland Bank Executor and Trustee Co Ltd and others [1970] 2 All ER 471; [1971] 1 QB 113; (1970) 114 SJ 225; [1970] 3 WLR 273 CA Solicitor not advising of unusual clause in lease negligent (but nominal damages for breach of contract if client does not prove negligence led to acting as did).

Sykes and others v Midland Bank Executor and Trustee Co, Ltd and others [1969] 2 All ER 1238; (1969) 119 NLJ 297t; [1969] 2 QB 518; (1969) 113 SJ 243; [1969] 2 WLR 1173 HC QBD Solicitor negligent for failing to draw unusual terms in lease to client's attention: cause of action once rent payable; appropriate damages.

Taittinger v Allbev (1993) 143 NLJ 332; [1993] TLR 62 HC ChD 'Elderflower Champagne', a non-alcoholic, carbonated drink produced and marketed in England unlikely to adversely impinge on goodwill in name 'champagne' of real champagne producers.

Takaro Properties Ltd, Rowling and another v [1988] 1 All ER 163; [1988] AC 473; (1988) 132 SJ 126; [1988] 2 WLR 418 PC Minister exercising statutory duty not liable for negligence despite judicial review finding that he considered irrelevant material as opinion was still reasonable.

Talbot Motor Co Ltd, British Broadcasting Corporation v (1981) 131 NLJ 237 HC ChD Successful passing off action restraining defendants from using same name in respect of same product which plaintiffs had tested some years previously.

Talbot v Berkshire County Council [1993] 4 All ER 9; (1993) 143 NLJ 402; [1994] QB 290; [1993] RTR 406; [1993] TLR 168; [1993] 3 WLR 708 CA Rule barring action where one already brought by co-plaintiff for same cause against same defendant applies to personal injuries.

Tallent v Coldwell [1938] Ch 653; (1937-38) LIV TLR 564 HC ChD Post-copyright infringement damages for conversion.

Tallerman v Dowsing Radiant Heat Company [1900] 1 Ch 1; [1900] LXIX (1) LJ 46 CA No injunction to stop inventor circulating publication which quoted from another's article on similar process of treating disease without mentioning other's name as was no passing off.

Tallerman v The Dowsing Radiant Heat Company (Limited) (1899-1900) 48 WR 146 HC ChD No injunction to stop inventor circulating publication which quoted from another's article on similar process of treating disease without mentioning other's name as was no passing off.

Tamworth Borough Council v Fazeley Town Council (1978) 122 SJ 699 HC ChD Injunction to prevent operation of new market on same day as franchise market on basis that holding former constituted nuisance.

Tan Chye Choo and others v Moi (Chong Kew) [1970] 1 All ER 266; (1969) 113 SJ 1000; [1970] 1 WLR 147 PC No right of action where defect in vehicle not result of negligence.

Tanter, General Accident, Fire and Life Assurance Corporation v (1984) 134 NLJ 35/82 HC QBD Broker owed duty of care to underwriter to whom gave signing down indication.

Targett v Torfaen Borough Council [1992] 3 All ER 27; (1991) 141 NLJ 1698 CA Landlord responsible for design/construction of house under duty of care to ensure house free from injurious defects even where known to victim if victim unable to avoid danger.

Tarlo, Gregory v (1964) 108 SJ 219 HC QBD Damages awarded against solicitor for failure to prosecute client's claim within statutorily allowed period.

Tarmac Civil Engineering Ltd and another, Spalding v [1966] 1 WLR 156 CA On liability of persons hiring crane to another for negligence of driver supplied with crane (construction of exceptions clause).

Tarmac Civil Engineering Ltd, Arthur White (Contractors) Ltd v (1967) 111 SJ 831; [1967] 1 WLR 1508 HL Exceptions clause excluding liability for negligence of driver supplied along with hired equipment to hirer valid and enforced.

Tarrant v Ramage and others [1997] TLR 434 HC QBD Shipowners must take reasonable care of crew members on ship operating in war zone.

Tarrant v Rowlands and another [1979] RTR 144 HC QBD Inadequate drainage by highway authority of area where water habitually collected after rain meant authority liable for accident occasioned thereby; person causing collision by driving so fast that fails to observe pool of water and drives into same losing control of car is negligent.

Tarrant, Randall v [1955] 1 All ER 600; (1955) 105 LJ 168; (1955) 99 SJ 184; [1955] 1 WLR 255 CA Driver of moving vehicle must show not negligent where strikes obvious non-moving vehicle; trespass by driver in field adjoining highway did not mean trespass/nuisance on highway.

Tarratt, Rogers v (1931) 72 LJ ccr43 CyCt Person failing to establish title to near-abandoned property that adjoined own held to have trespassed on near-abandoned property.

Tarry v Chandler (1935) 79 SJ 11 HC ChD Noisy manner in which stadium was operated was a nuisance.

Taylor, Edwards v (1922-23) 67 SJ 248 HC KBD Husband not liable where wife fraudulently represents that she is authorised to act for him.

Taylor, Finlayson v (1983) 133 NLJ 720; [1983] TLR 259 HC QBD Landlord liable in detinue/conversion for seeking to exercise lien over goods bailed with him by tenant where latter owed arrears of rent.

Taylor, Glasgow Corporation v [1921] All ER 1 HL Public authority negligent in allowing children into public playground where knew poisonous berries to be growing.

Taylor, Ogwo v [1987] 1 All ER 668; [1988] AC 431 (also HL); (1987) 137 NLJ 99; (1987) 131 SJ 506; [1987] 2 WLR 988 CA Negligent starter of fire liable to fireman for any foreseeable injuries suffered.

Taylor, Ogwo v [1987] 3 All ER 961; [1988] AC 431 (also CA); (1987) 137 NLJ 1110; (1987) 131 SJ 1628; [1987] 3 WLR 1145 HL Negligent starter of fire owes duty of care to firemen for injuries suffered extinguishing fire.

Taylor, Smith v (1965-66) 116 NLJ 1518 HC QBD Exclusion clause could not be relied on because not adequately brought to plaintiff's notice.

Taylor, Taylor and others v [1984] TLR 247 CA On relevant factors when deciding whether or not to disapply time limitation in personal injuries action.

TE Hopkins and Son, Ltd, Baker and another v [1958] 3 All ER 147; (1958) 102 SJ 636 HC QBD Master owed duty of care to doctor seeking to rescue servant; fatal accident damages not to be reduced by portion of estate made up of policy money.

TE Hopkins and Son, Ltd, Ward v; Baker and another v TE Hopkins and Son, Ltd [1959] 3 All ER 225; [1959] 1 WLR 966 CA Employer liable in negligence to servant also liable to doctor seeking to rescue same: no novus actus interveniens/volenti non fit injuria.

Teasdale v Williams and Co (1983) 133 NLJ 105 HC QBD Successful negligence suit against solicitor whose negligent failure to advise client of landlord's application for interim rent meant client failed to apply for new lease.

Tebbit and another, Lonrho plc v [1992] 4 All ER 280 CA Private action for negligence may arise if Secretary of State fails to release firm from undertaking to Secetary regarding purchase of shares.

Tebbit and another, Lonrho plc v [1991] 4 All ER 973; (1991) 141 NLJ 1295 HC ChD Striking-out application not appropriate forum for deciding legal points in new field of law; duty of care may arise in respect of discharge of statutory powers implementing, but not deciding policy even where purely economic loss; action against minister rather than judicial review permissible.

Tebbit, Bookbinder v [1989] 1 All ER 1169; (1989) 139 NLJ 112; [1989] 1 WLR 640 CA Plaintiff withdrawing allegation of general slander meant defendant could not rely on general charge to support justification plea.

Tedesco, Venn v (1926) 90 JP 185; [1926] 2 KB 227; [1926] 95 LJCL 866; (1926) 135 LTR 108; (1925-26) 70 SJ 709; (1925-26) XLII TLR 478 HC KBD In action under Lord Campbell's Act 1846 limitation period against public authorities is limitation prescribed in that Act.

Television New Zealand Ltd, Prebble (Richard William) v [1995] 1 AC 321; (1994) 144 NLJ 1131; (1994) 138 SJ LB 175; [1994] TLR 393; [1994] 3 WLR 970 PC On praying in aid Parliamentary proceedings to justify alleged defamation.

Telfair Shipping Corporation v Inersea Carriers SA [1985] 1 WLR 553 HC QBD Claim under indemnity clause over/under six years after stowage/discharge was statute-barred.

Telnikoff v Matusevitch [1990] 3 All ER 865; [1991] 1 QB 102; (1990) 134 SJ 1078; [1990] TLR 423; [1990] 3 WLR 725 CA Court may look to broader context in deciding if material libellous; plea of fair comment raises presumption that comment an honest expression of opinion unless counter-claim of malicious publication.

Telnikoff v Matusevitch [1991] 4 All ER 817; [1992] 2 AC 343; (1991) 141 NLJ 1590; [1991] TLR 513; [1991] 3 WLR 952 HL Letter in reply to article to be looked at in isolation when jury deciding if fair comment/libel; fair comment must be objectively fair.

The Dunlop Pneumatic Tyre Company (Limited) v Maison Talbot, the Earl of Shrewsbury and Talbot, and DM Weigel; Clipper Pneumatic Tyre Company v Same (1903-04) 48 SJ 156; (1903-04) XX TLR 88 HC KBD Injunction to restrain slander of title before actual damage transpires is available.

The Dunlop Pneumatic Tyre Company, Limited v The Dunlop Motor Company [1907] AC 430; (1907-08) XCVII LTR 259; (1906-07) 51 SJ 715; (1906-07) XXIII TLR 717; (1907) WN (I) 187 HL No passing off by latter party to case; nobody enjoys right to sole use of name 'Dunlop'.

The Earl of Craven v Pridmore and others (1900-01) XVII TLR 399 HC KBD Neighbour's longtime repairing of fence/cutting of trees in ditch bounding rented land (actions known to tenant but not to landlord of rented land) held to rebut presumption that fence was on landlord's land.

The Earl of Craven v Pridmore and others (1901-02) XVIII TLR 282 CA Neighbour's longtime repairing of fence/cutting of trees in ditch bounding rented land (actions known to tenant but not to landlord of rented land) did not rebut presumption that fence was on landlord's land.

The Earl of Harrington v The Mayor, &c, of Derby [1905] 1 Ch 205; (1905) 69 JP 62; (1904) 39 LJ 686; (1904-05) XXI TLR 98; (1904) WN (I) 210 HC ChD Consideration of Public Authorities Protection Act 1893, s 1, in context of nuisance action.

The East London Harbour Board v The Caledonia Landing, Shipping, and Salvage Company (Limited) and The Colonial Fisheries Company (Limited) (1907-08) XXIV TLR 516 PC Harbour board liable for not re-securing tug and coal hulk which had previously moved.

The Eastern and Australian Steamship Company (Limited), Fowles v (1916-17) 115 LTR 354; (1915-16) XXXII TLR 663 PC Queensland government not liable for negligence of shipping pilots it provided.

The Economist and another, University of Glasgow v; University of Edinburgh v The Economist and another [1990] TLR 533 HC QBD Defendant had to prove foreign libel laws different where plaintiff raised presumption that were the same.

The Embassy Hotel, Wright v (1935) 79 SJ 12 HC KBD Innkeeper not liable for theft of property of patron who had been negligent as regards care of same.

The Fen Reeves of the Biggleswade Common (by Frederick Gee, Acting Fen Reeve) v MO Seward and Son (1912) CC Rep I 48 CyCt On extent of liability of Fen Reeves — here found not to be liable in negligence.

The Fine Cotton Spinners' and Doublers' Association (Limited) and John Cash and Sons (Limited) v Harwood Cash and Co (Limited) [1907] 2 Ch 184; (1907-08) XCVII LTR 45; (1906-07) XXIII TLR 537; (1907) WN (I) 127 HC ChD Injunction granted to prevent new company using name of existing company.

The Freshfield (Owners) and others, Arthur Guinness, Son and Company (Dublin) Ltd v; The Lady Gwendolen (Limitation) (1965) 109 SJ 336; [1965] 3 WLR 91 CA Duty of person whose secondary business is that of shipowner is same as that of shipowner for whom is principal business.

The Friendly Society of Operative Stonemasons of England, Ireland and Wales and others, Read v [1902] 2 KB 88; [1902] 71 LJCL 634 HC KBD Good faith/absence of malice not enough to justify interfering with contract: only defence is having same/better right than that of person interfered with.

The Friendly Society of Operative Stonemasons of England, Ireland and Wales and others, Read v [1902] 2 KB 732; (1902) 37 LJ 543; [1902] 71 LJCL 994; (1902-03) XIX TLR 20 CA Earlier agreement not enough to justify interfering with contract.

The Governors of St Bartholomew's Hospital, Hillyer v (1909) 73 JP 501; [1909] 2 KB 820; (1909) 44 LJ 483; [1909] 78 LJKB 958; (1909-10) 101 LTR 368; (1908-09) 53 SJ 714; (1909) WN (I) 188 CA Hospital governors not liable for injury allegedly sustained by plaintiff at hands of hospital workers.

The Grand Priory in the British Realm of the Venerable Order of the Hospital of St John of Jerusalem, Shiffman v [1936] 1 All ER 557; (1936) 80 SJ 346 HC KBD Negligent for non-continuous attention to flagpole (occasioning injury to child allured thereby) erected in public place.

The Kite [1933] All ER 234 HC PDAD If can explain act in way that is no less likely than negligence burden reverts to plaintiff to show act was negligent; plaintiffs not allowed recover in tort for negligence for which under their contract with defendants, defendants not liable.

The Koursk [1924] All ER 168 CA To be joint tortfeasor must be some sort of connection/common plan between tortfeasors.

The Law Society, Hambrook v (1967) 111 SJ 195 HC QBD Non-malicious answers to Ministry of Labour questionnaire enjoyed qualified privilege.

The Lloyds Investment Trust Company (Limited) and others, Lloyds Bank Limited v (1911-12) XXVIII TLR 379 HC ChD Injunction granted upon application of Lloyds Bank prohibiting use of name Lloyds in connection with banking-finance or together with word 'Trust'.

The London and Northern Bank (Limited) v George Newnes (Limited) (1899-1900) XVI TLR 76 HC ChD Injunction granted to restrain publication of unfounded statement that particular bank was in liquidation.

The London County Council, Price's Patent Candle Company (Limited) v (1908) 72 JP 315; (1908) 43 LJ 302; [1909] 78 LJCh 1 (also CA); (1907-08) XXIV TLR 607; (1908) WN (I) 131 HC ChD Council not to create nuisance in course of sewage treatment.

The London County Council, Price's Patent Candle Company (Limited) v [1908] 2 Ch 526; (1908) 72 JP 429; (1908) 43 LJ 524; [1909] 78 LJCh 1 (also HC ChD); (1908-09) XCIX LTR 571; (1907-08) XXIV TLR 823; (1908) WN (I) 188 CA Council not to create nuisance in course of sewage treatment.

The London Evening Newspapers Company (Limited), George Outram and Co (Limited) v (1910-11) 55 SJ 255; (1910-11) XXVII TLR 231 HC ChD Injunction to use same newspaper name refused where use of name would not result in any confusion/injury.

The London Express Newspaper, Ltd, Knupffer v [1942] 2 All ER 555; [1943] KB 80; (1943) 93 LJ 125; [1943] 112 LJ 176; (1942) 167 LTR 376; (1942) 86 SJ 367; (1942-43) LIX TLR 31; (1942) WN (I) 206 CA Cannot claim individually libelled by class/group libel unless can show words refer to one as individual.

The London General Omnibus Company (Limited), Clark v (1906) 41 LJ 492; [1906] 75 LJKB 907; (1906-07) XCV LTR 435; (1905-06) 50 SJ 631; (1905-06) XXII TLR 691 CA Funeral expenses of unmarried daughter living with father irrecoverable as fatal accident damages by father.

The London General Omnibus Company (Limited), Hase v (1906-07) XXIII TLR 616 HC KBD Not negligent of bus driver to turn bus close to kerb and so occasion injury to upstairs passenger struck by small obstruction avoidable by wider turn.

The London General Omnibus Company (Limited), Simon v (1906-07) XXIII TLR 463 HC KBD Not negligent where passenger struck by obstruction as bus rounded corner as not proven driver could reasonably have seen obstruction/have foreseen it would injure passenger.

The London Motor-Cab Proprietors Association and the British Motor-Cab Company (Limited) v The Twentieth Century Press (1912) (Limited) (1917-18) XXXIV TLR 68 HC ChD Injunction on publication pending libel trial refused where would be to no effect (was no intent to publish any more)/action was wrongly framed/publication in issue might not be privileged.

The Mayor, &c, of Brighton, Heath v (1908) 72 JP 225; (1908) XCVIII LTR 718; (1907-08) XXIV TLR 414 HC ChD Noise from electric generator/transformer annoying churchgoers not enough to merit injunction for nuisance.

The Mayor, &c, of Chichester v Foster (1905-06) XCIII LTR 750; (1905-06) XXII TLR 18; (1905-06) 54 WR 199 HC KBD Recovery of damages from driver of traction engine who in driving along road crushed water mains leading to waterworks.

The Mayor, &c, of Derby, The Earl of Harrington v [1905] 1 Ch 205; (1905) 69 JP 62; (1904) 39 LJ 686; (1904-05) XXI TLR 98; (1904) WN (I) 210 HC ChD Consideration of Public Authorities Protection Act 1893, s 1, in context of nuisance action.

The Mayor, &c, of Exeter, Stanbury v (1906) 70 JP 11; (1905-06) XCIII LTR 795; (1905-06) XXII TLR 3; (1905-06) 54 WR 247 HC KBD Local authority not liable where vet whom they employed carried out duties imposed on him, not them under Diseases of Animals Act 1894.

The Valentine Meat Juice Company v The Valentine Extract Company (1900-01) LXXXIII LTR 259; (1899-1900) XVI TLR 522 CA Successful action to injunct opponent from using own name as part of product name where claimant contended confusion would arise as to identity of manufacturer.

The Valley Printing Company and Rankine, Mansell v (1908) 43 LJ 90; (1908) 77 LJCh 397; (1907-08) XXIV TLR 311 HC ChD Injunction/damages available to author of unpublished matter against anyone who infringes exclusive right to publish/not to publish.

The Valley Printing Company, Mansell v (1908) 43 LJ 448; (1908) 77 LJCh 742; (1907-08) XXIV TLR 802 CA Injunction/damages available to author of unpublished matter against anyone who infringes exclusive right to publish/not to publish.

The Vanguard Motorbus Co (Limited), Isaac Walton and Co v; Gibbons v The Vanguard Motorbus Co (Limited) (1908) 72 JP 505; (1908-09) 53 SJ 82; (1908-09) XXV TLR 13 HC KBD Bus striking permanent structure (in first case) could be due to negligence of driver (and in second case) was negligent use of nuisance placed on highway.

The Vectis (1928-29) XLV TLR 384 HC PDAD Common law principles of negligence applicable in Admiralty action arising from collision.

The Wagon Mound (No 2); Overseas Tankship (UK), Ltd v The Miller Steamship Co Pty Ltd and another [1966] 2 All ER 709; [1967] AC 617; (1966) 110 SJ 447; [1966] 3 WLR 498 PC Negligent where fail to prevent foreseeable injury; foreseeability of injury essential for recovery in nuisance.

The War Office and another, Browning v (1962) 112 LJ 849; [1963] 1 QB 750; (1962) 106 SJ 957; [1963] 2 WLR 52 CA Disability pension deductible from personal injury damages; damages for negligence are intended to compensate victim not punish tortfeasor.

The War Office, Adams v [1955] 3 All ER 245; (1955) 105 LJ 666; (1955) 99 SJ 746; [1955] 1 WLR 1116 HC QBD Crown exemption from tortious liability.

The War Office, Waldon v [1956] 1 All ER 108; (1956) 106 LJ 26; (1956) 100 SJ 33 CA On consideration of relevant awards of damages by judge.

The Winkfield [1900-03] All ER 346; [1902] 71 LJP 21; (1901-02) 46 SJ 162; (1901-02) XVIII TLR 178; (1901-02) 50 WR 246 CA Bailee liable to bailor for damages recovered from third party for negligent loss of goods.

Theaker v Richardson [1962] 1 All ER 229; (1962) 112 LJ 136; (1962) 106 SJ 151 CA Could be anticipated/natural and probable result of writing letter to person that would be opened by spouse.

Theodore Goddard and Co, Frisby v [1984] TLR 127 CA On concealment of right of action as ground for striking out claim.

Thevannasan son of Sinnapan and others, Heng (Chop Seng) v [1975] 3 All ER 572; [1976] RTR 193 PC Bad parking does not raise presumption of negligence; reasonable foreseeability of collision necessary.

Theyer v Purnell [1918] 2 KB 333; [1919] 88 LJCL 263; (1918-19) 119 LTR 285; (1918) WN (I) 174 HC KBD Recovery of damages consequent upon trespass of sheep: doctrine of scienter inapplicable.

Thomas and another v British Railways Board and others [1976] 3 All ER 15; [1976] QB 913; (1976) 120 SJ 334; [1976] 2 WLR 761 CA Juxtaposition of railway/footpath imposed duty of care on Board to provide stile but local authority liable for repair.

Thomas and Clark, Fenton Textile Association, Limited v (1928-29) XLV TLR 113 HC KBD Liability of solicitors for conversion of client's funds.

Thomas and Evans, Limited v Mid-Rhondda Co-operative Society, Limited [1941] 1 KB 381; [1941] 110 LJ 699; (1940) 84 SJ 682; (1940-41) LVII TLR 228 CA Non-liability of riparian owner in negligence/nuisance or under Rylands v Fletcher for flooding consequent upon pulling down of flood wall which had itself erected.

Thomas and others v National Union of Mineworkers (South Wales Area) and others [1985] 2 All ER 1 HC ChD Peaceful/responsible picketing not watching or besetting/nuisance even if secondary picketing.

Throgmorton Publications Ltd and another, S and K Holdings Ltd and others v [1972] 3 All ER 497; (1972) 116 SJ 375; [1972] 1 WLR 1036 CA Plaintiff cannot sever allegedly defamatory parts of article; defendant can plead justification in respect of whole.

Thrower v Thames Valley and Aldershot Bus Co Ltd [1978] RTR 271 CA Precautionary measures plaintiff suggested bus company should have taken were unrealistic: plaintiff failed to establish collision arose from negligence of bus company.

Thurgood, Larby v (1992) 136 SJ LB 275; [1992] TLR 493 HC QBD Refusal to order interview between plaintiff and employment consultant in order that plaintiff's real employment prospects might be gauged.

Thurston v Charles (1904-05) XXI TLR 659 HC KBD Substantial damages available for wrongful conversion/detention where published another's private correspondence but privilege in communication not destroyed so no libel.

Tidball, Day v (1929) 68 LJ ccr24 CyCt Damages available from CyCt in action for trespass following order by court of summary jurisdiction pursuant to the Small Tenements Recovery Act 1838.

Tideway Investment and Property Holdings Ld v Wellwood; Same v Orton; Same v Jones; Same v Friedentag; Same v Thornley [1952] Ch 791 (also CA); (1952) 96 SJ 579; [1952] 1 TLR 1177 HC ChD Erection of flue pipes on undemised portion of premises was trespass (albeit minor).

Tideway Investment and Property Holdings Ld v Wellwood; Same v Orton; Same v Jones; Same v Friedentag; Same v Thornley [1952] 2 TLR 365 CA Erection of flue pipes on undemised portion of premises was trespass (albeit minor).

Tidy and another v Battman [1933] All ER 259; [1952] Ch 791 (also HC ChD); [1934] 1 KB 319; (1934) 77 LJ 28; (1934) 103 LJCL 158; (1934) 150 LTR 90; (1933) WN (I) 276 CA No rule of law that one must be negligent if one collides with stationary vehicle.

Tilbury Contracting and Dredging Company (1906), Limited, London General Omnibus Company, Limited v (1907) 71 JP 534 HC ChD Successful action for damage to building effected by negligent laying of sewers.

Till, Attorney-General v (1909) 44 LJ 130; [1909] 78 LJKB 708; (1909) C LTR 275 CA Negligence in delivery does not open one to prosecution for refusal/neglect to deliver taxable income statement pursuant to the Income Tax Act 1842, s 55.

Tilley v Stevenson [1939] 4 All ER 207; (1939) 88 LJ 298; (1939) 83 SJ 943 CA Where burst pipe must show person claimed against knew/ought to have known water being fed to pipe.

Tillstone, Callow v (1900-01) LXXXIII LTR 411 HC QBD Negligent certification by vet that unsound meat is fit for consumption can ground conviction for aiding and abetting in sale of unsound meat.

Time Out Ltd and another, Brent Walker Group plc and another v [1991] 2 All ER 753; [1991] 2 QB 33; [1991] 2 WLR 772 CA Fair comment defence based on privileged material must give fair/accurate report of occasion of privilege.

Times Newspapers Ltd and another, DDSA Pharmaceuticals Ltd v [1972] 3 All ER 417; (1972) 122 NLJ 609t; [1973] QB 21; (1972) 116 SJ 585; [1972] 3 WLR 582 CA Particulars in pleadings in libel actions.

Times Newspapers Ltd and others (Schilling and Lom (a firm), third party), Watts v [1996] 1 All ER 152; [1995] TLR 488; [1996] 2 WLR 427 CA Respective liability of publisher and client for libel committed in course of apology for earlier libel must be considered separately where qualified privilege may arise in relation to either party.

Times Newspapers Ltd and others, Derbyshire County Council v [1992] 3 All ER 65; (1992) 142 NLJ 276; [1992] QB 770; [1992] TLR 69; [1992] 3 WLR 28 CA Trading/non-trading corporation with corporate reputation may sue for libel/slander but local authority may not unless actual financial loss.

Times Newspapers Ltd and others, Derbyshire County Council v [1993] 1 All ER 1011; [1993] AC 534; (1993) 143 NLJ 283; (1993) 137 SJ LB 52/81; [1993] TLR 87; [1993] 2 WLR 449 HL Local authority cannot sue for defamation.

Times Newspapers Ltd and others, Derbyshire County Council v [1991] 4 All ER 795; [1991] TLR 175 HC QBD Local authority may sue for libel even if no financial loss/property affected.

Times Newspapers Ltd and others, Electrical, Electronic, Telecommuncation and Plumbing Union v [1980] QB 585; (1980) 124 SJ 31; [1980] 3 WLR 98 HC QBD Trade union could not bring action for libel of itself per se or for libel of all of its members.

Times Newspapers Ltd and others, Rothermere and others v [1973] 1 All ER 1013; (1973) 123 NLJ 250t; (1973) 117 SJ 266; [1973] 1 WLR 448 CA Prolonged examination of documents (not complexity/length of trial) can justify no jury but need not.

Times Newspapers Ltd, De L'Isle (Viscount) v [1987] 3 All ER 499; (1988) 132 SJ 54; [1988] 1 WLR 49 CA Finding of fact and not a discretion whether trial by judge preferable to trial by jury where many documents/accounts.

Times Newspapers Ltd, Prager v [1988] 1 All ER 300; (1987) 137 NLJ 810; (1988) 132 SJ 55; [1988] 1 WLR 77 CA Cannot plead wider meaning of words used where if proved would not create less damnable form of statement made; can plead justification of any alternative meaning that might convince jury.

Times Publishing Co, Godman v [1926] 95 LJCL 747 HC KBD On pleading justification.

Times Publishing Company, Limited, Godman v [1926] 2 KB 273; (1926) 61 LJ 384; (1926) 135 LTR 291; (1925-26) 70 SJ 606 CA On pleading justification.

Times Publishing Company, The Aga Khan v [1924] 1 KB 675; (1924) 59 LJ 90; [1924] 93 LJCL 361; (1924) 130 LTR 746; (1923-24) XL TLR 299; (1924) WN (I) 54 CA On 'rolled-up plea' of fair comment.

Times Publishing, Ltd, Webb v [1960] 2 All ER 789; (1960) 110 LJ 590; [1960] 2 QB 535; (1960) 104 SJ 605 HC QBD Qualified privilege attaches to newspaper reports of foreign legal actions if accurate/fair/without malice/of real public interest.

Timmis v Pearson [1934] LJNCCR 115 CyCt Overcrowding by tenant need not of itself render tenant guilty of nuisance.

Timothy Whites Ltd v Byng [1934] LJNCCR 47 CyCt Animal owners under positive duty to restrain their animals trespassing on another's property.

Tims v John Lewis and Co, Ltd [1951] 1 All ER 814; (1951) 115 JP 265; [1951] 2 KB 459; (1951) 101 LJ 203; (1951) 95 SJ 268; [1951] 1 TLR 719; (1951) WN (I) 188 CA Upon arrest must be taken to police officer/justice of the peace forthwith.

Tims, John Lewis and Co, Ltd v [1952] 1 All ER 1203; [1952] AC 676; (1952) 116 JP 275; (1952) 102 LJ 262; (1952) 96 SJ 342; [1952] 1 TLR 1132; (1952) WN (I) 241 HL Not false imprisonment where store detectives take arrested party before police within reasonable time (not forthwith).

Tingle Jacobs and Co (a firm) v Kennedy [1964] 1 All ER 888; (1964) 108 SJ 196; [1964] 1 WLR 638 CA Traffic lights presumed to be working properly unless contrary evidence.

Tinling (CT) and Co, Ltd, Hobbs v; Hobbs v Nottingham Journal, Ltd [1929] All ER 33; (1929) 67 LJ 290; (1929) 98 LJCL 421; (1929) WN (I) 89 CA On libel; on mitigation of damages where are of bad character.

Tinling (CT) and Company, Limited, Hobbs v; Hobbs v Nottingham Journal, Limited [1929] 2 KB 1 HC KBD On procedure in libel action; on mitigation of damages where are of bad character.

Titchmarsh v Royston ater Company Limited (1899-1900) LXXXI LTR 673 HC ChD Injunction granted to halt trespass on private road.

Titley, Stewart v [1939] LJNCCR 89 CyCt Innkeeper liable for theft of patron's car from car park left in forecourt though not delivered to innkeeper/her car park attendant.

Toal (Pauper) v North British Railway Company [1908] AC 352; (1908) 77 LJPC 119; (1908-09) XCIX LTR 173; (1907-08) XXIV TLR 673 HL Leaving railway door open as train pulled from station could be negligent.

Tocci v Hankard and another (1966) 110 SJ 835 CA Overtaking when passing side road deemed not to be negligent.

Todd (by his next best friend Anne Todd) v Davison [1971] 1 All ER 449; (1971) 115 SJ 144; [1971] 1 WLR 267 Assizes Infant's right of action expires if reasonable parents would have brought action.

Todd, Ladbroke and Co v (1914-15) 111 LTR 43 HC KBD Is negligent for banker without making inquiries to open account for person presenting cheque marked 'Account payee only'.

Tolhurst and others, Ashley v [1937] LJNCCR 78 CyCt Car-park owners liable for breach of contract of bailment for reward and in conversion where handed car to person who did not produce ticket for same and who it emerged was not the owner.

Tolleth, Ashingdon v (1951) 101 LJ 235 CyCt Failed action in negligence against osteopath.

Tolley v Fry (JS) and Sons, Limited [1930] 1 KB 467; (1929) 68 LJ 429; (1930) 99 LJCL 149; (1930) 142 LTR 270; (1929) 73 SJ 818; (1929-30) XLVI TLR 108; (1929) WN (I) 272 CA Something innocently stated could not through circumstance of publication be defamatory.

Tolley v Fry (JS) and Sons, Ltd [1931] All ER 131; [1931] AC 333; (1931) 71 LJ 277; (1931) 100 LJCL 328; (1931) 145 LTR 1; (1931) 75 SJ 220; (1930-31) XLVII TLR 351; (1931) WN (I) 87 HL Something innocently stated may through circumstance of publication be defamatory.

Tolley v Morris [1979] 1 All ER 71; (1978) 128 NLJ 712t; (1978) 122 SJ 436; [1979] 1 WLR 205 CA Court would not dismiss for inaction suit of infant plaintiff brought in extended limitation period.

Tolley v Morris (1979) 129 (1) NLJ 518; (1979) 123 SJ 353; [1979] 1 WLR 592 HL Non-dismissal for inaction of suit of infant plaintiff brought in extended limitation period.

Tollitt, Aerators, Ltd v [1900-03] All ER 564 HC ChD Action dismissed as name complained of was commonplace words/unconfusing.

Tom Pettifer Ltd et al, Hoare v (1984) 134 NLJ 284c CA Extension of time allowed that service of writ might be acknowledged.

Tomkies and others, Calvet v [1963] 3 All ER 610; (1963) 113 LJ 722; (1963) 107 SJ 791; [1963] 1 WLR 1397 CA Evidence of actual loss suffered not admitted as general pecuniary loss claimed.

Tomlin and others, Secretary of State for Foreign and Commonwealth Affairs v [1990] TLR 758 CA Extended limitation period of thirty years applied to disused embassy building from which Foreign Secretary sought to evict squatters who claimed adverse possession of building.

Tomlinson, Norris (an infant) and Norris v [1941] LJNCCR 211 CyCt Butcher liable for injury occasioned to child-licensee who placed hand in sausage machine (an allurement/trap) while was running.

Tomlinson, Williamson v (1933) 76 LJ ccr6 CyCt Lorry driver negligent as did not drive with additional carefulness expected of driver of large vehicle.

Tong (Chan Wai) and another v Sum (Li Ping) [1985] AC 446; (1985) 129 SJ 153; [1985] 2 WLR 396 PC On appropriate damages for personal injuries; on damages for loss of future earnings.

Tong (Goh Chok), Jeyaretnam (Joshua Benjamin) v (1989) 133 SJ 1032; [1989] 1 WLR 1109 PC Comments of politician at press conference deemed to be fair comments and not defamatory.

Toogood v Wright [1940] 2 All ER 306; (1940) 84 SJ 254 CA Absent scienter was no special duty in relation to racing greyhounds.

Toong Fong Omnibus Co, Ltd, Singh (an infant) v [1964] 3 All ER 925; (1965) 115 LJ 24; (1964) 108 SJ 818; [1964] 1 WLR 1382 PC On uniformity of awards/interference by appellate court in level of damages.

Toperoff v Mor [1973] RTR 419 HC QBD Front-seat passenger not wearing seat belt deemed one-quarter liable for injuries suffered.

Tophams, Ltd and Capital and Counties Property Co, Ltd [1965] 3 All ER 1, Sefton (Earl) v [1965] Ch 1140 (also HC ChD); [1965] 3 WLR 523 CA Size of money offered evidenced inducement to breach contract.

Toplis and Harding and Russell, Old Gate Estates, Ltd v [1939] 3 All ER 209; (1939) 88 LJ 11; (1939) 161 LTR 227; (1939) 83 SJ 606 HC KBD No recovery for pure economic loss.

Trexapalm, Tavener Rutledge Ltd v (1975) 125 NLJ 869t; (1975) 119 SJ 792 HC ChD Suspended interlocutory judgment granted in favour of 'Kojapop' manufacturers against 'Kojak' lollipop manufacturers.

Trinder v Great Western Railway Company (1918-19) XXXV TLR 291 HC KBD Bus company not liable for injury to passenger on upper level hit by tree which had been cut back by company and where driver not negligent/company unaware was overhanging tree.

Triplex Safety Glass Co, Ltd, Evans v [1936] 1 All ER 283 HC KBD Delay between buying car/windscreen smashing; chance to examine windscreen; possible cause other than manufacturer's negligence meant manufacturer not liable in negligence for occurrence.

Trist and others, Draper v [1939] 3 All ER 513 CA On damages for passing-off.

Trollope Colls Cementation Overseas Ltd and another, Jones v [1990] TLR 62 CA Foreign Limitation Periods Act 1984 inapplicable where to apply it would be more unfair than fair.

Troman, Stansbie v [1948] 1 All ER 599; [1948] 2 KB 48; (1948) 98 LJ 175; [1948] 117 LJR 1206; (1948) LXIV TLR 226; (1948) WN (I) 117 CA Decorator owed duty to safeguard premises from thieves when leaving temporarily.

Troman, Stansbie v [1947] LJNCCR 134 CyCt Decorator owed duty to safeguard premises from thieves when leaving temporarily.

Trotman v British Railways Board (1974) 124 NLJ 1030t; (1975) 119 SJ 65 HC QBD Rail board one-third liable for injury to rail workman injured by train whose driver probably did not sound warning.

Trowbridge Urban District Council, Stancomb v [1910] 2 Ch 190; (1910) 102 LTR 647 HC ChD Injunction to restrain council discharging sewage into stream.

Trubyfield and another v Great Western Railway Company [1937] 4 All ER 614; (1937) 84 LJ 420; (1938) 158 LTR 135; (1937) 81 SJ 1002; (1937-38) LIV TLR 221; (1938) WN (I) 12 HC KBD On appropriate fatal accident damages to administrator of infant daughter's estate where daughter killed through negligence of rail company's driver.

Truckell v Stock [1957] 1 WLR 161 CA That footings extended beyond boundary of wall (wall rested on footings) was trespass.

Trucks and Spares, Ltd v Maritime Agencies (Southampton), Ltd [1951] 2 All ER 982 CA Bills of lading proper proof of title justifying interim delivery order.

Truro Corporation v Rowe [1902] 71 LJCL 974 CA Successful claim by corporation against oyster fisherman who trespassed upon foreshore in course of trade.

Truscott and another v McLaren and another [1982] RTR 34 CA Person on major road was negligent in not taking reasonable steps to avoid collision with car whom saw approaching on minor road.

Trustees of Upwell Branch of Independent Order of Oddfellows and Overland, Walker v [1934] LJNCCR 426 CyCt Failed action for trespass against landlord entering onto property following non-payment of rent (not estopped by letter had sent from entering onto said property).

Trznadel v British Transport Commission [1957] 3 All ER 196 CA On engine-drivers' responsibilities to railway employees on track.

Tsikata v Newspaper Publishing plc [1997] 1 All ER 655 CA Report of government special inquiry was 'public proceeding' so fair and accurate statements concerning the report per se were privileged.

Tsikata v Newspaper Publishing plc [1994] TLR 569 HC QBD Report of government special inquiry was 'public proceeding' so fair and accurate statements concerning the report per se were privileged.

Tuck, Harry and Co v (1912) CC Rep I 60 CyCt Dog-owner not liable for injury occasioned by dog absent interference by owner.

Tuddenham, Lawson v [1945] LJNCCR 141 CyCt Failed claim in nuisance/trespass arising from allegedly excessive user of right of way.

Tudor-Hart v British Union for the Abolition of Vivisection [1937] 4 All ER 475; [1938] 2 KB 329; [1938] 107 LJCL 501; (1938) 158 LTR 162; (1937) 81 SJ 1020; (1937-38) LIV TLR 154 CA Cannot apply for particulars of facts as is application for evidence.

Tuey v Clarke [1940] LJNCCR 31 CyCt Driver liable in negligence for colliding with cyclist during black-out even though cyclist did not have required red rear-light as driver not going at such speed that could pull up to avoid collision.

Tugwell (an infant), Bennett v [1971] 2 All ER 248; (1971) 121 NLJ 129t; [1971] 2 QB 267; [1971] RTR 221; (1971) 115 SJ 289; [1971] 2 WLR 847 HC QBD Apparent acceptance of risk raises volenti non fit injuria even if in mind does not really accept.

Tuley and others, Canadian Pacific Wine Co v [1921] LJPC 233 PC Police not rendered trespassers by seizing goods absent search warrant in course of lawful search/seizure.

Tully, Short v [1943] LJNCCR 208 CyCt On liability of cattle-owner for road traffic collision occurring where cattle escape/are driven onto highway.

Tunbridge Wells Gas Company, Batcheller v (1901) LXXXIV LTR 765; (1900-01) 45 SJ 577; (1900-01) XVII TLR 577 HC ChD Gas company liable in nuisance for leak from gas mains into water pipes which contaminated water.

Tunnicliffe and Hampson (Limited), West Leigh Colliery Company (Limited) v (1907-08) 52 SJ 93; (1907-08) XXIV TLR 146 HL On appropriate damages for damage caused by subsidence.

Tunnicliffe and Hampson, Limited v West Leigh Colliery Company, Limited [1905] 2 Ch 390 HC ChD On appropriate damages for damage caused by subsidence.

Tunnicliffe and Hampson, Limited v West Leigh Colliery Company, Limited [1906] 2 Ch 22; (1906) XCIV LTR 715 CA On appropriate damages for damage caused by subsidence.

Tunstall, Newall v [1970] 3 All ER 465; (1971) 115 SJ 14 Assizes No interest where order made not order against defendant.

Turley v Daw (1906) XCIV LTR 216 HC KBD Judgment debtor cannot during duration of committal order bring action against County court bailiff for non-service of judgment summons.

Turley v King (1944) 108 JP 73; (1944) 170 LTR 247; (1943-44) LX TLR 197; (1944) WN (I) 51 HC KBD Landlord must comply with order to abate statutory nuisance (war-damaged houses) notwithstanding Landlord and Tenant (War Damage) Act 1939.

Turnball v Wieland (1916-17) XXXIII TLR 143 HC KBD Employer liable for unlicensed cattle drover's negligence.

Turnbull, Northumberland Hotels, Ltd v [1943] LJNCCR 50 CyCt Tenant not liable for trespass where remains in property after date specified in invalid notice to quit.

Turnbull, Robertson v (1981) 131 NLJ 1211 HL Refusal of damages (expenses/solatium) to husband whose wife suffered non-fatal injury in road accident.

Turner (an infant) v Felton and others [1940] LJNCCR 300 CyCt Absent reasonable basis for questioning person going to police station for questioning in belief that was required to go could claim damages from police for false imprisonment.

Turner (otherwise Robertson) v Metro-Goldwyn-Mayer Pictures, Ltd [1950] 1 All ER 449; (1950) 94 SJ 145 HL That motivated by financial interest need not mean malicious; opinion need only be genuine not right — here honest views absent malice so qualified privilege remained.

Turner and another v Deal Corporation (1967) 111 SJ 685 HC QBD Successful action in nuisance for damage to property in course of road-widening.

Turner Manufacturing Co Ltd, Doughty v [1964] 1 All ER 98; (1964) 114 LJ 73; (1964) 108 SJ 53; [1964] 2 WLR 240 CA Not liable for unforeseen consequences of unforeseen accident.

Turner v Arding and Hobbs, Ltd [1949] 2 All ER 911 HC KBD Vegetable matter on shop floor an unusual danger in consequence of which were found liable to invitee.

Turner v Civil Service Supply Association Limited (1926) 134 LTR 189 HC KBD Non-liability of (non-common) carriers for loss of goods through fire caused by own servant's negligence as had exempted selves from liability in contract.

Turner v Coates [1916-17] All ER 264; [1917] 1 KB 670; [1917] 86 LJCL 321; (1916-17) 115 LTR 766; (1916-17) XXXIII TLR 79 HC KBD Owner liable in negligence for injuries arising from putting uncontrolled/unbroken colt on road.

Tysoe v Davies [1983] Crim LR 684; [1984] RTR 88; [1983] TLR 434 HC QBD Were (80%) to blame for accident arising directly from driving with thick clouds of smoke coming from exhaust; person with whom collided (20%) liable for not keeping proper look-out notwithstanding smoke.

UBAF Ltd v European American Banking Corp [1984] 2 All ER 226; [1984] QB 713; (1984) 128 SJ 243; [1984] 2 WLR 508 CA Cause of action following entry into contract on foot of fraudulent misrepresentation might run from later date than that of entry into contract.

Udale v Bloomsbury Area Health Authority [1983] 2 All ER 522; (1983) 127 SJ 510; [1983] TLR 113; [1983] 1 WLR 1098 HC QBD Damages unavailable for birth after sterilisation but can recover for distress, pain, suffering and effect on family finances.

Ulster Weaving Co, Ltd, Cavanagh v [1959] 2 All ER 745 HL Expert evidence of trade practice not definite as regards negligence: issue properly left to jury.

Umek v London Transport Executive (1984) 134 NLJ 522 HC QBD Rail Board one-third liable for fatal accident involving member of staff crossing certain point of line (after told not to) as did not advise trains on approaching said point to slow down.

Underwood (AL), Limited v Bank of Liverpool and Martins, Limited (1922-23) XXXIX TLR 606 HC KBD Bank's negligent disposal of cheques was conversion.

Underwood (AL), Ltd v Bank of Liverpool and Martins; Same v Bank (Barclays) [1924] All ER 230; (1924) 131 LTR 271; (1923-24) XL TLR 302 CA Bank's negligent disposal of cheques was conversion.

Unicos Property Corporation, Ltd, Robinson and others v [1962] 2 All ER 24 CA Limitation applied despite amendment to claim as was still same action.

Union Bank of Australia, Limited v McClintock and Others [1922] 1 AC 240; [1922] 91 LJPC 108; (1922) 126 LTR 588 PC Action failed as if ratified act of manager so as to have cause of action would also ratify later conversion.

Union Cartage Co, Ltd, Donovan v [1932] All ER 273; [1933] 2 KB 71; (1933) 102 LJCL 270; (1933) 148 LTR 333; (1933) 77 SJ 30; (1932-33) XLIX TLR 125 HC KBD Strict duty of care on owner of unattended vehicle which is allurement to children only if vehicle is dangerous per se.

Union Transport Finance Limited v British Car Auctions Ltd (1977) 127 NLJ 1247b CA Could be conversion of hire purchase item where bailee so acted as to open up right to immediate possession of relevant article by bailor.

Union-Castle Mail Steamship Company, Limited, Taylor (J) and Sons, Limited v (1931-32) XLVIII TLR 249 HC KBD Shipowners not liable for not warning that in course of carriage castor seed had been mixed with maize (thus rendering latter unsuitable for animal feed).

United Australia, Ltd v Barclays Bank, Ltd [1939] 1 All ER 676; [1939] 2 KB 53; (1939) 87 LJ 180; [1939] 108 LJCL 477; (1939) 160 LTR 259; (1938-39) LV TLR 457; (1939) WN (I) 81 CA Mere bringing of action in contract waives right to sue in tort.

United Australia, Ltd v Barclays Bank, Ltd [1940] 4 All ER 20; [1941] AC 1; [1940] 109 LJCL 919 HL Earlier contractual action not bar to tortious action as no judgment obtained.

United Automobile Services, Limited, and others, Ingram v [1943] 2 All ER 71; [1943] KB 612; [1943] 112 LJ 447; (1943) 169 LTR 72; (1942-43) LIX TLR 295; (1943) WN (I) 126 CA Trial judge's apportionment of damages between joint tortfeasors will rarely be interfered with by CA if agrees that both parties are tortfeasors.

United Bank of Kuwait plc, Gold Coin Joailliers SA v (1996) TLR 4/11/96 CA Bank not under duty of care when providing reference over telephone regarding financial status of customer to ensure person in respect of whom enquiry was made was actually the person dealing with the enquirer.

United Bank of Kuwait v Hammoud and others (1987) 137 NLJ 921 HC QBD On close proximity of relationship between solicitor/client necessary before former liable to latter for loss occasioned through former's inadequate supervision of worker/junior lawyer.

United Dairies (London) Ltd, Cutter v [1933] All ER 594; [1933] 2 KB 297; (1933) 76 LJ 56; (1933) 102 LJCL 663; (1933) 149 LTR 436; (1933) WN (I) 166 CA On liability for acts of (here tame) animal.

W Truman (Limited) v Attenborough (Robert) (1910-11) 103 LTR 218; (1909-10) 54 SJ 682; (1909-10) XXVI TLR 601 HC KBD On passing of property under approbation contract — on whether estopped from denying title.

W v Commissioner of Police of the Metropolis [1997] TLR 403 CA Failed action in negligence by woman police constable against her superiors for their breach of (non-existent) duty of care towards her.

W v Egdell [1990] Ch 359 (also HC ChD); (1990) 134 SJ 286; [1990] 2 WLR 471 CA On duty of confidentiality owed (and liability for breach of same) by psychiatrist to mental patient at whose instruction prepare mental health report.

W v Egdell and others [1990] Ch 359 (also CA); (1989) 133 SJ 570; [1989] 2 WLR 689 HC ChD On duty of confidentiality owed (and liability for breach of same) by psychiatrist to mental patient at whose instruction prepare mental health report.

W v Meah; D v Meah and another [1986] 1 All ER 935; (1986) 136 NLJ 165 HC QBD Damages for trespass primarily compensatory.

W Woodward (Limited) v Boulton Macro (Limited); Re W Woodward (Limited) (1915) 50 LJ 147; [1916] 85 LJCh 27; (1914-15) XXXI TLR 269; (1915) WN (I) 124 HC ChD Passing off action failed where not proved that 'gripe water' had come to identify plaintiffs' product alone.

Wagner v West Ham Corporation (1920-21) XXXVII TLR 86 HC KBD Tram owners not liable for tram being started on passenger's prompting (unless conductor's not prompting was negligent).

Wah Tat Bank Ltd and another v Kum (Chan Cheng) [1975] 2 All ER 257; [1975] AC 507; (1975) 125 NLJ 133; (1975) 119 SJ 151; [1975] 2 WLR 475 PC Joint tortfeasor not sued to judgment could be sued again.

Wainwright, Ashton and others v [1936] 1 All ER 805; (1936) 81 LJ 313 HC KBD Solicitor negligent in allowing client open club after clerk's wrongful refusal to register it rather than advise client to seek mandamus order.

Waite v Redpath Dorman Long Ltd [1971] 1 All ER 513 HC QBD No interest on order made under RSC Ord 22, r 5.

Wakeford v Wright (1922-23) XXXIX TLR 107 CA Absent special damage clergyman could not bring action for words spoken of him in capacity of clergyman unless holding office/in receipt of temporal words spoken when words uttered.

Walcroft Property Co Ltd and another, Anns and others v [1976] QB 882; (1976) 120 SJ 216; [1976] 2 WLR 512 CA Cause of action from time building defects discovered/ought to have been discovered.

Walder v The Mayor, Aldermen and Burgesses of the Borough of Hammersmith [1944] 1 All ER 490; (1944) 108 JP 224; (1945) 95 LJ 111 HC KBD No duty of care towards (child) trespasser.

Walder, Hardy v [1984] RTR 312 CA Motorcyclist (two-thirds) and driver (one-third) liable for collision where former drove too fast/overtook at blind corner and latter did not stop/look before turning from minor on to main road.

Waldock and another, Zoernsch v (1964) 108 SJ 278 CA Ex-President of European Commission on Human Rights enjoyed privilege in respect of allegedly negligent acts done when acting in official capacity.

Waldock v Winfield [1901] 2 KB 596 CA Master liable for negligence of servant has on hire to another.

Waldon v The War Office [1956] 1 All ER 108; (1956) 106 LJ 26; (1956) 100 SJ 33 CA On consideration of relevant awards of damages by judge.

Waldorf Toilet Saloons, Ltd, Dobbin v [1937] 1 All ER 331 Assizes Negligent permanent waving of bleached/dyed hair by hairdresser.

Waldron, O'Connor v [1934] All ER 281; [1935] AC 76; (1934) 78 LJ 416; (1935) 152 LTR 289; (1934) 78 SJ 859; (1934-35) LI TLR 125; (1934) WN (I) 213 PC Words spoken by commissioner of administrative tribunal in discharge of duties not privileged.

Wales and another, Wales v (1967) 111 SJ 946 HC QBD On appropriate personal injury damages (following negligent road traffic collision) following great delay in litigation.

Wales v Wales and another (1967) 111 SJ 946 HC QBD On appropriate personal injury damages (following negligent road traffic collision) following great delay in litigation.

Walford and others v Richards (1975) 125 NLJ 1023t CA Limitation period disapplied in light of plaintiff's unawareness of material fact of decisive nature.

Walker and another v Manchester and Liverpool District Banking Company Limited (1913) 108 LTR 728; (1912-13) 57 SJ 478 HC KBD Customer could recover amounts bank paid out on foot of forged cheques though customer had not checked pass-book when from time to time was returned to him.

Walker and another, Oakley v (1977) 121 SJ 619 HC QBD Personal injury damages available for collapse of marriage consequent upon negligent road traffic accident.

Walker and Lake (Trustees) and Crisp, Howard and Wife v [1947] KB 860; [1947] 116 LJR 1366; (1947) 177 LJR 326; (1947) 91 SJ 494; (1947) LXIII TLR 518; (1947) WN (I) 216 HC KBD Landlord not liable to invitee of tenant injured while on tenanted property.

Walker and Stanger, Melton v (1981) 131 NLJ 1238; (1981) 125 SJ 861 HC ChD Date of cause of action ran from date negligently drafted document was signed.

Walker v Crabb (1916-17) 61 SJ 219; (1916-17) XXXIII TLR 119 HC KBD Person employing services of auctioneer not liable for negligence of same as auctioneer not person's servant.

Walker v John McLean and Sons Ltd [1979] 2 All ER 965; (1979) 129 (1) NLJ 294; (1979) 123 SJ 354/374; [1979] 1 WLR 760 CA Damages to reflect value of money; need not be reduced to counter inflation.

Walker v Linom [1907] 2 Ch 104; [1907] 76 LJCh 500; (1907-08) XCVII LTR 92; (1906-07) 51 SJ 483 HC ChD Legal estate of negligent trustees second to equitable interest of purchaser of property who through negligence of trustees bought property without notice of settlement.

Walker v Northumberland County Council [1995] 1 All ER 737; (1994) 144 NLJ 1659; (1995) 139 SJ LB 19 HC QBD Employer owes duty of care not to cause workers psychiatric damage by reason of work burden or character.

Walker v Trustees of Upwell Branch of Independent Order of Oddfellows and Overland [1934] LJNCCR 426 CyCt Failed action for trespass against landlord entering onto property following non-payment of rent (not estopped by letter had sent from entering onto said property).

Walker, De Parrell v (1932) 76 SJ 850; (1932-33) XLIX TLR 37 HC KBD Employer of clock-winder who stole property from house to which sent deemed negligent in hiring criminal person as clockwinder.

Walker, Howard v [1947] 116 LJR 1366; (1947) 177 LTR 326; (1947) 91 SJ 494 HC KBD Tenant (but not landlord) liable for injury to tenant's invitee where injured self on negligently maintained forecourt before tenant's shop.

Walker, Lowery v [1909] 2 KB 433; (1909) 44 LJ 356; [1909] 78 LJKB 874; (1909-10) 101 LTR 78; (1908-09) 53 SJ 544; (1908-09) XXV TLR 608; (1909) WN (I) 130 HC KBD Owner not liable for injuries to trespassers by vicious animal.

Walker, Lowery v [1910] 1 KB 173; (1909) 44 LJ 745; (1910) 79 LJKB 297; (1909-10) 101 LTR 873; (1909-10) 54 SJ 99; (1909-10) XXVI TLR 108; (1909) WN (I) 249 CA Owner not liable for injuries to trespassers by vicious animal.

Walker, Lowery v [1911] AC 10; (1910) 45 LJ 738; (1911) 80 LJCL 138; (1910-11) 103 LTR 675; (1910-11) 55 SJ 62; (1910-11) XXVII TLR 83; (1910) WN (I) 241 HL Owner who had erected warning notice liable for injuries to trespassers by vicious animal.

Walker, McKinnon Industries, Ltd v (1951) 95 SJ 559; (1951) WN (I) 401 PC Injunction merited to restrain discharge of noxious vapours/matter from defendant's works onto plaintiff's land.

Walker, Sherbourne v [1955] Crim LR 184 HC QBD Successful action for damages against policeman guilty of assault/wrongful imprisonment/malicious prosecution.

Walkers (a firm) and Another, Lee and Another v (1940) 162 LTR 89; (1939) 83 SJ 925 HC KBD Owner not liable for injury caused by dog whom knew to pose a risk where person injured by dog brought injury upon themselves through their own interference.

Walkin v South Manchester Health Authority [1995] 4 All ER 132; [1995] TLR 380; [1995] 1 WLR 1543 CA Limitation period on claims for physical injury or economic loss arising from unwanted pregnancy after failed sterilisation runs from date of personal injury i.e., date of conception.

Walkley v Fox (1914) CC Rep III 66 CyCt Prescription Act 1832 deemed inapplicable insofar as Dean Forest Re-afforestation Act 1668 applied so person acquired no right of user after forty years.

Walkley v Precision Forgings Ltd [1979] 2 All ER 548; (1979) 129 (1) NLJ 520; (1979) 123 SJ 354; [1979] 1 WLR 606 HL Courts will rarely disapply limitation to enable second action where earlier action begun in time but allowed lapse.

Walkley v Precision Forgings Ltd [1979] 1 All ER 102; [1978] 1 WLR 1228 CA Plaintiff may ask for disapplication of limitation period in respect of second action even if first dismissed for want of prosecution.

Wall, Corelli v (1905-06) XXII TLR 532 HC ChD Interim injunction on publication of picture postcards refused as alleged libel insufficiently made out.

Wallace v Clayton (1962) 112 LJ 208 CyCt Successful action for nuisance occasioned by growing of poplar trees (damages plus suspended injunction).

Wallace-James, Baird v [1916] 85 LJPC 193 HL Letter from president of parish charity to chair of parish council criticising parish medical officer's under-use of nurse provided by charity was privileged.

Wallach, Ward v [1937] LJNCCR 86 CyCt Where bolt connecting car and trailer simply fell out there was a presumption of negligence which person owning car/trailer which became detatched was required to rebut.

Wallbank, Searle v [1947] 1 All ER 12; [1947] AC 341; (1947) 97 LJ 9; [1947] LJNCCR 34; [1947] 116 LJR 258; (1947) 176 LTR 104; (1947) 91 SJ 83; (1947) LXIII TLR 24; (1947) WN (I) 60 HL No duty to highway users to maintain fence to prevent animals straying onto highway; no duty to prevent undangerous animals straying onto highway.

Waller (Eric) Ltd and another, Kearney v [1965] 3 All ER 352; [1966] 2 WLR 208 HC QBD Contractors did not owe occupiers' liability to non-employee injured in area under occupation/control of sub-contractors.

Waller v Lawton (1981) 131 NLJ 1134 HC QBD On appropriate damages for person who suffered inter alia serious brain damage when struck by motor vehicle.

Waller v Levoi (1968) 118 NLJ 1004t; (1968) 112 SJ 865 CA Driver who parked car on bend in road was 20% liable for injuries suffered by careless motorcyclist who leaped from bike to avoid colliding with car.

Waller, Hanson v [1901] 1 QB 390; [1901] 70 LJK/QB 231; (1900-01) 49 WR 445 HC QBD Master not liable for servant's falsely imprisoning third party.

Wallersteiner v Moir; Moir v Wallersteiner and others [1974] 3 All ER 217; (1974) 124 NLJ 525t; [1974] 1 WLR 991 CA Libel action used to gag party an abuse of process; consideration of sub judice company affairs at company meeting not contempt.

Wallis, Cotton v [1955] 3 All ER 373; (1955) 105 LJ 712; [1955] 1 WLR 1168 CA Low price of building merited architect's certification at lower standard than otherwise.

Wallis, Morgan and another v (1916-17) XXXIII TLR 495 HC KBD Qualified privilege where solicitor in dictating bill of costs included without malice as a point of information a statement that was in fact defamatory.

Walpole and another v Partridge and Wilson (a firm) [1994] 1 All ER 385; [1994] QB 106; [1993] 3 WLR 1093 CA Collateral attack on final decision in earlier proceedings not necessarily abuse of process.

Walsall Metropolitan Borough Council, S v [1986] 1 FLR 397; (1985) 135 NLJ 986; (1985) 129 SJ 685; [1985] 1 WLR 1150 CA Local authority not vicariously liable for negligence of foster parents.

Walsh v Holst and Co, Ltd, and others [1958] 3 All ER 33; (1958) 108 LJ 537; (1958) 102 SJ 545 CA Brick falling from construction site and hitting passer-by raised res ipsa loquitur (but was defeated here).

Walsh v Redfern and another [1970] RTR 201 HC QBD Person on main road to give way to person on minor road if necessary to avoid accident; lorry driver not contributorily negligent where was driving at reasonable speed on main road and collided with car emerging from minor road without paying heed to warning signs.

Walter Scott Motor Co v Horwitt [1937] LJNCCR 30 CyCt Person on whose property tree grew not liable in nuisance when branches overhanging another's property fell and occasioned damage.

Walter v Alltools, Limited (1944) 171 LTR 371; (1944-45) LXI TLR 39; (1944) WN (I) 214 CA On relevant factors when gauging appropriate damages for false imprisonment.

Walter v Ashton [1902] 2 Ch 282; [1902] 71 LJCh 839; (1902-03) LXXXVII LTR 196; (1902) WN (I) 66 HC ChD On granting injunctions for unauthorised use of name: injunction to restrain sale of cycles in such a way that they appeared to be connected with 'The Times' newspaper.

Walter v Yalden [1902] 2 KB 304 HC KBD Lease to expire before limitation ran/lessor could enter property on which trespasser with Statute of Limitations title against lessee.

Walters v WH Smith and Son, Ltd [1911-13] All ER 170; (1914) 78 JP 118; [1914] 1 KB 595; [1914] 83 LJKB 335; (1914) 110 LTR 345; (1913-14) 58 SJ 186; (1913-14) XXX TLR 158; (1913) WN (I) 359 HC KBD Private person must to defeat false imprisonment claim show reasonable suspicion that person whom arrested committed an offence that was effected.

Walters, Kensington Borough Council v [1960] Crim LR 62; (1959) 103 SJ 921; [1959] 3 WLR 945 HC QBD On expeditious recovery by local authority (pursuant to London Government Act 1939, s 181(3)) of damages for costs incurred by it following road traffic accident.

Waltham Forest Health Authority, Hughes v [1990] TLR 714 CA That surgical decision erroneous or that other surgeons critical of decision did not preclude finding that surgeons being sued not negligent.

Walthamstow Borough Council, Purkis v [1934] All ER 64; (1934) 98 JP 244 CA Child using playground swing a licensee.

Walton and Hemingway, Paul E Schweder and Co v (1910-11) XXVII TLR 89 HC KBD Non-recovery for losses country broker incurred on sale of shares (without consulting clients) following advice from their agent, a London stockbroker firm.

Walton v Jacob (1938) 82 SJ 586 HC KBD On assessing apppropriate damages for loss of expectation of life for healthy twenty-one year old man killed in negligent road traffic collision.

Walton, Daish (an infant by his next friend Albert Edward Daish) v [1972] 1 All ER 25; (1971) 121 NLJ 928t; [1972] 2 QB 262; (1971) 115 SJ 891; [1972] 2 WLR 29 CA Damages not to be reduced by National Health Service benefits.

Wandsworth Health Authority, Forbes v [1996] 4 All ER 881; (1996) 146 NLJ 477; [1997] QB 402; (1996) 140 SJ LB 85; (1996) TLR 21/3/96; [1996] 3 WLR 1108 CA On when possess adequate knowledge for limitation period to commence running.

Wandsworth, Wimbledon and Epsom District Gas Company v Grant (1926) 62 LJ ccr70 CyCt Failed action in trespass against gas company which laid gas mains along road without agreement of soil-owner.

Waple v Surrey County Council [1997] 2 All ER 836 HC QBD Information passed by solicitor of one party to solicitor of other party upon latter solicitor's request was absolutely privileged.

War Office, Blount v (1953) 97 SJ 388; [1953] 1 WLR 736 HC QBD War office liable for theft of goods left (bailed) with War Office's agreement in requisitioned house despite transfer of requisition to Ministry of Agriculture.

War Office, Browning v (1962) 106 SJ 452 HC QBD Veterans' benefits payable to injured US military employee disregarded when assessing personal injuries damages payable to same.

Warbey and others, Monk v (1934) 151 LTR 100; (1933-34) L TLR 263 HC KBD Owner of car liable towards person injured by car when driven by individual accompanying person to whom car loaned.

Warbey and others, Monk v (1935) 152 LTR 194; (1934-35) LI TLR 77 CA Owner of car liable towards person injured by car when driven by individual accompanying person to whom car loaned.

Warboys (JH) v Sherburn (JA) (1977) 127 NLJ 1151b CA On best means of assessing appropriate damages in negligence actions (by reference to medical reports not law reports).

Ward v Cannock Chase District Council [1986] Ch 546; (1986) 130 SJ 316; [1986] 2 WLR 660 HC ChD On damages available upon damage to house resulting from council's disrepair of neighbouring buildings/vandalism consequent upon neglect.

Ward v Hertfordshire County Council (1969) 133 JP 514; (1969) 119 NLJ 272t; (1969) 113 SJ 343; [1969] 1 WLR 790 HC QBD Local education authority liable at common law for failure to adequately protect schoolchildren from reasonably foreseeable risk when playing in schoolyard before school hours.

Ward v Hertfordshire County Council (1970) 134 JP 261; (1970) 120 NLJ 13t; (1970) 114 SJ 87; [1970] 1 WLR 356 CA Local education authority not liable at common law for injury suffered by child playing in schoolyard before school began — not inherently dangerous area/providing warder would not have prevented accident.

Ward v James [1965] 1 All ER 563; (1965) 115 LJ 228; (1965) 109 SJ 111; [1965] 2 WLR 455 CA On damages/when jury trial appropriate in personal cases.

Ward v Lewis and others [1955] 1 All ER 55; [1955] 1 WLR 9 CA No connection between alleged slander and special damage meant could be no conspiracy to slander.

Ward v London County Council [1938] 2 All ER 341; (1938) 85 LJ 310; (1938) 82 SJ 274 HC KBD Fire engine driver bound by traffic light regulations.

Ward v TE Hopkins and Son, Ltd; Baker and another v TE Hopkins and Son, Ltd [1959] 3 All ER 225; [1959] 1 WLR 966 CA Employer liable in negligence to servant also liable to doctor seeking to rescue same: no novus actus interveniens/volenti non fit injuria.

Ward v Tesco Stores Ltd [1976] 1 All ER 219; (1976) 120 SJ 555; [1976] 1 WLR 810 CA Absent explanation of apparent failure of duty of care court could infer breach thereof.

Ward v Wallach [1937] LJNCCR 86 CyCt Where bolt connecting car and trailer simply fell out there was a presumption of negligence which person owning car/trailer which became detatched was required to rebut.

Ward, Adam v [1916-17] All ER 157; [1917] AC 309; (1917) 52 LJ 126; [1917] 86 LJCL 849; (1917-18) 117 LTR 34; (1916-17) XXXIII TLR 277 HL Letter defaming another but without malice was privileged.

Ward, Adam v (1914-15) XXXI TLR 299 CA Letter defaming another but without malice and under moral compulsion was privileged.

Ward, Chapman v (1974) 124 NLJ 988t; [1975] RTR 7; (1974) 118 SJ 777 HC QBD Front seat passenger without seat belt not guilty of contributory negligence as regards injuries suffered in accident.

Ward, Harrison v [1939] LJNCCR 160 CyCt Doctor liable for increased suffering caused to patient by his negligent treatment of same.

Ward, Philips v [1956] 1 All ER 874; (1956) 106 LJ 281; (1956) 100 SJ 317; [1956] 1 WLR 471 CA Damages for negligent survey/valuation were difference between real value and value in report; damages to be measured at date of report.

Ward, Robinson v (1958) 108 LJ 491 HC QBD On elements of slander of office of honour.

Ward, Thompson v (1953) 97 SJ 352; [1953] 2 WLR 1042 CA Tenant who had abandoned premises and lost entitlement to possession could not sustain trespass action against occupier.

Ward, Wisbech Rural District Council v (1927) 91 JP 166; (1926-27) XLIII TLR 739; (1927) WN (I) 236 HC KBD Architect in certificating building work was under terms of particular contract not acting in quasi-/arbitral role and so could be (and was) liable in negligence.

Ward, Wisbech Rural District Council v (1927) 91 JP 200 CA Architect in certificating building work was not negligent.

Wardell-Yerburgh v Surrey County Council [1973] RTR 462 HC QBD Emergency vehicle driver (here one-third liable for collision which occurred) owes that duty of care to public which regular driver owes.

Warden and Co Ltd and others, Crowne v (1968) 112 SJ 824 CA Was just possible that newspaper headline and bold introduction could be defamatory though overall article was not.

Warden, Burnett, Hood and Hampton v [1935] LJNCCR 245 CyCt That medical treatment given in error did not mean administration of same was perforce negligent.

Wardley v Margolis (1981) 131 NLJ 447 HC QBD Damages from solicitor who negligently allowed personal injuries action with every chance of success to lapse.

Wards Mobility Services Ltd, Hodgkinson and Corby Ltd and another v [1994] TLR 446; [1994] 1 WLR 1564 HC ChD Must be deception for there to be passing off (no deception here so no passing off).

Ware and De Freville, Ltd v Motor Trade Association and others [1920] All ER 387; [1921] LJCL 949 CA Absent special circumstances statement that intend to do lawful act cannot be defamatory.

Ware v Garston Haulage Co, Ltd [1943] 2 All ER 558; [1944] KB 30; (1944) 94 LJ 109; [1944] 113 LJ 45; (1944) 170 LTR 155; (1943-44) LX TLR 77 CA Unlit motor vehicle on unlit nighttime road a nuisance.

Waring v Kenyon and Co (1927) Limited [1935] LJNCCA 155; (1935) 79 SJ 306 CA Valid finding that person injured in collision between car (in which was passenger) and parked, unlit lorry.

Warner v Clark, Islip et al (1984) 134 NLJ 763c CA Exemplary damages available where breach of contract proved as liability in tort thereby set up.

Warner v Elizabeth Arden, Ltd (1939) 83 SJ 258; (1939) WN (I) 41 HC KBD Beauty salon not liable in negligence or as bailees for necklace removed from handbag left unattended without notice of contents to salon.

Warran, Darbishire v [1963] 3 All ER 310; (1963) 107 SJ 631; [1963] 1 WLR 1067 CA Damages greater than cost of replacing damaged chattel irrecoverable.

Warren and another v King and others [1963] 3 All ER 521; (1963) 113 LJ 705; [1964] 1 WLR 1 CA On proper direction on/level of damages (for paralysed infant) and rôle of appellate court regarding jury awards.

Warren and Phillips, Harris v (1918) 53 LJ 213; [1918] 87 LJCh 491; (1918-19) 119 LTR 217; (1917-18) 62 SJ 568; (1917-18) XXXIV TLR 440; (1918) WN (I) 173 HC ChD Failed passing off action against persons who had acquired copyright over old song newly publishing same.

Warren v Railway Executive (1950) 100 LJ 344; (1950) 94 SJ 457 HC KBD Rail company liable where invitee-passenger got into unlighted train waiting on platform and injured self while looking for seat.

Warrington Corporation, McLoughlin v (1911) 75 JP 57 CA Town corporation could be found negligent where through defective repair of fountain person was injured when another climbing on fountain dislodged stone therefrom.

Warrington Health Authority, Lybert v [1995] TLR 290 CA On appropriate warning pre-sterilisation operation as to possibility of pregnancy post-sterilisation operation (here warning inadequate).

Warwick (John), White v [1953] 2 All ER 1021; (1953) 97 SJ 740; [1953] 1 WLR 1285 CA Hire contract exception clause found to exclude contractual but not tortious liability.

Warwick and another v Jeffery (1983) 133 NLJ 912 HC QBD On awarding of damages following road traffic accident in actions under Fatal Accidents Act 1976/Law Reform (Miscellaneous Provisions) Act 1934 in actions brought by ex-wife (who bore children by deceased) and co-habitee (who bore one child by deceased).

Warwick Tyre Company, Limited v New Motor and General Rubber Company, Limited [1910] 1 Ch 248; (1910) 45 LJ 36; [1910] 79 LJCh 177; (1909-10) 101 LTR 889; (1910) WN (I) 8 HC ChD Injunction to stop use of name 'Warwick' in respect of motor tyres as calculated to deceive consumers that defendant's tyres produced by plaintiffs.

Water Commissioners of the City of London and the Corporation of the City of London (Ontario), Saunby v [1906] AC 110; [1906] 75 LJPC 25 PC Allowed seek injunction for trespass (arbitration requirements in Ontario Act inapplicable).

Waterfield v Goodwin (1955) 105 LJ ccr332 CyCt Successful action in nuisance against neighbours (in semi-detached house) whose music lessons/practising of music/fondness for gramophone and radio music created a nuisance by noise.

Waterhouse v Waterhouse (1906) XCIV LTR 133; (1905-06) 50 SJ 169 HC ChD On father's obtaining injunction against trespass in father's house by his son.

Waterlow and Sons Limited, Bradshaw v [1914-17] All ER 36; [1915] 3 KB 527; [1916] 85 LJKB 318; (1915-16) 113 LTR 1101; (1914-15) XXXI TLR 556; (1915) WN (I) 292 CA No want of reasonable and probable cause found.

Waterman, Turner v (1961) 105 SJ 1011 HC QBD Landlord failed in duty of care owed to all visitors as did not take adequate safeguards with regard to floorboards exposed to dry rot.

Waters and Co, Allen v [1924-35] All ER 671; [1935] 1 KB 200; [1935] LJNCCA 86; (1935) 152 LTR 179; (1934-35) LI TLR 50; (1934) WN (I) 201 CA Damages untouched though included amount for debt recoverable from but unpaid by person awarded damages.

Waters v Sunday Pictorial Newspapers [1961] 2 All ER 758; (1961) 111 LJ 518; (1961) 105 SJ 492 CA On pleading in libel action.

Watford Rural District Council, Phillimore v [1913] 2 Ch 434; (1913) 77 JP 453; (1913-14) 109 LTR 616 HC ChD Injunction to restrain sewage farm discharging effluent into private ditch/ sewer of another; damages also awarded for nuisance by smell/underground passage of sewage.

Watkins v City of Birmingham (1976) 126 NLJ 442b CA On relationship necessary before milk distributors could be vicariously liable for actions of milk deliverers.

Watkins v Moffatt and others (1967) 111 SJ 719 CA Person who emerged from side road and drove onto main road at speed was guilty of negligence.

Watkins v Moffatt and others [1970] RTR 205 CA Driver on main road not contributorily negligent where collided with driver suddenly emerging from side road without paying heed to warning signs.

Watney, Combe, Reid, and Co (Limited), Jones v (1911-12) XXVIII TLR 399 HC KBD Can/cannot recover for aggravation of personal injury in respect of which claiming where aggravation due to own carelessness/natural causes.

Watson (Sir Patrick H) v Jones (Mrs JP) or M'Ewan et é contra; Watson (Sir Patrick H) v Jones (James) [1905] AC 480; [1905] 74 LJPC 151; (1905-06) XCIII LTR 489; (1905) WN (I) 130 HL Witness privilege in witness box against later slander action extends to communications to solicitor/client in preparing for trial.

Watson and others v People's Refreshment House Association Ld [1952] 1 KB 318; (1952) 96 SJ 150; [1952] 1 TLR 361; (1952) WN (I) 74 HC KBD Non-liability of innkeeper for damage to coach parked outside hospitium of inn with his permission but not at his invitation.

Watson Burton (a firm), Ochwat and another v (1997) 141 SJ LB 163 HC QBD Failed action in negligence against solicitors.

Watson v Buckley, Osborne, Garrett and Co, Ltd, and Wyrovoys Products, Ltd [1940] 1 All ER 174; (1940) 89 LJ 45 HC KBD Donoghue v Stevenson applied to goods distributors.

Watson v Fowles [1967] 3 All ER 721 CA Damages awarded as one sum: need not be divided under headings; actuarial approach undesirable.

Watson v Heslop [1971] RTR 308; (1971) 115 SJ 308 CA Negligent to park car in narrow, busy road at night; negligent not to have slowed down as soon as dazzled by oncoming lights.

Watson v Murray and Co [1955] 1 All ER 350 HC QBD Sheriff committed trespass in taking exclusive possession of party's store/in preparing to hold sale in store; were liable in negligence for goods stolen from store.

Watson v Powles (1967) 117 NLJ 758t; [1968] 1 QB 596; (1967) 111 SJ 562; [1967] 3 WLR 1364 CA On gauging damages in personal injury actions.

Watson v Smith (1983) 133 NLJ 641 HC QBD On appropriate damages for personal injuries suffered by motor cyclist in road traffic accident with lorry being driven by defendant.

Watson v Thomas S Whitney and Co, Ltd and another [1966] 1 All ER 122; (1966) 130 JP 109; (1966) 110 SJ 73; [1966] 1 WLR 57 CA Person walking near to kerb not contributorily negligent when struck by vehicle.

Watson, Haimes v [1981] RTR 90 CA Horse rider not negligent where collision occurred after horse shied.

Watson, Liffen v [1940] 2 All ER 213; [1940] 1 KB 556; (1940) 89 LJ 183; [1940] 109 LJCL 367; (1940) 84 SJ 368; (1939-40) LVI TLR 442; (1940) WN (I) 100 CA Damages for traumatic neurosis and for loss of board and lodging at place of employment.

Watson, Liffen v (1939) 161 LTR 351; (1939) 83 SJ 871 HC KBD Taxi-driver was negligent where could not explain why had braked and skidded when knew was likely to skid when so braked.

Watson, Martin v [1994] 2 All ER 606; (1994) 144 NLJ 463; [1994] QB 425; (1994) 138 SJ LB 55; [1994] TLR 45; [1994] 2 WLR 500 CA That a defendant is not technically the prosecutor precludes finding of malicious prosecution where a prosecution undertaken was a natural and intended consequence of false and malicious actions by defendant.

Watson, Martin v [1995] 3 All ER 559; [1996] 1 AC 74; (1995) 145 NLJ 1093; (1995) 139 SJ LB 190; [1995] TLR 408; [1995] 3 WLR 318 HL That a defendant is not technically the prosecutor does not preclude a finding of malicious prosecution where a prosecution undertaken was a natural and intended consequence of false and malicious actions by defendant.

Watson, Tylden-Wright v [1938] LJNCCR 107 CyCt Allowing gypsies to camp on land was not an unnatural user/was transitory so injunctive relief inappropriate/rendered land-owner liable for trespass of gypsies' horses onto land of another.

Watt (Julia), Watt (Lady Violet) v [1905] AC 115; [1904-07] All ER 840 HL Court cannot without defendant's agreement threaten re-trial unless plaintiff agrees to reduced damages where jury award absurd.

Watt (Lady Violet) v Watt (Julia) [1905] AC 115; [1904-07] All ER 840 HL Court cannot without defendant's agreement threaten re-trial unless plaintiff agrees to reduced damages where jury award absurd.

Watt and Scott, Limited, City of Montreal v [1922] 2 AC 555; (1923) 128 LTR 147; (1922) WN (I) 271 PC Municipal authority's liability for overflowing sewer reduced where another was contributorily negligent in causing same.

Watt v Hertfordshire County Council [1954] 2 All ER 368; (1954) 118 JP 377; (1954) 98 SJ 372; [1954] 1 WLR 835 CA Not liable in negligence to fireman for injury resulting from risk that ought reasonably be assumed by fireman.

Watt v Hertfordshire County Council [1954] 1 All ER 141; (1954) 118 JP 97; (1954) 104 LJ 376; [1954] 1 WLR 208 HC QBD Fireman has heavier burden to discharge in proving what asked to do shows employer not taking reasonable care of him.

Watt v Longsdon [1929] All ER 284; [1930] 1 KB 130; (1929) 68 LJ 76; (1929) 98 LJCL 711; (1930) 142 LTR 4; (1929) 73 SJ 544; (1928-29) XLV TLR 619 CA Absent common interest must be duty on maker's side and interest meriting protection on recipient's side for occasion of statement to be privileged.

Watt v Longsdon (1928-29) XLV TLR 419 HC KBD Absent common interest bona fide voluntary revelation of information believed to be true and pertaining to interest meriting protection on recipient's side is privileged.

Watt v Watt (1904-05) 49 SJ 400; (1904-05) XXI TLR 386; (1905) WN (I) 60; (1904-05) 53 WR 547 HL Excessive damages in tort action can only be reduced by court where parties agree to same.

Watts and another, Andrews v [1971] RTR 484 HC QBD Cattle owner who did not provide adequate lighting (two-thirds) liable and driver who did not slow down when signalled to do so (one-third) liable for collision with cattle herd on nighttime road.

Watts v Aldington; Tolstoy v Aldington [1993] TLR 655 CA Settlement agreement between victim and one tortfeasor did not free other tortfeasor from liability.

Watts v Times Newspapers Ltd and others (Schilling and Lom (a firm), third party) [1996] 1 All ER 152; [1995] TLR 488; [1996] 2 WLR 427 CA Respective liability of publisher and client for libel committed in course of apology for earlier libel must be considered separately where qualified privilege may arise in relation to either party.

Watts-Russell v Eayrs [1934] LJNCCR 324 CyCt Recovery of damages for loss of sheep through negligence of a shepherd provided by person from whom had acquired grazing rights on certain estate.

WE and E Jackson (a firm), Povey v [1970] 2 All ER 495; (1970) 114 SJ 269; [1970] 1 WLR 969 CA On quantum of damages appeals.

Weait and another v Jayanbee Joinery, Ltd [1962] 2 All ER 568 CA Can amend defence to show not liable if evidence so showing first emerges after limitation.

Wealden Woodlands (Kent) Ltd v National Westminster Bank Ltd [1983] TLR 182 CA Company not estopped (by not itself noticing same) from bringing action against bank for clearance of forged cheques drawn on its account.

Weardale Steel, Coal and Coke Company, Limited and Others, Herd v [1913] 3 KB 771 HC KBD Action for false imprisonment as defendant not under contractual duty to facilitate exit so that was denied same not imprisonment.

Weardale Steel, Coal and Coke Company, Limited and Others, Herd v [1915] AC 67; (1914) 49 LJ 411; (1913) 48 LJ 391; [1915] 84 LJKB 121; (1914-15) 111 LTR 660; (1913-14) XXX TLR 620; (1914) WN (I) 289 HL Party denied relief for false imprisonment on volenti non fit injuria basis.

Weardale Steel, Coal and Coke Company, Limited and Others, Herd v [1913] 3 KB 771 (also HC KBD); [1913] 82 LJKB 1354 CA Action for false imprisonment as defendant not under contractual duty to facilitate exit so that was denied same not imprisonment.

Wearmouth Coal Co, Ltd and Sunderland Gas Co, Hanson v [1939] 3 All ER 47; (1939) 87 LJ 411; (1939) 83 SJ 397; (1938-39) LV TLR 747 CA Gas company negligent in placing mains upon ground being mined underneath; mining company not liable Donoghue v Stevenson-style for loss to other upon ground subsiding.

Weaver v Commercial Process Company, Limited , and others (1947) LXIII TLR 466 HC KBD Apportionment of respective negligence of suppliers/receivers of defective jar of nitric acid which resulted in injury to employee of receivers.

Weaver, More v [1928] All ER 160; [1928] 2 KB 520; (1928) 66 LJ 124; (1928) 97 LJCL 721; (1929) 140 LTR 15; (1928) 72 SJ 556; (1928) WN (I) 207 CA Absolute privilege attaches to communications between solicitor/client in matters pertinent to that relationship.

Weaver, More v (1928) 72 SJ 319; (1928) WN (I) 158 HC KBD Absolute privilege attaches to communications between solicitor/client in matters pertinent to that relationship.

Webb and another v Sandown Urban District Council (1925) 60 LJ 606 CyCt Person did not by virtue of occasional trespass of cattle upon another's land for under twelve years acquire title to same to exclusion of owner.

Webb and another, Stubbings v [1993] 1 All ER 322; [1993] AC 498; [1993] 2 FCR 699 (also CA); [1993] 1 FLR 714; (1993) 143 NLJ 166; (1993) 137 SJ LB 32; [1992] TLR 619; [1993] 2 WLR 120 HL Claim for damages arising from mental ill-health following childhood rape/indecent assault an action for trespass to person and hence subject to six-year limitation period.

Webb and another, Stubbings v [1991] 3 ALL ER 949; [1993] 2 FCR 699 (also HL); [1992] 1 FLR 296; [1992] QB 197; [1991] TLR 171; [1991] 3 WLR 383 CA Cause of action for personal injury on foot of sexual abuse ran from date plaintiff realised personal injury attributable to sexual abuse.

Webb v Baldwin (1911) 75 JP 564 HC ChD On proving dedication of highway to public (and so no trespass).

Webb v Knight; Hedley v Webb [1901] 70 LJCh 663 HC ChD Action for trespass effected in course of constructing sewage system.

Webb v Times Publishing, Ltd [1960] 2 All ER 789; (1960) 110 LJ 590; [1960] 2 QB 535; (1960) 104 SJ 605 HC QBD Qualified privilege attaches to newspaper reports of foreign legal actions if accurate/fair/without malice/of real public interest.

Webb, Mansel v [1918-19] All ER 794; [1919] 88 LJCL 323 CA Rylands v Fletcher-style liability for emission of sparks from locomotive engine travelling along highway.

Webber v Gasquet, Metcalfe and Walton (1982) 132 NLJ 665 HC ChD Recovery of damages for negligence of solicitors vis-à-vis safeguarding plaintiff's property rights during divorce action.

Webber v McCausland (1948) 98 LJ 360 CyCt Hairdresser liable in negligence for sale of dangerous hair dye (though plaintiff contributorily negligent in not fully reading warning on bottle).

Weber v Birkett [1925] All ER 244; (1925) 60 LJ 464; (1925) 133 LTR 598; (1924-25) XLI TLR 451 CA Non-apportionment of damages meant had not been separate verdict on each issue: mistrial.

Weber v Birkett [1925] 1 KB 720; (1925) 60 LJ 294; (1925) WN (I) 77 HC KBD Non-apportionment of damages meant had not been separate verdict on each issue: mistrial; unsatisfactory mode of apology.

Weber, Simpson v (1925) 133 LTR 46; (1924-25) XLI TLR 302 HC KBD Growing of creeper in such a way as blocked another's gutter was trespass for which damages available.

Webster v Bakewell Rural District Council (1916) 80 JP 437 HC ChD Trespass action (for minor trespass) an abuse of process: dismissed with costs.

Webster, Bradford Corporation and another v (1920) 84 JP 137; [1920] 2 KB 135; [1920] 89 LJCL 455; (1920) 123 LTR 62; (1919-20) XXXVI TLR 286; (1920) WN (I) 80 HC KBD Corporation could recover wages/special pension from tortfeasor for injury to constable in corporation's service.

Weeds v Blaney and another (1976) 120 SJ 333 HC ChD Negligence did not preclude rectification of contract.

Weeks, Thornhill v (1914) 78 JP 154 HC ChD Injunction to restrain trespass where trespassers failed to establish public right of way.

Wegg-Prosser, Hayward and another v (1978) 122 SJ 792 HC QBD Libel action stayed where plaintiffs sought to rely on documents inadvertently obtained by them after they were disclosed by solicitor to court officer in course of taxation.

Weigall v Westminster Hospital [1936] 1 All ER 232; (1936) 80 SJ 146; (1935-36) LII TLR 301 CA Hospital negligent towards mother of patient/invitee slipping on mat on polished floor when entering hospital room for consultation with surgeon.

Weigall v Westminster Hospital (Governors) (1935) 79 SJ 560; (1934-35) LI TLR 554 HC KBD Hospital negligent towards mother of patient/invitee slipping on mat on polished floor when entering hospital room for consultation with surgeon.

Weinbaum, La Radiotechnique v (1927) 64 LJ 121; (1928) 97 LJCh 17; (1927) 71 SJ 824; (1927) WN (I) 211 HC ChD On when HC will order particulars of defence.

Weiner v Harvey and Co, Ltd [1936] LJNCCR 94 CyCt Injunction refused where further incident of passing off (of tobacco blend) not likely; on entrapment of person guilty of passing off.

Weingarten Brothers v Bayer and Co [1904-07] All ER 877; (1905) XCII LTR 511; (1904-05) XXI TLR 418 HL Passing-off found where used another's distinctive logo on own products.

Weingarten Brothers v Charles Bayer and Co (1903) LXXXVIII LTR 168; (1902-03) XIX TLR 239 HC ChD Injunction granted prohibiting sale of goods not made by plaintiff under plaintiff's distinctive trade-name where was possibility of confusion among buyers.

Weingarten Brothers v Charles Bayer and Company (1903-04) LXXXIX LTR 56; (1902-03) XIX TLR 604 CA Reversal of injunction granted by HC KBD prohibiting sale of goods not made by plaintiff under plaintiff's distinctive trade-name where was possibility of confusion among buyers.

Weisz and others, Paley (Princess Olga) v (1928-29) XLV TLR 102 HC KBD Failed action in detinue/conversion by Russian exile against defendants who purchased property confiscated by Soviets.

Weisz and others, Paley (Princess Olga) v (1928-29) XLV TLR 365 CA Failed action in detinue/conversion by Russian exile against defendants who purchased property confiscated by Soviets.

Welch v Bank of England and another [1955] Ch 508; (1955) 99 SJ 236; [1955] 2 WLR 757 HC ChD On negligence as basis for estoppel in banking stock transfer action.

Welch, Greenwell v (1904-05) 49 SJ 538 HC KBD Not allowed to treat as distress what have dealt with as trespass.

Welch, Grunnell v [1905] 2 KB 650; (1905-06) 54 WR 216 HC KBD Trespass ab initio in proceeding under first trespass warrant.

Welch, Grunnell v (1905-06) 54 WR 581 CA Trespass ab initio in proceeding under first trespass warrant.

Weld-Blundell v Stephens [1920] All ER 32; (1920) 55 LJ 206; [1920] 89 LJCL 705; (1920) 123 LTR 593; (1919-20) 64 SJ 529; (1919-20) XXXVI TLR 640 HL Nominal damages where ultimate cause of action was one's own behaviour/where recovery sought for consequences that were not natural/probable consequences of acts of party against whom claiming.

Weld-Blundell v Stephens [1919] 1 KB 520; [1919] 88 LJCL 689 (also HC KBD); (1919) 120 LTR 494; (1918-19) 63 SJ 301; (1918-19) XXXV TLR 245 CA Nominal damages where ultimate cause of action was one's own behaviour.

Weld-Blundell v Stephens [1918] 2 KB 742; [1919] 88 LJCL 689 (also CA); (1917-18) XXXIV TLR 564; (1918) WN (I) 254 HC KBD Non-recovery of damages where ultimate cause of action was one's own.

Weldon v 'The Times' Book Company (Limited) (1911-12) XXVIII TLR 143 CA Book distributors not liable for alleged libel in book distributed where did not know/were not negligent in not knowing of same and need not have been on inquiry as to same.

Weldon v Home Office [1990] 3 All ER 672; [1992] 1 AC 58 (also HC QBD/HL); [1990] TLR 269; [1990] 3 WLR 465 CA Intentional unreasonable deprivation by prison authorities of residual liberty of prisoner is false imprisonment.

Wellaway v Courtier [1916-17] All ER 340; (1917) CC Rep VI 94; [1918] 1 KB 200; (1917) 52 LJ 451; [1918] 87 LJCL 299; (1918) 118 LTR 256; (1917-18) 62 SJ 161; (1917-18) XXXIV TLR 115; (1917) WN (I) 368 HC KBD Crop-purchaser can maintain action in trespass.

Weller and Co and another v Foot and Mouth Disease Research Institute [1965] 3 All ER 560; [1966] 1 QB 569; (1965) 109 SJ 702; [1965] 3 WLR 1082 HC QBD Research Institute liable to farmers but not auctioneer at local cattle mart for escape of foot and mouth virus from laboratory.

Weller, Blaker v [1964] Crim LR 311t HC QBD Successful action against police for false imprisonment/malicious prosecution.

Wellingborough Council v Gordon (1991) 155 JP 494; [1990] TLR 713 HC QBD Prosecution arising from noise at Friday night birthday party to which all neighbours invited, most attended and none complained, an extreme reaction: nonetheless was no 'reasonable excuse' for noise (Control of Pollution Act 1974, s 58).

Wells v Cooper [1958] 2 All ER 527; (1958) 108 LJ 377; [1958] 2 QB 265; (1958) 102 SJ 508 CA Occupier not liable for injury sustained through own failure at everyday repair if exercised skill of competent carpenter.

Wells v Metropolitan Water Board (1938) 102 JP 61; (1937-38) LIV TLR 104 HC KBD Water board liable in negligence for injury caused to child by way of open valve-box lid, it being known to Board that lids were commonly interfered with.

Wells v Wells; Thomas v Brighton Health Authority; Page v Sheerness Steel Co plc [1997] 1 All ER 673; (1996) 140 SJ LB 239; (1996) TLR 24/10/96; [1997] 1 WLR 652 CA On gauging damages for future expenses and losses in personal injury cases.

Wellwood, Tideway Investment and Property Holdings Ld v; Same v Orton; Same v Jones; Same v Friedentag; Same v Thornley [1952] Ch 791 (also CA); (1952) 96 SJ 579; [1952] 1 TLR 1177 HC ChD Erection of flue pipes on undemised portion of premises was trespass (albeit minor).

Wellwood, Tideway Investment and Property Holdings Ld v; Same v Orton; Same v Jones; Same v Friedentag; Same v Thornley [1952] 2 TLR 365 CA Erection of flue pipes on undemised portion of premises was trespass (albeit minor).

Welsh and others, Ferguson v [1987] 3 All ER 777; (1987) 137 NLJ 1037; (1987) 131 SJ 1552; [1987] 1 WLR 1553 HL Usually occupier not liable to contractor's employees but exceptionally may be.

697

West Ham Borough Council, Dalby v (1945) 109 JP 180; (1945) 173 LTR 191; (1945) 89 SJ 270; (1944-45) LXI TLR 467 HC KBD Invitors liable for scalding of invitee using shower-bath (even though he had not tested water temperature) as he had not been told how to use same properly/not been warned about dangers of same/had through usage come to expect water of certain temperature.

West Ham Corporation, Wagner v (1920-21) XXXVII TLR 86 HC KBD Tram owners not liable for tram being started on passenger's prompting (unless conductor's not prompting was negligent).

West Hartlepool Steam Navigation Co, Ltd, Morris v [1956] 1 All ER 385; (1956) 100 SJ 129 HL Non-closure of hatch of hold through which party fell was negligent.

West Herts Group Hospital Management Committee, Edwards v [1957] 1 All ER 541; (1957) 121 JP 212; (1957) 107 LJ 169 CA Hospital committee not liable as invitor/master or via implied term in employment contract with house physician for personal belongings stolen from staff hostel.

West Leigh Colliery Company (Limited) v Tunnicliffe and Hampson (Limited) (1907-08) 52 SJ 93; (1907-08) XXIV TLR 146 HL On appropriate damages for damage caused by subsidence.

West Leigh Colliery Company, Limited, Tunnicliffe and Hampson, Limited v [1905] 2 Ch 390 HC ChD On appropriate damages for damage caused by subsidence.

West Leigh Colliery Company, Limited, Tunnicliffe and Hampson, Limited v [1906] 2 Ch 22; (1906) XCIV LTR 715 CA On appropriate damages for damage caused by subsidence.

West Lindsey District Council and others, Richardson v [1990] 1 All ER 296; (1989) 139 NLJ 1263; [1990] 1 WLR 522 CA Local authority does not normally owe duty of care to see that building project complies with building regulations.

West Midland Passenger Executive, Howell v (1973) 123 NLJ 13t CA Limitation period disapplied where unaware of rights until shortly before instigated action.

West Midlands Gas Board, Lloyd v [1971] 2 All ER 1240; (1971) 115 SJ 227; [1971] 1 WLR 749 CA Retrial where plaintiff succeeded on facts did not plead; res ipsa loquitur inapplicable as defective object in premises of plaintiff.

West Midlands Regional Health Authority, Maynard v [1985] 1 All ER 635; (1983) 133 NLJ 641; (1984) 128 SJ 317; [1983] TLR 316; [1984] 1 WLR 634 HL Doctor not proved negligent simply because was reputable body of opinion that disagreed with action he took as well as body of opinion that agreed with action he took.

West Riding of Yorkshire County Council, Parkinson v (1921-22) 66 SJ 488 HC KBD Council liable for misfeasance of highway where accident arose as result of state in which workmen left road overnight.

West Suffolk County Council, Burton v [1960] 2 All ER 26; (1960) 124 JP 273; [1960] 2 QB 72; (1960) 104 SJ 349 CA Highway authority not negligent where did not warn of ice on road.

West v Bristol Tramways Co [1908-10] All ER 215; (1908) 72 JP 243; [1908] 2 KB 14; [1908] 77 LJCL 684; (1908-09) XCIX LTR 264; (1907-08) 52 SJ 393; (1907-08) XXIV TLR 478; (1908) WN (I) 95 CA Rylands v Fletcher applied to creosoting as non-natural user of land.

West v Bristol Tramways Company (Limited) (1908) 72 JP 145; (1907-08) 52 SJ 264; (1907-08) XXIV TLR 299 HC KBD Rylands v Fletcher applied to creosoting as non-natural user of land.

West v Hughes of Beaconsfield Ltd and another [1971] RTR 298 HC QBD On liabilities of van driver and following car for injuries to cyclist whom former knocked down and latter ran over (latter act not novus actus interveniens).

West Wiltshire District Council v Garland and others; Cond and others (third parties) [1993] Ch 409; [1993] TLR 112; [1993] 3 WLR 626 HC ChD On duty of care owed by district auditors when auditing local authority accounts.

West Wiltshire District Council v Garland and others; Cond and others (third parties) [1995] Ch 297; (1995) 139 SJ LB 18; [1994] TLR 622; [1995] 2 WLR 439 CA On duty of care owed by district auditors when auditing local authority accounts.

WH Smith and Son, Ltd, Walters v [1911-13] All ER 170; (1914) 78 JP 118; [1914] 1 KB 595; [1914] 83 LJKB 335; (1914) 110 LTR 345; (1913-14) 58 SJ 186; (1913-14) XXX TLR 158; (1913) WN (I) 359 HC KBD Private person must to defeat false imprisonment claim show reasonable suspicion that person whom arrested committed an offence that was effected.

WH Smith and Son, Robinson v (1900-01) XVII TLR 235 HC KBD Dangerous employment (newspaper boys at railway station having to cross lines) put special duty of care on employers which may not have discharged.

WH Smith and Son, Robinson v (1900-01) XVII TLR 423 CA Dangerous employment (newspaper boys at railway station having to cross lines) put special duty of care on employers which may not have discharged.

WH Smith and Son, The Attorney-General v (1910) 74 JP 313; (1910) 45 LJ 390; (1910-11) 103 LTR 96; (1909-10) XXVI TLR 482 HC ChD Whether user of public street in front of business place a nuisance depends on circumstances (here was not).

WH Smith and Sons, Ltd, Smith v [1952] 1 All ER 528; (1952) 96 SJ 181 CA On damages/costs where both parties equally to blame.

Wharton v Sweeney (1961) 105 SJ 887 CA On appropriate damages for loss of eye.

Wheat v E Lacon and Co, Ltd [1966] 1 All ER 582; [1966] AC 552; (1965-66) 116 NLJ 611; (1966) 110 SJ 149; [1966] 2 WLR 581 HL Husband and wife running split premises occupied whole; no occupiers' liability where accident reasonably avoidable.

Wheat v E Lacon and Co, Ltd and others [1965] 2 All ER 700; (1965) 115 LJ 464; [1966] 1 QB 335; (1965) 109 SJ 334; [1965] 3 WLR 142 CA Brewer not in control of part of inn run as private boarding-house so not occupier.

Wheeler and another v JJ Saunders Ltd and others [1995] 2 All ER 697; [1996] Ch 19; [1995] TLR 3; [1995] 3 WLR 466 CA Planning consent does not preclude action for nuisance.

Wheeler and another v New Merton Board Mills, Ltd [1933] All ER 28 CA Cannot be volenti non fit injuria in action for breach of statutory duty.

Wheeler v Copas [1981] 3 All ER 405; (1981) 131 NLJ 367 HC QBD Damages for worker given unsuitable ladder for work by farmer but damages halved given that worker understood danger but used ladder anyway.

Wheeler v Morris [1914-15] All ER 1196; (1915) CC Rep IV 53; (1915) 50 LJ 335; [1915] 84 LJKB 1435; (1915-16) 113 LTR 644 CA Shopowner not liable for injury to party caused by two men pulling on external sun-blind as was not reasonably foreseeable/had taken all reasonable steps.

Wheeler v Morris [1915] 84 LJKB 269; (1915) 112 LTR 412 HC KBD Shopowner could be liable for injury to party caused by two men pulling on external sun-blind in respect of which inadequate precautions taken.

Wheeler v Somerfield and others [1966] 2 All ER 305; (1965-66) 116 NLJ 837; [1966] 2 QB 94; [1966] 2 WLR 1006 CA Libel damages for injury to health possible (but not here); could be that to include articles of certain section of publication might carry innuendo but not here.

Wheeler v Somerfield and others (1965) 109 SJ 875 HC QBD Failed claim of innuendo in one article based on other articles.

Wheeler, Beer v (1965) 109 SJ 133 HC QBD Experienced bull-manager ought to have been instructed as to all steps in new bull-keeping procedure but in light of experience was half-liable for accident.

Wheeler, Beer v (1965) 109 SJ 457 CA Experienced bull-manager did not have to be instructed in all steps in new bull-keeping procedure.

Whichello v Medway and Gravesend Hospital Management Committee and another (1964) 108 SJ 55 HC QBD Decision not to take step which might have proved more fruitful approach to treating patient was not actually negligent.

Whitbread (Wales) Ltd, Knight v (1980) 130 NLJ 116c CA Defendant pub-owners liable as occupiers to barmaid for failing to provide safe means of access to garage in which pub watchdog kept.

White and another v Eastaugh (1921) CC Rep X 11 CyCt Order for possession available against tenant who through refusal to quit property upon cessation of tenancy renders self a trespasser.

White and another v Jones and another [1995] 2 AC 207 (also CA); [1995] 3 FCR 51; (1995) 145 NLJ 251; (1995) 139 SJ LB 83; [1995] TLR 89; [1995] 2 WLR 187 HL Solicitor owed duty of care to intended beneficiary whom it was reasonably foreseeable would suffer loss through solicitor's negligence in relation to preparation of will.

White and another v Jones and others [1993] 3 All ER 481; [1995] 2 AC 207 (also HL); (1993) 143 NLJ 473; [1993] TLR 124; [1993] 3 WLR 730 CA Non-preparation of will following instruction makes solicitor liable to disappointed beneficiary where instructor dies before will prepared/executed.

White and another v London General Omnibus Co (1914) 49 LJ 114; (1913-14) 58 SJ 339; (1914) WN (I) 78 HC ChD Nuisance by noise/smell from garage not permanent injury to reversion.

White and another v Metropolitan Police Commissioner [1982] TLR 221 HC QBD Exemplary damages from Police Commissioner for false imprisonment/assault/malicious prosecution by police officers.

White and Co (a firm), Ford and another v (1964) 114 LJ 554; (1964) 108 SJ 542; [1964] 1 WLR 885 HC ChD On quantifying damages available where property purchased on foot of solicitor's negligent advice.

White and others, Demerara Electric Company Limited v [1907] AC 330; (1907) XCVI LTR 752; (1906-07) 51 SJ 497 PC No nuisance condition in lighting order extended to contemporaneous granting of tramways licence.

White and Sons, Dulieu v [1900-03] All ER 353; [1901] 2 KB 669; [1901] 70 LJK/QB 837; (1901-02) LXXXV LTR 126; (1900-01) 45 SJ 578; (1900-01) XVII TLR 555; (1901-02) 50 WR 76 HC KBD Damages recoverable where nervous shock followed by physical injury.

White and Wife v Steadman [1913] 3 KB 340; [1913] 82 LJKB 846; (1913-14) 109 LTR 249; (1912-13) XXIX TLR 563; (1913) WN (I) 172 HC KBD Stable keeper liable to wife injured as result of behaviour of horse rented to husband.

White Hudson and Co, Ltd v Asian Organisation, Ltd [1965] 1 All ER 1040; (1964) 108 SJ 937; [1964] 1 WLR 1466 PC Can be passing-off by get-up even though writing on items distinguishes them.

White v Blackmore and others [1972] 3 All ER 158; (1972) 122 NLJ 561t; [1972] 2 QB 651; (1972) 116 SJ 547; [1972] 3 WLR 296 CA Volenti non fit injuria inapplicable to motor racecourse visitor injured through race organisers' shortcomings; exclusion clause valid.

White v J and F Stone Lighting and Radio, Limited [1939] 3 All ER 507; [1939] 2 KB 827; [1939] 108 LJCL 868; (1939) 161 LTR 107; (1939) 83 SJ 603; (1938-39) LV TLR 949; (1939) WN (I) 280 CA On what constitutes a privileged occasion.

White v London Transport Executive (1982) 126 SJ 277 HC QBD Assessment of fatal accident damages.

White v St Albans City and District Council [1990] TLR 196 CA On extent of liability of occupier towards trespasser.

White v Warwick (John) [1953] 2 All ER 1021; (1953) 97 SJ 740; [1953] 1 WLR 1285 CA Hire contract exception clause found to exclude contractual but not tortious liability.

White, Barry Railway Company v (1900-01) XVII TLR 644 HL On negligence/contributory negligence in action for personal injuries suffered at level crossing.

White, Holden v [1982] 2 All ER 328; (1981) 131 NLJ 476; [1982] QB 679; (1982) 126 SJ 230; [1982] TLR 165; [1982] 2 WLR 1030 CA Not visitor if using public/private right of way.

Whiteford v Hunter (1950) 94 SJ 758; (1950) WN (I) 553 HL Surgeon found not to be negligent in his mis-diagnosis of patient's ailment.

Whiteley, Hue v (1928) 66 LJ 304; (1929) 98 LJCh 227; (1929) 140 LTR 531; (1928) WN (I) 257 HC ChD On inferring right of way from traditional user of pathway/roadway (in action for injunction to restrain alleged trespass).

Whiteley, Limited v Hilt [1918] 2 KB 115; (1918) CC Rep VII 37; (1917-18) XXXIV TLR 402 HC KBD Third party buying hire-purchase item from hirer thereby repudiating hire-purchase of same could be successfully sued in detinue/conversion.

Whiteley, Limited v Hilt [1918] 2 KB 808; (1917-18) XXXIV TLR 592 CA Third party buying hire-purchase item from hirer thereby repudiating hire-purchase of same acquired interest of hirer.

Whiting v Hillingdon London Borough Council (1970) 114 SJ 247 HC QBD Highway authority not occupier of footpath/not liable in negligence for person who injured self on concealed tree stump.

Whitmore and another v Euroways Express Coaches Ltd and others [1984] TLR 290 HC QBD Damages recoverable for shock of being in hospital with/seeing hurt spouse (albeit that were not affected medically/in psychiatric manner by the shock).

Whitmores (Edenbridge), Limited v Stanford [1909] 1 Ch 427 HC ChD Rylands v Fletcher inapplicable to owner of land on which another keeps/impounds water (or other dangerous element) for that other's purposes; injunction to restrain interference (inter alia by trespass) with full use and enjoyment of stream.

Whittaker v Bailey (1925) 60 LJ 521 CyCt Where house sold and conveyance did not mention existing right of way use of the way held to pass to buyer of house.

Whittaker v London County Council (1915) 79 JP 437; [1915] 2 KB 676; (1915-16) 113 LTR 544; (1915) WN (I) 212 HC KBD Recovery of damages for injuries sustained when wrongfully ejected physically from tramway.

Whittle, Robinson v [1980] 3 All ER 459; (1980) 124 SJ 807; [1980] 1 WLR 1476 HC QBD Faulty application within 21 days to state case may be amended anytime before High Court hearing; could not plead defence in respect of killing birds under Protection of Birds Act 1954, s 4(2) (a) where charged with laying poison to kill birds.

Whittle, Taylor v (1931) 72 LJ ccr39 CyCt Other negligent party to road traffic collision could not plead contributory negligence of husband-driver as defence to action brought against him by wife-passenger.

Whitworth and another, Smoldon v (1996) TLR 18/12/96 CA On duty of care owed towards rugby player by rugby referee.

Whitworth and another, Smoldon v (1996) TLR 23/4/96 HC QBD Rugby referee owes duty of care in policing scrums to ensure that are conducted safely.

Whymark v Abrahams (1922) CC Rep XI 58 CyCt Owner of house not liable for injury occurring to passer-by when brick fell from defective chimney unless proved that owner let house with defect/was under contractual duty to keep chimney in repair.

Wickett v Port of London Authority [1929] 1 KB 216; (1929) 98 LJCL 222; (1928) 138 LTR 668 HC KBD Dock authority exemption clause applicable where injury sustained by person on barge being assisted into London docks by authority servants.

Wickham Holdings Ltd v Brooke House Motors Ltd [1967] 1 WLR 295 CA Finance company could only recover outstanding amount due under hire-purchase agrement where hirer wrongfully sold goods hired.

Wiehe v Dennis Brothers (1912-13) XXIX TLR 250 HC KBD Person from whom buying horse and with whom left horse for few days during which horse injured liable in negligence as gratuitous bailee who could not show were not negligent.

Wieland v Cyril Lord Carpets, Ltd [1969] 3 All ER 1006 HC QBD Damages available for second injury on foot of original negligence.

Wieland, Turnball v (1916-17) XXXIII TLR 143 HC KBD Employer liable for unlicensed cattle drover's negligence.

Wiffen v Bailey and others [1914-15] All ER 967; (1915) 79 JP 145; [1915] 1 KB 600; (1914) 49 LJ 674; [1915] 84 LJKB 688; (1914-15) 59 SJ 176; (1914-15) XXXI TLR 64; (1914) WN (I) 434 CA Malicious prosecution action failed where could not show damage to frame; imperilling of life/limb/liberty; financial loss.

Wilks and another v Cheltenham Homeguard Motor Cycle and Light Car Club and another (1971) 115 SJ 127 HC QBD Motor cycle race participant owes duty of care to spectators not to be reckless; race organisers not liable for injuries which could not reasonably have foreseen/prevented.

Willcox v Kettell [1937] 1 All ER 222; (1937) 83 LJ 58 HC ChD Leave to underpin wall did not prevent extension of foundations thereof onto other's property being trespass.

Willett and another, Goke v (1973) 123 NLJ 274t; [1973] RTR 422 CA Liability in negligence where failed to give hand-signal when about to undertake dangerous turn.

Willetts v Chaplin and Co (1922-23) XXXIX TLR 222 HC KBD Was reasonable for warehousemen to sell all furniture deposited with them by plaintiff and not just enough to cover the unpaid costs of storage.

William A Jay and Sons v Veevers (JS), Ltd [1946] 1 All ER 646 Assizes Apportionment of liability for contributory negligence on Admiralty Division principles.

William Cuenod and Company v Charles John Leslie and Wife (1908-09) 53 SJ 14; (1908-09) XXV TLR 2 HC KBD Husband liable for torts of judicially separated wife committed during coverture.

William Davis and Co (Leicester) Ltd, Home Brewery plc v [1987] 1 All ER 637; [1987] QB 339; (1987) 131 SJ 102; [1987] 2 WLR 117 HC QBD Lower land occupier taking steps to prevent water flowing from higher land liable in nuisance to higher land occupier if steps unreasonable and cause damage.

William Edge and Sons, Limited v William Nicholls and Sons, Limited [1911] AC 693; (1910-11) 55 SJ 737; (1911) WN (I) 176 HL Injunction granted to restrain passing off by get-up.

William Henderson Sons, Ltd, Murphy v; McBride v Same (1963) 107 SJ 534 CA Occupiers liable in negligence for having fire doors open or for not closing them as soon as possible after became aware of fire.

William Leitch and Co Limited v Leydon; AG Barr and Co Limited v Macgheoghean (1930) 70 LJ 375; (1931) 100 LJPC 10; (1931) 144 LTR 218 HL Water vendor did not owe duty of care to aerated water manufacturer (with whom had no contract) to ensure that bottles supplied for vendor to fill were not those of said manufacturer/put to use of which said manufacturer did not approve.

William Nash, Ltd, Stevens v [1966] 3 All ER 156; (1965-66) 116 NLJ 1203; (1966) 110 SJ 710; [1966] 1 WLR 1550 CA Generally CA will not seek to examine personal injuries.

William Nicholls and Sons, Limited, William Edge and Sons, Limited v [1911] AC 693; (1910-11) 55 SJ 737; (1911) WN (I) 176 HL Injunction granted to restrain passing off by get-up.

William Summers and Co Limited v Boyce and Kinmond and Co (1907-08) XCVII LTR 505 HC ChD Injunction granted to restrain disclosure of company secrets by ex-employee to new employer — damages from ex-employee/new employer for disclosures which had occurred.

William Whiteley, Limited, Phillips v (1938) 82 SJ 196; (1937-38) LIV TLR 379 HC KBD On duty of care owed by ear-piercer.

William Whiteley, Ltd, Philips v [1938] 1 All ER 566 HC KBD Surgeon's standard of care not expected of jeweller doing ear-piercing.

William Willett Ltd and another, Driver v [1969] 1 All ER 665; (1969) 119 NLJ 248 Assizes On deciding whether sufficient closeness of relationship to give rise to duty of care.

Williams and another v Luff (1978) 122 SJ 164 HC QBD Duty of care owed towards child en ventre sa mère injured in road traffic collision.

Williams and another v Natural Life Health Foods Ltd and another (1996) 140 SJ LB 43; [1997] TLR 24 HC QBD Company director found liable for tortious acts of company.

Williams and another, London Borough of Southwark v; London Borough of Southwark v Anderson and another [1971] 2 All ER 175; [1971] Ch 734; [1971] 2 WLR 467 CA Trespass on foot of homelessness not justifiable as necessity.

Williams and Co, Teasdale v (1983) 133 NLJ 105 HC QBD Successful negligence suit against solicitor whose negligent failure to advise client of landlord's application for interim rent meant client failed to apply for new lease.

Willis, Lane v; Same v Beach (1972) 116 SJ 102; [1972] 1 WLR 326 CA Case properly stayed where plaintiff refused to undergo medical examination.

Willmett and Co and another, Jolliffe v [1971] 1 All ER 478; (1970) 120 NLJ 707t; (1970) 114 SJ 619 HC QBD Person entering home of separated spouse (not family home) with permission of other spouse is trespasser; employer not responsible for torts of independent contractor unless commssioned tort/negligence in choosing same led to tort.

Willmett and Co, Nandreph Ltd v [1978] 1 All ER 746; (1978) 122 SJ 744 HC ChD Benefit arising from negligence may be deduced from damages if appropriate.

Willmott, Munro v [1948] 2 All ER 983; [1949] 1 KB 295; (1948) 98 LJ 657; [1949] 118 LJR 471; (1948) LXIV TLR 627; (1948) WN (I) 459 HC KBD Appropriate damages for conversion/detinue.

Willoughby, Baker v [1969] 2 All ER 549; (1969) 113 SJ 37; [1969] 2 WLR 489 CA Equal blameworthiness: appropriate damages.

Willoughby, Baker v [1968] 2 All ER 236; (1968) 118 NLJ 277t; [1969] 1 QB 38; (1968) 112 SJ 234; [1968] 2 WLR 1138 HC QBD Post-personal injury wounding with which original injury merged did not disentitle one to damages for original injury.

Willoughby, Baker v [1969] 3 All ER 1528; [1970] AC 467; (1968) 118 NLJ 1197t; (1970) 114 SJ 15; [1970] 2 WLR 50 HL Respective duty of motorists/pedestrians to be road wary; personal injury damages are for loss occasioned by injury — here no new loss after second injury so no further damages.

Wills v TF Martin (Roof Contractors) Ltd [1972] RTR 368; (1972) 122 NLJ 81t; (1972) 116 SJ 145 HC QBD Placing skip on highway not proven negligent and though a nuisance person who collided with same, not skip-owner was liable.

Willson v Ministry of Defence [1991] 1 All ER 638 HC QBD 'Chance of serious deterioration': 'chance' means something more than fanciful/'serious deterioration' more than ongoing deterioration and greater than ordinary deterioration.

Wilmshurst and others, Greenlands (Limited) v (1912-13) XXIX TLR 64 HC KBD Statements of person acting as confidential agent of member of trade association not privileged.

Wilmshurst and the London Association for Protection of Trade and another, Greenlands, Limited v [1913] 3 KB 507; (1913) 48 LJ 471; [1914] 83 LJKB 1; (1913-14) 109 LTR 487; (1912-13) 57 SJ 740; (1912-13) XXIX TLR 685 CA Statements of person acting as confidential agent of member of trade association not privileged.

Wilsher v Essex Area Health Authority [1986] 3 All ER 801; (1986) 136 NLJ 1061; [1987] QB 730; (1970) 130 SJ 749; [1987] 2 WLR 425 CA Health authority can be liable in failing to provide competent medics; 'team negligence' non-existent; standard of care that of ordinary skilled person; burden of proof not transferred by showing step that ought to have been taken not taken; negligence if heightened risk because of action even if other risks present.

Wilsher v Essex Area Health Authority [1988] 1 All ER 871; [1988] AC 1074; (1988) 138 NLJ 78; (1988) 132 SJ 418; [1988] 2 WLR 557 HL Must prove causation between injury and negligent act — not enough that negligent act one of a number of possible causes.

Wilson and another v Hodgson's Kingston Brewery Company (Limited) (1916) 80 JP 39; [1916] 85 LJKB 270; (1915-16) 113 LTR 1112; (1915-16) 60 SJ 142; (1915-16) XXXII TLR 60; (1915) WN (I) 352 HC KBD Brewery/tenant of tied pub not liable for injury suffered by independent deliverer who elected to deliver beer by particular route.

Wilson and another, Gammell v [1980] 2 All ER 557; [1982] AC 27 (also HL); (1980) 130 NLJ 510; (1980) 124 SJ 329; [1980] 3 WLR 591 CA Estate can sue for lost earnings in lost years; gravestone is funeral expense; sum for loss of life expectation changeable/not constantly reviewable.

Wilson and another, Hall v [1939] 4 All ER 85; (1939) 88 LJ 276; (1939) 83 SJ 961; (1939-40) LVI TLR 15 HC KBD Allowance for risk of death in war made when gauging fatal personal injury damages.

Winfield, Waldock v [1901] 2 KB 596 CA Master liable for negligence of servant on has hire to another.

Wing v London General Omnibus Co [1908-10] All ER 496; (1909) 73 JP 429; [1909] 2 KB 652; [1909] 78 LJKB 1063; (1909-10) 101 LTR 411; (1908-09) 53 SJ 713; (1908-09) XXV TLR 729 CA Skidding not per se evidence of negligent driving; on res ipsa loquitur; Rylands v Fletcher applies to unnatural user of highway for traffic.

Wing v London General Omnibus Company Limited (1909) 73 JP 170; (1909) C LTR 301; (1908-09) 53 SJ 287 HC KBD Recovery of damages for personal injuries sustained by passenger when bus skidded (not proved that passenger knew of/had accepted risk of skidding).

Wing, Heath and Co and others, Coolee, Limited v (1930-31) XLVII TLR 78 HC KBD Successful action against negligent insurance brokers.

Winkworth v Raven [1931] All ER 847; (1931) 71 LJ 119; (1931) 100 LJCL 206; (1931) 144 LTR 594; (1931) 75 SJ 120; (1930-31) XLVII TLR 254; (1931) WN (I) 42 HC KBD Responsibilites of innkeeper to guest: no liability as no negligence shown.

Winnick, Hines v [1947] 2 All ER 517; [1947] Ch 708; [1948] 117 LJR 187; (1947) 91 SJ 560; (1947) LXIII TLR 520; (1947) WN (I) 244 HC ChD Stage name of musician protected in passing off action.

Winnifrith and Leppard, Piper v (1917) CC Rep VI 93; (1917-18) XXXIV TLR 108; (1917) WN (I) 358 HC KBD Joint savaging of sheep by two dogs owned by two different owners did not mean owners joint tortfeasors.

Winnipeg Electric Company v Geel (Jacob) [1932] AC 690; (1932) 101 LJPC 187; (1933) 148 LTR 24; (1931-32) XLVIII TLR 657 PC Matter for jury whether motor vehicle owner has negatived presumption of negligence under Manitoban law where motor vehicle injures another.

Winnipeg, Selkirk and Lake Winnipeg Railway Company, Pronek v [1933] AC 61; (1933) 102 LJPC 12; (1933) 148 LTR 193 PC On duty of railway company operating its cars in part on a highway.

Winsbury-White, Morris v [1937] 4 All ER 494 HC KBD Visiting surgeon not liable for negligence of resident surgeons/nurses (did not act as agents); post-operation finding of tube in patient's body not res ipsa loquitur.

Winslade, Simons v [1938] 3 All ER 774; (1938) 86 LJ 142; (1938) 82 SJ 711 CA Person quitting pub for outside toilet to rear of pub is still invitee.

Winstanley v Bampton [1943] 1 All ER 661; [1943] KB 319; (1944) 94 LJ 108; [1943] 112 LJ 430; (1943) 168 LTR 206; (1942-43) LIX TLR 183; (1943) WN (I) 55 HC KBD Privileged letter to plaintiff's commanding officer lost privilege through malice.

Winter and another, Morriss v (1926-30) XXVIII Cox CC 687; [1930] 1 KB 243; (1930) 142 LTR 67; (1928-29) XLV TLR 643 HC KBD No right to early discharge where earn remission marks so no false imprisonment thereafter.

Winters and another, Burton v [1993] 3 All ER 847; [1993] 1 WLR 1077 CA Common law right to self-redress for trespass by encroachment if urgency requires it/legal action unmerited.

Wintle v Bristol Tramways and Carriage Company Limited (1917) 81 JP 55; [1917] 86 LJCL 240; (1917) 116 LTR 125; (1916-17) 61 SJ 183; (1917) WN (I) 7 HC KBD Though only required to have one lamp by statute driving petrol lorry in instant circumstances with one lamp was negligent.

Wintle v Bristol Tramways and Carriage Company Limited (1917) 52 LJ 188; [1917] 86 LJCL 936; (1917-18) 117 LTR 238; (1917) WN (I) 163 CA Though only required to have one lamp by statute driving petrol lorry in instant circumstances with one lamp could be negligent.

Wiper Supply Services, Ltd and another, Knight v (1965) 109 SJ 358 HC QBD On appropriate damages for above the knee amputee injured after went through green light by person turning from side-road..

Wisbech Rural District Council v Ward (1927) 91 JP 166; (1926-27) XLIII TLR 739; (1927) WN (I) 236 HC KBD Architect in certificating building work was under terms of particular contract not acting in quasi-/arbitral role and so could be (and was) liable in negligence.

Wood, Crow v [1970] 3 All ER 425; [1971] 1 QB 77; (1970) 114 SJ 474; [1970] 3 WLR 516 CA Party failing in duty to maintain walls cannot complain of cattle trespass by neighbour's sheep.

Wood, Nelson, Murdoch and Co v (1921) CC Rep X 76; (1922) 126 LTR 745; (1921-22) XXXVIII TLR 23 HC KBD Improper sale of hire-purchase piano not per se a repudiation of hire-purchase contract and as finance company had not accepted repudiation/terminated contract transfer of piano was not conversion.

Wood, North v (1914) CC Rep III 18; [1914] 1 KB 629; [1914] 83 LJKB 587; (1914) 110 LTR 703; (1913-14) XXX TLR 258; (1914) WN (I) 38 HC KBD Father not liable for act of infant daughter's savage dog.

Wood, Pilkington v [1953] 2 All ER 810; [1953] Ch 770; (1953) 103 LJ 555; (1953) 97 SJ 572; [1953] 3 WLR 522 HC ChD Duty of mitigation does not require bringing complex litigation; unforeseeable damages irrecoverable; no need for resale of land to gauge actual loss caused by solicitor's negligence in purchase.

Wood, Pontin and another v [1961] 3 All ER 992 HC QBD Writ set aside where sought to amend outside limitation period and no special reason justifying disapplication of limitation.

Woodall Duckham Construction Co Ltd, James v [1969] 2 All ER 794; (1969) 113 SJ 225; [1969] 1 WLR 903 CA Damages for loss of earnings reduced where delay deferred return to work.

Woodfield, Morey v [1963] 3 All ER 533; (1963) 107 SJ 651; [1964] 1 WLR 16 CA On appeals concerning personal injury damages.

Woodland and others, Salsbury v [1969] 3 All ER 863; (1969) 119 NLJ 365t; [1970] 1 QB 324; (1969) 113 SJ 327; [1969] 3 WLR 29 CA No negligence if employ competent person to do work not in itself dangerous.

Woodman and Son (Builders), Ltd and others, Clayton v [1961] 3 All ER 249; [1962] 2 QB 533 (also CA); (1961) 105 SJ 889 HC QBD Architects owe duty of care to builders to watch out for their safety and are liable for physical (not economic) loss occasioned by breach of duty.

Woodman and Son (Builders), Ltd and others, Clayton v [1962] 2 All ER 33; (1962) 112 LJ 288; [1962] 2 QB 533 (also HC QBD); (1962) 106 SJ 242; [1962] 1 WLR 585 CA Architect not liable for manner in which builder performs work.

Woodman Matthews and Co, RP Howard Ltd v (1983) 133 NLJ 598 HC QBD Solicitor liable in negligence for failure to seek new tenancy for client under terms of Landlord and Tenant Act 1954, Part II.

Woodman v Pwllbach Colliery Company Limited (1914-15) 111 LTR 169 CA No common law right or easement pursuant to lease of colliery to create nuisance..

Woodman v Richardson (1937) 84 LJ 144; (1937) 81 SJ 70 CA Non-liability of invitor towards invitee for not reasonably foreseeable course of events (not instigated by invitor's employees) that resulted in injury to invitee.

Woodman, Pwllbach Colliery Co, Ltd v [1914-15] All ER 124; [1915] AC 634; (1915) 50 LJ 117; [1915] 84 LJKB 874; (1915-16) 113 LTR 10; (1914-15) XXXI TLR 271; (1915) WN (I) 108 HL Authorisation to carry on business not per se authorisation to carry on nuisance (unless cannot otherwise be carried on).

Woods v Duncan and others; Duncan and another v Hambrook and others; Duncan and another v Cammell Laird and Co, Ltd [1946] 1 All ER 420; [1946] AC 401; [1947] 116 LJR 120; (1946) 174 LTR 286; (1945-46) LXII TLR 283 HL Resolution of negligence action; on res ipsa loquitur.

Woods v Martins Bank, Ltd and another (1958) 108 LJ 665 HC QBD Bank and manager liable for negligent advice regarding investments given by manager to plaintiff.

Woods, Great Northern Railway Company v (1917) CC Rep VI 50 CyCt Rail company liable in negligence for carriage of sheep in overcrowded conditions.

Woodward and another v Mayor of Hastings and others [1944] 2 All ER 565; (1945) 109 JP 41; [1945] KB 174; [1945] 114 LJ 211 (also HC KBD); (1945) 172 LTR 16; (1944-45) LXI TLR 94; (1944) WN (1) 239 CA Grammar school governors not public authority/were liable for caretaker's negligence.

Woodward and another v Mayor of Hastings and others [1944] 2 All ER 119; (1944) 108 JP 247; [1944] KB 671; (1945) 95 LJ 111; [1945] 114 LJ 211 (also CA); (1944) 171 LTR 231; (1943-44) LX TLR 404 HC KBD Suing school governors subject to public authority limitation.

Woodward and others v Hutchins and others (1977) 121 SJ 409; [1977] 1 WLR 760 CA Refusal to grant injunction restraining disclosure of confidential information obtained in course of employment.

Woodward v Mayor of Hastings and Others; Same v Same (1945) 172 LTR 16; (1944) WN (I) 239 CA School governors not entitled to protection of public authority limitation period in negligence action.

Wooldridge v Sumner and another [1962] 2 All ER 978; (1962) 112 LJ 520; [1963] 2 QB 43; (1962) 106 SJ 489 CA Sports participant not liable in negligence to viewing public injured through non-reckless errors of judgment; volenti non fit injuria not relevant.

Woolerton and Wilson Ltd v Richard Costain (Midlands) Ltd (1969) 119 NLJ 1093t HC ChD Postponed injunction granted against party guilty of trespass when swung crane to and fro.

Woolfall v Knowlsey Borough Council [1992] TLR 319 CA Local authority liable for injury to child occasioned by explosion of aerosol can which had been part of rubbish left uncleared by local authority on foot of industrial dispute.

Woollahra Municipal Council, Dunlop v [1981] 1 All ER 1202; [1982] AC 158; (1981) 125 SJ 199; [1981] 2 WLR 693 PC Can only recover for illegal act not null act; absent malice passing of null act not misfeasance and misfeasance essential to abuse of public office.

Wooller v London Transport Board and another [1976] RTR 206 CA That single passenger thown to floor did not mean bus driver negligent in travelling too close to lorry in front and having to brake suddenly when lorry braked so as to avoid collision.

Woollerton and Wilson Ltd v Richard Costain Ltd [1970] 1 All ER 483; (1969) 119 NLJ 1093t; (1970) 114 SJ 170; [1970] 1 WLR 411 HC ChD Postponed injunction granted against party guilty of trespass when swung crane to and fro.

Woolley and others, Briess and others v [1954] AC 333; [1954] 2 WLR 832 HL Shareholders vicariously liable for fraudulent misrepresentation of agent whom they appointed to sell their shares.

Woolmer v Delmer Price, Ltd [1955] 1 All ER 377; [1955] 1 QB 291; [1955] 2 WLR 329 HC QBD Could not rely on exception clause where no explanation of disappearance of bailed goods offered: must show either negligence or no negligence.

Woolwich Borough Council, Barnett v (1910) 74 JP 441 HC ChD Failed action for injunction to restrain nuisance as was brought out of time allowed under Public Authorities Protection Act 1893.

Woolwich Borough Council, Craib v (1919-20) XXXVI TLR 630 HC KBD Sewer authority not liable for non-feasance that gives rise to nuisance.

Woor, Clark and another v [1965] 2 All ER 353; (1965) 109 SJ 251; [1965] 1 WLR 650 HC QBD Action not barred where concealment by fraud led to late discovery of damage; damages measured from date of discovery.

Wootton and Kelley (trading as the Stoneleigh Quarry Company), Leake v (1923) CC Rep XII 68 CyCt Failed action against quarrying company for damages after cattle got sick drinking water polluted (but only inter alia) by local quarry.

Wootton v Sievier [1911-13] All ER 1001; [1913] 3 KB 499; (1913) 48 LJ 374; [1913] 82 LJKB 1242; (1913-14) 109 LTR 28; (1912-13) 57 SJ 609; (1912-13) XXIX TLR 596; (1913) WN (I) 187 CA Particulars required when justification pleaded.

Worboys v Acme Investments Ltd (1969) 119 NLJ 322t CA On proving professional negligence on part of architect.

Worlock v SAWS and Rushmoor Borough Council (1981) 131 NLJ 1054 HC QBD Building contractor (breach of contract) and council (breach of building regulations) liable to plaintiff for damages suffered as result of defective building work.

Wormald v Cole [1954] 1 All ER; (1954) 104 LJ 201; [1954] 1 QB 614; (1954) 98 SJ 232; [1954] 2 WLR 613 CA Cattle owner liable for personal injury caused to neighbour upon trespass of quiet cattle.

Worsfold v Howe [1980] 1 All ER 1028; (1980) 130 NLJ 140; [1980] RTR 131; (1980) 124 SJ 646; [1980] 1 WLR 1175 CA Contributory negligence where collision between motorcyclist on main road and driver edging from lesser road.

Worsley (E) and Co, Ltd v Cooper [1939] 1 All ER 290; (1939) 87 LJ 103 HC ChD Misrepresenting that another business (of same kind as one's own) had ceased was (absent malice/special damage) passing off.

Worsley v Hollins and another (1991) 141 NLJ 425t; [1991] RTR 252; [1991] TLR 153 CA Full service undertaken/MoT certificate issued six weeks/one month before collision negatived presumption of res ipsa loquitur.

Worsley, Frayne v [1934] LJNCCR 40 CyCt That chattels taken from bailiff when in walking possession of same did not per se mean bailiff had been negligent.

Worsley, Rondel v [1967] 3 All ER 993; [1969] 1 AC 191; (1967) 111 SJ 927; [1967] 3 WLR 1666 HL Counsel immune from negligence action for all work in conduct of/pending litigation; solicitor immune for advocacy work/in settling case.

Worsley, Rondel v [1966] 3 All ER 657; [1967] 1 QB 443 (also HC QBD); (1966) 110 SJ 810; [1966] 3 WLR 950 CA Solicitor acting as advocate can be sued for negligence; barrister cannot be sued for acts done pending/in course of litigation.

Worsley, Rondel v [1966] 1 All ER 467; (1965-66) 116 NLJ 501; [1966] 2 WLR 300 HC QBD Counsel not liable in negligence for acts of advocacy.

Worthing Gas Light and Coke Company, Schweder v [1912] 1 Ch 83 HC ChD Injunction to prevent trespass by laying pipes through/against plaintiff's premises.

Worthington's Cash Stores (1930), Limited, Slater v [1941] 1 All ER 245; (1941) 91 LJ 100; [1942] 111 LJ 91 (also CA); (1941) 165 LTR 293; (1940-41) LVII TLR 294; (1941) WN (I) 26 HC KBD Nuisance/negligence liability where had not removed snow from roof four days after heavy snowstorms ended.

Worthington's Cash Stores (1930), Ltd, Slater v [1941] 3 All ER 28; [1941] 1 KB 488; [1942] 111 LJ 91 (also HC KBD); (1940-41) LVII TLR 468 CA Nuisance/negligence liability where had not removed snow from roof four days after heavy snowstorms ended.

Wragg v Grout and London Transport Board (1965-66) 116 NLJ 752t CA Bus driver/company not liable for injuries sustained by passenger on bus where fell because camber of road suddenly changed.

Wray v Essex County Council (1936) 82 LJ 296; (1936) 155 LTR 494; (1936) 80 SJ 894 CA Oil can not inherently dangerous: failed negligence action arising from loss of eye occasioned by one pupil running into spout of oil can being carried by another pupil under teacher's instructions to certain part of school.

Wright and another v Anderton (1909) C LTR 123; (1908-09) 53 SJ 135; (1908-09) XXV TLR 156; (1908) WN (I) 258 HC KBD Relationship of innkeeper and guest (with liability that entails for former) begins where is intent to supply and to take accommodation.

Wright and another, Haringey London Borough Council v (1969) 113 SJ 900 VacCt Interim injunction restraining two onetime students of college of art from returning to same.

Wright and ors, Anthony and ors v (1994) 144 NLJ 1452i HC ChD Investors who did not act on auditor's work could not sue auditor for non-discovery of misuse of trust money.

Wright v British Railways Board [1983] 2 AC 773; (1983) 133 NLJ 681; (1983) 127 SJ 478; [1983] TLR 454; [1983] 3 WLR 211 HL On gauging amount of interest due on personal injuries award.

Wright v Cheshire County Council [1952] 2 All ER 789; (1952) 116 JP 555; (1952) 102 LJ 581; (1952) 96 SJ 747; [1952] 2 TLR 641; (1952) WN (I) 466 CA Test of reasonable care in sports activities is what is customary practice.

Wright v Dunlop Rubber Co Ltd and ICI Ltd; Cassidy v Same (1971) 121 NLJ 361 HC QBD Factory owners liable for negligent exposure of workers to carcinogen (liable from moment discovered its effects); manufacturers of chemical liable in negligence for not withdrawing it from sale.

Wright v Hearson (1916) 51 LJ 284; (1916) WN (I) 216 HC KBD Counsel for plaintiff in personal injuries action arising from allegedly negligent driving by defendant ought not to have asked latter if was insured.

714

Wyman or Ferguson (Pauper) v Paterson and others [1900] LXIX (3) LJ 32; (1900) LXXXII LTR 473; (1899-1900) XVI TLR 270 HL Trustees liable for trust funds lost through their gross negligence.

X and others v Bedfordshire County Council [1994] 1 FLR 431; (1993) 143 NLJ 1783; [1993] TLR 590 HC QBD Failed attempt by children to sue local authority for injuries suffered through authority's alleged negligence/breach of statutory duty as regarded exercise of its care functions.

X v Bedfordshire County Council (1995) 145 NLJ 993 HL To ground action for careless performance of duty must prove that common law duty of care arose in circumstances of case.

Yachuk and Another v Oliver Blais Co, Ld [1949] 2 All ER 150; [1949] AC 386; (1949) LXV TLR 300; (1949) WN (I) 186 PC No contributory negligence by young child purchaser of petrol: seller thereof completely liable for later injuries suffered by child.

Yager v Fishman and Co and Teff and Teff [1944] 1 All ER 552 CA Solicitor did not owe client duty to state that latest date for option to determine approaching.

Yalden, Walter v [1902] 2 KB 304 HC KBD Lease to expire before limitation ran/lessor could enter property on which trespasser with Statute of Limitations title against lessee.

Yardley and Robinson, Yardley v (1956) 106 LJ ccr412 CyCt Where tenant did not know/could not reasonably have known of personal danger to plaintiff neither he nor landlord were liable in personal injuries action brought by plaintiff.

Yardley v Coombes (1963) 107 SJ 575 HC QBD On assessing appropriate damages to be awarded against negligent solicitor.

Yardley v Yardley and Robinson (1956) 106 LJ ccr412 CyCt Where tenant did not know/could not reasonably have known of personal danger to plaintiff neither he nor landlord were liable in personal injuries action brought by plaintiff.

Yardy v Greenwood [1935] LJNCCA 218; (1935) 79 SJ 363 CA Inappropriate staying of action for assault so that prosecution for causing grievous bodily harm with intent/causing grievous bodily harm might be brought.

Yates and another, Elliott v (1899-1900) 44 SJ 591 CA Was lawful to levy distress after financial year ended for taxes that became owing during the last financial year.

Yates, Bland v (1913-14) 58 SJ 612 HC ChD Excessive manure (which gave off smell and attracted flies) was nuisance even though area in which located was market gardening area.

Yates, Roach v [1938] 1 KB 256; [1938] 107 LJCL 170; (1937) 81 SJ 610 CA On assessment of personal injury damages for person rendered unable to look after self.

Yeatman and others v Homberger and Co (1912-13) 107 LTR 742; (1912-13) XXIX TLR 26 CA Not to repeat action not satisfactory response to passing off complaint: must seek to redress damage done.

Yeatman v L Homberger and Co (1912-13) 107 LTR 43; (1911-12) 56 SJ 614 HC ChD Injunction granted to restrain passing off in price circular of one wine as another.

Yeomans v Davies and Camden and Islington Area Health Authority (1981) 131 NLJ 210 HC QBD Damages following negligently performed vasectomy operation.

Yeun Kun Yeu and others v Attorney-General of Hong Kong [1988] AC 175; (1987) 137 NLJ 566; (1987) 131 SJ 1185; [1987] 3 WLR 776 PC Hong Kong Commissioner of Deposit-taking Companies did not owe duty of care to individual depositors for losses suffered through misbehaviour of deposit-taking company registered by Commissioner.

Yewen and the Croydon Rural District Council, Newcombe v (1912-13) XXIX TLR 299 HC KBD Council could reach indemnity agreement with contractor.

Yianni v Edwin Evans and Sons [1981] 3 All ER 592; (1981) 131 NLJ 1074; [1982] QB 438; (1981) 125 SJ 694; [1981] 3 WLR 843 HC QBD House purchaser's relying on negligent surveyor's valuation of house (for building society) were owed duty of care by surveyor.

York House Trading Ltd and another, Merrill Lynch Futures Inc v [1984] TLR 340 CA That stockbroker made losses on stock market not per se evidence that stockbroker negligent.

York Montague Ltd, South Australia Asset Management Corporation v; United Bank of Kuwait plc v Prudential Property Services Ltd; Nykredit Mortgage Bank plc v Edward Erdman Group Ltd (formerly Edward Erdman) (an unlimited company) [1996] 3 All ER 365; [1997] AC 191; (1996) 146 NLJ 956; (1996) 140 SJ LB 156; (1996) TLR 24/6/96; [1996] 3 WLR 87 HL Damages available where relied on negligent valuation given by surveyor were for losses which mistake in valuation could foreseeably entail.

Yorkshire Electricity Board v British Telecommunications plc (1970) 130 SJ 613; [1986] 1 WLR 1029 HL Cause of action where owning undertakers' apparatus damaged by operating undertakers did not run from date of damage but date owning undertakers suffered expense of repair.

Yorkshire Electricity Board, Bridlington Relay, Ltd v [1965] 1 All ER 264; [1965] Ch 436; (1965) 115 LJ 107; (1965) 109 SJ 12; [1965] 2 WLR 349 HC ChD On interference with television signals as nuisance.

Yorkshire Electricity Board, Naylor v [1966] 3 All ER 327; (1965-66) 116 NLJ 1032t/1432; [1967] 1 QB 244; (1966) 110 SJ 528; [1966] 3 WLR 654 CA Appropriate damages for loss of life of young, engaged man.

Yorkshire Fire and Civil Defence Authority, Church of Jesus Christ of Latter-Day Saints (Great Britain) v (1996) TLR 9/5/96 HC QBD Fire brigade does not owe duty of care to owner of burning property.

Yorkshire Traction Co, Ltd and others, Holling and another v [1948] 2 All ER 662 Assizes Blowing of smoke across road so that view obscured a nuisance.

Youde v Chester Corporation [1934] LJNCCR 44 CyCt Matter at issue deemed to be res judicata in second negligence action arising from road traffic incident; could not plead were not at all negligent and that other was contributorily negligent.

Young and another, Cameron and others (paupers) v (1908) 77 LJPC 68 HL On liability of Scots landlord vis-à-vis his tenants in negligence.

Young v Buckles [1952] 1 KB 220 CA Recoverability of professional charges in excess of that for which building licence allowed (Defence (General) Regulations 1939, r56(4) applied).

Young v Chester [1974] RTR 70 CA Seeking to start car broken down on carriageway with self-starter (which dimmed/extinguished lights) was negligent in that obviated warning to others of presence.

Young v Chester [1973] RTR 319 HC QBD Seeking to start car broken down on carriageway with self-starter (which dimmed/extinguished lights) was negligent in that obviated warning to others of presence but so was other's driving too fast with dimmed lights.

Young v Edward Box and Co, Limited [1951] 1 TLR 789 CA Person allowed by foreman to be carried in defendant's lorry by their employee was licensee not trespasser.

Young v Purdy [1997] 1 FCR 632; [1996] 2 FLR 795 CA Solicitor not liable in damages for negligent actions of client consequent upon solicitor's breach of contract by way of termination of retainer.

Young, Hay (or Bourhill) v [1942] 2 All ER 396; [1942] 111 LJ 97; (1943) 93 LJ 108; (1942) 167 LTR 261; (1942) 86 SJ 349; [1943] AC 92 HL Tortfeasor in motor vehicle collision not liable to bystander for nervous shock as not reasonably foreseeable.

Youngs, Ryan v [1938] 1 All ER 522; (1938) 82 SJ 233 CA Employer not liable in negligence/ nuisance for collision occasioned by act of God (worker in apparent good health dying at wheel).

Youssoupoff v Metro-Goldwyn-Mayer Pictures, Limited (1934) 78 SJ 617; (1933-34) L TLR 581 CA Defamation via ('talking') cinema film is libel; allegation that woman has been seduced is defamatory of her; on appropriate damages for libel.

Yusuf-Ud-Din (Syed Mahamad) v The Secretary of State for India in Council (1902-03) XIX TLR 496 PC Where person released on bail after arrest under warrant which is later set aside the time for bringing false imprisonment action runs from date of release on bail.

Zimmer Manufacturing Co Ltd, Zimmer Orthopaedic Ltd v (1968) 118 NLJ 1053t; [1968] 1 WLR 1349 CA Claim and counterclaim dismissed for want of prosecution in action involving inter alia passing off.

Zimmer Orthopaedic Ltd v Zimmer Manufacturing Co Ltd (1968) 118 NLJ 1053t; [1968] 1 WLR 1349 CA Claim and counterclaim dismissed for want of prosecution in action involving inter alia passing off.

Zoernsch v Waldock and another (1964) 108 SJ 278 CA Ex-President of European Commission on Human Rights enjoyed privilege in respect of allegedly negligent acts done when acting in official capacity.